D0741884

GRUHN'S GUIDE TO VINTAGE GUITARS

An Identification Guide for American Fretted Instruments, 2nd Edition

GEORGE GRUHN
AND
WALTER CARTER

Miller
Freeman
Books

San Francisco

Published by Miller Freeman Books
600 Harrison Street, San Francisco, CA 94107
Publishers of *Keyboard, Bass Player,* and *Guitar Player* magazines

ın Miller Freeman
A United News & Media publication

Distributed to the book trade in the U.S. and Canada by Publishers Group West, 1700 Fourth Street, Berkeley, CA 94710

Distributed to the music trade in the U.S. and Canada by Hal Leonard Publishing, P.O. Box 13819, Milwaukee, WI 53213

Cover Design: Greene Design
Interior Design and Composition: Leigh McLellan

Library of Congress Cataloging-in-Publication Data:
Gruhn, George.
   Gruhn's guide to vintage guitars : an identification guide for American fretted instruments / By George Gruhn & Walter Carter. – 2nd ed.
         p.   cm.
   ISBN 0-87930-422-7
   1. Stringed instruments—United States—Collectors and collecting Catalogs. 2. Stringed instruments—United States—History. 3. Guitar—United States—Collectors and collecting Catalogs. 4. Guitar—United States—History. I. Carter, Walter. II. Title.
ML1000.G78 1999
787.87'1973'075—DC21   98-43711
                                                        CIP

Printed in the United States of America
99 00 01 02 03 04   5 4 3 2 1

CONTENTS

CONTENTS

Before the first edition of *Gruhn's Guide to Vintage Guitars* was off the presses, we had a file folder full of new information. We had two goals in mind for future editions. On the "micro" level, we wanted to extend the depth of our research for the models covered in the original edition. On the "macro" level, we wanted to broaden the scope of the book to include more models and more makers.

We made many, many micro-changes and additions, although most will probably go unnoticed. Only those readers with a scrutinizing interest in Epiphone Zephyr Deluxes, for example, will see that we've narrowed a "circa…" or a "by…" down to an exact year and that we've broken down a previously lumped-together group of changes into a more detailed chronological series. Nevertheless, that kind of detail represents the original inspiration for this work, and we're pleased to be able to carry it on.

The macro-changes and additions are easy to see: all-new, full-blown model listings for Guild, Ovation, Mosrite, Epiphone banjos, OAI/OMI Dobros, Gibson banjos and Gibson amplifiers, plus updated model listings for all the makers covered in the first edition.

In short, this second edition is just like the first edition except that it has more of everything—more details, more models and more makers.

Obviously, we're still a long way from including every model and maker that generates interest from a collector or player. On the other hand, we're a long way *beyond* our original goal, which was to provide a guide for vintage models only. In a strict vintage sense, that meant no CBS Fenders, no Norlin Gibsons, no Indian rosewood Martins, etc. Our plan was thwarted, ironically, by the lack of information readily available on the recent non-vintage, non-collectible models. If for no other reason than to provide the means to distinguish an original vintage model from newer versions of the same model, we decided to follow through to current production in the original edition. And it's good that we did. Interest in new models has *increased* in the last few years. Over a million people own guitars that were made in the last 25 years, and we've talked to most of them, or so it seems, in Gruhn's role as proprietor of Gruhn Guitars and Carter's position as Gibson company historian from 1993–98. They want to know more about these recent models.

The unpredictability of the vintage market gave us another compelling reason for bringing the new edition up to date. Some models that had no vintage value (which we define as an instrument's value beyond its utility value as a playable used guitar) seven years ago have now become collectible. Since no one can predict exactly which models will gain vintage or collectible status, we have once again attempted to include models introduced right up to press time.

Updating the model listings was the least enjoyable part of this new edition. In earlier eras, in any given year, there would be one Stratocaster or one D-28 or four distinct Les Paul models. This edition lists over 40 variations on the Les Paul Standard alone, over 40 D-28s and more than 80 Stratocaster models. In putting together the first edition, we had seen ourselves as researchers and historians; by the time this new edition was finished, we were feeling more like list makers.

The number of variations on basic models prompted a change in format that should help readers better understand a manufacturer's product line. The variations of the Martin D-28, for example, are all listed with abbreviated descriptions, noting only those specs that differ from the standard D-28 specs. To distinguish the variation models from basic models, the basic model name is printed in a type size slightly larger than that of the variation models.

We did enjoy adding the new manufacturer sections. The subject of Gibson banjos probably has the highest ratio of interest to available information of any type of vintage instrument. There is virtually nothing—only a few old magazine articles—to help the banjo collector, and the Gibson banjo section was probably the most-requested addition to this guide. We've also expanded the sections on two other makers—Guild and Ovation—from serial number lists to complete model descriptions. And we've added Mosrite to our list of makers.

With these additions, we need to add our thanks to Tom Gray and John Quarterman, who generously offered us their Dobro research prior to publishing it in their own book; James Werner, who sent us an advance copy of his monumental list of Fender serial numbers; Lynn Wheelwright and Mike Newton, whose information on Gibson contract (budget) brands more than doubled the content of that section, and for many, many details of prewar guitars and amplifiers from Gibson and National-Dobro; Hans Moust and Jay Pilzer, who both painstakingly proofed the Guild section line by line; Stan Jay, for D'Aquisto information; and Elaine Frizzell, for Mosrite help. Once again, we thank the sales and repair staff at Gruhn Guitars: Dan Mills (general manager), Keith Gregory, Paul Johnson, Troy Lacey, Calvin Minner, Ethan Pilzer, John Hedgecoth, Sam Calveard, Bill Baldock, Andy Jellison and Ben Burgette.

We've received a number of queries and, in a few cases, complaints regarding the independent makers included in the first edition. We included D'Angelico, D'Aquisto and Stromberg, of course, because of the considerable vintage interest in their guitars. We chose Benedetto, Collings and Gilchrist because we knew them well, and we felt sure their instruments would endure. Although many independent makers have established good reputations in the last few years, we have only added one long-established maker to this edition—John Monteleone—using the same uneven, subjective criteria.

Although we have gone beyond our original concept, we probably will never reach our grand vision. We had intended to use this as a blueprint upon which to build an all-encompassing, encyclopedic work. If you wanted to know about the Gibson ES-335, for example, you would find—in one book, in one entry—all the specs, along with photographs of instruments and other appropriate information. Now, for identification, dates and specs, you can look in this book. But for photographs and an in-depth discussion of the model in the context of Gibson electrics (up through the 1960s, at least), you should look to *Gibson Electrics: The Classic Years*. For photographs and a sense of the model in the context of American electric guitars, we would refer you to *Electric Guitars and Basses* or *American Guitars*. And to get a feel for the ES-335 in the broader contexts of Gibson history and the musical instrument industry, you should look to *Gibson Guitars: 100 Years of an American Icon*. No discussion of the ES-335 would be complete without the musicians who played the model, and that would involve another half-dozen books. (And we haven't even touched on the issue of values.)

The vintage guitar bookshelf is growing faster than anyone could have imagined a decade ago. In the first edition, we listed eight books for recommended reading. By the time we started work on the revised edition, there were 18 books on Fender alone. The first book devoted to a single model, Tom Van Hoose's *The Gibson Super 400: Art of the Fine Guitar*, was published just before our book, and since then we've seen two books devoted to Gibson Les Pauls, and two devoted to one single variation of one Les Paul model—the cherry sunburst Les Paul Standard of 1958–60.

Clearly, no amount of research and revision will make *Gruhn's Guide to Vintage Guitars* the be-all and end-all for the vintage instrument enthusiast, but with this revised edition, and with future editions, we believe it will continue to be the best and most accurate primary source of information on vintage fretted instruments.

George Gruhn
Walter Carter
Nashville
May 1999

Since 1960, interest in vintage instruments and, not surprisingly, values of vintage instruments have multiplied many times over. With prices for a single instrument ranging from a few hundred dollars to tens of thousands, accurate information is crucial to the instrument buyer or seller. A Martin D-45 made prior to World War II, for example, can be worth more than 20 times as much as a recent issue D-45, even though there is relatively little difference in design. A 1966 Fender Stratocaster is very similar in appearance to its 1964 counterpart, but Fender instruments made after the company's sale to CBS in 1965 are worth significantly less than pre-CBS examples. Obviously, a buyer or seller must know how to tell the difference.

The question asked most often of the staff at Gruhn Guitars is "How much is my instrument worth?" To know the value of an instrument, one must first know what it is, when it was made and how original its condition is. With literally thousands of models made by the major American manufacturers in the twentieth century, simply identifying and dating a model can often be a great mystery.

We have assembled the best information from every available source—original catalogs and literature, information already in print, the unpublished knowledge of many dedicated collectors and the actual instruments we have personally seen in our day-to-day business. We have seen thousands upon thousands of instruments, yet we still frequently come across one unlike any that we have ever seen or heard of before. We occasionally come across a model that we had previously seen only in catalogs, and conversely, we have seen numerous examples of some models that we've never found in catalogs.

We have incorporated new information into this book right up to press time, and we believe that the information here is the best available. We also know from the experience of compiling this book that more and more information will surface. We will continue to revise and refine this work for future editions, and we welcome any new information.

As the vintage market grows, it becomes increasingly subject to the same factors that influence the stock market: currency exchange rates, fad buying and panic selling, for example. Also, the vintage market is still small enough that a few wealthy collectors can exert a profound influence by taking a sudden interest—or sudden lack of interest—in a certain model. Not only the value of some specific models but the vintage market as a whole could change drastically during the time it takes to turn a manuscript into a book. Consequently, we will not attempt to provide market prices for any models, but we do assess the relative merits of various models in the Comments sections.

For some manufacturers, we have drawn heavily from information found in familiar sources, which are listed separately in a bibliography. In addition, we would like to thank these friends for sharing their expertise in the following areas: Dobro: Mike Cass; Epiphone: Hans Moust; Fender: Gary Bohannon, A.R. Duchossoir, Richard Smith and John Sprung; Gibson: Ray Atwood, Julius Bellson, Gary Burnett, Dave Patrick, J.T. Riboloff, Tim Shaw and Tom Van Hoose; Gretsch: Mayner Greene, Duke Kramer, Jay Scott and Danny Thorpe; Guild: Hans Moust; Larson Brothers: Robert Hartmann and Dennis Watkins; National: Bob Brozman, Mike Newton and Dennis Watkins; Rickenbacker: John Hall and Richard Smith; pot codes: Hans Moust. A special thanks is due Mike Longworth for his painstaking, line-by-line proofreading of the Martin section. For their valuable input, we would also like to thank the sales staff at Gruhn Guitars: Dan Green, Dan Mills, Hank Sable, David Sebring and Dennis Watkins.

George Gruhn
Walter Carter
Nashville
Spring 1991

SCOPE

The purpose of this book is to provide information by which to identify, date and determine the originality of vintage American fretted instruments.

Not all American manufacturers are included. Some that produced great quantities of instruments, such as Kay and Harmony, are omitted because the majority of their instruments were cheaply made and those that survive are generally not of great significance in the vintage and used instrument market. Other makers are omitted simply because we do not yet have enough information to put together a useful identification section.

If an instrument is not in this book, then one of the following explanations probably applies:

1. It varies from catalog descriptions. Catalog photos and descriptions do not always match the actual instruments. In fact, the descriptions do not always match the instruments shown in the accompanying photos. Manufacturers have been known to use photos as much as 10 years out of date. Non-standard but factory original parts may have been installed as a result of shortages or surpluses at the factory. Some instruments announced and placed in catalogs were never actually produced and sold.

2. It is a custom-order instrument, a prototype or an obscure model that never appeared in a catalog or in literature.

3. It is a limited-run variation of a standard model.

4. It is of too recent vintage to be listed in this book.

5. It is a non-original instrument. Parts have been changed, it has been refinished, it has been customized with non-original inlay, electronics, etc.

ORGANIZATION

Instruments are organized by manufacturer. An alphabetical index of models, by manufacturer, is provided at the end of the book.

A General Information section at the beginning of each manufacturer's chapter details design changes that affect most or all models in the line. Protocol in the General Information sections is the same as that of the individual model descriptions (see Model Descriptions, following). Serial number information is included at the end of General Information sections.

Instruments by each manufacturer are grouped according to type and in the following order: acoustic archtop guitars, flat tops, electric archtops, solidbody electrics, basses, steels, mandolins and other instruments. Within these sections, they may be further grouped by general style or period of manufacture. The groupings are listed under the Section Organization heading at the beginning of each section.

KEYS

At the beginning of most model sections is a model identification key. The key is organized like an outline. Each level of indent is a yes-or-no question. If yes, go to the next level of indent; if no, then proceed at the same level of indent until the answer is yes.

MODEL DESCRIPTIONS

The major models are usually listed in chronological order. Models within subsections may be in chronological order, alphanumeric order or simply grouped in a logical way based on the relationship of the models. For example, the Gibson L-5P, which is a cutaway version of the L-5, is found with the L-5 description and not in its own separate, chronological place. On the other hand, Gibson's ES-125T, a thinbody version of the ES-125 hollowbody electric, is found with other thinlines and not with the ES-125 and other full-depth models.

The following example from the Epiphone Electric Archtops section illustrates the conventions used in model descriptions:

Zephyr De Luxe:[1] 17 3/8" wide, spruce top, 1 pickup with slot-head screw poles and oblong housing in bridge position, volume and tone control on 1 shaft with circular *Mastervoicer* control plate, Frequensator[2] tailpiece, 5-ply top and back binding, triple-bound pickguard, 5-piece maple/walnut neck, bound rosewood fingerboard with 2 inlaid white lines, cloud inlay,[3] block inlay at 15th fret, triple-bound peghead, vine peghead inlay, pearl logo, gold-plated hardware, blond finish, tenor (with metal peghead logo plate) and plectrum models available[4]
Introduced (first listed as **Deluxe Zephyr Spanish Electric**): **Dec. 1, 1941**[5]
2 knobs on circular *Mastervoicer* plates on line at right angle to strings:[6] **1942**
Pickup in middle position, some with sunburst finish: **by**[7] **1947**
Large rectangular metal-covered pickup: **by 1948**
Pickup in neck position: **1949**
New York pickup, 2 pickups optional, 3-way slide switch on 2-pickup model, 2 knobs near edge, *Mastervoicer* control plates on 1-pickup model only, sunburst or blond finish:[8] **1950**
Knobs on line parallel to strings: **1951**
Discontinued:[9] **by 1954**

Zephyr De Luxe Regent:[10] 17 3/4" wide, rounded cutaway, laminated spruce top, large rectangular pickup in middle position, 2 knobs near edge, circular *Mastervoicer* control plates...

1. Specifications for each model generally follow this protocol: body shape and size, body wood, pickups, controls, bridge and tailpiece, pickguard, binding, neck and fingerboard, fingerboard inlay, peghead, metal plating, finish. Thus, the finish color should always be at the end of a description. The bridge and tailpiece specs should always be somewhere after the electronics and before the fingerboard inlay.
2. Many tailpieces, pickups and other parts whose descriptions are not self-explanatory are described in more detail in the manufacturer's General Information section.
3. *Inlay* refers to fingerboard inlay unless specified as peghead inlay, soundhole inlay, etc.
4. Tenors and other variations of the same instrument have the same ornamentation unless otherwise specified.
5. Introduction date is the earliest appearance, whether in a catalog, in literature or as evidenced by an actual instrument.
6. Only the specs that change are listed. Inlay, for example, continues to be cloud pattern. Some dates, especially in the General Information sections, signify a range of years, such as 1955–59 or 1973–current, and in those cases the relevant specifications apply only to that range of years.

7. *By* in front of a date means that that date is the earliest that a change or an introduction has been documented. Although we believe the "by" dates are accurate within a year or two, the changes could conceivably have been implemented any time after the previously listed date.

8. Where multiple specification changes are listed, those changes may not have all been made at exactly the same time. It is common practice for manufacturers to use up old supplies before instituting new specs. Some transitional instruments may have new-style pickups, for example, but still retain the old-style fingerboard inlay. In the case of Gibson's changeover from "patent-applied-for" humbucking pickups to patent-number pickups, some instruments were fitted with one of each. Changes in Gretsch models are so difficult to pinpoint that collectors say, only half-jokingly, that all Gretsch models are transitional.

9. *Discontinued* usually refers to the year the model was dropped from the company catalog. Where shipping records differ from catalog listings, years when the model was *Last made* or *Shipped through* may also be included. *Available* is used when a model did not change through its entire production period.

In some cases, the *total* number of instruments shipped over a model's entire production run is indicated. Production figures not specified as *total* are for that year only.

10. Variations of basic models are listed with the basic model. The model name of the variation is printed in smaller type than that of the basic model.

COMMENTS

The authors' comments at the end of each section are intended to be a general guideline for models that may be highly regarded by collectors. The vintage market, like any other market for collectibles, is constantly changing. The models noted as collectible are likely to remain so, even though prices may fluctuate. Some models that are not currently considered to be desirable, and thus are not mentioned in Comments, could become collectible in the future.

A FINAL CAUTION

We urge you to use all the information available here and elsewhere to cross-check model descriptions with serial number lists, with manufacturer's specs and with other similar instruments. No book or catalog can take the place of in-hand experience.

Again, information may be conflicting in some cases. If a serial number was affixed to an instrument at some length of time before the instrument was completed, then the specifications of the instrument may conflict with the year in which a serial number list indicates it was made. Instruments may be numbered before they are finished, as in the case of the 1963 Gibson Flying Vs and Explorers that bear 1958 serial numbers. Instruments may be numbered after they are finished, as in the case of a Gibson mandolin we have seen with a 1952 serial number but with specs indicating that it was almost certainly built in 1949. In addition, accepted serial number lists are not always completely reliable. We have seen, for example, several Gretsch guitars with a sales receipt from a year earlier than the date given in the generally accepted Gretsch serial number list. We have also seen two Gretsch Model 6120s with consecutive serial numbers, but with earlier features on the example with the later number.

So be careful. The information in this book may not keep you from being surprised by something new, but it should keep you from being fooled.

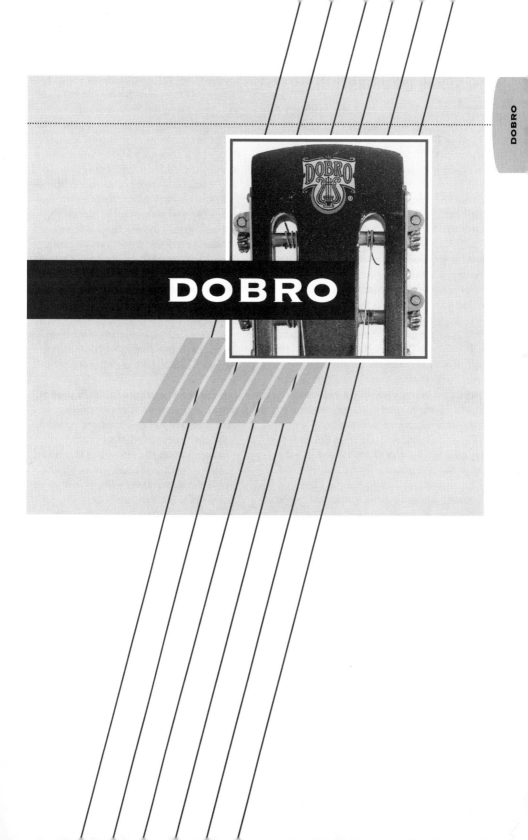

GENERAL INFORMATION

The Dobro brand name has been identified with resonator guitars since 1929 and is currently owned by Gibson Guitar Corp. Despite its registered-trademark status, the Dobro name has at times been used generically to refer to woodbodied instruments with 1) an aluminum cone or "resonator" mounted so that the cone opens toward the top of the instrument and 2) an 8-armed spider assembly supporting the bridge. And, contrary to the generic use of "Dobro," owners of the Dobro brand have used it on metalbody resonator guitars with various resonator systems and on non-resonator instruments as well as on woodbody, spider-resonator instruments.

The Dobro name derives from the *Do*pyera *Bro*thers—John, Rudy, Emil (Ed), Robert and Louis—who played various roles in the design, manufacture and financing of Dobro instruments. John Dopyera and his brothers formed the National String Instrument Company in Los Angeles in 1926 (see National section) and incorporated with more partners in 1928. John Dopyera said he split from National and made the first Dobro brand instruments in 1928, although his official resignation from National did not come until February 19, 1929. It is likely that no more than a few prototype Dobros were made in 1928, and regular production began in 1929.

Louis and Robert Dopyera retained their interest in National after John left. After a legal dispute National and Dobro merged in 1932. That same year National-Dobro granted a license to Regal, a Chicago-based manufacturer and distributor, to make instruments using a Dobro resonator, and Regal introduced its first models in June 1933. Dobros were then made concurrently by National-Dobro in California and by Regal in Chicago until 1937, at which time Regal gained the exclusive right to market Dobro, and National-Dobro moved to Chicago.

Other prewar brands: In addition to the Regal brand, Dobro made instruments in California under the Norwood Chimes brand. Some California-made examples of the Angelus model have *Angelus* on the peghead as a brand name, although it was a standard model in the Dobro line. Dobro also made instruments in California for other distributors who sold them under their own brands. Brands probably made in California include Broman (student models), Penetro (a lap-size model with a small mandolin-size resonator) and Ward (for the Montgomery Ward mail-order house). Brands probably made by Regal include Alhambra (metalbody), Bruno, More Harmony (not a brand of the Harmony company) and Orpheum (metalbody and woodbody). Magn-o-tone brand resonator guitars may have been made both in California and by Regal in Chicago.

According to Ed Dopyera, National-Dobro made no resonator instruments from 1940 until after World War II. National-Dobro reorganized as Valco by 1942 and retained rights to the Dobro brand name, but the company made no more instruments under the Dobro brand.

DB Original: Ed and Rudy Dopyera may have made some resonator instruments in the 1950s with leftover prewar Dobro parts. They began making Dobros on a regular basis in 1962 under the DB Original brand.

In 1964 Ed Dopyera's son Emil and a group of partners were granted a license to manufacture instruments with the Dobro brand, and in 1965 they began making Dobros in Gardena, CA.

Mosrite: In 1966, Semi Moseley of Mosrite (see Mosrite section) bought Dobro. Dobros from the Mosrite period have markedly different characteristics than those of the previous and following periods (although the Mosrite/Dobro style actually originated with the Dopyera's 1965 instruments).

Replica 66: During the first year that Mosrite owned Dobro, the Dopyeras made resonator guitars under the Replica 66 brand.

Hound Dog/OMI/OAI: In 1967, Ed and Rudy Dopyera, their sister Gabriela Lazar, and their nephew Ronald Lazar formed the Original Music Instrument company in Huntington Beach, CA. OMI initially made resonator guitars under the Hound Dog brand and banjos under the Dopera's Original brand.

OMI regained rights to Dobro in 1970 and resumed production of Dobro-brand instruments in Huntington Beach, CA, in 1971 (while continuing for a short time to make instruments under the Hound Dog and Dopera's Original brands). The OMI line included models with the Dobro-style "spider bridge" resonator system and with the National-style "biscuit bridge" resonator system. The Dopyeras sold OMI to Chester and Mary Lizak in 1985.

Gibson Guitar Corp. purchased OMI in 1993. In early 1997 Gibson moved the OMI division to Nashville and made it a part of a new bluegrass-oriented division called Original Acoustic Instruments. OAI produced a few Dobros in 1997 from work-in-progress and resumed production on a limited basis in 1998.

RESONATOR COVERPLATE

PAT PEND, low-rise design, 12 screws with "clock-point" arrangement (directly below fingerboard is 12 o'clock): **1928 only**

PAT PEND, high-rise design, 12 screws with "clock-point" arrangement (directly below fingerboard is 12 o'clock): **1929–31**

PAT PEND, low-rise design, 12 screws with "clock-point" arrangement (directly below fingerboard is 12 o'clock), poinsettia pattern holes, double-cyclops models only: **1932 only**

Pat #1872633, 12 screws with "clock-point" arrangement (directly below fingerboard is 12 o'clock): **1932 only**

Pat #1896484, other patents pending, screws at 11:30 and 12:30 positions (directly below fingerboard is 12 o'clock, no screw at 12 o'clock), California and Regal models: **1933–39**

Some with *Pat #1896484*, poinsettia pattern, Regal only: **1933–39**

COVERPLATE PATTERNS

Standard guitar and tenor guitar: 4 semi-circular groups of holes, 17 holes in each group, California-made and Regal-made models

"Poinsettia": 4 groups of holes, 7 holes in each group arranged in a sunrise pattern, California-made and Regal models

Standard Regal metalbody: 4 groups of holes, 2 rows of 4 semi-rectangular holes in each group

Moon-and-stars: holes shaped like stars and crescent moons, Regals only (some mandolins, ukes and a few guitars)

Standard mandolin coverplate: 6 semi-circular groups of holes, 13 round holes in each group

Standard uke coverplate: 4 semi-circular groups of holes, 13 round holes in each group

BODY

3 top holes (at end of fingerboard)...
California-made: most with beveled (countersunk) hole edges
Regal-made: square edges on holes

Except for No. 45 (spruce-top version), most slot-head Regals and almost all solid-head Regals have no small holes in top.

Thick top: California-made student models with 1/2" thick top and no sound well, poplar body, routed "ledge" around top hole for cone, most with neck tongue mounted between 2 V-blocks and additional block at opposite end of sound well, some with normal neck block, some with Martin-type top bracing pattern in upper chamber, no room at end of fingerboard for another fret...
Some No. 27s, serial numbers in 3000s: **1929**
Some "Cyclops" models (see model descriptions): **1930–31**

Binding...
California-made, thick body binding: **1929–34**
California-made, thin body binding: **1934–37**
Regal-made, thick body binding: **1933–39**
A few Regals with wood binding: **1933–39**

DOBRO

DIMENSIONS

	WIDTH		LENGTH	DEPTH	
UPPER		LOWER		HEEL	ENDPIN
California, 1929–c. 1934					
10 1/2"		14 1/4"	19 1/8"	2 7/8"	3 1/8"
California, c. 1935–37					
10 1/2"		14 1/4"	19 1/8"	3"	3 1/4"
Regal, screen holes, 12 frets clear of body					
Large (California) size					
10 1/2"		14"	19 1/8"	3 1/4"	3 1/4"–3 1/2"
Smaller size					
10"		14 1/4"	19 1/8"	3 1/4"	3 1/4"–3 1/2"
Regal, *f*-holes					
10"		14 1/4"	19 1/8"	3 1/4"	3 1/4"–3 1/2"
Regal, 14 frets clear of body (6-strings and tenors)					
9 1/2"		14"	17 3/4"	3 1/4"	3–3 1/2"

RESONATOR CONE

Spun aluminum, spin marks barely visible, no "lugs" (indentions near widest part of cone to support spider bridge): **prototypes**

Stamped aluminum, no "lugs": **1929–c. 1932**

Stamped aluminum, 4 or 8 "lugs": most California-made and virtually all Regals (after Regals introduced): **1931–39**

Spun aluminum, spin marks visible, no "lugs" (indentions near widest part of cone to support spider bridge), some California-made examples with serial number range 8000–9000: **1937**

4 holes near narrowest part of resonator cone: many examples of all models throughout prewar production

SPIDER (BRIDGE SUPPORT)

Long spider, 8 arms rest on edge of cone, flat middle section and #14 stamp: **1929**

Long spider, 8 arms rest on edge of resonator, rounded (half-spherical) middle section…
California-made: **1930**
Some Regals: **1933–39**

Short spider, 8 arms rest on "lugs" (indentions near widest part of cone)…
All California-made: **1931–37**
Some Regals: **1933–39**

Short spider, 4-arms: Angelus and mandolin models only: **1929–39**

Coverplates, cones, and spiders are interchangeable. Various players prefer various combinations of equipment. Most prefer cones with the 4 holes at the narrowest part of the cone, and some have had these added. A competent metalworker can make these newly cut cones indistinguishable from those that originally had holes. The only cones that can safely be assumed to be original are those that have never been removed from the instrument. These usually bear evidence of small tacks (similar in size to the 5th-string "spikes" sometimes installed on banjo fingerboards) and the original glue that held them in place.

SOUND WELL, CALIFORNIA-MADE

3-ply wood, very thick sound well construction, thick kerfing around top and back edges (usually thicker around top than back), 9, 11 or 13 round holes (13-hole examples have holes very close together; 9-hole examples typically have holes unevenly spaced with more holes on the upper side toward the top screen-holes), hand-bored holes with edges rounder than Regal-made machine-punched holes: **1929**

Stamped parallelogram-shaped holes: **1930–37**

Some with no kerfing around back edge: **mid to late 1930s**

A few with triangular-shaped holes: **throughout**

Sound Well, Regal-Made

Thin sound well approximately same thickness as top,
9 round machine-punched holes with square edges:
1933–39
Some Regals made for Broman with 1 hole in sound
well for neck tongue; some with hole for neck
tongue plus 2 holes in lower body area (at 5 and
7 o'clock positions): **mid 1930s**
Many Regals with no sound well, routed "ledge"
around top hole for cone: **mid 1930s**
Most Regal models with *f*-holes (instead of screen
holes) have no sound well.
All Regal metalbody guitars have no sound well.
Some Regal mandolins and ukes have no sound well.

Neck

14 frets clear of body: Regal-made
Neck heel…
California-made roundnecks: heel reaches at least
to back binding
Regals: neck-heel does not reach binding
Fingerboard…
"Red bean" wood: **1929 only**
No dot at 17th fret: **1929 only**
Dot at 17th fret: **1930 and after**
California-made, most with unbound fingerboard: **after
1934**
Most California-made have room at end of fingerboard
for another fret, except for cyclops and thick-top
models.
All Regal-made have no room at end of fingerboard for
another fret.

Peghead

California-made…
Sawn slots with square slot-ends: **1929–37**
Some No. 27s with upper slot-ends that are round
(routed) but still ramped: **1937**
Regal-made…
Routed slots with rounded slot-ends, upper slot-
ends square to top (not ramped): **1933–39**
Dobro decal, many examples: **1934–39**
Green oval decal with *Regal* and crown, many
examples: **1933–39**
Solid peghead, many examples: **1935–39**
Dobro and lyre decal…
Yellow border: **1928 only**
No yellow border, red is bright, all California-made
and some Regals: **1929–39**
Similar to 1929, but with browner red color (OMI-
made): **1970–72**
Circled *R* (trademark registration symbol): **1972–
current**

Prototypes

Prototypes typically have no serial number and a peghead length of 6" from top to nut (1/4" shorter than
production models).

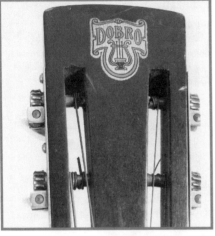

Peghead of 1929 Dobro. Like most California-made Dobros, the slots are cut with a saw and have square ends. Slot-ends are also "ramped" (angled) rather than cut perpendicularly into the peghead. The logo decal is one of the very earliest, with a yellow border around the edge.

Peghead of 1980s OMI Dobro. Like all postwar Dobros and all prewar Regal-made Dobros, the slots are routed, with round ends cut perpendicularly into the peghead. The postwar decal differs from the prewar style, with a larger letter B, different black areas of the lyre figure and the circled-R trademark registration symbol.

Neck and body area of a 1929 Dobro No. 45. The coverplate screw is at the "12 o'clock" position," the 3 holes near the neck have beveled edges for a countersunk look, there is no room at the end of the fingerboard for another fret and no inlay at the 17th fret.

Neck and body area of a 1980s Dobro. The coverplate screws are in the "11:30 and 12:30" positions, the 3 holes near the neck are only slightly beveled and there is a dot at the 17th fret.

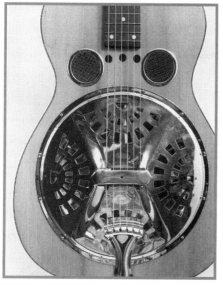

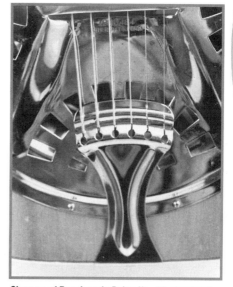

Body of a Regal-made Dobro No. 45 from the mid 1930s. The coverplate is the standard Dobro pattern, and the 3 holes near the neck have right-angle edges. Many Regals have no holes near the neck. Most have room for another fret at end of fingerboard.

Close-up of Regal-made Dobro No. 45, showing the standard Dobro tailpiece and the standard mid 1930s coverplate with patent #1,896,484 and notice of other patents pending.

Regal-made Dobro mandolin with moon-and-stars pattern coverplate.

SERIAL NUMBERS

1929–37

Serial numbers are stamped into the top of the peghead. No factory serial number records are available.

Most Regal-brand Dobros have no serial number.

This list was originally compiled by Mike Cass, with updated information from John Quarterman and Tom Gray.

NUMBER	YEAR
800s–1400s	1929
1400s–2000s	1930
2000s–2600s	1931
2600s–3200s	1932
3200s–3900s	1933
4000s	1933 Regal-made, a few California-made
5000s–5600s	1933 California-made
5700s–7600s	1934–36 California-made and Regal-made
8000s–9000s	1936–37
L9000s	1937 Regal-made
A prefix	1936
B prefix or suffix	1932–33 usually with 3 digits, most Cyclops models
M prefix	mid 1930s

EL MONTE, 1962–64

Number is pressed into top of peghead. Series begins with 001. Production is estimated at 31 or 32 per month. No number list is available.

GARDENA, 1965–66

Number is pressed into top of peghead. "Screens" in upper bouts have punched diamond-shape holes. No number list is available.

MOSRITE, 1966–69

Number is pressed into the fingerboard near the body end. No number list is available.

OMI/OAI

1970–74

NUMBER	YEAR
101–401	1967–70
402–712	1971
713–1427	1972
1428–2296	1973
2297–2372	Jan.–Feb. 1974

1974–79

Configuration: **y (#)### D**

Single numeral **y** at beginning is last digit of year. Although some models are stamped with a 3 for 1973, they were not completed until 1974.

3 or 4 numerals **(#)###** in center are serial number ranking for the year, beginning each year with 101.

Final letter **D** is body type: D = wood, B = brass, M = sheet metal or mandolin, X = Model 114
Example: 8 304 D = 1978 woodbody

1980–mid 1988

Configuration: **y #### yD**
First numeral **y** is decade of manufacture: 8 = 1980s, 9 = 1990s.
Numerals **####** in center (may be 2, 3 or 4 numerals) are serial number ranking for the year.
Numeral **y** before final letter is last digit of year.
Final letter **D** is body type: D = wood, B = metal.
Example: 8 5002 6B on a 1986 model 33S (metalbody)

Mid 1988–94

Configuration: **A# #### yyD**
Letter and numeral **A#** at beginning (some models have 2 numerals or a single letter at beginning) are model designation.
Numerals **####** in center (may be 3, 4 or 5 numerals) are ranking.
2 numerals **yy** before final letter are last 2 digits of year.
Final letter **D** refers to body type: D = wood, B = metal, H = Hound Dog model, P = solid peghead
Example: R5 262 90D on a 1990 model D60S (woodbody)

1995–97

Configuration: **A(A) (#)### yy**
First letter(s) **A(A)** refer to model.
Numerals **(#)###** in middle are ranking.
Final 2 numerals **yy** are last 2 digits of year.
Example: BA 104 95 on a 1995 model 33S

1998–current

8 digits with configuration **ymmddrry**
First **y** is last digit of year.
mm is month.
dd is day of month.
rr is ranking.
Final **y** is decade.
Example: 80429119 = 1998, 4th month, 29th day, 11th instrument that day

1929–41 KEY

Metal body
    Yellow-brown sunburst finish = **No. 32, 1935–37**
    Silver and black 2-tone finish = **No. 32, 1937–38**
    Silver finish with gold highlights = **No. 46, 1935–37**
    Mahogany- or maple-grain paint finish = **No. 46, 1937–38**
    Rosewood-grain paint finish = **No. 35**
Plated body
    Engraved borders = **Leader (No. 14)**
    Banner engraved across back = **Professional (No. 15)**
    Dobro or *Regal* engraved on back = **Artist (No. 16)**
    Spanish dancer/garden scene = **No. 62**
    Other ornamental engraving = **No. 65**

1921–41 Key *(continued)*
Woodbody
  2 screen holes in upper bouts (unjoined)
    Sandblasted French scroll design
      D on back = **No. 60**
      No *D* on back
        No body binding = **No. 65/66**
        Bound top and back = **No. 66-B**
    Walnut top
      2-piece back = **No. 106**
      4-piece back = **No. 126**
      Gold-plated hardware = **No. 156**
    Spruce top
      Mahogany back and sides
        Flat back = **No. 45, 1933–37**
        Arched back = **No. 55, 1933–34**
      Walnut back and sides
        Nickel-plated hardware = **No. 175**
        Gold-plated hardware = **No. 206**
    Mahogany top
      Standard coverplate
        No engraving on coverplate = **No. 45, 1933–37**
        Engraved coverplate or inlaid celluloid logo = **No. 85/86**
      4 clusters of holes in coverplate = **No. 15**
    Birch, maple, magnolia or poplar top
      No 3 holes in top
        Flat top = **No. 27, 1933–39; No. 32 1939–41**
        Arched top = **Regal, no model name**
      3 holes in top
        No binding
          Walnut stain finish = **No. 45, 1929–34**
          Black finish = **No. 36**
        Bound fingerboard
          Decal logo = **No. 55, 1929–34**
          Celluloid inlaid logo = **No. 76**
  Joined screen holes = **Double Cyclops**
  1 screen hole
    Shaded or brown finish = **Cyclops No. 27**
    Rosewood-grain finish = **Cyclops No. 45**
    Sandblasted French scroll design = **Cyclops No. 60**
  f-holes
    Angelus on peghead = **No. 19/Angelus**
    Regal or Dobro brand
      Shaded finish
        4 dots on fingerboard = **No. 6**
        Standard dot inlay = **No. 25, 1937–38; No. 27, 1939–41**
      Natural finish maple or spruce top = **Regal, no model name**

1929–41

Dobro model numbers and specs may be inconsistent. Model names were not stamped on instruments. Model numbers typically correspond to retail price, and prices varied from one distributor to another as well as from one period to another. Some numbers were used for several different models, and some models had several different model numbers.

Unless otherwise specified, all guitar models have 3-ply woodbody construction, 2 round screen holes in the upper bouts and the standard Dobro coverplate.

Regal-made models may have a Dobro brand or a Regal brand.

SECTION ORGANIZATION

California-Made Models
Regal-Made Woodbody Models
Dobro/Regal "Silver Guitar" Series
Other Dobro/Regal Metalbody Models
Tenortropes
Mandolins
Ukuleles
Electrics

CALIFORNIA-MADE MODELS

No. 45: unspecified wood, no binding, roundneck or squareneck, silver-painted metal parts specified but some with mixture of painted and plated parts, dark walnut stain finish
Introduced: **1929**
Variation: painted mahogany-color coverplate and tailpiece, serial numbers for this variation range from 1200–1300
Available as Cyclops model (see following): **1932–33**
Discontinued: **by 1934**
Model number continues in California-made line and in Regal-made line, but with different specs (see following)

No. 55/56: referred to as **Standard**, unspecified hardwood, unbound top and back, roundneck or squareneck, bound fingerboard, chrome-plated hardware, walnut finish
Introduced as **No. 55: 1929**
Renamed **No. 56:** birch body, no binding, mahogany neck, squareneck or roundneck, bound red bean fingerboard, nickel-plated hardware: **1932**
Discontinued: **by mid 1934**

No. 50: tenor, smaller mandolin-size resonator and coverplate, otherwise same specs as No. 55
Available: **1931–early 1934**

No. 65/66: sandblasted French scroll design on top, back and sides, some with sandblasted design on peghead, no body binding, bound fingerboard (earliest with red bean fingerboard)
Introduced as **No. 65: 1929**
Renamed **No. 66:** birch body, mahogany neck, chrome-plated hardware: **1932**
Discontinued, replaced by No. 60 (see following): **mid 1933**

No. 66B: bound top and back, otherwise same as No. 66: **1932–33**

No. 60: similar to No. 66-B but with large *D* in center of back, bound red bean fingerboard: **mid 1933–1936**

No. 85/86/Professional: ribbon-grain Tabasco mahogany body, engraved coverplate, fleur-de-lis on handrest, triple-bound top and back, mahogany neck, bound "Cardinal wood" fingerboard, roundneck or squareneck
Introduced as **No. 85: 1929**
Renamed **No. 86:** rosewood fingerboard, engraved tuner buttons, celluloid peghead inlay, chrome-plated hardware, 2-tone reddish brown finish: **1932**
Discontinued: **by mid 1934**

No. 125/De Luxe: 5-ply black walnut construction with 4-way matched burl, *Dobro De Lux* engraved on handrest, triple-bound top and back with black line on side of binding, black walnut neck, roundneck or squareneck, triple-bound ebony fingerboard, celluloid inlaid logo, nickel-plated hardware, natural finish
Introduced: **1929**
Discontinued: **by mid 1934**

CUSTOM WALNUT MODELS

Custom walnut-body Dobros with gold-plated hardware were introduced at a trade show in 1929. The original trade show examples have serial numbers below 2000.

No. 106/100: black walnut body, 2-piece book-matched back, engraved coverplate, triple-bound top and back, walnut neck, roundneck or square-neck, bound ebony fingerboard, diamond-and-arrows fingerboard inlay, celluloid inlaid logo, chrome-plated hardware
Introduced as **No. 106: 1930**
Renamed **No. 100: mid 1933**
No engraving on coverplate: **by 1936**
Discontinued: **1937**

No. 100: tenor: **1932**

No. 156/150: black walnut body with 2-piece back (some with 4-piece back), engraved coverplate, triple-bound top and back, walnut neck, roundneck or squareneck, bound ebony fingerboard, diamond-and-arrows fingerboard inlay, engraved pearl logo, engraved gold-plated hardware
Introduced: **1930**
Discontinued: **by mid 1934**

No. 206: spruce top, black walnut back and sides with 4-piece back, engraved coverplate, triple-bound top and back, gold-sparkle top border, walnut neck, roundneck or squareneck, bound ebony fingerboard, diamond-and-arrows fingerboard inlay, engraved pearl logo, some with gold-sparkle border around peghead, engraved gold-plated hardware, spruce top, engraved gold-plated hardware
Introduced: **1930**
Discontinued: **by mid 1934**

No. 36: magnolia body, no binding, mahogany neck, roundneck only, macawood (macacauba) fingerboard, silver-painted hardware (some with plated hardware), black lacquer finish
Introduced: **1932**
Discontinued: **by mid 1934**

No. 76: poplar or birch body, ivoroid bound top and back, bound ebony fingerboard, pearl dot inlay, 12 frets clear of body, inlaid celluloid peghead logo, 2-tone reddish brown finish
Available: **1932–33**
Model number reintroduced on a standard guitar model in Regal-made series (see following)

No. 75: tenor version of No. 76
Introduced: **by 1932**
Discontinued: **1934**

No. 175: referred to as **Special De Luxe** model, spruce top, nickel-plated metal parts
Introduced: **1932**
Discontinued: **by mid 1934**

"Cyclops" No. 27: single screen hole in body at end of fingerboard, no binding, roundneck or squareneck, some squarenecks with flush frets, nickel-plated hardware, some with "silver high-lighted" 2-toned Duco finish, some with brown finish
Available: **mid 1932–mid 1933**
Model number continues in California-made series and in Regal-made series with standard double-screen-holes (see following)

"Cyclops" No. 45: single screen hole in body at end of fingerboard, bound top, back and neck, nickel-plated hardware, rosewood-grain paint finish
Available: **mid 1932–mid 1933**
Model number continues in California-made series and in Regal-made series with different specs (see following)

"Cyclops" No. 60: single screen hole in body at end of fingerboard, sandblasted French scroll design on top, sides and back, bound top and back, bound fingerboard, chrome-plated hardware, ebony 2-tone finish
Variations: some with 1/2"-thick top, some with black finish
Available: **mid 1932–mid 1933**
Model number continues in California-made series and in Regal-made series with slightly different specs (see following)

"Double-Cyclops": 2 screen holes joined together, some with bound top and fingerboard (no back binding), some with no binding anywhere, some (sold through Montgomery Ward) with poinsettia coverplate
Available: **mid 1933**

No. 19/Angelus: birch body, *f*-holes, 12 large round holes in coverplate, some with binding, some with painted top and back edges to simulate binding, 12 or 14 frets clear of body, slotted peghead, some with *Angelus* on peghead, 2-tone walnut finish
Introduced (also made by Regal): **mid 1933**

California production discontinued: **1937**
Model 19 continues in Regal-made series (see following)

No. 27G: unspecified hardwood body (birch, mahogany or maple), no holes in top at end of fingerboard, bound top, unbound back, unbound fingerboard, dot inlay
Introduced (also made by Regal as No. 27): **mid 1933**
California production discontinued: **1937**
Model 27 continues in Regal-made series (see following)

No. 37G: mahogany body, some with no holes in top near fingerboard, bound top and back, bound fingerboard, dot inlay
Introduced (also made by Regal as No. 37): **mid 1933**
Variation: poplar body, no holes in top at end of fingerboard, bound top, unbound back and fingerboard, square neck with 12 or 14 frets clear of body, Regal-type fingerboard with no room at end for another fret, slotted peghead with Regal-type routed slots, double-sunburst top finish (sunburst above and below resonator), teardrop sunburst pattern on back, sunburst peghead finish: **1937**
California production discontinued: **1937**
Model 37 continues in Regal-made series (see following)

No. 45G: mahogany body, spruce top, dot inlay
Introduced (also made by Regal as No. 45): **mid 1933**
California production discontinued: **1937**
Model 45 continues in Regal-made series (see following)

Dobro Jr.: budget flat top model (non-resonator), trapeze tailpiece, 14 frets clear of body, sunburst finish
Introduced: **by 1934**
Discontinued: **by 1937**

REGAL-MADE WOODBODY MODELS

Regal-Dobros may have 12 or 14 frets clear of body, roundneck or squareneck, slotted or solid peghead, Regal or Dobro decal logo.

Regal No. 27: birch, mahogany or maple body, no holes in top at end of fingerboard, bound top, 2-tone walnut finish

Introduced (also produced in California-made series): **mid 1933**
Specs change to those of Regal No. 25, 3-segment *f*-holes in upper bouts (see following): **1939**
Earlier No. 27 specs continue on Regal No. 32 (see following)
Discontinued: **1942**

No. 27 1/2: tenor, similar specs to Regal No. 27: **mid 1933–37**

Regal No. 37: mahogany body, bound top and back, some with bound fingerboard
Available (also produced in California-made series): **mid 1933–37**

No. 37 1/2: tenor, similar specs to Regal No. 37: **mid 1933–37**

Regal No. 45: spruce top, mahogany back and sides, 4-ply top binding, single-bound back, unbound ebonized (black stain) fingerboard
Available (also produced in California-made series): **mid 1933–37**

No. 45 1/2: tenor, similar specs to Regal No. 45: **mid 1933–37**

Angelus: birch body, 3-segment *f*-holes in upper bouts, 12 large round holes in coverplate, slotted peghead, painted top and back edges to simulate binding, 12 frets clear of body, roundneck or squareneck, some with *Angelus* on peghead, dull walnut finish (later with natural finish or orange-to-brown sunburst finish
Available (also available in California-made series): **mid 1933–36**

Regal No. 55: spruce top, mahogany back and sides, arched back, bound top and back, roundneck or squareneck, fancy inlay, chrome-plated hardware
Available: **mid 1933–34**

No. 6: birch body, 3-segment *f*-holes in upper bouts, mandolin-size resonator, moon-and-stars or 12-diamond pattern coverplate, trapeze tailpiece, 4 dot inlays, roundneck, squareneck or tenor neck, 2-tone shaded finish
Available: **1937–41**

DOBRO

No. 25: 3-segment *f*-holes in upper bouts, bound top and back, 14 frets clear of body, roundneck or squareneck, slotted peghead, 2-tone walnut finish
Available: **1937–38**

Tenor No. 25 1/2: specs similar to No. 25 guitar: **late 1930s**

Unknown Regal model: 15 1/2" wide, birch body, archtop, bound top and back, 3-segment *f*-holes, various coverplates (moon-and-stars, poinsettia or standard Dobro style), ebonized (black stain) fingerboard, 4 dot inlays, 13 frets clear of body, nickel-plated hardware, sunburst finish
Available: **1938–39**

No. 5: 3-segment *f*-holes in upper bouts, mandolin-size resonator, 12 diamond-shaped holes in coverplate, plate tailpiece, roundneck, 4 dot inlays, blond finish
Available: **1939–41**

No. 32: same as Regal No. 27, body, roundneck, squareneck or tenor available, mahogany-grain paint finish
Available: **1939–41**

No model number: maple body, some with spruce top, 3-segment *f*-holes in upper bouts, black binding on top and back, 12 frets clear of body, ebonized (black-stain) fingerboard, 4 dot inlays, natural finish
Available: **1941**

DOBRO/REGAL "SILVER GUITAR" SERIES

All have 5-segment *f*-holes, 4 groups of 8 semi-rectangular holes in coverplate, 3 cutouts in tailpiece, 14 frets clear of body, solid peghead, Hawaiian setup (H) optional. Models were made by Dobro in California and by Regal in Chicago (from parts supplied by Dobro).

Leader (14M or 14H): nickel-plated brass body, engraved borders, roundneck or squareneck, rosewood fingerboard, solid peghead, pearl logo
Available: **1934–35**

Professional (15M or 15H): engraved "German silver" (nickel alloy) body, diagonal banner and

Dobro logo across back, roundneck or squareneck, solid peghead, white pearloid peghead veneer
Available: **1934–35**

Artist (16M or 16H): engraved German silver (nickel alloy) body, roundneck or squareneck, ebony fingerboard, floral or diamond inlay, more engraving than No. 15, back engraved with *Dobro* or (later) *Regal*, solid peghead
Available: **1934–35**

Unknown Regal model: similar to Regal No. 32 metalbody, tortoise-grain plastic pickguard, gold sparkle peghead veneer (some with rhinestones inlaid), solid peghead, Dobro logo, yellow-to-brown sunburst finish
Available: **1934–35**

OTHER DOBRO/REGAL METALBODY MODELS

All have "violin" or "fiddle" edges (curled edge with top extending over sides), Dobro or Regal logo. Models were made by Dobro in California and by Regal in Chicago (from parts supplied by Dobro) until 1937, after which all were produced by Regal. Models were originally catalogued with round "window" soundholes (with a cross in the middle) in upper bouts. After production moved exclusively to Regal, some examples have 5-segment *f*-holes in upper bouts.

No. 32/35: sheet metal body, 14 frets clear of body, solid peghead, yellowish brown sunburst paint finish
Introduced as **No. 32: 1935**
Silver and black 2-tone finish: **by 1937**
Listed as **No. 35: 1939**
Discontinued: **1942**

No. 46: all-aluminum Dobro-lite or Luma-lite body, 14 frets clear of body, slotted peghead, silver finish with gold highlights
Introduced as **No. 46: 1935**
Mahogany-grain or maple-grain paint finish: **by 1937**
Listed as **No. 47: 1939**
Discontinued: **1942**

No. 62: nickel-plated brass body, Spanish dancer in garden etched on back, solid peghead
Introduced as **No. 62: 1935**

Rosewood fingerboard specified: **by 1937**
Listed as **No. 65: 1939**
Discontinued: **1942**

TENORTROPES

Tenortropes have a circular body with a tenor guitar
neck.
Tenor guitars with standard guitar body are listed with
their corresponding guitar models.

Tenortrope No. 45/50: specs similar to No. 55
guitar of same period, mahogany finish
Introduced as **No. 45** or **No. A45: 1929**
Listed as **No. 50: 1932**
Discontinued: **1934**

Tenortrope No. 60/75/Professional: specs
similar to No. 65 guitar
Introduced as **No. 60: 1929**
Listed as **No. 75: 1932**
Discontinued: **1934**

Tenortrope No. 75/100/De Luxe: specs simi-
lar to No. 125 guitar of same period,
Introduced as **No. 75: 1929**
Listed as **No. 100** (No. 75 listed with specs formerly
assigned to No. 60): **1932**
Discontinued: **1934**

MANDOLINS

Mandolin No. 5: unspecified top and back, magno-
lia sides, mahogany neck, bound 19-fret red bean
fingerboard, chrome-plated hardware, 2-tone finish
Available: **1929–33**

Mandolin No. 7: birch top and back, magnolia
sides, sandblasted French scroll pattern, engraved
coverplate, mahogany neck, bound 24-fret rosewood fingerboard, chrome-plated hardware
Available: **1929–33**

Mandolin No. 10: walnut body, triple-bound top
and back, walnut neck, walnut neck, bound 24-fret
ebony fingerboard, engraved coverplate and tailpiece
Available: **1929–33**

Mandolin No. 37M: specs similar to No. 37G
guitar, mahogany body (see preceding)
Available: **1934–37**

Mandolin No. 45M: specs similar to No. 45 gui-
tar, spruce top (see preceding)
Available: **1934–37**

Mandolin No. 60/210: specs similar to No. 60
guitar, sandblasted French scroll design (see pre-
ceding)
Introduced: **1934**
Listed as **No. 210: 1939**
Discontinued: **1942**

Mandolin No. 250: specs similar to Regal No. 25
guitar, *f*-holes, 2-tone finish
Available: **1934–38**

Mandolin No. 270: mahogany-grain paint finish
Introduced: **1934**
f-holes (same specs as earlier mandolin No. 250;
specs for No. 270 assigned to mandolin No. 320):
1939
Discontinued: **1942**

Mandolin No. 370: specs similar to Regal No. 37
guitar, mahogany body (see preceding)
Available: **1934–37**

Mandolin No. 450: specs similar to Regal No.
45, spruce top (see preceding)
Available: **1934–37**

Mandolin No. 320: specs similar to No. 32 gui-
tar (specs previously assigned on mandolin No.
270, mahogany-grain paint finish)
Available: **1939-41**

Mandolin No. 210: ebonized fingerboard, 2-tone
shaded finish, moon-and-stars coverplate
Available: **1939-41**

UKULELES

Uke No. 30: 1 screenhole (cyclops style), no binding
Available: **1931–33**

Uke No. 40: 1 screenhole (cyclops style), bound
top and back
Available: **1931–33**

Uke No. 15: mahogany body and neck, 2 screen-

holes, coverplate with 4 hole clusters, rosewood fingerboard
Introduced, made by Dobro in California and Regal in Chicago: **1934**
Produced in Chicago only: **1937**
Unspecified wood, mahogany finish: **1938**
Discontinued: **1942**

Regal ukulele (no model number): unspecified body, f-holes in upper bout, moon-and-stars coverplate, cone not specified as genuine Dobro, mahogany neck, rosewood fingerboard, sold through Montgomery Ward
Available: **1936–37**

ELECTRICS

All-Electric: standard Style 37 body and neck (all-mahogany body, bound top and back, bound fingerboard), slant-mounted pickup with metal bar polepiece, horseshoe magnet pickup mounted on aluminum bracket that spans soundwell (first 3 or 4 examples with no visible evidence of pickup, no control knob, pickup rests on back of guitar, 2 posts from pickup to bridge functioning as bridge support), no resonator cone, 1 control knob on lower treble bout near tailpiece, bound top and back, bound fingerboard, no holes in coverplate, *Dobro* and lightning bolts etched on coverplate diagonally under strings, jack on side or on top, most with square neck, 12 frets clear of body
Available: **mid-to-late 1933**
Some assembled from parts, straight-mounted pickup, 14-fret roundneck: **c. 1936–37**

Electric resonator model: similar to All-Electric except for inclusion of a resonator cone, straight-mounted pickup sits on back of guitar, 2 posts from pickup through cone to bridge functioning as bridge support, 12 frets clear of body, round neck
Available: **early-to-mid 1934**

No. 1 Hawaiian Guitar: cast aluminum body, large circular lower body with 4 "panels" (indented sections) on top, no upper f-holes, split-blade pickup in oblong housing, no knobs on top, large Dobro lyre logo between pickup and neck, 20-fret ebony fingerboard, dot inlay, 2 cutouts in peghead, 6 or 7 strings
Introduced: **1935**

2 knurled pickup height-adjustment screws, 1 volume knob (tone knob added on later examples), elongated f-holes next to neck (lyre logo and f-holes are part of casting pattern), some with 26-fret fingerboard extending over lyre logo: **c. 1936**
Discontinued: **1938**

No. 2/Electric Standard/Spanish Electric: body and neck made by Regal, 15 1/2" wide, spruce top, laminated maple back and sides, 3-segment f-holes, blade pickup in oblong housing, pickup stamped *Pat. Appl'd.,* pickup cover section points toward bridge, pickup in bridge position, volume control and jack on top next to tailpiece (some late examples of this version have jack on rim), trapeze tailpiece, single-bound top, unbound back, dovetail neck joint, bound rosewood fingerboard, multiple dots-and-diamonds inlay, rosewood peghead veneer, Harmony-made tuners with metal "butter-bean" buttons, block-letter logo across peghead
Introduced as **Standard Guitar: early 1935**
Tone control added, jack on rim on treble side: **late 1935**
Extended pickup mounting "ears" with 2 knobs to adjust pickup height, *Pat. Pending* stamped on pickup coil housing, pickguard cut out to accommodate pickup, knobs on opposite sides, dot inlay with 3 dots at 7th and 9th frets, Harmony Tone-Rite tuners with hexagonal baseplates and pentagonal metal buttons: **early 1936**
Pickup cover section points toward neck, volume and tone knobs on lower treble bout: **early to mid 1936**
Volume and tone knobs on upper bass bout, bound tortoiseshell celluloid pickguard with engraved flower, pickguard stops short of pickup, screw-on jack on lower bass bout: **mid 1936**
Ebonoid pickguard (black celluloid), large pearl block inlay, larger peghead with angled corners, ebonoid peghead veneer with binding simulated by beveled edge, engraved peghead logo: **late 1936**
Rectangular pickup bolted to saddle and suspended through top, volume and tone knobs on lower treble bout, shorter ebonoid pickguard, triple-bound top, non-angled corners on peghead, open-back Kluson tuners with metal buttons: **mid 1937**
Renamed **Spanish Electric Guitar**, body made by Kay, no soundholes, blade pickup in bridge position, bound pickguard, 7-ply neck by National-Dobro,

bolt-on neck tenon (similar to woodbody Dobro neck), standard dot inlay: **late 1937**
Last made (catalogued into 1940 but all known examples have a B-prefix serial number): **1937**

Woodbody Hawaiian: square-end body, smooth graduation to neck, knobs on opposite sides, rectangular metal pickup cover extends under knobs, screw-on jack on bass side, 23" scale, ebonoid (black celluloid) fingerboard and peghead veneer, parallelogram markers with Roman numerals, block-letter logo reads upside down to player, mahogany stain finish
Available: **1937–41**

Electric Mandolin: standard woodbody mandolin construction, arched top, flat back, blade pickup with oblong housing
Available: **1935–41**

Amplifier: cabinet made by Bulwin (a Los Angeles case company), approx. 18" wide, 18" high, 18" deep, black Keratol (vinyl) covering, metal bumpers on all corners, round leather handle with ring ends, round speaker opening approx. 9" in diameter, grille similar to Dobro guitar coverplate, stamped logo just below center of coverplate, 8" Lansing speaker, 5 tubes, 2 inputs, volume control
Introduced: **mid-to-late 1933**
18" wide, 10" high, 8" deep, round leather handle with ball ends, oval wood veneer grille approx. 14" by 7" with cutout *Dobro* and lyre design, internal specs unavailable, probably with 2 6" speakers: **1934**
Discontinued: **late 1934**

COMMENTS

California-made woodbody Dobros are the models most highly regarded by players and collectors, although several of the best-known musicians play Regal-made models. Squareneck models bring more than roundnecks.
Regal woodbody models with *f*-holes are generally not highly regarded by players or collectors.
Regal metalbody models are not considered by players to be as good as National metalbody models, but because of their rarity and ornamentation, they do have some appeal to collectors.
The All-Electric is one of the earliest electric guitars and is thus of some historic interest. All electric Dobros are of interest primarily to collectors for historic reasons rather than utility.

1962–70

SECTION ORGANIZATION

DB Original
Dobro, Inc. (Gardena)
Mosrite
Mobro
Replica 66
Hound Dog
Dopera's Original

DB ORIGINAL

Ed and Rudy Dopyera made some guitars in the 1950s under the DB Original Brand. The 1950s logo decal is a blue and yellow shield with stars, the letters *D* and *B*, and a diagonal banner with *Original*.
They began making resonator guitars on a regular basis in El Monte, CA, in 1962, under the DB Original brand, distributed by Standel. Production is estimated at 31 or 32 per month. Serial numbers begin with 001.

Specs include: ash, walnut or maple body, 14 frets clear of body, roundneck or squareneck, dot inlay, dots off-center to the treble side on frets 3 and 9, dot off-center to the bass side on fret 7.
In addition to basic models, a model with mahogany finish was sold as the Uncle Josh Model, and a model with dark shaded mahogany finish, anodized coverplate and dots in the center of the fingerboard was sold as the Deacon Brumfield Model.
The 1960s DB Original logo decal is a shield with *Original* running vertically between the letters *D* and *B*.

DOBRO, INC. (GARDENA)

Dobro, Inc., moved production to Gardena, CA, in January 1965 with the specs that would be associated with the Mosrite period of ownership (see following). Dobro was sold to Mosrite in 1966.

MOSRITE

Semie Moseley of Mosrite (see Mosrite section) acquired the Dobro name in 1966. Dobros pictured in a 1966 flier may not have been made until 1967 (Mosrite/Dobro #DB0001 is documented as having been ordered in January 1967 and received in May 1967). Production ceased in 1969 when Moseley went into bankruptcy. Moseley later made resonator guitars under the Mosrite and Mobro brands (see following).

An estimated 100–150 early examples were made from old parts in Gardena, and these may have a serial number on the end of the peghead. Later examples made at the Mosrite facility in Bakersfield, CA, have a number on the fingerboard near the body.

Custom features available include: engraved coverplate, gold or silver plating, custom fingerboard inlay, custom finish

MOSRITE/DOBRO SPECS

Note: These specs also apply to the 1965 Dobros made by Dobro, Inc., in Gardena, CA (see preceding).

Soundholes: All have upper bout soundholes filled with a seive-like, diamond-hole plate (replacing the screen holes in prewar Dobros), neck adjustable by tilt screw, trapeze tailpiece, most with exposed bridge, some high-nut models with aluminum nut

Resonators: Mosrite/Dobro model names begin with a C or D, which designates the resonator style:

D resonator: traditional Dobro style cone, traditional Dobro style coverplate with 4 fan-pattern groupings of holes but with 3 rows of holes (plus single hole) in each grouping (prewar Dobro plates have 2 rows of holes plus single hole in each grouping), coverplate covers bridge, spider type bridge support, screw behind bridge rather than through bridge, middle legs of spider bent to compensate for offset bridge, pressed cone

C resonator: inverted cone with biscuit, coverplate with 6 groupings of 4 rectangular holes, exposed bridge, ribs on cone

Logo: metal logo plate

MOSRITE MODELS

The following models were introduced in 1965 by Dobro, Inc., prior to Mosrite's acquisition of the Dobro brand (see preceding).

D-50/The Richmond: 14 3/4" wide, 3 5/16" deep, D resonator and coverplate, ribbon-grained African mahogany or curly maple body, traditional Dobro-style coverplate, double-bound top, bound back, 24 5/8" scale, unbound rosewood fingerboard, 20 frets
Available: **1965–69**

D-50E: pickup with adjustable polepieces, 2 knobs: **1965–69**

D-50S/The Uncle Josh: squareneck, bound fingerboard, inlaid frets, high bone nut, top tuners
Introduced: **1965**
Bound fingerboard specified on roundneck models, metal tuner buttons specified, unbound fingerboard pictured on squareneck: **1968**
Last produced: **1969**

D-50SE/The Uncle Josh Electric: same as D-50S but with adjustable-pole pickup, 2 knobs: **1965–69**

C-60/The Avalon: C resonator and coverplate, single-bound top and back, rosewood fingerboard, dot inlay, deep candy apple red or dark metallic blue finish
Available: **1965–67**

C-60E: adjustable-pole pickup, 2 knobs: **1965–67**

D-40/The Texarkana: D resonator and coverplate, unbound fingerboard, dot inlay, deep candy apple red, dark metallic blue, or rich mahogany sunburst finish
Available: **1965–67**

D-40E/The Texarkana Electric: adjustable-pole pickup, 2 knobs: **1965–67**

D-40S/The Blue Grass: squareneck, bound fingerboard, bone nut, inlaid frets, top tuners
Available: **1965–67**

D-40SE/The Blue Grass Electric: adjustable-pole pickup, 2 knobs: **1965–67**

C-3/The Monterey: 3/4 size, 14 1/4" wide, mahogany back and sides, maple top, C resonator and coverplate, double-bound top, single-bound back, 23 1/4" scale, unbound rosewood fingerboard, dot inlay
Available: **1965–69**

C-3E/The Monterey Electric: adjustable-pole pickup, 2 knobs: **1965–69**

D-100/The Californian: double cutaway, 1 7/8" deep, D resonator and coverplate 2 pickups, 2 knobs and 1 switch, 24 1/2" scale, bound fingerboard, 22 frets, metal tuner buttons
Available: **1965–69**

D-100-12/Californian 12-string: slotted peghead: **1965–69**

D-100B, Californian Bass: solid peghead: **1967–69**

C-65/The Plainsman: narrow upper bouts, ribbon grained African mahogany body, maple body, or mahogany back and sides with maple top, D resonator and coverplate, double-bound top, single-bound back, rosewood fingerboard, dot inlay
Available: **1966–67**

C-65E/The Plainsman Electric: adjustable-pole pickup, 2 knobs: **1966–67**

D-12/The Columbia: 12-string, ribbon grained African mahogany or curly maple body, D resonator and coverplate, unbound rosewood fingerboard, dot inlay, slotted peghead, natural finish
Available: **1966–67**

D-12E/The Columbia Electric: adjustable-pole pickup, 2 knobs: **1966–67**

D-12S/The Lexington: squareneck, bound fingerboard, high bone nut, inlaid frets, top tuners: **1966–67**

D-12SE/The Lexington Electric: adjustable-pole pickup, 2 knobs: **1966–67**

D-8/The Memphis: 5-string banjo neck, 3/4 body size, maple top, mahogany back and sides, C resonator and coverplate, optional pickup, single-bound top and back, 26" scale, unbound rosewood fingerboard, 22 frets
Available: **1968–69**

MOBRO

Mosrite lost rights to the Dobro name by 1970. After bankruptcy, a reorganized Mosrite offered resonator models under the Mosrite and Mobro brands. The following numbers and descriptions are from a 1975 catalog from Pacific Music Supply Co., Mosrite's exclusive distributor.

Mobro Standard Guitar (21405): traditional Dobro-style coverplate, exposed bridge, optional humbucking pickup (**21405-E**), bound fingerboard, dot inlay, solid peghead, natural or cherry finish
Available: **1975**

Mobro Steel Guitar (21404): slotted peghead, top tuners, optional humbucking pickup (**21404-E**)
Available: **1975**

REPLICA 66

After selling the Dobro name to Mosrite in 1966, Ed and Rudy Dopyera made resonator guitars in Gardena, CA, under the Replica 66 brand.
Specs include thick-waisted body, plastic coverplate with hole pattern reversed (fan opens to the center of the plate rather than to the outside), some with plastic fingerboard, some with fiberglass body.
The three basic models are delineated by unbound body of unspecified wood, bound mahogany body and bound mahogany body with blond top.

HOUND DOG

Hound Dog was the brand name of Original Musical Instruments, Inc., formed by the Dopyeras and others in Gardena in 1967. The Hound Dog brand also appeared in the mid 1970s on a line of Japanese flat top, non-resonator guitars and in the 1990s in the regular OMI line.

Hound Dog Logo
Hound dog's face looking at 3/4 angle, guitar neck bent over dog's head: **1967**
Hound dog looking straight ahead, *Original Hound Dog* over dog's head: **1968–71**
Hound dog looking straight ahead, *Original Hound Dog* over dog's head ("Original" not underlined): **1990s**

DOPERA'S ORIGINAL

The Original Musical Instruments company, owned by the Dopyeras, reacquired rights to the Dobro name in 1970 but continued to use the Hound Dog brand and also introduced the Dopera's Original brand on a metalbody guitar (made from a prewar National Triolian die) with a spider bridge and standard Dobro resonator.

Some models continue under 60 Classic and DW60 designation (see preceding)

60A: roundneck (**60A**) or squareneck (**60A-S**), rosewood fingerboard, dot inlay, slotted peghead, brass hardware, amber sunburst finish: **1981–95** (amber finish available after 1995 on 60 Classic, see preceding)

60B: roundneck version of 60BS: **1985–95**

60B-S: mahogany body, bound top and back, engraved coverplate, squareneck, ebony fingerboard and peghead veneer, pearl diamond inlay, slotted peghead, black finish: **1981–95**

60CL: cyclops model (see following)

60G: figured maple body, roundneck or squareneck (**60G-S**), slotted peghead, gold-plated hardware: **1986**

60M/62: mahogany body, engraved coverplate, roundneck or squareneck (**60M-S**) bound ebony fingerboard, floral inlay, pearl logo, bound slotted peghead, natural mahogany finish, also listed as **Model 62: 1981–95**

60PH-S: purple-heart body, lyre on coverplate, squareneck, ebony fingerboard, pearl inlay, pearl peghead inlay: **1983–late 1980s**

60W: roundneck version of 60W-S: **1987–95**

60WC: pointed cutaway, screen holes, 12 frets clear of body, ebony fingerboard, black chrome hardware, black binding, roundneck, white finish: **1993–96**

60W-S/64: walnut body, engraved coverplate with lyre pattern, bound top and back, squareneck, bound ebony fingerboard, tree-of-life inlay, abalone logo, ebony peghead veneer, slotted peghead, bound peghead, also listed as **Model 64: early 1980s–95**

60ZSC: pointed cutaway, lattice-pattern holes in upper bouts (similar to holes in National tri-cones), poinsettia coverplate, 12 frets clear of body, ebony fingerboard, abalone seagull inlay, black binding, roundneck, dark sunburst finish, solid peghead: **1993–96**

PS60MG: "pinstriped," diagonally striped panels of mahogany and maple, roundneck or squareneck: **1992–96**

PS60WL: "pinstriped," diagonally striped panels of walnut and maple, roundneck or squareneck: **1992–96**

S60C Curly Maple Special: solid curly maple body and neck, engraved coverplate, triple bound top, back and fingerboard, roundneck or squareneck, ebony fingerboard, pearl diamond inlay: **1994–95**

S60K Koa Special: solid koa body, engraved coverplate and tailpiece, triple bound top and back, mahogany neck, roundneck or squareneck, triple-bound ebony fingerboard, tree-of-life inlay, triple-bound peghead, pearloid peghead veneer: **1994–95**

S60M Mahogany Special: solid mahogany body, engraved coverplate, triple-bound top and back, roundneck or squareneck, triple-bound rosewood fingerboard, dot inlay, triple-bound peghead: **1994–95**

S60R Rosewood Special: solid rosewood back and sides, solid spruce top, engraved coverplate, triple bound top and back, mahogany neck, roundneck or squareneck, triple-bound ebony fingerboard, lyre inlay, bound peghead, rosewood peghead veneer: **1994–95**

ZS60MG: zebra striped, wide diagonal alternating mahogany stripes on front and back, roundneck or squareneck, slotted peghead: **1992–96**

ZS60WL: zebra striped, wide diagonal alternating walnut and maple stripes, roundneck or squareneck, slotted peghead: **1992–96**

C-60: cyclops model, 1 screenhole, unbound top, squareneck, dark walnut sunburst finish
Introduced: **1985**
Referred to as **60C: 1989**
Roundneck (**C-60**) or squareneck (**C-60S**): **1990**
Discontinued: **1996**

F-60/"F" Hole Classic: laminated maple body, upper-bout *f*-holes holes, bound top and back, rosewood fingerboard, dot inlay, slotted peghead, roundneck (**F-60**) or squareneck (**F-60S**), brown finish
Introduced: **by 1986**
Dark burst finish optional, roundneck (**F-60D**) or squareneck (**F-60DS**): **1988**
Renamed **"F" Hole Classic**, roundneck or squareneck, vintageburst, blackburst or darkburst finish: **1994**
No production: **1997**

Production resumed: **1998**
Still in production

Model 62: see 60M, preceding

Model 63: 8-string, trapeze tailpiece, bound top and back, squareneck, brown sunburst finish
Available: **1973–1996**

Model 64: see 60W-S, preceding

Model 66: sandblasted design on top and back similar to prewar Model 65 (see 1928–41 section), roundneck, slotted peghead, sunburst finish
66: roundneck, slotted peghead
66-S: squareneck, slotted peghead
P66: roundneck, solid peghead
P66-S: squareneck, solid peghead
Available: **1972–95**

Model 12/Ye Olde Wooden: 12-string version of Model 60, trapeze tailpiece, roundneck, slotted peghead, brown sunburst finish
Introduced as variation of **Ye Olde Wooden DOBRO: 1972**
Named **Model 12: 1973**
Discontinued: **1994**

Model 10: 10-string version of Model 60, trapeze tailpiece, bound top, squareneck, solid peghead, brown sunburst finish
Available: **1973–93**

Model 114/Blues Special: roundneck, solid peghead, natural top finish, 3-tone sunburst finish back, sides and peghead, solid peghead, optional acoustic pickup (**114A**) or acoustic/magnetic pickup (**114B**)
Introduced: **1973**
Referred to as **Blues Special: late 1970s**
Discontinued: **by 1985**
Reintroduced, ƒ-holes, roundneck (**114**) or squareneck (**114S**), slotted peghead, dark sunburst finish: **1990**
Discontinued: **1995**

114C: pointed cutaway, ƒ-holes, natural finish, black binding on top and back, slotted peghead:
by 1993–95

Model 27: poinsettia coverplate, no holes in top at end of neck, no binding, squareneck only, slotted peghead or solid peghead, brown sunburst finish
Available: **1976–94**

P27: solid peghead: **1970s–91**

27 Deluxe: figured maple top, poinsettia coverplate, parallelogram soundwell holes, no holes in top at end of neck, squareneck, bound ebony fingerboard, lyre inlay, bound solid peghead, engraved pearl logo, dark stain finish
Available: **1995–96**

Model 45-S: mahogany back and sides, spruce top, mahogany neck, triple-bound body, ebony fingerboard, chrome-plated hardware, squareneck only, slotted peghead
Available: **1987–92**

Model 50: spruce top, walnut back and sides, roundneck or squareneck, ebony fingerboard, lyre inlay, slotted peghead
Available: **1992**

Woodbody 90 (WB90)/14-fret: ƒ-holes, 9 1/2" resonator cone with biscuit bridge, seive-hole coverplate, roundneck or squareneck, 14 frets clear of body, slotted peghead, satin (non-gloss) sunburst finish on unbound model, gloss sunburst finish available with white binding
Introduced as **14-fret: 1990**
Discontinued: **1997**

90S/Soft Cutaway: maple body, rounded cutaway, small holes in upper bouts in diamond pattern, diamond-hole coverplate, no binding, roundneck, 9 1/2" cone, slotted peghead, natural finish: **1993–96**

Hula Blues: ƒ-holes, 9 1/2" resonator cone with biscuit bridge, seive-hole coverplate with holes in diamond pattern, no binding, roundneck or squareneck, 12 frets clear of body, slotted peghead, stenciled palm tree scenes, blue, green or brown/yellow 2-tone finish
Introduced: **1987**
Black/yellow or maple/peach 2-tone finish: **1995**
No production: **1997**
Production resumed: **1998**
Still in production

Soft Cutaway: see 90 Woodbody, preceding

Zephyr: flamed maple body, available with solid or laminated body, lattice-pattern soundholes in upper bout (similar to National tricone style), poinsettia coverplate, ebony fingerboard, dot inlay, pearl *Dobro* inlaid at 12th fret, woodbody, roundneck (**Zephyr**) or squareneck (**Zephyr-S**), solid peghead
Available: **1987–94**

Zephyr Deluxe: flamed maple body, solid top, maple neck, 12 frets clear of body, ebony fingerboard, *D-O-B-R-O* inlay: **1990**

Hound Dog 101: Dobro cone with spider resonator, no soundwell, no binding, roundneck or squareneck (**Hound Dog 101-S**), maple fingerboard, slotted peghead, light sunburst finish
Available: **1990–94**

33 Wood: woodbody version of Model 33 (see Metalbody Models, following), upper bout *f*-holes, 10 1/2" resonator cone with biscuit bridge, radiused fingerboard
Available: **1996**

SIGNATURE MODELS

Jerry Douglas: squareneck, internal soundposts and tonebars, mahogany body and neck, 25" scale, bound rosewood fingerboard, engraved pearl logo, limited run of 200 with signature on peghead, also available without signature, natural finish
Introduced: **1995**
Production suspended: **1997**
Production resumed: **1998**
Still in production

Al Perkins: squareneck, *f*-holes, poinsettia coverplate, engraved palmrest, bound fingerboard, 24 1/2" scale, single-dot inlay at frets 5, 7, 9, 12 and 17, engraved pearl logo, limited run of 200 with signature on peghead, also available without signature, gold-plated hardware, dark brown finish
Introduced: **1995**
Production suspended: **1997**

Josh Graves: similar to Graves' 1930s No. 37 squareneck, mahogany body, no holes in top at end of fingerboard, 25" scale, solid peghead, limited run of 200 with signature on peghead, also available without signature, sunburst finish
Introduced: **1995**
Production suspended: **1997**

Pete "Oswald" Kirby: similar to Kirby's 1930s model, roundneck, parallelogram soundwell holes, no holes in top at end of fingerboard, V-neck, 24 1/2" scale, metal high-nut adapter, limited run of 200 with signature on peghead, also available without signature, sunburst finish
Introduced: **1995**
Production suspended: **1997**

Tom Swatzell: engraved coverplate, 24 1/2" scale, bound ebony fingerboard, diamond inlay, engraved pearl logo, limited run of 200 with signature on peghead, also available without signature, fireburst finish
Introduced: **1995**
Production suspended: **1997**

NON-RESONATOR WOODBODY MODELS

Kona: elongated acoustic guitar body, no resonator, round soundhole, dot inlay, transducer or magnetic pickup optional
Available: **1996**

Kahuna: Dobro guitar body shape, no resonator, 4 crescent-shaped soundholes, dot inlay, transducer or magnetic pickup optional
Available: **1996**

Troubadour: standard flat-top guitar body, similar shape to Gibson L-00, mahogany top, back and sides, round soundhole, no resonator, rectangular bridge, rosewood fingerboard, dot inlay, transducer or magnetic pickup optional
Available: **1996**

Spruce Troubadour: spruce top: **1996**

METALBODY MODELS

Model 20/The Deco: chrome-plated bell brass body, etched Art Deco figures, bound fingerboard, diamond inlay, bound peghead, etched pearl logo
Available: **1971–late 1970s**

Model 30: steel body, enamel paint finish in gold, blue or red
Available: **early 1970s**

Model 33: chrome-plated bell brass body, upper-bout *f*-holes, etched ornamentation on body, radiused fingerboard, dot inlay, solid peghead

33/90: Hawaiian Duolian, inverted cone with biscuit bridge, maple neck, roundneck or squareneck, rosewood fingerboard
Introduced: **1972**
Renamed **Model 90** (see following): **1973**

33D/Dobro: etched diamond pattern design on front, *D* on back
Introduced: **1971**
Floral design on front, script *D* on back, roundneck with 10 1/2" resonator cone with biscuit bridge (**33D**), roundneck with Dobro cone and spider bridge (**33D-1**) or squareneck with Dobro cone and spider bridge (**33D-S**): **by 1975**
Discontinued: **1987**
Reintroduced, etched lattice design on front, script *D* on back: **1995**
Discontinued: **1997**

33H/Hawaiian: etched Hawaiian scenes, roundneck with 10 1/2" resonator cone with biscuit bridge or standard Dobro cone with spider bridge (**33H**), roundneck with Dobro cone and spider bridge (**33H-1**) or squareneck with Dobro cone and spider bridge (**33H-S**)
Introduced: **by 1973**
Roundneck (**33H**) or squareneck(**33H-S**), both versions available with biscuit or spider bridge: **1990**
Discontinued: **1997**

33S/Sailboat: etched sailboat on back, roundneck: **1971–80s, 1994**

33 The Mesa: Southwestern etching design, roundneck, ebony fingerboard, dot inlay: **1996**

33 California Girl: women etched on top and back, roundneck, ebony fingerboard, dot inlay: **1996**

33 10-string: spider or biscuit resonator, special order only: **mid 1980s**

33 Painted/Model 88/33 Steel: steel body, paint finish
Introduced as **33 Painted: by 1986**

Discontinued: **by 1993**
Reintroduced as **Model 88**; optional spider bridge (**88-1**) or spider bridge with squareneck and flat fingerboard (**88S-1**): darkburst or yellowburst finish: **1995**
Renamed **33 Steel (DS33)**, amberburst and darkburst finish: **1995**
Discontinued: **1997**

33TP: triplate, 3 resonator cones under standard Dobro coverplate, roundneck (**33TP**) or squareneck (**33TP-S**): **1990**

Model 36/The Rose: chrome-plated bell brass body, upper-bout *f*-holes, engraved rose-pattern ornamentation, unbound radiused fingerboard, dot inlay, solid peghead, roundneck with 10 1/2" resonator cone and biscuit bridge (**36**), roundneck with Dobro cone and spider bridge (**36-1**) or squareneck with Dobro cone and spider bridge (**36-S**)
Introduced: **1970s**
Roundneck (**36**) or squareneck (**36-S**), both versions available with biscuit or spider bridge: **1990**
Discontinued: **1997**

36-12: 12-string, spider bridge, roundneck: **1970s–94**

36 10-string: spider or biscuit resonator: **by 1985**

36TP: triplate, 3 resonator cones under standard Dobro coverplate, roundneck (**36TP**) or squareneck (**36TP-S**), few if any made: **1990**

Model 75/The Lily of the Valley: chrome-plated bell brass body, engraved with lily of the valley pattern, maple neck, unbound ebony fingerboard and peghead veneer, pearl logo, pearl inlay, roundneck with 10 1/2" resonator cone and biscuit bridge (**75**), roundneck with Dobro cone and spider bridge (**75-1**) or squareneck with Dobro cone and spider bridge (**75-S**)
Introduced as **Custom Deluxe: by 1972**
Roundneck (**75**) or squareneck (**75-S**), both versions available with biscuit or spider bridge: **1990**
Discontinued: **1997**

75 10-string: spider or biscuit, special order only: **by 1985**

75TP: triplate, 3 resonator cones under standard Dobro coverplate, roundneck (**75TP**) or squareneck (**75TP-S**), few if any made: **1990**

Model 88: see 33 Painted, preceding

Model 90/Duolian/Bottleneck: chrome-plated
bell brass body, *f*-holes, etched Hawaiian scene, 9
1/2" resonator cone with biscuit bridge, moon-and-
stars coverplate hole pattern, roundneck or square-
neck,14 frets clear of body, flat fingerboard,
unbound fingerboard, dot inlay, slotted peghead
Introduced as **Model 33, Hawaiian Duolian: 1971**
Renamed **Model 90: 1972**
Renamed **Bottleneck Special: 1986**
Painted body: **1987**
Painted model listed as **Model 95** (see following);
Model 90 listed with plain chrome-plated body,
plain, etching or engraving optional: **1988**
Optional painted body: **1990**
Renamed **Bottleneck 90**, *Duolian* peghead decal: **1994**
Discontinued: **1997**

90 Deluxe: nickel-plated bell brass body, bound
fingerboard, diamond inlay, decal logo: **1996**

90 10-string: special order only: **by 1985**

Model 95: *f*-holes, 9 1/2" resonator cone with biscuit bridge, powder-coat (non-gloss finish)
Available: **1988–early 90s**

Model 1000/The Dobro Special: chrome-
plated bell brass body, 10 1/2" resonator cone with
biscuit bridge or Dobro cone with spider bridge,
floral engraving on top and sides, shield engraving
on back, ebony fingerboard and peghead veneer,
cloud inlay, bound peghead, etched pearl logo,
roundneck with biscuit bridge (**1000**), roundneck
with spider bridge (**1000-1**) or squareneck with spider bridge (**1000-2**)
Introduced as **Super Custom Deluxe: by 1972**
Roundneck (**1000**) or squareneck (**1000-S**), both
versions available with biscuit or spider bridge:
1990
Discontinued: **1997**

1000 10-string: special order only: **by 1985**

1000TP: triplate, 3 resonator cones under standard
Dobro coverplate, roundneck (**1000TP**) or squareneck (**1000TP-S**), few if any made: **1990**

Model 3000/The Chrysanthemum: etched

chrysanthemum pattern, bound ebony fingerboard, diamond inlay, bound peghead, etched
pearl logo
Available: **1996**

ELECTRICS

E-45 lap steel: squared bottom of body, pickup
with 2 bars, tone and volume knobs on opposite
sides, 23" scale, dot inlay, anodized aluminum hardware (appears gold), 6-string (**E45-6**), 7-string
(**E45-7**), 8-string (**E45-8**) or 10-string (**E45-10**)
Available: **late 1970s–86**

E3: solidbody, 2 humbucking pickups, laminated
neck-through-body, rosewood fingerboard
E3B: maple body, black finish
E3M: maple body, natural finish
E3P: padauk body
ESPH: purple heart body
E3W: walnut body
Available: **late 1970s–1986**

Oahu: lap steel, elongated guitar-shaped body, semi-
hollow construction, upper-bout *f*-holes, 2 metal-
covered mini-humbucking pickups (Gibson Firebird
style), 4 knobs, dot inlay
Available: **1996**

Oahu Deluxe: fancy inlay: **1996**

Bluesmaker: double cutaway with rounded horns,
mahogany body, 3-piece mahogany neck-through-
body construction, 2 pickups, dot inlay, vintageburst, blackburst, blueburst, greenburst,
purpleburst or wineburst finish
Available: **1996**

BluesMaker Deluxe: figured maple top: **1996**

DobroLektric: semi-hollowbody, single rounded
cutaway, upper-bout *f*–holes, seive-hole coverplate
with diamond configuration (no resonator), 2 pickups, 3 knobs on coverplate, flat or radiused fingerboard, dot inlay, vintageburst, blackburst, blueburst,
greeenburst, purpleburst or wineburst finish
Available: **1996–current**

ValPro: electric solidbody, map-shaped body similar
to National/Valco map-shapes of early 1960s,

2 metal-covered mini-humbucking pickups (Gibson Firebird style), some with cream soapbar (Gibson P-100) pickups, 4 knobs, asymmetrical peghead, *ValPro* logo, sea foam green, coral pink, cherry red, light sky blue or black finish
Available: **1996**

ValProJr.: smaller body: **1996**

BASSES

Upright Portable Bass: violin-style upright bass, *f*-holes, removable neck, no other specs available
Available: **1974–85**

D Bass: guitar body, screen holes, standard spider bridge and resonator, bound top and back, 34" scale, solid peghead, fretless model (**D Fretless**) available, darkburst or natural finish
Available: **1995–96**

F Bass: guitar body, *f*-holes, standard spider bridge and resonator, unbound back, 34" scale, darkburst finish: **1995–96**

F Deluxe Bass: guitar body, *f*-holes, standard spider bridge and resonator, bound top and back, 34" scale, fretless model (**F Deluxe Fretless**) or 5-string (**F Deluxe 5-string**) available, darkburst or natural finish: **1995–96**

MISC. MODELS

5-string: 5-string banjo neck, maple body, circular lower bout, narrow shoulders with no soundholes, moon-and-stars coverplate, round holes in body surrounding coverplate, unbound fingerboard, peghead dips in center
Available: **1984–96**

Mahogany 5-string: mahogany body: **1996**

Model 15(D)/Ampliphonic Mandolin: mandolin, 11 3/4" wide, 13 3/4" scale, moon-and-stars coverplate, solid peghead, brown sunburst finish
Introduced as **Ampliphonic Mandolin: by 1974**
Renamed **Model 15: by 1978**
Discontinued: **1995**

15G: flame maple body: **1984–86**

COMMENTS

Most players of woodbody Dobros prefer the prewar instruments. Recent metalbody Dobros with the National-style resonator and biscuit bridge have gained a degree of respect among players. The fancier engraved models have some appeal to collectors, although not as much as the original prewar National tricones on which the new Dobro designs are based.

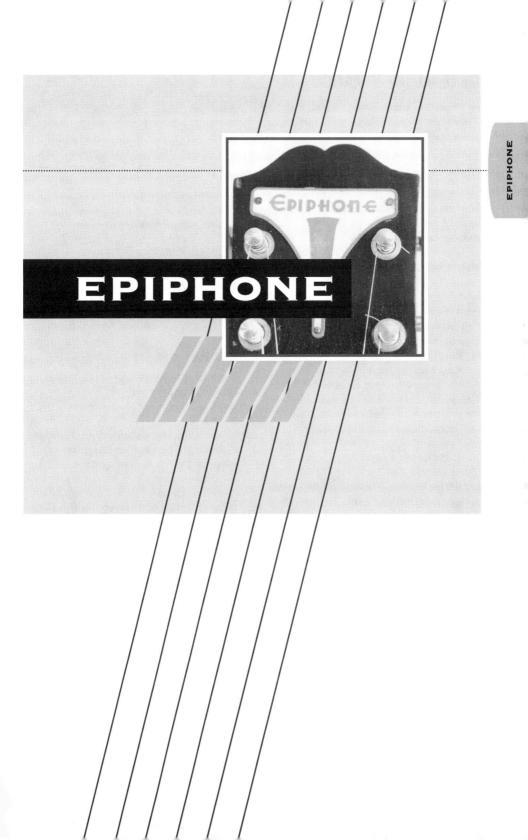

EPIPHONE

GENERAL INFORMATION

Epiphone traces its history to Anastasios Statho-poulo, who began making violins, lutes and lioutos (tradtional Greek instruments) in Sparta, Greece, in 1873 (according to company literature from the 1930s, although he would have only been 10 years old). Stathopoulo's family relocated to Smyrna, Turkey, in 1877, where he eventually established an instru-ment manufacturing business. To escape persecution he moved to New York in 1903.

Stathopoulo's instruments bore the label *A. Statho-poulo*. After his death in 1915, his sons Epaminondas (Epi), Orpheus (Orphie) and Frixo carried on the busi-ness and began using the House of Stathopoulo brand name in 1917. They incorporated in 1923 and concen-trated on banjos, introducing the Epiphone Recording Series banjos (named after Epi) in 1924. The company name was changed to Epiphone Banjo Corporation in 1928.

Epiphone was best known in the 1920s for the highly ornamented Recording banjos. In the 1930s Epiphone became virtually the only banjo company to make a successful changeover to guitars as its pri-mary product. Epiphone also supplied guitars for other distributors under the Sorrentino and Howard brands. The name of the company was changed in 1935 to Epiphone, Inc.

Epi Stathopoulo died of leukemia in 1943, and the company never fully recovered from his death or from the effects of World War II. The C.G. Conn Company, a band instrument manufacturer and instrument dis-tributor, acquired some control over Epiphone distrib-ution and production in 1953 and moved production in part to Philadelphia, although labels continued to say New York. Orphie Stathopoulo regained control in 1955, but few instruments were made from 1956–57.

Chicago Musical Instrument Co., which owned Gib-son, acquired Epiphone in 1957 and moved produc-tion to a facility near the Gibson factory in Kalamazoo, MI. Gibson introduced new Epiphone models at the annual trade show in 1958 and began shipping Epi-phones in 1959. In 1960 production was moved to the newly expanded Gibson factory at 225 Parsons St.

Epiphone was included in the takeover of Chicago Musical Instrument by the ECL company in December 1969. Shipping records show a little over 800 Epi-phones shipped from Kalamazoo in 1970. That same year, ECL (soon to be renamed Norlin) outsourced all Epiphone production to Japanese suppliers. In 1979 Norlin began moving Epi production to Korea, and by the mid 1980s almost all Epiphones were made in Korea.

Epiphone and Gibson (headquartered in Nashville since 1984) were acquired in 1986 by Henry Juszkie-wicz, David Berryman and Gary Zebrowski. By the early 1990s, Epiphone had become a leading import brand. Occasional limited runs have been produced in Gibson's Nashville and Montana facilities.

MODEL NAMES

In addition to the Zephyr and Zephyr Regent models, Epiphone applied the two terms to other models to signify electric or cutaway models:
Zephyr = electric
Regent = cutaway

LABELS

A. Stathopoulo: **1903–16**
House of Stathopoulo: **1917–28**
Epiphone Banjo Corporation, Long Island City, N.Y.: **1928–35**
Masterbilt label, several different label styles, all with *Masterbilt* in fancy lettering: **1931–1937**
Silver oval label, *The Epiphone Corp.* on banner, *New York* and *Builders of Art Musical Instruments* below banner: **1932–33**
Rectangular label, white paper with blue or blue-green border and *Epiphone, Inc., New York, N.Y., U.S.A.:* **1935–57**
Gibson-made: rectangular label, blue paper, epsilon (slashed-*C*) logo and *Epiphone, Inc., Kalamazoo, Michigan:* **1958–70**
Japanese-made, blue label: similar if not identical to Gibson-made label of 1958–70, some with *Made in Kalamazoo*, serial numbers typically have 7 digits, most model names and numbers inconsistent with 1958–70 model designations: **1970–early 1980s**
Japanese-made, light brown rectangular label: **1980s**

NEW YORK-MADE PICKUPS

Rickenbacker-type horseshoe, magnets wrap over strings: **1935–36**
Oblong shape with bar magnet: **1937–c. 1943**
"Truebalance": oblong shape with large slot-head screwpoles: **1937–47**

Oblong shape with fat oblong bar magnet: **1940s**

Tone Spectrum, rectangular, metal-covered...

> Phillips-head screwpoles, no mounting rings, mounted by 4 screws in corners of metal cover: **c. 1946–47**

> Yellow mounting ring covers part of top of pickup: **1948**

> 1 1/2" x 3 1/8", Phillips-head screwpoles, poles not in center but not as close to edge as New York style (see following), yellow frame surrounds pickup, some with no poles and black frame: **1948–51**

> 1 1/8" x 2 13/16" (3 5/8" wide including mounting blocks), referred to as "New York" style after changeover to Gibson-made pickups (see following), small slot-head screwpoles very close to edge, mounted to top by screws through cream-colored "blocks" or side extensions (some pickups on low-end models have no visible poles and black mounting blocks): **1949–61**

DeArmond: black or white face, 6 evenly spaced poles, poles adjustable by 6 separate screws (very similar to standard pickup on Gretsch models of the period), some Epi examples: **1953–57**

DeArmond: black plastic cover, oval chrome plate in center, chrome mounting ring: **1953-57**

Gibson-made (see following): **late 1950s–70**

GIBSON-MADE PICKUPS

The first Gibson-made electrics were fitted with left-over "New York" pickups from Epiphone's stock. As these were used up, Gibson began using 3 different pickup styles:

Mini-humbucking: not used on any Gibson models until 1969 on Les Paul Deluxe, smaller than standard Gibson humbucking pickup, 1 1/8" x 2 5/8", double-coil, rectangular metal-covered, slot-head screwpoles close to edge, black plastic frame, slightly smaller than New York style Epi pickups

P-90: standard on some low-end Gibson models, single-coil, poles across center, attached by screws through triangular "ears" extending from each end, some models with a rectangular (no ears) "soap-bar" P-90

Melody Maker: standard on low-end Gibson models, single-coil, narrow oblong shape, plastic cover, no polepieces

TAILPIECES

Standard trapeze, all models: **1920s–c. 1937**

Heavy trapeze with 4 cutouts, Emperor and De Luxe: **late 1935–late 1937**

Frequensator: double-trapeze design, allows for a longer string length on the 3 bass strings, shorter string length on the 3 treble strings, sometimes reversed by players to accommodate short strings or to reverse tone qualities, used on high-end models: **late 1937–1970**

Vibrato: flat-arm, strings wrap around metal cylinder of graduated diameter, wooden plate with epsilon (slashed-C) logo: **1961–70**

TRUSS RODS

No truss rod: **before 1937–39**

Truss rod adjustment at body end of fingerboard...
> Introduced on Emperor and high-end models: **1937**
> All models: **1939–51**

Truss rod adjustment at peghead: **1951–52 and after**

Metal truss rod cover with ridge in center, some models: **1954–57**

Celluloid truss rod cover: **1958–70**

LOGOS

Script: Most Epiphone guitars of the pre-Gibson period have a script logo with a standard script E. A few early models have a block-letter logo. The script logo continued into the Gibson period until Gibson had used up the stock of New York-made necks (with laminated construction).

epsilon (slashed-C): The logo beginning with a lower-case Greek letter *epsilon* (which looks like a Roman letter C with a horizontal slash) appeared by 1939 in literature and on metal peghead plates.

Models with inlaid or paint logos changed to Gibson necks and the epsilon logo around 1961. On flat tops, the Gibson neck can be distinguished by a wider flare toward the top of the peghead. By the 1963 catalog, all solidbody guitars, all basses, and all flat top guitars are pictured with the epsilon logo. In the 1965 catalog, all models have the epsilon logo except the Deluxe and Triumph (acoustic) and Emperor and Broadway (electric).

EPIPHONE

EPIPHONE

Epiphone metal peghead logo plate. The plate and the epsilon (slashed-C) logo were first used on electric models in the 1930s. The epsilon character eventually appeared on tuners and pickguards as well as on the modern peghead logo.

Epiphone script logo with script E, on a 1948 Blackstone. The vertical oval inlay figure appeared on many later models.

"New York" pickup, standard on most models in the 1950s and for several years after Gibson's acquisition of Epiphone in 1957.

Oblong pickup with large slot-head screws, appears on many models from 1939–43.

Large metal-covered pickup on a Zephyr Deluxe Regent, circa 1950.

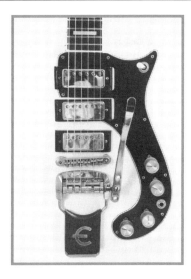

Gibson-made mini-humbucking pickups on a Crestwood Deluxe. This instrument is fitted with the unique Epiphone vibrato (unlike any vibrato on Gibson models) with the vibrato shaft increasing in diameter from the 1st to the 6th string to match the increasing string gauges. The rosewood tailpiece insert has the epsilon (slashed-C) logo.

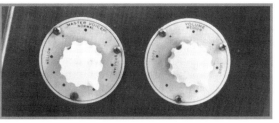

Large knobs on Mastervoicer plates.

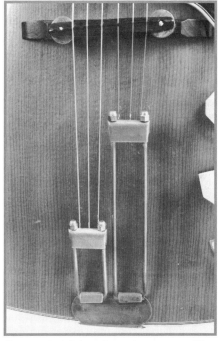

Frequensator tailpiece. Some players reversed the Frequensator to accommodate short string lengths or to reverse the tonal effect of the different tailpiece lengths.

Smaller, 8-sectioned knobs with pointers.

EARLY GIBSON-MADE EPIPHONES

After Gibson bought Epiphone, Epi parts were used up before Gibson parts were utilized. In addition to "New York" pickups (see preceding), some models—both acoustic and electric—feature a New York neck of laminated construction with more of a V shape than Gibson necks. The New York Epi peghead shape is also different from that of later Gibson-made necks.

MODEL NUMBERS

Model numbers date from Epiphone's ownership by Conn in 1953 until Gibson moved Epi production to Japan in 1970.

Letters preceding model numbers: A = acoustic archtop, BV = bass violin, E = electric archtop, EB = electric bass or Epiphone banjo, EC = Epiphone classical, EM = Epiphone mandolin, FT = flat top, SB = solidbody

Letters after numbers: C = cherry or cutaway, D = double pickup, E = electric, MV = maestro vibrola, N = natural finish, T = thinbody, V = vibrato

MODEL NUMBER	PREFIX	MODEL
7P	EA	Professional
8P	EA	Professional with amplifier
28	FT	Caballero tenor
30	EC	Madrid
30	FT	Caballero
44	EB	Campus banjo
45	FT	Cortez
66	EM	Venetian mandolin
77	ETB	Tenor banjo
79	FT	Texan
85	FT	Serenader
88	EB	Minstrel banjo
90	EC	Entrada
90	FT	El Dorado
95	FT	Folkster
98	FT	Troubadour
100	EC	Seville
110	FT	Frontier
111, 112	E	Emperor (blond, sunburst)*
111, 112	A	Emperor cutaway (blond, sunburst)*
112	FT	Bard
120	FT	Excellente
121, 122	A	Emperor non-cutaway (blond, sunburst)*
150	EC	Classic
188	EB	Plantation banjo
200	EC	Espana
210	FT	Deluxe Cutaway
211, 212	E	Deluxe, pre-1957 (blond, sunburst)
211, 212	E	Sheraton, 1958–70 (blond, sunburst)*
211, 212	A	Deluxe cutaway (blond, sunburst)*
221, 222	A	Deluxe non-cutaway (blond, sunburst)*
230	E	Casino

MODEL NUMBER	PREFIX	MODEL
231, 232	EB	Rivoli (blond, sunburst)*
232	SB	Crestwood Deluxe
251, 252	E	Broadway (blond, sunburst)*
300	EC	Barcelona
311, 312	E	Zephyr cutaway (blond, sunburst)*
311, 312	A	Broadway cutaway (blond, sunburst)*
321, 322	E	Zephyr non-cutaway (blond, sunburst)*
321, 322	A	Broadway non-cutaway (blond, sunburst)*
332	SB	Crestwood Custom
351, 352	E	Windsor (blond, sunburst)*
360	E	Riviera
411, 412	A	Triumph cutaway (blond, sunbust)*
421, 422	A	Triumph non-cutaway (blond, sunburst)*
421, 422	E	Century (blond, sunburst)*
432	SB	Wilshire
444	E	Granada
451, 452	E	Sorrento (blond, sunburst)*
521, 522	A	Devon (blond, sunburst)*
533	SB	Coronet
621, 622	A	Zenith (blond, sunburst)*
721	SB	Olympic Special
722	SB	Olympic
Caiola		Caiola
EBDL		Embassy Deluxe
EBS		Newport
EBV		Rivoli
HR-SE		Howard Roberts Standard
HR-CE		Howard Roberts Custom

* In 1961 Gibson began using only the even-numbered model designation for sunburst, blond or any other finish.

SERIAL NUMBERS

Lists of numbers for acoustic guitars from 1932–44 and for acoustic and electric guitars from 1951–56 were originally compiled by Tom Wheeler from the records of Petty Music of Pittsburgh and revised by Jim Fisch and L.B. Fred. Additional number lists for pre-Gibson (pre-1958) instruments were compiled by Fisch and Fred.

ACOUSTICS, 1920s–1950

Serial numbers typically appear on a label inside the body. This list does not include banjos.

RANGE	YEAR	RANGE	YEAR
1–999	late 1920s	11000s	1937
1000s	1931	12000s	1938
5000s	1932	13000s–14400s	1939
6000s	1933	14500s	1940
7200s	1934	16000s–17400s	1941
8000s–9000s	1935	17500s–18100s	1942
10000s	1936	18200s–18900s	1943

RANGE	YEAR	RANGE	YEAR
19000s–20000s	1944	56000s	1947
50000s–52000s	1944	57000s	1948
52000s–54000s	1945	58000s	1949
54000s–55000s	1946		

ELECTRICS, 1935–44

RANGE	YEAR	RANGE	YEAR
000–249	1935	3500–4999	1940
250–749	1936	5000–6499	1941
750–1499	1937	6500–7499	1942
1500–2499	1938	7500–8299	1943
2500-3499	1939	8300–9000	1944

ELECTRICS, 1945–50

Numbers on electric instruments from 1945–50 are coded by model, with the first 2 digits signifying the model and the final 3 digits signifying a ranking within that model's production.

FIRST 2 DIGITS	MODEL
15	Century Hawaiian (possibly all Hawaiians)
25	Zephyr Spanish
26	Zephyr Spanish
60	Century Spanish
75	Zephyr De Luxe
85	Zephyr De Luxe Regent

ACOUSTICS AND ELECTRIC, 1950–57

RANGE	YEAR	RANGE	YEAR
59000s	1950	67000s	1954
60000s–63000s*	1951	68000s	1955
64000s	1952	69000s	1957
64000s–66000s	1953		

*Many instruments throughout the 1930s have numbers in the 60000s and 61000s.

1958–61

Hollowbody models

Serial number on label, with *A* prefix.
Note: This Epiphone A-number series is different from the A-series used on Gibson instruments of the same period.

RANGE	YEAR
A 1000s	1959
A 2000s	1959–60
A 3000s–A4312	1960–early 1961

Solidbody models

Serial number inked on back of peghead with configuration **y ###** or **y ####**.
As with Gibson solidbody models of the same period, the first digit **y** corresponds to the last digit of the year.
Example: 9 2506 = 1959

1961–70

Beginning in 1961, Epiphone serial numbers follow Gibson's number series (see Gibson Serial Numbers section).

1977–CURRENT, U.S.-MADE

Starting in the late 1970s, occasional limited runs of Epiphones have been made in Kalamazoo, Nashville or Bozeman, MT (site of Gibson's flat top production). Serial numbers on these models follow Gibson's regular serial number system:

8-digit number impressed into back of peghead: **ydddynnn**

yy (1st and 5th digits) = year of manufacture

ddd (digits 2–4) = day of the year; 001 = Jan. 1, 365 = Dec. 31

nnn (digits 6-8) = rank of the instrument that day. All instruments made at the Kalamazoo, MI, factory (1977–84) and guitars made at the Bozeman, MT, factory (1989–current) are numbered beginning with 001 each day. Instruments made at the Nashville factory are numbered each day beginning with 500 or 501.

Examples:

80012005 = the 5th instrument made in Kalamazoo (1977–84) or Bozeman (1989 or later) on the first day of 1982

82569625 = the 125th or 126th instrument made in Nashville on the 256th day of 1989

1970–CURRENT, FOREIGN-MADE

Almost all Epiphones from 1970 to the mid 1990s were made in Japan or Korea. Many have a 7-digit serial number for which no list is available.

Beginning in the late 1980s, some examples have a number in which the first digit corresponds to the last digit of the year, or the first 2 digits correspond to the last 2 digits of the year.

In the 1990s, some models have a number beginning with a letter signifying the manufacturing facility, followed by a digit corresponding with the last digit of the year.

Examples:

S3456789 = 1993, made by Samick

R4567890 = 1994, made by Aria

ACOUSTIC ARCHTOPS KEY

Upper treble bout with lopped-off appearance, model letter on peghead
Dot inlay = **Recording A** (flat top)
Large engraved-block inlay
Cross engraving on inlay = **Recording D**
Floral engraving on inlay = **Recording E**
Small paired-diamond inlay
Black binding = **Recording B** (flat top)
3-ply binding = **Recording C**
Standard guitar body shape
Cloud inlay = **De Luxe, 1935–70**
Block inlay
Dip in peghead = **Broadway, 1934–58**
Rounded-peak peghead = **Apollo**
3-segment V-block = **Emperor**
Slotted-block inlay
Vertical oval peghead inlay = **Howard Roberts**
Vine peghead inlay = **Howard Roberts Custom**

Standard guitar body shape *(continued)*

 Notched-block inlay = **Spartan 1936–48**

 Single-parallelogram inlay = **Blackstone, 1936–48**

 Oval inlay

  Mahogany back and sides = **Devon**

  Maple back and sides = **Zenith, 1958–68**

 Varied floral, notched-triangle and notched-diamond inlay

  Rope-pattern top marquetry = **De Luxe, 1931–late 1935**

  Triple-bound top = **Tudor**

 Notched-diamond inlay = **Triumph, 1934–70**

 4-point star inlay = **Broadway, 1931–33**

 Small paired-diamond inlay = **Triumph, 1931–33**

 Dot inlay

  Round hole

   Fixed bridge = **Numbered Series**

   Trapeze tailpiece = **Spartan, 1934–35**

  f-holes

   Bound fingerboard

    Maple back and sides = **Blackstone, 1931–33, 1936–48**

    Walnut back and sides = **Royal, 1933–35**

    Mahogany back and sides

     Sharply peaked peghead = **Blackstone, 1934–35**

     Rounded-peak peghead = **Royal, 1931–32**

   Unbound fingerboard

    Maple back and sides

     White binding = **Zenith, 1931–33, 1949–58**

     Tortoiseshell celluloid binding = **Ritz**

    Mahogany back and sides

     Rounded peak peghead

      Archtop = **Olympic**

      Flat top = **Beverly**

     Center-dip peghead = **Byron**

    Walnut back and sides = **Zenith, 1933–49**

ACOUSTIC ARCHTOPS

SECTION ORGANIZATION

Recording Series
Numbered Series
Masterbilt Series
Later New York-Made Models
Sorrentino Models
Howard Models
Gibson-Made Models

RECORDING SERIES

All have asymmetrical body, cutaway bout slopes for a "lopped off" appearance, round soundhole, spruce top, movable bridge on fixed base, trapeze tailpiece, neck with 3 center laminates, 25" scale, 13 frets clear of body, engraved celluloid peghead veneer with *Epiphone* banner across top, *Recording* banner across middle and ornate initial letter of model name, banjo-style (straight-through) tuners, amber-to-red sunburst finish, available in concert (13 5/8" wide) or auditorium (15 1/2") size.

Bridge variations: glued bridge with staggered bridge pins and no tailpiece, glued bridge with strings passing under retainer and anchoring in trapeze tailpiece

Recording A: flat top and back, 3-ply figured maple back and sides (some mahogany), black body binding, rosewood fingerboard, dot inlay, rounded peghead peak

Recording B: flat top, arched back, 3-ply figured maple back and sides (some mahogany), black body binding, rosewood fingerboard with white binding, small paired slotted-diamond inlay in zigzag pattern, green leaves engraved on peghead, pointed peghead peak

Recording C: carved top, 3-ply figured maple back and sides, later examples with elevated pickguard, triple-bound top and back, bound pointed-end ebony fingerboard, small paired slotted-diamond inlay in zigzag pattern, gold celluloid peghead veneer with black engraving, green leaves engraved on peghead

Recording C variation: flat top, conventional symmetrical body shape, celluloid block inlay with floral engraving

Recording D: carved top, 3-ply figured maple back and sides, bound top and back, violin purfling around edges, elevated pickguard follows body contour, bound pointed-end fingerboard, large celluloid block inlay with cross-like engraving

Recording E: carved top, 3-ply figured maple back and sides, ebony and ivory bridge, elevated black pickguard follows contour of body, triple-bound top and back, bound pointed-end fingerboard, large celluloid block inlay with floral engraving, mother-of-pearl tuner buttons, sparkle-tint peghead veneer, engraved gold-plated hardware

Recording series introduced: **by 1928**

Last listed: **1931**

NUMBERED SERIES

Models 0, 1, 2, 3 and **4:** 13 5/8" wide, flat top or archtop, round hole, fixed bridge, staggered bridge pin alignment, pickguard covers part of soundhole, lower models with flat mahogany back, higher models with arched back of laminated maple, model number on peghead, higher models with celluloid peghead veneer

Available: **late 1920s–early 1930s**

MASTERBILT SERIES

All have arched spruce top, f-holes, rosewood fingerboard.

Some models have Masterbilt peghead: *Epiphone*

across top, *Masterbilt* across bottom, model name slanted across center, asymmetrical peghead with dip on treble side.

Masterbilt series announced: **June 1931**

De Luxe: 16 3/8" wide, curly maple back and sides, 3-segment f-holes, single-bound pickguard, trapeze tailpiece, 4-ply top binding with rope-pattern purfling, triple-bound back, bound fingerboard with curved end, varied diamond-and-triangle-pattern inlay, pearl rectangle at 14th fret, Masterbilt peghead with flowers, bound peghead, gold-plated hardware, sunburst finish

Introduced: **1931**

Straight-end fingerboard, floral and notched-diamond inlay pattern, pearl rectangle at 15th fret, vine peghead inlay, block-letter logo, white pickguard: **1934**

17 3/8" wide, multiple binding, tortoise pickguard extends below bridge, single-bound "cello" f-holes with squared edge at each corner, flat-plate tailpiece with 4 cutouts, segmented cloud inlay, script logo, earliest labeled **Super De Luxe: late 1935**

Single-piece (non-segmented) cloud inlay: **by 1936**

Frequensator tailpiece, truss rod adjustable at end of fingerboard: **late 1937**

Center-dip peghead, natural finish optional: **1939**

Some with unbound f-holes: **1950**

f-holes with pointed corners: **1951**

Single flower on peghead, truss rod cover on peghead: **1952**

Some examples 18 1/2" wide, same body shape and size as Emperor, flower peghead inlay: **mid 1950s**

Discontinued: **1957**

De Luxe Regent: cutaway, some with flower peghead inlay

Introduced: **by 1948**

Some with unbound f-holes: **1950**

f-holes with pointed corners: **1951**

Single flower on peghead, truss rod cover on peghead: **1952**

Renamed **Deluxe Cutaway: 1953**

Gibson-Epiphone De Luxe (see following): **1958**

Empire: tenor version of Deluxe, 15 1/2" wide, 23" scale, otherwise same specs and changes

Introduced: **1931**

Discontinued: **by 1937**

Broadway: 16 3/8" wide, laminated walnut back, solid walnut sides, 3-segment or standard *f*-holes, trapeze tailpiece, unbound pickguard, triple-bound top and back, 5-piece maple/mahogany neck, bound ebony fingerboard with rounded end, 4-point star-shaped inlay, Masterbilt peghead with flower inlay, sunburst finish
Introduced: **1931**
Carved (solid) walnut back, bound pickguard, square-end fingerboard, large block inlay, no inlay at 1st fret, wandering vine peghead inlay, block-letter logo, unbound peghead, gold-plated hardware: **1934**
17 3/8" wide, pickguard extends even with bridge, "cello" *f*-holes with squared edge at each corner, flat-plate tailpiece with 4 cutouts, multiple-bound top, inlay at 1st fret, multiple-bound peghead, script logo, gold-plated hardware: **1936**
Frequensator tailpiece: **late 1937**
Maple back and sides, center-dip peghead: **1939**
Blond finish optional: **early 1941**
Transition from vine peghead inlay to flower inlay: **1945–46**
f-holes with pointed corners: **1951**
Broadway acoustic discontinued (Broadway electric continued in Gibson line, see Hollowbody Electrics): **1958**

Broadway Regent: single cutaway
Introduced: **by 1948**
f-holes with pointed corners: **1951**
Renamed **Broadway Cutaway: by 1953**
Some with paint "binding" around *f*-holes: **c. 1954**
Discontinued: **1958**

Bretton: tenor version of Broadway, 15 1/2" wide, 23" scale, otherwise same specs and changes
Introduced: **1931**
Renamed **Broadway Tenor**, plectrum available: **1937**
Discontinued: **1949**

Tudor: 16 3/8" wide, maple back and sides, trapeze tailpiece, triple-bound top and back, 5-piece maple/mahogany neck, single-bound fingerboard with curved end, notched-triangle and notched-diamond inlay, unbound Masterbilt peghead with inlaid banners, gold-plated hardware
Introduced: **c. 1933**
Bound pickguard, block-letter logo, wandering vine peghead inlay: **1934**
Discontinued: **by 1937**

Triumph: 15 1/4" wide, laminated walnut back, walnut sides, unbound pickguard, trapeze tailpiece, 3-segment *f*-holes, triple-bound top and back, unbound fingerboard with curved end, paired slotted diamond inlay in zigzag pattern, Masterbilt peghead, nickel-plated hardware, sunburst finish
Introduced: **1931**
16 3/8" wide, laminated maple back and sides, single-bound top and back, dot inlay: **1933**
Solid maple back and sides, single-bound fingerboard, notched-diamond inlay, unbound rounded-peak peghead, block-letter logo, peghead inlay of floral ornament with fleur-de-lis design at top: **1934**
Script logo: **1935**
17 3/8" wide, "cello" *f*-holes with squared edge at each corner, triple-bound top, single-bound back, bound pickguard extends below bridge, single-bound peghead, flat-plate tailpiece with 4 cutouts: **1936**
Frequensator tailpiece, center-dip peghead: **late 1937**
Blond finish optional: **early 1941**
Fat columnlike peghead inlay: **by 1947**
epsilon (slashed-*C*) on pickguard: **1947**
f-holes with pointed corners: **1950**
Discontinued: **by 1958**

Triumph Regent: single cutaway
Introduced: **by 1948**
f-holes with pointed corners: **1950**
Renamed **Triumph Cutaway: by 1953**
Gibson-Epi Triumph (see following): **1958**

Hollywood: tenor version of Triumph, 23" scale, otherwise same specs and changes
Introduced: **1931**
Renamed **Triumph tenor**, plectrum model (27" scale) also available: **1937**
Discontinued: **1958**

Royal: 15 1/2" wide, mahogany back and sides, 3-segment *f*-holes, unbound pickguard, single-bound top and back, single-bound fingerboard, dot inlay, Masterbilt peghead, sunburst finish
Introduced: **1931**
Walnut back and sides, rounded-peak peghead: **1933**
Last made: **1935**

Spartan: 16 3/8" wide, laminated maple back, maple sides, round hole, unbound pickguard, trapeze tailpiece, single-bound top and back, triple-bound

fingerboard, dot inlay, stickpin peghead inlay, block-letter logo, rounded-peak peghead, sunburst finish
Introduced: **1934**
f-holes with pointed corners, walnut back and sides, triple-bound top, bound fingerboard, notched-block inlay, bound peghead, Greek column peghead inlay, script logo: **by 1936**
Center-dip peghead: **1939**
Blond finish, prima vera wood (light mahogany) back and sides, optional: **early 1941**
Plastic inlay material (not pearl) on fingerboard and peghead, notched elongated diamond peghead inlay: **by 1947**
Discontinued: **by 1949**

Regent: tenor companion to Spartan, 15 1/2" wide, *f*-holes, mahogany back and sides, bound top and back, trapeze tailpiece, 23" scale, bound fingerboard, dot inlay, block-letter logo, stickpin peghead inlay, rounded-peak peghead, sunburst finish
Introduced: **1934**
Discontinued, replaced by **Spartan Tenor** (see following): **1937**

Spartan Tenor: same specs and changes as Spartan, plectrum (27" scale) also available
Introduced (replacing Regent): **1937**
Discontinued: **by 1949**

Blackstone: 14 3/4" wide, maple back and sides, unbound pickguard, single-bound top and back, single-bound fingerboard, dot inlay, engraved pearloid peghead veneer, three-on-a-strip tuners, ebony finish
Introduced: **1931**
Rounded-peak peghead with inlaid Masterbilt banners, sunburst finish on top, back and sides: **1933**
15 1/2" wide, mahogany back and sides, block-letter logo, stickpin peghead inlay, unbound peghead with sharp peak: **1934**
16 3/8" wide, maple back and sides, "cello" *f*-holes with squared edge at each corner, trapeze tailpiece, parallelogram inlay, elongated notched-diamond peghead inlay, script logo: **by 1936**
Tenor and plectrum available: **1937**
Center-dip peghead: **1939**
Blond finish optional: **early 1941**
Abalone notched-oval peghead inlay, abalone logo: **by 1945**

Notched-diamond peghead inlay, plastic (not pearl) inlay material: **1946**
Discontinued: **by 1949**

Zenith: 13 5/8" wide, maple back and sides, 3-segment *f*-holes, Masterbilt banner peghead
Introduced: **1931**
Single-bound top and back, black elevated pickguard, unbound rosewood fingerboard with square end, dot inlay, rounded-peak peghead, *Zenith* engraved diagonally into wood peghead face: **1933**
14 3/4" wide, walnut back and sides, block-letter logo, stickpin peghead inlay, 3-on-a-strip tuners, sunburst top finish: **1934**
16 3/8" wide, "cello" *f*-holes with squared edge at each corner, elongated notched-diamond peghead inlay, script logo, individual tuners: **1936**
Tenor and plectrum available: **1937**
Center-dip peghead: **1939**
Maple back and sides, blond finish optional: **by 1949**
f-holes with pointed corners: **1950**
Vertical oval peghead inlay: **1951**
Gibson-Epi Zenith (see following): **1958**

Melody: tenor companion to Zenith, 13 1/4" wide, 23" scale, bound top and back
Introduced: **1931**
Walnut back and sides (does not increase in size with Zenith): **1934**
Discontinued: **1937**

Zenith Tenor: same specs as Zenith, plectrum (27" scale) also available, replaces Melody: **1937–58**

Olympic: 13" wide, mahogany back and sides, 3-segment *f*-holes, no binding, rounded top of peghead, no logo
Introduced: **1931**
13 5/8" wide, trapeze tailpiece, rounded-end fingerboard, dot inlay, sunburst finish: **by 1933**
Decal logo with *Epiphone* on banner and *Masterbilt* underneath banner: **1934**
15 1/4" wide, "cello" *f*-holes with squared edge at each corner, single-bound top and back, no *Masterbilt* banner on peghead: **by 1936**
Tenor and plectrum available: **1937**
Center-dip peghead, script decal logo with tail underneath: **1939**
Script decal logo with no tail (like inlaid version), some with pearl logo: **by 1943**
Discontinued: **by 1949**

Beverly: 13" wide, flat top, laminated arched mahogany back, mahogany sides, 3-segment *f*-holes, adjustable bridge, trapeze tailpiece, elevated pickguard, no body binding, dot inlay, rounded-top peghead, some with no logo, some with decal or impressed logo, 3-on-a-strip tuners, brown finish, tenor and Hawaiian available
Introduced: **1931**
Discontinued: **by 1937**

LATER NEW YORK-MADE MODELS

Emperor: 18 1/2" wide, maple back and sides, plate tailpiece with 4 cutouts (earliest with cutouts forming arrow shape) and *Epiphone*, elongated pickguard, 13-ply binding on top and back, triple-bound "cello" *f*-holes with squared edge at each corner, 7-piece maple/mahogany neck, single-bound ebony fingerboard with 2 white lines inlaid along edges, 3-segment V-block pearl inlay, triple-bound peghead, vine peghead inlay, triangular peghead inlay next to nut, dip on top treble side of peghead, clipped peghead corners, gold-plated hardware, sunburst finish
Introduced: **late 1935**
Frequensator tailpiece: **late 1937**
Center-dip peghead with clipped corners, natural finish optional: **1939**
Abalone wedge in 3-segment V-block inlay: **c. 1939**
Rosewood fingerboard: **by 1946**
Pearl (not abalone) wedge in 3-segment V-block fingerboard inlay, inlays segmented by wood spaces, no triangle inlay on peghead: **by 1945**
Pearl block inlay with abalone V insert (non-segmented): **by 1948**
f-holes with pointed corners: **1951**
epsilon (slashed-*C*) on pickguard: **1950**
Truss rod cover on peghead: **1952**
Discontinued: **mid 1950s**

Soloist Emperor: rounded cutaway with slight ledge on treble side of neck, *f*-holes with pointed corners, pearl block inlay with abalone wedge (non-segmented): **1941–42**

Emperor Regent, rounded cutaway, introduced: **by 1948**
f-holes with pointed corners: **1951**

epsilon (slashed-*C*) on pickguard: **1950**
Renamed **Emperor Cutaway: by 1953**
Truss rod cover on peghead: **1952**
Gibson-Epi Emperor (see following): **1958**

Concert: trapezoidal soundhole, based on custom-made guitar for Johnny Smith, natural or sunburst finish, as many as 8 made: **late 1940s**

Apollo: 13 5/8" wide, sycamore back and sides, 3-segment *f*-holes, "outlined" pickguard (edge painted to simulate binding), bound rosewood fingerboard, block inlay, rounded-peak peghead, banner decal logo, plastic tuner buttons, sunburst finish, available only in England
Available: **1937–early 1940s**

Byron: 15 3/8" wide, mahogany back and sides, trapeze tailpiece, unbound pickguard, single-bound top and back, rosewood fingerboard, dot inlay, script decal logo with tail underneath, center-dip peghead
Available possibly as early as: **1939**
First listed: **1949**
Discontinued from catalog: **by 1954**
Last made, metal peghead plate: **1955**

Ritz: 15 1/2" wide, laminated maple back and sides, "cello" *f*-holes with squared edge at each corner, unbound pickguard, tortoiseshell celluloid binding on top and back, trapeze tailpiece, cherry neck, rosewood fingerboard, dot inlay, center-dip peghead, logo inlaid or decal, blond finish, tenor available
Introduced: **1940**
Discontinued: **by 1949**

Devon: 17 3/8" wide, laminated mahogany back, mahogany sides, Frequensator tailpiece, single-bound pickguard with epsilon (slashed-*C*), *f*-holes with points at each corner, triple-bound top, single-bound back, single-bound rosewood fingerboard, oval inlay, notched-oval peghead inlay, script logo, nickel-plated hardware sunburst finish
Introduced: **1949**
Blond finish, prima vera (light mahogany) back and sides optional: **by 1954**
Metal peghead plate: **1955**
Discontinued: **1957**

SORRENTINO MODELS

In the mid 1930s Epiphone made guitars under the Sorrentino brand for distribution by the Chicago Musical Instrument Co. The following models were listed in the 1935 CMI catalog. Sorrentino models typically have a different peghead design than their Epiphone equivalent.

Luxor: similar to De Luxe but with block inlay and wood marquetry around top

Premier: similar to Tudor except for peghead

Artist: combines features of Broadway and Triumph, walnut body

Avon: similar to Blackstone but with walnut body and fancier inlay

Lido: similar to Zenith but with bound fingerboard

Arcadia: similar to Olympic but with walnut body

HOWARD MODELS

Epiphone may have made guitars for distribution under the Howard brand in the mid 1930s. One example is similar to the Broadway model but with a fleur-de-lis peghead inlay and *Howard* etched into the peghead banner inlay.

GIBSON-MADE MODELS

Emperor: 18 1/8" wide, rounded cutaway, Frequensator tailpiece, multiple binding, ebony fingerboard, 3-segment V-block inlay with abalone wedge, vine peghead inlay, gold-plated hardware, sunburst or natural finish
Introduced (continued from earlier Epi line): **1958**
Available by special order only: **1963**
Discontinued: **1970**

Deluxe: 17 3/8" wide, rounded cutaway, Frequensator tailpiece, single-bound *f*-holes, multiple-bound top and pickguard, triple-bound back, multiple-bound ebony fingerboard, cloud inlay, triple-bound peghead, vine peghead inlay, gold-plated hardware, sunburst or natural finish
Introduced (continued from earlier Epi line): **1958**

Available by special order only: **1965**
Discontinued: **1970**

Triumph: 17 3/8" wide, rounded cutaway, Frequensator tailpiece, bound top and back, rosewood fingerboard, notched-diamond inlay, fat column peghead inlay, sunburst or natural finish
Introduced (continued from earlier Epi line): **1958**
Available by special order only: **1965**
Discontinued: **1970**

Zenith: 16 3/8" wide, non-cutaway, trapeze tailpiece, single-bound top and back, rosewood fingerboard, oval inlay, vertical oval peghead inlay, sunburst finish
Introduced (continued from earlier Epi line): **1958**
Available by special order only: **1965**
Discontinued: **1970**

Howard Roberts and Howard Roberts
Custom: offered in catalog as acoustic models without pickup, most built with pickup, cherry or sunburst finish (see Epiphone Electric Archtops): **1965–68**

COMMENTS

Recording models were Epiphone's earliest high quality guitars. They are hard to find in good condition and are sought more by blues players and collectors than by jazz or folk players.

Pre-1937 Epis are of very high quality and are generally much scarcer than later models. They are of considerable interest to collectors. They have a smaller body and a less modern neck feel than later models and consequently are less sought by players for utility use.

Models made from 1937 (when body sizes were increased) to the end of New York production in the mid 1950s are the most highly regarded by collectors. Most desirable are the professional grade models on which the company built its reputation: Emperor, De Luxe, Broadway and Triumph. These models, along with Gibsons, are considered by most collectors and musicians to be the best factory-made archtop guitars ever produced. Low-end models are generally regarded as excellent instruments for serious amateurs.

FLAT TOPS KEY

MODELS WITH UNUSUAL FEATURES

Sloped cutaway with "lopped off" appearance = **Recording Series** (listed and keyed in the Acoustic Archtops section).

Staggered bridge pin alignment, "snakehead" peghead (narrower toward top), number from 0 to 4 on peghead = **Numbered Series**

2 *f*-holes = **Beverly**

4 *f*-holes = **Madrid, 1931–35**

Circular body = **Tenor Lute**

MODELS WITH CONVENTIONAL FEATURES

No inlay (classical models)
  Treble-side fingerboard extension
    Bound fingerboard
      Gold-plated hardware = **Concert**
      Nickel-plated hardware = **Alhambra**
    Unbound fingerboard = **Seville, 1938–41**
  Symmetrical fingerboard
    Mahogany back and sides
      Rounded peghead corners = **Classic**
      Pointed peghead corners
        Fan bracing
          25 1/2" scale = **Seville** or **Seville Electric, 1961–70**
          22 3/4" scale = **Entrada**
        Non-fan bracing = **Madrid, 1962–70**
    Maple back and sides
      Gold-plated hardware = **Barcelone**
      Nickel-plated hardware = **Espana**
Dot inlay
  Mahogany top
    No binding = **F.T. 30**
    Tortoiseshell celluloid binding = **Caballero (FT 30)**
  Spruce top
    Mahogany back and sides
      6-string
        Cutaway body = **EM30 E/A**
        Staggered bridge pins **or** flush frets = **Navarre**
        Masterbilt on peghead **or** trapeze tailpiece = **F.T. 27**
        Tortoiseshell celluloid binding = **F.T. 50**
        Metal peghead logo plate = **Cortez**
        2 white pickguards, flat fingerboard = **Folkster**
        8-digit serial number = **EM10**
      12-string
        16 1/4" wide = **Bard**
        14 1/4" wide = **Serenader**
    Walnut back and sides
      15 1/2" wide = **F.T. 37**
      14 1/2" wide = **F.T. 45**
    Rosewood back and sides = **EM20**

Engraved celluloid block inlay (E on peghead) = **Recording E**
Cloud inlay
  Non-cutaway
    Maple body = **F.T. De Luxe**
    Rosewood body = **Excellente**
  Cutaway = **De Luxe Cutaway**
Slotted-block inlay
  Cutaway = **Zephyr Regent style**
  Non-cutaway
    Tortoiseshell celluloid pickguard or no pickguard
      Square-shouldered dreadnought
        Maple body = **Frontier (FT 110)**
        Walnut body = **F.T. 79, 1941–48**
        Rounded shoulders = **Madrid, 1936–40**
      2 white pickguards = **Troubadour**
Single-parallelogram inlay
  Maple body
    Stickpin peghead inlay = **F.T. 75**
    Vertical oval peghead inlay = **F.T. 79, 1954–58**
  Mahogany body
    Square-shouldered dreadnought = **El Dorado**
    Round-shouldered dreadnought = **Texan**
    Non-dreadnought shape (thin waist) = **F.T. 79, 1949–57**

FLAT TOPS

SECTION ORGANIZATION

New York-Made Steel-String Models
Gibson/U.S.-Made Steel-String Models, 1958–95
12-Strings
New York-Made Classicals
Gibson-Made Classicals

NEW YORK-MADE STEEL-STRING MODELS

Recording Series: asymmetrical body with lopped-off cutaway on upper treble bout. Higher models have carved top. For description of entire series, see Epiphone Acoustic Archtops section, preceding.

Recording A: flat top and back, 3-ply figured maple back and sides (some mahogany), black body binding, rosewood fingerboard, dot inlay, rounded peghead peak

Recording B: flat top, arched back, 3-ply figured maple back and sides (some mahogany), black body binding, rosewood fingerboard with white binding, small paired slotted-diamond inlay in zigzag pattern, green leaves engraved on peghead, pointed peghead peak

Recording C variation: flat top (standard Recording C has carved top), conventional symmetrical body shape, celluloid block inlay with floral engraving
Recording series introduced: **by 1928**
Last listed: **1931**

Numbered Series: 13 5/8" wide, flat top or archtop, round hole, fixed bridge, staggered bridge pin alignment, pickguard covers part of soundhole, lower models with flat mahogany back, higher models with arched back of laminated maple, model number on peghead, higher models with celluloid peghead veneer
Models 0, 1, 2, 3, 4, available: **late 1920s–early 1930s**

Tenor Lute: tenor guitar, circular body, paired slotted-diamond inlay in zigzag pattern
Available: **late 1920s**

Beverly: 13" wide, arched back, laminated back, mahogany sides, 3-segment *f*-holes, adjustable bridge, trapeze tailpiece, elevated pickguard, no body binding, dot inlay, rounded top of peghead, some with no logo, some with decal or impressed logo, 3-on-a-strip tuners, brown finish, tenor and Hawaiian available

Introduced: **1931**

Discontinued: **by 1937**

Madrid: 4 *f*-holes (no round soundhole), maple back and sides, bound top and back, staggered bridge pins, multiple-bound top, single-bound back, 14 frets clear of body, bound rosewood fingerboard, dot inlay, rounded-peak peghead, white celluloid peghead overlay with engraved banners, shaded brown finish, Spanish or Hawaiian (high nut) setup

Introduced: **1931**

Offered in Hawaiian style only, 16 1/2" wide, glued pickguard, round hole, 12 frets clear of body, slotted-block inlay, celluloid frets flush with fingerboard (some with Spanish setup), pearl script logo, cherry sunburst finish: **by 1936**

Classical-type bridge with strings through bridge, trapeze tailpiece, center-dip peghead, dark cherry red sunburst finish: **1939**

Discontinued: **by 1941**

Model name reintroduced in Gibson-made classical line (see following): **1962**

Navarre: mahogany back and sides, staggered bridge pins, bound soundhole, bound top and back, 14 frets clear of body, bound rosewood fingerboard, dot inlay, rounded-peak peghead, banner logo, shaded brown finish

Introduced: **1931**

Hawaiian style only, 16 1/2" wide, bridge pins in straight line, glued pickguard, 12 frets clear of body, unbound fingerboard, celluloid frets flush with fingerboard (some with Spanish setup), center-dip peghead, pearl script logo: **by 1936**

Fixed bridge with strings passing under retainer bar, trapeze tailpiece, center-dip peghead: **1939**

Discontinued: **1940**

F.T. 75: 16 1/2" wide, maple back and sides, tortoise pickguard, triple-bound top and soundhole, bound back, 14 frets clear of body, bound rosewood fingerboard, single-parallelogram inlay, squared-off

peghead, notched-stickpin peghead inlay, pearl script logo, dark cherry sunburst finish

Introduced: **1935**

Fixed bridge with strings passing under retainer bar, trapeze tailpiece, single-bound top and back, center-dip peghead: **1939**

Blond finish optional: **early 1940**

Discontinued: **by late 1941**

F.T. 37: 15 1/2" wide, walnut back and sides, tortoise pickguard, single-bound top and back, 14 frets clear of body, dot inlay, squared-off peghead, banner peghead decal, yellow sunburst top finish

Introduced: **1934**

Fixed bridge with strings passing under retainer bar, trapeze tailpiece, single-bound top and back, center-dip peghead, script logo, natural finish optional: **1939**

Discontinued: **1942**

F.T. 27: 14 1/2" wide, mahogany back and sides, tortoise pickguard, 2 routings in bridge parallel to strings, ebony saddle, bound top, unbound back, 14 frets clear of body, dot inlay, squared-off peghead, peghead decal with block-letter logo on banner arching over *Masterbilt*, 3-on-a-strip tuners, sunburst top finish

Introduced, earliest labeled **F.T. No. 1: 1934**

Fixed bridge with strings passing under retainer bar, trapeze tailpiece, single-bound top and back, center-dip peghead, script logo, natural finish optional: **1939**

Discontinued: **1942**

F.T. De Luxe: 16 1/2" wide, maple back and sides, engraved tortoise pickguard, fixed bridge with strings passing under retainer bar, trapeze tailpiece, multiple-bound top and back, maple neck, multiple-bound rosewood fingerboard, cloud inlay, block inlay at 15th fret, bound peghead, vine peghead inlay, gold-plated hardware, sunburst or natural finish

Available: **1939–41**

De Luxe Cutaway flat top introduced (see following): **early 1950s**

Concert, Seville, and **Alhambra,** see New York-Made Classicals (following)

F.T. 110: 15 7/8" wide, 5 3/16" deep, square-shouldered dreadnought, maple back and sides, multiple-bound top, single-bound back, single-bound fingerboard, cherry neck, slotted-block inlay, center-dip peghead, pearl script logo, vertical oval peghead inlay, enclosed tuners
Introduced: **1941**
Body shape with more rounded shoulders and thinner waist, laminated maple back and sides, arched back, epsilon (slashed-*C*) on pickguard, finish options: all-natural, natural top with stained back and sides, sunburst: **1949**
16" wide, compensating saddle: **1954**
Model number continued by Gibson as **Frontier** (see following): **1958**

F.T. 79: 15 7/8" wide, 5 3/16" deep, square-shouldered dreadnought, walnut back and sides, rosewood pin bridge, double-bound top, single-bound back, cherry neck, single-bound rosewood fingerboard, slotted-block inlay, single-bound center-dip peghead, stickpin peghead inlay
Introduced: **1941**
Body shape with more rounded shoulders and thinner waist, laminated maple back and sides, arched back, epsilon (slashed-*C*) on pickguard, single-parallelogram inlay, vertical oval peghead inlay: **1949**
16" wide, triple-bound top and back specified (some single-bound), mahogany neck, stain finish on back and sides: **1954**
Model number continued by Gibson as **Texan** (see following): **1958**

F.T. 50: 14 1/2" wide, mahogany back and sides, tortoiseshell celluloid binding on top and back, cherry neck, unbound rosewood fingerboard, dot inlay, center-dip peghead, pearl script logo, natural top finish, brown finish on back and sides
Introduced: **1941**
Discontinued: **by 1949**

F.T. 45: 14 1/2" wide, walnut back and sides, bound top and back, cherry neck, unbound rosewood fingerboard, dot inlay, natural top finish, brown finish on back and sides
Introduced: **1941**
Discontinued: **by 1949**
Model number reintroduced by Gibson as **Cortez** (see following): **1958**

F.T. 30: 14 1/2" wide, all-mahogany body, no binding, cherry neck, dot inlay, script logo, 3-on-a-strip tuners, mahogany finish
Introduced: **1941**
Discontinued: **by 1949**
Model number reintroduced by Gibson as **Caballero** (see following): **1958**

Deluxe Cutaway (flat top), some labeled **Deluxe Regent:** 17 3/8" wide, single rounded cutaway, laminated curly maple back and sides, arched back, tortoise pickguard extends to edge of cutaway bout, 8-ply binding on top and back, single-bound rosewood fingerboard, curved fingerboard end follows shape of soundhole, cloud inlay, flower peghead inlay (some with vine), gold-plated hardware, natural top (some sunburst)
Introduced: **1954**
Discontinued: **by 1957**

Model name unknown: 17 3/8" wide, single rounded cutaway, less fancy than Deluxe Cutaway flat top, slotted-block inlay
Introduced: **early 1950s**
Discontinued: **by 1957**

Gibson/U.S.-Made Steel-String Models, 1958–95

See Gibson, General Information, for illustration of round-shouldered and square-shouldered dreadnought body shapes.

Frontier: 16 1/4" wide, square-shouldered dreadnought, maple back and sides, 7-ply top binding, 5-ply back binding, epsilon (slashed-*C*) logo on pickguard, 25 1/2" scale, bound fingerboard, slotted-block inlay, pearl logo, gold-plated hardware, walnut finish back and sides, natural or sunburst top finish
Introduced (model number FT 110 continued from Epi line): **1958**
Vertical oval peghead inlay: **1961**
Adjustable saddle: **1962**
Large pointed pickguard with rope and cactus design: **1963**
Teardrop pickguard: **1965**
Some with laminated back: **c. 1968**
Discontinued: **1970**

Limited run of 30 made by Gibson Montana, square-shouldered dreadnought, rosewood back and sides, upper belly bridge, large pickguard with extended point and rope-and-cactus engraving, multiple-bound top and back, bound rosewood fingerboard, slotted block inlay, unbound peghead, vertical oval peghead inlay, nickel-plated tuners with plastic keystone buttons, antique chocolate finish on back and sides with natural top, or natural finish: **1994**

Texan: 16 1/4" wide, round-shouldered dreadnought, mahogany back and sides, epsilon (slashed-*C*) on pickguard, 25 1/2" scale, rosewood fingerboard, single-parallelogram inlay, pearloid tuner buttons, sunburst or natural top finish
Introduced (model number FT 79 continued from Epi line): **1958**
Vertical oval peghead inlay: **1961**
Adjustable rosewood saddle: **1962**
Metal tuner buttons: **by 1967**
Discontinued: **1970**
Limited run of 170 made by Gibson Montana, round-shouldered dreadnought, mahogany back and sides, rosewood bridge with upper belly, squared-teardrop pickguard with epsilon (slashed-*C*) logo, multiple-bound top and back, unbound rosewood fingerboard, single-parallelogram inlay, epsilon (slashed-*C*) on truss rod cover, nickel-plated Grover tuners, vertical oval peghead decal, decal logo, antique natural or vintage sunburst finish: **1993–95**

Cortez: 14 1/4" wide, mahogany back and sides, 24 3/4" scale, dot inlay, epsilon (slashed-*C*) logo on pickguard, metal peghead logo plate, sunburst or natural top finish
Model number FT 45 continued from Epi line: **1958**
Sunburst finish only: **1959**
Natural top optional, adjustable saddle on natural top only: **1962**
Discontinued: **1970**

Caballero: 14 1/4" wide, all mahogany body, tortoiseshell celluloid binding, epsilon (slashed-*C*) logo on pickguard, 24 3/4" scale, dot inlay
Model number FT 30 continued from Epi line: **1958**
No logo on pickguard: **1961**
Adjustable saddle: **1963**

Tenor available: **1963–68**
Discontinued: **1970**

Excellente: 16 1/4" wide, square-shouldered dreadnought, rosewood back and sides, tune-o-matic bridge, large pointed pickguard with eagle, multiple-bound top and back, 25 1/2" scale, multiple-bound ebony fingerboard, cloud inlay, large pearl and abalone peghead inlay, single-bound peghead, gold-plated hardware, natural top finish
Available: **1963–69**
Limited run of 23 made by Gibson Montana, square-shouldered dreadnought, rosewood back and sides, bridge style similar to Gibson Dove but with 2 points (no upper points) and 2 pearl dots, pickguard engraved with eagle landing, multiple-bound top and back, 25 1/2" scale, maple neck, bound ebony fingerboard, cloud inlay, bound peghead with large unengraved pearl inlay, epsilon (slashed-*C*) on truss rod cover, gold-plated tuners with keystone buttons, antique natural or vintage sunburst finish: **1994–95**

El Dorado: 16 1/4" wide, square-shouldered dreadnought shape, mahogany back and sides, multiple-bound top and back, 25 1/2" scale, bound fingerboard, single-parallelogram inlay, vertical oval peghead inlay, metal tuner buttons
Introduced: **1963**
Adjustable saddle: **1965**
Discontinued: **1970**

Troubadour: 16 1/4" wide, square-shouldered dreadnought shape, maple back and sides, 2 white pickguards, multiple-bound top, single-bound back, 12 frets clear of body, classical fingerboard width, 24 3/4" scale, slotted-block inlay, solid peghead, gold-plated hardware, walnut finish back and sides
Available: **1963–69**

Folkster: 14 1/4" wide, mahogany back and sides, 2 white pickguards, 12 frets clear of body, classical fingerboard width, 24 3/4" scale, dot inlay
Available: **1966–69**

EM10: mahogany back and sides, dot inlay, natural or vintage sunburst finish, limited run of 51 made in Bozeman, MT (only specs available)
Available: **1993**

EM20: rosewood back and sides, dot inlay, natural or vintage sunburst finish, limited run of 57 made in Bozeman, MT (only specs available)
Available: **1993**

EM30 A/E: cutaway, Accu-Voice piezo pickup system, natural or vintage sunburst finish, limited run of 16 made in Bozeman, MT (only specs available)
Available: **1993**

12-STRINGS

Bard: 16 1/4" wide, mahogany back and sides (maple back and sides with walnut finish listed as option), adjustable saddle, epsilon (slashed-*C*) on pickguard, multiple-bound top and back, 24 3/4" scale, dot inlay, vertical oval peghead inlay
Available: **1962–69**

Serenader: 14 1/4" wide, mahogany back and sides, adjustable saddle, slashed-*C* logo on pickguard, 24 3/4" scale, dot inlay, walnut finish on back and sides
Available: **1963–69**

NEW YORK-MADE CLASSICALS

Concert: 16 1/2" wide, maple back and sides, multiple-bound top and back, rosewood bridge, 12 frets clear of body, 14-fret neck optional, single-bound rosewood fingerboard, treble-side fingerboard extension over soundhole, slotted peghead with dip in top center, gold-plated hardware, clear finish
Available: **Nov. 1938–late 1941**

Alhambra: 14 3/8" wide, maple back and sides, single-bound top and back, fixed rosewood bridge, 12 frets clear of body, 14-fret neck optional, single-bound rosewood fingerboard, treble-side fingerboard extension over soundhole, slotted peghead with dip in top center, nickel-plated hardware, clear finish
Introduced: **1938**
14-fret neck discontinued: **1941**
Discontinued: **late 1941**

Seville: 14 3/8" wide, mahogany back and sides, rosewood bridge, 12 frets clear of body, 14 fret-neck optional, unbound rosewood fingerboard, treble-side fingerboard extension over soundhole, slotted peghead with dip in top center, clear finish
Introduced: **1938**
14-fret neck discontinued: **1941**
Discontinued: **late 1941**
Model name reintroduced by Gibson (see following): **1961**

GIBSON-MADE CLASSICALS

All are 14 1/4" wide with 25 1/2" scale, fan bracing.

Seville: mahogany back and sides, tortoiseshell celluloid binding, standard rounded neck heel, pointed peghead corners
Introduced: **1961**
French heel (sharp back edge): **1965**
Discontinued: **1970**

Seville Electric: 1961–63

Barcelone: maple back and sides, black binding, French heel (sharp back edge), pearloid tuner buttons, gold-plated hardware, rosewood finish on back and sides
Available: **1963–68**

Espana: maple back and sides, black binding, French heel (sharp back edge), walnut finish on back and sides
Available: **1962–68**

Classic: mahogany back and sides, French heel (sharp back edge), tortoiseshell celluloid binding
Introduced: **1963**
Standard heel: **1965**
Discontinued: **1970**

Entrada: 13 1/4" wide, 22 3/4" scale, standard rounded neck heel, pointed peghead corners
Available: **1963–68**

Madrid: mahogany back and sides, tortoiseshell celluloid binding, standard rounded neck heel, ladder-braced top, pointed peghead corners
Available: **1962–69**

EPIPHONE

ELECTRIC ARCHTOPS

EPIPHONE

COMMENTS

During the New York era, Epiphone made flat tops of good quality, but they never achieved the recognition of Epi archtops or the flat top guitars made by Gibson and Martin. Gibson-made Epi flat tops are better known, partly because so many were sold. They are fully equivalent in quality to similar Gibson models of the same period. However, because Gibson quality declined in the 1960s, very few Gibson-Epis are highly sought by collectors today.

Jumbo size models are the most highly regarded, especially those from 1958–61 with New York-style neck and non-adjustable saddle. Most desirable is the Excellente, which is fancier than any Gibson dreadnought flat top of its time and rivaled only in the Gibson line by the super jumbo J-200.

ELECTRIC ARCHTOPS KEY

Dot inlay
 Non-cutaway
  Full-depth body
   Electar peghead logo
    14 3/4" wide = **Electar Model M Spanish**
    13 1/2" wide = **Electar Model C Spanish**
   Epiphone logo
    Mahogany back and sides = **Kent**
    Maple back and sides
     14 3/8" or 13 1/2" wide = **Coronet**
     15 1/4" wide = **Harry Volpe**
     16 3/8" or 15 1/4" wide = **Century, c. 1939–58**
  Thinbody
   Knobs into pickguard = **Granada**
   Knobs into top
    24 3/4" scale = **Century, 1958–70**
    22" scale = **Century 3/4**
  Pointed cutaway
   24 3/4" scale
    Knobs into top = **Sorrento, 1960–62**
    Knobs mounted on pickguard = **Granada Cutaway**
   22" scale = **Sorrento 3/4**
  Double-cutaway
   Knobs into top = **Casino, 1961–62**
   Knobs and switches on arc-shaped plate = **Caiola Standard**
Cloud inlay
 Non-cutaway = **Zephyr De Luxe**
 Cutaway = **Zephyr Deluxe Regent**
V-block 3-piece inlay
 Non-cutaway = **Deluxe Electric**
 Single-cutaway
  Full-depth body
   1 or 2 pickups = **Zephyr Deluxe Regent**
   3 pickups = **Zephyr Emperor Regent, Emperor Electric**
  Thinbody = **Emperor**
 Double-cutaway = **Sheraton**

Single-parallelogram inlay
  Knobs into pickguard = **Professional**
  Knobs into top
    Mini-humbucking pickups = **Riviera**
    P-90 pickup(s) = **Casino, late 1962–70**
Block or slotted-block inlay
  Non-cutaway = **Zephyr, 1937–58**
  Single rounded cutaway
    Full-depth body
      2 pickups = **Broadway**
      1 pickup = **Zephyr Regent (Zephyr Cutaway)**
    Thinbody = **Zephyr, 1958–70**
  Pointed cutaway
    Vertical oval peghead inlay = **Howard Roberts**
    Vine peghead inlay = **Howard Roberts Custom**
  Double-cutaway = **Caiola** or **Caiola Custom**
Oval inlay
  Gold-plated hardware = **Windsor**
  Nickel-plated hardware = **Sorrento, 1962–70**

ELECTRIC ARCHTOPS

SECTION ORGANIZATION

New York-Made Models, 1935–57
Gibson-Made Models, Hollowbody
Gibson-Made Models, Semi-Hollowbody

NEW YORK-MADE MODELS, 1937–57

Electar Model M Spanish: 14 3/4" wide, laminated maple body, flat back, horseshoe pickup, 2 knobs (earliest with 1 volume knob incorporating on/off switch), jack on top, cloth-covered access plate on back, single-bound top and back, neck extension flush with top (not elevated), single-bound rosewood fingerboard, dot inlay, point at top of peghead, *Electar* peghead logo, sunburst top, brown finish on back and sides, tenor and plectrum available
Introduced: **1935**
"Rhythm" control (third knob for additional tone control) added: **1937**
Oblong pickup with screwpoles, neck extension raised off of top: **later 1937**
Discontinued: **by 1939**

Electar Model C Spanish: 13 1/2" wide, laminated maple body, flat top and back, blade pickup in oblong housing, 2 knobs (earliest with 1 knob), jack on top, cloth-covered access plate on back, single-

bound top and back, unbound rosewood fingerboard, dot inlay, point at top of peghead, *Electar* peghead logo, sunburst top, brown finish on back and sides, tenor and plectrum available
Introduced: **1935**
"Rhythm" control (third knob for additional tone control) added: **mid 1937**
Discontinued: **by 1939**

Century: 14 3/4" wide, laminated maple back and sides, mid-point of *f*-holes even with pickup, blade pickup with oblong housing in bridge position, metal pickup cover/handrest, 2 knobs near edge, jack on top, trapeze tailpiece, single-bound top and back, cloth-covered access plate on back, bound rosewood fingerboard, dot inlay, center-dip peghead, metal peghead logo plate, highlighted walnut finish, tenor and plectrum available
Introduced: **by 1939**
15 1/4" wide, top of *f*-holes even with pickup, no handrest, jack on side: **1941**
16 3/8" wide, oblong pickup with fat blade in neck position, square control plates with radial markings, no back access plate, unbound fingerboard: **mid 1940s**
Large rectangular pickup with non-adjustable poles in neck position, knobs on a line that crosses strings, epsilon (slashed-*C*) logo on pickguard, highlighted mahogany finish: **by 1949**

New York pickup with no poles and black mounting
blocks: **1950**

Some with DeArmond pickup with rectangular black
housing and oblong chrome plate, blond finish
available: **1953**

Gibson-Epi Century (see following): **1958**

Coronet: 14 3/8" wide (some 13 1/2" wide), laminated mahogany body, mid-point of *f*-holes even
with pickup, blade pickup with oblong housing in
bridge position, cord hard-wired through top, 2
knobs on line parallel to strings, trapeze tailpiece,
single-bound top and back, cloth-covered access
plate on back, unbound rosewood fingerboard, dot
inlay, metal peghead logo plate, brown sunburst
finish, Spanish or Hawaiian setup

Introduced: **by 1939**

Top of *f*-holes even with pickup, knobs close to edge,
jack on side: **1941**

Discontinued: **by 1949**

Model name revived (see Electric Solidbodies): **1958**

Zephyr: 16 3/8" wide, laminated curly maple body,
mid-point of *f*-holes even with pickup, 1 oblong
pickup with large screwpoles in bridge position,
metal pickup cover/handrest, 2 knobs on circular
Mastervoicer plates, knobs on line parallel to
strings, jack on top, trapeze tailpiece, 3-ply top
binding, single-bound back, cloth-covered access
plate on back, 3-piece maple/mahogany neck,
single-bound rosewood fingerboard, pearl block
inlay, metal peghead logo plate, blond finish, tenor
and plectrum available

Introduced: **1939**

Top of *f*-holes even with pickup, no handrest, knobs
close to edge, jack on side: **1941**

Longer pickguard cutout for pickup: **1943**

Top-mounted pickup in middle position, single-bound
top and back, some with laminated spruce top,
some with sunburst finish: **c. 1944**

17 3/8" wide, large rectangular metal-covered pickup
with polepieces: **by 1947**

No more with laminated spruce top, New York pickup
in neck position, 3-piece cherry/maple neck: **1949**

Frequensator tailpiece, knobs on line parallel to
strings, sunburst or blond finish: **1950**

Some with DeArmond pickup and clear plastic barrel
knobs, knobs on line that crosses strings: **1953**

Catalogued as **Zephyr Electric**, available in non-cutaway

or cutaway, some cutaways labeled **Zephyr Cutaway**,
tenor available as non-cutaway only: **1954**

Gibson-Epi Zephyr (see following): **1958**

Zephyr Regent: rounded cutaway, sunburst finish
only, introduced: **1950**

Sunburst or blond finish, some with DeArmond pickup
and clear plastic barrel knobs, knobs on line that
crosses strings: **1953**

Catalogued as **Zephyr Electric**, available in non-
cutaway or cutaway, some labeled **Zephyr Cutaway:**
1954

Gibson-Epi Zephyr (see following): **1958**

Zephyr De Luxe: 17 3/8" wide, laminated spruce
top, 1 pickup with slot-head screwpoles and oblong
housing in bridge position, volume and tone control
on 1 shaft with circular *Mastervoicer* control plate,
Frequensator tailpiece, 5-ply top and back binding,
triple-bound pickguard, 5-piece maple/walnut neck,
bound rosewood fingerboard with 2 inlaid white
lines, cloud inlay, block inlay at 15th fret, triple-
bound peghead, vine peghead inlay, pearl logo, gold-
plated hardware, blond finish, tenor (with metal
peghead logo plate) and plectrum models available

Introduced, first listed as **Deluxe Zephyr Spanish
Electric: Dec. 1, 1941**

2 knobs on circular *Mastervoicer* plates on line at right
angle to strings: **1942**

Pickup in middle position, some with sunburst finish:
by 1947

Large rectangular metal-covered pickup: **by 1948**

Pickup in neck position: **1949**

New York pickup, 2 pickups optional, 3-way slide
switch on 2-pickup model, 2 knobs near edge,
Mastervoicer control plates on 1-pickup model
only, sunburst or blond finish: **1950**

Knobs on line parallel to strings: **1951**

Discontinued: **1954**

Zephyr De Luxe Regent: 17 3/4" wide, rounded cutaway, laminated spruce top, large rectangular
pickup in middle position, 2 knobs near edge, circular *Mastervoicer* control plates, slotted switch, Frequensator tailpiece, 7-ply binding on top and back,
triple-bound rosewood fingerboard, pearl block inlay
with abalone V insert (some with inverted V, some
with cloud), triple-bound peghead, vine peghead
inlay, gold-plated hardware, sunburst or blond finish

Introduced: **1948**

2 pickups optional, knobs on line parallel to strings
3-way slider switch: **1949**

2 New York pickups (no single-pickup model): **1950**

5-ply top and back binding, triple-bound pickguard:
1951

Knobs on line that crosses strings: **by 1953**

Renamed **Deluxe Electric**, specified with laminated
maple top, some with single-flower (Broadway
type) peghead inlay: **1954**

Some 18 1/2" wide with single-bound f-holes and
nickel-plated hardware: **mid 1950s**

Discontinued: **1958**

Kent: 15 3/8" wide, laminated mahogany back and
sides, laminated maple top, flat back, large rectangular pickup with non-adjustable poles in bridge
position, 2 knobs on a line that crosses strings,
trapeze tailpiece, bound top and back, epsilon
(slashed-C) on pickguard, unbound rosewood
fingerboard, dot inlay, metal peghead logo plate,
sunburst top finish, brown finish on back and
sides

Introduced: **1949**

Discontinued: **by 1954**

Zephyr Emperor Regent: 18 1/2" wide,
rounded cutaway, laminated spruce top, laminated
maple back and sides, 3 New York pickups, 2
knobs, control plate with 6 small pushbuttons, 7-
ply binding on top and back, 3-ply binding on f-
holes, single-bound rosewood fingerboard with 2
white lines inlaid near edges, pearl block inlay with
abalone V insert, triple-bound peghead, vine peghead inlay, sunburst or blond finish

Introduced as **Zephyr Emperor Vari Tone: 1950**

Some with DeArmond pickups: **1953–57**

Renamed **Emperor Electric**, laminated maple top: **1953**

Gibson-Epi Emperor (see following): **1958**

Harry Volpe: 15 1/4" wide, laminated white
mahogany body, extra-wide string spacing, black
rectangular pickup, oblong chrome plate in center
area of pickup, pickup in neck position, knobs on
line that crosses strings, epsilon (slashed-C) logo
on pickguard, trapeze tailpiece, single-bound top
and back, unbound rosewood fingerboard, dot
inlay, 5-sided metal peghead logo plate with model
name, 3-on-a-strip tuners, sunburst finish

Available: **March 1955–57**

GIBSON-MADE MODELS, HOLLOWBODY

Emperor: 18 1/2" wide, single rounded cutaway,
thinbody, 3 New York pickups, 4 knobs, tune-o-
matic bridge, Frequensator tailpiece, multiple binding, ebony fingerboard, 25 1/2" scale, 3-piece
V-block inlay with abalone wedge, vine peghead
inlay, stairstep tuner buttons, gold-plated hardware,
sunburst or natural finish

Model name continued from Epi line: **1958**

Mini-humbucking pickups: **by 1961**

Available by special order only: **1963**

Sunburst finish only: **1965**

Discontinued (later in Japanese- and Korean-made
lines with different specs): **1969**

Broadway: 17 3/8" wide, single rounded cutaway,
full-depth body, 2 New York pickups, rosewood
bridge, Frequensator tailpiece, single-bound pickguard, 25 1/2" scale, block inlay, fat columnlike
peghead inlay, deluxe plastic tuner buttons, sunburst or natural finish

Continued from Epi line: **1958**

Mini-humbucking pickups: **by 1961**

Tune-o-matic bridge: **1963**

Cherry finish optional, only year shipped: **1967**

Natural finish optional: **1968**

Discontinued: **1970**

Century: 16 3/8" wide, non-cutaway, thinbody, 1
New York pickup, rosewood bridge, trapeze tailpiece, unbound tortoiseshell celluloid pickguard, 25
1/2" scale, dot inlay, metal peghead logo plate, sunburst finish

Model name continued from Epi line: **1958**

P-90 pickup: **1959**

Royal burgundy finish: **1961**

No peghead plate: **1963**

Sunburst finish only: **1968**

Discontinued (later in Japanese-made line): **1970**

Century 3/4: 3/4-size, 22" scale: **1961–67**

Zephyr: 17 3/8" wide, single rounded cutaway, thinbody, 2 New York pickups, trapeze tailpiece,
unbound tortoiseshell celluloid pickguard, slotted-
block inlay, metal peghead logo plate, natural or
sunburst finish

Model name continued from Epi line: **1958**

No peghead plate: **1960**

Mini-humbucking pickups: **by 1961**
Discontinued: **1964**

Windsor: 16 3/8" wide, single pointed cutaway, thinbody, 1 New York pickup in neck position, 2 New York pickups optional, rosewood bridge, trapeze tailpiece, unbound tortoiseshell celluloid pickguard, 24 3/4" scale, oval inlay, metal peghead logo plate, gold-plated hardware, sunburst or natural finish
Introduced: **1959**
No peghead plate: **1960**
Mini-humbucking pickup(s): **by 1961**
Discontinued: **1962**

Sorrento: 16 1/4" wide, single pointed cutaway, thinbody, 1 or 2 mini-humbucking pickups, pickup in neck position on single-pickup model, tune-o-matic bridge, vibrato optional, trapeze tailpiece, unbound tortoiseshell celluloid pickguard, 24 3/4" scale, dot inlay, metal peghead logo plate, nickel-plated hardware, sunburst, natural or royal olive finish
Introduced: **1960**
Oval inlay: **1962**
Vibrato discontinued: **1962**
No peghead plate: **by 1963**
Cherry or sunburst finish: **1968**
Discontinued: **1970**

Sorrento 3/4: 3/4 size, 22" scale: **1961–62**

Casino: 16" wide, rounded double cutaway, thinbody, 1 P-90 pickup in middle position or 2 P-90 pickups, tune-o-matic bridge, trapeze tailpiece, vibrato optional, white 3-ply pickguard with beveled edge, single-bound top and back, 24 3/4" scale, 16 frets clear of body, single-bound fingerboard, dot inlay, sunburst or royal tan finish
Introduced: **1961**
Vibrato optional: **1962**
Single-parallelogram inlay: **late 1962**
Chrome pickup cover(s): **by 1963**
Cherry finish optional: **1967**
Discontinued (later in Japanese-made line): **1970**

Granada: 16 1/4" wide, non-cutaway thinbody, 1 *f*-hole, 1 oblong single-coil pickup (Gibson Melody Maker style) mounted into pickguard, rosewood bridge, trapeze tailpiece, controls built into pickguard

(like Gibson ES-120T), pickguard surrounds pickup, 24 3/4" scale, dot inlay, sunburst finish
Available: **1962–69**

Granada Cutaway: single pointed cutaway: **1965–70**

Caiola Custom: Al Caiola model, 16" wide, double rounded cutaway, thin body, 2 mini-humbucking pickups, ebony adjustable bridge, trapeze tailpiece with wood center insert, *Caiola Model* inlaid on trapeze insert, arc-shaped control plate with 2 knobs and 5 switches plus pickup selector switch, 7-ply top binding, 5-ply back binding, 5-ply pickguard binding, *Custom* on block at body end of fingerboard, 25 1/2" scale, single-bound rosewood fingerboard, zero fret, block inlay, single-bound peghead, fat column peghead inlay, mahogany red (walnut) or royal tan (yellow sunburst) finish
Introduced as **Caiola: 1963**
Tune-o-matic bridge: **by 1965**
Renamed **Caiola Custom: 1966**
Walnut finish only: **1968**
Discontinued: **1970**

Caiola Standard: 2 P-90 pickups, otherwise same electronics as Caiola Custom, single-bound top and back, dot inlay, unbound peghead, no peghead ornament
Introduced: **1966**
Cherry or sunburst finish: **1968**
Discontinued: **1970**

Howard Roberts: 16 1/4" wide, single pointed cutaway, full-depth body, carved spruce top, single-bound oval soundhole, no soundhole ring, 1 floating mini-humbucking pickup, single-bound top and back, plate tailpiece with 3 raised parallelograms and pointed ends, white 3-ply pickguard with beveled edge, rosewood bridge, bound rosewood fingerboard, slotted-block inlay, vertical oval peghead inlay, chrome-plated hardware, cherry finish
Introduced: **1964**
Triple-bound top: **1965**
Natural or sunburst finish optional: **1965–67**
Natural or sunburst finish standard, cherry not listed: **1968**
Tune-o-matic bridge: **1967**
Discontinued: **1970**

Howard Roberts Custom: tune-o-matic bridge (pictured in catalog with adjustable rosewood bridge), triple-bound top, single-bound back, single-bound pickguard, single-bound ebony fingerboard, triple-bound peghead, vine peghead inlay, walnut finish
Introduced: **1965**
Natural finish optional, only year (6 shipped): **1966**
Multiple-bound top and pickguard, triple-bound back, multiple-bound peghead, black finish optional: **late 1960s**
Discontinued: **1970**
Reintroduced with changes in Gibson line (see Gibson Electric Archtops): **1974**

GIBSON-MADE MODELS, SEMI-HOLLOWBODY

Sheraton: 16" wide, double rounded cutaway, 2 New York pickups, tune-o-matic bridge, Frequensator tailpiece, optional Epi vibrato with epsilon (slashed-*C*) logo on tailpiece, multiple-bound top and back, multiple-bound pickguard, 24 3/4" scale, bound fingerboard, V-block inlay, metal tuner buttons (early with New York style tuners), multiple-bound peghead, vine peghead inlay, gold-plated hardware, sunburst or natural finish
Introduced: **by 1958**
Mini-humbucking pickups, vibrato standard: **by 1961**
Cherry finish optional: **1965**
Discontinued (later in Japanese- and Korean-made lines): **1970**
Limited run of 250 made in Nashville: **1993–94**

Professional: 16" wide, double rounded cutaway, 1 mini-humbucking pickup, 2 knobs on treble side, 3 knobs and numerous switches on bass side (companion amplifier has no control knobs and is controlled from the guitar), all controls mounted through symmetrical pickguard, tune-o-matic bridge, Frequensator tailpiece, single-bound top and back (catalog specifies multiple binding), single-parallelogram inlay, multi-prong jack and standard 1/4" jack, mahogany finish
Available: **1962–66**

Riviera: 16" wide, double rounded cutaway, 2 mini-humbucking pickups, tune-o-matic bridge, Frequensator tailpiece, single-bound top and back (catalog specifies multiple binding), single-bound tortoiseshell celluloid pickguard, 24 3/4" scale, single-bound fingerboard, single-parallelogram inlay, royal tan finish
Introduced: **1962**
Sunburst finish standard: **1965**
White 3-ply pickguard with beveled edge, cherry finish optional: **1966**
Vibrato optional: **1967**
Discontinued (later in Japanese-made line): **1970**
Limited run of 250 made in Nashville: **1993–94**

Riviera 12-string: symmetrical peghead
Introduced: **1965**
White 3-ply pickguard with beveled edge, cherry finish optional: **1966**
Discontinued: **1970**

COMMENTS

New York-made Epiphone electrics are interesting but generally are not nearly as highly regarded as the equivalent acoustics, which have solid carved tops and backs rather than the laminated construction of the electrics. In addition, the electronics on New York Epis are not of high quality compared to Gibsons of the same period or to the later Gibson-made Epiphones. Consequently, New York Epi electrics bring less than Gibsons of the same period or equivalent Epi acoustics.

Early Gibson Epis with New York pickups are of interest to collectors. Most hollowbody Epi electrics bring less than the equivalent Gibson models.

Double-cutaway thinbody electrics are the most highly sought, particularly the rare Emperor (66 total made) and the early blond-finish Sheraton. Some seek Sheratons with New York pickups, though not for sound. The Sheraton brings fully as much and sometimes more than the equivalent Gibson ES-355 of the same period. The Riviera, though equal in playability and sound, is not nearly as sought after and brings less than the equivalent ES-335. The Casino is associated with the Beatles and brings as much or more than the equivalent ES-330.

ELECTRIC SOLIDBODIES KEY

Body shaped like map of U.S. = **Map shape promo model**
Single cutaway
    2 pickups = **Olympic Double, 1960–62**
    1 pickup
        Standard scale = **Olympic, 1960–62**
        3/4 scale = **Olympic 3/4, 1960–62**
Symmetrical double cutaway
    2 pickups
        Carved (arched) top = **Spirit**
        Flat top
            Gold-plated hardware = **Crestwood (Custom), c. 1958–62**
            Nickel-plated hardware = **Wilshire, c. 1958–62**
    1 pickup
        Poles visible on pickup = **Coronet, c. 1958–62**
        No pickup poles = **Olympic Special, 1963–65**
Asymmetrical double cutaway, bass-side horn longer than treble-side
    Block inlay
        3 pickups = **Crestwood Deluxe**
        2 pickups = **USA Coronet**
    Oval inlay = **Crestwood Custom, 1963–70**
    Offset dot inlay = **USA Pro I**
    Dot inlay in center of fingerboard
        2 pickups
            Poles visible on pickups = **Wilshire, 1963–70**
            No pickup poles = **Olympic Double, 1963–70**
        1 pickup
            Poles visible on pickups
                epsilon (slashed-*C*) on truss rod cover = **Coronet, 1963–70**
                Dwight on truss rod cover or peghead = **Dwight**
            No pickup poles
                All frets clear of body = **Olympic, 1963–70**
                Some frets over body = **Olympic Special, 1965–70**

ELECTRIC SOLIDBODIES

All Epiphone solidbody electrics are double-cutaway with 24 3/4" scale, unless otherwise specified.

All were listed by 1963 as available in the following custom colors: sunset yellow, California coral and Pacific blue.

Crestwood (Custom): symmetrical slab body (square body edges), 1 3/4" deep, 2 New York pickups, tune-o-matic bridge, asymmetrical pickguard with epsilon (slashed-*C*) logo, rosewood fingerboard, dot inlay, metal peghead logo plate, gold-plated hardware, cherry finish
Introduced: **by 1958**

1 3/8" deep, rounded body edges, symmetrical pickguard: **c. 1959**

Renamed **Crestwood Custom: 1959**

2 mini-humbucking pickups, vibrato, oval inlay, no pickguard logo, no peghead plate, pearl peghead logo: **1961**

White finish optional: **by 1962**

Asymmetrical body with upper bass horn slightly longer than upper treble, vibrato optional, asymmetrical pickguard, 6-on-a-side tuner arrangement, nickel-plated hardware: **1963**

Vibrato standard: **1965**

Discontinued: **1970**

Crestwood Deluxe: asymmetrical body with bass horn slightly longer than treble, rounded body edges, 1 3/8" deep, 3 mini-humbucking pickups, tune-o-matic bridge, vibrato, asymmetrical pickguard, bound ebony fingerboard, block inlay, triple-bound peghead, 6-on-a-side tuner arrangement, cherry or white finish
Available: **1963–69**

Coronet: symmetrical slab body (square body edges), 1 3/4" deep, 1 New York pickup, asymmetrical pickguard, combination bridge-tailpiece, dot inlay, metal peghead logo plate, cherry finish (some black)
Introduced: **1958**
P-90 pickup: **c. 1959**
1 3/8" deep, rounded body edges, symmetrical pickguard: **c. 1960**
No peghead plate: **1961**
Vibrato optional: **1962**
Asymmetrical body with upper bass horn slightly longer than upper treble, metal covered P-90 pickup, 6-on-a-side tuner arrangement, silver fox finish optional: **1963**
No vibrato: **1966**
Discontinued: **1970**
Reintroduced as **USA Coronet:** active electronics, 1 NSX single-coil pickup, 1 L-6 humbucking pickup, tune-o-matic bridge or Floyd Rose vibrato, maple neck, 24 3/4" scale, bound rosewood fingerboard, block inlay, gold-plated hardware with tune-o-matic bridge, chrome-plated hardware with Floyd Rose bridge, bullion gold, candy apple blue or candy apple purple finish: **1990**
Black chrome or gold-plated hardware, candy apple blue finish optional: **1991**
Discontinued: **1992**

Wilshire: symmetrical slab body (square body edges), 1 3/4" deep, 2 white soapbar P-90 pickups, symmetrical pickguard, tune-o-matic bridge, vibrato optional, dot inlay, pearl logo, cherry finish
Introduced: **1959**
1 3/8" deep, rounded body edges: **c. 1960**
Black soapbar P-90 pickups, epsilon (slashed-*C*) on pickguard, no vibrato: **1961**
2 mini-humbucking pickups, Maestro vibrato optional: **mid 1962**
Asymmetrical body with upper bass horn slightly longer than upper treble, 6-on-a-side tuner arrangement: **1963**

Red fox finish (cherry stain with yellow filler) optional: **1965**
Vibrato not offered: **1966**
Discontinued: **1970**

Wilshire 12-string, center-dip peghead: **1966–68**

Olympic: single cutaway, 1 single-coil pickup with no poles in oblong black housing (Gibson Melody Maker style), stud-mounted bridge/tailpiece, rosewood fingerboard, dot inlay, narrow peghead, script decal logo reads upside-down to player, sunburst finish
Introduced: **1960**
Asymmetrical double cutaway with upper bass horn slightly longer than upper treble, epsilon (slashed-*C*) between pickups: **1963**
6-on-a-side tuner arrangement: **1964**
Maestro vibrato optional: **1964**
Vibrato standard: **1965**
Cherry finish optional: **1966–69**
Discontinued: **1970**

Olympic Double: 2 pickups: **1960–69**

Olympic 3/4: 3/4 size, 22" scale: **1960–63**

Olympic Special: symmetrical body (like Gibson Melody Maker of the same period) with sharper cutaway tips than other Epi models, 1 single-coil pickup with no poles in oblong black housing (Gibson Melody Maker style), pickguard extends around pickup, vibrato optional, dot inlay, narrow peghead, logo reads upside down to player, sunburst finish
Introduced: **1962**
Maestro vibrato optional: **1964–65**
Asymmetrical body with bass horn slightly longer than treble (still with sharper tips than other Epis), vibrato standard: **1965**
Discontinued: **1970**

Dwight: made for dealer, same specs and model number as Coronet (see preceding) but with *Dwight Model* on truss rod cover or peghead, no Epiphone logo on peghead
75 shipped: **1963**
36 shipped: **1967**

Spirit: double cutaway, carved top, 2 humbucking pickups, 4 knobs, toggle switch, similar to Japanese- or Korean-made Genesis, made in Kalamazoo
Available: **1979**

Map shape: mahogany body (3-piece "pancake" style with maple center laminate) shaped like map of the United States, 2 humbucking pickups, 4 knobs, 1 switch, tune-o-matic bridge, dot inlay, pearl script logo, promotional model, companion to Gibson Map promotional model, made in U.S. Available: **1983**

USA Pro I: double-cutaway poplar body with extended horns, contoured top and back, Gibson L-8 humbucking pickup in bridge position, slant-mounted Gibson SC-2 single-coil pickup in neck position, 2 knobs, 1 switch, Floyd Rose vibrato, 25 1/2" scale, maple bolt-on neck, 24-fret ebony finger-board, offset dot inlay, *PRO* inlaid at 24th fret, *USA* on truss rod cover, 6-on-a-side tuner arrangement Available: **1989–91**

COMMENTS

Some collectors are interested in early solidbody models with New York pickups but not for their sound. Later solidbodies with mini-humbucking pickups bring less money than their Gibson equivalents with standard humbucking pickups. None is especially valuable, although the workmanship on Epiphones is fully equivalent to that of Gibson models of the same period.

ELECTRIC BASSES KEY

Solidbody
Adjustable bridge saddles = **Embassy Deluxe**
Non-adjustable saddle = **Newport**
Semi-hollowbody = **Rivoli**

ELECTRIC BASSES

Rivoli: thin semi-hollowbody, symmetrical double cutaway, *f*-holes, vibrato optional (rare), 1 large rectangular pickup with polepieces, dot inlay, banjo-style tuners, vertical oval peghead inlay, natural or sunburst finish
Introduced: **1959**
Right-angle tuners: **c. 1960**
Discontinued: **1962**
Reintroduced, sunburst finish only: **1963**
Natural finish optional: **1965**
Cherry finish optional: **1966**
Discontinued: **1969**
Reintroduced with 2 pickups: **1970**
Last made: **1970**

Newport: solidbody, asymmetrical double cutaway with bass horn longer than treble, 1 large rectangular pickup with polepieces, combination bridge-tailpiece, metal hand rest over strings, 30 1/2" scale, dot inlay, 2-on-a-side tuner arrangement, cherry finish
Introduced: **1961**
2 pickups optional: **1961–63**
Fuzz-tone available: **1962**
6-string model available: **1962–65**
4-on-a-side tuner arrangement: **1963**
Red fox finish (cherry stain with yellow fill) optional: **1965**
Discontinued: **1970**

Embassy Deluxe: solidbody, asymmetrical double cutaway with bass horn longer than treble, 2 pickups with no polepieces (like Gibson Thunderbird basses), metal handrest and bridge cover, tune-o-matic bridge, 34" scale, dot inlay, 4-on-a-side tuner arrangement, cherry finish
Available: **1963–69**

COMMENTS

Epiphone electric basses are not especially sought by collectors or players, although their workmanship and playability is fully equivalent to Gibson instruments of the same period. The Embassy Deluxe is the Epiphone equivalent to the highly sought Gibson Thunderbird basses, and it has the potential to gain some of appeal that Thunderbirds hold for collectors and players.

STEELS KEY

Singleneck
  Teardrop body shape
    Electar peghead logo = **Electar Hawaiian, 1935**
    Epiphone peghead logo = **Century, 1939–49**
  Guitar-shaped body
    Eharp on peghead = **Eddie Alkire Eharp**
    Electar on peghead = **Electar Model C Hawaiian**
    Epiphone peghead logo
      White pickguard = **Coronet**
      No pickguard
        No binding = **Kent**
        Bound top = **Century, 1950–57**
  Straight-line body edges
    Electar peghead logo = **Electar Model M Hawaiian**
    Epiphone peghead logo = **Zephyr**
  Rectangular body shape
    Pitch changing levers = **Varichord**
    No pitch changing levers = **Solo Console**
Doubleneck
  Rectangular body shape = **Duo Console, Double Console**
  Angled body corners = **Rocco**
Tripleneck = **Console Triple Neck**

STEELS

Most pre-World War II Epiphone lap steels have a rectangular plate on the back of the peghead with 7 (or more) patent numbers licensed from Miessner Inventions, Inc., of Millburn, NJ.

Electar Hawaiian: teardrop body shape, horseshoe-magnet pickup wraps over strings, 1 knob, dot markers, amplifier and guitar in same case
Only appearance: **Dec. 1935**

Electar Model M Electric Hawaiian:

stairstep body shape, Art Deco ornamentation etched on metal top piece, horseshoe-magnet pickup wraps over strings, 2 knobs on opposite sides, bound rosewood fingerboard, colored dot markers, *Electar* peghead plate, black-on-black finish, 6, 7 or 8 strings
Introduced: **1936**
Third knob (additional tone control) added: **mid 1937**
Pickup with large slot-head screwpoles, chrome-plated pickup cover/handrest, blue and black top finish, gray body finish: **1938**

Third knob removed: **mid 1938**
Discontinued: **1939**

Electar Model C Electric Hawaiian: guitar shape, oblong bar pickup, 2 knobs on opposite sides with treble knob mounted through pickguard, bound top, dot markers, *Electar* peghead plate, sunburst finish
Available: **1936–38**

Rocco: Anthony Rocco model, doubleneck, rectangular body with angled corners, metal top, horseshoe-magnet pickups wrap around strings, 2 volume knobs on opposite sides, 1 tone knob between necks (later 2 tone controls), jack on top, string dampers, geometric pattern markers, *Electar* logo plate and *Rocco Model* between necks, standard setup with 7-string and 8-string neck, combinations of 6, 7 or 8 strings available by special order
Available: **1936–38**

Zephyr: maple body with square end, oblong pickup with large slot-head screwpoles, metal pickup cover/handrest, 2 knobs on opposite sides on circular *Mastervoicer* plates, black metal fingerboard, fancy markers, metal *Epiphone* peghead logo plate, black body finish, white plastic top, 6, 7 or 8 strings
Introduced: **1939**
Bottom corners scooped out (still straight across bottom edge), knobs on same side, metal-covered pickup, metal pickup/bridge cover with epsilon (slashed-*C*), bound top and back, varied-color fingerboard markers, enclosed tuners, sunburst finish: **by 1950**
Knobs on rectangular control plate: **by 1954**
Discontinued: **1957**

Century: maple body, teardrop body shape with belly across bottom edge, 2 knobs on opposite sides, blade pickup, metal pickup cover/handrest, black plastic pickguard, metal fingerboard, bowtie markers, metal peghead logo plate, black finish, 6, 7 or 8 strings
Introduced: **1939**
Rounded guitar-like bouts, bottom corners scooped out, straight line across bottom edge, knobs on same side, metal pickup/bridge cover with epsilon (slashed-*C*), bound top and back: **by 1950**
Discontinued: **1957**

Coronet: maple guitar-shaped body, blade pickup with oblong housing, knobs on opposite sides, hard-wired cord, white pickguard, rosewood fingerboard with frets, pearl dot inlay, metal *Epiphone* peghead logo plate, black finish, 6-string only
Introduced: **1939**
Jack on side, metal fingerboard, bowtie markers: **by 1941**
Discontinued: **by 1949**

Solo Console: rectangular maple body with prima vera (white mahogany) laminated on sides and top, oblong pickup with large slot-head screwpoles, removable pickup cover, 2 knobs on opposite sides, black binding, black metal fingerboard/control plate, bowtie markers, *Electar* logo between neck and pickup, metal peghead logo plate, 6, 7 or 8 strings
Introduced: **1939**
Enclosed tuners: **by 1941**
Metal-covered pickup: **1950**
Discontinued: **by 1954**
Duo Console: doubleneck, rectangular maple body

with prima vera (white mahogany) laminated on sides, gold-painted metal plate on top, 2 oblong pickups with large slot-head screwpoles, 2 knobs on circular *Mastervoicer* plates between pegheads, large screwed-down pickup cover/handrest, 2 bar-like string dampers, black celluloid and white mahogany binding, black metal fingerboards, metal logo plate at extreme peghead end of body, 2 8-string necks standard, any combination of 6-, 7- or 8-string necks available by special order
Introduced: **1939**
Chrome top plate, knobs between necks near bridge, tortoiseshell celluloid binding, enclosed tuners: **1941**
Rounded corners, no metal top plate, metal-covered pickups, metal bridge/pickup covers with epsilon (slashed-*C*) logo: **1950**
Renamed **Double Console: 1954**
Discontinued: **1958**

Console Triple-Neck: 3 necks, tortoiseshell celluloid bridge covers, otherwise same as Duo Console, sunburst or natural finish
Introduced: **1950**
Renamed **Triple-Neck Console: 1954**
Discontinued: **1958**

Electar Grande: wooden stand (not an instrument) for Solo or Duo Console, prima vera wood (white mahogany), Electar-style script *E* in relief on front panel, wheels, breaks down to 2 luggage-like carrying cases
Introduced: **1939**
Discontinued: **by 1949**

Varichord: rectangular body of prima vera wood (white mahogany), pickup with large slot-head screwpoles, wood bridge cover does not extend over pickup, 2 knobs on circular *Mastervoicer* plates, 7 strings, 7 pitch-changing levers on top
First sold: **1939**
First appearance in literature: **1941**
Discontinued: **by 1943**

Kent: maple guitar-shaped body, New York pickup with no poles and black mounting frames, metal handrest, 2 knobs on same side on plastic plate, no binding, metal fingerboard, bowtie markers, metal *Epiphone* peghead logo plate (some with decal script logo with tail underneath)
Available: **1949–53**

Eddie Alkire Eharp: guitar-shaped body, 10 strings, metal-covered pickup with screwpoles, yellow pickup mounting ring, 1 round knob and 1 lever knob, knobs on treble side, raised plastic semicircular handrest on bass side, asymmetrical rosewood fingerboard, dot markers, model name on peghead logo plate, no Epiphone logo, epsilon (slashed-*C*) on tuner enclosures, white top finish
Available (never catalogued): **early 1950s**

COMMENTS

Epiphone lap steels were good utility instruments for their time, but their pickups make them less desirable today than some Fender, Gibson, Rickenbacker, National and Supro models. The models of greatest interest to collectors are those that are rare, aesthetically appealing or historically interesting, such as the Model M, Rocco and Varichord.

MANDOLINS

SECTION ORGANIZATION

Mandolins
Mandolas
Mandocellos
Electric Mandolins
Gibson-Made Model

MANDOLINS

Mandolins pictured in Epiphone catalogs do not change from 3-segment *f*-holes to standard *f*-holes until 1939, and that is the date listed in the following model descriptions. However, it is highly likely that they changed to "cello" *f*-holes (with squared edge at each corner) at the same time the guitar models did, in 1936.

Windsor: symmetrical 2-point body, carved top and back, "curly" maple back and sides, 3-segment *f*-holes, bound elevated pickguard, triple-bound top and back, checkered purfling around top, 5-piece maple/mahogany neck, 13 7/8" scale, bound ebony fingerboard with asymmetrical treble-side extension, inlay of two diagonal diamonds separated by dot, asymmetrical peghead with *Masterbilt*, *Windsor* and *Epiphone* on banners, peghead triple-bound on front and back including volute, gold-plated hardware, sunburst finish
Introduced: **1932**
Rosewood fingerboard, diagonally placed four-point-star inlay: **1933**
2-point Windsor model discontinued, Windsor name continues with specs previously assigned to Windsor Special (see following): **by 1937**

Windsor Special: scroll body, carved top and back, "curly" maple back and sides, 3 segment *f*-holes, bound elevated pickguard, triple-bound top and back, checkered purfling around top, 5-piece maple/mahogany neck, 13 7/8" scale, bound ebony fingerboard with treble-side extension, diagonally placed four-point-star inlay, Masterbilt peghead, gold-plated hardware, sunburst finish
Introduced: **1934**
Renamed **Windsor**, "flame" maple back and sides, no checkered purfling: **by 1936**
"Cello" *f*-holes with squared edge at each corner, pickguard cutout to accommodate bridge, rosewood fingerboard, slotted-block inlay, pearl script logo, vine peghead inlay, dip on treble side of peghead: **1939**
Discontinued: **by 1949**

Strand: symmetrical 2-point body, carved top and back, walnut back and sides, 3-segment *f*-holes, unbound elevated pickguard, triple-bound top and back, engraved tailpiece cover, mahogany neck, 13 7/8" scale, single-bound fingerboard with rounded end, paired slotted-diamond inlay in zigzag pattern, asymmetrical peghead with *Masterbilt*, *Strand* and *Epiphone* on banners, nickel-plated hardware, sunburst finish
Introduced: **1932**
Triple-bound top, single-bound back, rounded-peak peghead, block letter logo, stickpin peghead inlay: **1935**
"Cello" *f*-holes with squared edge at each corner, pickguard dips around bridge, plain tailpiece cover,

rosewood fingerboard with square end, single-parallelo-gram inlay, center-dip peghead, script logo: **by 1939**
Oval hole, epsilon (slashed-*C*) on pickguard, pick-guard does not extend below bridge, cherry neck, vertical oval peghead inlay: **by 1950**
Discontinued: **1958**

Artist: scroll body, same as 1937 Windsor but with "curly" maple back and sides, single-bound top and back, mahogany neck, 13 7/8" scale, nickel-plated hardware, sunburst top finish, deep red finish on back and sides
Introduced: **1936**
"Cello" *f*-holes with squared edge at each corner, single-parallelogram inlay, wandering vine peghead inlay: **1939**
Discontinued by: **1949**

Rivoli: symmetrical pear-shaped body (like Gibson A-style), laminated walnut back and sides, 3-segment *f*-holes, triple-bound top and back, mahogany neck, 13 7/8" scale, bound rosewood fin-gerboard, dot inlay, rounded-top peghead with model name between *Epiphone* and *Masterbilt* banners, sunburst top finish, walnut finish on back and sides
Introduced: **1932**
Single-bound top and back: **by 1934**
Solid carved back, "cello" *f*-holes with squared edge at each corner, pickguard dips around bridge, center-dip peghead, stickpin peghead inlay, script logo: **by 1939**
Oval hole, vertical oval peghead inlay: **by 1950**
Discontinued: **1958**

Adelphi: symmetrical pear-shaped body (like Gib-son A-style), laminated maple back and sides, 3-segment *f*-holes, unbound elevated pickguard, single-bound top and back, mahogany neck, 13" scale, unbound rosewood fingerboard with square end, dot inlay, rounded-peak peghead with model name between *Epiphone* and *Masterbilt* ban-ners, yellow-to-cherry sunburst top finish, cherry finish on back and sides
Introduced: **1932**
Maple neck: **1934**
"Cello" *f*-holes with squared edge at each corner, pick-guard dips around bridge, center-dip peghead, script logo with tail underneath, no other peghead ornamentation: **by 1939**
Discontinued: **by 1949**

MANDOLAS
Windsor: similar specs to Windsor mandolin: **1932–49**

Strand: similar specs to Strand mandolin: **1932–49**

Rivoli: similar specs to Rivoli mandolin: **1932–49**

Adelphi: similar specs to Adelphi mandolin: **1932–49**

Artist: similar specs to Artist mandolin: **1937-49**

MANDOCELLOS
All have symmetrical pear-shaped body (like Gibson A-style mandolin and K-1 mandocello.

No. 1: same wood and ornamentation as Blackstone guitar: **1932–48**

No. 2: same wood and ornamentation as Triumph guitar: **1932–48**

No. 3: same wood and ornamentation as De Luxe guitar: **1932–48**

ELECTRIC MANDOLINS
Electar Model M: symmetrical pear-shaped body (like Gibson A-style), no soundholes, laminated curly maple top, back and sides, oblong pickup with large slot-head screwpoles, 1 volume control and jack on treble side, 2 tone controls on bass side, single-bound top and back, single-bound rosewood fingerboard, maple neck, dot inlay, pointed top of peghead, metal *Electar* peghead plate
Available: **1937–38**

Zephyr: symmetrical pear-shaped body (like Gibson A-style), "cello" *f*-holes with squared edge at each corner, laminated maple top, back and sides, oblong pickup with large slot-head screwpoles, 2 white knobs on opposite sides, knobs on circular *Mastervoicer* plates, jack into top, bound rosewood fingerboard, slotted block inlay (some with dots), center-dip peghead, metal peghead logo plate, blond finish
Introduced: **1939**
Metal covered pickup, knobs on same side, no

Mastervoicer plates, cherry neck, sunburst finish optional: **by 1950**
Discontinued: **1958**

Century: symmetrical pear-shaped body (like Gibson A-style), no *f*-holes, laminated maple top, back and sides, oblong blade pickup mounted on large rectangular plate, 2 knobs on opposite sides, jack into top, black pickguard, bound top and back, cherry neck, bound rosewood fingerboard, dot inlay, metal *Epiphone* peghead logo plate, pointed-top peghead, sunburst finish
Introduced: **1939**
"Cello" *f*-holes with squared edge at each corner, no plate under pickup, tortoiseshell celluloid pickguard, center-dip peghead: **1941**
Discontinued: **by 1949**

GIBSON-MADE MODEL

Venetian: symmetrical pear-shaped body (like Gibson A-style), similar to Gibson A-50, maple back

and sides, bound fingerboard, dot inlay, sunburst finish
Introduced: **1961**
Electric model available: **1966**
Discontinued: **1970**

COMMENTS

The Windsor, Windsor Special and Artist mandolins, along with all Epiphone mandola and mandocello models, are extremely rare—so rare, in fact, that it is questionable whether any were made beyond the examples in catalog photographs. They are of great interest to collectors as well as players.

Of the models made in significant numbers the relatively rare Strand garners the most interest from collectors. The Strand and Rivoli are regarded by players as quality instruments. The Adelphi is the most commonly seen Epiphone mandolin and is not highly regarded.

ACOUSTIC BASSES

All have laminated bodies.
All are 3/4-size (the most common, "standard" upright bass size) with 42" scale.

SECTION ORGANIZATION

New York-Made Models
Gibson-Made Models

NEW YORK-MADE MODELS

B-4: fine-grain spruce top, highly figured maple back and sides, black-white-black binding on top and back, rosewood fingerboard and tailpiece, lacquered brass tuners, colored (later described as light golden brown) or blond finish
Introduced: **June 1940**
Metal logo plate on tailpiece: **1942**
Ebonized maple tailpiece: **1954**
B-4 continued in Gibson line (see following): **1958**

B-3: select spruce top, "highly figured" maple back and sides, inlaid purfling, rosewood fingerboard and tailpiece, brass tuners, Cremona brown sunburst finish with highlights on top, back, and sides

Introduced: **June 1940**
Metal logo plate on tailpiece: **1942**
Discontinued: **by 1949**

B-2: spruce top, "good curly maple" back and sides, rosewood fingerboard and tailpiece, nickel-plated tuners, light cherry sunburst finish
Introduced: **June 1940**
Metal logo plate on tailpiece: **1942**
Discontinued: **by 1949**

B-1: plain maple back and sides, ebonized rosewood fingerboard and tailpiece, dark cherry red sunburst finish
Introduced: **June 1940**
Metal logo plate on tailpiece: **1942**
Discontinued: **by 1949**

B-5 Artists Model: fine-grain spruce top, highly figured maple back and sides, rosewood fingerboard and tailpiece, triple-bound top and back, engraved gold-plated tuner plates, light golden brown or blond finish
Introduced: **Jan. 1941**

Metal logo plate on tailpiece: **1942**
Ebonized maple tailpiece: **1954**
Continued in Gibson line (see following): **1958**

GIBSON-MADE MODELS

B5/The Artist: continued from Epi line, Van Eps
adjustable bridge, gold-plated tuners, natural (**B5N**)
or shaded (**B5S**) finish
Available: **1958–64**

B4/The Professional: continued from Epi line,
Van Eps adjustable bridge, polished brass tuners,
natural (**B4N**) or shaded (**B4S**) finish
Available: **1958–64**

BV/The Studio: student model, shaded finish
Available: **1958–64**

SHIPMENTS OF GIBSON-MADE EPI BASSES, 1958–64

B5N	37
B5S	40
B4N	46
B4S	166
BV3	55

COMMENTS

Epiphone basses are considered by players to be
among the finest laminated-construction upright
basses. It was Epi's bass production capability that
sparked Gibson's initial interest in acquiring Epiphone in 1957. Although Gibson shipping records
show a fair number of basses produced (344 total),
Gibson-made Epi basses are seldom seen.

BANJOS

SECTION ORGANIZATION

General Information
Recording Series
Budget Models
Electric Models
Gibson-Made Models

GENERAL INFORMATION

Epiphone began making banjos possibly as early as
1917. Early examples have a block-letter logo arced
across the top of the peghead. They resemble the
banjos made by the William Lange company of New
York, with open back, Lange-type tone ring and
often with a large head (larger than 11" in diameter).
The banjos for which Epiphone is most highly
regarded are those of the Recording Series of circa
1925 to circa 1935. Recording models resemble
Paramount banjos of the same period, not only in
ornamentation but in model nomenclature. Paramount models run from A to F; first letters of Epiphone model names run from A to E.
Production on Epiphone acoustic banjos ceased by the
mid 1930s, but all models—Recording series and
budget models—were catalogued through 1942. All
Epiphone pre-World War II models were catalogued
as tenor or plectrum; 5-strings were not listed but
were available, although they are very rare.
Production of Epiphone banjos did not resume after
World War II until after Gibson's acquisition of Epiphone in 1957.

MISC. SPECS

Many have *House of Stathopoulo* decal on back of
peghead.
Most have 11" head diameter; a few early examples are
larger.
Flanges...
Die-cast flange with egg-shaped holes: **pre-1925**
Hexagonal flange holes longer and narrower than
earlier egg-shape holes: **1925-27**
Cross-shaped flange holes: **1927–1930s**
No metal coordinator rod through body: **early
1920s–1925**
Metal coordinator rod through body: **1925–1930s**
X-shaped openings under armrest: **1929–1930s**

RECORDING SERIES

Recording models often vary from catalog
specifications.

Recording: walnut resonator and neck, dragon on
resonator (later with wood marquetry forming 3

concentric rings and inverted-V), carved neck heel, ebony fingerboard, multi-ply peghead, dragon peghead inlay winding through *Epiphone* and *Recording*, engraved gold-plated hardware
Introduced: **by 1925**
Discontinued: **1927**

Artist: walnut resonator with 1 holly-and-ebony inlaid ring, walnut neck with 3 holly-and-ebony laminate strips, bound ebony fingerboard, fingerboard inlay of paired slotted-diamond inlay in zigzag pattern, ebony peghead veneer with *A* and fancy pearl inlay, nickel-plated hardware
Available: **1925–c. 1935**

Alhambra: resonator covered in silver pearloid with 2 inlaid rings, 5-ply walnut neck, silver pearloid fingerboard with tinted cross-pattern figures, silver pearloid peghead veneer, model name on peghead, silver-plated hardware
Available: **1927–c. 1935**

Bandmaster: rosewood neck, ebony fingerboard, engraved pearl 4-pointed star inlay, dragon figure inlay on peghead, gold-plated hardware
Introduced: **1925**
Single-bound fingerboard with multi-colored marquetry on side, amber pearloid-covered resonator, ebony peghead veneer with *B* and fancy pearl inlay, amber pearloid veneer on back of peghead: **1927**
Discontinued: **c. 1935**

Concert: carved neck heel, rosewood neck, varied-pattern fingerboard inlay, dragon figure inlay on peghead, engraved gold-plated hardware
Introduced: **1925**
Resonator covered in amber pearloid with 3 inlaid rings and 2 inlaid lines, pearloid fingerboard with engraved and tinted floral-pattern markers, pearloid peghead veneer with model name, pearl tuner buttons: **1927**
Variation: resonator covered in dark green pearloid, blue floral-design resonator inlay, checkered and/or gold-sparkle borders on resonator and fingerboard, non-engraved gold-plated hardware
Discontinued: **c. 1935**

Concert Special: white holly resonator with 3 inlaid rings and 2 straight lines, resonator sides

covered in pearloid, pearloid fingerboard with engraved and tinted markers, white holly neck, carved neck heel, pearloid peghead veneer with model name, engraved gold-plated hardware
Available: **1927–c. 1935**

DeLuxe: inner circle on resonator covered with white pearloid with engraved and tinted floral-pattern ring, wide outer ring on resonator covered with black pearloid, resonator sides covered with pearloid, ebony neck, carved neck heel, fingerboard of alternating black and white pearloid, dragon figure inlay on peghead, engraved gold-plated hardware
Introduced: **1925**
Non-dragon peghead with model name: **1927**
Discontinued: **c. 1935**

DeLuxe Art: varied pattern fingerboard inlay, custom artistic resonator design, black finish: **1925–c. 1935**

Dansant: inner circle on resonator covered with silver-sparkle pearloid, crest design on inner resonator circle, wide outer ring on resonator covered with gold-sparkle pearloid, floral pattern on outer ring, white holly neck with laminates of red, black and blue, carved neck heel, alternating white pearloid and tortoiseshell celluloid fingerboard, engraved and tinted pearloid peghead veneer with model name, engraved gold-plated hardware
Available: **1927–c. 1935**

Emperor: resonator covered in white pearloid with large floral ring engraved and tinted, floral ornamentation on side of resonator and back of peghead, ebony neck with 9 laminates, carved neck heel, alternating white and black pearloid fingerboard, blue and orange floral patterns on white fret areas, pearloid peghead veneer with rhinestone border, model name on peghead, engraved gold-plated hardware
Available: **1927–c. 1935**

BUDGET MODELS

Note: Epiphone also made banjos similar to some of the following budget models for distributors under other brand names.

Professional: original list price $90, also available as banjo-ukulele, no other specs available
Available: **mid 1920s**

Wonder: original list price $50, also available as banjo-ukulele, no other specs available
Available: **mid 1920s**

Mayfair: walnut resonator with binding and small circular ornament, walnut neck, ebony fingerboard, dot inlay, pearloid peghead veneer with model name
Available: **1928–c. 1935**

Rialto: walnut resonator with ebony purfling, bound ebony fingerboard, dot inlay, pearloid peghead veneer with model name
Available: **1928–c. 1935**

Peerless: walnut veneer resonator with 1 holly-and-ebony ring, bound ebony fingerboard, dot inlay, pearloid peghead veneer with model name
Available: **1928–c. 1935**

ELECTRIC MODELS

Electar Banjo: maple top, horseshoe-magnet pickup wraps over strings, trapeze tailpiece, pickguard covers upper treble quadrant of top, 2 knobs on opposite sides, jack on side, bound top, rosewood fingerboard, block inlay, *Electar* peghead logo, tenor or plectrum, sunburst finish
Introduced: **late 1936**
Oblong pickup with slot-head screwpoles, metal pickup cover/handrest: **1937**
Discontinued: **1939**

Century: blade pickup, metal pickup cover/handrest, inlaid pickguard covers upper treble quadrant of top, trapeze tailpiece, jack on top, block inlay, metal *Epiphone* peghead logo plate, sunburst finish
Introduced: **1939**
No handrest, jack on side, dot inlay: **1941**
Discontinued: **by 1949**

Zephyr: oblong pickup with slot-head screwpoles, metal pickup cover/handrest, knobs on large circular *Mastervoicer* plates, pickguard covers upper treble quadrant of top, trapeze tailpiece, jack on top, bound top, bound rosewood fingerboard, block inlay, metal peghead logo plate, natural finish: **1939**
No handrest, jack on side: **1941**
Discontinued: **by 1949**

GIBSON-MADE MODELS

Minstrel: 5-string, Gibson Mastertone flat head tone ring, 26 1/4" scale, single-parallelogram inlay (double-parallelogram at 11th fret), resonator, plastic tuner buttons
Introduced: **1961**
1 plectrum Minstrel shipped: **1967**
Discontinued: **1970**

Campus: 5-string longneck, raised-head tone ring (simple brass hoop like Gibson RB-100, not a Mastertone tone ring), 32" scale, no resonator, dot inlay, plastic tuner buttons
Available: **1962–70**

Plantation: 5-string longneck, Gibson Mastertone flat head tone ring, 32" scale, dot inlay, no resonator, metal tuner buttons
Available: **1962–68**

Tenor: 4-string, raised-head tone ring (simple brass hoop like Gibson RB-100, not a Mastertone tone ring), 22 2/3" scale, dot inlay, resonator, plastic tuner buttons
Available: **1964–69**

COMMENTS

Early models (pre-Recording Series) are well-made instruments, but because of their early design features—open back, short scale (tenors), large head, lighter tone ring and lack of metal coordinating rod—they are of interest primarily for historical reasons.

Recording Series banjos, particularly those made from 1927 to circa 1935 with the metal coordinating rod and heavier flange, are regarded by tenor players as among the finest of the period, as fine or finer than the Paramounts of the same period. For collectors, they represent the golden age of the banjo, and they are among the most ornate and most highly sought banjos of their period. The very rare 5-string examples are highly regarded by collectors but not so much by musicians, due to the overwhelming preference of 5-string players for the sound of the Gibson Mastertone models.

Of the Gibson-made Epiphone banjos, only those with Mastertone tone ring (Minstrel and Plantation) appeal to players.

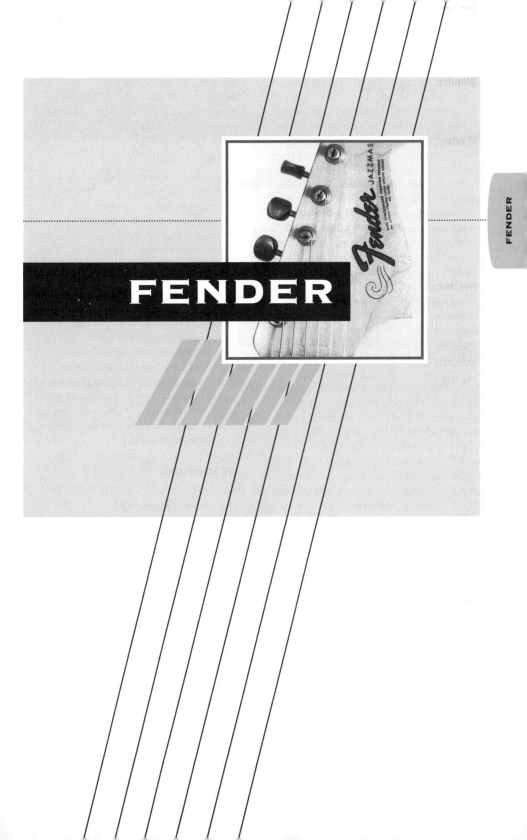

FENDER

GENERAL INFORMATION

eo Fender and Doc Kauffman began making K&F brand lap steels and amplifiers in Fullerton, CA, in the fall of 1945. Kauffman left in early 1946, and Fender continued as Fender Electric Instrument Company.

With the introduction of the Esquire and Broadcaster (soon to be Telecaster) in 1950, Fender became the first company to successfully market solidbody electric guitars. The first commercially successful solidbody bass, the Precision, was introduced in late 1951 and was even more revolutionary than Fender's solidbody guitars. The Stratocaster, introduced in 1954, went on to become one of the all-time classic guitar designs. Fender amplifiers played a key role in the success of the company and in the growth of the electric guitar market. By the mid 1950s Fender rivaled Gibson as the leading maker of electric guitars, a rivalry that continues today.

Fender was sold to CBS on January 4, 1965. Although the instrument lines continued to expand until the end of the decade, the sale to CBS marked the beginning of a decline in Fender quality that lasted through the 1970s.

Bill Shultz (formerly of Yamaha) was hired as president of Fender in 1981 and began a large scale modernization of the factory that caused a sharp decline in production. Concurrently, in an effort to capitalize on the growing market for imported copies of Fender models, Fender and Japanese partners formed Fender Japan in May 1982. Initially Fender Japan made a line of vintage reissues marketed only in Japan and Europe. These were marked with a small *Made in Japan* peghead decal. A lower-priced line, labeled Squier, was introduced in October 1983 for U.S. distribution.

In March 1985 CBS sold Fender to a group headed by Schultz, which incorporated as Fender Musical Instruments Corp. Production facilities were not included in the sale, however, and through most of 1985 Fenders were made only overseas. U.S. production resumed in late 1985 in new facilities in Corona, CA, with a successful new line of American Standard models. Amplifier production was consolidated in Lake Oswego, OR, in 1985.

Fenders are now produced in several countries, including the United States, Mexico, Japan, China and Korea. Corporate offices and a custom amplifier production facility are located in Scottsdale, AZ. Fender began construction of a new manufacturing facility in Corona in 1997.

TERMS

Bakelite: Bakelite is a trade name for a molded phenolic resin. It has become a generic term used for all similar materials, such as the Phenolite used for black pickguards on early Telecasters and Esquires. Bakelite is most common in black, brown or white. It is somewhat similar in appearance to modern postwar thermal plastics, but is less shiny and more brittle. Although Bakelite should properly be capitalized, the term *bakelite* (lower case) is commonly used in reference to Fenders and is used here to refer to Phenolite and to similar material used on early Stratocasters.

Maple neck/rosewood fingerboard: The term *maple neck* refers to a 1-piece, fretted neck/fingerboard unit (with no separate fingerboard). The term *rosewood fingerboard* refers to a maple neck with a rosewood fingerboard. The maple neck with separate maple fingerboard is described as *maple neck with maple fingerboard.*

BODY WOOD

Ash...
  All models: **1950–mid 1956**
  Blonde finish with woodgrain showing through:
    mid 1956–current
Alder, custom color finishes: **mid 1956–current**
Mahogany, a few Telecasters and Stratocasters: **early 1960s**
Basswood, many Japanese-made models, some U.S.-made models: **1990–current**
Poplar, some Mexican-made models: **1992–current**
Exceptions: Rosewood Telecaster, Walnut Strat, etc.

FINISH

Nitrocellulose lacquer on non-custom colors: **1950–68**
Custom colors, any available Dupont Duco (nitrocellulose lacquer) or Dupont Lucite (acrylic lacquer, available from 1957 onward) color: **1950–58**
Custom colors standardized, high-end models (see Stratocaster section): **1958–current**
Polyurethane finish: **1968–current**

WIRE

Cloth-covered wire: **1950–68**

Transition to plastic-covered wire: **1968–69**

Plastic-covered wire: **1968–current**

NECK POCKET

Fully painted: **1950–late 1962**

Area on bass-side unpainted (except for yellow stain): **1962 onward**

BODY DATES

In body routings (many instruments): **1950–c. 1963**

On bottom of pickups: **1964–late 1970s**

PICKUPS, 1990S

"Original" series: reproductions of vintage pickups

American Standard: "Delta Tone" system, slightly hotter than vintage style

Custom Shop Custom '54 Strat: reissues of 1954–59 Stratocaster pickups

Texas Special: higher output

Tex-Mex: Alnico magnets, overwound for higher ouput

Fat '50s Strat: overwound '54 Stratocaster pickup

Lace Sensor: proprietary design by Don Lace, produced by Actodyne company, available (from lowest inductance to highest) in gold, silver, blue and red

NECK AND FINGERBOARD

1-piece maple, no truss rod, no "skunk stripe" on back, early Esquire: **1950 only**

1-piece maple, walnut "skunk stripe" on back (to fill truss rod routing): **1950**

Rosewood fingerboard, introduced on Jazzmaster: **mid to late 1958**

"Slab" rosewood fingerboard, flat–milled on back side (1-piece maple neck/fingerboard still available as replacement or special order): **Sept. 1959**

"Curved" rosewood fingerboard, thinner than "slab," curved back side: **mid 1962**

Thinner, veneer-like rosewood board: **mid 1963**

Separate maple fingerboard, no "skunk stripe"...

Available as early as: **1963**

Catalogued option on Telecaster, Telecaster Custom, Stratocaster, Jaguar, Esquire, Esquire Custom, Precision Bass, Jazz Bass, all 2-pickup Coronado 6-strings, all Coronado basses: **1967**

1-piece maple with skunk stripe, acrylic finish, optional on Telecaster, Telecaster Custom, Stratocaster, Jaguar, Esquire, Esquire Custom, Precision

Bass, Jazz Bass, all 2-pickup Coronado 6-strings, all Coronado basses: **1969**

Slab rosewood fingerboard (with Biflex truss rod): **1980s**

4-screw neckplate introduced: **1950**

3-screw neckplate introduced...

Stratocaster, Telecaster Thinline, Custom Telecaster, Telecaster Bass: **1971**

Telecaster Deluxe (from introduction): **1972**

Jazz Bass: **1975**

Starcaster (from introduction): **1976**

4-screw neckplate reintroduced...

Anniversary Stratocaster: **1979**

All Stratocasters: **1980**

All other models: **1981**

Neckplate stamp...

Plain: **1949–c. Aug. 1965**

F on neckplate: **c. Aug. 1965–1982**

Script *Fender* or Custom Shop logo: **1982–current**

Truss rod

Rod adjustment at body end: **1950**

Tilt-neck, allen nut adjustment on peghead, some models: **1971**

Biflex truss rod: **1980s**

NECK DATES AND STAMPS

Information for 1969–80 was compiled by Greg Gagliano and published in *20th Century Guitar* magazine.

1950–Mar. 1962

Penciled date.

Mar. 1962–69

Stamped code with month and year.

Configuration: **s MON yy A**

s = neck style (model)

s(s) = neck style (model), examples:

3	Telecaster
5	Precision Bass
22	Stratocaster

MON = 3-letter abbreviation for month

yy = year

A = neck width:

A	1 1/2"
B	1 5/8"
C	1 3/4"
D	1 7/8"

Example 3JUN63B = Telecaster (3) made in June 1963 with 1 5/8" width.

1969–71

6, 7 or 8 digits followed by letter

Configuration: **s(s)###m(m)yA**

significance unknown

m(m) = month

y = last digit of year.

A = neck width, see preceding).

Example: 3320119B = Telecaster (3) made in November (11) 1959 (9)

1972–80

8 digits

Configuration: **ssnnwwyd**

ss = neck style (model), examples:

01	Precision Bass
02	Jazz Bass
09	Stratocaster
13	Telecaster

nn = neck code:

00 . . . rosewood fingerboard

01 . . . rosewood fingerboard

03 . . . "skunk stripe" maple neck (1-piece maple construction or with rosewood fingerboard)

10 . . . fretless maple neck

ww = week

y = last digit of year

d = day of the week (1 = Monday, 2 = Tuesday, etc.)

1982–current

Date stamp returns, first on the reissue models of 1982 and then across the line.

PEGHEAD

Peghead matches body color on custom color Jazzmaster, Jaguar and Jazz Bass models, except for blond and shoreline gold finish.

STRING GUIDES

Single round guide for high-E and B strings: **1950**

Butterfly clip: **mid 1956**

Metal spacer between clip and peghead: **1959**

2 butterfly clips...

Stratocaster, Telecaster, Telecaster Deluxe, Custom Telecaster, Esquire: **1971**

Mustang: **1976**

4 strings through guide, Starcaster (from introduction): **1976**

2 pin clips, non-vintage Strats and Teles only: **1983**

TUNERS

"Single line," *Kluson Deluxe* on back, patent pending notice, button shaft does not go through gear enclosure: **1950–early 1951**

Kluson, no writing on tuner cover, button shaft does not go through gear enclosure: **early 1951–54**

"Single line," *Kluson Deluxe* on back, button shaft goes through gear enclosure: **1956**

"Double line," *Kluson Deluxe* on each line: **1964**

Fender tuners with *F* logo: **1966**

Fender stamped on back: **1981**

LOGO

Montego and LTD archtop models have a pearl logo rather than the standard decal.

"Spaghetti" logo, gold or silver outlined in black, unconnected *nde* in *Fender*...

Model name under logo: **1950**

Model name after logo, Stratocaster only: **1954**

New models as introduced: **1950s**

"Transition" logo, gold (silver on Precision only), connected *nde* in *Fender*, model name after logo...

New models as introduced: **1960–68**

Jazz Bass: **1960**

Jaguar, Precision Bass: **by 1962**

All other models except Telecaster and Esquire: **Jan. 1965**

Telecaster: **1967**

Esquire: **1968**

Black logo...

All models except following: **1968**

Stratocaster: **July 1968**

Telecaster Bass, Mustang: **1972**

Mandolin: **by 1974**

Musicmaster, Mustang Bass: **by 1976**

Musicmaster Bass: **by 1978**

Trademark registration symbol, circled-*R* with logo: **1966**

New transition-type logo, silver (Lead I and II) or gold (Stratocaster, Precision Bass Special): **1980**

New transition-type logo, silver outlined in black: **1983**

Spaghetti or transition logos on reissue models: **1982–current**

OTHER PEGHEAD DECALS

All Fender solidbody guitars have the model name on the peghead except for the following: "No Caster" (see Telecaster), Rosewood Telecaster, Telecaster

Thinline from 1968–71, Swinger and a few custom color Jaguars, Jazzmasters and Jazz Basses.

Patent numbers on peghead: **1961–76**

Serial number and *Made in USA* on peghead, no patent numbers: **1976–current**

CASES FOR HIGH-END MODELS

"Thermometer," bulbous peghead area: **1950**

"Contour," 1 edge follows body contour, 1 edge straight: **1953**

Rectangular, center pocket, tweed cover: **mid 1954**

Side pocket, tweed cover, red lining: **mid 1955**

Side pocket, tweed cover, orange lining: **late 1958**

Brown Tolex cover, burnt orange lining: **1960**

Brown Tolex cover, reddish orange lining: **mid 1962**

White or black Tolex cover, black leather ends, reddish orange lining, logo on case: **late 1962–65**

Black Tolex cover, no logo: **1965–67**

Black Tolex cover, logo: **1968–current**

Tweed cases, some reissues: **1980s–current**

MODEL SERIES, LATE 1990S

By the late 1990s, Fender was offering dozens of different variations of Stratocasters and Telecasters. Following is a general organizational guide to Fender's model system, although more exceptions may exist than are noted:

Standard: made in Mexico, poplar body, standard hardware, white/black/white pickguard

Deluxe: made in Mexico (except Lyte models made in Japan), popular after-market options as standard equipment, vintage style hardware, 3-ply pickguard

Collectable: reissue models made in Japan (except '69 Tele Thinline made in Mexico), basswood body, vintage hardware

California: alder body, Tex-Mex pickups, vintage hardware, deluxe gig bag

American Standard: made in USA, white/black/white pickguard, medium jumbo frets, Micro-tilt neck adjustment (accessible through hole in neckplate), straplock buttons, die-cast tuners, molded case

Hot Rodded American: includes Roadhouse Strat, Lone Star Strat, U.S. Fat Tele (none with "Hot Rodded" in model name), made in USA, alder body, medium jumbo frets, tortoiseshell plastic pickguard, straplock buttons, die-cast tuners, black Tolex case

American Deluxe: ash or alder body, aged plastic parts, deluxe hardware, straplock buttons, black Tolex case

American Vintage: reissue models made in USA, vintage hardware and pickups, tweed case

"Slab" rosewood fingerboard, used from 1959–62. The maple neck is planed flat, and the line between fingerboard and neck is straight.

"Curved" rosewood fingerboard, used from 1962 to current time. Maple neck surface is curved, fingerboard is uniform width, and the line between fingerboard and neck is curved.

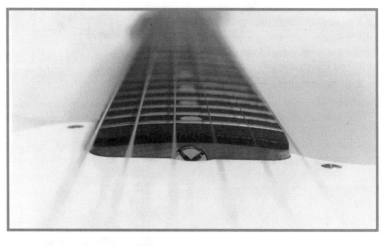

Jazzmaster pickup.

Closeup of Jazzmaster pickup, with "notched" pickup frames.

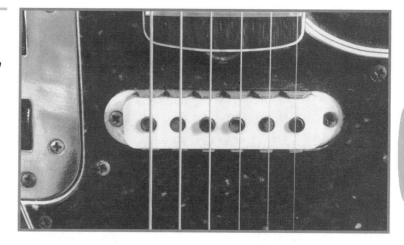

FENDER

Fender humbucking pickup on a Telecaster Thinline.

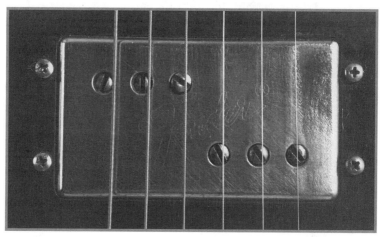

FENDER

Jaguar body, with standard Jazzmaster-type tremolo.

Telecaster body, with slab body style.

Stratocaster body, with rounded body edges.

Musicmaster body, with anodized aluminum (gold colored) pickguard.

Spaghetti logo on a 1956 Stratocaster, small Strat peghead.

Transition logo on a 1965 Jazzmaster.

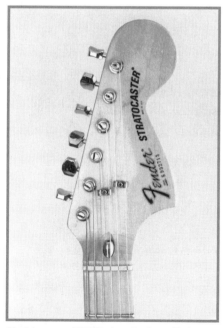

Black logo on a 1979 Stratocaster, large Strat peghead used from 1965–81, bullet truss rod.

Telecaster peghead with 1970s-style logo.

SERIAL NUMBERS

Fender guitars have a serial number on the bridgeplate, neckplate or peghead decal. Serial numbers are not strictly chronological, as is evident by the wide range of overlapping numbers from year to year, but they do fall into rough chronological groups.

Exceptions:

1950–late 1954: Telecasters and Esquires have a single series, Precision Basses (beginning in 1951) have their own series and Stratocasters (1954) have their own series.

LTD guitars, acoustic guitars, mandolins and lap steels have their own number series.

Coronados have their own number series.

Bass Vs have their own number series, virtually all in the 600000s.

Mavericks, Customs and Swingers have their own number series.

Many special editions and vintage reissues have non-standard number series.

For information on neck and body stamps, see General Information section.

Serial number lists are based on a list of numbers and neck dates compiled by James Werner. Other sources include A.R. Duchossoir, Tony Bacon and Paul Day.

NUMBER PLACEMENT

On bottom end of bridgeplate (lap steels): **1946–49**

On bridgeplate near bridge...

Lap steels: **1950–80**

Guitars and Precision bass: **1950–54**

On back tremolo plate, earliest Stratocasters: **1954**

On upper edge of back neckplate: **1954–mid 1976**

On lower edge of back neckplate, some examples: **1959–60**

Double-stamped, some examples: **late 1957–early 1959**

On peghead decal: **mid 1976–current**

On backplate, reissue models: **1982–current**

ESQUIRE AND BROADCASTER/NO-CASTER/TELECASTER, 1950–54

Number on bridge. Neck dates on Broadcasters, No-casters and early Telecasters may overlap.

NUMBER RANGE	YEAR		NUMBER RANGE	YEAR
33–860	1950–52		1343–2885	1950–54
0005–0746	1950–52		2911–5368	1951–54
0748–1331	1951–52			

PRECISION BASS, 1951–54

Number on bridge.

NUMBER RANGE	YEAR		NUMBER RANGE	YEAR
161–357	1951		0161–0470	1951–52
299–619	1952		0475–0840	1952–53
0001–0160	1952		0848–1897	1953–54

STRATOCASTER, 1954

NUMBER RANGE   **YEAR**
Under 6000 1954

ELECTRIC MODELS, 1954 AND AFTER

Number on neckplate.

GENERAL RANGE	LOWEST	HIGHEST	YEAR OF NECK DATE
0001–6000s	0001	10146	late 1954
7000s–8000s	3152	10798	1955 (some preceded by 0)
01000s–08000s			1954–63
09000s–16000s	7895	16957	1956
17000s–24000s	10604	28522	1957 (some preceded by – or 0)
25000s–33000s	022526	40644	1958 (some preceded by 0)
34000s–43000s	022878	51593	1959
44000s–58000s	39993	66626	1960
59000s–70000s	55531	77754	1961
71000s–93000s	69520	96203	1962
94000s–99000s	81977	99924	1963

L-SERIES

A few examples			1962
L00001–L19000s	L00001	L60330	1963
L20000s–L59000s	L08825	L92560	1964
L60000s–L99000s	L23537	L99944	1965

F-SERIES, F ON NECKPLATE

100000–110000s	100173	158977	1965
120000s–170000s	112172	261343	1966
180000s–210000s	156657	263115	1967
220000s–251000s	204352	262774	1968
252000s–291000s	224160	290835	1969
292000s–298000s	278916	304089	1970
299000s–344000s	261863	331031	1971
345000s–370000s	258495	654030	1972
380000s–530000s	316987	602615	1973
540000s–590000s	417024	677199	1974
600000s–656000s	595121	717257	1975
657000s–660000s			1976
670000s-700000s			1971–76

CROSS-CHECK F-SERIES LIST

GENERAL RANGE	YEAR OF NECK DATE
400000s	Apr. 1973–Sept. 1976
500000s	Sept. 1973–Sept. 1976
600000s	Aug. 1974–Aug. 1976
700000s	Sept. 1976–Dec. 1976

FENDER

FENDER

NUMBER ON PEGHEAD DECAL

GENERAL RANGE	YEAR OF NECK DATE	GENERAL RANGE	YEAR OF NECK DATE
7600000 (76 in boldface)	1976–77	E400000s	1984, 1985, 1987
800000s	1979–81	E800000s	1988, 1989
1000000s–8000000s	1976–81 (7-digits)	E900000s	1989, 1990
S100000s–S600000s	1979–82	N900000s	1990
S700000s–S770000s	1977	N000000s	1990
S740000s–S800000s	1978	N100000s	1991
S810000s–S870000s	1979	N200000s	1992
S880000s–S980000s	1980	N300000s	1993
S950000s–S990000s	1981	N400000s	1994
E000000s–E100000s	1979–82	N500000s	1995
E110000s–E120000s	1980–83	N600000s	1996
E200000s	1982	N700000s	1997
E300000s–E310000s	1983	N800000s	1998
E320000s–E390000s	1984–85		

CROSS-CHECK NUMBER LIST, S OR E PREFIX

NUMBER	PERIOD	NUMBER	PERIOD
S7	Jan. 1977–Apr. 1978	N9	1990
S8	Dec. 1977–Dec. 1978	N0	1990–91
S9	Nov. 1978–Aug. 1981	N2	1992
E0	June 1979–Dec. 1981	N3	1993
E1	Dec. 1980–Jan. 1982	N4	1994
E2	Dec. 1981–Jan. 1983	N5	1995
E3	Dec. 1982–Jan. 1985	N6	1996
E4	Dec. 1983–early 1988	N7	1997
E8	1988–89	N8	1998
E9	1989–90		

JAPANESE-MADE FENDERS

PREFIX	PERIOD	PREFIX	PERIOD
JV	1982–84	I	1989–90
SQ	1983–84	J	1989–90
E	1984–87	K	1990–91
A	1985–86	L	1991–92
B	1985–86	M	1992–93
C	1985–86	N	1993–94
F	1986–87	O	1994–95
G	1987–88	P	1995–96
H	1988–89		

OTHER FENDER NUMBERS

25#### = Anniversary Stratocaster: **mid 1979–early 1980s**

AMXN prefix: AMX = made in Mexico and America, N = decade (1990s)

C prefix: **1982**

CA, CB, CC, CD or CE prefix, collectors series: **Dec. 1981–Dec. 1982**

D prefex: **late 1981–early 1982**

GO prefix: **early 1980s**

MN prefix: M = Mexican made, N = decade (1990s): **1990s**

SE prefix, Signature Edition model: **1982–current**

V###### = Vintage reissues: **1982–current**

4-digit decal on back of peghead, custom order: **1987–current**

ESQUIRES AND TELECASTERS

SECTION ORGANIZATION

Esquires

Telecasters

Esquire and Telecaster Finishes, 1950–69

Telecaster Reissues

Misc. Telecaster Models

Artist Signature Models

Acoustic/Electric Models

Squiers

ESQUIRES

Esquire: single cutaway, ash body, 1 pickup with flush poles, 2 dome knobs (some smooth, some rimmed on top), 2-position toggle switch, white pickguard with 5 slot-head screws, 3 brass paired-string adjustable saddles (early with steel saddles), strings anchor through body, maple neck, no truss rod, slot-head neck bolts, round string guide, logo below string guide, black finish

Announced in *Musical Merchandise* magazine: **June 1950**

Routed for 2 pickups, no routing channel between pick-ups, some examples with 2 pickups, short round-cap 3-way tone selector switch, black bakelite pickguard, butterscotch blond finish: **summer 1950**

No Esquires made: **late Sept. 1950–Jan. 1951**

Reintroduced, 1 pickup, truss rod, butterscotch blond finish (later finish changes and options listed after Telecaster, following): **Jan. 1951**

Routing channel between pickup routings: **late summer 1951**

Phillips-head neck bolts: **early 1952**

Phillips-head pickguard screws: **mid to late 1952**

White celluloid pickguard: **late 1954**

Staggered-height pickup poles, "top-hat" switch (thin top, rounded base), serial number on neckplate,

butterfly-clip string guide: **late 1955**

Logo above string guide: **July or Aug. 1956**

Threaded steel saddles: **late 1958**

Strings anchor at bridge: **late 1958**

8 screws in pickguard: **by summer 1959**

Strings anchor through body: **early 1960**

White laminated pickguard: **1965**

Last produced: **early 1970**

Esquire Custom: same as Esquire but with alder body, bound top and back, rosewood fingerboard, sunburst finish

Introduced: **mid 1959**

3-ply pickguard: **1960**

Discontinued: **early 1970**

TELECASTERS

Broadcaster/No-caster/Telecaster: same body shape as Esquire, single-cutaway, ash body, 2 pickups, flush poles on bridge pickup, serial number stamped on housing of bridge pickup, no routing channel between pickup routings, 2 dome knobs (some smooth, some rimmed on top), short round-cap pickup selector switch, black bakelite pickguard with 5 slot-head screws, 3 brass paired-string adjustable saddles, strings anchor through body, maple neck, truss rod with slot-head adjustment, slot-head neck fastening bolts, round string guide, logo below string guide

Introduced as **Broadcaster**, 300–500 made: **late Oct. (or early Nov.) 1950–Feb. 1951**

Phillips-head truss rod adjustment: **early 1951**

Model name removed from peghead (Gretsch had been marketing a Broadkaster drum continuously since the 1920s), referred to by collectors as **No-caster: Feb. 1951**

Renamed **Telecaster:** routing channel between pickup routings (a few No-casters routed between pickups), model name on peghead decal: **early 1951**

Phillips-head neck fastening bolts: **early 1952**

Phillips-head pickguard screws: **late 1952**

White plastic pickguard: **late 1954**

Staggered-height poles on bridge pickup, "top-hat" switch (thin top, rounded base), serial number on neckplate, butterfly-clip string guide: **late 1955**

Logo above string guide: **July or Aug. 1956**

Alder body for custom colors, ash body for blond finish: **mid 1956**

Threaded steel saddles: **late 1958**

Strings anchor at bridge: **late 1958**

8 screws in pickguard: **1959**

Strings anchor through body: **early 1960**

White laminated pickguard: **by late 1963**

Bigsby vibrola optional: **1967–74**

2 string guides on peghead: **1972**

Black laminated pickguard: **1975**

White laminated pickguard: **1981**

Renamed Standard Telecaster (see following): **1982**

ESQUIRE AND TELECASTER FINISHES, 1950–69

"Butterscotch," whitish yellow to show woodgrain, tendency to yellow over time: **1950**

"Tele blond," translucent whitish yellow, somewhat gray on heavily figured ash bodies, less yellowing over time: **mid 1955**

More opaque yellow finish, less woodgrain visible: **1960–68**

Cimarron red, a few custom orders, some sprayed over blond or sunburst: **1955–60**

Sunburst, most common custom finish (but still rare) …

2-tone: **1957**

3-tone: **1958–59**

Black, very few (less than 10) Esquires in 1950, later Teles and Esquires: **late 1958–early 1959**

Any available Dupont Duco (nitrocellulose lacquer) or Dupont Lucite (acrylic lacquer, available from 1957 onward) color: **1950–58**

Standardized custom colors (see Stratocaster section): **1959 and after**

Pink paisley and blue floral (preprinted sheets applied to body and then oversprayed) optional: **1968–69**

TELECASTER REISSUES

'50s Relic Nocaster: Custom Shop model, swamp ash body, cosmetically aged honey blond finish

Available: **1997–current**

'50s Telecaster (USA): Custom Shop model, ash body, vintage pickups, white pickguard, maple neck, nickel- or gold-plated hardware, "white-washed" blond, 2-tone sunburst or black finish

Available: **1997–current**

'50s Telecaster (Japan): made in Japan, bass-wood body, 3-saddle bridge, maple neck with tinted finish, 21 frets, black pickguard, blond finish on body

Introduced: **1992**

Blond, 2-tone sunburst, black or candy apple red finish: **1995**

Slight V-neck, chrome- or gold-plated hardware, black, blond, 2-tone sunburst, candy apple red, shell pink or sonic blue finish: **1997**

Still in production

'52 Telecaster: reissue of 1952 Telecaster, ash body, serial number on bridgeplate, vintage style pickups, cloth-covered wire, black pickguard, rosewood fingerboard or maple neck, 21 frets, spaghetti logo, butterscotch blond finish

Announced as **Vintage Telecaster** but not produced: **Jan. 1981**

Introduced as **'52 Telecaster: Jan. 1982**

First production: **mid 1982**

Black, butterscotch blond or copper finish: **1997**

Still in production

Custom Classic '52 Left-Handed Tele: USA Custom Shop model, left-handed version of '52 Telecaster (reissue): **1996–current**

Paisley Tele: made in Japan, basswood body, maple neck, vintage 6-saddle bridge, maple neck, nickel-plated hardware, pink paisley finish

Introduced as limited run model: **1994**

Still in production

MISC. TELECASTER MODELS

Standard Telecaster: continuation of original Telecaster model, 6 standard and 7 custom finishes: **1982**

6-saddle bridge with asymmetrical saddles and top-loading strings, single-ply white pickguard with 5 screws (earliest with 8 screws): **1983**

Marble-ized "bowling ball" finish in red, gold or blue, 25 produced in each finish: **1984**

Discontinued: **1985**

Reintroduced, made in Mexico, poplar body, white pickguard, 6-saddle bridge, strings through body, maple neck, 21 frets, Lake Placid blue, black, crimson red metallic, brown sunburst or Arctic white finish: **by 1991**

Still in production

Telecaster Custom: alder body (a few ash), 3-ply pickguard, single-bound top and back, rosewood fingerboard, sunburst finish, a few custom color examples

Introduced: **mid 1959**

A few with white finish and black binding: **1965–72**

Last made: **spring 1972**

'60s Telecaster Custom: USA Custom Shop model, alder body, bound top and back, Texas Tele pickups, rosewood fingerboard, 21 frets, nickel- or gold-plated hardware, 3-tone sunburst, black or custom color finish

Available: **1997–current**

'72 Tele Custom: made in Japan, humbucking neck pickup, 2 volume controls, 2 tone controls, 3-way selector switch, vintage 3-saddle bridge, black/white/black pickguard, maple neck, 21 frets, bullet truss rod, 3-tone sunburst or black finish

Available: **1997–current**

'90s Telecaster Custom: finish applied in Mexico, basswood body, double-bound top and back, marble-ized celluloid pickguard, vintage style pickups and electronics, 6-saddle bridge with strings through body, oval neck profile, rosewood fingerboard, 21 frets, gold-plated hardware, Olympic white or black finish

Available: **1995–97**

Telecaster Thin Line: ash or mahogany body, hollow on bass side, 1 *f*-hole, no *Thin Line* decal on peghead, natural finish, sunburst and other custom color finishes available

Introduced: **late 1968**

2 humbucking pickups, *Thin Line* decal on peghead: **late 1971**

Discontinued: **1980**

'69 Telecaster Thinline: made in Japan, mahogany body, hollow on bass side, 1 *f*-hole, 2 single-coil pickups, white pearloid pickguard, maple neck, natural finish

Available: **1997–current**

'72 Telecaster Thinline: made in Japan, ash body, hollow on bass side, 1 *f*-hole, 2 Telecaster humbucking pickups, white pearloid pickguard, strings through body, maple neck, bullet truss rod, natural finish

Available: **1997–current**

'90s Tele Thinline: ash body, hollow on bass side, 1 *f*-hole, same pickups and hardware as American Standard, double-bound top, 3-tone sunburst, black, natural Foto Flame (simulated woodgrain) or crimson transparent finish, black Tolex case with red lining

Available: **1997–current**

Rosewood Telecaster: rosewood body, 3-ply black pickguard, serial number beginning with *A*

First made for George Harrison, 2-piece top, 2-piece back, thin maple laminate between top and back sections: **Dec. 1968**

Introduced: **1969**

Some with chambered body: **1971–72**

Last made: **1972**

Japanese-made reissue, limited production: **late 1980s–94**

Custom Telecaster: (also called Telecaster Custom in literature) standard Tele bridge pickup, humbucking neck pickup, 4 knobs, 3-position toggle switch on upper treble bout, 6-saddle bridge (earliest with 3 saddles), elongated pickguard surrounds all controls, rosewood fingerboard or maple neck, bullet truss rod

Available: **March 1970–81**

'62 Custom Telecaster: made in Japan, basswood body, vintage 3-saddle bridge, white/black/white pickguard, bound top and back, rosewood fingerboard, 21 frets, chrome-plated hardware, 3-tone sunburst or candy apple red finish

Available: **1997–current**

FENDER

Deluxe Telecaster: poplar body, contoured back, 2 humbucking pickups, 4 knobs, 3-position toggle switch on upper treble bout, 6-saddle bridge, maple neck, 21 frets, bullet truss rod, large Strat-like peghead
Introduced: **late 1972**
Antigua finish (cream-to-brown sunburst) available: **1977–79**
Discontinued: **1982**

'90s Telecaster Deluxe: finish applied in Mexico, alder body with Strat-style contours, basswood top cap with Foto Flame finish (simulated woodgrain), 2 Strat-style pickups in neck and middle position, vintage Tele pickup in bridge position, 5-way selector switch, 6-saddle bridge, white pearloid pickguard, maple neck with Foto Flame finish (simulated woodgrain) rosewood fingerboard, 21 frets, 3-tone sunburst, black, candy apple red or sonic blue finish
Introduced as **'90s Telecaster Deluxe Foto Flame: 1995**
Discontinued: **1997**
Reintroduced, alder body (no basswood cap), maple neck (no Foto Flame), 22 frets: **fall 1997**
Still in production

American Deluxe Tele: made in USA, alder or ash body, contoured back, Vintage-Noiseless Tele pickups plus Vintage-Noiseless Strat pickup in middle position, 7-way switch, white pickguard, bound top, rosewood fingerboard or maple neck, 22 frets, alder body available with 3-tone sunburst, black or crimson red stain finish, ash body available with white blond, teal green transparent or purple transparent finish
Available: **1998–current**

Black and Gold: black finish, 6-saddle bridge, black peghead face, gold-plated hardware
Available: **mid 1981– mid 1983**

Sparkle: poplar body, white pickguard, brass saddles, strings through body, champagne sparkle, gold sparkle or silver sparkle finish
Available: **1993–95**

Elite: alder body, 2 white plastic-covered humbucking pickups with no visible poles, 4 knobs and 3-way switch, active electronics, bridge with 6

saddles and drop-in string loading, bound top, 2 string guides, natural or sunburst finish
Available: **June 1983– early 1985**

Gold Elite: pearloid tuner buttons, gold-plated hardware: **June 1983– early 1985**

Walnut Elite: black walnut body, walnut neck with maple skunk stripe, ebony fingerboard, pearloid tuner buttons, gold-plated hardware: **June 1983– early 1985**

American Standard: similar to Standard Telecaster but with 9.5"-radius fingerboard (more rounded than standard 12"-radius fingerboard), alder body, 6-saddle bridge with symmetrical saddles, 22-fret neck, rosewood fingerboard or maple neck, black, Caribbean mist, lipstick red, midnight blue, midnight wine, sunburst or vintage white finish
Introduced: **Jan. 1988**
Metal *40th Anniversary* logo: **1994 only**
Black, candy apple red, Inca silver or brown sunburst finish: **1997**
Still in production

American Standard Aluminum Body: hollow aluminum body, blue marble, purple marble or red/silver/blue graphic American flag finish: **1994**

American Standard B-Bender: maple neck, Parsons/White B-string bender, Olympic white, black, candy apple red or brown sunburst finish: **1995–97**

40th Anniversary: based on American Standard Telecaster, ash body, bookmatched flame maple top, bound top, ivoroid pickguard, curly maple neck, abalone inlay, pearloid tuner buttons, antique 2-tone sunburst, natural or translucent red finish, limited run of 300
All American Standard Telecasters from 1994 have a 40th Anniversary metal logo plate but are easily distinguishable from the 40th Anniversary model by their lack of a maple top cap and lack of binding.
Available: **summer 1988–early 1990**

Contemporary: made in Japan, 2 single-coil and 1 humbucking pickup or 2 humbuckers with 3-way switch and coil tap, 3 knobs, vibrato, rosewood fingerboard, 22 frets, black chrome hardware
Available: **1985–87**

TelecasterPlus Standard: Lace blue neck pickup, dual Lace red pickup in bridge position, coil tap switch, 22 frets, rosewood fingerboard or maple neck
Available: **1990–92**

TelecasterPlus Deluxe: Strat-style tremolo, roller nut, locking Schaller tuners: **1990–92**

Telecaster Plus: alder body, alder body, ash veneer on top and back, 3 Lace Sensor pickups, white binding on top and back, rosewood fingerboard or maple neck, 22 frets, chrome-plated hardware, black, crimson burst, blue burst, antique burst or teal green metallic finish: **1995–97**

Set Neck Telecaster: mahogany body with cavities to lighten weight, bound top, glued-in mahogany neck, painted peghead, curly maple top, 22-fret fingerboard, antique burst, autumn gold, transparent crimson, transparent ebony or transparent sapphire blue finish, available in 3 versions:

- 2 DiMarzio humbucking pickups with exposed coils, Brazilian rosewood fingerboard
  Introduced: **summer 1990**
  Pau ferro fingerboard: **1993**
  Discontinued: **1996**

- Strat-style tremolo, ebony fingerboard, roller nut: **1990–95**

- 2 humbucking and 1 single-coil pickup, Floyd Rose tremolo, ebony fingerboard: **1990–95**

Set Neck Tele CA: USA Custom Shop model, humbucker in neck position with coil tap, standard Tele single-coil pickup in bridge position, 2 knobs mounted into top, glued-in mahogany neck, ebony fingerboard, small tortoiseshell celluloid pickguard covers only upper right quadrant, sunset orange transparent, natural, silver sparkle or gold sparkle finish: **1992**

Set Neck Tele Jr.: USA Custom Shop model, mahogany body with 11 tone chambers, 2 Seymour Duncan Hot Soapbar P-90 single-coil pickups, American Standard Strat style 6-saddle bridge, tortoiseshell celluloid pickguard, glued-in neck, pau ferro fingerboard, 21 frets, natural, antique burst, crimson transparent or vintage white finish: **1997–current**

HMT Telecaster: made in Japan, basswood body, maple top, ƒ-hole on bass side, 2 DiMarzio humbucking pickups, coil tap, standard bridge, 2 knobs, no pickguard, bound top, black chrome hardware, 3-tone sunburst, Olympic white, natural or crimson stain finish
Available: **1992**

HMT Telecaster Floyd Rose: made in Japan, 1 DiMarzio humbucking pickup with coil tap, 1 blue Fender-Lace pickup, 2 knobs, 3-way switch, Floyd Rose tremolo, triangular sharkstooth inlay, angled peghead without scroll at top, bold script logo, 3-tone sunburst, natural, midnight blue, chrome red or crimson stain finish: **1992**

Foto Flame: made in Japan, alder body, basswood top cap, vintage style electronics, 3-saddle bridge, rosewood fingerboard, Foto Flame treatment (simulated woodgrain) on top and neck, natural, aged cherry sunburst, autumn burst or 3-tone transparent sunburst finish
Available: **1995**

California "Fat" Tele: finish applied in Mexico, alder body, Tex/Mex humbucking neck pickup, Tex/Mex single-coil bridge pickup, 5-way switch with coil tap, 6-saddle bridge, maple neck with tinted finish, 21 medium jumbo frets, chrome-plated hardware, black, brown sunburst, candy apple red, fiesta red or vintage white finish
Available: **1997–98**

California Tele: Tex/Mex Strat neck pickup, Tex/Mex Tele bridge pickup, rosewood fingerboard or maple neck: **1997–98**

American Classic: Custom Shop model, 2 Texas Special Strat pickups and 1 Texas Tele bridge pickup, American Standard Tele bridge, pickguard, rosewood fingerboard or maple neck, 22 frets, chrome- or gold-plated hardware, 3-tone sunburst, blond, 2-tone sunburst, Olympic white or custom color finish
Available: **1996–current**

Bajo Sexto Telecaster: Custom Shop model, baritone guitar, 2-piece ash body, black pickguard, 30.2" scale, lightly figured maple neck, 2-tone sunburst or honey blond finish
Available: **1993–current**

81

Telecaster XII: Custom Shop model, 12-string, 2-piece swamp ash body, figured maple neck with C profile, 2 Texas Tele single-coil pickups wired in series, strings mount through body, rosewood fingerboard or maple neck, 3-tone sunburst, 2-tone sunburst, vintage blond or sea foam green finish
Available: **1997–current**

Telecaster Special: made in Mexico, poplar body, ash top, maple fingerboard, 22 frets, 1 single-coil and 1 humbucking pickup, natural finish
Available: **1994–96**

Tex-Mex Tele Special: made in Japan, poplar body, 1 Tex/Mex single-coil and 1 Tex/Mex humbucking pickup, maple neck, 21 frets: **1997**

Traditional Telecaster: made in Mexico, poplar body, vintage 6-saddle bridge, maple neck, chrome-plated hardware, Arctic white, black or Torino red finish
Available: **1997**

Deluxe Nashville Tele: made in Mexico, alder body, 2 Tex/Mex Tele pickups and 1 Tex/Mex Strat pickup in middle position, 5-way switch, 6-saddle bridge, strings through body, rosewood fingerboard or maple neck, 21 frets, black, candy apple red, brown sunburst or Arctic white finish
Available: **1997–current**

Nashville B-Bender Tele: made in USA, alder body, American Standard Tele pickups plus Texas Special Strat pickup in middle position, B-string bender, 6-saddle bridge, 5-way switch, white pearloid pickguard, rosewood fingerboard or maple neck, 22 frets, 3-tone sunburst, Olympic white, black or candy apple red finish
Available: **1998–current**

1998 Collectors Edition: made in USA, ash body, American Vintage Tele pickups, single-ply white pickguard, maple neck with V profile, 21 frets, oval pearl inlay at 12th fret engraved with *1998*, gold-plated hardware, sunburst finish, brown Tolex case with gold lining, limited run of 1,998, ranking on neckplate
Available: **1998**

Tele-Sonic: made in USA, mahogany body with tone chambers, 2 DeArmond single-coil pickups (similar to 1950s Gretsch style), 4 knobs mounted into top, switch on upper bass bout, stop tailpiece, pickguard does not surround neck pickup, 24 3/4" scale, rosewood fingerboard, 22 frets, sunburst or crimson transparent finish
Available: **1998**

U.S. Fat Tele: alder body, American Standard bridge pickup, Fender humbucking neck pickup (1 row of 6 polepieces), 5-way switch with coil tap, 6-saddle bridge, strings through body, rosewood fingerboard or maple neck, 22 frets, 3-tone sunburst, Olympic white, black or candy apple red finish
Available: **1998–current**

ARTIST SIGNATURE MODELS

James Burton: ash body, 3 black Lace pickups, 5-way switch, 6-saddle bridge, maple neck, 21 frets, 4 finish and hardware variations:
- Black with silkscreened gold paisley, gold-plated hardware
- Black with silkscreened candy red paisley, black chrome hardware
- Pearl white finish (no paisley), gold-plated hardware
- Frost red finish (no paisley), black chrome hardware
Available: **January 1990–current**

James Burton Standard: made in Mexico, white pickguard, Texas Tele pickups, 6-saddle bridge, maple neck, 2-tone sunburst, black, vintage white or candy apple red finish: **1995–current**

Albert Collins: USA Custom Shop model, ash body, Gibson-type humbucking pickup in neck position, 6-saddle bridge, glitter contact paper on bridge cover, white binding on top and back, maple neck with maple fingerboard, 21 frets, natural finish, natural Foto Flame finish (simulated woodgrain)
Available by custom order only: **June 1990–current**

Jerry Donahue: USA Custom Shop model, ash body, bird's eye maple top and back, Stratocaster pickup in neck position (but closer to bridge than on other Teles), custom Tele-style bridge pickup, black pickguard, bound top and back, maple neck with slight V profile, 21 frets, gold-plated hardware, dark 2-tone sunburst finish, 3-tone sunburst, sap-

phire blue transparent or crimson transparent finish
Available by custom order only: **1992–current**

J.D.: Jerry Donahue model, made in Japan, basswood body, Stratocaster pickup in neck position, vintage style bridge with brass saddles, 5-position switch, maple neck, 3-tone sunburst, black, sapphire blue transparent or crimson transparent finish:
Available: **1992–current**

Danny Gatton: Custom Shop model, based on 1953 Tele, swamp ash body, 2 Barden double-blade humbucking pickups, bent switch, angled stainless steel saddles, notched bridge side plate, maple neck, 22 frets, cubic zirconium side dots, unfinished back of neck, honey blond or frost gold finish, tweed case
Available: **June 1990–current**

Clarence White: Custom Shop model, Texas Tele bridge pickup, white '54 Strat neck pickup, tortoise-shell celluloid pickguard, maple neck, 21 frets, Scruggs/Keith tuners on both E strings, B-bender, 2-tone sunburst finish, tweed case
Available: **1994–current**

Waylon Jennings Tribute Series: Custom Shop model, based on 1963 Tele, leather "White Rose" inlay on body, Texas Tele pickups, 6-saddle bridge, maple neck, 21 frets, Scruggs/Keith tuner on low E string, maple neck, "Flying W" logo inlaid at 12th fret, black finish
Available: **1995–current**

Merle Haggard Tribute Series: Custom Shop model, highly figured maple top, Duncan bridge pickup, Texas special neck pickup, 4-way switch, bound top, ivoroid pickguard, glued-in maple neck, 22 frets, special "Tuff Dog Tele" peghead inlay, pearl tuner buttons, gold-plated hardware
Available: **1997–current**

Nokie Edwards Limited Edition: made in Japan, laminated body of ash, basswood and rock maple with flame maple top, 2 Seymour Duncan humbucking pickups, black pickguard, ebony fingerboard, 22 frets plus zero-fret, gold-plated hardware, 3-tone sunburst or transparent finishes
Available: **1996**

Hellecasters Will Ray Jazz-a-caster: made in Japan, basswood body, 2 Seymour Duncan reverse-wound Jazzmaster pickups (rectangular with white covers), pearloid pickguard, Hip Shot Will Ray model B-string bender, "Vintique" knob on master volume control, vintage 6-saddle bridge, rosewood fingerboard, 22 frets, triangular pearloid inlay, small Strat-style peghead, gold foil-leaf finish, custom colors available, limited run
Available: **1997**

Will Ray "Mojo": Custom Shop model, ash body, custom Jazzmaster pickups (rectangular with white covers), Hip Shot Will Ray model B-string bender, 3 knobs with black "Vintique" knob in middle, 3-saddle bridge, oval pearloid pickguard, rosewood fingerboard, 22 frets, voodoo skull inlay, gold-leaf pattern finish in ultra marine blue, cadmium orange or lime green
Available: **1998–current**

John Jorgensen: Custom Shop model, korina body, double-coil pickups (vintage Tele-style), 3-saddle bridge, pickguard matches finish, African rosewood fingerboard with champagne sparkle or silver sparkle finish, ebony fingerboard with black body finish
Available: **1998–current**

Buck Owens: made in Japan, basswood body, Vintage Tele pickups, gold pickguard, rosewood fingerboard, 22 frets, gold-plated hardware, red-silver-and-blue sparkle finish on body and peghead
Available: **1998–current**

ACOUSTIC/ELECTRIC MODELS

HMT Acoustic/Electric: made in Japan, *f*-hole in bass bout, silver Fender-Lace pickup mounted at angle in neck position, piezo pickup in acoustic-style pin bridge, 3 knobs, 3-tone sunburst, Olympic white, natural or crimson stain finish
Available: **1992**

Telecoustic Standard: made in Japan, spruce top, oval soundhole, basswood body, piezo pickup in rosewood acoustic-style pin bridge, 3 slide controls for volume, treble and bass, rosewood fingerboard, antique burst, black or natural finish
Available: **1993–95**

Telecoustic Custom: made in Japan, bound top, mahogany back, active electronics, pau ferro and ebony bridge, mahogany neck, pau ferro fingerboard, pearl tuner buttons, antique burst or natural finish: **1993–95**

Telecoustic Deluxe: made in Japan, mahogany back, mahogany neck, rosewood fingerboard, pearl tuner buttons: **1993–95**

Telecaster Acoustic-Electric: made in Japan, semi-hollow basswood body, spruce top, 1 *f*-hole, piezo bridge pickup, slant-mounted single-coil neck pickup, 3 knobs, active electronics, rosewood bridge with strings through body, bound top and back, rosewood fingerboard, 22 frets, 25 1/4" scale, 3-tone sunburst or black finish
Available: **1995–97**

Telecaster Classical Thinline: made in Japan, nylon strings, piezo pickup, 2 knobs, rosewood fingerboard, 22 frets
Available: **1995–97**

SQUIERS

Telecaster Squier: made in Japan
Available: **1983–94**

Squier—Made in U.S.A. Telecaster: body and neck made in USA, finish applied in Mexico, final assembly in USA
Available: **1990–91**

COMMENTS

Esquires, Telecasters and Stratocasters (see following section) played a major role in the popularization of the solidbody electric guitar. Examples made from their introduction into the late 1960s are highly regarded by players and collectors. Generally, the earlier the example, the more highly sought.

STRATOCASTERS

SECTION ORGANIZATION

Stratocaster with Detailed Specs
Reissues
Anniversary Stratocasters
Misc. Stratocasters
Signature Stratocasters

STRATOCASTER WITH DETAILED SPECS

Stratocaster: asymmetrical double cutaway body shape, body contoured on back and on lower bass bout, 3 single-coil pickups, jack angled into top, tremolo standard, see following for more detailed specs
Introduced: **spring 1954**
First non-tremolo models: **Mar. 1955**
A few with bound fingerboard: **1965–67**
Referred to in literature as **Standard Stratocaster** (no *Standard* on peghead): **1982**
The term *Standard Stratocaster* was used by Fender to distinguish the basic current Stratocaster from variations and reissues. However, among collectors and dealers, the term is commonly used as if it were a separate model designation, referring to the Stratocaster (official model name) with the following specs:
2 knobs, jack in 3rd-knob position, 90-degree jack angle, 1-piece tailpiece with drop-in string loading, single-ply white pickguard, black, sienna sunburst, brown sunburst or ivory finish: **1983**
Marblized "bowling ball" finishes available: **late 1984**
Standard Stratocaster discontinued: **Jan. 1985**
Basic American-made Stratocaster reintroduced as **American Standard Stratocaster** (see following): **1986**
Standard Stratocaster name reintroduced on Mexican-made model (see following): **1992**

Body

Wood...
> Ash...
>> All finishes: **1954–mid 1956**
>> Blond finish only: **mid 1956–current**
> Alder: **mid 1956–current**
> Basswood: many Japanese-made models: **1992–current**
> Poplar: some Mexican-made models: **1992–current**
> Exceptions: Walnut Stratocaster, laminate-body models, etc.

Gold-plated hardware optional: **1956–67**

Back plate (tremolo spring cover)...
> Round string holes: **1954–early 1955**
> Oval string holes: **1955 and after**

No back plate (different type tremolo systems), Standard and Elite: **mid 1983–85**

Knobs and pickup covers...
> White bakelite, some knobs with parallel sides, some with steep-sloped sides: **1954**
> White plastic (some bakelite pickup covers in 1956 and 1957): **1956**
> White plastic pickup covers, black knobs: **1976**
> Black or white plastic pickup covers and knobs: **by 1977**

Pickups...
> Staggered-height poles: **1954**
> Flush-pole pickups: **late 1974**

Pickguard...
> Single-layer white bakelite, 8 screws: **1954**
> Single-layer white plastic: **1955**
> Anodized aluminum, some examples: **1954–58**
> 3-layer celluloid, white-black-white, greenish tint, 11 screws: **1959**
> 3-layer plastic, no greenish tint: **Aug. or Sept. 1965**
> Tortoise grain plastic (rare): **early 1960s**
> 3-layer, black-white-black: **1975**

Pickguard, middle screwhole on bass side...
> Screwhole near middle pickup: **1954**
> Screwhole midway between neck pickup and middle pickup: **1959**
> Screwhole near middle pickup: **mid 1963**

Shoulder on control cavity routing: **1959 and after**

Finishes, 1954–82

2-tone sunburst, yellow to black: **1954–58**, some in **1959** and **1960**

Blond and black available as custom colors, any

Dupont Duco (nitrocellulose lacquer) or Dupont Lucite (acrylic lacquer, available from 1957 onward) color: **1954–58**

3-tone sunburst, yellow to red to black: **mid 1958**

Custom colors standardized (some custom colors have sunburst underneath): **March 1958**

COLOR	YEARS
Fiesta red	1958–69
Olympic white	1958–80
Gold metallic	1958–59
Lake Placid blue metallic	1958–59
Dakota red	1958–69
Black	1958–84
Daphne blue	1960–65
Shoreline gold metallic	1959–65
Burgundy mist metallic	1960–65
Foam green	1960–69
Inca silver metallic	1960–65
Shell pink	1960–63
Sherwood green metallic	1960–65
Sonic blue	1960–72
Surf green	1960–65
Candy apple red metallic	1963–73
Blue ice metallic	1965–69
Charcoal frost metallic	1965–69
Firemist gold metallic	1965–71
Firemist silver metallic	1965–71
Ocean turquoise metallic	1965–71
Teal green metallic	1965–69
Blond	April 1970–82
Natural	1972–82

Peghead Size

Small peghead: **1954**

Enlarged peghead official: **Dec. 19, 1965**

Transition period to larger peghead: **late 1965–early 1966**

Small peghead revived: **1981**

Decals

Configuration of *Stratocaster with synchronized tremolo*...
> Small letters, straight line: **1954**
> Bold letters, curved line: **July 1968**
> No *with synchronized tremolo*: **1970**
> Small letters: **1980**

Original contour body...
> No patent notice: **1954**

Pat. Pend added: **1961**

Patented replaces *Pat. Pend*: **1968**

Decal discontinued: **1976**

Made in USA: **1976–current**

Numbers on Decal

No number: **1954**

2 PAT numbers, both beginning with 2: **1961**

3 PAT numbers: **spring 1962**

4 PAT numbers: **mid–1964**

5 PAT numbers: **mid–1965**

2 PAT numbers, 1 DES number: **Feb. 1966**

2 PAT numbers, 2nd begins with 3: **mid 1968**

1 PAT number beginning with 2: **mid 1970**

1 PAT number beginning with 3: **mid 1972**

Serial number, no patent number: **1976–current**

REISSUES

'50s Stratocaster: Collectables model, made in Japan, V-neck with skunk stripe, single-ply 8-screw pickguard, maple neck, 21 frets, aged hardware, 2-tone sunburst, Olympic white, black, candy apple red, shell pink or sonic blue finish

Available: **1992–current**

1954 Stratocaster: USA Custom Shop model, ash body, flame maple top optional, Custom '50s pickups, vintage style tremolo, 3-position switch, white pickguard, lightly figured maple neck/fingerboard, soft-V neck profile, 21 frets, chrome- or gold-plated hardware

Finishes for ash body: 2-tone sunburst, vintage blond or Aztec gold

Finishes for maple body: 2-tone sunburst, natural or aged cherry

Available: **1997–current**

'57 Stratocaster: reissue of 1957 Strat, alder body, staggered polepieces, cloth-wrapped wire, white single-layer pickguard, maple neck/fingerboard, 2-tone lacquer sunburst finish standard, vintage custom colors available (candy apple red, vintage white, black, Lake Placid blue, fiesta red), serial number beginning with *V*, tweed case

Introduced: **Jan. 1982**

Translucent blond finish optional (limited edition): **June 1987**

Shoreline gold finish optional: **1997**

Still in production

'58 Stratocaster: USA Custom Shop model, ash body, Fat '50s pickups, vintage style tremolo, 3-way switch, aged knobs and pickguard, '58 neck shape, maple neck/fingerboard, 21 frets, chrome- or gold-plated hardware, 3-tone sunburst, black or blond finish

Available: **1997–current**

1960 Stratocaster: USA Custom Shop model, alder body, 3 Texas Special pickups with aged covers, rosewood fingerboard, 21 frets, optional gold-plated hardware, brown Tolex-covered case, 3-tone sunburst, Olympic white or black

1960 Stratocaster FMT: bookmatched 2-piece flamed maple top, 3-tone sunburst, natural or aged cherry sunburst: **1997–current**

'60s Stratocaster: Collectables model, made in Japan, basswood body, U-shaped neck, slab rosewood fingerboard, 21 frets, vintage tuners and tremolo, aged hardware, 3-tone sunburst, Olympic white, black, blue Foto Flame (simulated woodgrain), crimson Foto Flame, candy apple red, shell pink or sonic blue finish

Introduced: **1992**

Foto Flame finishes discontinued: **1995**

Still in production

'60s Strat Natural: Collectables model, made in Japan, alder body, basswood top, natural or Foto Flame (simulated woodgrain) finish: **1994–95**

'62 Stratocaster: reissue of 1962 Strat, alder body, staggered polepieces, cloth-wrapped wire, 3-ply pickguard, rosewood fingerboard, 3-tone lacquer sunburst finish standard, vintage custom colors available (candy apple red, vintage white, black, Lake Placid blue, fiesta red), serial number beginning with *V*, tweed case

Introduced: **Jan. 1982**

Translucent blond finish optional (limited edition): **June 1987**

Shoreline gold finish optional: **1997**

Still in production

'68 Stratocaster: Collectables model, made in Japan, ash body, white 3-ply pickguard, gloss-finished U-shaped maple neck, 21 frets, large peghead, 3-tone sunburst, natural or vintage white finish

Available: **1997–current**

'69 Stratocaster: Custom shop model, alder body, 3 custom-wound '69 pickups, staggered polepieces, rosewood fingerboard or maple neck, 21 frets, large peghead, 3-tone sunburst, Olympic white or black finish
Available: **1997–current**

Paisley Strat: made in Japan, ash body with offset waists, maple neck, body covered with pink paisley printed material
Available: **1993**

Blue Flower Strat: made in Japan, ash body with offset waists, maple neck, body covered with blue floral printed material
Available: **1993**

Relics: Custom Shop models, alder body, aged and worn body and hardware

Relic '50s Stratocaster: maple neck, vintage blond finish
Introduced: **1996**
2-tone sunburst finish optional: **1997**
Still in production

Relic '60s Stratocaster: slab rosewood fingerboard, nickel- or gold-plated hardware optional
Standard finishes: 3-tone sunburst or Olympic white
Custom finish colors: Lake Placid blue, daphne blue, burgundy mist metallic or fiesta red
Available: **1996–current**

Relic Floyd Rose: Seymour Duncan '59 humbucking pickup in bridge position, Floyd Rose Original locking tremolo, maple neck, large peghead, Olympic white or black finish: **1998–current**

ANNIVERSARY STRATOCASTERS

Anniversary: commemorates 25th anniversary of model, bridge cover, 4-bolt maple neck, Sperzel tuners, 6-digit serial number beginning with 25, *Anniversary* on bass horn, silver metallic finish (around 500 early examples with white pearlescent finish), standard case and form fit case
Approx. 10,000 made: **1979–80**

35th Anniversary: Custom Shop model, quilted maple/alder body, Lace Sensor pickups, standard tremolo, white pickguard, bird's eye maple neck, ebony fingerboard, pearl dot inlay, 22 frets, locking tuners, active electronics, 3-tone sunburst finish, standard case and form fit case
500 made: **1989–91**

40th Anniversary: reissue of 1954 model, tweed case, 1,954 made: **1994**

Fender's 50th Anniversary Model: maple top, staggered-height pickup poles, American Standard tremolo, rosewood fingerboard, 2 string trees on peghead, gold-plated hardware, spaghetti logo
2,500 made: **1996**

MISC. STRATOCASTERS

Rosewood Stratocaster: "sandwich body" with rosewood top and back, thin maple center laminate
2 made for Jimi Hendrix but never delivered: **1969**

The Strat: alder body, hotter bridge pickup than standard, 9 tone control combinations, heavier brass bridge assembly than standard, locking-nut vibrato system optional, 4-bolt neck, 21 frets, smaller peghead than Standard Strat but unlike original Strat design, gold-plated hardware, candy apple red, Lake Placid blue or Arctic white finish
Available: **1980–July 1983**

Walnut Strat: black walnut body, 1-piece walnut neck/fingerboard with maple skunk stripe, pearloid tuner buttons, natural finish
Available: **1981–July 1983**

Gold Stratocaster: standard pickups and pickguard, maple neck, pearloid tuner buttons, gold-plated metal parts, metallic gold finish
Available: **1981–July 1983**

Smith Strat: alder body, 4-bolt neck, rosewood fingerboard, 21 frets, small peghead
Available: **1981–82**

Elite Stratocaster: active electronics, white plastic pickup covers with no visible poles, jack on side, special design tremolo with piece covering adjustment screw-heads, no back cavity for tremolo springs, snap-on tremolo arm, drop-in string loading, maple neck, 21 frets
Available: **May 1983–84**

Walnut Elite Stratocaster: walnut body and neck, ebony fingerboard, pearloid tuner buttons, gold-plated hardware: **mid 1983–84**

Gold Elite Stratocaster: pearloid tuner buttons, gold-plated hardware: **mid 1983–84**

Contemporary Strat: made in Japan, alder body, locking vibrato, rosewood fingerboard, black peghead face, chrome-plated hardware, 3 versions:

- 1 humbucking pickup with exposed coils, 1 knob, white pickguard
- 2 humbucking pickups, 2 knobs, 3-way switch, coil tap, black pickguard
- 2 single-coil and 1 humbucking pickup, 2 knobs, 5-way switch, coil tap

Introduced: **1985**

Discontinued: **1989**

Reintroduced as Custom Shop model, down-sized alder body, contoured heel, figured maple top optional, deluxe tremolo or Fender Floyd tremolo, Texas Special pickups in neck and middle position, Seymour Duncan double-screw JB humbucker in bridge position, rosewood fingerboard or maple neck

Alder finishes: shoreline gold metallic, black pearl or ice blue metallic

Maple-top finishes: natural, aged cherry sunburst or teal green transparent

Available: **1997–current**

American Standard: alder body, 5-way switch standard, reverse-wound middle pickup for hum-canceling effect, 3-ply white pickguard, redesigned saddles (without bar saddles of original design), 2-piece tremolo tailpiece with 2 bearing points, rosewood fingerboard or maple neck, 22 frets, silver transition logo, truss rod adjustment at peghead (not bullet style), 2 string trees, Arctic white, black, brown sunburst, Caribbean mist, lipstick red, midnight blue or midnight wine finish

Introduced: **Nov. 1986**

Blond, Olympic white, black, candy apple red, natural Foto Flame (simulated woodgrain), Inca silver or brown sunburst finish: **1997**

"Hard-Tail" non-tremolo version optional: **1998**

Still in production

American Standard Aluminum Body: hollow aluminum body, anodized finish of blue marble, purple marble or red/silver/blue flag graphic: **1994**

Limited Edition American Standard: alder body, American Standard tremolo, 3 American Standard pickups, tinted neck, 22 frets, 1950s style peghead decal, ocean turquoise or candy apple red finish with matching peghead finish: **1995**

American Standard Strat GR Ready: Roland GK2 pickup system, Olympic white, black, candy apple red or brown sunburst finish: **1995–97**

U.S. Strat Plus: alder body, ash veneer optional, 3 gold Lace Sensor pickups, LSR roller nut, pearloid pickguard, American Standard tremolo, rosewood fingerboard or maple neck, Schaller locking tuners, graffiti yellow, Arctic white, black, black pearl dust, blue pearl dust, brown sunburst, Caribbean mist, lipstick red, midnight blue or midnight wine finish

Introduced as **Strat Plus: 1987**

Renamed **U.S. Strat Plus: 1992**

Lake Placid blue, Olympic white, black, candy apple red, natural, Inca silver or brown sunburst finish: **1997**

Discontinued: **1998**

U.S. Deluxe Strat Plus: alder body, ash veneer top and back, red, blue and silver Lace Sensor pickups, Fender/Floyd Rose tremolo, tortoiseshell celluloid pickguard, rosewood fingerboard or maple neck, black, crimson burst, blue burst, antique burst or shoreline gold metallic finish: **1992–97**

U.S. Strat Ultra: alder body, figured maple top and back veneer, Fender-Lace Sensor pickups, Fender/Floyd tremolo, pearloid pickguard, ebony fingerboard, pearl dot inlay, locking tuners, LSR roller nut, black, crimson burst, blue burst or antique burst finish

Available: **1990–97**

Stratocaster XII: 12-string, alder body, white pickguard, rosewood fingerboard, 22 frets, 6-on-a-side tuner arrangement, candy apple red finish

Available: **1988–95**

H.M. Strat: made in Japan, basswood body, black pickups with no covers, Kahler vibrato, jack in side, 25.1" scale, rosewood fingerboard or maple neck, 24 frets, black peghead face, large *Strat* logo, black chrome hardware, black, blue, red or white finish, 4 pickup configurations:

- 1 humbucker, no pickguard
- 2 humbuckers, no pickguard

- 1 single-coil, 1 humbucker, pickguard
- 2 single-coils, 1 humbucker, no pickguard

Introduced: **1988**

Redesigned: angled peghead without scroll at top, bold script *Fender* logo, 3-tone sunburst, midnight blue, chrome red, brite white, blackstone, bluestone or redstone finish, 2 versions: **1992**

- 2 DiMarzio humbucking and 1 single-coil pickups, coil tap, 5-position selector switch, 3 knobs, black pickguard, Floyd Rose Pro tremolo
- 1 DiMarzio humbucking pickup and 2 single-coil pickups, coil tap, no pickguard, Floyd Rose Original tremolo

Discontinued: **1993**

H.M. Strat Ultra: figured maple top and back, 4 black-covered Lace Sensor pickups (2 together as double-coil in bridge position), 3 knobs, 5-way switch, mini-switch, ebony fingerboard, split-triangle inlay, pearl peghead logo: **1990–92**

HRR '50s Stratocaster: made in Japan, basswood body, 2 single-coil and 1 DiMarzio humbucking pickup, coil tap, Floyd Rose tremolo, maple neck, 22 frets, black, blue Foto Flame (simulated woodgrain), crimson Foto Flame, Olympic white or 2-tone sunburst finish

Available: **1990–95**

HRR '60s Stratocaster: rosewood fingerboard: **1990–94**

Standard Stratocaster: made in Mexico, poplar body, rosewood fingerboard or maple neck, 21 frets, also available left-handed with basswood body

Introduced: **1992**

Lake Placid blue, black, crimson red metallic, brown sunburst or Arctic white finish: **1997**

Still in production

Standard Roland Ready Stratocaster: Roland GK-2A pickup system, 2 white pushbuttons between knobs and selector switch, rosewood fingerboard: **1998–current**

Set Neck: Custom Shop model, mahogany body, figured maple top, 4 Lace Sensor pickups (humbucker configuration in bridge position), active electronics, glued-in neck, ebony fingerboard, pearl dot inlay, 22 frets, antique burst, natural, transparent crimson or transparent ebony finish

Introduced: **1992**

Ash body, highly figured maple top, Texas Special pickups in neck and middle position, Seymour Duncan double-screw JB humbucker in bridge position, rosewood fingerboard, natural or antique burst finish: **1996**

Still in production

Set Neck Floyd Rose Strat: 2 single-coil and 1 humbucking pickup, Floyd Rose tremolo: **1992–95**

American Classic: Custom Shop version of American Standard, alder body, 3 Texas Special pickups, American Standard tremolo, pearloid pickguard, rosewood fingerboard, 22 frets, nickel- or gold-plated hardware, 3-tone sunburst, blond, 2-tone sunburst or Olympic white finish, black Tolex-covered case

Available: **1993–current**

Short Scale Strat: made in Japan, offset body waists, ash body, white pickguard, 24" scale, rosewood fingerboard or maple neck, 22 frets, Arctic white, 3-tone sunburst, black or frost red finish

Available: **1993**

Stratocaster Special: made in Mexico, ash veneer body, 1 single-coil and 1 humbucking pickup, rosewood fingerboard or maple neck, black brown sunburst, crimson transparent or vintage blond finish

Available: **1994**

Foto Flame: Collectables model, made in Japan, alder body, basswood top, aged cherry sunburst, autumn burst, natural or 3-tone transparent finish, Foto Flame (simulated woodgrain) finish on top cap and back of neck: **1994–95**

Aluminum Body: hollow aluminum body, anodized finishes, 3 versions:

- Chrome finish, black pickguard and peghead
- Green finish with gold and black swirls
- Jet black finish, chrome pickguard

Available: **1994**

Tex-Mex Strat: made in Mexico, poplar body, Tex-Mex Trio single-coil pickups, vintage style tremolo, white pickguard, rosewood fingerboard or maple

neck, 21 frets, black, brown sunburst, candy apple red, sonic blue or vintage white finish
Available: **1996–97**

Tex-Mex Strat Special: 1 single-coil and 1 humbucking Tex-Mex pickup: **1997**

Lone Star Strat: alder body, Texas Special pickups in bridge and middle position, Seymour Duncan Pearly Gates humbucker in bridge position, rosewood fingerboard or maple neck, 22 frets, 3-tone sunburst, Olympic white, black, candy apple red, shoreline gold metallic or teal green metallic finish
Available: **1996–current**

California Strat: shaping and final assembly in U.S., painted in Mexico, Tex-Mex Trio pickups, alder body, tinted maple neck or rosewood fingerboard, medium jumbo frets, black, candy apple red, brown sunburst, fiesta red or vintage white finish
Available: **1997–98**

California Fat Strat: humbucking pickup in bridge position, black candy apple red brown sunburst, fiesta red or vintage white finish: **1997–98**

Fat Strat Floyd Rose: Tex-Mex humbucking pickup in bridge position, 2 Tex-Mex single-coil pickups in neck and middle positions, 5-way switch, Floyd Rose locking tremolo, rosewood fingerboard, 21 frets, black plastic parts, large peghead, black or Arctic white finish: **1998–current**

Double Fat Strat Floyd Rose: 2 Tex-Mex humbucking pickups in bridge and middle positions, Tex-Mex single-coil in neck position: **1998–current**

Roadhouse Strat: poplar body, 3 Texas Special pickups, 5-way selector switch, pearloid or tortoiseshell celluloid pickguard, American Standard hardware, rosewood fingerboard or maple neck, 22 frets, 3-tone sunburst, Olympic white, black, candy apple red, shoreline gold metallic or teal green metallic finish
Available: **1997–current**

Big Apple Strat: 2 Seymour Duncan humbuckers, 5-way switch, tremolo, pearloid or tortoiseshell celluloid pickguard, rosewood fingerboard or maple neck, 22 frets, 3-tone sunburst, Olympic white,

black, candy apple red, shoreline gold metallic or teal green metallic finish
Introduced: **1997**
"Hard-Tail" non-tremolo version optional: **1998**
Still in production

Carved Top Strat (HSS): Custom Shop model, ash body, carved bookmatched flame maple top, Seymour Duncan double-screw JB humbucking pickup in bridge position, Texas Special pickups in neck and middle positions, 2 knobs, rosewood fingerboard or maple neck, natural, aged cherry sunburst, antique burst, crimson transparent or teal green transparent finish, tweed case
Introduced: **1997**
Renamed **Carved Top Strat HSS: 1998**
Still in production

Carved Top Strat HH: 2 Seymour Duncan humbucking pickups with chrome-plated covers, black pickup mounting rings: **1998–current**

Traditional Stratocaster: made in Mexico, 3-ply white pickguard, rosewood fingerboard or maple neck, 21 frets, black, Torino red or Arctic white finish
Available: **1997**

Traditional Fat Stratocaster: humbucking pickup in bridge position: **1997**

1997 Collector's Edition: 1962 style, 3 Texas Special pickups, tinted neck, medium jumbo frets, oval pearl inlay at 12th fret, gold-plated hardware, 3-color sunburst finish of nitrocellulose lacquer, serial number on neck plate, limited run 1,997 made: **1997**

Deluxe Powerhouse Strat: made in Mexico, poplar body, Powerhouse "super quiet" pickup system with active mid-boost, white pearloid pickguard, tremolo, rosewood fingerboard or maple neck, 21 frets, Lake Placid blue, black, candy apple red or Arctic white finish
Introduced: **1997**
Catalogued as **Powerhouse Strat: 1998**
Still in production

Deluxe Super Strat: made in Mexico, ash body, 3 Super Fat Super Strat pickups, 7 pickup combina-

tions, tortoiseshell celluloid pickguard, rosewood fingerboard or maple neck, 21 frets, gold-plated hardware, black, brown sunburst, crimson transparent or honey blond finish
Introduced: **1997**
Catalogued as **Super Strat: 1998**
Still in production

American Deluxe: made in USA, alder or ash body, fingerboard or maple neck, 22 frets, abalone dot inlay, aged plastic parts, 3-tone sunburst, black or crimson red transparent finish with alder body, white blond, teal green transparent or purple transparent with ash body
Available: **1998–current**

American Deluxe Fat Strat: Fender DH-1 humbucking pickup in bridge position, standard tremolo or Fender Deluxe locking tremolo, LSR roller nut: **1998–current**

N.O.S. Strat: Custom Shop model, mid-1960s styling using original tooling and production techniques, alder body, replicas of 1965 pickups hand-wound and signed by Abigail Ybarra (Fender employee since 1959), rosewood fingerboard, 21 frets, 3-tone sunburst, black or Olympic white finish
Available: **1998–current**

Classic Player Strat: Custom Shop model, vintage tremolo, gold anodized aluminum pickguard, rosewood fingerboard or maple neck, V-neck or C-neck, 22 frets, Sperzel tuners, black, aged cherry burst or teal green transparent finish
Available: **1998–current**

Signature Stratocaster Models
Jimi Hendrix

Jimi Hendrix Limited Edition: right-handed Strat with additional contour on top, ash body, maple neck with truss rod adjustment at body end of neck, 21 frets, reverse peghead, mirror-image decal, white finish
Approximately 25 made: **1980**

Jimi Hendrix Tribute: left-handed guitar strung right-handed, maple neck with separate maple fingerboard, 21 frets, reverse peghead, mirror image decal, Olympic white finish: **1996–current**

Jimi Hendrix Monterey: reverse peghead, red and green psychedelic finish, backstage pass on lower bout, 210 made: **1997**

Jimi Hendrix Voodoo: made in USA, right-handed guitar, reverse staggered pickup polepieces, bridge pickup mounted at reverse angle, maple neck, 21 frets, engraved neckplate, reverse peghead, 3-tone sunburst, Olympic white or black finish: **1998–current**

Stevens LJ: Custom Shop model, highly figured top, 2 special humbucking pickups, set neck, Brazilian rosewood fingerboard, autumn gold, antique burst, crimson stain or ebony stain finish
35–40 made, including 2 prototypes designated Stevens LJ II and 2 designated Stevens LJ III: **1987**

Mary Kaye '57: based on '57 reissue, gold-plated hardware, translucent white finish
Available: **1987–89**

Mary Kaye '62: based on '62 reissue, gold-plated hardware, translucent white finish: **1987–89**

Eric Clapton: made in USA, similar to '57 reissue, alder body, 3 gold Fender-Lace sensor pickups, active electronics, mini-switch on earliest examples, tremolo blocked, maple neck, 22 frets (earliest with 21 frets), Olympic white, black pewter, Torino red or candy green finish
Available: **spring 1988–current**

Yngwie Malmsteen: made in USA, alder body, DiMarzio pickups in bridge and neck position, vintage Strat pickup in middle position, DiMarzio vintage replacement tuners, American Standard Strat bridge and tremolo, rosewood fingerboard or maple neck, 21 frets, fingerboard scalloped between frets, brass nut, large peghead, candy apple red, vintage white or sonic blue finish
Available: **summer 1988–current**

HLE/Homer Haynes: Homer Haynes Limited Edition, similar to '57 reissue, gold anodized pickguard, gold-plated hardware, gold finish, numbered Custom Shop run of 500
Available: **1988**

Jeff Beck: alder body, 4 gold Lace Sensor pickups (2 at bridge), 3 knobs, 5-way switch, switch for bridge-pickup selection, special design bridge/tremolo unit, laminated pickguard with 11 screws, rosewood fingerboard, 22 frets, roller nut, locking tuners, signature on peghead, vintage white, surf green or midnight purple finish
Available: **1991–current**

Robert Cray: Custom Shop model, alder body, "hard tail" non-trem bridge, 3-ply white pickguard with 11 screws, truss rod adjustment at body end of neck, custom neck shape, rosewood fingerboard, 21 frets, 1 string guide, signature on peghead, gold-plated hardware, brown Tolex case, 3-tone sunburst, Inca silver or violet finish
Available: **1991–current**

Stevie Ray Vaughan: made in USA, alder body, Texas Special pickups, left-handed tremolo unit, laminated black pickguard with 8 screws, *SRV* on pickguard, oval neck profile, truss rod adjustment at body end of neck, Brazilian rosewood fingerboard, 21 frets, clay dot inlay, 1 string guide, gold-plated hardware, 3-tone sunburst finish
Introduced: **1992**
Pau ferro fingerboard replaces rosewood, transitional period: **late 1992–early 1993**
Still in production

Floyd Rose

Floyd Rose Classic (HSS): made in USA, alder body, Dimarzio PAF Pro humbucker in bridge position, 2 American Standard pickups in neck and middle positions, 5-way selector switch, Floyd Rose Original tremolo, locking nut, rosewood fingerboard or maple neck, 22 frets, vintage tuners, 3-tone sunburst, black, candy apple red or vintage white finish
Introduced: **1992**
Discontinued: **1997**
Reintroduced, Fender DH-1 humbucking pickup in bridge position: **1998**
Still in production

Floyd Rose Classic HH: 2 Fender DH-1 humbucking pickups in bridge and neck positions, American Standard single-coil pickup in middle position: **1998–current**

Floyd Rose Standard: made in Mexico, poplar body, Floyd Rose II tremolo, 2 single-coil and 1 humbucking pickup, 21 frets, chrome-plated hardware, black or Arctic white finish
Available: **1994–current**

Floyd Rose Standard Foto Flame: made in Mexico, basswood body, antique Foto Flame (simulated woodgrain), blue Foto Flame or crimson Foto Flame finish: **1994–95**

Freddie Tavares Aloha: hollow aluminum body, anodized finish with Hawaiian scene
153 made: **1993–94**

Richie Sambora

Richie Sambora: alder body, DiMarzio PAF double-coil pickup in bridge position, 2 Texas Special single-coil pickups in neck and middle positions, Floyd Rose Original tremolo, mid-range tone boost, maple neck, star inlay, cherry sunburst or Arctic white finish
Available: **1993–current**

Richie Sambora Standard: made in Mexico, poplar body, Floyd Rose II tremolo, rosewood fingerboard dot inlay, Lake Placid blue, black, crimson red metallic or Arctic white finish
Available: **1994–current**

Richie Sambora Black Paisley: made in Japan, 2 RS Special single-coil and 1 custom-wound humbucking pickup, black paisley finish: **1996**

Harley Davidson: hollow aluminum body with engraved Harley Davidson logo, chrome finish, first 60 with diamond emblem on peghead
109 made: **1993**

Bill Carson: same as '57 Stratocaster reissue but with neck profile specified by Bill Carson, Cimarron red finish, tweed case
41 made for Music Trader (dealer), 59 for general sale: **mid 1990s**

Dick Dale: Custom Shop model, alder body, vintage tremolo, reverse peghead, reverse-angle bridge pickup, rosewood body, brown Tolex case, chartreuse sparkle finish
Available: **1994–current**

Playboy 40th Anniversary: maple neck, black
pearl bunny inlay, gold-plated hardware, Marilyn
Monroe centerfold graphic finish, red leather strap,
red leather gigbag
175 made: **1994**

Hank Marvin: fiesta red finish, European distribution only
164 made: **1995–96**

Buddy Guy: ash body, 3 gold Lace Sensor pickups,
preamp, 5-way selector switch, vintage-style
tremolo, white pearloid pickguard with sunburst
finish, tortoiseshell celluloid pickguard with blond
finish, custom maple neck with V profile, 1950s-
style logo decal, 2-tone sunburst or honey blond
finish, tweed case
Available: **1995–current**

Ventures Limited Edition: light ash body, 3
Lace Sensor gold pickups, active electronics,
pearloid pickguard, vintage style tremolo, rosewood
fingerboard, white block inlay, 22 frets, midnight
black transparent finish
Available: **1996 only**

Bonnie Raitt: alder body, Texas special pickups,
pearloid pickguard, narrow neck, rosewood fingerboard, flatter fingerboard radius than standard,
22 frets, large peghead, 3-tone sunburst or desert
sunset finish
Available: **1996–current**

Jimmie Vaughan Tex Mex: made in Mexico,
poplar body, Tex Mex pickups in neck and middle
positions, hotter Tex Mex pickup in bridge position,
1 volume and 2 tone controls, white pickguard,
tinted maple neck, special neck profile, 21 medium
jumbo frets, U.S. vintage hardware, Olympic white
finish
Available: **1997–current**

Ritchie Blackmore: made in Japan, basswood
body, partially scalloped fingerboard, 2 Seymour
Duncan Quarter Pound pickups, no middle pickup
(cover only), 1970s style tremolo, rosewood fingerboard, oversized peghead, Olympic white finish
Available: **1997**

Hellecasters Jerry Donahue: made in Japan,
basswood body, Seymour Duncan custom Tele-
voiced pickup at bridge, steel tone plate under pickguard, custom-wired 5-way selector switch with
added 2-positon rotary switch, blue sparkle pickguard, maple fingerboard, Wilkaloid self-lubricating
nut, sapphire blue transparent finish
Available: **1997**

Hellecasters John Jorgensen: made in
Japan, Seymour Duncan custom-voiced split-coil
single-coil pickups, gold sparkle pickguard, 2-pivot
point tremolo, back routed for extra tremolo travel,
rosewood fingerboard, 22 frets, gold-sparkle dot
inlays, Wilkaloid self-lubricating nut, reverse headstock, Schaller locking tuners, gold-leaf foil finish
Available: **1997**

Mathias Jabs: made in Japan, alder body, Sey-
mour Duncan JB humbucking pickup in bridge
position, 2 Custom Shop '50s single-coil pickups in
middle and neck positions, vintage-style tremolo,
rosewood fingerboard, Saturn inlay, candy apple
red finish, limited edition
Available: **1998–current**

COMMENTS

Stratocasters from the 1950s and early 1960s are
highly regarded by collectors and players, with custom colors bringing more than standard finishes.
The demand for custom color models extends past
CBS's acquisition of Fender, into the late 1960s.
In the late 1980s, vintage Strats became so popular
that the buying craze was dubbed Strat-mania. By
1990 the market had collapsed as fast as it had
risen. Prices for vintage Strats have since risen and
stabilized.

FENDER

FENDER

ELECTRIC GUITARS, MANDOLIN AND VIOLIN

ELECTRIC GUITARS, MANDOLIN AND VIOLIN

SECTION ORGANIZATION
Solidbody Guitars
Other Solidbody Instruments
Hollowbody Guitars

SOLIDBODY GUITARS

Esquire: see Esquires and Telecasters section, preceding

Broadcaster/"No-Caster"/Telecaster: see Esquires and Telecasters section, preceding

Stratocaster: see Stratocasters section, preceding

Duo-Sonic: 3/4 size, double-cutaway, non-offset waists, straight-mounted bridge pickup, angled neck pickup, plastic pickup covers, no pickup poles, 2 knobs, 1 switch, 3 paired-string adjustable bridge saddles, anodized aluminum pickguard, 22 1/2" scale, blond (beige) finish
Introduced: **mid 1956**
Plastic pickguard: **c. 1960**
Restyled like Mustang (see following), contoured body (earliest with slab body), offset body waists, 2 angled pickups, 2 switches, 24" scale optional, red, white or blue finish: **1964**
22 1/2"-scale only (models with 24" scale labeled Duo-Sonic II): **1965**
Discontinued: **1969**
Reintroduced: made in Mexico, poplar body, offset body waists, 3-segment saddle, maple neck, black, Torino red or Arctic white finish: **1994**
Discontinued: **1998**

Duo-Sonic II: Duo-Sonic with 24" scale: **1965–69**

Musicmaster: 3/4 size, same body as Duo-Sonic, 1 slant-mounted pickup near neck with plastic cover and no poles, 2 knobs, 3 paired-string adjustable bridge saddles, anodized aluminum pickguard, 22 1/2" scale, 21 frets, blond finish
Introduced: **mid 1956**
Plastic pickguard: **late 1959**
Restyled like Mustang, offset body waists, 24" scale optional, red, white, or blue finish: **1964**

22 1/2"-scale only (models with 24" scale labeled Musicmaster II): **1965**
24" or 22 1/2" scale: **late 1969**
24" scale only, 22 frets, black or white finish: **1975**
Last made: **1980**

Musicmaster II: Musicmaster with 24" scale: **1965–69**

Jazzmaster: contoured body with offset waists, 2 rectangular white-covered pickups (a few early with black pickup covers), 3-position toggle switch, volume and tone roller knobs on bass side of pickguard, 2 white plastic knobs (early with chrome-plated barrel knobs) on treble side, chrome-plated control plates, floating tremolo and bridge, anodized aluminum pickguard, individual bridge saddles, 25 1/2" scale, rosewood fingerboard, clay dot inlay, large Strat-like peghead, sunburst finish, custom colors available
Introduced: **mid 1958**
Tortoiseshell celluloid pickguard: **late 1959**
Bound fingerboard: **late 1965**
Block inlay: **mid 1966**
Black pickup covers: **1977**
Last made: **1980**
Reintroduced as **'62 Jazzmaster:** made in Japan, basswood body, rosewood fingerboard, 3-tone sunburst, candy apple red or vintage white finish: **1996**
Still in production

The Ventures Limited Edition Jazzmaster: made in Japan, ash body, Seymour Duncan JM single-coil pickups, white pearloid pickguard, bound rosewood fingerboard, 22 frets, block inlay, midnight black transparent finish: **1996**

Jaguar: similar body and peghead shape to Jazzmaster, 2 white oblong Strat-like pickups with notched metal side plates, 2 knobs and 3 slide switches on treble side, selector switch and 2 roller knobs on bass side, string mute, Jazzmaster-type floating tremolo and bridge, 24" scale, sunburst finish, custom colors available
Introduced: **mid 1962**
Last made: **1975**
Reintroduced as **'62 Jaguar:** made in Japan, bass-

94

wood body, rosewood fingerboard, 3-tone sunburst, candy apple red or vintage white finish: **1996**
Still in production

Mustang: offset waists, 2 slant-mounted pickups, plastic pickup covers, no visible pickup poles, 2 on/off switches, master tone knob, master volume knob, tremolo, 24" scale (22 1/2" optional but rare), 1 string guide, plastic tuner buttons, red, white or blue finish
Introduced: **Aug. 1964**
2 string guides, metal tuner buttons: **1975**
Discontinued: **1982**
Reintroduced as **'69 Mustang:** made in Japan, basswood body, rosewood fingerboard, 24" scale, sonic blue or vintage white finish: **1996**
Renamed **Mustang: 1997**
Discontinued: **1998**

Competition Mustang: red, burgundy or orange finish with racing stripes: **1969–73**

Marauder: 4 concealed pickups, some with visible pickups and slanted frets
Available (very rare): **1965**

Electric XII: 12-string, split single-coil pickups, rosewood fingerboard, dot inlay, "hockey stick" peghead shape, 6 tuners per side, sunburst or blond finish standard, custom colors available
Introduced: **mid 1965**
Bound fingerboard: **late 1965**
Block inlay: **mid 1966**
Discontinued: **1969**

Bronco: offset waists, slab body, 1 Strat-like pickup slant-mounted near bridge, tremolo, white pickguard with 13 screws, 24" scale, red finish
Introduced: **1967**
Pickguard with 15 screws: **1970**
Black laminated pickguard: **c. 1975**
Last made: **1980**

Musiclander/Swinger/Arrow: same model under different names, designed to use up spare parts from other models, body scooped out at strap button, Musicmaster electronics, Mustang neck with 24" scale, dot inlay, 6-on-a-side tuner configuration, pointed peghead with straight edges on tre-

ble and bass side, no model name on peghead, variety of finish colors
Introduced (necks dated 1966-68): **mid 1969**
Discontinued: **1972**

Custom/Maverick: same model under different names, asymmetrical double cutaway, body pointed at strap button, 2 split pickups (from Electric XII), pointer knob, 4-way switch, tremolo, bound fingerboard, block inlay, Electric XII-style "hockey stick" peghead with 3-on-a-side tuner arrangement, sunburst finish
Available (necks dated 1966–68): **mid 1969–71**

Lead I: double-cutaway, non-offset waists, alder body, 1 pickup with 12 polepieces, 2 knobs, 2 2-way selector switches, controls and jack on pickguard, laminated pickguard with 11 screws, 6-saddle bridge, strings through body, rosewood fingerboard or maple neck, 2 string guides, black or brown finish
Available: **1979–92**

Lead II: 2 pickups, 2-way switch and 3-way switch: **1979–92**

Lead III: 2 pickups, 2 3-way switches: **1982**

Bullet: single-cutaway body similar to Telecaster, 2 pickups with black or white covers, 2 knobs, 3-way switch, jack into top, pickguard surrounds all controls, 6-saddle bridge, raised lip of pickguard forms tailpiece, white or black painted metal pickguard with 6 screws, rosewood fingerboard or maple neck, 1 string guide, small Tele-style peghead, Star bullet logo, red or white finish, assembled in U.S. from Korean parts
Introduced: **1981**
No Korean parts: **late 1981**
Bullet model expanded into Bullet series (see following), double-cutaway alder body, offset waists, white pickups, white pickguard, maple neck: **1983**
Bullet series last made: **1983**

Bullet H1: 1 humbucking pickup, pushbutton coil-tap: **1983**

Bullet H2: 2 humbucking pickups, 3-way switch, 2 pushbutton coil-tap switches, strings through body, sunburst, walnut, red or white finish: **1983**

Bullet S2: 2 white single-coil pickups, pickups, 6-saddle bridge, strings through body, white laminated pickguard with 9 screws, maple neck, sunburst, walnut, red or white finish: **1983**

Bullet S3: 3 white single-coil pickups, 5-way switch, 6-saddle bridge, strings through body, white laminated pickguard with 9 screws, maple neck, sunburst, walnut, red or white finish: **1983**

Bullet Deluxe: mahogany body, single cutaway, 6-saddle bridge, strings through body, white or black laminated pickguard with 8 screws: **1981–83**

Prodigy: double cutaway with horns more pointed than typical Fender, offset waists, poplar body, 2 single-coil and 1 uncovered humbucking pickup, 2 knobs, 5-way switch, controls and jack on pickguard, 6-saddle bridge, tremolo, black laminated plastic pickguard with 8 screws, rosewood fingerboard or maple neck, 1 string guide, chrome-plated hardware, Arctic white, black, crimson red metallic or Lake Placid blue finish
Available: **1991–95**

Prodigy II: no vibrato, locking nut, no string guide, black chrome hardware: **1991–95**

Robben Ford: symmetrical double cutaway, solid alder body with tone chambers, carved spruce top, 2 humbucking pickups with exposed coils, 4 knobs, coil tap, bridge and tailpiece similar to Gibson tune-o-matic bridge and TP-6 fine-tune tailpiece, glued-in mahogany neck, multiple-bound ebony fingerboard, split-corner block inlay, bound peghead, 3-on-a-side tuner configuration, ebony tuner buttons, gold-plated hardware, antique burst, autumn gold or black finish
Available: **1989–94**

Robben Ford Ultra: Custom Shop model, symmetrical double cutaway, solid mahogany body with tone chambers, carved top of maple (**Ultra FM**) or spruce (**Ultra SP**), 2 Seymour Duncan humbucking pickups with metal covers, 4 knobs, selector switch and jack on top near control knobs, bridge and tailpiece similar to Gibson tune-o-matic bridge and TP-6 fine-tune tailpiece, glued-in mahogany neck, multiple-bound ebony fingerboard, split-corner block inlay, engraved pearl scroll peghead inlay, 3-on-a-side tuner configuration, top of peghead

comes to a point on bass side, maple top available in 3-tone sunburst or crimson transparent finish, spruce top in 3-tone sunburst, black or crimson transparent finish: **1994–current**

Robben Ford Elite: Custom Shop model, hand carved figured maple top, solid mahogany body, unbound pao ferro fingerboard, small abalone dot inlay: **1994–current**

Jag-Stang: made in Japan, designed by Kurt Cobain of Nirvana, basswood body similar to Jaguar but with longer treble horn, humbucking pickup in bridge position, vintage Strat pickup in neck position, 2 3-way switches, volume and tone control, Mustang style tremolo, 24" scale, rosewood fingerboard, oversized 1960s Strat-style peghead, fiesta red or sonic blue finish
Available: **1996–current**

Cyclone: body shape similar to Duo-Sonic with offset waists, uncovered Atomic Humbucker in bridge position, Tex-Mex Strat single-coil pickup in neck position, 2 knobs, 3-way toggle switch on upper treble bout, vintage Strat-style tremolo, tortoiseshell celluloid or white pearloid pickguard, rosewood fingerboard, 22 frets, 24 3/4" scale, dot inlay, large peghead, black, candy apple red, brown sunburst or vintage white finish
Available: **1998–current**

Toronado: body shape similar to Jazzmaster but not as elongated, 2 Atomic Humbucker pickups with chrome-plated covers, 4 knobs, 3-way toggle switch on upper bass bout, "hard-tail" bridge (nontremolo) with strings through body, tortoiseshell celluloid pickguard, rosewood fingerboard, 22 frets, 24 3/4" scale, dot inlay, large peghead, black, candy apple red, brown sunburst or vintage white finish
Available: **1998–current**

Showmaster: undersized Stratocaster body, carved maple top, Seymour Duncan '59 Trembucker humbucking pickup in bridge position, 2 Fat '50s single-coil pickups in middle and neck positions, 2 knobs, 2-point tremolo or locking tremolo, figured maple neck, 22 frets, abalone dot inlay, aged cherry sunburst, teal green transparent, bing cherry transparent or cobalt blue transparent finish
Available: **1998–current**

OTHER SOLIDBODY INSTRUMENTS

Mandolin: 4 strings, 1 oblong pickup with reddish/brown plastic cover, no pickup poles, maple neck, anodized aluminum pickguard, logo decal (no other decal) on peghead, sunburst or Tele-type translucent blond finish

Introduced: **early 1956**

Tortoiseshell celluloid pickguard, rosewood fingerboard, *Original contour body* peghead decal: **late 1959**

No *Original contour body* decal: **by 1970**

Sunburst finish only: **by 1972**

3-ply black pickguard: **by 1974**

Discontinued: **1976**

Electric Violin: exaggerated body waists, maple body, internal pickup, 2 knobs, jack on bass side of top, detachable maple neck, ebony fingerboard, peghead shape similar to Fender guitar pegheads but with single slot, enclosed geared tuners all on bass side, decal logo on treble side of peghead, sunburst finish

Introduced: **1958**

Discontinued: **1959**

Reintroduced, peghead with center routing for tuners, ebony tuning pegs: **1969**

Discontinued: **1976**

HOLLOWBODY GUITARS

Coronado: 16 1/8" wide, symmetrical double cutaway, thinbody, bridge similar to Gibson tune-o-matic with individually adjustable saddles, tremolo optional, bolt-on neck, standard Fender peghead with 6-on-a-side tuner configuration

Wildwood colors optional (see Acoustic Flat Tops) on Coronado II and XII only; *Wildwood I, Wildwood II,* etc. up to *VI* on peghead to designate color

Coronado I: 1 rectangular pickup with adjustable poles, single-bound top and back, some with checkered binding, dot inlay, sunburst or cherry finish: **Jan. 1966–69**

Coronado II: 2 pickups, tremolo optional, some with checkered binding, bound *f*-holes, bound fingerboard, block inlay: **Jan. 1966–69**

Coronado XII: 12-string, bound fingerboard, block inlay, bracket-type string guide: **Jan. 1966–69**

Antigua II: Coronado II with silver-to-black sunburst finish: **late 1967–70**

Antigua XII: Coronado XII with silver-to-black sunburst finish: **late 1967–70**

LTD: 17" wide, single cutaway, full-depth body, carved top and back, highly figured maple back and sides, 1 floating humbucking pickup, 2 knobs mounted on pickguard, wood bridge, multiple-bound top and back, *F* on tailpiece, bolt-on neck, 25 1/2" scale, single-bound fingerboard, diamond-in-block inlay, bound peghead, 3 outline heart-pattern peghead inlays, 3-on-a-side tuner arrangement, gold-plated hardware, 3-tone sunburst finish

Available: **1969–75**

Montego: 17" wide, single cutaway, full-depth body, bound *f*-holes, bolt-on neck, diamond-in-block inlay, 6-piece vase-like peghead inlay, bound peghead, chrome-plated hardware, sunburst or natural finish

Montego I: 1 humbucking pickup mounted on top, 2 knobs mounted into body: **1969–75**

Montego II: 2 humbucking pickups mounted on top, 4 knobs mounted into body: **1969–75**

Starcaster: asymmetrical double cutaway, thin body, humbucking pickups, 5 knobs, 1 switch on upper treble bout, beveled treble-side edge of peghead

Available: **1976–80**

D'Aquisto: designed by James L. D'Aquisto (also see D'Aquisto section under Independent Makers)

D'Aquisto Standard: made in Japan, 15 3/4" wide, single cutaway, laminated maple body, *f*-holes with center-point on only one side, 2 humbucking pickups, 4 knobs, solid ebony tailpiece and pickguard, set neck, rosewood fingerboard, 20 frets, block inlay, bound peghead, 6-piece vase-like peghead inlay, ebony tuner buttons, gold-plated hardware, black, natural or violin sunburst finish: **1984**

D'Aquisto Elite: made in Japan, 15 3/4" wide, single cutaway, laminated maple back and sides, spruce top, *f*-holes with center-point on outer edge only, 1 humbucking pickup, 2 knobs, solid ebony tailpiece and pickguard, bound top, set maple neck, ebony fingerboard, 22 frets, block inlay, bound peghead, 6-piece vase-like peghead inlay, ebony tuner buttons, gold-plated hardware, black, natural or violin sunburst finish: **1984, 1989–94**

D'Aquisto Deluxe: Custom Shop model, 15 3/4" wide, single cutaway, solid maple body, solid carved spruce top, *f*-holes with center-point on only one side, humbucking pickup with metal cover and black mounting ring, 2 knobs, solid ebony tailpiece and pickguard, multiple binding, set maple neck, bound ebony fingerboard, 22 frets, block inlay, 6-piece vase-like peghead inlay, chrome-plated hardware, natural Foto Flame, antique burst or crimson transparent finish: **1994–current**

D'Aquisto Ultra: Custom Shop model, 15 3/4" wide, single cutaway, laminated figured maple back and sides, carved spruce top, *f*-holes with center-point on only one side, optional Armstrong floating pickup, solid ebony tailpiece and pickguard, multiple binding, bound ebony fingerboard, 22 frets,

block inlay, 6-piece vase-like peghead inlay, ebony tuner buttons, gold-plated hardware, natural or antique burst finish: **1994–current**

COMMENTS

For most collectors and players, pre-CBS instruments are more desirable than later examples, although the demand for custom color examples has extended into the late 1960s.

Low-end Fender solidbodies are not generally highly regarded by collectors or players.

Coronados are not highly regarded by collectors or players, although the wildwood models have some aesthetic appeal.

Montego and LTD models are fairly rare and have some appeal to collectors.

ACOUSTIC FLAT TOPS

SECTION ORGANIZATION

Flat Tops, 1963–70
Other Flat Top Lines

FLAT TOPS, 1963–70

All have 2 screws in pickguard, 6-on-a-side tuner arrangement (except Classic and Folk), bolt-on neck with metal plate on back.

"Broomstick" models: The first 200–300 flat tops were made with no support rod through the body. All later large-body models (King, Shenandoah) and many smaller body models have a support rod of aluminum aircraft tubing and are sometimes referred to as broomstick models.

King/Kingman: 15 5/8" wide, 20" long body, dreadnought shape, spruce top, mahogany back and sides standard, optional back and sides of Brazilian rosewood, Indian rosewood, zebrawood or vermillion, multiple-bound top and back, adjustable saddles, 25 1/2" scale, bound fingerboard, 21 frets, dot inlay, chrome-plated tuner buttons, natural top finish
Introduced: **late 1963**
Renamed **Kingman**, sunburst or natural top: **1966**
Maple, rosewood or vermillion back and sides optional, antigua finish (silver-to-black sunburst) optional, black and custom color finishes optional: **1968**

Discontinued: **1971**

Wildwood: Kingman with dyed beechwood back and sides, 3-ply beveled-edge pickguard, block inlay, peghead color coordinates with body: green, gold and brown, gold and purple, dark blue, purpleblue or blue-green
Available: **1966–70**

Concert: 15 3/8" wide, 19" long body, spruce top, mahogany back and sides standard, optional back and sides of Brazilian rosewood, Indian rosewood, zebrawood or vermillion, single-ply pickguard, 25 1/2" scale, unbound fingerboard, 20 frets
Introduced: **late 1963**
Sunburst finish optional: **1968**
Discontinued: **by 1970**

Classic: classical nylon string, back and sides of Indian rosewood, Brazilian rosewood or maple, strings tie to bridge, no pickguard, 19-fret fingerboard, slotted peghead
Available: **late 1963–65**

Folk: similar to Classic but designed for steel strings, tortoiseshell celluloid pickguard
Available: **late 1963–64**

Shenandoah: Kingman 12-string, 15 3/8" wide, mahogany back and sides, checkered top binding and soundhole ring, crest-shaped neckplate with *F*, 25 1/2" scale, unbound rosewood fingerboard, dot inlay
Introduced: **1965**
Antigua finish (silver-to-black sunburst) optional: **1967**
5-ply top binding, bound back, 5-line soundhole ring, bound fingerboard, large block inlay: **by 1968**
Square neckplate, sunburst or black finish optional: **1968**
Discontinued: **1971**

Malibu: 14 7/8" wide, mahogany back and sides, single-bound top, 25 1/2" scale, dot inlay, sunburst, mahogany or black finish
Available: **1965–70**

Villager: Malibu 12-string, 25 1/2" scale
Introduced: **1965**
Sunburst finish optional: **1969**
Discontinued: **1971**

Palomino: 15 3/8" wide, triple-bound top and back, 25 1/2" scale, dot inlay, plastic tuner buttons, sunburst, mahogany or black finish
Available: **1968–70**

Newporter: 14 3/8" wide, spruce top, mahogany back and sides, single-bound top, unbound back, 25 1/2" scale, dot inlay, mahogany stain top finish
Introduced: **1965**
Mahogany top, 3-ply pickguard, black finish optional: **by 1968**
Discontinued: **1971**

Redondo: 14 3/8" wide, Newporter with spruce top, mahogany back and sides, 25 1/2" scale, natural finish
Available: **1969–70**

OTHER FLAT TOP LINES
Harmony-made series: various styles made by Harmony, stenciled Fender logo
Available: **early 1960s**

F-series: Japanese made, 3–5 screws in pickguard, standard neck heel, 2 or 4 outline shapes on peghead, 3-on-a-side tuner arrangement, various steel-string and classical models
Introduced: **by 1969**
No screws in pickguard, Martin-style teardrop pickguard, dip at top center of peghead, Fender script logo: **by 1972**
Discontinued: **by 1979**

Tarrega Classics: Swedish-made
Available: **1963–69**

1990s
Made in Asia, various body styles, electric-style 6-on-a-side tuner arrangement (except 12-string): **by 1991**
Conventional acoustic guitar pegheads with 3-on-a-side tuner arrangement: **by 1995**

COMMENTS
American-made Fender flat tops are not highly regarded by players, although the Wildwood models have some aesthetic appeal.

BASSES

SECTION ORGANIZATION
Precision, Standard Models
Precision Reissues
Misc. Precisions
Jazz, Standard Models
Jazz Reissues
Signature Jazz Models
Misc. Jazz Models
Other Models

PRECISION, STANDARD MODELS
Precision (P-bass): asymmetrical double cutaway, slab (non-beveled) body, black single-coil pickup with level polepieces, 2 knobs, 2 pressed-fiber saddles, strings through body, earliest with serial number on bridgeplate, black bakelite pickguard covering both upper sides of body, slot-head pickguard screws, metal bridge and pickup covers, 34" scale, maple neck, dot inlay, slot-head neck bolts, thin Tele-like peghead, blond finish

99

Introduced: **Nov. 1951**

Phillips-head neck bolts: **early 1952**

Phillips-head pickguard screws: **mid to late 1952**

Beveled body (a few leftover slab bodies as late as 1957): **1954**

2-color sunburst finish with white pickguard standard, blond finish with black pickguard optional: **1954**

Staggered height polepieces, steel saddles: **1955**

Custom Dupont colors officially offered, white pickguard standard with blond or custom finish: **1956**

Split double-rectangular pickup with raised A-string pole, strings anchor through bridge unit, smaller pickguard of anodized aluminum, wider Strat-like peghead with point on treble side: **mid 1957**

3-tone sunburst standard (some 2-tones produced in 1959 and 1960): **mid 1958**

Level pickup polepieces: **late 1958**

Slab rosewood fingerboard: **mid 1959**

Tortoiseshell celluloid pickguard with standard finishes, laminated white pickguard with custom finishes (some aluminum pickguards into mid 1960): **late 1959**

Curved rosewood fingerboard: **mid 1962**

Thinner veneer-like fingerboard: **mid 1963**

Maple neck with separate maple fingerboard (no skunk stripe) optional: **1968**

Maple neck optional, narrow neck width optional: **late 1969**

Fretless fingerboard optional: **1970**

Black pickguard: **c. 1975**

Thumbrest on bass side: **by 1976**

Antigua model available, silver-to-black sunburst finish, matching finish on pickguards: **1977–79**

Replaced by **Standard Precision: 1981**

Standard Precision: alder body, white split-coil pickup, white or black laminated pickguard

Introduced, replacing Precision: **1981**

White pickguard, truss rod adjustment at peghead: **1983–85**

Made in Mexico, poplar body, rosewood fingerboard, Lake Placid blue, black, crimson red metallic or Arctic white finish: **by 1995**

Still in production

American Standard Precision: made in USA, alder body, graphite reinforced neck, strings-through-body bridge, rosewood fingerboard or maple neck, fretless rosewood fingerboard (with fret lines) optional

Introduced: **1988**

Lake Placid blue, Olympic white, black, candy apple red, Inca silver or brown sunburst finish: **by 1995**

Still in production

PRECISION REISSUES

'50s Precision: Collectables model, made in Japan, basswood body, white pickguard, maple neck, black, candy apple red, Olympic white, sonic blue or 3-tone sunburst finish

Available: **1992–95**

'51 Precision: Collectables model, made in Japan, similar to 1951 Precision, slab body, 1 Tele-style pickup, vintage 2-saddle bridge, maple neck

Available: **1997**

'57 Precision: made in USA, reissue of 1957 Precision, ash body, threaded bridge saddles, anodized aluminum pickguard, maple neck, 2-tone sunburst, vintage custom colors optional (Lake Placid blue, black, candy apple red, fiesta red, vintage white), tweed case

Introduced: **1982**

Alder body: **1989**

Standard finishes: 2-tone sunburst, black or vintage white: **by 1994**

Still in production

'60s Precision: Collectables model, made in Japan, basswood body, tortoiseshell celluloid or white pickguard, rosewood slab fingerboard, black, candy apple red, Olympic white, sonic blue, Foto Flame (simulated woodgrain) or 3-tone sunburst finish

Available: **1994–95**

'62 Precision: made in USA, reissue of 1962 Precision, alder body, laminated tortoiseshell cellluloid pickguard, rosewood fingerboard, 3-tone sunburst, vintage custom colors optional (Lake Placid blue, black, candy apple red, fiesta red, vintage white), tweed case

Introduced: **1982**

Standard finishes: 2-tone sunburst, black or vintage white: **by 1994**

Still in production

'75 Precision: made in Japan, ash body, 2 knobs on metal plate, black pickguard, maple fingerboard
Available: **1994**

OTHER PRECISION MODELS

Precision Special: alder body, active electronics, visible-pole pickups, 3 knobs, mini-switch, white pickguard, maple neck, gold-plated hardware, red, blue or white finish
Available: **1980–83**
Reintroduced, made in Mexico, poplar body, ash veneer top, 1 P-bass and 1 Jazz pickup, black pickguard, 3 knobs, black, brown sunburst, crimson burst or vintage blonde finish
Available: **1997**

Walnut Precision Special: black walnut body, walnut neck (no separate fingerboard) with maple skunk stripe, black pickguard: **1980–83**

Elite Precision I: ash body, 1 white split-coil pickup with no visible poles, 2 knobs, active electronics, white pickguard, rosewood fingerboard: **1983–85**

Elite Precision II: 2 pickups, 3 knobs, 3-way mini switch, rosewood fingerboard or maple neck: **1983–85**

Gold Elite I: 1 pickup, 2 knobs, gold-plated hardware: **1983–85**

Gold Elite II: 2 pickups, 3 knobs, 3-way mini switch, gold-plated hardware: **1983–85**

Walnut Elite I: black walnut body, 1 pickup, 3 knobs, series/parallel switch, walnut neck with maple skunk stripe, ebony fingerboard, gold-plated hardware: **1983–85**

Walnut Elite II: 2 pickups: **1983–85**

U.S. Plus: alder body, split-coil pickup and Jazz-type pickup, black pickup covers, 2 knobs, 4-saddle bridge with fine tuners, white laminated pickguard, 3-way selector switch, pushbutton switch on pickguard, rosewood slab fingerboard or maple neck, truss rod adjustment at peghead
Available: **1989–92**

U.S. Plus Deluxe: split-coil pickup and Jazz-type pickup, active electronics, 2 concentric knobs, jack in side, rosewood fingerboard or maple neck, truss rod adjustment at peghead: **1991–94**

James Jamerson Tribute: limited run of 100: **1991**

Precision Acoustic/Electric: made in Japan, hollow basswood body, spruce top, bound top, f-hole on bass side, Lace Sensor pickup and piezo bridge pickup, 3 knobs, fretless rosewood fingerboard, 20-fret fingerboard optional, antique burst or natural finish
Available: **1992–93**

Vintage Precision Custom: Custom Shop model, 2-piece slab body of swamp ash, vintage P-bass pickup in middle position, vintage J-bass pickup in bridge position, 2 knobs with 1951-style control plate, semi-figured rock maple neck, small Tele-style peghead, vintage nickel-plated hardware, 2-tone sunburst or honey blonde finish
Available: **1993–current**

Precision Deluxe: smaller body of alder with ash veneer on top and back, vintage P-bass split-coil pickup in middle position, humbucking pickup in bridge position, 4 knobs, controls include 3-band Active EQ, optional strings-through-body bridge or top-load bridge, graphite reinforced neck, rosewood fingerboard or maple neck, black, crimson burst, blue burst, antique burst, shoreline gold metallic or teal green metallic finish
Available: **1995–current**

Precision Lyte (Standard): made in Japan, basswood body, smaller and lighter than standard model, beveled edges in cutaways, 1 P-bass pickup and 1 J-bass pickup with no visible polepieces and script *Fender* on cover, 4 knobs for pan, active bass boost/cut, active treble boost/cut, volume and pickup selection, die-cast bridge unit mounted into body, no pickguard, slim neck profile, rosewood fingerboard, 22 frets, graphite nut, Goto mini tuners, gold-plated hardware
Introduced: **1992**
Chrome-plated hardware, antique burst, frost red, frost white or Montego black finish: **1995**
Still in production

Precision Lyte Deluxe: mahogany body, humbucking bridge pickup, gold-plated hardware, natural Foto Flame (simulated woodgrain) finish
Introduced: **1995**
Natural (non-Foto Flame) finish: **1998**
Still in production

Foto Flame Precision: made in Japan, alder body with basswood cap, white pearloid pickguard, split-coil pickup, 1960s-style 4-saddle bridge, rosewood fingerboard, Foto Flame (simulated woodgrain) finish on top of body and back of neck, natural, aged cherry sunburst, autumn burst or 3-tone sunburst finish:
Available: **1995**

Traditional Precision: made in Mexico, poplar body, rosewood fingerboard, split-coil pickup, black, Torino red or Arctic white finish
Available: **1996–97**

California P-Bass Special: alder body, Jazz Bass neck, 1 vintage P-bass pickup and 1 vintage J-bass pickup, vintage-style bridge, gold anodized pickguard, rosewood fingerboard or maple neck, black, candy apple red, brown sunburst or vintage white finish
Available: **1997–current**

American Deluxe Precision: made in USA, alder or ash body, 1 humbucking pickup in bridge position and 1 P-bass pickup in middle position, active electronics, 4 knobs, 3-band active EQ, optional strings-through-body bridge or top-load bridge, graphite neck reinforcement, rosewood fingerboard or maple neck, 22 frets, alder body available in 3-tone sunburst black or crimson red transparent finish, ash body available in white blond, teal green transparent or purple transparent finish
Available: **1998–current**

Donald "Duck" Dunn Precision: made in Japan, alder body, vintage P-bass pickup, vintage bridge, gold anodized aluminum pickguard, maple neck, candy apple red finish
Limited run available: **1998**

JAZZ, STANDARD MODELS

Jazz: offset body waist indents, 2 rectangular pickups, 2 concentric ("stacked") volume/tone knobs, individual string mutes, 34" scale, slab rosewood fingerboard, tapered fingerboard narrow at nut
Introduced: **1960**
Blond or custom finishes available: **1962**
3 non-stacked knobs (2 volume and 1 tone): **early 1962**
Curved fingerboard: **mid 1962**
No string mutes: **by 1963**
Bound fingerboard: **late 1965**
Block inlay: **late 1966**
Maple fingerboard optional with black binding and black block inlay: **1969**
Pearloid blocks and white binding optional on maple fingerboard: **by mid 1970s**
3-bolt neck, "bullet" truss rod adjustment at peghead: **1975**
Replaced by Standard Jazz: **1981**

Standard Jazz: white pickup covers, 4-bolt neck, rosewood fingerboard maple neck, fretless fingerboard available
Introduced: **1981**
Made in Mexico, poplar body, rosewood slab fingerboard, 2 J-bass pickups with black covers, 2 volume controls, 1 tone control, white-black-white pickguard, slab rosewood fingerboard, fretless fingerboard optional, chrome-plated hardware, polyester finish in Lake Placid blue, black, crimson red metallic, brown sunburst, or Arctic white finish: **1995**
5-string optional: **1998**
Still in production

Jazz Bass Gold: Standard Jazz Bass with gold-plated hardware, gold finish: **1981–84**

American Standard Jazz: vintage style pickups, bridge with strings-through-body, 3 knobs for individual pickup volume and master tone, graphite reinforced neck, rosewood fingerboard or maple neck, Arctic white, black, brown sunburst, Caribbean mist, lipstick red, midnight blue or midnight wine finish
Introduced: **1988**
Lake Placid blue, Olympic white, black, candy apple red or brown sunburst finish: **by 1995**
Inca silver finish optional: **1997**
5-string optional, pau ferro fingerboard: **1998**
Still in production

Jazz Reissues

'60s Jazz: Collectables model, made in Japan, basswood body, white pickguard, finger rest, rosewood fingerboard, black, candy apple red, Olympic white, sonic blue, natural Foto Flame (simulated woodgrain) or 3-tone sunburst finish
Available: **1994–95**

'60s Relic Jazz: Custom Shop model, replica of early 1960s model cosmetically aged, non-concentric knobs, 3-tone sunburst or Olympic white finish
Available: **1996–current**

'62 Jazz: made in USA, reissue of 1962 Jazz, alder body, concentric knobs, 3-tone sunburst finish standard, vintage custom colors optional (Lake Placid blue, black, candy apple red, fiesta red, vintage white)
Introduced: **1982**
Optional tortoiseshell celluloid or white-black-white pickguard: **1995**
Available: **1982–current**

Limited Edition '62 Jazz: gold-plated hardware, translucent blond finish: **1987–89**

'75 Jazz: Collectables model, made in Japan, ash body, 2 volume controls, master tone control, bridge cover with *F* logo, 20 frets, rosewood fingerboard or maple neck, block inlay, 3-tone sunburst or natural Foto Flame (simulated woodgrain) finish
Available: **1995–current**

Signature Jazz Models

Jaco Pastorius Jazz: limited run of 100: **1991**

Noel Redding Limited Edition Jazz: 1965 specs, alder body, 2 single-coil pickups, tortoiseshell celluloid pickguard, 2 volume controls, master tone control, rosewood fingerboard, 20 frets, 3-tone sunburst finish
Available: **1997–current**

The Ventures Limited Jazz: light ash body, pearloid pickguard, finger rest, rosewood fingerboard, block inlay, gold-plated hardware, midnight black transparent finish
Available: **1996**

Geddy Lee Jazz: made in Japan, alder body, 2 '62 U.S. Jazz pickups, BadAss II bridge, bakelite knobs, white-black-white pickguard, maple neck with black binding, black block inlay, black finish
Limited run available: **1998**

Marcus Miler Jazz: made in Japan, ash body, 2 vintage J-bass pickups, 4 knob, 2-band active EQ with bypass switch, extended pickguard covers most of lower treble quadrant, metal handrest over middle-position pickup, maple neck, white block inlay, 3-tone sunburst, Olympic white or natural finish
Limited run available: **1998**

Misc. Jazz Models

Contemporary Jazz: ash body, rosewood fingerboard, fretless fingerboard available, 1 J-style and 1 P-style pickup, 2 knobs
Available: **1987**

Jazz Plus: alder body, ash body optional, concentric knobs and rotary selector switch, jack on side, active electronics, rosewood fingerboard or maple neck, 22 frets, Arctic white, black, black pearl burst, blue pearl burst, brown sunburst, Caribbean mist, lipstick red, midnight blue, midnight wine or natural finish
Available: **1990–94**

Jazz Plus V: 5-string: **1990–95**

American Classic Jazz: USA Custom Shop model, downsized ash body, 2 standard pickups, 4 knobs for volume/treble, midrange, bass and pan, tortoiseshell celluloid pickguard, finger rest, graphite reinforced neck, rosewood fingerboard or maple neck, pearloid block inlay, 3-tone sunburst or natural finish
Available: **1995–96**

Jazz Special: made in Japan, basswood Precision-style body, 1 P-bass and 1 J-bass pickup, no pickguard, Jazz-style neck, graphite nut, black chrome hardware
Available: **1990s**

Jazz Power Special: active electronics, laminated neck of maple, graphite and rosewood: **1990s**

FENDER

BASSES

FENDER

BASSES

Foto Flame Jazz: made in Japan, alder body with basswood top, white pearloid pickguard, 1960s-style 4-saddle bridge, rosewood fingerboard, Foto Flame (simulated woodgrain) finish on top cap and back of neck, natural, aged cherry sunburst, autumn burst or 3-tone sunburst finish:
Available: **1995**

Jazz Bass Deluxe (Active): smaller body of alder with ash veneer on top and back, 2 single-coil pickups, 4 knobs, controls include 3-band Active EQ , graphite reinforced neck, rosewood fingerboard or maple neck, fretless fingerboard optional, black, crimson burst, blue burst, antique burst or 3-tone transparent finish
Introduced: **1995**
Renamed **Deluxe Active Jazz:** made in Mexico, standard size poplar body, J-bass pickups, active electronics, 4 knobs, rosewood fingerboard, black, candy apple red, brown sunburst or Arctic white finish: **1997**
Renamed **Active Jazz: 1998**
Still in production

Jazz Bass Deluxe V (Active): 5-string, otherwise same specs and finishes as Jazz Bass Deluxe
Introduced: **1995**
Not offered: **1997**
Reintroduced as **Active Jazz Bass V**, made in Mexico, same electronics and finishes as Active Jazz: **1998**
Still in production

Traditional Jazz: made in Mexico, poplar body, rosewood fingerboard, Arctic white, black or Torino red finish
Available: **1997**

American Deluxe Jazz: made in USA, alder or ash body, 2 J-bass pickups, active electronics, 4 knobs, 3-band active EQ, optional strings-through-body bridge or top-load bridge, graphite reinforced neck, rosewood fingerboard or maple neck, 22 frets, fretless rosewood fingerboard available, 5-string neck available, alder body available in 3-tone sunburst black or crimson red transparent finish, ash body available in white blond, teal green transparent or purple transparent finish
Available: **1998–current**

OTHER BASSES

Bass VI: 6-string, body shape similar to Jazzmaster guitar, 3 Strat-like pickups with metal frames, 3 on/off switches, master volume and tone knobs, 6 adjustable bridge saddles, Jazzmaster-type floating tremolo, 30" scale, rosewood fingerboard, dot inlay, sunburst finish, approximately 300-400 sold, pre-CBS
Introduced: **late 1961**
Foam rubber mute, Jaguar-like pickups with notched metal sidepieces, 4th "strangle switch" (condenser): **late 1963**
Bound fingerboard: **late 1965**
Block inlay: **mid 1966**
Black pickguard: **1974**
Discontinued: **1975**
Reintroduced as Collectables model, made in Japan, alder body, master tone and volume knobs, 3 on/off switches, low-end cut switch, floating tremolo with trem-lock, tortoiseshell celluloid pickguard, 30 1/4" scale, 3-tone sunburst finish: **1995**
Discontinued: **1998**

Bass V: 5-string (designed for high 5th string), elongated double cutaway body, 1 split pickup, 2 knobs, finger rest, 34" scale, bound rosewood fingerboard, 15 frets, dot inlay
Introduced: **June 1965**
Block inlay: **mid 1966**
Discontinued: **1970**

Mustang Bass: 1 split-coil pickup, 30" scale, red, white or blue finish
Introduced: **1966**
Offset waist indents: **1969**
Competition red, burgundy, orange or blue finishes with racing stripes, or sunburst finish: **1970**
Sunburst, natural, walnut, black, white or blond finish: **1976**
White, black, natural, Antigua, wine or tobacco sunburst finish: **by 1979**
Discontinued: **1981**

Coronado Bass I: thin hollowbody, double cutaway with rounded horns, 1 pickup, unbound *f*-holes, 2 finger rests, 34" scale, dot inlay
Introduced: **1966**
Wildwood finish (dye injected into beechwood) optional: **1967**

Antigua finish (silver-to-black sunburst) optional: **1968**
Discontinued: **1970**

Coronado Bass II: thin hollowbody, double cutaway with
rounded horns, 2 pickups, bound *f*-holes, 2 finger
rests, 34" scale, bound fingerboard, block inlay
Introduced: **1967**
Wildwood finish (dye injected into beechwood)
optional: **1967**
All finishes discontinued except Antigua: **1970**
Antigua discontinued: **1972**

Telecaster Bass: slab body like 1951–53 Precision, 1 single-coil gray pickup (early P-bass style),
white pickguard, finger rest on treble side, 34"
scale, maple neck, slender Telecaster-like peghead,
peghead decal of *Telecaster* in block letters followed
by *Bass* in script, blond finish standard, custom
colors available
Introduced: **1968**
Pink paisley or blue floral finish available: **1968–69**
Fretless neck optional: **late 1970**
Humbucking pickup: **Feb. 1972**
Discontinued: **1979**

Musicmaster Bass: 1 oblong pickup with plastic
cover and no visible poles, 30" scale, dot inlay, red,
white or blue finish
Introduced: **1970**
White or black finish only: **by 1976**
Discontinued: **1983**

Bullet Bass: alder body, 1 split-coil pickup, 2
knobs, maple neck, small Tele-style peghead,
brown sunburst, ivory, red or walnut finish

Bullet B30: 30" scale, 19 frets: **1982–83**

Bullet B34: 34" scale: **1982–83**

Bullet B40: 30" scale, 20 frets: **1982–83**

HM Bass Ultra: made in USA, basswood body,
figured maple top and back, 3 J-style pickups, 5-
position selector switch, 2 knobs, rosewood
fingerboard, black peghead, black chrome hardware, 3-tone sunburst, midnight blue, chrome red,
brite white, blackstone, bluestone or redstone
finish
Available: **1990–92**

HM Bass: made in Japan, basswood body: **1992**

HM Bass V: 5-string: **1992**

JP-90: poplar body, 1 P-style and 1 J-style pickup,
2 knobs, 3-way selector switch, black pickguard,
rosewood fingerboard, Arctic white, black or Torino
red finish
Available: **1990–94**

Prodigy Active: poplar body, 1 P-style and 1 J-
style pickup, 2 concentric knobs for volume/pan
and treble/bass control, active electronics, rosewood fingerboard, Arctic white, black, crimson red
metallic or Lake Placid blue finish
Available: **1992–95**

HMT Bass: made in Japan, acoustic/electric, P-
bass shape, *f*-hole on bass side, basswood body,
figured maple top, silver Lace Sensor pickup with
P-style split coil configuration, piezo bridge pickup,
wood bridge, 2 knobs, rosewood fingerboard, triangular sharkstooth inlay, angled peghead without
scroll at top, bold script logo
Available: **1992**

Stu Hamm "Urge" Bass: made in USA, contoured alder body, shape similar to Precision but
smaller and with wider treble-side cutaway, 2 custom J-bass pickups in bridge and middle positions,
custom P-bass pickup between J-bass pickups, no
pickup poles, active electronics, 3 knobs mounted
into top, pearloid pickguard, 32" scale, pao ferro
fingerboard, 24 frets, no inlay, white blonde, Sherwood metallic, Montego black or burgundy mist
metallic finish
Available: **1992–current**

Stu Hamm "Urge" Standard Bass: made in Mexico,
poplar body, 2 J-bass pickups, active electronics,
2 knobs mounted into top, 32" scale, rosewood
fingerboard, 24 frets, dot inlay, Lake Placid blue,
black, crimson red metallic or Arctic white finish:
1994–current

MB: made in Japan, body shape similar to Precision
but with narrower horns, basswood or poplar body,
1 P-bass pickup and 1 J-bass pickup, master volume, master tone and pan pot controls, rosewood

fingerboard, maple neck, non-standard peghead, 2-and-2 tuner configuration with straight string pull, black, brown sunburst, chrome red or Arctic white finish
Available: **1994–95**

MB-5: 5-string, 2 rectangular single-coil pickups, 3-and-2 tuner configuration: **1994–95**

Prophecy: made in Japan, single-coil pickup, 2 knobs, finger rest

Prophecy I: basswood body, white pickguard, maple neck, 20 frets, blond or custom color finish: **1994**

Prophecy II: ash body, active electronics, gold-plated hardware: **1994**

Prophecy III: alder/walnut/bubinga body, active electronics, maple neck-through-body, gold-plated hardware: **1994**

Performer Elite: 2 white single-coil pickups, 3 knobs, active electronics, white pickguard, rosewood fingerboard, sunburst finish
Available: **1985–88**

Roscoe Beck V Bass: 5-string, alder body, shape between Precision and Jazz, 2 double J-bass

pickups, 2 knobs, 2 mini-toggle switches, 5-way switch, black non-vintage pickguard, rosewood fingerboard, dot inlay, string guide for highest 3 strings, 4-and-1 tuner configuration, 3-tone sunburst, candy apple red, shoreline gold metallic or teal green metallic finish
Introduced: **1995**
Pau ferro fingerboard: **1997**
Still in production

COMMENTS

The Precision was the first commercially successful fretted electric bass and for almost four decades was the standard by which all other basses were judged. Early P-basses are highly sought by collectors, although they do not bring as much as Telecasters, Esquires and Stratocasters of the same period. P-basses with split-coil pickups (mid 1957 and after) are more highly regarded by players than those with earlier pickups.

The P-bass sound has traditionally been more highly regarded by players than the Jazz model. However, by 1990 the sound of the Jazz bass had become the preferred sound, and demand switched accordingly from P-bass to Jazz. Early Jazz basses with concentric knobs are highly sought by collectors.

STEELS

GENERAL INFORMATION

Scale length on non-pedal models: 22 1/2", except some Stringmasters
Patent pending notice on tuner assembly: **1950–62**
Patent number on tuner assembly: **1963 and after**

Serial numbers: Each model has its own number series.

SECTION ORGANIZATION

Non-Pedal Models
Pedal Models

NON-PEDAL MODELS

K and F brand: made by Doc Kauffman and Leo Fender, straight sides, rectangular pickup with

patent pending, strings through pickup, 2 small white knobs, symmetrical control plate, painted dot markers and fret lines, bone nut, right-angle tuners, no peghead plate, black finish
Introduced: **1945**
Large brown knobs, metal nut, *K and F* on peghead plate, gray crinkled finish: **later**
Curved body sides: **later**
Asymmetrical metal fingerboard, Roman numeral markers: **later**
Discontinued: **by mid 1946**

Organ Button: similar shape to later K&F style, body bouts join neck at 17th fret, rectangular pickup, strings through pickup, 2 non-domed Broadcaster-type knobs, 1 red pushbutton for organ-like tonal effect, asymmetrical control plate,

asymmetrical metal fingerboard, Roman numeral markers, right-angle tuners, lightning bolt on peghead plate, most with non-lacquer waxlike finish
Available: **1946–47**

Princeton: longer body bouts than Organ Button, body bouts join neck at 12th fret, rectangular pickup, strings through pickup, 1 knob, hardwired cord, asymmetrical control plate, asymmetrical metal fingerboard, Roman numeral markers, right-angle tuners, lightning bolt on peghead plate, serial number begins with *A*
Available: **1946–48**

Deluxe: longer body bouts than Organ Button, body bouts join neck at 12th fret, rectangular pickup, strings through pickup, 2 knobs, asymmetrical control plate, asymmetrical metal fingerboard, Roman numeral markers, lightning bolt on peghead plate, right-angle tuners, non-lacquer waxlike finish, serial number on early examples begins with *B*
Introduced: **1946**
Light or dark-stain lacquer finish: **c. 1947**
Trapezoid-shaped pickup with bass end wider than treble end, strings through pickup: **late 1948**
Bound top and back (in catalog photo): **1949 only**
Straight-line body sides (no bouts), block letter logo on metal plate on treble side of fingerboard, symmetrical fingerboard, dot and diamond markers, peghead routed for tuner assembly, top tuners, walnut or blond finish, available as **Deluxe 6** (6-string) or **Deluxe 8** (8-string): **1950**
Walnut finish described as dark finish: **1951**
Script logo on plate: **1956**
Stringmaster model features (see following), 2 understring pickups, control knob for pickup balance under bridge cover, rectangular bridge cover, 3 legs optional: **by 1957**
Dark (walnut) finish discontinued: **by 1972**
White or black finish: **by 1976**
Discontinued: **by 1981**

Dual 8 Professional: 2 8-string necks, rectangular pickups, strings through pickups, *Dual Professional* in block letters on metal plate between necks (no Fender logo), 2 diamond-shaped plates on front, Roman numeral markers, peghead routed for tuner assembly, top tuners, 3 legs optional, walnut or blond finish, serial number on early examples begins with *D*

Introduced: **1946**
Trapezoid-shaped pickups with bass end wider than treble end, strings through pickups, *Fender* on logo plate: **very late 1948**
Walnut finish described as "dark" finish: **1951**
Dots-and-diamonds markers: **1953**
Script logo on plate: **1956**
Stringmaster features (see following), 2 understring pickups per neck, control knob for pickup balance under bridge cover, rectangular bridge cover, script logo decal on front, 22 1/2" scale standard, 24 1/2" scale optional, 4 legs optional: **1957**
Discontinued: **1957**

Dual 6 Professional: 2 6-string necks, all other specs and changes same as Dual 8 Professional
Introduced: **1950**
Dark (walnut) finish discontinued: **1973**
White or black finish: **by 1976**
Discontinued: **by 1981**

Champion/Student: symmetrical 2-bout body, Telecaster-style flat-pole pickup, non-domed Broadcaster-type knobs, symmetrical bridge cover, dot and diamond markers, right-angle tuners, white plastic tuner buttons, peghead narrows toward top, lightning bolt on peghead plate, felt on back, slot-head screws, body covered in yellow or blue pearloid
Note: Blue pearloid Champions were produced only in occasional runs in 1949, 1952–53 and possibly at other times. Blue examples may look green as a result of aging. Yellow examples may vary in color as a result of aging and different batches of pearloid.
Officially introduced: **summer 1949**
First produced: **late 1949**
A few with painted blond finish: **late 1949**
Listed only as **Student** model, domed Telecaster-type knobs, Phillips-head screws: **1952**
Discontinued, replaced by **Champ** (see following): **mid 1955**

Champ: straight-line body sides, understring pickup with black plastic cover, black knobs, bevel from fingerboard to body edges, rectangular markers, script logo decal near fingerboard, peghead routed for tuner assembly, top tuners, black tuner buttons, desert fawn (tan-blond) finish
Introduced: **mid 1955**
White or black finish: **by 1976**
Discontinued: **by 1981**

White: named after Fender plant manager Forrest White, no Fender brand, white plastic pickup cover and 2 knobs, symmetrical metal fingerboard, block markers, peghead routed for tuner assembly, *White* logo on body facing player, white finish, 3 legs, matching amp available
Available: **1955–c. 1957**

Studio Deluxe: 1 pickup, white pickup cover, chrome knobs, script logo decal next to finger-board, dots-and-diamonds markers, peghead routed for tuner assembly, top tuners, white tuner buttons, blond finish, 3 legs
Introduced: **by Jan. 1956**
Metal logo plate next to fingerboard: **by 1970**
White or black finish: **by 1976**
Discontinued: **by 1981**

Custom: 3 8-string necks, trapezoid-shaped pickups with bass end longer than treble end, strings through pickups, block-letter logo on metal plate between necks, 2 diamond-shaped plates on front, Roman numeral markers, top tuners, 3 legs optional, walnut or blond finish
Introduced: **1949**
Walnut finish replaced by "dark" finish: **1951**
Dots-and-diamonds markers, no diamond plates on front, script logo decal on front: **1953**
Discontinued: **by 1958**

Stringmaster: 2, 3 or 4 necks, 8-string necks stan-dard, 6-string necks optional, 2 plastic-covered pickups per neck (early with metal pickup covers like Telecaster neck pickup), control knob for pickup balance under bridge cover, script logo on metal plate, 2 diamond-shaped plates and logo decal on front, 26" scale standard, block markers, blocks with arrowheads at frets 12 and 24, peghead routed for tuner assembly, dark or blond finish, 4 legs optional
Introduced: **1953**
22 1/2" scale standard, 24 1/2" scale optional: **1955**
Walnut or blond finish: **by 1973**
White or black finish: **by 1976**
4-neck Stringmaster discontinued: **by 1969**
24 1/2" scale standard, 22 1/2" discontinued: **by 1979**
All Stringmasters discontinued: **by 1981**

PEDAL MODELS

1000: 2 8-string necks, 8 pedals standard, up to 10 pedals optional, 24 1/2" scale, cable pitch-changing mechanism, aluminum-magnesium frame, natural blond finish
Introduced: **mid 1957**
Black and white finish: **by 1960**
Sunburst finish: **1963**
String mute: **by 1970**
Discontinued: **by 1976**

400: 1 8-string neck, 4 pedals standard, up to 10 pedals optional, cable pitch-changing mecha-nism, natural blond finish
Introduced: **spring 1958**
Black and white finish: **by 1960**
Sunburst finish: **1963**
Discontinued: **by 1976**

2000: 2 10-string necks, 10 or 11 pedals, cable pitch-changing mechanism, sunburst finish
Introduced: **1964**
String mutes: **by 1970**
Discontinued: **by 1976**

800: 1 10-string neck, 6 pedals standard, up to 11 pedals optional, cable pitch-changing mecha-nism, sunburst finish
Introduced: **1964**
String mute: **by 1970**
Discontinued: **by 1976**

PS 210: 2 10-string necks, 5 pedals standard, up to 8 pedals optional, 1–4 knee levers, walnut burl fin-ish, 6 prototypes produced
Catalogued but never in production: **1970–76**

Artist Dual 10: 2 10-string necks, 8 pedals, 4 knee levers, rod pitch-changing mechanism, black or mahogany finish
Introduced: **by 1976**
Discontinued: **by 1981**

Artist Single 10: 10-string neck, 3 pedals, 4 knee levers, rod pitch-changing mechanism, black or mahogany finish
Introduced: **by 1976**
Discontinued: **by 1981**

Student Single 10: 10-string neck, 3 pedals, 1 knee lever, rod pitch-changing mechanism, black vinyl finish
Introduced: **by 1976**
Discontinued: **by 1981**

COMMENTS

Fender and K&F lap steels from pre-1950 are sought by collectors for their historical value. Champion,

Studio Deluxe and Deluxe 8 are the models most highly regarded by players. Multi-neck models have some historical appeal.

Most Fender pedal steels are not highly regarded because of their cable pitch-changing design. Later models with rod mechanism are more highly regarded but are quite rare. Most pedal steel players prefer modern instruments.

AMPLIFIERS, GENERAL INFORMATION

EARLY CABINET STYLES

Hardwood; cabinet finish dark (stained mahogany, oak or cherry), medium (stained oak) or light (natural maple, some oak); grille cloth colors gold (yellow), red, blue or mauve (purple); 3 chrome strips on front, slot-head screws, most early examples with *RM* penciled on chassis (initials of co-designer Ray Massie), Professional, Deluxe Model 26, Princeton (Student): **mid 1946**
"TV front" with rounded grille corners, no chrome strips (except V-front Super): **1948**
Upper back panel extends almost halfway down to protect tubes: **1951**
Grille corners squared, wide front panels above and below grille, narrow front panels to left and right of grille (chrome strip removed from Super): **mid to late 1952**
Upper and lower front panels narrowed, grille enlarged: **mid to late 1954**

CABINET COVERS

No cover, stained hardwood finish, Professional, Deluxe Model 26 and Princeton (Student): **mid 1946–48**
Tweed airplane luggage linen...
　Vertical tweed lines, fuzzy mohair-like grille cloth...
　　Dual Professional (from introduction): **1946**
　　All models except Champion (800 or 600): **1948**
　Diagonal tweed lines...
　　All models except Champion 600 (Champ):
　　early to mid 1949
　　Champion 600 (Champ): **1953**
Gray linen, Champion 800: **1948**
2-tone marbled leatherette, Champion 600: **1949–52**

Brown Tolex...
　Vibrasonic (from introduction): **mid 1959**
　Bandmaster, Concert, Pro, Super, Twin: **1960**
　Princeton, Deluxe, Tremolux, Vibrolux, Vibroverb:
　　1961
　No Champ or Harvard in brown or blond Tolex
Blond Tolex, coarse texture...
　Bandmaster and Bassman: **early 1961**
　Showman (from introduction): **1961**
Blond Tolex, smooth texture...
　Showman, Bandmaster, Bassman: **1963**
Black Tolex...
　Concert, Deluxe, Princeton, Pro, Reverb, Super, Twin, Vibrolux, Vibroverb: **mid to late 1963**
　All other models: **Aug. 1964**

LOGOS AND MODEL NAMES, TWEED-COVERED MODELS

FENDER in block letters, *Fullerton, California* in small letters...
　Deluxe, Pro, Super, Bandmaster, Twin, Bassman:
　　pre-1955
　Champ, Princeton: **pre-1956**
Fender in script, no model name, no *Fullerton*...
　Deluxe, Pro, Super, Tremolux: **1955–56**
　Vibrolux: **1956 only**
　Champ, Princeton: **1956, 1959 and after**
Fender in script, model name, no *Fullerton*...
　Bassman, Bandmaster, Twin: **1955 and after**
　Champ, Princeton: **1957 only**
　All other models: **1957 and after**
Fender in script, no model name, *Fullerton, California,* Champ, Princeton: **1958–60**
Fender in script, model name, *Fullerton, California,* Deluxe, Tremolux, Vibrolux, Harvard: **1960 and after**

FENDER

AMPLIFIERS

FENDER

LOGOS AND MODEL NAMES, TOLEX-COVERED MODELS

Script *Fender* with tail underlining, logo plate attached to grille cloth, brown control plate on models with brown Tolex cover, "blackface" control plate on blond and black Tolex-covered models, script model name and *-Amp* on control plate (except no -*Amp* on Bandmaster), FENDER ELECTRIC INSTRUMENT COMPANY (sometimes abbreviated in various forms) under model name (except for Champ and Vibro Champ): **1959**

FENDER MUSICAL INSTRUMENTS under model name, transitional period: **Apr.–Aug. 1965**

"Silverface" control plate with block letter model name and -*Amp* (except no -*Amp* on Super Reverb), transitional period: **Apr. 1967–fall 1967**

No -*Amp* on control faceplate: **1972**

No tail underlining *Fender:* **1976**

Circled-R (trademark registration symbol) above letter *r* in *Fender, Made in U.S.A.* underneath letters *en*, blackface control plate with script model name (except block letter model name on Harvard): **1982**

Model name on plate attached to grille cloth, some new models: **1983 and after**

NUMBERS

Fender amp models have their own separate number series. No number lists are available. However, most models can be accurately dated by their specs and by various codes.

Model Code, 1951–60s

Model code is stamped on label, 3 or 4 characters. Configuration: **dA#(#)**

1st digit **d** denotes decade
5 . . . . 1950s
6 . . . . 1960s

2nd character **A** denotes year
A 1951
B 1952
C 1953
D 1954
E 1955–early 1960s
G . . . . early 1960s

3rd digit or 3rd and 4th digits denote model

1 . . . . Champ
2 . . . . Princeton
3 . . . . Deluxe
4 . . . . Super
5 . . . . Pro
6 . . . . Bassman
7 . . . . Bandmaster
8 . . . . Twin
9 . . . . Tremolux
10 . . . . Harvard
11 . . . . Vibrolux
12 . . . . Concert
13 . . . . Vibrasonic
14 . . . . Showman
15 . . . . Reverb unit
16 . . . . Vibroverb

2-letter code, May 1953–67

Code is ink stamped on tube chart.

1ST LETTER	2ND LETTER
A 1951	A . . . . January
B 1952	B . . . . February
C 1953	C . . . . March
D 1954	D . . . . April
E 1955	E . . . . May
F. 1956	F. . . . . June
G 1957	G . . . . July
H 1958	H . . . . August
I. 1959	I . . . . September
J. 1960	J. . . . . October
K 1961	K . . . . November
L 1962	L . . . . December
M. 1963	
N 1964	
O, black ink . 1965	
O, green ink . 1966	
P 1966	
Q 1967	

Examples: DG = July 1954; KB = February 1961

Chassis Codes
1960–late 1970s
Configuration: **A##wwyy**
ww = week
yy = year
Example: C412265 = 22nd week of 1965

Late 1970s–early 1980s
Configuration: **yyww**
4 digits *reversed* denote week and year.
Example: 1831 = 13th week of 1981

Codes on Parts

Speakers, transformers and potentiometers may be stamped with a 6- or 7-digit code that includes a manufacturing date for that part. See Appendix, Pot Codes section.

Dates

An uncoded date in the 1960s is not a manufacture date but a service date.

AMPLIFIERS

K&F: made by Doc Kauffman and Leo Fender, stenciled K&F logo or brass nameplate, 3 models, 8", 10" or 15" speaker
Available: **late 1945–mid 1946**

Princeton: also referred to as **Student** model, wood cabinet, 3 vertical chrome strips on front, 8" Jensen speaker (some with Utah), no controls, most with no serial number, brown cord, 4.5 watts
Introduced: **mid 1946**
Tweed cover, TV front, brown grille, 2 pointer knobs: **1948**
Wide panel cabinet, top control panel: **1952**
Narrow panel cabinet: **1954**
Brown Tolex cover, light brown grille, brownface panel, 4 knobs, 10" Jensen speaker, 12 watts: **1961**
Black Tolex cover, silver grille, blackface control panel: **1963**
5 knobs: **1964**
Silverface control panel: **1969**
Discontinued: **1980**

Princeton Reverb: black Tolex cover, silver grille, blackface control panel, 6 knobs: **Aug. 1964–1979**

Princeton Reverb II: solid state, black Tolex cover, silver grille, blackface control panel, 8 knobs, 12" speaker, 20 watts
Available: **1982–85**

Princeton 112: solid state, 12" speaker, black Tolex cover, silver grille, black control panel, 9 knobs, 40 watts: **1993–95**

Princeton 112 Plus: solid state, 12" speaker, black Tolex cover, silver grille, black control panel, 9 knobs, 65 watts: **1995–current**

Princeton 112SE: 12" speaker, 160 watts: **1995**

Princeton Chorus: solid state, 2 10" Eminence speakers, black Tolex cover, black grille, black control panel, 11 red knobs, 2x25 watts
Introduced: **1989**
Black grille, black knobs: **1992**
Replaced by **Princeton Stereo Chorus**, silver grille: **1995**
Still in production

Model 26/Deluxe: 10" speaker, wood cabinet, 3 vertical chrome strips on front, 3 inputs, 3 controls (mic volume, tone, inst. volume), brown cord, gold anodized (possibly painted) Jensen speaker with no writing or markings except for 1001 written vertically on square magnet, tubes hang down, no extra mounting screw for chassis, 6F6 power tubes, tube configurations vary, serial number range 1–c. 285
Introduced as **Model 26: mid 1946**
Serial number range c. 286–1250, silver Jensen speaker with Jensen stenciled on round magnet, speaker code 220632 (a few exceptions), tubes mounted horizontally with base toward front of amp, usual tube configuration (from left) 6SC7, 6N7, 6V6, 6V6, 5Y3, extra top mounting screw on chassis
Model 26 replaced by **Deluxe**: 12" speaker, tweed cover, TV front, 3 knobs, 10 watts: **1948**
15 watts: **1954**
Brown Tolex cover, 6 knobs: **1961**
Black Tolex cover, 8 knobs, 20 watts: **mid 1963**
Discontinued: **1967**

Deluxe Reverb: 9 knobs: **1963–79**

'65 Deluxe Reverb: reissue of blackface version, 22 watts: **1993–current**

Deluxe Reverb II: solid state, blackface, 11 knobs, 20 watts: **1982–85**

Solid State Deluxe Reverb: black Tolex cover, silver grille, aluminum panel, 9 knobs, 12" speaker, 25 watts
Introduced: **1967**
32 watts: **1969 only**
Discontinued: **1971**

Deluxe 85: solid state, 12" speaker, black Tolex cover, silver grille, 11 red knobs, 65 watts: **1988–93**

Deluxe 112: solid state, 12" speaker, black Tolex cover, silver grille, 10 knobs, 65 watts: **1992–95**

Deluxe 112 Plus: solid state, 12" speaker, black Tolex cover, silver grille, 10 knobs, 90 watts: **1996–current**

Professional/Pro: 15" Jensen speaker, some with field coil speaker (no permanent magnet), wood cabinet, 3 vertical chrome strips on front, 15 watts
Introduced as **Professional: mid 1946**
Renamed **Pro,** tweed cover, brown grille, TV front, 3 pointer knobs: **1948**
Wide panel cabinet: **1952**
Narrow panel cabinet, 26 watts: **1954**
Brown Tolex cover, light brown grille, brownface panel, 9 knobs, 25 watts: **1960**
Black Tolex cover, silver grille, blackface control panel: **1963**
Discontinued: **1965**

Pro Reverb: black Tolex cover, silver grille, blackface control panel, 2 12" speakers, 9 knobs, 40 watts
Introduced: **1965**
Silverface control panel: **1969**
45 watts: **1972**
10 knobs: **1976**
Blackface control panel, 12 knobs, 70 watts: **1981**
Discontinued: **1983**

Solid State Pro Reverb: black Tolex cover, silver grille, aluminum panel, 10 knobs, 2 12" speakers, 50 watts: **1967–70**

Pro 185: solid state, black Tolex cover, black grille, black control panel, 14 red knobs, 2 12" Eminence speakers, 160 watts
Introduced: **1989**
Black knobs, silver grille: **1993**
Discontinued: **1986**

Dual Professional/Super: V-Front, 2 10" silver Jensen speakers aimed at different angles, 1 chrome strip on front, tweed cover, speakers usually with date code 220632, crude (looks hand-printed) tube chart, 4 inputs (2 inst., 1 mic, lo gain), tube configuration (from left) 5U4, 6L6, 6L6, 6SJ7, 6SJ7, 6SJ7, 16 watts
Introduced as **Dual Professional: mid 1946**
Renamed **Super: early 1947**
Wide panel cabinet, tweed cover, brown grille, top panel, 3 pointer knobs, speakers in same direction, 20 watts: **early 1952**
Narrow panel cabinet, 4 knobs: **1954**
Brown Tolex cover, brown grille, brownface panel, 9 knobs, 30 watts: **1960**
Some with 45 watts: **1962**
Discontinued: **1964**
Super reintroduced: black Tolex cover, silver grille, blackface control panel, 12 knobs, 4 10" speakers with Alnico magnets, 60 watts: **1992**
Discontinued: **1997**

Super Reverb: 4 10" speakers: **1963**

Solid State Super Reverb: black Tolex, silver grille, aluminum panel, 9 knobs, 4 10" speakers, 50 watts: **1967–70**

Super 60: black Tolex cover, black grille, black control panel, 8 red knobs, 12" Eminence speaker, 60 watts
Introduced: **1989**
Black knobs: **late 1989**
Discontinued: **1994**

Super 112: similar to Super 60 but with different controls, including overdrive and notch filter, optional Celestion speakers: **1988–93**

Super 210: same as Super 112 but with 2 10" Eminence speakers: **1988–93**

Super Six Reverb: black Tolex cover, silver grille, silverface control panel, 12 knobs, 6 10" speakers, 100 watts: **1970–79**

Super Bassman: see Bassman section, following

Super Champ: see Champ section, following

Super Showman: see Showman section, following

Super Twin: see Twin section, following

Dual Professional: Custom Shop model, 3 10" speakers, cream Tolex cover, black grille, brownface control panel, 10 knobs, tube reverb, fat switch, vibrato, 100 watts: **1994–current**

Champion 800: TV front, 8" speaker, gray linen cover, hammerloid (gray-green) chassis color, 3 tubes, 1 volume control, 4 watts
Introduced (about 100 made): **1948**
Replaced by **Champion 600:** 6" speaker, 2-tone marbled leatherette cover, early examples with 800 crossed out, 3 watts: **1949**
Renamed **Champ**, tweed cover: **1953**
4 watts: **1954**
8" speaker, 3 knobs, black Tolex cover: **1964**
5 watts: **1965**
6 watts: **1972**
Discontinued: **1980**

Vibro-Champ: black Tolex cover, silver grille, blackface control panel, 5 knobs, 8" speaker, tremolo, 4 watts
Introduced: **1964**
Silverface control panel, 5 watts: **1969**
6 watts: **1972**
Discontinued: **1980**

Champ II: 10" speaker, 4 knobs, 18 watts: **1982–85**

Champ 12: 12" speaker, 6 red knobs, 12 watts: **1986–92**

Champ 25: hybrid tube/solid state, 12" speaker, 10 knobs, 25 watts: **1992–95**

Champion 110: solid state, black Tolex cover, 10" speaker, 7 knobs, reverb, 25 watts: **1993–current**

Super Champ: black Tolex cover, silver grille, blackface control panel, 6 knobs, 10" speaker, Electro-voice speaker optional, 18 watts: **1982–85**

Bassman: 15" speaker, 26 watts
Introduced: **1951**
50 watts: **1954**
4 10" speakers, 2 inputs: **1954**
4 inputs, mid-range control, plastic handle: **by mid 1957**
Piggyback design, 1 12" speaker: **1961**
2 12" speakers, cabinet dimension 32" x 21": **1962**
Cabinet dimension 40" x 29 1/2": **1968**
2 15" speakers: **late 1968**
Discontinued: **1980**

Bassman Ten: 4 10" speakers, 8 knobs, 50 watts
Introduced: **1972**
70 watts: **1981**
Discontinued: **1983**

Bassman Compact: solid state, 1 15" speaker, 6 knobs, 50 watts: **1981–85**

Bassman 20: 1 15" speaker, 4 knobs, 20 watts: **1982–85**

Bassman 50: 2 15" speakers, 6 knobs, 50 watts
Introduced: **1972**
Master volume added: **1974**
Discontinued: **1977**

Bassman 60: Fender Japan model, solid state, 1 15" speaker, 5 knobs, 60 watts: **1990–94**

'59 Bassman: tweed cover, brown grille, top-mounted controls, metal panel, 6 pointer knobs, 4 inputs, 4 10" speakers, 45 watts: **1990–current**

Bassman 70: 2 15" speakers, 7 knobs, 70 watts: **1977–79**

Bassman 100: 4 12" speakers, 8 knobs, 100 watts: **1972–79**

Bassman 135: piggyback style, 4 10" speakers, 9 knobs, 135 watts: **1979–83**

Solid State Bassman: black Tolex cover, silver grille, aluminum panel, 4 knobs, 3 12" speakers, 100 watts: **1968–70**

Transistor Bassman: same as Solid State Bassman

Super Bassman: black Tolex cover, silver grille, silverface control panel, 7 knobs, 2 15" speakers, 100 watts: **1970–72**

Super Bassman II: Super Bassman with 2 cabinets, also called Bassman 100 (see preceding)

Twin: wide panel cabinet, tweed cover, brown grille, 4 knobs, 2 12" Jensen speakers, 15 watts
Introduced: **1952**
Narrow panel cabinet, 50 watts: **1954**
Presence knob: **1955**
Brown Tolex cover, maroon or light brown grille, brownface panel, 9 knobs, 90 watts: **1960**
Discontinued: **1963**
Reintroduced, 2 12" speakers, black Tolex cover, silver grille, blackface control panel, 14 numbered knobs,

FENDER

AMPLIFIERS

FENDER

spring reverb, output control for 100 watts or
25 watts: **1996**
Still in production

Twin Reverb: black Tolex cover, blackface control
panel, 11 knobs, 2 12" Jensen speakers, 85 watts
Introduced: **1963**
Silverface control panel: **1964**
Push-pull master volume: **1976**
Blackface control panel, 135 watts: **1981**
Discontinued: **1983**
Reverb model reintroduced as Twin, see preceding:
1996

'65 Twin Reverb: reissue, black Tolex, silver grille,
blackface control panel, 11 numbered knobs, 2 12"
speakers, 85 watts: **1992–current**

Twin Reverb II: black Tolex cover, silver grille, blackface control panel, 12 knobs, 2 12" speakers, channel switching and effects loop, 105 watts: **1983–85**

Super Twin: black Tolex cover, black grille with white
border, blackface control panel, 12 knobs, 2 12"
speakers, 180 watts
Introduced: **1976**
No border on grille: **1981**
Discontinued: **1982**

The Twin: black Tolex cover, optional white, grey, red
or snakeskin cover, black grille, black control panel,
11 red knobs, 2 12" special design Fender speakers,
100 watts
Introduced: **1987**
Silver grille, black knobs, Eminence speakers: **1992**
Still in production

Bandmaster: 1 15" speaker, 15 watts
Introduced: **mid 1953**
3 10" speakers: **1957**
30 watts: **1960**
Piggyback design, 1 12" speaker, 40 watts: **1961**
45 watts: **1970**
Discontinued: **1975**

Bandmaster Reverb: piggyback design, 2 12" speak-
ers, 45 watts
Introduced: **1970**
Diagonal speaker configuration: **1976**
70 watts: **1981**
Discontinued: **1982**

Tremolux: narrow panel cabinet, tweed cover, brown

grille, 12" speaker, tremolo, 5 knobs, 15 watts
Introduced: **1955**
Piggyback design, cream Tolex cover, maroon grille,
brownface panel, 8 knobs, 10" speaker, 30 watts:
1961
2 10" speakers: **1962**
Black Tolex cover, blackface control panel: **1964**
Discontinued: **1966**

White: student model, companion to lap steel,
named after Fender general manager Forrest White,
narrow-panel cabinet, blue/grey cloth cover, blue
grille, top controls, 2 knobs, 8" speaker, *White*
nameplate (no Fender nameplate), 3 watts, blue
leather handle
Available: **1955–c. 1957**

Vibrolux: narrow panel cabinet, tweed cover, brown
grille, 4 pointer knobs, 10" Jensen speaker, tremolo,
10 watts
Introduced: **mid 1956**
Brown Tolex cover, light brown grille, brownface panel,
8 knobs, 12" speaker, 30 watts: **1961**
Black Tolex, silver grille, blackface control panel: **1964**
Discontinued: **1965**

Vibrolux Reverb: black Tolex cover, silver grille, black-
face control panel, 9 knobs, 2 10" speakers, 35 watts
Introduced: **Aug. 1964**
Silverface control panel, 40 watts: **1970**
Discontinued: **1979**
Reintroduced, blackface features, 2 10" blue speakers
with Alnico magnets, 9 white knobs, 40 watts: **1996**

Solid State Vibrolux Reverb: black Tolex cover, silver
grille, aluminum panel, 9 knobs, 2 10" speakers,
35 watts: **1967–70**

Custom Vibrolux Reverb: Custom Shop model, blond
Tolex, tan grille, 2 10" blue Alnico speakers,
40 watts: **1995**

Harvard: tweed cover, brown grille, 10" speaker,
2 pointer knobs, 10 watts
Introduced: **mid 1956**
10" speaker: **1958**
Discontinued: **1961**
Reintroduced, solid state, black Tolex cover, silver
grille, blackface control panel, 4 knobs, 10" speaker,
20 watts: **1979**
Discontinued: **1983**

Harvard Reverb II: solid state, black Tolex cover, black-face control panel, 7 knobs, 20 watts: **1982–85**

Vibrasonic: brown Tolex cover (some cream), brown grille, brownface panel, 9 knobs, 15" JBL speaker, 25 watts
Available: **late 1959–62**

Vibrasonic Reverb: black Tolex cover, silver grille, silverface control panel, 12 knobs, 15" speaker, 100 watts: **1972–79**

Vibro-Champ: see Champ section, preceding

Custom Vibrasonic: Custom Shop model, blackface control panel, 15" speaker, fat switch on guitar channel, sweet switch on steel channel, 100 watts: **1995**

Concert: 4 10" speakers, 9 knobs, 40 watts
Introduced: **1960**
Discontinued: **1965**
Reintroduced, 12" speaker, 12 knobs, 60 watts: **1992**
Still in production

Concert 112: 12" speaker, 11 knobs, 60 watts: **1982–85**

Concert 210: 2 10" speakers, 11 knobs, 60 watts: **1982–85**

Concert 410: 4 10" speakers, 11 knobs, 60 watts: **1982–85**

Showman 12: piggyback design, white Tolex cover, maroon grille, brownface panel, 9 knobs, 12" JBL speaker, 85 watts
Introduced: **1961**
Gold grille: **1963**
Black Tolex cover, blackface control panel, silver grille: **1964**
Discontinued: **1967**

Showman 15: piggyback design, white Tolex cover, maroon grille, brownface panel, 9 knobs, 15" JBL speaker, 85 watts
Introduced: **1961**
Gold grille: **1963**
Black Tolex cover, blackface control panel, silver grille: **1964**
Discontinued: **1968**

Super Showman: solid state, black Tolex cover, black-face control panel, 18 knobs, 4 12" speakers or 8 10" speakers, 140 watts: **1969–71**

Showman 112: solid state, black Tolex cover, black-face control panel, silver grille, 12 knobs, 12" speaker, 200 watts: **1983–86**

Showman 115: 15" speaker: **1983–86**

Showman 210: 2 10" speakers: **1983–86**

Showman 212: 2 15" speakers: **1983–86**

Double Showman: piggyback design, white Tolex cover, maroon grille, brownface panel, 9 knobs, 2 15" JBL speakers, 85 watts
Introduced: **Dec. 1962**
Renamed **Dual Showman: mid 1963**
Black Tolex cover, blackface control panel: **1964**
Discontinued: **1969**
Dual Showman reintroduced, optional speaker cabinets, 10 red knobs, 100 watts: **1987–94**

Dual Showman Reverb: black Tolex cover silver grille, silverface control panel, 11 knobs, 2 15" speakers, 100 watts
Introduced: **1969**
Master volume added: **1972**
Distortion switch added: **1976**
Discontinued: **1980**

Fender Reverb Unit: rough brown Tolex cover, leather handle, flat logo, a few early examples with grille cover that looks like back panel (no grille cloth visible) later with tan grille cloth, brownface panel, brown knobs, brown plastic domed switch, 2-spring pan, foot switch with 1/4" jack
Inroduced: **1961**
Rough white Tolex cover (some with brown Tolex through early 1964), oxblood grille, some with 6V6 insted of 6K6 power tubes: **mid 1962**
Tan grille, spring handle (plastic strap), white knobs, a few with 3-spring pan: **late 1962**
Smooth white Tolex cover, blackface control panel, 3-spring pan: **mid 1963**
Black Tolex cover: **mid 1964**
Silverface control panel, silver/black amp-type knobs: **1966**
Discontinued: **1972**

'63 Fender Reverb: reissue of brown Tolex version, mix and tone control: **1995–current**

Custom Tweed Reverb: Custom Shop model, tweed cover, chicken head knobs: **1995**

Vibroverb: brown Tolex cover, light brown grille, brownface panel, 9 knobs, 2 10" speakers, 35 watts
Introduced: **1963**
Black Tolex cover, silver grille, blackface control panel, 15" speaker: **1964**
Discontinued: **1965**

'63 Vibroverb: reissue, brown Tolex cover, light brown grille, brownface panel, 9 knobs, 2 10" speakers, 40 watts: **1990–current**

Bronco: similar to Vibro Champ but with red nameplate, 8" speaker, 7 pointer knobs, 60 watts, 5 knobs, 5 watts
Introduced: **1968**
6 watts: **1972**
Discontinued: **1975**
Reintroduced, tweed cover, solid state, top-mounted controls, chrome panel, 3 pointer knobs, 15 watts: **1993**
Blond Tolex cover optional: **1995 only**
6 pointer knobs: **1996**
Still in production

Musicmaster Bass: black Tolex cover silver grille, silverface control panel, 2 knobs, 12" speaker, 12 watts
Available: **1970–83**

Quad Reverb: black Tolex cover, silver grille, silverface control panel, 12 knobs, 4 12" speakers, 100 watts
Available: **1970–79**

Scorpio: black Tolex cover, silver grille, black control panel, 10 knobs, 2 12" JBL speakers, 56 watts
Available: **1970–72**

Taurus: black Tolex cover, silver grille, black control panel, 10 knobs, 2 10" JBL speakers, 42 watts
Available: **1970–72**

Libra: solid state, black Tolex cover, black control panel, 10 knobs, 4 12" speakers, 105 watts
Available: **1970–72**

Capricorn: 3 12" speakers, 10 knobs, 105 watts
Available: **1970–72**

Bantam Bass: 10" Yamaha speaker with plastic cone, 50 watts
Available: **1970–72**

Sidekick: Japanese made line, companion to Squier guitar line

400 PS Bass: black Tolex cover, black foam grille, black control panel, 11 knobs, 18" speaker horn cabinet, 435 watts
Available: **1970–75**

300 PS: black Tolex cover, black foam grille, black control panel, 12 knobs, 4 12" speakers, 300 watts
Available: **1976–79**

Studio Bass: black Tolex cover, silver grille, blackface control panel 12 knobs, 15" Electrovoice speaker, 200 watts
Available: **1977–82**

Studio Lead: solid state, black Tolex cover, silver grille, blackface control panel, 11 knobs, 12" speaker, 50 watts: **1983–85**

Studio 85/85: solid state, black Tolex cover, silver grille, blackface control panel, 9 red knobs, 12" Eminence speaker, 65 watts: **1988–96**

140: amp head, black Tolex cover, blackface control panel, 8 knobs, 135 watts
Available: **1979–82**

B300: solid state bass amp head, no nameplate, black control panel, 10 black knobs, 300 watts, logo painted on front panel
Available: **1979–82**

30: black Tolex cover, silver grille, blackface control panel, 9 knobs, 2 10" speakers or 1 12" speaker, 30 watts
Available: **1979–82**

75: black Tolex cover, silver grille, blackface control panel, 8 knobs, 15" speaker, 75 watts
Available: **1979–83**

Yale Reverb: solid state, black Tolex cover, silver grille, blackface control panel, 7 knobs, 12" speaker, 50 watts
Available: **1982–85**

London Reverb: solid state, black Tolex cover, silver grille, blackface control panel, 12 knobs, 100 watts

London Reverb 112: 12" speaker: **1983–85**

London Reverb 210: 2 10" speakers: **1983–85**

London Reverb Top: piggyback design: **1983–85**

London 185: solid state head only, black Tolex cover black grille, black control panel, 160 watts: **1988–92**

Montreux: solid state, black Tolex cover, silver grille, black control panel, 12 knobs, 12" speaker, 100 watts
Available: **1983–85**

Stage Lead: solid state, black Tolex cover, silver grille, blackface control panel 11 knobs, 12" speaker, 100 watts
Available: **1983–85**

Stage Lead 212: 2 12" speakers: **1983–85**

Stage 112 SE: black Tolex, silver grille, black control panel, 10 knobs, 12" speaker, 160 watts: **1989–current**

BXR: solid state bass amps, black Tolex cover, black grille

BXR Dual Bass 400 Head: 4 red knobs, 2x200 watts: **1987–current**

BXR 15: 8" speaker, 4 black knobs, 15 watts: **1994–96**

BXR 25: 10" speaker, 4 black, knobs, 25 watts: **1992–current**

BXR 60: 12" speaker, 5 black, knobs, 60 watts: **1994–current**

BXR 100: 15" speaker, 3 black knobs, 7-band EQ, 100 watts: **1993–current**

BXR 200: 15" Eminence speaker, also available as separate head and speaker enclosures with 1 15", 2 10" or 4 10" speakers, 5 black knobs, 9-band EQ, 200 watts: **1995–current**

BXR 300: 15" speaker, also available as separate head and cabinet, 5 red knobs, 300 watts
Introduced: **1987**
Black knobs: **1993**
Still in production

85: solid state, black Tolex cover, silver grille, blackface control panel, 9 knobs, 12" Eminence speaker, 85 watts
Available: **1988–92**

HOT: solid state, gray carpet cover, black grille, black control panel, 3 red knobs, 10" speaker, 25 watts
Introduced: **1990**
Black cover, black knobs: **1992**
Discontinued: **1996**

JAM: solid state, 12" speaker, gray carpet cover, black grille, black control panel, 5 red knobs, 25 watts
Introduced: **1990**
Black cover, black knobs: **1992**
Discontinued: **1996**

RAD: solid state, gray carpet cover, black grille, black control panel, 2 red knobs, 18" speaker, 20 watts
Introduced: **1990**
Black carpet cover, black knobs: **1992**
Discontinued: **1996**

RAD Bass: solid state, gray carpet cover, black grille, black control panel, 4 red knobs, 10" speaker, 25 watts
Introduced: **1992**
Black carpet cover, black knobs: **1992**
Renamed **BXR 25**, see preceding: **1994**

M-80 Bass: solid state, gray carpet cover, black grille, black control panel, 12" speaker, 90 watts, available as combo amp or head only
Introduced: **1989**
15" speaker or piggyback with 2 15" speakers, 6 red knobs, 160 watts: **1991**
Black cover, black knobs: **1992**
Discontinued: **1995**

Power Chorus: solid state, black Tolex cover, black grille, black control panel, 15 red knobs, 2 12" speakers, 2x65 watts
Available: **1991–95**

Ultra Chorus: solid state, black Tolex cover, silver grille, black control panel, 14 knobs, 2 12" speakers, 2x65 watts: **1993–95**

Ultimate Chorus: solid state, black Tolex cover, silver grille, black control panel, analog chorus, 14 knobs, 2 12" speakers, 65 watts: **1995–current**

Performer 1000: hybrid tube/solid state, black Tolex cover silver grille, blackface control panel, 11 knobs, 12" speaker or piggyback versions with 12" speaker or 4 12" speakers, 100 watts
Available: **1993–95**

Performer 650: 12" speaker, 70 watts: **1995**

Blues Deluxe: tweed cover, 12" speaker, 7 pointer knobs, 40 watts
Introduced: **1993**
Blond Tolex cover optional: **1995 only**
Discontinued: **1998**

Blues de Ville: tweed cover, 4 10" speakers, 7 pointer knobs, 60 watts
Introduced: **1993**
2 12" speakers optional: **1994**
Blond Tolex cover optional: **1995 only**
Discontinued: **1997**

Blues Junior: tweed cover, top mounted controls, metal panel, 1950s-style nameplate, 12" speaker, fat switch, spring reverb, 6 pointer knobs, 15 watts
Introduced: **1995**
Black Tolex cover, silver grille: **1996**
Still in production

Pro Junior: tweed cover, top mounted controls, metal panel, 1950s-style nameplate, 10" speaker, 2 pointer knobs, 15 watts
Introduced: **1995**
Blond Tolex cover optional: **1995 only**
Black Tolex cover, silver grille: **1996**
Still in production

Tone-Master: Custom Shop model, piggyback design, cream Tolex cover, brownface panel, 4 12" or 2 12" speakers, 9 knobs, 100 watts
Available: **1993–current**

Vibro-King: Custom Shop model, cream Tolex cover, black control panel, 3 10" vintage blue speakers with Alnico magnets, 9 knobs, tube reverb, tremolo, fat switch, 60 watts
Available: **1993–current**

Bullet: solid state, black Tolex cover, black control panel, 8" speaker, 6 knobs, 15 watts
Available: **1993–current**

Bullet Reverb: 7 knobs: **1995–current**

Hot Rod: black Tolex cover, silver grille, top mounted controls, metal panel, 1950s-style nameplate

Hot Rod DeVille 410: 4 10" speakers, 8 pointer knobs, 60 watts

Hot Rod Deville 212: 2 12" speakers, 8 pointer knobs, 60 watts

Hot Rod Deluxe: 1 12" speaker, 8 pointer knobs, 40 watts
Introduced: **1996**
Tweed cover optional: **1998**
Still in production

Rumble Bass: Custom Shop model, separate head and cabinet, 4 10" speakers, cream Tolex cover, oxblood grille, 9 knobs, 300 watts
Available: **1996–current**

Prosonic: combo design with 2 12" Celestion speakers or separate head with 4 12" Celestion speakers, black Tolex, silver grille, black control panel, 8 black knobs, 60 watts
Available: **1996–current**

Pro Junior: see Blues models, preceding

Frontman: solid state, black Tolex cover, black metal grille, blackface control panel with white border

Frontman 15G: 8" speaker, 6 knobs, 15 watts: **1996–current**

Frontman 15R: 8" speaker, 7 knobs, reverb, 15 watts: **1996–current**

Frontman 25R: 10" speaker, 7 knobs, reverb, 25 watts: **1996–current**
Frontman 15B: bass amp, 8" speaker, 4 knobs, 15 watts: **1996–current**

Roc•Pro: solid state, black Tolex cover, aluminum panel
Roc•Pro 700: 12" speaker, 10 black knobs, 70 watts

Roc•Pro 1000: solid state, available as combo with 12" speaker or as separate head, 12 black knobs, 100 watts

GE-112: 12" speaker cabinet for Roc•Pro 1000 head

GE-412: 4 12" speaker cabinet for Roc•Pro 1000 head
Available: **1996–current**

Automatic SE: solid state, 12" speaker, black Tolex
cover, silver grille, black control panel, 5 knobs,
4 pushbutton presets, reverb, chorus, 25 watts
Available: **1997–current**

Automatic GT: solid state, 12" speaker, black Tolex
cover, black grille, aluminum panel, 5 knobs,
4 pushbutton presets, reverb, chorus, 25 watts:
1997–current

Amp Can: black cylinder shape, battery powered,
6" speaker, 4 knobs, 15 watts
Available: **1997–current**

Squier/SKX/Sidekick: Japanese (or Mexican-
made) line

COMMENTS

Fender amplifiers powered the guitar revolution of the
1950s and '60s. The majority of guitarists used
Fender amps, regardless of the brand of guitar they
played. Fender bass amps made the use of the electric bass possible.

Tweed-covered and earlier Fender amps are among the
most highly sought by collectors. The more powerful tweed-covered models are also highly sought by
players. The tweed Bassman with 4 10" speakers
and 4 inputs (mid 1957–60) is considered by many
players to be the finest rock and roll guitar amp
ever made.

Brown Tolex-covered, blond Tolex-covered and blackface models are highly regarded by players.

Silverface and later models are regarded as fine utility
amps.

FENDER

GIBSON

GENERAL INFORMATION

Orville H. Gibson began making instruments as early as 1894 in Kalamazoo, MI. He applied the violin concept of a carved, arched top to the mandolin and guitar, resulting in instruments that were louder and more durable than those of his contemporaries. His only patent, granted in 1898, was for a mandolin design with the sides and neck carved from a single piece of wood.

By 1902 demand for "The Gibson" exceeded Orville's production capacity, and he sold the rights to his name and patent to five Kalamazoo businessmen who formed The Gibson Mandolin-Guitar Manufacturing Co., Ltd., on October 10, 1902. Orville owned stock and trained workers for a brief time, but by the end of 1903 he was no longer involved with the Gibson company (although there is evidence that he did continue to make instruments). He was paid a monthly pension until his death in 1918.

With aggressive marketing built around a system of "teacher-agents" instead of traditional retail store distribution, Gibson quickly became the leading mandolin maker. After World War I, however, the tenor banjo began to overshadow the mandolin. In an attempt to revive the mandolin market, Gibson introduced the Master Model series of 1922, designed by acoustic engineer Lloyd Loar. Loar's F-5 mandolins are considered by most American musicians to be the finest mandolins ever made, and his L-5 guitar set the standard for the *f*-hole models that would dominate the early 1930s, but they were initially only moderately successful.

Gibson bowed to the changing instrument market, shifting emphasis to banjo production and dropping "Mandolin-Guitar" from the company name in 1923 to become Gibson, Inc. By the late 1920s Gibson was a leading banjo maker, and when the guitar rose into prominence in the 1930s, Gibson's archtop *f*-hole models played an influential role.

During the 1930s and early '40s Gibson made instruments under various brands including Kalamazoo, Mastertone and Oriole (Gibson's in-house budget brands), Recording King and Ward (for Montgomery-Ward), Cromwell, Capital, Kel Kroydon and others.

The Chicago Musical Instrument company (CMI), a major distributor, bought Gibson in 1944 and continued making instruments in Kalamazoo. CMI bought the Epiphone company of New York in 1957 and moved Epiphone production to Gibson facilities in Kalamazoo. Epiphone production was moved overseas in 1970 (see Epiphone section).

The Ecuadorian Company Ltd. (ECL) took over CMI in December 1969. In 1970 the company was renamed Norlin, a combination of the names of Norton Stevens and M.H. Berlin, presidents of ECL and CMI, respectively. Norlin built a Gibson plant in Nashville in 1974 and split production between Kalamazoo and Nashville until 1984, when the Kalamazoo plant was closed and all production moved to Nashville.

Gibson began a long decline in the 1970s, as did the entire guitar industry. In January 1986, Gibson was sold to Henry Juszkiewicz, David Berryman and Gary Zebrowski, three former classmates at Harvard business school, who incorporated as Gibson Guitar Corp. The sale included Gibson's Strings & Accessories division (located in Elgin, IL) and Epiphone. The company acquired the Flatiron mandolin company in May 1987, and moved Gibson mandolin production to the Flatiron facility in Bozeman, MT. In 1989 Gibson built a new Flatiron factory and moved production of all Gibson mandolins and flat top guitars to Bozeman. In 1999 Gibson broke ground on a new facility in Memphis to manufacture the ES line of electric hollowbody guitars.

With Juszkiewicz as chairman and Berryman as president, Gibson expanded with the acquisition of Steinberger, Tobias, Slingerland drums, OMI (Dobro-brand instruments), Kramer guitars, Trace Elliott amps and Opcode Systems (computer software and hardware). Gibson has also had distribution or other business relationships with Oberheim synthesizers, Dawn Pro Audio, RedBear amps, Mapex drums and Ramirez guitars.

Though still incorporated as Gibson Guitar Corp., the company began doing business under a new name and logo, Gibson Musical Instruments, in late 1994.

Gibson history can be divided into the following periods:

Late 1800s–circa 1904: "Orville style" instruments, made by or in the style of Orville Gibson. These typically have a very steep peghead angle (20° or greater), large long neck volute, wide paddle-shaped peghead, friction tuning pegs, pickguard inlaid into the top, integral one-piece neck and sides, and back carved with a steep angle at the sides and flat across the middle.

Circa 1905–circa 1909: Transition from original Orville-style designs to better playability. By circa 1905 Gibsons have modern-style back carving, smaller peghead and geared tuners. From circa 1906–08 the bridge height gradually increases on both mandolins and guitars. Body shapes and designs become more refined. Neck and sides are separate pieces with a dovetail neck joint. The elevated pickguard is introduced.

Circa 1909–early 1920s: The classic mandolin era. The modern artist mandolin is introduced, and its development peaks with the introduction of the F-5 in 1922. The Master Model concept carries over to the guitar line with the introduction of the first *f*-hole archtop, the L-5. Primitive banjo models are introduced in 1917.

Mid 1920s–1933: The banjo era. Gibson banjo design evolves rapidly from trapdoor resonator style to one-piece flange Mastertone models. Guitars continue to have relatively small dimensions. The *f*-hole archtop design is developed, and Gibson's first flat top models are introduced.

Late 1934–World War II: The beginning of the guitar era. To give guitars added volume in big band settings, archtop guitar body widths are "advanced" (increased) by 1" to 17", and the 18"-wide Super 400 is introduced in late 1934. New and larger flat top designs are introduced with the Jumbo (round-shouldered dreadnought) in 1934 and Super Jumbo (soon to be the SJ-200) in late 1937. Electric lap steels are introduced in late 1935, followed by electric archtops in 1936. Cutaway archtops and an optional natural finish are introduced in 1939. From 1939–42 Gibson adds a violin, viola, cello and bass to the line.

World War II: Production is limited due to restrictions on materials and Gibson's production of war products. No electric guitars or banjos are made.

Late 1940s–1965: The electric guitar dominates. Gibson's first solidbody electric, the Les Paul Model, is introduced in 1952. New pickup and bridge systems are developed. New designs for hollowbody electrics include laminated construction and the "thinline" body depth. Semi-hollow electrics with double-cutaway bodies are introduced in 1958.

1966–69: Quality begins to fall.

1970–84: Quality continues to fall in the Norlin era. Many new models are introduced. Some are experimental; most are short-lived. The 1970s are perceived as a period of high production with less attention to quality. By the late 1970s Gibson faces growing financial problems.

1985–current: Under new ownership, quality improves as Gibson works to regain its past reputation. Many classic models are reissued with more attention to original specs than reissue models of earlier periods. Gibson has a difficult time establishing new models, such as the M-III, Nighthawk and Starburst, but is successful with numerous variations and limited-run versions of familiar models such as the Les Paul, SG, J-200, etc. (although the lack of information available from Gibson on many limited-run models undermines the collectible appeal associated with a limited run).

GIBSON ELECTRICS, MANDOLINS AND BANJOS

Gibson electrics, mandolins and banjos each have a separate General Information section preceding their respective model listings.

LABELS

Many low-end acoustic instruments and all solidbody instruments have no label.

White rectangular label, *O.H. Gibson*, photo of Orville Gibson and lyre-mandolin: **1890s–late 1902**

White rectangular label, *Gibson Mandolin-Guitar Mfg. Co. Ltd.*, photo of Orville Gibson and lyre-mandolin, 1898 patent date, no serial number or model name: **late 1902–c. 1903**

White oval label, photo of Orville Gibson and lyre-mandolin, *Gibson Mandolin-Guitar Mfg. Co. Ltd.*, *Patent February first, 1898*, serial number, no model name: **c. 1903–c. 1908**

White oval label, *Gibson Mandolin-Guitar Co.*, no photo of Orville Gibson or lyre-mandolin, 1898 and 1906 patent notices…
  Serial number and model name hand-inked or pen ciled: **c. 1908–32**
  Serial number hand-written, model name ink-stamped, some examples: **1917–32**

White oval label, *Gibson Inc.* in typeset lettering (no *Mandolin-Guitar Co.*), serial number and model name ink-stamped: **1933–55**

Master models: Style 5 and Style TL (mando-lute) only…

GIBSON

Label signed and dated by Lloyd Loar (in addition to Master Model label): **June 1, 1922–Dec. 21, 1924**

Master Model label: **1922–27** (and later reissues)

Orange oval label, postwar modern *Gibson* logo on label, serial number (beginning c. 20000) and model name: **early 1955–early 1970**

Square label, *Gibson Inc.*, label divided into 4 triangles; small black, purple and white label on archtops, large orange and white label on flat tops, model name, no serial number: **early 1970–83**

White oval label...

Thin script logo, serial number and model name: **1983–89**

Gibson U.S.A., block-letter logo, serial number and model name: **1983–89**

Beige oval label: serial number and model name, electrics with *Gibson U.S.A.*, acoustics with *Gibson Guitar Corp., Bozeman, Montana*: **1989–current**

Orange oval label, replica of 1955–70 style, some reissue models: **1992–current**

BODY WIDTHS OF CATALOG STYLES

Standard . . . . 12 1/2"
Concert . . . . 13 1/2"
Auditorium . . . . 14 3/4"
Grand concert, pre–WWII . . . . 16"
Grand concert, post–WWII . . . 14 1/4"
Grand auditorium . . . . 16"
Advanced archtop . . . . 17"
Super 400/300 . . . . 18"
Jumbo flat top . . . . 16"
Super jumbo flat top . . . . 17"

MODEL NUMBERS AND NAMES

Model names before World War II often signify the list price of the model. For example, the J-200 listed for $200, the Super 400 for $400 and the L-37 for $37.50. Model names did not change when prices increased.

From 1971–76, Gibson added *Artist*, *Custom* or *Deluxe* to the model names of many flat tops: J-200 Artist, Dove Custom, J-50 Deluxe, for example. These names, which appear on labels, are *not* different models unless noted as such in the model descriptions.

ARCHTOP BRIDGES AND TAILPIECES

Glued down bridge: **1902**

Non-compensating maple bridge, trapeze tailpiece with pins anchored in tortoiseshell celluloid crosspiece: **c. 1905**

Compensating ebony bridge, all models except Style U harp guitar (maple bridge and 1 long ebony saddle on Style U): **1918**

Height-adjustable bridge...

Ebony (some with straight non-compensating underside so bridge can be turned over for Hawaiian playing): **late 1921**

Rosewood: **1935**

Trapeze tailpiece with no pins, strings loop under tailpiece...

L-5: **1923**

L-4, L-3: **1924**

Strings straight through trapeze: **late 1920s**

Wooden crosspiece on trapeze, some examples: **1942–46**

FLAT TOP BRIDGES AND TAILPIECES

The J-200, prewar J-100, prewar J-55 and some postwar J-200 variations have bridges that do not conform to these specs.

Pyramid ends...

All models except Lucas: **1926–27**

Lucas (from introduction): **1928–30**

Short, tiered 2-piece construction, straight-bevel ends, slight belly, all models except Lucas and L-2...

Extra bridge pin in belly area: **1928**

No extra bridge pin in belly area: **1929**

Trapeze tailpiece, adjustable bridge...

L-2, most examples: **1929–30, 1932–34**

Lucas, examples with rosewood back and sides: **1932–33**

Longer 1-piece with modern type bevels...

Lucas, examples with maple back and sides: **1931, 1934–41**

L-2: **1931**

All other models: **1931–WWII**

2 pearl dots on bridge: **late 1930s–1960s**

Martin-type belly bridge (belly below bridge)...

Some banner-logo examples: **1942–46**

Standard on most models: **late 1968 (or early 1969)–1984**

Upper belly (above bridge pins): **c. 1950–late 1968**

Adjustable bridge saddle...

J-160E (from introduction): **1954–70**

Rare option on some other models: **1956–60**

Standard on many models: **1960–70**

Trapeze tailpiece, glued-down bridge, B-45-12 and B-25-12: **1961, 1965–early 1969**

No pearl dots, transitional period: **1960s**

Plastic bridge, all models below SJ: **1965–67**
Upper "reverse" belly, most models: **1984–current**
Flying bird, rounded ends: **1992–current**
Bird-and-beak, rounded ends, point in middle:
1997–current

BINDING

Plain (ungrained) plastic: **pre–1909**
Grained ivoroid: **c. 1909–24**
Return to plain (ungrained) plastic…
L-5 and K-5: **1924 and after**
All other models: **1925 and after**
Grained ivoroid reintroduced only on F-5L and later
longneck mandolins: **1978**

NECKS

Truss rod…
Introduced on all models except Jr. (some early flat
tops and some examples made during World
War II have no truss rod; all models made by
Gibson under other brands have no truss rod):
late 1922
Double-action rod installed on Montana-made flat
tops only, 1/4" nut (slightly smaller than standard Gibson truss rod nut): **1994–95**
High-end models: L-5, L-12, Super 400, J-200, etc.…
2-piece with 1 laminate stripe, referred to by Gibson as 3-piece: **1922–mid 1961**
3-piece with 2 laminate stripes, referred to by Gibson as 5-piece: **late 1961–current**
Mid-line models: L-7, J-50, Les Pauls SGs, ES-335
series, non-reverse Firebirds, etc.…
1-piece mahogany: **1910s–early 1969**
Some examples with laminated neck: **1942–46**
3-piece mahogany, no laminate stripes: **mid 1969–74**
3-piece maple, no laminate stripes, Les Pauls, ES-
335 series, new models, basses: **Sept. 1974-
early 1980s**
Some walnut and walnut-maple necks: **1978 and after**
Transition period to 1-piece mahogany (current
construction), Les Pauls, ES-335 series: **1980–83**
Low-end models: Melody Makers, SG-100s, LGs, etc.…
1-piece mahogany: **into early 1970s**
1-piece maple: **early 1970s–current**

PEGHEADS

Wide "paddle" peghead: **1890s–c. 1906**
Slotted peghead: **by 1907**

Solid peghead (except Classical models): **1908–current**
"Snakehead," peghead narrows toward top…
Introduced: **1923**
Discontinued on all models except L-5: **1927**
Discontinued on L-5: **1934**
Fiber peghead veneer replaces wood veneer: **late 1970**
MADE IN THE USA, impressed on back of peghead,
instruments made for export only: **late 1920s–50s**
MADE IN U.S.A.…
Impressed on back of peghead, all models:
1970–mid 1975
On decal on back of peghead: **mid 1975–mid 1977**
Impressed on back of peghead, most models:
mid 1977–current
Exceptions with no MADE IN U.S.A.: some mandolins,
L-5, Super 400 and Johnny Smith models from
1970s and 1980s; many mandolins, banjos, His-
toric Collection and Custom Shop examples from
the 1990s
Original Gibson Prototype stamp on back of peghead,
applied to first 3 or 4 examples of new models, in-
cluding Les Paul 25/50, ES-347, The Paul, The SG,
Explorer II, ES-335 Pro and F-5L: **1978–early 1990s**
Peghead pitch, non-grafted and non-spliced
pegheads…
20° or greater: **1890s–c. 1904**
Less than 20°, eventually to 17°: **1904–late 1965**
14°: **late 1965–73**
17°, some models: **1973**
Volute on back of peghead…
Introduction period (varies according to model):
late 1969–74
L-5, L-5CES, Byrdland, Super 400, Super 400CES
and Johnny Smith: **Sept. 1974**
Discontinued, all models: **March 1981**
Peghead thickness…
Thickness (depth) of peghead narrows toward top:
until mid 1950
Uniform thickness: **mid 1950–current**

LOGOS

No logo, crescent and star inlay: **1890s–c. 1902**
Some with The Gibson logo (slanted or straight
across), some with no logo: **c. 1903–c. 1907**
The Gibson slanted: **c. 1908-late 1920s**
The Gibson straight across peghead, all flat tops,
some archtops: **late 1920s**
Transition to Gibson logo (varies by model): **1928–34**
Script Gibson…

Pearl inlaid, high-end models: **1933–42, 1946**

White silkscreen, low-end models: **1928–43**

Thicker *Gibson*, Super 400 and other high-end
models: **mid 1930s**

Thicker *Gibson*, all models: **by late 1930s**

Gold script *Gibson*...

All models made during WWII, low-end postwar
models: **1943–early 1947**

Only a Gibson Is Good Enough on banner, most ex
amples of LG-2, J-45 and SJ, a few L-50s: **1943–46**

"Modernized" script with tail on *G* and *N*, low-end
models...

Gold silkscreen, closed *b* and *o*: **early 1947–c. 1954**

Gold decal: **c. 1954–current**

"Modernized" script with tail on *G*, high-end models,
pearl-inlaid...

Transitional period, some examples with modern
logo, some with script: **early 1947**

Dot on *i* connected to *G*, open *b* and *o*, lower link
between *o* and *n*: **early 1947–51**

Dot on *i* free from *G*, open *b* and *o*, lower link
between *o* and *n*: **1951–68**

"Pantograph" logo, large rectangular pearl inlay (pearl
is not cut) with paint stenciled around *Gibson* ...

Dot on *i* free from *G*, closed *b* and *o* (some with
open *b* and *o* in 1969), lower link between *o* and
n: **1968 only**

No dot on *i*, lower link between *o* and *n*: **late 1968–
late 70**

Smaller, thinner logo, pre-sunk into fiber peghead veneer...

No dot on *i*, lower link between *o* and *n*: **late
1970–72**

Dot on *i* reintroduced (some without dot through
1981): **1972–current**

Upper link between *o* and *n*: **1981–current**

Pre-WWII script logos reintroduced...

Some banjos, all mandolins: **1970**

Some high-end guitars, Mark series: **1970s**

Decal *The Gibson Guitar Company, U.S.A.*, Sonex 180,
GGC 700 and other low-end solidbody electrics:
1982 only

FINISH COLORS, 1902–20s

Orange or ebony top (some old stock still available as
late as 1920): **1902–18**

Uniform red mahogany (described as shaded from
golden red to mahogany), L-3, L-4, Style O, A-4,
F-2, F-4, H-4, and K-4: **1914–17**

Red mahogany sunburst, L-3, L-4, Style O, A-4, F-2, F-

4, H-4, and K-4: **1917–late 1920s**

Sheraton brown introduced: **1918**

Old ivory (white) top optional, L-3, A-3, H-2, K-2:
1918–22

Cremona brown sunburst introduced, Style 4 mandolin family (most examples with red mahogany
sunburst throughout 1920s): **early 1921**

LLOYD LOAR, MASTER MODELS, VIRZI TONE-PRODUCER

Lloyd Loar joined Gibson as an acoustic engineer in
1919. Among the features introduced during his
tenure: *f*-hole mandolins and guitars, elevated
fingerboards on guitars and mandolins, and a
longer neck (not longer scale) on mandolins. The
series of instruments with these innovations was
named Style 5 and promoted as the Master Model
series (the name was also appropriated for the
Mastertone banjo line). Loar personally inspected
and signed labels on an estimated 250 instruments.
A second special label identified these as Master
Model instruments.

Many Loar-signed instruments from 1924 were fitted
with the Virzi Tone-Producer, an oval-shaped wood
sounding board suspended from the top. Many of
these have been removed.

Loar left Gibson in December 1924 to pursue other
interests, particularly the development of electric
instruments. In the early 1930s, he formed the Vivi-
Tone company to market electric guitars.

WARTIME MODELS

During World War II, from sometime in 1942 until late
1945, Gibson ceased production on all electric
instruments and most acoustic instruments. Limited quantities of the following models were available: L-00, LG-2, J-45, Southerner Jumbo, L-50,
L-7 and special uncatalogued archtops. Some
examples of the LG-2, J-45, SJ and L-50 have a
banner peghead logo that reads *Only a Gibson Is
Good Enough*. Many examples have 3-on-a-plate
tuners and (on archtops) a wooden crosspiece on
the trapeze tailpiece. Some flat tops have no truss
rod; archtops do have a truss rod. Some examples
have a laminated neck. Due to materials shortages,
specifications may vary greatly from standard catalog descriptions on models produced during and
immediately after the war.

J-200 from 1990 with body shape referred to by collectors as jumbo.

SJ from circa 1945, with teardrop pickguard and body shape referred to by collectors as round-shouldered dreadnought.

Hummingbird from 1990 with square-shouldered dreadnought body shape.

L-0 from the 1930s, with prewar small-body shape (14 3/4" wide) and prewar pickguard shape.

B-25 from circa 1968, with body shape of postwar small-body (14 3/4" wide) flat tops, including LG-series. Large pickguard with point was introduced circa 1955. Bridge is "belly above bridge" design with height-adjustable saddle.

LG-2 3/4, with 3/4-size body shape.

Gibson peghead before mid-1950, with thinner depth towards top.

Gibson peghead from mid 1950 and after, with uniform thickness.

SERIAL NUMBERS

Gibson instruments made before 1977 may have a serial number or a factory order number (or code letter), or both, or neither. Due to the various serial number systems employed, some numbers may be duplicated on several instruments.

Gibson instituted a new number system in 1977, used on most but not all guitar models, with which it is possible to determine the exact day a number was stamped on an instrument.

NUMBER CONFIGURATION AND PLACEMENT

1902–1947

No serial number or model name on label, photo of Orville Gibson and lyre-mandolin on label, date sometimes penciled under top: **1902–c. 1908**

Serial number and model name on white paper label, number range 0100-99999…
Hand-inked or penciled (some overlap with previous style): **c. 1908–32**
Ink-stamped: **1932–47**

Factory order number stamped on neck block inside body: **1908–c. 1930**

Some low-end models with no number: **c. 1927–mid 1930s**

3-digit number ink-stamped on neck block, some flat tops: **c. 1927–mid 1930s**

Factory order number containing letter A–G, ink-stamped on inside back, on neck block (flat tops) or on label: **1935–41**

Factory order number beginning with letter D–H impressed into back of peghead: **1938–41**

Factory order number of 3 or 4 digits, followed by hyphen, followed by 1 or 2 digits, ink-stamped on neck block (flat tops) or inside back: **1942–47**

1947–61

Hollowbody instruments…
Number preceded by letter *A* on white oval label: **1947–early 1955**
Number preceded by letter *A* on orange oval label: **early 1955–61**
Factory order number of 3 or 4 digits, followed by hyphen, followed by 1 or 2 digits, ink-stamped on inside back: **1947–52**

Factory order number beginning with letter Q–Z, ink-stamped on inside back: **1952–61**

Solidbody instruments...

No number: **1952–late 1953**

4 digits impressed into top of peghead, space after 1st digit, 1st digit is 3: **late 1953**

Number inked on back of peghead, 5-digit number with space after first digit or 6-digit number (used late in each year) with no space between digits: **late 1953–early 1961**

1961–77

3, 4 or 5 digits inked (thinner type style than 1950s inked number) or lightly impressed into peghead: **1961–63**

6 digits inked or lightly impressed into peghead (no *MADE IN USA* stamp on peghead): **1963–69**

6 digits impressed into peghead, *MADE IN USA* on peghead: **1970–75**

8-digit number on decal: **1975–77**

Other configurations on special or limited edition models: **1971–77**

1977–current

8-digit number impressed into peghead: **1977–current**

Number also on beige oval (old style) label, hollow and semi-hollow models: **1989–current**

Vintage 1950s and 1960s style numbers, on peghead or paper label, reissue models: **1977–current**

Letter followed by space followed by 3 digits, ink-stamped, limited edition and early Chet Atkins models:

1982–current

SERIAL NUMBERS, 1902–47

Series starts with 1000.

YEAR	APPROX. LAST NUMBER	YEAR	APPROX. LAST NUMBER
1903	1500	1926	83600
1904	2500	1927	85400
1905	3500	1928	87300*
1906	5500	1929	89750*
1907	8300	1930	90200
1908	9700	1931	90450
1909	10100	1932	90700
1910	10600	1933	91400
1911	10850	1934	92300
1912	13350	1935	92800
1913	16100	1936	94100
1914	20150	1937	95200
1915	25150	1938	95750
1916	32000	1939	96050
1917	39500	1940	96600
1918	47900	1941	97400
1919	53800	1942	97700
1920	63650	1943	97850
1921	69300	1944	98250
1922	71400	1945	98650
1923	74900	1946	99300
1924	81200	1947	99999
1925	82700		

* Most Nick Lucas models from 1928–33 have a 1928 or 1929 serial number.

FACTORY ORDER NUMBERS, 1908–23

Numbers consist of a 3-digit, 4-digit or 5-digit batch number followed by a 1-digit or 2-digit number (from 1–40) ranking the instrument. This information was compiled by Roger Siminoff.

YEAR	SELECTED BATCH NUMBERS	YEAR	SELECTED BATCH NUMBERS
1908	259	1916	2667, 3508
1909	309	1917	3246, 11010
1910	545, 927	1918	9839, 11159
1911	1260, 1295	1919	11146, 11212
1912	1408, 1593	1920	11329, 11367
1913	1811, 1902	1921	11375, 11527
1914	1936, 2152	1922	11565, 11729
1915	2209, 3207	1923	11973

FACTORY ORDER NUMBERS AND LETTER CODES, 1935–41

Many instruments from 1935–41 have a letter designating the year of production.

1935–37: Letter is between the batch number and the instrument number. Code is ink-stamped on the inside back.

1938–41: 2 or 3 letters precede instrument ranking number. Code is either ink-stamped onto the label or impressed into the back of the peghead (or, on lap steels, impressed into the back of the body near the neck). Second letter indicates brand of instrument: G = Gibson, K = Kalamazoo, W = Recording King (Montgomery Ward). Third letter (if there is one) is E for electric.

DA, EA, FA prefix: Some high-end guitar models and a few banjos and electric Hawaiians have the letter *A* added to the prefixes D, E or F. Several examples of the L-5 and Super 400 have EA-prefix numbers, suggesting 1939 production, along with a separate serial number on a paper label indicating 1940 or 1941 production. However, based on a banjo example with FA-prefix and a 1940 sales receipt, it is probable that DA, EA and FA prefixes do indicate 1938, 1939 and 1940, respectively, and that a later serial number indicates that the instrument was not completed until a later time.

LETTER	YEAR	LETTER	YEAR
A	1935	E	early 1941 (E, with no other letter)
B	1936		
C	1937	F, FA	1940
D, DA	1938	G	1941
EX	1939 (E, followed by any other letter)	H	1942

A-SERIES NUMBERS, 1947–61

Series starts Apr. 28, 1947 with A 100. Last number was assigned on Feb. 21, 1961.

YEAR	APPROX. LAST NUMBER	YEAR	APPROX. LAST NUMBER
1947	A 1304	1955	A 21909
1948	A 2665	1956	A 24755
1949	A 4413	1957	A 26819
1950	A 6597	1958	A 28880
1951	A 9419	1959	A 32284
1952	A 12462	1960	A 35645
1953	A 16101	1961	A 36147
1954	A 18667		

GIBSON

EPIPHONE A-SERIES, 1958–61

Epiphone hollow and semi-hollow models made by Gibson from 1958–61 have their own serial number series. From 1961–69, Gibson and Epi models are numbered in the same series.

YEAR	APPROXIMATE RANGE
1958	A 1000s
1959	A 2000s
1960	A 3000–A 3186

FACTORY ORDER NUMBERS, 1947–51

A wide range of inconsistent numbers appears in 1948 and early 1949. By the end of 1949, the system becomes more orderly.

RANGE	YEAR	RANGE	YEAR
700s–1000s	1947	2000s	late 1949
1100s–3700s	1948	3000s–5000s	1950
3700s–4500s	early 1949	6000s–9000s	1951

FACTORY ORDER CODE LETTERS, 1952–61

Code letter precedes batch number.

LETTER	YEAR	LETTER	YEAR
Z	1952	U	1957
Y	1953	T	1958
X	1954	S	1959
W	1955	R	1960
V	1956	Q	1961

SOLIDBODY NUMBERS, 1953–61

Number is inked on peghead.

Configuration: **y nnnn** or (late in each year) **ynnnnn**.

y = last digit of year

nnnn or **nnnnn** = ranking among solidbody models

1961–70

Series begins Feb. 1961 with 100. Many numbers from 1963–69 appear on more than one instrument. This list was originally compiled by A.R. Duchossoir from Gibson records.

NUMBER RANGE	YEAR(S)	NUMBER RANGE	YEAR(S)
100–42440	1961		
42441–61180	1962	106100–106899	1963
61450–64222	1963	109000–109999	1963, 1967
64240–71040	1964	110000–111549	1963
71041–96600	1962, a few from	111550–115799	1963, 1967
	1963, 1964	115800–118299	1963
96601–99999	1963	118300–120999	1963, 1967
000001–099999	1967	121000–139999	1963
100000–106099	1963, 1967		

NUMBER RANGE	YEAR(S)	NUMBER RANGE	YEAR(S)
140000–140100 . . . . 1963, 1967		503405–520955 . . . . 1965, 68	
140101–144304 1963		520956–530056 1968	
144305–144380 1964		530061–530850 . . . . 1966, 1968–69	
144381–149864 1963		530851–530993 1968–69	
149865–149891 1964		530994–539999 1969	
149892–152989 1963		540000–540795 . . . . 1966, 1969	
152990–174222 1964		540796–545009 1969	
174223–176643 . . . . 1964, 1965		555000–556909 1966	
176644–250335 1964		558012–567400 1969	
250336–305983 1965		570087–570643 1966	
306000–310999 . . . . 1965, 1967		570645–570755 1966–67	
311000–320149 1965		570857–570964 1966	
320150–320699 1967		580000–580080 1969	
320700–329179 1965		580086–580999 . . . . 1966–67, 1969	
329180–330199 . . . . 1965, 1967		600000–600998 . . . . low-end models, 1966,	
330200–332240 . . . . 1965, 1967–68			some 1967, 1968
332241–348092 1965		600000–606090 . . . . high-end models, 1969	
348093–349100 1966		700000–700799 . . . . 1966–67, 1969	
349121–368638 1965		750000–750999 1968–69	
368640–369890 1966		800000–800999 1966–69	
370000–370999 1967		801000–812838 . . . . 1966, 1969	
380000–385309 1966		812900–819999 1969	
390000–390998 1967		820000–820087 . . . . 1966, 1969	
400001–406666 1966		820088–823830 1966	
406667–409670 1966–68		824000–824999 1969	
409671–410900 1966		828002–847488 . . . . 1966, 1969	
410901–419999 . . . . no entries in ledger		847499–858999 . . . . 1966, 1969	
420000–429193 1966		859001–895038 1967	
500000–500999 . . . . 1965–66, 1968–69		895039–896999 1968	
501009–501600 1965		897000–898999 . . . . 1967, 1969	
501601–501702 1968		899000–899999 1968	
501703–502706 . . . . 1965, 1968		900000–901999 1970	
503010–503109 1968		910000–999999 1968	

1970–75

6-digit number, *Made in USA* on back of peghead
Exception: 1990s reissues of 1960s solidbody models (see following)

NUMBER RANGE	YEAR(S)	NUMBER RANGE	YEAR(S)
6 digits + A 1970		800000s. 1973–75	
000000s. 1973		900000s. 1970–72	
100000s. 1970–75		A + 6 digits 1973–75	
200000s. 1973–75		B + 6 digits 1974–75	
300000s. 1974–75		C + 6 digits 1974–75	
400000s. 1974–75		D + 6 digits 1974–75	
500000s. 1974–75		E + 6 digits. 1974–75	
600000s. 1970–72, 1974–75		F + 6 digits. 1974–75	
700000s. 1970–72			

1975–77

Number on peghead decal, 2-digit prefix followed by 6-digit number

PREFIX	YEAR
99	1975
00	1976
06	1977

1977–CURRENT

8-digit number impressed into back of peghead with configuration **ydddynnn**

yy (1st and 5th digits) = year of manufacture

ddd (digits 2–4) = day of the year; 001 = Jan. 1, 365 = Dec. 31

nnn (digits 6-8) = rank of the instrument that day. Serial number stamp is applied in mid-production, at the point when the neck is attached to the body. All instruments made at the Kalamazoo factory (1977–84) and guitars made at the Bozeman factory (1989–current) are numbered beginning with 001 each day. Instruments made at the Nashville factory from 1977–89 were numbered each day beginning with 500 or 501. Beginning in 1990, regular production models continued to be numbered in Nashville each day beginning with 500 or 501, but some models were also numbered in the 300s, 400s, 700s, 800s and 900s.

Examples:

80012005 = the 5th instrument made in Kalamazoo on the first day of 1982

82569625 = the 125th or 126th instrument made in Nashville on the 256th day of 1989

EXCEPTIONS

Vintage reissues, see following.

Special runs, 1970s and 1980s: Some examples, such as the Les Paul Spotlight Special, are numbered with configuration **yy nnnn**, with **yy** = year, **nnnn** = ranking.

Les Paul Classic, 1990–current: Les Paul Classics have a 1950s-style inked-on serial number with the first digit corresonding to the last digit of the year of manufacture.

1994 electrics: In 1994 only, the Nashville plant numbered all instruments that normally would have received an 8-digit number with configuration **94nnnnnn**. The final 6 digits denote the ranking of each instrument over the entire year's production.

Centennial electric models, 1994: inked-on number with configuration **yyyy-mm**.

yyyy = ranking of the model according to the years of the centennial (1894 corresponds to #1, 1994 corresponds to #101)

mm = month of the model within the series, ranging from 1-14 (only 12 models were actually produced; 2 more were prototyped).

Dove in Flight and J-200 Montana Gold, 1996: configuration **DFynnny** or **MGynnny**, respectively.

yy = year

nnn = ranking.

Mandolins, 1987–current: Beginning with Bozeman, MT, production, mandolins have a different numbering system. See Gibson Mandolins, General Information.

Banjos: in most periods, banjos have their serial number system. See Gibson Banjos, General Information.

VINTAGE REISSUES, 1982–LATE 1992

Heritage series Flying V and Moderne, also early Chet Atkins CE, late 1981–83: inked-on number with configuration **A nnn**.

First letter **A** may range from A–K.

Digits **nnn** are ranking. Most series return to 001 after 099 (example: A 098, A 099, B 001, B 002, etc.), but some examples have ranking of 100 and higher.

Heritage series Explorer, 1982–83: inked-on number with configuration **1 ####**.

First digit is **1**.

Digits **####** after space are ranking.

Les Paul reissues, 1970s–1993, and Historic Collection reissues, 1992: Beginning with custom-ordered dealer reissues of the Les Paul Standard in the 1970s, Les Paul reissues have a 1950s-style inked-on serial number (see Solidbody Numbers, preceding). On some dealer reissues, the first digit is a 9 or 0, corresponding to a 1959 or 1960 neck, respectively (or in the case of a Leo's model, a letter *L*). On other dealer reissues and on all regular production reissues through late 1992, the first digit corresponds to the last digit of the year of manufacture.

VINTAGE REISSUES, LATE 1992–CURRENT

Les Pauls and other reissues of 1952–60 solidbodies

Configuration **m ynnn**

m = model code

y = last digit of year of manufacture

nnn = ranking

MODEL CODE EXAMPLES	MODEL(S)	MODEL CODE EXAMPLES	MODEL(S)
2	1952 Les Paul	8	1958 Les Paul, Explorer
4	1954 Les Paul	9	1959 Les Paul, Flying V
6	1956 Les Paul	0	1960 Les Paul
7	1957 Les Paul, Futura		

Reissues of 1961–69 Solidbody Models

Number system begins in 1997. Number is pressed into back of peghead.

Configuration **yynnnm**

yy = year of manufacture

nnn = ranking

m = model code (year of reissue)

MODEL CODE EXAMPLES	MODEL
1	SG/Les Paul
3	1963 Firebird I
4	1964 Firebird III
5	1965 Firebird V and VII
8	1968 Les Paul Custom

Historic Series ES Models (Hollow or Semi-hollow Electrics)

Number system begins in 1995.

Configuration **A-mynnn**

A or B designates Historic Series

m = model (year of reissue)

y = last digit of year of manufacture

nnn = ranking

GIBSON

MODEL CODE
EXAMPLES   **MODEL**
2 . . . . 1952 ES-295
3 . . . . 1963 ES-335 block inlay
4 . . . . 1964 ES-330
5 . . . . 1965 ES-345
9 (A prefix) . . . . 1959 ES-335 dot inlay
9 (B prefix) 1959 ES-355

CUSTOM SHOP INK-STAMPED NUMBERS, 1993–CURRENT

Configuration **y-9nnn** or (if ranking exceeds 999) **y9nnnn**

y = last digit of year of manufacture

9 = designation for a Custom Shop guitar

nnn(n) = ranking

ACOUSTIC ARCHTOPS KEY

Oval hole
  Paddle-shaped peghead
    Pearl and ebony top binding = **O-2**
    Green and white top binding = **O-3**
    Celluloid top binding
      Bound back = **O-1**
      Unbound back (no pickguard) = **Style O, 1902–07**
  Peghead with dip in center of top
    Scroll body = **Style O, 1908–23**
    Symmetrical body
      Split-block inlay = **Super 400 Western Sky Oval Hole**
      Dot inlay
        13 1/2" wide = **L-3, c. 1927–28**
        16" wide = **L-4, 1912–32**
Round hole
  Single black soundhole binding = **L-Jr.**
  3-ply white-black-white soundhole ring = **L-50, 1932–34**
  4 thin black soundhole rings = **L-2, 1924–26**
  7-ply white-and-black soundhole rings
    Maple back and sides = **L-4, 1929-35, 1937**
    Mahogany back and sides = **L-75, 1935–39**
  1 colored-wood inlaid soundhole ring = **L**
  2 rope-pattern soundhole rings = **L-1, 1903–c. 1920**
  2 5-ply soundhole rings = **L-1, c. 1920–24**
  3 wood-inlaid soundhole rings
    Unbound fingerboard = **L-2, 1902**
    Bound fingerboard = **L-3, 1902–08**
  Herringbone or checkered soundhole ring = **L-3, 1908–27, 1929–33**
f-holes
  Peghead spec unavailable, 17" wide, fancy inlay = **Special No. 7**
  Celluloid peghead veneer = **L-75, 1933–34**

Flowerpot (torch) peghead inlay
    Non-cutaway = **L-5**
    Cutaway
        Full-depth body = **L-5C**
        Thin body = **L-5CT**
Double-handled vase peghead inlay = **L-75, late 1934–35**
5-piece split-diamond peghead inlay
    Non-cutaway = **Super 400**
    Cutaway
        18" wide (*Super 400* on tailpiece) = **Super 400C**
        17" wide (*Johnny Smith* on tailpiece) = **Johnny Smith**
7-piece diamond-shape peghead inlay = **L-12, 1934–41**
Fleur-de-lis peghead inlay
    Cloud fingerboard inlay = **Citation**
    Varied-pattern fingerboard inlay
        Inlay at first fret = **L-4, 1937–46**
        No inlay at first fret = **L-7, 1934**
Other ornamental peghead inlay
    Double-triangle fingerboard inlay = **L-10, late 1934–39**
    Varied pattern fingerboard inlay
        Black finish = **L-10, 1933–late 1934**
        Sunburst finish
            Nickel-plated hardware = **L-7, 1934–42**
            Gold-plated hardware = **L-12, 1932–34**
    Double-parallelogram fingerboard inlay
        Triple-bound peghead = **L-12, 1941–42**
        Single-bound peghead
            17" wide
                Gold-plated hardware
                    Non-cutaway = **L-12, 1947–55**
                    Cutaway = **L-12C**
                Nickel-plated hardware
                    Non-cutaway = **L-7, 1942–56**
                    Cutaway = **L-7C**
            18" wide
                Non-cutaway = **Super 300**
                Cutaway = **Super 300C**
        Unbound peghead
            Non-cutaway = **L-4, 1947–56**
            Cutaway = **L-4C**
No peghead ornament other than logo
    16" wide
        Black finish
            Pearl logo = **L-10, 1931–33**
            Arched back = **Black Special No. 4**
            Silkscreen logo = **wartime model** (name unknown)
        Sunburst finish
            Mahogany sides = **L-48**
            Maple sides = **L-50, 1935–1966**
        Special No. 5 (no other specs available)

f-holes, no peghead ornament other than logo *(continued)*

14 3/4" wide

Pearl logo = **L-50, 1934-35**

Silkscreen logo

Tortoiseshell celluloid body binding = **L-47**

White body binding

Bound pickguard = **L-37**

Unbound pickguard

Arched back = **L-30**

Flat back = **L-75, 1932**

Black Special No. 2 (no other specs available)

Special No. 3 (no other specs available)

ACOUSTIC ARCHTOPS

Some instruments made by Orville Gibson, beginning in 1894 and prior to the formation of the Gibson company, have a star and crescent inlaid on the peghead. Some are dated on the underside of the top.

"Orville-style" instruments, made in the early years of the Gibson company, have a carved back that is flat across the middle.

Even though early Gibson catalogs specify maple back and sides, virtually all pre-1908 guitars have walnut back and sides. Virtually all guitars from 1908 through the mid 1920s have birch back and sides. The L-5 has maple back and sides by 1925. Other models make the change to maple by circa 1927.

STYLE 0: oval soundhole, 2 inlaid wood rings around soundhole, fixed bridge with pyramids at ends, single-bound top, single-bound fingerboard and peghead, dot inlay, solid paddle-shaped peghead with rounded top, peghead veneer with pearl inlay, friction pegs, black top finish, dark mahogany finish on back and sides, available in standard (12 1/2"), concert (13 1/2") or grand concert (16") size

Variation: catalog picture shows 2 rope-pattern soundhole rings with solid ring between, unbound fingerboard and peghead, no peghead inlay

Introduced: **1902**

Slotted peghead, pointed-end fingerboard: **1906**

Some examples 18" wide, fixed bridge with pyramids at ends, bound fingerboard, bound peghead, slotted or solid peghead with geared tuners, inlaid peghead ornament or slanted *The Gibson* logo: **c. 1906–07**

Body style commonly referred to by collectors as **Style 0 Artist**, 16" wide, pointed cutaway, carved scroll

on upper bass bout, 2 rope-pattern soundhole rings with solid ring between, asymmetrical fingerboard with treble-side extension, trapeze tailpiece with pins anchored in tortoiseshell celluloid crosspiece, solid peghead, right-angle tuners, fleur-de-lis inlay at top of peghead: **1908**

First catalog reference to Artist's Model, elevated pickguard with single support, pickguard does not cover entire treble side of soundhole: **1911**

Uniform mahogany (slightly shaded) or golden orange finish: **1914**

Larger pickguard with 2 supports, pickguard covers treble side of soundhole, fleur-de-lis inlay at center of peghead, *The Gibson* logo, red mahogany sunburst finish: **1918**

Last catalogued: **1922**

Last made: **1925**

0-1: bound oval soundhole, 2 soundhole rings of fancy wood with pearl border, bound top and back, bound ebony fingerboard, pearl fingerboard inlays and side inlays, solid paddle-shaped peghead with rounded top, peghead veneer with pearl inlay, black top finish, dark mahogany back and sides finish, available in standard (12 1/2"), concert (13 1/2") or grand concert (16") size

Only catalog appearance: **1902**

0-2: bound oval soundhole, 2 soundhole rings of fancy colored wood with pearl border, pearl and ebony rope-pattern top binding, mahogany bridge with pearl inlays, inlaid bridge pins, bound ebony fingerboard, pearl dot fingerboard inlays and side inlays, pointed peghead with star and crescent inlay, black top finish, dark mahogany finish on back and sides, available in standard (12 1/2"), concert (13 1/2") or grand concert (16") size

Only catalog appearance: **1902**

O-3: bound oval soundhole, 2 soundhole rings of fancy colored wood with pearl border, mahogany bridge with pearl inlays, green and white rope-pattern top binding with fancy wood purfling, bound ebony fingerboard, pearl fingerboard inlay, peghead veneer with pearl binding, friction tuners with pearl buttons, black top finish, dark mahogany finish on back and sides, available in standard (12 1/2"), concert (13 1/2") or grand concert (16") size

Only catalog appearance: **1902**

STYLE L: 12 1/2" wide, round soundhole with ring of colored woods, bound top and back, ebony fingerboard, dot inlay, black peghead veneer, orange top finish, dark mahogany finish on back and sides

Introduced: **1902**

Unbound soundhole, single soundhole ring, slotted peghead: **by 1906**

Discontinued: **1907**

L-1: single-bound round soundhole with 2 rope-pattern wood rings, single-bound top, ebony fingerboard, dot inlay, peghead veneer, orange top finish, dark mahogany finish on back and sides, available in standard (12 1/2") or concert (13 1/2") size

Introduced: **1902**

13 1/2" wide, narrower waist, trapeze tailpiece with pins anchored in tortoiseshell celluloid crosspiece, elevated pickguard, 13 frets clear of body, bound fingerboard, standard peghead with slanted *The Gibson* logo: **1908**

No pickguard: **c. 1912**

Pickguard: **1914**

Sheraton brown finish: **1918**

2 5-ply soundhole rings: **by 1920**

Discontinued: **1925**

Model number reintroduced as flat top (see Gibson Flat Tops section): **1926**

L-2: round soundhole, 3 inlaid soundhole rings of colored wood, single-bound top, unbound fingerboard, pearl fingerboard inlay, peghead veneer with pearl inlay, orange top finish, dark mahogany finish on back and sides, available in standard (12 1/2"),

concert (13 1/2") or grand concert (16") size

Introduced: **1902**

Discontinued: **by 1907**

Reintroduced, 13 1/2" wide, round soundhole, plain 4-ring soundhole inlay, catalog specifies multiple-bound top and single-bound peghead but virtually all with single-bound top and unbound peghead, single-support pickguard, bound back, bound ebony fingerboard, dot inlay, trapeze tailpiece, amber finish: **1924**

Discontinued: **1926**

Model number reintroduced as flat top (see Flat Tops section): **1929**

L-3: round soundhole with 3 inlaid rings of fancy colored wood, bound top, 13 frets clear of body, bound ebony fingerboard, pearl fingerboard inlay, peghead veneer with pearl inlay, orange top finish, dark mahogany back and sides finish, available in standard (12 1/2"), concert (13 1/2") or grand concert (16") size

Introduced: **1902**

13 1/2" wide, herringbone middle soundhole ring, trapeze tailpiece with pins anchored in tortoiseshell celluloid crosspiece: **1908**

Floral peghead inlay, pickguard, slanted *The Gibson* logo: **1911**

Red mahogany (slightly shaded) finish: **1914**

Red mahogany sunburst finish standard, ivory finish by special order: **1918**

Trapeze tailpiece with no pins: **1924**

Maple back and sides: **by late 1920s**

Oval soundhole: **c. 1927**

Round soundhole, checkered or diamond pattern on middle soundhole ring: **1929**

Raised fingerboard: **by 1932**

Discontinued: **1933**

L-4: 16" wide, oval soundhole, 3-ring soundhole inlay with diamond-pattern middle ring, trapeze tailpiece with pins anchored in tortoiseshell celluloid crosspiece, elevated pickguard with 2 supports, bound top and back, 12 frets clear of body, single-bound ebony fingerboard with pointed end, fingerboard extends over soundhole, pearl dot inlay, single-bound peghead, front and back peghead veneers, slanted *The Gibson* logo, black top finish

Introduced: **1912**

Solid middle ring in soundhole inlay shown in catalogs

(most examples from 1914–20 with diamond pattern), red mahogany (slightly shaded) finish standard, black or orange available by special order: **1914**

Red mahogany sunburst finish: **1918**

Diamond-pattern soundhole ring shown again in catalogs, single pickguard support, straight *The Gibson* logo: **by 1920**

Trapeze tailpiece with no pins: **1923**

Checkered outer soundhole rings, solid middle ring: **1927**

Round soundhole, 7-ply black and white soundhole ring, single-bound top and back, unbound pickguard, single-bound rosewood fingerboard with square end, 14 frets clear of body, dot inlay, unbound peghead: **by early 1928**

Unbound fingerboard, *Gibson* logo: **mid 1928**

Bound fingerboard, diamond peghead inlay: **by late 1933**

f-holes, raised diamond on trapeze tailpiece, single-bound pickguard, varied-pattern inlay beginning at 1st fret, single-bound peghead, fleur-de-lis peghead inlay, sunburst finish: **1935**

Round soundhole optional: **1937 only**

Unbound pickguard: **1937**

Natural finish optional: **1940**

Unbound peghead: **1941**

Triple-bound top and back, bound pickguard: **1946**

Double-parallelogram inlay, laminated beveled-edge pickguard, crown peghead inlay: **1947**

Discontinued: **1956**

L-4C: pointed cutaway, pointed-end tailpiece plate with 3 raised parallelograms, laminated pickguard, double-parallelogram inlay, crown peghead inlay, sunburst or natural finish: **1949–71**

L-Jr.: budget version of L-1, 13 1/2" wide, round soundhole with single black binding, trapeze tailpiece with pins anchored in tortoiseshell celluloid crosspiece, ebony fingerboard, dot inlay, amber top finish specified, most with uniform brown finish on top, back and sides

Available: **c. 1919–1926**

L-5: 16" wide, birch back, maple sides, early with Virzi Tone-Producer standard, trapeze tailpiece, triple bound top and back, triple-bound pickguard (early with unbound pickguard), single-bound ebony fingerboard with pointed end, dot inlay, triple-bound peghead, flowerpot peghead inlay,

slanted logo, 3-on-a-plate tuners, snakehead peghead narrower at top, *The Gibson* logo, silver-plated hardware, Cremona brown sunburst finish all over, *Gibson Master Model* label and Lloyd Loar signature label

Introduced: **late 1922**

Last Loar label: **Dec. 1924**

Gold-plated hardware: **1925**

Maple back and sides, triple-bound fingerboard with black line on side: **by 1925**

Straight *The Gibson* logo: **by 1927**

Last Master Model label: **1927**

Block inlay (many pearloid) beginning at 3rd fret, individual tuners: **early 1929**

Square-end fingerboard: **mid 1929**

"Advanced" body 17" wide, thin or thick X-braced top, 3/4" bridge with thin top, 1 1/4" bridge with thick top, flat plate tailpiece with engraved *L-5*, 5-ply top binding, triple-bound back, 5-ply pickguard binding, unbound *f*-holes, 25 1/2" scale, pointed-end fingerboard with 5-ply binding, block inlay beginning at 1st fret, wider (non-snakehead) peghead with 5-ply binding: **late 1934**

Bound *f*-holes: **by 1936**

Gold-plated tailpiece with silver center insert, 3 engraved diamonds on tailpiece, Grover enclosed tuners with stairstep buttons: **1937**

Wider tailpiece with small hole at bottom center for allen wrench tension adjustment, no hinge on tailpiece, natural finish optional: **1939**

Parallel top bracing, 1 standard top thickness: **mid 1939**

Some with white pearloid pickguard: **1939 only**

Discontinued: **1958**

L-5 Premier/L-5C: rounded cutaway

Introduced as **L-5P: 1939**

Renamed **L-5C: c. 1948**

Discontinued: **1982**

L-5CT: George Gobel model (built for popular comedian of the late 1950s and early '60s), thin body, 24 3/4" scale, cherry red finish, otherwise same specs as L-5C of the same period

Introduced: **Dec. 1958**

Discontinued (43 total shipped, some with "McCarty" pickguard/pickup, a few with humbucking pickups): **1961**

Reintroduced, Custom Shop model, quilted maple top, back and sides, 2 1/2" deep, 1 floating pickup,

Brazilian rosewood pickguard, fingerboard and peghead veneer: **1983 only**

L-5 '34 non-cutaway: reissue with features from c. 1934, 16" wide, parallel top braces, trapeze tailpiece, unbound *f*-holes, block inlay, Cremona brown sunburst finish, Historic Collection model: **1995–current**

L-10:
16" wide, strings loop over trapeze tailpiece, single-bound top and back, single-bound ebony fingerboard, dot inlay, nickel-plated hardware, black finish

Introduced: **1929**

First catalogued: **1931**

Single-bound top and pickguard, ornate rectangle-enclosed inlay, single-bound peghead, double-handled vase peghead inlay: **1933**

17" wide, X-braced top, raised diamond on tailpiece, black-and-white checkered binding on top, double-triangle inlay, single-bound peghead, ornate vase and curlicues peghead inlay, red mahogany sunburst finish: **late 1934**

Diamond-and-curlicues peghead inlay: **1935**

Discontinued: **1939**

L-12:
16" wide, trapeze tailpiece, single-bound top and back, bound pickguard (some early unbound), single-bound fingerboard, ornate rectangle-enclosed inlay, no inlay at 1st fret, single-bound peghead, double-handled vase and curlicues peghead inlay, gold-plated hardware, red mahogany sunburst finish

Introduced: **1930**

First catalogued: **1932**

17" wide, X-braced top, triple-bound top and pickguard, bound back, double-parallelogram inlay, triple-bound peghead, 7-piece diamond/star-shaped peghead inlay, sunburst finish: **late 1934**

Flat-plate tailpiece with cutouts: **1937**

Parallel top bracing: **mid 1939**

Single-bound pickguard, single-bound peghead, crown peghead inlay, sealed tuners, keystone tuner buttons: **1941**

Laminated beveled-edge pickguard: **1948**

Discontinued: **1955**

L-12 Premier: rounded cutaway: **1947–50**

L-7:
16" wide, trapeze tailpiece, single-bound top and back, single-bound pickguard (some early

unbound), single-bound rosewood fingerboard, varied-pattern inlay beginning at 3rd fret, single-bound peghead, fleur-de-lis peghead inlay, earliest with *The Gibson* logo, sunburst finish

Introduced: **1932**

Double-handled vase and curlicues peghead inlay: **mid 1934**

17" wide, X-braced top: **later 1934**

Ornate rectangle-enclosed inlay beginning at 1st fret: **later 1934**

Tailpiece with pointed ends and raised arrowheads: **1934**

Flat plate tailpiece with cutout (still with pointed ends), some with engraved *L-7* on tailpiece base: **1937**

Natural finish available: **1939**

Parallel top bracing: **mid 1939**

Triple-bound top, double-parallelogram inlay, crown peghead inlay: **1942**

Standard trapeze tailpiece: **by 1944**

Wood crosspiece on tailpiece, 3-on-a-plate tuners, some examples: **1943–46**

Laminated beveled-edge pickguard: **1948**

Discontinued: **1956**

TG-7: tenor: 1934–40

L-7C: cutaway, sunburst or natural finish

Introduced: **1948**

Tailpiece with pointed ends and 2 raised diamonds: **1957**

Discontinued: **1972**

L-7E and L-7CE: "McCarty" pickguard/pickup unit with 1 or 2 pickups mounted on pickguard (only models with "McCarty" pickup to have separate model designations): 1948–54

L-50:
14 3/4" wide, 17 1/2" long body, flat back (some with arched back), round soundhole (some with *f*-holes), ebony bridge, short trapeze tailpiece, pickguard glued to top, single-bound top, unbound back, dot inlay, pearl *Gibson* logo, dark mahogany sunburst finish

Introduced: **1932**

19 1/4" long, *f*-holes (some with round soundhole), standard trapeze tailpiece, bound top and back, elevated pickguard, pearl logo: **1934**

16" wide: **1935**

Arched back: **later 1935**

Tailpiece with raised diamond: **1936**

Wood crosspiece on tailpiece, 3-on-a-plate tuners, paint or decal logo, some with banner logo: **1943**

Single-bound pickguard, single-bound fingerboard, pearloid trapezoid inlay, decal logo: **c. 1946**

Laminated beveled-edge pickguard: **1949**

Discontinued: **1971**

TG-50: tenor, dot inlay throughout production: **1934–57**

L-75: 14 3/4" wide, 17 1/2" long body, flat back, maple back and sides, short trapeze tailpiece, bound top and back, dot inlay, white silkscreen logo

Introduced: **1932**

Mahogany back and sides, bound fingerboard, white pearloid fingerboard and peghead veneer, ornate rectangle-enclosed inlay, notched-diamond peghead inlay: **1933**

19 1/4" long, standard trapeze tailpiece, single-bound rosewood fingerboard, dot inlay, double-handled vase peghead inlay: **1934**

16" wide, arched back, round soundhole, elevated pickguard, 3-piece column-like peghead inlay: **1935**

Discontinued: **1939**

Super 400: 18" wide, body shape like early Style O with 12 1/2" upper bout width, figured maple back and sides, thin or thick X-braced top, 3/4" bridge with thin top, 1 1/4" bridge with thick top, triangular inlay at ends of bridge base, tailpiece with Y-shaped center section and model name on crosspiece, 7-ply top binding, triple-bound back, triple-bound *f*-holes, brown pearloid pickguard with 5-ply binding, pointed-end ebony fingerboard, triple-bound fingerboard, 24 3/4" scale, single- and double-split block inlay, 5-ply peghead binding, 5-piece split-diamond peghead inlay, 3-piece split-diamond inlay on back of peghead, model name on heelcap, engraved open-back Grover tuners, gold-plated hardware, Cremona brown sunburst finish

Introduced: **1934**

Upper bout 13 5/8" wide, 25 1/2" scale: **c. 1936**

Sealed Grover tuners optional, model name on heelcap: **c. 1937**

Stairstep tuner buttons: **1938**

Rounded Y shape on tailpiece with hole at bottom center for allen wrench tension adjustment, no hinge on tailpiece, Kluson tuners with metal keystone-shaped buttons, natural finish optional: **1939**

Parallel top bracing: **mid 1939**

Amber plastic tuner buttons: **mid to late 1939**

No model name on heelcap: **1942**

White plastic tuner buttons: **by 1947**

Rosewood fingerboard: **1949**

Ebony fingerboard: **1953**

Metal tuner buttons: **by 1957**

Discontinued: **1955**

Super 400 Premier/Super 400C: rounded cutaway, same changes as non-cutaway model

Introduced as **L Super 400P: 1939**

Renamed **Super 400C: c. 1948**

Discontinued: **1982**

'39 Super 400, reissue of non-cutaway 1939 version, Historic Collection model: **1993–current**

'39 Super 400 Premier, reissue of cutaway 1939 version, Historic Collection model: **1993–current**

Super 400 Western Sky Oval soundhole: oval soundhole, gold-plated hardware, pearl white or heritage cherry sunburst finish, Historic Collection model: **1993–95**

L-30: 14 3/4" wide, flat back, adjustable bridge, elevated unbound pickguard, single-bound top and back, dot inlay, silkscreen logo, black finish

Introduced: **1935**

Dark mahogany brown sunburst top finish, mahogany finish on back and sides: **late 1936**

Discontinued: **1943**

L-37: 14 3/4" wide, flat back, adjustable bridge, single-bound top and back, single-bound pickguard, dot inlay, red mahogany sunburst finish

Introduced: **1935**

Brown sunburst top finish, chocolate brown back and sides: **1937**

Discontinued: **1941**

L-47: 14 3/4" wide, flat back, tortoiseshell celluloid binding on top and back, white binding on pickguard, natural or sunburst finish

Available: **1940–42**

L-48: 16" wide, mahogany back and sides, mahogany top (early with spruce top), single-bound top and back, dot inlay (a few early with trapezoid), silkscreen logo, sunburst finish

Introduced: **c. 1946**

Spruce top, maple back, mahogany sides, single-ply tortoiseshell celluloid pickguard, 3-on-a-plate Kluson Deluxe tuners: **1952**
Laminated mahogany top and sides, laminated maple back specified in catalog but most with mahogany back: **by 1957**
Discontinued: **1971**

Super 300: 18" wide, triple-bound top and back, tailpiece with 3 cutouts, laminated beveled-edge pickguard, single-bound fingerboard with square end, double-parallelogram inlay, single-bound peghead, crown peghead inlay, sunburst finish
Available: **1948–55**

Super 300C, rounded cutaway: **1954–57**

NON-CATALOG SPECIALS

Black Special No. 4: L-50 size, 16" wide, black finish
Available: **1937–40**

Black Special No. 2: L-30 size, 14 3/4" wide, black finish
Available: **1937–40**

Special No. 7: 17" wide, spruce top, maple back and sides, carved back, bound pickguard, bound fingerboard with fancy inlay (fingerboard and peghead inlays vary), maple neck, sunburst finish, dealer net $38.50, limited run dealer special
Available: **Mar. 1941**

Special No. 5: L-50 size, 16" wide (no other specs available), dealer net $24.50, limited run dealer Christmas special
Available: **1940–Dec. 1941**

Special No. 3: L-30 size, 14 3/4" wide (no other specs available), dealer net $18.50, limited run dealer Christmas special
Available: **1940–Dec. 1941**

Wartime special (name unknown): 16" wide, spruce top, maple back and sides, flat back, trapeze tailpiece, single-bound top and back, large V-shaped neck, dot inlay, silkscreen logo, black finish available: **c. 1943–c. 1946**

COMMENTS

Gibson invented the archtop guitar and has remained the preeminent maker of archtops. The only vintage models more highly sought by collectors and players are those by individual makers such as D'Angelico, D'Aquisto and Stromberg, whose instruments represent refinements of such Gibson innovations as carved top and back, tone bars (and later X-braced top), fingerboard raised off top, adjustable bridge, elevated pickguard, large body size, cutaway body shape and adjustable truss rod.

Pre-1910: While of considerable interest to collectors because of their innovative design, aesthetic and artistic appeal, and great rarity, these instruments leave much to be desired for players.

1910–23: These have better playability than guitars of the earlier period. They are suitable for the styles of their period, such as ragtime, early blues and early jazz, but they do not command as much interest from players as from collectors.

1924–early 1930s: The L-5 is the first Gibson guitar of great interest to musicians as well as collectors. The early Loar-signed models, although they do not have such modern characteristics as a large body, slim neck, cutaway or high degree of ornamentation, are nevertheless exceptionally fine instruments by modern standards. The other models of the period, all with oval or round soundhole, are of less interest.

Early 1930s–World War II: This is the classic period of Gibson archtops. The *f*-hole, advanced (17" or wider) models from late 1934 onward defined what an archtop guitar is today. Except for a Loar-signed L-5, the prewar Super 400 and advanced body L-5 are the most highly sought Gibson archtops by collectors and players alike, with cutaways bringing more money than the equivalent non-cutaways and natural finish bringing more than sunburst.

1946–1950s: Postwar Gibson archtops are fine instruments, though not as highly sought as those of the classic prewar period.

1960s–1980s: Instruments from this period, while still good instruments, are not as highly regarded by players or collectors as those of earlier periods.

1990s: Reissues of the L-5 and Super 400, made by Gibson's Custom, Art, Historic division, are excellent instruments.

HARP GUITARS

Although Gibson catalogs specified maple back and sides on all harp guitars, pre-1908 instruments are virtually all made of walnut. Later instruments are made of birch.

Style R: 6 strings on neck, 6 sub-bass strings, 17 7/8" wide, scroll on upper bass bout with pearl in scroll, maple back and sides, oval soundhole, 2 soundhole rings of fancy colored wood, fixed mahogany bridge with scroll at each end, nickel-plated metal strap tailpiece described in catalog but not in catalog illustration, inlaid bridge pins, single-bound top, 25 1/2" scale, asymmetrical ebony extended fingerboard with treble-side extension, friction keys, orange top finish, dark mahogany back and sides finish

Only catalog appearance: **1902**

Style R-1: 6 strings on neck, 6 sub-bass strings, 17 7/8" wide, scroll on upper bass bout with pearl in scroll, maple back and sides, bound soundhole, 2 soundhole rings of fancy colored wood with pearl border, fixed mahogany bridge with scroll at each end, nickel-plated metal strap tailpiece described in catalog but not in catalog illustration, inlaid bridge pins, pearl and ivory rope-pattern top binding, pearl dot in scroll, 25 1/2" scale, asymmetrical ebony extended fingerboard with treble-side extension, dot inlay, friction keys, scroll on peghead, black top finish, dark mahogany back and sides finish

Only catalog appearance: **1902**

Style U-1: 6 strings on neck, 12 sub-bass strings, 21" wide, scroll on upper bass bout with pearl dot in scroll, maple back and sides, bound soundhole, 2 soundhole rings of fancy colored wood with pearl border, fixed mahogany bridge with scroll at each end, silver-plated metal strap tailpiece, inlaid bridge pins, white and green rope-pattern top binding, 27 1/4" scale, asymmetrical ebony extended fingerboard with treble-side extension, dot inlay, friction keys, scroll on peghead, bound peghead, adjustable extension rod for upright playing, black top finish, dark mahogany back and sides finish

Only catalog appearance: **1902**

Style U: 6 strings on neck, 12 sub-bass strings,

21" wide, scroll on upper bass bout with pearl dot in scroll, maple back and sides, bound soundhole, 2 soundhole rings of fancy colored wood with pearl border, fixed mahogany bridge with scroll at each end, metal strap tailpiece, nickel-plated extension bridge support, inlaid bridge pins, pearl and ivory rope-pattern top binding, pearl in scroll, 27 1/4" scale, asymmetrical ebony extended fingerboard with treble-side extension, dot inlay, friction keys, sub-bass tuners in 2-2-2-2-2-2 configuration, scroll on peghead, adjustable extension rod for upright playing (described but seldom if ever seen), black top finish, dark mahogany back and sides finish

Introduced: **1902**

6 strings on neck, 10 sub-bass strings, 2 black-and-white rope-pattern soundhole rings with solid ring in between, single-bound top and back, single-bound fingerboard, 25 1/2" scale, slanted *The Gibson* pearl logo, right-angle tuners on guitar neck, sub-bass tuners in 1-2-2-2-2-1 configuration, no extension rod for upright playing: **c. 1906**

18 1/4" wide, moveable 1-piece maple bridge with ebony saddle piece, double-trapeze tailpiece with pins mounted on tortoise grain celluloid plate: **c. 1907**

2 checkered soundhole rings with diamond-pattern ring in between, single-bound top and back, bone saddle piece for 6 strings, 24 3/4" scale, sub-bass tuners in 2-3-3-2 configuration, rounded peghead with scroll on peghead extension: **1908**

Cedar neck specified: **1911**

18 3/4" wide, elevated pickguard with 2 supports, Mexican mahogany neck, dark mahogany top finish: **1913**

Red mahogany sunburst top finish standard, golden orange or ebonized (black) by special order only: **1914**

1 pickguard support, ebony saddle piece: **1915**

Honduras mahogany neck: **1918**

Compensating adjustable bridge for 6 strings, separate bridge for sub-bass strings, no pearl in body scroll: **by early 1920s**

Discontinued from catalog: **1939**

Boehm Style: named after musician Walter Boehm, 21" wide, 30" long body (3 1/2" longer than Style U), no other specs available

Only reference: **1923**

COMMENTS

The Style U with 10 sub-bass strings is the only commonly seen Gibson harp guitar model. Although Gibson carried Style U in the catalog until 1939, it is unlikely that any were manufactured after circa 1924.

The few musicians playing harp guitars today prefer flat top instruments such as those made with the Dyer brand (see Larson Brothers section). Gibson harp guitars are interesting oddities for aesthetic, artistic and historical reasons.

FLAT TOPS KEY, 15 7/8" OR WIDER

No fingerboard inlay (cutaway body) = **Bossa Nova**
Custom inlay, fan-shaped bridge, gold-plated tuners = **Mark 99**
Inlay in shape of Harley Davidson shield logo = **Harley Davidson**
Small cross fingerboard inlay = **Chicago 35**
King's crown inlay = **Elvis Presley "King of Rock"**
Elvis Presley fingerboard inlay = **Elvis Presley Signature**
Autumn-leaf fingerboard inlay
    Jumbo body shape = **J-2000/Custom**
    Thin dreadnought shape = **CL-50 Supreme**
Angel-wing fingerboard inlay
    Angel-wing peghead inlay
        Non-cutaway = **CL-40 Artist**
        Cutaway = **CL-45 Artist Cutaway**
    Crown peghead inlay = **Dove Artist**
Cloud fingerboard inlay = **J-250 Presentation**
Floret fingerboard inlay
    Non-cutaway
        Floret peghead inlay = **CL-30 Deluxe**
        Crown peghead inlay = **Songbird Deluxe**
    Cutaway
        Jumbo body = **EC-20 Floret**
        Slim dreadnought body = **CL-35/Songbird Deluxe Cutaway**
Notched-diamond fingerboard inlay = **CL-20 Standard Plus**
Double-parallelogram fingerboard inlay
    Rounded cutaway = **EC-30/Blues King Electro/J-185 EC Cutaway**
    Non-cutaway
        Plain pickguard
            Dreadnought body shape
                Unbound fingerboard = **Southerner Jumbo, 1942-46**
                Bound fingerboard
                    Black backstripe = **Hank Williams Jr.**
                    No black backstripe
                        Sunburst = **Southerner Jumbo (SJ), 1942–72**
                        Natural = **Country-Western Jumbo** or **SJN**
                Jumbo (round) body shape = **J-185**
            Dove on pickguard = **Dove**
            Hummingbird on pickguard = **Hummingbird, 1960–73, 1984-current**
            2 white pickguards = **Folk Singer Jumbo**
    Small block fingerboard inlay = **J-160E, 1972–78**

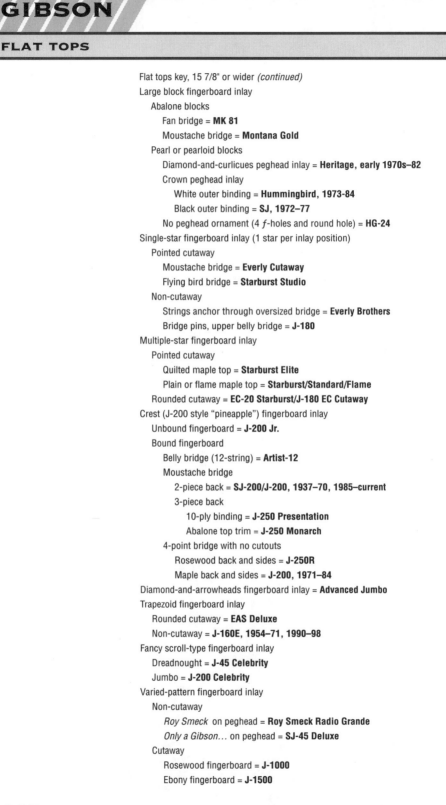

Flat tops key, 15 7/8" or wider *(continued)*
Large block fingerboard inlay
  Abalone blocks
    Fan bridge = **MK 81**
    Moustache bridge = **Montana Gold**
  Pearl or pearloid blocks
    Diamond-and-curlicues peghead inlay = **Heritage, early 1970s–82**
    Crown peghead inlay
      White outer binding = **Hummingbird, 1973-84**
      Black outer binding = **SJ, 1972–77**
    No peghead ornament (4 *f*-holes and round hole) = **HG-24**
Single-star fingerboard inlay (1 star per inlay position)
  Pointed cutaway
    Moustache bridge = **Everly Cutaway**
    Flying bird bridge = **Starburst Studio**
  Non-cutaway
    Strings anchor through oversized bridge = **Everly Brothers**
    Bridge pins, upper belly bridge = **J-180**
Multiple-star fingerboard inlay
  Pointed cutaway
    Quilted maple top = **Starburst Elite**
    Plain or flame maple top = **Starburst/Standard/Flame**
  Rounded cutaway = **EC-20 Starburst/J-180 EC Cutaway**
Crest (J-200 style "pineapple") fingerboard inlay
  Unbound fingerboard = **J-200 Jr.**
  Bound fingerboard
    Belly bridge (12-string) = **Artist-12**
    Moustache bridge
      2-piece back = **SJ-200/J-200, 1937–70, 1985–current**
      3-piece back
        10-ply binding = **J-250 Presentation**
        Abalone top trim = **J-250 Monarch**
    4-point bridge with no cutouts
      Rosewood back and sides = **J-250R**
      Maple back and sides = **J-200, 1971–84**
Diamond-and-arrowheads fingerboard inlay = **Advanced Jumbo**
Trapezoid fingerboard inlay
  Rounded cutaway = **EAS Deluxe**
  Non-cutaway = **J-160E, 1954–71, 1990–98**
Fancy scroll-type fingerboard inlay
  Dreadnought = **J-45 Celebrity**
  Jumbo = **J-200 Celebrity**
Varied-pattern fingerboard inlay
  Non-cutaway
    Roy Smeck on peghead = **Roy Smeck Radio Grande**
    Only a Gibson... on peghead = **SJ-45 Deluxe**
  Cutaway
    Rosewood fingerboard = **J-1000**
    Ebony fingerboard = **J-1500**

Dot fingerboard inlay
  Banner logo
    Round-shouldered dreadnought
      Pearl banner = **Buddy Holly**
      Silkscreen banner = **J-45, 1942–45**
    Square-shouldered dreadnought
      Non-cutaway = **J-30 Montana**
      Cutaway = **J-30C**
  Prewar script logo and model name = **Roy Smeck Stage Deluxe**
  Prewar script logo
    Unbound fingerboard
      White silkscreen logo = **J-35**
      Gold silkscreen logo = **J-45, 1942–47**
      Pearl logo
        Belly bridge = **J-60**
        Rectangular bridge = **Jumbo**
        Moustache bridge = **Jumbo Deluxe**
        Asymmetrical fan-shaped bridge
          Rosewood body = **MK-72**
          Maple body = **MK-53**
          Mahogany body
            6-string = **MK-35**
            12-string = **MK-35-12**
    Bound fingerboard
      Square-end fingerboard = **Jumbo 55, 1939–42**
      Pointed-end fingerboard = **Super Jumbo 100**
  Postwar block-letter logo
    Molded synthetic back and sides
      3-band EQ = **OP-25**
      No electronics = **J-25**
    Maple back and sides
      Double cutaway = **EAS Classic Double-Cutaway**
      Rounded cutaway
        Belly above bridge = **EAS Classic/Standard**
        Bird-and-beak bridge **= EC-10 Standard**
      Pointed cutaway = **The Star**
      Non-cutaway
        Dove on peghead = **Gospel**
        No peghead ornament
          17" wide super jumbo (rounded) shape = **J-100, 1985–97**
          16" wide jumbo (rounded) shape = **Working Musician 180**
          Square-shouldered dreadnought shape = **J-35, 1985–87**
    Rosewood back and sides
      Ebony fingerboard = **Heritage, 1965–early 1970s**
      Rosewood fingerboard
        Non-cutaway
          6-string = **Blue Ridge**
          12-string = **Blue Ridge 12**
        Cutaway = **Les Paul Jumbo**

Dot fingerboard inlay, postwar block-letter logo *(continued)*
    Mahogany back and sides
        12-string
            No peghead ornament = **JG-12**
            2-piece peghead inlay = **B45-12**
        6-string
            Jumbo shape
                Teardrop or scalloped-edge pickguard = **J-100Xtra**
                J-200-style pickguard (with points) = **J-100, 1970–74**
                Thin-shouldered dreadnought = **WM-10 Songwriter**
            Square-shouldered dreadnought
                No-pin bridge = **J-40**
                Arched back = **J-55**
                 Unbound back = **JG-0**
                Pin bridge, flat back, bound back
                    Belly above bridge = **J-30, 1985–93**
                    Belly below bridge
                        Sunburst top = **J-45, 1969–81**
                        Natural top = **J-50, 1969–81**
            Round-shouldered dreadnought
              Gold-plated tuners
                24 3/4 scale = **Formula 1-S**
                25 1/2 scale = **Formula 1-L**
              Nickel- or chrome-plated tuners
                Bird-and-beak bridge = **CL-10**
                Belly bridge
                    Sunburst top = **J-45, 1947–69, 1984–current**
                    Natural top
                        White outer binding = **J-50, 1947–69**
                        Black binding = **Working Man 45/Songbird**

FLAT TOPS KEY, 14 3/4" OR NARROWER

This key does not include classical models.

No logo, no peghead ornament = **GY (Army-Navy)**
Torch peghead ornament = **L-20 Special**
Vase-over-dot peghead ornament (prewar logo)
    Dot inlay = **L-00 Blues King**
    Block inlay = **Blues King Special**
Prewar logo or wartime banner logo, no other ornament
    Black top
        Unbound back = **L-00, 1932–mid 1930s**
        Bound back
            Spanish setup (slanted saddle) = **L-0, 1937–42**
            Hawaiian setup (straight saddle) = **HG-0**
    Argentine gray sunburst top (gold sparkle binding) = **L-2, 1931**

Natural, amber or brown-stain top (uniform finish)
    Mahogany back and sides
        Mahogany top = **L-0, 1928–33**
        Spruce top
            4 *f*-holes and round hole = **HG-20**
            Round hole
                12 frets clear of body = **L-1, 1926–28**
                14 frets clear of body
                    Teardrop (Martin-style) pickguard = **LG-3, 1942–55**
                    Pickguard follows body edge = **L-00, 1941–45**
    Maple back and sides = **L-0, 1926–28**
    Rosewood back and sides = **L-2, 1932–34**
Brown sunburst top
    Varied-pattern fingerboard inlay
        Wood fingerboard = **Nick Lucas Model**
        Celluloid fingerboard
            14 frets clear of body = **Century (L-C)**
            12 frets clear of body = **HG-Century**
    Dot inlay
        Rosewood back and sides = **L-2, 1929–30**
        Mahogany (or maple) back and sides
            No pickguard (Hawaiian setup)
                Round hole = **HG-00**
                4 *f*-holes and round hole = **HG-22**
            Teardrop (Martin-style) pickguard shape = **LG-2, 1943–47**
            Pickguard follows contour of body edge
                Black bridge pins and end pin = **L-00, 1933–45**
                White bridge pins and end pin = **L-1, 1928–37**
Pearl postwar logo
    Floret inlay = **L-130**
    Angel wing inlay = **L-140**
    Autumn leaf inlay = **L-150**
White postwar logo = **WM-00 Bluesbender/L-00, 1999–current**
Gold postwar logo
    Mahogany top = **LG-0**
    Brown sunburst top
        Cutaway
            No pickup = **CF-100**
            Pickup = **CF-100E**
        Non-cutaway
            6-string
                Straight "ladder" bracing
                    14 3/4" wide = **LG-1**
                    12 3/4" wide = **LG-2 3/4, 1949–62**
                X bracing = **LG-2, early 1947–62**
            12-string = **B-25-12**

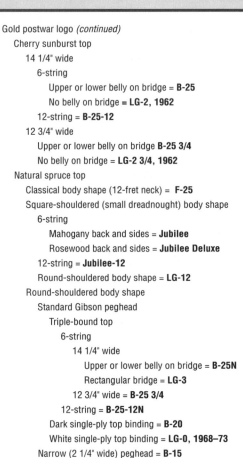

Gold postwar logo *(continued)*
Cherry sunburst top
14 1/4" wide
6-string
Upper or lower belly on bridge = **B-25**
No belly on bridge **= LG-2, 1962**
12-string = **B-25-12**
12 3/4" wide
Upper or lower belly on bridge **B-25 3/4**
No belly on bridge = **LG-2 3/4, 1962**
Natural spruce top
Classical body shape (12-fret neck) = **F-25**
Square-shouldered (small dreadnought) body shape
6-string
Mahogany back and sides = **Jubilee**
Rosewood back and sides = **Jubilee Deluxe**
12-string = **Jubilee-12**
Round-shouldered body shape = **LG-12**
Round-shouldered body shape
Standard Gibson peghead
Triple-bound top
6-string
14 1/4" wide
Upper or lower belly on bridge = **B-25N**
Rectangular bridge = **LG-3**
12 3/4" wide = **B-25 3/4**
12-string = **B-25-12N**
Dark single-ply top binding = **B-20**
White single-ply top binding = **LG-0, 1968–73**
Narrow (2 1/4" wide) peghead = **B-15**

FLAT TOPS

BODY STYLES

Gibson names

Gibson gave most 16"-wide (and larger) flat tops a J or Jumbo designation, regardless of body style.

Prior to World War II, Gibson used *super jumbo* for the 17"-wide SJ-200 and *jumbo* for all 16"-wide flat tops, regardless of body shape. In the early 1950s, the SJ designation shifted to the Southerner Jumbo dreadnought, as the SJ-200 became the J-200. The SJ-200 name was revived in the 1990s on reissues.

Gibson continued to call all 16" models *jumbo* well into the 1980s. By the 1990s Gibson had begun to use the terms that collectors use (see following), referring to 16" and 17" models with the circular lower bout as *jumbo* models and referring to traditional dreadnought-shaped models as *sloped-shouldered* or *square-shouldered.*

Collectors' names

Gibson jumbo shape refers to models with a thin waist and a circular lower bout, such as the 17" J-200 or the 16" J-185 and Everly Brothers models.

Round-shouldered dreadnought refers to models such as the Advanced Jumbo, pre-1969 J-50 or pre-1963 SJ, with a relatively flat bottom edge, a thick waist and upper bouts that appear to be more rounded or sloped than the Martin style dread-nought shape.

Square-shouldered dreadnought refers to models such as the Hummingbird and post-1963 Southerner Jumbo, with relatively square, Martin style upper bouts.

Large-bodied guitars are divided here according to collectors' terms for *jumbo* (16" or 17" inches wide) and *dreadnought*.

Dreadnought styles

Gibson has made dreadnought-size guitars in three different body styles: round-shouldered, square-shouldered and "slim" or "thin-shouldered."

	Round D	Square D	Slim D
Upper bout	11 1/2"	11 13/16"	11 7/16"
Waist	10 1/2"	11"	10 1/4"
Lower bout	16"	16"	16"
Depth at neck	3 7/8"	3 3/4"	3 7/8"
Depth at endpin	4 3/4"	4 3/4"	4 3/4"

Arched top and back: A few early flat top examples have a carved, arched back in the style of Gibson's archtop acoustic guitars. Early catalog listings specify a slightly arched top and/or back, but this description refers to a flat top or back that may be arched very slightly by the bracing. These specs are noted in model descriptions, but there is no easily discernible difference between "slightly arched" and the later flat specification. Beginning with the J-55 and Gospel models of 1973, some models have a laminated back with a noticeable arch.

Tenors and plectrums: Any standard guitar model was available with tenor or plectrum neck by special order. Only those offered as catalog models are listed here.

SORS electronics: Symbiotic Oriented Receptor System, piezo pickup, 2 knobs on upper bass bout, available on some models: **1985–89**

1994 labels: All Gibson Montana flat tops in 1994, plus some with serial numbers from late 1993, bear a label with Gibson's Centennial logo.

SECTION ORGANIZATION
Pre-WWII Models, 14 1/2" or Narrower
Hawaiians
Traditional Dreadnoughts
J-200s and Related Jumbos

Other Jumbos
Mark Series
LG and B-25 Series
Other Small-Bodied Models Introduced After WWII
Starburst, EAS and EC Models
Custom Line Thin-Shouldered Dreadnoughts
Working Musician Series
Classicals
Special Limited-Run Series

PRE-WWII MODELS, 14 1/2" OR NARROWER

Postwar reissues of prewar small-body models (L-00, Blues King, L-0, L-1, L-2, L-C and Nick Lucas) are listed with the original prewar model.

GY (Army-Navy): 13 1/2" wide, flat top version of L-Jr. archtop, slightly arched top and back, maple back and sides, maple bridge, trapeze tailpiece with pins anchored in tortoiseshell celluloid crosspiece, no binding, no logo, ebony fingerboard, dot inlay, Sheraton brown finish

Because of the GY's low-budget design, Gibson ads stated that although the GY was made by Gibson, it was "not a Gibson." Ads also recommended that the GY be set up for Hawaiian playing.

Introduced: **Dec. 1918**
Discontinued (case listed but instrument not listed): **1921**

L-1: (earlier archtop, see Gibson Acoustic Archtops section) 13 1/2" wide, circular lower bout, slightly arched top, earliest with H-pattern top bracing, maple back and sides, earliest with arched back, fixed ebony bridge with pyramids at ends, black bridge pins, 3 evenly spaced rings around soundhole, bound soundhole, 3-ply top binding (earliest single-bound), single-bound back, 12 frets clear of body, 25" scale, earliest with no truss rod, unbound ebony fingerboard with square end, dot inlay at frets 5, 7 and 9, *The Gibson* paint logo straight across peghead, light amber top finish, Sheraton brown finish on back and sides

Introduced: **1926**
Mahogany back and sides, short rosewood bridge with slight belly and straight-bevel ends, white bridge pins, extra pin below bridge pins, unbound soundhole, 1 multi-ply ring around soundhole (may vary),

single-bound top and back, unbound or bound rosewood fingerboard, dot inlay to 15th fret, brown sunburst finish: **1928**

No belly on bridge: **1929**

No extra pin on bridge: **later 1929**

14 3/4" wide, body more squared at bottom, longer modern type bridge with 2 pearl dots, 24 3/4" scale, unbound fingerboard: **by 1931**

14 frets clear of body: **1932**

Top and back not specified as slightly arched, firestripe tortoiseshell celluloid pickguard, *Gibson* logo: **1933**

Flat top and back specified: **1934**

Discontinued: **by 1937**

Reintroduced, 13 1/2" wide, circular lower bout, mahogany back and sides, ebony bridge with pyramid ends, bound top and back, 24 3/4" scale, unbound ebony fingerboard, dot inlay, *The Gibson* logo, nickel-plated tuners with metal buttons, vintage sunburst finish, limited run of 100: **1991**

Renamed **L-1 1992 Edition: 1992**

Discontinued as production model: **1993**

Reintroduced as **L-1**, same specs as 1991 model: **1994**

Last made (3 shipped): **1995**

TG-1: 4-string tenor, 12 5/8" wide, slightly arched top, mahogany back and sides, short straight-beveled rosewood bridge on large base, extra pin in bridge base, bound top and back, 23" scale, bound rosewood fingerboard with pointed end, dot inlay, peghead ornament with 4-point pattern and curlicues, thin *The Gibson* logo, sunburst finish

Introduced: **1927**

14 3/4" wide, longer modern type bridge with no extra pin, *Gibson* logo, no peghead ornament: **1930**

Unbound fingerboard, sunburst finish, other specs same as L-1: **1933**

Discontinued (1 shipped in 1938, 1 in 1940): **1937**

PG-1: plectrum neck, 26 1/4" scale (specified as 27" in catalog), otherwise same as TG-1: **1928–38**

L-1 Custom Club: prototype for L-1 1992 Edition, highly flamed maple back and sides, checkered marquetry around body, neck and peghead, pyramid bridge with faceted jewel-like inlay, antique natural finish: **1993**

L-1 International Special: Robert Johnson model, Estate Edition, pearl Robert Johnson signature on 12th fret, pearl truss rod cover, black finish, black

alligator case with Robert Johnson CD in pocket, special series for Guitar Center: **Sept. 1993–94**

L-1 Curly Maple Montana Special: curly maple back and sides, Nick Lucas style varied-pattern inlay, flowerpot peghead inlay, guitar of the month: **Feb. 1993**

L-0: 13 1/2" wide, circular lower bout, slightly arched top and back, maple back and sides, 2-and-1 soundhole ring configuration (may vary), ebony belly bridge with pyramids at ends, black pins, bound top and back, 25" scale, earliest with no truss rod, 12 frets clear of body, ebonized fingerboard, dot inlay at frets 5, 7, and 9, angled *The Gibson* silkscreen logo, amber brown finish

Introduced: **1926**

Mahogany top, back and sides, short rosewood bridge with slight belly and straight-bevel ends, black bridge pins, extra white pin below bridge pins, ebony saddle, ebonized rosewood fingerboard, dot inlay to 15th fret, ebony nut, amber finish: **1928**

No belly on bridge: **1929**

No extra pin on bridge: **1929**

14 3/4" wide, body more square at bottom, white-black-white soundhole ring, longer modern type bridge, 24 3/4" scale, unbound fingerboard: **1931**

Top and back not specified as slightly arched, 14 frets clear of body, some with *Gibson* logo: **1932**

Discontinued: **1933**

Reintroduced, spruce top, mahogany back and sides, bound top and back, black bridge pins and end pin, tortoiseshell celluloid pickguard, some with white pickguard, black finish: **1937**

Discontinued: **1942**

TG-0: 12 5/8" wide, mahogany top, back and sides, slightly arched top, short straight-beveled rosewood bridge, no bridge base, black bridge pins, 23" scale, unbound rosewood fingerboard with pointed end, thin *The Gibson* logo in silver paint, light amber finish

Introduced: **1927**

14 3/4" wide, longer modern type bridge with no extra pin, *Gibson* logo, no peghead ornament: **1930**

Discontinued: **1933**

Reintroduced (see LG-0, following): **1960**

HG-0: Hawaiian setup, straight (non-slanted) saddle, 12 frets clear of body, heavier bracing: **1937–42**

Nick Lucas Model (Gibson Special): 13 1/2"

wide, deeper than other models (4 1/2" or more at neck and endpin), mahogany back and sides, slightly arched top and back, 2 multi-ply soundhole rings, rosewood bridge with pyramids at ends, slight belly on bridge, extra pin below bridge pins, triple-bound top and back, triple-bound rosewood fingerboard, small varied-pattern inlay, 12 frets clear of body, Grover tuners with metal buttons, *The Gibson* logo, special round Nick Lucas label, sunburst finish

Most examples have serial numbers suggesting 1928 or 1929 production but have features of later versions. These should be dated according to specs rather than by serial number.

Introduced: **1928**

Larger varied-pattern inlay with notched diamond at 3rd fret, fleur-de-lis peghead inlay: **later 1928**

14 3/4" wide, 3-ply soundhole ring, rectangular bridge (no pyramids) *Gibson* logo: **1929**

Rosewood back and sides, 13 frets clear of body: **c. 1930**

Catalogued with mahogany back and sides but most are rosewood, pin bridge listed as standard, adjustable bridge and trapeze tailpiece listed as optional but most examples with adjustable bridge and trapeze, most with elevated pickguard, some with pickguard glued to top, ebony fingerboard raised off of top (catalogued with rosewood fingerboard): **1932**

Catalogued with rosewood back and sides: **1933**

Flat top and back, maple back and sides specified (some with mahogany), pickguard glued to top, 14 frets clear of body, rosewood shade sunburst finish on back and sides: **1934**

Discontinued from catalog: **1938**

Last shipped (2 instruments): **1941**

Reintroduced, rosewood, curly koa or curly maple back and sides, 14 5/8" wide, rectangular rosewood bridge, 25 1/2" scale, rosewood fingerboard, varied-pattern inlay, prewar script logo, fleur-de-lis peghead inlay, vintage sunburst finish, introduced as limited edition of 100 with label numbered and signed by Ren Ferguson: **1991**

Discontinued: **1992**

Reintroduced, flamed maple back and sides: **1999**

Still in production

1928 Nick Lucas: 1934 styling, maple back and sides: **1993–94**

'29 Nick Lucas Special: 14 3/4" wide, 1934 styling, maple back and sides: **1998**

Nick Lucas Elite: abalone trim, abalone inlay: **1999–current**

Nick Lucas Maple: maple back and sides: **1994**

Nick Lucas Rosewood Montana Special: rosewood back and sides, back of peghead painted black with brass limited edition plate: **1993–95**

L-2: (earlier archtop, see Acoustic Archtops section)

14 3/4" wide, slightly arched top and back, rosewood back and sides, short bridge with straight-beveled ends specified, most with height-adjustable bridge and trapeze tailpiece, no pickguard, triple-bound top and back, 13 frets clear of body, double-bound ebony fingerboard, dot inlay, pearl *The Gibson* logo, sunburst finish specified, most examples with natural top finish

Introduced: **June 1929**

Some with gold-sparkle binding: **1930**

Mahogany back and sides, longer modern-type pin bridge, gold-sparkle binding around top and soundhole borders, 12 frets clear of body, 6-point flame peghead inlay (resembles court jester's head), Argentine gray sunburst finish: **1931**

Flat top specified, rosewood back and sides, no sparkle trim, adjustable bridge and trapeze tailpiece (listed as optional), elevated pickguard, rosewood fingerboard raised off of top, 13 frets clear of body, *Gibson* logo, natural top finish: **mid to late 1932**

Pin bridge, no tailpiece, pickguard glued to top (some still with adjustable bridge and trapeze tailpiece): **1933**

14 frets clear of body, some with no peghead ornament: **1934**

Discontinued: **1935**

1929 L-2: Jan. 1994 Centennial model, L-00 size, rosewood back and sides, ebony vintage style bridge, gold-sparkle soundhole ring, elevated pickguard, 12 frets clear of body, ebony fingerboard, 6-point flame peghead inlay: **1994**

L-00/Blues King: 14 3/4" wide, mahogany back and

sides, bound top, unbound back, rectangular rosewood bridge, black bridge pins and endpin, dot inlay, 14 frets clear of body, *The Gibson* logo, black finish

Introduced as **L-00: 1932**

Gibson logo, some with white pickguard: **1932**

Tortoiseshell celluloid pickguard follows contour of body edge, sunburst top, red mahogany finish back and sides, black finish still available: **1933**

Bound back: **by 1937**

Black finish discontinued: **1938**

Natural finish optional: **1941**

Only a Gibson Is Good Enough peghead banner (some with white silkscreen logo in 1943), some with no truss rod: **1943**

Discontinued: **1946**

Reintroduced, mahogany back and sides, prewar style firestripe tortoiseshell celluloid pickguard follows contour of body edge, rectangular bridge, single-bound top and back, 25 1/2" scale, bound rosewood fingerboard, dot inlay, prewar script logo in cream paint, antique ebony or vintage sunburst finish: **1991**

Antique natural, antique walnut or vintage sunburst finish: **1992**

Antique ebony finish optional: **1994**

Renamed **Blues King L-00:** tortoiseshell celluloid pickguard, unbound fingerboard, prewar script decal logo, gold decal peghead ornament of 2-handled vase over dot, nickel-plated tuners with metal buttons: **1994**

Discontinued: **1997**

Reintroduced as **L-00: 1999**

Still in production

TG-00: 14 3/4" wide, rectangular bridge, 23" scale, Gibson logo, black finish

Introduced: **1932**

Unbound fingerboard, sunburst finish: **1933**

Discontinued: **1943**

PG-00: plectrum neck, 26 1/4" scale (specified as 27" in catalog), otherwise same as TG-00: **1932–37**

HG-00: Hawaiian setup, straight (non-slanted) saddle, 12 frets clear of body, heavier bracing: **1937–42**

L-00 3/4: 35 total shipped: **1938–39**

WM-00: see WM-00 Bluesbender 90, Working Musician Series, following

Blues King Special: L-00 body, 14 3/4" wide, rosewood back and sides, belly bridge, prewar style tortoiseshell celluloid pickguard follows contour of body edge, 25 1/2" scale, bound ebony fingerboard, pearl block inlay, multiple-bound top and back, bound peghead, peghead inlay of 2-handled vase

inlay over dot, prewar script logo, nickel-plated tuners with metal buttons, antique natural or vintage sunburst finish: **1994**

L-C/Century: named after Century of Progress Exposition in Chicago, 14 3/4" wide, curly maple back and sides, triple-bound top and back, triple-bound fingerboard, white pearloid fingerboard and peghead veneer, notched-diamond inlay within rosewood rectangles (some with banjo style hearts-and-flowers or wreath-pattern inlay), 14 frets clear of body, notched-diamond peghead inlay, sunburst finish on top, back and sides

Introduced: **1932**

Single-bound top and back, rosewood peghead veneer, unbound peghead, stickpin (elongated diamond) peghead inlay, black truss rod cover (rare version): **1938**

Variation: bound peghead, notched-diamond peghead inlay, pearloid truss rod cover: **1938**

L-C discontinued (3 shipped in 1940, 1 in 1941): **1939**

HG-Century: Hawaiian setup, straight-mounted saddle, 12 frets clear of body, heavier bracing: **1937–38**

L-C 3/4: 1 shipped: **1939**

1933 Century: Feb. 1994 Centennial model, curly maple back and sides: **1994**

HAWAIIANS

By 1920 Gibson offered steel guitar equipment—"nut adjuster," high saddle, steel and picks—to convert any model to Hawaiian setup. Some height-adjustable bridges in the early 1920s have a saddle with a straight bottom side so that the saddle can be turned over for Hawaiian playing. Any model could also be ordered as a Hawaiian (designated by an H after the model name). Only catalogued models are listed here.

Contrary to catalog specs for HG-series guitars, virtually all examples were set up for Spanish style play, with 14-fret neck and standard frets. Roy Smeck models were all originally Hawaiian setup with inlaid fret markers flush with the fingerboard, although many have been converted to Spanish.

HG-24: 16" wide, dreadnought shape, rosewood back and sides, inner side "wall" does not meet back of guitar, conventional round soundhole plus

4 *f*-holes, single-bound top and back, 14 frets clear of body, single-bound fingerboard elevated off top, pearloid block inlay, fleur-de-lis peghead inlay, *The Gibson* logo, natural top or sunburst finish (rare model)

HG-22: 14 1/2" wide, dreadnought shape (thick-waisted), maple back and sides, inner side "wall" does not meet back of guitar, conventional round soundhole plus 4 *f*-holes, tortoiseshell celluloid pickguard, single-bound top and back, unbound rosewood fingerboard elevated off top, 14 frets clear of body, 24 3/4" scale, white paint logo, 3-on-a-plate tuners, sunburst top finish (very rare model)

HG-20: 14 1/2" wide, dreadnought shape (thick-waisted), maple back and sides, inner side "wall" does not meet back of guitar, conventional round soundhole plus 4 *f*-holes, 14 frets clear of body, 24 3/4" scale, unbound fingerboard, dot inlay, silkscreen logo, brown finish (rare model)
HG series introduced: **by 1929**
Only catalog appearance: **1932**
Discontinued: **1933**

Roy Smeck Stage Deluxe: 16" wide, round-shouldered dreadnought shape, mahogany back and sides, single-bound top and back, pickguard follows contour of body edge, 12 frets clear of body, ivoroid fret markers flush with fingerboard, dot inlay, silkscreen model name and logo on peghead, sunburst finish
Introduced: **1934**
Varied-pattern inlay: **1938**
Discontinued: **1943**

Roy Smeck Radio Grande: (also see Roy Smeck Special, preceding) 16" wide, round-shouldered dreadnought shape, rosewood back and sides, bound top and back, bound fingerboard, 12 frets clear of body, ivoroid fret markers flush with fingerboard, varied-pattern inlay (like Nick Lucas model) with notched diamond at 3rd fret, silkscreen model name and logo on peghead, natural top finish
Introduced: **1934**
Discontinued from catalog: **1937**
Last shipped (26 instruments): **1939**

Variations
- Some with mahogany back and sides and sunburst top
- 1 example with Smeck body and L-Century style pearloid fingerboard and peghead veneer
- 1 example with short body, 14 3/4" wide, 17 1/2" long (same as Kalamazoo model KG-11), maple back and sides, ladder-braced top, rectangular bridge, straight saddle, 14 frets clear of body, Spanish style neck, pearloid fingerboard, L-Century style inlay, pearloid peghead veneer and truss rod cover, *Roy Smeck Radio Grande* stenciled on peghead, possibly Roy Smeck Special model, which appears in shipping ledgers in 1936 but specs unavailable

1934 Roy Smeck Radio Grande: rosewood back and sides, 12 frets clear of body, wide rosewood fingerboard, Nick Lucas style varied-pattern inlay, set up for standard play, high nut and high saddle included, antique natural finish: **1994**

HG-Century: Hawaiian version of L-C (see preceding)

HG-00: Hawaiian version of L-00 (see preceding)

HG-0: Hawaiian version of L-0 (see preceding)

LG-H: Hawaiian version of LG-1 (see following)

TRADITIONAL DREADNOUGHTS

Jumbo: 16" wide, round-shouldered dreadnought, mahogany back and sides, near-uniform body depth as deep as 4 1/2", rectangular bridge with no pearl dots, bound top and back, 24 3/4" scale, unbound rosewood fingerboard, dot inlay, 1 3/4" nut width, pearl logo, Grover tuners with metal buttons, sunburst finish on top, back, sides and neck
Available: **1934–35**

1934 Jumbo: Mar. 1994 Centennial model, modeled after custom-made Jumbo, rosewood back and sides, elevated pickguard, flower and leaf inlay, bound peghead, pearl logo, vintage cherry sunburst finish: **1994–95**

Trojan: 16" wide, round-shouldered dreadnought, mahogany back and sides, near-uniform body depth as deep as 4 1/2", rectangular bridge with

2 pearl dots, bound top, unbound back, 24 3/4"
scale, French heel (neck heel sharp rather than
rounded), unbound rosewood fingerboard, dot
inlay, white silkscreen logo, sunburst finish
39 made: **Oct.–Dec. 1936**

Jumbo 35: 16" wide, round-shouldered dreadnought, mahogany back and sides, rectangular
bridge with 2 pearl dots outside of bridge pins, single-bound top and back, earliest with 14 1/2 frets
clear of body, wide neck heel, 24 3/4" scale, dot
inlay, silkscreen logo, 3-on-a-plate tuners on
square-end plates, plastic tuner buttons, sunburst
top finish, red mahogany finish on back and sides
Introduced: **late 1936**
Pearl dots in bridge within width of bridge pins,
V-shaped neck: **late 1930s**
Natural finish optional, at least 2 examples with cherry
sunburst finish, at least 2 with opaque blond top
finish: **1939**
Discontinued: **1943**
Model name reintroduced on square-shouldered
dreadnought (see J-35, following): **1985**
Prewar style J-35 reintroduced, round-shouldered
dreadnought, ebony fingerboard, large pearl prewar
logo, limited edition of 250: **1995**

Advanced Jumbo: 16" wide, round-shouldered
dreadnought, rosewood back and sides, firestripe tortoiseshell celluloid pickguard, single-bound top and
back, 25 1/2" scale, bound rosewood fingerboard,
diamond-and-arrowheads inlay, unbound peghead,
vertical diamond-and-arrowheads peghead inlay,
Grover tuners with metal buttons, sunburst finish
Introduced: **late 1936**
Discontinued (2 shipped): **1940**
Reintroduced, 16 1/16" wide, rectangular Brazilian rosewood bridge, firestripe pickguard follows contour of
body edge, single-bound top and back, 25 1/2" scale,
bound Brazilian rosewood fingerboard, unbound
peghead, pearl prewar logo, nickel-plated Grover
G-98 tuners, vintage sunburst finish: **April 1990**
Antique natural finish optional: **1992–93**
Renamed **1936 Advanced Jumbo:** sunburst finish, pro-
duction limited to approximately 100 per year: **1997**
Discontinued: **1999**

Advanced Jumbo Montana Special: herringbone top
border, antique natural finish, guitar of the month:
Mar. 1993

Advanced Jumbo Curly Maple Montana Special:
curly maple back and sides, abalone top border,
guitar of the month: **Oct. 1993**

Advanced Jumbo Birdseye: birdseye maple back and
sides: **1995–96**

Montana Advanced Jumbo: rosewood back and sides,
herringbone top border, abalone inlay: **1995**

Jumbo Deluxe: 16" wide, round-shouldered
dreadnought, mahogany back and sides, moustache-shaped bridge with cutouts at bridge ends,
height-adjustable saddle bearings, 4 semi-
rectangular pearl inlays and 2 pearl dots on bridge,
single-bound top and back, unbound fingerboard,
dot inlay, pearl logo, sunburst finish
3 shipped: **1938**

Jumbo 55: 16" wide, round-shouldered dreadnought, mahogany back and sides (at least 1 with
rosewood back and sides), scalloped-edge pickguard, moustache bridge (smaller than SJ-200 or
SJ-100 bridge) with cutouts at bridge ends and 2
pearl dots, 1-piece saddle, 25 1/2" scale, bound
"coffeewood" fingerboard, dot inlay, pearl logo,
stairstep peghead shape, sunburst finish
Introduced: **1939**
Rosewood bridge with beveled edges and 3 points and 3
pearl dots, 24 3/4" scale, rosewood fingerboard, standard Gibson peghead shape (non-stairstep): **1941**
Discontinued: **1943**
Reintroduced as J-55 with different specs (see following): **1973**
Prewar style reintroduced as **J-55R LE**, rosewood back
and sides, firestripe pickguard with scalloped edge,
moustache bridge with open ends and no pearl
inlay, unbound stairstep peghead, prewar script
logo, gold-plated Grover Imperial tuners, limited
run of 250: **1995**

1940 Jumbo 55: July 1994 Centennial model, mahogany back and sides, ebony moustache bridge, scalloped pickguard, ebony fingerboard, stairstep
peghead, vintage Advanced Jumbo style (Waverly)
tuners: **1994**

J-45: 16" wide, round-shouldered dreadnought,
mahogany back and sides (some wartime with
maple back and sides, some with mahogany top),
black bridge pins, belly bridge with 2 pearl dots,

firestripe celluloid teardrop pickguard, single-bound top and back (some early with multiple binding), 24 3/4" scale, rosewood fingerboard, 20 frets, dot inlay, *Only a Gibson Is Good Enough* peghead banner, sunburst finish

Introduced: **Aug. 1942**

Some with maple back and sides, some with mahogany top, some with no truss rod: **1943–44**

Tortoiseshell celluloid teardrop pickguard, black stripe down back center seam: **1943**

Rectangular bridge: **1943**

No black backstripe: **1944**

Belly bridge: **1946**

No peghead banner: **mid 1946**

Upper belly on bridge: **by 1949**

Triple-bound top: **by 1950**

3-ply top, a few with 4-piece top: **1950 only**

Longer pickguard with point at upper bout, 20 frets: **1955**

Adjustable bridge saddle optional: **1956**

No dots on bridge: **c. 1961**

Cherry sunburst finish: **1962**

Some with screwed-down pickguard and black finish: **1968**

A few with cherry red finish: **late 1960s**

Logo on pickguard: **later 1968**

Belly below bridge: **1969**

Square-shouldered dreadnought shape, black teardrop pickguard with no logo, 25 1/2" scale: **late 1969**

Non-adjustable saddle, double-X bracing: **1970**

J-45 Deluxe on label (no change in specs): **early to mid 1970s only**

Longer pickguard with point at upper bout, 4-ply top binding with tortoiseshell celluloid outer layer, single-layer tortoiseshell celluloid back binding: **by 1975**

J-45/50: label applied to J-45 and J-50: **c. 1976 only**

White-black-white top binding: **by 1981**

Discontinued: **1982**

Reintroduced, round-shouldered dreadnought, upper belly on bridge, tortoiseshell celluloid teardrop pickguard, triple-bound top, single-bound back, 24 3/4" scale, unbound rosewood fingerboard, dot inlay, decal logo, sunburst, natural or ebony finish: **1984**

Multiple-bound top and back, antique walnut or vintage sunburst finish: **1989**

Antique ebony finish optional: **1990 only**

Vintage cherry finish optional: **1991 only**

Antique cherry, antique ebony, antique walnut or vintage sunburst finish: **1993**

Renamed **J-45 Western**: triple-bound top and back,

Only a Gibson Is Good Enough peghead banner, gold decal logo, plastic keystone tuner buttons, vintage sunburst finish: **1994**

Renamed **Early J-45**: triple-bound top, single-bound back, no peghead banner, decal logo, nickel-plated closed-back tuners with metal keystone buttons, sunburst finish: **1997**

Renamed **J-45**: **1999**

Still in production

J-45 Celebrity: rosewood back and sides, ebony bridge, 25 1/2" scale, bound ebony fingerboard, fancy abalone scroll inlay, fern peghead inlay, natural top finish, limited edition of 90, 90th anniversary label: **1985**

J-45 Custom Vine: customer-selected wood for back and sides, abalone trim, vine fingerboard inlay: **1999–current**

J-45 International Special: maple back and sides, abalone soundhole ring, rosewood fingerboard, no inlay, special series for Guitar Center: **1994**

J-45 Koa: koa back and sides, natural or vintage sunburst finish: **1992–93, 1995–96**

J-45 Montana Special: no specs available: **1996**

J-45 Rosewood: rosewood back and sides: **1995–96**

J-45 Rosewood (2nd version): rosewood back and sides, ebony fingerboard and bridge, abalone inlay: **1999–current**

J-45 Rosewood Custom: rosewood back and sides, abalone binding, ebony fingerboard and bridge, abalone inlay, bound fingerboard and peghead: **1999–current**

J-45 VS Yamano Reissue: made for Japanese distribution only, same as J-45 Yamano Special (see following) but with white plastic tuner buttons: **1996**

J-45 Yamano Special: made for Japanese distribution only, single soundhole ring, vintage style bridge with pearl dots, vintage sunburst finish: **1993**

SJ-45: see Southerner Jumbo, following

WM-45/Working Man 45: see Working Musician Series, following

Buddy Holly: based on wartime J-45, mahogany back and sides, rectangular bridge with 2 pearl dots, teardrop pickguard, triple-bound top, single-bound back, pearl logo, rosewood fingerboard, dot inlay, pearl peghead banner engraved with *Only a Gibson Is Good Enough*, nickel-plated tuners, vintage sunburst finish, production limited to 250 in 1995, 750 through 1997

Available: **1995–98**

J-50: same as J-45 except for double-bound top, natural top finish (some early possibly with sunburst top)

First shipped: **July 1942**

None shipped: **1943–44**

Production resumed: **1945**

Specs and changes same as J-45 except for:

Triple-bound top: **by 1950**

Some with laminated back (no center seam): **late 1960s**

J-45/50: label applied to J-45 and J-50: **c. 1976 only**

Discontinued: **1982**

Style reintroduced as J-45 natural, round-shouldered dreadnought, see preceding: **1984**

J-50 name reintroduced on existing J-45 natural: **1990**

Discontinued: **1995**

Limited run for Japanese distribution: **1998**

Reintroduced into regular production: **1999**

Still in production

1955 J-50: 1950s style pickguard with point at upper treble bout, 1 shipped: **1994**

J-50 Yamano: no specs available: **1996**

Southerner Jumbo/SJ/Country-Western/Hank Williams Jr.: 16 1/8" wide,

round-shouldered dreadnought, first batch (all with factory order batch number 910) with rosewood back and sides, all later with mahogany back and sides (except a few wartime with maple), rectangular bridge with 2 pearl dots, teardrop pickguard, 7-ply top binding, multiple-bound back, some with black stripe down back seam, 24 3/4" scale, unbound rosewood fingerboard, pearl double-parallelogram inlay, *Only a Gibson Is Good Enough* banner on peghead, sunburst finish

Introduced, some early with no truss rod: **Jan. 1944**

Belly below bridge, bound fingerboard, pearloid double-parallelogram inlay, no banner on peghead: **1946**

Modern decal logo: **1948**

Upper belly on bridge: **1949**

Natural finish optional: **1954**

Longer pickguard with point at upper bout: **c. 1955**

Crown peghead inlay, pearl logo: **1956**

Natural finish named **Country-Western Jumbo: 1956**

Country-Western renamed **SJN: 1960**

A few with cherry sunburst finish: **1961**

Adjustable saddle: **c. 1961**

SJN renamed **SJN Country Western: 1962**

Square-shouldered dreadnought shape, 3-point pickguard: **late 1962**

Belly below bridge: **1969**

Non-adjustable saddle: **1970**

Double-X bracing, 25 1/2" scale, teardrop pickguard: **1971**

Unbound fingerboard, small block inlay, 3-point pickguard: **1972**

4-ply binding with black outer layer on top and back, black backstripe, 2-ply fingerboard binding with black outer layer: **by 1974**

SJ and SJN Country Western discontinued (4 SJs shipped): **1978**

Reintroduced as **SJ**, round-shouldered dreadnought, mahogany back and sides, multiple-bound top and back, tortoiseshell celluloid teardrop pickguard, 24 3/4" scale, rosewood fingerboard, double-parallelogram inlay, *Only a Gibson...* peghead banner, vintage sunburst finish: **1991**

Discontinued: **1992**

Reintroduced, **1994**

Discontinued: **1995**

3 shipped: **1996**

Reintroduced as **Hank Williams Jr.:** upper belly on bridge, teardrop pickguard, multiple-bound top and back, black backstripe, single-bound fingerboard, decal logo, vintage nickel-plated tuners, vintage sunburst finish: **1997**

Renamed **Southern Jumbo: 1999**

Still in production

SJ Rosewood: rosewood back and sides, 1999 version with firestripe pickguard and *Only a Gibson...* peghead banner: **1991, 1994, 1999**

SJ-45: teardrop pickguard, 2 pearl dots on bridge, vintage sunburst finish: **1991**

SJ-45 Deluxe: abalone top border, belly bridge with 2 pearl dots, tortoiseshell celluloid teardrop pickguard, bound rosewood fingerboard, varied-pattern floral inlay, bound peghead, gold engraved pearl *Only a Gibson Is Good Enough* peghead banner, plated tuners with metal buttons, antique natural or special vintage sunburst finish: **1994–96**

SJ-45 Deluxe Special: no specs available: **1995–96**

Country Western: see Southerner Jumbo, preceding

J-40: square-shouldered dreadnought, mahogany back and sides, double-X bracing, no bridge pins, black teardrop pickguard, unbound rosewood fingerboard, dot inlay, no peghead veneer, decal logo, Kluson Deluxe tuners with keystone buttons, natural top finish, walnut back and sides finish
Introduced: **1971**
Larger pickguard with point, black peghead: **1977**
Tortoiseshell celluloid binding: **by 1981**
Discontinued: **1982**

J-55: square-shouldered dreadnought, laminated mahogany back and sides, arched back, double-X bracing, tortoiseshell celluloid pickguard with point at upper bout, tortoiseshell celluloid binding, 25 1/2" scale, rosewood fingerboard, dot inlay, Kluson Deluxe tuners with keystone buttons, pearl logo, natural top finish, walnut finish on back and sides
Introduced: **1973**
White-black-white top binding: **by 1979**
Discontinued: **1982**

J-55R LE: see Jumbo 55 (prewar model), preceding

J-160E: 16" wide, round-shouldered dreadnought, solid spruce top, laminated mahogany sides, mahogany back, ladder bracing, 1 single-coil adjustable-pole pickup at end of fingerboard, straight upper edge of pickup, point on lower edge of pickup, 2 knobs, upper belly on bridge, adjustable saddle with large adjustment knobs, 2 large dots inlaid on bridge, bound top and back, small prewar style pickguard follows contour of body edge, 24 3/4" scale, 19 frets, 15 frets clear of body, bound rosewood fingerboard, pearloid trapezoid inlay, crown peghead inlay, pearl logo, sunburst finish
Introduced: **1954**
Laminated spruce top: **1955**
20 frets: **1955**
Smaller saddle adjustment screws: **by 1960**
2 sets of soundhole rings: **1963**
Cherry sunburst finish: **mid 1960s**
Screwed-down pickguard: **1968 only**

Belly below bridge: **1969**
Square-shouldered dreadnought shape, no dots on bridge, longer pickguard with point at upper treble bout, no pickguard screws: **1969**
Non-adjustable saddle, slight extension on upper edge of pickup to meet neck, straight lower edge of pickup, teardrop pickguard: **1970**
Pickup not visible, control knobs on bridge, 4-point bridge shape, non-adjustable saddle, 3-point pickguard, small block inlay: **1972**
Discontinued: **1979**
Reintroduced as **J-160:** solid spruce top, solid mahogany back and sides, P-100 stacked-coil humbucking pickup, upper belly on bridge with no height-adjustable saddle, pickguard follows contour of body, 24 3/4" scale, 15 frets clear of body, bound rosewood fingerboard, pearloid trapezoid inlay, crown peghead inlay, pearl logo, nickel-plated tuners with plastic keystone buttons, vintage sunburst finish: **1990**
Discontinued: **1997**

J-160E Montana Special: no specs available: **1995**

J-160E Yamano Reissue: made for Japanese distribution only, laminated spruce top, adjustable bridge, P-90 pickup: **1996**

J-160E John Lennon: set of 3 models replicating Lennon's J-160E at various times in his career, limited run of 47 sets
Fab Four: sunburst finish, original early 1960s style
Magical Tour: swirl-pattern finish in purple, blue and red, pickup moved to edge of soundhole nearest bridge
Bed In: natural finish, pickup returned to original position, screw holes from pickup mounting of previous version, line drawing of John and Yoko Ono on top, Indian-pattern woven strap
Introduced: **Jan. 1998**

Hummingbird: 16" wide, square-shouldered dreadnought, mahogany back and sides, pickguard with 2 points on upper treble bout and and 1 point level with bridge, engraved hummingbird on pickguard, adjustable bridge saddle, upper belly on bridge, multiple-bound top, 24 3/4" scale, bound rosewood fingerboard, double-parallelogram inlay, crown peghead inlay, pearl logo, pearloid keystone tuner buttons, gold-plated hardware, cherry sunburst finish
Introduced: **1960**

Some with maple back and sides: **c. 1962–63**

Natural finish optional: **1963**

Some with laminated sides: **1965 only**

25 1/2" scale: **1965**

Screwed-down pickguard: **1968 only**

Belly below bridge: **1969**

Grover Rotomatic tuners with metal buttons: **1968–71**

Chrome-plated tuners: **by 1970**

Non-adjustable saddle: **1970**

Hummingbird Custom on label (no change in specs):
early to mid 1970s only

Double-X bracing, block inlay: **1971**

24 3/4" scale, returns to double-parallogram inlay: **1984**

Single-X bracing: **1985**

Belly above bridge, antique cherry or vintage sunburst finish: **by 1989**

25 1/2 scale: **1989**

Antique ebony finish optional: **1992**

Heritage cherry finish optional: **1994**

Renamed **Early '60s Hummingbird,** upper belly bridge, 6-ply top binding, 3-ply back binding, 24 3/4 scale, unbound peghead: **1997**

Renamed **Hummingbird: 1999**

Still in production

Hummingbird Custom: multi-colored inlay and engraving on pickguard, pearl peghead inlay of engraved birds and flowers, abalone logo: **1993, 1999**

Hummingbird Koa Montana Special: koa back and sides: **1993**

Hummingbird Quilted International Special: quilted maple back and sides, vintage cherry finish, special for Guitar Center: **Mar. 1993**

Hummingbird Montana Special: koa back and sides, abalone soundhole ring, guitar of the month: **Aug. 1993**

1963 Hummingbird Century: Nov. 1994 Centennial model, maple back and sides, holly peghead veneer, heritage cherry sunburst finish: **1994–1995**

Hummingbird Montana Special: no specs available: **1995–96**

Songbird: see Songwriter Dreadnought, Working Musician Series, folllowing: **1999–current**

B-45-12: 12-string, 16 1/4" wide, round-shouldered dreadnought, mahogany back and sides, rectangular bridge with adjustable ebony saddle, trapeze tailpiece, long pickguard with point at upper bout, triple-bound top, single-bound back, 24 3/4" scale, unbound rosewood fingerboard, dot inlay, fingerboard 2" wide at nut, pearloid peghead inlay of vertical double-triangle with rounded points, Kluson Deluxe tuners with white plastic buttons, cherry sunburst finish

Introduced: **1961**

Square-shouldered dreadnought, 16" wide, upper belly on bridge, bridge pins, natural top (**B-45-12N**) optional: **1962**

Upper belly on bridge, no bridge pins, no tailpiece: **c. 1963**

Upper belly on bridge, trapeze tailpiece: **c. 1965**

Pearl peghead inlay with pointed ends: **by mid 1960s**

Rectangular bridge, trapeze tailpiece: **1966**

Belly below bridge with pins, no tailpiece: **1970**

12 frets clear of body: **early 1970s**

Discontinued: **1979**

Reintroduced, rosewood back and sides, upper belly bridge, antique cherry, vintage sunburst or natural finish: **1991**

Antique ebony finish optional: **1993**

Natural finish discontinued: **1994**

Discontinued: **1995**

Dove: 16 1/4" wide, square-shouldered dreadnought, maple back and sides, tune-o-matic bridge, abstract dove-shaped inlays on bridge ends, pickguard with 2 points toward bridge and 1 toward upper treble bout, pearl dove inlay on pickguard, multiple-bound top and back, 25 1/2" scale, bound rosewood fingerboard, double-parallelogram inlay, unbound peghead, crown peghead inlay, pearl logo, Grover Rotomatic tuners, cherry sunburst or natural finish

Introduced: **1962**

Grover tuners with metal keystone buttons: **1965**

Some with laminated back and sides: **1965**

Screwed-down pickguard: **1968 only**

Grover Rotomatic tuners: **1968**

Belly below bridge, adjustable saddle: **1969**

Non-adjustable bridge saddle: **1970**

Dove Artist on label (no change in specs): **early to mid 1970s only**

Double-X bracing: **1971**

Ebony fingerboard: **1975**

Single-X bracing: **1984**

Antique cherry, ebony or vintage sunburst finish: **1986**

Antique natural, alpine white or vintage sunburst finish: **1987**

Antique cherry or vintage sunburst finish: **1988**

Antique ebony finish optional: **1991**

Gold-plated tuners with metal keystone buttons, heritage cherry finish optional: **1994**

Renamed **'60s Dove:** 6-ply top binding, 3-ply back binding, 25 1/2" scale, unbound peghead: **1997**

Renamed **Dove: 1999**

Still in production

Dove Artist: continuation of CL-40 Artist (see following), slim-dreadnought body, rosewood back and sides, ebony belly bridge, multiple-bound top, triple-bound back, ebony fingerboard, abalone angel wing inlay, crown peghead inlay, gold-plated tuners: **1999–current**

Dove Artist Cutaway: rounded cutaway: **1999–current**

Dove Custom Club: quilted maple back and sides, abalone top border, vine inlay in fingerboard, doves in flight on peghead and bridge, bound peghead: **1993**

Dove Rosewood: rosewood back and sides: **1993**

Dove Montana Special: rosewood back and sides, pearl top border, pearl truss rod cover, back of peghead painted black with limited edition brass plate, guitar of the month: **Apr. 1993**

Dove Rosewood International Special: rosewood back and sides, pearl soundhole ring, pearl top border, vintage cherry finish, special series for Guitar Center: **Aug. 1994**

Dove Commemorative: antique cherry or heritage cherry finish: **1994–96**

Dove Montana Special: no specs available: **1995–96**

Dove in Flight: highly figured maple back and sides, 3-piece maple neck with 1960-style slim profile, bound rosewood fingerboard, pearl double-parellogram inlay, pearl peghead inlays of 4 flying doves, gold-plated tuners with metal keystone buttons, enhanced antique cherry finish, natural top, limited run of 200, certificate of authenticity included, serial number configuration DF + 5 digits: **1996**

New Doves in Flight: similar to Dove in Flight, customer-selected wood for back and sides: **1999**

Folk Singer Jumbo (FJN): 16 1/4" wide, square-shouldered dreadnought, mahogany back and sides, belly above bridge, straight-mounted saddle, double white pickguards, multiple-bound top, 24 3/4" scale, 12 frets clear of body, bound fingerboard, 2" nut width, double-parallelogram inlay, crown peghead inlay, pearl logo, natural top finish, deep red finish on back and sides

Available: **1963–67**

Heritage: 16 1/4" wide, square-shouldered dreadnought, solid rosewood back and sides, ebony bridge with upper belly, adjustable ebony saddle, elongated teardrop pickguard of tortoiseshell celluloid, tortoiseshell celluloid binding on top and back, 25 1/2" scale, unbound ebony fingerboard, dot inlay, no peghead ornament, decal logo, natural top

Introduced: **1965**

Laminated rosewood back and sides, black pickguard, multiple-bound top and back with white outer layer, diamond-and-curlicues peghead inlay: **1968**

Belly below bridge: **1969**

Non-adjustable saddle: **1970**

Double-X bracing: **1971**

Black outer binding: **by 1975**

White outer binding, Gibson/Schaller tuners: **1979**

Discontinued: **1982**

Heritage-12: 12-string, rectangular ebony bridge with no pins, trapeze tailpiece, metal tuner buttons: **1968–70**

Heritage Custom: solid rosewood back and sides, large ebony bridge with pointed ends and curlicue inlays, ivory saddle, dark body binding, ebony fingerboard, pearl block inlay: **c. 1972**

Heritage Deluxe: specs unavailable, 2 shipped: **1968**

Blue Ridge: 16 1/4" wide, square-shouldered dreadnought, laminated back and sides with rosewood outer layer and maple inner, upper belly on bridge, adjustable rosewood saddle, black teardrop pickguard, bound top and back, 25 1/2" scale, rosewood fingerboard, dot inlay, decal logo, no peghead ornament, metal tuner buttons, walnut stain finish on peghead

Introduced: **1968**

Belly below bridge: **1969**

Non-adjustable saddle: **1970**

Oval low-impedance pickup optional (1 shipped): **1973**
Discontinued: **1979**
Reintroduced, round-shouldered dreadnought, triple-
bound top, double-parallelogram inlay: **1989**
Discontinued: **1990**

Blue Ridge-12: 12-string, 12 frets clear of body:
1970–78

Les Paul Jumbo: 16 1/4" wide, square-shouldered dreadnought with rounded cutaway, rosewood back and sides, oval low-impedance pickup,
4 knobs, belly below bridge, backstripe, 19 frets,
dot inlay, decal logo
Introduced: **1969**
Catalogued with maple back and sides: **1971**
Discontinued: **1973**

JG-0: square-shouldered dreadnought, mahogany
back and sides, bound top, unbound back, dot
inlay, decal logo, natural top finish
Available: **1970–72**

JG-12: 12-string version of JG-0: **1970**

Bossa Nova: classical electric, 16 1/4" wide, dreadnought size and shape, single cutaway, rosewood
back and sides, ceramic piezo bridge pickup, height-
adjustable bridge, flat rosewood fingerboard, no
inlay, slotted peghead with wriggle-edge top
Available, 7 listed on shipping records: **1971–73**

Gospel: 16 1/4" square-shouldered dreadnought,
double-X bracing, arched back, laminated maple
back and sides, ebony belly bridge, long tortoiseshell celluloid pickguard with point at upper bout,
4-ply top binding with tortoiseshell celluloid outer
layer, single-layer tortoiseshell celluloid back binding, 25 1/2" scale, ebony fingerboard, dot inlay, flying dove decal on peghead, chrome-plated tuners
with metal keystone buttons, natural finish
Available: **1973–79**
Reintroduced, arched back, laminated mahogany back
and sides, upper belly bridge, teardrop pickguard,
multiple-bound top and back, unbound rosewood
fingerboard, dot inlay, nickel-plated tuners with
plastic keystone buttons, flying dove decal on peghead, decal logo, antique natural or vintage sunburst finish: **1992**
Rosewood belly bridge, prewar style tortoiseshell

celluloid pickguard follows contour of body edge,
2-handled vase over dot decal on peghead, prewar
script decal logo, plastic keystone tuner buttons,
antique natural, vintage sunburst or antique walnut
finish: **1994**
Blue or red finish optional: **1995**
Discontinued: **1997**

Gospel Montana Special: no specs available: **1996**

J-25: 16 1/4" wide, round-shouldered dreadnought,
laminated spruce top, molded synthetic back and
sides, tortoiseshell celluloid teardrop pickguard,
rosewood belly bridge, multiple-bound top with
dark outer layer, 24 3/4" scale, unbound rosewood
fingerboard, dot inlay, pearloid keystone tuner buttons, decal logo, natural or sunburst top finish
Available: **1983–85**

J-35: 15 15/16" wide, square-shouldered dreadnought, maple back and sides, upper belly on bridge,
tortoiseshell celluloid teardrop pickguard, bound top
and back, 3-piece maple neck, 25 1/2" scale,
unbound rosewood fingerboard, dot inlay, decal
logo, nickel-plated hardware, cherry sunburst finish
Available: **1985–86**

J-35 reissue: reissue of prewar Jumbo 35, see
preceding: **1995**

J-30: 15 15/16" wide, square-shouldered dreadnought, mahogany back and sides, upper belly on
bridge, tortoiseshell celluloid teardrop pickguard,
bound top and back, 24 3/4" scale, unbound rosewood fingerboard, dot inlay, decal logo, nickel-
plated tuners with plastic keystone buttons, antique
white, wine red or vintage cherry sunburst finish
Introduced: **1985**
Antique ebony, antique walnut with natural top or vintage sunburst finish: **1989**
Pearl logo: **1993**
Renamed **J-30 Montana**, *Only a Gibson Is Good
Enough* peghead banner: **1994**
Discontinued: **1997**

J-30 Cutaway: rounded cutaway, upper belly on bridge,
tortoiseshell celluloid teardrop pickguard, multiple
bound top and back, unbound rosewood fingerboard, dot inlay, *Only a Gibson Is Good Enough* banner decal, gold decal logo, plastic keystone tuner

buttons, antique walnut or sunburst finish Available: **1990–95**

J-30 Koa: koa back and sides: **1995**

J-30 Mahogany Top: all-mahogany body: **1992**

J-30 Montana Special: no specs available: **1995**

J-30 Rosewood: rosewood back and sides: **1992–93, 1995–96**

J-30 Western: no specs available: **1994**

J-60: 16" wide, square-shouldered dreadnought, rosewood back and sides, ebony bridge with lower belly, tortoiseshell celluloid teardrop pickguard, 2 soundhole rings in groups of 3 and 7, multiple-bound top, triple-bound back, 25 1/2" scale, unbound ebony fingerboard, no inlay, pearl dot markers on side of fingerboard only, pearl prewar script logo, nickel-plated tuners with metal buttons, antique natural or vintage sunburst finish
Introduced: **1992**
Vintage sunburst finish optional: **1995**
Renamed **J-60 Traditional** (catalogued with thin-shouldered dreadnoughts in CL Custom Line but not a thin dreadnought), dot inlay, pearl prewar script logo, gold-plated tuner buttons: **1997**
Discontinued: **1999**

J-60 12-string: vintage sunburst: **1992**

J-60 Curly Maple, Montana Special: curly maple back and sides, back of peghead painted black with brass limited edition plate: **1993, 1996**

J-60 Maple International Special: maple back and sides, special series for Guitar Center: **1993–94**

J-60 Montana Special: curly maple back and sides, tortoiseshell celluloid binding, guitar of the month: **May 1993**

OP-25: round-shouldered dreadnought, molded fiberglass back (left over from J-25, see preceding), model name derives from "oil pan" look of fiberglass back, dot inlay, transducer pickup, 3-band EQ control
Approximately 200 made: **late 1991–early 1992**

Chicago 35: round-shouldered dreadnought, mahogany back and sides, rectangular bridge, prewar style tortoiseshell celluloid pickguard follows contour of body edge, unbound rosewood finger-board, small cross inlays, unbound peghead, 2-handled-vase over dot silkscreened on peghead, gold prewar script decal logo, nickel-plated tuners with metal buttons, antique natural or special vintage sunburst finish
Available: **1994–95**

Formula 1-S: round-shouldered dreadnought, arched back of laminated mahogany, rosewood fingerboard, 24 3/4" scale, dot inlay, pearl logo, gold-plated hardware, satin (non-gloss) finish

Formula 1-L: 25 1/2" scale
Approx. 100 of each model produced: **1996**

J-200s and Related Jumbos

Super Jumbo/J-200: 16 7/8" wide, rosewood back and sides (at least 1 with maple back and sides), double-X bracing pattern, large moustache-shaped ebony bridge with cutouts at bridge ends, 4 pearl ribbon inlays on bridge, height-adjustable individual saddle bearings, pickguard with engraved flower motif, multiple-bound top and back, maple neck, 25 1/2" scale (earliest with 26" scale), single-bound ebony fingerboard with pointed end, crest ("pineapple") inlay, triple-bound peghead, crown peghead inlay, stairstep tuner buttons, strap-fastening bracket on back of peghead and at endpin, gold-plated hardware, sunburst finish
Prototypes, some labeled L-5 Spec., varying specs: **1937**
First **Super Jumbo** shipped: **Aug. 1938**
Renamed **Super Jumbo 200**, 17" wide, center-stripe marquetry on back: **1939**
1-piece saddle, rosewood fingerboard, pearloid keystone tuner buttons: **1941**
Single-X bracing: **1942**
Catalogued as **J-200** (labeled **SJ-200** into early 1950s), maple back and sides, single-bound peghead, no strap brackets: **1947**
Natural finish optional: **1948**
5" deep: **by 1950s**
At least 1 with rosewood back and sides: **mid 1950s**
Grover Rotomatic tuners with oval buttons: **1959**
Adjustable bridge saddle optional: **1960**
Tune-o-matic bridge, 4 pearl inlays in bridge cutouts (in addition to previous inlays): **1961**
Keystone tuner buttons: **1963**
Grover Rotomatic tuners: **1968**

Height-adjustable saddle (not tune-o-matic) standard: **1969**

No pearl dots on bridge: **by 1970**

Ebony fingerboard: **by 1971**

J-200 Artist on label (no change in specs): **early to mid 1970s only**

Bridge with points at 4 corners (no moustache ends) and pearl curlicue inlays below pins, non-adjustable saddle: **1970**

Rosewood fingerboard: **1979**

Moustache bridge with 1 cutout at each end and 2 pearl ribbon inlays below pins, multiple-bound peghead: **1985**

2 inlays below pins (none above), antique ebony, natural or vintage sunburst finish: **1989**

4 3/4" deep: **by 1990s**

Custom cherry finish optional: **1990–91**

Antique cherry finish optional: **1992**

Antique cherry, antique ebony, natural, custom cherry or vintage sunburst finish: **1994**

4 pearl ribbon inlays on bridge: **1995**

Renamed **'50s Super Jumbo 200: 1997**

Renamed **SJ-200 Reissue**, flamed maple back and sides, Madagascar rosewood fingerboard, 1950s styling: **1999**

Still in production

'38 SJ-200: May 1994 Centennial model, maple back and sides, ebony moustache bridge, height-adjustable individual saddle bearings, prewar pickguard with multi-colored celluloid dots, multiple-bound fingerboard, white-bordered truss rod cover, antique natural finish, available: **1994–95**

'48 SJ-200N: August 1994 Centennial model, highly figured maple back and sides, rosewood bridge, white-bordered truss rod cover, antique natural finish, available: **1994**

1952 J-200: no specs available: **1994**

1952 J-200 Reissue Montana Special: eastern curly maple back and sides, prewar style bridge, Imperial (stairstep) tuners, guitar of the month: **June 1993**

J-200 12-string: solid (non-cutout) moustache bridge with 4 pearl inlays filling ends of moustache, ebony fingerboard, double-crest peghead inlay, gold-plated tuners with metal buttons, antique natural finish: **1990–96**

J-200 Birdseye: birdseye maple back and sides, limited edition of 250: **1995**

J-200 Celebrity: rosewood back and sides, smaller pickguard with no engraving, mahogany neck, bound ebony fingerboard, ornate scroll-type inlay, fern peghead inlay, limited edition of 90, 90th anniversary label

Prototype **J-200 Elite** made for John Denver: **1984**

J-200 Celebrity introduced: **1985**

Standard J-200-type pickguard: **1986**

Discontinued: **1987**

J-200 Commemorative: antique natural finish (no other specs available): **1990–95**

J-200 Custom: tree-of-life fingerboard inlay and peghead inlay: **1993**

J-200 Custom Cherry: cherry finish: **1995–96**

J-200 Custom Club: based on Ray Whitley's late-1930s J-200, Brazilian rosewood back and sides, 9-ply binding plus purfling on top and back, 5-ply binding on fingerboard, pearl block inlay engraved with Western scenes, *Ray Whitley* on peghead, 37 made: **1994–95**

J-200 Deluxe Maple: maple back and sides, 4 abalone bridge inlay ribbons, abalone pearl border on top and back, tortoiseshell celluloid pickguard with pearl inlay, ebony fingerboard, abalone fingerboard inlay, gold-plated Grover Imperial tuners, vintage sunburst or antique natural: **1994–95**

J-200 Deluxe Rosewood: rosewood back and sides, 4 abalone bridge inlay ribbons, abalone top border, ebony fingerboard, abalone fingerboard inlay, gold-plated Grover Imperial tuners, vintage sunburst or antique natural: **1993–96**

J-200 Elite: flamed maple back and sides, ebony fingerboard and bridge, abalone inlay: **1999–current**

J-200 International Special: abalone soundhole ring, Grover Imperial tuners, vintage cherry finish, special for Guitar Center: **Jan. 1994**

J-200 Koa: koa back and sides, antique natural finish Available: **1991–93**

Reintroduced, abalone inlay, gold-plated Imperial (stairstep) tuners, limited edition of 250: **1995**

J-200 Koa Custom Club: guitar of the month model, koa back and sides: **1993**

J-200 Koa International Special: koa back and sides, abalone inlay, *International Collectors Series* on brass plate, brass truss rod cover, green felt case lining with pink insert under peghead, special for Guitar Center: **Oct. 1993–94**

J-200 Koa Montana Special: koa back and sides, abalone top border, abalone soundhole ring, abalone inlay on fingerboard, peghead and bridge, Imperial (stairstep) tuners, back of peghead painted black with limited edition brass plate, guitar of the month: **Dec. 1993**

J-200 Montana Special: no specs available: **1996**

J-200 Quilted: quilted maple back and sides, sunburst or natural finish: **1995–96**

J-200 Rose: Dec. 1994 Centennial model, based on Emmylou Harris' J-200 customized by Danny Ferrington, rose pickguard, gold-plated tuners, ebony finish: **1994–95**

J-200 Rose Gold: ebony fingerboard, gold pearl inlay on fingerboard, peghead and bridge: **1995**

J-200 Rosewood: rosewood back and sides: **1991**, **1994–96**

J-200 Rosewood Montana Special: rosewood back and sides, prewar style bridge, Imperial (stairstep) tuners, gold-plated hardware, back of peghead painted black with gold-plated limited edition plate, guitar of the month: **Jan. 1993, 1995**

J-200 Special International Special: rosewood back and sides, pearloid peghead veneer and pickguard, gold-plated truss rod cover, Imperial (stairstep) tuners, special for Guitar Center: **July 1993–94**

J-200 Yamano Reissue: made for Japanese distribution only, 4 ribbon inlays in bridge, larger floral pattern on pickguard: **1996**

SJ 200: vintage sunburst finish, 1950s specs, limited run of 100: **1991**

Western Classic SJ-200: rosewood back and sides, double-bound top and back, historic inlay: **1999–current**

SJ-200 Custom Vine: customer-selected wood for back and sides, vine fingerboard inlay: **1999–current**

Montana Gold: J-200 body, maple back and sides, ebony moustache bridge with 4 pearl ribbon inlays, pickguard engraved with model name and wheat, multiple-bound top and back, maple neck, bound ebony fingerboard, pearl block inlay, bound peghead, engraved pearl peghead inlay of model name on banner around sheaf of wheat, Custom Shop peghead logo, gold-plated Imperial (stairstep) tuners, Montana harvest gold finish, limited run of 200, serial number configuration MG + 5 digits: **1996**

Elvis Presley Signature: modeled after Elvis' oldest J-200, abstract pickguard design, *Elvis Presley* and 2 stars inlaid on fingerboard, gold-plated keystone tuners, antique natural finish, limited run of 250
Introduced: **1996**

Elvis Presley "King of Rock": J-200, black pickguard with king's crown inlay, ebony bridge, ebony fingerboard with king's crown inlays, king's crown peghead inlay, limited run of 250
Introduced: **1996**

Ron Wood J-200: double pickguards, gold pearl and abalone inlay, pearl signature inlay on peghead, first 100 labels signed, limited edition
Introduced: **1997**

J-200 Jr.: 16" wide, maple back and sides, moustache bridge with cutouts and 2 pearl ribbon inlays, multiple-bound top and back, 25 1/2" scale, unbound rosewood fingerboard, crest ("pineapple") inlay, crown peghead inlay, pearl logo, nickel-plated tuners, antique ebony, natural or custom cherry finish
Introduced: **1991**
Vintage sunburst finish optional: **1993**
Discontinued: **1996**

J-200 Jr. 12-string: antique ebony, natural or vintage sunburst finish, available: **1992–93**

J-200 Jr. Custom Club: koa back and sides, Christmas tree sparkle binding, mother-of-pearl and abalone inlay on fingerboard and peghead: **1993–1994**

J-200 Jr. International Special: rosewood back and sides, J-2000 style marquetry, mahogany neck, white-black-white fingerboard binding, special for Guitar Center: **Apr. 1993**

J-200 Jr. Koa: koa back and sides, antique natural finish: **1991–92**

J-200 Jr. Rosewood: rosewood back and sides, antique natural or vintage sunburst finish: **1991–92**

J-250R: same as J-200 but with rosewood back and sides
20 shipped: **1972–78**

J-250 Presentation: Schmetterling spruce top with bear claw pattern, flamed maple back and sides, 3-piece back, 10-ply binding on top and back, checkered marquetry, bound pickguard does not come to a point, 5-ply binding on pickguard, fossilized mammoth bone saddle, endpin and bridge pins, square neck heel, triple-bound fingerboard, cloud inlay, triple-bound peghead on front and back, pearl stairstep tuner buttons, limited edition of 101
Available: **1995–96**

J-250 Monarch: 3-piece Brazilian rosewood back, abalone trim all around, engraved gold-plated tuners, ebony fingerboard and bridge, king's crown inlay of pearl and abalone, volute on back of neck, abalone truss rod cover
Available: **1995–98**

J-250 Monarch Custom: antique natural finish, 1 with special sunburst finish (no other specs available): **1994–95**

J-1000: rounded cutaway, rosewood back and sides, rosewood moustache bridge, herringbone top border, bound rosewood fingerboard, Nick Lucas style varied-pattern inlay, bound peghead, gold-plated tuners, vintage sunburst finish
Introduced: **1992**
Antique natural finish optional: **1993**
Discontinued (1 made): **1994**

J-1500: rounded cutaway, rosewood back and sides, abalone soundhole ring, checkered marquetry, bound ebony fingerboard, abalone Nick Lucas style varied-pattern inlay, abalone fleur-de-lis

peghead inlay, gold-plated tuners, antique natural or vintage sunburst finish
Available: **1992**

J-2000/Custom: maple back and sides (**J-2000M**) or rosewood back and sides (**J-2000R**), gold-plated tuners, antique natural or Alpine white finish (no other specs available)
Available: **1986**
Reintroduced, 17" wide, rounded cutaway, rosewood back and sides, abalone top border, abalone sound-hole ring, ebony flying bird bridge with abalone angel-wing inlays, 25 1/2" scale, bound ebony fingerboard, abalone angel-wing inlay, bound peghead, angel-wing peghead inlay, prewar script logo, gold-plated tuners, antique natural or vintage sunburst finish: **1992**
Renamed *J-2000 Custom*: **1993**
Discontinued (2 shipped): **1996**
Reintroduced as **J-2000 Custom Cutaway: 1999**
Still in production

OTHER JUMBOS

Super Jumbo 100: 17" wide, mahogany back and sides, scalloped-edge pickguard, large moustache-shaped bridge with cutouts at bridge ends, height-adjustable individual saddle bearings, 2 pearl dots on bridge, wide triple-binding on top, single-bound back, backstripe, maple neck, scale length almost 26", bound ebony fingerboard with pointed end, dot inlay, pearl logo, stairstep peghead shape, sealed-back Kluson tuners with butterfly buttons, sunburst finish
Introduced: **1939**
Rosewood bridge with beveled edges and 3 points and 3 pearl dots, 1-piece saddle, standard Gibson peghead, round tuner buttons: **1941**
Discontinued: **1943**
Reintroduced with different specs (see J-100, following): **1985**

1939 SJ-100: June 1994 Centennial model, mahogany back and sides, ebony moustache bridge, scalloped pickguard, bound ebony fingerboard, stairstep peghead, Grover Imperial tuners, vintage sunburst finish: **1994**

J-185: 16 1/4" wide, 5 1/4" deep, maple back and sides, upper belly on bridge, 2 Maltese-cross inlays

on bridge, triple-bound top and back, 24 3/4" scale, single-bound rosewood fingerboard, double-parallelogram inlay, crown peghead inlay, gold-plated hardware, natural or sunburst finish
Introduced: **1951**
4 15/16" deep: **by 1955**
Discontinued (28 natural shipped): **1958**
Reintroduced, 25 1/2" scale, mahogany neck with shaded finish on first run only, non-shaded neck finish thereafter on examples with natural top finish, chrome-plated hardware: **1990**
Reintroduced, antique natural, vintage sunburst: **1990**
Produced in limited run of 100: **1991**
Discontinued: **1995**
Reintroduced: **1999**
Still in production

1951 J-185: Oct. 1994 Centennial model, maple back and sides, Maltese cross inlays on bridge, smaller peghead, holly peghead veneer, small crown peghead inlay: **1994–95**

J-185 EC Cutaway: continuation of EC 30 Blues King Electro (see following): **Jan. 1999–current**

J-185 Koa: koa wood body, 6 with Nick Lucas style fingerboard inlays and snowflake inlay on bridge ends: **1991–94**

J-185 Reissue International Special: highly figured maple back and sides, antique cherry back and sides finish, natural top finish, special for Guitar Center: **May 1993**

J-190 EC Cutaway: continuation of EC 20 Blues King Electro (see following), block inlay, crown peghead inlay, onboard electronics: **Jan. 1999–current**

Everly Brothers/J-180: 16 1/4" wide, 4 3/8" deep, maple back and sides, oversized bridge with 3 pearl dots, strings anchor through bridge (no pins), adjustable saddle, double tortoiseshell celluloid pickguards extend below bridge, 24 3/4" scale, single-bound rosewood fingerboard, star inlay, star peghead inlay, black finish
Introduced as **Everly Brothers: late 1962**
Natural top with red back and sides optional (46 shipped): **1963 only**
Natural top standard (no black), walnut stain back and sides, black pickguards, pickguards do not extend below bridge: **1968**

4 3/4" deep: **by 1970**
Discontinued: **1972**
Reintroduced as **J-180**, non-adjustable saddle, double oversized pickguards (at least 1 example with single teardrop pickguard), rosewood bridge with upper belly, black finish: **1986**
Thinner pickguards: **1989**
Nickel-plated tuners, antique ebony finish: **1989**
Discontinued: **1991**
Reintroduced as **Everly Bros**: **1992**
Cherry finish optional: **1993**
Renamed **The Everly:** moustache bridge with 6 stars below pins, star on peghead, bound peghead, Grover tuners, antique ebony or heritage cherry finish: **1994**
Renamed **J-180:** 5-ply top binding, 3-ply back binding, moustache bridge with no star inlays, gold-plated tuners, ebony finish only, first 100 labels signed by Don Everly: **1996**
Upper belly bridge: **1997**
Still in production

Everly Cutaway: pointed cutaway, Accu-voice pickup system, double pickguards with points at upper and lower ends, rosewood moustache bridge with 6 stars, gold-plated Grover tuners, antique ebony finish (pictured with cherry sunburst): **1994–96**

J-180 '50s Reissue Montana Special: no specs available: **1993–94**

J-180 Artist: rosewood moustache bridge (J-100 style), tortoiseshell celluloid binding on top, back and fingerboard, rosewood fingerboard, gold pearl inlay, black-white-tortoiseshell celluloid binding on peghead, gold pearl star peghead inlay, antique ivory finish: **1993**

J-180 Artist Montana Special: tortoiseshell celluloid binding on top, back, fingerboard and peghead, gold pearl inlay, guitar of the month: **Nov. 1993**

J-180 EC Cutaway: continuation of EC-20 Starburst (see following), crown peghead inlay: **Jan. 1999–current**

J-180 International Special: pinless bridge, pearloid pickguard, J-200 binding and soundhole ring, ebony fingerboard, pearloid peghead veneer, Grover Imperial tuners, black finish, limited edition brass plate on back of peghead, special series for Guitar Center: **Nov. 1993**

J-180 Montana Special: reissue of original Everly Brothers, thick pickguards, pinless bridge, guitar of the month: **July 1993**

J-180 Yamano Special: pinless bridge with adjustable saddle, upside-down star inlay at 17th fret, grayburst finish: **1992–93**

Working Musician J-180: single-pickguard, dot inlay, gloss top finish only: **1999–current**

Artist-12: 17" wide, maple back and sides, oval hole, belly bridge, elevated maple pickguard follows contour of body edge, multiple-bound pickguard, multiple-bound top and back, backstripe marquetry, pearloid heel cap, 5-piece neck, 12 frets clear of body, bound rosewood fingerboard with pointed end, 17 frets, J-200-type crest ("pineapple") inlay, large crown peghead inlay, pearl logo, sunburst or natural finish

1 instrument shipped: **1970**

J-300 Artist: 17" wide, rosewood back and sides, J-200 bridge and pickguard, fleur-de-lis peghead inlay

Available: **1970–71**

J-100: 17" wide, mahogany back and sides, cedar top, black teardrop pickguard, rosewood belly bridge, 4-ply top binding with black outer layer, black-bound back, mahogany neck, 25 1/2" scale, dot inlay, crown peghead inlay, pearl logo

Introduced as **J-100 Custom: 1970**

Some with moustache bridge, stairstep peghead: **1972**

Discontinued (4 shipped in 1975): **1974**

Reintroduced, maple back and sides, spruce top, belly above bridge, tortoiseshell celluloid teardrop pickguard, multiple-bound top, bound back, maple neck, 25 1/2" scale, unbound rosewood fingerboard, dot inlay, no peghead ornament, decal logo, nickel-plated tuners with plastic keystone buttons, sunburst or natural finish: **1985**

Antique ebony or vintage sunburst finish: **1989**

Limited Edition, some with stairstep peghead, moustache bridge and prewar style scallop pickguard: **1991**

Antique walnut or vintage sunburst finish: **1992**

Vintage sunburst finish only: **1993**

Discontinued: **1997**

J-100 Xtra: 17" wide, mahogany back and sides, rosewood moustache bridge with cutouts but no pearl inlays, J-200 style tortoiseshell celluloid pickguard with no engraving, multiple-bound top and back, 25 1/2" scale, unbound rosewood fingerboard, dot inlay, decal logo with *Only a Gibson Is Good Enough* banner, nickel-plated tuners, natural top finish with antique walnut finish on back and sides or vintage sunburst finish

Introduced: **1991**

Crest peghead decal, no banner on peghead, antique natural finish optional: **1994**

Discontinued: **1997**

Reintroduced: **1999**

Still in production

J-100 Xtra 12-string: antique natural or vintage sunburst finish: **1995–96**

J-100 Xtra Chakte Kok: "Smartwood" materials certified by Rainforest Alliance, chakte kok back and sides (from Yucatan peninsula in Mexico): **1995–96**

J-100 Xtra Cutaway: rounded cutaway: **1994**

J-100 Xtra Montana Special: no specs available: **1995**

Harley Davidson: 16" wide, *Harley Davidson* in script on pickguard, pearl inlay in shape of Harley Davidson shield logo, antique ebony finish, limited run of 1500 available only through Harley Davidson dealers: **1994–95**

Blues King Electro (Blues Maestro)/EC-30:

15 7/8" wide, rounded cutaway, arched back of laminated flamed maple, solid maple sides, piezo bridge pickup, rosewood belly bridge, prewar style tortoiseshell celluloid pickguard follows contour of body edge, multiple-bound top and back, 24 3/4" scale, bound rosewood fingerboard, double-parallelogram inlay, bound peghead, pearl peghead inlay of 2-handled vase over dot, prewar script logo in pearl, Grover tuners with metal buttons, nickel-plated hardware, natural top finish with chocolate or walnut back and sides, or cherry sunburst or vintage sunburst finish

Introduced (listed on production records as **Blues Maestro Electric**): **1994**

Antique natural finish available with gold-plated hardware: **1996**

Renamed **EC-30 Blues King Electro**, see EC series, following: **1997**

Blues King Electro Montana Special: 25 1/2" scale: **1995–96**

Blues King Electro Quilted Top: quilted maple top, antique natural finish: **1996**

Blues Maestro Electric Quilted Top: quilted maple top, amber finish available: **1996**

MARK SERIES

Mark models were designed by Michael Kasha and Richard Schneider. All have 16 3/16"-wide body, narrower at the waist than dreadnought models, and 25 1/2" scale. Special design features include modified fan-pattern bracing, asymmetrical fan-shape bridge wider on bass end than treble, removable pickguard, optional saddles, narrow peghead shape with points at upper corners (similar to snakehead shape of the 1920s), and old style script logo.

Early experimental examples have serial numbers with *GSKX* prefix.

MK-99: handcrafted and signed by luthier Richard Schneider, gold-plated hardware, steel-string or classical, available by special order only, 1 listed on shipping records, 1 example with "No. 1 of 12" on label
Available: **late 1975–78**

MK-81: rosewood back and sides, multiple-bound top and back, 3-piece ebony/rosewood/ebony fingerboard, abalone block inlay, gold-plated hardware, natural or sunburst finish
Available: **late 1975–78**

MK-72: rosewood back and sides, black binding on top and back, 3-piece ebony-rosewood-ebony fingerboard, dot inlay, nickel-plated hardware, natural or sunburst finish
Available: **late 1975–78**

MK-53: maple back and sides, multiple-bound top and back, rosewood fingerboard, dot inlay, nickel-plated hardware, sunburst or natural top finish, walnut-stain finish on back and sides
Available: **late 1975–78**

MK-35: mahogany back and sides, black binding

on top and back, rosewood fingerboard, dot inlay, nickel-plated hardware, natural or sunburst finish
Available **late 1975–78**

MK-35-12: 12-string MK-35, 12 shipped **1977**

LG AND B-25 SERIES

LG-2: 14 1/8" wide, mahogany back and sides, X-braced top, rectangular bridge with 2 pearl dots, black bridge pins, firestripe teardrop pickguard, single-bound top and back (some with multiple-bound top), 24 3/4" scale, 19 frets, rosewood fingerboard, dot inlay, silkscreen or decal logo, *Only a Gibson Is Good Enough* peghead banner, 3-on-a-plate tuners, sunburst finish
Introduced: **Aug. 1942**
Tortoiseshell celluloid teardrop pickguard: **1943**
Some with sunburst mahogany top, some with maple back and sides: **1943–46**
No peghead banner: **1946**
Larger pickguard with point at upper treble bout, 20 frets: **1955**
No pearl dots on bridge: **c. 1961**
Cherry sunburst finish: **1961**
White bridge pins, adjustable saddle: **1962**
Discontinued, replaced by B-25 (see following): **1962**

LG-2H: Hawaiian, straight saddle: **1945–mid 1950s**

LG-2 3/4: often stamped *LG 3/4*, 12 3/4" wide, mahogany back and sides, straight-across ladder bracing, some with triple-bound top, 22 3/4" scale, rosewood fingerboard, dot inlay, decal logo, 3-on-a-plate tuners, sunburst top finish
Introduced: **1949**
Larger pickguard with point at upper treble bout: **c. 1955**
No pearl dots on bridge: **c. 1961**
Plastic bridge with upper belly, cherry sunburst finish: **1962**
Discontinued, replaced by B-25 3/4 (see following): **1962**

LG-3: 14 1/8" wide, mahogany back and sides, X-braced top, white bridge pins, triple-bound top, 24 3/4" scale, 19 frets, rosewood fingerboard, dot inlay, decal logo, earliest with *Only a Gibson Is Good Enough* peghead banner, 3-on-a-plate tuners, natural finish
Introduced: **Aug. 1942**

Larger pickguard with point at upper treble bout,
20 frets: **1955**
Adjustable saddle: **1961**
Belly above bridge: **1962**
Plastic upper-belly bridge: **later 1962**
Discontinued, replaced by B-25N (see following): **1963**

LG-1: 14 1/8" wide, mahogany back and sides,
straight-across ladder-braced top, no lengthwise
center seam on inside back, black bridge pins,
24 3/4" scale, 19 frets, rosewood fingerboard, dot
inlay, silkscreen or decal logo, 3-on-a-plate tuners,
sunburst finish
Introduced: **Apr. 1943**
Larger pickguard with point at upper treble bout,
20 frets: **1955**
Upper belly on bridge: **1962**
Last appearance on shipping records (25 shipped): **1968**
Examples as late as: **1974**

LG-0: 14 1/8" wide, all-mahogany body, mahogany
top, straight-across ladder bracing, rectangular
rosewood bridge, black bridge pins, screwed-on
teardrop pickguard, tortoiseshell celluloid binding
on top and back, 24 3/4" scale, 20 frets, rosewood
fingerboard, dot inlay, decal logo, 3-on-a-plate
tuners, natural mahogany finish
Introduced: **1958**
Plastic bridge with upper belly, adjustable saddle: **1962**
Screwed-down pickguard: **1960**
Rosewood bridge with upper belly: **1968**
Spruce top specified (some later with mahogany top),
white binding: **1968**
Discontinued: **1974**

TG-0: tenor version of LG-0
Introduced: **1960**
White bridge pins: **1962**
Upper belly on bridge: **1963**
Discontinued (3 shipped): **1974**

LG-12: 12-string, 14 1/8" wide, mahogany back and
sides, large belly bridge with bridge pins, adjustable
saddle, long pickguard with point at upper bout
(some with teardrop pickguard), single black
soundhole ring, single-bound top, unbound back,
3-piece neck, 18 frets, 12 frets clear of body,
24 3/4" scale, rosewood fingerboard, dot inlay, no
peghead veneer, natural top finish, light mahogany
finish on back and sides

Introduced (does not appear on shipping totals until
1970): **1967**
Non-adjustable saddle, teardrop pickguard: **1970**
Discontinued (2 shipped): **1973**

B-25: 14 1/4" wide, mahogany back and sides, long
pickguard with point at upper treble bout, upper
belly on bridge, adjustable saddle, triple-bound top,
single-bound back, 24 3/4" scale, rosewood finger-
board, dot inlay, decal logo, cherry sunburst finish
or natural top (**B-25N**)
Introduced: **1962**
Plastic bridge: **1963**
Belly below bridge: **1969**
Non-adjustable saddle, no peghead veneer: **1970**
Black outer layer of binding: **1972**
B-25 discontinued (6 shipped): **1977**

B-25 3/4: 12 3/4" wide, X-braced top (some with
straight-across ladder bracing, possibly leftover
LG-2 3/4 bodies), adjustable saddle, 22 3/4" scale,
cherry sunburst finish
Introduced: **1962**
Plastic bridge: **1963**
Rosewood bridge: **by 1968**
Natural top available: **1966**
Discontinued: **1968**

TG-25: tenor, sunburst finish or natural top (**TG-25N**),
otherwise same specs and changes as B-25:
1962–70

B-25-12: 12-string, 14 1/2" wide, mahogany back and
sides, long pickguard with point at upper bout,
oversized pin bridge with upper belly, adjustable
saddle, single-bound top and back, 24 3/4" scale,
14 frets clear of body, unbound rosewood fingerboard, dot inlay, decal logo, cherry sunburst or natural finish (**B-25-12-N**) on top
Introduced: **1962**
Upper belly on bridge, no bridge pins, no tailpiece:
c. 1963
Larger upper-belly bridge, no bridge pins, trapeze tailpiece, triple-bound top: **1965**
Rectangular bridge, trapeze tailpiece: **1965**
Screwed-down pickguard: **1968**
Belly below bridge, bridge pins, no tailpiece, 3-piece
neck: **1969**
Cherry sunburst finish discontinued: **1970**
Natural top finish only: **1971**
Discontinued (2 shipped): **1977**

OTHER SMALL-BODIED MODELS INTRODUCED AFTER WORLD WAR II

CF-100: 14 1/8" wide, pointed cutaway, solid spruce top, mahogany back and sides, X-braced top, bound top and back, tortoiseshell celluloid teardrop pickguard, upper belly on bridge, 24 3/4" scale, bound rosewood fingerboard, trapezoid inlay, crown peghead inlay, pearl logo (earliest with no peghead inlay and decal logo), sunburst finish
Available: **1950–58**

CF-100E: same as CF-100 except for 1 single-coil adjustable-pole pickup at end of fingerboard, small prewar style pickguard follows contour of body edge: **1951–58**

1950 CF-100E: Sept. 1994 Centennial model, mahogany back and sides, P-90 pickup, vintage style barrel knobs, rosewood bridge with lower belly, rosewood fingerboard: **1994**

F-25 Folksinger: 14 1/2" wide, classical body shape, mahogany back and sides, belly above bridge, double white pickguards, 24 3/4" scale, 12 frets clear of body, dot inlay, fingerboard 2" wide at nut, natural top, walnut stain finish on back and sides
Introduced: **1963**
Jubilee body shape (small dreadnought), belly below bridge: **1969**
No pickguard: **1970**
Discontinued: **1971**

B-15: 14 1/2" wide, student model, spruce top, laminated mahogany back and sides, large belly below bridge (some with large rectangular bridge), adjustable saddle, black teardrop pickguard, single-bound top (some with no binding), unbound back, 24 3/4" scale, unbound rosewood fingerboard, dot inlay, narrow peghead, black decal logo, satin (non-gloss) finish
Available: **1967–70**

Jubilee: 14 1/4" wide, body shape similar to square-shouldered dreadnought but smaller, laminated mahogany back and sides, belly bridge with adjustable rosewood saddle, black teardrop pickguard, triple-bound top, single-bound back, 24 3/4" scale, unbound rosewood fingerboard, dot inlay, decal logo, 3-on-a-plate Kluson Deluxe tuners, natural top finish, black finish on back, sides and neck
Available: **1969–70**

Jubilee-12: 12-string, 12 frets clear of body, available: **1969–70**

Jubilee Deluxe: laminated rosewood back and sides, light-colored backstripe, triple-bound top, single-bound back, decal logo, natural top finish: **1970**

B-20: 14 1/2" wide, mahogany back and sides, black binding, standard peghead size
Available: **1971–72**

L-20 Special: 14 3/4" wide, L-00 shape, rosewood back and sides, transducer pickup, ebony bridge with upper belly, no pickguard, multiple-bound top and back, V-neck profile, 24 3/4" scale, bound ebony fingerboard, pearl block inlay, bound peghead, torch peghead inlay, gold-plated tuners with plastic keystone buttons, antique natural or vintage sunburst finish
Available: **1993–94**

L-20 Koa International Special: koa back and sides, pearl soundhole ring, ivoroid binding, pearl truss rod cover, special for Guitar Center: **June 1993–94**

Blues King and Blues King Special:
see L-00

L-130: 14 3/4" wide, bubinga back and sides, Nick Lucas body (4" deep), abalone soundhole ring, multiple-bound top and back, rosewood fingerboard, abalone floret inlay, gold-plated tuners
Available: **1999–current**

L-140: 14 3/4" wide, rosewood back and sides, Nick Lucas body (4" deep), multiple-bound top, triple-bound back, ebony fingerboard, abalone angel wing inlay, abalone angel wing peghead inlay, gold-plated tuners
Available: **1999–current**

L-150: 14 3/4" wide, customer-selected wood for back and sides, Nick Lucas body (4" deep), triple-bound top and back, abalone top border, single-bound ebony fingerboard, abalone autumn leaf inlay, bound peghead, abalone autumn leaf peghead inlay, gold-plated tuners
Available: **1999–current**

STARBURST, EAS AND EC MODELS

The Star: 16" wide, pointed cutaway, standard 3-ply pickguard, rosewood fingerboard, dot inlay, star inlay on peghead, antique ebony finish
Introduced: **1991**
Sunburst finish optional: **1992 only**
Discontinued: **1994**

Starburst/Standard/Flame: 16" wide, pointed cutaway, solid figured maple back and sides, transducer pickup and preamp, rosewood flying bird bridge with no beak, 3 star inlays on bridge, no pickguard, multiple-bound top and back, unbound rosewood fingerboard, multiple-star inlay, gold-plated tuners, 3 star inlays on peghead, nickel- or gold-plated tuners, amber, aquamarine, black cherry, black, blue, green, gray (electric only), mauve, peach, purple, red or vintage sunburst finish
Introduced as **Starburst: 1992**
Renamed **Starburst Standard** or **Starburst Flame**, depending on finish color: **mid 1992**
Starburst Standard finishes: antique natural, red, amber or vintage sunburst
Starburst Flame finishes: black cherry, blue, cherry, green, gray, peach or purple
Discontinued: **1994**

Starburst Elite: 16" wide, pointed cutaway, quilted maple top, solid maple back and sides, transducer pickup and preamp, ebony flying bird bridge with no "beak" (point), 3 star inlays on bridge, no pickguard, triple-bound top and back, bound ebony fingerboard, multiple-star inlay, 4 star inlays on peghead, bound peghead, pearl logo, gold-plated tuners, amber, cherry or vintage sunburst finish
Introduced: **1992**
Antique natural finish optional: **1993**
Discontinued: **1994**

Starburst Studio: 16" wide, pointed cutaway, spruce top, solid maple back and sides, transducer pickup and preamp, rosewood flying bird bridge with no "beak" (point), 3 star inlays on bridge, multiple-bound top and back, unbound rosewood fingerboard, single-star inlay (2 at 12th fret), 4 star inlays on peghead, nickel-plated tuners, antique natural, cherry, ebony or vintage sunburst finish
Introduced: **1992**
Discontinued (1 ebony shipped): **1995**

EAS Deluxe: 16" wide, thinbody, rounded cutaway, solid flamed maple top, arched back of laminated maple, transducer pickup and preamp, rosewood bridge with upper belly, cream pickgard with straight edge next to waist, cream binding on top and back, 24 3/4" scale, bound rosewood fingerboard, trapezoid inlay, nickel-plated tuners with plastic buttons, *Deluxe* on truss rod cover, crown peghead inlay, pearl logo, vintage cherry sunburst finish
Available: **1992–94**

EAS Classic/Standard: 16" wide, thinbody, rounded cutaway, spruce top, arched back of laminated maple, transducer pickup and preamp, prewar style tortoiseshell celluloid pickguard follows contour of body edge, belly above bridge, single-bound top and back, 24 3/4" scale, unbound rosewood fingerboard, dot inlay, nickel-plated tuners with plastic keystone buttons, antique ebony, cherry or ivory finish
Introduced: **1992**
Renamed **EAS Standard:** metal tuner buttons, a few with gold-plated tuners, antique natural, vintage cherry, vintage sunburst, antique ebony or cherry finish: **1993**
Vintage cherry finish discontinued: **1994**
Discontinued: **1995**

EAS Classic Double Cutaway: double rounded cutaway: **1993 only**

EC-30 Blues King Electro/J-185 EC Cutaway: 15 7/8" wide jumbo body, rounded cutaway, 4 3/4" deep at endpin, spruce top, laminated maple back and sides, arched back, transducer pickup, controls on rim, ebony bird-and-beak bridge, 4-ply top binding with white outer layer, single-bound back, 24 3/4" scale, maple neck, ebony fingerboard, double-parallelogram inlay, peghead inlay of double-handled vase over dot, gold-plated tuners, antique natural finish
Introduced as EC-30 Blues King Electro: **1997**
Renamed **J-185 EC Cutaway**, crown peghead inlay: **Jan. 1999**
Still in production

EC-20 Starburst/J-180 EC Cutaway: 15 7/8" wide jumbo body, rounded cutaway, 4 3/4" deep at endpin, spruce top, laminated maple arched back, solid maple sides, transducer pickup, controls on rim, rosewood bird-and-beak bridge with 3 star inlays, multiple-bound top, single-bound back, 24 3/4" scale, rosewood fingerboard, multiple-star inlay, star inlay

on peghead, gold-plated tuners, antique natural, translucent cherry or blue gloss finish
Introduced as EC-20 Starburst: **1997**
Renamed **J-180 EC Cutaway**, crown peghead inlay: **Jan. 1999**
Still in production

EC-20 Floret: no bridge inlay, floret fingerboard inlay, floret peghead inlay: **1998**

EC-10 Standard: 15 7/8" wide jumbo body, rounded cutaway, 3 1/16" deep at endpin, spruce top, laminated maple arched back, solid maple sides, transducer pickup, controls on rim, rosewood bird-and-beak bridge, black-bound top with white line, unbound back, 24 3/4" scale, rosewood fingerboard, dot inlay, silver silkscreen logo, nickel-plated tuners, ebony, blue or red finish
Introduced: **1997**
Emerald forest green finish optional: **1998**
Discontinued: **late 1998**

CUSTOM LINE THIN-SHOULDERED DREADNOUGHTS

All have thin-shouldered dreadnought shape, transducer pickup, 25 1/2" scale, abalone soundhole ring, 2-point tortoiseshell celluloid pickguard

CL-50 Supreme: rosewood back and sides, ebony bird-and-beak bridge, triple-bound top and back, abalone top border, single-bound ebony fingerboard, abalone autumn leaf inlay, bound peghead, abalone autumn leaf peghead inlay, gold-plated tuners
Introduced: **Jan. 1997**
Tree-of-life inlay optional: **1998**
Discontinued: **late 1998**

CL-40 Artist/Dove Artist: rosewood back and sides, ebony bird-and-beak bridge, multiple-bound top, triple-bound back, ebony fingerboard, abalone angel wing inlay, abalone angel wing peghead inlay, gold-plated tuners
Introduced as **CL-40 Artist**: **Jan. 1997**
Renamed **Dove Artist**, listed in square-shouldered dreadnought line but retains slim-dreadnought shape, belly bridge, crown peghead inlay: **Jan. 1999**
Still in production

CL-45 Artist Cutaway/Dove Artist Cutaway: rounded cutaway
Introduced as **CL-45 Artist Cutaway: 1998**
Renamed **Dove Artist Cutaway**, listed in square-shouldered dreadnought line but retains slim-dreadnought shape, crown peghead inlay: **Jan. 1999**
Still in production

J-60 Traditional: catalogued in Custom Line but not a thin-shouldered dreadnought, see J-60 in Dreadnoughts section, preceding

CL-30 Deluxe/Songbird Deluxe: laminated back and sides of chechen, michiche, bubinga or tslan, arched back, rosewood bird-and-beak bridge, multiple-bound top and back, rosewood fingerboard, abalone floret inlay, gold-plated tuners
Introduced as **CL-30 Deluxe: Jan. 1997**
Renamed **Songbird Deluxe**, listed in square-shouldered dreadnought line but retains slim-dreadnought body shape, laminated rosewood back and sides, belly bridge, crown peghead inlay: **Jan. 1999**
Still in production

CL-35 Deluxe Cutaway/Songbird Deluxe Cutaway: rounded cutaway
Introduced as **CL-35 Deluxe Cutaway: 1998**
Renamed **Songbird Deluxe Cutaway**, listed in square-shouldered dreadnought line but retains slim-dreadnought body shape, laminated rosewood back and sides, belly bridge, crown peghead inlay: **Jan. 1999**
Still in production

CL-20 Standard Plus: laminated back and sides of chechen, michiche, bubinga or tslan, arched back, rosewood bird-and-beak bridge, 4-ply top binding with tortoiseshell celluloid outer layer, tortoiseshell celluoid binding on back, rosewood fingerboard, abalone notched-diamond inlay, nickel-plated tuners
Available: **Jan. 1997–98**

CL-10: laminated mahogany back and sides, arched back, rosewood bird-and-beak bridge, 4-ply top binding with black outer layer, black-bound back, rosewood fingerboard, dot inlay, silver silkscreen logo, nickel-plated tuners, semi-gloss finish
Available: **Jan. 1997–98**

WM-10: see Working Musician Series, following

WORKING MUSICIAN SERIES

All have solid mahogany back and sides with scalloped bracing, dark binding on top and back, black teardrop pickguard, dovetail neck joint, slender neck profile, unbound rosewood fingerboard, dot inlay, white silkscreen logo, non-gloss finish.

WM-45 Working Man 45: round-shouldered dreadnought, non-gloss finish

Introduced: **1998**

Gloss top finish, moved to J-45 line: **1999**

Still in production

WM-10 Songwriter Dreadnought/Songbird: thin-shouldered dreadnought, non-gloss finish

Introduced: **1998**

Renamed **Songbird**, listed in square-shouldered line but retains slim-dreadnought body, gloss top finish: **Jan. 1999**

Still in production

WM-00 Bluesbender 98: 14 7/8" wide with circular lower bout (same body shape as 13 1/2"-wide early L-1), non-gloss finish

Introduced: **1998**

Gloss top finish: **1999**

Still in production

Working Musician 180: see Everly Brothers/J-180, preceding

CLASSICALS

GS stands for Gut String.

GS-85: 14 1/2" wide, rosewood back and sides, rosewood bridge with rounded ornamental ends and 2 ornamental pearl inlays, 2 pearl ribbon inlays on bridge below strings, multiple-bound top, bound back, ebony fingerboard, solid peghead

27 shipped: **1939–42**

GS-35: 14 1/2" wide, mahogany back and sides, rosewood bridge with rounded ornamental ends and 2 ornamental pearl inlays, 2 rectangular pearl bridge inlays below strings, single-bound top and back, ebony fingerboard, solid peghead

39 shipped: **1939–42**

GS-1: 14 1/2" wide, mahogany back and sides (some rosewood), black soundhole rings in groups of 2-3-2, 2 ribbon inlays and 2 Maltese-cross inlays on bridge, triple-bound top, bound back, rosewood fingerboard, bone nut with lengthwise groove to create zero fret, solid peghead, white tuner shafts, natural top finish

Available: **1950–56**

GS-2: 14 1/4" wide, maple top, maple back and sides, triple-bound top, single-bound back, slotted peghead, decal logo

Introduced: **1954**

Variation: spruce top, 2 Maltese crosses inlaid on bridge, 2 rectangular bridge inlays, zero fret, black peghead veneer: **1955**

Discontinued: **1957**

GS-5 Custom Classic/C-5: 14 1/4" wide, rosewood back and sides, 2 Maltese cross inlays on bridge, multiple-bound top and back, slotted peghead, engraved tuner plates, decal logo

Introduced: **1954**

Referred to as **C-5**, 14 1/4" wide: **1957**

Discontinued: **1960**

C-1 (early example): 14 1/2" wide, mahogany back and sides, 2 rectangular bridge inlays, 2 multi-ply soundhole rings, tortoiseshell celluloid binding on top and back, rosewood fingerboard, zero fret (earliest without zero fret), ebony nut, slotted peghead with center dip at top, black peghead overlay, no logo, rectangular paper label: **c. 1951**

Introduced in literature, 14 1/4" wide, mahogany back and sides, plain soundhole ring: **1957**

Wide decal rosette (soundhole rings), unbound back, decal peghead logo: **1964**

Discontinued: **1971**

C-1E: ceramic piezo pickup built into bridge: **1960–67**

C-1S: "petite" size, 13 1/4" wide: **1961–66**

C-1D: soundhole ring with broken line in center, ladder bracing, inlaid rosette, black binding on top and back, narrow slotted peghead with dip in center of top: **1963–71**

C-2: 14 1/4" wide, maple back and sides, 3 rings around soundhole, bound top and back, rosewood

fingerboard, zero fret (earliest without zero fret), slotted peghead with dip in center of top, reddish body finish (later walnut)
Introduced: **1957**
2 rectangular bridge inlays under strings: **1960**
Soundhole ring narrower than C-1 with broken line in center, narrower peghead, decal logo: **1964**
Discontinued: **1971**

C-6 Custom/Richard Pick: 14 1/4" wide,
Richard Pick model, rosewood back and sides, 3/4"-wide rosewood soundhole ring, tortoiseshell celluloid binding, ebony fingerboard, zero fret, slotted peghead, rosewood veneer on peghead, no logo, pearloid tuner buttons, gold-plated hardware
Introduced: **1958**
2 pearl ribbon bridge inlays under strings: **1966**
Discontinued: **1971**

C-0: 14 1/4" wide, mahogany back and sides, black top binding, unbound back, wide decal soundhole ring, rosewood fingerboard, ebony nut, zero fret, slotted peghead, satin (non-gloss) finish
Available: **1962–70**

Lyon & Healy Anniversary C-0: commemorating 100th anniversary of Lyon & Healy instrument makers, oval label with *Lyon & Healy Anniversary*, C-0 model name and standard Gibson serial number: **1964**

C-4: 14 1/4" wide, maple back and sides, 2 pearl ribbon bridge inlays under strings, rosewood fingerboard, zero fret, slotted peghead, rosewood-stain finish on back and sides
Available: **1962–67**

C-8: 14 1/4" wide, rosewood back and sides, 2 pearl ribbon bridge inlays under strings, ebony fingerboard, zero fret, narrow slotted peghead, rosewood peghead veneer, no logo
Available: **1962–68**

Flamenco 2: 14 1/4" wide, cypress back and sides, thinner body than classicals, 2 pearl ribbon bridge inlays behind strings, 2 white pickguards between soundhole and bridge, zero fret, slotted peghead
Available: **1963–67**

Bossa Nova: see Dreadnoughts (preceding)

C-L: student model, mahogany back and sides, non-gloss finish (no other specs available)
Available: **1969–70**

C-1000: rosewood back and sides, no other specs available
Available: **late 1969–70**

C-800: rosewood back and sides, no other specs available
Available: **late 1969–70**

C-100: labeled "Master Style," standard-width slotted peghead, ebony fingerboard, satin non-gloss finish
Available: **1970–71**

C-500: rosewood back and sides, "decorative Spanish purfling," abalone and ivory bridge inlays, laminated mahogany/ebony neck, ebony fingerboard, narrow peghead with dip in center of top, gold-plated hardware

C-400: same as C-500 but with chrome-plated hardware
Available: **1971–72**

C-300: mahogany back and sides, wood binding, wider soundhole ring than C-100, rosewood fingerboard, narrow peghead with dip in center of top
Available: **1971–72**

C-200: mahogany back and sides, same as C-100 but with gloss finish
Available: **1971–72**

Special Limited-Run Series

Custom Club Models, 1993–94
Limited edition series, CC# in model code
1. L-1 flamed maple
2. Dove quilted maple
3. J-200 Jr. koa
4. J-200 rosewood Ray Whitley

Montana Special Series, 1993
Guitar-of-the-month program. All have *MS* and month in model code.

Examples: ACHBMS8 = 8th month, ACAJMS10 = 10th month

January: J-200, rosewood back and sides, prewar bridge, Imperial tuners

February: L-1, curly maple back and sides, Nick Lucas inlay, flowerpot peghead inlay

March: Advanced Jumbo, herringbone top border, natural finish

April: Dove, pearl top border, pearl truss rod cover

May: J-60, curly maple back and sides, tortoiseshell celluloid binding

June: J-200 1952 reissue, prewar bridge, Imperial (stairstep) tuners

July: J-180 reissue (Everly Brothers), thick pickguard, pinless bridge

August: Hummingbird, koa back and sides, abalone soundhole ring

September: no model, L-1 Robert Johnson Estate Edition was announced but ultimately offered in the International Series (see following)

October: Advanced Jumbo, curly maple back and sides, abalone top border

November: J-180 Artist (Everly Brothers), tortoiseshell celluloid binding on top, back, neck and peghead, gold pearl inlay, black finish

December: J-200, koa back and sides, abalone top border, abalone soundhole ring, abalone inlay in fingerboard, bridge and peghead, abalone truss rod cover, Imperial tuners

International Series, 1993–94

Guitar-of-the-month series for Guitar Center retail chain. All have *IS* plus number suffix in model code.

March (No. 3), 1993: Hummingbird, quilted maple back and sides, vintage cherry finish

April (No. 4): J-200 Jr., rosewood back and sides, J-2000 marquetry, mahogany neck, white-black-white fingerboard binding

May (No. 5): J-185, highly figured maple back and sides, antique cherry back and sides finish, natural top finish

June (No. 6): L-20 Koa, ivoroid binding, pearl soundhole ring and truss rod cover

July (No. 7): J-200, pearloid pickguard and peghead veneer, gold truss rod cover, Grover Imperial tuners

August (No. 8): Dove, rosewood back and sides, pearl top binding, pearl soundhole ring, vintage cherry finish

September (No. 9): L-1 Estate Edition: pearl Robert Johnson signature at 12th fret, pearl truss rod cover, black finish, black alligator case with Robert Johnson CD in pocket

October (No. 10): J-200 koa, abalone inlay

November (No. 11): J-180, black finish, pearloid pickguard, pearloid peghead veneer, J-200 binding and soundhole ring, ebony fingerboard, pinless bridge, Grover Imperial tuners

December (No. 12): J-60, curly maple back and sides, tortoiseshell celluloid binding

January, 1994: Centennial J-200, vintage cherry, abalone soundhole ring, black peghead, Grover Imperial tuners

February, 1994, Centennial L-1, curly maple back and sides.

Centennial Series, 1994

Guitar-of-the-month program commemorating Gibson's centennial year of 1994. Each model was produced in a limited run of no more than 100.

Centennial models from Gibson Montana (unlike the electric Centennial series from Gibson Nashville) are based on historic models but are not totally accurate reissues. Production ranged from late 1993 into 1995, depending on the model. Descriptions are with the model listings.

All Gibson Montana flat tops in 1994 bear a label with Gibson's Centennial logo, but only the following models were part of the Centennial program.

January: 1929 L-2
February: 1933 Century
March: 1934 Jumbo
April: 1934 Smeck Radio Grande
May: 1938 SJ-200
June: 1939 SJ-100
July: 1940 Jumbo 55
August: 1948 SJ-200N
September: 1950 CF-100E
October: 1951 J-185
November: 1963 Hummingbird
December: J-200 Rose, based on Emmylou Harris' customized J-200, rose pickguard, gold-plated tuners, ebony finish

COMMENTS

Gibson began as a maker of carved-top instruments only and was disdainful of flat tops, referring to them in advertising as "old style" instruments. With the exception of the Nick Lucas model, Gibson's earliest flat tops were designed as budget or student-grade instruments.

In the 1930s Gibson developed professional quality flat tops, incorporating such features as adjustable truss rod, adjustable saddle and larger bodies. Although workmanship in general on pre-World War II Gibsons is not as neat and clean as on Martins of the same period, Gibsons are very well-designed and lightly constructed so as to have a distinctive tone. Many players prefer Gibsons of this period to all other flat tops. Of the prewar models, those considered to be classics are the Nick Lucas, SJ-200 and all jumbos, especially the Advanced Jumbo.

Flat tops of the late 1940s and '50s are well-made, highly regarded instruments. The most highly sought models of the 1950s are the J-200 and J-185, with all dreadnoughts highly regarded by players.

Many acoustic players consider the guitars of the 1960s to be inferior in tone due to the adjustable bridges used at the time, although in other respects construction is similar in quality to that of the 1950s. The Everly Brothers model is highly sought. The Dove also has some appeal to collectors. Many stage performers who desire an instrument with visual appeal regard the Hummingbird, Dove, Everly Brothers and J-200 highly enough that prices for 1960s examples of these models rival prices for 1950s instruments.

Flat tops from the 1970s are mediocre by consensus of players, collectors and even the Gibson company. Workmanship was at a low point, and the double-X bracing pattern used at the time was detrimental to tone.

The quality of Gibson flat tops rose after manufacturing was moved to Bozeman, MT, in 1989. In the mid 1990s the institution of a double-truss rod system (eventually discontinued) and finish-checking problems (due to the use of insufficiently dried wood) eroded Gibson's reputation for flat tops. Quality control efforts in the late 1990s were successful in improving Gibson flat top quality.

Limited runs: In the mid 1990s Gibson Montana produced numerous limited- and special-run models. Specifications for some of these models are not well-documented. Additionally, in some cases the limited-run versions of a model were produced in greater numbers than the regular production version, undermining to some degree the collectible value associated with a limited-run model.

ELECTRICS, GENERAL INFORMATION

MODEL NAMES

Letters usually denote the following: E = electric; S = Spanish; H = Hawaiian; T (before number) = tenor; T (after number) = thinline; D = double pickup; C = cutaway or (at end) cherry finish; N = natural finish

Pre-World War II model numbers were often derived from the cost of a guitar and amplifier set. For example, the ES-150 guitar was originally listed with Model EH-150 amp for $150.

ELECTRIC ARCHTOP BODIES

1936–42: all models have solid spruce top, solid maple back and sides.

1946–current: most models have laminated maple top, back and sides.

Exceptions

L-4CES, L-5CES, L-5CT (Gobel), Byrdland and Super 400CES...

Solid spruce top, solid maple back and sides:
1946–59, 1970–current

Laminated maple back identifiable by the lack of a center seam: **1960–69**

Johnny Smith, Citation, Kalamazoo Award (floating-pickup models): solid spruce top, solid maple back and sides throughout production

Barney Kessel...

Most with laminated spruce top: **1961–64**

A few with solid spruce top and solid maple back: **mid 1960s**

PICKUPS

"Charlie Christian": identified with jazz guitarist Charlie Christian but never officially named, hexagonal shape with V-ends, black housing, white binding around blade and outer edge of housing (EH-150 lap steels have no binding around outer edge of pickup), large magnet (not visible) with 3 mounting screws through top...

Lap steels: single blade for 3 bass strings, 3 blades for treble strings: **1935–38**

Guitars, variation #1: single blade straight across pickup: **1936–39**

Guitars, variation #2: single blade with notch under B-string (overlaps with variation #1): **1938–39**

Guitars, variation #3: single blade for 3 bass strings, 3 blades for treble strings: **1939–40**

Guitars, ES-250 variation: 6 non-adjustable blades, triple-bound: **1938–40**

Christian pickup available by custom order: **mid 1950s–1960s**

Christian pickup standard on ES-175DCC: **1978–80**

ES-100 type: single blade, rectangular white housing, large magnet (not visible) with 3 mounting screws through top: **1938–40**

ES-125 type (prewar): rectangular metal-covered, 6 screwpoles on Spanish guitars, no poles on lap steels: **1940–42**

ES-300 type: oblong, tortoiseshell celluloid housing, adjustable poles, diagonally mounted (large 7" size, then to 4 1/8" within a few months), used on ES-300 and on lap steels: **1940–42**

P-90...

ES-125 type (postwar): non-adjustable poles, a few with no visible poles, black plastic rectangular cover with extension "ears" to attach to top (oval housing with no cover on lap steels): **c. 1946–50**

"Dog-eared": single coil, adjustable poles, rectangular housing with extension "ears" to attach to top: **1946–current**

"Soapbar": same coil as P-90 but with rectangular cover (no "dog ears"), updated version later called HP-90: **1952–current**

Finger rest: first catalogued as "conversion" pickup, referred to by collectors as McCarty pickup, pickup and controls integrated into pickguard, available with 1 or 2 non-adjustable-pole pickups for L-7, L-5 and Super 400; units factory-fitted or available as accessory, factory-fitted models designated with *E* in model name until 1954 (examples: L-7E for single pickup, L-7CED for cutaway with 2 pickups): **1948–71**

Alnico V: single-coil, 6 rectangular adjustable magnet-

poles (Alnico V is the alloy used for the magnet)...

Dog-eared style, high-end archtops (and reissues): **1952–mid 1957, 1996–current**

Soapbar style, Les Paul Custom and reissues (neck pickup only): **1954–mid 1957, 1971, 1991–current**

Humbucking: 2 coils, 1 1/2" x 2 3/4", metal cover with 1 row of adjustable poles...

Steel guitar style: 3 rows of polepieces (3 coils) with 4-6-4 configuration: **1956**

No markings on back of pickup (not visible without removing pickup), brass screw: **Feb. 1957**

PATENT APPLIED FOR ("PAF") sticker on back, nickel-plated screw: **1957–62**

Patent number decal (patent granted July 28, 1959) on back: **mid 1962–75**

Transition to patent number decal, many examples with 1 PAF sticker and 1 patent number decal: **mid 1962–early 1963**

Patent number stamped onto back (engineering order dated 1974, first appearance 1975): **1975–early 1991**

Numerous variations in windings and magnet type, including Velvet Brick (black and white "zebra" bobbins, active copper coil), Dirty Fingers (extra windings), Series 7 (potted Dirty Fingers): **late 1970s–current**

Reissue of PAF style, *PAT APP'D FOR* on sticker, original-style wire, magnet and number of turns, small cross in top of bobbin, introduced with Les Paul Heritage 80 and then on other vintage-related models (ES-335DOT, ES-175): **1980–current**

Some with decal on back, some stamped *Gibson USA:* **early 1991–current**

Melody Maker: oblong shape, narrow coil, plastic cover, no visible poles...

7/8" wide: **1959 only**

5/8" wide: **1960–73, 1977–81**

Firebird humbucking, "Super Deluxe": smaller than standard humbucking, metal cover, no visible poles, used on Firebirds (and reissues) and later on Nighthawks and other models: **1963–69, 1972–current**

Les Paul low-impedance: relatively large, oblong shape: **1968–c. 1973**

Mini-humbucking: 2 coils, 1 1/16" x 2 9/16" (introduced on Epiphone models, see Epiphone section), metal cover, visible poles: **1969–85**

Bill Lawrence: Bill Lawrence worked for Gibson

designing pickups throughout the 1970s and
1980s. Lawrence-design pickups include the poleless 5-sided humbuckers (L-5S), blade set in clear
epoxy (Marauder) pickups and the sidewinder
poleless black plastic-covered (Les Paul Studio)

P-100: same appearance as P-90 (with "ear" extensions or soapbar) but with stacked double-coil
design: **1990–current**

NSX: single coil, black oval housing, slug (non-
adjustable polepieces): **1991–current**

Blues 90: cream soapbar covers, slug (non-adjustable
polepieces): **1996–current**

Gibson embossed on pickup covers…
Les Paul Professional, Personal, Recording and
Signature models; L-5S (as introduced): **1969-75**
Melody Maker pickups: **late 1970-72**
Humbucking and P-90 pickups: **1971–72**

SELECTED PICKUP SPECS

Pickup	Magnets	Inductance Henries	Peak khz	Resistance* Ohms (K)
Original HB	1 Alnico V	4.95	5.6	7.8
Super	1 Indox VII ceramic	4.7	5.8	7.8
PAF	1 Alnico II	4.45	10.3	7.8
Deluxe (mini)	1 Alnico V	2.58	8	6.5
Super Deluxe	1 Indox V ceramic	5.9	3.9	7.5
Dirty Fingers	3 Indox VII	8.6	6.0	16.0
Velvet Brick	1 ceramic	4.7	5.8	7.8
P-90	2 Alnico V	7.5	4.8	16.0

* Resistance at 1000cps

KNOBS

Smooth rounded top, bumps around top edge, some
with arrow across top, 1 black and 1 brown:
1935–39

Smooth top, 8-sided, arrow across top, 1 black and
1 brown: **1936–42**

"Radio," 3 sets of ridges on sides: **1936–42**

"Barrel," 5/8" high, straight-sided…
Clear with no numbers: **1946–49**
Clear with numbers 0–10 visible through knob:
1949–early 1953

"Speed" knobs, 1/2" high, clear, barrel shape with
numbers visible through knob: **mid 1953–mid 1955**

"Bonnet," flared base…
Plain top, numbers visible through knob: **late
1955–mid 1960**
Metal *Tone* and *Volume* caps: **mid 1960–67**
Opaque, numbers imprinted, grooved side, sharper
angle at base: **1967–early 1970s**

Reissues of older style knobs: **early 1970s–current**

BRIDGES AND TAILPIECES

Combination trapeze bridge/tailpiece…
Strings loop under bridge, Les Paul Model only:
mid 1952–53
Strings loop over bridge, ES-295 and ES-225 only:
1952–59

Stud-mounted bridge/tailpiece, non-compensated
Les Paul Model: **late 1953–late 1955**
Les Paul Jr (from introduction) and other low-end
solidbody models: **mid 1954–62**

Stud-mounted bridge/tailpiece, compensating raised
ridge: **1962–71**

ABR-1 tune-o-matic bridge: individually adjustable
metal saddles, oblong base…
No retaining wire between screw-heads and
base, stamped *ABR-1* : **1954–61**
Retaining wire between screw-heads and base:
1961–71
No *ABR-1* stamp: **mid 1960s–91**
Nylon saddles, models with chrome-plated hard
ware, some examples: **1961–71**
Metal saddles, no retaining wire between screw
heads and base: **1971–current**
ABR-1 stamp returns: **1991–current**

Larger tune-o-matic, rectangular base: **1971–82**

"Nashville" wide-travel tune-o-matic, slightly wider
base to allow for greater string-length adjustment:
1977–current

TP-6 tailpiece, fine-tuners on tailpiece: **1978–current**

Combination bridge/tailpiece with individual string
adjustments (similar to Bad-Ass aftermarket unit):
1983–85

Bigsby vibrola: optional on many models: **1952–current**

SW vibrato: sideways action, large coverplate with
engraved lyre: **late 1958–mid 1963**

Gibson vibrola: U-shaped spring, 3 mounting screws,
white plastic tip on vibrato arm …
Low-end models, no coverplate: **1961–early 1970s**
High-end models, large coverplate with engraved
lyre: **mid 1963–early 1970s**

Kahler-licensed: **1981–1990**
Floyd Rose-licensed: **1987–current**
Steinberger-licensed: **1988–90**

HARDWARE

Nickel-plated parts began to be replaced by chrome-plated in 1965. The changeover was accomplished faster on the more popuplar models.

KLUSON TUNERS, 1950S–1960S

Many Gibson models (including Les Paul Standard, ES-335, ES-345, Explorer, and Byrdland) were fitted with Kluson tuners with plastic tuner buttons, flared to resemble a tulip.
Single ring around button base: **1950s–early 1960s**
Double ring around button base, introduced…
 Models with nickel-plated hardware: **very late 1960**
 Models with gold-plated hardware: **c. 1962**

SPECIAL MODEL SERIES

1991 Celebrity Series

Guitar-of-the-month series, black finish, white pickguard, gold-plated hardware, Celebrity Series decal on back of peghead, certificate of authenticity
July: Les Paul Classic
Aug.: SG Standard
Sept.: Firebird V
Oct.: Chet Atkins SST

1988 Showcase Edition

Guitar-of-the-month series, all with EMG pickups and active electronics except for Les Paul Pro, limited runs of 200 for domestic distribution, 50 for foreign distribution
Mar.: Les Paul Custom, ruby finish
Apr.: SG '62, blue finish
May: ES-335, beige finish
June: Les Paul Standard, silverburst finish
July: Chet Atkins CE, vintage sunburst finish
Aug.: Les Paul Custom Lite, goldtop finish
Sept.: WRC SR-71, white finish
Oct.: SG Custom, Ferrari red finish
Nov.: U-2
Dec.: Les Paul Pro, P-90 pickups, goldtop finish

1994 Centennials

Guitar-of-the-month series, initially offered to dealers as 3 different series but only one series produced, all models with diamond dot over letter *i* in Gibson logo, serial number from 1894–1994 raised on tailpiece, row of diamonds forms first numeral *1* of tailpiece number, gold-plated hardware, gold medallion on back of peghead, serial number inked on back of peghead followed by month designation, month designations go to 14, as two announced models were not produced, package includes framed 16" x 20" photo of individual instrument, felt peghead cover, black leather-covered case, gold signet ring, limited runs of 101 maximum

Month	Suffix	Model
Jan.	1	Les Paul Special DC, heritage cherry sunburst
*	2	Les Paul Special, single-cutaway, gold finish
*	3	Les Paul Special, single-cutaway, TV yellow finish
Feb.	4	Les Paul Classic, goldtop finish
Mar.	5	ES-350T, vintage sunburst finish
Apr.	6	Explorer, antique gold finish
May	7	EDS-1275, ebony finish
June	8	ES-355, vintage sunburst finish
July	9	Flying V, antique gold finish
Aug.	10	ES-335, cherry finish
Sept.	11	Firebird VII, vintage sunburst finish
Oct.	12	Les Paul Standard, vintage sunburst finish
Nov.	13	Les Paul '57 Black Beauty 3-pickup, ebony finish
Dec.	14	L-5CES, ebony finish

* Prototypes made but never put into production.

ES-150 style "Charlie Christian" pickup (installed on an ES-250).

Finger-rest pickup unit on an L-7ED.

ES-125 type pickup with non-adjustable poles.

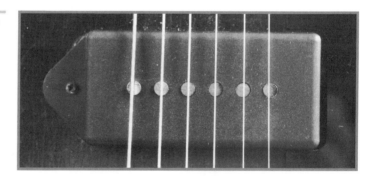

P-90 pickup on a Les Paul Jr.

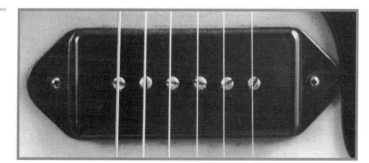

GIBSON

Metal-covered P-90 pickup on an ES-330.

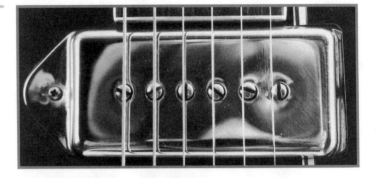

Soapbar P-90 pickup on a 1952 Les Paul.

Humbucking pickup on a Byrdland.

Mini-humbucking pickup on a Les Paul Deluxe.

Firebird mini-humbucking pickup.

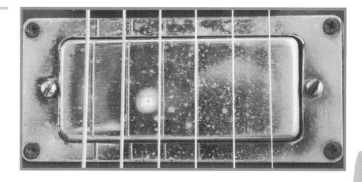

Pickup on a CF-100E, also found on J-160E (early version).

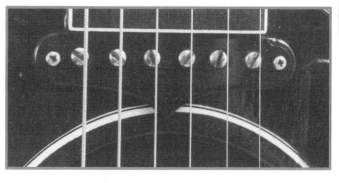

Wide (early version) Melody Maker pickup.

Narrower (later) Melody Maker pickup.

Low-impedance pickup with embossed logo on a Les Paul Recording.

Trapeze bridge/tailpiece on a 1952 Les Paul.

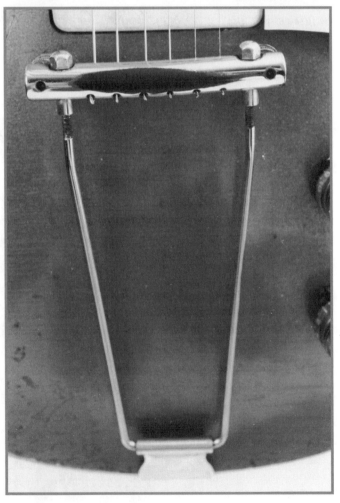

Early 1970s-style pickup with plastic cover, on an SG-II.

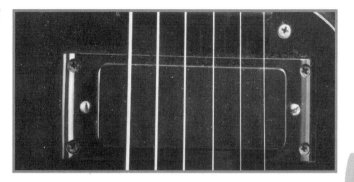

Stud-mounted bridge/tail-piece on a 1960s Melody Maker.

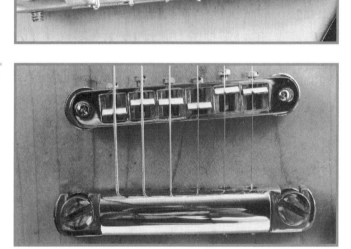

Tune-o-matic bridge (with no retaining wire between screw-heads and base) and stopbar tailpiece on a Les Paul Deluxe.

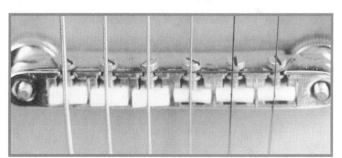

Tune-o-matic bridge with retaining wire between screw-heads and base, and nylon saddles, used on some models from 1961–71.

Late 1960s Melody Maker with a replacement (non-Gibson) bridge, a common retrofit item on Gibson models with stud bridge/ tailpiece.

Slant-mounted ES-300 type pickup on an EH-150 from the early 1940s, knobs with rounded top, arrow and bumps around edges (one of several pre-World War II knob styles).

Stud bridge with "lightning bolt" compensating ridges, vibrato system on a 1964 Firebird III.

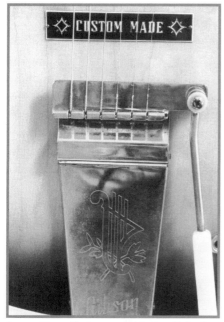

Lyre-and-logo vibrato cover and Custom Made plate on an early 1960s ES-335.

Clear barrel knobs on a late 1940s ES-125.

Barrel knobs with numbers, 5/8" high, on a 1952 Les Paul.

Speed knobs, barrel shape with numbers, 1/2" high, on a 1953 Les Paul.

Clear (gold-backed) bonnet knobs with plain top and numbers visible through knobs, on a late 1950s CF-100E.

Clear bonnet knobs with tone and volume caps on a 1960s ES-335.

Black bonnet knobs on a late 1960s ES-330.

Clear barrel knobs (black-backed) on a late 1970s Les Paul Artisan.

ELECTRIC ARCHTOPS KEY

Non-cutaway
    Full-depth body
        Double-parallelogram, open-book, or fancy varied-pattern inlay
            Oblong pickup, slant-mounted = **ES-300, 1940–42**
            Blade pickup = **ES-250**
            Pole pickup(s) with ears = **ES-300, 1946–52**
        Trapezoid inlay
            Bound fingerboard
                16 1/4" wide = **ES-135**
                17" wide = **ES-150, 1950–57**
            Unbound fingerboard = **ES-125, 1946–50**
        Dot inlay
            14 1/4" wide
                Pole pickup = **ES-100/ES-125, 1940–42**
                Blade pickup = **ES-100, 1938–40**
            16 1/4" wide
                Prewar script logo = **ES-150, 1936–42**
                Postwar block letter logo = **ES-125, 1950–70**
            17" wide = **ES-150, 1946–50**
    Thinline body
        Melody Maker pickup (oblong) = **ES-120T**
        P-90 pickup (rectangular with ears)
            16 1/4" wide = **ES-125T**
            12 3/4" wide = **ES-125T 3/4**
Single cutaway
    ES-135 decal on peghead = **ES-135, 1991–current**
    Chet Atkins decal on peghead = **Chet Atkins Tennessean**
    Flying bird peghead inlay = **Kalamazoo Award**
    Crest with half-moons and castle = **Crest (L-5CEST variation)**
    Split-diamond peghead inlay
        Pickups mounted in top
            18" wide = **Super 400 CES**
            17" wide = **Super V**
        Floating pickup(s)
            1 pickup
                Square-end fingerboard = **Johnny Smith**
                Pointed-end fingerboard = **Super V/BJB**
            2 pickups = **Johnny Smith Double**
    Flowerpot peghead inlay
        Wide plate tailpiece = **L-5 CES**
        Tubular tailpiece = **Byrdland**
    Vine peghead inlay
        Rosewood fingerboard = **Howard Roberts Custom**
        Ebony fingerboard = **Howard Roberts Artist**
    Double-crown peghead inlay = **Tal Farlow**
    Fleur-de-lis peghead inlay = **Citation**

Single cutaway *(continued)*
  Crown peghead inlay
    Double-parallelogram fingerboard inlay
      Bound peghead
        Full-depth body = **ES-350**
        Thinline body
            23 1/2" scale = **ES-350T, 1955–63**
            25 1/2" scale = **ES-350T, 1977–81**
      Unbound peghead
        Gold finish = **ES-295**
        Non-gold finish
          Full-depth body
            Spruce top = **L-4CES**
            Maple top
               1 adjustable-pole pickup = **ES-175**
               2 adjustable-pole pickups = **ES-175D**
               1 blade (Christian) pickup = **ES-175CC**
          Thinline body = **ES-175T**
      Pearl block fingerboard inlay
        4 knobs = **ES-5**
        6 knobs = **ES-5 Switchmaster**
      Red blocks on bass side = **Chet Atkins Country Gentleman**
      Dot inlay = **Howard Roberts Fusion**
  No peghead ornament
    Full-depth body
      16 1/4" wide
        1 pickup = **ES-125C**
        2 pickups = **ES-125CD**
      12 3/4" wide = **ES-140 3/4**
    Thinline body
      Bound fingerboard
        1 pickup = **ES-225T**
        2 pickups = **ES-225TD**
      Unbound fingerboard
        16 1/4" wide
          1 pickup = **ES-125 TC**
          2 pickups = **ES-125TDC**
        12 3/4" wide = **ES-140 3/4T**
Double cutaway, rounded horns
  Winged-*f* peghead inlay = **ES-Artist**
  5-piece split-diamond peghead inlay
    Pickups mounted into top = **ES-355TD**
    Floating pickups = **Crest**
  Double-triangle peghead inlay = **ES-335-12**
  Les Paul on peghead = **Les Paul Signature**
  Lucille peghead inlay
    No Varitone = **B. B. King Standard**
    Varitone = **B. B. King Custom** or **B. B. King Lucille**

Custom Shop logo on peghead
  Dot inlay = **ES-336**
  Double-parallelogram inlay = **ES-346**
Crown peghead inlay
  Small block inlay
    Full-depth body = **ES-150DC**
    Thinline body
      TP-6 tailpiece, brass nut
        Mono, no master volume = **ES-335TD CRR**
        Stereo, master volume = **ES-335TD CRS**
      Stopbar, trapeze or Bigsby tailpiece; bone nut
        Master volume and master mixer controls = **ES-340TD**
        Tone and volume for each pickup
          Coil tap switch on upper treble bout = **ES-335, 1977–81**
          Coil tap switch near control knobs = **ES-240**
          No coil tap = **ES-335TD, 1962–76, 1995–96 (LE)**
  Large block inlay
    f-holes = **ES-347TD**
    No *f*-holes = **ES-357**
  Single parallelogram inlay = **ES-335TD, 1969**
  Double-parallelogram inlay = **ES-345TD**
  Dot inlay
    f-holes
      Pickup covers
      Exposed pickup coils = **ES-335Pro**
        Orange oval label = **ES-335TD, 1958-62**
        Beige or white oval label = **ES-335DOT**
    No *f*-holes
      2 pickups = **ES-335 Studio**
      3 pickups = **ES-337**
No peghead ornament
  P-90 pickup(s)
    1 pickup = **ES-330T**
    2 pickups = **ES-330TD**
  Melody Maker pickups = **ES-320TD**
  Mini-humbucking pickups = **ES-325**
  Standard humbucking pickups
    6-on-a-side tuner arrangement = **Trini Lopez Standard**
    3-on-a-side tuner arrangement = **ES-369**
Double cutaway, pointed horns
  Bowtie inlay = **Barney Kessel Custom**
  Double-parallelogram inlay = **Barney Kessel Regular**
  Slashed-diamond inlay = **Trini Lopez Deluxe**

ELECTRIC ARCHTOPS

SECTION ORGANIZATION

Full-Depth Models
Thinlines, Non-cutaway
Thinlines, Single Cutaway
Double Cutaway, Semi-hollowbody
Double Cutaway, Fully Hollowbody
Double Cutaway, Routed Back
Artist Models
Acoustic Archtops with Optional Pickups

FULL-DEPTH MODELS

ES-150: 16 1/4" wide, X-braced top, flat back, slender *f*-holes, Charlie Christian blade pickup, single-ply binding around pickup and around blade, 3 pickup adjustment screws through top, 2 knobs, jack at tailpiece base, trapeze tailpiece with raised diamond, single-bound pickguard, single-bound top and back, single-bound rosewood fingerboard, dot inlay, pearl logo, sunburst finish

Introduced: **Dec. 1936**

Triple-bound pickup: **1938**

Arched back, rectangular metal-covered adjustable-pole pickup near bridge, jack on side, unbound fingerboard: **1940**

Production ceased for WWII: **1942**

Reintroduced, 17" wide, laminated maple body (at least one example with maple top and mahogany back and sides), P-90 pickup in neck position, jack on side, laminated beveled-edge pickguard, bound top and back, dot inlay, silkscreen logo: **June 1947**

Trapezoid inlay, bound fingerboard: **1950**

Discontinued (6 shipped): **1956**

EST-150: tenor version of ES-150, 16 1/4" wide, arched back, jack on side

Introduced: **1937**

Renamed **ETG-150: 1940**

Production ceased for World War II: **1942**

Reintroduced, 16 1/4" wide (electric version of TG-50), 1 P-90 pickup, laminated beveled-edge pickguard, bound fingerboard, dot inlay, no peghead ornament: **1947**

Discontinued: **1971**

ESP-150: plectrum version of ES-150: **1937–42**

ES-100/ES-125: 14 1/4" wide, X-braced carved spruce top, flat back, blade pickup with white rectangular housing, pickup in neck position, jack on side, some with 2 sound posts inside, single-bound top and back, rosewood fingerboard, dot inlay, silkscreen logo, no peghead ornament, sunburst finish

Introduced as **ES-100: 1938**

Rectangular metal-covered pickup with adjustable poles, pickup in bridge position: **1940**

ES-100 renamed **ES-125: 1941**

Production ceased for World War II, last instruments shipped: **1943**

Reintroduced, 16 1/4" wide, black P-90 pickup with 6 non-adjustable poles, some with no visible poles, pickup in neck position, tortoiseshell celluloid pickguard, trapeze tailpiece with raised diamond, single-bound top and back, unbound fingerboard, pearloid trapezoid inlay, silkscreen logo, sunburst finish: **1946**

Some with all-mahogany body, dot inlay: **1946**

Plain tailpiece, dot inlay: **by 1950**

Standard P-90 pickup: **c. 1951**

Discontinued: **1970**

ES-125C: 16 1/4" wide, pointed cutaway, 1 P-90 pickup: **1966–70**

ES-125CD: 2 pickups: **1966–70**

ES-125T, ES-125T 3/4: See Thinlines, Non-Cutaway, following

ES-125TC: See Thinlines, Single Cutaway, following

ES-250: 17" wide, X-braced carved spruce top, arched maple back (most pressed rather than carved), triple-bound Christian pickup with 6 blades, most with bound pickup blade, jack at tailpiece base, large non-engraved Super 400 style tailpiece, triple-bound pickguard, wide triple-binding on top and back, 2-piece maple neck with stripe down middle, single-bound rosewood fingerboard, open-book inlay, carved stairstep peghead, back of peghead painted black coming to a point below nut, metal tuner buttons, pearl logo, sunburst finish

Variations:
- Unbound non-stairstep peghead
- Single-bound non-stairstep peghead with fancy inlay
- Double-parallelogram inlay, plate tailpiece with pointed ends and raised diamond and arrows
- Fancy rectangular-enclosed inlay (like 1937 L-7),

plate tailpiece with pointed ends and raised diamond and arrows
- P-90 pickup (bodies and necks probably prewar stock), postwar logo, plate tailpiece with pointed ends and raised diamond and arrows

Introduced: **1939**
Natural finish available: **1939**
Discontinued: **1940**

ES-300: 17" wide, parallel-braced carved spruce top, most with dowel supports under bridge, carved maple back, large (7" long) slant-mounted oblong pickup with adjustable poles, jack on side, pictured with L-5 style plate tailpiece with center insert missing, most with plate tailpiece with pointed ends and raised diamond and arrows, some with trapeze tailpiece with 1 raised diamond, triple-bound top and back, bound tortoiseshell celluloid pickguard, 2-piece maple neck with stripe down middle, double-parallelogram inlay, single-bound peghead, back of peghead painted black coming to point below nut, crown peghead inlay (first Gibson model with crown), pearl logo, natural finish

Variation: 7-piece split-diamond peghead inlay
Introduced: **1940**
Smaller (4 1/8" long) slant-mounted pickup in bridge position, some with single-ply binding, natural or sunburst finish: **1941**
Production ceased for World War II: **1942**
A few produced, black finish, P-90 pickup: **late 1945**
Reintroduced, laminated maple body, P-90 pickup in neck position, trapeze tailpiece with pointed ends and 3 raised parallelograms (early with plate tailpiece with 2 ƒ-hole cutouts), laminated beveled-edge pickguard (early with bound tortoiseshell celluloid pickguard), triple-bound top and back, bound peghead, 1-piece mahogany neck, bound rosewood fingerboard, double-parallelogram inlay, crown peghead inlay, plastic keystone tuner buttons, sunburst or natural finish: **mid 1946**
Early postwar variation: 5-ply laminated mahogany top, back and sides, sunburst finish on top, reddish-brown finish on back, sides and neck
2 P-90 pickups, 2 volume knobs on lower treble bout, master tone knob on upper treble bout: **1948**
Discontinued: **1952**

ES-350 (originally **ES-350 Premier**): rounded cutaway version of ES-300, 17" wide, 1 P-90 pickup,

trapeze tailpiece with pointed ends and 3 raised parallelograms, laminated beveled-edge pickguard (early with bound tortoiseshell celluloid pickguard), triple-bound top and back, 2-piece maple neck with stripe down center, single-bound fingerboard, double-parallelogram inlay, single-bound peghead, back of peghead painted black coming to a point below nut, crown peghead inlay, plastic keystone tuner buttons, gold-plated hardware, sunburst or natural finish

Introduced: **1947**
2 P-90 pickups (single-pickup model pictured in ads into 1949 but not offered in catalog), 2 volume knobs on lower treble bout, master tone knob on cutaway bout: **1948**
4 knobs, toggle switch: **1952**
Tune-o-matic bridge: **1956**
Discontinued as full-depth model, replaced by **ES-350T**, see Thinlines, Single Cutaway, following: **1956**

ES-5/Switchmaster: 17" wide, rounded cutaway, 3 P-90 pickups, 3 volume controls, 1 master tone knob on cutaway bout, trapeze tailpiece with pointed ends and 3 raised parallelograms, laminated beveled-edge pickguard, triple-bound top and back, bound ƒ-holes (a few early with unbound ƒ-holes), 2-piece maple neck with stripe down center, pointed-end rosewood fingerboard with 5-ply binding, large pearl block inlay, single-bound peghead, back of peghead painted black coming to a point, crown peghead inlay, gold-plated hardware, sunburst or natural finish

Introduced as **ES-5**, earliest with L-5P Spec. or ES-350 Spec. designation: **June 1949**
Tune-o-matic bridge, Alnico V pickups specified (but virtually all with P-90s), 5-ply top and back binding: **by 1955**
Renamed **ES-5 Switchmaster**, 3 P-90 pickups, 6 knobs, separate volume and tone controls for each pickup, 4-way slotted switch on cutaway bout: **late 1955**
Tubular tailpiece with double-loop design: **1956**
Humbucking pickups: **mid 1957**
Pointed cutaway: **late 1960**
Discontinued: **1962**

ES-5 Reissue: 3 P-90 pickups: **1996–current**

Switchmaster Reissue: 3 humbucking pickups: **1996–current**

Switchmaster Reissue Alnico: 3 Alnico V pickups: **1996–current**

ES-175: 16 1/4" wide, pointed cutaway, 1 P-90 pickup in neck position, 2 knobs, trapeze tailpiece with pointed ends and 3 raised parallelograms, laminated beveled-edge pickguard, triple-bound top, single-bound back, single-bound fingerboard, double-parallelogram inlay, crown peghead inlay, sunburst or natural finish
Introduced: **1949**
Some with Alnico V pickup (rare): **early to mid 1950s**
Some with 2 pickups (see ES-175D, following): **1951–53**
Humbucking pickup: **Feb. 1957**
Discontinued: **1971**

ES-175D: 2 P-90 pickups
Earliest labeled *ES-175*, 2 volume controls on lower treble bout, master tone control on cutaway bout (no toggle switch): **1951–53**
ES-175D introduced, 2 tone controls and 2 volume controls on lower treble bout, toggle switch: **1953**
Some with Alnico V pickup(s) (rare): **early to mid 1950s**
Humbucking pickups: **Feb. 1957**
Tailpiece with T in center and zigzag tubes on sides: **1958**
Back to original pointed-end tailpiece: **early 1970s**
Tune-o-matic bridge: **by 1977**
Mahogany back and sides, antique natural or vintage sunburst finish: **1983**
Alpine white finish optional, gold-plated hardware optional with Alpine white only: **1987**
Gold-plated hardward standard with Alpine white and ebony finish: **1988**
Nickel-plated hardware with antique natural or vintage sunburst finish, optional with ebony finish: **1990**
Maple back and sides: **late 1990**
Renamed **ES-175 Reissue**, Historic Collection, nickel-plated hardware, antique natural or vintage sunburst finish: **1991**
Listed as limited-run model: **1993**
Still in production

ES-175CC: Charlie Christian pickup, 3 screws into top, adjustable rosewood bridge, sunburst or walnut stain finish: **1978–79 only**

ES-175D CMT: curly maple top, bound ebony finger-

board, bound peghead, gold-plated hardware: **1989–90**

ES-175T: see Thinlines, Single Cutaway, following

ES-775 Classic Beauty: laminated figured maple body, 2 humbucking pickups, 3-ply maple neck, ebony fingerboard, slotted-block inlay, gold-plated hardware, antique natural, vintage sunburst or ebony finish
Introduced: **1990**
Wine red finish available: **1992**
Discontinued: **1993**

ES-140 (3/4): 12 3/4" wide, pointed cutaway, 1 P-90 pickup, trapeze tailpiece, single-bound top and back, 22 3/4" scale, dot inlay, sunburst finish
Introduced: **1950**
Natural finish optional (rare): **1953**
Discontinued as full-depth model, replaced by **ES-140 3/4T**, see Thinlines, Single Cutaway, following: **1957**

L-5CES: electric version of L-5C, 17" wide, rounded cutaway, solid carved spruce top, carved maple back, maple sides, 2 P-90 pickups, single-bound *f*-holes, multiple-bound top, back, fingerboard and peghead, pointed-end ebony fingerboard, block inlay, flowerpot peghead inlay, sunburst or natural finish
Introduced: **1951**
Alnico V pickups: **1954**
Humbucking pickups: **late 1957**
Pointed cutaway, 1-piece laminated maple back: **mid 1960**
Rounded cutaway, solid 2-piece back: **mid to late 1969**
Natural or vintage sunburst finish: **1986**
Ebony or wine red finish optional: **1991**
Still in production

L-5CES Centennial: guitar of the month, ebony finish, serial number in raised numerals on tailpiece, numeral *1* of serial number formed by row of diamonds, letter *i* of logo dotted by inlaid diamond, gold medallion on back of peghead, gold-plated hardware, limited run of no more than 101 serial numbered from 1894–1994, package includes 16 x 20 framed photograph and gold signet ring: **Dec. 1994**

L-5S: see Gibson Solidbodies section

L-5 Studio: 2 humbucking pickups, 4 knobs, switch on cutaway bout, tune-o-matic bridge, trapeze tailpiece, "ice cube marble" pattern celluloid pickguard, black binding on top and back, unbound ebony fingerboard, dot inlay, pearl logo, translucent blue or translucent red finish: **1996–current**

Super V CES: similar to L-5 CES but with Super 400 neck and peghead, 6-finger tailpiece, antique sunburst or natural finish
Introduced: **1978**
Natural or vintage sunburst finish: **1986**
Ebony or wine red finish optional: **1991**
Discontinued: **1993**

Super V/BJB: same as Super V CES but with 1 floating pickup: **1978–83**

Super 400CES: electric version of Super 400C, 18" wide, rounded cutaway, solid carved spruce top, carved maple back, maple sides, 2 P-90 pickups, multiple-bound top, back, *f*-holes, fingerboard and peghead, ebony fingerboard, split-block inlay, 5-piece split-diamond peghead inlay, sunburst or natural finish
Introduced: **1951**
Alnico V pickups: **1954**
Humbucking pickups: **late 1957**
Pointed cutaway, 1-piece laminated maple back (at least 1 with 2-piece laminated back): **mid 1960**
Rounded cutaway, solid 2-piece back: **mid to late 1969**
Natural or vintage sunburst finish: **1986**
Ebony or wine red finish optional: **1991**
Still in production

Super 400C 50th Anniversary: BJB floating pickup, engraved heelcap, binding on back of peghead comes to point (similar to Citation binding but with no volute), *Super 400 1935 50th Anniversary 1984* engraved in abalone inlay on back of peghead, Kluson Sealfast tuners with pearl buttons: **1984**

Chet Atkins Super 4000: thinbody Super 400, carved spruce top, figured maple back and sides, floating full-size humbucking pickup, 5-piece maple neck, heritage cherry sunburst finish
Prototype made for Chet Atkins: **1995**
Limited run of 25 announced: **1997**

ES-295: ES-175 body and neck, 16 1/4" wide, pointed cutaway, 2 P-90 pickups with white covers, clear pickguard back-painted with white background and gold floral design, trapeze bridge/tailpiece combo with strings looping over bridge, triple-bound top, single-bound back and fingerboard, 19-fret fingerboard, double-parallelogram inlay, crown peghead inlay, gold-plated hardware, gold finish
Introduced: **1952**
20-fret fingerboard: **1955**
Humbucking pickups: **late 1958**
Last shipped: **late 1958**
Reintroduced, bullion gold finish: **1990**
Bigsby vibrato: **1992**
Historic Collection model: **1993**
Discontinued: **1995**

Super 300CES: acoustic model Super 300C, some with pickup(s) added at factory: **1954**

ES-130/ES-135: 16 1/4" wide, 1 P-90 pickup mounted 1" from fingerboard, trapeze tailpiece with raised diamond, laminated beveled-edge pickguard, single-bound top and back, mahogany neck, 24 3/4" scale, single-bound fingerboard, trapezoid inlay, decal logo, no peghead ornament, sunburst finish
Introduced as **ES-130: late 1954**
Renamed **ES-135: mid 1956**
Discontinued: **1958**
Reintroduced as thinbody model (see following)

L-4CES: 16 1/4" wide, pointed cutaway, solid spruce top, Christian pickup, bound rosewood fingerboard, double-parallelogram inlay, crown peghead inlay
Available by special order: **1958 only**
9 shipped: **1969**
Reintroduced, carved spruce top, mahogany back and sides, 2 humbucking pickups, 4 knobs, 1 switch on upper bass bout, tune-o-matic bridge, L-5 style plate tailpiece, multiple-bound pickguard, triple-bound top and back, gold-plated hardware, transparent amber or vintage sunburst finish: **mid 1986**
Ebony finish optional: **1987**
Wine red finish optional: **1991**
Still in production

ES-150DC: double rounded cutaway, 3" deep, 2 humbucking pickups, 4 knobs on lower treble bout, master volume knob on upper treble bout, triple-bound top, single-bound back, single-bound fingerboard, small block inlay, crown peghead inlay, natural, walnut, or cherry finish

Available: **1969–74**

Le Grand: see Johnny Smith, following

THINLINES, NON-CUTAWAY

ES-125T: thinline ES-125, 16 1/4" wide, P-90 pickup, trapeze tailpiece, single-bound top and back, unbound fingerboard, dot inlay, decal logo, sunburst finish

Available: **1956–68**

ES-125T 3/4: 12 3/4 " wide, 22 3/4" scale: **1957–68**

ES-125TD: 2 pickups: **1957–63**

ES-120T: 16 1/4" wide, 1 *f*-hole, Melody Maker pickup mounted on pickguard, knobs and jack mounted on pickguard, single-bound top and back, dot inlay, decal logo, sunburst finish

Available: **1962–70**

THINLINES, SINGLE CUTAWAY

ES-225T: 16 1/4" wide, pointed cutaway, P-90 pickup in middle position, trapeze bridge/tailpiece combination with strings looping over bridge, laminated beveled-edge pickguard, single-bound top and back, single-bound fingerboard, dot inlay, pearl logo, no peghead ornament, sunburst or natural finish

Available: **1955–58**

ES-225TD: 2 pickups: **1956–58**

Byrdland: Billy Byrd/Hank Garland model, thinbody short-scale version of L-5CES, 17" wide, rounded cutaway, 2 1/4" deep, carved maple back, 2 Alnico V pickups, triple-loop tubular tailpiece with no engraving, tortoiseshell celluloid pickguard (a few early with pearloid), 7-ply top binding, triple-bound back, 7-ply pickguard binding, single-bound *f*-holes, ebony fingerboard with pointed end, 5-ply fingerboard binding, 23 1/2" scale, narrow neck, narrow string spacing and narrow pickup pole spacing, block inlay, flowerpot peghead inlay, 7-ply peghead binding, gold-plated hardware, sunburst or natural finish

Introduced: **1955**

Humbucking pickups: **late 1957**

A few with humbucking bridge pickup and Charlie Christian neck pickup: **late 1957–71**

A few with double rounded cutaway: **1958–62**

Byrdland engraved on crosspiece of tailpiece: **1959**

Pointed cutaway, 1-piece laminated maple back: **late 1960**

Some with stereo wiring and Vari-tone switch (rare): **late 1960–68**

Rounded cutaway, solid 2-piece back: **mid to late 1969**

Ebony or wine red finish optional: **1991**

Available with rounded cutaway or pointed cutaway: **late 1998**

Still in production

ES-350T (later renamed TD): 17" wide, rounded cutaway, 2 P-90 pickups, tune-o-matic bridge, tailpiece with W-shape tubular design and *ES-350T* on oblong crosspiece, laminated beveled-edge pickguard, triple-bound top and back, neck-body joint at 14th fret, 23 1/2" scale, single-bound fingerboard and peghead, double-parallelogram inlay, crown peghead inlay, gold-plated hardware, sunburst or natural finish

Introduced: **1955**

Humbucking pickups: **mid 1957**

Pointed cutaway: **late 1960**

Discontinued: **1963**

Reintroduced, rounded cutaway, 2 humbucking pickups, tune-o-matic bridge, tubular triple-loop tailpiece with engraved *ES-350T*, neck-body joint at 14th fret, 25 1/2" scale, sunburst, fireburst (redder than standard sunburst) or natural finish: **1977**

Fireburst finish discontinued: **1979**

Discontinued: **1981**

Reintroduced, vintage sunburst finish, limited runs: **1992**

Still offered

ES-350T Centennial: guitar of the month, vintage sunburst finish, serial number in raised numerals on tailpiece, numeral *1* of serial number formed by row of diamonds, letter *i* of logo dotted by inlaid diamond, gold medallion on back of peghead, gold-plated hardware, limited run of no more than 101 serial numbered from 1894–1994, package includes 16" x 20" framed photograph and gold signet ring: **Mar. 1994**

ES-140 3/4T: 12 3/4" wide, pointed cutaway, 1 P-90 pickup, single-bound top and back, 22 3/4" scale, dot inlay, no peghead ornament, sunburst or natural finish

Introduced, replacing ES-140 3/4 full-depth model: **1957**

Natural finish discontinued: **1959**

Discontinued: **1968**

L-5 CEST: electric version of L-5CT (see Acoustic Archtops section), rounded cutaway, 2 humbucking pickups, cherry or sunburst finish

4 examples recorded as "L-5 special thin model": **1954**

Introduced: **1959**

Discontinued: **1962**

Offered as **L-5CT**, Custom Shop model, quilted maple top, back and sides, 2 1/2" deep, 1 floating pickup, Brazilian rosewood pickguard, fingerboard and peghead veneer: **1983 only**

Crest Special: custom variations of L-5CT, some labeled *L-5CT Spec.*, pointed cutaway, ebony fingerboard, slashed-block (Super 400 style) inlay, Varitone, gold-plated crest-shaped insert in trapeze tailpiece, crest peghead inlay with 3 crescent moons and castle, at least 6 examples special-ordered by Gibson sales representative Andy Nelson

Available: **1961–63**

ES-125TC: ES-125T with pointed cutaway, 16 1/4" wide, P-90 pickups, single-bound top and back, unbound fingerboard, decal logo, sunburst finish

Introduced: **1960**

Cherry sunburst finish: **1961**

Discontinued: **1970**

ES-125TCD: 2 P-90 pickups

Introduced: **1960**

Renamed **ES-125TDC: 1961**

Discontinued: **1971**

ES-175T: 16" wide, pointed cutaway, 1 7/8" deep, 2 humbucking pickups, 4 knobs on lower treble bout, 1 switch on upper bass bout, laminated beveled-edge pickguard, tune-o-matic bridge, trapeze tailpiece with pointed ends and 3 raised parallelograms, triple-bound top and back, single-bound rosewood fingerboard, double-parallelogram inlay, crown peghead inlay, pearl logo, wine red,

natural, or sunburst finish

Available: **1976–79**

ES-135: (also see full-depth version, preceding) 16" wide, pointed cutaway, laminated maple body with Chromyte (balsa) center block, 2 P-100 stacked-coil humbucking pickups, tune-o-matic bridge, trapeze tailpiece, maple neck, unbound rosewood fingerboard, dot inlay, model name decal on peghead, decal logo, chrome-plated hardware, cherry ebony or vintage sunburst finish

Introduced: **mid 1991**

Limited run with '57 Classic humbucking pickups, gold-plated hardware with wine red or natural finish, chrome-plated with vintage sunburst or ebony finish: **late 1998–99**

Still in production

ES-135 Gothic: 2 '57 Classic humbucking pickups with no covers, black pickguard, ebony fingerboard, moon-and-star inlay at 12th fret, no other inlay, white outline of logo on peghead, black chrome hardware, flat black finish

Available: **late 1998–current**

DOUBLE CUTAWAY, SEMI-HOLLOWBODY

All are 16" wide, 1 5/8" deep, with 24 3/4" scale. All have maple block down middle of body. From Dec. 1972–Aug. 1975 (dates of Gibson engineering orders; dates of implementation may be several months later) maple block extends only from tailpiece to endpin.

ES-335TD: 2 humbucking pickups, 2 tone and 2 volume knobs, 1 switch, tune-o-matic bridge, stop tailpiece, Bigsby vibrato optional (most models fitted with Bigsby have *CUSTOM MADE* plate covering original tailpiece holes; some without holes or plate), laminated beveled-edge pickguard extends below bridge, single-bound top and back, neck-body joint at 19th fret, single-bound rosewood fingerboard, dot inlay, crown peghead inlay (early with unbound fingerboard and no peghead ornament), sunburst or natural finish

Introduced: **spring 1958**

Cherry finish optional: **late 1959**

Shorter pickguard does not extend below bridge: **early 1961**

Small pearloid block inlay: **mid 1962**

Trapeze tailpiece (some with stop tailpiece in 1965): **late 1964**

Some with single-parallelogram inlay: **1963**, **1967**, **1969**

Walnut finish optional: **1969**

Coil-tap switch on upper treble bout: **1977**

Discontinued, replaced by ES-335 DOT: **late 1981**

ES-335 DOT/Reissue: reissue of 1960 ES-335, 4 knobs, 1 switch, tune-o-matic bridge, stop tailpiece, dot inlay, nickel-plated hardware

Introduced as **ES-335 DOT**, replacing ES-335TD: **late 1981**

Pearl white offered as Custom Shop finish, gold-plated hardware: **1984 only**

Cherry, antique natural, Alpine white, ebony or vintage sunburst finish: **1986**

Gold-plated hardware optional with Alpine white finish: **1987**

Gold-plated hardware standard with Alpine white: **1988**

Renamed **ES-335 Reissue**, classic white finish optional: **1990**

Cherry or vintage sunburst finish only: **1991**

Natural finish optional: **1994**

Brunswick blue finish, gold-plated hardware, limited Custom Shop run: **1994**

Optional translucent brown finish with gold-plated hardware or ebony finish with nickel-plated hardware, metal tuner buttons: **late 1998**

Limited runs with black binding, ebony fingerboard, small block inlay, translucent blue, natural or translucent red finish: **late 1998–1999**

Still in production

ES-335 DOT CMT: Custom Shop model, highly figured maple top and back, 2 PAF humbucking pickups, full-length maple centerblock, mahogany neck, antique natural or vintage sunburst finish: **1983–85**

ES-335 Showcase Edition: guitar of the month series, EMG pickups, beige finish, limited run of 200 for U.S. distribution, 50 for overseas: **Apr. 1988**

Custom Shop ES-335: figured maple back, long pickguard, thick 1959-style neck, replica orange oval label: **1995–current**

ES-335-12: 12-string, double-triangle peghead inlay with rounded points, otherwise same specs and changes as ES-335

Introduced: **1965**

Double-triangle peghead inlay with sharp points: **1968**

Discontinued: **1971**

ES-335TD CRS: Country Rock Stereo model, 2 pickups, stereo electronics, coil-tap switch, master volume control, TP-6 tailpiece, brass nut, country tobacco or Dixie brown (pink-to-brown sunburst) finish, 300 made: **1979**

ES-335TD CRR: Country Rock Regular model, 2 Dirty Fingers humbucking pickups with exposed coils, coil-tap switch, brass nut, antique sunburst finish, 300 made: **1979**

ES-335 Centennial: guitar of the month, cherry finish, serial number in raised numerals on tailpiece, numeral *1* of serial number formed by row of diamonds, letter *i* of logo dotted by inlaid diamond, gold medallion on back of peghead, gold-plated hardware, limited run of no more than 101 serial numbered from 1894–1994, package includes 16 x 20 framed photograph and gold signet ring: **Aug. 1994**

ES-335 Custom: Custom Shop model, similar to ES-335 DOT but with thick 1958-style neck: **1996–current**

ES-335 Gothic: 2 '57 Classic humbucking pickups with no covers, black pickguard, ebony fingerboard, moon-and-star inlay at 12th fret, no other inlay, white outline of logo on peghead, black chrome hardware, flat black finish: **late 1998–current**

ES-335S: see Gibson Solidbody section

ES-335 Pro: 2 Dirty Fingers humbucking pickups with exposed coils, tune-o-matic bridge, stop tailpiece, bound fingerboard, dot inlay, crown peghead inlay, antique sunburst or cherry red finish: **1979–81**

ES-335 Studio: no *f*-holes, 2 Dirty Fingers humbucking pickups with covers (earliest with exposed-coil PAF humbuckers), single-bound top and back, mahogany neck, unbound rosewood fingerboard (earliest with ebony), dot inlay, no peghead ornament, decal logo, ebony or cherry finish

Introduced: **1986**

Wine red finish optional, classic white replaces alpine white: **1990**

Renamed **ES Studio: 1991**

Discontinued: **late 1991**

ES-337: no *f*-holes, 3 P-90 pickups, mahogany neck, bound ebony fingerboard, dot inlay, nickel-plated hardware

1 instrument made for Gibson employee Bruce Bolen:
c. 1984

ES-340TD: identical in appearance to ES-335 except for laminated maple neck (ES-335 has mahogany neck during entire production period of ES-340), 2 humbucking pickups, master volume control and master mixer control, walnut or natural finish
Available: **1969–73**

ES-240: identical to ES-335 except for coil-tap switch on lower bass treble bout near tone and volume knobs, stopbar tailpiece, wine red finish on 1 example
Shipping records show 3 instruments: **1977–1978**

ES-345TD: 2 humbucking pickups, stereo electronics (separates pickups and necessitates a Y-chord), Vari-tone rotary tone selector, black ring around Vari-tone switch, tune-o-matic bridge, stop tailpiece, laminated beveled-edge pickguard extends below bridge, triple-bound top, bound back, neck-body joint at 19th fret, single-bound rosewood fingerboard, double-parallelogram inlay, crown peghead inlay, gold-plated hardware, sunburst or natural finish
Introduced: **1959**
Cherry finish optional: **late 1959**
Shorter pickguard does not extend below bridge: **early 1961**
Gold ring around Vari-tone switch: **1960**
Last natural finish shipped: **1960**
Trapeze tailpiece with raised diamond: **late 1964**
Walnut finish optional: **1969**
Stop tailpiece: **1982**
Discontinued: **1983**

ES-347TD: 2 humbucking pickups, 4 knobs and 1 pickup selector switch on lower treble bout, coil-tap switch on upper treble bout, tune-o-matic bridge, TP-6 tailpiece, laminated beveled-edge pickguard, single-bound top and back, single-bound ebony fingerboard, large block inlay, single-bound peghead, crown peghead inlay, pearl logo
Introduced: **1978**
Not listed: **1986**
Listed as **ES-347S**, gold-plated hardware, ebony, vintage sunburst or Country Gentleman brown finish: **1987**
Multiple-bound peghead: **1987**

Antique natural finish optional, Country Gentleman brown finish discontinued: **1988**
Last listed: **1990**
Last made: **1993**

ES-355TD: 2 humbucking pickups, mono circuitry, tune-o-matic bridge, Bigsby vibrato (available without vibrato but extremely rare), SW vibrato (sideways action) optional, multiple-bound pickguard extends below bridge, multiple-bound top, triple-bound back, single-bound f-holes, neck-body joint at 19th fret, single-bound ebony fingerboard, large block inlay, multiple-bound peghead, 5-piece split-diamond peghead inlay, Grover Rotomatic tuners, cherry finish
Introduced: **1958**
Stereo electronics (separates pickups and necessitates a Y-chord) with Vari-tone rotary tone selector (**ES-355 TDSV**) optional but more common than mono, round Vari-tone knob in catalog photos through 1962 but virtually all with pointed knob: **1959**
Shorter pickguard does not extend below bridge: **early 1961**
SW vibrato (with sideways action) standard: **1961**
Kluson tuners: **1961**
Gibson vibrato with lyre on coverplate: **1963**
Grover tuners: **by 1967**
Walnut finish optional: **1969**
Bigsby vibrato: **1969**
Non-stereo, non-Vari-tone (ES-355TD) version discontinued: **1970**
Gibson vibrato with lyre on coverplate: **by 1978**
Discontinued: **1982**
Reintroduced, mono electronics, some with Varitone, pickguard extends below bridge (1959 style), some with Bigsby vibrato, replica orange oval Kalamazoo replica label, cherry sunburst, cherry, antique natural or vintage sunburst, limited runs from Custom Shop: **1994**, **1997**

ES-355 Centennial: guitar of the month, vintage sunburst finish, serial number in raised numerals on tailpiece, numeral *1* of serial number formed by row of diamonds, letter *i* of logo dotted by inlaid diamond, gold medallion on back of peghead, gold-plated hardware, vintage sunburst finish, limited run of no more than 101 serial numbered from 1894–1994, package includes 16" x 20" framed photograph and gold signet ring: **June 1994**

ES-357: Mitch Holder model, 2" deep, curly maple top, no ƒ-holes, 3 black soapbar P-90 pickups or 3 P-90 pickups with humbucking covers (pole-pieces across center of pickup cover), TP-6 fine-tune tailpiece, 4 knobs (3 volume, 1 master tone), selector switch, mini-toggle switch for middle pickup control, single-bound top and back, 3-piece maple neck, bound ebony fingerboard, pearl block inlay, crown peghead inlay, bound peghead, metal tuner buttons, gold-plated hardware, natural finish, black finish on back of peghead

7 made in Kalamazoo Custom Shop: **1983–84**
A few made in Nashville: **c. 1984**

ES-320TD: 2 Melody Maker pickups with embossed logo, oblong metal control plate with 2 knobs and 2 slide switches, tune-o-matic bridge, nickel-plated bridge cover with logo, black plastic pickguard, bound top and back (black-painted edges to simulate binding on natural finish models), rosewood fingerboard, dot inlay, decal logo, natural, walnut, or cherry finish
Introduced: **1971**
Discontinued (10 shipped in 1975): **1974**

ES-325TD: 1 ƒ-hole, semi-circular plastic control plate, 4 knobs, 2 mini-humbucking pickups with no visible poles, tune-o-matic bridge, trapeze tailpiece with pointed ends, single-bound top and back, dot inlay, cherry or walnut finish
Introduced: **1972**
Pickups with polepieces, wine red finish optional: **1976**
Discontinued (2 shipped in 1979): **1978**

ES-Artist: 1 3/4" deep, no ƒ-holes, 2 humbucking pickups, active electronics, 3 knobs (bass, treble, volume), 3-way selector switch, 3 mini-toggle switches (bright, compression/expansion, active on/off), tune-o-matic bridge, TP-6 tailpiece, laminated beveled-edge pickguard, multiple-bound top and back, single-bound ebony fingerboard, dot inlay positioned close to bass edge of fingerboard, winged-ƒ peghead inlay, pearl logo, gold-plated hardware, cherry sunburst, ebony or antique fireburst finish
Available: **1979–85**

ES-369: 2 Dirty Fingers pickups with exposed coils, 4 speed knobs, 1 selector switch, 1 mini-toggle coil-tap switch, tune-o-matic bridge, TP-6 tailpiece, single-ply cream-colored pickguard, single-bound top and back, single-bound rosewood fingerboard, pearloid trapezoid inlay, snakehead peghead, old-style script logo
Available: **1982**

DOUBLE CUTAWAY, FULLY HOLLOWBODY

ES-330TD: double rounded cutaway, shorter neck than 335 series, 2 black plastic-covered P-90 pickups, tune-o-matic bridge, trapeze tailpiece, single-bound top and back, bound fingerboard, dot inlay, pearl logo, no peghead ornament, sunburst or natural finish
Introduced: **1959**
Cherry finish optional, natural discontinued: **by 1962**
Chrome pickup cover(s), block inlay: **1962**
Sparkling burgundy finish optional: **1967–69**
Walnut finish optional: **1968**
Full-length neck (ES-335 style): **1969**
Discontinued: **1972**

ES-330T: 1 black plastic-covered P-90 pickup in middle position: **1959–62**

ES-150DC: see Full Depth Models, preceding

Crest: (also see Crest Special, preceeding) double rounded cutaways, flat back (some with arched back), laminated Brazilian rosewood body, 2 floating mini-humbucking pickups, multiple-bound rosewood pickguard, adjustable rosewood bridge, multiple-bound top, triple-bound back, single-bound ƒ-holes, backstripe marquetry, neck-body joint at 16th fret (like ES-330), fingerboard raised off of top, block inlay, multiple-bound peghead, 5-piece split-diamond peghead inlay, gold-plated (**Crest Gold**) or silver-plated (**Crest Silver**) hardware
Available: **1969–71**

DOUBLE-CUTAWAY, ROUTED BACK

ES-336: 13 3/4 wide, body lines similar to ES-335, routed mahogany back with solid center area, back beveled on bass side, solid carved maple top, ƒ-holes, 2 '57 Classic humbucking pickups, 4 knobs, Nashville tune-o-matic bridge, bound top and back, offset-V neck profile, bound rosewood fingerboard with compound radius, dot inlay, tapered peghead with straight string-pull, decal

logo, Custom Shop decal logo on peghead, sealed-back tuners, chrome-plated hardware, inked-on serial number with first digit corresponding to last digit of year of manufacture, emberglow or wine red finish, Custom Shop model
Available: **1996–current**

ES-346: fancier version of ES-336, flamed maple top, multiple-bound top, double-parallelogram inlay, gold-plated hardware, emberglow, faded cherry or gingerburst finish
Available: **1997–current**

Artist Models

Byrdland: Billy Byrd and Hank Garland model (see Thinlines, Single Cutaway, preceding)

Johnny Smith/Le Grand: 17" wide, 3 1/8" deep (not as deep as L-5), single rounded cutaway, X-braced carved spruce top, maple back and sides, 1 floating mini-humbucking pickup, knobs on pickguard, adjustable ebony bridge, L-5 style tailpiece with model name on center insert, multiple-bound top and back, 25" scale, multiple-bound ebony fingerboard with square end, split-block inlay, multiple-bound peghead, 5-piece split-diamond peghead inlay, gold-plated hardware, sunburst or natural finish
Introduced: **1961**
6-finger tailpiece: **by 1979**
Discontinued: **1989**
Reintroduced as **Le Grande:** chablis, dark wineburst, sunrise orange or translucent amber finish: **1993**
Vintage sunburst finish optional, sunrise orange discontinued: **1995**
Tri-burst finish optional: **1997**
Still in production

Johnny Smith Double: 2 floating mini-humbucking pickups
Introduced: **1963**
6-finger tailpiece: **by 1979**
Discontinued: **1989**
Listed as **Chet Atkins (JS) Double**, 1 prototype made, several made with experimental floating pickups: **Mar. 1989–Mar. 1991**

Barney Kessel Regular: 17" wide, full-depth body, most with laminated spruce top, double

pointed cutaways, 2 humbucking pickups, tune-o-matic bridge, trapeze tailpiece with raised diamond, model name on wood tailpiece insert, laminated beveled-edge pickguard, triple-bound top and back, mahogany neck, 25 1/2" scale, bound rosewood fingerboard, double-parallelogram inlay, bound peghead, crown peghead inlay, nickel-plated hardware, cherry sunburst finish
Introduced: **1961**
Laminated maple top: **1965**
A few with solid spruce top and solid maple back: **mid 1960s**
Discontinued: **1974**

Barney Kessel Custom: maple neck, bowtie inlay, musical note peghead inlay, gold-plated hardware: **1961–73**

Tal Farlow: full-depth body, deep rounded cutaway, binding material inlaid in cutaway to simulate scroll, 2 humbucking pickups, 4-point single-bound pickguard, toggle switch just below pickguard, tune-o-matic bridge, trapeze tailpiece with raised diamond, model name on wood tailpiece insert, triple-bound top, 25 1/2" scale, bound fingerboard, fingerboard inlay like inverted J-200 crest inlay, bound peghead, double-crown peghead inlay, viceroy brown finish
Introduced: **1962**
Discontinued: **1971**
TF-7: no specs available, listed: **April 1991**
Reintroduced, nickel-plated hardware, wine red or viceroy brown finish: **1993**
Still in production

Trini Lopez Standard: ES-335 thinline body, 16" wide, double rounded cutaways, diamond-shaped soundholes, 2 humbucking pickups, tune-o-matic bridge, trapeze tailpiece with raised diamond, model name on wood tailpiece insert, laminated beveled-edge pickguard, single-bound top and back, 24 3/4" scale, bound fingerboard, slashed-diamond inlay, 6-on-a-side tuners, no peghead ornament, decal logo, cherry finish standard, many with sparkling burgundy finish, a few with Pelham blue finish
Available: **1964–70**

Trini Lopez Deluxe: full-depth body, double pointed cutaways (like Barney Kessel models), diamond-shaped soundholes, 2 humbucking pickups, 3-way pickup selector on treble cutaway bout,

standby switch on bass cutaway bout, tune-o-matic bridge, trapeze tailpiece with raised diamond, model name on wood tailpiece insert, bound pickguard, pickguard cutout for switch, triple-bound top and back, bound fingerboard and peghead, slasheddiamond inlay, 6-on-a-side tuner arrangement, no peghead ornament, cherry sunburst finish
Available: **1964–70**

Les Paul Signature: 16" wide, thin body, bassside cutaway rounded similar to ES-335, trebleside cutaway more pointed like Les Paul Standard (solidbody), 2 oblong low-impedance humbucking pickups with white covers, 4 knobs (volume, treble tone, midrange tone, in/out phase switch), 3-way selector on upper bass bout, 2 jacks (high impedence on top, low-impedance on rim), large rectangular tune-o-matic bridge, bound rosewood fingerboard, trapezoid inlay, sunburst or gold finish
Introduced: **1973**
Rectangular pickups with embossed *Gibson*: **mid 1974**
High/low impedance humbucking pickups: **1976**
Sunburst finish discontinued: **1976**
Discontinued: **1978**

Howard Roberts Custom: 16" wide, full-depth body, pointed cutaway, laminated maple top, oval hole, 1 floating humbucking pickup, heightadjustable ebony bridge, multiple-bound pickguard, multiple-bound top and back, single-bound rosewood fingerboard, slotted-block inlay, multiple-bound peghead, vine-pattern peghead inlay, chrome-plated hardware, sunburst or cherry finish
Reintroduced from Epiphone line (with changes): **1974**
Some labeled *Howard Roberts Artist* (see General Information, Model Names): **1974–76**
Sunburst or wine red finish: **1975**
Discontinued: **1981**

Howard Roberts Artist: ebony fingerboard, gold-plated hardware, sunburst, natural, or wine red finish: **1976–80**

Howard Roberts Artist Double Pickup: bridge pickup mounted into top with mounting ring: **1979-80**

Howard Roberts Fusion: 14 7/8" wide, semihollowbody, 2 5/16" deep, cutaway shape similar to

Les Paul solidbody models, 2 humbucking pickups, 4 knobs, tune-o-matic bridge, TP-6 tailpiece, triplebound top, bound back, dot inlay, crown peghead inlay, chrome-plated hardware, sunburst, fireburst, or ebony finish
Introduced: **1979**
Ebony, cherry or vintage sunburst finish: **1985**
Renamed **Howard Roberts Fusion IIL: late 1988**
6-finger tailpiece: **1990**
Renamed **Howard Roberts Fusion III**, gold-plated hardware: **1991**
Cherry finish discontinued: **1993**
Still in production

B.B. King Standard: no *f*-holes, 2 PAF humbucking pickups, stereo electronics with 2 jacks, Nashville tune-o-matic bridge, TP-6 tailpiece, laminated beveled-edge pickguard, multiple-bound top and back, single-bound rosewood fingerboard, dot inlay, *Lucille* peghead inlay, chrome-plated hardware, ebony or cherry finish
Introduced: **1980**
Renamed **Lucille Standard: 1981**
Discontinued: **1985**

B.B. King Custom/Lucille: no *f*-holes, 2 PAF humbucking pickups, Vari-tone rotary tone selector switch, stereo wiring with 2 jacks, tune-o-matic bridge, TP-6 tailpiece, multiple-bound top and back, single-bound pickguard, ebony fingerboard, large block inlay, *Lucille* peghead inlay, gold-plated hardware, ebony or cherry finish
Introduced as B.B. King Custom: **1980**
Renamed **Lucille Custom: 1981**
Renamed **B.B. King Lucille: 1986**
Still in production

B.B. King "Little Lucille": see Blueshawk in Korinas, Firebirds, Misc. Solidbodies and Doublenecks section

Chet Atkins Country Gentleman (350XT, 3535): 17" wide, rounded cutaway, thinline semi-hollowbody, 2 humbucking pickups, 3 knobs (2 volume, 1 master tone) and 3-way selector switch on lower treble bout, master volume knob on cutaway bout, tune-o-matic bridge, ebony bridge base with pearl inlay, Bigsby vibrato with curved tubular arm, 7-ply top binding, 5-ply back

binding, single-bound *f*-holes, laminated maple neck, 25 1/2" scale, 21 frets, unbound ebony fingerboard, red rectangular inlays positioned on bass edge of fingerboard, 1 3/4" nut width, unbound peghead, crown peghead inlay, metal tuner buttons, gold-plated hardware, ebony or wine red finish

Prototype named Chet Atkins 350XT, introduced as **Chet Atkins 3535: June 1986**
Renamed **Chet Atkins Country Gentleman: Oct. 1986**
Sunrise orange finish optional: **1990**
Bigsby vibrato optional: **by 1993**
Ebony finish discontinued: **1995**
Still in production

Chet Atkins Tennessean: 16 1/4" wide, 1 5/8"

deep, single rounded cutaway, laminated maple back and sides with Chromyte (balsa) center block, 2 humbucking pickups, tune-o-matic bridge, stopbar tailpiece, clear pickguard with silver paint on back and model name stenciled in black, single-bound top and back, 25 1/2" scale, unbound ebony fingerboard, dot inlay positioned closer to bass edge of fingerboard, 1 3/4" nut width, clear plastic truss rod cover back-painted silver, Chet Atkins signature peghead decal, plastic tuner buttons, sunrise orange, wine red, Country Gentleman brown or ebony finish
Introduced: **1990**
Ebony finish discontinued: **1993**
Still in production

Chet Atkins (JS) Double: same as Johnny

Smith Double, 1 prototype made, several made with experimental floating pickups
Listed: **Mar. 1989–Mar. 1991**

ES-165 Herb Ellis: similar to single-pickup ES-

175, 16" wide, full-depth, pointed cutaway, 1 humbucking pickup, 24 3/4" scale, rosewood fingerboard, double-parallelogram inlay, model name and signature on peghead, decal logo, gold-plated hardware, cherry, ebony or vintage sunburst finish
Introduced: **1991**
Vintage sunburst finish only: **1995**
Still in production

Wes Montgomery: L-5CES with 1 humbucking

pickup in neck position, gold-plated hardware, vintage sunburst or wine red finish, Historic Collection model
Available: **1993–current**

Wes Montgomery Heart: reissue of one of Wes Montgomery's personal L-5s, heart-shaped pearl inlay with engraved *Wes Montgomery* in cutaway bout, special leather case, certificate, limited run of 25: **1997**

ACOUSTIC ARCHTOPS WITH OPTIONAL PICKUPS

Citation: 17" wide, full-depth body, rounded cutaway, solid spruce top, solid maple back and sides, 1 or 2 floating mini-humbucking pickups (some without visible polepieces), wood pickguard with fleur-de-lis inlay, control knob(s) on pickguard, fancy tailpiece, multiple-bound top and back, 5-ply maple neck, 25 1/2" scale, bound ebony fingerboard with pointed end, cloud inlay, multiple-bound peghead, fleur-de-lis inlays on front and back of peghead and on bridge, gold-plated hardware, varnish (non-lacquer) finish in sunburst or natural
Available: **1969–70**
Catalogued: **1975**
New series available: **1979–83**
Reintroduced, limited production: **1993**
Still offered

Kalamazoo Award: 17" wide, full-depth body, rounded cutaway, solid carved spruce top, solid maple sides, carved maple back, 1 floating mini-humbucking pickup (some without visible polepieces), adjustable ebony bridge with pearl inlays, wood pickguard with abalone inlay, knobs mounted on pickguard, multiple-bound top and back, bound *f*-holes, bound ebony fingerboard, abalone block inlay, multiple-bound peghead, flying bird peghead inlay, gold-plated hardware, varnish (non-lacquer) finish in antique sunburst or natural
Available: **1978–84**

Kalamazoo Award 100th Anniversary: 2 made for Yamano (Japanese distrubutor): **1991**

COMMENTS

Prewar: Gibson was the first company to manufacture a commercially viable hollowbody electric. Unlike the earliest efforts of Rickenbacker, Epiphone or National, the earliest Gibson electrics are still considered to be superb jazz guitars. The ES-150 and ES-250, both of which were used by Charlie Christian, are more highly regarded than any other prewar electric guitar.

Postwar full-depth: Non-cutaway models, except for the early postwar ES-300, were generally designed as student models and do not command high prices. Deluxe models, such as the L-5CES and Super 400CES, are considered by musicians and collectors to be among the finest instruments of their type ever produced. The laminated-body models, originally cheaper than the L-5CES and Super 400CES, are also fine instruments. Early ES-350s and ES-5s (without toggle switch or slide switch) have somewhat less utility than later versions but are fine instruments. The ES-5 Switchmaster, ES-350 (with toggle switch, 1952–56), ES-175 and ES-295 are very highly regarded.

Thinlines, fully hollow, single cutaway: The Byrdland is unsurpassed in quality, but because of its short scale and narrow neck, it brings much less than the extremely rare L-5CEST. The ES-350T was popularized by Chuck Berry, but is also somewhat limited in market appeal by its narrow, short-scale neck. Other single-cutaway thinlines are much less in demand.

Thinlines, double cutaway: The thinline design, double-cutaway body shape and semi-hollow construction are Gibson innovations that have been widely copied by other makers. Early ES-335, ES-345, and ES-355 models are highly sought. The ES-335, which had the lowest list price of the three, brings the highest price on the vintage market. The early version with PAF humbucking pickups, dot inlay and stop tailpiece is considered one of Gibson's classic models. The Vari-tone system of the ES-345 and the vibrato that was standard on the ES-355 make them less desirable than the ES-335. Natural finish models bring higher prices than sunburst or cherry. Fully hollow thinlines have never had the market appeal of the semi-hollow models.

Artist models: All are of fine quality. The Tal Farlow is the most highly sought. The Johnny Smith and others with acoustic construction and floating pickups are very highly regarded. Kessel and Lopez models have never had a great market appeal.

The Citation is one of the most modern Gibson models to be revered by collectors, with market prices among the highest for acoustic or electric-acoustic Gibsons from any period. The Kalamazoo Award is also highly regarded.

LES PAULS, SGs AND MELODY MAKERS KEYS

Not all model variations are included in this key.

CARVED TOP, SINGLE-CUTAWAY MODELS

All are **Les Paul** models

2 oblong low-impedance pickups
    Block inlay
        Guitar jack on top = **Recording**
        Mic jack and guitar jack on side = **Personal**
        Trapezoid inlay = **Professional**
2 mini-humbucking pickups
        Trapezoid inlay = **Deluxe**
        Dot inlay = **L.P. XR-II**

1 P-90 and 1 Alnico V pickup

  Custom, 1954–mid 1957

  Custom '54

  Custom Black Beauty '54 Reissue

2 soapbar pickups

  Ebony fingerboard = **Pro-Deluxe**

  Rosewood fingerboard

    Gibson on pickup covers = **Standard '58**

    Plain pickup covers

      Unbound top = **Studio Gem**

      Uniform binding depth

        Les Paul Model, 1952–mid 1957

        Goldtop Reissue, 1990-current

      Deeper cutaway binding

        Chrome-plated hardware = **Standard**

        Gold-plated hardware = **(40th) Anniversary**

2 black pickups with no polepieces = **Studio Lite, 1987–90**

2 EMG pickups

  Flat back = **Custom Showcase Edition**

  Contoured back = **Custom Lite Showcase Edition**

2 standard-size humbucking pickups

  Flame, tree-of-life or "harp" inlay = **Ultima**

  Hearts-and-flowers inlay = **Artisan**

  Corvette script inlay = **'60 Corvette**

  Slashed-block inlay

    25/50 on peghead = **25th Anniversary Les Paul**

    Split-diamond peghead inlay

      LE on truss rod cover = **Super Custom**

      No *LE* on truss rod cover = **Custom/400**

  Abalone block inlay = **The Les Paul**

  Pearl block inlay

    f-holes = **Bantam Elite/Florentine**

    Diamond-shaped soundholes = **Elite Diamond Sparkle**

    No soundholes

      Script *LP* peghead inlay = **L.P. Artist**

      5-piece split-diamond peghead inlay

        Contoured back = **Custom Lite**

        Flat back = **Custom**

  Abalone trapezoid inlay = **Elegant**

  Pearl trapezoid inlay

    Exposed-coil pickups

      Rosewood fingerboard = **Kalamazoo**

      Ebony fingerboard = **Standard Special**

    Covered pickups

      Les Paul signature on peghead

        Gold-plated hardware = **Heritage 80 Award**

        Nickel-plated hardware = **30th Anniversary**

      Custom Shop logo inlay on peghead = **Catalina**

GIBSON

2 standard-size humbucking pickups *(continued)*

Pearloid trapezoid inlay (full-size)

Walnut center piece in top = **Spotlight Special**

Explorer-style peghead, 6-on-a-side tuners = **Les Paul XPL**

Ebony fingerboard

Unbound top

Pickup covers = **Studio, 1990–98**

No pickup covers = **Studio Lite, 1990–98**

Multiple-bound top = **Black Beauty 82**

Chechen fingerboard = **Smartwood**

Rosewood fingerboard

No name on truss rod cover

Goldtop

Plain pickguard

Les Paul Model, mid 1957–mid 1958

Goldtop Reissue

Flowers on pickguard = **'57 Goldtop Mary Ford**

Any other finish

Uniform binding depth

Serial number begins with digit

Standard, mid 1958–60

Les Paul Reissue

Strings and Things Reissue

Guitar Trader Reissue

Serial number begins with *L*: **Leo's Reissue**

Deeper binding in cutaway = **CMT**

Classic on truss rod cover = **Classic**

Heritage 80 on truss rod cover

Rosewood fingerboard = **Heritage 80**

Ebony fingerboard = **Heritage 80 Elite**

Jimmy Wallace on truss rod cover = **Jimmy Wallace Reissue**

North Star on truss rod cover = **Les Paul North Star**

O-L-D H-I-C-K-O-R-Y inlay = **Old Hickory**

Standard on truss rod cover = **Standard, 1976–current**

Standard 82 on truss rod cover = **Standard 82**

St*udio* on truss rod cover = **Studio, 1996–98**

Small (3/4-scale) trapezoid inlay

Lightweight body (with tone chambers) = **Standard Lite**

Solid body = **Studio, 1999–current**

Dot inlay

Single-bound top

No coil-tap switch = **Studio Standard**

Coil-tap switch = **L.P. XR-II**

Multiple-bound top

Gold-plated hardware = **Studio Custom**

Chrome-plated hardware = **SM**

Unbound top

Gold-plated hardware = **Smartwood Exotic**

Chrome-plated hardware
    Walnut body = **The Paul**
    2-piece mahogany body = **The Paul Deluxe**
    3-piece mahogany body = **The Paul II/SL**
    Maple (or alder) top
        No coil-tap switch = **Studio**
        Coil-tap switch
            Rosewood fingerboard = **L.P. XR-I**
            Ebony fingerboard = **Studio Lite**
2 single-coil and 1 humbucking pickup
    Trapezoid inlay = **Classic with M-III electronics**
    Dot inlay = **Studio Lite/M-III electronics**
3 humbucking pickups
    Block inlay
    Custom
    Custom Black Beauty '57 Reissue
    Lightning bolt inlay = **Ace Frehley**
    Hearts & flowers inlay = **Artisan**

CARVED TOP, DOUBLE-CUTAWAY MODELS

SG body shape, pointed horns = **Les Paul '63 Corvette Sting Ray**
Non-SG body shape, rounded horns
    Explorer peghead, 6-on-a-side tuners
        2 pickups = **Les Paul Double-Cutaway XPL**
        3 pickups = **Les Paul Double-Cutaway XPL/400**
    Peghead tapered for straight string-pull = **Les Paul DC Pro**
    Standard Gibson center-dip "dove wing" peghead
        K-II on truss rod cover = **Les Paul K-II**
        No *K-II* on truss rod cover
            Dot inlay = **Les Paul DC Studio**
            Trapezoid inlay = **Les Paul Standard-DC**

FLAT TOP, SINGLE-CUTAWAY MODELS

1 pickup with no visible poles
        24 3/4" scale **= Melody Maker, 1959–60**
        22 3/4" scale = **Melody Maker 3/4, 1959–60**
1 pickup with visible poles
    Standard peghead
        Sunburst or cherry finish
        24 3/4" scale
            Stud bridge/tailpiece
            Les Paul Jr., 1954–mid 1958
            1957 Les Paul Jr. Single Cutaway
            bridge = **Les Paul Jr., 1986–92**
        22 3/4" scale = **Les Paul Jr. 3/4, 1956–mid 1958**
        Limed mahogany finish
        TV, 1955–mid 1958
        1957 Les Paul Jr. Single Cutaway
    Narrow peghead = **Melody Maker, 1986–92**

Flat top, single cutaway *(continued)*
2 pickups with no visible poles = **Melody Maker D**
2 pickups with visible poles
  Rosewood fingerboard
    1 mini-switch (coil-tap)
      Unbound top = **L.P. XR-I**
      Bound top = **L.P. XR-II**
    3 mini-switches = **Les Paul Special 400**
    No mini-switches
      Stud bridge/tailpiece
        Les Paul Model on peghead = **Les Paul 55**
        Les Paul Special on peghead
          Les Paul Special, 1955–mid 1958
          1957 Les Paul Special Single Cutaway
      Tune-o-matic bridge
        Dot inlay = **Les Paul Jr. II/Special**
        Mini-trapezoid inlay = **Jr. Special**

FLAT TOP, NON-SG STYLE, DOUBLE-CUTAWAY MODELS

Horns point into neck

1 pickup with visible poles
  Cherry finish
    Stud bridge/tailpiece
      24 3/4" scale
        Les Paul Jr., mid 1958–early 1961
        1960 Les Paul Jr. Double Cutaway
      22 3/4" scale = **Les Paul Jr. 3/4, mid 1958–early 1961**
    Tune-o-matic bridge = **Les Paul Jr. Double Cutaway**
  Limed mahogany finish
    Les Paul TV, mid 1958–early 1961
    1960 Les Paul Jr. Double Cutaway
1 pickup with no visible poles
  24 3/4" scale = **Melody Maker, 1961–65**
  22 3/4" scale = **Melody Maker 3/4, 1961–65**
2 pickups with visible poles
  Mini-trapezoid inlay = **Les Paul Jr. Lite**
  Dot inlay
    Les Paul Special on peghead
      24 3/4" scale
        Stud bridge/tailpiece
          Les Paul Special, early to mid 1959
          1960 Les Paul Special Double Cutaway
        Tune-o-matic bridge = **Special Double Cutaway**
      22 3/4" scale = **Les Paul Special 3/4**
    No *Les Paul* on peghead
      Bound fingerboard
        24 3/4" scale = **SG Special, late 1959–early 1961**
        22 3/4" scale = **SG Special 3/4, late 1959–early 1961**
      Unbound fingerboard = **All American II**

2 pickups with no visible poles

   Stud bridge/tailpiece = **Melody Maker D, 1961–65**

   Tune-o-matic bridge = **Melody Maker Double, 1977–82**

Flat Top, SG Style, Double-Cutaway Models

Horns point into neck

1 single-coil P-90 pickup (with visible poles)

   Les Paul on peghead = **SG/Les Paul Jr.**

   No *Les Paul* on peghead

      Cherry finish = **SG Jr.**

      White finish = **SG TV, 1961–68**

1 black plastic-covered pickup, mini-humbucking size = **SG I**

1 oblong pickup with no visible poles

   Controls into pickguard

      24 3/4" scale = **Melody Maker, 1966–71**

      22 3/4" scale = **Melody Maker 3/4, 1966–70**

   Oblong metal control plate = **SG-100**

1 humbucking pickup

   Dot inlay

      Coil tap = **All American I/SG-X**

      No coil tap = **Special I/SG Special**

   Split-diamond inlay = **SG 90 Single**

   Sting Ray inlay = **Les Paul '63 Corvette Sting Ray**

1 humbucking and 1 single-coil (or stacked double-coil) pickup

   Stopbar tailpiece = **SG 90 Double**

   Strings through body = **SG-Z**

2 humbucking pickups (metal-covered or exposed-coil)

   Trapezoid inlay

      Les Paul on truss rod cover = **SG/Les Paul Standard**

      No Les Paul on truss rod cover

         Vibrato = **SG Standard, late 1963–70**

         No vibrato

            Chrome-plated hardware = **SG Standard, 1988–current**

            Nickel-plated hardware = **SG Reissue**

         Gold-plated hardware = **SG Standard Korina**

   Block inlay

      Coil tap controlled by rotary knob = **SG Exclusive**

      Coil tap controlled by toggle = **SG Elite**

      No coil tap

         Semi-circular control plate = **SG Deluxe, 1971**

         No control plate

            Rectangular bridge base = **SG Deluxe, 1981–83**

            Oblong bridge base = **SG Standard, 1972, 1983–86**

   Dot inlay

      2 toggle switches = **SG R-1/Artist**

      1 toggle switch

         3 knobs = **SG Studio; Special II/SG Special, 1981–96**

         4 knobs

            Large pickguard = **SG Special, 1996–current**

2 humbucking pickups, dot inlay, 4 knobs *(continued)*
    Small pickguard
        Walnut body and neck = **The SG (Standard)**
        Mahogany body = **The SG (Deluxe), SG Standard 1981–83**
2 oblong single-coil pickups with non-adjustable poles = **AA II**
2 oblong pickups with no visible poles
    Controls mounted through pickguard
        6-string = **Melody Maker D, 1966–70**
        12-string = **Melody Maker-12**
    Controls on oblong metal control plate
        Cherry, walnut or black finish = **SG-200**
        Cherry sunburst finish = **SG-250**
2 soapbar pickups
    Knobs mounted into top
        Dot or block inlay = **SG Special**
        Split-diamond inlay = **SG Supreme**
    Knobs on semi-circular control plate = **SG Pro**
2 rectangular black plastic-covered pickups
    Block inlay
        Bound fingerboard = **SG Standard, 1973–80**
        Unbound fingerboard = **SG Special, 1973–78**
    Dot inlay
        Triangular wing-shaped pickguard
            Cherry or walnut finish = **SG II**
            Cherry sunburst finish = **SG III**
        3-point pickguard = **SG Special, 1972**
2 single-coil pickups and 1 humbucking pickup = **SG Special 400**
3 humbucking pickups with visible poles
    Les Paul plate on body near neck = **SG/Les Paul Custom**
    No *Les Paul* on instrument = **SG Custom**
3 mini-humbucking pickups with no visible poles = **SG-Deluxe**
3 oblong pickups = **Melody Maker III**

LES PAULS, SGs AND MELODY MAKERS

SECTION ORGANIZATION

GENERAL MODEL DIFFERENCES

Although the appearance of a 1950s Les Paul is different from a 1960s SG, the relationship between models is generally the same. In later decades Gibson did not adhere to these model delineations with respect to inlay patterns, binding and electronics.

Junior: 1 black dog-eared P-90 pickup, wraparound bridge/tailpiece, unbound rosewood fingerboard, dot inlay, nickel-plated hardware, decal logo

Special: same body as Junior of equivalent year, 2 black soapbar P-90 pickups, wraparound bridge/tailpiece, single-bound rosewood fingerboard, dot inlay, pearl logo, nickel-plated hardware

Standard: 2 pickups (originally soapbars, then humbucking pickups as soon as available), various bridges/tailpieces (changing as new designs become available), single-bound rosewood fingerboard, pearloid trapezoid inlay, pearl logo, nickel-plated hardware

Custom: originally with 2 pickups but with 3 as soon as humbuckings become available, tune-o-matic bridge, single-bound ebony fingerboard, pearl block inlay, low frets (until 1975), multiple-bound peghead, 5-piece split-diamond peghead inlay, pearl logo, gold-plated hardware

These general differences—number of pickups, type of bridge and style of fingerboard—also apply to the four models in the original reverse-body Firebird series (see Korinas, Firebirds, Misc. Solidbodies & Doublenecks section): Junior = Firebird I, Special = Firebird III, Standard = Firebird V, Custom = Firebird VII.

COMMON COLLECTORS TERMS

SG/Les Paul: Bodies on Les Paul models changed to SG-style double-cutaway, pointed-horn bodies in late 1960 and early 1961, but the model names (except for the Special) did not change until 1963. These models, with SG body and *Les Paul* on the peghead or on a body plate, are commonly referred to as SG/Les Pauls.

Les Paul Standard: *Standard* was not officially used until the introduction of the cherry sunburst finish in 1958. However, most collectors also refer to 1952–58 goldtop (officially called the Les Paul Model) as Les Paul Standard.

SG NECK-BODY JOINT

Joint at 22nd fret, smooth joint, immediate bevel (no lip): **1961**

Joint at 22nd fret, smooth joint, straight lip on back of neck at 21st fret: **1962**

Joint at 22nd fret, ledge around joint, curved lip on back of neck extends to 18th fret: **1962–66**

Joint at 19th fret, ledge at joint, lip extends to 16th fret: **1967–c. 1971**

Joint at 17th fret, ledge around joint, immediate bevel (no lip): **c. 1971–78**

Joint at 18th fret, smooth joint, lip extends to 16th fret: **1979–c. 1985**

Joint at 22nd fret, step around joint, lip extends to 20th fret: **c. 1986–current**

LES PAUL STANDARDS

Les Paul Model/Standard: carved 3-piece maple top, mahogany back and neck, 2 soapbar P-90 pickups with cream-colored cover, trapeze bridge/tailpiece combination with strings looping under bridge, single-bound top, binding inside cutaway same depth as binding around rest of top, single-bound rosewood fingerboard (earliest with unbound fingerboard), trapezoid inlay, pearl logo, *Les Paul* signature and *MODEL* silkscreened on peghead, Kluson Deluxe tuners, plastic keystone tuner buttons with single ring near tuner shaft, yellow silkscreened model name, no serial number, nickel-plated hardware, gold top finish, some with gold back and sides, a few with red top finish

Introduced as **Les Paul Model: mid 1952**

Serial number on back of peghead: **mid 1953**

Stud bridge/tailpiece: **late 1953**

Tune-o-matic bridge: **mid to late 1955**

Humbucking pickups, a few with all-mahogany body: **mid 1957**

Renamed **Les Paul Standard:** 2-piece bookmatched maple top, cherry sunburst finish: **mid 1958**

Jumbo frets, by #9 0348: **mid 1959**

Slimmer neck: **1960**

Metal caps on tone and volume knobs, plastic tuner buttons with double ring near tuner shaft: **very late 1960**

SG body, side-pull Deluxe Gibson vibrato, *Les Paul Model* on peghead, cherry finish: **very early 1961**

Les Paul on truss rod cover, crown peghead inlay, no *Les Paul Model* on peghead: **by mid 1961**

A few with pearl-inlaid ebony tailblock: **1962**

Discontinued, renamed **SG Standard** (see SGs, following): **late 1963**

Les Paul Standard reintroduced, 2-piece top, soapbar pickups, tune-o-matic bridge, deeper binding inside cutaway than on the rest of top (a few early with uniform-depth binding), small peghead, gold top finish: **1968**

Wider peghead: **early 1969**

Discontinued: **1969**

Not catalogued as Les Paul Standard but available as Les Paul Deluxe (see following) with optional full-size humbucking pickups, *Standard* on truss rod cover: **1972–76**

Les Paul Standard reintroduced, 4-piece pancake body (2 layers of mahogany with thin maple layer in middle, maple top), 3-piece top, 2 full-size humbucking pickups, tune-o-matic bridge, wider binding inside cutaway than on rest of top, *Standard* on truss rod cover, peghead decal with *Les Paul* signature and *MODEL*, plastic tuner buttons, serial number stamped on back of peghead, wine red, sunburst, cherry sunburst or natural top finish offered in catalog, tobacco sunburst finish also shipped: **late 1975**

2-piece body (solid mahogany back, 2-piece maple top), natural, cherry sunburst, dark sunburst, wine red, ebony or goldtop finish: **1978**

Alpine white, ebony, wine red, cherry sunburst or vintage sunburst finish: **1986**

Ebony, heritage cherry sunburst or vintage sunburst finish: **late 1987**

Silverburst finish optional: **mid 1988 only**

TV yellow finish optional: **1990 only**

Standard finishes: ebony, honey burst, heritage cherry sunburst or vintage sunburst: **1990**

Optional natural finish with gold-plated hardware, limited run: **late 1991–92**

Wine red finish optional: **1993**

Some Les Paul Reissues (see following) with less attractive woodgrain top downgraded from Reissue to Standard, inked-on serial number, *Standard* on truss rod cover: **early 1990s**

Still in production

Variations and Limited Runs

Blue, green and other custom color finishes, finished on top, back, sides and neck, made in Kalamazoo plant (last 3 digits of serial number below 500): **1980**

Red or blue metallic finish, finished on top, back, sides and neck, ebony fingerboard, metal tuner buttons with string-winders, 4-digit number under standard 8-digit serial number, gold-plated hardware: **1982**

P-100 pickups, goldtop finish: **1989**

Translucent yellow finish, limited edition Colours series: **Aug. 1990**

Translucent blue finish, exposed cream pickup coils, gold-plated hardware, limited edition Colours series: **Sept. 1990**

Translucent black finish, limited edition Colours series: **Oct. 1990**

Translucent purple finish, gold-plated hardware, limited edition Colours series: **Nov. 1990**

3-piece curly maple top: **1992**

Gold-plated bridge, tailpiece and pickup covers, black chrome tuners and knobs, ebony finish: **1993**

Les Paul Standard '58: mahogany back, maple top cap, similar to 1954 Les Paul Standard, 2 soapbar pickups with *Gibson* embossed on covers, wraparound bridge/tailpiece, 1-piece neck with no volute, goldtop finish

Introduced: **1971**

Discontinued from catalog: **1973**

Last shipped: **1975**

CMT: curly maple top, metal jack plate, deeper binding inside cutaway than other top binding, stamped 8-digit serial number, made primarily for Sam Ash stores: **1986–mid 1989**

Custom Shop Standard: Custom Shop model, 1 zebra-coil pickup, 1 black-coil pickup, no pickup covers, Grover tuners, faded cherry sunburst finish, Classic-style inked-on serial number (first digit corresponds to last digit of year of manufacture): **early 1997–current**

Standard 83: Custom Shop model, highly figured maple top, PAF-reissue humbucking pickups, ABR-1 tune-o-matic bridge, 1-piece mahogany neck, rosewood fingerboard, pearl trapezoid inlay, nickel-plated hardware, antique natural, vintage cherry sunburst or vintage sunburst finish: **1983**

Studio Standard: see Studios, following

Standard Lite: see **Double-Cutaway Carved-Top Les Pauls**, following

Standard Showcase Edition: guitar of the month series, EMG pickups, silverburst finish: **June 1988**

Standard Birdseye: birdseye maple top: **1993–96**

Standard Plus: figured maple top, honey burst, heritage cherry sunburst or vintage sunburst finish: **1995–97**

Standard Special: Custom Shop model, 2 PAF humbucking pickups, cream binding, bound ebony fingerboard, pearl trapezoid inlay, metal keystone tuner buttons, gold-plated hardware, cardinal red finish: **1983**

Studio Standard: see Studios, following

Standard Centennial: guitar of the month, vintage sunburst finish, limited serial number in raised numerals on tailpiece, numeral *1* of serial number formed by row of diamonds, letter *i* of logo dotted by inlaid diamond, gold medallion on back of peghead, gold-plated hardware, run of no more than 101 serial numbered from 1894–1994, package includes 16" x 20" framed photograph and gold signet ring
Available: **Oct. 1994**

Standard Reissues

The earliest Les Paul Standard Reissues were special-ordered by Gibson dealers. Typically, these have a highly figured top and uniform-depth binding in the cutaway, but other features of 1958–60 Standards—such as peghead size, body size and deep-dish top carving—may not be accurately reproduced.

Strings and Things Reissue: special order by Strings and Things, a Gibson dealer in Memphis, curly top, uniform-depth binding in cutaway, 28 produced
Available: **1975-78**

Jimmy Wallace Reissue: *Jimmy Wallace* on truss rod cover, special order by musician/dealer Jimmy Wallace, working from 1978–81 at Arnold & Morgan in Dallas, then through his own store at Sound Southwest in Sunnyvale, TX
Available: **1978-97**

Leo's Reissue: special order by Leo's Music, a Gibson dealer in Oakland, CA, made in Nashville, inked-on serial number starts with letter *L* followed by a space
Available: **1982–mid 1980s**

Guitar Trader Reissue: special order by Guitar Trader, a Gibson dealer in Redbank, NJ, serial number begins with 9, except for a few beginning with 0 (with thinner 1960-style neck), less than 50 made
Available: **1982–mid 1980s**

Heritage 80: 2-piece highly flamed maple top, binding inside cutaway same depth as rest of top binding, 3-piece neck, *Heritage 80* on truss rod cover, earliest with 4-digit serial number (0001, 0002, etc.), small peghead, nickel-plated hardware
Available: **1980–82**

Heritage 80 Elite: 1-piece neck, ebony fingerboard, *Heritage 80 Elite* on truss rod cover, chrome-plated hardware: **1980–82**

Heritage 80 Award: 1-piece mahogany neck, ebony fingerboard, pearl trapezoid inlay, gold-plated hardware, oval pearl medallion on back of peghead with limited edition number: **1981**

Standard 82: made in Kalamazoo plant (Heritage and Reissue were produced in Nashville plant), flamed maple top, uniform-depth binding in cutaway, 1-piece neck, *Standard 82* on truss rod cover, nickel-plated hardware
Available: **1982**

30th Anniversary: 2 PAF humbucking pickups, ABR-1 tune-o-matic with spring retainer, uniform-depth binding in cutaway, 3-piece mahogany neck, 1-piece neck optional, pearl trapezoid inlay, *30th Anniversary* engraved on inlay at 19th fret, nickel-plated hardware, all-gold finish, serial number with A-, B- or C-prefix followed by 3 digits
Available: **1982–83**

Les Paul Reissue/Flametop: copy of 1959 Les Paul Standard, deep-dish top carving, highly flamed maple top, plastic jack plate, binding inside cutaway same depth as other top binding, no model name on truss rod cover, inked-on 1950s-style serial number with 1st digit corresponding to last digit of year (earliest with 9 as 1st digit, standard 8-digit serial number in control cavity), heritage cherry sunburst, heritage dark sunburst or goldtop finish (goldtop described separately, see following)
Introduced: **1983**
Renamed **Les Paul '59 Flametop Reissue** (with thick 1959-style neck) and **Les Paul '60 Flametop Reissue** (with thin-profile Les Paul Classic-style neck): **late 1991**
"Replica" model with more accurate reproduction of originals, smaller peghead, elongated neck tenon (visible under neck pickup), floor of control cavity routed parallel to top of guitar, serial number beginning with 9 or 0 (for '59 or '60, respectively), 1st digit after space corresponds to year, *R9* or *R0* stamped in control cavity: **1993**
Available with plain top, quilt top, killer top or "distressed" treatment (finish checking, metal tarnishing, playing wear, etc.) by Tom Murphy; distressed

model available only from Vintage World in Cranston, RI; package for all models includes reissue brown case with pink plush lining and copy of book *Beauty of the Burst*: **early 1999**
Still in production

Les Paul '58 Plaintop: same specs as '59 Reissue except for plain maple top, heritage cherry sunburst or heritage red finish
Available: **1994–early 1999**

Les Paul '58 Figured Top: same specs as '59 Reissue except for less-figured top (more figured than '58 Plaintop)
Introduced: **1996**
Butterscotch or vintage red finish optional: **1997**
Discontinued: **early 1999**

Les Paul Reissue Goldtop: same as Les Paul Reissue (see preceding) but with goldtop finish
Introduced: **1983**
Soapbar P-100 pickups (same in appearance as P-90 but with humbucking with stacked-coil design): **early to mid 1990**
Renamed **Les Paul '56 Goldtop Reissue: late 1991**
Still in production

Les Paul '57 Goldtop: 2 humbucking pickups, nickel-plated hardware: **1993–current**

'57 Goldtop Mary Ford: '57 Reissue with ES-295 style gold leaves stenciled on pickguard, custom armrest on lower bass bout, 2 humbucking pickups, goldtop finish: **1997–current**

Les Paul '54: Custom Shop model, '57 Classic pickups with exposed black coils, wraparound tailpiece, nickel-plated hardware, oxblood finish: **1997**

OTHER STANDARD-RELATED LES PAULS

Carved top, 2 pickups and/or chrome-plated hardware.

Deluxe: 4-piece pancake body (2 layers of mahogany with thin maple layer in middle, carved maple top cap), 2 mini-humbucking pickups (some with soapbar pickups), rosewood fingerboard, trapezoid inlay, *Deluxe* on truss rod cover, *Les Paul* signature and *MODEL* silkscreened on peghead, gold top finish: **1969**
3-piece neck: **1969**
Cherry sunburst finish available: **1971**
Cherry finish available: **1971–75**
Walnut finish available: **1971–72**

Peghead decal with *Les Paul* signature and *MODEL*: **mid 1972**
Tobacco sunburst finish available (some years on left-handed model only): **1972–79**
Standard humbucking pickups optional, *Standard* on truss rod cover: **1972–76**
Natural finish optional: **1975**
RR red sparkle top finish optional: **1975 only**
BB blue sparkle top finish: **1975–77**
Wine red finish optional: **1975–85**
2-piece body, solid mahogany with maple top: **1977**
Discontinued: **1985**
Hall of Fame edition, all gold finish: **1991 only**
Reintroduced, limited run, natural finish: **1992 only**

Pro-Deluxe: 2 soapbar P-90 pickups, tune-o-matic bridge, cream binding, ebony fingerboard, trapezoid inlay, Schaller M-6 tuners, chrome-plated hardware, goldtop, ebony, tobacco sunburst or cherry sunburst finish
Available: **1978–81**

Pro Showcase Edition: guitar of the month, P-90 pickups, goldtop finish, limited run of 200 for U.S. distribution, 50 for overseas: **Dec. 1988**

North Star: multiple-bound top, single-bound fingerboard, trapezoid inlay, star peghead inlay, *North Star* on truss rod cover
Available: **1978**

Kalamazoo: Les Paul Standard made in Kalamazoo plant (regular production at this time was in Nashville), 2-piece top, 2 exposed-coil humbucking pickups with cream-colored coils, speed knobs, large rectangular tune-o-matic bridge, stop tailpiece, examples from first run with *Custom Made* plate nailed onto top below tailpiece, pearl trapezoid inlay, *Les Paul KM* on truss rod cover, antique sunburst, natural or cherry sunburst finish
Limited edition of 1500: **1979**

Spotlight Special: 3-piece top with curly maple outer pieces and walnut center, 2 PAF humbucking pickups, multiple cream-brown-cream top binding, rosewood fingerboard, trapezoid inlay, walnut peghead veneer, oval pearloid tuner buttons, gold-plated hardware, antique natural finish, serial number of 83 followed by a space and 4-digit ranking, production at least as high as 211 instruments
Optional antique sunburst finish with cream top binding,

ebony peghead veneer and keystone tuner buttons
Available: **1983–84**

XPL: Explorer peghead with 6-on-a-side tuner
configuration
Available: **1984**

Classic: based on 1960 model, no pickup covers,
1960 on pickguard, uniform-depth binding inside
cutaway, low-profile neck, *Les Paul Model* on peghead *Classic* on truss rod cover, inked on 1960
style serial number with 1st digit corresponding to
last digit of year, nickel-plated hardware, heritage
cherry sunburst, bullion gold, vintage sunburst or
honey burst finish
Introduced (some with 1989 serial number): **1990**
Last 4-digit number (0 999) of 1990, later numbers in
1990 are 5-digit with no space after 0: **late Nov.
1990**
Bullion gold (all gold) or ebony finish only: **1992**
Bullion gold, heritage cherry sunburst or honey burst
finish: **1993**
Les Paul Classic on peghead: **late 1993**
"Colors" series, translucent finishes, available: **late
1995**
No sunburst finishes: **1998**
Discontinued, limited run produced with Nashville
tune-o-matic bridge and Grover Rotomatic tuners,
goldtop version continues as Classic Plus (see following): **late 1998**

Classic Celebrity Series: black finish, white pickguard, gold-plated hardware: **July 1991**

Classic with M-III electronics: 1 humbucking and
2 single-coil pickups, introduced as limited run
model: **late 1991–93**

Classic Plus: figured maple top, translucent red,
translucent amber or translucent purple finish
Introduced: **late 1991**
Honey burst, heritage cherry sunburst or vintage sun-
burst finish optional: **1992**
Vintage sunburst finish discontinued, translucent
amber finish added: **1993**
Discontinued: **1996**
Reintroduced, figured top with translucent amber or
translucent red finish, starndard carved maple top
with bullion gold top finish: **1999**
Still in production

Classic Premium Plus: highly figured maple top
(flame runs all the way to the edge), honey burst,

heritage cherry sunburst or translucent amber
finish: **1993–97**

Classic Birdseye: birdseye maple top: **1993**

Classic Centennial: guitar of the month, goldtop finish, serial number in raised numerals on tailpiece,
numeral *1* of serial number formed by row of diamonds, letter *i* of logo dotted by inlaid diamond,
gold medallion on back of peghead, gold-plated
hardware, limited run of no more than 101 serial
numbered from 1894–1994, package includes 16 x
20 framed photograph and gold signet ring:
Feb. 1994

Anniversary: 2 P-100 stacked coil humbucking
pickups with cream soapbar covers, *40th Anniversary* engraved in 12th fret inlay, gold-plated hardware, black finish, limited run of no more than 300
Available: **1992–93**

Mahogany: mahogany body (no maple top), P-90
pickups
Available: **1993**

'60 Corvette: top scooped out to simulate side
scoops on 1960 Chevrolet Corvette automobile,
Corvette stylized script inlay, crossed racing flags on
peghead, cascade green, tuxedo black, horizon blue,
Roman red, sateen silver or ermine white finish
Available: **1995–97**

Bantam Elite/Florentine Standard: Custom
Shop model, '57 Classic humbucking pickups,
ebony fingerboard, pearl block inlay, 5-piece split-
diamond peghead inlay, gold-plated hardware, *f*-
holes with vintage sunburst, wine red or black finish,
diamond-shaped soundholes with gold, red or silver
sparkle finish, other sparkle finishes made in small
numbers as prototypes
Introduced as **Bantam Elite**: **1995**
Paint-finish models renamed **Florentine Standard**,
sparkle finish models renamed **Elite Diamond
Sparkle** (see following): **late 1995**
Discontinued: **1998**

Bantam Elite Plus/Florentine Plus: figured maple top,
gold-plated hardware, heritage cherry sunburst,
antique natural or emberglow finish standard, early
examples also in purple, emerald green, faded blue,
midnight blue, rosa red and translucent black finish
Introduced as **Bantam Elite Plus: 1995**

Renamed **Florentine Plus: late 1995**
Last offered: **1998**

Elite Diamond Sparkle: diamond-shaped soundholes, sparkle (metalflake) gold, red or silver finish standard, early examples with ice blue, Brunswick blue, black, copper or lavender sparkle finish
Available: **1995–97**

Elegant: Custom Shop model, highly flamed maple top, ebony fingerboard with compund radius, abalone trapezoid inlays, abalone Custom Shop peghead inlay, nickel-plated hardware, heritage darkburst or firemist finish
Available: **1996–current**

Variations
Quilt: quilted maple top: **1997**
Double Quilt: quilted maple top, figured mahogany back: **1997**
Super Double Quilt: highly quilted maple top, highly figured mahogany back, antique natural or butterscotch finish: **1997**

Ultima: Custom Shop model, highly flamed maple top, abalone top border, trapeze tailpiece, optional fingerboard inlay patterns of flame, tree of life or harp (from an early Gibson harp guitar fingerboard inlay), pearl tuner buttons, gold-plated hardware, heritage cherry sunburst finish
Available: **1996–current**

Catalina: Custom Shop model, ebony fingerboard with compound radius, pearl trapezoid inlay, pearl Custom Shop logo inlay on peghead, nickel-plated hardware, black pearl, canary yellow or Riverside red finish
Available: **1996–current**

Smartwood (Standard): Les Paul Standard with wood certified by the Rainforest Alliance, chechen fingerboard, pearl trapezoid inlay, gold-plated hardware, natural finish
Available: **1996–current**

Smartwood Exotic: see The Paul, following

Tie-Dye: top hand-finished by artist George St. Pierre in simulated tie-dyed pattern, limited run of about 100, each one unique
Available: **summer 1996**

Korina: figured maple top, korina back and neck, nickel-plated hardware
Available: **1997**

SIGNATURE MODELS

Jimmy Page: push/pull knobs control phasing and coil tapping, standard .050" fret height, Grover tuners with kidney-bean buttons, gold-plated hardware
Introduced: **1995**
After approximately 500 shipped: locking nut added to bridge height-adjustment, fret height lowered to .038", Kluson tuners with keystone buttons
Still in production

Joe Perry: curly maple top, specially wound bridge pickup, no binding, push/pull tone control to activate mid-boost, black burst stain finish
Introduced as limited run Custom Shop model: **1996**
Regular production model: **1997**
Still in production

Slash: Custom Shop model, Slash image carved into top, cranberry finish
Limited run of 50: **1997**

Ace Frehley: 3 DiMarzio pickups, multiple-bound top, bound fingerboard and peghead, lightning bolt inlay, signature at 12th fret, Ace graphic on peghead, heritage cherry sunburst finish
Introduced as limited run Custom Shop model: **1997**
Regular production model: **1997**
Still in production

LES PAUL CUSTOMS

Custom: 1-piece mahogany body with carved top, Alnico V neck pickup, black soapbar P-90 bridge pickup, tune-o-matic bridge, stop tailpiece, optional Bigsby (listed as a separate catalog model), multiple-bound top and back, single-bound ebony fingerboard, pearl block inlay, low frets (nicknamed The Fretless Wonder), *Les Paul Custom* on truss rod cover, 5-piece split-diamond peghead inlay, pearl logo, closed-back Kluson tuners, plastic tulip-shaped tuner buttons, gold-plated hardware, ebony finish (nicknamed The Black Beauty)
Introduced: **late 1953**
3 humbucking pickups (a few with 2 pickups): **mid 1957**

Grover Rotomatic tuners: **by 1959**

SG body, 3 humbucking pickups, side-pull Deluxe Vibrato, *Les Paul Custom* on plastic plate between fingerboard and pickup, white pickguard, white finish: **early 1961**

Note: The Custom's change to SG body came later than the Standard's. Many examples of single-cutaway "Black Beauty" Les Paul Customs exist with 1961 serial numbers.

Some with pearl-inlaid ebony tailblock (rare): **1962**

Renamed **SG Custom** (see SG section, following): **late 1963**

Les Paul Custom reintroduced, 7-ply top binding, low frets, *Les Paul* on truss rod cover, gold-plated hardware, black finish: **1968**

4-piece pancake body (2 layers of mahogany with thin maple layer in middle, maple top): **1969**

Neck volute: **1970**

Cherry or cherry sunburst finish optional: **1971**

3 pickups optional (see separate model listing, following)

Tobacco sunburst finish optional: **1972**

Twentieth Anniversary engraved in block letters on the 15th-fret inlay, black or white finish: **1974**

Standard jumbo frets, white or natural finish optional: **1975**

Wine red finish available: **1976**

2-piece body (solid mahogany with maple top): **1977**

Walnut finish optional: **1977–78 only**

Silverburst finish with chrome-plated hardware available: **1979–82**

No neck volute: **by 1980**

Ebony, Ferrari red or pewter finish available with chrome-plated hardware; ebony, Alpine white, wine red, cherry sunburst or vintage sunburst finish with gold-plated hardware: **1986**

Gold-plated hardware only, ebony, Alpine white, cherry sunburst or vintage sunburst finish: **late 1987**

Honey burst finish optional: **1990**

Translucent red finish, limited edition Colours series: **July 1990**

Translucent white finish, limited edition Colours series: **Dec. 1990**

Antique white or wine red finish: **1991**

Ebony finish available in limited runs: **1994**

Ebony, wine red or Alpine white finish: **1999**

Still in production

Custom 20th Anniversary: all Les Paul Customs in

1974 have *Twentieth Anniversary* engraved in block letters on the 15th-fret inlay, black or white finish: **1974**

Custom/maple fingerboard: 4-piece pancake body (2 layers of mahogany with thin maple layer in middle, maple top), carved maple top, 2 humbucking pickups, black pickguard, maple fingerboard, gold-plated hardware, ebony or natural finish: **1975–81**

Custom/nickel-plated parts: 4-piece pancake body (2 layers of mahogany with thin maple layer in middle, maple top), nickel-plated hardware, ebony or wine red finish

Offered as Special Edition model: **1976 only**

Introduced as catalog model: **1979**

Chrome-plated hardware: **1985**

Discontinued: **1987**

Wine red finish, 3 '57 Classic pickups, nickel plated hardware, limited Custom Shop run: **1996**

Custom/3 pickups: 3 pickups available as option on standard (2 pickup) Les Paul Custom: **1971–73, 1978**

3 pickups offered as "Special Edition Custom with 3 pickups," natural, ebony, or wine red finish: **1976 only**

Custom Showcase Edition: guitar of the month series, EMG pickups, ruby finish, limited run of 200 for U.S. distribution, 50 for overseas: **Mar. 1988**

Custom Plus: figured maple top, honey burst, heritage cherry sunburst or vintage sunburst finish

Introduced: **1991**

Dark wine finish optional: **1992**

Discontinued: **1998**

Custom '54: reissue of 1954 Les Paul Custom, Alnico V neck pickup, P-90 bridge pickup, standard 6-digit serial number with *LE* prefix

Introduced: **1972**

Discontinued: **1973**

Shipping records show 3 in 1975, 1 in 1977

Custom 25th Anniversary: *25th Anniversary* engraved in script on tailpiece, *Les Paul* signature on pickguard, chrome-plated hardware, metallic silver finish

Available: **1977**

Black Beauty '82: multi-ply cream binding, unbound ebony fingerboard, trapezoid inlay, speed tuners, gold-plated hardware, black finish, 4-digit serial number, some with additional standard 8-digit serial number
Available: **1982–83**

Super Custom: prototypes for Steve Perry model, earliest made in Kalamazoo factory, then in Nashville, 1 humbucking pickup with cover, 1 exposed-coil humbucking pickup, curly maple top, back and sides covered with curly maple veneer, multiple-bound top, 3-piece maple neck, single-bound fingerboard, Super 400-style slashed-block inlay, *LE* on truss rod cover, cherry sunburst finish all over
Available: **1984**

Custom Lite: 1 3/8" deep (5/8" thinner than Les Paul Custom), contoured back, 2 PAF humbucking pickups, 2 volume knobs, master tone knob, coil-tap switch, pickup selector switch on upper bass bout, ebony fingerboard, block inlay, Floyd Rose vibrato or tune-o-matic bridge and stopbar tailpiece, gold-plated hardware except for chrome-plated tuner buttons, metallic sunset, ebony, Ferrari red or pewter finish available wih chrome-plated hardware; Alpine white, metallic sunset, ebony, wine red, heritage cherry sunburst or vintage sunburst finish with gold-plated hardware
Introduced: **1987**
Gold-plated hardware only, metallic sunset, ebony or heritage cherry sunburst finish: **1988**
SW-5 sidewinder pickup in neck position, L-8 humbucking pickup in bridge position, black pickup covers with no visible poles, black chrome hardware: **1989**
Discontinued: **1990**

Custom Lite Showcase Edition: EMG pickups, active electronics, goldtop finish, limited run of 200 for U.S. distribution, 50 for overseas: **Aug. 1988**

Custom 35th Anniversary: 3 humbucking pickups, *35th Anniversary* etched on middle peghead inlay, 1959-style inked-on serial number
Available: **1989**

Custom/400: Custom Shop model, Super 400-style slashed-block fingerboard inlay, ebony or antique white finish, limited run
Available: **late 1991–92**

Custom Black Beauty '54 Reissue: reissue of 1954 model, Alnico V and P-90 pickups, Bigsby vibrato optional, ebony finish
Available: **1991–current**

Custom Black Beauty '57 Reissue: reissue of 1957 model, 2 or 3 humbucking pickups, Bigsby vibrato optional, ebony finish
Available: **1991–current**

'57 Black Beauty 3-Pickup Centennial: guitar of the month, 3 pickups, ebony finish, serial number in raised numerals on tailpiece, numeral *1* of serial number formed by row of diamonds, letter *i* of logo dotted by inlaid diamond, gold medallion on back of peghead, gold-plated hardware, limited run of no more than 101 serial numbered from 1894–1994, package includes 16" x 20" framed photograph and gold signet ring
Available: **Nov. 1994**

Mahogany Custom: Custom Shop model, 1-piece mahogany body with carved top, 3 '57 Classic humbucking pickups, gold plated hardware, faded cherry finish
Available: **1997**

Old Hickory Les Paul: tulip poplar body from 274-year-old tree on the grounds of The Hermitage (Andrew Jackson's residence in Nashville) felled by a tornado on April 16, 1998, Les Paul Custom trim, first 3 with timeline banner on top of guitar, hickory fingerboard, *Old Hickory* pearl fingerboard inlay, Andrew Jackson's image on peghead inlay (same image as on a $20 bill), image of The Hermitage on pickguard
Limited run of 200 introduced: **1998**

LOW-IMPEDANCE LES PAUL MODELS

Les Paul Personal and Les Paul Professional models were designed for use with the Les Paul LP-12 amplifier, which is equipped with low- and high-impedance inputs. For use with a standard high-impedance amp, a transformer cord is necessary.
Most Les Paul low-impedance models have different body dimensions than other Les Paul models. The last version of the Recording model has the same size body as the Standard and Custom.

Model	Width	Length	Depth
Standard, Custom	13"	17 3/8"	2"
Personal, Professional	14"	18 1/4"	2"
Recording	13 1/2"	17 3/4"	1 3/4"

Les Paul Personal: single cutaway, carved top, mahogany body, contoured back, 2 oblong low-impedance pickups mounted at a slant, *Gibson* embossed on pickup covers, microphone input jack on side of upper bass bout, mic volume control knob and 1 switch on upper bass bout, guitar input jack on side of lower treble bout, 4 knobs and 2 slide switches on lower treble bout, tune-o-matic bridge, Gibson Bigsby vibrato optional, low frets, block inlay (earliest with dot inlay), 5-piece split-diamond peghead inlay, gold-plated hardware, walnut finish
Available: **1969–70**

Les Paul Professional: single cutaway, carved top, 3-piece body of mahogany with center maple laminate, contoured back, 2 oblong low-impedance pickups mounted at a slant, *Gibson* embossed on pickup covers, pickup selector switch on upper bass bout, 4 knobs, slide switch for in/out phase, 3-position slide switch for tone, 3-prong jack, tune-o-matic bridge, Gibson Bigsby tailpiece optional, rosewood fingerboard, trapezoid inlay, chrome-plated hardware, walnut finish
Introduced: **1969**
Standard jack, no contour on back of body: **by 1970**
Discontinued: **1971**

Les Paul Recording: replaces Personal and Professional, 2 oblong low-impedance pickups mounted at a slant with embossed *Gibson*, 4 knobs (volume, treble, bass, "decade" tone control) and pickup selector on control plate, high/low imped-ance selector switch (transformer built into guitar), 3-way tone control and 2-way phase control on control plate, jack on top into control plate, tune-o-matic bridge, small block inlay, 5-piece split-diamond peghead inlay, walnut finish
Introduced: **1971**
White finish optional: **1975**
Selector switch on upper bass bout, 2 jacks in side: **by 1978**
Large tune-o-matic bridge in rectangular housing, ebony or cherry sunburst finish optional: **1978**
Discontinued: **1980**

Les Paul Signature: See Gibson Electric Arch-tops section

MISC. LES PAULS WITH CARVED TOP AND/OR HUMBUCKING PICKUPS

The Les Paul: solid maple top on maple back, 2 super humbucking pickups, 5-sided rosewood pickup covers, rosewood knobs and switch, rosewood pickguard, rosewood control plates on back, rose-wood outer binding, green- and red-stained wood inner bindings, maple neck, 3-piece ebony-rose-wood-ebony fingerboard, abalone block inlay, 5-piece split-diamond peghead inlay, pearl tuner buttons, pearl plate on back of peghead with limited edition number, gold-plated hardware, natural or rosewood finish
Introduced: **1976**
Large tune-o-matic bridge in rectangular housing, TP-6 tailpiece: **by 1978**
Natural finish only: **1979**
Discontinued: **1980**

Les Paul Artisan: carved maple top, 2 humbuck-ing pickups, 3 pickups optional, tune-o-matic bridge, TP-6 tailpiece, single-bound ebony finger-board, multiple-bound peghead, hearts-and-flowers inlay, hearts-and-flowers peghead inlay, pearl logo in thin pre-war style script, gold-plated hardware, walnut, tobacco sunburst, or ebony finish
Introduced: **1976**
3 humbucking pickups standard: **1979**
Large tune-o-matic bridge with rectangular base: **1980**
Discontinued: **1982**

The Paul (Standard): walnut body, 2 exposed-coil humbucking pickups, black mounting rings, selector switch near control knobs, tune-o-matic bridge, no pickguard, walnut neck, unbound ebony fingerboard, dot inlay, decal logo
Introduced: **1978**
First shipped: **1979**
Firebrand model, logo branded onto peghead (no inlay): **May 1981**
Discontinued: **1982**

The Paul Deluxe: mahogany body, beveled edges around lower treble bout, 2 exposed-coil humbuck-ing pickups, selector switch below tailpiece, no pickguard, unbound ebony fingerboard, dot inlay,

some with *Firebrand* on truss rod cover but not a Firebrand (branded logo) model, natural or antique natural finish
Introduced: **by 1980**
Ebony or wine red finish: **1985**
Discontinued: **1986**

The Paul II/SL: 3-piece mahogany body (not sandwich), carved top, 2 humbucking pickups, rosewood fingerboard, dot inlay, ebony or wine red finish
Introduced as **The Paul II** in All American series: **July 1996**
Moved to Les Paul line, renamed **The Paul SL** (SL for Sans Lacquer), polyurethane finish specified but many with lacquer finish: **1998**
Still in production

Smartwood Exotic: The Paul II with body of exotic wood certified by the Rainforest Alliance, mahogany back, top cap options include curupay, taperyva guasu, cancharana, peroba, banara or ambay guasu, 2 humbucking pickups, 2 knobs, 1 switch, curupay fingerboard, dot inlay, gold-plated hardware, SL (Sans Lacquer) matte polyurethane finish specified available: **1998–current**

25th Anniversary Les Paul: limited edition to mark 25th anniversary of model, 50th anniversary of Les Paul's career, carved maple top, 2 humbucking pickups, coil-tap switch, black barrel knobs, tune-o-matic bridge, TP-6 tailpiece, bound fingerboard and peghead, slashed-block inlay, brass nut, *25* over *50* inlaid on peghead, metal keystone tuner buttons, gold-plated hardware, cherry sunburst, black, wine red or natural finish, regular serial number and limited edition number on back of peghead, at least 1842 produced
Available by special order (some with 1978 number): **1979**

L.P. Artist: also referred to as Les Paul Active, 2 humbucking pickups (3 pickups optional), active electronics, 3 knobs (volume, treble, bass), 3 mini switches (expansion, compression, brightness), tune-o-matic bridge, TP-6 fine-tune tailpiece, multiple-bound top, bound ebony fingerboard, large block inlay, brass nut, triple-bound peghead, script *LP* peghead inlay, gold-plated hardware, sunburst finish

Introduced: **1979**
Fireburst or ebony optional: **1980**
Discontinued: **1982**

L.P. XR-1: flat top, 2 exposed-coil Dirty Fingers humbucking pickups, coil-tap switch, unbound top, 3-piece maple neck, unbound rosewood fingerboard, dot inlay, tobacco sunburst, cherry sunburst or goldburst finish
Introduced: **1981**
Discontinued: **by 1983**

L.P. XR-II: flat or carved top of figured maple, laminated mahogany body, 2 super humbucking pickups specified, examples with metal-covered mini-humbucking pickups with no polepieces and *Gibson* embossed on pickup covers, coil-tap switch, Nashville tune-o-matic bridge, bound top, 3-piece maple or 2-piece mahogany neck, unbound rosewood fingerboard, dot inlay, pearl logo, metal tuner buttons, chrome-plated hardware, honey sunburst or vintage cherry sunburst finish
Available: **1981–82**

L.P. Session/XR-III: specs unavailable
Introduced as **L.P. Session: 1982**
Renamed **L.P. XR-III: May 1982**
Discontinued: **late 1982**

Les Paul Silver Streak: dot inlay, all silver finish
Available: **1982**

LES PAUL STUDIOS

Les Paul SM: possible prototype for Les Paul Studio, made in Kalamazoo factory, contoured back, 2 humbucking pickups, coil tap, multiple-bound top, bound fingerboard, dot inlay, *SM* on truss rod cover, silverburst finish
Available: **1980**

Les Paul Studio: alder body, carved top, 2 PAF humbucking pickups with covers, 4 knobs, selector switch on upper bass bout, tune-o-matic bridge, black pickguard, no binding anywhere, 1-piece maple neck, rosewood fingerboard, dot inlay, pearloid keystone tuner buttons, *Studio* on truss rod cover, *Les Paul Model* decal on peghead, decal logo, plastic keystone tuner buttons, chrome-plated hardware, natural, electric blue, pewter or tobacco sunburst finish

Introduced: **1983**

Ebony, white or wine red finish: **1984**

Night violet offered as Custom Shop finish, gold-plated hardware: **1984–85**

Ebony fingerboard: **1986**

Mahogany neck, trapezoid inlay, gold-plated hardware optional, TV yellow finish optional but available with chrome-plated hardware only: **1990**

TV yellow finish discontinued, Alpine white finish available only with gold-plated hardware: **1991**

Rosewood fingerboard: **1994**

Rosewood or ebony fingerboard (ebony fingerboard only with Alpine white finish): **1996**

Limited run of 90 for Guitar Center, P-90 pickups, white finish, gold-plated hardware: **1997**

Rosewood fingerboard, medium (3/4-size) trapezoid inlay, chrome- or gold-plated hardware, ebony, emerald or ruby finish: **1999**

Still in production

Miller Genuine Beer Les Paul: Miller Genuine logo, approx. 20 made: **1992**

Les Paul Studio Synthesizer: Roland 700
synthesizer system, Alpine white or ebony finish

Only listing: **1985**

Studio Standard: cream binding on top, cream-
bound rosewood fingerboard, dot inlay, sunburst, cherry sunburst, or white finish

Introduced: **1984**

Ferrari red finish only: **1986**

Discontinued: **1988**

Studio Custom: multiple-bound top, bound rose-
wood fingerboard, gold-plated hardware, Alpine white, cherry sunburst, sunburst or ebony finish

Available: **1984–85**

Studio Lite: 1 3/8" deep, contoured back, 2 special
pickups, 2 knobs, coil-tap switch, tune-o-matic bridge, stop tailpiece, unbound ebony fingerboard, dot inlay, *Les Paul Model* peghead decal, pearl logo, plain truss rod cover, ebony, Alpine white or nuclear yellow finish

Introduced: **1987**

"Sidewinder" humbucking pickup in neck position, L-8

humbucking pickup in bridge position, black pickup covers with no visible polepieces, Floyd Rose vibrato, ebony, Alpine white or candy apple red finish: **1989**

Black chrome hardware, jade, black, heritage cherry sunburst, vintage sunburst or translucent red finish: **1990**

Humbucking pickups with exposed coils, trapezoid inlay, translucent black, translucent blue or translucent red finish: **1991**

Vintage sunburst or heritage cherry sunburst finish available with gold-plated hardware: **1992**

Black chrome hardware with translucent blue finish, gold-plated hardware with vintage sunburst or heritage cherry sunburst finish: **1993**

Discontinued: **1998**

Studio Lite/lightly figured maple top: 2-piece or 3-piece top of figured maple, 2 humbucking pickups with exposed coils, trapezoid inlay, translucent red or translucent amber finish, limited run: **late 1991**

Studio Lite/M-III electronics: 2 humbucking pickups and 1 single coil pickup, 2 knobs, 1 slide switch, 1 mini-switch, introduced as limited run but then offered as catalog model: **late 1991–94**

Studio Gem: 2 P-90 cream soapbar pickups, rose-
wood fingerboard, trapezoid inlay, *Studio* on truss rod cover, pearl logo, gold-plated hardware, ruby red, emerald green, topaz yellow, sapphire blue or amethyst purple finish

Available: **1996–97**

Double-Cutaway Carved-Top Les Pauls

K-II: double cutaway, carved top, 2 humbucking pickups

Available: **1980**

Double-Cutaway XPL: does not say *Les Paul*
anywhere, symmetrical double-cutaway, carved top, 2 humbucking pickups, 4 knobs, selector switch above knobs, Gibson/Kahler Supertone vibrato or tune-o-matic bridge, bound top, 24 3/4" scale, bound ebony fingerboard, 22 frets, dot inlay, 6-on-a-side tuner configuration, peghead points to treble side, decal logo, chrome-plated hardware, heritage cherry sunburst or heritage dark sunburst finish,

Custom Shop model

Introduced: **1984**

Rosewood fingerboard, Ferrari red finish optional:
1985

Discontinued: **1987**

Double-Cutaway XPL/400: 400-series electronics, 1 Dirty Fingers humbucking pickup and 2 single-coil pickups, master tone and master volume knob, 3 mini-switches for on/off pickup control, push/pull volume control for coil tap, rosewood fingerboard, cream binding

Introduced: **1984**

Ebony fingerboard, white binding: **mid 1984**

Discontinued: **1985**

DC Pro: Custom Shop model, double-cutaway body shape like 1959 Les Paul Jr., rounded horns, carved highly figured maple top, 2 humbucking pickups with tune-o-matic or wraparound bridge, or 2 P-90 white soapbar pickups with wraparound bridge, 24 3/4" or 25 1/2" scale, tapered peghead for straight string-pull, nickel-plated hardware, translucent black, translucent indigo, butterscotch, heritage darkburst or faded cherry finish

Available: **1997–98**

DC Studio: double-cutaway body shape like 1959 Les Paul Jr., rounded horns, carved maple top, 2 humbucking pickups, 2 knobs, wraparound tailpiece, unbound top and back, 24 3/4" scale, unbound rosewood fingerboard, dot inlay, standard peghead shape, chrome-plated hardware, ebony, heritage cherry sunburst, emerald green or ruby finish

Introduced: **1997**

Tune-o-matic bridge: **1998**

Discontinued: **late 1998**

Standard-DC/DC Standard: double-cutaway body shape like 1959 Les Paul Jr., rounded horns, carved flame maple top, 2 humbucking pickups, 2 knobs, switch near bridge, tune-o-matic bridge, unbound top, unbound back, 24 3/4" scale, bound rosewood fingerboard, trapezoid inlay, standard peghead shape, pearl logo, no Les Paul designation on peghead or truss rod cover, chrome- or gold-plated hardware, translucent finish colors: amber serrano, blue diamond, black pepper, red hot

tamale or green jalapeno; limited edition finish colors: tangerine burst or lemon burst

Introduced: **1998**

Discontinued, similar model introduced as Standard Lite, see following: **1999**

Standard Lite: double-cutaway body shape like 1959 Les Paul Jr., rounded horns, 2 humbucking pickups with covers, no binding, rosewood fingerboard, medium (3/4-size) trapezoid inlay, no Les Paul designation on peghead or truss rod cover, gold-plated hardware, translucent amber, translucent red or translucent blue finish

Available: **1999–current**

Les Paul Juniors

Les Paul Jr.: flat top, slab mahogany body, single cutaway, 1 black P-90 pickup, stud-mounted bridge/tailpiece, tortoiseshell plastic pickguard, 16 frets clear of body, unbound rosewood fingerboard, dot inlay, yellow silkscreen logo and model name on peghead, nickel-plated hardware, sunburst finish

Introduced: **mid 1954**

Double cutaway with rounded horns, 22 frets clear of body on regular Jr., 15 frets clear on Jr. 3/4, cherry red finish: **mid 1958**

SG body, laminated pickguard, *Les Paul Jr.* on peghead, cherry finish: **early 1961**

Maestro vibrato optional: **by 1962**

Renamed **SG Jr.** (see SG section, following): **late 1963**

Les Paul Jr. reintroduced, single-cutaway, P-90 pickup with black "dog-ear" cover, tune-o-matic bridge, gold knobs, rosewood fingerboard, dot inlay, model name on peghead, decal logo, metal tuner buttons, chrome-plated hardware, heritage cherry or tobacco sunburst finish: **1986**

Black knobs: **early 1987**

Pearl white finish optional: **late 1987**

P-100 stacked-coil humbucking pickup with dog-eared cover, heritage cherry, tobacco sunburst or TV yellow finish: **1990**

Discontinued from price list: **late 1991**

Last made: **early 1992**

Reintroduced as **1957 Les Paul Jr. Single Cutaway**, P-90 pickup, vintage sunburst, faded cherry or TV yellow finish, Custom Shop model: **1998**

Still in production

Les Paul Jr. 3/4: same body size and shape as Les Paul Jr., shorter neck, shorter 22 3/4" scale, 14 frets clear of body, introduced: **1956**
Jr. 3/4 discontinued: **early 1961**

Les Paul TV: Les Paul Jr. with limed mahogany finish (name derives either from popular TV cabinet finishes of the day or from the belief that the finish would show up better than sunburst on black-and-white TV), a few early examples are natural finish mahogany
Introduced: **1954**
Finish described as natural in price list and as limed oak in catalog: **1956**
Limed mahogany finish in catalog description: **1957**
Double cutaway with rounded horns: **mid 1958**
Renamed **SG TV**, still with rounded cutaway horns: **late 1959**
SG body shape, white finish (see SG section, following): **early 1961**

Les Paul Jr. Double Cutaway: double-cutaway with rounded horns, P-90 pickup with black "dog-ear" cover, tune-o-matic bridge, 22 frets, 24 3/4" scale, rosewood fingerboard, dot inlay, model name on peghead, decal logo, metal tuner buttons, chrome-plated hardware, heritage cherry or tobacco sunburst finish
Introduced: **1987**
Pearl white finish optional: **late 1987**
Ebony, coral or luna silver finish: **1988**
Plastic tuner buttons, sunburst finish optional: **1989**
Discontinued: **mid 1989**
Limited run of 200, P-100 stacked-coil humbucking pickup with dog-eared cover, nickel-plated hardware, TV yellow finish, Hall of Fame series: **1990–92**
Reintroduced, P-90 pickup, heritage cherry or TV yellow finish: **1995**
Discontinued: **1996**
Reintroduced as **1957 Les Paul Jr. Double Cutaway**, P-90 pickup, faded cherry or TV yellow finish, Custom Shop model: **1998**
Still in production

Jr. DC SP: Les Paul Special double cutaway reissue, see following

Jr. II: reissue of single-cutaway Les Paul Special (model name derives from internal product code for 2-pickup Jr.), see Les Paul Specials, following

Jr. Special: single-cutaway Les Paul Special, see Les Paul Specials, following

Junior Lite: double-cutaway Les Paul Special, see Les Paul Specials, following

LES PAUL SPECIALS

Special: flat top, slab body, single cutaway, 2 black soapbar P-90 pickups, neck pickup next to fingerboard, stud bridge/tailpiece, laminated beveled-edge pickguard, 4 knobs, toggle switch on upper bass bout, single-bound rosewood fingerboard, dot inlay, pearl peghead logo, yellow silkscreen model name, nickel-plated hardware, limed mahogany finish (a few very early with natural finish)
Introduced: **1955**
Double cutaway with rounded horns, switch near bridge, 22 frets clear of body, cherry red finish optional: **early 1959**
Space between neck pickup and fingerboard, switch farther away from bridge: **mid 1959**
Renamed SG Special: **late 1959**
SG body (see SG section, following): **early 1961**
Single-cutaway and double-cutaway versions reintroduced, see following

Special 3/4: same body shape and size as double-cutaway Les Paul Special, shorter 22 3/4" scale, 15 frets clear of body, cherry finish
Introduced: **1959**
Renamed SG Special 3/4: **late 1959**
SG body (see SG section, following): **early 1961**

Les Paul 55: single cutaway, slab mahogany body, 2 black soapbar pickups, tune-o-matic bridge (earliest with wraparound bridge/tailpiece), mahogany neck, 23 frets, 24 3/4" scale, bound rosewood fingerboard, dot inlay, *Les Paul Model* on peghead, pearl logo, plastic keystone tuner buttons, sunburst or wine red finish
Introduced: **1974**
Sunburst or limed mahogany finish: **1977**
Wine red finish optional: **1979**
Discontinued: **1981**

Special Double Cutaway: reissue of double-cutaway Les Paul Special, rounded horns, 2 black soapbar P-90 pickups, switch on treble side near bridge, tune-o-matic bridge, mahogany neck, 22 frets, 24 3/4" scale, bound rosewood fingerboard, *Les Paul Model* on peghead, bound rosewood fingerboard, dot inlay, metal tuner buttons, chrome-plated hardware, sunburst, cherry or limed mahogany finish

Introduced as limited edition, *LE* with serial number: **1976**

Regular production model, ebony, tobacco sunburst, sunburst or wine red finish: **1978**

Cherry, limed mahogany or sunburst finish: **1979**

Not listed: **1986–87**

Listed as **Les Paul Jr. Double Cutaway Special: 1988**

Discontinued: **1989**

Reintroduced as **Les Paul Special Double Cutaway**, Custom Shop model, 2 P-90 pickups, vintage neck joint, wraparound tailpiece, nickel-plated hardware, offered first as limited run of 300, then put into regular production: **late 1993**

Discontinued: **1995**

Reintroduced as **1960 Les Paul Special Double Cutaway**, 2 P-90 pickups, bound fingerboard, faded cherry or TV yellow finish, Custom Shop model: **1998**

Similar model reintroduced in regular production as Jr. Lite (see following)

Still in production

Special Double Cut Centennial: guitar of the month, serial number in raised numerals on tailpiece, numeral *1* of serial number formed by row of diamonds, letter *i* of logo dotted by inlaid diamond, gold medallion on back of peghead, gold-plated hardware, heritage cherry finish, limited run of no more than 101 serial numbered from 1894–1994, package includes 16" x 20" framed photograph and gold signet ring

Available: **Jan. 1994**

Jr. Lite: double-cutaway Special, contoured back on bass side, 2 P-100 pickups, 4 knobs, selector switch near bridge, tune-o-matic bridge, unbound rosewood fingerboard, mini-trapezoid (1/2-scale) inlay, *Les Paul Special* signature decal on peghead, ebony, natural or cinnamon finish

Available: **1999–current**

Special 400: single cutaway, 400-series electronics, 1 Dirty Fingers humbucking pickup and 2 sin-

gle-coil pickups, master tone and master volume knob, 3 mini-switches for on/off pickup control, push/pull volume control for coil tap, vibrato, early with rosewood fingerboard and creme binding, later with ebony fingerboard and white binding

Available: **1985**

Junior II/Special (single-cutaway): reissue of single-cutaway Les Paul Special (model name derives from Gibson internal code for Special as 2-pickup Jr.), single cutaway, slab mahogany body, 2 black soapbar P-100 pickups, tune-o-matic bridge, bound rosewood fingerboard, *Les Paul Special* on peghead, heritage cherry, tobacco sunburst or ebony finish

Introduced as **Junior II: early 1989**

Renamed **Special**, heritage cherry, tobacco sunburst, or TV yellow finish: **late 1989**

Run of 300 with *LE* serial number, P-100 pickups: **1990**

Ebony finish optional: **1992 only**

Renamed **Special SL:** SL for Sans Lacquer, unbound fingerboard, polyurethane finish specified but many with lacquer: **1998**

Renamed **1960 Les Paul Special Single Cutaway**, 2 P-90 pickups, bound fingerboard, faded cherry or TV yellow lacquer finish, Custom Shop model: **1998**

Similar model continues in regular production as Jr. Special (see following)

Still in production

Les Paul Special Single Cutaway Centennial: serial number in raised numerals on tailpiece, numeral *1* of serial number formed by row of diamonds, letter *i* of logo dotted by inlaid diamond, gold medallion on back of peghead, gold-plated hardware, gold finish (serial number with 2-suffix) or TV yellow finish (serial number with 3-suffix)

Announced as models in Centennial guitar of the month program, but never put into production or offered for public sale, prototypes used for promotions: 1 TV yellow for CompuServe promo, a few gold for Aerosmith promo, 1 gold for Six Flags promo: **1994**

Jr. Special: contoured back on bass side, 2 P-100 stacked-coil humbucking pickups, 4 knobs, selector switch on upper bass bout, tune-o-matic bridge, unbound rosewood fingerboard, mini-trapezoid inlay (1/2-size), *Les Paul Special* signature decal on

peghead, ebony, cinnamon or natural finish:
1999–current

SG Standard/Deluxe

SG Standard: Les Paul Standard changes to SG
body shape, 2 humbucking pickups, 4 knobs, selector switch by pickguard, side-pull Deluxe Gibson
vibrato, *Les Paul* on truss rod cover, crown peghead inlay (prototypes with *Les Paul Model*
silkscreened on peghead), pearl logo, cherry finish:
very late 1960
Some with pearl-inlaid ebony tailblock (rare): **1962**
Renamed **SG Standard:** Maestro vibrato (up-and-
down pull) with lyre and logo on coverplate, no *Les
Paul* on truss rod cover: **late 1963**
Larger pickguard surrounds pickups, no pickup
frames: **1966**
Discontinued, replaced by **SG Deluxe** (see following):
1971
Reintroduced, 2 metal-covered humbucking pickups, no
space between neck pickup and end of fingerboard,
large rectangular tune-o-matic bridge, old-style 3-
point pickguard, barrel knobs, unbound rosewood
fingerboard, small block inlay, crown peghead inlay,
cherry, walnut or natural finish: **late 1972**
Black plastic-covered humbucking pickups: **1973**
Oval tune-o-matic bridge base: **1975**
Bigsby vibrato standard, stop tailpiece optional, cherry,
walnut, white or tobacco sunburst finish: **1976**
Bigsby optional: **1977**
Toggle switch near knobs, jack into side: **1980**
Discontinued, name continues on The SG (Standard),
see following: **1981**
Reintroduced, metal-covered humbucking pickups,
small block inlay, cherry or sunburst finish: **1983**
Discontinued: **1987**
Reintroduced, space between neck pickup and end of
fingerboard, selector switch near lower edge of
body, jack in side, small pickguard, trapezoid inlay,
metal tuner buttons, ebony or wine red finish: **1988**
Heritage cherry, candy apple red, ebony, silver luna or
candy apple blue finish: **1990**
Large pickguard, jack into top, silver luna finish dis-
continued, TV yellow added: **1991**
Limited runs of candy apple blue and candy apple red
finish: **1992**
Ebony or heritage cherry finish only: **1993**
Limited run with natural burst finish: **late 1998**
Still in production

SG Standard Celebrity Series: black finish, white
knobs, white pickguard, gold-plated hardware: **Aug.
1991**

SG Standard Korina: korina (African limba wood)
body, 3-piece sandwich body with rosewood center
laminate, gold-plated hardware, antique natural
finish, limited run of 500: **1993–94**

SG Deluxe: replaces SG Standard, non-beveled
cutaways, 2 humbucking pickups, 4 black bonnet
knobs, triangular pickguard (Les Paul Standard-
style) flush with top, tune-o-matic bridge, Gibson
Bigsby vibrato, semi-circular control plate, bound
rosewood fingerboard, small block inlay (some with
dots), natural, cherry or walnut finish
Introduced: **1971**
Discontinued (SG Standard reintroduced): **1972**
16 shipped: **1973–74**
Reintroduced, large tune-o-matic bridge in rectangular
housing: **by 1981**
Discontinued: **1985**
Reintroduced with different specs, see Misc. SG Models, following: **1988**

The SG (Standard): solid walnut body, 1 standard humbucking pickup, 1 super humbucking "velvet brick" pickup, no pickup covers, black mounting
rings, tune-o-matic bridge, 4 speed knobs, small
pickguard, walnut neck, ebony fingerboard, dot
inlay, chrome-plated hardware, natural walnut finish
Introduced: **1979**
Firebrand model, logo branded onto peghead (no
inlay): **May 1980**
Renamed **SG Standard**, pearl logo, wine red, walnut,
or ivory finish: **1981**
Discontinued, name continues on reintroduction of
earlier-style SG Standard (see preceding): **1983**

The SG (Deluxe): solid mahogany body, 1 standard
humbucking pickup, 1 Super humbucking "velvet
brick" pickup, no pickup covers, black mounting
rings, tune-o-matic bridge, 4 speed knobs, small
pickguard, walnut neck, ebony fingerboard, dot
inlay, chrome-plated hardware, antique mahogany
or natural mahogany finish
Introduced: **1979**
Walnut finish only: **1982**
Ebony or wine red finish only: **1982**
Discontinued: **1985**

SG Reissue: 2 humbucking pickups, space between neck pickup and end of fingerboard, tune-o-matic bridge, stop tailpiece, selector switch near pickguard, small early-1960s style pickguard, jack in top, bound rosewood fingerboard, trapezoid inlay, crown peghead inlay, plastic keystone tuner buttons, nickel-plated hardware, heritage cherry finish
Introduced: **1986**
Renamed **SG '62 Reissue: 1988**
Discontinued: **1991**
Reintroduced as **Les Paul SG '61 Reissue: 1993**
Still in production

SG '62 Showcase Edition: guitar of the month, EMG pickups, blue finish, limited run of 200 for U.S. distribution, 50 for overseas: **Apr. 1988**

SG CUSTOMS

SG Custom: Les Paul Custom changes to SG body, 3 humbucking pickups, side-pull Deluxe Vibrato, white laminated pickguard with 3-point shape, *Les Paul Custom* on plastic plate between neck and pickup, ebony fingerboard, block inlay, 5-piece split-diamond peghead inlay, white finish: **early 1961**
Some with pearl-inlaid ebony tailblock (rare): **1962**
Les Paul Custom renamed **SG Custom**, no *Les Paul Custom* plate: **late 1963**
Deluxe vibrato (up-and-down pull) with lyre and logo on coverplate: **late 1963**
Larger pickguard surrounds pickups, no pickup frames: **1966**
Walnut finish: **by 1969**
Wing-shaped pickguard (Les Paul Standard style) mounted directly onto top, black pickup mounting rings, knobs, switch and jack on semi-circular control plate, Bigsby vibrato: **1972**
Old-style 3-point pickguard, large tune-o-matic bridge in rectangular housing, no vibrato: **late 1972**
Cherry finish optional: **1972**
White finish or white finish with black binding optional: **1974**
Wine red, white, or walnut: **1975**
Black finish available (7 shipped): **1975 only**
Bigsby vibrato standard, stop tailpiece optional: **1976**
Bigsby optional: **1977**
Tobacco sunburst and cherry finish optional: **1978**
Walnut or white finish standard: **1979**
Discontinued: **1980**

Reintroduced as **SG '62 Custom:** 3 PAF humbucking pickups, tune-o-matic bridge, antique ivory finish: **1986**
Renamed **SG Les Paul Custom: 1987**
Classic white finish: **1990**
Discontinued: **1991**
Reintroduced, Custom Shop model, 3 '57 Classic pickups, gold plated hardware, classic white finish: **1997**

SG Custom Showcase Edition: EMG pickups, Ferrari red finish, 200 made for U.S. distribution, 50 for overseas: **Oct. 1988**

30th Anniversary SG Custom: 3 '57 Classic humbucking pickups, block inlay, pearl peghead inlay with engraved *30th Anniversary*, TV yellow finish (darker than traditional TV yellow), limited run of no more than 300: **1991**

1967 SG Custom: large 4-point pickguard, wine red finish, limited run: **late 1991**

Les Paul SG '67 Custom: gold-plated hardware, wine red or classic white finish: **1992–1993**

Tony Iommi Les Paul SG: endorsed by Black Sabbath guitarist, 2 Iommi signature humbucking pickups, ABR-1 tune-o-matic bridge, small pickguard, slim neck profile, bound ebony fingerboard, 24 frets, horizontal cross inlays of sterling silver beginning at 1st fret and extending to 23rd fret, signature on peghead, Kluson deluxe tuners, chrome-plated hardware, black finish, limited run
Available: **1998**

SG JR. AND SG TV

SG Jr.: Les Paul Jr. changes to SG body, 1 P-90 pickup, laminated pickguard, *Les Paul Junior* on peghead, cherry finish: **early 1961**
Maestro vibrato optional: **by 1962**
Renamed **SG Jr.:** no model name on peghead: **late 1963**
Vibrato standard: **1965**
Black soapbar pickup, pickguard surrounds pickup: **1966**
Discontinued: **1971**
Reintroduced, ebony or wine red finish, limited run: **late 1991**
Cherry or wine red finish: **1992**
Discontinued: **1994**

SG TV: Les Paul TV renamed **SG TV**, double cutaway with rounded horns, 1-P-90 pickup, limed mahogany finish: **late 1959**

SG body, white finish: **late 1961**

Maestro vibrato optional: **by 1962**

Vibrato standard: **1965**

Soapbar pickup, pickguard surrounds pickup: **1966**

SG TV discontinued: **1968**

All American I/SG-X: 1 humbucking pickup, 2 knobs, coil tap, decal logo, ebony finish

Introduced as **All American I**, trade show special: **January 1995**

Reintroduced as part of All American series: **July 1996**

Renamed **SG-X**, ebony or dark wineburst finish standard, Caribbean blue, coral or corona yellow finish in limited runs: **summer 1998**

Limited runs in army green, chocolate brown or rust finish: **late 1998–99**

Still in production

SG SPECIALS

SG Special: Les Paul Special and Les Paul Special 3/4 renamed **SG Special** and **SG Special 3/4:** double cutaway with rounded horns, space between neck pickup and fingerboard, no model name on peghead, cherry or cream finish (similar to limed finish but more opaque): **late 1959**

SG body, cherry or white finish (described as cream finish in catalog): **early 1961**

Maestro vibrato optional: **by 1962**

Vibrato standard: **1965**

Pickguard surrounds pickups, no frames on pickups: **1966**

Discontinued, replaced by **SG Pro** (see following): **1971**

Reintroduced: 2 black mini-humbucking pickups with visible poles, old-style 3-point pickguard, 3-way selector switch, large tune-o-matic bridge in rectangular housing, unbound rosewood fingerboard, dot inlay, no peghead ornament, cherry or walnut: **late 1972**

Smaller tune-o-matic, small block inlay SG on truss rod cover, pearl logo: **1973**

Discontinued (6 shipped 1978–79): **1978**

SG Special 3/4: Les Paul Special 3/4 renamed SG Special 3/4, double cutaway with rounded horns, neck pickup next to fingerboard, 22" scale, no

model name on peghead, cherry finish: **late 1959**

SG body: **early 1961**

Discontinued: **early 1961**

Special I/SG Special: 1 exposed-coil humbucking pickup, combination bridge/tailpiece with individual string adjustments, 2 knobs, jack into top, unbound rosewood fingerboard, dot inlay, *Special* on truss rod cover, silver finish standard, ebony, ivory, antique sunburst or cherry finish optional (for upcharge)

Special II: 2 pickups

Introduced: **1983**

Renamed **Gibson Special**, then **SG Special**, 1 or 2 exposed-coil humbucking pickups, black pickup rings, 2 knobs with single-pickup, 3 knobs and selector switch with double-pickup, jack into top, combination bridge-tailpiece with individual string adjustments, black Kahler Flyer vibrato optional, no pickguard, unbound rosewood fingerboard, 22 frets, dot inlay, *Special* on truss rod cover, plastic keystone tuner buttons, decal logo, Ferrari red, pewter or panther pink finish: **mid 1985**

Tune-o-matic bridge: **by late 1985**

Floyd Rose tremolo with black chrome hardware optional, Ferrari red, pewter or Alpine white finish: **1986**

2 PAF humbucking pickups with exposed coils (1-pickup version no longer available), 3 knobs (2 volume, 1 master tone), 3-way selector switch, no pickguard, ebony fingerboard, dot inlay, *SG* on truss rod cover, plastic tuner buttons: **1986**

Ferrari red or pewter finish: **1989**

Alpine white or TV yellow finish optional: **1990**

Large 4-point pickguard, candy apple red, candy apple blue, ebony, heritage cherry or TV yellow finish: **1991**

TV yellow finish discontinued, metallic teal finish available in limited run: **1993**

Ferrari red, ebony or Alpine white finish: **1994**

Discontinued: **1996**

Reintroduced as **SG Special**, All American series, 2 humbucking pickups, 4 knobs, large pickguard, unbound ebony fingerboard, dot inlay, decal logo, ebony or Ferrari red finish: **July 1996**

Moved to SG line: **1998**

Limited runs in ebony stain, plum or cream finish, gold-plated hardware with cream finish: **late 1998–99**

Still in production

GIBSON

Generation Swine SG Special: promotional guitars for Motley Crue's *Generation Swine* CD and tour, ebony finish, red pickguard with "Generation Swine" logo, 5 guitars given away at Guitar Center stores and 1 given away nationally: **mid 1997**

SG Pro: replaces SG Special, 2 black soapbar P-90 pickups with mounting rings, semi-circular control plate, wing-shaped pickguard (Les Paul Standard-style) fastened directly onto top, tune-o-matic bridge in large rectangular housing, Gibson Bigsby vibrato, single-bound rosewood fingerboard, dot inlay, pearl logo, cherry, walnut or natural mahogany finish
Introduced: **late 1971**
Discontinued (SG Special reintroduced): **1972**
25 shipped: **1973–74**

SG Special 400: 400-series electronics, 1 Dirty Fingers humbucking pickup and 2 single-coil pickups, master tone and master volume knob, 3 mini-switches for on/off pickup control, push/pull volume control for coil tap, vibrato, bound rosewood fingerboard, dot inlay, black hardware
Available as special order SG Special: **1985**
Introduced as **SG 400**, ebony, Ferrari red or pewter finish: **1986**
Discontinued: **1987**

MISC. SG MODELS

SG Studio: similar to SG Special Reissue of 1985, 2 humbucking pickups, 3 knobs, 1 toggle switch, no pickguard, dot inlay, some with satin finish
Available: **1978 only**

SG Exclusive: 2 humbucking pickups with or without covers, coil tap controlled by rotary knob (volume knob on standard SG), white pickguard, bound rosewood fingerboard, block inlay, pearl logo, crown peghead inlay, ebony finish
Available: **1979**

SG-R1/Artist: thicker body than standard SG, active solid-state electronics, 4 knobs (2 numbered 0-5-0), 3-way toggle, 2-way toggle, no pickguard, unbound ebony fingerboard, dot inlay, crown peghead inlay
Introduced as **SG-R1: 1980**
Renamed **SG Artist: 1981**
Discontinued: **1982**

SG Elite: mahogany body, 2 Spotlight humbucking pickups, coil-tap switch, tune-o-matic bridge, TP-6 fine-tune tailpiece, 24 3/4" scale, bound ebony fingerboard, block inlay, locking nut, crown peghead inlay, gold-plated hardware, pearl white or metallic sunset finish
Available: **1987–89**

SG 90 Single: 1 humbucking pickup with black cover, pearloid pickguard, strings mounted through body, Floyd Rose vibrato optional, unbound ebony fingerboard, 25 1/2" scale, 2-piece split-diamond inlay, crown peghead inlay, pearl logo, Alpine white, metallic turquoise, or heritage cherry finish

SG 90 Double: 1 oblong single-coil pickup mounted diagonally in neck position, 1 black-covered humbucking pickup in bridge position, 2 knobs, push/pull for coil tap, selector switch between knobs, pearloid pickguard surrounds neck pickup
Available: **1988–90**

Les Paul '63 Corvette Sting Ray: top carved to resemble back split-window of 1963 Chevrolet Corvette Stingray, maple body and neck, 1 humbucking pickup with no polepieces, ebony fingerboard, *Sting Ray* inlay, crossed racing flags on peghead, nickel-plated hardware, Riverside red, ilver or black finish
Available: **late 1995–97**

SG Deluxe: (also see earlier style) 3 Firebird-style humbucking pickups with no polepieces, 2 knobs, 6-way rotary selector switch, pearloid pickguard, unbound rosewood fingerboard, dot inlay, decal logo, chrome-plated hardware, ebony, ice blue or hellfire red finish
Introduced: **1998**
Ebony fingerboard, small block inlay, Maestro (Bigsby style) vibrato: **early 1999**

SG-Z: 1 stacked-coil and 1 standard humbucking pickup, 2 knobs, selector switch between knobs, tune-o-matic bridge, Z-shaped tailpiece with strings through body, small pickguard, bound rosewood fingerboard, split-diamond inlay, 3-piece reverse-Z pearl peghead inlay, black chrome hardware, platinum or verdigris finish
Available: **1998**

SG Supreme: mahogany back, flamed maple top cap, 2 P-90A soapbar pickups with black covers, 4 knobs, bound ebony fingerboard, split-diamond inlay, bound peghead with 5-piece split-diamond (SG Custom style) inlay, gold-plated hardware, fireburst (3-tone sunburst) finish
Available: **early 1999–current**

MELODY MAKERS, SG-100 SERIES AND SG-I SERIES

Melody Maker: slab body, 1 3/8" deep, single rounded cutaway (Les Paul Jr. shape but 3/8" thinner), 7/8"-wide oblong pickup with black plastic cover and no visible poles, wraparound bridge/tailpiece, pickguard surrounds pickups, knobs mounted into pickguard, unbound rosewood fingerboard, dot inlay, narrow (2 1/4") peghead, decal logo, sunburst finish
Introduced: **1959**
Pickup width narrows to 5/8": **1960**
Symmetrical double cutaway with rounded horns, horns point away from neck, slightly rounded body edges: **1961**
Maestro vibrato optional: **1962**
Body edges more rounded, horns point slightly farther away from neck, cherry finish: **1963**
SG body, pointed horns, horns point into neck, white pickup covers, enlarged white pickguard covers most of upper body, knobs mounted into top, Gibson vibrato standard, fire engine red or Pelham blue finish: **1965**
Walnut finish optional: **1968**
Walnut finish only, wider peghead: **1970**
Replaced by **SG-100** (see following): **1971**
Reintroduced, single cutaway, slab body, high-output PAF humbucking pickup near bridge, tune-o-matic bridge, 2 knobs mounted into pickguard, 22 frets, 24 3/4" scale, rosewood fingerboard, dot inlay, narrow peghead, chrome-plated hardware, Ferrari red or ebony finish: **mid 1986**
Antique white finish optional: **1988**
Discontinued: **1993**

MM 3/4: 22 3/4" scale, 12 frets clear of body: **1959–70**
Same changes as MM except for optional sparkling burgundy finish: **1967**

MM-D/Melody Maker Double: 2 pickups: **1960–70**
Same changes as MM except for:

Optional sparkling burgundy finish: **1967**
Standard peghead size: **late 1969**
Discontinued, replaced by **SG-200** and **SG-250**: **1971**
Reintroduced as **Melody Maker Double**, slab body, double cutaway with rounded horns, horns point away from neck, 2 Melody Maker pickups, tune-o-matic bridge (earliest with stud-mounted wraparound bridge/tailpiece), 4 knobs, switch near tailpiece, jack on top, black pickguard, earliest with bolt-on neck, laminated mahogany neck, 22 frets, 24 3/4" scale, rosewood fingerboard, dot inlay, narrow peghead, metal tuner buttons, chrome-plated hardware, cherry or sunburst finish: **early 1977**
Discontinued: **1983**

MM-III: 3 pickups: **1967–71**
Same changes as MM except for optional sparkling burgundy finish: **1967**

MM-12: 12-string, 2 pickups, no vibrato: **1967–71**
Same changes as MM except for optional sparkling burgundy or Pelham blue finish: **1969**

All American II: early 1960s-style MM body with short pointed horns, 2 oblong single-coil pickups with non-adjustable polepieces, see Korinas, Firebirds, Miscellaneous Solidbodies and Doublenecks section

SG-100 Series: poplar body specified, examples with mahogany body, double pointed cutaways, oblong Melody Maker type pickup(s), large pickup mounting plate, metal bridge cover with engraved *Gibson*, oblong control plate, no pickguard shown in catalog photo, some with triangular Les Paul-type pickguard, some with large SG-type pickguard, unbound rosewood fingerboard, dot inlay, standard Gibson peghead shape

SG-100: 1 pickup, cherry or walnut finish

SG-200: 2 pickups, 2 slide switches, cherry, walnut or black finish

SG-250: 2 pickups, 2 slide switches, cherry sunburst finish
Introduced, replacing Melody Maker series (no SG-250s shipped until 1972): **1971**
SG-100 available with P-90 pickup: **1972**
Discontinued, replaced by **SG I, SG II, SG III** (see following): **late 1972**

SG I Series: double pointed cutaway, beveled edges, mahogany body, triangular wing-shaped pickguard, black plastic-covered mini-humbucking pickup(s) with no poles, semi-circular control plate, dot inlay, standard Gibson peghead shape

SG I: 1 pickup, 2 knobs, wraparound bridge/tailpiece, cherry or walnut finish

SG II: 2 pickups, 2 knobs, 2 slide switches, cherry or walnut finish

SG III: 2 pickups, 2 slide switches, tune-o-matic bridge, cherry sunburst finish

Introduced: **late 1972**

SG I available with P-90 pickup: **1972 only**

All discontinued: **1974**

SG II available with standard humbucking pickups, 61 shipped: **1975**

SG I, SG II, SG III shipped as late as: **1979**

COLOURS SERIES, 1990

July: Les Paul Custom, translucent red finish

August: Les Paul Standard, translucent yellow finish

September: Les Paul Standard, exposed cream pickup bobbins, gold-plated hardware, translucent blue finish

October: Les Paul Standard, translucent black finish

December: Les Paul Custom, translucent white finish

COMMENTS

The cherry sunburst Les Paul Standard from 1958–60 is (along with the 1958 Flying V and Explorer) the most highly sought solidbody production model Gibson on the vintage market. Among goldtops from 1952–58, the last version (with humbucking pickups) is most highly regarded by players and collectors, with earlier versions having progressively less appeal.

Les Paul Customs from 1954–60 are highly sought. Special, Jr., and TV models from the same period bring prices several times more than their value as utility instruments, with TV-finish models especially sought by collectors.

Most limited edition models bring prices above those of standard issue from the same period. However, Gibson's documentation of some limited runs is poor, and in some cases (the Guitar Trader Les Paul Reissue compared to a Gibson production Reissue of the same period, for example) the limited-run model is almost indistinguishable from the regular model. Consequently, the collectible value of limited-run models may be undermined.

Les Paul Recording series models are of some historical interest but are not highly regarded by players.

The Les Paul Deluxe, with smaller mini-humbucking pickups, is regarded strictly as a utility instrument.

Early SG/Les Paul models appeal to collectors and players. SG models through 1965 are well-regarded, but most collectors (except for fans of guitarist Angus Young of the group AC/DC) do not seek those made after 1965.

Melody Makers, SGs from the early 1970s and most of the non-Standard and non-Custom models through the 1970s and 1980s have little appeal to collectors.

KORINAS, FIREBIRDS, MISC. SOLIDBODIES AND DOUBLENECKS

SECTION ORGANIZATION

Flying Vs

Explorers

Modernes

Firebirds, Original Reverse-Body Series

Firebirds, Non-Reverse Body

Later Firebirds

Misc. Models Introduced 1972–81

Chet Atkins Models

Misc. Models Introduced 1982–93

Nighthawks

All American Series

Doublenecks

Flying V: Korina (African limba wood) body, 2 humbucking pickups, 3 knobs in straight line, strings anchor through body, V-shaped string anchor plate, white pickguard (a few black), body shoulders square at neck, all frets clear of body, raised plastic peghead logo, black ridged-rubber strip on side of lower treble bout, triangular peghead with rounded top, gold-plated hardware, natural finish, brown case with pink or red plush lining

Available: **1958**

Shipping records show 81 in 1958, 17 in 1959

Examples with 1958 body (some with ink-stamped serial number, some with oversized impressed serial number), patent-number pickups, nickel-plated hardware, black case with yellow plush lining: **1962–63**

Mahogany body, 2 humbucking pickups, large pickguard surrounds pickups, no frames around pickups, triangular knob configuration, selector switch above knobs, jack below knobs (into pickguard), tune-o-matic bridge, simple spring vibrato, sloped shoulders, shoulders meet neck at 17th fret, no rubber strip on side, 24 3/4" scale, rosewood fingerboard, 22 frets, dot inlay, logo embossed on oversized truss rod cover, most with shorter peghead than 1958 model, most with no serial number on back of peghead, chrome-plated hardware, cherry or sunburst finish, medallion on case, shipping records show 2 in 1965, 111 in 1966, 15 in 1969, 47 in 1970

Mahogany body, medallion on top (some without medallion) with *Limited Edition Reissue*, Gibson logo and numerical ranking, 2-piece mahogany body, 2 humbucking pickups with frames, large white-black-white pickguard surrounds pickups, channel routing under pickguard, black tapered knobs with triangular configuration, selector switch and jack below knobs, tune-o-matic bridge, no vibrato, sloped shoulders, shoulders meet neck at 17th fret, no rubber strip on side, 24 3/4" scale, rosewood fingerboard, 22 frets, dot inlay, logo embossed on oversized truss rod cover, shorter peghead than 1966 version, sunburst or cherry finish, shipping records show 350 in 1971, 2 in 1973, 1 in 1974

Uncovered pickups, natural mahogany, black, tobacco sunburst, or white finish: **1975**

Discontinued (model style continues as Flying V I/83, see following): **1980**

Flying V I/83: alder body, sloped shoulders, shoulders meet neck at 17th fret, 2 Dirty Fingers exposed-coil humbucking pickups, triangular knob

configuration, tune-o-matic bridge, several vibrato systems optional, no pickguard, maple neck, unbound ebony fingerboard, dot inlay, decal logo, chrome-plated hardware, ebony or ivory finish

Introduced as **Flying V I: 1981**

Renamed **Flying V 83**, ebony fingerboard, some with combination bridge/tailpiece with individual string adjustments: **1983**

Rosewood fingerboard standard, ebony optional (for upcharge): **Nov. 1983**

Renamed **Flying V:** vibrato optional, locking-nut system optional, ebony, Alpine white or red finish, custom and designer finishes optional: **by June 1984**

Scorpion graphic finish available: **1985 only**

Night violet finish available, gold-plated hardware: **1985 only**

Ebony, Ferrari red, panther pink or pewter finish: **1985**

Alpine white finish optional, panther pink discontinued: **1986**

Pewter finish discontinued: **late 1987**

Discontinued: **1988**

Flying V Left Hand: ebony or red finish: **June 1984–87**

Flying V Black Hardware: Kahler vibrato standard, black hardware, otherwise same specs as Flying V model of June 1984 (see preceding), only listing: **early 1985**

Flying V 400/400+: 400-series electronics, 1 Dirty Fingers humbucking pickup and 2 single-coil pickups, master tone and master volume knob, 3 mini-switches for on/off pickup control, push/pull volume control for coil tap, Kahler Flyer vibrato, black chrome hardware, Alpine white, ebony, Ferrari red or pewter finish: **1985–late 1986**

Flying V Reissue/'67 (1990s): mahogany body, knobs in triangular configuration, switch and jack into pickguard below knobs, ebony, cherry, vintage sunburst or classic white finish, chrome-plated hardware

Introduced: **1990**

Renamed **Flying V '67: 1991**

Cadillac gold finish, gold-plated hardware, limited run: **1993 only**

Still in production

Flying V Centennial: guitar of the month, serial number in raised numerals on tailpiece, numeral *1* of serial number formed by row of diamonds, letter *i* of logo dotted by inlaid diamond, gold medallion on back of peghead, gold-plated hardware, antique gold finish, limited run of no more than 101 serial numbered from 1894–1994, package includes 16 x 20 framed photograph and gold signet ring: **July 1994**

Flying V II: walnut or maple top, 5-piece maple/walnut body, beveled top and back body edges, boomerang-shaped pickups, tune-o-matic bridge, ebony fingerboard, dot inlay, gold-plated hardware, natural finish
Available: **1979–82**

Flying V Heritage: limited edition reissue of 1958 Flying V, Korina wood body, some with 1-piece body, body shoulders square at neck, shoulders meet neck at 21st fret, 2 PAF humbucking pickups, tune-o-matic bridge, bonnet knobs in straight line, V-shape string anchor plate, black pickguard, 3-piece Korina neck, rosewood fingerboard, 22 frets, dot inlay, raised peghead logo, plastic keystone tuner buttons, gold-plated hardware, antique natural, ebony, candy apple red, or white finish, serial number of letter followed by 3 digits (example: A 123)
Available: **late 1981–82**

Flying V Korina: continuation of Flying V Heritage, black barrel knobs, 8-digit serial number: **1983**

The V/Flying V CMT: maple body (earliest with mahogany body), curly maple top, 2 Dirty Fingers humbucking pickups with exposed creme coils, 3 knobs in curving line, selector switch between upper knobs, no pickguard, bound top, vibrato optional, maple neck, 22 frets, 24 3/4" scale, ebony fingerboard, dot inlay, pearl logo, gold-plated hardware, antique sunburst, antique natural or vintage cherry sunburst finish: **May 1981–85**

Flying V FF 81: made for Frankfurt (Germany) trade show available: **1981**

Flying V XPL: Kahler vibrato or combination bridge/tailpiece with individual string adjustments, maple neck, unbound ebony fingerboard, 22 frets, dot inlay, Explorer-style peghead, 6-on-a-side tuner arrangement, black hardware, night violet or plum wineburst finish
Introduced: **1984**

Tune-o-matic bridge optional, ebony, Ferrari red, pewter or regal blue finish: **1985**
Discontinued: **1987**

Flying V XPL Black Hardware: Kahler vibrola standard, ebony, Alpine white, or red finish, otherwise same specs as Flying V XPL
Only listing: **early 1985**

Flying V 90: 1 humbucking pickup, Floyd Rose vibrato optional, 25 1/2" scale, double-triangle inlay, pearl logo, black chrome hardware, Alpine white, ebony or nuclear yellow finish: **1988**

Flying V 90 Double: 1 single-coil and 1 double-coil pickup, 2 knobs, push/pull volume knob for coil tap, tune-o-matic bridge, Floyd Rose vibrato optional, 25 1/2" scale, double-triangle inlay, black chrome hardware, pearl logo, Alpine white, ebony or luna silver finish: **1989–90**

Jimi Hendrix '69 Flying V Custom: based on 1969 model, mahogany body, 490R and 490T humbucking pickups, signature on pickguard, mahogany neck, double-triangle inlay, gold-plated hardware, first run of 400 numbered on truss rod cover, Hall of Fame series logo on back of peghead, ebony finish
Available: **late 1991–1993**
25 promotional instruments made for RCA: **1995**

1958 Korina Flying V: replica of 1958 style, gold-plated hardware, antique natural finish
Introduced: **1992**
First 21 numbered with 9 followed by space followed by last digit of year and ranking (9 y### configuration) with odd-numbered ranking: 001, 003, 005, etc., companion to Korina Explorers with even-numbered ranking: **1991–93**
Still in production

Lonnie Mack Flying V: mahogany body, 1958-style control arrangement, Bigsby vibrato with anchor bar between lower bouts: **1993–94**

Flying V Primavera: primavera wood (light mahogany), gold-plated hardware with antique natural finish, chrome-plated hardware with brite translucent red, sunset metalic, translucent purple, translucent green or translucent blue finish, Custom Shop limited run: **1994**

Flying V '98: mahogany body, 2 ceramic-magnet humbucking pickups with exposed coils, 1958-style controls (3-in-line knob configuration, switch above knobs, jack in lower treble bout), Grover tuners with metal buttons, natural or natural burst finish with gold-plated hardware or translucent purple finish with chrome-plated hardware, limited run: **late 1998**

Flying V '98 Gothic: 2 '57 Classic humbucking pickups with no covers, Flying V '98 control configuration with 3-in-line knobs, black pickguard, ebony finger-board, moon-and-star inlay at 12th fret, no other inlay, white outline of logo on peghead, black chrome hardware, flat black finish: **late 1998–current**

EXPLORERS

Explorer: Korina (African limba wood) body, straight body lines, elongated upper treble bout and lower bass bout, 2 humbucking pickups, knobs in straight line, tune-o-matic bridge, stop tailpiece, white pickguard, scimitar-shape peghead curves to treble side, pearl logo (a few early with forked peg-head and raised plastic logo), rectangular brown case with red or pink plush lining
Available: **1958**
Shipping records do not list Explorer specifically. Records show "Korina (Mod. Gtr)," 19 shipped in 1958, 3 in 1959.
Models with 1958 body (some with ink-stamped serial number), patent number pickups, nickel-plated hardware, black case with yellow plush lining, shipped: **into 1963**
Reintroduced, mahogany body, gold bonnet knobs, white pickguard, gold-plated hardware, pearl logo, natural, white, or black finish: **1975**
Limited run with Korina body: **1976**
Discontinued: **1980**

Explorer I/83: alder body, 2 Dirty Fingers hum-bucking pickups, 2 volume controls and 1 master tone control, knobs in straight line, selector switch on upper treble horn, tune-o-matic bridge, stop tail-piece, black Kahler Flyer vibrato, maple neck, 24 3/4" scale, unbound rosewood fingerboard, 22 frets, dot inlay, decal logo, chrome-plated hardware
Introduced: **1981**
Renamed **Explorer 83:** several vibrato systems

optional, maple neck, ebony fingerboard: **1983**
Rosewood fingerboard standard, ebony optional (for upcharge): **Nov. 1983**
Renamed **Explorer**, triangular knob configuration, selector switch near knobs, no pickguard, custom graphic and original artist finishes optional, night violet offered as Custom Shop finish: **mid 1984**
Scorpion graphic finish available: **1985 only**
Night violet finish available, gold-plated hardware: **1985 only**
Ebony, Ferrari red, panther pink or pewter finish: **1985**
Alpine white finish optional, panther pink discontinued: **1986**
No vibrato, ebony fingerboard: **by 1987**
Pewter finish discontinued: **late 1987**
Discontinued: **1989**

Explorer Left Hand, listed: **June 1984–87**

Explorer Black Hardware: Kahler vibrato standard, black hardware, only listing: **early 1985**

Explorer Synthesizer: Roland 700 synthesizer system, Alpine white or ebony finish: **1985**

Explorer 400/400+: 400-series electronics, 1 Dirty Fin-gers humbucking pickup and 2 single-coil pickups, master tone and master volume knob, 3 mini-switches for on/off pickup control, push/pull vol-ume control for coil tap, Kahler Flyer vibrato, black chrome hardware, Alpine white, ebony, Ferrari red or pewter finish: **1985–late 1986**

Explorer Reissue/'76: mahogany body, chrome-plated hardware, ebony, cherry, vintage sunburst or classic white finish
Introduced: **1990**
Renamed **Explorer '76: 1991**
Natural burst or natural finish available in limited runs: **late 1998**
Still in production

Explorer Centennial: guitar of the month, serial num-ber in raised numerals on tailpiece, numeral *1* of serial number formed by row of diamonds, letter *i* of logo dotted by inlaid diamond, gold medallion on back of peghead, gold-plated hardware, antique gold finish, limited run of no more than 101 serial numbered from 1894–1994, package includes 16 x 20 framed photograph and gold signet ring: **Apr. 1994**

Explorer Gothic: 2 '57 Classic humbucking pickups with no covers, black pickguard, ebony fingerboard, moon-and-star inlay at 12th fret, no other inlay, white outline of logo on peghead, black chrome hardware, flat black finish
Available: **late 1998–current**

The Explorer/Explorer CMT: maple body,
bound curly maple top, 2 Dirty Fingers humbucking pickups with exposed coils, 3 knobs in straight line, knobs mounted into top, 3-way selector switch into pickguard on upper treble horn, tune-o-matic bridge, TP-6 tailpiece, maple neck, 22 frets, 24" 3/4 scale, unbound ebony fingerboard, dot inlay, some with *E/2* on truss rod cover, pearl logo, gold-plated hardware, antique sunburst, vintage cherry sunburst, antique natural
Available as limited edition model: **1976**
Available as regular production model: **May 1981–84**

Explorer II: walnut or maple top, 5-piece walnut
and maple body, beveled body edges, 2 humbucking pickups with exposed coils, 3 knobs in straight line, knobs mounted into top, 3-way selector switch into pickguard on upper treble horn, tune-o-matic bridge, TP-6 tailpiece, 22 frets, 24" 3/4 scale, unbound ebony fingerboard, dot inlay, *E/2* on truss rod cover, gold-plated hardware, natural finish
Available: **1979–83**

Explorer Korina: similar to 1958 Explorer and
Explorer Heritage (see preceding), gold knobs, Nashville tune-o-matic bridge, metal buttons, standard 8-digit serial number, candy apple red, ebony, ivory, or antique natural finish
Available: **1982–84**

Explorer Heritage: limited edition reissue of
1958 Explorer, Korina wood body, 2 PAF humbucking pickups, black knobs, 3-piece Korina neck (first 8 examples with 1-piece neck), rosewood fingerboard, dot inlay, pearloid keystone tuner buttons, pearl logo, gold-plated hardware, serial number of *1* followed by a space and 4 digits, antique natural, ebony or ivory finish
100 made: **1983**

Explorer III: alder body, 3 soapbar HP-90 pickups,
2 knobs, 2 selector switches, tune-o-matic bridge, locking nut vibrato system optional, maple neck, 24 3/4" scale, rosewood fingerboard, dot inlay, decal logo, metal tuners, chrome-plated hardware, ebony, red, Alpine white or military-style camouflage finish
Available: **mid 1984–mid 1985**

Explorer III Black Hardware: Kahler vibrato standard, black hardware: **early 1985**

EXP 425: 1 humbucking and 2 single-coil pickups,
no pickup covers, 2 knobs, 3 mini-toggle switches, Kahler vibrato, ebony fingerboard, black hardware
Available: **1985–86**

XPL Custom: see Misc. Models Introduced
1982–93, following

Explorer 90: 1 humbucking pickup, 2 knobs,
lightning-bolt tailpiece with strings through body, Floyd Rose vibrato optional, 25 1/2" scale, ebony fingerboard, 24 frets, double-triangle inlay, black chrome hardware, Alpine white, ebony or luna silver finish
Available: **1988**

Explorer 90 Double: 1 single-coil pickup in neck position and 1 double-coil pickup in bridge position, 2 knobs, push/pull volume knob for coil tap, tune-o-matic bridge, selector switch between knobs, lightning-bolt tailpiece with strings through body, Floyd Rose vibrato optional, 25 1/2" scale, ebony fingerboard, 24 frets, double-triangle inlay, black chrome hardware, pearl logo, Alpine white, ebony or luna silver finish, black peghead finish
Available: **1989–90**

1958 Korina Explorer: replica of original, Korina
body and neck, gold-plated hardware, antique natural finish
Introduced, first 11 numbered with 9 followed by space followed by last digit of year and ranking (9 y### configuration), all with even-numbered ranking: 002, 004, 006, etc., companion to Korina Flying Vs with odd-numbered ranking: **1993**
5 with "split" V-shaped peghead, numbered 8 9401 through 8 9405: **1994**
Still in production

Futura: swooping cutout on bass side, see Misc.
Models Introduced 1972–81, following

GIBSON

Futura Reissue: reissue of 1958 Explorer proto-
type (slightly different body shape), mahogany
body, narrower treble horn than Explorer, asymmetrical split-V peghead shape, limited run of 100
Available: **1996**

MODERNES

Moderne: Korina (African limba wood) body, bass
side of body like Flying V, treble side scooped out,
asymmetrical peghead longer on treble side
The Moderne design was patented along with the
Explorer and Flying V in 1958. Gibson shipping
records note a total of 22 instruments shipped in
1958 and 1959 as "Korina (Mod. Gtr)," but this is
generally accepted as the Explorer (both the
Explorer and the Flying V were described in the
1958 price list as Modernistic Guitars). The Moderne never appeared in a price list, catalog or shipping record. According to eyewitnesses, Gibson did
display a Moderne at a trade show in 1958, but no
original Moderne is known to exist now.

Moderne Heritage: limited edition, issued with
Flying V Heritage and Explorer Heritage reissues, 2
humbucking pickups,3 barrel knobs, tune-o-matic
bridge, unbound rosewood fingerboard, dot inlay,
string guides on peghead, gold-plated hardware,
serial number of letter followed by 3 digits (example: D 001), natural finish, production of 500
announced, approximately 143 made, all with D
prefix: **1982**
Red, white or ebony finish available: **1982–1983**

FIREBIRDS, ORIGINAL
REVERSE-BODY SERIES

All with reverse body, treble horn larger than bass
horn, neck-through-body construction with side
wings glued on, raised middle section of body, Firebird humbucking pickups with nickel-plated covers
and metal mounting rings, 3-ply white-black-white
pickguard with beveled edge, beveled peghead
edge, large Kluson banjo style tuners all on treble
side of peghead with high E-string nearest nut, logo
on extended truss rod cover, sunburst finish
Custom colors available: golden mist, silver mist, Kerry
green, Polaris white, Pelham blue, frost blue, ember
red, Inverness green, cardinal red, heather poly
Firebird line introduced: **mid 1963**

Peghead reversed, pegs on bass side: **1965**
Variations of Firebird I and Firebird III: non-beveled peg-
head, right-angle tuners, black P-90 pickups: **1965**
Discontinued: **May 1965**

Firebird I: 1 pickup, no switch, 2 knobs, wraparound bridge with raised integral saddles, no
vibrato,
(a few with Firebird III vibrato), unbound rosewood
fingerboard, dot inlay

Firebird III: 2 pickups, 3-way toggle switch, wraparound bridge with raised integral saddles, simple
spring vibrato with flat arm, single-bound fingerboard, dot inlay

Firebird V: 2 pickups, 3-way toggle switch, tune-o-
matic bridge, Deluxe vibrato (tubular lever arm
with plastic end cap, metal tailpiece cover engraved
with Gibson and leaf-and-lyre), single-bound fingerboard, trapezoid inlay

Firebird VII: 3 pickups, 3-way toggle switch, tune-
o-matic bridge, Deluxe vibrato (tubular lever arm
with plastic end cap, metal tailpiece cover engraved
with Gibson and leaf-and-lyre decoration), single-
bound ebony fingerboard, block inlay beginning at
1st fret, gold-plated hardware

FIREBIRDS, NON-REVERSE SERIES

All with non-reverse body, body and peghead shape
opposite of original Firebirds, bass horn larger than
treble horn, glued-in neck with visible joint, black
sliding selector switch, no pickup mounting rings,
white pickguard surrounding pickups with red Firebird logo on upper left, unbound rosewood fingerboard, dot inlay, non-beveled peghead (similar to
Fender shape), right-angle tuners, sunburst finish,
custom colors available

Non-reverse Firebird I: 2 black soapbar P-90
pickups, wraparound bridge with raised integral
saddles, short-arm vibrato with tubular lever and
plastic tip

Non-reverse Firebird III: 3 black soapbar P-90
pickups, wraparound bridge with raised integral saddles, vibrato with tubular lever arm and plastic tip:
1965–69

GIBSON

Non-reverse Firebird V: 2 Firebird mini-humbucking pickups, tune-o-matic bridge, Deluxe vibrato (tubular lever arm with plastic end cap, metal tailpiece cover engraved with Gibson and leaf-and-lyre decoration), nickel-plated hardware: **1965–69**

Firebird V 12-string: 1966–67

Non-reverse Firebird VII: 3 Firebird mini-humbucking pickups, tune-o-matic bridge, Deluxe Vibrato (tubular lever arm with plastic end cap, metal tailpiece cover engraved with Gibson and leaf-and-lyre decoration), gold-plated hardware: **1965–69**

LATER FIREBIRDS

Firebird (V): reissue of Firebird V, *LE* limited edition medallion, reverse body shape, logo embossed on pickup covers
366 shipped: **1972–73**

Firebird 76: reverse body, neck-through-body construction, 2 pickups, 4 knobs, selector switch, tune-o-matic bridge, red-and-blue Bicentennial Firebird figure (with stars) on pickguard near switch, 22 frets, 24 3/4" scale, unbound rosewood fingerboard, dot inlay, straight-through banjo tuners with metal buttons, gold-plated hardware, sunburst, natural mahogany, white or ebony finish
Introduced: **1976**
Not listed: **1979**
Reintroduced as **Firebird**, 1-piece neck-through-body, cherry, ebony or natural finish: **1980**
Discontinued: **1981**

Firebird V: 2 mini-humbucking pickups with no visible poles, Gibson/Kahler Supertone vibrato optional, rosewood fingerboard, pearloid trapezoid inlay, nickel-plated hardware, tobacco sunburst or heather poly finish
Listed: **June 1986–Mar. 1987**

Firebird Reissue: reverse body slightly different from original reverse body, 7-piece neck-through-body construction, same general specs as 1964 Firebird V but with pickups 0.1" wider than originals, no vibrato, tune-o-matic bridge, stop tailpiece, tuners on

treble side of peghead, chrome-plated hardware, vintage sunburst, cherry or classic white finish
Introduced: **1990**
Cardinal red finish optional: **1991**
Still in production

Firebird V Celebrity Series: reverse body, black finish, white pickguard, gold-plated hardware: **Sept. 1991–93**

Firebird II: maple body with figured maple top cap, 2 full-size Series VI active humbucking pickups, 4 black barrel knobs, selector switch near knobs, 2 mini-switches for standard/active and brightness control, tune-o-matic bridge, TP-6 fine-tune tailpiece, bound top, large backplate for electronics access, 3-piece maple neck, 22 frets, 24 3/4" scale, unbound rosewood fingerboard, dot inlay, pearl logo at tip of peghead, antique sunburst or antique fireburst finish
Available: **July 1981–82**

Firebird I: reverse body, 1 pickup, gold-plated hardware, red, vintage sunburst or frost blue finish, Custom Shop limited run available: **late 1991–92**

Firebird VII: reverse body, 3 pickups, aged inlay, chrome-plated hardware, vintage sunburst or frost blue finish, Custom Shop limited run available: **late 1991–93**

Firebird VII Centennial: guitar of the month, vintage sunburst finish, serial number in raised numerals on tailpiece, numeral *1* of serial number formed by row of diamonds, letter *i* of logo dotted by inlaid diamond, gold medallion on back of peghead, gold-plated hardware, limited run of no more than 101 serial numbered from 1894–1994, package includes 16" x 20" framed photograph and gold signet ring: **Sept. 1994**

MISC. MODELS INTRODUCED 1972–81

L-5S: 13 1/2" wide, single cutaway, carved maple top, contoured back, 2 large oblong low-impedance pickups with metal covers and embossed logo, 4 knobs, large rectangular tune-o-matic bridge, large L-5 style plate tailpiece with silver center insert, no pickguard, 7-ply top binding and 3-ply back binding with black line on side, maple control cavity cover, 5-piece neck

(3 maple pieces with mahogany laminates), 5-ply fingerboard binding with black line on side, 22 frets, 24 3/4" scale, 17 frets clear of body, bound ebony fingerboard with pointed end, abalone block inlay, 5-ply peghead binding, flowerpot peghead inlay, gold-plated hardware, natural, cherry sunburst or vintage sunburst finish

First listed: **mid 1972**

First shipped: **1973**

Humbucking pickups, vintage sunburst finish discontinued, fireburst finish added: **1974**

Stop tailpiece: **late 1975**

TP-6 tailpiece: **mid 1978**

Discontinued: **1985**

L-6S/Custom: 13 1/2" wide, 1 1/8" deep, single cutaway, maple body, 2 5-sided humbucking pickups with ceramic magnets and no visible poles, 3 knobs (volume, midrange and tone), 6-position rotary tone selector switch for parrallel and phase selection, large rectangular tune-o-matic bridge, stop tailpiece, early with pointed pickguard, 24-fret fingerboard, 18 frets clear of body, 24 3/4" scale, unbound maple fingerboard with natural finish, unbound ebony fingerboard with tobacco sunburst finish, small block inlay, narrow peghead with similar shape to snakehead L-5 of late 1920s, chrome-plated hardware, natural or cherry finish

Introduced: **1973**

Rectangular pickups, dot inlay: **1975**

Renamed **L-6S Custom**: **1975**

Discontinued: **1980**

L-6S Deluxe: same body shape as L-6S, beveled top around bass side, 2 5-sided humbucking pickups with black covers, 3 screws in pickup mounting rings, 2 knobs, no 6-position tone selector, 3-way pickup selector switch, large rectangular tune-o-matic bridge, strings anchor through body, string holes on a line diagonal to strings, unbound rosewood fingerboard, small block inlay, metal tuner buttons

Introduced: **1975**

Dot inlay: **1978**

Discontinued: **1981**

Midnight Special: same body shape as L-6S, non-beveled top around bass side, 2 humbucking pickups with metal covers and no polepieces, 2 knobs, 2-way

tone switch, jack into top, large rectangular tune-o-matic bridge, strings anchor through body on a diagonal line, bolt-on maple neck, maple fingerboard, decal logo, metal tuner buttons, chrome-plated hardware, black, white, natural or wine red finish

Available: **1974–79**

Marauder: 12 3/4" wide, Les Paul-shape single cutaway, maple or mahogany body, humbucking pickup in neck position, blade pickup in bridge position, pickups set in clear epoxy, 2 knobs, rotary tone selector switch between knobs, large pickguard covers entire upper body and extends around lower treble bout, bolt-on maple neck, unbound rosewood fingerboard, dot inlay, triangular peghead with rounded top, decal logo

Introduced: **1975**

Maple fingerboard: **1978**

Some with selector switch on cutaway bout: **1978**

Discontinued: **1982**

Marauder Custom: same as Marauder but with 3-way selector switch on cutaway bout, bound fingerboard, block inlay, tobacco sunburst finish: **1976–77**

S-1: 12 3/4" wide, Les Paul-shape single cutaway, 3 single-coil pickups with center bar, pickups set in clear epoxy, 2-way toggle on cutaway bout (selects bridge pickup alone), 4-position rotary switch for pickup selection, 2 knobs (volume, tone), large rectangular tune-o-matic bridge, stop tailpiece, large pickguard covers entire upper body and extends around lower treble bout, bolt-on neck, maple fingerboard (some early with rosewood), dot inlay, triangular peghead with rounded top

Introduced: **1976**

Black pickup covers: **by 1978**

Rewired to allow selection of bridge pickup alone: **1978**

Discontinued: **1980**

RD: double cutaway, 14 5/8" wide, upper treble horn longer than upper bass horn, lower bass horn larger than lower treble horn

RD Standard: 2 humbucking pickups, 4 knobs, 1 selector switch, tune-o-matic bridge, 25 1/2" scale, rosewood fingerboard, dot inlay, model name on truss rod cover, decal logo, chrome-plated hardware, natural, tobacco sunburst or walnut finish

First made: **1977**

First appearance on shipping records: **1978**

Discontinued: **1979**

RD Custom/77 Custom: same as RD Standard, but with active electronics, 4 knobs (standard Gibson controls), 3-way pickup selector switch, 1 selector switch, 2-way mini switch for mode selection (neutral or bright), large backplate, maple fingerboard, natural or walnut finish

First made, named **RD Custom: 1977**

First appearance on shipping records: **1978**

Renamed **RD 77 Custom: 1979**

Discontinued: **1979**

RD Artist/79: active electronics, 2 humbucking pickups, 4 knobs (standard Gibson controls), 3-way pickup selector switch, 3-way switch for mode selection (neutral, bright, front pickup expansion with back pickup compression), tune-o-matic bridge, TP-6 tailpiece, large backplate, 3-piece mahogany neck, 24 3/4" scale, bound ebony fingerboard (some unbound), block inlay, multiple-bound peghead, winged-*f* peghead inlay, pearl logo, gold-plated hardware

Introduced: **1978**

2 mini-switches (bright, expansion/compression): **1979**

Listed as **RD: 1981**

Discontinued: **1982**

RD Artist/77: 25 1/2" scale, available by special order: **1980**

RD Artist CMT: maple body, bound curly maple top, gold speed knobs, TP-6 fine-tune tailpiece, maple neck, 24 3/4" scale, bound ebony fingerboard, block inlay, chrome-plated hardware, antique cherry sunburst or antique sunburst finish, limited run of 100 or less: **Apr. 1981**

GK-55: Les Paul body size and shape, single cutaway, slab mahogany body, 2 Dirty Fingers pickups with exposed coils, 4 knobs, rectangular tune-o-matic bridge, TP-6 tailpiece or stop tailpiece, no pickguard, bolt-on neck, unbound rosewood fingerboard, dot inlay, model name on truss rod cover, decal logo, tobacco sunburst finish

1,000 made: **1979–80**

335-S Deluxe: double rounded cutaway, solid mahogany body narrower than ES-335, 2 Dirty Fin-

gers exposed-coil humbucking pickups, coil-tap switch, tune-o-matic bridge, TP-6 tailpiece, triangular wing-shaped pickguard, bound ebony fingerboard, dot inlay, brass nut

Available: **1980–82**

335-S Standard: no coil tap

Introduced: **1980**

Branded peghead logo (some routed for inlay but no inlay): **Apr. 1980**

Discontinued: **1981**

335-S Custom: coil tap, unbound rosewood fingerboard

Introduced: **1980**

Branded peghead logo (some routed for inlay but no inlay): **Apr. 1980**

Discontinued: **1981**

KZ-II: body shape of double-cutaway Melody Maker with rounded horns, made in Kalamazoo factory, 2 humbucking pickups, tune-o-matic bridge, dot inlay, metal tuner buttons, chrome-plated hardware, standard Gibson peghead size, *KZ-II* on truss rod cover, walnut stain with satin non-gloss finish

Available: **1980–81**

Sonex-180 (Deluxe): Les Paul body size and shape, beveled edge on bass side, single cutaway, Multi-Phonic body (wood core, resin outer layer), 2 exposed-coil Velvet Brick humbucking pickups, 3-way selector switch, tune-o-matic bridge, pickguard covers 3/4 of body, bolt-on 3-piece maple neck, 24 3/4" scale, rosewood fingerboard, 22 frets, dot inlay, metal tuners, decal logo chrome-plated hardware, ebony

Introduced as Sonex 180: **1980**

Renamed Sonex-180 Deluxe: **1981**

Sonex by Gibson logo decal: **June 1982**

The Gibson Guitar Co. logo decal: **July 1982**

Standard Gibson logo, ebony, candy apple red, silverburst or antique fireburst finish: **late 1982**

Discontinued: **1984**

Sonex-180 Deluxe Left Hand: 1982

Sonex-180 Custom: coil-tap switch, Japanese-made neck, ebony fingerboard, ebony or white finish

Introduced: **late 1980**

U.S.-made neck: **early 1982**

Discontinued: **mid 1982**

Sonex Artist: active electronics, 2 standard humbucking pickups, 3 mini-switches (bright, compression, expansion), TP-6 tailpiece, no pickguard, 3-piece maple neck, 22 frets, 24 3/4" scale, rosewood fingerboard, dot inlay, *Artist* on truss rod cover, *The Gibson Guitar Company* decal logo, candy apple red, silver or ivory finish
Introduced: **1981**
Standard Gibson logo: **1982**
Discontinued: **1985**

GGC-700: Les Paul shape, flat top, beveled edge on bass side, 2 humbucking pickups with exposed zebra coils, 4 black barrel knobs, selector switch near bridge, coil tap switch, jack into top, tune-o-matic bridge, large black pickguard covers 3/4 of body, unbound rosewood fingerboard, dot inlay, *The Gibson Guitar Company* decal logo, metal keystone tuner buttons, chrome-plated hardware, ebony finish
Available: **1981–82**

Victory MV-2 or **MV-II:** maple body, 13" wide, asymmetrical double cutaway with extended horns, horns come to a point, Velvet Brick zebra-coil neck pickup, special design black-coil humbucking bridge pickup, 2 knobs, coil-tap switch, 3-position slide switch, wide-travel "Nashville" tune-o-matic bridge, 3-piece bolt-on maple neck, 22 frets, 24 3/4" scale, bound rosewood fingerboard, dot inlay positioned near bass edge of fingerboard, 6-on-a-side tuner arrangement, peghead points to bass side, decal logo and *Victory* decal near nut, chrome-plated hardware, candy apple red or antique fireburst finish

Victory MV-10 or **MV-X:** 2 zebra-coil humbucking pickups and 1 stacked-coil humbucking pickup (middle position), 2 knobs, master coil-tap switch, 5-position slide switch, bound ebony fingerboard, antique cherry sunburst, candy apple red or twilight blue finish
Available: **Aug. 1981–84**

CHET ATKINS MODELS

Chet Atkins Standard CE: classical electric, 14 1/2" wide, chambered mahogany back, spruce top, simulated round soundhole, soundhole insert with signature and prewar script logo, transducer

pickup, roller knobs recessed into upper bass side, individual trim pots accessible internally, rectangular bridge, multiple-bound top with brown outer layer, 25 1/2" scale, unbound rosewood fingerboard, 1.8" nut width (also specified as 1 13/16" and 1 7/8"), slotted peghead, scalloped top edge of peghead, no peghead logo, gold-plated hardware, antique natural or Alpine white finish

Chet Atkins CEC: ebony fingerboard 2" wide at nut
First 1000 examples (approx.) have serial number of letter + 3 digits: A 001–A 100, B 001–B 100, etc., through K 100 (no letter/ prefix)
First made: **Dec. 1981**
Introduced: **1982**
Ebony or wine red finish optional: **1990**
A few with Chromyte (balsa) center: **c. 1991**
Alpine white discontinued: **1993**
Bridge with flared ends, standard Gibson center-dip peghead, gold decal logo (modern style): **1993**
Cedar top optional: **1994–95**
Ebony fingerboard (both models): **1996**
Still in production

Chet Atkins CE Showcase Edition: guitar of the month, vintage sunburst finish, limited run of 200 for U.S. distribution, 50 for overseas: **July 1988**

Chet Atkins SST: steel-string electric, single cutaway, spruce top, mahogany body with Chromyte (balsa) center, transducer bridge pickup with built-in preamp, simulated round soundhole, soundhole insert with signature and prewar script logo, transducer pickup, 2 knobs on top, ebony bridge, bound top, mahogany neck, 21 frets, 25 1/2" scale, unbound ebony fingerboard, dot inlay, 1 11/16" nut width, solid peghead, scalloped top edge of peghead, no peghead logo, gold-plated hardware, antique natural, Alpine white or ebony finish
Introduced: **1987**
Wine red or antique natural finish optional: **1990**
Small inlays at bridge ends, standard Gibson center-dip peghead shape, crown peghead inlay, prewar script logo: **1991**
Alpine white finish discontinued: **1993**
No soundhole, knobs on rim, bridge with upper belly and bridge pins, star inlay at bridge ends, signature decal on upper bass bout next to fingerboard, multiple bound top, square-end ebony fingerboard, star

fingerboard inlay, star peghead inlay, black peghead veneer, pearl logo in postwar script: **1993**

Heritage cherry sunburst finish optional: **1994**

Still in production

Chet Atkins Celebrity Series: gold-plated hardware, ebony finish: **Oct. 1991–93**

Chet Atkins SST 12-string: controls on rim, star fingerboard inlay, scalloped top edge of peghead, prewar script logo, gold-plated hardware, antique natural, Alpine white, wine red or ebony finish

Introduced: **1990**

Ebony finish only: **1993**

Last made: **1994**

Chet Atkins SST 12-string Brett Michaels Edition: antique gold finish, 2 made: **1992–93**

Chet Atkins SST w/ Flame Top: flamed maple top, antique natural, heritage cherry sunburst or translucent amber finish: **1993–95**

Chet Atkins CGP: contoured mahogany body, 2 single-coil pickups tapped for normal and high output, 2 knobs (volume and tone), 2 mini-toggles for ohm tap, 3-way selector switch, flat-mount bridge/tailpiece with individual string adjustments, bolt-on maple neck, neck/body joint at 17th fret, ebony fingerboard, 22 frets, 25 1/2" scale, Kahler Flyer vibrato optional, gold-plated hardware, wine red finish

Catalogued but never in production: **mid 1986–early 1987**

Chet Atkins Studio Classic: single cutaway, hollow mahogany body, fan-braced spruce top, controls on rim, no soundhole, flared bridge ends, abalone top border, cocobolo wood bindings, top inlaid at end of fingerboard with rosewood and abalone fleur-de-lis, 26 1/4" scale, V-end ebony fingerboard 2" wide at nut, small *CGP* inlay at 7th fret, no other fingerboard inlay, slotted peghead, peghead narrows toward top, rosewood peghead veneer, prewar style *The Gibson* logo in pearl, logo slanted, small fleur-de-lis peghead inlay, gold-plated hardware, antique natural finish

Introduced: **1991**

Small oval abalone inlays in bridge ends, large abalone block inlaid in bridge, asymmetrical fingerboard

with treble-side extension, abalone top trim extends around fingerboard end, no top inlay, modern pearl logo: **1993**

Discontinued: **1994**

Chet Atkins Studio CE: single cutaway, hollow mahogany back, spruce top, controls on rim, individual string volume controls accessible internally, no soundhole, flared bridge ends, 26" scale, unbound ebony fingerboard with treble-side extension, signature on upper bass bout near fingerboard, multiple-bound top with black outer layer, slotted peghead, decal logo, gold-plated hardware, antique natural finish

CEC: ebony fingerboard 2" wide at nut

Available: **mid 1993–current**

Chet Atkins Phasar: asymmetrical double cutaway, 2 narrow humbucking pickups with no visible poles, 1 pickup straight-mounted in middle position and 1 slant-mounted in bridge position, 2 knobs, rosewood fingerboard, 25 1/2" scale, dot inlay, 6-on-a-side tuner arrangement, wine red, ebony or sunrise orange finish

6 instruments made (3 with vibrato, 3 without): **1987**

MISC. MODELS INTRODUCED 1982–93

Futura: neck-through-body construction, cutout along entire bass side of body, cutout on upper treble side, deep cutout from bottom end almost to bridge, 2 humbucking pickups with no visible poles, 2 knobs, Gibson/Kahler Supertone vibrato optional, TP-6 tailpiece, 24 3/4" scale, 6-on-a-side tuners, gold-plated hardware, ebony, ultra violet or pearl white finish

Available: **1982–84**

Futura Reissue (1958 Explorer prototype), see Explorers, preceding

Corvus I: neck-through-body construction, cutout along entire bass side of body, cutout on upper treble side, deep V-shaped cutout from bottom end almost to bridge, 1 humbucking pickup with black cover and no visible poles, pickup dipped in epoxy, 2 knobs, combination bridge/tailpiece with individual string adjustments, bolt-on maple neck, 24 3/4" scale, unbound rosewood fingerboard, dot inlay, 6-on-a-side tuners, decal logo, chrome-plated hardware, silver finish standard, antique natural, ebony (single-pickup only), tangerine, fire red, yellow mist or electric blue finish optional (for upcharge) Available: **1982–84**

Corvus II: 2 pickups, 3 knobs: **1982–84**

Corvus III: 3 high-output single-coil pickups, 2 knobs, 5-way switch: **1982–84**

Challenger I: Les Paul style single cutaway, slab top, 1 humbucking pickup with black cover and no visible poles, 2 knobs, pickguard surrounds pickup(s), combination bridge/tailpiece with individual string adjustments, bolt-on maple neck, unbound rosewood fingerboard, dot inlay, standard peghead shape, decal logo, chrome-plated hardware, silver finish standard, antique natural, ebony (single-pickup only), tangerine, fire red, yellow mist or electric blue finish optional (for upcharge) Available: **1983–84**

Challenger II: 2 pickups, 3 knobs: **1983–84**

Invader: Les Paul-type single cutaway, mahogany body, beveled bass-side edge, 2 ceramic magnet humbucking pickups with exposed zebra coils, 4 knobs, 3-way selector switch mounted with control knobs, tune-o-matic bridge, stop tailpiece, bolt-on maple neck, ebony fingerboard, dot inlay, standard Gibson peghead shape, decal logo, chrome-plated hardware
Introduced (prototype as early as 1980): **1983**
Alpine white, ebony or Ferrari red finish: **by 1986**
Discontinued: **1988**

Invader-style buildout models: model names unknown, designed to use up Invader bodies:
• 1 narrow pickup, 2 knobs, Kahler vibrato, set maple neck, ebony fingerboard, dot inlay, crown peghead inlay, black chrome hardware: **1988**
• 2 humbucking pickups with black plastic covers and no visible polepieces, 2 knobs, 1 switch, Kahler Flyer vibrato, pearloid pickguard covers most of treble side of body, jack into pickguard, set neck, unbound ebony fingerboard, dot inlay, Explorer-style peghead with 6-on-a-side tuner arrangement, black chrome hardware: **1989**

Map-shape: limited run promotional model, mahogany body shaped like United States, 2 humbucking

pickups, 4 knobs, 1 switch, combination bridge/tailpiece with individual string adjustments, 3-piece maple neck, ebony fingerboard, dot inlay, crown peghead inlay, pearl logo, some with Epiphone logo (made in USA), metal tuner buttons, natural mahogany finish standard, 9 made with American flag finish
Available: **1983**

Spirit I: double cutaway with rounded horns, carved top, bass horn slightly longer than treble, body meets neck at 20th fret, 1 exposed-coil humbucking pickup with creme coils, 2 barrel knobs, combination bridge/tailpiece with individual string adjustments, tortoiseshell celluloid pickguard, 3-piece maple neck, 24 3/4" scale, unbound rosewood fingerboard, 22 frets, dot inlay, plastic keystone tuner buttons, decal logo, chrome-plated hardware, silver finish standard, ebony, vintage wineburst or antique sunburst optional (for upcharge)
Introduced: **1982**
Curly maple top available, vintage wineburst or antique sunburst finish: **1983 only**
Discontinued: **1988**

Spirit II: 2 pickups, 3 knobs, selector switch below knobs, no pickguard, bound top: **1982–87**

Spirit I XPL: 1 pickup with creme coils, Kahler Flyer vibrato, bound top, bound fingerboard, Explorer-style peghead with 6-on-a-side tuner arrangement: **1985–86**

Spirit II XPL: 2 pickups, 3 knobs, selector switch below knobs: **1985–86**

Black Knight Custom: Les Paul single cutaway body shape with beveled edges, 2 humbucking pickups, 4 knobs, 3-way selector switch near knobs, Kahler vibrato, bolt-on neck, rosewood fingerboard, dot inlay, 6-on-a-side tuner arrangement, black chrome-plated hardware, Grover tuners, ebony finish
Available: **1984**

Q Series/Alpha Series: body shape similar to Victory MV series (see preceding), bolt-on neck

Q-100: 1 Dirty Fingers humbucking pickup, tune-o-matic bridge, optional Kahler Flyer vibrato, ebony

fingerboard, dot inlay, 6-on-a-side tuner arrangement, chrome-plated hardware without Kahler, black chrome hardware with Kahler, ebony finish
Introduced: **1985**
Ebony or panther pink finish: **late 1985**
Discontinued: **1986**

Q-200: 1 HP-90 single-coil pickup in neck position, 1 Dirty Fingers humbucking pickup in bridge position, coil tap, Kahler Flyer vibrato, ebony fingerboard, dot inlay, 6-on-a-side tuner arrangement, black chrome or chrome-plated hardware, ebony or Alpine white finish
Introduced: **1985**
Renamed **Q-2000**, ebony, Ferrari red or panther pink finish: **late 1985**
Discontinued: **1986**

Q-300/3000: 3 HP-90 single-coil pickups, 2 knobs, selector switch, "mid" switch, Kahler Flyer vibrato, no pickguard, ebony fingerboard, dot inlay, 6-on-a-side tuner arrangement, black chrome or chrome-plated hardware, ebony or red finish
Introduced as **Q-300: 1985**
Renamed **Q-3000**, 2 knobs for volume and tone control, 3 mini-switches for on/off pickup control, rosewood fingerboard, ebony, Ferrari red or panther pink finish: **late 1985**
Discontinued: **1986**

Q-4000/400: 1 humbucking pickup, 1 Dirty Fingers humbucking pickup and 2 single-coil pickups, master tone and master volume knob, 3 mini-switches for on/off pickup control, push/pull volume control for coil tap, Kahler Flyer vibrato, earliest with neck-through-body construction, later with bolt-on neck, ebony fingerboard, dot inlay, decal logo, black hardware, ebony, Ferrari red or panther pink finish
Introduced as **Q-4000: late 1985**
Renamed **Q-400**, ebony finish: **1986**
Discontinued: **1987**

XPL Standard: "sculptured" body, small Firebird shape, 2 Dirty Fingers humbucking pickups, tune-o-matic bridge or Kahler Flyer vibrato, chrome-plated or black chrome hardware, ebony, Kerry green or Alpine white finish
Available: **1985**

XPL Custom: body shape somewhat similar to Explorer but with sharply pointed horns, cutout at lower tre-

ble horn, bound curly maple top, 2 Dirty Fingers exposed-coil humbucking pickups, 2 knobs, 1 switch, locking nut vibrato system, bound top, dot inlay, cherry sunburst or Alpine white finish:
1985–86

US-1: double cutaway body shape similar to Fender Stratocaster, maple top, mahogany back, Chromyte (balsa) core, 3 humbucking pickups (2 with stacked-coil design) with no visible poles, 3 mini-switches for on/off pickup control, 2 knobs (push/pull volume control for coil tap), tune-o-matic bridge or Kahler locking nut vibrato system, bound top and back, maple neck, 24 frets, 25 1/2" scale, bound ebony fingerboard, double-triangle inlay, bound peghead, 6-on-a-side tuner arrangement, large raised plastic logo, mini-Grover tuners, gold-plated hardware with tune-o-matic bridge, black chrome hardware with Kahler vibrato, pearl white, ebony or heritage cherry sunburst finish
Introduced: **mid 1986**
Inlaid pearl logo: **1987**
Natural top with black back, antique gold or heritage cherry sunburst finish: **1988**
Discontinued: **1991**

U-2/Mach II: asymmetrical double cutaway body shape similar to Fender Stratocaster, basswood body, contoured back, 2 single-coil pickups and 1 HPAF humbucking pickup, 2 Spotlight humbucking pickups optional, Floyd Rose vibrato, 2 knobs, 3 mini-switches, bound top, maple neck, 25 1/2" scale, unbound rosewood fingerboard, 24 frets, dot inlay, unbound peghead, 6-on-a-side tuner arrangement, large raised plastic logo, black chrome hardware, ebony or Ferrari red finish
Introduced as **U-2: 1987**
Metallic turquoise finish optional: **mid 1988**
Ebony fingerboard, candy apple red finish optional, Ferrari red discontinued: **1989**
Renamed **Mach II: 1990**
Discontinued: **1991**

U-2 Showcase Edition: guitar of the month series, EMG pickups, limited run of 200 for U.S. distribution, 50 for overseas: **Nov. 1988**

WRC: designed by Wayne Charvel, alder body, body shape similar to Fender Stratocaster, beveled lower bass bout, 1 humbucking pickup and 2 stacked-coil humbucking pickups with black covers and no polepieces, 3 on/off mini-switches, push/pull volume control for coil tap, Floyd Rose vibrato, bolt-on maple neck, 25 1/2" scale, ebony fingerboard, dot inlay, 6-on-a-side tuner arrangement, point on treble side of peghead, *WRC* or *WC* on truss rod cover, prewar script logo, earliest with Charvel decal on peghead, ebony, honey burst or Ferrari red finish

Introduced: **mid 1987**
Black Kahler Spider vibrato: **late 1988**
Discontinued: **1989**

WRC Showcase Edition: guitar of the month series, 3 EMG pickups (1 humbucking, 2 single-coil), 3 knobs, 4 toggle switches, Kahler vibrato, Sperzel tuners, white finish, up to 200 made for U.S. distribution, 50 for foreign distribution: **Sept. 1988**

SR-71: designed by Wayne Charvel, body shape similar to Fender Stratocaster, 1 humbucking and 2 single-coil pickups, Floyd Rose locking nut vibrato system, glued-in maple neck, 25 1/2" scale, 6-on-a-side tuner arrangement, point on treble side of peghead, prewar script logo, ebony, nuclear yellow or Alpine white finish, Custom Shop model, 250 made, limited edition number on truss rod cover
Available: **1987–89**

Junior Pro: single cutaway mahogany body (Les Paul shape), beveled waist on treble side, slim-coil humbucking pickup with black cover and no visible polepieces, small pickguard extends from treble-side waist to end of fingerboard, 2 knobs, Steinberger KB-X locking-nut vibrato, ebony fingerboard, dot inlay, decal logo, black chrome hardware
Available: **1988**

M-III/M-IV: swooping double cutaway with extended bass horn, beveled lower bass bout, pickguard extends up bass horn, 25 1/2" scale, 24 frets, peghead points to bass side, 6-on-a-side tuner arrangement with tuners all on treble side, logo reads upside down to player

M-III Standard: poplar body, 2 ceramic magnet humbucking pickups with no covers in neck and bridge positions, NSX single-coil pickup with slug polepieces in middle position, 2-way toggle switch and 5-way slide switch for 10 pickup combinations, Floyd Rose vibrato, maple neck and fingerboard, black arrowhead inlay flush with bass side, Alpine white, ebony or candy apple red finish
Introduced: **1991**
Ebony finish only: **1993**
Discontinued: **1996**

M-III Standard, no pickguard: translucent red or translucent amber, Custom Shop limited edition
Introduced: **late 1991**
Regular production model: **1993**
Discontinued: **1996**
Reintroduced in All-American series (see following): **July 1996**

M-III Deluxe: laminated body of maple/walnut/poplar, same electronics as M-III Standard, Floyd Rose vibrato, maple neck and fingerboard, arrowhead inlay flush with bass side, antique natural finish, limited run: **1991–92**

M-III-H (Standard): 2 humbucking pickups, no pickguard, translucent red or translucent amber finish, Custom Shop limited run: **late 1991–92**

M-III-H Deluxe: 5-ply body with walnut top, curly maple back and poplar core, 2 humbucking pickups, 6-way switch, no pickguard, satin (non-gloss) neck finish, antique natural finish, Custom Shop limited run: **late 1991**

M-III Stealth: black limba wood body (similar to walnut), Floyd Rose vibrato, black chrome hardware, satin neck finish: **late 1991**

M-IV S Standard: Steinberger vibrato, black chrome hardware, ebony finish: **1993–95**

M-IV S Deluxe: Steinberger vibrato, natural finish: **1993–95**

The Graceland: single cutaway, mahogany body, spruce top, 2 black soapbar pickups, custom pickguard with modern-art design from Elvis Presley's custom J-200 acoustic
Available: **1995–96**

NIGHTHAWKS

All have single cutaway, mahogany back, flat maple top, low profile bridge with strings through body, 25 1/2" scale.

Nighthawk Special: 1 Firebird mini-humbucking pickup in neck position, 1 NSX single-coil pickup in middle position, 1 slant-mounted humbucking pickup, master volume, push/pull master tone, 5-way switch, optional 2-pickup version with no single-coil and no push/pull tone control, rosewood fingerboard, dot inlay, gold-plated hardware, ebony, heritage cherry or vintage sunburst finish

Available: **1993–98**

Nighthawk Standard: 1 Firebird mini-humbucking pickup in neck position, 1 NSX single-coil pickup in middle position, 1 slant-mounted humbucking pickup in bridge position, master volume, push/pull master tone, 5-way switch, optional 2-pickup version with no single-coil and no push/pull tone control, rosewood fingerboard, double-parallelogram inlay, gold-plated hardware, fireburst, translucent amber or vintage sunburst finish

Introduced: **1993**

Floyd Rose vibrato available on 3-pickup model only: **1994**

Discontinued: **late 1998**

Nighthawk Custom: 1 Firebird mini-humbucking pickup in neck position, 1 NSX single-coil pickup in middle position, 1 slant-mounted humbucking pickup, master volume, push/pull master tone, 5-way switch, optional 2-pickup version with no single-coil and no push/pull tone control, ebony fingerboard, trapezoid inlay, gold-plated hardware, antique natural, fireburst or translucent amber finish

Introduced: **1993**

Floyd Rose vibrato available on 3-pickup model only: **1994**

Discontinued: **late 1998**

Landmark: 2 Firebird mini-humbucking pickups, 2 knobs, 3-way slide switch with coil-tap capability, combination bridge/tailpiece with individual string adjustments, strings mount through body, single-bound top, unbound rosewood fingerboard, dot inlay, pearl logo, gold-plated hardware, Glacier blue, Sequoia red, Mojave burst, Navajo turquoise or Everglades green finish

Available: **July 1996–97**

The Hawk: All American series (see following)

Available: **July 1996–97**

Blueshawk: semi-hollow poplar body, f-holes, 2 special design Blues 90 pickups with cream soapbar covers and non-adjustable poles, 2 knobs (with push/pull to disable Varitone), slide switch, 6-position Vari-tone control, combination bridge/tailpiece with individual string adjustments, strings through body, single-bound top, unbound rosewood fingerboard, diamond inlay, stacked-diamond peghead inlay, pearl logo, gold-plated hardware, ebony or cherry finish

Introduced: **1996**

Maestro vibrato (Bigsby style) optional: **1998**

Still in production

B.B. King "Little Lucille": Blueshawk with B.B. King Lucille features, circular mounting plate for Varitone control with numbered positions, TP-6 fine-tune tailpiece, gold-plated truss rod cover engraved with *B.B. King*, black finish, *Little Lucille* on upper bass bout next to fingerboard

Available: **1999–current**

ALL AMERICAN SERIES

All American I/SG-X: SG-style double cutaway, 1 humbucking pickup, coil tap, ebony finish

Introduced as limited trade show special: **Jan. 1995**

Reintroduced as part of All American series: **July 1996**

Renamed SG-X: **1998**

Still in production

All American II: double cutaway with rounded horns, similar to early 1960s Melody Maker, 2 oblong single-coil pickups with non-adjustable polepieces, vibrato, ebony or deep wine red

Introduced as trade show special: **Jan. 1995**

Reintroduced as part of All American series: **July 1996**

Discontinued: **1998**

The Hawk: Nighthawk body shape, no top cap, no binding, dot inlay, ebony or wine red finish

Available: **July 1996–97**

SG Special: 2 humbucking pickups, ebony or Ferrari red finish

Introduced in All American series: **July 1996**

Moved to SG line: **1998**

Still in production

M-III: 3 humbucking pickups, ebony or wine red finish
Available: **July 1996–97**

The Paul II: Les Paul body shape but thinner body
(see The Paul), carved top, ebony or wine red finish
Introduced in All American series: **July 1996**
Moved to Les Paul line: **1998**
Still in production

DOUBLENECKS

Doublenecks were initially available by custom order
with any combination of necks. Several double
6-strings (with 2 standard 6-string necks) exist.
At least one early style (hollowbody) example has
an 8-string mandolin neck and a 4-string tenor
guitar neck.

EDS-1275 Double 12: 12-string and 6-string
necks, double pointed cutaways, hollow body with
maple back and sides and carved spruce top, no
soundholes, 2 humbucking pickups for each neck,
2 knobs for each neck, 1 switch on treble side,
1 switch on bass side, 1 switch between bridges,
tune-o-matic bridges, triple-bound top and back, 24
3/4" scales, bound rosewood fingerboards, double-
parallelogram inlay, no peghead ornament, sunburst, white or black finish
Introduced (custom order only): **1958**
SG-shape solid mahogany body, double pointed cutaways, beveled edges, 4 knobs on lower treble
bout, 1 switch between tailpieces, 1 switch on
upper treble bout: **c. 1962**
Discontinued (110 total shipped): **1968**
Reintroduced, decal logo, sunburst, walnut, or white
finish: **1977**
Walnut, white or cherry sunburst finish: **1982**
Longer headstock on 12-string neck, heritage cherry
finish optional, cherry sunburst discontinued: **1986**
Pearl logo, walnut finish discontinued: **1987**
Gold-plated hardware with Alpine white finish: **mid
1988**
Historic collection model: **1991**
Returned to regular line: **1995**
Still in production

EDS-1275 Centennial: guitar of the month, ebony finish, serial number in raised numerals on tailpiece,
numeral *1* of serial number formed by row of diamonds, letter *i* of logo dotted by inlaid diamond,

gold medallion on back of peghead, gold-plated
hardware, limited run of no more than 101 serial
numbered from 1894–1994, package includes
16 x 20 framed photograph and gold signet ring:
May 1994

EMS-1235 Double Mandolin: octave (short)
6-string guitar neck (a few with 8-string mandolin
neck) and standard 6-string guitar neck, double
pointed cutaways, hollow maple body with carved
spruce top, no soundholes, 1 humbucking pickup
for short neck, 2 humbucking pickups for standard
neck, height-adjustable bridge for short neck, 15
1/2" scale on short neck (longer than standard
mandolin scale), 24 3/4" scale on guitar neck,
bound rosewood fingerboards, double-parallelogram inlay, no peghead ornament, sunburst, white
or black finish
Introduced (custom order only): **1958**
SG-shape solid mahogany body, double pointed cutaways, beveled edges, 4 knobs on lower treble
bout, 1 switch between tailpieces, 1 switch on
upper treble bout: **c. 1962**
Discontinued (61 total shipped): **1968**

EBSF-1250: bass and 6-string, double pointed cutaways, SG-shape solid mahogany body, beveled
edges, 2 humbucking pickups for each neck, knobs
on lower treble bout, 1 switch between tailpieces,
1 switch on upper treble bout, fuzz-tone on bass,
cherry red finish
Introduced (special order only): **1962**
Sunburst, white or black finish (no cherry): **1963**
Discontinued (22 total shipped): **1968**

COMMENTS

Original 1958–59 Flying Vs and Explorers, as well as
1962–63 examples with 1958-59 body, are the
most highly sought of any solidbody Gibson production model (with the possible exception of the
1958–60 sunburst Les Paul Standard with highly
figured top). Due to their extremely high value, they
have been copied by skilled forgers. Various later
versions appeal to players for aesthetic reasons or
for their modern vibrato systems. Of the later models, only the Heritage Korina reissues have special
appeal to collectors.

Original reverse-body Firebirds are very highly regarded by collectors. Non-reverse models bring less but still have some appeal to collectors, particularly in custom colors.

Of the other solidbody styles in this section, the L-5S has some collector appeal based on its maple body, and the map-shaped promotional model has some value as a conversation piece. The Chet Atkins CE is highly regarded by players. In general, all the other models from the L-6S through the M-series are of interest primarily in the context of Gibson company history.

Doublenecks with carved tops are unlike any other Gibson guitar design and are especially desirable for their sound as well as for their rarity.

ELECTRIC BASSES KEY

Semi-hollowbody
    Single cutaway
        Chrome-plated hardware = **EB-650**
        Gold-plated hardware = **EB-750**
    Symmetrical double cutaway
        1 pickup
            6 strings = **EB-6, 1960–61**
            4 strings
                Plastic-covered pickup = **EB-2, 1958–61**
                Metal-covered pickup = **EB-2, 1964–72**
        2 pickups = **EB-2D**
    Asymmetrical double cutaway = **Les Paul Signature**
Solidbody
    Explorer guitar body shape = **Explorer**
    Flying V guitar body shape = **Flying V**
    Firebird body shape
        1 pickup = **Thunderbird II**
        2 pickups
            Mahogany body
                Handrest and bridge cover
                    Thunderbird IV, 1963–69
                    Thunderbird 76
                    Thunderbird 79
                    Thunderbird III
                No handrest or bridge cover = **Thunderbird IV, 1986–current**
            Curly maple top = **Firebird II**
    Single cutaway
        Oblong pickups = **Les Paul Triumph**
        Rectangular pickups
            Trapezoid inlay
                Gold-plated tuners = **Les Paul Smartwood**
                Chrome-plated tuners = **Les Paul Standard (LPB-3)**
                Black chrome tuners = **Les Paul Deluxe (LPB-2)**
            Dot inlay = **Les Paul Special (LPB-1)**

Violin-shaped body
> Brown plastic pickup cover, banjo tuners = **EB, 1953–58**
> Chrome pickup cover, right-angle tuners = **EB-1, 1970–72**

Double cutaway with rounded horns = **EB-0, 1959–early 1961**

Double cutaway with pointed horns (SG-style)
> 1 pickup with visible poles
>> 30 1/2" scale
>>> Crown peghead inlay
>>>> No fuzztone = **EB-0, early 1961–69, 1972–79**
>>>> Fuzztone = **EB-0F**
>>> No peghead ornament
>>>> Solid peghead = **EB**
>>>> Slotted peghead **= EB-0, 1969–72**
>> 34 1/2" scale
>>> 3-position slide switch = **EB-4L**
>>> No slide switch = **EB-0L**
> 1 pickup with no visible poles
>> 30 1/2" scale = **SB-300**
>> 34 1/2" scale = **SB-400**
> 2 pickups with visible poles
>> 6 strings = **EB-6 after 1961**
>> 4 strings
>>> 30 1/2" scale = **EB-3**
>>> 34 1/2" scale = **EB-3L**
> 2 pickups with no visible poles
>> Split-diamond inlay = **EB-Z**
>> Dot inlay
>>> 30 1/2" scale = **SB-350**
>>> 34 1/2" scale = **SB-450**

Asymmetrical double-cutaway, longer bass horn
> Standard Gibson peghead = **Ripper/L9-S**
> Triangular peghead with rounded top
>> Inlay in center of fingerboard
>>> 1 movable pickup = **Grabber**
>>> 3 pickups = **G-3**
>> Inlay closer to bass side of fingerboard
>>> 4 strings = **Gibson IV**
>>> 5 strings = **Gibson V**
> Peghead points to bass side (4-on-a-side tuners)
>> 2 pickups
>>> Battery pocket on back = **Victory Artist**
>>> No battery pocket on back = **Victory Custom**
>> 1 pickup = **Victory Standard**
> Peghead points to treble side = **Q-80, Q-90**

Asymmetrical double cutaway, longer treble horn
> Active electronics = **RD Artist**
> Standard (passive) electronics = **RD Standard**

Straight-line body edges, 90-degree angles = **20/20**

GIBSON

ELECTRIC BASSES

<u>SECTION ORGANIZATION</u>

Solidbody Models Introduced 1953–68
Thunderbirds
Solidbody Models Introduced 1969 and After
Hollowbody Models

SOLIDBODY MODELS INTRODUCED 1953–68

Gibson Electric Bass/EB-1: violin-shaped mahogany body, carved top, painted-on purfling and *f*-hole, Alnico magnet pickup with poles close to bridge side, brown Bakelite pickup cover, barrel knobs, elevated pickguard, screw-in end pin, telescopic end pin also provided for upright playing, 30 1/2" scale, Kluson banjo style tuners, exposed bridge, crown peghead inlay, brown stain finish, brown contoured case with plush pink lining

Introduced as **Gibson Electric Bass: 1953**
Discontinued, 546 total shipped: **1958**
Reintroduced as **EB-1:** humbucking pickup with poles across middle, chrome pickup cover, chrome bridge cover, black bonnet knobs, standard right-angle tuners, rectangular case: **1970**
Discontinued: **1972**

EB-0: slab mahogany body, double cutaway with rounded points (like 1959 Les Paul Jr.), 1 black plastic-covered humbucking pickup, neck-body joint at 17th fret, 30 1/2" scale, rosewood fingerboard, dot inlay, Kluson banjo style tuners, cherry red finish

Introduced: **1959**
Pickup poles across middle of pickup: **1960**
Right-angle tuners: **early 1961**
SG-style double cutaway with pointed horns, beveled top edges, unbeveled cutaway edges: **early 1961**
Metal-covered pickup, string mute: **c. 1962**
Slotted peghead, no crown on peghead: **late 1969**
Walnut finish optional: **by 1971**
Black finish available (11 shipped): **1971–75**
Solid peghead, crown peghead inlay: **1972**
Natural finish available (5 shipped): **1973**
Discontinued (6 shipped): **1979**

EB-0F: built-in fuzztone: **1962–65**

EB-0L: 34 1/2" scale: **late 1969–79**

EB-3: mahogany body, SG-style double cutaway with pointed horns, 2 humbucking pickups (large neck pickup, small bridge pickup), black plastic cover on neck pickup, metal cover on bridge pickup, hand-rest between pickups, 4-position rotary tone switch with pointer knob, string mute, neck-body joint at 17th fret, 30 1/2" scale, rosewood fingerboard, dot inlay, crown peghead inlay, solid peghead cherry red finish

Introduced: **1961**
2 metal pickup covers: **1962**
No handrest, metal bridge cover, slotted peghead, no crown on peghead: **late 1969**
Walnut finish optional: **by 1971**
Natural finish available on EB-3 (49 total shipped):
  1971–73
Solid peghead, crown peghead inlay: **1972**
White finish available on EB-3 (69 total shipped):
  1976–79
Discontinued: **mid 1979**

EB-3L: 34 1/2" scale, available: **1969–72**

EB-6: introduced as semi-hollowbody (see following), body changes to SG-style double cutaway with pointed horns, dot inlay, 2 humbucking pickups, larger metal tuning keys, cherry red finish: **1962**
Discontinued (135 total shipped): **1966**

Melody Maker: SG-style double cutaway with pointed horns, 1 pickup, dot inlay
Introduced: **1967**
Last made, replaced by EB (see following): **1970**

THUNDERBIRDS

Thunderbird II: companion to Firebird I guitar, reverse body shape, neck-through-body construction, 1 metal-covered pickup with no visible poles, 2 knobs, 34" scale, dot inlay, right-angle tuners all on bass side of peghead, sunburst finish standard, custom colors available

Introduced: **1963**
Non-reverse body, glued-in neck with visible joint: **mid 1965**
Discontinued: **1969**
Reintroduced, reverse body, 40 made: **1983–84**

Thunderbird IV: companion to Firebird III, same as Thunderbird II but with 2 pickups, 4 knobs
Introduced: **1963**
Non-reverse body, glued-in neck with visible joint: **mid 1965**
Discontinued: **1969**
Reintroduced, reverse body, 2 humbucking pickups, 3 knobs, bass tune-o-matic bridge with 3-point support, no handrest, no bridge cover, black chrome hardware, tobacco sunburst or heather poly finish: **mid 1986**
Black chrome hardware: **1988**
Tobacco sunburst, ebony or classic white finish: **1990**
Cardinal red finish optional: **1991**
Vintage sunburst finish only: **1993**
Natural, natural burst or ebony stain finish offered in limited runs: **late 1998**
Still in production

Thunderbird 76: companion to Firebird 76 guitar, reverse body, red-and-blue Centennial Thunderbird figure (with stars) on pickguard, 2 pickups, 3-point adjustable bridge/tailpiece, 34 1/2" scale, rosewood fingerboard, dot inlay, sunburst, natural mahogany, white or ebony finish
Available: **1976**

Thunderbird 79: reverse body, 2 pickups, natural mahogany, ebony, or tobacco sunburst finish
500 made: **1979**

Firebird II: reverse body, curly maple top, mahogany body, flat top, glued-in neck, antique sunburst, vintage cherry sunburst or antique natural finish
Available: **1982 only**

Thunderbird III: reverse body, 2 pickups, 3 knobs, handrest and bridge cover, Thunderbird figure on pickguard, unbound rosewood fingerboard, dot inlay
Available: **1979–82**

SOLIDBODY MODELS INTRODUCED 1969 AND AFTER

Les Paul Bass/Triumph: mahogany body (companion to Les Paul Professional and Les Paul Personal), single cutaway, carved top, 2 oblong low-impedance pickups mounted straight across, 3 knobs (master volume, bass, treble), high/low impedance switch, oblong control plate, 30 1/2" scale, unbound fingerboard, dot inlay, crown peghead inlay, walnut finish
Introduced as **Les Paul Bass: 1969**
Renamed **Les Paul Triumph**, semi-circular control plate, 3 knobs (master volume, bass, treble), high/low impedance switch, phase switch, 3-position tone switch, jack on top, small block inlay, 5-piece split-diamond peghead inlay, white finish optional: **1971**
Discontinued (44 shipped): **1979**

EB: maple body, SG-style double cutaway with pointed horns, 1 large humbucking pickup, 2 knobs, long pickguard extends below bridge, neck-body joint at 15th fret, dot inlay, 30 1/2" scale, decal logo, no peghead ornament
Available: **1970**

EB-1: see Gibson Electric Bass, preceding

EB-4L: mahogany body, SG-style double cutaway with pointed horns, 1 large humbucking pickup, 2 knobs, 3-position slide switch, string damper, rosewood fingerboard, dot inlay, 34 1/2" scale, cherry or walnut finish
Listed: **1972–75**
Last shipped (including 1 black finish): **1979**

SB-400: mahogany body, SG-style double cutaway with pointed horns, 1 black plastic-covered mini-humbucking pickup, 34 1/2" scale
Available: **1971–73**

SB-300: SB-400 with 30 1/2" scale: **1971–73**

SB-450: mahogany body, SG-style double cutaway with pointed horns, 2 black plastic-covered mini-humbucking pickups (earliest with oval pickups with embossed Gibson), 2 knobs and 2 push switches mounted on control plate, string damper, no pickguard, thumbrest near fingerboard (earliest with no string damper, no thumbrest), rosewood fingerboard, dot inlay, 34 1/2" scale, cherry or walnut finish
Available: **1972–74**
Last shipped: **1978**

SB-350: SB-450 with 30 1/2" scale: **1972–74**

L9-S/Ripper: solid maple body, asymmetrical double cutaway, 2 humbucking pickups, 3 knobs (volume, midrange rolloff, treble rolloff), 4-position rotary tone switch, strings anchor through body, 34 1/2" scale, bolt-on maple neck, maple fingerboard with natural finish, ebony fingerboard with sunburst finish, dot inlay, standard Gibson peghead, decal logo, natural maple or sunburst finish

Introduced as **L9-S: 1973**

Renamed **Ripper: 1974**

Alder body, glued-in neck, sunburst finish discontinued, ebony finish (with ebony fingerboard) optional: **1975**

Discontinued: **1982**

L9-FS: fretless version of Ripper, alder body, glued-in neck, ebony or tobacco sunburst finish: **1975–81**

Grabber (G-1): solid maple body, asymmetrical double cutaway, 1 movable pickup with *Gibson* embossed on plastic cover, 2 knobs, 34 1/2" scale, bolt-on maple neck, maple fingerboard, dot inlay, triangular peghead with rounded top, decal logo, wine red or ebony finish

Introduced: **late 1974**

Alder body: **1975**

Natural finish available: **1976**

Discontinued: **1982**

Grabber III (G-3): solid alder body, asymmetrical double cutaway, 3 single-coil pickups wired for humbucking capability, 2 knobs, 1 switch, transparent pickup covers, 34 1/2" scale, bolt-on maple neck, maple fingerboard, dot inlay, triangular peghead with rounded top, nickel-plated hardware, natural, sunburst or ebony finish

Introduced: **1975**

Black pickup covers: **1976**

Strings anchor through body, chrome-plated hardware: **1979**

Discontinued: **1982**

RD Standard: companion to RD guitars, asymmetrical double cutaway with extended treble horn, 2 humbucking pickups with black covers and no visible poles, 3 knobs, strings anchor through body, unbound maple fingerboard with natural finish model, unbound ebony fingerboard with ebony finish model, dot inlay, decal logo, no peghead ornament, standard Gibson peghead, dot inlay, natural or ebony finish

Available: **1977–79**

RD Artist: maple body, asymmetrical double cutaway with extended treble horn, 2 Series V humbucking pickups with black covers and no visible poles, 4 knobs (standard Gibson controls), 3-way pickup selector switch, 3-way mode selector switch (neutral, bright, front pickup expansion with back pickup compression), active electronics, strings anchor through body, laminated maple neck, maple fingerboard with natural finish model, ebony fingerboard with all other finishes, dot inlay, winged-*f* peghead inlay, pearl logo, standard Gibson peghead, natural, antique sunburst, ebony or fireburst finish with ebony fingerboard

Introduced: **1977**

Mode switch replaced by 2 mini switches (brightness, expansion/compression): **1980**

Discontinued: **1982**

RD Artist 6-string: 6 produced: **c. 1980**

Victory Standard: companion to Victory guitars, maple body, asymmetrical double cutaway with extended horns, horns come to a point, 1 slant-mounted humbucking pickup, 2 knobs, 1 mini-switch, 3-piece bolt-on maple neck, 34" scale, rosewood fingerboard, asymmetrical fingerboard extension on treble side, fretless fingerboard optional, dot inlay positioned closer to bass edge of fingerboard, brass nut, 4-on-a-side tuners, peghead points to bass side, decal logo and *Victory Bass* decal near nut, chrome-plated hardware, silver or candy apple red finish

Available: **1981–86**

Victory Artist: 2 humbucking pickups, neck pickup mounted at slant, 3 knobs, 2 mini-switches, active electronics, battery pocket on back, antique fireburst or candy apple red finish: **1981–85**

Victory Custom: same as Victory Artist but with passive electronics, no battery pocket on back, no more than 250 made

Listed: **1982–84**

Last made: **1987**

Flying V: companion to Flying V guitar, bound or

unbound fingerboard, blue stain, ebony or silverburst finish
Available: **late 1981–82**

Explorer: companion to Explorer guitar, alder body,
2 humbucking pickups with black covers and no
visible polepieces, 3 knobs in straight line, bridge
with individually adjustable saddles, 3-piece maple
neck, 32" scale, rosewood fingerboard, 21 frets,
brass nut, chrome-plated hardware
Introduced: **1984**
Custom graphics available: **1985 only**
Chrome-plated or black chrome hardware, Alpine
white, ebony or Ferrari red finish: **1985**
Discontinued: **1987**

Explorer Shadow: "Shadow" piezo bridge pickup:
1985–86

Q-80/Q-90: same body shape as Victory series,
2 pickups, 3 knobs, no pickguard, square-end rosewood fingerboard, dot inlay in center of fingerboard, peghead points to treble side, black chrome
hardware, ebony, Ferrari red or panther pink finish
Introduced as **Q-80: 1986**
Renamed **Q-90**, ebony or coral finish: **1988**
Discontinued: **1990**

Q-90 Nylon String: available with frets or fretless,
alpine white, ebony or darkburst finish: **1989–90**

Q-90 Combo: ebony, candy apple red, candy apple
blue, honey burst or darkburst finish: **1990**
Darkburst finish discontinued: **1991**
Discontinued: **1992**

Gibson IV: asymmetrical double cutaway, mahogany body, 2 humbucking pickups, 3 knobs in
straight line (2 volume, 1 tone), no pickguard,
mahogany neck, 22 frets, 34" scale, ebony fingerboard, dot inlay positioned closer to bass side of
fingerboard, peghead narrows toward top, black
chrome hardware, heather poly, pearl white, Ferrari
red or natural finish
Available: **1986–88**

Gibson V: 5-string: **1986–88**

20/20: designed by Ned Steinberger, straight-line
body edges with 90-degree angles, extended bass
horn, maple body, 2 humbucking pickups, active

electronics, 3 knobs, maple neck, 24 frets,
34" scale, ebony fingerboard, dot inlay, small rectangular peghead, 2-on-a-side tuners with offset
configuration, Sperzel tuners, black chrome hardware, luna silver or Ferrari red finish
Available: **1987–88**

WRC I: companion to WRC guitar designed by
Wayne Charvel, asymmetrical double cutaway, 1
pickup, ebony or nuclear yellow finish
Listed but never in production: **1988**

WRC II: 2 pickups, ebony or metallic turquoise finish,
not produced

Les Paul Special Bass (LPB-1): single cutaway, slab mahogany body, 2 TB-Plus Thunderbird
pickups with black plastic covers, mahogany neck,
34" scale, ebony fingerboard, dot inlay, flowerpot
peghead inlay, black chrome hardware, ebony, heritage cherry or TV yellow finish
Introduced: **late 1991**
Ebony finish discontinued, tobacco sunburst optional:
1992
Ebony, classic white or heritage cherry finish: **1993**
5-string optional: **1993**
No flowerpot inlay on peghead: **1994**
Still in production

Les Paul Deluxe Plus Bass (LPB-2): single
cutaway, mahogany body, carved maple top, 2 Bartolini pickups with active electronics, mahogany
neck, 34" scale, ebony fingerboard, trapezoid inlay,
flowerpot peghead inlay, black chrome hardware,
translucent black, translucent blue, translucent red
or translucent amber finish
Introduced: **late 1991**
Heritage cherry sunburst or translucent amber finish
only: **1993**
No flowerpot inlay on peghead: **1994**
Still in production

Les Paul Deluxe Premium Plus Bass: highly figured
maple top, 5-string optional: **1993–current**

Les Paul Standard Bass (LPB-3): single cutaway, mahogany body, carved maple top, 2 TB-Plus
Thunderbird pickups with black plastic covers,
mahogany neck, 34" scale, ebony fingerboard,
trapezoid inlay, flowerpot peghead inlay, chrome-

plated hardware, ebony, honey burst, heritage cherry sunburst or vintage sunburst finish

Introduced: **late 1991**

Ebony, heritage cherry sunburst or translucent amber finish: **1993**

5-string optional: **1995**

Still in production

Les Paul Standard Premium Plus Bass: highly figured maple top, 5-string optional, heritage cherry sunburst or translucent amber finish

Introduced: **1993**

No flowerpot inlay on peghead: **1994**

Discontinued: **1995**

Les Paul Smartwood Bass: wood certified by Rainforest Alliance, single cutaway, semi-hollow mahogany body, flat maple top, 2 Gibson TB Plus pickups, active Bartolini electronics, 4 knobs, no binding, chechen fingerboard, pearl trapezoid inlay, antique natural, heritage cherry sunburst, earthburst, emerald or ebony finish

Available: **1998–current**

EB-Z: double cutaway with pointed horns (SG body shape), mahogany body, 2 Z-bass humbucking pickups with black covers and no polepieces, 3 knobs in straight-line configuration, 2 mini switches for coil tap and pickup selector, black pearloid pickguard, 34" scale, unbound wenge fingerboard, split diamond inlay, 3-piece split-diamond peghead inlay, black chrome hardware, heritage cherry or ebony finish

Available: **1998–current**

HOLLOWBODY MODELS

EB-2: ES-335 type semi-hollowbody, double rounded cutaway, *f*-holes, 1 humbucking pickup with poles across center of pickup (earliest with single-coil pickup), black plastic pickup cover (a few early with brown cover), stud bridge/tailpiece, single-bound top and back, 30 1/2" scale, dot inlay, crown peghead inlay, Kluson banjo style tuners with large holes through shafts, sunburst or natural finish

Introduced: **spring 1958**

Baritone pushbutton control: **1959**

Some with black finish: **May 1959**

String mute: **by 1960**

Some with cherry finish: **March 1960**

Right-angle Kluson tuners: **late 1960**

Discontinued (32 EB-2 and 7 EB-2N total shipped): **1961**

Reintroduced, metal pickup cover with poles across middle, string mute, sunburst finish: **1964**

Cherry finish optional: **late 1965**

Walnut or sparkling burgundy finish optional: **by 1969**

Discontinued: **1972**

EB-2D: 2 humbucking pickups (1 standard bass pickup in neck position, smaller pickup in bridge position), selector switch, pushbutton baritone control, sunburst or cherry finish

Introduced: **1966**

Walnut or sparkling burgundy finish optional: **by 1969**

Discontinued: **1972**

EB-6: 6 strings, tuned an octave below standard guitar, ES-335 type semi-hollow body, double rounded cutaway, *f*-holes, 1 humbucking guitar pickup, string spacing like guitar, 30 1/2" scale, crown peghead inlay, right-angle tuners, plastic keystone tuner buttons, sunburst finish

Introduced: **1960**

Solidbody, SG-style double cutaway with pointed horns, dot inlay, 2 humbucking pickups, larger metal tuning keys, cherry red finish: **1962**

Discontinued (135 total shipped): **1966**

Les Paul Signature: semi-hollowbody, asymmetrical double cutaway with rounded horns, 1 oblong low-impedance humbucking pickup, trapezoid inlay, sunburst or gold finish

Introduced: **1973**

High impedance pickup, gold finish only: **1976**

Discontinued (58 shipped): **1979**

EB-650: single cutaway, arched top, laminated maple body with Chromyte (balsa) center block, 2 TB-Plus Thunderbird pickups with black plastic covers, diamond soundholes, maple neck, 34" scale, ebony fingerboard, dot inlay, flowerpot peghead inlay, chrome-plated hardware, translucent black, translucent blue, translucent red, translucent purple or translucent amber finish

Available: **late 1991–93**

EB-750: single cutaway, arched top, laminated maple body with Chromyte (balsa) center block, 2 Bartolini pickups with active electronics, diamond soundholes, maple neck, 34" scale, ebony finger-

board, abalone dot inlay, gold-plated hardware, antique natural, ebony or vintage sunburst finish
Available: **late 1991–93**

COMMENTS

Reverse-body Thunderbird basses are considered to be the best electric basses ever made by Gibson and are the most highly sought by collectors.

The early version of the violin-shaped bass (later named EB-1) is highly regarded by collectors. Early versions of the EB-2, EB-0 and EB-3 have some appeal to collectors. The EB-6 is very rare and considered to be of high quality.

In general, Gibson basses never achieved the respect or success of Fenders. Virtually all Gibson basses made after 1965 have no more than average value as utility instruments.

STEELS KEY

No pedals
  Singleneck
    Symmetrical body, 2 rounded bouts (guitar shape)
      No control plate (knobs into top)
        Green and gray bridge/pickup cover = **Royaltone, 1956–57**
        No pickup cover
          Shoulders join neck at an angle
            Metalbody = **E-150 metalbody**
            Woodbody = **E-150 woodbody**
          Shoulders taper into neck
            Hexagonal or oblong pickup = **EH-150, 1936–42**
            Rectangular white pickup = **EH-100, 1936–40**
      Metal plate extends under fingerboard to form peghead
        Sunburst finish = **EH-185**
        Natural finish = **EH-275**
      5-sided metal control plate
        Natural mahogany finish = **EH-100, 1940–41**
        Sunburst finish
          Single-bound top = **EH-125**
          Triple-bound top = **EH-150, late 1942**
      Gold plastic control plate and bridge/pickup cover
        Curlicue design on bridge cover = **BR-4**
        Plain bridge cover = **BR-6, 1949–60**
      White control plate and bridge cover = **BR-6, 1947–49**
    Symmetrical body with points on upper bouts = **Royaltone, 1950–52**
    Symmetrical 3-bout body = **BR-9**
    Symmetrical square-end body (1 bout) = **Century, 1966–67**
    Straight-line body on bass side only
      Bittersweet (salmon) finish = **Century, 1955–65**
      Black finish = **Century, 1948–55**
      Any other paint finish = **Ultratone**
      Natural finish korina wood
        Custom Deluxe on peghead = **Skylark Deluxe**
        No *Custom Deluxe* on peghead = **Skylark**

No pedals *(continued)*
Doubleneck
Rosewood fingerboards
Rectangular body = **Console Grand, 1939–42**
Guitar-shaped body = **EH-150 doubleneck**
Silver back-painted plastic fingerboards
Sunburst finish = **Console Grand, 1946–66**
Natural finish = **CGN**
Black back-painted plastic fingerboards = **CG 520**
Korina wood fingerboards and body = **Consolette**
Maple fingerboards and body = **CG 530**
Tripleneck
Sunburst = **CGT**
Natural = **CGTN**
4 pedals
Maple body, contoured top = **Electraharp, 1949–56; EH-630 1956–67**
"Limed oak" butcher block body = **EH-610**
6 pedals
Maple and walnut cabinet = **Electraharp, 1939–42**
No cabinet
Doubleneck = **EH-620**
Tripleneck = **Multiharp**
8 pedals
Singleneck = **EH-810**
Doubleneck = **EH-820**

STEELS

SECTION ORGANIZATION

Lap Models Introduced Before World War II
Lap Models Introduced After World War II
Console Models
Pedal Models

LAP MODELS INTRODUCED BEFORE WORLD WAR II

E-150: cast aluminum guitar-shaped body, shoulders angled into neck at a sharper angle than EH-150 and all later models, Charlie Christian pickup with bound blade and separate poles under treble strings, 2 knobs on opposite sides, unbound ebony fingerboard with V-end (a few rosewood, white) inlaid fret markers, metal nut black paint logo, open-back tuners with metal buttons
98 total shipped: **Oct. 1, 1935–36**

Electric Hawaiian EH-150: hollow guitar-shaped body, shoulders taper into neck, all maple construction, screwed-on back, Charlie Christian

pickup with bound blade and unbound outer edge, 2 knobs on opposite sides, triple-bound top (early with single-bound top), bound rosewood fingerboard with V-end, pearl dot markers, pearl logo, no peghead ornament, sunburst finish, 6 or 7 strings (later 8, 9, or 10 strings optional, at least 1 with 13 strings)
Introduced: **Jan. 1, 1936**
Transition of features, **late 1936–37:**
Bound outer edge of pickup (some with unbound outer edge through 1937)
4-piece diamond peghead inlay
Knobs on same side, 1 black knob, 1 brown knob
Bound back
Glued-on back, pickup blade split in middle (pickup magnet underneath top changes to horseshoe shape), triple-bound top and back: **early 1938**
Chrome-plated bridge cover: **early 1938**
ES-300 type oblong pickup mounted at a slant (a few with metal mounting plate): **Nov. 1939**
Fleur-de-lis peghead inlay: **late 1940**
Square-end metal fingerboard, fancy markers: **1941**
Specs identical to EH-125 except for triple-bound top:

solid mahogany body, 5-sided metal control plate, metal-covered pickup with raised center (some with tortoiseshell celluloid material in center), knobs on opposite sides, triple-bound top, single-bound back, metal fingerboard, fleur-de-lis peghead inlay: **Oct. 1942**

Discontinued: **1943**

Doubleneck Electric Hawaiian: 2 necks, otherwise similar to EH-150

Available: **1937–38**

Roy Smeck Special: hollow guitar-shaped body, shoulders taper into neck, Charlie Christian pickup with bound blade, 2 knobs on opposite sides, black body binding, V-end ebony fingerboard with white and black binding, dot inlay, black peghead binding, model name on peghead, white finish, custom-ordered by Roy Smeck for Roy Smeck School of Music, approx. 14 produced, some shipped with white-covered amplifier with *Smeck* stenciled on front (also see EH-275, following)

First shipped: **Mar. 6, 1936**

Last shipped, probably natural finish, tortoiseshell celluloid binding, white-painted hardware: **1941**

EH-100: hollow guitar-shaped body, shoulders taper into neck, all maple construction, blade pickup with white rectangular housing, 1 knob on treble side, bound top, rosewood fingerboard with square end, dot inlay, silkscreen logo, black finish, 6 or 7 strings

Introduced: **early 1936**

2 knobs on opposite sides: **later 1936**

Sunburst finish: **1937**

2 knobs on treble side: **by late 1937**

Solid mahogany body, metal-covered pickup, 5-sided control plate surrounds knobs and pickup, knobs on opposite sides, no body binding, square-end metal fingerboard with fancy markers (some with rosewood fingerboard and pearl dot inlay), peghead tapers to point (like Kalamazoo models), silkscreen logo, natural mahogany finish: **1940**

Discontinued: **1941**

EH-125: solid mahogany guitar-shaped body, shoulders taper into neck, metal-covered pickup, 5-sided metal control plate, metal bridge cover, single-bound top and back (triple-bound top listed as

EH-150, see preceding, late 1942), metal fingerboard, fancy markers, fleur-de-lis peghead inlay, pearl logo, sunburst finish

Available: **1940–42**

EH-185: hollow guitar-shaped body of curly maple, shoulders taper into neck, Charlie Christian pickup with triple-bound edge, triple-bound top and back, 1-piece metal plate extends from peghead to bridge (under fingerboard) covering most of lower bout, peghead is part of metal plate, plate is thicker under fingerboard, wood neckpiece bolts on to back of metal plate, non-slip material in shape of diamonds applied to back of neck and body, single-bound rosewood fingerboard with V-end, dot inlay, slotted peghead with 1/2"-wide slots, top tuners with metal buttons, sunburst or natural (**EH-185N**) finish, metal plate painted glossy black, available with 6, 7, 8 or 10 strings and left-handed

Introduced: **Sept. 1939**

Transition of features, late **1939–40**:

Metal plate with uniform thickness from fingerboard area to body area, plate painted crinkled brown

Black line on side of fingerboard binding

Some with 5/8"-wide peghead slots

ES-300 type oblong pickup with polepieces, pickup mounted at a slant, black-gray crinkle paint on metal plate: **late 1940**

Discontinued: **1942**

EH-275 (EH-250): hollow guitar-shaped body of curly maple, shoulders taper into neck, ES-300 type pole pickup mouted at a slant, 1-piece metal plate extends from peghead to bridge (under fingerboard) covering most of lower bout, peghead is part of metal plate, wood neckpiece bolts on to back of metal plate, tortoiseshell celluloid binding on top and back, rosewood fingerboard with V-end, white fingerboard binding, white and yellow block inlay, multi-colored inlaid fret markers (some with EH-185 fingerboard with dot inlay), slotted peghead, top tuners, natural finish, brown crinkle paint finish on metal plate, available with 6, 7 or 8 strings

Introduced (first 6 examples designated **EH-250**): **Sept. 1940**

Discontinued (approx. 25 total shipped, approx. 3 designated *Roy Smeck* models): **1942**

GIBSON

LAP MODELS INTRODUCED AFTER WORLD WAR II

BR-3: catalog specs unavailable, 1 example with guitar-shaped body, pickup with non-adjustable poles, tortoiseshell celluloid bridge/pickup cover and jackplate, tuners with rivet shaft bases
Introduced: **Jan. 1946**
Replaced by BR-4: **1947**

BR-4: solid mahogany guitar-shaped body, P-90 pickup with non-adjustable poles, knobs on opposite sides, large gold plastic plate covers lower bouts, curlicue design on pickup cover, binding varies (some with none, some with top only, some with top and back), rounded neck, sunburst finish
Available: **1947**

BR-1/Ultratone: solidbody with straight-line bass side, rounded extension around knobs on treble side, maple body, pickup with non-adjustable poles, 3 knobs, coral bridge/pickup cover with lyre design and *Ultratone*, plastic fingerboard back-painted silver, fingerboard widens along bass side, dot markers, coral rectangular tuner buttons, gray and silver peghead cover, 6 strings, white finish
Introduced as **BR-1: Mar. 1946**
Renamed **Ultratone: late 1946**
Adjustable pickup poles: **c. 1950**
Straight body edge around knobs, flower on pickup cover, fingerboard back-painted blue, bass edge of fingerboard parallel to strings, some with *Century* at end of fingerboard, no peghead cover, curlicue peghead ornament, logo straight across peghead, dark blue finish: **c. 1953**
Beige fingerboard, peghead cover with floral design, seal brown finish: **by 1955**
Bound top, clay colored tuner buttons, ivory top finish, natural mahogany back and sides finish: **1956**
Humbucking pickup, flower design on pickup cover: **1958**
Discontinued: **1959**

Ultratone 7: 7 strings: **1947–55**

BR-6: solid mahogany guitar-shaped body, knobs on opposite sides, plastic control plate back-painted white, white bridge/pickup cover, square neck, white open-block markers with numbers, black finish
Introduced: **July 1946**

Gold plastic control plate and pickup cover, string ends visible, single-bound top and back, metal fingerboard, gold-painted markers, round neck, sunburst finish: **1948**
Knobs on same side: **1949**
Discontinued: **1960**

BR-6B: specs unavailable, possibly BR-6 with black finish, 77 shipped: **1956–59**

BR-9: solidbody with graduated 3-bout shape, brown plastic pickup/bridge cover, 2 white radio knobs on same side, pickup with non-adjustable poles, open-block markers with numbers, beige finish, brown or reddish brown fingerboard and trim
Introduced: **1947**
Adjustable pickup poles: **c. 1950**
Discontinued: **1959**

Century-6: solidbody, straight-line bass side of body, rounded extension around knobs on treble side, maple body, pickup with non-adjustable poles, 3 knobs, silver fingerboard, no peghead cover, curlicue figure on peghead, peghead points slightly to treble side, oval tuner buttons, black finish
Introduced: **1948**
Some Ultratone examples (see preceding) with *Century* at end of fingerboard: **c. 1953**
P-90 soapbar pickup matching finish, plastic bridge cover does not hide pickup, 3 knobs, beach white (beige) fingerboard, dot markers, 1-color plastic peghead cover, bittersweet (salmon or clay color) finish: **by 1955**
Slightly asymmetrical body with square end, mini-humbucking pickup with no poles, rectangular metal pickup cover, control plate extends up neck, dark fingerboard, red and yellow markers, logo reads upside down to player, red finish: **by 1966**
Discontinued: **1968**

Century 10: 10 strings, design suggested by musician Eddie Alkire (see Epiphone Eharp) but never officially endorsed, black finish, 90 shipped: **1948–55**

Century D: specs unavailable, 20 shipped: **1956–59**

Royaltone: solid symmetrical body with points on upper bouts, maple top, 2-tone dark brown and black bridge cover, natural top finish, brown back and sides finish
Available: **1950–52**

Guitar-shaped body, plastic pickup cover, colored dot markers, olive-mustard finish: **1956–57**

Skylark (EH-500): solid Korina (African limba wood) body, square-end body with straight line on bass side, slant-mounted pickup, control plate has shoulder to include knob, body beveled around fingerboard, open-block markers with numbers, peghead points slightly to treble side, raised plastic logo reads upside down to player, natural finish
Introduced: **1956**
8-string available: **1958**
Discontinued: **1968**

Skylark Deluxe: same as Skylark except for dot markers, *Custom Deluxe* stenciled on peghead: **1958–59**

CONSOLE MODELS

Console Grand: doubleneck, hollow rectangular body of flamed maple, staggered tiers, Charlie Christian pickups with triple-bound edge, bound blade with individual poles, lever mutes, chrome-plated bridge covers, triple-bound top and back, bound rosewood fingerboards with V-ends, dot inlay (some with block inlay), 7- and 8-string combinaton standard, any combination of 6, 7 or 8 strings optional, sunburst finish, a few natural finish, optional maple stand with wheels
Introduced: **April 1938**
Screw-on legs: **Oct. 1938**
Metal plate extends under both fingerboards (EH-185 style), no mutes: **Aug. 1939**
Production suspended for World War II: **1942**
Reintroduced, contoured top (some with prewar body), 3 knobs, oblong P-90 pickups, Lucite fingerboard back-painted silver, double 8-string standard, sunburst or natural (**CGN**) finish: **1948**
4 legs: **by 1953**
Large humbucking pickups with 4-8-4 pole configuration: **1956**
Discontinued: **1967**

CGT: Console Grand tripleneck, sunburst finish, 4 legs
Introduced: **1951**
Natural finish (**CGTN**) introduced: **1953**
Replaced by **CG 523**, optional legs: **1956**
Discontinued: **1957**
Last shipped: **1959**

Consolette: rectangular korina (African limba wood) body, 2 8-string necks, staggered tiers, white P-90 pickups, white bridge/pickup covers, 2 knobs and switch between necks, natural finish (described in catalog as "mahogany type finish")
Introduced: **1952**
Discontinued, name continues on laminated maple model C-530 (see following): **1956**
Last korina Consolettes shipped: **1957**

CG-520: 2 8-string necks, pickups with 4-8-4 pole configuration, 2 knobs, 2 push switches, 3-way switch, 4-way tone selector switch on each neck, black binding, black fingerboard, tuners arranged in pairs, raised black logo on front, natural finish, 4 non-adjustable legs optional
Available: **1956–66**

Console (C-530): listed as Consolette (see preceding), 2 8-string necks, laminated maple body, humbucking pickups with 2 rows of visible poles, mute and tone-boost pushbuttons, maple fingerboards, natural finish, 4 legs optional
Introduced (2 shipped in 1955): **1956**
Listed as Console (C-530): **1957**
Last shipped: **1966**

PEDAL MODELS

Electraharp/EH-630: 6 pedals, 8 strings, maple top, maple cabinet with walnut panels, slant-mounted ES-300 style oblong pickup with screw-poles, heavy metal bridge and tuner covers (some wood), bound rosewood fingerboard with V-end, dot inlay, tuners at pickup end, natural finish
Introduced: **early 1941**
4 pedals, maple body, top beveled around fingerboard, 4 aluminum legs, pedals anchored on legs, sunburst finish: **1949**
Renamed **EH-630: 1956**
Humbucking pickup: **1956**
Mute and tone-boost pushbuttons: **1960**
Discontinued: **1967**

EH-620: 6 pedals
Introduced: **1955**
Humbucking pickup: **1956**
Mute and tone-boost pushbuttons on EH-630 and EH-620: **1960**
Discontinued: **1967**

EH-610: 4 pedals, 6 strings, rectangular "limed oak" butcher block body, non-contoured top, humbucking pickup
Available: **1957–66**

EH-820: doubleneck, 8 pedals on rack across front, humbucking pickup, Vari-Tone rotary tone selector switch, cherry finish
Available: **1960–66**

EH-810: singleneck version of EH-820, 8 pedals
Available: **1961–66**

Multiharp: 3 necks, 6 pedals on middle neck, ebony finish
Available: **1957–65**

COMMENTS

Prewar models with the Charlie Christian pickup are the most highly regarded by collectors and players. The metalbody model, which is Gibson's first electric instrument and the only metalbody of any kind ever made by the company, is very rare and highly sought. Prewar models with the oblong slant-mounted pickup are also highly regarded, especially the EH-185 and the extremely rare natural finish EH-275. Low-end models, especially those with metal-covered pickup, are of considerably less interest.

Most postwar lap and console models are regarded as fine utility instruments. The Ultratone and Century models are among the most visually appealing of any Gibson instruments. The early Consolette and the Skylark, with Korina wood bodies, are sought by collectors for their association with the Korina Explorer and Flying V guitars.

The prewar Electraharp, which is the first modern, professional quality pedal steel, is extremely rare and quite a conversation piece.

Postwar pedal steels are, ironically, more primitive and cumbersome in design than the prewar Electraharp (due to a patent dispute) and have limited appeal to collectors or players.

UKULELES

Uke-1: 6" wide, mahogany body, black and white rope-pattern soundhole ring, no body binding, 12-fret ebonized (black-stained) fingerboard with pointed end, all frets clear of body, small dot inlay, ebony nut and saddle, peghead tapers to point at top, *The Gibson* silkscreen logo, black tuner buttons, light amber finish
Introduced: **late 1926**
17-fret rosewood fingerboard extends to soundhole: **1928**
Gibson logo: **by mid 1930s**
White-black-white soundhole ring, single-bound top, unbound back, 12-fret fingerboard, 11 frets clear of body, larger pearl dot inlay, darker finish: **1937**
Unbound top: **by 1955**
Discontinued (2 shipped): **1967**

Uke-2: 6" wide, mahogany body, rope-pattern soundhole ring, triple-bound top, single-bound back, 12-fret rosewood fingerboard with pointed end, all frets clear of body, bone nut and saddle, small dot inlay, peghead tapers to point at top, *The Gibson* silkscreen logo, white tuner buttons, light amber finish
Introduced: **late 1926**
17-fret fingerboard extends to soundhole: **1928**
Discontinued: **1937**

Uke-3: 6" wide, mahogany body, colored-wood rope-pattern soundhole ring, multiple-bound top and back, bound rosewood fingerboard with pointed end, 17-fret fingerboard extends to soundhole, bone nut and saddle, varied-pattern inlay, peghead tapers to point at top, pearl ornamental peghead inlay, *The Gibson* silkscreen logo, black tuner buttons, brown mahogany waxed finish
Introduced: **late 1926**
Pearl logo, white tuner buttons (some catalogs specify black buttons and ivoroid saddle): **1928**
Discontinued: **1937**

Custom models: During the late 1920s and early 1930s, virtually any ornamentation was available on a Gibson ukulele by custom order. Several examples exist with red poinsettia flowers on the top, ivoroid fingerboard, ivoroid peghead veneer, and pearl logo. Other fancy variations exist.

TU: tenor ukulele, 9" wide, mahogany back and sides, mahogany top specified but many with spruce top, tiered belly bridge with sharp-bevel ends and extra pin, white-black-white soundhole ring, single-bound top and back (some with 3-ply binding0, 18-fret rosewood fingerboard with square end, 12 frets clear of body, small dot inlay, peghead tapers to point at top, *The Gibson* logo, dark finish

Introduced: **1927**

Spruce top specified, *Gibson* logo: **1937**

Mahogany top: **1938**

Renamed **TU-1: 1949**

Unbound top and back: **by 1962**

Discontinued (2 shipped): **1965**

ETU: electric TU-1, 88 total shipped: **1949–53**

TU-3: specs unavailable, 205 shipped: **1950–55**

BU-1: baritone ukulele, 10" wide, mahogany body, pin bridge, rosewood fingerboard, dot inlay, truss rod, dip in center of peghead

Available: **1961–67**

COMMENTS

Gibson ukuleles are regarded as excellent instruments. Style 2 and Style 3 are rare and sought by collectors.

MANDOLINS, GENERAL INFORMATION

MANDOLIN FAMILY STYLES

A-style: A, C or D model designation, 10 1/4" wide (early examples are wider), symmetrical rounded body, 13 7/8" scale

A-style exceptions:

A-1 and A-50: 11 1/4" wide with 14 1/2" scale, 1937–42 only

A-5: Florentine 2-point body shape, 1957–70; F-style body shape with lump scroll, 1970–79

A-12: F-style with "lump" scroll body shape, 1971–80 (throughout production)

F-style: F model designation, 10" wide (early examples are wider), scroll on upper bass bout, pre-1910 models with 3 body points, later models with 2 points

Mandola: H model designation, 12" wide pre-1908; 11" wide 1908 and after; 15 3/4" scale, tuned a fifth below mandolin

Mandocello: K model designation, 14" wide, 24 3/4" scale, tuned an octave below mandola

Mando-bass: J model designation, 24" wide, 42" scale, standard bass tuning

GENERAL DESIGN EVOLUTION, 1890s–1920s

1890s–late 1902: made by Orville Gibson prior to the formation of the Gibson company, a wider and deeper body than later models, 3-point body shape on F models, walnut back and sides, flat back with carved edge, 1-piece neck heel and sides, pick-guard inlaid into top, pearl dot inlaid in scroll on F models, long neck volute at peghead, shallow neck set, large "paddle" peghead on A models, fric-

tion tuners on F models and *O. H. Gibson* on label

Late 1902–c. 1904: "Orville-style" early Gibson company models have the same design as Orville-made models but with the Gibson company label. Although models were catalogued, many examples do not conform to catalog specs.

c. 1904–07: carved curved back, low bridge, neck separate from sides, shallow neck set, no peghead volute, geared tuners, *The Gibson* logo (by 1907), standard (non-paddle) peghead on A models

1908–09: birch back and sides except for maple F-4 and a few maple F-2s, narrower and shallower body, higher bridge, elevated pickguard, 2 pick-guard clamps, no pearl dot in scroll

1910 and after: 2-point body shape on F models, modern bridge height, 1 pickguard clamp

Mid 1922: introduction of Style 5 Master Models (see Lloyd Loar section in Gibson General Information), maple back and sides, many features different from other F-models (see model descriptions)

Circa 1926–27: maple back and sides on all models

By late 1929: lacquer finish, heavier construction

1930s–42: design experimentation beginning in 1937 with larger body on A-1 and A-50, introduction of electric mandolin EM-150.

1942–46: mandolin production ceased for World War II

Late 1940s–60s: introduction of longneck F-12, larger peghead on F models, introduction of Florentine solidbody electric model

1970–77: major restyling of F-style in an attempt to revive older designs; smaller peghead, new carving pattern, bound pickguard, fancy fingerboard and peghead inlay, non-dovetail neck joint, pearl or pearloid tuner buttons

1978–current: modern era begins with introduction of F-5L, production moves from Kalamazoo to Nashville in 1984, then to the Flatiron facility in Belgrade, MT, in 1987, then back to Nashville in 1997 (see Gibson General Information)

CONTRADICTIONS TO CATALOG

Back and sides: Catalogs from 1903 through the mid 1920s describe all mandolins as having maple back and sides. However, the only early models with maple back and sides are the F-4, F-5 and H-4, plus some F-2 examples from c. 1906–09. Virtually all other mandolins, mandolas and mandocellos have walnut back and sides until c. 1907. From c. 1908 to the mid to late 1920s, all (except F-4, F-5, H-4 and H-5) have birch back and sides. The K-5 mandocello changes from birch to maple with the L-5 guitar by 1925. All other models switch to maple in the mid to late 1920s. A few later models are mahogany.

Pickguards: The 1902 catalog describes all A models as having a tortoiseshell pickguard inlaid into the top, with pearl ornament inlaid into the pickguard and pearl "binding" or border around the pickguard. The A is pictured, however, with no pickguard; the A-1, A-2 and A-3 are shown with a plain tortoiseshell pickguard; only the A-4 is shown with the pickguard as described. Many examples from 1903–07 have a pickguard inlaid into the top with pearl or plastic binding material around the edge of the pickguard.

Tailpieces: Catalogs as late as 1963 show all mandolins with clamshell tailpiece. More accurate dates are provided in this section and in the model descriptions.

TOP BRACING

Oval or round hole models: 1 small transverse brace
f-hole models: 2 lengthwise tone bars

BRIDGES

1-piece low bridge: **1890s–c. 1907**
Bridge height raised but not to modern height: **1908–09**
Bridge height raised to modern height, moveable individual string saddles: **1910–16**
1-piece compensating bridge (no separate saddles): **1917–early 1921**
Height-adjustable…

Small base, bottom edge flush with top of instrument, 2 extensions on top of base for adjustment screws, adjustable alumimum top, adjustment wheels 3/8" in diameter: **early 1921 only**
Larger base with 2 feet, 2 extensions on top of base for adjustment screws, ebony base and top, adjustment wheels 3/8" in diameter: **mid 1921–late 1930s**
Larger bridge with 2 feet, 2 extensions on top of base for adjustment screws, adjustment wheels 1/2" in diameter: **late 1930s–1942**
Bottom edge of bridge flush with top of instrument (no feet), flat top of base (no extensions for screws), adjustment wheels 5/8" in diameter: **1946–current**
1920s style bridges with small adjustment wheels, Style 5 models: **late 1980s–current**

TAILPIECE COVERS

Top edge with slight points, deep indents on sides near top, engraved *The Gibson*, ornamental pattern above logo: **1902–07**
Wriggle top edge, small indents on sides near top, engraved *The Gibson*, ornamental pattern above logo…
Stamped ornamentation, all models except Style 5: **1908–42**
Engraved ornamentation, Style 5 only: **1922–27**
A few with engraved ornamentation, various models: **early 1930s**
Clamshell shape, no logo…
A-0 (throughout production): **1927–34**
A-1: **1941–42**
A-50: **1946–early 1960s**
A-40 (from introduction): **1948–early 1960s**
EM-150: **1948–early 1960s**
Clamshell shape with logo…
Florentine electric (from introduction): **1954–c. 1960**
A-5 (from introduction): **1957–c. 1960**
F-5, F-12: **1948–late 1950**
Wriggle top edge pattern, modern *Gibson* logo, no ornamental pattern above logo…
F-5, F-12: **late 1950–70**
All other models: **by 1965–70**
Replicas of earlier tailpieces, ornamental pattern above logo, engraved ornamentation: **1970–current**

PICKGUARDS

Inlaid into top: **1890s–1907**
Elevated, 2 clamps around side of body on models

with 3-point body shape, 1 clamp on models with 2-point body, spike attachment to bridge, pointed shape at cutout for bridge: **1908–16**

Elevated, no point at bridge cutout: **late 1916–21**

Elevated, right-angle support screwed into side of body, no spike attachment to bridge: **mid 1921–current**

Exceptions: C-1 has painted-on pickguard; oval hole A-00 (1933 only) and A-C (Century model) have pickguard glued to top.

NECKS

Cherry neck specified: **pre-1912**

3-piece mahogany neck: **1912–23**

1-piece mahogany neck, all models except F-5 and postwar F-12 (see following): **1923–1970**

1-piece mahogany, all models except F-5 and F-12: **1946–70**

1-piece maple, all models: **1970–current**

Longneck models have fingerboard extension support as integral part of neck: **1970–78**

Fingerboard extension support is not part of neck: **1978–current**

F-5…

2-piece maple with laminate stripe: **1922**

1-piece maple: **very late 1922–1942**

1-piece mahogany: **1949–late 1950**

2-piece maple with laminate stripe: **early 1950s–1960**

5-piece maple with 2 laminate stripes: **late 1961–69**

F-12, 1949–70…

1-piece mahogany: **1949–early 50s**

2-piece maple with laminate stripe: **early 1950s–1960**

5-piece maple with 2 laminate stripes: **late 1961–69**

The term *longneck* (not longer scale) refers to a neck design with more frets clear of body. On longneck models, the body binding meets the neck at approximately the 15th fret. On standard shortneck models, the body binding meets the neck at approximately the 12th fret.

PEGHEADS

Tuners…

Friction pegs, F models (most have been replaced by standard tuners): **1890s–c. 1904**

German-made, gear wheel above shaft, A models: **1890s–1925**

German-made, gear wheel above shaft, F models: **c. 1904–25**

Waverly, gear wheel below shaft: **1926–42**

Kluson Deluxe, enclosed gears, 4 on a plate: **1946–c. 1971**

Schaller: **c. 1971–current**

Tuner buttons…

Inlaid on A-3, A-4, all F models, and corresponding mandolas and mandocellos: **pre–1918**

Ivoroid (ivory-grained celluloid), all models except Style 5: **1918–mid 1930s**

Plain celluloid, all models except those with pearl buttons (see following): **mid 1930s–current**

Mother-of-pearl tuner buttons…

Style 5: **1922–42, 1970–current**

F-12: **1934–37**

Truss rod (except A-Jr., A-0), introduced: **late 1921**

Tuner plates angling toward each other at top: **1923–27**

Tapered snakehead peghead, A models: **1923–27**

PATENT DATES ON PARTS

Pickguard: Mar. 30, 1909

Pickguard clamp: July 4, 1911

Adjustable bridge: Jan. 18, 1921

SERIAL NUMBERS, 1902–87

Mandolins, mandolas and mandocellos have serial numbers in the same series as guitars (see Gibson General Information).

SERIAL NUMBERS, 1987–CURRENT

7 digits with configuration **ynnnmmz**

y = last digit of year of manufacture

nnn = the rank of the instrument within its style series (see following)

mm = month of manufacture

z = decade of manufacture

Example: 0280089 was made in August (08), 1990, and is the 280th instrument of its style. For easier interpretation, put the last digit first. The transposed example, 9028008, shows the year (90) followed by the rank (280) followed by the month (08).

Style series: The F-5L, Army-Navy, and H-5 models each have their own number series. The A-5G and A-5L are numbered together in a single series. Rankings do not start over at the beginning of each year.

Model A from 1917.

F-4 from 1919 with 2-point scroll body, inlaid tuner buttons, long flowerpot peghead inlay, binding line (hidden by pickguard) meeting neck at 12th fret.

F-5L from 1991 with fern peghead inlay, longneck design with binding line meeting neck at 15th fret.

Florentine electric from 1969 with carved top, solid-body design.

ACOUSTIC MANDOLINS KEY

Scroll body with 3 points
  Fancy inlay = **"Artist Model"**
  Dot inlay
    1 rope-pattern soundhole ring = **F**
    2 rope-pattern soundhole rings
      Pearl and ebony top binding = **F-2, 1902–c. 1904**
      White and green top binding
        Silver-plated hardware = **F-3**
        Gold-plated hardware = **F-4, 1902–c. 1904**
      Single ivoroid top binding
        Bound peghead = **F-4, c. 1904–09**
        Unbound peghead = **F-2, c. 1904–09**
Scroll body with 2 points
  Oval hole
    Bound peghead = **F-4, 1910–34**
    Unbound peghead
      Diamond peghead inlay = **F-4, 1935–43**
      No peghead ornament = **F-2, 1910–34**
  ƒ-holes
    Flowerpot (torch), fern or other floral peghead inlay
      Dot inlay
        Bound fingerboard
          Gold-plated hardware = **F-5, early 1925–late 1929** or **F-5L**
          Silver-plated hardware
            Bill Monroe signature label = **F-5L Bill Monroe**
            No Monroe label = **F-5, 1922–early 1925** or **F-5L, 1989–90**
        Unbound fingerboard = **F-5G**
      Block or other fancy inlay = **F-5, late 1929–1979**
    Crown peghead inlay = **F-12, 1948–69**
    Fleur-de-lis or 2-handled vase with curlicues peghead inlay
      Longneck = **F-12, 1970–80**
      Shortneck
        Square-end fingerboard = **F-7**
        Asymmetrical extended fingerboard
          Gold-plated hardware (sunburst finish) = **F-12, 1934–36**
          Nickel-plated hardware (black finish) = **F-10**
"Lump" scroll body, large bass-side horn but no scroll cutout
  Fleur-de-lis peghead inlay = **A-5, 1970–79**
  No peghead ornament = **A-12**
Symmetrical body with 2 body points
  Hollowbody = **A-5, 1957–69**
  Solidbody electric = **Florentine (EM-200)**
Symmetrical body, no points
  Oval hole
    1 rope-pattern soundhole ring
      Unbound top = **A, 1902–07**
      Bound top = **A-1, 1902–07** or **A, 1908–19**

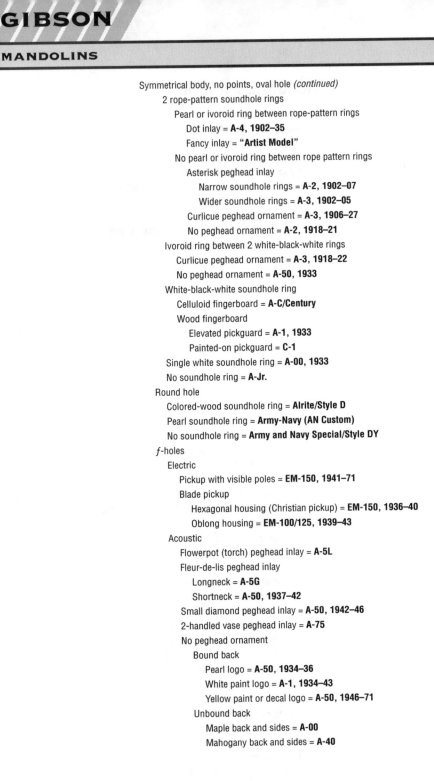

Symmetrical body, no points, oval hole *(continued)*

2 rope-pattern soundhole rings

Pearl or ivoroid ring between rope-pattern rings

Dot inlay = **A-4, 1902–35**

Fancy inlay = **"Artist Model"**

No pearl or ivoroid ring between rope pattern rings

Asterisk peghead inlay

Narrow soundhole rings = **A-2, 1902–07**

Wider soundhole rings = **A-3, 1902–05**

Curlicue peghead ornament = **A-3, 1906–27**

No peghead ornament = **A-2, 1918–21**

Ivoroid ring between 2 white-black-white rings

Curlicue peghead ornament = **A-3, 1918–22**

No peghead ornament = **A-50, 1933**

White-black-white soundhole ring

Celluloid fingerboard = **A-C/Century**

Wood fingerboard

Elevated pickguard = **A-1, 1933**

Painted-on pickguard = **C-1**

Single white soundhole ring = **A-00, 1933**

No soundhole ring = **A-Jr.**

Round hole

Colored-wood soundhole ring = **Alrite/Style D**

Pearl soundhole ring = **Army-Navy (AN Custom)**

No soundhole ring = **Army and Navy Special/Style DY**

f-holes

Electric

Pickup with visible poles = **EM-150, 1941–71**

Blade pickup

Hexagonal housing (Christian pickup) = **EM-150, 1936–40**

Oblong housing = **EM-100/125, 1939–43**

Acoustic

Flowerpot (torch) peghead inlay = **A-5L**

Fleur-de-lis peghead inlay

Longneck = **A-5G**

Shortneck = **A-50, 1937–42**

Small diamond peghead inlay = **A-50, 1942–46**

2-handled vase peghead inlay = **A-75**

No peghead ornament

Bound back

Pearl logo = **A-50, 1934–36**

White paint logo = **A-1, 1934–43**

Yellow paint or decal logo = **A-50, 1946–71**

Unbound back

Maple back and sides = **A-00**

Mahogany back and sides = **A-40**

MANDOLAS KEY

Symmetrical body with no points
- *f*-holes
  - Square-end fingerboard = **H-0**
  - Extended fingerboard = **M-5**
- Oval hole
  - 1 rope-pattern soundhole ring = **H**
  - 2 rope-pattern soundhole rings
    - Pearl or ivoroid ring between rope rings = **H-2**
    - No pearl or ivoroid ring between rope rings = **H-1**

Scroll body
- Oval soundhole = **H-4**
- *f*-holes = **H-5**

MANDOCELLOS KEY

Symmetrical pear-shaped body
- 1 rope-pattern soundhole ring = **K**
- 2 rope-pattern soundhole rings
  - Pearl or ivoroid ring between rope rings = **K-2**
  - No pearl or ivoroid ring between rope rings = **K-1**

Scroll body = **K-4**
Guitar body = **K-5**

MANDOLINS

SECTION ORGANIZATION

Symmetrical Body Mandolins
Asymmetrical Body Mandolins
Electric Mandolins
Mandolas
Madocellos
Other Mandolin Family Instruments

SYMMETRICAL BODY MANDOLINS

A: oval soundhole, colored-wood soundhole ring, unbound ebony fingerboard, dot inlay, large rounded paddle-shaped peghead, golden orange top finish, reddish finish on back and sides
Introduced: **1902**
Smaller non-paddle peghead: **c. 1905**
Single-bound top: **by 1906**
Elevated pickguard, no peghead logo: **by 1908**
Brown finish standard: **1918**
Snakehead peghead: **1923**
Standard peghead: **1928**
Discontinued: **1933**

A-1: bound oval soundhole with 2 wood-inlaid rings, pickguard inlaid into top, single-bound top, unbound ebony fingerboard, dot inlay, large rounded paddle-shaped peghead, golden orange top finish, reddish finish on back and sides
Introduced: **1902**
Smaller non-paddle peghead, *The Gibson* logo: **c. 1905**
Elevated pickguard: **1908**
Discontinued: **1918**
Reintroduced, 1 ring around soundhole, single-bound top and back, no logo (some with silver paint logo), black top finish, brown back and sides finish: **1922**
Snakehead peghead: **1923**
Discontinued: **1927**
Reintroduced, bound top, unbound back, white silkscreen logo, standard center-dip peghead shape, sunburst finish: **1933**
f-holes, bound top and back: **1934**
11 1/4" wide, 14 1/2" scale: **1937**
10 1/4" wide, 13 7/8" scale, clamshell tailpiece cover: **1941**
Discontinued: **1943**

A-2/A2-Z: bound oval soundhole with 2 wood-inlaid rings, pickguard inlaid into top, single-bound top and back, bound ebony fingerboard, dot inlay, large rounded paddle-shaped peghead, veneer on peghead, asterisk peghead inlay, golden orange top finish, reddish finish on back and sides
Introduced as A-2: **1902**
Discontinued: **by 1908**
Reintroduced, bound oval soundhole with 2 narrow wood-inlaid rings, elevated pickguard, bound top and back, bound ebony fingerboard, dot inlay, pearl *The Gibson* logo, brown finish: **1918**
Renamed **A2-Z:** double-bound top, single-bound back, double-bound soundhole, black-white-black soundhole ring, bound fingerboard, amber top finish, brown back and sides finish: **1922**
Snakehead peghead: **1923**
A2-Z renamed **A-2: 1927**
Discontinued: **1928**

A-3: bound oval soundhole with 2 wood-inlaid rings, pickguard inlaid into top, single-bound top and back, bound ebony fingerboard, dot inlay, large rounded paddle-shaped peghead, veneer on peghead, asterisk peghead inlay, golden orange top finish, reddish finish on back and sides
Introduced: **1902**
Smaller non-paddle peghead, ornamental curlicue peghead inlay, *The Gibson* peghead logo, inlaid tuner buttons: **by 1906**
Elevated pickguard: **1908**
Wide white soundhole ring between 2 black-white-black rings, ivoroid pickguard, ivory top finish: **1918**
Discontinued: **1922**

A-4: bound oval soundhole with 2 wood-inlaid rings, single-bound top and back, ornamental inlay in pickguard, bound ebony fingerboard, dot inlay, black top finish, reddish finish on back and sides
Introduced: **1902**
Solid white soundhole ring between 2 ivoroid-and-wood rope-pattern rings, elevated pickguard with point at bridge cutout, smaller peghead, fleur-de-lis peghead inlay, *The Gibson* logo, inlaid tuner buttons: **by 1908**
Treble-side fingerboard extension: **1912**
Uniform red mahogany finish (slightly shaded) standard, black or orange top finish optional: **1914**
No tuner button inlay: **1918**

Dark mahogany sunburst top finish only: **by 1918**
Snakehead peghead: **1923**
Standard peghead: **1928**
Straight *The Gibson* logo: **1928**
Gibson logo, amber red mahogany sunburst top finish: **1934**
Discontinued: **1935**

"Artist Model": does not appear in literature or company records, similar to A-4 except for ornate fingerboard inlay, some with A-3 style curlicue peghead inlay, some with fleur-de-lis, many with F-style body (see following)
Available: **c. 1904–07**

Alrite/Style D: flat top and back, no body taper at neck, round hole, ebony bridge, elevated pickguard, colored wood inlay around top edge and soundhole, white plastic binding, ebony fingerboard, dot inlay, no peghead logo, special round label with model name, golden orange top finish, reddish finish on back and sides
Available: **1917**

Army and Navy Special, Style DY: flat top and back, round hole, elevated pickguard anchored to bridge, dot inlay, peghead veneer, no logo, special round label with model name, brown stain finish
Available: **1918–22**
Reintroduced as Army-Navy (AN Custom) with different specs (see following): **June 1988**
Discontinued: **1997**

A Jr.: oval soundhole, black binding around soundhole, elevated pickguard, no body binding, ebony fingerboard, special round Jr. label, dark brown stain finish
Introduced: **c. 1919**
Snakehead peghead: **1923**
Discontinued, replaced by A-0: **1927**

A-0: oval soundhole, no binding or soundhole ornamentation, clamshell tailpiece cover, dot inlay, brown finish
Available: **1927–33**

C-1: flat top, oval soundhole, mahogany back and sides, painted-on "pickguard," clamshell tailpiece

cover, bound top, unbound back, ebony finger-board, silkscreen logo, natural top finish
Only catalog appearance: **1932**

A-00: oval soundhole, carved top, flat back, non-adjustable ebony bridge, pickguard glued to top, bound top, ebony fingerboard, dot inlay, *The Gibson* logo, brown sunburst finish
Introduced: **1933**
f-holes, elevated pickguard, clamshell tailpiece cover, *Gibson* logo: **1934**
Arched back, interior back brace (A-1 of the same period does not have interior back brace): **1936**
Adjustable bridge, single-bound top and back, sunburst finish: **1939**
Discontinued: **by 1943**

A-50: oval soundhole, bound top and back, single-bound fingerboard, fingerboard raised off of top, dot inlay, silkscreen *Gibson* logo, dark red mahogany sunburst finish
Introduced: **1933**
f-holes: **1934**
11 1/4" wide, bound pickguard, 14 1/2" scale, fingerboard flush with top, varied-pattern inlay similar to Nick Lucas guitar model (see Flat Tops section), fleur-de-lis peghead inlay (a few with flowerpot), pearl logo, brown sunburst finish: **mid 1937**
10" wide, 13 7/8" scale, clamshell tailpiece cover, dot inlay, small diamond peghead inlay: **1942**
Yellow silkscreen script logo: **1946**
No peghead ornament: **early 1947**
Modern logo: **later 1947**
Laminated beveled-edge pickguard: **late 1947**
Discontinued: **1971**

A-C/Century: oval soundhole, flat back, pickguard glued to top, bound top and back, bound pearloid fingerboard, double- and triple-diamond pearl inlay set into rosewood, pearloid peghead veneer, slotted-diamond pearl peghead inlay set into rosewood
Available: **1934–36**

A-75: *f*-holes, bound top and back, fingerboard raised off of top, single-bound fingerboard, dot inlay, 2-handled vase peghead inlay, slanted *Gibson* logo, brown mahogany sunburst finish
Available: **1934–36**

A-40: *f*-holes, arched top and back, laminated mahogany back with cross brace, clamshell tail-

piece cover, single-bound top, rosewood fingerboard, dot inlay, natural or sunburst finish
Available: **1948–70**

A-5: oval soundhole, Florentine symmetrical 2-point body, maple back and sides, laminated beveled-edge pickguard, clamshell tailpiece cover with *Gibson*, bound rosewood fingerboard with treble-side extension, dot inlay, scroll peghead shape, crown peghead inlay, pearl logo, golden sunburst finish
Introduced: **1957**
4 made with violin-scroll peghead: **1960**
Cherry sunburst finish: **early 1960s**
F-style 2-point body shape with lump scroll (no scroll cutout), longneck, fleur-de-lis peghead inlay, script *Gibson* logo: **1970**
Discontinued: **1979**

A-5L: based on custom-made 1923 A-5 signed by Lloyd Loar, body shape shorter and more rounded than Loar example, same ornamentation and construction as F-5L (see following) but with A-style body, longneck, fingerboard raised off of top, flowerpot peghead inlay (Loar example has fleur-de-lis), snakehead peghead shape, sunburst finish
Available: **early 1988–current**

A-5G: same body and neck style as A-5L but with single-bound top, unbound fingerboard, unbound peghead, abalone fleur-de-lis peghead inlay
Available: **early 1988–96**

Army-Navy (AN Custom): reissue of Army and Navy Special (see preceding), flat top, flat back, round soundhole, pearl soundhole ring, non-adjustable ebony bridge, triple-bound top and back, longneck, bound ebony fingerboard with pointed end, ornamental curlicue peghead inlay, script *The Gibson* logo inlaid in pearl
Available: **June 1988–96**

ASYMMETRICAL BODY MODELS

F: 3-point body, oval soundhole, pearl dot in scroll, bound top, pickguard inlaid into top, pearl inlay in pickguard, ebony fingerboard with treble-side extension, dot inlay, scroll peghead shape, veneer on peghead, friction pegs, golden orange top finish
Only catalog appearance: **1902**

F-2: 3-point body, oval soundhole, pearl dot in scroll, pickguard inlaid into top, ornate pearl inlay on pickguard, bound soundhole with 2 wood-inlaid rings, pearl and ebony rope-pattern top binding, ebony fingerboard with treble-side extension, dot inlay, scroll peghead shape, star and crescent peghead inlay, front and back peghead veneer, friction pegs, black top finish, reddish finish on back and sides
Introduced: **1902**

Single-bound top and fingerboard, *The Gibson* peghead inlay, right-angle tuners, inlaid tuner buttons, tuner plates angle away from each other at top: **c. 1904**

Ivoroid and wood soundhole rings, elevated pickguard with point and 2 clamps, golden orange top finish optional (most examples black): **1908**

2-point body: **1910**

Uniform red mahogany finish (slightly shaded) standard, black or orange top finish optional: **1914**

No inlay on tuner buttons, dark mahogany sunburst finish: **1918**

Truss rod: **late 1922**

1-piece neck, rounded neck heel, arrow-end tuner plates: **1923**

Round-end tuner plates: **1926**

Maple back and sides: **c. 1927**

Discontinued: **1934**

F-3: 3-point body, oval soundhole, pearl dot in scroll, pearl-bound pickguard inlaid into top, ornate pearl inlay in pickguard, bound soundhole with 2 wood-inlaid rings, white and green rope-pattern top border with pearl binding, ebony fingerboard with treble-side extension, dot inlay, scroll peghead shape, front and back peghead veneer, friction pegs, inlaid tuner buttons, black top finish, reddish finish on back and sides
Only catalog description (no illustration): **1902**

F-4: 3-point body, oval soundhole, pearl dot in scroll, pearl-bound pickguard inlaid into top, pearl inlay in pickguard, bound soundhole with 2 rope-pattern wood-inlaid rings, white and green rope-pattern top border with pearl binding, bound ebony fingerboard with treble-side extension, dot inlay, scroll peghead shape, pearl peghead binding, front and back peghead veneer, friction pegs, black top finish, reddish finish on back and sides
Introduced: **1902**

Ivoroid and wood soundhole rings, elevated pickguard with point and 2 clamps, single-bound top and back, pearl nut, ivoroid-bound peghead, ornate long-flowerpot peghead inlay of abalone and wire, no logo, right-angle tuners, inlaid tuner buttons, notched-end tuner plates angle away from each other at top, black top finish standard, golden orange top finish optional (most examples are golden orange): **by 1908**

2-point body: **1910**

Double-flowerpot peghead inlay, slanted *The Gibson* logo: **1911**

Uniform red mahogany finish standard, black or orange finish optional: **1914**

No pickguard point at bridge cutout: **1917**

No inlay on tuner buttons, dark mahogany sunburst finish: **1918**

Truss rod, single-flowerpot peghead inlay (earliest with truss rod have double flowerpot cut by truss rod routing): **late 1922**

1-piece neck, rounded neck heel, arrow-end tuner plates: **1923**

Round-end tuner plates: **1926**

Pointed-end fingerboard, unbound peghead, large diamond peghead inlay, yellow-to-brown sunburst top, brown back and sides finish: **1935**

2 checkerboard (black and white plastic) outer soundhole rings with white middle ring: **c. 1936**

Discontinued: **1943**

"Artist Model": not mentioned in literature or records, 3-point body (some with A-4 styling), walnut back and sides, oval soundhole with pearl and wood rings, pickguard inlaid into top, fancy pearl inlay in pickguard, some with top border of alternating pearl-and-ebony blocks, some with single-bound top, ornate fingerboard inlay similar to F-5 of 1970s, unbound peghead, *The Gibson* logo, no peghead ornament, black top finish
Available: **c. 1904–07**

F-5: 2-point body, *f*-holes, triple-bound top and back, triple-bound pickguard, pickguard follows body point, right-angle pickguard support screwed into side of body, pickguard support of triple black-and-white binding material, hand-engraved tailpiece cover, truss rod, longneck, 2-piece maple neck with laminate stripe, bound ebony fingerboard with treble-side extension, black line on side of fingerboard binding, dot inlay, bound peghead, black line on side of peghead binding, flowerpot peghead inlay, *The Gibson* logo, notched-end tuner plates, pearl tuner buttons, silver-plated hardware, Cremona shaded brown (sunburst) finish, *Master Model* and Loar-signature labels

The F-5 is first Gibson model with the following features (which would become standard on modern mandolins and modern archtop guitars): parallel top braces, bound pickguard, right-angle pickguard support screwed into side of body, maple neck, fingerboard raised off of top, longneck design with 15 frets to body binding line

Introduced: **June 1922**

Narrower 1-piece maple neck, arrow-end tuner plates: **late 1922**

Some examples with black line on side binding (rather than on top): **1923**

Many examples with Virzi Tone-Producer (internal soundboard, see Gibson General Information), some examples with fern peghead inlay (most with flowerpot): **1924**

Ivoroid body binding, plain celluloid fingerboard binding with black line on side, triple-bound peghead: **by mid 1924**

A few with fern peghead inlay, a few with gold-plated hardware: **late 1924**

No Virzi Tone Producer except for 1 example, no Loar label, fern peghead inlay standard, sunburst finish lighter and more golden than Loar period, gold-plated hardware: **early 1925**

Metal pickguard bracket, Waverly tuners (rounded ends) with shafts above gear wheels: **early 1927**

No Master Model label, stamped (not engraved) *The Gibson* on tailpiece cover, dot inlay from 3rd fret, darker finish: **c. 1928**

Block inlay from 3rd fret, heavier construction: **late 1929**

Gibson logo: **c. 1932**

Block inlay from 1st fret, flowerpot peghead inlay: **by late 1930s**

A few with fleur-de-lis peghead inlay: **c. 1940**

Discontinued: **1943**

Reintroduced, laminated beveled-edge pickguard, clamshell tailpiece cover with *Gibson*, single-bound top and back, triple-bound fingerboard with black line on side, 1-piece mahogany neck, block inlay from first fret, triple-bound peghead, flowerpot peghead inlay, plastic tuner buttons, standard postwar logo, smaller prewar size peghead: **late 1949**

Wriggle-edge tailpiece with postwar logo, triple-bound top and back, 2-piece maple neck with ebony laminate stripe, larger peghead: **late 1950**

5-piece neck: **late 1961**

Redesigned, different carving pattern and structural features, triple-bound pickguard, ornate abalone fingerboard inlay (similar to early "Artist" models), flowerpot peghead inlay like top half of F-4 double-flowerpot from 1911–21 (fancier than Loar-period F-5 flowerpot), script *The Gibson* logo, small peghead, special F-5 label: **1970**

Discontinued: **1980**

F-5L: reissue of Loar F-5 (actually closer to 1925 F-5), fern peghead inlay, gold-plated hardware

Introduced: **1978**

Optional silver-plated hardware, flowerpot peghead inlay, available: **1988–early 1991**

Still in production

F-5L Bill Monroe: same as F-5L (preceding) but with black line on side of body binding rather than on top, flowerpot peghead inlay, logo lower on peghead than standard F-5L, label signed by Bill Monroe, optional varnish finish, replica 1923 style case

Available: **early 1991–96**

F-5G: single-bound top, unbound back, unbound fingerboard and peghead, pearl logo, flowerpot peghead inlay, brown burst finish on top, brown finish on back, sides and neck

Available: **1993–current**

F-12: 2-point body, *f*-holes, single-bound top and back, single-bound pickguard, no point on pickguard at body point, single-bound fingerboard with treble-side extension, fingerboard raised off of top, scroll-type inlay, single-bound peghead, 2-handled vase and curlicues peghead inlay, pearl tuner buttons, gold-plated hardware, red mahogany sunburst top finish, deep red finish on back and sides

First made: **1931**

First catalog appearance: **1934**

Discontinued: **1937**

Reintroduced, point on pickguard, clamshell tailpiece cover, mahogany neck, longneck, bound rosewood fingerboard with square end, fingerboard flush with top, dot inlay, small prewar size peghead, unbound peghead, crown peghead inlay, Cremona brown sunburst top finish, uniform brown finish on back and sides: **1948**

Wriggle-edge tailpiece cover, fingerboard raised off of top, larger peghead: **late 1950**

Triple-bound top and back, treble-side fingerboard extension, fleur-de-lis peghead inlay, *The Gibson* script logo: **by 1970**

Discontinued: **1980**

F-7: 2-point body, *f*-holes, single-bound top and back, bound pickguard, no point on pickguard at body point, single-bound square-end fingerboard, fingerboard raised off of top, varied-pattern inlay (similar to Nick Lucas guitar, see Flat Tops section), single-bound peghead, fleur-de-lis peghead inlay or 2-handled vase and curlicues peghead inlay, sunburst finish

Available: **1934–39**

F-10: 2-point body, *f*-holes, single-bound top and back, bound pickguard, no point on pickguard at body point, single-bound fingerboard with treble-side extension, fingerboard raised off of top, scroll-pattern inlay, single-bound peghead, 2-handled vase and curlicues peghead inlay, ivoroid tuner buttons, nickel-plated hardware, black finish

Available: **1934–36**

A-5: 2-point body with lump scroll (no scroll cutout), *f*-holes, longneck, rosewood fngerboard, dot inlay, fleaur-de-lis paghead inlay

Available: **1970–79**

A-12: 2-point body with lump scroll (no scroll cutout), *f*-holes, laminated beveled-edge pickguard, longneck, rosewood extension fingerboard, no peghead ornament, sunburst finish

Available: **1970–79**

Electric Mandolins

EM-150: A-00 body, 10" wide, carved top and back, Charlie Christian pickup with no binding, single-bound pickguard, pickguard cutout for pickup, bound top and back, knobs on opposite sides of body, dot inlay, brown sunburst top finish

Introduced: **1936**

Rectangular screwpole pickup, knobs on same side: **1941**

P-90 pickup, laminated beveled-edge pickguard, clamshell tailpiece cover, bound fingerboard (same specs as postwar A-50): **c. 1949**

Golden sunburst finish: **by 1956**

Discontinued: **1971**

EM-100/125: blade pickup with oblong housing (3 screws in top), plain tailpiece

Introduced as EM-100: **1938**

Renamed **EM-125: 1941**

Discontinued: **1943**

Florentine/EM-200: solid mahogany body, symmetrical 2-point shape, carved top (similar to Les Paul electric guitar), soapbar P-90 pickup, metal saddle, laminated beveled-edge pickguard follows body point, single-bound top, single-bound rosewood fingerboard, dot inlay, scroll peghead shape, crown peghead inlay, gold-plated hardware, sunburst top finish

Introduced as **Florentine: 1954**

Renamed **EM-200: 1960**

Renamed **Florentine: 1962**

Pickguard surrounds pickup: **by 1966**

Discontinued: **1971**

Mandolas

H: mandola, same features as Style A mandolin

Only catalog appearance: **1902**

H-1: same features and changes as A-2 mandolin

Introduced: **1902**

Same features as A-1 mandolin but with treble-side fingerboard extension, bound fingerboard: **1908**

Same features as A-2 mandolin: **1918**

2 wood-inlaid soundhole rings: **1922**

No peghead change (no snakehead shape): **1923–27**

Black top finish: **1925**

Same features as Style A mandolin: **1927**

Discontinued: **1936**

H-2: same features and changes as A-4 mandolin

Introduced: **1902**

Ivory finish available by special order: **1918**

Discontinued: **1922**

H-4: same features and changes as F-4 mandolin

Introduced: **1910**

Last made: **late 1920s**

Discontinued from catalog: **1940**

H-5: same features and changes as F-5 mandolin, *f*-holes
Introduced: **1923**
Last made: **late 1920s**
Discontinued from catalog: **1936**
A few produced: **1990–91**

H-0: A-style body, 11" wide, *f*-holes, flat back, square-end rosewood fingerboard, dot inlay, silkscreen logo, sunburst finish
Introduced: **1936**
Arched back: **1940**
Discontinued: **1943**

M-5: A-style, *f*-holes
Available: **1994–97**

MANDOCELLOS

K: same features as Style A mandolin
Only catalog appearance: **1902**

K-1: same features and changes as H-1 mandola
Introduced: **1902**
Discontinued (very rare after 1930): **1943**

K-2: same features and changes as Style A-4 mandolin and H-2 mandola
Introduced: **1902**
Ivory finish available by special order: **1918**
Discontinued: **1922**

K-4: same features and changes as F-4 mandolin and H-4 mandola
Introduced: **1912**
Last produced: **late 1920s**
Discontinued from catalog: **1940**

K-5: L-5 guitar body, 16" wide, birch back and sides, asymmetrical fingerboard with treble-side extension, F-5 type tailpiece mounted onto trapeze tailpiece, L-5 type peghead, flowerpot peghead inlay, same ornamentation and changes as L-5 guitar
Introduced: **1924**
Maple back and sides, peghead inlay remains flowerpot pattern (when F-5 and K-5 go to fern): **1925**
Last made: **late 1920s**
Discontinued from catalog: **1936**

OTHER MANDOLIN FAMILY INSTRUMENTS

Mando-Bass, Style J: 4 strings, A-style body, 24" wide, carved top and back, bound round soundhole, 2 rope-pattern soundhole rings, maple bridge with 2 slots for individual string saddles, trapeze tailpiece with pins mounted on tortoiseshell celluloid crosspiece, bound top, unbound back, 42" scale, asymmetrical fingerboard with treble-side extension, dot inlay, elevated arm rest optional, extension endpin (upright bass style) from side, pearl *The Gibson* logo, red mahogany sunburst top finish, black or orange top finish optional
Introduced: **1912**
Brown finish: **1918**
Black top finish: **1923**
Adjustable bridge, 1-piece ebony saddle, no arm rest, square-end fingerboard, silver silkscreen logo, black top finish, brown finish on back and sides: **by 1928**
Last made: **c. 1930**
Discontinued from catalog: **1940**

Tenor Lute, Style TL-1: 4 strings, carved top and back, A-style mandola body, *f*-holes, elevated pickguard, single-bound top, square-end fingerboard raised off of top, tenor banjo scale, dot inlay, banjo style peghead and tuners (a few with 8 strings and mandolin style tuners), pearl *The Gibson* logo, natural top finish, brown finish on back and sides, *Master Model* label
Introduced: **by 1924**
Discontinued: **c. 1926**

COMMENTS

Very early mandolins made by or in the style of Orville Gibson generally do not have a very good sound and appeal primarily to collectors.

Mandolins from c. 1904–09 have a more modern design than those of the earlier period, but they still do not have a powerful enough sound to appeal to players. They do have some historical appeal, and the more ornate models have aesthetic appeal as well.

The three-point F-style models from 1909 are the first with a good "modern" sound. High-end models from 1910 (the advent of two-point F styles) into the 1920s, in both A and F styles, are considered excellent utility instruments for classical, old-time or jazz music, but they lack the power of the F-5 design.

The F-5 of the 1920s is considered by players and collectors to be the pinnacle of mandolin design. These command some of the highest prices on the vintage market of any production instrument, with Loar-signed examples bringing more than those without the Loar signature.

In the 1930s, due to the lack of demand for mandolins, F-5s are as rare as Loar-signed models, but they are not regarded as having the quality of sound or construction of 1920s models. The F-7, F-10 and F-12 are sought because of their rarity. Because of their shortneck design, however, they do not bring as much as the F-5.

Postwar models of all styles are generally not highly regarded until the introduction of the F-5L in 1978. The F-5L and the A-5L are regarded by players as instruments of high quality and are considered to be Gibson's best mandolins since the late 1920s.

Mandolas and mandocellos are increasing sought by players of classical and "new acoustic" music. With the exception of Loar-signed instruments, mandolas and mandocellos bring prices slightly higher than the equivalent mandolins. The Loar-signed mandolin is so highly sought that it brings more than Loar-signed mandolas or mandocellos.

The mando-bass is rare and has great appeal as a conversation piece.

The mando-lute is rare and is the only non-Style 5 instrument to bear the *Master Model* label, but it is sought by collectors primarily as a curiosity.

Of the electric mandolins, the EM-150 has some historical appeal (as do all Gibson instruments with the Charlie Christian pickup). The Florentine has some appeal based on its unusual carved solid-body design.

BANJOS, GENERAL INFORMATION

Name	Type	Strings	Intro	Scale	Head diameter
TB	Tenor	4	10/9/18	19": 1918–24 21" optional: 1922–24 21" or 23": 1925–1930s 23": 1930s–current	Some TB: 12", 1918–23 Styles 0, 1, 2, TB: 10" 1/2" thru 1924 Styles 0, 1, 2, TB: 11", 1925 and after Styles 3 and higher: 11"
MB	Mandolin banjo	8*	4/19	14 3/4"	10 1/2", 1919–c. 1922, 1925–c. 1929 9", 1923–24 11", c. 1929 and after
GB	Guitar banjo	6	10/9/18	24 3/4"	14", 1918–24 11", 1925 and after
CB	Cello banjo	4	by 9/19	24 3/4"	14"
UB	Ukulele banjo	4	1924	Style UB*: 14 3/4" Style 1: 12 1/4" All other styles: 13 3/4"	Style UB*: 9" Style 1: 6" All other styles: 8"
RB	Regular	5	1924	25 5/16", 1924 26 1/4"**, late 1920s–current	Same as TB
PB	Plectrum	4	1924	26 1/4"**	Same as TB
PT	Plectrum/tenor	4	late 1927	24 1/2"	Same as TB

* The 4-stringed Style UB was catalogued as a ukulele-banjo but it has the scale and neck of a mandolin-banjo.

** Plectrum and Regular (5-string) models were catalogued with 26 3/4" scale length, but actual scale is 26 1/4".

MODEL NAMES

First part of name designates type of instrument: TB = tenor banjo, PB = plectrum banjo, etc.

Second part of name (after hyphen) is style: 00, 0, 1, 11, 2, 3, 4…

MISCELLANEOUS SPECS

Rim support and adjustment…

Dowel stick: **1918**

Dowel stick and coordinator rod: **1919–20**

Nut and coordinator rod…

All non-Mastertone models: **1921–42**

All models: **1950s–60s**

2 coordinator rods, Style 3 and higher: **1923–42, 1970–current**

Tension hoop…

Grooved: **1918–1926**

Notched (except UB and some GBs): **1927 onward**

Adjustable truss rod in neck…

All models except Style 1: **late 1921–current**

Style 1 (with 1-piece flange): **c. 1930 onward**

Elevated celluloid pickguard…

Pictured in catalogs: **mid 1921–24**

Optional: **into 1930s**

Tone Projector, "resonator plate," "trap door": **Mar. 1922–24**

Pyralin resonator, Styles 4 and 5 only (trap door still optional): **1923**

Thin 1/2" rim, tone ring overhangs rim, brass hoop put in tone ring for added width: **mid 1960s–1969**

RIMS AND FLANGES

Diagrams © *Pickin'* magazine, courtesy Roger Siminoff.

Diagram 1. Hollow rim with wood spacers, open tone chamber between rim plies, head rests directly on rim (no tone ring), brackets pass through a tube: **1918–22**

Diagram 2. Ball bearing. Hollow tube tone chamber rests on ball bearings, holes drilled in chamber tube, brackets pass through tube: **by Mar. 1923**

Diagram 3. Spring-loaded ball bearing. Springs under ball bearings, slightly shorter lip on side of rim, otherwise very similar in outward appearance to earlier non-spring ball bearing: **by early 1925**

Diagram 4. Later spring-loaded ball-bearing (larger springs and bearings). Beveled or arched appearance around outer edge of head, tube-and-plate flange, solid rod on top of tone chamber tube, holes in tone chamber, bracket nuts flush with bottom of rim, outer rim support (metal sheath look) between lip and head, holes in outer rim support: **Feb. 1925**

No holes in outer rim support (sheath): **1926**

Diagram 5. Archtop. Cast tone chamber, flat side viewable from inside rim, small lip, tube and plate flange, bracket nut not flush with bottom of rim, arch of top more pronounced than ball bearing style, no holes in tone chamber, grooved stretcher band: **c. 1927**

40 holes in tone chamber: **1928 onward**

Diagram 6. Archtop, one-piece flange. No rounded "lip" on side of rim: **1929**

Diagram 7. Flat-head. Head stays flat (no fall-off at edge), cast tone chamber (except earliest version), 1-piece cast flange with no tube, most with 20 holes in tone chamber

Variations, in chronological order:

• Low profile, tone chamber of bent brass (not cast) similar to Bacon & Day tone chambers of the period, interchangeable with archtop tone ring, extremely rare

• Low profile, light weight, interchangeable with archtop tone ring

• High profile, tone ring slightly higher than earlier style, light weight, slightly shorter lip, not interchangeable with archtop

• High profile, heavy weight (most highly sought version)

• Postwar styles, some with 19-hole tone ring

Introduced as option on Styles 6, Bella Voce, Florentine, All American (non-cast version, extremely rare): **1927**

First appearance of cast flat-head tone ring: **1928**

Optional on Styles 3, 4, 5 and Granada: **Oct. 1929**

Standard on Top Tension models (see following): **1937–42**

Standard on all Mastertone models: **1970–current**

Diagram 8: Shoes-and-plate. Wood flange and brackets supported by wooden "shoes" connected by bolts through rim, used on low-end models and banjo-ukes with diamond-hole and wavy flanges: **late 1920s–30s**

Diagram 9. Top tension. Head tension adjustment from top, flat-head tone ring, 1-piece flange, Styles 7, 12 and 18: **1937–42 and reissues**

GIBSON

Diagram 1. Hollow rim with wood spacers: 1918–22

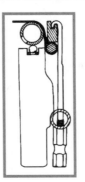

Diagram 2. Ball bearing: by Mar. 1923

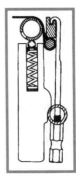

Diagram 3. Spring-loaded ball bearing: by early 1925

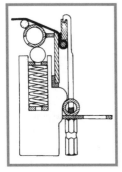

Diagram 4. Later spring-loaded ball-bearing : Feb. 1925

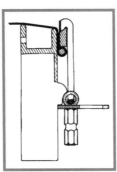

Diagram 5. Archtop, tube and plate flange: c. 1927 onward

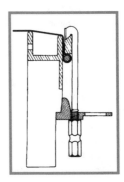

Diagram 6. Archtop, one-piece flange 1929

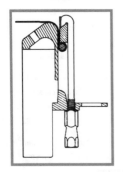

Diagram 7. Flat-head: 1928–42, 1970–current

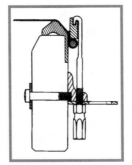

Diagram 8: Shoes-and-plate: late 1920s–30s

Diagram 9. Top tension: 1937–42 and reissues

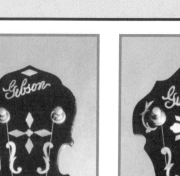

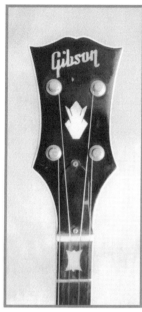

Fiddle peghead.

Double-cut peghead.

Guitar-style peghead on a 1950s RB-250.

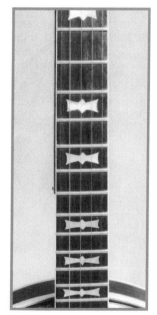

Wreath inlay.

Hearts and flowers inlay.

Bowtie inlay.

Single coordinator rod and neck fastening nut, flat-head 20-hole tone ring, thin rim, on a 1960s RB-250.

Double coordinator rods, archtop tone ring with no holes, on a 1927 Style 3.

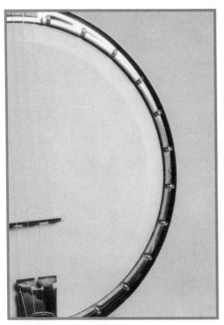

Beveled appearance around edge of head, showing archtop tone ring.

Top tension style, with head-tension nuts accessible without removing resonator, flat-head tone ring.

Diamond-hole flange on a late 1920s UB-4.

Tube-and-plate flange, with tension hooks going through metal tube.

One-piece flange (with flat-head tone ring), with tension hooks going through flange.

SERIAL NUMBERS

1918–34

The 4- or 5-digit numbers in the following list are batch numbers. They are typically followed by 1 or 2 digits.

NUMBER RANGE	YEAR	NUMBER RANGE	YEAR
100s–900s, open back	1918–c. 1922	9100s	1930
100s–200s, resonator	1935	9200s	1931
300s–900s	1936	9300s	1932
1000s	1937	9400s–9500s	1933
2000s	1938	9600s–9700s	1934
7000s	1922–24	9800s–9900s	1935
8000s–8200s	1925	11000s	1922–Feb. 1925
8300s–8500s	1926	D + 4 digits	1938
8600s–8800s	1927	E + 4 digits	1939
8900s	1928	F + 4 digits	1940
9000s	1929	G + 4 digits	1941

1950s

Many banjos in the late 1950s have no serial number and must be dated by specs.

Serial numbers from the 1950s have a similar configuration to Gibson solidbody electric guitars of the period:

####-## (a numeral followed by a space, followed by 3 or 4 more numerals). The first numeral corresponds to the last digit of the year.

Example: 6 0123-12 = 1956

1960s

Same as Gibson guitar numbering system: up to 6 digits impressed into the back of the peghead; no *MADE IN USA* on back of peghead. See Serial Numbers (after Gibson General Information section).

1970–87

Except for Earl Scruggs models (see following), banjos are numbered in the same system as guitars, with *MADE IN USA* on back of peghead. See Serial Numbers (after Gibson General Information section).

EARL SCRUGGS MODELS

Each model has its own number configuration and series, starting at introduction with 001 and continuing through current production. A year-by-year number list is not available. Production figure is current for Feb. 1999.

MODEL	CONFIGURATION	PRODUCTION
Standard	####	3622
'49 Classic	yy-##	122
Golden Deluxe	yy-##	32
Flint Hill Special	FH-yy-##	10
Special	ES-yy-##	52

yy = year

= ranking from beginning of model production

1988–CURRENT

Earl Scruggs Models

See preceding.

Style 250

Configuration **250-yy-##**

yy = year

= ranking for the year, each year begins with 001

Granada

Configuration **yy-mm-##**

yy = year

mm = month

= ranking for the year, each year begins with 01

Example: 98-05-10 = 10th Granada of 1998, made in May

Custom Models

MODEL	CONFIGURATION
Super 400	**S400-##**
Floral	**FL-yy-##**
Imperial	**MP-yy-##**

yy = year

= ranking from beginning of model production

All other models

All numbered styles (except 250, see preceding) have configuration **s(s)-yymm-##**

    s(s) = style

    yy = year

    mm = month

    ## = ranking for the year in that style

Example: 3-9507-12 = 12th Style 3 banjo of 1995

BANJOS

SECTION ORGANIZATION

Models with No Style Designation

Styles 1–5, Style 11

Budget Styles, Pre-World War II

High-End Styles Introduced Pre-World War II

Top-Tension Models

Models Introduced After World War II

Earl Scruggs Models

Custom Models

Ukulele Banjos

MODELS WITH NO STYLE DESIGNATION

TB: open back, ebony fingerboard, dot inlay, bound peghead, "moccasin" peghead shape comes to point at top (earliest with guitar-style peghead, with "dove-wing" dip in center), 2 notches on each side of peghead, veneer on front and back, slanted *The Gibson* logo in center of peghead, fleur-de-lis peghead inlay below logo, small ornamental inlay above logo

Introduced: **Sept. 1918**

Referred to as Deluxe style, optional pickguard extends

GIBSON

from rim to bridge, metal support rod for pickguard, optional metal armrest rod, engraved crown-shaped tailpiece cover, bound back of rim, 3-piece maple neck with ebony center laminate, 27 frets, 15 frets clear of body, bound ebony fingerboard with treble-side extension, dot inlay at frets 5, 7, 10, 12 (2), 17 · and 19, small dot inlay at frets 22 and 24, pearl nut, ivoroid tuner buttons, shaded mahogany finish on rim and neck, 24 frets: **by mid 1921**

Optional trapdoor resonator: **1922**

Renamed **TB-4** (see following): **Apr. 1923**

MB: similar specs to TB
Introduced: **by Apr. 1919**
Same specs as TB of mid 1921, except for symmetrical ebony fingerboard with pointed end, 18 frets, 12 frets clear of body, dot inlay at frets 5, 7, 10, 12 (2) and 15, 3 notches on each side of peghead: **by mid 1921**

Optional trapdoor resonator: **1922**

Renamed **MB-4** (see Style 4, following): **Apr. 1923**

GB: similar specs to TB
Introduced: **mid 1919**
Same specs as TB of mid 1921, except for pickguard and armrest available as option, guitar style trapeze tailpiece, no tailpiece cover, 24 frets, 17 frets clear of body, dot inlay at frets 5, 7, 9, 12, (2) and 15: **by mid 1921**

Renamed **GB-4** (see Style 4, following): **Apr. 1923**

CB: similar specs to TB, same body and neck size as GB but with 4 strings
Introduced: **by Sept. 1919**
Same specs as TB of mid 1921, except for pickguard and armrest available as option, no tailpiece cover, 25 frets, 17 frets clear of body, dot inlay at frets 5, 7, 9, 12 (2), and 15: **by mid 1921**

Renamed **CB-4** (see Style 4, following): **Apr. 1923**

PB and **RB:** not offered

STYLES 1–5, STYLE 11

Style 2

TB-2: also referred to as Melody model, open back, pickguard extends from end of fingerboard to bridge, metal pickguard support rod, metal armrest rod, no tailpiece cover, unbound ebony fingerboard with square end, 24 frets, 17 frets clear of body, dot inlay at frets 5, 7, 10, 12 (2) and 15, peghead tapers to point at top, no logo, black peghead veneer, Sheraton brown rim finish, natural neck and peghead finish

Introduced: **by Nov. 1920**

Trapdoor resonator: **1922**

Not pictured in catalogs: **1923–24**

Laminated maple resonator with amber brown finish, wavy-shape flange, rosewood fingerboard, varied-pattern inlay, simple flowerpot peghead inlay, slanted *The Gibson* logo: **1925**

Diamond-hole flange: **1926**

Walnut resonator, 1-piece flange, bound resonator and fingerboard, pearloid fingerboard and peghead veneer, black silkscreen markers, fiddle-shape peghead, *Gibson* logo, transitional period: **late 1929–30**

Small modified archtop tone ring, flat hooks, grooved stretcher band: **1930**

Celluloid covered resonator: **1932**

No celluloid on resonator: **by 1934**

Discontinued: **1937**

1 shipped: **1938**

MB-2: same specs as TB-2 except for no pickguard, no armrest, crown-shaped tailpiece cover, dot inlay
Introduced: **1920**
Not offered: **1924–25**
Discontinued: **1937**
Last shipped: **1938**

PB-2 introduced: **1922**
Discontinued (1 shipped): **1937**

RB-2: 1922–31

Style 1

TB-1: trapdoor resonator, ebony fingerboard, pearl dot inlay, nearly straight peghead sides, no peghead ornament, slanted *The Gibson* logo, nickel-plated hardware, brown sunburst finish

Introduced: **1922**

Rosewood fingerboard, fancy inlay, no resonator: **1925**

11" head diameter, maple resonator, shoes-and-plate flange: **1926**

Diamond flange holes, single-bound fingerboard and resonator, dot inlay, dark mahogany finish: **later 1926**

1-piece flange, bound fingerboard, bat inlay, multiple dots at frets 15 and 17, inverted flower peghead inlay, unbound fiddle-shape peghead: **by 1930**

Dot inlay at frets 1, 3, 5, 7, 10, 12 (2), 15 and 17, dark brown finish with no shaded areas: **1936**

Bat inlay with dots near body: **1938**
Last made: **1940**

RB-1 introduced: **1922**
Last shipped: **1940**
Reintroduced, parts interchangeable with Mastertone
parts, simple brass tone ring, rosewood fingerboard, dot inlay, slanted *Gibson* logo, fleur-de-lis
peghead inlay, double-cut peghead, nickel-plated
hardware, amber brown (Granada sunburst) or red
maple finish: **late 1990**
Discontinued: **1995**

MB-1 introduced: **1922**
Not offered: **by 1924**
Reintroduced: **1925**
Last made: **1937**

GB-1: 1922–40

PB-1: 1926–40

Style 3: trapdoor resonator, unbound ebony fingerboard, dot inlay, "moccasin" peghead shape comes
to point at top, 2 notches on each side of peghead,
nickel-plated hardware, mahogany sunburst finish

TB-3, RB-3, PB-3 and **MB-3** (see following) introduced:
May 1923
Laminated maple resonator, Mastertone construction,
ball-bearing tone ring, multiple-diamond inlay,
curlicues and cross peghead inlay, single-bound resonator and fingerboard, fiddle-shape peghead, *Mastertone* on peghead, red mahogany finish: **1925**
No *Mastertone* on peghead: **1926**
Mahogany resonator with 2 white-black-white concentric rings, single-bound resonator, 1-piece flange,
larger fancy inlay, 6-piece ornamental peghead inlay
with curlicues, double-cut peghead shape, transitional period: **late 1929–30**
Last TB-3, RB-3, PB-3 shipped, variation introduced as
Style 75, see following: **1937**

RB-3 reintroduced, mahogany resonator and neck,
2 concentric rings of binding material on resonator,
bound rosewood fingerboard, "standard" (varied-
pattern with 3 joined diamonds at 1st fret), wreath
or "Reno" inlay (flying eagle fingerboard inlay with
standard Style 3 peghead inlay), single-ply antiqued
binding, nickel-plated hardware, red brown mahogany finish, tenor and plectrum available: **mid 1988**
No plectrums: **1995**
No tenors: **1996**

RB-3 still in production

MB-3 introduced: **May 1923**
Diamond-hole flange: **1927**
1-piece flange, 11" head: **1928**
Last shipped: **1939**

GB-3: dot inlay
Listed: **by 1932**
Last shipped: **1937**

CB-3: not offered

Style 4: pyralin resonator (trapdoor optional), maple
neck, bound ebony fingerboard, pearl dot inlay,
slanted *The Gibson* logo, fleur-de-lis peghead inlay,
2 points on each side of peghead, silver-plated
hardware
TB, MB, CB and GB renamed **TB-4, MB-4, CB-4** (dot
inlay throughout production), **GB-4** (dot inlay
throughout production): **1923**
Elevated plastic pickguard, extension fingerboard
with 19" scale, non-extension fingerboard with
21" scale: **by 1924**
RB-4, PB-4 available: **by 1924**
Mahogany resonator, mahogany neck, black-and-
white-bound rosewood fingerboard, hearts-and-
flowers inlay, 2 inlaid rings on resonator,
triple-bound resonator, fiddle-shape peghead,
Mastertone on peghead, floral peghead inlay,
chrome-plated hardware: **1925**
No *Mastertone* on peghead: **1926**
Burl walnut resonator and neck, 1-piece flange, walnut
neck, flying eagle inlay (some early 1-piece flange
examples with hearts-and-flowers inlay), double-cut
peghead shape, chrome-plated hardware: **Oct. 1929**
Style 4 discontinued: **1937**
TB-4, RB-4 last shipped: **1937**
PB-4 last shipped: **1939**
RB-4 reintroduced, walnut resonator and neck, 2 concentric rings of marquetry inlaid on resonator,
bound rosewood fingerboard, flying eagle inlay,
multi-ply antiqued binding, nickel-plated hardware,
antique walnut finish: **1991**
Still in production

MB-4 (formerly MB): specs similar to TB-4
Introduced: **1923**
Small notched diamond peghead inlay, no fleur de lis:
1925-27
Discontinued: **1932**

GB-4, **CB-4**: specs similar to TB-4 except for dot inlay: **1923–31**

Style 5: Pyralin resonator, trapdoor optional, fern peghead inlay (similar to F-5 mandolin peghead inlay), gold-plated hardware

Introduced, no MB-5: **May 1923**

Elevated plastic pickguard, extension fingerboard with 19" scale, non-extension fingerboard with 21" scale, triple-bound tapered peghead with notches: **c. 1923**

Pearloid/ivoroid-covered rim, walnut resonator, 2 inlaid rings on resonator, fancy binding, wreath inlay, fiddle-shape peghead, *Mastertone* on peghead, marquetry on back of peghead, engraved gold-plated hardware: **1925**

No *Mastertone* on peghead: **1926**

Discontinued: **1929**

RB-5 reintroduced, walnut resonator and neck, 2 pearloid marquetry rings inlaid on resonator, bound rosewood fingerboard, wreath inlay, pearl nut, multiple antiqued binding with pearloid marquetry, 2-piece tube & plate flange, Kirshner tailpiece, amber tuner buttons, satin gold-plated hardware, antique walnut finish: **1995**

Still in production

PB-5: 1926–28

Style 11: maple resonator covered with pearloid, pearloid fingerboard and peghead cover with red-blue-black floral design, single-bound fingerboard and resonator, 4-petal stenciled ornament on peghead and resonator back, nickel-plated hardware, blue or black finish

TB-11, **RB-11**, **PB-11** available: **1931–42**

BUDGET STYLES, PRE-WORLD WAR II

Junior: no resonator, ebony fingerboard, dot inlay, narrow peghead, pictured with natural maple finish but virtually all with black finish

TB-Jr.: 10 1/2" head diameter, introduced: **May 1923**

MB-Jr., **RB-Jr.**, **PB-Jr.** introduced: **1924**

Junior line discontinued, replaced by Style 0: **1925**

Style 0: no resonator, 10 1/2" head diameter, ebonized maple fingerboard, dot inlay, antique mahogany finish

Introduced TB-0 and MB-0 only: **1925**

11" head diameter: **1926**

Resonator, hexagonal flange holes, bound fingerboard, dot inlay, peghead with points at pegs closest to nut, no peghead ornament: **by Sept. 1929**

Discontinued: **1931**

Oriole: tenor, 10 1/2" head diameter, no resonator, 21" scale, bound ebonized fingerboard, dot inlay, pointed-top peghead, script *Oriole* peghead logo (no *Gibson* logo), London grey finish

Introduced: **c. 1926**

Fleur-de-lis peghead ornament, mahogany finish: **c. 1927**

Discontinued: **by 1932**

Style 00: maple resonator and neck, 1-piece flange, most with 3/4" rim, some with 1/2" rim, rosewood fingerboard, dot inlay at frets 5, 7, 10, 12 (2), no peghead inlay, nickel-plated hardware, single-bound resonator and fingerboard, silkscreen logo, peghead tapers to a point, light shaded walnut finish

TB-00, **PB-00**, **RB-00**, **MB-00** available: **1932–42**

GB-00: 2 shipped: **1939, 1940**

HIGH-END STYLES INTRODUCED PRE-WORLD WAR II

Granada: maple resonator and neck, multiple-bound resonator, 2 inlaid rings on resonator, rosewood fingerboard, hearts-and-flowers inlay on fingerboard and peghead, *Mastertone* on peghead, engraved gold-plated hardware

TG (tenor) introduced: **1925**

No *Mastertone* on peghead: **1926**

PG (plectrum) available: **1926**

RG (5-string) available: **1932**

No rings on resonator: **by 1930**

1-piece flange, flying eagle inlay (some early 1-piece flange examples with hearts-and-flowers inlay), double-cut peghead: **1929**

Discontinued: **1937**

PG, RG last shipped: **1937**

TG last shipped: **1940**

RB-Granada reintroduced, maple resonator and neck,

bound rosewood fingerboard, flying eagle or hearts-and-flowers inlay, inlay below *Mastertone*, gold-plated hardware, rich amber brown finish, plectrum or tenor available: **1986**

No plectrums: **1995**

No tenors: **1996**

RB Granada still in production

Florentine: multiple wood and binding options, Renaissance scenes on pearloid fingerboard, carved crown and crest on resonator, carved neck heel, pearloid peghead veneer with rhinestone border and rhinestone inlays forming floral bouquet (commonly referred to as "ice cream cone"), some with butterfly pattern peghead inlay, engraved gold-plated hardware

Introduced: **1927**

Discontinued: **1937**

TB-Florentine, PB-Florentine last shipped: **1941**

Reintroduced: **1970**

Discontinued: **1986**

1 RB-Florentine produced: **1995**

Bella Voce: multiple wood and binding options, rosewood fingerboard, varied flower-pattern inlay, carved lyre on resonator, carved neck heel, ebony peghead veneer, engraved gold-plated hardware

Introduced: **1927**

Pearloid peghead veneer with rhinestone border and rhinestone inlays forming floral bouquet (same peghead as Florentine): **1928**

Discontinued: **1930**

A few TB-BV and PB-BV shipped through: **1939**

1 RB-Bella Voce produced: **1995**

Style 6: maple resonator and neck, no ornament on resonator, black and white checkered binding around resonator edges and fingerboard and peghead, some with gold-sparkle binding, hearts-and-flowers inlay, ebony fingerboard, floral peghead inlay, engraved gold-plated hardware, Argentine gray sunburst finish

Introduced: **late 1927**

Discontinued: **1937**

1 TB-6 electric, 1 PB-6 electric: **1937**

PB-6 last shipped: **1939**

TB-6 last shipped: **1940**

RB-6 Sparkle: figured maple resonator and neck, bound ebony fingerboard, vintage inlay, multiple binding with antique gold-sparkle, amber tuner buttons, gold-plated hardware, Argentine gray sunburst finish: **1995–Current**

RB-6 Checkerboard: checkered binding, pearl tuner buttons: **1995–Current**

All American: multiple wood and binding options, carved eagle on resonator and peghead, historical scenes on pearloid fingerboard, engraved gold-plated hardware

Introduced: **1930**

Discontinued: **1937**

A few TB-AA shipped through: **1941**

Reintroduced, RB, TB or PB available: **1970**

Discontinued: **1986**

1 RB-All American produced: **1995**

Style 75/Crowe: variation of Style 3 (see preceding), mahogany resonator and neck, rosewood fingerboard, varied-pattern inlay with 3 connected diamonds at 1st fret and 4-point star at 3rd, unbound double-cut peghead, floral peghead inlay, nickel-plated hardware

TB-75, **RB-75**, **PB-75** introduced: **1937**

8 PB-75s shipped: **1937–39**

Discontinued: **1943**

Reintroduced as **RB-75 Crowe:** replica of banjo owned by J.D. Crowe, mahogany resonator and neck, 2 concentric rings inlaid on resonator, bound rosewood fingerboard, varied-pattern inlay with 3 connected diamonds at 1st fret and 4-point star at 3rd, antique single-ply binding on resonator and fingerboard, special prewar style RB-75 tone ring, ivoroid tuner buttons, nickel-plated hardware, red brown mahogany finish: **1997**

Still in production

Electric Banjo: tenor (**ETB**), 5-string (**ERB**) or plectrum (**EPB**), circular wood body with flat maple top, screwed-on back, Charlie Christian pickup, 2 knobs on side, Style 12 banjo neck with large bowtie inlay on fingerboard and peghead, sunburst finish

Available: **1939–42**

TOP-TENSION MODELS

All have head tension adjustable from top, resonator carved on outside and flat on inside, arched (radiused) fingerboard, large peghead with notches above nut (shape unique to top-tension models).

Style 7: maple resonator, maple neck, single-bound rosewood fingerboard, slotted-bowtie inlay, single-bound peghead, slotted bowtie peghead inlay, nickel-plated hardware, dark brown finish

TB-7, **PB-7** introduced: **1937**
First **RB-7** shipped: **1938**
Large art deco semi-hexagonal inlay, fleur-de-lis peghead inlay: **1941**
Discontinued: **1943**

RB-7 reintroduced, carved maple resonator, maple neck, bound rosewood fingerboard with radius, bowtie inlay, single-ply white binding, ivoroid tuner buttons, nickel-plated hardware, rich chocolate finish: **1994**
Still in production

Style 12: black walnut resonator and neck, black walnut neck, triple-bound resonator, triple-bound rosewood fingerboard, large art deco semi-hexagonal inlay, triple-bound peghead, chrome-plated hardware, shaded walnut finish
Introduced: **1937**

TB-12, **PB-12** introduced: **1937**
First **RB-12** shipped: **1938**
Last made: **1939**

RB-12 reintroduced, carved walnut resonator with 3-ply antiqued binding, walnut neck, single-bound rosewood fingerboard with radius, large art deco semi-hexagonal inlay, triple-bound peghead, large vertical peghead inlay, amber tuner buttons, nickel-plated hardware, antique walnut finish: **1995**
Antique natural burst finish: **1997**
Still in production

Style 18: maple resonator with 3-ply binding, maple neck, triple-bound arched rosewood fingerboard, large art deco semi-hexagonal inlay, triple-bound peghead, large vertical peghead inlay, pearl tuner buttons, engraved gold-plated hardware, sunburst finish

TB-18, **PB-18** introduced: **1937**

RB-18 shipped: **1938–40**
Discontinued: **1943**

RB-18 reintroduced, carved figured maple resonator, figured maple neck, bound rosewood fingerboard with radius, vintage inlay, multiple antique binding, amber tuner buttons, engraved gold-plated hardware, amber brown finish: **1995**
Vintage sunburst finish: **1997**
Still in production

MODELS INTRODUCED AFTER WORLD WAR II

Style 100: maple resonator with white binding, 1-piece flange, mahogany neck, unbound rosewood fingerboard, dot inlay, center-dip "dove-wing" peghead, decal logo, "pancake" tuners with 3-1 ratio, sunburst finish

RB-100, **TB-100**, **PB-100** introduced: **1948**
2-piece flange, 3-piece mahogany neck, fiddle-shape peghead: **1969**
Discontinued: **1979**

Style 150: laminated mahogany resonator, 1-piece flange, simple brass hoop, no tone ring, white-black-white binding and 2 concentric rings on resonator, bound rosewood fingerboard, unbound center-dip "dove-wing" peghead, bowtie inlay, crown peghead inlay, Mastertone-style Kluson tuners with 12-1 ratio, walnut finish

RB-150, **TB-150**, **PB-150** introduced: **1948**
Discontinued: **1959**

Style 250: Mastertone model, laminated mahogany resonator, 2-piece flange, white-black-white binding and 2 concentric rings on resonator, 2-piece flange, no tone ring, bound rosewood fingerboard, bowtie inlay, *Mastertone* engraved in inlay at next-to-last fret, bound center-dip "dove wing" peghead, crown inlay

RB-250, **TB-250**, **PB-250** introduced: **1954**
Unbound fiddle-shape peghead, pearl script logo, peghead inlay of diamonds pointing in 4 directions and 2 curlicues: **late 1968–69**

Mahogany resonator and neck, 2-piece flange, 11-ply rim painted black, single-bound ebony fingerboard, 22 frets, varied-pattern inlay with 3 connected diamonds at 1st fret, nickel-plated hardware, red brown mahogany finish: **1970**
3-ply rim: **late 1970s**
1-piece flange: **1988**
Still in production

Style 170: no resonator, rosewood fingerboard, dot inlay, 4-point peghead shape, decal logo, "pancake" tuners with 3-1 ratio
Introduced: **1960**
11-ply rim painted black, fiddle-shape peghead: **1970**
Last listed (1 shipped): **1973**

Style 175: longneck RB-170, 5th string begins at 7th fret, no resonator, rosewood fingerboard, dot inlay, 4-point peghead shape, decal logo, "pancake" tuners with 3-1 ratio
Introduced: **1962**
11-ply rim painted black, fiddle-shape peghead: **1970**
Last listed (3 shipped): **1973**

Style 180: same as RB-175 but with Mastertone tone ring, bound fingerboard, Mastertone-style Kluson tuners with 12-1 ratio
Available: **1961–67**

Style 500: laminated maple resonator with wood marquetry, maple neck, multiple-bound, checkered marquetry on side of neck and resonator back, ebony fingerboard, bowtie inlay, bound 4-point peghead, crown peghead inlay, gold-plated hardware, optional finishes
Available: **1964–69**

Style 800: maple resonator, 1-piece flange, bound ebony fingerboard, flying eagle, hearts-and-flowers or wreath inlay, double-cut peghead, engraved gold-plated hardware, sunburst, cherry sunburst, Argentine gray, natural or viceroy brown finish
Introduced: **1964**
2-piece flange, 11-ply rim painted black, fiddle-shape peghead: **1970**
Shipping records show no Style 800 banjos: **1972–78**
Catalogued with wreath inlay standard, flying eagle or hearts-and-flowers inlay optional: **1975**

Cherry sunburst finish only: **1978**
Antique sunburst, Argentine gray, natural, vintage sunburst or sunburst finish: **1980**
Discontinued: **1986**

Style 350: bound mahogany resonator with decal of eagle clutching drum, 11-ply rim painted black, 3-piece mahogany neck, single-bound fingerboard, varied-pattern inlay with 3 connected diamonds at 1st fret, *Mastertone* engraved in inlay at next-to-last fret, fiddle-shape peghead, nickel-plated hardware, walnut stain finish
Available: **1974–76**
Shipping totals show 1 in 1974, 26 in 1976

Super 400: split-block inlay (Super 400 guitar style)
Available: **1998–current**

EARL SCRUGGS MODELS

Earl Scruggs (Exact Replica/Standard): curly maple resonator and neck, multiple binding, bound ebony fingerboard, hearts-and-flowers inlay, inlays at 1st and 15th frets, bound double-cut peghead, hearts-and-flowers peghead inlay, script Gibson logo, model name on truss rod cover, yellow-brown finish
The Earl Scruggs model was based on Scruggs' Granada as it was repaired by Gibson in 1984. It differed from original Granada specs in that it had an ebony fingerboard with 2 extra inlays, no rings on resonator and nickel-plated hardware. First-version Scruggs models also have the following features that differ from original Granadas: smaller peghead, parts not to prewar specs, yellowish finish color
Introduced, first 1,984 instruments signed by Earl Scruggs: **1984**
Larger prewar style peghead, hardware closer to prewar specs (flange manufactured from original 1930s die), "exact replica" finish (dark neck finish, sunburst resonator finish): **1988**
Referred to as **Earl Scruggs Exact Replica** or **Earl Scruggs Standard: 1992**
Still in production

Earl Scruggs Golden Deluxe: figured maple resonator and neck, *DeLuxe* engraved on tailpiece cover, bound ebony fingerboard, hearts-and-flowers inlay, multi-ply antiqued binding, unbound double-cut fiddle-shape peghead, hearts-and-flowers peghead inlay, script Gibson logo, satin gold-plated hardware, "exact replica" finish

Available: **1991–current**

Earl Scruggs '49 Classic: figured maple resonator and neck, bound rosewood fingerboard, bowtie inlay, multiple binding, unbound double-cut peghead, hearts-and-flowers peghead inlay, script Gibson logo, nickel-plated hardware, "exact replica" finish

Available: **1992–current**

Earl Scruggs Special: figured maple resonator and neck, abalone signature inlaid on resonator, *Special* engraved on tailpiece cover, multiple binding all around with abalone border, bound ebony fingerboard, hearts-and-flowers inlay, multiple binding, bound double-cut peghead, hearts-and-flowers peghead inlay, script Gibson logo, pearl tuner buttons, engraved gold-plated hardware, antique natural finish

Available: **1995–current**

Earl Scruggs Flint Hill Special: figured maple resonator and neck, triple-bound resonator, bound ebony fingerboard, hearts-and-flowers inlay, multiple binding with abalone trim, double-cut peghead bound with pearl, hearts-and-flowers peghead inlay, script Gibson logo, abalone truss rod cover, pearl tuner buttons, engraved nickel-plated hardware, antique natural finish

Available: **1997–current**

CUSTOM MODELS, 1998–CURRENT

Produced on a custom order basis. Specs vary according to customer order.

Floral: ripple pearl binding, heavily engraved and inlaid with floral pattern

Imperial: ripple pearl binding, heavily engraved and inlaid

UKULELE BANJOS

UB: mandolin scale, 9" head diameter, trapdoor resonator, 20 brackets, unbound ebony fingerboard with square end, dot inlay at frets 5, 7, 10, 12 (2)

and 15, maple neck, straight peghead sides (similar to later Jr. models), slanted *The Gibson* logo in center of peghead, no ornamental peghead inlay, front peghead veneer, black tuner buttons, natural finish

Available: **Dec. 1924–25**

UB-1: 6" head diameter, no support rod, unbound flat-plate resonator, 10 brackets, ebonized pearwood fingerboard, dot inlay at frets 5, 7 and 9 (some with dots at 5, 7 and 10)

Introduced: **1926**
Gibson logo: **by 1937**
Discontinued: **1942**

UB-2: 12 brackets, bound flat plate resonator, single support rod, ebonized pearwood fingerboard, dot inlay at frets 5, 7 and 10

Introduced: **by 1926**
17 frets: **1927**
Bound fingerboard, 14 frets, slanted *The Gibson* logo in center of peghead: **c. 1930**
Dot inlay at frets 5, 7, 10, and 12 (2), fleur-de-lis peghead inlay, small ornamental inlay above logo: **by 1932**
Discontinued: **1942**

UB-3: early example: trapdoor resonator, maple neck, 4-point star peghead inlay of diamond-shape figures (same inlay as MB-3): **c. 1924**

Introduced in catalog, bound flat-plate resonator, 14 brackets, 14 frets, bound fingerboard, multiple-diamond inlay at frets 5, 7, 10 and 12, slanted *The Gibson* logo, fleur-de-lis peghead inlay below logo, small ornamental peghead inlay above logo: **1926**
Resonator with diamond-hole flange: **1928**
15 frets: **1932**
Discontinued: **1937**
Last shipped: **1939**

UB-4: triple-bound maple resonator, diamond-hole flange, 16 brackets, mahogany neck, bound rosewood fingeboard, varied-pattern inlay at frets 5, 7, 9, 12, 14 and 17, straight *The Gibson* logo above tuning pegs, flowerpot peghead inlay, nickel-plated hardware

Introduced: **1927**
Varied-pattern inlay at frets 3, 5, 7, 10, 12 and 15, peghead ornament similar to sheaf of grain: **1928**
Gold-plated hardware: **1929**

15 frets, dot inlay to 15th fret, no peghead ornament:
1932

Last listed: **1936**

Shipping totals show 3 in 1937, 4 in 1938, 20 in 1940

UB-5: same specs as UB-4 except for gold-plated hardware

Available: **1927–28**

5 shipped: **1940**

Note: Gibson literature shows no distinction between the UB-5 and the gold-plated UB-4 (1929 and after). Consequently, most collectors refer to any gold-plated ukulele banjo as a UB-5

AMPLIFIERS

GENERAL INFORMATION

The earliest Gibson amplifiers were designed and built for Gibson by the Lyon & Healy company of Chicago. Prior to World War II, production amps had a chassis designed by Lyon & Healy (probably by audio engineer John Kutilek) with cabinet made by Geib, the company that supplied instrument cases to Gibson. All prewar amps came with a slip cover.

From World War II to 1967, Gibson amps were built in Kalamazoo. Beginning with the solid-state models of 1966–67, Gibson amplifier production was moved away from Kalamazoo. No amplifiers were produced or shipped from Kalamazoo after 1967.

CMI, Norlin and Gibson Guitar Corp. (Gibson's parent companies) continued to market amplifiers sporadically from the late 1960s into the early 1990s. Listings for those models may not be complete.

CABINET STYLES

Tweed "aeroplane" cloth cover with stripes or vinyl cover, round grille, round leather handle: **1936–42**

Flat leather "strap" handle first appears: **1940**

Metal handles first appear: **early 1950s**

Tweed vinyl cover, amber handle insert with *Gibson:*
1959

Trapezoidal cabinet shape: **1963–64**

Rectangular cabinet, black cover, silver grille cloth, silver plastic logo diagonally in upper right corner of grille: **1965–67**

Side panels extend approx. 1" above top panel:
1968–69

MAESTRO

In addition to the Gibson brand, the Maestro brand was used on a line of accordian amps. Most, if not all, Maestro-brand amps of the 1950s and '60s have the Gibson logo on the control plate. Maestro cabinet styles are similar to Gibsons of the same period, except that Maestros with a metal handle do not have the Gibson logo on the plastic handle insert.

SERIAL NUMBERS

Gibson amps do not follow the same series as guitars, and no serial number list is available. Amps must be dated by specifications and/or date codes on electronic parts (see Appendix).

SECTION ORGANIZATION

Pre-World War II Models
Post-World War II Tube Models
Solid-State Models, 1960s
Maestro Models
Gibson, 1970s
Lab Series
Genesis
Lab Series 2
Gibson Labs

PRE-WORLD WAR II MODELS

EH-150: 13 3/4" wide, 13 3/4" high, 7 1/4" deep, gold/brown tweed cover with orange and black vertical stripes in center, leather suitcase handle, leather corners, nickel-plated hardware, removable latched back, 8 7/8" round speaker opening, black metal grille, *Gibson* in lower right corner, cabinet sides 1/2" thick wood, front and back 1/4" thick, 4 tubes, 1 10" speaker, inside of cabinet covered in grained alligator material, control panel (from left): power cord, 1 1/4" glass fuse (screw-in house type), on/off toggle switch, pilot light, chassis finished in black textured paint, serial number usually penciled on speaker bell, 4 round rubber feet

Introduced: **Oct. 1935**

GIBSON

AC/DC version (**EH-160**) available: **early 1936**

Small fuse holder: **by Feb. 1936**

15 1/4" wide, 14 3/4" high, 8" deep, 6 tubes, control panel (from left), on/off, fuse, echo imput, mic volume, pilot light, instrument volume, 1 mic and 2 instrument imputs, normal/bass tone toggle, 4 stage amplification and 15 watt output: **Sept. 1936**

8 1/2" deep, front 3/4" thick, 7 tubes: **May 1937**

2 produced with white paint finish, *Smeck* in lower right corner: **1937**

16 1/2" wide, 15 3/8" high, 8 5/8" deep, sides round to top, front 5/8" thick, 10 5/8" round speaker hole, black metal grill, leather corners on bottom, 1-12" speaker, inside of cabinet covered with brown and black grained material: **Aug. 1937**

17 1/4" wide, 15 5/8" tall, 9" deep, speaker hole with rounded front edge, inside covered in cream colored paper, control panel (from left): power cord, on/off toggle, tone control, mic volume, instrument volume, 1 mic and 2 instrument inputs, pilot light, model and serial number: **Aug. 1941**

Last made: **1942**

Variations: 25 cycle, 25 cycle C, AC/DC, 230 volt, 60 cycle 115 volt, 50 cycle 250 volt, 30 watt, AC/DC 110/230 volt, New York band AC/DC

Echo Speaker: extension speaker, cabinet size the same as EH-150 of the same year, 1 10" inch speaker, closed removable back, cord caddy inside on bottom, *echo* in white marker on inside back

Available: **Sept. 1936–42**

Smeck: Roy Smeck model, variation of 1937 EH-150, white paint finish, see preceding

EH-100: square cornered open-back cabinet, black imitation leather cover, embossed double line follows front perimeter, most with metal bumpers on all corners, some with bumpers on bottom corners only, round speaker opening, metal grille, *Gibson* in white in lower right corner, 4 tubes, 1 10" speaker, control panel (from left): power cord, fuse, 2 inputs; leather suitcase handle

Introduced: **mid 1936**

14" wide, 12" high, tan aeroplane cloth cover with multiple vertical black stripes, 5 tubes, controls (from left), 2 instrument inputs,1 mic input, mic volume, fuse, cord, also available with AC/DC power (**EH-110**): **mid 1937**

14" wide, 12" high, 7 3/4" deep, dark brown aeroplane cloth cover with horizontal yellow stripes, chrome-plated metal bumpers on all corners, 8 3/4" round speaker opening, *Gibson* below opening, removable latched back, 6 tubes, 1 10" speaker: **Sept. 1938**

Green/gray cover, horizontal white lines: **mid 1939**

12" wide, 14 3/4" high, 8" deep, natural finished mahogany cabinet specified, most covered in green/gray aeroplane cloth, open back, top section (approx. three-quarters of unit) contains 1 10" speaker and lifts off of bottom chassis, 6 tubes, control panel (from left): 2 instrument inputs,1 mic input, mic volume control, fuse, on/off toggle switch, cord; leather strap handle: **mid 1940**

Discontinued: **1943**

Variations: 25 cycle, 25 cycle C, AC/DC 110/120, 230 volt

EH-185: tweed cover with black and orange vertical stripes down center, round speaker opening, oblong port above speaker opening, logo to upper left of grille, controls lift out of cabinet, 1 12" speaker, controls (from left to right): on/off toggle and extension speaker jack, treble tone, bass tone, pilot light, mic volume, instrument volume, 2 instrument inputs and 1 mic input

Variations: EH-185C, 25 cycle, natural finish, 6 volt, built-in vibrato

Introduced, approx. first 60 examples with *EH-150* stamped into plate, some with *EH-150* stamp scratched through and/or over-stamped; logged into shipping records as "new model 150," serial numbers begin with 15000: **July 1939**

Labeled EH-185: **Oct. 1939**

Control panel as EH-150 of the same period (from left): power cord, on/off toggle, tone control, mic volume, instrument volume, 1 mic and 2 instrument inputs, pilot light, model and serial number, serial numbers are from EH-150 series, beginning around 13800: **Oct. 1941**

Last made: **1942**

EH-195: variations of EH-185, AC/DC, built-in vibrato, 250 volt 50 cycle

Available: **1939–42**

EH-275: natural maple cabinet, tortoiseshell celluloid binding, round speaker opening, oblong port above speaker opening, logo to upper left of grille, con-

trols lift out of cabinet, same controls as EH-185
Available, approx. 30 shipped: **1940–42**

EH-250: specs unavailable, probably unbound version of EH-275 (see preceding)
2 shipped: **1940**

EH-125: 16 1/2" wide, 15 3/8" high, 8 5/8" deep, sides round to top, medium brown aeroplane cloth cover, leather suitcase handle, leather lower corners, removeable latched back, 10 5/8" round speaker opening with rounded front edge, black metal grille, *Gibson* in lower right hand corner, 1 12" speaker, 5 tubes, chassis does not extend to meet sides, brown crinkle paint finish on chassis, control panel (from left): 2 instrument inputs,1 mic input, 6 mic volume control, fuse, on/off toggle switch, cord
Introduced: **June 1941**
Dark avocado green aeroplane cloth cover, 5 tubes: **Feb. 1942**
Discontinued: **late 1942**

Variation: 25 cycle: **1941–42**

EH-126: 6-volt
5 shipped: **1941**

EH-135: AC/DC
7 shipped: **1941**

POST-WORLD WAR II TUBE MODELS

BR-1: brown leatherette cover, rectangular grille of perforated aluminum, stylized letter *G* on grille, logo above grille, leather handle, 12" Jensen field coil speaker, top-mounted chassis, 6 tubes, cream control panel mounted at angle, 15–18 watts, 8 tubes
Control panel: 3 inputs aligned vertically; 3 large brown knobs, mic volume, instrument volume, tone; pilot light, fuse cap and on/off switch aligned vertically
Available: **late 1945–49**

BR-3: cloth cover, round hole, modern letter *G* stenciled on grille cloth, hinged back, Utah field coil speaker, 3 inputs, 3 knobs, 7 tubes
Available: **Jan. 1946–1947**

BR-4: brown leatherette cover with wide center section of cream leatherette, rectangular grille, swirl-pattern grille cloth, 2 vertical wood strips over grille, *GIBSON* in block letters above grille, kitchen cabinet

handle, 12" Utah field coil speaker, bottom-mounted chassis, 6 tubes, 12–14 watts
Control panel: 3 inputs aligned vertically; 3 black pointer knobs for mic volume, instrument volume tone; pilot light, fuse cap and on/off switch aligned vertically
Available: **1946–47**

BR-6/GA-6/Lancer: vertical rectangular cabinet, brown leatherette cover, 3 horizontal rectangular speaker openings, swirl-pattern grille clothe, *GIBSON* below speaker openings, leather handle, 10" field coil speaker, bottom-mounted chassis, 5 tubes, cream control panel mounted at angle, 8–10 watts, catalogued with kitchen cabinet handle, examples with leather handle
Control panel: 2 inputs, volume control, fuse cap, on/off switch
Introduced as BR-6: **1946**
Horizontal cabinet shape, 2 rectangular grille openings, stylized letter *G* on center crosspiece, tan grille cloth, 10" dynamic speaker, 5 tubes, 3 inputs, 1 knob, *Gibson* logo to lower right of grille opening, 12 watts, leather handle: **1948**
Renamed: **GA-6**, 11 1/4" high, 20" wide, rectangular grille, mottled gray-brown fabric cover, *Gibson 6* above grille, 1 12" Jensen speaker, 4 inputs, 3 knobs, 10-12 watts: **1956**
20" wide, 16" high, dark leatherette cover, *Gibson* above grille, metal handle with plastic insert: **1958**
Named **Lancer**, tweed cover, *Gibson* in upper right corner of grille, 5 tubes, 14 watts: **1960**
Discontinued: **1962**

GA-25: dark brown leatherette cover, 2 round speaker openings, large chain-link pattern grille cloth, Gibson logo under smaller speaker, 1 12" Jensen and 1 8" Jensen speaker (permanent magnet), 6 tubes, 4 inputs, volume and tone knobs, 15 watts, leather handle, separate cover of dark green vinyl
Introduced: **late 1947**
Discontinued, replaced by GA-30 (see following): **1948**
Model number revived on GA-25RVT/Hawk (see following)

BR-9/GA-9: cabinet narrower at top, cream leatherette cover, round speaker opening, brown trim with 3 vertical strips over speaker opening,

289

Gibson logo below opening, 8" speaker (early with field coil speaker), 4 tubes, 2 inputs, volume control, on/off switch, fuse cap

Introduced as **BR-9: 1948**

Renamed **GA-9: 1954**

13" high, 17 1/2" wide, rectangular grille, tan fabric cover, *Gibson 9* above grille, 1 10" Jensen speaker, 4 tubes, 2 inputs, leather handle: **1956**

20" wide, 16" high, *Gibson* above grille, metal handle with plastic insert: **1958**

Discontinued: **1961**

GA-50: 26" wide, 20.5" high, mottled brown leatherette cover, 2 round speaker openings with vertical slats, removable back panel, 1 12" Jensen and 1 8" Jensen speaker (permanent magnet), 7 tubes, 4 inputs, 2 volume, bass tone, treble tone, 25 watts

Available: **1948–55**

GA-50T: tremolo, 8 tubes: **1948–55**

GA-30/Invader: light brown leatherette cover, rectangular grille, Gibson logo in middle of grille, 1 12" Jensen and 1 8" Jensen speaker (permanent magnet), 6 tubes, 14 watts, 4 inputs, 3 knobs (volume, "tone expander" switch, tone control)

Introduced as **GA-30: 1948**

22" wide, 20" high, rectangular grille, mottled grey/brown cover on lower part, dark brown leatherette above grille, *Gibson 30* above grille: **1956**

Gibson above grille, 3 knobs (2 volume, tone), tone expander switch, metal handle with plastic insert: **1958**

Named **Invader**, tweed cover, standby switch (pointer knob) added, *Gibson* in upper right corner of grille: **1960**

Discontinued: **1962**

GA-30RV: reverb, 4 round knobs: **1961**

GA-30RVT: reverb, tremolo, tweed cover, standby switch (pointer knob) added, *Gibson* in upper right corner of grille

Introduced: **1962**

Tan cover, brown grille, 8 tubes, 7 knobs: **1963**

Discontinued: **1967**

GA-CB: "Custom-Built" model, 26" wide, 20 1/2" high, 12" deep, mottled brown leatherette cover or brown aeroplane cloth cover with green piping, round speaker opening with vertical slats, grille of

metal screen with tan/gold material, Gibson logo on upper left, 1 15" coaxial Jensen speaker, 10 tubes, 4-position "frequency selector" switch on upper back panel, control panel (from left): logo, pilot light, on/off toggle switch, bass control, treble control, tremolo frequency, tremolo intensity, instrument gain, mic gain, 1 mic and 3 instrument inputs, hardwired foot switch for tremolo; 25–30 watts, leather handle or metal handle with plastic insert

Available: **1949–52**

GA-20/Crest: 17" high, 20" wide, brown leatherette cover, 2 rectangular grille openings, *G* in center of grill crosspiece, *Gibson* to upper right of grille, 1 12" speaker, top-mounted chassis, 6 tubes, 4 inputs 3 knobs, 12–14 watts, leather handle

Introduced as GA-20: **1950**

20" wide, 16 1/2" high, rectangular grille, mottled grey/brown fabric cover on lower part, dark brown leatherette above grille, *Gibson 20* above grille, 16 watts: **1955**

Gibson above grille, metal handle with plastic insert: **1958**

Named **Crest**, tweed cover, *Gibson* in upper right corner of grille: **1960**

Discontinued: **1962**

GA-40 Les Paul/GA-40T/Mariner: tremolo,

22" wide, 15 1/2" high, brown leatherette cover on lower part, dark brown leatherette on upper third, dark brown wicker pattern grille, grill insert with *LP* monogram, *Gibson* above grille, top-mounted controls, 1 12" Concert series Jensen speaker, 8 tubes, 4 inputs, foot switch with 15' cord

Introduced as **GA-40 Les Paul: 1952**

20" high, 22" wide, rectangular grille, mottled grey/brown cover on lower part, dark brown leatherette above grille, *Gibson 40* above grille, small oval *Les Paul* plate below grille, no monogram on grille, 1 12" Jensen speaker, 7 tubes, 4 inputs, 5 knobs, 14–16 watts, leather handle: **1955**

8 tubes: **1956**

Metal handle with plastic inserts: **1958**

Renamed: **GA-40T Les** Paul, tweed cover, *Gibson* in upper right corner of grille: **1960**

Renamed **Mariner**, tan cover, brown grille, 26" wide, 20" high, 1 12" speaker, 6 tubes, 4 inputs, 6 knobs, 25 watts

Discontinued: **1967**

GA-8 Gibsonette/Discoverer: 13" high, 17 1/2"
wide, tan fabric cover, rectangular grille, dark brown
grille cloth, *Gibsonette* above grille, 1 10" Jensen
speaker, 2 inputs, 1 knob, 8 watts, leather handle
Introduced as **Gibsonette: 1952**
20" wide, 16" high, gold fabric cover, *Gibson* above
grille, 9 watts, metal handle with plastic insert: **1958**
Gibson in upper right corner of grille: **1960**
Renamed **Discoverer**, 10 watts: **1962**
Discontinued: **1964**

GA-8T/Discoverer: tremolo, 20" wide, 16" high, gold
fabric cover, *Gibson* in upper right corner of grille, 1
10" Jensen speaker, 9 watts, metal handle with plastic insert
Introduced: **1960**
Tan cover, brown grille, 1 12" speaker, 5 tubes, 7 knobs,
15 watts: **1963**
Discontinued: **1967**

GA-90: bass amp, 24 1/2" wide, 20" high, rectangular
wicker-pattern grille, *Gibson 90* slightly right of center, dark brown cover, 6 8" Jensen speakers, 8 tubes,
preamp, 4 inputs, 2 channels, 7 knobs, gain control
switch, 25 watts, metal handle with plastic insert
Available: **1953–60**

GA-77/Vanguard: 20" high, 24" wide, rectangular
grille, mottled brown/grey cover on lower portion,
dark brown leatherette on portion above grille,
Gibson 77 on front, 6 tubes, 1 15" Jensen speaker,
4 inputs, monitor output jack, 5 knobs, 25 watts
Introduced as **GA-77: 1954**
22" wide, 20 1/8" high, *Gibson* above grille, 4 inputs,
6 knobs, off/standby/on knob, 35 watts, metal handle with plastic insert: **1958**
Renamed **Vanguard**, tweed cover, *Gibson* in upper
right corner of grille, 35 watts: **1960**
Discontinued: **1962**

GA-77RV: reverb, 6 knobs: **1961**

GA-77RVT: reverb, tremolo, 22" wide, 20 1/8" high,
Gibson in upper right corner of grille, 4 inputs,
6 knobs, off/standby/on knob, 35 watts, metal han-
dle with plastic insert
Introduced: **1962**
Tan cover, brown grille, 8 tubes, 4 inputs, 10 knobs:
1963
Last made: **1967**

GA-77RVTL: reverb, tremolo, JBL speaker: **1961–66**

GA-77RET: tremolo, reverb, 28" wide, 20 1/2" high,
black vinyl cover, silver grille, controls on front, *Gibson* on upper left grille, 2 10" speakers, 4 inputs, 13
knobs
Available: **1964–67**

GA-77RETL: 1 15" Lansing speaker
Available: **1964–67**

GA-55: 20" high, 26 1/2" wide, rectangular grille,
mottled grey/brown cover on lower part, dark brown
leatherette above grille, *Gibson 55* above grille, 2
12" speakers, 6 tubes, 4 control knobs, 20 watts
Available: **1954–58**

GA-55V: vibrato: **1954–48**

GA-7: specs unavailable
Available: **1954–56**

GA-70/Country and Western: 22" high, 20"
wide, vertical grille, *Gibson* and steer head on grille,
mottled grey-black cover on lower part, dark brown
leatherette on upper third, 1 15" Jensen speaker,
6 tubes, 4 inputs, 25 watts, metal handle with plastic insert
Available: **1955–58**

GA-15: specs unavailable
Available: **1955–56**

GA-20T/Ranger: tremolo, *Gibson 20T* logo, 7
tubes, 5 knobs, 16 watts
Introduced as **GA-20T: 1956**
Named **Ranger**, tweed cover, *Gibson* in upper right
corner of grille: **1960**
Discontinued: **1962**

GA-5/Les Paul Junior/Skylark: 13 1/2" wide,
11 1/2" wide, rectangular grille, *Gibson* above grille,
tan fabric cover, 5" x 7" oval speaker, 3 tubes, 2
inputs, volume control, Les Paul signature on control plate, 4 watts
Introduced: **1956**
Mottled brown finish, round speaker, Les Paul signature and *TV model* on control plate: **1957**
Renamed **Skylark**, 13 1/2" high, 13 1/2" wide, gold
cover, 1 8" Jensen speaker, 3 tubes, 2 inputs, volume control, 4 1/2 watts, leather handle: **1958**

19 1/2" wide, 15" high, tan cover, brown grille, 5 tubes, 2 inputs, 3 knobs, 10 watts: **1963**

17 1/4" wide, 14 3/4" high, black vinyl cover, silver grille cloth, controls on front, no logo on grille cloth, 3 tubes, 1 10" speaker, 2 inputs, 4 knobs: **1966**

Discontinued, model name continues as solid state model (see following): **1968**

GA-5T/SkylarkT: tremolo, 6 knobs (model name continues on solid state model, see following): **1960–67**

GA-Super 400: 28" wide, 20" high, rectangular grille, mottled grey/brown fabric cover on lower part, dark brown leatherette on upper third of cabinet, *Gibson 400* on grille, 2 12" speakers, 12 tubes, 3 channels, 6 jacks to left of knobs, 9 knobs, 60 watts, metal handle with plastic insert, cabinet handles on sides, 4-wheel dolly base

Introduced: **1957**

Vinyl tweed-pattern cover, no dolly base: **1960**

Jacks below knobs, small rectangular grille on back panel: **1962**

Discontinued: **1964**

GA-200 Rhythm King: bass amp, 28" wide, 20" high, rectangular grille, mottled grey/brown fabric cover on lower part, dark brown leatherette on upper third of cabinet, *Gibson 400* on grille, 2 12" speakers, 11 tubes, 2 channels, preamp, 4 jacks to left of knobs, 6 knobs, 60 watts, metal handle with plastic insert, cabinet handles on sides, 4-wheel dolly base

Introduced as **GA-200: 1957**

Renamed **Rhythm King**, vinyl tweed-pattern cover, no dolly base: **1960**

Jacks below knobs, small rectangular grille on back panel: **1962**

Discontinued: **1964**

GA-85: 17 3/4" wide, 26" high, rectangular grille, cover on front, dark cover on sides and back, gold grille cloth, *Gibson* on grille, 1 12" Jensen speaker, removable chassis, 6 tubes, 4 jacks, 5 knobs, on/standby/off knob, 25 watts, leather handle

Available: **1957–58**

GA-88S Stereo-Twin: 2 cabinets, 23 3/4" wide, 22" high, tweed cover, *Gibson* in upper right corner of grilles, removable controls, 2 12" speakers, 8 tubes, 6 knobs, on/standby/off knob, 35 watts

Available: **1959–61**

GA-86 Ensemble: 17 3/4" wide, 26" high, tweed cover *Gibson* on grille, 1 12" Jensen speaker, removable chassis, 7 tubes, 4 jacks, 6 knobs, on/standby/off knob, 35 watts, leather handle

Available: **1959–60**

GA-83S Stereo-Vib: 26 1/4" wide, 21 1/2" high, tweed cover, *Gibson* in upper right grille, additional speaker openings on sides and back, 4 8" and 1 12" speakers, 13 tubes, 4 inputs, 3 pointer knobs, 3 round knobs, 35 watts, metal handle with plastic insert

Available: **1959–61**

GA-80 Vari-Tone: tremolo, preset tones, 22" wide, 20" high, tweed cover, *Gibson* in upper right corner of grille, 1 15" Jensen speaker, 7 tubes, 4 inputs, 6 chicken-head knobs, 6 pushbuttons for preset tones, 2 round knobs, 25 watts, metal handle with plastic insert

Available: **1959–61**

Catalogued as **GA-80T** but none shipped: **1962**

GA-80: specs unavailable: **1959**

GA-79T: stereo, tremolo, trapezoidal cabinet shape, front panel 11" wide, back panel 25 3/4" wide, 18 3/4 high, side panels at 45-degree angle to front, speaker openings, 2 oblong openings on front panel, *Gibson 79* on front panel, 2-10" Jensen speakers, 9 tubes, 4 inputs, 6 knobs, 30 watts

Available: **1960–61**

GA-79RVT Multi-Stereo: stereo, reverb, tremolo, 5 inputs, 6 round knobs (2 tone, 2 volume, reverb depth, tremolo frequency), 2 stereo-out mini-jacks, *Multi-Purpose* on control plate

Introduced as **GA-79RVT: 1961**

Jensen speakers not specified

Named **Multi-Stereo**, black cover, silver grille cloth

Introduced: **1961**

Tan cover, brown grille: **1963**

Last made: **1967**

GA-79RV: stereo, reverb: **1961**

GA-18T Explorer: tremolo, 5 tubes, 3 inputs, monitor speaker jack (only specs available)

Introduced: **1956**

20" wide, 16 1/2" high, tweed cover, *Gibson* in upper right corner of grille, 1 10" speaker, 5 tubes, 3 inputs, 4 knobs, 14 watts, metal handle with plastic insert: **1961**
Discontinued: **1964**

GA-300RVT: chassis removable from cabinet, reverb, tremolo, 9 tubes, 4 inputs, 11 knobs
Available: **1962–63**

GA-60: 5 tubes, 2 inputs (only specs available)
Available: **1962–63**

GA-14 Titan: 20" wide, 16" high, vinyl tweed cover, *Gibson* in upper right corner of grille, 1 10" speaker, 5 tubes, 4 inputs, 3 knobs, 14 watts, metal handle with plastic insert
Available: **1959–61**

GA-100: bass amp, 22" wide, 20" high, vinyl tweed cover, *Gibson* in upper right grille, 1 12" speaker, removable chassis with 3 legs, 9 tubes, 2 inputs, 3 knobs, 35 watts, metal handle with plastic insert
Available: **1960–64**

GA-87: specs unavailable
Available: **1960**

GA-45RVT Saturn: not a Maestro model, reverb, tremolo, 25 1/2" wide, 17 1/2" high, black vinyl cover, silver grille cloth, *Gibson* in upper left of grille, 2 10" speakers, 10 knobs
Available: **1965–67**

GAV-1: vibrato unit, 6" wide, 6" high, brown cover
Available: **1955–60**

GA-78: Bell 30 Stereo model, tremolo, 8 tubes (only specs available)
Available: **1960**

GA-75: 24" high, 20" wide, mottled brown leatherette cover, round speaker grille with vertical slats, top-mounted controls, 1 15" speaker, 7 tubes, 5 inputs, 25 watts, logo in upper right corner, leather handle
Available: **1950–55**

GA-75 Recording: 20" wide, 22" high, controls mounted near back edge of top panel, black vinyl

cover, silver grille cloth, *Gibson* in upper right grille, 2 10" speakers, 4 inputs, metal handle with plastic insert
Available: **1964–67**

GA-75L: 1-15" Lansing speaker: **1964–67**

GA-8T: specs unavailable
Available: **1960**

GA-19RVT Falcon: tweed cover, 1 12" speaker, 7 tubes, 5 knobs
Introduced: **1961**
Tan cover, brown grille: **1963**
Discontinued, Falcon name continues on solid state model (see following): **1967**

GA-25RVT Hawk: reverb, tremolo, 26" wide, 20" high, tan cover, brown grille, 1 15" speaker, 7 tubes, 4 inputs, 7 knobs
Available (model name continues on solid state model, see following): **1963–67**

GA-17RVT Scout: reverb, tremolo, 22" wide, 18" high, tan cover, brown grille, 1 10" speaker, 6 tubes, 4 knobs
Available: **1963–65**

Titan I: piggyback design, tremolo, trapezoid-shape cabinet and head(wider at base than at top), 38" wide, 24 3/4" high, tan cover, brown grille, no logo on grille, model name above grille, 2 12" speakers, 11 tubes, 4 inputs, 11 knobs
Available: **1963–65**

Titan III: piggyback design, tremolo, trapezoid-shape cabinet and head (wider at base than at top), 38" wide, 24 3/4" high, tan cover, brown grille, no logo on grille, model name above grille, 1 15" and 2 10" speakers, 11 tubes, 4 inputs, 11 knobs
Introduced: **1963**
Rectangular cabinet and head, black cover, silver grille, model name above logo, 2 handles on speaker cabinet, cabinet mounted on wheels: **1965**
Last made: **1967**

Titan V: piggyback design, tremolo, trapezoid-shape cabinet and head (wider at base than at top), 38" wide, 24 3/4" high, tan cover, brown grille, no logo on grille, model name above grille, 2 15" JBL speakers, 11 tubes, 4 inputs, 11 knobs

Introduced: **1963**

Rectangular cabinet and head, black cover, silver grille, logo in upper right corner of grille, model name above logo, 2 15" Lansing speakers, 2 handles on speaker cabinet, cabinet mounted on wheels: **1965**

Last made: **1967**

Atlas IV: piggyback design, trapezoid-shape cabinet and head (wider at base than at top), 38" wide, 24 3/4" high, tan cover, brown grille, no logo on grille, model name above grille, 1 15" speaker, 5 tubes, 2 inputs, 4 knobs

Introduced: **1963**

Rectangular cabinet and head, black cover, silver grille, model name above logo, 1 15" speaker, 2 inputs, 4 knobs, 2 handles on speaker cabinet, cabinet mounted on wheels: **1965**

Last made: **1967**

Atlas IV L: Lansing speakers: **1967**

Mercury I: piggyback design, tremolo, trapezoid-shape cabinet and head (wider at base than at top), 38" wide, 24 3/4" high, tan cover, brown grille, no logo on grille, model name above grille, 2 12" speakers, 7 tubes, 4 inputs, 11 knobs

Available: **1963–65**

Mercury II: piggyback design, tremolo, trapezoid-shape cabinet and head (wider at base than at top), 38" wide, 24 3/4" high, tan cover, brown grille, no logo on grille, model name above grille, 1 15" and 1-10" speaker, 7 tubes, 4 inputs, 11 knobs

Introduced: **1963**

Rectangular cabinet and head, black cover, silver grille, model name above logo, 1 -15" and 1 10" speakers, 4 inputs, 11 knobs, 2 handles on speaker cabinet, cabinet mounted on wheels: **1965**

Last made: **1967**

Mercury 2L: Lansing speaker, 8 tubes (only specs available): **1967**

Mercury Medalist: specs unavailable

Available: **1964–66**

Atlas Medalist: 26 1/2" wide, 28 1/2" wide, black cover, silver grille, no logo on grille, controls on

front, *Atlas* on upper left control plate, 1 15" speaker, 2 inputs, 5 knobs, mounted on wheels

Available: **1964–67**

Custom 402A: recessed front control panel, 1 12" speaker, 4 knobs

Available: **1964**

GA-4RE: reverb/echo unit, black vinyl cover, silver grille cloth

Available: **1964–67**

GA-3RV: reverb unit, black vinyl cover, silver grille cloth

Available: **1964–67**

Titan Medalist: 1 15" speaker and 1 10" speaker, 11 tubes, tilt-back support

Available: **1964–67**

GA-15RVT Explorer: not a Maestro model, reverb, tremolo, 20" 1/2 wide, 16 3/4" high, black vinyl cover, silver grille cloth, *Gibson* in upper left grille, 1 10" speaker, 3 inputs, 7 knobs

Available: **1965–67**

GA-95RVT Apollo: tremolo, reverb, 28" wide, 20 1/2" high, black vinyl cover, silver grille clothe, logo in upper left of grille, 2 12" speakers, 4 inputs, 12 knobs

Available: **1965–67**

GA-95RVTL: Lansing speakers: **1966–67**

GA-55RVT Ranger: reverb, tremolo, 28" wide, 15 1/4" high, black vinyl cover, silver grille cloth, *Gibson* in top center of grille, 4 10" speakers, 4 inputs, 11 knobs

Available: **1965–67**

GA-55RVTL: Lansing speakers: **1967**

GA-29RVT: specs unavailable

Available: **1965–67**

GA-20RVT Minuteman: reverb, tremolo, 20" wide, 16 3/4" high, black vinyl cover, silver grille cloth, *Gibson* in upper left grille, 1 12" speaker, 4 inputs, 10 knobs

Available: **1966–67**

GA-35RVT Lancer: reverb, tremolo, 25 1/2" wide, 17 1/2" high, black vinyl cover, silver grille cloth, *Gibson* in upper left grille, 1 12" speaker, 4 inputs, 10 knobs
Available: **1966–67**

Duo Md. Lt.: specs unavailable
Available: **1967**

Medalist 410: 4 10" speakers (only specs available)
Available: **1967**

Thor: bass amp, 2 10" speakers (only specs available)
Available: **1967**

SOLID-STATE MODELS, 1960S

TR-1000T Starfire: transistor (solid state), tremolo, 22" wide, 18" high, charcoal cover, grey grille, 1 12" speaker, 7 knobs, 40 watts
Available: **1962–66**

TR-1000RVT: reverb, tremolo: **1963–65**

GSS-100: separate amp and 2 speaker cabinets, vibrato, tremolo, reverb, amp 24 1/2" wide, 11 1/2" high, speaker cabinets 24" wide, 12" high, black vinyl cover, silver grille, 2 10" speakers per cabinet, 4 inputs, 11 knobs, 100 watts
Available: **1966–67**

GSS-50: tremolo, reverb, 23 3/4" wide, 20" high, black vinyl cover, silver grille, 2 10" speakers, 4 inputs, 11 knobs, 50 watts
Available: **1966–67**

Plus-50: extension amp, 24" wide, 12" high, black vinyl cover, silver grille, 2 10" speakers
Available: **1966–67**

Skylark: 13 1/4" wide, 18 3/4" high, black vinyl cover, 1 10" speaker, 3 knobs
Available: **1968–69**

Skylark T: tremolo, 4 knobs: **1968–69**

Falcon: black vinyl cover, 1 12" speaker, 4 inputs, 9 knobs
Available: **1968–69**

Hawk: 14 3/4" wide, 24 1/2" high, black vinyl cover, 1 10" speaker, 4 knobs
Available: **1968–69**

MAESTRO MODELS

GA-45T Maestro Standard: accordian amp, tremolo, 22" wide, 20" high, rectangular grille, grey fabric cover on lower part, dark leatherette on upper part, gray grille cloth, *Maestro Accordian Amplifier* above grille (no Gibson logo), 4 8" Jensen speakers, 7 tubes, 4 inputs, 6 pointer knobs (2 volume, bass, treble, tremolo depth and "frequency"), 14 watts, metal handle with plastic insert
Introduced as **Maestro: 1955**
Maestro above grille: **1958**
Renamed **Maestro Standard**, tweed cover, *Maestro* on grille, 16 watts: **1960**
Discontinued: **1961**

GA-46T Super Maestro: accordian and bass amp, vibrato, 20" wide, 20" high, mottled grey/brown fabric cover on lower part, black leatherette on upper third, *Maestro Super* on grille, 2 12" speakers, 10 tubes, 4 inputs, 8 knobs, 60 watts, metal handle with plastic insert, 4-wheel dolly base
Introduced: **1957**
Tweed cover, no dolly base, cabinet handles on side: **1960**
Discontinued: **1962**

GA-16T Maestro Viscount: 20" wide, 16 1/2" high, vinyl tweed cover, *Maestro* in upper right grille, 5 tubes, 3 inputs, 4 pointer knobs (volume, tone, tremolo depth and frequency), 14 watts
Available: **1959–60**

GA-2RT Maestro Deluxe Reverb-Echo: reverb, tremolo, 20 wide, 16 high, vinyl tweed cover, *Maestro* on upper right grille, 7 tubes, 1 12" Jensen speaker, 4 inputs, 5 round knobs (2 volume, tone, reverb and stacked knob for tremolo control), 16 watts, metal handle with plastic insert
Available: **1961**

GA-1RT Maestro Reverb-Echo: reverb, tremolo, 18 3/4" wide, 13 1/2" high, vinyl tweed cover, *Maestro* on upper right grille, 3 tubes, 1 12"

Jensen speaker, 1 input, 2 pointer knobs (volume, tremolo speed), 8 watts, leather handle
Available: **1961**

GA-1: specs unavailable: **1961**

GA-1RVT: 4 tubes, 2 inputs, 3 knobs (volume, reverb, tremolo): **1961**

GA-87 Stereo Maestro: 23 3/4" wide, 22" high,
Maestro Stereo on grille, 2 12" speakers, 8 tubes, 4 inputs, 6 knobs, on/standby/off knob, 35 watts, metal handle with plastic insert
Available: **1961**

GA-78RV Maestro 30 Stereo: accordian amp,
stereo, reverb, trapezoidal cabinet shape, front panel 11" wide, back panel 25 3/4" wide, 18 3/4 high, side panels at 45-degree angle to front, speaker openings, 2 oblong openings on front panel, silver-flecked charcoal cover, *Maestro 30* on front panel, 2 10" Jensen speakers, 5 inputs, 6 round knobs, 2 stereo-out mini-jacks, 30 watts
Available: **1961**

GA-78RVT: Maestro model, reverb, tremolo (only specs available): **1961**

GA-78RVS: Maestro model, reverb, stereo (only specs available): **1961**

GA-45RV: reverb (only specs available)
Available: **1961**

Bell-15RV: reverb, 7 tubes (only specs available)
Available: **1961**

GA-15RVT: accordian amp, reverb, 22" wide, 20"
high, black vinyl cover, *Maestro 15RV* on upper right grille, 7 tubes, 4 inputs, 5 round knobs (2 volume, bass, treble, reverb), 14–16 watts, metal handle with plastic insert
Available: **1962**

M-1RVT: reverb, tremolo (only specs available)
Available: **1962–63**

M-2RVT: reverb, tremolo (only specs available)
Available: **1962–63**

M-216RVT: reverb, tremolo
Available: **1963**

M-202: no specs available
Available: **1963**

M-201: no specs available
Available: **1962–63**

GIBSON, 1970S

Most with black cabinet cover, black grille, logo in upper right corner of grille.

LP-12: Les Paul model, piggyback, cabinet 28" wide, 45 1/4" high, cabinet on casters, 4 12" speakers, 2 horns, high- and low-impedance inputs, 12 knobs, 190 watts
Available: **1970**

GSS-100: 2 speaker columns each with 4 -10" speakers: **1970**

GSS-100HC: 2 speaker columns each with 2 12" speakers and 1-14" horn: **1970**

GSS-100HCL: Lansing speakers: **1970**

Medalist 2/12: reverb, tremolo, 2 12" speakers,
100 watts: **1970**

Medalist 4/10: tube amp, reverb, tremolo, 4 10"
speakers: **1970**

Thor: bass amp, 18 3/4" wide, 31 1/4" high, 2 10"
speakers, 2 inputs, 3 knobs, 50 watts: **1970–74**

G-10: 20" wide, 15" high, 1 -10" speaker, 2 inputs, 5 knobs, 10 watts: **1972–75**

G-20: tremolo, 21" wide, 17" high, 1 10" speaker, 2 inputs, 6 knobs, 10 watts: **1972–75**

G-30: 22" wide, 19" high, 1 12" speaker, 2 inputs, 6 knobs, 15 watts: **1972**

G-40: tremolo, reverb, 24 1/2" wide, 20" high, 1 12" speaker, 2 inputs, 6 knobs, 20 watts: **1972**

G-50: tremolo, reverb, 24 1/2" wide, 20" high, 1 12" speaker, 4 inputs, 9 knobs, 40 watts: **1972**

G-60: tremolo, reverb, 27 1/2" wide, 22 1/2" high, 1 15" speaker, 4 inputs, 9 knobs, 60 watts: **1972**

G-70: tremolo, reverb, 27 1/2" wide, 22 1/2" high, 2 -12" speakers, 4 inputs, 9 knobs, 60 watts: **1972**

G-80: tremolo, reverb, 27 1/2" wide, 22 1/2" high, 4 10" speakers, 4 inputs, 9 knobs: **1972**

Super Thor: tremolo, reverb, 24 3/4" wide, 44 1/2" high, 2 15" speakers, 4 inputs, 6 knobs, 65 watts: **1972–74**

GA-5WTR: tremolo, reverb, 15 " wide, 17" high, 1 10" speaker, 2 inputs, 4 knobs, foot control, 5 watts: **1973–75**

GA-5WT: tremolo, no reverb, 3 knobs: **1973–75**

GA-5: 2 knobs: **1973–75**

G-115: 4 10" speakers, phase shift, 100 watts: **1975**

G-105: 2 12" speakers, phase shift, 100 watts: **1975**

G-100A: 2 12" speakers, no phase shift, 100 watts: **1975**

G-55: 1 12" speaker, phase shift, 50 watts: **1975**

G-50A: 1 12" speaker, no phase shift, 50 watts: **1975**

G-35: 1 12" speaker, 15 watts: **1975**

G-50B: bass amp, 1 15" speaker, 50 watts: **1975**
G-100B: bass amp, 2 15" speakers, 100 watts: **1975**

E-65: 1975

E-75: 1975

E-20B: bass amp, 1 -15" speaker, 3 knobs (volume, treble, bass): **1975**

GA-88S: 11 tubes, 2 cabinets, 22" high, 23 3/4" wide; 20 3/8" high, 22 1/2" wide, date unavailable

GA-83S: specs and date unavailable

LAB SERIES

Designed by Moog, a division of Norlin (Gibson's parent company). All have the following features: *LAB SERIES* logo plate in upper left corner of cabinet

(both speaker cabinet and amp cabinet on piggy-back models), compressor and master controls at right end of control plate, 3-band EQ controls
The following model series appeared in a 1979 brochure.

L-2: bass amp, piggyback, single channel, 1 15" speaker, 100 watts

L-3: guitar amp, combo, single channels, 1 12" speaker, 60 watts

L-4: bass amp, piggyback, two channels, 2 15" speakers, 200 watts

L-5: guitar amp, combo, two channels, 2 12" speakers, 100 watts

L-7: guitar amp, combo, two channels, 4 10" speakers, 100 watts

L-9: guitar amp, combo, two channels, 1 15" speaker, 100 watts

L-11: guitar amp, piggyback, two channels, 8 12" speakers, 200 watts

GENESIS

Gibson logo in upper left corner of grille.
The following models were listed in a circa 1980 brochure.

G10: 14" wide, 13.5" high, 1 8" speaker, 3-band EQ, 10 watts

G25R: 23" wide, 19 1/4" high, 1 10" speaker, 3-band EQ, 25 watts

G25: no reverb

G40R: 2 10" speakers, 40 watts

B40: bass amp, 18 3/4" wide, 19 1/4" high, 1 12" speaker, 3-band EQ, 40 watts

LAB SERIES 2

Gibson logo in upper left corner of grille.
The following models were listed in a circa 1980 brochure.

GA60R-10: 24 1/2" wide, 18" high, 1 10" speaker, 60 watts, also sold as head unit with separate 2 12" or 4 10" cabinets

GA60R-12: 24 1/2" wide, 18" high, 1 12" speaker, 60 watts

GA120R-10: 27 1/2" wide, 27" high, 4 10" speakers, 120 watts

GA120R-12: 27 1/2" wide, 20" high, 2 12" speakers, 120 watts

B79: 20 3/4" wide, 22" high, 1 15" speaker, 3-band EQ, 70 watts

B120: 26" wide, 27" high, 1 15" speaker, 6-band EQ, 120 watts, also sold as head unit with separate 1-15" cabinet

GIBSON LABS

All with gold/orange cover, gold grille, available in the early 1990s.

Classic Gold: tube preamp, 85 watts

Gold Chorus: 80 watts

GB 440: bass amp, 2 cabinets, 4 10" speakers, 1 15" speaker

COMMENTS

Prewar models are sought by collectors. Some models from the late 1940s and 1950s, particularly those with Jensen speakers, are sought by players and collectors. The early version of the Les Paul model, with *LP* grille insert, is collectible. Most postwar tube models are considered to be good utility amplifiers, although Gibson amps in general are not nearly as highly regarded as Fenders. Solid state models are generally not highly regarded.

OTHER BRANDS MADE BY GIBSON

Gibson was one of many manufacturers that supplied instruments to distributors and mail-order companies under various house brands. Gibson also marketed instruments under its own budget brands.

Unlike Martin and Epiphone, whose commercial-brand models typically have the same construction as regular line models but with different ornamentation, Gibson's commercial- and budget-brand models were designed to be less expensive to manufacture—primarily due to their lack of an adjustable truss rod in the neck—and thus different from the models that carried the Gibson brand. Also unlike Martin and Epiphone, Gibson devoted a significant percentage of its production effort to budget brands.

Gibson began commercial-brand production around 1929 for Montgomery Ward. The period of highest production lasted from the mid 1930s until 1942, when Gibson diverted almost all production activity to war products. The Kalamazoo brand was revived on a few models shortly after World War II and

again on a line of solidbody electrics from 1965–70. Gibson provided guitar bodies, necks and fingerboards to National/Valco (see National/Valco, General Information) from 1946 through the 1950s.

Kalamazoo (Gibson's in-house brand), Kel Kroydon, Recording King (Montgomery Ward) and Cromwell (used by various distributors) are the only Gibson-made brands that would not be considered rare. Gibson also made instruments under other brands for foreign distribution. Undoubtedly, more brands and models exist than are listed in this section.

DIFFERENCES BETWEEN GIBSON BRAND AND BUDGET BRAND MODELS

No Gibson budget brands have a Gibson stamp or logo.

No Gibson budget brand models have an adjustable truss rod, except for the postwar Kalamazoo guitars.

All budget brand archtops have a slightly smaller bridge and shorter *f*-holes than Gibson brand models.

Kalamazoo "roof top" peghead with straight edges coming to a point.

Kalamazoo peghead tapering to a sharp point.

Kalamazoo peghead and logo on a late 1960s electric bass.

Tapered peghead of a high-end Recording King, with crown and logo stenciled over pearl inlay.

GIBSON

Almost all budget brand flat tops have straight-across "ladder" top bracing. Dreadnoughts have X-braced tops, as do the L-2 size S.S. Stewart, Trujo Model B, Kel Kroydon KK-1 and KK-2, and possibly other models.

Exceptions: Gibson made occasional instruments in the late 1930s and early 1940s with the Gibson brand but with budget-brand specifications.

SECTION ORGANIZATION

Ambassador
Capital
Carson Robison
Coast Wholesale
Cromwell
Fascinator
Francis Day & Hunter
Grinnell
Hayden
Kalamazoo
Kel Kroydon
Liberty
Martelle
Marshall
Mason
Mastertone
Mitchell Brothers
Nouveau
Old Kraftsman
Oriole
Orville
Paynes
Recording King/Ward
Reznick Radio
Spiegel
S.S. Stewart
Tex Star
Trujo
Ward
Washburn
Werlein Leader

AMBASSADOR

Gretsch and Brenner sold instruments under the Ambassador brand. They were made by various makers, including Harmony, Kay and Gretsch. Gibson supplied a limited number of guitars in 1936. They may have a paper label inside with *Gretsch and Brenner*.

M-5: similar to Cromwell G-4, arched (not carved) top, 16" wide, mahogany back and sides: **1936**

M-7: specs unavailable

M-9: similar to early Cromwell G-5, arched (not carved) top with X-pattern bracing, 16 1/4" wide, 20 1/2" long, 3 1/2" deep at sides, mahogany back and sides, arched and braced back, triple-bound top, single-bound back, bound pickguard with straight sides, mahogany neck, bound rosewood fingerboard, slotted-diamond inlays, peghead tapers to a point, rosewood peghead veneer, pearl *Ambassador M-9* inlaid at an angle, Grover G-98 tuners with metal buttons, dark sunburst finish on top, back and sides: **1936**

M-11: specs unavailable, possibly similar to early style Cromwell G-6: **1936**

M-15: specs unavailable, possibly similar to early style Cromwell G-8: **1936**

C-5: specs unavailable, possibly similar to Kalamazoo KG-11: **1936**

G-7: specs unavailable, possibly similar to Kalamazoo KG-14: **1936**

CAPITAL

Capital was the house brand of J.W. Jenkins Sons Music Co., a Kansas City mail order house. Capital guitars have the Jenkins name on a small rectangular paper label.

Flat top: probably model J-1, L-0 size, 14 3/4" wide, mahogany back and sides, L-0 type pickguard with upper part cut off, single-bound soundhole, single-bound top and back, rosewood fingerboard, large dot inlay at frets 3, 5 and 7, plus 2 small dots inlaid at 12th fret, line inlaid down center of fingerboard, peghead tapers to a point, script *Capital* peghead logo stenciled in white, sunburst finish
Available: **1936–38**

J-1: flat top, probably similar to Cromwell G-1 or Kalamazoo KG-11

JTG-1: tenor

GIBSON

J-2: archtop, probably similar to Cromwell G-4

JTG-2: tenor

J-3: archtop, probably similar to Cromwell G-3 or Kalamazoo KG-21

J-4: archtop, probably similar to Cromwell G-4 or Kalamazoo KG-22

J-15: specs unavailable: **1938**
J-16: specs unavailable: **1938**
J-20: specs unavailable: **1938**
J-17: specs unavailable
J-18: specs unavailable
J-20: specs unavailable: **1938**

JM-2: mandolin, similar to Cromwell GM-2 or Kalamazoo KM-11

JM-4: mandolin, similar to Cromwell GM-4 or Kalamazoo KM-21

EJ-H: lap steel, similar to Cromwell EG-H, pear-shaped maple body, screw-on back, blade pickup in oval housing, knobs on opposite sides, rosewood V-end fingerboard, dot inlay, center stripe down fingerboard, peghead tapers to a point, pearl script *Capital* peghead logo, sunburst finish

EJ-5: electric Spanish, similar to Cromwell EG-5

EJ-M: electric mandolin, similar to Cromwell EG-M

EJ-A: amplifier, similar to Cromwell amplifier

CARSON ROBISON:

See Recording King, following

COAST WHOLESALE

See Mason, following

CROMWELL

Cromwell instruments were distributed by several mail order companies, including Grossman, Richter and Phillips, and Continental.

1935–36: Gibson pickguards, pickguard brackets and tailpieces, large dot inlays on the fingerboard (a few with a white line of binding material down center of fingerboard), "roof top" peghead with straight edges coming to a point,

1937–late 1939: Most with line of binding material down the center of the fingerboard and *Cromwell* in block letters straight across the peghead.

G-1: flat top, similar to Kalamazoo KG-11, 14 3/4" wide, 17 1/2" long body, mahogany back and sides, "roof top" peghead with straight edges coming to a point, white stenciled logo
Available: **1935–36**

G-2: 14 3/4" wide, flat top, L-0 size, similar to Kalamazoo KG-14, mahogany back and sides, rectangular bridge, white bridge pins, bound top and back, Gibson prewar type pickguard with upper part cut off, rosewood fingerboard, "roof top" peghead with straight edges coming to a point, white stenciled logo, sunburst finish
Introduced: **1935**
Peghead tapers to point at top, described in Continental catalog as gleaming black finish but pictured with sunburst top: **1938**
Discontinued: **late 1939**

GT-2: tenor version of G-2: **1935–late 1939**

G-3: arched (not carved) top, 14 3/4" wide, L-30 size, similar to Kalamazoo KG-21, pressed mahogany back, mahogany sides, bound top and back, white stenciled logo
Available: **1935–36**

G-4: 16" wide, arched (not carved) top, *f*-holes, similar to Kalamazoo KG-31, mahogany back and sides, adjustable bridge, trapeze tailpiece, double-bound top and back, unbound pickguard, unbound rosewood, "roof top" peghead with straight edges coming to a point, pearl logo, sunburst top finish, brown finish on back and sides
Introduced: **1935**
Peghead tapers to a point: **1938**
Discontinued: **late 1939**

GT-4: tenor version of G-4: **1935–late 1939**

G-5: 16" wide, carved X-braced top, *f*-holes, maple

back and sides, adjustable bridge, trapeze tailpiece, multiple-bound top, bound back, single-bound pickguard, single-bound fingerboard, "roof top" peghead with straight edges coming to a point, pearl logo, sunburst finish
Introduced: **1935**
Peghead tapers to point at top: **1937**
Discontinued: **late 1939**

EG-5: electric version of G-5, oval pickup with bar across middle, pickup in middle position, 3 screws in top between pickup and fingerboard, pickguard cutout to accommodate pickup, 2 knobs on treble side by *f*-hole, side jack, a few early examples with pearl logo, most with stenciled logo: **1937–38**

ETG-5: tenor version of EG-5: **1937–38**

G-6: 16" wide, carved top, *f*-holes, mahogany back (arched but not carved) and sides, adjustable bridge, trapeze tailpiece, double-bound top and back, checkered marquetry around top, elevated pickguard with checkered marquetry around edge, bound rosewood fingerboard with checkered marquetry on sides, pearl logo, "roof top" peghead with straight edges coming to a point, sunburst finish
Introduced: **1935**
Maple back and sides, adjustable bridge, trapeze tailpiece, double-bound top and back, double-bound pickguard, single-bound fingerboard, double-arrowhead inlay (like Gibson L-10 of same period), most with no center line down fingerboard, peghead tapers to a point at top, ornamental peghead inlay, pearl logo, metal tuner buttons, light brown sunburst finish: **1938**
Discontinued: **late 1939**

G-8: 16" wide, 4" deep, carved top, *f*-holes, mahogany back (pressed) and sides, bound top and back, bound pickguard, bound rosewood fingerboard, multiple small diamond inlay, "roof top" peghead with straight edges coming to a point
Available: **1935–36**

GM-2: mandolin, A-style body, round hole, flat top and back, mahogany back and sides, non-adjustable bridge, clamshell tailpiece cover, triangular pickguard glued to top, single-bound top and back, rosewood fingerboard, "roof top" peghead with straight lines coming to point, pearl logo, sunburst

top finish
Available: **1935–late 1939**

GM-4: mandolin, A-style body, *f*-holes, arched (not carved) top and back, mahogany back and sides, adjustable bridge, clamshell tailpiece cover, elevated pickguard, bound top and back, rosewood fingerboard, "roof top" peghead with straight lines coming to point, sunburst top finish
Available: **1935–late 1939**

EG-H: lap steel, pear-shaped body with narrow shoulders, curly maple top and back, blade pickup in oval housing with thick binding, 2 adjustment screws at ends of pickup, 2 knobs on opposite sides (shown in catalog with knobs on treble side), large rectangular bridge/tailpiece, bound top, unbound screw-on back, rosewood V-end fingerboard, dot inlay, center stripe down fingerboard, peghead tapers to a point, sunburst finish, early examples with pearl logo and metal tuner buttons, later with stenciled logo and white plastic buttons, 6 or 7 strings
Available: **1937–38**

EG Amplifier: dark brown cloth covering with horizontal yellow stripes, detachable back, metal corners, 10" speaker, 6 tubes, 3 inputs, 2 knobs for mic and instrument volume, 8–10 watts
Available: **1937–38**

FASCINATOR

The Fascinator line was distributed by Tonk Bros. Co. of Chicago. Peghead tapers to a sharp point at top. Peghead logo is stenciled on a pearl rectangle with *Fascinator* in block letters diagonally across. Descriptions and model numbers are from the 1935 Tonk Bros. catalog.

4960: L-0 size flat top, 14 3/4" wide, maple back and sides, bound top and back, rosewood fingerboard, dot inlay, sunburst finish

4970: 16" wide, arched top and back, *f*-holes, mahogany back and sides, adjustable non-compensating bridge, trapeze tailpiece, single-bound triangular pickguard, triple-bound top, single-bound back, rosewood fingerboard specified as bound but pictured without binding, dot inlay, 3 dots at 12th fret

4980: 16" wide, arched top and back, *f*-holes, mahogany back and sides, adjustable non-compensating bridge, trapeze tailpiece, single-bound triangular pickguard, single-bound top and back, single-bound rosewood fingerboard, varied-pattern inlay with 5-piece crosslike pattern at 3rd fret, peghead specified as bound but pictured without binding, V-shape peghead inlay with small diamond in V, sunburst finish

5284: A-style mandolin, *f*-holes, arched top and back, mahogany back and sides, adjustable non-compensating bridge, clamshell tailpiece cover, elevated pickguard, single-bound top and back, rosewood fingerboard, dot inlay, sunburst finish

FRANCIS DAY & HUNTER

Francis Day & Hunter was a British distributor.

FDH: also listed as FDH Special, similar to Cromwell G-6
Available: **1937–38**

GRINNELL

Flat top: model made for music store chain based in Detroit, flat tops similar to KG-14 and KGH-14 (Hawaiian)
Available: **1940**

HAYDEN

Flat top: similar to Cromwell G-2, "roof top" peghead with straight sides coming to a point, no other specs available
Available: **late 1936**

KALAMAZOO, 1933–42

Kalamazoo was Gibson's in-house budget brand.
Logos: The prewar Kalamazoo logo is stylized print, almost like script but with unjoined letters (letter *z* resembles numeral *3*). The postwar logo is script with joined letters.
Oriole: The Oriole brand was first used by Gibson in the late 1920s on budget banjos, which have *Oriole* on the peghead, no Gibson logo and no bird decal. The Oriole name was revived in 1940 for a line of Kalamazoo models with tortoiseshell celluloid binding and natural finish (tan finish on the lap steel).

Kalamazoo/Oriole models have *Kalamazoo* and a decal of a bird on the peghead.
Body sizes: Gibson catalogs specify L-0 and L-30 models as 14 3/4" wide. Kalamazoo flyers specify grand concert size as 14 1/2" wide. Unless otherwise specified, the Kalamazoos are, in fact, the same body size and shape as the Gibson equivalent.

KALAMAZOO PEGHEAD SHAPES, 1933–42

Square top of peghead, KG-11 Spanish: **1933–42**
"Roof top" peghead with straight edges leading to a point…
    All models except KG-11 Spanish, mandolins, mandolas and mando-bass: **1935–38**
    Mandolins, mandolas, and mando-bass, except Oriole models: **1937–42**
Peghead tapers to a sharp point, except for KG-11, Oriole guitars, all mandolins and mandolas: **1938–41**
Standard Gibson peghead with dip in center, Oriole models only: **1940–42**

KALAMAZOO FLAT TOPS

KG-10: see Kalamazoo, 1965–70, following

KG-11: flat top, 14 3/4" wide, 17 1/2" long body (1 3/4" shorter than 14-fret L-0 body size), mahogany back and sides, no pickguard, some with checkered soundhole ring, bound top, unbound back, dot inlay, squared-off peghead, sunburst top finish, dark mahogany back and sides finish,
Introduced: **1933**
Pickguard follows contour of body (but not as far into upper bout as Gibson models): **1936**
Discontinued: **1941**

Senior: same as KG-11 but with firestripe pickguard, *Senior* vertically on peghead under *Kalamazoo* logo: **1933–34**

KHG-11: Hawaiian, straight saddle, 12 frets clear of body, high nut, "roof top" peghead shape: **1936–40**

KTG-11: tenor: **1935–40**

KG-14: flat top, L-0 size, mahogany back and sides, bound top, pickguard follows contour of body (but not as far into upper bout as Gibson models), unbound back, unbound rosewood fingerboard, dot inlay, sunburst finish
Available: **late 1936–40**

GIBSON

KHG-14: Hawaiian, straight saddle, 12 frets clear of body, high nut: **late 1936–41**

KTG-14: tenor: **late 1936–40**

KG-3/4 Sport Model: 3/4-size flat top, 12 3/4" wide, mahogany back and sides, bound top, rosewood fingerboard, dot inlay, sunburst finish
Available: **1937–41**

KHG-3/4: Hawaiian, 12 frets clear of body: **1937–41**

KGN-12: Oriole model, L-0 size, mahogany back and sides specified, most with maple back and sides, pickguard follows contour of body (but not as far into upper bout as Gibson models), tortoiseshell celluloid binding on top and back, unbound fingerboard, dot inlay, bird decal on peghead, natural finish
Available: **1940–41**

KHG-12: Hawaiian, 12 frets clear of body, sunburst finish: **1939–41**

KTG-12: tenor: **1939–41**

KHGN-12: Hawaiian, 12 frets clear of body: **1940–41**

KTGN-12: tenor: **1940–41**

KG-12: sunburst finish, listed but few if any made: **1940–41**

KES-R: electric flat top, earliest with KG-11 style short body, later L-0 size, 2-segment blade pickup in black oval housing, pickup mounted on circular plate in soundhole, 2 pickup mounting screws through plate, 1 octagonal knob with pointer, rosewood fingerboard, dot inlay, shaded top finish, mahogany back and sides finish, tenor available (both body styles)
Available: **1938–40**

KG: 16 instruments on shipping totals, specs unavailable: **1953**

KALAMAZOO ARCHTOPS

KG-21: L-30 size, 14 3/4" wide, arched (not carved) spruce top and mahogany back, *f*-holes, L-30 size, adjustable bridge, trapeze tailpiece, unbound black pickguard, bound top, unbound rosewood fingerboard, dot inlay, sunburst finish on top only
Introduced: **early 1936**
Bound back, side position dots on neck, sunburst

finish on back and sides: **late 1936**
Discontinued: **1941**

KTG-21: tenor: **1935–39**

KHG-21: Hawaiian, 9 shipped: **1938–39**

KG-31: L-50 size, 16" wide, arched (not carved) spruce top and mahogany back, bound top and back, adjustable bridge, brown pickguard, trapeze tailpiece, unbound rosewood fingerboard, dot inlay, sunburst finish, tenor available
Introduced: **1935**
Bound top and back, bound pickguard, bound fingerboard: **late 1936**
Discontinued: **1940**

KTG-31: tenor: **1935–40**

KPG-31: plectrum, 1 shipped: **1938**

KG-22: L-50 size, 16" wide, carved spruce top, carved maple back, adjustable bridge, trapeze tailpiece, unbound pickguard, bound top and back, rosewood fingerboard, dot inlay, sunburst finish
Available: **1940–42**

KTG-22: tenor: **1937–39**

KHG-22: Hawaiian, 3 shipped: **1939**

KG-32: arched top and back, *f*-holes, L-50 size, 16" wide, spruce top, maple back and sides, adjustable bridge, trapeze tailpiece, single-bound pickguard, tortoiseshell celluloid binding on top and back, unbound rosewood fingerboard, dot inlay, ebony nut, sunburst finish
Available: **1939–42**

KGN-32: Oriole model, bird decal on peghead, natural finish: **1940–42**

KHG-32: Hawaiian, 1 shipped: **1940**

KG-16: arched top and back, *f*-holes, L-30 size, mahogany back and sides, adjustable bridge, trapeze tailpiece, unbound pickguard, bound top, unbound back, unbound rosewood fingerboard, dot inlay, mist brown finish
Available: **1939–41**

KES: electric, L-30 size, arched top and back, metal-covered pickup with no visible polepieces in bridge

position, 1 knob, bound top, unbound back, elevated pickguard, unbound rosewood fingerboard, dot inlay
Available: **1939–40**

KES-R: Oriole model, tortoiseshell celluloid binding, bird decal on peghead, natural finish: **1940**

KES-TG: tenor, 1 shipped: **1940**

KES-150: electric, L-50 size, no other specs available
1 shipped: **1940**
Appears on shipping totals, specs unavailable:
1949–52

KALAMAZOO ELECTRIC HAWAIIANS

KEH: lap steel, guitar-shaped maple body, 2-segment blade pickup with oval housing, 5-sided control plate, bound top, rosewood fingerboard, dot inlay, peghead tapers to a point, chocolate brown finish
Introduced: **1938**
7-string or 8-string optional: **1940**
5-sided control plate, rectangular metal covered pickup with raised center, knobs on opposite sides, metal fingerboard, cream crinkled paint finish with brown sunburst sides: **1941**
Discontinued: **1952**
Reintroduced, stairstep shape, metal fingerboard similar to Gibson BR-4, red-brown finish: **1946**
Discontinued: **1947**

KEHC: specs unavailable: **1940**

KEH-R: Oriole model, guitar-shaped mahogany body, 5-sided control plate, no binding, dot inlay, tan finish, bird decal on peghead
Introduced: **1940**
Metal pickup cover, dark-colored metal fingerboard, fancy markers, sunburst finish: **1941**
Discontinued: **1942**

KEA/KEH amp: 10" speaker, round grille, 60 cycle or 25 cycle
Available: **1938–41, 1946–52**

KEAC: amplifier, specs unavailable: **1939**

KALAMAZOO MANDOLIN FAMILY

KM-11: A-style, round hole, flat top and back (described as slightly arched), mahogany back and sides, brown pickguard glued to top, non-height

adjustable bridge, clamshell tailpiece cover, unbound rosewood fingerboard, dot inlay at frets 5, 7 and 9, squared-off peghead, sunburst top finish, brown back and sides finish
Introduced: **1935**
Height-adjustable bridge, bound fingerboard, "roof top" peghead shape: **late 1936**
Discontinued: **1941**

KM-21: A-style, f-holes, arched (not carved) spruce top and mahogany back, adjustable bridge, clamshell tailpiece cover, bound top, unbound pickguard, unbound rosewood fingerboard, dot inlay, sunburst finish
Introduced: **early 1936**
Bound top and back, bound pickguard, bound fingerboard: **late 1936**
Discontinued: **1940**

KH-21: mandola, same style as KM-21 mandolin, sunburst finish
Available: **1936–39**

KM-12: A-style, f-holes, maple back and sides, clamshell tailpiece cover, unbound pickguard, tortoiseshell celluloid binding on top and back, unbound fingerboard, dot inlay, sunburst finish
Available: **1939–42**

KMN-12: Oriole model, bird decal on peghead, natural finish: **1940–42**

KM-22: mandolin, A-style body, f-holes, maple back and sides, clamshell tailpiece cover, bound top and back, bound pickguard, bound fingerboard, dot inlay, sunburst finish
Available: **1939–42**

KH-22: mandola, same trim as KM-21 mandolin, sunburst finish
4 shipped: **1939**

KK-31: mandocello, same style as KG-31 guitar, 24 3/4" scale, sunburst finish
Available: **1936–38**

KK-32: mandocello, same body and trim as KG-32 guitar
2 shipped: **1940**

KJ: mando-bass, A-style body shape, *f*-holes, 24" wide, arched (not carved) spruce top and maple back, bound top, dot inlay, 42" scale, brown sunburst finish Available: **1936–38**

KALAMAZOO BANJOS

KTB: tenor, 11" maple rim, 23" scale, maple resonator and neck, no flange, unbound rosewood fingerboard, dot inlay, peghead tapers to a point Available: **1935–41**

KPB: plectrum: **1935–40**

KRB: 5-string: **1935–41**

KMB: mandolin banjo: **1935–41**

KALAMAZOO, 1965–70

Except for the KG-10 flat top, all Kalamazoo models from 1965–70 are electric solidbodies with the following general specs:

Asymmetrical double cutaway shape similar to many Fender models, Melody Maker pickup(s) with white cover, bolt-on neck, rosewood fingerboard, dot inlay, peghead shape similar to Fender with 6-on-a-side tuner arrangement, red, white or blue finish: **1965–c. 1968**

SG-body shape, symmetrical double cutaway with pointed horns, no bevels in cutaways, same peghead shape and tuner arrangment as earlier version: **c. 1968–70**

Serial numbers: Kalamazoo solidbody electrics have a 6-digit serial number impressed into the back of the peghead. Although the numbers appear to be standard Gibson numbers, they are inconsistent with numbers on Gibson brand instruments. Some numbers are from series that were used in more than one year; some numbers fall outside of recorded serial number ranges; some numbers have 000 as the first 3 digits (which on the Gibson line indicates a 1973 date of manufacture). These numbers are from a separate series that applies to Kalamazoos only.

KG-1: 1 pickup, no vibrato: **1965–69**

KG-1A: 1 pickup, flat-plate vibrato: **1965–69**

KG-2: 2 pickups, no vibrato: **1965–69**

KG-2A: 2 pickups, flat-plate vibrato: **1965–70**

KB: electric bass, 1 large rectangular pickup at neck, metal handrest, dot inlay, 4-on-a-side tuner arrangement, flame red, glacier white or Las Vegas blue finish: **1966–70**

KG-10: flat top, similar to LG-0, all mahogany, narrow peghead (like Melody Maker electric solidbody): **1968–69**

KALAMAZOO AMPS, 1965–67

1: 14" wide, 15 7/8" high, dark grey vinyl covering, 10" speaker, front control panel, 2 inputs, 2 knobs: **1965–67**

2: same as model 1 but with tremolo, 3 knobs: **1965–67**

3: solid state, 13" wide, 16 1/8" high, dark grey vinyl covering, 10" speaker, front control panel, 2 inputs, 2 knobs: **1965–67**

4: same as model 3 but with tremolo, 3 knobs

Reverb 12: tremolo, reverb, 18 1/2" wide, 16" high, black vinyl covering, 12" speaker, 5 tubes, front control panel, 2 inputs, 6 knobs: **1965–67**

Bass 30: 25 1/2" wide, 20" high, black vinyl covering, 2 10" speakers, tilt-out control panel, 4 tubes, 3 knobs, 30 watts: **1965–67**

Bass 50: 50 watts: **1965–67**

KEL KROYDON

Kel Kroydon was an in-house budget brand, introduced in 1930 and produced possibly as late as 1933. The significance of the name is unknown. The banjos are fairly common; guitar and mandolin models are relatively rare.

KK-1: flat top guitar, L-0 body, 14 3/4" wide, spruce top with 2 tropical birds stenciled, birds facing each other with tails curling under bridge and plumes curling around soundhole, mahogany back and sides, bound top, 12 frets clear of body, unbound ebonized (black-stained) fingerboard, dot inlay, orange logo

KK-2: flat top guitar, L-0 body, 14 3/4" wide, spruce top with Hawaiian scene stencil (2 volcanos, palm trees, and a boat), mahogany back and sides, bound top, 12 frets clear of body, pearloid fingerboard, art deco markers, *Kel* stenciled horizontally across top of peghead, *Kroydon* stenciled vertically, tenor available

KK-10: banjo, very similar to Gibson TB-1 (see Gibson banjos) except for logo, no truss rod

KK-11: banjo, pearloid fingerboard, very similar to Gibson TB-11 (see Gibson banjos) except for logo, no truss rod, black finish
Available: **early 1930s**

KK-20: mandolin, similar to Gibson C-1

KK-21: mandolin, pearloid fingerboard

LIBERTY

Flat top: short body, similar to Kalamazoo KG-11, squared-off peghead, *Liberty* brand in white silkscreen on peghead, brand/stamp on back of peghead reads *Fully Made by Gibson, Inc.* above *Kalamazoo, Mich.*, small area of sunburst finish on top
Available: **early 1930s**

MARSHALL

Flat top: similar to Kel Kroydon KK-2, volcano scene stenciled on top, bound top and back, black and orange geometric markers, *MarShall* stenciled horizontally across top of peghead, *Special* (beginning with *S* in *MarShall*) stenciled vertically
Available: **c. 1930**

MARTELLE

The distributor of the Martelle brand is unknown. Some Martelle-brand instruments were made by Regal.

Deluxe: flat top, 16" wide, round-shouldered dreadnought shape, laminated maple back and sides, rectangular pin bridge, elevated pickguard, 3-ply soundhole ring, single-bound top and back, celluloid fingerboard with black binding, rosewood dot inlay, small pearl slotted-diamonds inlaid into rosewood dots, wriggle-top peghead with protrusion in center, celluloid peghead veneer, *Martelle* stenciled in block letters horizontally across peghead, *Deluxe*

stenciled in block letters vertically, gold-plated planetary (banjo style) tuners, pearl tuner buttons, sunburst finish: **c. 1934**

Deluxe variation: flat top, 16" wide, round-shouldered dreadnought shape, similar to Gibson Roy Smeck Stage Deluxe, mahogany back and sides, Gibson peghead shape with *Martelle* stenciled in block letters horizontally across peghead, *Deluxe* stenciled in block letters vertically: **c. 1934**

MASON

Instruments with the Henry L. Mason brand were distributed by Coast Wholesale and produced by various makers. Gibson shipped limited numbers of instruments to Coast from 1936–39. Most models are similar to Cromwell models (see preceding). Only the CW-4 had production of more than 100 instruments.

CW-2: flat top, L-0 size, similar to Cromwell G-2 and Kalamazoo KG-14: **1936–39**

CWT-2: tenor version of CW-2, similar to Cromwell GT-2: **1937**

CW-4: archtop, L-50 size, mahogany back and sides, similar to Cromwell G-4 and Kalamazoo KG-22: **1936–39**

CWTG-4: tenor version of CW-4, similar to Cromwell GT-4: **1937**

CW-5: archtop, maple back and sides, similar to Cromwell G-5 and Kalamazoo KG-31: **1936–39**

CW-6: archtop, similar to Cromwell G-6: **1936–38**

CWM-2: mandolin, flat top and back, similar to Cromwell GM-2: **1936–38**

CWM-4: mandolin, arched top back, similar to Cromwell GM-4 and Kalamazoo KM-21: **1936–38**

CWM-6: specs unavailable

EG-5: similar to Cromwell EG-5

Amplifier: specs unavailable

GIBSON

MASTERTONE

Gibson introduced the Mastertone name in the 1920s as a model line for high-end Gibson banjos, and it continues as such today. In 1941 a Mastertone line of electrics was marketed as an in-house budget brand. Gibson also marketed a Hawaiian acoustic and possibly other acoustic Mastertone models.

Acoustic Hawaiian: flat top, 14 3/4" wide, 17 1/2" long (1 3/4" shorter than 14-fret L-0 body size), mahogany back and sides, 12 frets clear of body, brown finish: **1939–42**

MESG: electric flat top, all mahogany, metal-covered pickup mounted on round plate, plate in soundhole, 1 octagonal knob with pointer, bound top and back, bound fingerboard, dot inlay, *Mastertone Special* on peghead: **1939–42**

MEHG: lap steel, mahogany body, no binding, 5-sided control plate, cream-colored metal fingerboard, fancy markers, peghead tapers to point at top, *Mastertone Special* on peghead, tan ripple-spun finish: **1939–41**

Banjo: tenor, 5-string, plectrum and mandolin-banjo styles: **1937–41**

MITCHELL BROTHERS

Instruments with the Mitchell Brothers brand were available through Montgomery Ward. Model numbers are Ward's catalog numbers.

732/1586: banjo, maple resonator and neck, *Mitchell Bros.* stenciled on peghead, sunburst finish
Introduced as **732: late 1934**
Smaller logo or Ward logo: **early 1935**
Renumbered **1586: late 1935**
Discontinued: **late 1936**

NOUVEAU

Gibson introduced a line of flat top guitars under the *Nouveau by Gibson* brand in 1986. Nouveau bodies and necks were made in Japan and then shipped unassembled to the U.S., where they were then assembled and finished. Electric models joined the line in 1987.

Gibson moved the acoustic Nouveaus to the Epiphone line, under the brand *Nouveau by Epiphone,* by September 1987. Electrics were moved to Epiphone by February 1988. The entire Nouveau line was discontinued by early 1989.

NOUVEAU BY GIBSON

NV6: acoustic flat top, square-shouldered dreadnought, maple back and sides, Martin-style belly bridge and teardrop pickguard, bound fingerboard: **1986–87**

NV6R: rosewood back and sides: **1986–87**

NV6R-S: rosewood back and sides, solid spruce top: **1987**

NVT: NV6 with tortoiseshell celluloid binding: **1987**

NV12: 12-string: **1986–87**

NV185: acoustic flat top, jumbo size: **1986–87**

C7: F-style mandolin: **1986–87**

NVJ: full-depth *f*-hole archtop, 1 floating pickup, controls on pickguard, zigzag tailpiece: **1987**

Spotlight: solidbody electric, double-cutaway with short treble horn, 2 humbucking pickups, 1 knob, 2 switches, vibrato, V inlay: **1987**

X-1000: solidbody electric, double-cutaway similar to Fender Stratocaster, 1 humbucker and 2 single-coil EMG pickups, 2 knobs, 3 mini switches, locking nut vibrato, triangular inlay, 6-on-a-side tuner arrangement: **1987**

NOUVEAU BY EPIPHONE

Unless otherwise noted, specs are the same as for Nouveau by Gibson models.

NV6: 1988

NV6R: 1988

NV6RS: 1988

NVT: 1988

NV12: 1988

NV185: 1988

C7: 1988

NVJ: 1987

X-1000: 1987–88

Spotlight: 1987–88

Spotlight CMT: curly maple top: **1988**

Firebird 300: 1988

Firebird 500: 1988

OLD KRAFTSMAN

The Old Kraftsman brand was owned by the Spiegel mail-order company. Most Old Kraftsman instruments were made by Kay. Gibson-made instruments appeared in Spiegel catalogs only from fall 1936 through spring 1937.

Four-digit numbers are Spiegel catalog numbers; S-prefix numbers are Gibson numbers.

2154/8707: carved top, 16" wide, maple back and sides, bound top and back, bound pickguard, bound fingerboard, dot inlay, pictured in catalog with "roof top" peghead with straight sides coming to a point, stenciled vase and curlicues on peghead, *Old Kraftsman* stenciled in block letters across peghead
Introduced as 2154: **1936**
Renumbered **8707**, peghead tapers to a point, *Old* horizontally across peghead, *Kraftsman* vertically: **early 1937**
Discontinued: **late 1937**

8708: similar to Recording King M-5, carved top, 16" wide, maple back and sides, bound top and back, bound pickguard, bound fingerboard, inlay of diamond with 3 horizontal lines on each side to form rectangle, peghead tapers to a point, *Old* horizontally across peghead, *Kraftsman* vertically, additional lines and small diamonds on peghead around logo, sunburst finish
Available: **spring 1937**

S-34/8709: electric archtop, 16" wide, maple back and sides, oval pickup, volume control on upper

bass bout, hardwired cord coming out of tailpiece, bound top and back, bound pickguard, unbound fingerboard, dot inlay, some with *Old Kraftsman* in block letters across peghead with vase and curlicues ornament, some with *Old* horizontally across peghead, *Kraftsman* vertically
Available: **spring 1937**

S-36/8710: electric Hawaiian guitar and amp set, round body shape, bound top, screw-on back, oval pickup with no height adjustment screws, maple bridge/tailpiece, metal saddle, 1 knob on bass side, jack on bass side, unbound fingerboard, dot inlay, peghead tapers to a point, stenciled vase and curlicues on peghead, *Old Kraftsman* stenciled in block letters across peghead
Available: **spring 1937**

ORIOLE

Gibson first used the the Oriole brand in the 1920s on an inexpensive banjo. The Oriole designation was revived in the Kalamazoo line (see preceding) on models with natural finish, all of which have the *Kalamazoo* brand.

Oriole tenor banjo: 10 1/2" head diameter, no resonator, 21" scale, bound ebonized fingerboard, dot inlay, pointed-top peghead, script *Oriole* peghead logo (no *Gibson* logo), London grey finish
Introduced: **c. 1926**
Fleur-de-lis peghead ornament, mahogany finish: **c. 1927**
Discontinued: **by 1932**

ORVILLE

Instruments bearing the *Orville* or *Orville by Gibson* brand are *not* made by Gibson. Beginning around 1990, Gibson licensed the name to a Japanese distributor. Orville-brand instruments are approved copies of Gibson models, manufactured and distributed in Japan.

PAYNES

Flat top: similar to Kalamazoo KG-11
Available: **1937**

Recording King/Ward

Recording King and Ward were house brands used by the Montgomery Ward company from 1929–43. Some Recording King and Ward guitars were made by Gibson; others were made by Kay, Regal and Gretsch.

The Recording King brand was first used as a model name on instruments supplied by Gibson in 1929. By 1931 it was a brand name for a line of fretted instruments. In 1935 and 1936 the company used Ward as a brand name. The Recording King brand resumed in 1937, but many examples from 1935–37 have no brand.

From 1938 into spring 1940, Ward used the Recording King brand only on Gibson-made instruments. Those made by other companies had no brand.

Some Recording Kings have a Gibson style serial number stamped onto the back of the peghead or (in the case of lap steels) on the back of the body. These numbers have a 2- or 3-letter prefix, the 2nd letter of which is *W* for Ward. The Recording King crown logo is a king's crown and is quite different from the "crown" peghead inlay on later high-end Gibsons.

The catalog of spring 1940 marked the last of the Gibson-made Recording Kings. The brand continued in use until 1943 (on instruments mostly made by Kay), after which Ward switched to the Sherwood brand.

Model numbers are Ward's catalog numbers.

Recording King/Ward Guitar Peghead Shapes

Squared-off: **1931–late 1934**

"Roof top" with straight sides coming to a point
  All models: **early 1935–1936**
  Some models retain "roof top": **1936–40**

Curved sides, top tapers to a point, most models: **spring 1937–summer 1940**

Recording King Banjos

Recording King 505/506: *Recording King* is model name (not brand), tenor, similar to Gibson Style 6, maple rim, neck and resonator, 2-piece flange with hexagonal holes, checkered binding, hearts and flowers inlay, chrome-plated hardware
Introduced as model 505: **fall 1929**

Replaced by model **506**, lower price, unspecified wood, possibly mahogany: **late 1930**
Discontinued: **late 1931**

Studio King/772: plectrum (**641**) or tenor (**645**), mahogany rim, neck and resonator, 2-piece flange with hexagonal holes, similar to Gibson Style 4 of the same period (except for flange)
Variation: 1 example with 1-piece flange, 40-hole tone ring and similar construction to Gibson Style 3
Introduced: **late 1929**
Renumbered **772**: **early 1932**
Discontinued: **late 1932**

Recording King 803: tenor, walnut resonator and neck, inlay similar to Gibson Style 3: **early 1933–early 1934**

731: tenor, similar to Kalamazoo KTB, maple resonator, mahogany neck, guitar style peghead with straight edges coming to a point, sunburst finish: **early 1934–early 1935**

1586: tenor, maple resonator and neck, similar to Kalamazoo KTB, non-Mastertone tone ring, dot inlay, guitar style peghead with peak in center, Grover tuners with 2-1 gear ratio: **1935**

1593: tenor, maple resonator and neck, deeper resonator than model 1586, non-Mastertone tone ring, bound fingerboard, small diamond inlay, Grover tuners with 2-1 gear ratio: **1936–40**

1584: 5-string version of model 1593: **1938–40**

952: tenor, open-back: **early to mid 1940**

953: 5-string, open back: **early to mid 1940**

954: tenor, resonator, plain ornamentation: **early to mid 1940**

955: 5-string, resonator, plain ornamentation: **early to mid 1940**

956: tenor, resonator, fancier ornamentation: **early to mid 1940**

957: 5-string, resonator, fancier ornamentation: **early to mid 1940**

Recording King/Ward Flat Tops

Recording King flat top (807/811): same body style as Gibson Nick Lucas model, 14 3/4" wide, 4 5/8" deep, mahogany back and sides, rectangular bridge, some with X-braced top, some with ladder bracing, single-bound top and back, 12 frets clear of body, squared-off peghead, pearl block on peghead with etched *Recording King*, black finish

Introduced as model 807: **spring 1931**

Replaced by model **811**, maple back and sides, most with ladder-braced top, sunburst finish: **fall 1931**

Discontinued: **late 1932**

Carson Robison (926)/Model K: named after country songwriter, flat top, 14 3/4" wide, 17 1/2" long (1 3/4" shorter than 14-fret L-0 body size, same as Kalamazoo KG-11), mahogany back and sides, single-bound top, unbound back, triple-bound soundhole, rosewood fingerboard, dot inlay, squared-off peghead, *Carson J. Robison* signature stenciled on peghead in white (no other logo or peghead ornament), sunburst top finish, tenor available (**1204**)

Introduced: **fall 1933**

Renumbered **1201: fall 1935**

Renumbered **1281**, then **1115**, L-0 body size and shape, 14 3/4" wide, 19 1/4" long, single-bound top, unbound back, smaller pickguard than on Gibson models, ebonized rosewood fingerboard, dot inlay, Hawaiian (12 frets clear of body) or standard (14 frets): **fall 1936**

Renamed **Recording King Model K**, peghead tapers to point at top, stenciled crown on peghead, stenciled *Recording King* and *Carson J. Robison* signature on peghead: **spring 1938**

Discontinued: **fall 1939**

Carson Robison Hawaiian (1134): 12 frets clear of body: **spring 1938–fall 1940**

Carson Robison 3/4 (1135): short scale, 3/4 size: **fall 1938–fall 1939**

Carson Robison jumbo (1052): flat top, 16 1/4" wide, circular lower bout (small version of J-200, like postwar Gibson J-185, no flat top equivalent in pre-war Gibson line), rectangular bridge, bound top, unbound back, rosewood fingerboard, dot inlay, "roof top" peghead with straight sides coming to a point, stenciled crown, *Recording King* and *Carson J. Robi-*

son signature on peghead, sunburst finish

Available: **fall 1939–fall 1940**

Andy Sanella: 16" wide Hawaiian, round-shouldered dreadnought, mahogany back and sides, 12 frets clear of body, inlaid fret lines, *Andy Sanella* stenciled on peghead, sunburst top finish

Available: **fall 1935–early 1936**

Ray Whitley rosewood (1027): named after country recording star, body similar to Gibson Advanced Jumbo, 16" wide, round-shouldered dreadnought, rosewood back and sides, bridge with points at either end and at belly (like 1941 Gibson J-55), bridge beveled around edges, bound soundhole, no soundhole ornamentation, tortoiseshell celluloid pickguard with vine and leaf patterns engraved around edge, 5-piece maple neck, 24 3/4" scale, single-bound rosewood fingerboard, small diamonds inlaid on fingerboard in various patterns, no truss rod; peghead ornamentation from top to nut: pearl crown, large pearl rectangle with *Recording King* stenciled in black script, *Ray Whitley* signature stenciled at an angle; peghead tapers to point at top, sunburst finish

Available: **spring 1939–spring 1940**

Ray Whitley mahogany (1028): 16" wide, round-shouldered dreadnought, mahogany back and sides, rectangular bridge, single-bound top and back, mahogany neck, rosewood fingerboard, pearl dot inlay at 5, 7, 9 and 12 (2), peghead tapers to point

Variation: bridge with 3 points and beveled edges, no signature, pearl rectangle in peghead

Available: **fall 1939–fall 1940**

Recording King/Ward Archtops

853: 14 3/4" wide, 17 1/2" long body, carved top, maple back and sides, squared-off peghead, some with *Recording King* stenciled on peghead, sunburst finish: **spring 1933–early 1935**

681: L-30 size, 14 3/4" wide, round soundhole, maple back and sides, sunburst finish: **fall 1934–early 1935**

1007: L-30 size, 14 3/4" wide, similar to Kalamazoo KG-16, mahogany back and sides, bound top and back, peghead with straight sides coming to a point, may have Ward label, sunburst finish: **1935**

1205: L-30 size, 14 3/4" wide, mahogany back and sides, laminated spruce top, bound top, unbound back, peghead tapers to a point: **fall 1935–early 1936**

1203: tenor version of 1205

1002: specs unavailable, probably 16" wide, mahogany back and sides, may have Ward label: **1935**

1206: mahogany back and sides, bound top and back: **1935**

1241: mahogany back and sides, carved top, bound pickguard, dot inlay: **1935**

1242: mahogany back and sides, carved top, 4" deep, fancy fingerboard and peghead inlay, bound pickguard: **1935–spring 1936**

Tone Crest (1282): see M-3, following

1284: f-holes, 16" wide, maple back and sides, carved top, triple-bound top, single-bound back, bound pickguard, single-bound rosewood fingerboard, "roof top" peghead with straight edges coming to a point, narrow rectangular pearl inlay across upper part of peghead (no other peghead ornament or logo), round label inside with *WARDS* framed by stylized *M* and *W*, sunburst finish
Available: **1936–37**

M-2 (1254, 1136): carved top, f-holes, 16" wide, maple back and sides, single-bound pickguard, dot inlay, top of peghead with straight edges to point, pearl logo with *WARD* in stylized block letters, round label inside with *WARDS* framed by stylized *M* and *W*, sunburst finish
Introduced as model **1254: late 1936**
Recording King brand, bound top, unbound back, dot inlay: **1937**
Named **M-2 (1136)**, bound top, back and pickguard, rosewood fingerboard, dot inlay, peghead comes to a point, pearl block inlay and stenciled crown on peghead: **1938**
Discontinued: **1941**

M-3/Tone Crest (1282, 1283, 1228, 1137, 1103):
f-hole archtop, 16" wide, maple back and sides, laminated spruce top, tortoiseshell celluloid binding on top and back, bound fingerboard, cream pickguard, dot inlay, natural finish (**1283**); the **Tone Crest** model (**1282**) is probably the same model with sunburst finish
Introduced: **late 1936**
Renumbered **1228**, carved top: **1937**
Named **M-3 (1137)**, cream binding on top, back, pickguard and fingerboard, tortoiseshell celluloid pickguard, 5-piece maple neck (with 2 rosewood laminate stripes), peghead tapers to point at top, unbound peghead, pearl peghead inlay of crown (with stenciled ornamentation) and rectangular block with *Recording King* stenciled in black script, *Model M-3* stenciled in white block letters above nut, plastic tuner buttons, sunburst finish: **1938**
Optional natural finish with tortoiseshell celluloid binding (**1103**): **1940**
Discontinued: **1941**

M-4 (1123): f-holes, 16" wide, maple back and sides, carved top, mahogany neck, bound top and back, bound peghead, small diamond inlay, bound pickguard, peghead tapers to point at top, block at top of peghead
Introduced as model **1123: 1937–39**
Named M-4, 5-ply neck: **1938**
Discontinued: **1940**

M-5 (1285, 1124, 1121): f-hole archtop, 16" wide, 4" deep, maple back and sides, adjustable rosewood bridge, trapeze tailpiece, checkered top binding, single-bound back, bound rosewood fingerboard with checkered binding on sides, small diamond inlay, diamond and block inlay on peghead, checkered binding around peghead, metal tuner buttons, chrome-plated hardware, sunburst finish
Introduced as model **1285: 1936**
Renumbered **1124**, checkered binding around pickguard, 5-piece maple neck (with 2 rosewood laminate stripes), 3-piece pearl inlay of rectangle broken by dot in center, peghead tapers to point at top, single-bound peghead, black front of peghead; pearl peghead inlays (from top to nut): crown with stenciled black ornamentation, large rectangular block with *Recording King* stenciled in black script, verti-

cal rendering of fingerboard inlay pattern: **1937**

Named **M-5**: small vertical block inlay on peghead with *Model-M5* stenciled in black: **1938**

Renumbered **1121**, 17" wide, 4" deep, 2 pearl diamond inlays on bridge base, trapeze tailpiece with 4 vertical bars and crosspiece in middle, 5-ply top binding, triple-bound back, triple-bound pickguard, single-bound fingerboard, single black line around side of binding on body and fingerboard, large diamond inlay, unbound peghead with inverted crown cutout at top of peghead, rosewood peghead veneer, same peghead inlay as earlier version except for diamond (fingerboard inlay pattern) instead of broken rectangle: **1939**

Discontinued: **1941**

M-6 (1122): M-5 with gold-plated hardware
Available: **1938–39**

1150: 16" wide, probably similar to Kalamazoo KG-22, maple back and sides, bound top and back, sunburst finish
Available: **late 1939–mid 1940**

1070: similar to Kalamazoo KG-16, 14 3/4" wide, mahogany back and sides, bound top, unbound back
2 shipped: **1939**

RECORDING KING ELECTRIC SPANISH

1270, 1128: carved top, 16 1/4" wide, *f*-holes, maple back and sides, volume knob on bass side of pickup, bound top and back, bound pickguard, peghead tapers to point (earliest with "roof top" peghead with straight sides coming to a point), some with ornate vase stenciled on peghead
Introduced as model **1270: spring 1937**
Tone control added, mounted through pickguard: **fall 1937**
Discontinued: **1939**

Roy Smeck Professional Model (1141): guitar and amp set, specs unavailable
5 sets shipped: **late 1937**

Roy Smeck A 104 (1127): carved top, 16 1/4" wide, *f*-holes, maple back and sides, oval pickup at end of fingerboard, 3 screws in top, 2 knobs on upper bass bout, rosewood adjustable bridge,

trapeze tailpiece, single-bound black pickguard, single-bound top and back, dot inlay, peghead tapers to point, pearl block peghead inlay, stenciled crown, *Roy Smeck* and *Model A104* on peghead
Introduced: **1938**
Some with bound pickup, controls on treble side: **late 1938**
Bound pickup, pickguard cutout for pickup, bound fingerboard, pearl crown on peghead: **1939**
Discontinued: **late 1040**

Model A Spanish (1140): archtop, 16 1/4" wide, *f*-holes, mahogany back and sides, 2 knobs on bass side of pickup, bound top and back, pearl block on peghead, peghead tapers to point
Available: **1938**

Model D Spanish (1010, 1110, 1114): carved top, 16 1/4" wide, *f*-holes, maple back and sides, blade pickup in oblong black housing mounted in neck position, 2 knobs on upper bass bout, trapeze tailpiece, bound top and back, unbound rosewood fingerboard, dot inlay, peghead tapers to a point, crown stenciled above logo, sunburst finish
Introduced as model **1010: fall 1938**
Mahogany back and sides: **spring 1939**
Named **Model D** (1110): **fall 1939**
Maple back and sides optional (1114): **1940**
Discontinued: **1941**

RECORDING KING ELECTRIC HAWAIIAN

1271: pear-shaped body, screw-on back, 1 knob on bass side, maple bridge, no pickup height adjustment, bound top, square-end rosewood fingerboard, "roof top" peghead with straight sides coming to a point
Available: **1937**

Roy Smeck Professional Model: guitar and amp set, specs unavailable
2 sets shipped: **late 1937**

1129: pear-shaped body, screw-on back, 2 knobs on bass side, metal bridge, height-adjustable pickup
Available: **1937–38**

Model A (1139, 1008, 1021): stairstep body, square metal control plate, "roof top" peghead with straight

sides coming to a point, large block peghead inlay, brown finish
Introduced as model **1139: 1938**
Renumbered model **1008**, bound top and back, stenciled logo: **1938**
Renumbered model **1021**, pear-shaped body, bond top and back, square control plate, peghead tapers to a point: **1939**
Discontinued: **1940**

Roy Smeck AB 104 (1151, 1023): lap steel, pear-shaped body, blade pickup in oval housing, 2 octagonal knobs, no bridge cover, single-bound top, unbound screw-on back, square-end rosewood fingerboard, peghead tapers to point; peghead ornamentation from top to nut: crown stenciled in white, pearl rectangle with *Recording King* stenciled in black script, *Roy Smeck Model-AB104* stenciled in white; sunburst finish

Introduced as model **1151: 1938**
Renumbered model **1023**: wider shoulders, wider lower bout, glued-on back, bound top and back (a few with screw-on back and no back binding), bound fingerboard with V-end: **1939**
Discontinued: **1941**

Model D Hawaiian (1005, 1109): narrow pear-shaped body, blade pickup (1 or 2 segments) in oblong black housing, oblong control plate surrounds pickup, 2 octagonal knobs on opposite sides, painted top border to simulate binding, 22 1/2" scale, unbound rosewood fingerboard with square end, dot inlay, stenciled crown and logo on peghead, "roof top" peghead with straight sides coming to a point, brown finish

Introduced as model **1005: 1938**
Larger body, peghead tapers to a point: **1939**
5-sided control plate: **1940**
Discontinued: **1941**

Roy Smeck C (1024): console electric Hawaiian, bound rectangular maple body, blade pickup in oblong housing, 2 knobs on opposite sides, rosewood fingerboard, dot inlay, 8 strings, recessed tuners, crown and Smeck signature to bass side of tuners, sunburst finish

Available: **1939–40**

RECORDING KING AMPLIFIERS

All made with chassis by Lyon & Healy and cabinet by Geib.

Model A 10" amplifier (1271, 1128, 1149):
10" speaker, 5 tubes, brown Keratol covering, volume control, 3 inputs, electronics similar to Gibson EH-100
Introduced as model **1271: spring 1937**
Renumbered model **1128: fall 1937**
Some covered with black Keratol with gray horizontal stripes: **1938**
Renumbered model **1149**, black Keratol covering with gray horizontal stripes (some still labeled model 1128), 4 or 5 tubes: **spring 1938**
Named **Model A**, some with cream covering, some with brown covering: **fall 1938**
Discontinued: **fall 1939**

1143: specs unavailable, probably 12" speaker
25 shipped: **1939**

Model A/D 8" amplifier (1001): square size, 4 vertical-oval cutouts in front, 8" speaker, 4 tubes, 2 jacks, 7 watts, gray/black crackle-effect Keratol covering, slip cover also available
Introduced as **Model A (1001): spring 1938**
Renamed **Model D: fall 1938**
Discontinued: **1941**

1013: Roy Smeck model, brown and white Keratol covering, some with black Keratol and vertical gray stripes, round grille, 12" speaker, 7 tubes, 4 inputs, 12–15 watts, electronics similar to Gibson EH-150
Available: **1938–40**

RECORDING KING MANDOLINS

807/1610: A-style body shape, similar to Kalamazoo KM-11, flat top and back, round soundhole, mahogany back and sides, bound top and back, pickguard glued to top, mahogany neck, dot inlay, squared-off peghead, some with Ward label
Introduced as model **807: fall 1934**
Renumbered model **1610: fall 1935**
Discontinued: **mid 1936**

1607: A-style, *f*-holes, similar to Kalamazoo KM-21, mahogany back and sides, laminated spruce top,

bound top and back, mahogany neck, dot inlay, squared-off peghead
Available: **1935–36**

1642: A-style, *f*-holes, maple back and sides, carved top, bound top and back, bound pickguard, peaked peghead
Available: **1936–37**

969: A-style, *f*-holes, similar to Kalamazoo KMN-12, maple back and sides, tortoiseshell celluloid binding, natural finish
Available: **1940**

REZNICK RADIO

Flat top: similar to Kalamazoo KG-11
Available: **1937**

SPIEGEL

S-1: Spiegel model S-1 appears in Gibson shipping ledgers in 1937. Spiegel marketed guitars under the Old Kraftsman brand (see preceding), some of which were made by Gibson, but specs are not available for the S-1 model.

S.S. STEWART

S.S. Stewart was a prominent banjo maker in the late 19th and early 20th century. By the time Gibson supplied instruments under the Stewart brand, it was distributed by Buegeleisen & Jacobson.

Guitar: similar to Gibson L-2 of the same period, triple-bound spruce top with X-pattern bracing, mahogany back and sides, 3-ply soundhole ring, single-bound rosewood fingerboard, dot inlay, mahogany neck, 12 frets clear of body, squared-off peghead with rosewood veneer, pearl *S.S. Stewart* and delicate design on peghead
Available: **1931–32**

Banjo: similar to Gibson TB-11 and Kel Kroydon of the same period, back of resonator covered with pearloid with Kel Kroydon peghead-style stencil, pearloid fingerboard, red-and-black stenciled fret markers with inlaid rhinestones, peghead with black feathery stencil pattern down center and 6 inlaid rhinestones
Available: **1931**

TEX STAR

Flat top: distributed by San Antonio Music, similar to Kalamazoo KG-11
Available: **1936**

TRUJO

Gibson supplied guitars for the Trujo Banjo Co. of San Francisco.

Style A: similar to Kel Kroydon KK-1, S.S. Stewart and Gibson L-2 of the period, single-bound spruce top with X-pattern bracing, mahogany back and sides, 3-ply soundhole ring, mahogany neck, 12 frets clear of body, unbound rosewood fingerboard, dot inlay, squared-off peghead painted black, inlaid pearloid rectangle approx. 1 1/2" x 5/8" with *Trujo* stenciled in black, small carved and painted leaf designs in upper corners of peghead, open-back tuners with white buttons, natural finish
Available: **1929**

Style B: L-2 size, spruce top with X-pattern bracing, rosewood back and sides, triple-bound top and back, bound soundhole with 3-ply ring, mahogany neck, 12 frets clear of body, bound rosewood fingerboard with black line on side of binding, dot inlay, standard Gibson peghead shape, black peghead with inlaid pearloid rectangle approx. 1 1/2" x 5/8", *Trujo* stenciled in black, finely carved and painted designs in corners and down center of peghead, banjo tuners
Available: **1930**

WARD

See Recording King/Ward, preceding

WASHBURN

The Washburn brand was acquired by the Tonk Bros. Co. of Chicago from Lyon & Healy in the late 1920s. Gibson supplied a small number of Washburn-brand instruments from 1938–40. Earlier and later Washburns were supplied by Regal and may be difficult to distinguish from Gibson-made examples, except that the workmanship on the inside of the body is better on Gibson-made examples.
Gibson production for most models was in the 35–50

range. Model 5240 is the only Gibson-made model with production over 100.

Junior (5240): flat top, similar to Cromwell G-2 and Kalamazoo KG-14, 14 3/4" wide: **1938–40**

Classic (5241): flat top, similar to Ward's Carson Robison model 1052, 16 1/4" wide, circular lower bout (small version of J-200, like postwar Gibson J-185), no flat top equivalent in prewar Gibson line, mahogany back and sides, bound top, bound fingerboard, dot inlay, natural finish: **1939–40**

Collegian (5242): arched (not carved) top, 16 1/4" wide, similar to early Cromwell G-4 or Kalamazoo KG-22, mahogany back and sides, mahogany neck: **1938–40**

Aristocrat (5243): carved top, 16 1/4" wide, similar to early Cromwell G-5 or Kalamazoo KG-31, mahogany back and sides, bound top and back, mahogany neck, bound fingerboard, single-parallelogram inlay, sunburst finish: **1939–40**

Inspiration (5244): flat top, described as "extra super auditorium size," possibly 16 1/4" wide, 4" or more deep, mahogany back and sides, bound top and back, 5-ply maple/mahogany neck, unbound ebony fingerboard, pearl logo, sunburst finish : **1938–40**

Solo (5246): flat top, 15 1/2" wide, no equivalent body shape in the Gibson line, rosewood back and sides, 2-ply binding on top and back, ebony bridge, 5-ply maple/mahogany neck, unbound ebony fingerboard, dot inlay, pearl logo, small protrusion at top of peghead, natural top finish: **1938–40**

Superb (5248): carved top, "extra super auditorium size," probably 16 1/4" wide, 4" or more deep, similar to Cromwell G-8 and Recording King M-5, maple back and sides, bound top and back, checkered purfling around top, checkered binding on pickguard, 5-ply maple/mahogany neck, unbound ebony fingerboard, triple-parallelogram inlay, rosewood peghead veneer, pearl logo, sunburst finish: **1939**

Solo Deluxe (5249): flat top, "large super auditorium size," 16 1/4" wide, no Gibson equivalent (possibly Regal-made), rosewood back and sides,

triple-bound top and back, 5-ply maple/mahogany neck, triple-bound ebony fingerboard, block inlay, rosewood peghead veneer, vertical pearl logo, gold-plated Kluson tuners, sunburst top finish, dark finish on back, sides and neck: **1938–40**

Inspiration mandolin (5280): probably flat-back similar to Cromwell GM-2 or Kalamazoo KM-11: **1938–39**

Classic mandolin (5281): probably arched-back similar to cromwell GM-4 or Kalamazoo KM-21: **1938–39**

WERLEIN LEADER

Electric Hawaiian set: made for Philip Werlein, similar to Kalamazoo KEH and KEA electric Hawaiian and amplifier set
Available: **1941–42**

COMMENTS

High-end Recording King and Cromwell models are roughly equivalent in construction and ornamentation to midline Gibsons. The Ray Whitley rosewood dreadnought may bring about half the price of the highly sought Gibson Advanced Jumbo. The mahogany dreadnoughts (with X-braced tops) and the 5-M (with carved top) bring nearly as much as equivalent Gibson models.

The Kel Kroydon tenor banjo is sought for conversion to a 5-string, and it approaches the Gibson TB-11 in value.

High-end Kalamazoo archtop models from the prewar period rival the low-end Gibson models for sound and playability. Kalamazoo flat tops all have ladder bracing and generally do not compare favorably to the X-braced Gibson equivalents. Most Kalamazoo models bring less on the vintage market than their Gibson equivalent.

Kalamazoo postwar solidbody electrics are not highly regarded by players or collectors.

In general, all prewar brands made by Gibson are of some historical interest to collectors, but except for the models already noted, most bring prices based on their utility.

GRETSCH

GRETSCH

GENERAL INFORMATION

The Gretsch company was formed as a tambourine manufacturer in Brooklyn, NY, in 1883 by Friedrich Gretsch, a German immigrant. After the founder's unexpected death in 1895, his son, Fred Gretsch, Sr., headed the company. Fred Gretsch, Sr. retired in 1942, leaving management to his sons Fred Gretsch, Jr., who managed the operation briefly before serving in the Navy, and William Walter (Bill) Gretsch, who headed the company from 1942 until his death in 1948. Upon Bill Gretsch's death, his brother assumed the presidency and held the position until he sold Gretsch to the Baldwin company in 1967.

The Gretsch line was expanded to include banjos and ukes by 1910 and drums by the 1920s. The first guitars—a line of tenor models—were introduced in 1927. In 1930, the company opened a Chicago office for sales and distribution only (no manufacturing), and by the mid 1930s Gretsch was a full-line instrument distributor, offering various brands of stringed instruments, drums and band instruments.

Gretsch introduced the line of Gretsch-American archtop guitars in 1933. Also in the 1933 catalog was a wide selection of other instruments and brands, including ukes, banjos, flat top and archtop tenors, Rex brand budget instruments, Kay-Kraft guitars and Harmony instruments. In 1940 Gretsch acquired B&D banjos from the Bacon company.

In the late 1930s and 1940s Gretsch became known for guitars with fancy trim and design innovations such as cat's eye soundholes on archtops and a triangular soundhole on flat tops. By the mid 1950s Gretsch's emphasis had shifted to electrics. As with the earlier acoustic models, imaginative finish colors and ornamentation became trademarks of the Gretsch electric line in the 1950s and 1960s. Chet Atkins's signature line of electric guitars played a major role in the company's success.

In 1967 the Baldwin company of Cincinnati acquired Gretsch and consolidated Gretsch guitars, Gretsch drums, Baldwin guitars and Ode banjos into one company. Sho-Bro resonator guitars, previously made by the Sho-Bud company of Nashville, were incorporated into the Gretsch guitar line. Sho-Bud pedal steels were distributed by Gretsch.

Instrument production was moved to Booneville, AR, in 1970, and administration was moved to Cincinnati in August 1972. Due to two factory fires, few if any Gretsch guitars were made from January 1973 to spring 1974.

Gretsch bought Kustom in 1978. Shortly thereafter, Gretsch was sold to Charlie Roy and administration moved to Gallatin, TN. In 1980, administration was moved to the Kustom offices in Chanute, KS.

The last guitars from the Booneville plant were made in 1981. Some guitars were assembled in Mexico until around 1983.

In 1985 Gretsch was acquired by Fred Gretsch (son of Bill Gretsch). Gretsch debuted a new guitar line in early 1990 assembled overseas from parts made in the U.S., Canada and Germany. Gretsch revived its traditional high-end Synchromatic 400/Eldorado archtop model, made by the Heritage company of Kalamazoo, MI, in 1991 and added four more models, made in the U.S. by luthier Gene Haugh, in 1995.

LABELS

Beginning in the late 1940s, labels have model number and serial number. On flat tops the label is visible through the soundhole. On open-hole archtops, the label is visible through the bass-side *f*-hole. On solidbodies and closed-hole hollowbodies, the label is on the underside of the control cover plate or in the control cavity.

White rectangular label: *The Fred Gretsch Mfg. Co.— 60 Broadway, Brooklyn, N.Y.*, no T-roof logo, serial number in red, model number in blue/black... Introduced, some models: **1940s** All models: **c. 1954**

T-roof logo: **1955**

Gray top part, orange background for *The Fred Gretsch Mfg. Co.*, beginning with serial number 25001: **1957–64**

No label, serial number on peghead: **1964–72**

That Great Gretsch Sound across bottom of label, most with 5-digit serial number beginning with 1 or 2: **c. late 1960s**

White label with black border, *Gretsch Guitars*, no address: **1972–c. 1983**

Label signed by Jim Duerloo and other principals of Heritage company, Synchromatic model: **1991–97**

GRETSCH

ARCHTOP BODY WIDTHS

Auditorium Special: 16"
Super Auditorium: 17"
Auditorium Grand: 18"

MODEL NAMES

Synchromatic, inlaid on the peghead of many models, refers to models with "synchronized" stairstep bridge and "chromatic" harp-shaped tailpiece.

In a 1939 brochure, Gretsch put *Synchromatic* after a model number—for example, No. 400 Synchromatic. In the 1949 catalog, some references to Synchromatic models have *Synchromatic* before the model number—for example, Synchromatic 400. The latter form is the one commonly used by collectors for models of all periods and is used in this section for all periods.

The 1949 catalog uses both Synchromatic model numbers and the 6000-series model numbers. A 1951 brochure uses *Synchromatic* with the 6000-series numbers only (no 100, 400, etc.), even though the 17" and 18" models are shown with a *G* tailpiece rather than the harp tailpiece that was standard equipment on Synchromatic models. In a 1952 brochure, the term *Synchromatic* is not used.

Electromatic refers to any Gretsch electric archtop from 1940–55.

PICKUPS

DeArmond: Gretsch Dynasonic, Fidela-tone, single-coil, black face, poles adjustable by a separate set of screws: **1949–57**

Filter 'Tron: double-coil, 2 rows of poles…
No markings on cover, smooth plastic frame: **very late 1957–58**
PAT. APPLIED FOR stamped on cover, ridged plastic frame: **1958–60**
Patent number on cover, ridged plastic frame: **1960–70**
Black face, no cover markings, height adjustable, metal frame: **1970–81**

Project-o-sonic stereo, optional…
Split pickups: each pickup with 3 poles and 1 bar for remaining 3 strings, bass/treble split…
White Falcon: **1958 only**
Country Club: **1958–59**
4-switch system: 4 switches on upper bass bout,

numerous tone combinations possible…
White Falcon: **1959–80**
Country Club: **1960–62**
1 pickup per channel, Double Anniversary only: **1960–62**

Hi-Lo 'Tron: single coil in humbucking case, polepieces through black face, low-end models: **1961–80s**
Super 'Tron: 2 metal bars (no screwpoles): **1964–80s**
Humbucking: screwpoles, metal cover: **1976–80s**

KNOBS

Clear plastic, barrel shape: **1949–c. 1954**
Steel, cross-hatch pattern on sides…
Plain top: **1954**
Arrow on top: **early 1955–57**
Arrow through *G* on top: **1957–mid 1967**
Aluminum, parallel ridges on sides, arrow through *G* on top…
Low-end models: **1966–80s**
High-end models: **mid 1967–80s**
Steel, cross-hatch pattern on sides, arrow through *G* on top, new models: **1990s**

BRIDGES

Ebony bridge with bone nut: **1933–late 1930s**
"Synchronized," rosewood, extended stairstep on bass side, height-adjustable (Synchromatic models): **late 1930s–53**
Rosewood height-adjustable (low-end models): **throughout**
Melita "Synchrosonic," individually adjustable saddles…
Electric hollowbodies: **1951–58**
Electric solidbodies: **1953–59**
Compensating metal, non-height-adjustable, Atkins models: **1954**
Metal bar, height-adjustable only, Atkins and some low-end models: **1955–80s**
Space Control, "roller," individual string rollers: **late 1957–80s**
Floating "tuning fork" bridge, unattached to body, tuning fork extends through hole in top into body, always used with roller bridge: **1965–72**
Adjustamatic, similar to Gibson tune-o-matic, individually adjustable string saddles: **1970–80s**
Terminator…
Similar to Fender Stratocaster bridge, spring-loaded string adjustments, Committee and Beast:

1975–80s
Standard Terminator, bridge/tailpiece unit,
adjustable saddles: **1976–80s**

TAILPIECES

Trapeze: **1933–83**
"Chromatic," harp-shaped (Synchromatic models):
late 1930s–54
G tailpiece: **1951–83**
Bigsby vibrato, *Bigsby* on base…
Arm does not rotate side-to-side, up-and-down
action only: **1955**
Arm rotates side-to-side: **1956–59**
Gretsch Bigsby, *Gretsch* and *Bigsby* on base, V-shaped
cutout: **late 1959–80s**
Burns vibrato, 3-sided pyramid protrusion at base:
1963 and after
Palm vibrato, short arm: **1963–68**

MUTES ("MUFFLERS")

Single mute with 1 rotary knob, Chet Atkins Hollow
Body: **mid 1961–63**
Single mute with 1 small lever-action knob…
Chet Atkins Hollow Body (Nashville): **1963–72**
Some Country Clubs: **1963–65**
All hollowbody basses: **1963–73**
Country Gentleman: **c. 1965–71**
Viking: **1968–69**
Double mute with 2 large rotary knobs…
White Falcon: **1960–early 1963**
Country Gentleman: **1961–early 1963**
Double mute with 2 small lever-action knobs…
Country Gentleman: **early 1963–66**
White Falcon: **early 1963–c. 1972**

NECK AND PEGHEAD

Thin "miracle neck" patented: **1949**
Script logo…
Introduced: **late 1930s**
Solidbody electrics: **1953–54**
Last script logos and Synchromatic pegheads:
late 1950s
T-roof logo (top of *T* extends from *G* to *H*) introduced…
In literature, on some drum models and (with
shorter *T*) on Broadkaster guitar: **by 1933**
New Yorker (archtop): **mid 1940s**
Model 6003 (flat top): **1951**

All models except White Falcon, White Penguin,
Eldorado and Fleetwood: **1954**
White Falcon and White Penguin: **1957**
Eldorado and Fleetwood: **by 1959**
Truss rod…
No truss rod cover or adjustment (non-adjustable
support rod concealed in neck): **1933–c. 1951**
Truss rod adjustment at body end of neck:
c. 1951–52
Truss rod adjustment at peghead…
Small truss rod cover on peghead: **1953–55**
Larger truss rod cover on peghead: **1956–70**
No truss rod cover on peghead (except Broadkaster),
Burns gearbox with cover on neck heel: **1970–80s**
Square metal peghead plate with engraved model
name (White Falcon and Country Gentleman also
have serial number on plate until 1965)…
Country Gentleman: **1958–70**
Anniversary: **c. 1958-70**
White Falcon: **1959–70**
Tennessean, Nashville: **by 1964–70**
Viking, Monkees: **mid 1960s–70**
Van Eps, Roc Jet, Streamliner: **late 1960s–70**
Made in U.S.A. stamped next to serial number: **June
1967–73**
Zero fret introduced…
Chet Atkins models: **1959**
Duo-Jets: **1962**
White Falcon, Country Club: **1963**
Sal Salvador, Astro Jet: **1965**
12-string, Viking, Double Anniversary, Rally,
Broadkaster (hollow and solid), short-scale
(single cutaway) basses, Rancher, Folk, Sun
Valley: **1968**

BOONEVILLE SPECS

Several across-the-line design changes were made
between Gretsch's acquisition by Baldwin in 1967
and the move to Booneville, AR, in 1970. These
changes include new wiring schemes, new pickup
styles, the introduction of the adjustamatic bridge
and a pickguard shape with straight lines (as
opposed to the rounded, teardrop-like shape of earlier pickguards). Old parts were used up before new
ones were implemented, so many transitional
examples were made during 1970.

DeArmond pickup with slot-head screws to adjust pole height, 1949–57.

Filter 'Tron pickup with patent-applied-for notice, used on high-end models, 1958–60.

GRETSCH

Filter 'Tron pickup with patent number, used on high-end models, 1960–70.

Hi-Lo 'Tron pickup, used on low-end models, 1961–80s.

321

Filter 'Tron pickups with no plates between poles, 1970–80s.

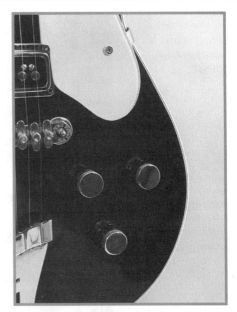

Metal knobs with plain top, 1954 only.

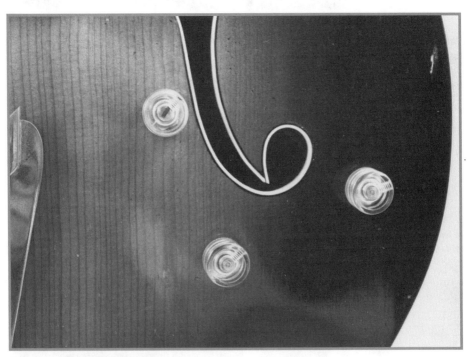

Clear plastic knobs, 1949–circa 1954.

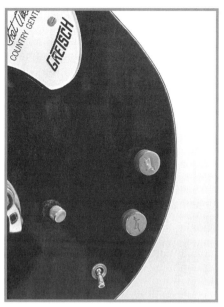

Metal knobs with arrow and G on top. Knobs from early 1955–57 have arrow only. Arrow through G appears in 1957.

Aluminum knobs with G and arrow, introduced on low-end models in 1966, on high-end models in mid 1967.

Synchromatic equipment on a 1952 Model 6192 (forerunner of Country Club): Synchronized bridge with stairstep extensions, Chromatic harp-shape tailpiece.

1961 Chet Atkins Country Gentleman with Gretsch Bigsby tailpiece, straight bar bridge 1/2" in diameter.

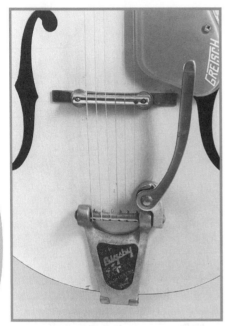

1958 Anniversary with Bigsby tailpiece, straight bar bridge 3/8" in diameter.

1955 Duo-Jet with Melita bridge, used on various models from 1951–59, and G tailpiece, first used in 1951.

Script logo, introduced in the late 1930s and used on some models into the late 1950s.

Space Control roller bridge, 1957–80s.

T-roof logo, used on a few guitar models from the 1940s, on almost all models beginning in 1954.

MODEL NUMBERS

Number approximating retail price: **1933–48**

6000-series: **1948–71**

7000-series (some overlap into 8000 series): **1971–80**

8000-series: **1979–83**

G-prefix, made overseas (except for U.S.-made G410 and G410M): **1990–current**

1955-suffix, U.S.-made reissues: **1995–current**

This list includes only U.S.-made models.

NUMBER	MODEL
410	Eldorado reissue
6000	Classic Hauser, inlaid peghead
6001	Classic Hauser, plain peghead
6002	Folk, sunburst top
6003	Model 6003, 1951–55
	Grand Concert, 1955–59
	Jimmie Rodgers, 1959–63
	Folk Singing, 1963–65
	Folk, natural top, 1965–75
6004	Burl Ives, 1952–55
	Folk, mahogany top, 1970–75
6005	Ozark Soft String
6006	Electro Classic
6007	Synchromatic Sierra
6008	Wayfarer Jumbo
6009	Jumbo Flat Top
6010	Sun Valley
6014	Synchromatic 100, sunburst, 1948–49
	Synchromatic 6014 (sunburst), 1949–55
	Corsair, sunburst, 1955–59
6015	Synchromatic 100, natural, 1948–49
	Synchromatic 6015 (natural), 1949–55
	Corsair, natural, 1955–59
6016	Corsair, Bordeaux burgundy
6020	12-string flat top
6021	Jumbo Synchromatic (Model 125F), 1948–55
6022	Rancher
6023	Bikini guitar
6024	Bikini bass
6025	Bikini doubleneck
6028	Synchromatic 160, sunburst
6029	Synchromatic 160, natural

NUMBER	MODEL
6030	Synchromatic 6030 (sunburst), 1951–55
	Constellation, sunburst, 1955–59
	Sho-Bro Spanish, 1969–71
6031	Synchromatic 6031 (natural), 1951–55
	Constellation, natural, 1955–59
	Sho-Bro Hawaiian, 1969–71
6036	Synchromatic 300, sunburst, 1948–51
	Synchromatic 6036 (sunburst), 1951–55
6037	Synchromatic 300, 1948–51
	Synchromatic 6037 (natural), 1951–55
6038	Synchromatic 6038 (sunburst), 1951–55
	Fleetwood, sunburst, 1955–59
	17" Eldorado, sunburst, 1959–68
6039	Synchromatic 6039 (natural), 1951–55
	Fleetwood, natural, 1955–59
	17" Eldorado, natural, 1959–68
6040	Synchromatic 400, sunburst, 1948–51
	Synchromatic 6040 (sunburst), 1951–55
	18" Eldorado, sunburst, 1955–70
6041	Synchromatic 400, natural, 1948–51
	Synchromatic 6041 (natural), 1951–55
	18" Eldorado, natural, 1955–70
6042	Synchromatic 400F (flat top)
6050	New Yorker
6070	Hollowbody bass, long scale, 1 pickup
6071	Hollowbody bass, short scale, 1 pickup
6072	Hollowbody bass, long scale, 2 pickups

GRETSCH

MODEL NUMBERS

NUMBER	MODEL
6073	Hollowbody bass, short scale, 2 PUs
6075	12-string electric, sunburst
6076	12-string electric, natural
6079	Van Eps 7-string, sunburst
6080	Van Eps 7-string, walnut
6081	Van Eps 6–string, sunburst
6082	Van Eps 6-string, walnut
6100	Black Hawk, sunburst
6101	Country Club, stereo, sunburst, 1959–63
	Black Hawk, black, 1968–72
6102	Country Club, stereo, natural, 1959–63
	Streamliner double cutaway, sunburst, 1969–75
6103	Country Club, stereo, Cadillac green, 1959–63
	Streamliner double cutaway, cherry, 1969–75
6104	Rally, green
6105	Rally, bamboo yellow/copper mist
6106	Princess
6111	Double Anniversary, stereo, sunburst
6112	Double Anniversary, stereo, 2–tone smoke green
6115	Rambler
6117	Double Anniversary, sunburst
	also, custom model, cat's eye sound-holes, 1965–68
6118	Double Anniversary, 2–tone smoke green
6119	Chet Atkins Tennessean
6120	Chet Atkins Hollowbody (Nashville, 1967–71)
6121	Chet Atkins Solid Body
6122	Chet Atkins Country Gentleman
6124	Anniversary, sunburst
6125	Anniversary, 2–tone smoke green
6126	Astro-Jet
6127	Duo-Jet tenor, 1959
	Roc Jet, Porsche pumpkin, 1969–71
6128	Duo-Jet
6129	Silver Jet
6130	Round Up, 1955–59
	Roc Jet, Mercedes black, 1969–73
6131	Jet Fire Bird
6132	Corvette solidbody, 1 PU, no vibrato

NUMBER	MODEL
6134	White Penguin, 1955–63
	Corvette solidbody, 1 PU, vibrato, 1963–68
6135	Corvette solidbody, 2 PUs
6136	White Falcon
6137	White Falcon, stereo
6145	Jet Airliner lap steel
6147	Jet Mainliner lap steel
6148	Jet Twin Console lap steel, no legs
6148L	Jet Twin Console lap steel, 4 legs
6152	Electromatic Student lap steel
6156	Electromatic Standard lap steel
6158	Electromatic Console lap steel
6182	Corvette hollowbody, sunburst
6183	Corvette hollowbody, natural
6184	Corvette hollowbody, jaguar tan
6185	Electromatic Spanish, sunburst, 1949–55
	Clipper, 2 PUs, sunburst, c. 1972–74
6185N	Electromatic Spanish, natural
6186	Clipper
6187	Electro II, non-cutaway, sunburst, 1951–55
	Corvette, ivory top, grey mist body, 1957
	Corvette-style, cutaway, ivory top, grey mist body, 1958
	Clipper, natural, 1959–60
	Viking, sunburst, 1967–75
6188	Electro II, non-cutaway, natural, 1951–55
	Viking, natural, 1967–75
6189	16" electric cutaway, 2 PUs, early 1950s–55
	Streamliner single cutaway, bamboo yellow/copper mist, 1955–57
	Viking, Cadillac green, 1967–72
6190	16" electric cutaway, 1 PU, sunburst, early 1950s–55
	Streamliner single cutaway, sunburst, 1955–57
6191	16" electric cutaway, 1 PU, natural, early 1950s–55
	Streamliner single cutaway, natural, 1955–57
6192	Electro II, cutaway, sunburst, 1951–54
	Country Club, sunburst, 1955–71

GRETSCH

NUMBER	MODEL
6193	Electro II, cutaway, natural, 1951–54
	Country Club, natural, 1955–71
6196	Country Club, Cadillac green
6199	Convertible, 1955–58
	Sal Salvador, 1958–68
7176	Southern Belle
7505	Folk, sunburst
7506	Folk, natural
7514	Sun Valley, sunburst
7515	Sun Valley, natural
7525	Rancher
7535	Deluxe
7545	Supreme
7555	Clipper
7560	Double Anniversary, sunburst
7565	Streamliner, sunburst
7566	Streamliner, cherry
7575	Country Club, sunburst
7576	Country Club, natural
7577	Country Club, walnut
7580	Van Eps, 7-string, sunburst
7585	Viking, sunburst
7586	Viking, natural
7593	White Falcon, single cutaway
7594	White Falcon
7595	White Falcon, stereo
7600	Broadkaster solidbody, natural
7601	Broadkaster solidbody, sunburst
7603	Broadkaster hollowbody, Bigsby, natural
7604	Broadkaster hollowbody, Bigsby, sunburst
7605	Broadkaster bass, natural
7606	Broadkaster bass, sunburst
7607	Broadkaster hollowbody, no Bigsby, natural
7608	Broadkaster hollowbody, no Bigsby, sunburst
7609	Broadkaster hollowbody, red
7610	Roc Jet, black, 1971–75
7611	Roc Jet, Porsche pumpkin, 1971–75
	Roc Jet, black, 1975–80

NUMBER	MODEL
7612	Roc Jet, cherry
7613	Roc Jet, walnut
7615	Solidbody bass
7617	BST 1000, 2 pickups, walnut
7620	Country Roc, 1974–79
	BST 2000, walnut, 1979–80
7621	Roc II
7623	Corvette solidbody, 2 pickups
7624	TK 300, autumn red
7625	TK 300, natural
7626	TK 300 bass, autumn red
7627	TK 300 bass, natural
7628	Committee
7629	Committee bass
7632	Deluxe Corvette
7635	Roc I
7655	Tennessean
7660	Nashville
7667	Streamliner II
7670	Country Gentleman
7680	Deluxe Chet, autumn red, 1973–75
	Atkins Super Axe, red rosewood, 1976–80
7681	Deluxe Chet, walnut, 1973–75
	Atkins Super Axe, ebony, 1976–80
7685	Atkins Axe, ebony
7686	Atkins Axe, red rosewood
7690	Super Chet, autumn red
7691	Super Chet, walnut
7705	Sho-Bro Hawaiian, 6–string
7710	Sho-Bro Hawaiian, 7–string
7715	Sho-Bro Spanish
8210	BST 1000, 1 pickup, walnut
8211	BST 1000, 2 pickups, red
8215	BST 1000, 2 pickups, walnut
8216	BST 1000, 1 pickup, red
8217	BST 1000, 2 pickups, walnut
8220	BST 2000, walnut
8221	BST 2000, red
8250	BST 5000

SERIAL NUMBERS

SYNCHROMATICS, 1940–49

Synchromatic models with cat's eye soundholes have a serial number stamped on the back, visible through the bass-side soundhole. They are numbered in one consecutive series, with approximate range 007–900.

NUMBER PLACEMENT, 1949–65

Ink-stamped on inside back, some *f*-hole models: **1949–55**

On label, most *f*-hole models (label on inside back), all solidbody models with control plate on back (label in control cavity or on back of control plate): **1949–65**

Scratched onto control plate, some solidbody examples: **1953–65**

Small numbers impressed into top of peghead or near top of peghead on back, Tennessean, Corvette and some other solidbody models: **1961–64**

1949–65

No Gretsch serial number list for this period is totally reliable. Although all guitars are numbered in the same series, the numbers and labels were not necessarily applied in chronological and numerical order. Example: Chet Atkins Solid Body models #23453 and #23454. The later-numbered example has humptop block inlay and no zero fret (earlier specs), while the earlier-numbered example has thumbprint inlay and a zero fret—the opposite of what the serial numbers would indicate.

NUMBER	YEAR	NUMBER	YEAR
3000s	1949–50	27000s–30000s	1958
4000s–5000s	1951	30000s–34000s	1959
5000s–6000s	1952	34000s–39000s	1960
6000s–8000s	1953	39000s–45000s	1961
9000s–12000s	1954	46000s–52000s	1962
12000s–16000s	1955	53000s–63000s	1963
17000s–21000s	1956	63000s–77000s	1964
22000s–26000s	1957	77000s–84000s	1964–early 65

1965–72

Number on back of peghead, no hyphen:

First digit or first 2 digits = month (1–12)

Next digit = last digit of year (1965–72, no 3 or 4)

Remaining digits = rank of individual instrument

Examples:

106347 = Oct. 1966, 347th instrument

72084 = July 1972, 84th instrument

787 = July 1968, 7th instrument

MADE IN USA on back of peghead next to serial number: **June 1967–73**

1973–81

Hyphenated number impressed into back of peghead with configuration **m(m)-y###**

1 or 2 digits **m(m)** = month

First digit after hyphen **y** = last digit of year

Last 3 digits **###** = rank of instrument

Example: 11-4252 = Nov. 1974, 252nd instrument

ACOUSTIC ARCHTOPS KEY

Round hole
   Scroll peghead inlay with vertical lines = **No. 50R**
   Fern peghead inlay = **No. 100R**
Cat's eye soundholes
   Ebony fingerboard
      Gold-sparkle binding
         Sunburst finish = **Synchromatic 400 (6040)**
         Natural finish = **Synchromatic 400 (6041)**
      Non-sparkle binding
         Sunburst finish = **Synchromatic 300 (6036)**
         Natural finish = **Synchromatic 300 (6037)**
   Rosewood fingerboard
      Humptop block inlay = **Synchromatic 200**
      Rectangular block inlay
         Pearl blocks = **Synchromatic 160**
         Abalone blocks = **Synchromatic 6012**
ƒ-holes
   Non-cutaway
      Diamond inlay
         Bunting and scroll peghead inlay = **No. 50, late 1930s**
         Flowers and scroll peghead inlay = **No. 65**
         Fern peghead inlay = **No. 100F**
      Rectangular inlay
         Artist on peghead = **No. 150**
         Synchromatic on peghead
            Tortoiseshell celluloid binding = **Synchromatic 115**
            White outer binding
               Sunburst finish = **Synchromatic 100 (6014), 1946–55**
               Natural finish = **Synchromatic 6015**
         Banner logo and fern peghead inlay = **Synchromatic 75**
         T-roof logo only on peghead = **Corsair**
         T-roof logo through circle on peghead = **model name unknown**
      Slashed humptop block inlay
         Sunburst = **Synchromatic 6036**
         Natural = **Synchromatic 6037**
      Varied pattern or trapezoidal inlay
         Musical note on peghead = **No. 250**
         Fern peghead inlay = **Synchromatic 100, 1940–46**
      Dot inlay
         No binding = **No. 25**
         Bound top and back
            Jet '21' on peghead = **Jet '21'**
            New Yorker or T-roof logo on peghead = **New Yorker**
            Pearl scroll logo = **No. 35**
            Bunting and scroll peghead inlay = **No. 50, 1940–49**

f-holes (continued)
Cutaway
Rectangular inlay
Sunburst finish = **Synchromatic 6030**
Natural finish = **Synchromatic 6031**
Slashed humptop block inlay
Sunburst finish = **Synchromatic 6038**
Natural finish = **Synchromatic 6039**
Humptop block or thumbprint inlay
18" wide
Sunburst finish = **Eldorado 6040**
Natural finish = **Eldorado 6041**
17" wide
Humptop block inlay
Synchromatic on peghead
Sunburst finish = **Fleetwood 6035**
Natural finish = **Fleetwood 6036**
No *Synchromatic* on peghead
Sunburst finish = **Constellation 6030**
Natural finish = **Constellation 6031**
Thumbprint inlay
Sunburst finish = **Eldorado 6038**
Natural finish = **Eldorado 6039**
16" wide
Sunburst finish = **Corsair 6014, 1959**
Natural finish = **Corsair 6015, 1959**
Bordeaux burgundy finish = **Corsair 6016, 1959**

ACOUSTIC ARCHTOPS

SECTION ORGANIZATION

Gretsch American Orchestra Series, Models Introduced in Late 1933
16"-Wide Models Introduced in 1935 and After
Synchromatic Models and Other 17"- and 18"-Wide Models

GRETSCH-AMERICAN ORCHESTRA SERIES, MODELS INTRODUCED IN LATE 1933

At introduction, all models are 16" wide with *f*-holes, carved spruce top, arched back, maple back and sides, trapeze tailpiece, black Bakelite pickguard, 3-piece maple neck (2 pieces of maple with rosewood laminate stripe), 14 frets clear of body, 24 1/2" scale, ebony fingerboard with pointed end, rounded-peak peghead. Changes occur as specified.

No. 25: no body binding, non-adjustable ebony bridge, dot inlay, rosewood peghead veneer, pearl scroll logo diagonally across peghead, dark red-to-brown shaded finish
Introduced: **late 1933**
Discontinued: **by 1939**

No. 35: bound pickguard, non-adjustable ebony bridge, single-bound top and back, pearl dot inlay, rosewood peghead veneer, pearl scroll logo diagonally across peghead, dark red-to-golden amber shaded finish
Introduced: **late 1933**
Adjustable maple bridge with rosewood stain, black plastic peghead veneer: **1936**
3-ply pearloid-black-white top binding, pearloid strip around top border of sides, rosewood fingerboard, scroll logo across top of peghead, tortoiseshell

celluloid tuner buttons, nickel-plated hardware, brown-to-amber shaded finish: **by 1939**
Discontinued: **by 1949**

No. 65: 4-ply top and back binding, bound pickguard, adjustable ebony bridge, single-bound fingerboard, notched-diamond inlay, rosewood peghead veneer, vertical floral peghead inlay, pearl scroll logo across top of peghead, dark red-to-golden amber shaded finish
Introduced: **late 1933**
Adjustable maple bridge with rosewood stain, black plastic peghead veneer, center-dip peghead: **1936**
Discontinued: **by 1939**

No. 100F/Synchromatic 100/Corsair:

adjustable ebony bridge, trapeze tailpiece, single-bound pickguard, multiple-bound top and back, small diamond inlay, rosewood peghead veneer, bound peghead, fern peghead inlay, pearl scroll logo across top of peghead, Grover tuners with metal buttons, gold-plated hardware, dark red-to-golden amber shaded finish
Introduced as **No. 100F: late 1933**
Tortoiseshell celluloid pickguard, black plastic peghead veneer, center-dip peghead: **1936**
Renamed **Synchromatic 100:** stairstep bridge, harp tailpiece, pickguard extends below bridge, rosewood fingerboard, varied-pattern mirror-image inlay, rounded peak peghead with clipped "ears," larger fern-pattern peghead inlay, amber-to-brown shaded finish, natural finish available with tortoiseshell celluloid binding: **by 1939**
Double-bound top and back, bound pickguard and f-holes, large block inlay, unbound peghead, *Synchromatic* on peghead, rounded top of peghead, sunburst finish: **early 1946**
Single-bound rounded-peak peghead: **late 1947**
Synchromatic 100 designated model **6014**, sunburst: **1949**
Model **6015**, natural finish, available: **by 1951**
No binding on pickguard, f-holes, or peghead: **1952**
Renamed **Corsair:** 16" wide, *G* tailpiece, single-bound top and back, adjustable rosewood bridge, tan pickguard with no logo, single-bound peghead, sunburst (**6014**), natural, (**6015**) or Bordeaux burgundy (**6016**) finish: **1955**
Humptop block inlay: **by 1957**

Single cutaway, ebony bridge, thumbprint inlay: **by 1959**
Discontinued: **1960**

No. 100R: No. 100 with round hole: **late 1933–38**

16"-WIDE MODELS INTRODUCED IN 1935 AND AFTER

All are 16" wide with f-holes, maple back and sides, unless otherwise specified.

No. 150: multiple-bound top and back, bound tortoiseshell celluloid pickguard, floral engraving around pickguard borders, 24 1/2" scale, bound ebony fingerboard with pointed end, block inlay, peghead ornament covers most of peghead, *Artist* on peghead, center-dip peghead, engraved tuner buttons, gold-plated hardware, sunburst finish
Available: **1935–38**

No. 50: maple adjustable bridge with rosewood-stain finish, trapeze tailpiece, triple-bound Bakelite pickguard, triple-bound top, single-bound back, 3-piece neck, 24 1/2" scale, bound ebony fingerboard with pointed end, diamond inlay, black plastic peghead veneer, rounded-peak peghead, pearl scroll peghead inlay with vertical lines, tortoiseshell celluloid tuner buttons, nickel-plated hardware, brown-to-amber shaded finish
Introduced: **1936**
Back of avoidire wood (blond mahogany), bound rosewood fingerboard, crosspiece at middle of tailpiece, dot inlay, white tuner buttons: **late 1930s**
Rosewood fingerboard: **by 1940**
Discontinued: **by 1949**

No. 50R: No. 50 with round hole: **1936–39**

No. 250: adjustable ebony bridge, trapeze tailpiece with 4 tubular pieces lengthwise and 1 tubular crosspiece in middle, bound tortoiseshell celluloid pickguard with 2 pearl-inlaid musical notes, 5-ply binding on top and back, pearl border around top, some with bound f-holes, 24 1/2" scale, bound ebony fingerboard with pointed end, varied-pattern inlay (later trapezoid and broken trapezoid inlay), single-bound peghead, pearl peghead inlay of 2 large musical notes, peghead indents below E-string tuners, protrusion at top of peghead,

pearl tuner buttons, gold-plated hardware, sunburst finish
Available: **1936–38**

No. 240: tenor, adjustable ebony bridge, trapeze tailpiece, single-bound top and back, 23" scale, ebony fingerboard with pointed end, bound top and back, dot inlay, point at top of peghead, pearl scroll logo diagonally across peghead

Note: Any standard model was available in tenor style by special order.
Available: **1936–38**

Synchromatic 75: stairstep bridge, trapeze tailpiece, bound pickguard, single-bound top and back, unbound *f*-holes, 3-piece maple neck, 24 1/2" scale, bound pointed-end fingerboard, large block inlay, large floral peghead inlay, scroll logo across top of peghead, black plastic peghead veneer, bound center-dip peghead, metal tuner buttons, nickel-plated hardware, amber-to-brown shaded finish
Introduced: **by 1939**
Harp tailpiece, triple-bound tortoiseshell celluloid pickguard extends below bridge, 4-ply top and back binding, unbound peghead: **by 1940**
Discontinued: **by 1949**

No. 30: adjustable maple bridge with rosewood-stain finish, trapeze tailpiece, black Bakelite pickguard, bound top, unbound back, unbound *f*-holes, 24 1/2" scale, rosewood fingerboard, pearl dot inlay, 3-piece maple neck, rosewood peghead veneer, pearl scroll logo diagonally across peghead, rounded-peak peghead, nickel-plated hardware, dark red-to-brown shaded finish
Introduced: **by 1939**
Discontinued: **by 1949**

Synchromatic 115: See Synchromatics, following

16 1/4" archtop (model name unknown): body probably made by Harmony, 16 1/4" wide, *f*-holes, laminated spruce top, maple back and sides, wooden tailpiece, 4-ply top binding, single-bound back, single-bound rosewood fingerboard, block inlay, painted T-roof logo slanting through circle, painted stars and rectangles in vertical row under logo, 3-color sunburst top finish, 2-color sunburst finish on back and sides
Available: **mid to late 1940s**

New Yorker: 16" wide, adjustable rosewood bridge, trapeze tailpiece, tortoiseshell celluloid pickguard, triple-bound top, single-bound back, bound rosewood fingerboard with square end, block inlay, stenciled peghead logo of T-roof *Gretsch* through circle and *New Yorker* vertically, rounded-top peghead (not peaked) with rounded corners, sunburst finish
Introduced: **by mid 1940s**
Single-bound top and back, unbound fingerboard, dot inlay, T-roof logo, *New Yorker* and lightning bolt vertically on peghead (**6050**): **by 1949**
Rounded-peak peghead with sharper corners: **by 1955**
Some examples with rectangular (flat top style) peghead or *Gretsch* plaque on peghead: **late 1960s**
Discontinued: **1970**

Jet '21': 16" wide, *f*-holes, bound top and back, white pickguard, trapeze tailpiece with slanted string-anchor bar, unbound rosewood fingerboard dot inlay, round-top (not peaked) peghead with rounded corners, ebonoid peghead veneer with beveled edges to simulate binding, engraved T-roof logo, Jet '21' engraved at angle, 3-on-a-plate tuners, black finish
Available: **late 1940s**

SYNCHROMATIC MODELS AND OTHER 17"- AND 18"-WIDE MODELS

Most Synchromatic models made prior to World War II have solid maple back and sides. Most postwar examples are of laminated maple.

Synchromatic 100, Corsair: see Gretsch-American Series, preceding

Synchromatic 75: see 16"-Wide Models Introduced in 1935 and After, preceding

Synchromatic 160: 17" wide, maple back and sides, double-bound cat's eye soundholes, stairstep bridge, harp tailpiece, bound pickguard almost covers treble soundhole, triple-bound top and back, 5-piece maple/rosewood neck, 26" scale, bound rosewood fingerboard with square end, 4-ply fingerboard binding, large block inlay, black plastic peghead veneer, script *Gretsch* across top of peghead, *Synchromatic* above E-string posts, single-bound peghead, peghead indents above E-string

tuners, protrusion on top of peghead, metal tuner buttons, chrome-plated hardware, sunburst finish
Introduced: **1939**
Natural finish with tortoiseshell celluloid binding optional: **early 1940s**
Production stopped: **1943**
Reintroduced, some with ebony fingerboard, no peghead indents, gold-plated hardware: **fall 1947**
Sunburst (**6028**) or natural (**6029**) finish: **1948**
Discontinued: **1951**

Synchromatic 200: 17" wide, double-bound cat's eye soundholes, maple back and sides, stairstep bridge, harp tailpiece, double-bound pickguard almost covers treble soundhole, wide multiple binding on top and back, 26" scale, bound rosewood fingerboard with square end, humptop block inlay, black plastic peghead veneer, script *Gretsch* across top of peghead, *Synchromatic* above A- and B-string posts, peghead indents at E-string tuners, protrusion on top of peghead, engraved metal tuner buttons, gold-plated hardware, amber-to-brown shaded finish or natural finish
Introduced: **1939**
Discontinued: **by 1949**

Synchromatic 300: 17" wide, double-bound cat's eye soundholes, stairstep bridge, harp tailpiece, bound pickguard almost covers treble soundhole, multiple-bound top and back, ebony fingerboard with square end, 5-ply binding on fingerboard sides and single-binding on end, 5-piece maple/rosewood neck, 26" scale, gold-sparkle slashed humptop block inlay, script *Gretsch* across top of peghead, *Synchromatic* above A- and B-string posts, peghead indents at E-string tuners, protrusion on top of peghead, multiple-bound peghead, enclosed Grover tuners, stairstep tuner buttons, gold-plated hardware, sunburst finish
Introduced: **1939**
Natural finish: **by 1941**
Sunburst (**6036**) or natural (**6037**) finish: **by 1948**
Catalogued as **Synchromatic 6036**, **6037**: 17" wide, double-bound *f*-holes, stairstep bridge, *G* tailpiece, bound pickguard, triple-bound top and back, bound fingerboard, slashed humptop block inlay, *Synchromatic* on peghead, rounded-peak peghead, stairstep tuner buttons, gold-plated hardware: **1951**
Discontinued: **by 1955**

Synchromatic 400: 18" wide, double-bound cat's eye soundholes, stairstep bridge, harp tailpiece with gold and chrome plating, pickguard with white and gold-sparkle binding almost covers treble soundhole, wide multiple binding with gold-sparkle on top and back (some with tortoiseshell celluloid at outer edge), 5-piece maple/rosewood neck, 26" scale, square-end ebony fingerboard with white and gold-sparkle binding, slashed humptop block inlay, slanted script logo starts between A- and D-string posts, crossed *Synchromatic*-and-tusk peghead ornament, peghead indents at E-string pegs, protrusion at top of peghead, stairstep tuner buttons, gold-plated hardware, sunburst or natural finish
Variation: triangular soundhole, referred to as Johnny Smith model, at least 2 made
Introduced: **by 1940**
No crossed peghead ornament, sunburst (**6040**) or natural (**6041**): **by 1948**
Catalogued as **Synchromatic 6040**, **6041**, *f*-holes, *G* tailpiece, multiple-bound top and back, multiple-bound pickguard and *f*-holes, triple-bound fingerboard and peghead, crossed peghead ornament returns, no peghead indents, rounded-peak peghead, available by custom order: **1951**
Rounded-top peghead: **by 1952**
Replaced by **Eldorado** (see following): **by 1955**

Synchromatic 115: 16" wide, *f*-holes, stairstep bridge, harp tailpiece, tortoiseshell celluloid pickguard, tortoiseshell celluloid binding on top, back and fingerboard, block inlay, unbound peghead, *Synchromatic* on peghead above A- and B-string posts, translucent blond finish
Introduced: **1946**
Trapeze tailpiece with slanted string-anchor bar: **early 1947**
Synchromatic on peghead below A- and B-string posts: **1947**
Discontinued: **1949**

Synchromatic 6012: 17" wide, similar to Synchromatic 160 (see preceding) but with 4-ply binding, abalone block inlay
Available: **c. 1948**

Synchromatic 6030, 6031/Constellation: 17" wide, single cutaway, stairstep bridge, harp tailpiece, bound pickguard, triple-bound top and back,

double-bound *f*-holes, bound rosewood fingerboard, block inlay, *Synchromatic* on peghead, rounded-peak peghead, gold-plated hardware, sunburst (**6030**) or natural (**6031**) finish
Introduced as **Synchromatic: 1951**
Renamed **Constellation:** *G* tailpiece, ebony bridge, humptop block inlay, no *Synchromatic* on peghead: **by 1955**
Discontinued: **1960**

Synchromatic 6038, 6039: 17" wide, single cutaway, stairstep bridge, *G* tailpiece, double-bound *f*-holes, multiple-bound top and back, bound pickguard, bound fingerboard, slashed-humptop block inlay, bound rounded-peak peghead, *Synchromatic* on peghead, stairstep tuner buttons, gold-plated hardware, sunburst (**6038**) or natural (**6039**) finish
Introduced: **by 1951**
Renamed **Fleetwood** (see following): **by 1955**

Eldorado: previously Synchromatic 400, 18" wide, single cutaway, *f*-holes, stairstep bridge, *G* tailpiece, elongated pickguard, triple-bound top and back, trapeze tailpiece, ebony fingerboard, humptop block inlay with black-white-black slash, triple-bound fingerboard and peghead, slanted script logo, crossed *Synchromatic*-and-tusk peghead ornament, rounded-peak peghead, gold-plated hardware, sunburst (**6040**) or natural (**6041**) finish
Introduced, custom order only: **by 1955**
Thumbprint inlay shown in catalog photo (humptop block inlay through 1960), *Gretsch* only on peg-

head: **1959**
Natural (6041) discontinued: **by 1968**
Discontinued: **by 1970**
Reintroduced, shaded (**G410**) or natural (**G410M**), made by Heritage company of Kalamazoo, MI: **1991**
Last made: **1997**

Fleetwood: 17" wide, single cutaway, *f*-holes, *Synchromatic* on peghead, otherwise same as Eldorado, sunburst (**6038**) or natural (**6039**) finish
Introduced, custom order only: **by 1955**
Renamed **Eldorado 6038** and **6039**, thumbprint inlay, *Gretsch* only on peghead: **1959**
Discontinued: **by 1968**

COMMENTS

Gretsch's current reputation is based more on electric archtop models than acoustics, which appeal primarily to Gretsch collectors. The quality of Gretsch workmanship is generally not as high as that of Gibson and Epiphone instruments from the same period. Thus many of the Gretsch models that survive are not in good condition. The high-end models with cat's eye soundholes are visually appealing and rare, and they have been sought for music videos and photo sessions. While these guitars are not equal in sound or playability to Gibson's or Epiphone's top models, they will bring a good price. Other Gretsch archtop acoustics are much less sought by collectors and musicians.

FLAT TOPS KEY

Triangular hole
    Cross-like peghead ornament = **Synchromatic 400F**
    Script *Synchromatic* on peghead
        Pearloid block inlay = **Jumbo Synchromatic (125F)**
        Slashed humptop block inlay = **Synchromatic 300 flat top**
    75 on peghead = **Synchromatic Sierra (X75F)**
    Gretsch in block letters, no ornament on peghead
        Natural top = **Town and Country**
        Red or orange top = **Rancher**
Resonator
    Round neck = **Sho Bro Spanish**
    Square neck = **Sho Bro Hawaiian**

Round hole
   Round body = **Rhumba**
   Standard guitar shape
      Bridge pickup = **Electro Classic**
      16" wide
         No fingerboard inlay = **Ozark Soft String**
         Diamond inlay = **No. 40 Hawaiian**
         Dot inlay
            2 dots at 12th fret
               12-string = **12-string**
               6-string
                  Natural top = **Wayfarer Jumbo**
                  Sunburst top = **Jumbo Flat Top**
            3 dots at 12th fret
               Redwood top = **Deluxe**
               Spruce top = **Supreme**
      15 1/2" wide = **Sun Valley**
      14 1/4" or 14 1/2" wide
         Solid peghead
            Pearloid peghead veneer with *Artist* = **Broadkaster**
            Burl Ives on peghead = **Burl Ives**
            Gretsch on peghead = **Grand Concert/Jimmie Rodgers/Folk**
         Slotted peghead
            Pin bridge = **Castilian**
            Classical string-loop bridge
               Wood inlay on back = **Classic Hauser 6000**
               No wood inlay on back = **Classic Hauser 6001**

FLAT TOPS

Broadkaster: 14 1/2" wide, top and back specified as arched, mahogany top, mahogany back and sides, ebony pin bridge, no pickguard, mahogany neck, square-end ebony fingerboard, dot inlay, celluloid peghead veneer, *Gretsch* in block letters across top of peghead, *Artist* vertically on peghead, peghead tapers to point at top, natural mahogany finish
Introduced: **by 1933**
Discontinued: **by 1936**

Castilian: 14 1/2" wide, spruce top, mahogany back and sides, triple-bound top, rosewood pin bridge, no pickguard, rosewood fingerboard with square end, dot inlay, slotted peghead, natural top finish
Introduced: **by 1933**
Discontinued: **by 1936**

Rhumba: round body, round hole, maple back and sides, ebony bridge, short trapeze tailpiece, elevated pickguard with no side supports, maple neck, ebony fingerboard with pointed end, dot inlay, rosewood peghead veneer, pearl scroll logo diagonally across peghead, sunburst finish
Introduced: **by 1933**
Discontinued: **by 1936**

No. 40 Hawaiian: 16" wide, spruce top, mahogany back and sides, round hole, large bowtie-shape ebony pin bridge, triple-bound pickguard screwed onto top, double-bound top and back, bound ebony fingerboard, varied-size diamond inlay, fret markers flush with fingerboard, 12 frets clear of body, green/grey pearloid peghead veneer, *Gretsch* and *Hawaiian* etched on peghead banners, rounded-

peak peghead, tortoiseshell celluloid tuner buttons, shaded brown finish
Introduced: **1936**
Discontinued: **by 1949**

Synchromatic 400F: 18" wide, triangular sound-hole, arched back, maple back and sides, stairstep bridge, harp tailpiece, elevated pickguard, multiple-bound top and back with tortoiseshell celluloid outer layer, bound fingerboard, slashed humptop block inlay, slanted script logo, crossed *Synchromatic*-and-tusk peghead ornament, peghead indents below E-string tuners, protrusion at top of peghead, enclosed Grover tuners, natural top finish, sunburst back and sides finish
Introduced: **by 1947**
Height-adjustable bridge, large triangular rosewood bridge base, metal string-anchor piece mounted at a slant, non-elevated pickguard (**6042**): **by 1949**
Discontinued: **by 1955**

Synchromatic 300 flat top: custom built for artist Buddy Starcher, triangular soundhole, arched back, maple back and sides, stairstep bridge, harp tailpiece, elevated pickguard, multiple-bound top and back, bound fingerboard, slashed humptop block inlay, straight logo, *Synchromatic* on peghead above A- and B-string posts, bound peghead, protrusion at peghead top and indents below E-string tuners, natural top finish, dark finish on back and sides
Introduced: **by 1947**
Discontinued: **by 1955**

Jumbo Synchromatic (Model 125F): 17" wide, maple back and sides, triangular soundhole, arched back, multiple-bound top and back, height-adjustable bridge, triangular rosewood bridge base, metal string-anchor plate mounted at a slant, 26" scale, single-bound rosewood fingerboard, pearloid block inlay, *Synchromatic* on peghead above A- and B-string posts, natural top, sunburst finish on back and sides (**6021**)
Variation: translucent white finish, tortoiseshell celluloid binding on top, back, soundhole, fingerboard and peghead
Introduced: **by 1947**
Replaced by **Town and Country** and **Rancher** (see following): **by 1955**

Synchromatic X75F/Sierra: 16" wide, triangular soundhole, arched back, maple back and sides, trapezoid-shaped bridge, metal string-anchor plate mounted straight across, rosewood fingerboard, block inlay, script *Gretsch* and *75* on peghead, sunburst finish
Introduced as **Synchromatic X75F: by 1947**
Renamed **Synchromatic Sierra (6007): 1949**
Discontinued: **by 1955**

Model 6003/Grand Concert/Jimmie Rodgers/Folk: 14 1/4" wide, round soundhole, mahogany back and sides, pin bridge, teardrop pickguard, 4-ply top binding, single-bound back, rosewood fingerboard, dot inlay, silkscreen T-roof logo within circle and parallelogram, natural top finish (**6003**)
Introduced: **1951**
Named **Grand Concert (6003)**, slanted logo: **by 1955**
Renamed **Jimmie Rodgers** (endorsed by the folk-pop star of the 1950s and 1960s, not the country star of the 1930s): **1959**
Renamed **Folk Singing**, 14 1/2" wide, 24 1/2" scale: **1963**
Renamed **Folk: 1965**
Zero fret, straight-across T-roof decal logo: **1967**
Sunburst top finish (**6002**) or mahogany top (**6004**) optional: **1969**
Sunburst (6002) and mahogany (6004) models available by special order only: **1972**
Discontinued: **1975**

Burl Ives: 14 1/4" wide, round soundhole, mahogany back and sides, teardrop pickguard, double-bound top, single-bound back, 9-ply soundhole ring, rosewood fingerboard, dot inlay, black painted peghead front, slanted T-roof logo with *Burl Ives* on peghead and on inside label, natural top finish (**6004**)
Available: **1952–54**

Town and Country: previously Jumbo Synchromatic (see preceding), 17" wide, triangular soundhole, arched back, maple back and sides, multiple-bound top and back, height-adjustable bridge, triangular rosewood bridge base, metal string-anchor plate mounted at a slant, 25 1/2" scale, bound fingerboard, block inlay (no *Synchromatic* on peghead), natural top finish (**6021**)

Introduced, replacing Jumbo Synchromatic: **1954**
Discontinued: **by 1959**

Rancher: 17" wide, Western version of Town and
Country, triangular soundhole, arched back, laminated spruce top, maple back and sides, height
adjustable bridge, triangular rosewood bridge base,
slant-mounted metal string-anchor plate, *G* brand
on bass side of top, longhorn engraved on tortoiseshell celluloid pickguard, 4-ply top binding, double-
bound back, single-bound rosewood fingerboard,
25 1/2" scale, block inlay engraved with cows and
cactus, single-bound peghead, peghead inlay of
engraved longhorn head, gold-plated hardware,
golden red (orange) finish (**6022**)
Introduced: **1954**
Gold pickguard, humptop block inlay with no engraving: **by 1957**
Thumbprint inlay, plain tan pickguard: **1959**
No *G* brand, 4-ply binding on top and back, horseshoe
peghead inlay: **1961**
Zero fret: **1969**
Renumbered (**7525**): **1971**
Discontinued: **by 1973**
Reintroduced, pointed pickguard, *G* brand on treble
side, block inlay engraved with cows and cactus,
standard pin bridge, horseshoe peghead inlay: **1975**
3-piece saddle, semi-circular bridge pin configuration:
c. 1978
Discontinued: **1980**

Sun Valley: 15 1/2" wide, laminated Brazilian rosewood back and sides, round soundhole, pin bridge,
tortoiseshell celluloid pickguard, 4-ply top binding,
single-bound back, ornamental backstripe, 24 1/2"
scale, ebony fingerboard, dot inlay, pearl logo,
bound peghead, natural top finish (**6010**)
Introduced: **by 1959**
Renumbered (**7515**): **1971**
Sunburst finish optional (**7514**): **by 1973**
Discontinued: **by 1977**

Classic Hauser/Silver Classic: 14 1/4" wide,
mahogany back and sides, rosewood fingerboard,
slotted peghead, back marquetry and peghead inlay
(**6000**) or plain back and peghead (**6001**)
Introduced: **1961**
Model 6000 referred to as **Silver Classic: 1969**
Discontinued, available by special order only: **1972**

Ozark Soft String: 16" wide classical, rosewood
back and sides, double-bound top and back, rosewood bridge, rosewood fingerboard, no inlay, slotted peghead, natural finish (**6005**)
Introduced: **by 1965**
Discontinued: **by 1968**

Sho Bro Spanish: 16 1/2" wide, dreadnought
shape, pointed cutaway, non-cutaway optional, cutaway with thinner body depth than non-cutaway
model, spruce top, mahogany back and sides,
Dobro style resonator, screened soundholes in
upper bout, multiple-bound top and back, bound
rosewood fingerboard, mahogany neck, dot inlay,
bound peghead, *Sho Bro* on peghead (no *Gretsch*
on peghead), natural top finish (**6030**)
Introduced: **late 1969**
Renumbered (**7715**): **1971**
Discontinued: **by 1978**

Sho Bro Hawaiian: 16 1/2" wide, non-cutaway,
spruce top, maple back and sides, Dobro style resonator, screened soundholes upper bout, multiple-
bound top and back, squareneck, bound fingerboard,
white celluloid fingerboard covering with playing-
card markers, bound peghead, *Sho Bro* on peghead
(no *Gretsch* on peghead), natural top finish (**6031**)
Introduced: **late 1969**
Renumbered (**7705**): **1971**
7-string (**7710**) available: **by 1972**
Discontinued: **by 1978**

Electro Classic: piezo bridge pickup system by
Baldwin (some amps with separate classical guitar
input) (**6006**)
Introduced: **1969**
Renumbered (**7495**): **1971**
Discontinued: **1973**

Wayfarer Jumbo: 16" wide, dreadnought shape,
maple back and sides, multiple-bound top, bound
back, brown pickguard with model name and ship
figure, maple neck, triple-bound fingerboard of
ebonized (dyed) rosewood, slashed-block inlay,
triple-bound peghead, chrome-plated Grover
tuners, natural top finish, cherry finish on back and
sides (**6008**)
Available: **1969–71**

12-string flat top: 16" wide, dreadnought shape, mahogany back and sides, multiple-bound top, bound back, rosewood fingerboard, dot inlay, natural fnish (**6020**)
Available: **1969–72**

Jumbo Flat Top: sunburst finish (no other specs available) (**6009**)
Available: **1969–71**

Deluxe: 16" wide, redwood top, mahogany back and sides, ebony fingerboard, dot inlay, 3 dots at 12th fret, chrome-plated hardware (**7535**)
Available: **c. 1978**

Supreme: 16" wide, dreadnought shape, spruce top, mahogany or rosewood back and sides, 3-piece saddle, ebony fingerboard, dot inlay, 3 dots at 7th and 12th frets, gold-plated hardware (**7545**)
Available: **c. 1978**

COMMENTS

Gretsch flat tops have never had a reputation for good sound or playability. The orange Rancher with *G* brand and cows-and-cactus inlay is of interest to collectors primarily as an accessory to the Western-ornamented electric models 6120, 6130 and Round-Up. Triangular-hole models in general bring prices in excess of their intrinsic or utility value. Other Gretsch models, even those that are older and rarer, are of little interest to collectors or players.

ELECTRIC ARCHTOPS KEY

Model numbers change from 6000 series to 7000 series in 1971. See model descriptions for 1970s model numbers.

Non-cutaway
  1 pickup
    Zigzag pattern on peghead
      Sunburst finish = **Electromatic 6185**
      Natural finish = **Electromatic 6185N**
    No zigzag on peghead
      Sunburst finish = **Corvette hollow body 6182**
      Natural finish = **Corvette hollow body 6183**
      Jaguar tan finish = **Corvette hollow body 6184**
      Ivory top finish = **Corvette hollow body 6187**
  2 pickups
    Sunburst finish = **Electromatic 6187**
    Natural finish = **Electromatic 6188**
Single rounded cutaway, bass bout joins neck at angle toward body
  Fancy abalone inlay
    Autumn red finish
      No Bigsby = **Super Chet 7690**
      Bigsby vibrola = **Super Chet 7690-B**
    Walnut finish
      No Bigsby = **Super Chet 7691**
      Bigsby vibrola = **Super Chet 7691-B**
  Thumbprint inlay
    Autumn red finish = **Deluxe Chet 7680**
    Walnut finish = **Deluxe Chet 7681**

Single rounded cutaway, bass bout joins neck at right angle
- 2 "eared" Filter 'Tron pickups (gold-plated)
  - 7 strings
    - Sunburst finish = **Van Eps 6079**
    - Walnut finish = **Van Eps 6080**
  - 6 strings
    - Sunburst finish = **Van Eps 6081**
    - Walnut finish = **Van Eps 6082**
- 2 standard pickups
  - Red or black finish, cat's eye soundholes = **custom model 6117**
  - White finish
    - Old-style Filter 'Tron pickups, plates between pole rows
      - Knob on cutaway bout = **White Falcon 6136, c. 1955–63**
      - Switch on cutaway bout = **White Falcon 6137, 1959–63**
    - No plates on pickup face = **White Falcon 7593**
  - Stain finish: mahogany, walnut, amber or red
    - DeArmond or Filter 'Tron pickups
      - Peghead plate = **Chet Atkins Country Gentleman 6122, 1958–61**
      - Longhorn or horseshoe peghead inlay = **Chet Atkins 6120, 1954–61**
    - Hi-Lo 'Tron pickups = **Chet Atkins Tennessean, 1961–80**
  - Sunburst, natural or green finish
    - Gold-plated hardware
      - *Electromatic* on peghead = **Electromatic 6189**
      - No *Electromatic* on peghead
        - Standard pickups
          - Sunburst finish = **Country Club 6192**
          - Natural finish = **Country Club 6193**
          - Green finish = **Country Club 6196**
        - Stereo electronics (see General Information)
          - Sunburst finish = **Country Club 6101**
          - Natural finish = **Country Club 6102**
          - Green finish = **Country Club 6103**
    - Chrome-plated hardware
      - Standard electronics (non-stereo)
        - Sunburst finish
          - Thumbprint inlay = **Double Anniversary 6117**
          - Dot inlay = **Clipper 6185**
        - 2-tone green finish = **Double Anniversary 6118**
      - Stereo electronics (see General Information)
        - Sunburst finish = **Double Anniversary 6111**
        - 2-tone green finish = **Double Anniversary 6112**
- 1 pickup
  - Dot inlay in center of fingerboard
    - Sunburst finish = **Clipper 6186**
    - Ivory top finish = **Model 6187, 1958**
    - Natural finish = **Clipper 6187**
  - Dot inlay near fingerboard edges = **Chet Atkins Junior**

Single rounded cutaway, bass bout joins neck at right angle, 1 pickup *(continued)*

Non-dot inlay

DeArmond pickup

Knobs on pickguard = **Convertible 6199**

Knobs mounted on top

Zigzag on peghead

Sunburst finish = **Electromatic 6190**

Natural finish = **Electromatic 6191**

No zigzag on peghead

Yellow top or jaguar tan finish = **Streamliner 6189**

Sunburst finish = **Streamliner 6190**

Natural finish = **Streamliner 6191**

Filter 'Tron or Hi-Lo 'Tron pickup

Ivory finish = **Rambler, 1960**

Sunburst finish

Chrome-plated hardware = **Anniversary 6124**

Gold-plated hardware = **Sal Salvador 6199**

2-tone green finish = **Anniversary 6125**

Orange or red finish = **Chet Atkins Tennessean 6119, 1959–60**

Single pointed cutaway = **Rambler 6115**

Double cutaway

Gold-plated hardware

White finish

3 knobs, 3 switches = **White Falcon 6136, 1963–82**

Any other knobs/switches = **White Falcon 6137, 1963–82**

Sunburst finish = **Viking 6187**

Natural finish = **Viking 6188**

Green finish = **Viking 6189**

Uniform stain finish

4-ply binding = **Chet Atkins Country Gentleman 6122, 1962–83**

2-ply binding = **Chet Atkins 6120 (Nashville), 1961–80s**

Chrome-plated hardware

Triangular inlay = **12-string**

Double thumbprint inlay = **Monkees**

Thumbprint inlay

Super 'Tron pickups

Roller bridge

Sunburst finish = **Streamliner 6102**

Cherry finish = **Streamliner 6103**

Tuning fork bridge

Sunburst finish = **Black Hawk 6100**

Black finish = **Black Hawk 6101**

Hi-Lo 'Tron pickups

G soundholes = **Songbird**

f-holes

Green finish = **Rally 6104**

Yellow top finish, copper finish on sides = **Rally 6105**

Dot inlay = **Broadkaster Hollow Body**

ELECTRIC ARCHTOPS

SECTION ORGANIZATION

Electromatics (pre-1955) and Later Related Models (Country Club, Corvette, Streamliner)

Chet Atkins Models

Single Cutaway Models, Introduced in 1955 and After (including models that later change to double-cutaway shape)

Double Cutaway Models

ELECTROMATICS AND LATER RELATED MODELS

Electromatic models do not have specific model names until 1955.

Electromatic Spanish/Corvette: 17" wide, maple body, 1 pickup, 2 knobs, sunburst finish (no other specs available)

Introduced: **1940**

16" wide, non-cutaway (same body as New Yorker 6050 acoustic), *f*-holes, 1 DeArmond pickup, 2 knobs on lower treble bout, rosewood bridge, trapeze tailpiece, unbound beveled-edge pickguard, triple-bound top, bound back, 25" scale, unbound rosewood fingerboard, dot inlay, 2-ply black-white peghead veneer, T-roof logo etched into peghead veneer, *Electromatic* etched vertically into peghead over zigzag pattern, edges of peghead veneer beveled to simulate binding, peghead tapers to point at top, sunburst finish (**6185**): **1949**

Natural finish (**6185N**) optional: **by 1951**

Named **Corvette (hollowbody)**, double-bound top and back, *Electromatic* on peghead, truss rod cover, no zigzag pattern, rounded-peak peghead, sunburst (**6182**), natural (**6183**) or jaguar tan (**6184**) finish: **1955**

G tailpiece, ivory top finish with grey mist finish on back and sides finish (**6187**) optional: **1957**

Rounded cutaway on Model 6187: **late 1957**

All Corvette models discontinued: **1959**

Corvette name reintroduced as an electric solidbody (see Electric Solidbodies)

Electro II non-cutaway: 16" wide, *f*-holes, 2 DeArmond pickups, 3 knobs on lower treble bout, stairstep bridge, trapeze tailpiece, unbound beveled-edge pickguard, triple-bound top, bound back, bound fingerboard, block inlay, 2-ply black-white peghead veneer, T-roof logo etched into peghead veneer, *Electromatic* etched vertically into peghead over zigzag pattern, edges of peghead veneer beveled to simulate binding, peghead tapers to point at top, sunburst (**6187**) or blond (**6188**) finish

Available: **1951–54**

Electro II cutaway/Country Club: 17" wide, 3 3/8" deep, *f*-holes, 2 DeArmond pickups, 3 knobs on lower treble bout, stairstep bridge, harp tailpiece, bound tortoiseshell celluloid pickguard, multiple-bound top, bound back, single-bound fingerboard, block inlay, single-bound rounded-peak peghead, script logo, *Synchromatic* on peghead, gold-plated hardware, sunburst (**6192**) or natural (**6193**) finish

Introduced: **1951**

3 knobs on lower treble bout, 1 knob on cutaway bout, double-bound *f*-holes, 3-ply top and back binding, 4-ply pickguard binding: **1952**

Melita bridge, truss rod: **1953**

Triple-bound fingerboard and peghead: **c. late 1953**

Named **Country Club**, 1 pickup selector switch added on upper bass bout, Melita bridge, *G* tailpiece, unbound pickguard, 4-ply top and back binding, double-bound *f*-holes, 7-ply fingerboard binding, humptop block inlay, 4-ply peghead binding, no *Synchromatic* on peghead, T-roof logo, stairstep tuners, gold-plated hardware, sunburst (**6192**), natural (**6193**) or Cadillac green (**6196**) finish, some with 2-tone gray finish (also numbered **6196**): **1954**

Filter 'Tron pickups, 2 knobs on lower treble bout, 1 knob on cutaway bout, 2 switches on upper bass bout, roller bridge, triple-bound fingerboard, thumbprint inlay: **1958**

Project-O-Sonic stereo optional with bass-treble split, Filter 'Tron pickups with only 3 visible screwpoles, 2 knobs on lower treble bout, 1 switch on cutaway bout, 2 switches on upper bass bout: **1958**

Project-O-Sonic models given separate model numbers, sunburst (**6101**), natural (**6102**) or Cadillac green (**6103**) finish: **1959**

Project-O-Sonic models: pickups identical in outer appearance to standard Filter 'Trons (no half-pole, half-bar configuration), 4 switches on upper bass bout: **1960**

GRETSCH

Body 1 7/8" deep, 2 control knobs, 1 knob on cutaway bout, 2 switches, triple-bound top and back, single-bound fingerboard and peghead: **1960**

Body 2 7/8" deep: **1963**

Project-O-Sonic Country Clubs (6101, 6102, 6103) discontinued: **by 1963**

Mute, 2 control knobs, 1 mute knob and 1 switch on lower treble bout, 1 knob on cutaway bout, 2 switches on upper bass bout, zero fret, large non-stairstep tuner buttons, padded back: **1963**

No mute, 2 knobs and 1 switch on lower treble bout: **1965**

Green finish (6196) discontinued: **1968**

Models renumbered, sunburst (**7575**), natural (**7576**): **1971**

4 knobs on lower treble bout, 1 knob on cutaway bout, 1 switch on upper bass bout, wooden tailpiece insert with model name, block inlay: **1974**

Sunburst finish (7575) discontinued, antique maple finish (**7577**) available: **1977**

Model 7577 described with walnut stain: **1979 only**

Natural (7576) and antique maple (7577) discontinued: **1981**

Reintroduced as **1955 Country Club Custom Reissue** (**G6196-1955**), U.S.-made, solid spruce top, 3 1/2" deep, DynaSonic pickups, natural, blue sunburst or Cadillac green finish: **1995**

Still in production

Electromatic 16" cutaway/Streamliner: 16" wide, laminated spruce top, 1 or 2 DeArmond pickups, Melita bridge, single-bound top and back, single-bound fingerboard, block inlay, 2-ply black-white peghead veneer, T-roof logo etched into peghead veneer, *Electromatic* etched vertically into peghead over zigzag pattern, beveled edges of peghead veneer to simulate binding, 2 pickups (**6189**), 1 pickup sunburst finish (**6190**), or 1 pickup natural finish (**6191**)

Introduced: **1951**

Named **Streamliner**, maple top, 1 pickup, Melita bridge, *G* tailpiece, 2 knobs on lower treble bout, double-bound top and back, single-bound *f*-holes, 25 1/4" scale, single-bound fingerboard, yellow or sunburst finish pictured in catalog with block inlay (later with humptop block), natural finish pictured with humptop block inlay, metal tuner buttons, *Electromatic* on peghead veneer, no zigzag pattern, chrome-plated hardware, bamboo yellow top finish with copper mist finish on back and sides (available

in jaguar tan by special order) (**6189**), sunburst (**6190**) or natural finish (**6191**): **1955**

Double-bound top and back, double-bound *f*-holes, single-bound fingerboard and peghead: **by 1957**

Transition to Anniversary (see following), transitional Model 6189 like 1957 Streamliner model but with 1 Filter 'Tron pickup in neck position, 1 knob on upper treble bout, 1 switch on upper bass bout, 24 3/4" scale, unbound peghead, no *Electromatic* on peghead: **1958**

Streamliner last listed: **1959**

Streamliner name reintroduced as thinbody double cutaway (see following): **1969**

CHET ATKINS MODELS

Chet Atkins Hollow Body/Nashville: 16" wide (some as narrow as 15 5/8"), single cutaway, 2 7/8" deep, laminated spruce top, 2 DeArmond pickups, 3 knobs on lower treble bout, 1 knob on cutaway bout, 1 switch on upper bass bout, compensating metal bridge, Bigsby vibrato, signpost and signature on rounded-end pickguard, bound *f*-holes, *G* brand on top, double-bound top and back, double-bound *f*-holes, 24 3/4" scale, bound rosewood fingerboard, block inlay engraved with cactus and cows except for unengraved block at 1st fret, metal nut, single-bound peghead, longhorn peghead inlay, gold-plated hardware (except nut, bridge and Bigsby), amber red (orange) finish (**6120**), white leather case with Western motif tooled leather trim

Introduced as Chet Atkins Hollow Body (prototype with serial number 13753): **late 1954**

Maple top, engraved block at 1st fret: **1955**

Block inlay with no engraving on any block, horseshoe peghead inlay: **1956**

No *G* brand: **1957**

Humptop block inlay: **c. late 1957**

Ebony fingerboard: **c. early 1958**

Filter 'Tron pickups, 2 switches on upper bass bout, bar bridge 1/2" in diameter, thumbprint inlay, interior top and back braces meet to form soundpost-like structure: **mid 1958**

Gretsch Bigsby vibrato, zero fret, bone nut: **1959**

2 1/4" deep, 2 knobs and 1 switch on lower treble bout (total of 3 knobs and 3 switches): **early 1961**

Double cutaway, simulated (painted-on) *f*-holes, single mute, mute knob on lower treble bout, signature (no signpost) on pickguard, leather back pad: **mid to late 1961**

Standard Gretsch (non-white) case: **1962**

Named **Nashville**, nameplate on peghead, pebble grain vinyl backpad: **c. 1964**

Renumbered (**7660**): **1971**

Adjustamatic bridge, squared pickguard, no mute, no nameplate: **1972**

Open *f*-holes, red finish: **1973**

Curved tubular-arm Gretsch Bigsby vibrato, new pickup housing: **1975**

Flat-arm vibrato: **c. 1979**

Discontinued: **1980**

Reintroduced as **1955 Nashville Custom Reissue** (**6120-1955**), U.S.-made, solid maple top, Dyna-Sonic pickups, Bigsby vibrato, natural or ebony finish: **1995**

Still in production

1955 Western Nashville Custom Reissue (G6120W-1955): U.S.-made, G-brand on top, Western motifs: **1995–current**

Chet Atkins Country Gentleman/Southern Belle: 17" wide, single cutaway, 2" deep (depth varies), simulated *f*-holes (see following), 2 Filter 'Tron pickups, 2 knobs on lower treble bout, 1 knob on cutaway bout, 2 switches on upper bass bout, metal bar bridge 1/2" in diameter, Bigsby vibrato, signature and signpost on pickguard, 4-ply binding on top and back, 24 1/2" scale, bound ebony fingerboard, thumbprint inlay, metal nut, single-bound peghead, stairstep tuner buttons, nameplate with serial number on peghead, gold-plated hardware (except nut and Bigsby), mahogany finish (**6122**)

Soundholes vary on examples from introduction through 1961. Most early examples have simulated *f*-holes of inlaid black plastic; most later examples have painted-on *f*-holes. Some have the appearance of binding (either paint, glue seam or actual binding material). Some examples have open *f*-holes, bound or unbound.

Prototype with no *f*-hole simulation, plain pickguard, white finish, labeled **6122: 1957**

Introduced: **late 1957**

No signpost on pickguard, zero fret, bone nut: **1959**

Gretsch Bigsby vibrato: **late 1959**

Some with 15 frets clear of body: **c. 1960**

Double mute with 2 large mute knobs on either side of bridge, padded back: **late 1961**

Double cutaway, 1 standby switch added on lower treble bout: **late 1961**

Gold-plated Gretsch Bigsby vibrato: **by 1962**

Smaller lever-action mute knobs: **early 1963**

Non-stairstep tuner buttons, no serial number on nameplate: **c. 1965**

Single mute, 1 mute knob/lever: **1966**

1 Super 'Tron and 1 Filter 'Tron pickup: **1964**

2 Filter 'Tron pickups: **1970**

Renumbered **7670**, adjustamatic bridge, no mute, no nameplate, walnut finish: **1971**

Open *f*-holes: **1972**

Curved tubular-arm Gretsch Bigsby: **by 1975**

Flat-arm vibrato: **c. 1979**

Discontinued: **1981**

Late 1970s parts assembled in Mexico, marketed as **Southern Belle (7176): 1983**

Chet Atkins Tennessean: specfied in catalog as 16" wide, most vary from 15 5/8" to 15 7/8", 2 5/8" deep, single cutaway, open *f*-holes, 1 Filter 'Tron pickup in bridge position, 1 knob on cutaway bout, 1 switch on upper bass bout, metal bar bridge 1/2" in diameter, Bigsby vibrato, black pickguard with white signature signpost and Gretsch logo, double-bound top, single-bound back, unbound ebony fingerboard, 24 1/2" scale, pearl thumbprint inlay, unbound peghead, chrome-plated hardware, no peghead ornament, metal tuner buttons, cherry finish (**6119**)

Introduced: **1958**

Zero fret: **1959**

Gretsch Bigsby vibrato: **late 1959**

2 1/4" deep, large violin-style simulated (painted-on) *f*-holes with no white border, 2 Hi-Lo 'Tron pickups, 1 knob on cutaway bout, 2 switches on upper bass bout, 2 knobs on lower treble bout, double-bound top, unbound back, gray pickguard with Gretsch logo only, single-bound rosewood fingerboard, no zero fret, plastic tuner buttons, "dark cherry" walnut finish: **1961**

2" deep, thinner painted-on *f*-holes, standby switch on lower treble bout, Atkins signature and Gretsch logo on gray pickguard, zero fret, single-bound fingerboard, metal tuner buttons, mahogany finish (slightly redder than walnut finish of 1961): **1962**

White paint outline around simulated *f*-holes, pearloid thumbprint inlay, padded back: **1963**

Walnut top finish (some faded to amber), mahogany back and sides finish: **1964**

Nameplate on peghead: **c. 1964**

Metal bar bridge 3/8" in diameter, plastic knobs, uniform dark-stain finish on top, back and sides: **mid 1967**

Open *f*-holes, dark cherry stain finish: **1970**
Renumbered (**7655**): **1971**
No nameplate, adjustamatic bridge: **1972**
Discontinued: **1980**

Chet Atkins Junior: 12 3/4" wide, single cutaway,
1 Super 'Tron pickup mounted near bridge, 2 knobs
and 1 switch on lower treble bout, metal bar bridge
3/8" in diameter, Burns vibrato, gray pickguard with
logo and signature, unbound open *f*-holes, double-
bound top and back, 23 1/4" scale, single-bound
rosewood fingerboard, dot inlay positioned near
bass edge of fingerboard on frets 1, 3, 5, 7 and 9,
block inlay at 12th fret, dot inlay positioned near
treble edge of fingerboard at frets 15, 17 and 19,
zero fret, bone nut, unbound peghead, peghead
plate with model name, orange stain finish
Available: **1970**

Super Chet: 17" wide, 2 1/2" deep, rounded cutaway, upper bass bout joins neck at an angle
toward body, 2 pickups, 5 knobs (master volume
plus individual tone and volume) on pickguard,
abalone- tailpiece inlay, model name on pickguard,
binding material around middle of sides, 24 1/2"
scale, fancy abalone inlay on fingerboard and peghead, zero fret, gold-plated hardware, 25 1/2" scale
or wider neck optional, autumn red finish (**7690**),
autumn red with Bigsby vibrato (**7690-B**), walnut
finish (**7691**), walnut with Bigsby vibrato (**7691-B**)
Available: **late 1972–80**

Deluxe Chet: 17" wide, 2 1/2" deep, rounded cutaway, upper bass bout joins neck at an angle
toward body, top-mounted controls, Bigsby vibrato,
signature (no model name) on pickguard,
thumbprint inlay, autumn red (**7680**) or walnut
(**7681**) finish
Available: **1973–74**

Single Cutaway Models, Introduced 1955 and After

This section includes models that later changed to
double cutaway.

White Falcon: 17" wide, single cutaway, 2 7/8"
deep, 2 pickups, 3 knobs on lower treble bout, 1
knob on cutaway bout, 1 switch on upper bass
bout, Melita bridge, tubular tailpiece with V-shape
piece and *G*, Bigsby vibrato optional, falcon on

pickguard, 4-ply top and back binding, double-
bound *f*-holes; gold leaf paint to simulate binding
around sides of body, *f*-holes, fingerboard and
peghead; 25 1/2" scale, triple-bound ebony fingerboard, engraved humptop block inlay, stairstep
tuner buttons, *Gretsch* vertically on peghead in
gold, gold-sparkle wing-shaped peghead inlays,
gold-sparkle truss rod cover, V-top peghead shape,
double-bound peghead, gold-plated hardware,
white finish (**6136**), earliest examples with *The
White Falcon* on label and no model number
Introduced: **1955**

Transition to gold-sparkle plastic binding, some examples with some gold leaf and some gold-sparkle
(peghead logo is last part to get gold-sparkle):
1955

Filter 'Tron pickups, roller bridge, thumbprint inlay: **1958**
Horizontal logo, nameplate on peghead: **1959**
Project-O-Sonic stereo optional, 3 poles and 1 bar on
each pickup, bass-treble split, 2 knobs on lower treble bout, 1 switch on upper treble bout, 2 switches
on upper bass bout (**6137**): **1958**

Projecto-O-Sonic model: pickups identical in outward
appearance to standard Filter 'Trons, 4 switches on
upper bass bout, 1 switch on upper treble bout:
1959

2" deep, double mute with 2 large mute knobs on
either side of bridge, padded back: **1960**

Non-stereo model: 2 control knobs and 1 switch on
lower treble bout, 1 knob on upper treble bout,
2 switches on upper bass bout: **1960**

Gretsch Bigsby vibrato standard: **1962**
Small lever-action mute knobs: early **1963**
Double-cutaway, V-shape tailpiece, zero fret: **1962**
Gretsch vibrato with *G* plate and straight tubular arm
curving slightly at tip, large non-stairstep tuner but-
tons: **1964**

Adjustable nut on vibrato arm, T-zone tempered treble-
end fingerboard with dot inlay from 15th fret: **1965**

Stereo configuration: 2 large plastic control knobs and
4 switch knobs on lower treble bout, 1 switch on
upper treble bout, 1 switch on lower bass bout,
mute knobs on either side of bridge: **by 1965**

Tuning fork bridge: **1966–69**
Renumbered, non-stereo (**7594**), stereo (**7595**): **1971**
Curved tubular-arm Gretsch Bigsby vibrato: **1972**
Single cutaway (**7593**) reintroduced: 2 knobs on lower
treble bout, 1 knob on cutaway bout, 2 switches on
upper bass bout (some examples with stereo
wiring, same knob and switch configuration as

1967 stereo model): **early 1970s**

No mute, block inlay: **by early 1970s**

Non-stereo double cutaway (7594) and single cutaway (7593) models discontinued, stereo double cutaway model (7595) available by special order only: **1980**

Stereo White Falcon (7595) discontinued: **1981**

Reintroduced as **White Falcon I/1955 White Falcon Custom Reissue** (G-6136-1955), U.S.-made, single cutaway, solid spruce top, DynaSonic pickups, winged peghead inlay: **1995**

Still in production

Convertible/Sal Salvador: 17" wide, single cutaway, 1 DeArmond pickup mounted on top, 2 knobs mounted on oversized pickguard, multiple-bound top, triple-bound back, doubled-bound *f*-holes, *G* tailpiece, adjustable rosewood bridge, multiple-bound rosewood fingerboard, triple-bound peghead, humptop block inlay, stairstep tuner buttons, gold-plated hardware, lotus ivory top finish with copper mist body finish (**6199**), sunburst finish available by special order

Introduced as **Convertible: by 1955**

Ebony fingerboard, thumbprint inlay, bamboo yellow top finish, copper mist finish on back and sides: **late 1957**

Renamed **Sal Salvador:** Filter 'Tron pickup, triple-bound top and back, triple-bound fingerboard, thumbprint inlay, triple-bound peghead, sunburst finish (**6199**): **1958**

Knobs mounted into top, large block inlay, zero fret: **1965**

Discontinued: **1968**

Rambler: 13" wide, pointed cutaway, 1 DeArmond pickup, 2 knobs on lower treble bout, adjustable rosewood bridge, *G* tailpiece, single-bound top and back, 23" scale, rosewood fingerboard, dot inlay, single-bound peghead, ivory top finish, green or black finish on back and sides (**6115**)

Introduced: **by 1957**

Rounded cutaway, Hi-Lo 'Tron pickup, red truss rod cover: **1960**

Discontinued: **by 1961**

Clipper: 16" wide, 1 3/4" deep, 1 pickup with slothead screwpoles and oval cutout in pickup cover, 2 knobs on lower treble bout, adjustable ebony bridge, trapeze tailpiece, double-bound top and back, 24 1/2" scale, dot inlay, sunburst finish (**6186**)

Introduced: **by 1958**

Natural finish (**6187**) available: **1959**

Hi-Lo 'Tron pickup: **1960**

Natural finish (6187) discontinued: **1961**

Short-arm "palm" vibrato listed as standard but rare: **1963**

No vibrato: **1968**

Renumbered (**7555**): **1971**

Sunburst (6186) discontinued, 2-pickup model (**6185**) introduced: **1972**

2-pickup Clipper (6185) discontinued: **1975**

Anniversary: commemorates Gretsch's 75th Anniversary, 16" wide, 2 1/2" deep, 1 Filter 'Tron pickup, 1 knob on cutaway bout, 1 switch on upper bass bout, roller bridge, *G* tailpiece, single-bound top and back, 24 1/2" scale, unbound fingerboard, pearl thumbprint inlay, unbound peghead, sunburst (**6124**) or 2-tone smoke green (**6125**) finish

Introduced: **1958**

Nameplate on peghead: **mid 1959**

Hi-Lo 'Tron pickup: **1960**

Pearloid thumbprint inlay: **by 1963**

Short-arm "palm" vibrato listed as standard but rare: **1963**

Model 6125 also available in 2-tone tan finish (similar to lotus ivory and copper mist): **1963**

Discontinued: **1972**

Double Anniversary: 2 pickups, 2 knobs on lower treble bout, 1 knob on cutaway bout, 2 switches on upper bass bout, sunburst (**6117**) or 2-tone smoke green (**6118**) finish

Introduced: **1958**

Nameplate on peghead: **mid 1959**

Hi-Lo 'Tron pickups: **1960**

Stereo (1 pickup per channel, *not* Project-O-Sonic) optional, sunburst (**6111**) or green (**6112**) finish: **1961**

Short-arm "palm" vibrato listed as standard but rare: **1963**

Bound fingerboard: **1963**

Stereo models (6111 and 6112) discontinued, model 6118 available in 2-tone tan finish (similar to lotus ivory and copper mist): **1963**

No vibrato, zero fret: **1968**

Sunburst model renumbered 7560: **1971**

2-tone green model (6118) discontinued: **1972**

Smaller *f*-holes, adjustamatic bridge, no nameplate: **by 1972**

1 switch on upper treble bout, 3 knobs on lower bass
bout, trapeze tailpiece: **1973**
Block inlay: **1974**
Discontinued: **1975**

Custom model 6117 (model name unknown):
15 5/8" wide, 1 13/16" deep, single cutaway, 2 Hi-Lo
'Tron pickups, cat's eye soundholes, 4 knobs on
lower treble bout, 1 switch on upper treble bout,
roller bridge, *G* tailpiece, thumbprint inlay, zero fret,
bright red or black finish (**6117**, same model number as sunburst Double Anniversary)
200 made: **1964–68**

Van Eps: 17" wide, 6 or 7 strings, 2 "eared" Filter
'Tron pickups with extra-heavy covers, *G* tailpiece,
roller bridge, floating tuning fork bridge, triple-
bound top, triple-bound fingerboard and peghead,
25 1/2" scale, thumbprint inlay, zero fret, nameplate
on peghead, gold-plated hardware 7-string sunburst (**6079**) or walnut (**6080**) finish, 6-string
sunburst (**6081**) or walnut (**6082**) finish
Introduced: **1968**
Wood bridge, no tuning fork, tailpiece with straight-
across string anchors: **1969**
Super 'Tron pickups: **by 1971**
7-string sunburst renumbered 7580: **1971**
All but 7-string sunburst discontinued: **1972**
7-string sunburst (7580) listed but available by special
order only: **1977**
7-string sunburst (7580) no longer listed: **1980**

DOUBLE CUTAWAY MODELS

White Falcon and **Chet Atkins** double-cutaway
models: see Single Cutaway section, preceding

Monkees: 2 Super 'Tron pickups, *Monkees* guitar-
shaped logo on pickguard and truss rod cover,
bound top and back, bound *f*-holes and fingerboard, Gretsch Bigsby vibrato, thumbprint inlay
along both edges of fingerboard, peghead plate with
model name and *Rock 'n' Roll Model*, red finish
Available: **1966–68**

Viking: 17" wide, 2" deep, 2 Super 'Tron pickups,
2 control knobs and 1 switch on lower treble bout,
1 knob on upper treble bout, 2 switches on upper
bass bout, single mute with 1 small lever knob on
lower treble bout, roller bridge, floating tuning fork
bridge, model name on pickguard (earliest with

name and Viking ship on pickguard), ebony fingerboard, thumbprint inlay, T-zone tempered treble-
end fingerboard with dots from 15th fret, zero fret,
nameplate on peghead, padded back, gold-plated
hardware, sunburst (**6187**), natural (**6188**) or Cadillac green (**6189**) finish
Introduced: **1964**
Renumbered: sunburst **7585**, natural **7586: 1971**
No tuning fork, tubular-arm Gretsch Bigsby, green
finish (6189) discontinued: **1972**
Sunburst (7585) and natural (7586) discontinued: **1975**

Rally: 16" wide, 2" deep, 2 Hi-Lo 'Tron pickups, bar
bridge, 3 knobs and 1 switch on lower treble bout, 1
knob on upper treble bout, standby and treble
booster switches on upper bass bout, bar bridge
(some with roller bridge), plate on back for active
electronics, Gretsch Bigsby vibrato, rally stripe on
pickguard and truss rod cover, double-bound top,
single-bound back, single-bound rosewood fingerboard, thumbprint inlay, T-zone tempered treble-end
fingerboard with dot inlay from 15th fret, zero fret,
green finish (**6104**) or bamboo yellow top finish with
2-tone copper mist finish on back and sides (**6105**)
Available: **1967–69**

12 string: 16" wide, 17" wide model optional, 2
Super 'Tron pickups, 2 knobs and 1 switch on lower
treble bout, 1 knob on upper treble bout, 2 switches
on upper bass bout, *G* tailpiece with straight-across
string anchors, large triangular inlay, zero fret,
padded back on 17" model only, sunburst (**6075**) or
natural (**6076**) finish
Introduced: **by 1967**
Natural (6076) and sunburst (6075) discontinued,
sunburst (6075) available by special order: **1972**

Black Hawk: 16" wide, 2" deep, 2 Super 'Tron pick-
ups, 2 control knobs and 1 switch on lower treble
bout, 1 knob on upper treble bout, 2 switches on
upper bass bout, roller bridge, floating tuning fork
bridge, *G* tailpiece or Gretsch Bigsby vibrato, single-bound top and back, single-bound rosewood
fingerboard, 24 1/2" scale, thumbprint inlay, T-zone
tempered treble-end fingerboard with dot inlay from
15th fret, zero fret, nameplate on peghead, sunburst (**6100**) or black (**6101**) finish
Introduced: **1967**
Sunburst (**6100**) finish discontinued: **1970**
Black (6101) finish discontinued: **1972**

Streamliner double cutaway:
16" wide, 2" deep, 2 Super 'Tron pickups, roller bridge, *G* tailpiece, bound rosewood fingerboard, 24 1/2" scale, thumbprint inlay, T-zone tempered treble-end fingerboard with dot inlay from 15th fret, zero fret, nameplate on peghead, sunburst (**6102**) or cherry (**6103**) finish

Introduced: **1969**

No nameplate, no T-zone fingerboard: **by 1972**

Sunburst (6102) finish discontinued: **1973**

Cherry (6103) finish discontinued: **1975**

Broadkaster hollowbody:
16" wide, 2 Super 'Tron pickups, 4 knobs on lower treble bout, 1 knob on upper treble bout, 1 switch on upper bass bout, dot inlay, zero fret, with *G* tailpiece natural (**7607**) or sunburst (**7608**) finish, with Gretsch Bigsby vibrato natural (**7603**) or sunburst (**7604**) finish

Introduced: **1975**

Humbucking pickups, terminator bridge/tailpiece: **1976**

Red finish (**7609**) standard, all other Broadkasters (7603, 7604, 7607, 7608) discontinued: **1977**

Red finish (7609) discontinued: **1980**

COMMENTS

The collector's market for Gretsch instruments is based largely on hollowbody electrics made from the mid 1950s through the mid 1960s. This market has been fueled at various times by the use of Gretsches by such notable players as Chet Atkins, George Harrison, Neil Young, Stephen Stills and Brian Setzer.

Gretsch guitars tend to be either loved or hated. Many Gibson and Fender players feel that Gretsches are inferior in workmanship. Binding material and the resin glue used for necksets tend to deteriorate with age, frequently necessitating repair work to put a vintage Gretsch in playing order. In addition, Gretsch switch systems and pickups are not generally considered to be as versatile as those of other makers.

Despite the drawbacks, Gretsches have a visual appeal—particularly the Atkins models, Western-trim models and the White Falcon—quite unlike that of any other maker. Many players of rockabilly and early rock and roll music feel the DeArmond pickups as well as the later Filter 'Trons have a distinctive twang and tone that is perfect for that type of music.

The models most highly regarded by collectors are the single-cutaway versions (up to early 1961) of the Chet Atkins Hollow Body, Chet Atkins Country Gentleman and White Falcon.

Models from the 1960s generally bring more than their 1970s equivalents.

New Japanese-made models are generally not true reissues, but combine features from various years. Structurally they are quite good.

ELECTRIC SOLIDBODIES KEY

Non-standard body shape
    Rectangular body = **Bo Diddley**
    Abstract square-ish body = **Jupiter**
    Abstract body, more curved than Jupiter = **Thunderbird**
    Absract body, lower bass bout like auto tail fin = **Cadillac**
Hinged body sides
    Guitar = **Bikini 6023**
    Bass = **Bikini 6024**
Double-neck bass/guitar (detachable bodies) = **Bikini 6025**
Single cutaway
    Dot inlay
        1 pickup
            Walnut stain finish = **BST 1000 (8210)**
            Red stain finish = **BST 1000 (8216)**
        2 pickups
            Walnut stain finish = **BST 1000 (7617, 8215 or 8217)**
            Red stain finish = **BST 1000 (8211)**

Single cutaway *(continued)*
  Large block, humptop block or thumbprint inlay
    Flat top
      2 pickups = **Roc II**
      1 pickup = **Roc I**
    Carved top
      3 or 4 knobs
        Black top finish
          6 strings = **Duo Jet, 1953–61**
          4 strings = **Duo Jet Tenor**
        Stained maple or knotty pine top
          Belt buckle tailpiece = **Round-up**
          Bigsby tailpiece = **Chet Atkins Solid Body 6131**
        Red top finish, black body = **Jet Firebird, c. 1955–61**
        Silver sparkle top = **Silver Jet, c. 1955–61**
        White finish = **White Penguin**
        Green finish = **custom-ordered Duo Jet**
        Sparkle finish (except silver) = **custom-order Duo Jet**
      5 knobs
        Thumbprint inlay = **Roc Jet**
        Western inlay = **Country Roc**
Symmetrical double cutaway
  Dot inlay
    Maple/walnut neck through body = **Committee**
    Solid mahogany body
      Walnut stain = **BST 2000 (7620 or 8220)**
      Red stain = **BST 2000 (8221)**
  Thumbprint inlay
    Black top finish = **Duo Jet, c. 1961–71**
    Silver sparkle top = **Silver Jet, c. 1961–63**
    Red top finish = **Jet Fire Bird, c. 1961–71**
    Sparkle top (except silver) = **custom-order Duo Jet**
Pointed treble-side cutaway, slight cutaway on bass side
  Black control plate = **Super Axe**
  No control plate = **Atkins Axe**
Asymmetrical double cutaway
  No fingerboard inlay = **TK 300**
  Thumbprint inlay = **Astro-Jet**
  Dot inlay
    Maple/walnut neck through body = **BST 5000**
    Glued-in or bolt-on neck
      Deluxe Corvette (specs unavailable)
      Vibrato
        22 1/2" scale = **Princess**
        24 1/2" scale
          Glittered gold finish = **Gold Duke (Corvette)**
          Glittered silver finish = **Silver Duke (Corvette)**
          Platinum grey or mahogany finish
            1 pickup = **Corvette 6134**
            2 pickups = **Corvette 6135**
      No vibrato
        Natural maple finish = **Broadkaster**
        Mahogany or cherry finish = **Corvette 6132**
        Platinum grey finish = **Corvette 6133**

ELECTRIC SOLIDBODIES

Duo-Jet and Roc-Jet models (including Chet Atkins Solid Body and White Penguin) from the 1950s and 1960s are not fully solid, but are heavily routed underneath the top. Beginning in 1970, all solid-body models are fully solid.

SECTION ORGANIZATION

Original Duo-Jet Series (including Chet Atkins Solid Body and White Penguin)
Later Single-Cutaway Duo-Jet Style Models (Roc Series)
Bo Diddley Models
Other Models
BST "Beast" Models

ORIGINAL DUO-JET SERIES

Duo-Jet: 13 1/4" wide, 2" deep, single cutaway, mahogany body, 2 DeArmond pickups, 3 knobs (master tone and 2 individual volume) on lower treble bout, 1 master volume knob on cutaway bout, 1 pickup selector switch on upper bass bout, Melita bridge, *G* tailpiece, gray plastic pickguard, triple-bound top, single-bound fingerboard and peghead, 24 1/2" scale, block inlay, script logo, chrome-plated hardware, black top finish (**6128**), a few custom-order green finish (all with gold-plated hardware), sparkle finishes available (see following)
Introduced: **mid 1953**
T-roof logo: **1955**
Humptop block inlay: **late 1956**
Roller bridge, thumbprint inlay: **early 1958**
13 1/2" wide, Filter 'Tron pickups, 2 knobs on lower treble bout, 1 knob on cutaway bout, 2 switches on upper bass bout: **1958**
Zero fret: **1959**
Symmetrical double cutaway body: **1961**
Standby switch on lower treble bout, bent flat-arm Burns vibrato, gold plastic pickguard, gold-plated hardware: **1962**
Sparkle finishes (see Silver Jet, following) listed as custom Duo-Jet finishes: **1963**
Sparkle finishes discontinued: **1966**
Super 'Tron pickups, Gretsch Bigsby vibrato: **1968**
Discontinued, available by special order only: **1971**

Duo-Jet Tenor (6127): 1959–60

Silver Jet: same specs and changes as Duo-Jet, silver sparkle top finish (**6129**)
Introduced: **by 1955**
Optional sparkle finishes listed: gold, champagne, burgundy, or tangerine; all sparkle finishes available on Gretsch drums available on Duo-Jet guitar: **1962**
Silver Jet discontinued as separate model, all finishes listed as custom Duo-Jet finishes: **1963**

Jet Fire Bird: black pickguard, a few with no logo on pickguard, red top finish, ebony finish back and sides (**6131**), same specs and changes as Duo-Jet
Introduced: **by 1955**
Discontinued, available by special order only: **1971**

Round-Up: Duo-Jet body shape, maple top, some with knotty pine top, some with mahogany top, 2 DeArmond pickups, 3 knobs (master tone and 2 individual volume) on lower treble bout, 1 master volume knob on cutaway bout, 1 pickup selector switch on upper bass bout, Melita bridge, *G* tailpiece, string anchors covered by rectangular "belt-buckle" with Western scene, *G* brand on top, 4-ply top binding, unbound back, sides covered with Western-motif tooled leather, bound fingerboard, block inlay engraved with cows and cactus, no inlay at 1st fret, longhorn head etched on pickguard and inlaid on peghead, bound peghead, gold-plated hardware, orange-stain top finish (**6130**), tweed case
Introduced: **1954**
Inlay at 1st fret with no engraving: **early 1955**
Engraving on 1st fret inlay: **mid 1955**
Triple-bound top: **1956**
Appears on price list but not in catalog: **1959**
Discontinued: **1960**

Chet Atkins Solid Body: Duo-Jet body shape, maple top, some with knotty pine top, 2 DeArmond pickups, 2 knobs on lower treble bout, 1 knob on cutaway bout, 1 switch on upper bass bout, height-adjustable metal compensating bridge, Bigsby vibrato, pickguard with signpost and Chet Atkins signature, *G* brand on top, 4-ply top binding, unbound back, sides covered with Western-motif tooled leather, bound rosewood fingerboard, block inlay engraved with Western scenes, single-bound peghead, longhorn peghead inlay, metal nut, gold-plated hardware (except for Bigsby, bridge and nut), "brown mahogany" orange finish (**6121**), white case with tooled leather trim

Introduced: **by 1955**

3-ply top binding: **late 1955**

3 knobs on lower treble bout, no leather side covering, triple-bound top and back, ebony fingerboard, unengraved humptop block inlay: **1957**

Straight bar bridge 1/2" in diameter, 4-ply top and back binding: **early 1958**

Filter 'Tron pickups, 2 knobs on lower treble bout, 1 knob on cutaway bout, 2 switches on upper bass bout, thumbprint inlay, horseshoe peghead inlay: **1958**

Gretsch Bigsby: **1959**

Zero fret, bone nut: **late 1959**

Bound top and back: **1960**

Symmetrical double cutaway body, 4-ply top and back binding, orange top finish: **1961**

Standby switch added to lower treble bout, standard Gretsch case: **1962**

Discontinued: **1963**

White Penguin: solidbody companion to White Falcon (see Electric Archtops section), 2 DeArmond pickups, tubular tailpiece with V-shaped piece and *G*, penguin on pickguard; gold-sparkle binding on sides of body, fingerboard and peghead; ebony fingerboard, engraved humptop block inlay, white finish (**6134**)

Introduced: **1955**

Filter 'Tron pickups, stereo optional, roller bridge, thumbprint inlay: **1958**

Horizontal logo, nameplate on peghead: **1959**

Symmetrical double cutaway body: **by 1963**

Discontinued (less than 100 total made): **1964**

LATER SINGLE CUTAWAY DUO-JET STYLE MODELS

Roc Jet: Super 'Tron pickups, adjustamatic bridge, Porsche pumpkin (**6127**) or Mercedes black (**6130**) finish

Introduced: **late 1969**

Renumbered, Porsche pumpkin (**7611**), Mercedes black (**7610**)

Red (**7612**) or walnut-stained mahogany (**7613**) finish optional: **1971**

Porsche pumpkin finish (**7611**) discontinued, model number 7611 assigned to black finish: **by 1975**

Red finish (7612) discontinued: **by 1977**

Humbucking pickups: **1978**

Discontinued: **1980**

Country Roc: Western style Roc-Jet, *G* brand, block inlay with engraved Western scenes, horseshoe inlaid on peghead, tooled leather side trim (**7620**)

Available: **1974–78**

Roc II: solid mahogany body, flat top, 2 humbucking pickups, elliptical control plate with 4 knobs and 1 switch and jack, bound top and back, bound ebony fingerboard, thumbprint inlay (**7621**)

Available: **1974–mid 1977**

Roc I: 1 pickup (**7635**): **mid 1970s**

BO DIDDLEY MODELS

Bo Diddley: rectangular body shape, 2 DeArmond pickups, Melita bridge, *G* tailpiece, bound fingerboard, thumbprint inlay, red top finish, black back and sides finish, 4 instruments made for singer Bo Diddley

First instrument made: **1958**

Second instrument made: **1960**

Third and fourth instruments made: **1962**

Jupiter, Thunderbird, and **Cadillac:** custom models made for Bo Diddley, Jupiter with abstract square-ish body shape, Thunderbird with more curved body shape, Cadillac with lower bass bout resembling an automobile tail fin, all with 2 Filter 'Tron pickups, Jupiter and Thunderbird with red top finish and black back and sides finish, Cadillac with orange top finish and black back and sides finish

2 Cadillacs made: **1961**

2 Jupiters and 2 Thunderbirds made: **c. 1961**

OTHER MODELS

Bikini: removable neck-body shaft and foldup "butterfly" back and wings, Hi-Lo 'Tron pickups, dot inlay, black finish, guitar only (**6023**), bass only (**6024**) or doubleneck (**6025**)

Available: **1961–62**

Corvette solidbody/Gold Duke/Silver Duke: 13 1/2" wide, asymmetrical double cutaway with bass horn slightly longer, slab body, 1 Hi-Lo 'Tron pickup, 2 knobs, rosewood bridge, trapeze

tailpiece, rectangular plate next to neck, no binding, 24 1/2" scale, dot inlay, narrow peghead, mahogany (**6132**) or platinum grey (**6133**) finish
Introduced: **1961**
Platinum grey finish (6133) discontinued: **1963**
Beveled body edges, sharper cutaway points, bar bridge 3/8" in diameter, larger pickguard covers routing for metal plate, cherry red finish, 1 pickup and no vibrato (**6132**), 1 pickup with flat-arm vibrato (**6134**), or 2 pickups with Burns flat-arm vibrato (**6135**): **1963**
2 tuners on bass side, 4 on treble side: **1964**
Glittered silver finish available as **Silver Duke**, glittered gold finish available as **Gold Duke**, a few made: **c. 1966**
1-pickup models (6132 and 6134) discontinued: **by 1968**
Bigsby, Super 'Tron pickups: **1968**
2-pickup model (6135) discontinued, available by special order only: **1972**
2-pickup model listed, humbucking pickups (**7623**): **1976**
Discontinued: **1978**

Deluxe Corvette: specs unavailable (**7632**): **early 1977**

Princess: Corvette-style double cutaway with beveled body edges, 1 Hi-Lo 'Tron pickup, 2 knobs, bar bridge 3/8" in diameter, short-arm palm vibrato, trapeze tailpiece, padded back, 24 3/8" scale, dot inlay, gold-plated hardware (**6106**), optional body/pickguard colors: white/grape (lavender), blue/white, pink/white or white/gold
Available: **1963**

Astro-Jet: asymmetrical double cutaway, pointed horns, beveled body edges, 2 Super 'Tron pickups, 3 knobs, 3 switches, roller bridge, Burns straight-arm vibrato, thumbprint inlay, 4 tuners on bass side, 2 on treble side, red top finish, black finish on back and sides (**6126**)
Available: **1965–67**

Broadkaster solidbody: 13 1/2" wide, double cutaway similar to Fender Stratocaster shape, rounded horns, bass horn longer than treble horn, maple body, 2 Super 'Tron pickups, 2 knobs, 2 toggle switches, adjustamatic bridge, strings anchor on metal plate tailpiece (tailpiece screwed into top), bolt-on maple neck, maple fingerboard, black dot

inlay, no peghead veneer, natural (**7600**) or sunburst (**7601**) finish
Available: **1975–c. 1979**

Committee: 12 1/2" wide, symmetrical double cutaway, 5-piece walnut and maple body, neck-through-body construction, 2 humbucking pickups, clear symmetrical pickguard, single-bound rosewood fingerboard, dot inlay, bound peghead, walnut grain peghead veneer, natural finish (**7628**)
Available: **1975–80**

TK 300: 12" wide, asymmetrical double cutaway, maple body, slight cutout at endpin, 2 humbucking pickups, bridge pickup slant-mounted, 2 knobs, white pickguard, bolt-on neck, no fingerboard inlay, peghead shape similar to hockey stick blade, 6-on-a-side tuner arrangement, vertical block letter logo reads upside down to player, natural (**7625**) or autumn red stain (**7624**) finish
Available: **1975–80**

Atkins Super Axe: pointed cutaway, upper bass bout joins neck at angle toward body, 2 humbucking pickups, phaser and compressor electronics, black elliptical control plate, 5 knobs, small square inlay, red rosewood stain (**7680**) or ebony stain (**7681**) finish
Appears in ads as un-named model played by Roy Clark (later Clark prototypes have asymmetrical rounded double cutaway design, no control plate, knobs and switches in elliptical pattern)
Introduced as Atkins Super Axe: **1976**
Discontinued: **1981**

Atkins Axe: pointed cutaway, upper bass bout joins neck at angle toward body, 2 humbucking pickups, standard electronics, 4 knobs on lower treble bout, 1 switch on upper bass bout, small square inlay, ebony stain (**7685**) or red rosewood stain (**7686**) finish
Available: **1976–80**

BST "BEAST" MODELS

BST 1000: single cutaway, mahogany body, bolt-on neck, dot inlay, T-roof logo reads upside down to player
1 humbucking pickup: walnut stain (**8210**) or red stain (**8216**) finish
2 humbucking pickups with exposed coils: walnut stain (**7617**, **8215**, or **8217**) or red stain (**8211**) finish
Available: **1979–80**

BST 2000: symmetrical double cutaway, mahogany body, 2 humbucking pickups, bolt-on neck, dot inlay, T-roof logo reads upside down to player, walnut stain (**7620** or **8220**) or red stain (**8221**) finish
Available: **1979**

BST 5000: asymmetrical double cutaway body shape, neck-through-body construction, 5-piece walnut and maple construction, some with no separate fingerboard, 2 humbucking pickups, stud tailpiece, dot inlay, T-roof logo reads upside down to player, natural walnut/maple finish (**8250**)
Available: **1979–80**

COMMENTS

The appeal of solidbody Gretsch guitars is primarily aesthetic. The models of greatest appeal to collectors are those with ornamentation closely related to the most desirable hollowbody models. The rare White Penguin is one of the most highly sought of all vintage electric guitars. The Roundup and Chet Atkins Solid Body are also highly sought. The Duo-Jet, which has no hollowbody equivalent, is also highly regarded, with custom color and sparkle-top models bringing more than the standard black-top model.

Double-cutaway models from the 1960s—especially sparkle-top models—are sought by collectors and players but bring less than their single cutaway equivalents.

Later solidbody models are of little interest to collectors.

BASSES

SECTION ORGANIZATION

Hollowbody Models
Solidbody Models

HOLLOWBODY MODELS

Model 6070: 17" wide, double cutaway, painted *f*-holes, extension endpin, 1 pickup, roller bridge, mute, padded back, 34" scale, asymmetrical peghead, 2-on-a-side tuner arrangement, gold-plated hardware, sunburst finish
Introduced: **by 1963**
No extension endpin: **1965**
Discontinued, available by special order only: **1972**

Model 6072: same as Model 6070 but with 2 pickups: **1968–71**

Model 6071: 16" wide, single cutaway, 29" scale, painted *f*-holes, 1 pickup, roller bridge, mute, padded back, zero fret, 4-on-a-side tuner arrangement, red mahogany finish
Introduced: **1968**
Discontinued, available by special order only: **1972**

Model 6073: same as Model 6071 but with 2 pickups: **1968–71**

SOLIDBODY MODELS

Solid Body Bass: double cutaway, mahogany body, cutout through upper bass bout, 2 Super 'Tron pickups, 3 knobs, 1 switch, large rosewood-grain pickguard with beveled edges, 2 finger rests, bound rosewood fingerboard, dot inlay, asymmetrical peghead with point at top on bass side, 2-on-a-side tuner arrangement, natural mahogany finish (**7615**)
Introduced: **by 1972**
Discontinued: **by 1975**

Broadkaster Bass: asymmetrical double cutaway, similar shape to Fender Stratocaster, rounded horns, bass horn longer than treble, 1 Super 'Tron pickup, 2 knobs, bolt-on maple neck, maple fingerboard, black dot inlay, no peghead veneer, natural (**7605**) or sunburst (**7606**) finish
Available: **1975–79**

Committee Bass: 13" wide, symmetrical double cutaway, 5-piece walnut and maple body, neck-

through-body construction, 1 Super 'Tron pickup, clear pickguard, metal bridge cover, bound rosewood fingerboard, dot inlay, walnut-grain peghead veneer, bound peghead, natural finish (**7629**)
Available: **1977–80**

TK 300 Bass: asymmetrical double cutaway, slight cutout at endpin area, 1 Super 'Tron pickup, 2 knobs, white pickguard, bolt-on neck, no fingerboard inlay, block-letter logo reads upside down to player, 4-on-a-side tuner arrangement, peghead shape similar to hockey stick blade, natural (**7627**)

or autumn red stain (**7626**) finish
Introduced: **by 1977**
Natural (7627) discontinued: **1980**
Autumn red (7626) discontinued: **1981**

COMMENTS

Gretsch hollowbody basses have some visual appeal but are sought by very few players as utility instruments. Solidbody models have little appeal.

STEELS

With the exception of the Electromatic Hawaiian model, all Gretsch steel guitars were made by Valco (see National/Valco/Supro section). Like Valco-made National and Supro models, Gretsch lap steels typically have a small metal serial number plate nailed onto the back of the neck at the peghead. Serial numbers on Valco-made Gretsch lap steels and amps are part of the overall Valco number series.

Electromatic Hawaiian Guitar: mahogany body, symmetrical guitar shape, knobs on opposite sides, wooden pickup cover, rope-pattern top binding, wooden fingerboard, dot markers, 6-on-a-side Stauffer-style tuner arrangement (like early Martin guitars) with high E-string shaft longer then low E-string shaft, *Gretsch* and *Electromatic* diagonally across peghead, musical note ornament above logo, natural finish
Available: **1940–42**

Electromatic Standard Guitar: symmetrical body with two points near neck and belly below bridge (like Supro Supreme), square control plate, 1 round knob, 1 pointer knob, bound fingerboard, geometric-shape markers, 6-on-a-side tuner arrangement, peghead wider at top than at nut, brown pearloid covering (**6156**)
Introduced: **by 1949**
Discontinued: **by 1955**

Electromatic Student Guitar: straight-line

body sides, square bottom, beveled from fingerboard to body edges, square control plate, 1 round knob, 1 pointer knob, geometric-shape markers, peghead narrower at top than at nut, pearloid covering (**6152**)
Introduced: **by 1949**
Discontinued: **by 1955**

Electromatic Console Guitar: 2 6-string necks, straight-line body edges with wedge between necks, body beveled around fingerboard, 2 square pickup/control plate units, each plate with 1 round knob and 1 pointer knob, bound fingerboards, geometric-shape markers, 6-on-a-side tuner arrangement, brown pearloid covering (**6158**)
Introduced: **by 1949**
Discontinued: **by 1955**

Jet Twin Console: 2 6-string necks, asymmetrical bodies joined together, staggered tiers, heavy metal bridge covers with *Gretsch* and *Electromatic*, 2 metal knobs on front neck, 1 knob on rear neck, clear plastic fingerboards back-painted white, geometric-shape markers, 6-on-a-side tuner arrangement, black finish (**6148**), 4 legs optional (**6148L**)
Introduced: **by 1955**
Discontinued: **1963**

Jet Mainliner: 6 strings, asymmetrical body, 2 metal knobs, heavy metal bridge cover with *Gretsch* and *Electromatic*, clear plastic fingerboard back-painted white, geometric-shape markers, 3-on-a-side tuner arrangement, asymmetrical peghead longer on treble side, black finish (**6147**)

Introduced: **by 1955**

Discontinued: **1963**

Jet Airliner: 6-strings, symmetrical body, 2 knobs on opposite sides, control plates shaped like rocket fins (similar to National Rocket 110), plastic bridge/pickup cover, painted-on frets, geometric-shape markers, symmetrical peghead, 3-on-a-side tuners, black finish (**6145**)

Introduced: **by 1955**

Discontinued: **1963**

COMMENTS

The Electromatic Hawaiian of the early 1940s and the Jet series of the 1950s have some aesthetic appeal for collectors.

Unlike Gretsch electric guitars, the postwar lap steels have Valco electronics, which are sought by some players for blues-related music.

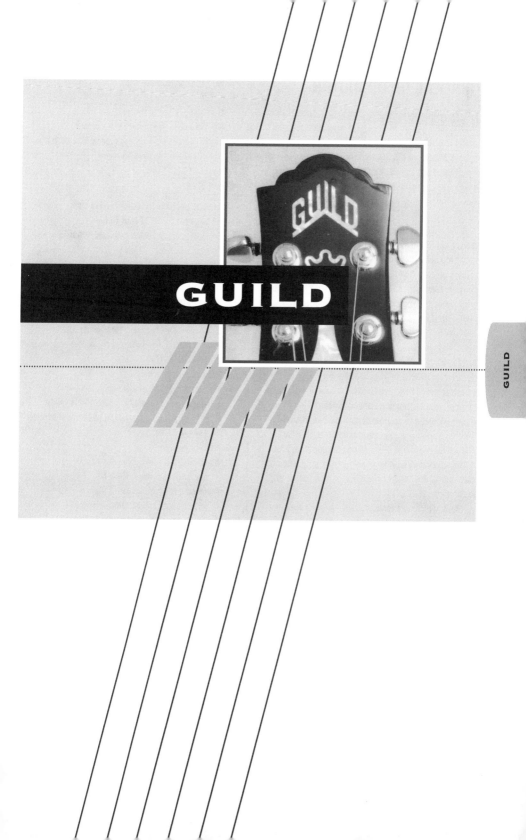

GUILD

GENERAL INFORMATION

Guild Guitars, Inc. was founded in New York in 1952 by Alfred Dronge, a musician, teacher and music store owner who had been born in Poland. Many key employees were former employees of Epiphone, which had moved production from New York to Philadelphia that year. In 1956 Guild moved from Manhattan across the Hudson River to Hoboken, NJ.

Guild built its reputation in the 1950s on archtop guitars but was able to successfully switch emphasis to flat top acoustics during the 1960s.

Dronge sold Guild to Avnet, an electronics company, in 1966 and stayed on as president. Production was moved to Westerly, RI, over a period from 1966–69. Dronge died in the crash of his private plane in 1972. Leon Tell, Dronge's vice president since 1963, became president, a position he held until 1983.

Avnet sold Guild in August 1986 to a group of investors headed by Jere Haskew, a banker from Chattanooga, and including Nashville vintage guitar dealer George Gruhn as vice president of product development and artist relations (Gruhn left in early 1988). The new corporation, Guild Music Corporation, was under a court-ordered financial restructuring when it was sold to the FAAS Corporation of New Berlin, WI, in January 1989.

FAAS, which was renamed U.S. Music Corporation by 1993, discontinued most electric models, concentrating on the flat top models. U.S. Music sold Guild to the Fender Musical Instrument Corp. in November 1995, and a Custom Shop was opened in Nashville shortly thereafter. Production models are still made in Westerly.

LABELS

Vertical rectangular, guitar silhouette...
  New York 3, N.Y.: **1953–54**
  New York 7, N.Y.: **late 1954–1956**
  Hoboken, N.J.: **1956–59**
  Some classicals with Hoboken label: **1965–69**
Horizontal rectangular, ghost figure playing guitar:
  1959–60
Oval, G-shield logo...
  Hoboken, no *USA:* **1961–64**
  Hoboken, USA: **1965–c. 1969**

No *Hoboken:* **c. 1969–72**
Oval, script *Guild*...
  Guarantee: **late 1972–74**
  No guarantee, *Westerly:* **1975–current**
2nd label, square label on neck block, Nashville Custom Shop model: **1996–current**

DATE STAMP

Most flat tops made in Westerly have a date stamp...
  On back brace: **1973–mid 1990s**
  On treble side of neck block: **mid 1990s–current**

PICKUPS

Guild single-coil...
  White or black plastic cover with rounded mounting "ears" (except on M-75 and M-65, which have no ears), screwpoles: **1953–early 1960s**
  White, rectangular, 6 magnet poles, low-end models: **1966–c. 1970**
DeArmond single-coil...
  No poles, low-end models only: **1958–61**
  6 magnet poles, white face: **late 1950s–1960**
  6 magnet poles, 6 pole-height adjustment screws: **1961–mid 1960s**
Guild humbucking...
  Metal cover, 6 screwpoles, 2 pickup-height adjustment screws: **1962-69**
  Metal cover, 6 screwpoles, 3 pickup-height adjustment screws: **1969–current**
DiMarzio: humbucker, 2 exposed white bobbins, open-end polepieces: **1977–80s**
California: Korean-made humbucker, 2 exposed black bobbins: **1983–89**

KNOBS

Clear barrel: **1953–58**
Amber/yellow top hat with Guild logo insert in chrome or gold: **1959–63**
Black top hat...
  Guild logo, numbers, tone or volume designation: **1964–72**
  Guild logo, numbers, no tone or volume designation: **1973–current**
  Guild logo, no numbers, no tone or volume designation: **1980s**

PICKGUARD

Stairstep pickguard introduced...

Johnny Smith/Artist Award: **1956–86**

Acoustic models with floating DeArmond: **late
1950s–c. 1987**

All other electric archtops: **1963**

SCALE LENGTH

Guitars: Scale lengths specified as 25 5/8" are actually
25 1/2".

Basses: Scale lengths specified as 30 1/2" are actually
30 3/4".

PEGHEAD SHAPE

Dip in center of top, all models except Johnny Smith:
1953–62

Peghead raised in center of top...

Transitional period: **1962–64**

All models: **by 1965**

Snakehead shape (tapers in at middle): acoustics and
Nightbirds: **1984–current**

Pegheads with all tuners on one side...

"Spade," concave curve on treble side, rounded tip,
script logo with lower-case letter *g*, tail of *g*
underlines *uild:* **1983–87**

Charvel-type, straight sides, treble side goes
directly to point, severe angle to treble side,

standard Guild peaked logo, underline goes
through letter *G:* **1985**

Charvel-type, straight sides, bass side goes directly
to point: **1984–87**

Bass side goes directly to point, treble side makes
curve at point: **1987–89**

Exceptions include Brian May, Thunderbird.

PEGHEAD LOGO

Peaked *Guild*...

Triangle under letters, all elements in a single piece:
c. 1953

Triangle under letters, each letter and triangle a
separate piece: **c. 1954**

Line under letters, no triangle: **c. 1955–current**

Script *Guild*, low-end models: **1953–early 1960s**

Simple *G* (no shield on lower half of *G*), some midline
models: **c. 1955–57**

Angular script *Guild*, pegheads with 4- or 6-on-a-side
tuner arrangement: **1987–93**

"Chesterfield" column-and-crown inlay (similar to the
design on a pack of Chesterfield cigarettes)...

Three vertical lines engraved in column: **1957–
early 1970s**

No engraving in column: **early 1970s–current**

GENERAL INFORMATION

F-style body with circular lower bout and thin waist, on an F-44.

D-style dreadnought body with flat lower bout and thick waist, on a D-60.

G-shield logo and narrow "snake-head" peghead on an F-44.

Pearl block fingerboard inlay with abalone V inserts, on an X-2000.

Chesterfield peghead inlay on a Songbird.

SERIAL NUMBERS

From 1953–65 and from 1970–79, Guild guitars are numbered in one consectutive series.

From 1965–69 most guitars are numbered with a 2-letter prefix and a separate number series for each model. However, a few (approximately 89) from 1966–69 are numbered in the original series.

Beginning November 1, 1970, all models return to a single number series.

Numbers for 1953–58 were compiled by Hans Moust. Numbers from 1959–86 are from Guild records.

Most Guild flat tops made in Westerly have a date stamp on the back brace from 1973 to the mid 1990s, and on the treble side of the neck block thereafter.

1953–79, SINGLE SERIES

YEAR	APPROX. LAST NUMBER	YEAR	APPROX. LAST NUMBER
(Numbers begin with 1000)			
1953	1500	1967	46637
1954	2200	1968	46656
1955	3000	1969	46695
1956	4000	1970	50978
1957	5700	1971	61463
1958	8300	1972	75602
1959	12035	1973	95496
1960	14713	1974	112803
1961	18419	1975	130304
1962	22722	1976	149625
1963	28943	1977	169867
1964	38636	1978	195067
1965	46606	1979	211877
1966	46608		

1965–70

Models are alphabetized by serial number prefix. Numbers are last number for that year. All series start with 101. This numbering system continued into 1970, but 1970 numbers are not available.

MODEL	PREFIX	1965	1966	1967	1968	1969
Artist Award	AA	101	113	139	157	167
A-50	AB	136	162	203	240	
D-44	AC	166	318	435	488	570
F-50	AD	119	190	291	355	418
F-212XL	AE	n/a	n/a	n/a	n/a	n/a
A-500	AF		102	none	115	
F-20	AG	316	1534	2499	2793	2822
M-20	AH	n/a	n/a	n/a	n/a	2000
F-30	AI	351	1142	1855	2270	2554
A-150	AI				108	113
D-40	AJ	333	1136	2244	2825	3218
F-47	AK	128	218	418	488	583
D-50	AL	192	301	513	584	698
F-212	AN	228	810	1558	2009	2271
F-312	AS	141	230	335	376	497

GUILD

SERIAL NUMBERS

MODEL	PREFIX	1965	1966	1967	1968	1969
SF-Bass	BA	177	654	1696	1946	2043
M-85	BB			109	194	241
Mark I	CA	316	996	1973	2156	
Mark II	CB	247	967	1173	2018	
Mark III	CC	252	666	992	1203	
Mark IV	CD	128	292	491	541	
Mark V	CE	120	137	195		
Mark VI	CF		128	175	197	
X-500	DA	106	138	180	235	244
SF-6	DB	101	174	274	329	339
SF-12	DC		586	896	897	910
M-75	DD			138	237	395
X-50	EA	202	326	491	502	506
T-50	EB	196	391	558	607	652
M-65 3/4	EC	182	267	322	334	
M-65	ED	160	194	270	335	414
T-100	EE	601	1939	2794	3003	3109
CE-100	EF	211	396	649	719	760
X-175	EG	107	160	239	322	346
DE-400	EH	126	233	275	301	
DE-500	EI	107	116	136	none	141
SF-2/SF-3	EK	387	2098	2819	3028	3098
SF-4	EL	276	1167	1840	2223	2272
SF-5	EN	194	927	1807	2141	2278
ST	ES				275	318
F-112	OA				511	695
F-412	OB				110	114
F-512	OC		(starts with 201)	206	223	
A-350	OD				109	112
M-20 3/4	OE					102
George Barnes	OF					104
D-25	OG				192	233
CA-100	OH				113	114
D-55	OI				105	113
D-35	OJ				1003	1592
S-50	SA	201	490	584		
S-100	SB	169	220	251	269	
S-200	SC	101	153	166	191	
Jet Star Bass	SD	108	327	343		

1979–86

Numbering by separate model series resumes on October 1, 1979. Numbers listed are last number for that year.

MODEL	PREFIX	1979	1980	1981	1982	1983	1984	1985	1986
D-212	AA			101085	101529	101895	102114	102395	102796
S-250	AB			100154	100236	100250			
S-25	AC			100159	100293	100339			
X-79	AD			100304	101342	101509	101705	101790	

MODEL	PREFIX	1979	1980	1981	1982	1983	1984	1985	1986
SB-201/202	AE				100109	100452			
S-275	AF					100110			
DE-500	AG					100019	100148	100153	100169
D-15	AH					100617	100924	101371	101815
S-26	AJ					100002			
Ashbury Bass	AJ								23
S-260	AK					100030			
D-17	AL						100092	100402	100575
B-50	BA	100002	100012	100168	100212	100249	100269	100306	100326
B-301/302 mah	BB	100400	100846						
B-301/302 ash	BC	100061	100196	100235					
B401/402	BD		100212	100335					
SB-600/602/603	BE					100050	100456	100135	101726
FS-46CE Bass	BF					100008			
SB-608	BG						100068	100116	
SB-604	BH					100226	100616		
Brian May	BHM						150	286	316
Bluesbird	BJ							100060	100215
SB-605	BK								100177
Nightbird	BL							100104	100324
Mark II	CA	100005	100246	100424	100510	100570	100657	100689	100733
Mark III	CB	100014	100163	100283	100305	100367	100406	100425	100461
Mark IV	CC	100017	100101	100199	100218	100232	100253	100270	
Mark V	CD	100021	100064	100089	100124	100137	100156	100176	100184
MKS-10CE	CE						100046	100056	
D-25	DA	100914	105752	109433	111910	112936	113675	114523	115528
D-35	DB	100503	102097	103268	103743	104078	104288	104477	104697
D-40	DC	100247	101105	101638	101782	101889	101972	102066	102190
D-50	DD	100212	100944	101382	101588	101737	101789	101878	101928
D-55	DE	100236	100661	101058	101186	101247	101298	101374	101406
G-37	DF	100052	100814	101339	101579	101774	101890	101990	102135
D-40C	DG		100542	100818	100959	101002	101032	101068	
G-212	DH	100035	100248	100398	100419	100436			
G-312	DJ	100014	100164	100235	100263	100281	100287		
D-44M	DK								
D-46	DL		100131	100622	n/a	100839	100887		
S-300 mah	EA	100054	100112	100468	100470				
S-300 ash	EB	100023	100039	100229	100230				
S-60D	EC	100019	100169	100207					
S-60/65	ED	100050	100349	100499	100500				
S-70	EE	100019	100104	100246					
D-70	EF			100151	100208	100250	100263	100280	
D-80	EG	100014	100017	100019					
D-25C	EH						100098	100101	
FS-46CE	EJ					100205	100306	100370	100401
D-52	EK					100034	100054		
D-15-12	EL					100064	100144	100211	
F-20	FA	100051	100244	100394	100490	100524	100545	100595	100663

GUILD

GUILD

SERIAL NUMBERS

MODEL	PREFIX	1979	1980	1981	1982	1983	1984	1985	1986
F-30	FB	100073	100235	100382	100440	100472	100509	100527	
F-40	FC	100015	100197	100381	100393				
F-50	FD	100018	100286	100424	100484	100535	100600	100650	100693
F-50R	FE	100025	100261	100340	100426	100431	100462	100479	100505
F-112	FF	100199	100277	100286	100294				
F-212	FG	100014	100194	100308	100324	100342	100358	100382	
F-212C	FH	100001	100056	100424					
F-212XL	FJ		100233	100401	100486	100525	100545	100567	
F-412	FK	100045	100221	100342	100385	100405	100445	100476	100506
F-512	FL	100040	100225	100362	100440	100477	100519	100543	100569
SF-4	GA	100051	100439	100686	100713	100842	100898	100911	100982
F-45CE	GB				100006	100409	100533	100683	100839
D-17-12	GC						100026		
G-45	GD				100002	100050	100053	100080	
D-47CE	GE					100026	100047	100049	
DS-48CE	GF					100024	100026		
F-30R	GG		100123	100174	100203	100207			
FS-46CE-12	GH					100005	100027		
F-45C-12	GJ						100030		
S-285	GK								100011
Studio 24	GL								100030
M-80	HA		100003	100229	100339	100350			
T-50	HB				100019				
S-280/281	HC					100050	100481	101039	101493
X-80	HD					100023	100129	100172	
S-282	HE						100047		
X-88	HF						100285	100457	
S-284	HG						100101	100435	100637
X-92	HH						129		
X-100	HJ						100004	100095	
T-250	HK								100123
X-170	HL							100014	100076
Artist Award	JA	100012	100043	100067	100097	100107	100122	100127	100133
X-500	JB	100036	100082	100136	100144	100148	100165	100178	100194
X-175	JC	100013	100114	100177	100184	100205	100217		
X-701/702	JD				100174	100234	100235		
SB-902	JE								
X-82	JF			100107	100311	100430	100460		
CE-100	KA	100015	100077	100136	100159	100169	100175		
D-62	KB						100046	100060	
D-64	KC						100030	100050	100193
D-66	KD						100110	100162	100208
F-42	KG						100036	100065	
F-44	KH						100078	100186	100249
F-46	KJ						100029	100089	100121
Prototypes	LL		100031	100108	100147	100198	100228	100234	100237

1987–93

MODEL	PREFIX	1987	1988	1989	1990	1991	1992	1993
Ashbury Bass	AJ	1109	1235					
D-17	AL	100886	100888					
B-30	B3	00100	00230	00310	00373	00425	00590	00727
B-50	BA	100212	100249	300310				
Nightbird I	BE	100083	100103					
SB-602	BE	102702	103519	103826	103981	104111	104420	104434
SB-604	BH	100725	100744					
Bluesbird	BJ	100216						
SB-605	BK	100435	100524		100569	100594	100748	100783
Nightbird II/Cst	BL	100426	100489	100530	100597	100626	100634	
Brian May	BM							20022
Mark II	CA	100743						
Mark III	CB	100463						
Mark V	CD	100185						
D-4	CF					000323	003381	006541
JF-4	CG						000746	0001572
D-4-12	CH						000631	001045
F-25E/F-4	CJ						000597	002255
F-4CE	CK						000003	
X-2000/4000	CL						000053	000054
D-40/D-40C	D040	0223						
D-60	D060	0113						
D-65	D065	0012						
D-15	D15	00642	1898	1898	2418	2700	3183	3484
D-225	D225	768						
D-25-12	D225					1372	1570	1630
D-25	D25				3561	3790	4482	4666
D-25-12	D25			1005	1271			
D-25-12	D2512	467						
D-30	D30	00367	0719	0921	1140	1259	1458	1709
D-40/D-40C	D40			400640	0824	0857	0884	
D-50	D50		00447	00478	0703	0782	0964	1104
D-60	D60		0234	0306	0308			
D-25	DA	001232						
D-25	DA25		2265	2986				
D-35	DB	104754						
D-40/D-40C	DC40		0482					
D-50	DD	101210						
D-55	DE	101407	n/a	101376				
D-312	DJ	100300						
D-80	EG	100024						
D-100	EG				100073	100085	100105	100148
DV52/DV62	EK							100611

GUILD

SERIAL NUMBERS

MODEL	PREFIX	1987	1988	1989	1990	1991	1992	1993
F-44	F044	0017						
F-45	F045	0311						
F-15	F15				0054	0167	0254	
F-30CE	F30						00130	00242
F-35	F35				0029	0038	0049	
F-45	F45		0535	0664	0816	0860	0918	
F-48	F48						0006	
F-65CE	F65						0062	0120
F-20	FA				100818	100874	100890	
F-50R/GF-50R	FE	100515						
JF-55	FE			100562	1--658	100707	10069	101037
JF-65R	FE			100516				
Prototypes	FF			000006	000015	000019	000036	000057
JF212XL	FJ			100612				
F-412	FK	100578						
F-512/JF-55-12	FL				100603	100621	100660	100708
SF-4	GA	100982			101002	101072	101115	101147
G-45	GD	100089						
GF-25	GF25	0409	0715	0845	0935	0946	0948	0999
GF-30	GF30	0269	0498	0604	0699	0766	0836	0845
GF-40	GF40	0082	0086					
GF-50	GF50	0212	0290	0322	0337			
GF-50-12	GF5012	0043						
GF-55	GF			100002	100069	100103	100126	100166
GF-60M	GF60	0048	0082					
GF-60R	GF60				277			
GF-60R	GF60R	0087	0206	0275				
F-30R	GG							100118
X-160	HJ		000005	000126				
GX Series	HJ				000771			000772
X-160/161	HJ				000154	000176	000261	000302
T-250	HK	100211						
X-170	HL	100230	100471	100558	100636	100660	100717	100765
JF-30-12	J23		0398	0561	0820	0970	1262	
JF-65-12	J26		5153					
Artist Award	JA	100147	100203	100227	100274	100280	100328	100379
X-500	JB	100214	100312	100341	100373	100389	100421	100173
SB-902	JE		1000153	000186	000195			
SB-905	JF		000009					
JF-30-12	JF23				0820	0970	1262	1502
JF-65-12	JF265			5227	5352	5427	5544	5635
JF-30	JF30	0234	0618	0663	1099	1224	1528	1880
JF-30-12	JF3012	0198						
JF-50	JF50	0050	0112					
JF-50-12	JF5012	0007						
JF-65M	JF65	0031						
JF-65R	JF65R	0019						
JF-65R-12	JF65R	0018						

MODEL	PREFIX	1987	1988	1989	1990	1991	1992	1993
JF-65-12	JF6512	0064						
S-284	JG	100638						
Detonator	JH				000605			
Standard	JH				000089	000120	000172	
SB-905	JJ	000008						
Classic	JK				000025	000038	000044	
Excellence	JL				000011	000016	000037	
S-4CE	KE						000042	
B-500CE	KF						000018	000061
Songbird	KK				001267	001352	001847	002243
D6/D7	KL							001210
JF4-12	LA							000166
CE-100	LB							000069
N'bird Std/Dlx	LC				000015	000020		
B-4E	LD							000271
F-5	LE							000122
FF5/FF5CE	LF							000046
DCE-1	LH							000003
Prototypes	LL	100238						

1994–97

MODEL	PREFIX	1994	1995	1996	1997
Artist Award	AA	000039	000089	000105	158
B-4E	AB04	0487	0714	1044	1257
B-30/B-30E	AB30	0132	0207	0286	1249
D-4/D-4E/D-25	AD04	2116	4518	8099	1129
D-6/D-6E/DV6	AD06	0701	1343	2106	2419
D-100/D-100C	AD10	0014	0022	0039	0049
DC-1/DCE-1	AD11	0841	1713	3572	4800
D-26	AD26		0458		
D-30	AD30	0184	0301	0348	0784
D-30 blond	AD30			0348	
D4-12/D25-12	AD42	0368	0802	1507	1738
DV-52	AD52	0445	0945	1850	2272
D-55	AD55	0114	0220	0412	0691
D-60	AD60	0028	0043		
DV-62	AD62	0145	0146		
DV-72	AD72	0197			
DV-73	AD73	0014	0052		
DV-74	AD74		0007	0022	
DV-76	AD76	0019			
S-4CE	AE04	0103	0343	0540	0672
F-4CE	AF04	0801	1355	2131	2598
F-5CE	AF05	0200	0353	0614	0660
FF-5CE	AF15	0119	0143		
A-25	AF25		0271	0893	0896
F-20	AF20	0049	0131		

SERIAL NUMBERS

MODEL	PREFIX	1994	1995	1996	1997
F-30	AF30	0151	0153		
F-50	AF50	0012	0015		
A-50	AF50		0078	0194	0209
F-65CE	AF65	0118	0237	0398	0556
Starfire IV	AG00	0014	0023	0219	0937
Starfire II/III	AG30				1083
JF-4/JF-4E	AJ04	0387	0424		
JF-100C	AJ10		0027	0041	0046
JF-100	AJ11	0121	0127		
JF100-12C	AJ12		0004	0012	
JF-30	AJ30	0329	0779	1720	2129
JF30-12	AJ32	0240	0592	1101	1291
JF4-12	AJ42	0064			
JF55-12	AJ52	0062	0175	0253	0300
JF-55	AJ55	0129	02093	0483	0613
JF65-12	AJ62	0090	0188	0304	0369
X-150	AK15				0004
X-160	AK16	0031			
X-170	AK17	0059	0138	0401	0799
X-500	AK50	0008	0010		
X-700	AK70			0118	0213
Pro4	AL04	0139			
Pro5	AL05	0078	0096		
Brian May Std.	BHD	00039			
Brian May Spec.	BHM	30114			
BM01/BM01 Std.	BHP	00003	00057		
Brian May	BM	00415			
BB Bluesbird	CL			0152	1013
D-15	D15	3520			
D-50	D50	1106	1107		
Crossroads	FA	000097			
Prototypes	FB	000004			
S-100/Songbird	FB00	0132	0194	0378	0770
DC-5	FC05	0298	0578	0964	1258
DC-130	FD	000019	000022		
GV-52	FE00	0225			
G-45 Hank Wms.	FG45	0004			
G-45 Hank Wms.	FG00	0067			
GV-70	FJ00	0059			
JV-52	FJ52	0028			
JV-72	FJ72	0018	0023		
DV-82	FK	000001			
D-65	GC	000020			
Prototypes	JJ		000009		
Brian May Sig.	ME	00316			

CUSTOM SHOP MODELS, 1997

The 45th Anniversary, Deco and Finesse models, made in Guild's Custom Shop in Nashville, have a 7-digit serial number with configuration **rrrymmy**.

rrr is a serial ranking, beginning with 500.

yy corresponds to the last 2 digits of the year, but in reverse order.

mm is the month.

Example: 5107019 = the 10th instrument made in January 1997

In addition, the ranking of each instrument in its own limited run is on the back of the peghead.

MODEL	NUMBER RANGE WITHIN SERIES
45th Anniversary	2–33 (of 45)
Deco	2–12
Finesse	2–11

ACOUSTIC ARCHTOPS KEY

Non-cutaway = **A-50 Granada/Cordoba**
Pointed cutaway = **CA-100 Capri**
Rounded cutaway
    Pearl block inlay with abalone V inserts
        f-holes
            Large pearl block on peghead = **Johnny Smith Award/Artist Award**
            G-shield peghead inlay = **A-500/550 Stuart/A-500B**
        Oval soundhole = **A-600**
    Block inlay
        Gold-plated hardware = **A-350/375 Stratford/A-350B**
        Nickel-plated hardware = **A-150 Savoy**

ACOUSTIC ARCHTOPS

All models were available with DeArmond pickup.

A-50 Granada/Cordoba: 16 1/4" wide, non-cutaway, laminated maple body, rosewood bridge, trapeze tailpiece, 3-piece mahogany/maple neck, 24 3/4" scale, unbound rosewood fingerboard, dot inlay, nickel-plated hardware, sunburst finish
Introduced as **A-50 Granada: 1956**
1-piece mahogany neck: **1959**
A-50B, blonde finish optional: **1959**
Renamed **A-50 Cordoba: 1961**
Discontinued: **1972**

A-150 Savoy: 17" wide, rounded cutaway, laminated maple back and sides, solid spruce top, rosewood adjustable bridge, harp tailpiece (early with trapeze tailpiece), 3-piece mahogany/maple neck, 24 3/4" scale, bound rosewood fingerboard, pearloid block inlay, Chesterfield (column and crown) peghead inlay, nickel-plated hardware, sunburst or blond finish
Available: **1958–73**

A-350 Stratford: 17" wide, rounded cutaway, solid curly maple back and sides (some with laminated back), solid spruce top, rosewood bridge, harp tailpiece, 3-piece maple/walnut neck, 24 3/4" scale,

bound rosewood fingerboard, pearl block inlay, *G* peghead inlay, gold-plated hardware, sunburst finish
Introduced: **c. 1956**
G-shield peghead inlay: **1959**
Ebony bridge and fingerboard: **by 1960**
Discontinued: **1973**

A-375 Stratford/A-350B: blond version of A-350
Introduced as **A-375 Stratford: c. 1956**
Renamed **A-350B: by 1960**
Ebony bridge and fingerboard: **by 1960**
Discontinued: **1973**

A-500 Stuart: 17" wide, rounded cutaway, solid
curly maple back and sides, solid spruce top, rosewood bridge, engraved harp tailpiece, 3-piece maple/walnut neck, 24 3/4" scale, bound rosewood fingerboard, pearl block inlay with abalone V inserts, G-shield peghead inlay, gold-plated hardware, sunburst finish
Introduced: **c. 1956**
Ebony bridge and fingerboard, 5-piece maple/walnut neck: **1959**
Discontinued: **1969**

A-550 Stuart/A-500B: blond version of A-500
Introduced as **A-550 Stuart: c. 1956**
Ebony bridge and fingerboard, 5-piece maple/walnut neck: **1959**
Renamed **A-500B: c. 1960**
Discontinued: **1969**

CA-100 Capri: 16 3/8" wide, pointed cutaway, laminated maple back and sides, solid spruce top, rosewood adjustable bridge, 3-piece mahogany/maple neck, 24 3/4" scale, bound rosewood fingerboard, pearloid block inlay, *G* peghead inlay, nickel-plated hardware, sunburst or blond finish
Introduced: **1956**
Chesterfield (column and crown) peghead inlay: **1957**
Harp tailpiece: **by 1960**
Discontinued: **1973**

CA-100B, blonde finish: **1961–72**

A-600: oval soundhole, checkered binding, pearl
block inlay with abalone V inserts
1 made, blond finish, labeled A-600B: **1968**
Listed, but none produced: **1970–73**

Johnny Smith Award: see Electric Archtops

Artist Award: see Electric Archtops

COMMENTS

In Guild's very early period, the company was best known for acoustic and electric archtops. Although emphasis soon shifted to flat tops, Guild maintained a high quality standard in acoustic archtop production. Guild archtops are highly respected as utilitarian instruments and because of their high quality are possible "sleepers" in the vintage market.

GUILD FLAT TOPS KEY

Some model variations are not listed, including those with optional pickup, designated by an E suffix.

Doubleneck = **Crossroads Double E**
Coral/turquoise/silver ornamentation in Southwestern motif = **DV-74**
Custom stone inlays
    Dreadnought body shape (thick waist) = **DV-72**
    Non-dreadnought body (thin waist) = **GV-72**
Deco inlay with oval abalone center piece
    Dreadnought body, thick waist = **Deco**
    Non-dreadnought body, thin waist = **Valencia, 1998–current**
Varied-pattern fingerboard inlay
    17" wide = **Custom F-512**
    18" wide = **Custom F-612**

Pearl block inlay, abalone V inserts, ebony dividing strips = **45th Anniversary**
Pearl block inlay with abalone V inserts
    Cutaway = **F-65CE**
    Non-cutaway
        Dreadnought body shape, 15 3/4" wide
            Abalone soundhole ring = **D-60, 1998–current**
            Non-abalone soundhole ring
                Rosewood back and sides = **TV Model D-55/D-65**
                Maple back and sides = **Hank Williams Jr.**
        Non-dreadnought body shape, rounded lower bout, thin waist
            6-string
                Maple back and sides = **Navarre F-50, 1957–87/JF-65**
                Rosewood back and sides
                    15" wide = **Aragon F-30R, 1976 onward**
                    17" wide = **Navarre F-50R/JF-65R**, JF-55
            12-string
                Maple back and sides = **Custom F-412/JF-65M-12**
                Rosewood back and sides = **Custom F-512/JF-65R-12/JF55-12**
Pearloid block inlay (no V inserts)
    Mahogany back and sides
        16" wide = **Bluegrass F-47**
        17" wide = **Navarre F-48**
    Maple back and sides
        Cutaway body = **Excellence**
        Non-cutaway body
            16" wide = **Valencia F-40/Bluegrass F-40, 1954–82**
            17" wide = **Navarre F-50, 1954–56**
Humptop trapezoid inlay
    Dreadnought body, thick waist
        Koa back and sides = **DK-70**
        Rosewood back and sides
            Abalone top edge border
                Plain neck heel = **D-80/D-100**
                Carved neck heel = **D-100C**
            No abalone top edge border
                Plain neck heel = **D-70**
                Carved neck heel = **D-70NT carved**
    Non-dreadnought body, rounded lower bout, thin waist
        6-string = **JF-100**
        12-string
            Carved neck heel = **JF-100-12C**
            Plain neck heel = **JF-100-12**
Small notched-diamonds and squares inlay
    Dreadnought body, thick waist = **D-62**
    F-style, rounded lower bout, thin waist = **F-42**

Guild flat tops key *(continued)*

Notched-diamond inlay

    Dreadnought body, thick waist

        Maple back and sides = **D-64**

        Rosewood back and sides = **D-66/D-60, 1984–89**

    Non-dreadnought body, rounded lower bout, thin waist

        Double cutaway = **Studio 24/S-60 Studio**

        Single cutaway = **GF-60C**

        Non-cutaway

            Rosewood back and sides = **F-46/GF-60R/GF-55**

            Maple back and sides = **F-44/GF-60M**

Snowflake inlay

    Dark binding = **A-25**

    Multi-ply binding = **A-50**

Abalone dot inlay (and peghead inlay), F (non-dreadnought) body = **GV-70**

Mother-of-pearl dot inlay

    Single cutaway, similar to Fender Tele = **CR-1 Crossroads Single E**

    Dreadnought body shape, thick waist

        Pearwood back and sides = **Bluegrass Jubilee D-44**

        Ash back and sides = **D-46**

        Maple back and sides

            Ebony fingerboard = **D-44M**

            Rosewood fingerboard = **G-37** or **D-30**

        Rosewood back and sides

            Cutaway = **DCE-5**

            Non-cutaway

               15" wide, "3/4-size dreadnought" = **G-75**

               15 3/4" or 16" wide

                   Chrome-plated tuners

                       6-string = **Bluegrass Special D-50**

                       12-string = **D-50-12**

                   Gold-plated tuners

                       Herringbone edge trim = **DV-62**

                       Non-herringbone edge trim = **DV-52**

                       Tortoiseshell celluloid binding = **Finesse**

        Mahogany back and sides

            Mahogany top

               Bound top and back

                   Cutaway = **D-25C**

                   Non-cutaway

                       6-string = **Bluegrass D-25, D-17** or **D-4M**

                       12-string = **D-17-12**

               Unbound top and back

                 6-string = **D-15** or **D-16**

                 12-string = **D-15-12**

Spruce top
   Pointed cutaway
      Oval hole
         Solidbody = **DS-48CE**
         Hollow body = **D-47CE**
      Round hole = **D-40C**
   Rounded cutaway
      Rosewood fingerboard = **DCE-1 True American**
      Ebony fingerboard = **DCE-2 True American**
   Non-cutaway, 17" wide = **G-41**
   Non-cutaway 15 5/8" or 16" wide
      No peghead ornament
         White binding
            Gold-plated tuners = **D-6**
            Chrome-plated tuners
               Arched (laminated) back
                  6-string **= D-25M**
                  12-string = **D-212/D-25-12**
               Flat back = **Bluegrass D-35**
         Dark binding
            6-string
               Natural top = **D-48** or **D-4**
               Mahogany stain top finish = **D-25**
            12-string = **D-4-12**
      Chesterfield peghead ornament
         Herringbone soundhole ring = **DV-6**
         Non-herringbone ring = **Bluegrass Jubilee D-40**
Non-dreadnought body shape, rounded lower bout, thin waist
   Solid mahogany back (routed)
      Oval hole
         3-on-a-side tuners
            Bound fingerboard = **FS-46**, **DS-48**
            Unbound fingerboard = **FS-20CE**
         6-on-a-side tuners
            6-string
              Piezo pickup = **FS-46-6**
              Piezo and hidden humbucker = **FS-48CE Deceiver**
            12-string = **FS-46-12**
      Round hole
         Classical string-tie bridge = **MKS-44**
         Pin bridge
            Blue or crimson finish = **S4CE-BG**
            Other finish
               Chrome-plated hardware = **S4-CE Songbird**
               Gold-plated hardware = **Songbird Custom**

Pearl dot inlay, non-dreadnought body shape *(continued)*
    Hollowbody, mahogany back and sides
        Rounded cutaway horn
            Spruce top = **F-25CE/F-4CE**
            Mahogany top = **F4-CEMH**
        Pointed cutaway horn
            6-string
                Piezo pickup = **F-45CE, 1983–84**
                No pickup = **GF-25C**
            12-string = **F-45C-12**
        Non-cutaway
            17" wide = **JF-4**
            16" wide
                Arched back
                    6-string = **F-45**
                    12-string = **F-45-12**
                Flat back
                    Dark binding = **GF-25**
                    Multiple binding = **GF-40**
            15" wide
                Spruce top = **Aragon F-30, 1959–current**
                Mahogany top = **Del Rio M-30**
            13 3/4" wide **Economy M-20**
    Maple back and sides
        Rounded cutaway
            Oval soundhole = **F-30CE**
            Round soundhole
                Black finish = **Standard**
                Blond finish = **Classic**
        Pointed cutaway
            Oval hole = **F-45CE/GF-45CE, 1985–91**
            Round soundhole
                Full-depth body
                    16" wide = **GF-30C**
                    17" wide = **JF-30C**
                Thin body
                    Maple back and sides = **Classic**
                    Curly maple back and sides = **Excellence**
        17" wide
            Non-cutaway
                6-string = **JF-30**
                12-string = **JF-30-12**
            Cutaway = **JF-30C**
        16" wide = **GF-30**
        15" wide = **Aragon F-30, 1954–58**
        13 3/4" wide, 24 3/4" scale = **Troubadour F-20**
        13 1/8" wide, 22 1/2" scale = **Troubadour F-20 3/4**

Rosewood back and sides
    Cutaway
        3" deep = **F-5CE**
        4 1/2" deep = **FF5-CE**
    Non-cutaway
        17" wide
            Non-herringbone soundhole ring = **JF-50R**
            Herringbone soundhole ring = **JV-52**
        16" wide
            Unbound fingerboard = **GV-52**
            Bound fingerboard = **GF-50**
        15" wide
            Abalone soundhole ring = **A-50**
            Non-abalone ring = **Aragon F-30R, 1973–75**
No fingerboard inlay
   12-string
      Dreadnought body shape
         Mahogany back and sides = **G-212**
         Rosewood back and sides = **G-312**
      Non-dreadnought body shape, thin waist
         Mahogany back and sides
            15 1/4" wide (F shape) = **Standard F-112**
            16" wide (non-F shape)
                Non-cutaway = **F-212**
                Cutaway = **F-212C**
            17" wide = **Standard F-212XL**
         Rosewood back and sides = **Artist F-312**
   6-string
      Cutaway
         Full-depth hollow body = **MKS-11**
         Thin hollow body = **CCE-100**
         Thin solidbody (routec)
            Slotted peghead = **MKS-10**
            Solid peghead = **MKS-44**
      Dreadnought body = **Mark 50**
      Non-dreadnought (non-cutaway) body
         Rosewood fingerboard
            Non-cutaway
                Mahogany top = **Mark I**
                Spruce top
                    Satin (non-gloss) finish = **Mark II**
                    Gloss finish = **Mark III**
         Ebony fingerboard
            Non-engraved tuners = **Mark IV**
            Engraved tuners
               25 1/2" scale
                  Ebony binding = **Mark V**
                  Natural wood binding = **Mark VI**
               26 1/4" scale = **Mark VII Custom**

GUILD

FLAT TOPS

Solidbody models with acoustic flat top styling and
transducer bridge pickup, such as the Songbird and
MKS-10, are included in this section.

MODEL NAMES, 1954–87

Most Guild flat tops have either the "F" body shape
with circular lower bout and thin waist or the "D"
(dreadnought) shape with flatter lower bout and thick
waist.

However, Guild model names are confusing and disorganized. The F and D body lines were developed
independent of each other so that F-body model
numbers usually do not correspond to D-body
model numbers. For example, the F-50 and D-50 do
not have similar specs, although the JF-50 and D-
50 do have the same specs in 1987.

PREFIXES

A: F shape, 15" wide: **1996–current**
D: dreadnought, thick waist, flat across bottom end:
1963–current
F: circular lower bout…
All sizes with F body shape: **1954–86**
Oval-hole cutaway models, 16" wide: **1991–current**
G: wide array of models, some with a maple dread-
nought body, others with odd body shapes and
sizes, and 12-strings
GF: F shape, 16" wide: **1987–89**
JF: F shape, 17" wide: **1987–current**
M: F shape with all-mahogany body: **mid 1960s–1978**

GRUHN-DESIGN, 1984–86

In 1984 George Gruhn designed a new group of models
that represented the first attempt at correlating
model numbers across body styles with respect to
wood and ornamentation. These models marked the
beginning of the narrower "snakehead" peghead that
most Guild dreadnoughts (except JF models) still
have today. The last digit of the model designates the
style. Dreadnought styles were numbered in the 60s;
F-style models were numbered in the 40s.

F-42/D-62: mahogany back and sides, plain ivoroid
binding on top and back, raised pearloid logo,
unbound rosewood fingerboard, small slotted
diamonds-and-squares inlay, earliest with inlays
only at frets 5, 7 and 9

F-44/D-64: maple back and sides, multiple black and
white lines of wood purfling, multiple binding with
ivoroid outer layer of binding, ivoroid-bound ebony
fingerboard, large slotted-diamond inlays (to
smaller, uniform-size inlays c. 1986)
F-46/D-66: rosewood back and sides, otherwise same
trim as model 4

LATE 1986–1987

Beginning in late 1986, Guild flat tops were reorganized into a number system that was consistent
across body styles with respect to wood and ornamentation. All styles were conceivably available
with D, GF or JF body, although some combinations
were never listed.

Style 15: laminated arched mahogany back, mahogany
top
Style 25: laminated arched mahogany back, spruce top
Style 30: laminated arched maple back, multi-ply binding
Style 40: solid mahogany back and sides, multi-ply
body binding, unbound rosewood fingerboard dot
inlay, Chesterfield peghead inlay
Style 50: rosewood back and sides, multi-ply body
binding, unbound ebony fingerboard, dot inlay,
Chesterfield peghead inlay
Style 60: rosewood (60R) or maple (60M) back and
sides, multiple black and white lines of wood purfling
with ivoroid outer binding, ivoroid-bound ebony
fingerboard, uniform-size slotted-diamond inlays
(same trim as earlier 44/64 and 46/56 models)
Style 65: rosewood back and sides, similar to earlier
D-55 and F-50, pearl block inlay with abalone
V inserts

1988–CURRENT

Following Gruhn's departure from Guild in 1988, the
system became disorganized again. For example,
by 1989 the D-65 had returned to its earlier designation of D-55, and its F-body companion, the
JF-65, also changed to the 55 number to become
the JF-55, even though prior to 1987 it had been
the F-50. In 1997, with the JF-55 still in production,
the JF-65 model name reappeared on a new and
different model.

SECTION ORGANIZATION

F-Body and Other Non-Dreadnought Models
Dreadnought Models
Solidbody Models
12-Strings
Classicals
Ukuleles

F-BODY AND OTHER NON-DREADNOUGHT MODELS

All have circular lower bout, thin waist.

Navarre F-50/JF-65: 17" wide, 4 1/2" deep, rounded lower bout, laminated arched maple back, tortoiseshell celluloid pickguard, rosewood belly bridge, 3-piece mahogany neck, 25 1/2" scale, bound rosewood fingerboard, pearloid block inlay, *G* peghead inlay, gold-plated tuners
Introduced as **Navarre F-50: 1954**
Maple neck with walnut laminate strip, pearl block inlay, G-shield peghead inlay: **1956**
Pearl block inlay with abalone V inserts: **1957**
Ebony fingerboard: **c. 1962**
Cloud bridge (2 points on belly): **1966**
Body 5" deep: **1967**
Ebony bridge (many with rosewood), black pickguard: **c. 1972**
Renamed **JF-65M: 1987**
Discontinued: **late 1987**

JF-65 reintroduced, maple back and sides, abalone soundhole ring, black pickguard, bound ebony fingerboard, pearl block inlay with abalone V inserts, bound peghead, G-shield peghead inlay, gold-plated Grover tuners: **1997**
Still in production

Navarre F-50R/JF-65R: 17" wide, 4 1/2" deep, rounded lower bout, rosewood back and sides, tortoiseshell celluloid pickguard, ebony belly bridge, wood marquetry backstrip, 3-piece mahogany/maple neck, 25" 1/2 scale, multiple-bound ebony fingerboard, pearl block inlay with abalone V inserts, G-shield peghead inlay, gold-plated tuners
Introduced: **1965**
Some with laminated rosewood back: **late 1960s**
Some with 3-piece padouk/maple neck: **early to mid 1970s**
Cloud bridge (2 points on belly): **1966**

Body 5" deep: **1967**
Ebony bridge (many with rosewood), black pickguard: **c. 1972**
Renamed **JF-65R: 1987**
Discontinued: **1987**
Reintroduced as JF-55 (see following)
Style 50 model number continues on JF-50R, with different specs (see following)

JF-55: continuation of rosewood version of JF-65R, 17" wide, rosewood back and sides, scalloped bracing, abalone soundhole ring, multiple-bound top and back, 3-piece mahogany neck, 25 5/8" scale, bound ebony fingerboard, pearl block inlay with abalone V inserts, bound peghead, G-shield peghead inlay, gold-plated tuners, natural or sunburst finish
Introduced: **1989**
Abalone soundhole ring: **c. 1995**
Still in production

F-65CE: 16" wide, 3" deep, rounded cutaway, oval soundhole, laminated flame maple back and sides, arched back, multiple body binding, transducer pickup with preamp, 25 5/8" scale, bound ebony fingerboard, pearl block inlay with abalone V inserts, bound peghead, G-shield peghead inlay, gold-plated tuners, sunburst or blond finish
Available: **1992–current**

Bluegrass F-40/Valencia: 16" wide, rounded lower bout, laminated arched maple back, small tortoiseshell celluloid pickguard, rosewood bridge (belly or straight), 3-piece mahogany/maple neck, 25 1/2" scale, bound rosewood fingerboard, pearloid block inlay beginning at 3rd fret, *G* peghead inlay
Introduced: **1954**
Chesterfield peghead inlay: **c. 1957**
Larger pickguard, block inlay beginning at 1st fret: **c. 1957**
Discontinued: **1963**
Reintroduced as **Bluegrass F-40: 1973**
Maple neck: **1976**
Discontinued: **1983**
Reintroduced as **Valencia:** solid maple back and sides, abalone top border, abalone soundhole ring, 5-piece maple neck, 25 5/8" scale, bound ebony fingerboard, deco pearl inlay with abalone center piece, G-shield peghead inlay, gold-plated hard-

ware, sunburst finish, Custom Shop model: **1998**
Still in production

Aragon F-30: 15" wide, laminated arched maple
back, rosewood belly bridge, small pickguard, 3-
piece mahogany/maple neck, 25 1/2" scale,
unbound rosewood fingerboard, dot inlay
Introduced: **1954**
Larger pickguard, *G* peghead inlay: **c. 1957**
Mahogany back and sides, 24 3/4" scale: **1959**
Chesterfield peghead inlay: **early 1960s**
Silkscreen peghead logo: **c. 1969**
15 1/2" wide, 25 1/2" scale: **c. 1970**
Discontinued: **1986**
Model name reintroduced as **F-30:** solid mahogany
back and sides, 24 3/4" scale, snakehead peghead,
handrubbed or gloss finish: **1998**
Still in production

Aragon F-30R: 15 1/2" wide, rosewood back and sides
Available: **1973–late 1975**
Reintroduced, multiple-bound ebony fingerboard,
pearl block inlay with abalone V inserts, G-shield
peghead inlay: **1976**
Discontinued: **1978**
Reintroduced as **F-30R:** solid rosewood back and
sides, 24 3/4" scale, gloss finish: **1998**
Still in production

Del Rio M-30: same as F-30 but with all-mahogany
body, satin (non-gloss) finish: **1959–64**

Troubadour F-20: 13 3/4" wide, maple back and
sides, rosewood bridge, small upper part of pickguard, bound top, unbound back, mahogany neck,
24 3/4" scale, rosewood fingerboard, dot inlay, sunburst finish
Introduced: **1956**
Natural finish available: **by 1958**
Mahogany back and sides: **1959**
25 1/2" scale: **1976**
Discontinued: **1987**

F-20 3/4: 13 1/8" wide, 22 1/2" scale: **1969–77**

Economy M-20: same as F-20 but with all-mahogany
body, satin (non-gloss) finish
Available: **1958–72**
Reintroduced as **M-20S: 1977**
Discontinued: **1978**

Bluegrass F-47: 16" wide, mahogany back and
sides, rosewood bridge, horses and horseshoe on
pickguard, 3-piece mahogany neck, 25 1/2" scale,
bound rosewood fingerboard, pearloid block inlay,
Chesterfield peghead inlay
Introduced: **1963**
Tortoiseshell celluloid pickguard: **1964**
Discontinued: **1976**

Navarre F-48: 17" wide, mahogany back and
sides, tortoiseshell celluloid pickguard, rosewood
bridge, 3-piece mahogany/maple neck, 25 1/2"
scale, bound rosewood fingerboard, pearloid block
inlay, Chesterfield peghead inlay
Available: **1972–75**

F-45CE: 16" wide, arched laminated mahogany
back, pointed cutaway, Fishman TASS pickup, dot
inlay, natural or sunburst finish
Introduced: **1983**
Curly maple back and sides, oval soundhole, bound
rosewood fingerboard, Chesterfield peghead logo:
1985
Renamed **GF-45CE,** snakehead peghead: **early 1987**
Renamed **F-45CE: April 1987**
Discontinued: **1992**

F-42: 16" wide, mahogany back and sides, plain
ivoroid binding on top and back, rosewood fingerboard, unbound rosewood fingerboard, small slotted diamonds-and-squares inlay, earliest with inlay
only at frets 5, 7 and 9, snakehead peghead, raised
pearloid logo
Available: **1984–85**

F-44: 16" wide, maple back and sides, multiple-
bound top and back, bound ebony fingerboard,
notched-diamond inlay, snakehead peghead, G-
shield peghead inlay, chrome-plated tuners
Introduced: **1984**
Renamed **GF-60M** (see following): **1987**

F-46: 16" wide, rosewood back and sides, bound
ebony fingerboard, notched-diamond inlay, snakehead peghead, G-shield peghead inlay, chrome-
plated tuners
Introduced: **1984**
Renamed **GF-60R** (see following): **1987**

Studio 24/S-60 Studio: double-cutaway, oval soundhole, maple back and sides, notched-diamond inlay, snakehead peghead
Introduced as **Studio 24: 1986**
Renamed **S-60 Studio: 1987**
Discontinued: **1989**

GF-25: 16" wide, rounded lower bout, mahogany back and sides, dark binding on top and back, mahogany neck, 25 5/8" scale, rosewood fingerboard, dot inlay, snakehead peghead, peaked logo, sunburst, mahogany, woodgrain red, natural or black finish
Introduced: **1987**
Sunburst or natural finish only: **1989**
Discontinued: **1992**

GF-25C: pointed cutaway, Chesterfield peghead inlay: **1988–91**

GF-30: 16" wide, maple back and sides, scalloped bracing, multiple-bound top and back, maple neck, 25 5/8" scale, rosewood fingerboard, dot inlay, snakehead peghead, Chesterfield peghead inlay
Available: **1987–91**

GF-30C: cutaway: **1987–89**

GF-40: 16" wide, mahogany back and sides, flat back, scalloped bracing, multiple-bound top and back, mahogany neck, 25 5/8" scale, dot inlay, snakehead peghead, Chesterfield peghead inlay
Available: **1987–88**

GF-50: 16" wide, rosewood back and sides, scalloped bracing, multiple-bound top and back, mahogany neck, 25 5/8" scale, unbound ebony fingerboard, dot inlay, snakehead peghead, Chesterfield peghead inlay
Available: **1987–91**

GF-60/GF-55: continuation of F-44 and F-46 (see preceding), 16" wide, rosewood back and sides (**GF-60R**) or maple back and sides (**GF-60M**), scalloped bracing, multiple binding, mahogany neck, 25 5/8" scale, bound ebony fingerboard, notched-diamond inlay, bound snakehead peghead, G-shield peghead inlay, gold-plated tuners
Introduced: **1987**

GF-60M discontinued: **1989**
GF-60 (rosewood) renamed **GF-55: 1990**
Discontinued: **1991**

GF-60C: rosewood back and sides, pointed cutaway: **1989**

JF-30: 17" wide, laminated arched maple back, solid maple sides, scalloped bracing, multiple-bound top and back, maple neck, 25 5/8" scale, rosewood fingerboard, dot inlay, snakehead peghead, Chesterfield peghead inlay, chrome-plated tuners, blond, sunburst, black or woodgrain finish
Introduced: **1987**
Gold-plated tuners: **1991**
Chrome-plated tuners: **1992**
Still in production

JF-30C: cutaway: **1988**

JF-30E: transducer pickup: **1994–97**

JF-50R: 17" wide, rosewood back and sides, multiple-bound top and back, mahogany neck, 25 5/8" scale, ebony fingerboard, dot inlay, snakehead peghead, Chesterfield peghead inlay
Available: **1987–88**

JF-65: see Navarre F-50, preceding

JF-4: 17" wide, laminated arched mahogany back, solid mahogany sides, bound top, 25 5/8" scale, rosewood fingerboard, dot inlay, snakehead peghead, peaked logo, chrome-plated tuners, natural satin (non-gloss) finish
Available: **1992–95**

JF-4E: transducer pickup: **1992–95**

JF-100: 17" wide, rosewood back and sides, scalloped bracing, multiple binding with maple outer layer and abalone border, abalone soundhole ring, 25 5/8" scale, 3-piece mahogany/maple neck, bound ebony fingerboard, abalone crown (humped trapezoid) inlay, bound peghead, abalone G-shield peghead logo, gold-plated tuners
Available: **1992–current**

JF-100C: carved neck heel: **1994–95**, **1997**

GF-100C: 16" wide: **c. 1995**

GUILD

JV-52: 17" wide, rosewood back and sides, scalloped bracing, bone saddle, cream binding, herringbone soundhole ring, ebony fingerboard, dot inlay, bone nut, ebony fingerboard, dot inlay, Chesterfield peghead inlay, gold-plated tuners, natural satin (non-gloss) finish
Available: **1994–95**

Standard: thinbody, rounded cutaway, maple back and sides, round soundhole, bound top, transducer pickup, dot inlay, large peghead, black finish
Available: **1990–91**

Classic: thinbody, rounded cutaway, maple back and sides, round soundhole, multiple binding, transducer pickup, pearl block inlay with abalone V inserts, large peghead, Chesterfield peghead inlay, blonde finish
Available: **1990–91**

Excellence: thinbody, rounded cutaway, curly maple back and sides, round soundhole, multiple binding, large peghead, transducer pickup, natural or sunburst finish
Available: **1990–91**

F-25CE: 16" wide, 3" deep, rounded cutaway, oval soundhole, laminated mahogany back, solid mahogany sides, transducer pickup with preamp, volume control, concentric treble/bass control, 25 5/8" scale, rosewood fingerboard, dot inlay, snakehead peghead, Chesterfield peghead inlay, chrome-plated tuners, sunburst, black, blond or woodgrain finish
Available: **1991–92**

F-30CE: 16" wide, 3" deep, rounded cutaway, oval soundhole, laminated flamed maple back, solid maple sides, multiple binding, transducer pickup with preamp, 25 5/8" scale, rosewood fingerboard, dot inlay, snakehead peghead, Chesterfield peghead inlay, gold-plated tuners, sunburst, black, blond or woodgrain finish
Available: **1992–95**

F-4CE: 16" wide, 3" deep, rounded cutaway, oval soundhole, laminated arched mahogany back, solid mahogany sides, transducer pickup with preamp, 24 3/4" scale, rosewood fingerboard, dot inlay, snakehead peghead, peaked logo, chrome-plated tuners, natural satin (non-gloss) finish
Available: **1992–current**

F4-CEMH: mahogany top, high-gloss finish: **1992–95**

F-5CE: 16" wide, 3" deep, rounded cutaway, oval soundhole, laminated arched rosewood back, solid rosewood sides, transducer pickup with preamp, 24 3/4" scale, rosewood fingerboard, dot inlay, snakehead peghead, peaked logo, gold-plated tuners, natural, sunburst or black finish
Available: **1992–current**

FF5-CE: deep body, 4 1/2" deep: **1992–95**

GV-52: 16" wide, rosewood back and sides, scalloped bracing, bone saddle, multiple body binding with cream outer layer, herringbone soundhole ring, ebony fingerboard, dot inlay, bone nut, ebony fingerboard, dot inlay, Chesterfield peghead logo, gold-plated tuners, natural satin (non-gloss) finish, some with gloss finish
Available: **1994–95**

GV-70: same as GV-52 but with abalone soundhole ring, abalone dot inlay, abalone G-shield peghead inlay and logo, gloss finish
Available: **1994–95**

GV-72: 16" wide, rosewood back and sides, herringbone top trim, ebony fingerboard, exotic stone inlays in soundhole ring, fingerboard and G-shield peghead inlay
Available: **1993**

A-25HG: 15" wide, mahogany back and sides, black body binding, unbound rosewood fingerboard, snowflake inlay, snakehead peghead, peaked logo, natural or antique burst high-gloss lacquer finish
Available: **1995–97**

A-25 (HR): hand-rubbed satin (non-gloss) finish: **1995–97**

A-50: 15" wide, rosewood back and sides, abalone soundhole ring, multiple body binding, unbound ebony fingerboard, abalone snowflake inlay, snakehead peghead, abalone peaked logo
Available: **1996–97**

45th Anniversary: concert body, maple back and sides, multiple body binding, abalone trim, ebony fingerboard and bridge, pearl block inlay with abalone V inserts and ebony dividing strips between pearl and abalone sections, rectangular pearl block at 12th fret with engraved *45th Anniversary*, limited run of 45 from Nashville Custom Shop
Available: **1997**

DREADNOUGHT MODELS

All with thick body waist.

Bluegrass Jubilee D-40: 15 3/4" wide, mahogany back and sides, rosewood bridge, 3-piece mahogany neck, 25 1/2" scale, unbound rosewood fingerboard, dot inlay, Chesterfield peghead inlay
Introduced: **1963**
Snakehead peghead: **1987**
Discontinued: **1992**

D-40E: pickup: **1968**

D-40C: pointed cutaway: **1975–91**

Bluegrass Special D-50: 15 3/4" wide, rosewood back and sides, rosewood bridge, multiple-bound top and back, 3-piece mahogany neck, 25 1/2" scale, unbound ebony fingerboard, dot inlay
Introduced: **1963**
Chesterfield peghead inlay: **c. 1968**
1-piece mahogany neck: **c. 1974**
Ebony bridge: **c. 1975**
Scalloped bracing, snakehead peghead: **1987**
Discontinued: **1993**

Bluegrass Jubilee D-44: 15 3/4" wide, pearwood back and sides, rosewood bridge, 25 1/2" scale, unbound ebony fingerboard, dot inlay
Available: **1965–72**

D-44M: maple back and sides
Introduced: **c. 1971**
Ebony bridge: **1973**
Discontinued: **1979**

TV Model D-55/D-65: 15 3/4" wide, rosewood back and sides, rosewood bridge, multiple body binding, 3-piece mahogany/maple neck, 25 1/2" scale, bound ebony fingerboard, pearl block inlay with abalone V inserts, bound peghead, G-shield peghead inlay, sunburst or natural finish, special order only
Introduced as **TV Model D-55: 1968**
Ebony bridge: **c. 1972**
3-piece padouk/maple neck: **c. 1973**
Regular production model: **1974**
Renamed **D-65: 1987**
Discontinued: **late 1987**
Reintroduced as **D-55:** 25 5/8" scale, large peghead, gold-plated tuners, natural or sunburst finish: **1990**
Abalone soundhole ring: **1996**
Still in production

Bluegrass D-25: 15 3/4" wide, all-mahogany body, rosewood bridge, small pickguard, tortoise-shell celluloid top and back binding, mahogany neck, 25 1/2" scale, unbound rosewood fingerboard, dot inlay, black peghead veneer with inlaid peaked peghead logo, natural or cherry red finish
Introduced: **1968**
Larger pickguard, no peghead veneer, silkscreen logo: **1969**
Spruce top (stained mahogany) or mahogany top, arched laminated mahogany back or solid flat mahogany back, black top and back binding, shaded mahogany or cherry finish: **1976**
Black or sunburst finish optional: **1980**
Sunburst, mahogany, woodgrain red, natural or black finish: **1987**
Still in production

D-25C: rounded cutaway: **1983–85**

Bluegrass D-35: 15 3/4" wide, spruce top, mahogany back and sides, rosewood bridge, small pickguard, tortoiseshell celluloid top and back binding, mahogany neck, 25 1/2" scale, unbound rosewood fingerboard, dot inlay, black peghead veneer with inlaid peaked peghead logo
Introduced: **1968**
Larger pickguard, no peghead veneer, silkscreen logo: **1969**
Discontinued: **1987**

G-37: 15 3/4" wide, laminated arched maple back, rosewood bridge, mahogany neck, 25 1/2" scale, unbound rosewood fingerboard, dot inlay, sunburst or natural top finish, sunburst finish on back and sides
Introduced: **1972**

Laminated maple neck, Chesterfield peghead inlay:
  c. 1976
Renamed **D-30**, see following: **1987**
Still in production

G-41: 17" wide, mahogany back and sides, rosewood bridge, mahogany neck, 26 1/4" scale, unbound rosewood fingerboard, dot inlay
Available: **1974–77**

G-75: 15" wide, "3/4-size dreadnought" with thick waist, rosewood back and sides, ebony bridge, black pickguard, mahogany neck, 25 1/2" scale, unbound ebony fingerboard, dot inlay, Chesterfield peghead inlay
Available: **1975–77**

D-70: limited edition, 15 3/4" wide, rosewood back and sides, ebony bridge, ivory saddle, pearl soundhole ring, multiple-bound top and back with maple outer layer, scalloped bracing, mahogany neck, 25 5/8" scale, bound ebony fingerboard, humptop trapezoid inlay, ivory nut, bound peghead, G-shield peghead inlay, ebony truss rod cover, gold-plated tuners
Available: **1981–85**

D-70 Carved: carved neck: **1983–85**

D-80/D-100: rosewood back and sides, scalloped bracing, multiple wood binding with abalone border, abalone soundhole ring, 25 5/8" scale, bound ebony fingerboard, abalone humptop trapezoid inlay, bound peghead, G-shield peghead inlay
Introduced as **D-80: 1983**
Discontinued: **1987**
Reintroduced as **D-100: 1990**
Still in production

D-80 carved/D-100C: carved neck heel
Introduced as **D-80 carved: 1983**
Discontinued: **1987**
Reintroduced as **D-100C**, abalone peghead inlay: **1990**
Still in production

D-46: ash back and sides, black pickguard, multiple-bound top, ash neck, unbound ebony fingerboard, dot inlay, Chesterfield peghead inlay, chrome-plated tuners, natural or sunburst finish
Available: **1980–85**

G-45 Hank Williams Jr: 15 3/4" wide, maple back and sides, scalloped bracing, *Hank Williams Jr.* pickguard inlay, bound ebony fingerboard, pearl block inlay with abalone V inserts, G-shield logo, blond finish
Available: **1982–86**
Reintroduced, snakehead peghead: **1993**
Discontinued: **1996**
Reintroduced as D-60 (see following) without Williams' endorsement: **1998**

D-47CE: 15 3/4" wide, oval soundhole, pointed cutaway, mahogany back and sides, 24 3/4" scale, Fishman TASS pickup, rosewood fingerboard, dot inlay, Chesterfield peghead inlay, natural, sunburst or black finish
Available: **1983–85**

D-52: 15 3/4" wide, rosewood back and sides, scalloped top bracing, herringbone soundhole ring, mahogany neck, 25 5//8 scale, unbound ebony fingerboard, dot inlay, Chesterfield peghead inlay
Available: **1983–84**

Mahogany Rush Series: 15 3/4" wide, dreadnought, mahogany back and sides, mahogany top, mahogany neck, 25 5/8" scale, rosewood fingerboard, dot inlay, peaked logo

D-15: unbound top and back, mahogany or woodgrain red finish, satin finish
Introduced: **1983**
Gloss finish: **1987**
Discontinued: **1988**

D-16: unbound top and back, natural mahogany gloss finish
Introduced: **1983**
Renamed D-15: **1987**
Discontinued: **1988**

D-17: bound top and back, natural mahogany gloss finish
Available: **1983–86**

D-62: mahogany back and sides, rosewood fingerboard, small slotted squares-and-diamonds inlay, earliest with inlay only at frets 5, 7 and 9, snakehead peghead
Available: **1984–85**

D-64: maple back and sides, multiple-bound top and back, bound ebony fingerboard, notched-diamond inlay, bound snakehead peghead, G-shield peghead inlay, chrome-plated tuners
Available: **1984–86**

D-66: 15 3/4" wide, rosewood back and sides, multiple-bound top and back, scalloped bracing, mahogany neck, 25 5/8" scale, bound ebony fingerboard, slotted-diamond inlay, bound snakehead peghead, G-shield peghead inlay
Introduced: **1984**
Renamed **D-60** (see following): **1987**

D-30: continuation of G-37 (see preceding), 15 3/4" wide, laminated arched maple back, solid maple sides, scalloped bracing, multiple-bound top and back, maple neck, 25 5/8" scale, rosewood fingerboard, dot inlay, Chesterfield peghead inlay
Introduced: **1987**
Gold-plated tuners, blond, sunburst, black or woodgrain finish: **1992**
Black, blond or antique burst finish: **1997**
Still in production

D-30E: transducer pickup: **1994–95**

D-60: continuation of D-66 (see preceding), 15 3/4" wide, rosewood back and sides, multiple-bound top and back, scalloped bracing, mahogany neck, 25 5/8" scale, bound ebony fingerboard, slotted-diamond inlay, bound snakehead peghead, G-shield peghead inlay
Introduced: **1987**
Discontinued: **1990**
Model name reintroduced, continuation of G-45 Hank Williams Jr. (see preceding), maple back and sides, abalone soundhole ring, bound ebony fingerboard, pearl block inlay with abalone V inserts, large peghead, G-shield logo: **1998**
Still in production

D-48: solid mahogany sides, laminated arched mahogany back, dark body binding, unbound rosewood fingerboard, dot inlay, natural satin (nongloss) finish
Available: **1992**

D-4: 15 3/4" wide, laminated arched mahogany back, solid mahogany sides, tortoiseshell celluloid pickguard, dark binding around top, 25 5/8" scale, rosewood fingerboard, dot inlay, chrome-plated tuners, snakehead peghead, dark peaked logo, natural satin (non-gloss) finish
Available: **1992–current**

D-4E: transducer pickup: **1992–97**

D-4HG: high-gloss natural or sunburst finish: **1992**

D-4G: gloss finish: **1998–current**

D-4M: solid mahogany top: **1998–current**

D-6 (S): 15 3/4" wide, mahogany back and sides, scalloped bracing, rosewood fingerboard, dot inlay, snakehead peghead, peaked logo, gold-plated tuners, natural satin (non-gloss) finish
Available: **1992–95**

D-6E: transducer pickup: **1992–95**

D-6HG: high-gloss natural or sunburst finish: **1992–95**

D-6HGE: high-gloss finish, transducer pickup: **1992–95**

DV-6: 15 3/4" wide, mahogany back and sides, scalloped bracing, herringbone soundhole ring, tortoiseshell celluloid pickguard, 25 5/8" scale, rosewood fingerboard, dot inlay, snakehead peghead, Chesterfield peghead inlay, black peghead finish, gold-plated tuners, natural satin (non-gloss) finish or high gloss finish (**DV6HG**)
Introduced: **1995**
High gloss finish optional (DV6HG no longer listed separately): **1998**
Still in production

DV-52: rosewood back and sides, scalloped bracing, bone saddle, multiple body binding with cream outer layer, herringbone soundhole ring, bone nut, unbound ebony fingerboard, dot inlay, snakehead peghead, gold-plated tuners, natural satin (non-gloss) finish (**DV-52S**) or high gloss finish (**DV-52HG**)
Introduced: **1992**
Abalone soundhole ring: **1996**
Listed as DV-52 with optional satin or gloss finish: **1998**
Still in production

DV-62: rosewood back and sides, scalloped bracing, bone saddle, cream binding, herringbone top bor-

der, herringbone soundhole ring, ebony fingerboard, dot inlay, bone nut, Chesterfield peghead inlay, gold-plated tuners, natural or sunburst finish
Available: **1993–95**

DV-72: rosewood back and sides, herringbone top trim, ebony fingerboard, exotic stone inlays in soundhole ring, fingerboard and G-shield peghead inlay
Available: **1993**

DCE-1 True American: rounded cutaway, laminated arched mahogany back, solid mahogany sides, transducer pickup with preamp, rosewood fingerboard, dot inlay, snakehead peghead, gold-plated tuners, natural satin (non-gloss) finish
Introduced: **1993**
High gloss finish optional (DCE-1HG not listed separately): **1998**
Still in production

DCE-1HG: high gloss black or antique sunburst lacquer finish: **1997**

DCE-2 True American: rounded cutaway, mahogany back and sides, transducer pickup with preamp, ebony fingerboard, dot inlay, snakehead peghead, gold-plated tuners, natural or sunburst finish
Available: **1993–94**

DCE-5: single cutaway, laminated arched rosewood back, solid rosewood sides, transducer pickup with preamp, multiple body binding, ebony fingerboard, dot inlay, snakehead peghead, gold-plated tuners, natural or sunburst finish
Available: **1994–current**

DV-74: rosewood back and sides, Southwestern motif, limited edition
Available: **1995–96**

DK-70: koa body, ebony fingerboard, humptop trapezoid inlay, abalone peghead logo
Available: **1995–96**

Finesse: rosewood back and sides, ebony bridge, tortoiseshell celluloid binding, 3-piece mahogany neck, bound ebony fingerboard, dot inlay, gold-plated tuners, Custom Shop model
Available: **1997–current**

Deco: rosewood back and sides, ebony bridge, multiple binding, 3-piece mahogany/maple neck, bound ebony fingerboard, deco pearl inlay with oval abalone center piece, bound peghead, Custom Shop model
Available: **1997–current**

SOLIDBODY MODELS

FS-46: 16" wide, pointed cutaway, routed oval soundhole, mahogany back, Fishman TASS pickup, 24 3/4" scale, bound rosewood fingerboard, dot inlay, 3-on-a-side tuners, natural, sunburst or black
Available: **1983–86**

FS-46-6: Fishman TASS pickup, maple fingerboard, 6-on-a-side tuners, natural, sunburst or black: **1983–85**

FS-48CE Deceiver: pointed cutaway, oval soundhole, hidden EMG humbucking pickup, piezo bridge pickup, maple fingerboard, black dot inlay, 6-on-a-side tuners
Available: **1985**

FS-20CE: pointed cutaway, routed mahogany back, spruce top, oval soundhole, Fishman TASS pickup
Available: **1986–early 1987**

DS-48CE: 15 3/4" wide, pointed cutaway, routed mahogany back, oval soundhole, Fishman TASS pickup, natural, sunburst or black
Available: **1983–84**

MKS-10: 14 3/4" wide, rounded cutaway, routed mahogany back, round soundhole, nylon strings, Fishman TASS pickup, 24 3/4" scale, rosewood fingerboard 2" wide, no inlay, slotted peghead, natural, sunburst or black finish
Available: **1984–86**

MKS-44: 14 3/4" wide, rounded cutaway, oval soundhole, mahogany back, Fishman TASS pickup, classical string-tie bridge, 24 3/4" scale, bound rosewood fingerboard, dot inlay, solid peghead, Chesterfield peghead logo, natural, sunburst or black finish
Available: **1984**

Songbird/S4-CE: designed by George Gruhn, 1-piece routed mahogany back, X-braced spruce top, pointed cutaway, round soundhole, transducer pickup with preamp, volume control, concentric treble/bass control, triple-bound top, rosewood fingerboard, dot inlay, snakehead peghead, Chesterfield peghead inlay, chrome-plated tuners, natural, black or white finish
Introduced as **Songbird: 1987**

S4-CE listed with satin finish; Songbird listed with natural, black or white gloss finish: **1992**
High gloss finish (**S4CE-HG**) or handrubbed natural finish (**S4CE-HR**): **1998**
Still in production

S4CE-BG: Barry Gibb (of the BeeGees) model, metallic blue or crimson finish, limited run: **1998**

Songbird Custom: gold-plated tuners, white, black or red top finish with black finish on back and sides
Available: **1989 only**

CR-1 Crossroads Single E: single cutaway, spruce top, 1-piece routed mahogany back and sides, curly maple top, EMG S2 pickup and transducer pickup, cream binding, rosewood fingerboard, dot inlay, gold-plated tuners, amber, black or woodgrain finish
Available: **1993–94**

CR-1 Crossroads Double E: Slash (of Guns 'N Roses) model, doubleneck, combination of acoustic 12-string neck and solidbody 6-string neck, routed mahogany back, bound maple top, soundhole on 12-string side, 12-string side has transducer pickup with unbound rosewood fingerboard and dot inlay, 6-string side has 2 EMG pickups with bound ebony fingerboard and pearl/abalone V-block inlay, both pegheads bound with G-shield inlays, Custom Shop model
Available: **1993, 1998–current**

12-STRINGS

F-212: 16" wide, jumbo shape with flat lower bout (non-dreadnought), mahogany back and sides, tortoiseshell celluloid pickguard, rosewood bridge, 3-piece mahogany/maple neck, 25 1/2" scale, unbound rosewood fingerboard, no inlay
Available: **1964–85**

F-212E: electric, pickup at end of fingerboard, 2 knobs on upper treble bout: **1965–74**

F-212C: pointed cutaway: **1976–81**

Artist F-312: 15 7/8" wide, flat lower bout but not dreadnought shape, rosewood back and sides, tortoiseshell celluloid pickguard, ebony bridge, 3-piece mahogany neck, 25 1/2" scale, unbound ebony fingerboard, no inlay
Introduced: **1964**
Chesterfield peghead inlay: **c. 1968**
Rosewood bridge: **1969**
Discontinued: **1974**

Standard F-112: 15 1/4" wide, rounded lower bout, mahogany back and sides, tortoiseshell celluloid pickguard, rosewood bridge, mahogany neck, 25 1/2" scale, unbound rosewood fingerboard, no inlay, peaked logo
Introduced: **1968**
Chesterfield peghead inlay: **1969**
Discontinued: **1982**

Standard F-212XL: 17" wide, rounded lower bout, mahogany back and sides, tortoiseshell celluloid pickguard, rosewood bridge, 3-piece mahogany/maple neck, 25 1/2" scale, unbound ebony fingerboard, no inlay, Chesterfield peghead inlay
Introduced: **1966**
Ebony bridge: **1977**
Discontinued: **1986**

Custom F-412/JF-65M-12/JF65-12:

12-string version of F-50, 17" wide, rounded lower bout, maple back and sides, black pickguard, rosewood bridge, 3-piece maple neck with walnut strip, 25 1/2" scale, bound ebony fingerboard, pearl block inlay with abalone V inserts, bound peghead, G-shield peghead inlay, gold-plated tuners
Introduced, special order only: **1968**
Regular production: **1974**
Renamed **JF-65M-12: 1987**
Renamed: **JF65-12:** 17" wide, laminated arched maple back, solid maple sides, multiple-bound top and back, maple neck, 25 5/8" scale, single-bound ebony fingerboard, pearl block inlay with abalone V inserts, multiple-bound peghead, G-shield peghead inlay, gold-plated tuners, natural or sunburst finish: **1987**
Still in production

Custom F-512/JF-65R-12/JF55-12: 12-string version of F-50R, 17" wide, rounded lower bout, rosewood back and sides, black pickguard, rosewood bridge, 3-piece mahogany neck with maple strip, 25 1/2" scale, bound ebony fingerboard, pearl block inlay with abalone V inserts (early with varied-pattern inlay with lyre at 1st fret), bound peghead, G-shield peghead inlay, gold-plated tuners
Introduced as **F-512**, special order only: **1968**
3-piece padouk/maple neck: **c. 1973**
Regular production: **1974**
Some with ebony bridge: **1976**
3-piece mahogany/maple neck: **1977**
Renamed **JF-65R-12: 1987**
Discontinued: **late 1987**
Reintroduced as **JF55-12:** scalloped bracing, abalone soundhole ring, multiple-bound top and back, 3-piece mahogany neck, natural or sunburst finish: **1991**
Still in production

Custom F-612: 18" wide, rounded lower bout, rosewood back and sides, tortoiseshell celluloid pickguard, rosewood bridge with 2 snowflake inlays, checkered purfling around top and sound-hole, 3-piece mahogany/maple neck, 26 1/4" scale, bound ebony fingerboard, varied-pattern inlay with lyre at 1st fret, bound peghead with checkered purfling, G-shield peghead inlay, gold-plated tuners, special order only
Available: **1970–late 1973**

D-212/D-25-12: 12-string version of D-25, laminated arched mahogany back, solid mahogany sides, rosewood fingerboard, dot inlay, chrome-plated tuners, natural, sunburst or black finish
Introduced as **D-212: 1981**
Renamed **D-25-12: 1987**
Discontinued: **1992**
Reintroduced, natural, sunburst, mahogany, cherry or black finish: **1996**
Still in production

G-212: 12-string version of D-40, 15 3/4" wide, dreadnought, mahogany back and sides, tortoiseshell celluloid pickguard, rosewood bridge, mahogany neck, 25 1/2" scale, unbound rosewood fingerboard with no inlay, Chesterfield peghead inlay, natural or sunburst finish
Available: **1974–83**

G-312/D-312/D-50-12: 12-string version of D-50, 15 3/4" wide, dreadnought, rosewood back and sides, black pickguard, rosewood bridge, 3-piece mahogany neck, 25 1/2" scale, unbound rosewood fingerboard with no inlay, Chesterfield peghead inlay
Introduced as **G-312: 1974**
Discontinued: **1985**
Reintroduced as **D-312: 1986**
Renamed **D-50-12:** scalloped bracing, multiple-bound top and back, 1-piece mahogany neck, 25 1/2" scale, unbound ebony fingerboard, dot inlay, Chesterfield peghead inlay: **1987**
Discontinued: **1987**

FS-46-12: solidbody, 16" wide, pointed cutaway, oval soundhole, solid mahogany back, Fishman TASS pickup, 24 3/4" scale, rosewood fingerboard, dot inlay, 6-on-a-side tuner arrangement, natural, sunburst or black finish
Available: **1983–85**

D-15-12: Mahogany Rush series, 15 3/4" wide, dreadnought, mahogany back and sides, mahogany top, mahogany neck, 25 5/8" scale, rosewood fingerboard, dot inlay, peaked logo, mahogany or woodgrain red finish, satin finish
Available: **1983–85**

D-17-12: Mahogany Rush series, all-mahogany body, natural mahogany gloss finish or cherry satin (non-gloss) finish
Available: **1984**

F-45C-12: 16" wide, pointed cutaway, arched laminated mahogany back, Fishman TASS pickup, 24 3/4" scale, rosewood fingerboard, dot inlay, Chesterfield peghead inlay, natural, sunburst or black finish
Available: **1984**

JF30-12: 17" wide, laminated arched maple back, solid maple sides, scalloped bracing, multiple-bound top and back, maple neck, 25 5/8" scale, unbound rosewood fingerboard, dot inlay, Chesterfield peghead inlay, chrome-plated tuners, amber, sunburst, black or woodgrain finish
Introduced: **1987**
Gold-plated tuners: **c. 1991**
Woodgrain finish discontinued: **1992**
Still in production

D4-12S: laminated arched mahogany back, solid mahogany sides, dark binding, rosewood fingerboard, dot inlay, peaked logo, chrome-plated tuners, natural satin (non-gloss) finish
Introduced: **1992**
Renamed **D4-12:** handrubbed finish: **1997**
Still in production

D4-12E: transducer pickup: **1992–95**

JF100-12: rosewood back and sides, scalloped bracing, multiple wood binding with abalone border, abalone soundhole ring, bound ebony fingerboard, abalone humptop-trapezoid inlay, bound peghead, abalone peghead inlay
Available: **1992–95**

JF-100-12C: carved neck heel: **1994–current**

CLASSICALS

Mark I: 14 1/2" wide, all-mahogany body, rosewood bridge, 3-piece mahogany neck, 25 1/2" scale, rosewood fingerboard, satin (non-gloss) finish
Available: **1961–72**

Mark II: 14 1/2" wide, mahogany back and sides, rosewood bridge, red-black-white soundhole ring, tortoiseshell celluloid top and back binding, 3-piece mahogany neck, 25 1/2" scale, rosewood fingerboard, rosewood peghead veneer, satin (non-gloss) finish
Available: **1961–86**

Mark III: 14 1/2" wide, mahogany back and sides, rosewood bridge, tortoiseshell celluloid top and back binding, floral-pattern soundhole ring, 3-ply binding with tortoiseshell celluloid outer layer, 3-piece mahogany neck, 25 1/2" scale, rosewood fingerboard, rosewood peghead veneer, nickel-plated tuners
Available: **1961–86**

Mark IV: 14 1/2" wide, rosewood or flamed pearwood back and sides, ebony bridge, 4-ply binding with tortoiseshell celluloid outer layer, 3-piece mahogany neck, 25 1/2" scale, ebony fingerboard, ebony peghead veneer, gold-plated tuners
Introduced: **1961**
Flamed maple back and sides optional, rosewood discontinued: **1962**

Flamed maple back and sides discontinued, pearwood only: **1963**
Rosewood bridge: **c. 1966**
Rosewood back and sides: **1978**
Discontinued: **1986**

Mark V: 14 1/2" wide, rosewood or flamed maple back and sides, ebony bridge, ebony top and back binding, 3-piece mahogany neck, 25 1/2" scale, ebony fingerboard, ebony peghead veneer, engraved gold-plated tuners
Introduced: **1961**
Rosewood back and sides only: **1964**
Rosewood bridge: **c. 1966**
Discontinued: **1987**

Mark VI: 14 1/2" wide, rosewood back and sides, ebony bridge, natural wood top and back binding, 3-piece mahogany neck, 25 1/2" scale, ebony fingerboard, ebony peghead veneer, engraved gold-plated tuners
Introduced: **1962**
Rosewood bridge with pearl inlays: **c. 1966**
Discontinued: **1987**

Mark VII Custom: 14 1/2" wide, rosewood back and sides, ebony bridge, ebony top and back binding, 3-piece mahogany neck, 26 1/4" scale, ebony fingerboard, ebony peghead veneer, engraved gold-plated tuners
Introduced: **1962**
Rosewood bridge with pearl inlays: **c. 1966**
Discontinued: **1987**

Mark 50: dreadnought body size, Jose Feliciano model, maple (**Mark 50M**) or rosewood (**Mark 50R**) back and sides, slotted peghead, natural or sunburst finish
Available: **1985**

MKS-10: see Solidbody (preceding)

MKS-11: not a solidbody (despite S in model name), 14 3/4" wide, pointed cutaway, oval soundhole, mahogany back and sides, nylon strings, Fishman TASS pickup, 24 3/4" scale, rosewood fingerboard 2" wide, no inlay, slotted peghead, natural, sunburst or black finish
Available: **1984**

MKS-44: see Solidbody (preceding)

CCE-100: thin solidbody classical (nylon string), cutaway, routed mahogany back, oval soundhole routing, wood inlay soundhole ring, transducer pickup with preamp, classic-style soundhole ornamentation, slotted peghead, natural satin (non-gloss) finish or high gloss (**CCE-100HG**) finish

Available: **1993**

UKULELES

B-11/U-11 Baritone Ukulele: 10 3/8" wide, all-mahogany body, 20 1/4" scale, rosewood fingerboard, geared right-angle tuners, satin finish

Introduced: **1963**

Some with spruce top, some with gloss brown or cherry finish: **early 1970s**

Discontinued: **1976**

U-21: deluxe chrome-plated tuners

COMMENTS

Guild has been remarkably consistent in quality throughout its existence and has neither a "golden era" nor a period of falling quality. Flat tops from all periods are regarded as good utility instruments. A few models, such as the F-50 and F-40 from the 1950s, are collectible. Guild's 12-strings of the 1960s are more highly regarded than those of any other maker and have achieved something of a cult following.

ELECTRIC ARCHTOPS KEY

Non-cutaway
    Block inlay
        1 pickup = **X-100/X-110**
        2 pickups = **X-200/X-220**
    Dot inlay
        2 7/8" deep = **Granada X-50 (Cordoba)**
        2" deep = **Cordoba T-50 Slim**
Double-cutaway with rounded horns
    Chrome-plated hardware
        Bigsby vibrato
            Switch on upper bass bout = **Bert Weedon Model**
            No switch on upper bass bout = **Starfire V**
        Harp tailpiece
            6-string = **Starfire IV**
            12-string = **Starfire XII**
    Gold-plated hardware
        G-shield peghead inlay = **Starfire VI**
        Large pearl block on peghead = **Custom 7/Deep Starfire**
Double-cutaway with pointed horns
    1 pickup = **Studio 301**
    2 pickups
        Harp tailpiece
            1 7/8" deep = **Studio 302**
            2 7/8" deep = **Studio 402**
        Bigsby vibrato = **Studio 303**

Single-cutaway with rounded horn
    1 pickup
        Block inlay with abalone V insert = **Johnny Smith Award/Artist Award**
        Block inlay with no V insert
            Full-depth body
                1953 date = **X-300/X-330**
                1954 or after = **Savoy X-150**
            Dot inlay
                24 3/4" scale = **Freshman M-65**
                22 3/4" scale = **M-65 3/4**
    2 pickups
        No *f*-holes
            Controls on pickguard
                17" wide = **George Barnes AcoustiLectric**
                13 1/2" wide = **George Barnes Guitar in F**
            Controls into top
                Single-coil pickups = **Aristocrat M-75**
                Humbucking pickups
                    Gold-plated hardware
                        Ebony fingerboard = **M-75 Deluxe**
                        Rosewood fingerboard = **BluesBird M-75**
                  Chrome-plated hardware = **M-75 Standard**
        f-holes
            Gold-plated hardware
                2 knobs = **Nightingale** (routed solidbody, see Solidbodies)
                4 knobs
                    Switch on upper bass bout
                        Block inlay with V inserts = **Duane Eddy Deluxe/DE-500**
                        Block inlay with no inserts = **Manhattan X-170**
                    No switch on upper bass bout
                      Block inlay with V inserts
                        3 1/4" deep **= Stuart X-500/X-550, Stuart X-700**
                        2" deep = **T-500**
            Nickel- or chrome-plated hardware
                3 1/4" deep
                    1953 date = **X-400/440**
                    1954–84 = Manhattan **X-175**
                    1989–93 = **Savoy X-160/X-161**
                    1998 and after = **Savoy X-150D**
                2" deep = **Duane Eddy Standard/DE-400**
    3 pickups
        Gold-plated hardware
            Block inlay with no V inserts = **Stratford X-350/X-375**
            Block inlay with abalone V inserts = **X-600/X-660**
        Chrome-plated hardware = **Stratford Starfire/SF-350**
Single-cutaway with pointed horn
    Block inlay = **Capri CE-100**
    Dot inlay
        Rosewood bridge
            1 pickup = **Slim Jim T-100**
            2 pickups = **T-100D**
        AdjustoMatic bridge, harp tailpiece
            1 pickup = **Starfire I**
            2 pickups = **Starfire II**
        Bigsby (metal) bridge and vibrato = **Starfire III**

GUILD

ELECTRIC ARCHTOPS

NON-CUTAWAY MODELS

X-100/X-110: 17" wide, laminated maple back and sides, laminated spruce top, 1 pickup, 2 knobs, bound rosewood fingerboard, block inlay, *G* peghead inlay, nickel-plated hardware, sunburst (**X-100**) or blond (**X-110**) finish
Available: **1953–54**

X-200/X-220: 17" wide, laminated maple back and sides, laminated spruce top, 2 pickups, bound rosewood fingerboard, block inlay, nickel-plated hardware, sunburst (**X-200**) or blond (**X-220**) finish
Available: **1953–54**

Granada/Cordoba X-50: 16 3/8" wide, laminated maple top, back and sides, 1 single-coil pickup, 2 knobs, 3-piece mahogany neck, 25 1/2" scale, unbound rosewood fingerboard, dot inlay, chrome-plated hardware, sunburst finish
Introduced: **1954**
Renamed **Cordoba X-50: late 1961**
24 3/4" scale: **c. 1956**
1-piece mahogany neck: **1959**
Discontinued: **1970**

X-50BI: blond finish: **1958–70**

Cordoba T-50 Slim: thinbody, 2" deep: **c.1961–late 1973**

SINGLE CUTAWAY MODELS

X-300/X-330: 17" wide, rounded cutaway, laminated maple back and sides, laminated spruce top, 1 pickup, 2 knobs, bound rosewood fingerboard, block inlay, *G* peghead inlay, nickel-plated hardware, sunburst (**X-300**) or blond (**X-330**) finish
Available: **1953–54**

X-400/X-440: 17" wide, rounded cutaway, 2 pickups, nickel-plated hardware, sunburst (**X-400**) or blond (**X-440**) finish
Available: **c. 1953–54**

Stuart X-500/X-550: 17" wide, rounded cutaway, laminated maple back and sides, laminated spruce top, 2 single-coil pickups with black covers, 4 knobs, selector switch on upper treble bout, 25 1/2" scale, bound rosewood fingerboard, pearl block inlay with abalone V insert, *G* peghead inlay, gold-plated hardware
Introduced as **X-500** (sunburst) and **X-550** (blond): **1953**
Stuart added to model name, white pickup covers: **1954**
X-550 renamed **X-500B: c.1960**
DeArmond pickups: **1961**
Humbucking pickups: **1963**
Master volume control: **c.1971**
Discontinued, replaced by X-700 (see following): **1994**

T-500: thinbody 2" deep, available: **c. 1961**

X-600/X-660 (sunburst/blond): 17" wide, rounded cutaway, laminated maple back and sides, laminated spruce top, 3 pickups, bound rosewood fingerboard, pearl block inlay with abalone V insert, *G* peghead inlay, gold-plated hardware
Only appearance: **1953**

Stratford X-350/X-375: 17" wide, rounded cutaway, laminated maple back and sides, laminated spruce top, 3 single-coil pickups with black covers, 2 knobs, 6 pushbutton switches, 25 1/2" scale, bound rosewood fingerboard, block inlay, unbound peghead, *G* peghead inlay, gold-plated hardware
Introduced as **X-350** (sunburst) and **X-375** (blond): **1953**
White pickup covers: **1954**
Bound peghead: **1955**
24 3/4" scale: **by 1958**
Maple top: **1958**
X-375 renamed **X-350B: 1958**
Ebony fingerboard: **1961**
DeArmond pickups: **1962**
Humbucking pickups: **1963**
Discontinued: **1965**

Johnny Smith Award/Artist Award: 17" wide, single-cutaway, highly figured maple back and sides, solid spruce top, floating DeArmond pickup, knob and jack in pickguard, engraved harp tailpiece,

multiple-bound top and back, 24 3/4" scale, multiple-bound ebony fingerboard, pearl block inlay with abalone V insert, multiple-bound peghead, model name engraved on large pearl peghead inlay, Grover Imperial tuners, gold-plated hardware, sunburst or blond finish
Introduced as **Johnny Smith Award: 1956**
Renamed **Artist Award: 1961**
Model name engraved on pickup: **1961**
Adjustable polepieces on pickup: **1965**
25 1/2" scale: **c. 1969**
18" model available by special order: **1970–72**
Floating humbucking pickup: **c. 1980**
Pickguard comes to point at body waist: **1989**
Still in production

Stratford Starfire SF-350: 17" wide, 3 1/8"
deep, rounded cutaway, laminated mahogany body, 3 single-coil DeArmond pickups, 2 knobs, 6 pushbuttons, ebony bridge or AdjustoMatic bridge, harp tailpiece, 24 3/4" scale, 3-piece mahogany/maple neck, bound ebony fingerboard, block inlay, G-shield peghead inlay, chrome-plated hardware
Introduced: **1961**
Humbucking pickups: **1963**
Discontinued: **1964**

Savoy X-150: 17" wide, rounded cutaway, maple
back and sides, spruce top, 1 pickup, 2 knobs, trapeze tailpiece, 3-piece mahogany neck, 25 1/2" scale, bound rosewood fingerboard (some early with unbound fingerboard), pearloid block inlay, *Guild* logo, nickel-plated hardware, sunburst (**X-150**), blond (**X-150B**) or sparkling gold (**X-150G**) finish
Introduced: **1954**
Harp tailpiece: **1955**
24 3/4" scale, *G* peghead inlay: **c. 1956**
Sparkling gold finish discontinued: **1959**
Humbucking pickup: **1963**
Discontinued: **1965**
Reintroduced as **X-150 Savoy**, Chesterfield peghead inlay: **1998**
Still in production

X-150D Savoy: 2 humbucking pickups (reissue of X-175), Chesterfield peghead inlay: **1998–current**

X-160 Savoy: 16 5/8" wide, rounded cutaway, lam-
inated maple body, soundposts, 2 humbucking

pickups, Bigsby vibrato tailpiece optional, chrome-plated hardware, black or sunburst finish
Available: **1989–93**

X-161/X-160B Savoy: Bigsby vibrato
Introduced as **X-161: 1990**
Renamed **X-160B: 1992**
Discontinued: **1994**

Manhattan X-175: 17" wide, rounded cutaway,
laminated maple back and sides, laminated spruce top, 2 single-coil pickups, 2 knobs, 3-way switch on cutaway bout, 3-piece mahogany/maple neck, 25 1/2" scale, bound rosewood fingerboard, pearloid block inlay, chrome-plated hardware, sunburst (**X-175**) or blond (**X-175B**) finish
Introduced: **1954**
24 3/4" scale, *G* peghead inlay: **c. 1956**
Chesterfield peghead inlay: **1957**
Extra volume and tone control added (4 knobs): **1958**
Humbucking pickups: **1963**
Blond finish X-175B discontinued: **1976**
Master volume control added to cutaway bout, selector switch on upper bass bout: **by 1981**
Discontinued: **1985**
Reintroduced as **X-150D Savoy** (see preceding): **1998**

X-170 Mini-Manhattan: 16 5/8" wide, rounded
cutaway, laminated maple body, soundposts, 2 humbucking pickups, selector switch on upper bass bout, engraved harp tailpiece, 24 3/4" scale, bound rosewood fingerboard, pearl block inlay, Chesterfield peghead inlay, gold-plated hardware, sunburst or blond finish
Introduced: **1985**
Renamed **Manhattan: 1987**
Still in production

X-170B: Bigsby tailpiece: **1995–current**

Aristocrat/BluesBird M-75 (Standard): 13
1/2" wide, rounded cutaway, thinbody, no *f*-holes, mahogany back and sides, spruce top, 2 single-coil pickups, 4 knobs, selector switch on upper bass bout, 3-piece mahogany/maple neck, 24 3/4" scale, neck/body joint at 18th fret, bound rosewood fingerboard, pearloid block inlay at 10 frets, gold-plated hardware, sunburst finish
Introduced as **Aristocrat M-75: 1954**
Inlay at 8 frets: **1959**

Natural blond top optional: **1959**

Optional mahogany top with cherry red finish: **1961**

Discontinued: **1963**

Reintroduced as **BluesBird M-75:** spruce, maple or mahogany top, humbucking pickups, neck/body joint at 16th fret: **1967**

Most with laminated maple back and sides: **1968**

Some with DeArmond pickups: **1970**

Renamed **M-75 Standard (M-75S)**, chrome-plated hardware: **1970**

Solidbody version available, distinguishable from hollowbody by stop tailpiece (see Solidbodies section): **1970**

Phase switch optional: **c. 1971**

Discontinued: **1972**

M-75 Deluxe (M-75G): ebony fingerboard, gold-plated hardware, phase switch optional: **1970–71**

Capri CE-100: 16 1/4" wide, pointed cutaway, maple top, back and sides, 1 single-coil soapbar pickup, 2 knobs, 3-piece mahogany/walnut neck, 24 3/4" scale, bound rosewood fingerboard, pearloid block inlay, chrome-plated hardware, sunburst finish

Introduced: **1956**

Chesterfield peghead inlay: **1957**

Humbucking pickup: **1963**

3-piece maple/mahogany neck: **1976**

CE-100 standard with 2 pickups: **1983**

Discontinued: **1985**

CE-100B: "Black Beauty," black finish: **1958**

CE-100D: 2 pickups: **1959–82** (CE-100 standard with 2 pickups beginning in 1983)

Slim Jim T-100/T-100D: 16 1/4" wide, 2" deep, pointed cutaway, maple top, back and sides, 1 or 2 single-coil pickups, 2 knobs (1 pickup) or 4 knobs (2 pickups), rosewood bridge, bound top, unbound back, 1-piece mahogany neck, 24 3/4" scale, bound rosewood fingerboard, dot inlay, chrome-plated hardware, sunburst or blond finish

Introduced: **1958**

Blond finish discontinued: **1971**

Discontinued: **late 1973**

Freshman M-65: 13 1/2" wide, 2" deep, rounded cutaway, maple top, mahogany back and sides, 1 single-coil pickup, 2 knobs, bound top, unbound back, 1-piece mahogany neck, 24 3/4" scale, bound

rosewood fingerboard, dot inlay, chrome-plated hardware, sunburst or blond top finish

Introduced: **1959**

Unbound fingerboard: **c. 1965**

Mahogany top with cherry red finish standard: **1961**

Blond finish discontinued: **1969**

Discontinued: **late 1973**

M-65 3/4: 22 3/4" scale, otherwise same specs and changes as Freshman M-65: **1959–73**

Starfire (single cutaway): 16 1/4" wide, 2" deep, pointed cutaway, laminated maple or laminated mahogany top, back and sides, bound top, unbound back, 1-piece mahogany neck, 25 1/2" scale, bound rosewood fingerboard, dot inlay, Chesterfield peghead inlay, chrome-plated hardware

Starfire I: 1 single-coil pickup, 2 knobs, AdjustoMatic bridge, harp tailpiece, Starfire red finish

Introduced: **1960**

Bound back: **1962**

Emerald green, honey amber, ebony grain finishes optional: **1962**

Humbucking pickups: **1963**

Discontinued: **1964**

Starfire II: 2 pickups, 4 knobs, 3-way switch on upper bass bout, AdjustoMatic bridge, harp tailpiece, Starfire red finish

Introduced: **1960**

Bound back: **1962**

Emerald green, honey amber, ebony grain finishes optional: **1962**

Humbucking pickups: **1963**

Rosewood bridge: **late 1973**

Discontinued: **1976**

Reintroduced, 2 humbucking pickups, harp tailpiece, 24 3/4" scale, chrome-plated hardware, black, blond or antique burst finish: **1997**

Still in production

Starfire III: 2 pickups, 4 knobs, 3-way switch on upper bass bout, metal bridge, Bigsby vibrato, Starfire red finish

Introduced: **1960**

Bound back: **1962**

Emerald green, honey amber or ebony grain finishes optional: **1962**

Humbucking pickups: **1963**

Discontinued: **1974**

Reintroduced, 2 humbucking pickups, Bigsby vibrato, 24 3/4" scale, chrome-plated hardware, black, blond, transparent red or antique burst finish: **1997**
Still in production

George Barnes AcoustiLectric: 17" wide, no

f-holes, single-cutaway, curly maple back and sides, solid spruce top, 2 humbucking pickups mounted on internal bar, 4 knobs mounted on pickguard, 3-way switch on cutaway bout, multiple-bound top, back, 5-piece maple/walnut neck, 24 3/4" scale, multiple-bound ebony fingerboard, pearl block inlay with abalone V insert, bound peghead, model name engraved on truss rod cover, gold-plated hardware, sunburst or blond finish
Available: **1962–72**

George Barnes Guitar in F: 13 1/2" wide, 2

7/8" deep, rounded cutaway, no f-holes, mahogany back and sides, spruce top, 2 humbucking pickups mounted on internal bar, 4 knobs mounted on pickguard, 3-way switch on cutaway bout, 1-piece mahogany neck, 22 3/4" scale, bound rosewood fingerboard, 6-piece pearloid block inlay at 10 frets, chrome-plated hardware, sunburst or cherry sunburst finish
Introduced: **1963**
Cherry sunburst finish discontinued: **1968**
Discontinued: **1973**

Duane Eddy Deluxe/DE-500: 17" wide, 2"

deep, rounded cutaway, laminated maple back and sides, laminated spruce top, 2 single-coil DeArmond pickups with white covers, 4 knobs, master volume knob on cutaway bout, selector switch on upper bass bout, Bigsby vibrato, signature on pickguard, 3-piece maple/walnut neck, 24 3/4" scale, bound ebony fingerboard, abalone block inlay with V insert, bound peghead, G-shield peghead inlay, signature on truss rod cover, gold-plated hardware, sunburst or blond finish
Introduced: **1962**
Humbucking pickups, stairstep pickguard with signature, no signature on truss rod cover: **1964**
No signature on pickguard: **1968**
Discontinued: **1974**
Reintroduced, old-stock DeArmond pickups with white covers: **1984**
Discontinued: **1987**

Duane Eddy Standard/DE-400: 17" wide, 2"

deep, rounded cutaway, laminated maple or mahogany back and sides, laminated spruce, maple or mahogany top, 2 single-coil DeArmond pickups with white covers, 4 knobs, master volume knob on cutaway bout, selector switch on upper bass bout, Bigsby vibrato, signature on pickguard, 3-piece mahogany/maple neck, 24 3/4" scale, bound rosewood fingerboard, pearloid block inlay, Chesterfield peghead inlay, signature on truss rod cover, chrome- and nickel-plated hardware, sunburst or blond finish
Introduced (earliest labeled *Duane Eddy Jr.*): **1963**
Humbucking pickups, cherry finish optional: **1964**
No signature on pickguard, cherry finish discontinued: **1968**
Discontinued: **1974**

X040/X-3000 Nightingale: single-cutaway,

carved top with f-holes, solid mahogany body with sound chambers, see Solidbodies section

DOUBLE CUTAWAY MODELS

Starfire (double cutaway): 16 3/8" wide, semi-

hollowbody, 1 7/8" deep, laminated maple or laminated mahogany body, 2 humbucking pickups, 4 knobs, switch on upper treble bout, AdjustoMatic bridge

Starfire IV: 3-piece mahogany/maple neck (some 1-piece mahogany), neck joint at 16th fret, bound rosewood fingerboard, dot inlay, Chesterfield peghead inlay, chrome-plated hardware, sunburst or cherry finish
Introduced: **1963**
Neck joint at 18th fret: **1967**
Master volume added, block inlay: **c. 1973**
Discontinued: **1987**
Reintroduced, sunburst or blond finish: **1993**
Transparent red finish optional: **1997**
Black finish optional: **1998**
Still in production

Starfire XII: 12-string, rosewood bridge, harp tailpiece: **1966–73**

Starfire V: master volume control, Guild/Bigsby vibrato, 3-piece mahogany/maple neck, neck joint at 16th fret, bound rosewood fingerboard, block inlay, Chesterfield peghead inlay, chrome-plated hardware, sunburst or blond finish

Introduced: **1963**
Neck joint at 18th fret: **1967**
Some with single-coil DeArmond pickups: **c. 1970**
Discontinued: **1973**

Starfire VI: Guild/Bigsby vibrato, 3-piece maple/walnut neck, neck joint at 16th fret, bound ebony fingerboard, pearl block inlay with abalone V inserts, G-shield peghead inlay, gold-plated hardware, sunburst or blond finish
Introduced: **1964**
Neck joint at 18th fret: **1967**
Some with single-coil DeArmond pickups: **c. 1970**
Harp tailpiece, Guild/Bigsby vibrato optional: **c. 1976**
Blond finish discontinued: **1974**
Discontinued: **1979**

Bert Weedon Model: 16 3/8" wide, thin fully hollow body 2" deep, laminated mahogany body, 2 single-coil DeArmond pickups, 4 knobs, master volume knob on upper treble bout, switch on upper bass bout, metal bridge, Guild/Bigsby vibrato, rounded pickguard with signature, 3-piece mahogany neck, neck joint at 16th fret, bound rosewood fingerboard, pearloid block inlay, Chesterfield peghead inlay, signature on truss rod cover, chrome-plated hardware, cherry red finish
Introduced: **1963**
Humbucking pickups: **late 1963**
Discontinued: **c. 1965**

Studio: 16 3/8" wide, thin semi-hollowbody, pointed horns, laminated maple body, rosewood bridge, harp tailpiece, 3-piece mahogany neck (some 1-piece), bound rosewood fingerboard, Chesterfield peghead inlay, chrome-plated hardware, sunburst finish
Introduced: **1968**
Humbucking pickups standard: **1970**
Discontinued: **1971**

Studio 301: 1 7/8" deep, 1 single-coil pickup (hum-bucking pickup optional), 2 knobs, dot inlay: **1968–70**

Studio 302: 1 7/8" deep, 2 pickups, 4 knobs, switch on upper bass bout, dot inlay: **1968–70**

Studio 303: 1 7/8" deep, 2 pickups, 4 knobs, switch on upper bass bout, metal bridge, Guild/Bigsby vibrato, dot inlay: **1968–70**

Studio 402: 2 7/8" deep, 2 single-coil pickup (hum-bucking pickup optional), 4 knobs, switch on upper bass bout, pearloid block inlay: **1969–70**

Custom 7/Deep Starfire: 16 3/8" wide, 3 3/8" deep, flame maple back and sides, laminated spruce top, 2 humbucking pickups, 4 knobs, master volume control on upper treble bout, selector switch on upper bass bout, ebony bridge, harp tailpiece, 24 3/4" scale, 5-piece maple/mahogany neck, bound ebony fingerboard, pearl block inlay with abalone V inserts, Artist Award style large peghead with large pearl-block peghead inlay, Grover Imperial tuners, gold-plated hardware
Available: **1969–70**

X-700: 17" wide, rounded cutaway, laminated maple back and sides, solid spruce top, 2 single-coil pickups with black covers, 4 knobs, selector switch on upper treble bout, 25 1/2" scale, bound rosewood fingerboard, pearl block inlay with abalone V insert, *G* peghead inlay, gold-plated hardware
Introduced: **1994**
24 3/4" scale, ebony fingerboard: **1998**
Still in production

COMMENTS

Gulid's electric archtops are a very diverse group of models, and most are regarded as fine utility instruments. The DE-500, George Barnes, M-75, early X-550 and the high-end 1950s models are sought by collectors.

SOLIDBODY KEY

The following models are not included in the key, due to a lack of available specifications: S-260, S-282, X-84V, X-97V, X108V.
Not all variations of every model are included in this key.

Single-cutaway

  Arched or contoured top

    Pearl block inlay with abalone V insert

      2 pickups = **X-2000 Nightbird**

      3 pickups = **BluesBird, 1984–87**

    Block inlay

      Mahogany body = **BluesBird M-75 Solid Body, 1970–77**

      Maple top = **BluesBird, 1997–current**

    Notched diamond inlay

      No *f*-holes = **Nightbird (II)**

      f-holes = **X040/X-3000 Nightingale**

    Dot inlay = **Nightbird I**

  Slab top

    1 visible pickup (and 1 in bridge) = **Crossroads**

    2 pickups = **T-250 or T-200 Roy Buchanan**

Symmetrical double-cutaway

  Arched top = **M-80CS**

  Slab (flat) top

    Dot inlay = **S-284 Starling/Aviator**

    Rising sun inlay = **S-285 Aviator**

Asymmetrical double-cutaway body with 2 points on lower bout

  2 pickups

    Block inlay = **Thunderbird/S-200**

    Dot inlay = **Polara/S-100, 1963–69**

  1 pickup = **Jet-Star/S-50, 1963–69**

Double-cutaway with pointed horns (similar to Gibson SG shape)

  Block inlay

    Bigsby vibrato = **S-100 Deluxe**

    No Bigsby = **S-100 Standard**

  Dot inlay

    2 pickups = **S-90**

    1 pickup = **S-50**

Double-cutaway with extended rounded bass horn

  Standard peghead

    Chesterfield peghead inlay

      2 pickups

        Rosewood fingerboard = **S-300**

        Ebony fingerboard = **S-400**

      3 pickups = **S-70**

    No Chesterfield peghead inlay

      1 pickup = **S-60, S-65D**

      2 pickups = **S-60D**

  Peghead narrows toward top

    5-way switch = **Brian May Standard**

    6 switches

      Pickups evenly spaced

        Signature on back of peghead **= BHM-1/Brian May Signature**

        No signature on back of peghead = **Brian May Pro**

      Middle pickup near bridge pickup = **Brian May Special**

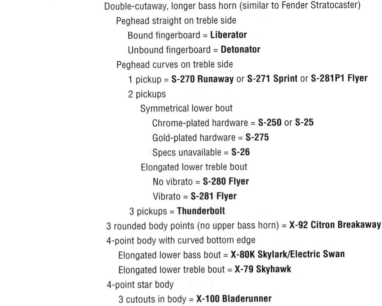

Double-cutaway, longer bass horn (similar to Fender Stratocaster)
Peghead straight on treble side
Bound fingerboard = **Liberator**
Unbound fingerboard = **Detonator**
Peghead curves on treble side
1 pickup = **S-270 Runaway** or **S-271 Sprint** or **S-281P1 Flyer**
2 pickups
Symmetrical lower bout
Chrome-plated hardware = **S-250** or **S-25**
Gold-plated hardware = **S-275**
Specs unavailable = **S-26**
Elongated lower treble bout
No vibrato = **S-280 Flyer**
Vibrato = **S-281 Flyer**
3 pickups = **Thunderbolt**
3 rounded body points (no upper bass horn) = **X-92 Citron Breakaway**
4-point body with curved bottom edge
Elongated lower bass bout = **X-80K Skylark/Electric Swan**
Elongated lower treble bout = **X-79 Skyhawk**
4-point star body
3 cutouts in body = **X-100 Bladerunner**
No cutouts
Star inlay = **X-88 Flying Star "Motley Crue"**
Dot inlay = **X-82 Nova/Starfighter**

SOLIDBODIES

Solidbody models with acoustic flat top styling and transducer bridge pickup, such as the Songbird, FS-46 and MKS-10, are listed in the Flat Tops section.

Aristocrat/BluesBird M-75 (Standard): 13 1/2" wide, rounded cutaway, no *f*-holes, thin hollowbody, see Electric Archtops

Thunderbird/S-200: asymmetrical double cutaway body with 2 points on lower bout, mahogany or alder body, "kickstand" built into back of body, 2 humbucking pickups, Hagstrom-made Adjusto-Matic bridge, vibrato, 4 knobs, 1 switch, 3 switches on oblong plate, mahogany neck 24 3/4" scale, bound rosewood fingerboard, block inlay, asymmetrical peghead, bird peghead inlay, chrome-plated hardware
Introduced: **1963**

Single-coil pickups: **c. 1966**
Standard peghead with Chesterfield inlay: **c. 1967**
Last made: **1968**

Polara/S-100: asymmetrical double cutaway body with 2 points on lower bout, mahogany or alder body, "kickstand" built into back of body, 2 single-coil pickups, Hagstrom-made AdjustoMatic bridge, vibrato, 4 knobs, 1 selector switch, mahogany neck 24 3/4" scale, unbound rosewood fingerboard, dot inlay, asymmetrical peghead, chrome-plated hardware
Introduced: **1963**
Discontinued, name continues on different style model (see following): **1970**

Jet-Star/S-50: asymmetrical double cutaway body with 2 points on lower bout, mahogany or alder body, 1 single-coil pickup, combination bridge/tailpiece with cover, 2 knobs, mahogany neck 24 3/4"

scale, unbound rosewood fingerboard, dot inlay, asymmetrical peghead, chrome-plated hardware
Introduced: **1963**
Vibrato optional: **1965**
Maple peghead veneer, 6-on-a-side tuner configuration: **1966**
Discontinued: **1970**

BluesBird M-75 solidbody: 13 3/4" wide,

rounded cutaway, arched top, mahogany body, 2 humbucking pickups, 4 knobs, selector switch on upper bass bout, AdjustoMatic bridge, stopbar tailpiece mounted at angle (hollowbody Bluesbird has harp or Bigsby tailpiece), mahogany neck, 24 3/4" scale, bound ebony fingerboard with gold-plated hardware (**M-75GS**) or bound rosewood fingerboard with chrome-plated hardware (**M-75CS**), block inlay, Chesterfield peghead inlay
Introduced: **1970**
Phase switch and master volume added: **c. 1972**
Discontinued: **1978**
Reintroduced, Brian Setzer design, poplar body, single cutaway, contoured top, 3 single-coil California pickups, master volume, master tone, 5-position slide switch, Kahler vibrato, no pickguard, maple neck, bound ebony fingerboard, 22 frets, pearl block inlay with abalone V insert, gold-plated hardware: **1984**
Options: flame maple body, 3 EMG single-coil pickups with "fat" control, 1 humbucker and 2 single-coil EMG pickups: **1986**
DiMarzio pickups, Guild/Mueller vibrato: **1987**
Discontinued: **1988**
Reintroduced with Nightbird styling (see following): **1997**

M-80CS/M-80: 13 3/4" wide, double cutaway,

arched maple top, mahogany body, 2 humbucking pickups, 4 knobs, master volume knob, phase switch, selector switch on upper bass bout, AdjustoMatic bridge, stopbar tailpiece mounted at angle, mahogany neck, 24 3/4" scale, bound rosewood fingerboard, block inlay, Chesterfield peghead inlay, chrome-plated hardware
Introduced as **M-80CS: 1975**
Discontinued: **1980**
Reintroduced as **M-80**: 2 humbucking pickups, coil tap or phase switch, bound top, unbound ebony fingerboard, dot inlay, candy apple red, red sunburst, black or sunburst finish: **1980**
Discontinued: **1984**

M-80CSD: Di Marzio PAF and SDHP pickups: **1978–79**

S-100 Standard: double cutaway body with

pointed horns (similar to Gibson SG shape), 2 humbucking pickups, 4 knobs, selector switch, AdjustoMatic bridge, vibrato, mahogany neck, 24 3/4" scale, bound rosewood fingerboard, block inlay, Chesterfield peghead inlay, chrome-plated hardware
Introduced: **c. 1970**
Stopbar tailpiece mounted at angle: **1971**
Phase switch: **1972**
Tailpiece moved closer to bridge: **c. 1975**
Discontinued: **1978**
Reintroduced: **1994**
Renamed **S-100 Polara: 1997**
Still in production

S-100 Deluxe: Bigsby vibrato: **1972–75**

S-100 Standard Carved: oak leaves and acorns carved into top of body: **1974–77**

S-100G: gold-plated hardware: **1994**

S-90: double cutaway, pointed horns (similar to Gib-

son SG shape), 2 humbucking pickups, 2 knobs, selector switch, combination bridge/tailpiece with cover, pickguard extends to bass side of body, mahogany neck, 24 3/4" scale, unbound rosewood fingerboard, dot inlay, chrome-plated hardware
Introduced: **1972**
AdjustoMatic bridge, stop tailpiece mounted at angle: **c. 1974**
Discontinued: **1977**

S-50: double cutaway, pointed horns (similar to Gib-

son SG shape), 1 single-coil pickup, 2 knobs, combination bridge/tailpiece with cover, pickguard on treble side of body only, mahogany neck, 24 3/4" scale, unbound rosewood fingerboard, dot inlay, chrome-plated hardware
Introduced: **1972**
Humbucking pickup, AdjustoMatic bridge, stop tailpiece mounted at angle: **c. 1974**
Discontinued: **1978**

S-300: 14 1/4" wide, double cutaway, extended

rounded bass horn, rounded bottom end, mahogany body, 2 humbucking pickups, 4 knobs, selector switch, phase switch, AdjustoMatic bridge, stop tailpiece mounted at angle, mahogany neck, 24 3/4"

scale, unbound ebony fingerboard, dot inlay, Chesterfield peghead inlay, chrome-plated hardware
Available: **1976–82**

S-300D: DiMarzio pickups (exposed cream coils): **1977–82**

S-300A: ash body: **1977–82**

S-300AD: ash body, DiMarzio pickups (exposed cream coils): **1977–82**

S-60: 14 1/4" wide, double cutaway, extended rounded bass horn, rounded bottom end, mahogany body, 1 humbucking pickup, 2 knobs, AdjustoMatic bridge, stop tailpiece mounted at angle, mahogany neck, 24 3/4" scale, unbound rosewood fingerboard, dot inlay, gold silkscreen logo, 3-on-a-plate tuners, chrome-plated hardware
Available: **1976–80**

S-60D: 2 DiMarzio pickups (exposed cream coils): **1977–81**

S-65D: 14 1/4" wide, double cutaway, extended rounded bass horn, mahogany body, 1 DiMarzio humbucking pickup, AdjustoMatic bridge, stop tailpiece mounted at angle, mahogany neck, 24 3/4" scale, unbound rosewood fingerboard, dot inlay, gold silkscreen logo, 3-on-a-plate tuners, chrome-plated hardware
Available: **1980–81**

S-70D: 14 1/4" wide, double cutaway, extended rounded bass horn, mahogany body, 3 DiMarzio single-pickups, AdjustoMatic bridge, stop tailpiece mounted at angle, mahogany neck, 24 3/4" scale, unbound rosewood fingerboard, dot inlay, Chesterfield peghead inlay, 3-on-a-plate tuners, chrome-plated hardware
Available: **1979–81**

S-70AD: ash body, ebony fingerboard, Chesterfield peghead inlay: **1979–81**

S-400: 14 1/4" wide, double cutaway, extended rounded bass horn, laminated mahogany body, 2 humbucking pickups, onboard EQ controls, 4 knobs, selector switch, phase switch, AdjustoMatic bridge, stop tailpiece mounted at angle, mahogany neck, 24 3/4" scale, unbound ebony

fingerboard, dot inlay, Chesterfield peghead inlay, chrome-plated hardware
Available: **early 1980–81**

S-400A: ash body: **late 1980–81**

Nightbird (II)/X-2000/Bluesbird: cutaway, carved spruce top, solid mahogany back routed for tone chambers, U-shaped chamber around outer edge of body, solid beneath tailpiece, routed under bridge, no soundholes, 2 Armstrong or EMG humbucking pickups (a few early with Seymour Duncan pickups), master volume, master tone, AdjustoMatic bridge, stopbar tailpiece multiple-bound top and pickguard, bound ebony fingerboard, notched-diamond inlay, multiple-bound snakehead peghead, G-shield peghead logo, black hardware
Introduced: **1985**
Optional maple top, coil tap, phaser switch, gold-plated hardware: **1986**
Renamed **Nightbird II: 1987**
Some with Guild HB-1 humbucking pickups: **1988**
Renamed **X-2000 Nightbird:** maple top, multiple binding, pearl block inlay with abalone V insert, woodgrain finish: **1992**
Discontinued: **1996**
Reintroduced as **Bluesbird,** arched maple top, AAA figured top optional, solid mahogany body routed for tone chambers, 2 humbucking pickups, 4 knobs, 1 switch on upper bass bout, tune-o-matic bridge, stopbar tailpiece, bound top, bound rosewood fingerboard, block inlay, Chesterfield peghead inlay, tobacco sunburst, cherry sunburst, gold black, crimson transparent or amber finish: **1997**
Still in production

Nightbird I: carved spruce top, 2 DiMarzio pickups, coil tap, phaser switch, master volume, master tone, multiple-bound top, unbound rosewood fingerboard, dot inlay, unbound snakehead peghead, Chesterfield peghead logo, chrome-plated hardware
Available: **1987–88**

X040/X-3000 Nightingale: same as Nightbird but with *f*-holes, multiple binding, ebony fingerboard, notched-diamond inlay, snakehead peghead, gold-plated hardware, woodgrain finish
Introduced as **X040 Nightingale: 1987**

Discontinued: **1989**

Reintroduced as **X-3000 Nightingale:** Seymour Duncan or EMG humbucking pickups: **1992**

Discontinued: **1996**

BHM-1/Brian May Signature: double cutaway, short treble horn, elongated bass horn, circular lower bout, mahogany body, Kahler vibrato, 3 custom single-coil DiMarzio pickups, power boost, 2 knobs, 6 switches, bound top and back, ebony fingerboard, dot inlay, blackface peghead narrows toward top, signature on back of peghead, red or green woodgrain finish

Introduced as **BHM-1 Brian May: 1984**

Maple top optional: **1986**

Discontinued: **1987**

Reintroduced as **Brian May Signature**, more authentic reproduction of May's personal guitar than earlier version, Seymour Duncan pickups, custom vibrato, red or green woodgrain finish, limited edition of 1,000: **1993**

Brian May Pro: same as Brian May Signature but with mahogany peghead veneer, no signature on back of peghead, black, white, red or green woodgrain finish: **1994–95**

Brian May Special: 3 single-coil pickups with middle pickup next to bridge pickup, 2 knobs, 6 switches: **early 1994–95**

Brian May Standard: 1 humbucking and 1 single-coil Seymour Duncan pickups, 2 humbucking or 3 single-coil pickups optional, no pickguard, 2 knobs, 5-way slide switch, black, vintage yellow, white, woodgrain red or woodgrain green finish:

Introduced: **1994**

3 single-coil pickups standard: **1995**

Discontinued: **1996**

S-275: double cutaway (similar to Fender Stratocaster shape), bound curly maple top, 2 humbucking pickups, 3 knobs, phase switch or coil tap, ebony fingerboard, 24 frets, dot inlay, Chesterfield peghead logo, gold-plated hardware, red sunburst or natural top finish

Available: **1982–83**

S-250: double cutaway (similar to Fender Stratocaster shape), 2 humbucking pickups, phase switch or coil tap, rosewood fingerboard, bound top, 24 frets, dot inlay, chrome-plated hadware, sunburst, black, candy apple red or metallic blue finish finish

Available: **1981–83**

S-25: double cutaway (similar to Fender Stratocaster shape), mahogany body, 2 humbucking pickups, volume and tone control, phase switch or coil tap optional, rosewood fingerboard, sunburst, black or metallic blue finish finish

Available: **1981–83**

S-26: specs unavailable: **1983**

S-260: specs unavailable: **1983**

S-282: specs unavailable: **1984**

X-79 Skyhawk: 4-point body with curved bottom end, elongated upper bass and lower treble bouts, 2 humbucking pickups, coil tap or phase switch, Kahler vibrato optional, unbound ebony fingerboard, 4-point star peghead shape, white, sunburst, black, candy apple red, metallic blue, black sparkle or purple finish

Introduced: **1981**

Custom color and graphic finishes available, including black-and-yellow striped "Twisted Sister": **1984**

Discontinued: **1986**

X-79-3: 3 single-coil pickups: **1981–85**

X-80(K) Skylark/Swan: 4-point body with rounded bottom end, elongated lower bass and upper treble bouts, 2 humbucking pickups, Kahler vibrato optional, black, candy apple red, pearl white or sunburst finish, custom and graphic finishes available

Introduced as **X-80 Skylark: 1982**

Renamed **Swan: Feb. 1985**

Renamed **Electric Swan: Oct. 1985**

Discontinued: **1986**

X-82 Nova/Starfighter: 4-point star body, bound top, 2 humbucking pickups, 3 single-coil pickups optional, 3 knobs, switch on upper treble bout, AdjustoMatic bridge, pickguard covers upper treble bout, unbound rosewood fingerboard, dot inlay, peghead narrows toward top, sunburst, black, candy apple red, metallic blue, black sparkle or purple finish

Introduced as **X-82 Nova: 1981**
Renamed **Starfighter:** Kahler vibrato optional, 6-on-a-side tuners, black, candy apple red, pearl white or sunburst finish, custom and graphic finishes available: **1984**
Discontinued: **1986**

X-84V: bolt-on neck, Guild or Kahler tremolo, no other specs available
Available: **1983**

X-97V: bolt-on neck, Guild or Kahler tremolo, no other specs available
Available: **1983**

X-108V: bolt-on neck, Guild or Kahler tremolo, no other specs available
Available: **1983**

X-88 Flying Star "Motley Crue": 4-point star body, Kahler vibrato optional, 1 humbucking pickup, unbound ebony fingerboard, arrowhead peghead comes to point, star inlay, black, candy apple red, pearl white or sunburst finish, custom and graphic finishes available
Introduced: **1984**
6-on-a-side tuners: **1985**
Discontinued: **1986**

X-88D: 2 humbucking pickups: **1984–87**

X-92 Citron Breakaway: body with 3 rounded points (no upper bass bout, somewhat similar to Gibson Moderne), 3 single-coil pickups, unbound rosewood fingerboard, dot inlay, peghead narrows toward top
Available: **1984**

T-200 Roy Buchanan: single cutaway (Fender Telecaster shape), 2 EMG single-coil pickups, brass bridge, bolt-on maple neck, rosewood fingerboard, dot inlay, peghead comes to a point
Available: **1986**

T-250: poplar body, single cutaway (Fender Telecaster shape), 2 EMG or 2 DiMarzio single-coil pickups, master volume, master tone, 3-way switch, bolt-on neck, 22 frets, rosewood fingerboard, 6-on-a-side tuners, chrome-plated hardware (gold-plated optional)

Introduced: **1986**
Optional offset peghead (original model style) or new style peghead: **1987**
Discontinued: **1988**

Detonator: poplar body, double cutaway with bass-side horn longer than treble-side (similar to Fender Stratocaster), 1 humbucking and 2 single-coil active DiMarzio pickups, EMG pickups optional, 5-position slide switch, Guild/Mueller tremolo, bolt-on maple neck, unbound rosewood fingerboard, dot inlay, 6-on-a-side tuners, black hardware
Available: **1987–88**

Detonator II: EMG pickups, Floyd Rose vibrato: **1988**

Liberator: poplar body, double cutaway with bass-side horn longer than treble-side, 1 humbucking and 2 single-coil DiMarzio pickups, 5-position slide switch, Guild/Mueller vibrato, set mahogany neck, bound ebony fingerboard, 24 frets, dot inlay, 6-on-a-side tuners, black chrome hardware
Available: **1987–88**

Liberator II: active EMG pickups, Floyd Rose vibrato, rising sun inlay: **1988**

Liberator Elite: flamed maple top, active Bartolini pickups, bound ebony fingerboard, rising sun inlay, gold-plated hardware: **1988**

S-280 Flyer: poplar body, double cutaway with bass-side horn longer than treble-side, 2 California humbucking pickups, 3 single-coil pickups optional, bolt-on maple or mahogany neck, 25 5/8" scale, unbound maple or rosewood fingerboard, dot inlay, 6-on-a-side tuners
Available: **1983–84**

S-281 Flyer: locking vibrato
Introduced: **1983**
Options: EMG humbuckers, "fat" control: **1987**
Discontinued: **1988**

S-281P1: 1 California humbucking pickup, 1 volume control, rosewood fingerboard
Introduced: **1985**
Renamed **S-281-1: 1987**
Discontinued: **1988**

S-284 Starling/Aviator: poplar body, symmetrical double cutaway, 1 humbucking and 2 single-coil

California pickups, master tone, master volume, jack into top, Kahler vibrato, rosewood fingerboard, dot inlay, 6-on-a-side tuners
Introduced as **S-284 Starling: 1984**
Renamed **S-284 Aviator: 1984**
Poplar or maple body, no pickguard, jack into side, ebony fingerboard: **1986**
DiMarzio pickups: **1987**
Options: flamed maple body, EMG pickups, "fat" control: **1987**
Discontinued: **1988**

S-285 Aviator: poplar body, 1 humbucking and 2 single-coil DiMarzio pickups, master tone, master volume, Kahler vibrato, bound ebony fingerboard, rising sun inlay, bound peghead
Options: flamed maple body, EMG pickups, "fat" control
Available: **1986–88**

S-270 Runaway: double cutaway (Fender Stratocaster shape), 1 EMG humbucking pickup, Kahler vibrato, bolt-on neck, unbound rosewood fingerboard, dot inlay, 6-on-a-side tuners
Available: **1985**

S-271 Sprint: 1 EMG pickup, Kahler vibrato (only specs available)
Available: **1986**

X-100 Bladerunner: poplar body, star body shape with 3 cutouts, 1 EMG humbucking pickup,

coil tap, "fat" control, Kahler vibrato, unbound ebony fingerboard, "Mercedes star" inlay
Available: **1985–87**

Thunderbolt: poplar body, asymmetrical double cutaway (similar to Fender Stratocaster shape), 1 humbucking and 2 single-coil DiMarzio pickups, coil tap, rosewood fingerboard, dot inlay, black chrome hardware
Available: **1987**

Crossroads CR-1 Single E: single cutaway, semi-hollow mahogany body, flat maple top, no soundholes, somewhat similar to Fender Telecaster, 1 humbucking pickup in neck position and 1 piezo pickup, 3 knobs, selector switch on upper bass bout, bound top, 25 1/2" scale, rosewood fingerboard, dot inlay, bound peghead, G-shield logo, chrome-plated hardware, black, woodgrain red, white, amber or natural finish
Available: **1994–96**

Crossroads CR-1 Double E: doubleneck, see Flat Tops

COMMENTS

Most Guild solidbodies are regarded as good utility instruments. The Nightbird and Nightingale are highly regarded. The later version of the Brian May models is collectible.

BASSES KEY

Flat top acoustic
  Non-cutaway = **B-50/B-30**
  Cutaway
    Hollowbody = **B-4E**
    Solidbody = **FS-46CE (FB-46)**
Semi-hollowbody archtop
  Single-cutaway (no soundholes)
    1 pickup = **M-85**
    2 pickups = **M-85 II**
  Double-cutaway
    1 pickup = **Starfire Bass**
    2 pickups = **Starfire Bass II**

Solidbody
  Single cutaway
    1 pickup = **M-85 I**
    2 pickups = **M-85 II**
  Symmetrical double cutaway, rounded horns
    1 pickup = **MB-801**
    2 pickups = **MB-802**
  Extended pointed horns, elongated (rounded) lower treble bout
    Chrome-plated hardware
      Dot inlay
        1 pickup = **SB-601 Pilot**
        2 pickups
          5 strings = **SB-605 Pilot**
          4 strings
            DiMarzio pickups = **SB-600 Pilot**
            EMG pickups
              Standard peghead = **SB-602 Pilot**
              "Offset" peghead = **SB-604 Pilot**
      Deluxe inlay
        4 strings = **SB-902 Advanced Pilot**
        5 strings = **SB-905 Advanced Pilot**
    Gold-plated hardware
      4 strings = **Pro4 Pilot**
      5 strings = **Pro5 Pilot**
  Extended rounded bass horn
    No onboard preamp
      1 pickup = **B-301**
      2 pickups = **B-302**
    Onboard preamp
      1 pickup = **B-401**
      2 pickups = **B-402**
  Rounded horns (similar to Fender Stratocaster guitar)
    1 pickup = **SB-201**
    1 split coil and 1 rectangular pickup = **SB-202**
    2 rectangular pickups = **SB-502E**
    3 pickups = **SB-203**
  Short pointed horns (body style similar to Gibson SG)
    1 pickup
      30 1/2" scale = **JS Bass I**
      34" scale = **JS I LS**
    2 pickups
      30 1/2" scale = **JS Bass II**
      34" scale = **JS II LS**
  4-point body, bottom side curves inward = **Jet-Star Bass**
  4-point star body
    Cutouts in body = **Blade Runner**
    No cutouts in body = **SB-608 Flying Star**
  4-point body with rounded bottom
    1 pickup = **X-701**
    2 pickups = **X-702**

BASSES

<u>SECTION ORGANIZATION</u>

Archtop Semi-Hollow Models
Solidbody Models
Flat Top Models

ARCHTOP SEMI-HOLLOW MODELS

Starfire Bass: 16 3/8" wide, thin semi-hollowbody 1 7/8" deep, double cutaway, laminated maple or laminated mahogany body, 1 Hagstrom-made single-coil pickup near bridge, 2 knobs, 2 finger supports, 1-piece mahogany neck, 30 1/2" scale, unbound rosewood fingerboard, 21 frets, dot inlay, Chesterfield peghead inlay, chrome-plated hardware, sunburst or cherry finish
Introduced: **1965**
Humbucking pickup: **1970**
Pickup near fingerboard: **by 1972**
Discontinued: **1975**

Starfire Bass II: 2 Hagstrom-made single-coil pickups, 4 knobs, selector switch and master volume knob on upper treble bout, pushbutton for bass boost, adjustable saddles
Introduced: **1967**
Humbucking pickups, tone switch replaces pushbutton: **1970**
Discontinued: **1978**
Reintroduced, 2 humbucking pickups, 30 1/2" scale, 20 frets, black, blonde, antique sunburst or transparent red finish: **1997**
Still in production

M-85: 13 1/2" wide, semi-hollowbody 2 3/4 deep, rounded cutaway, laminated maple back and sides, laminated spruce or maple top, 1 Hagstrom-made single-coil pickup, 2 knobs, adjustable saddles, 1-piece mahogany neck, 30 1/2" scale, unbound rosewood fingerboard, dot inlay, Chesterfield peghead inlay, chrome-plated hardware
Available: **1967–72**
Model name continues on solidbody (see following)

M-85 II: 2 Hagstrom-made pickups, 4 knobs, tone switch, master volume knob on cutaway bout, selector switch on upper bass bout: **1967–72**
Model name continues on solidbody (see following)

SOLIDBODY MODELS

Jet-Star Bass: asymmetrical body with short pointed horns on upper and lower bouts (similar to Thunderbird and Polara guitars), 1 Hagstrom-made humbucking pickup, 2 knobs, adjustable saddles, 2 finger rests, 3-piece mahogany/maple neck, 30 1/2" scale, unbound rosewood fingerboard, dot inlay, asymmetrical peghead, Chesterfield peghead inlay, chrome-plated hardware
Introduced: **1964**
4-on-a-side tuner arrangement, single-coil pickup: **1966**
Discontinued: **1970**

JS Bass I: double cutaway with pointed horns (similar to Gibson SG guitar style), humbucking pickup with metal cover, 2 knobs, 3-piece mahogany neck, 30 1/2" scale, rosewood fingerboard, dot inlay, Chesterfield peghead inlay, peaked logo
Introduced: **1970**
Renamed **JS Bass 1: late 1973**
"Carved" oak leaf design available: **1974–75**
Discontinued: **1976**

JS Bass II: 2 pickups, 4 knobs, mini-switch, selector switch
Introduced: **1970**
Renamed **JS Bass 2: late 1973**
"Carved" oak leaf design available: **1974–75**
Discontinued: **1977**

JS I LS: JS I with 34" scale: **1972–75**

JS II LS: JS II with 34" scale: **1972–77**

M-85 I: 13 3/4" wide, mahogany body, arched top, single cutaway, humbucking pickup with metal cover, bound top, 30 1/2" scale, rosewood fingerboard, dot inlay, Chesterfield peghead inlay, chrome-plated hardware
Available: **c. 1972–73**

M-85 II: 2 pickups
Introduced: **c. 1972**
Ebony fingerboard: **c. 1975**
Discontinued: **1976**

B Series: 14 1/4" wide, double cutaway body with extended rounded bass horn, laminated mahogany body, roller saddles, 3-piece mahogany neck, 34" scale, unbound ebony fingerboard, dot inlay, Chesterfield peghead inlay, chrome-plated hardware

B-301: 1 pickup: **1976–81**

B-301A: 1 pickup, ash body, maple neck: **1977–81**

B-302: 2 pickups: **1976–81**

B-302A: 2 pickups, ash body, maple neck: **1977–81**

B-401: 1 pickup, onboard preamp and EQ controls: **early 1980–81**

B-401A: ash body, maple neck: **late 1980–83**

B-402: 2 pickups and phase switch: **early 1980–82**

B-402A: ash body, maple neck: **late 1980–82**

SB-201: 13 7/8" wide, double cutaway, rounded horns, 1 split-coil pickup, 2 knobs, 34" scale, unbound rosewood fingerboard, dot inlay, Chesterfield peghead inlay, sunburst, purple, white, black, candy apple red, black sparkle or metallic blue finish Available: **1982–83**

SB-202: 1 split-coil and 1 single-coil pickup, 3 knobs, phase switch: **1982–83**

SB-203: 1 split-coil and 2 single-coil pickups, master volume, master tone, 3 mini-switches: **1983**

SB-502E: 13 7/8" wide, double cutaway, rounded horns, 2 rectangular pickups with metal mounting rings, active electronics, 2 knobs, 2 mini-knobs, 3 mini-switches (including phase switch, preamp on/off switch) Available: **1984–85**

MB-801: symmetrical double cutaway, rounded horns, mahogany back, carved maple top, 1 pickup, 34" scale, unbound ebony fingerboard, dot inlay, Chesterfield peghead inlay, chrome-plated hardware Available: **1981–82**

MB-802: 2 pickups: **1981–82**

Pilot/SB-600 Series: double cutaway with elongated pointed horns and elongated lower treble bout, P-J pickup configuration (1 split-coil Fender Precision-style, 1 single-coil Fender Jazz-style) maple neck, 34" scale, maple fingerboard

Pilot Pegheads

"Spade," concave curve on treble side, rounded tip, script logo with lower-case letter *g*, tail of *g* underlines *uild*: **1983–87**

Charvel-type, straight sides, treble side goes directly to point, severe angle to treble side, standard Guild peaked logo: **1985**

Charvel-type, straight sides, bass side goes directly to point, logo underline goes through letter *G:* **1984–87**

Bass side goes directly to point, treble side makes curve at point: **1987–89**

SB-601: poplar body, 1 pickup, sunburst, purple, white, black, candy apple red, black sparkle or metallic blue finish, available as SB-601 (no Pilot designation): **1983**

SB-602: 2 pickups
Introduced as SB-602: **1983**
Renamed **Pilot:** EMG pickups, rosewood fingerboard, dot inlay: **1984**
4-on-a-side tuners, options include maple body, fretless fingerboard and D-tuner: **1987**
Discontinued, replaced by Pro4 Pilot (see following): **1993**

SB-604 Pilot: same as SB-602 but with "offset" peghead: **1986–88**

SB-605 Pilot: 5-string, hipshot low D-tuner, 4-and-1 tuner configuration: **1986–93** (replaced by Pro5 Pilot, see following)

SB-600 Pilot: 2 DiMarzio pickups, optional maple body, rosewood fingerboard, optional fretless fingerboard, dot inlay, optional D-tuner: **1987–89**

SB-902 Advanced Pilot: maple body, active Bartolini pickups, maple neck, ebony fingerboard, deluxe inlay, amberburst, cherry sunburst or transparent charcoal finish: **1988–89**

SB-905 Advanced Pilot: 5-string, rosewood fingerboard: **1988–89**

Pro4 Pilot: solid maple body, beveled cutaways, 2 EMG active pickups (1 split-coil and 1 rectangu-

GUILD

lar), 4 knobs, gold-plated hardware, black, white, amber or woodgrain finish: **1993–95**

Pro5 Pilot: 5-string, 2 rectangular pickups: **1993–95**

X-701: 4-point body with elongated upper bass and lower treble bouts, curved bottom end, 1 pickup, 2 knobs, rosewood fingerboard, dot inlay, 4-point peghead shape, sunburst, purple, white, black, candy apple red, black sparkle or metallic blue finish
Available: **1982–84**

X-702: 2 pickups, 3 knobs: **1982–84**

SB-608 Flying Star: 4-point star body, 2 California pickups, EMG pickups optional, Kahler vibrato optional
Available: **1984–85**

Blade Runner: 4-point star body with 3 cutouts
Available: **1985–86**

Ashbory Bass: small 1-piece neck and body, 30" total length, 3 knobs, 1 switch, fretless neck, silicone strings, 18" scale, logo and model name on body, white, black, blue or red finish
Available: **1986–88**

FLAT TOP MODELS

B-50/B-30: 18" wide, arched laminated mahogany back, solid mahogany sides, spruce top, rosewood bridge, split saddle, 30 1/2" scale, unbound rosewood fingerboard, Chesterfield peghead inlay, chrome-plated tuners, natural (**NT**) or sunburst (**SB**)
Introduced as **B-50: 1975**
Renamed **B-30: 1987**
Discontinued: **1997**

B-50E/B-30E: transducer pickup, fretless fingerboard optional
Introduced as **B-50E: 1983**
Renamed **B-30E:** arched laminated mahogany back, solid mahogany sides: **1987**
Still in production

FS-46CE Bass (FB-46): bass version of FS-46CE guitar, 16" wide, single cutaway thinbody, round soundhole, spruce top, mahogany back, transducer pickup, 34" scale, mahogany or maple neck, rosewood or maple fingerboard, dot inlay, natural, sunburst or black
Only appearance: **late 1983**

B-4E: single cutaway, 16" wide, oval hole, arched laminated mahogany back, solid mahogany sides, multiple-bound top and back, 30 1/2" scale, unbound rosewood fingerboard, dot inlay, Chesterfield peghead inlay, chrome-plated tuners, satin (non-gloss) finish
Introduced: **1993**
Fretless fingerboard optional: **1997**
Still in production

BH4E HG: vintage white or black high gloss finish: **1994**

B-4 HG: no pickup, black gloss finish
Introduced: **1995**
Fretless fingerboard optional: **1997**
Still in production

B-4E MH: mahogany top: **1995–96**

COMMENTS

Guild basses are regarded as good utility instruments. The B-50 was one of the first commercially successful flat top acoustic basses and is highly regarded.

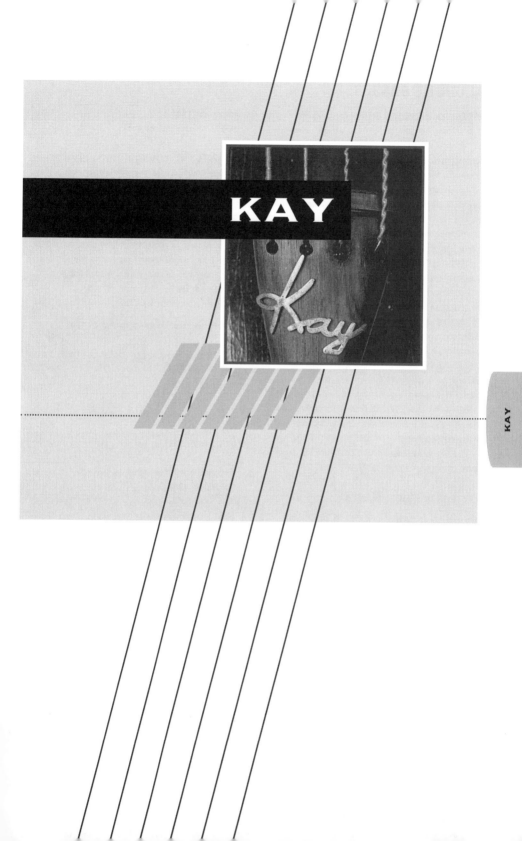

KAY

ACOUSTIC BASSES

The Kay company of Chicago began as the Groeschel Company in 1890, making bowlback mandolins. In 1918 the name was changed to the Stromberg-Voisinet company, which made the May-flower line of guitars and banjos. Henry K. Kuhrmeyer bought the company in 1928 and changed the name to Kay Musical Instruments in 1931. Making instruments under its own brand and for mail-order house brands, Kay claimed a production of almost 100,000 instruments per year by the mid 1930s.

Basses appeared in the Kay line in 1937 and were also marketed through others under the K. Meyer brand. According to company literature, Kay captured 20 percent of the U.S. bass market in its first year.

Kay was sold in 1955 to a group headed by Sydney Katz, formerly of Harmony. Many Silvertone brand guitars, sold through Sears, were made by Kay during this period. The Seeburg company, a jukebox manufacturer, bought Kay in 1965. In 1967, the company was sold to Robert Engelhardt, who also owned Valco (see National/Valco). Shortly thereafter, Kay went out of business and the name was acquired by an import instrument distributor.

All Kay basses have a laminated spruce top, laminated maple back and sides.

LETTERS IN MODEL NAMES

M = Maestro, originally top of the line, later midline and finally a student model
S = (chronologically) Slap, Swingmaster or Supreme
C = Concert, always a grade below Maestro

SIZES

Regulation or 3/4-size: 72" overall length, body depth 6 3/4"–7 3/4", 42" scale
Junior or 1/4-size (also referred to as 1/2-size): 62 1/4" overall length, 35 1/4" scale
Half-size: no specs available
Slap or Swingmaster: regulation size except for 2" thinner body depth, described as "quick in response to slapping, easy to twirl"

PRE-WORLD WAR II MODELS

Orchestra: ebonized fingerboard and tailpiece, shaded finish

Introduced: **1937**
Blond finish optional: **by 1941**

Concert: purfling on top and back, 2-piece back, rosewood fingerboard and tailpiece, brass tuner plates, shaded finish
Introduced: **1937**
Blond finish optional: **by 1941**

M-1: Maestro model, 2 black lines inlaid around top and back edges, ebony fingerboard and tailpiece, engraved brass tuner plates, shaded finish
Introduced: **1937**
Blond finish optional: **by 1939**

M-4: M-1 with blond finish, named: **by 1941**

S-1: Slap or swingmasters model, thin body, Orchestra model specs
Introduced: **1939**

S-3: Slap or swingmasters model, thin body, Concert model specs
Introduced: **1939**

S-4: thin body, Maestro model specs
Introduced: **1939**

S-5: Swingmaster dance band model, ebony fingerboard, purfling on top and back, bound *f*-holes, blond finish, full-depth body optional
Introduced: **1940**

S-6: same as S-5 with shaded finish, full-depth body optional

POST-WORLD WAR II MODELS

S-51: Chubby Jackson model, 5 strings, bound top and back, bound *f*-holes, ebony fingerboard and tailpiece, side position dots, nickel-plated tuning heads, shaded finish: **late 1945–late 1960s**

S-51B: blond finish: **late 1945–late 1960s**

M-1: Maestro "School Model," rosewood fingerboard and tailpiece with ebonized finish, black painted "binding" 5/8" wide, shaded finish

Introduced: **by 1952**
Discontinued: **late 1960s**

M-1B: blond finish

H-10: 1/4-size M-1 (64" overall length), shaded finish
Introduced: **by 1952**
Discontinued, replaced by M-2 or M-3: **by 1958**

M-2: 1/2 size M-1 (dimensions unavailable), rosewood fingerboard and tailpiece, violin brown finish
Introduced: **by 1958**
Discontinued: **1960**

M-3: 1/4 size M-1 (dimensions unavailable), single black line inlaid around top and back edges
Introduced: **by 1958**
Discontinued: **1960**

M-5: 5 strings, rosewood fingerboard and tailpiece, side position dots, brass tuning heads, shaded finish
Introduced: **by 1958**
Discontinued: **1960**

M-5B: blond finish

M-7 Selmer Kay: black-white-black purfling on top and back, triple-bound *f*-holes, ebony fingerboard and tailpiece, gold-plated tuner plates engraved with *Selmer-Kay*, golden brown finish
Available: **early 1950s**

C-1: Concert, rosewood fingerboard and tailpiece with natural finish, shaded finish
Introduced: **by 1952**
Discontinued: **1960**

S-8: Supreme, purfling of 2 thin black lines around top and back, 2 thin black lines around *f*-holes, ebony fingerboard and tailpiece, nickel-plated hardware, shaded finish
Introduced: **by 1952**
Renamed **S-1: 1958**
Discontinued: **late 1960s**

S-9: Swingmaster, thin body, inlaid purfling, nickel gears, ebony fingerboard and tailpiece, blond finish
Introduced: **by 1952**
Discontinued: **1960**

S-10: Swingmaster Mighty Midget, 1/3 smaller than S-9
Introduced: **by 1952**
Discontinued: **1960**

S-2: 1/2 size S-1 (dimensions unavailable), ebony fingerboard and tailpiece, golden brown finish
Introduced: **by 1958**
Discontinued: **1960**

S-3: 1/4 size S-1 (dimensions unavailable)
Introduced: **by 1958**
Discontinued: **late 1960s**

TV1: burnished gold finish
Introduced: **by 1955**
Discontinued: **late 1960s**

TV2: 2-tone copper and white finish
Introduced: **by 1955**
Discontinued: **late 1960**

COMMENTS

Kay acoustic basses were the most popular brand of laminated construction basses. They are highly regarded by players of popular music styles.

Prairie State
Guitars

LARSON

GENERAL INFORMATION

Carl and August Larson were born in Sweden and immigrated to Chicago in the 1880s. By the late 1890s they were building instruments for Robert Maurer, a music teacher and instrument retailer. Maurer began production of Champion and other brand instruments between 1882 and 1894. In 1897 he put the Maurer brand on all instruments.

In 1900, Maurer sold his shop to August Larson and others, with Carl probably kept on as an employee. Carl Larson later replaced all the other partners. They had essentially a two-man operation, with all other employees working only part-time. By circa 1904 the Larsons were making guitars for various distributors, including Wack, Stahl and Dyer. Also around 1904 the Larsons advertised a catalog of Maurer brand instruments. They added the Prairie State brand to their line, probably in the late 1920s. In the mid 1930s they discontinued the Maurer brand, replacing it with Euphonon.

Many Larson-made instruments were custom-ordered. Some were made for performers on the "WLS Barn Dance" radio program in Chicago. Instruments with a Larson brand are extremely rare.

August Larson died in 1944. Carl Larson retired in 1940 and died in 1946.

Total production of instruments made by Carl and August Larson is estimated at 11,000 to 12,000.

GENERAL CHARACTERISTICS

Braces: From the beginning Larson Brothers flat tops were designed for steel strings, pre-dating Martin and Gibson steel-string flat tops by more than 20 years. To support the top, the Larsons used an expanded version of Martin's X-pattern, often with laminated braces—spruce with a rosewood or ebony center laminate. Instruments made for Wack and Dyer typically have solid maple braces. Some Stahls have laminated braces; some have solid maple braces. The laminated bracing design was patented by August Larson in 1904.

Top and back: All tops and backs are "built under tension" and slightly arched.

Neck: Guitars have 12 frets clear of body until the early 1930s, 14 frets clear thereafter. Ebony fingerboard, bridge and peghead veneer are standard on all models.

Brand: Virtually no Larson Brothers model has a brand logo on the peghead. (At least one example exists with *Advance Music* on the peghead.) Maurer, Euphonon, and Prairie State logos are stamped on the center backstrip. About half of the Stahl brand instruments have a logo stamped on the inside backstrip; the others have a paper label. Except for the stamped Stahls, distributor brand instruments typically have a paper label on the inside back.

The Larsons had more variability in their model designs than any other major maker. They had a larger percentage of instruments that were unlabeled or bore misleading labels than any other highly respected maker.

MAURER

General features: 18 frets, 12 frets clear of body until early 1930s, 14 frets clear from the early 1930s onward.

Student models 487, 489, 491 and 493: lower quality woods and tuners, oak back and sides on lower models, mahogany on higher models, ladder bracing

Intermediate models (in order of ornamentation) 494, 525, 498, 495, 541, 551, 562, 562 1/2 and 564: X-braced top, mahogany back and sides on lower models, rosewood on higher, laminated necks and braces on higher models

Top of the line models 585, 587, 590 and 593: many with Brazilian rosewood back and sides, some with walnut

The Maurer brand was discontinued in the mid 1930s when the Euphonon brand was introduced.

EUPHONON

The Euphonon brand replaced the Maurer brand in the mid 1930s.

General features: 20 frets, 14 frets clear of body, solid peghead

Student models: 13 3/4" wide, mahogany back and sides, ladder bracing, single-bound body and fingerboard, ebony bridge and fingerboard, backstripe

Intermediate models: 15" and 16" wide, mahogany or rosewood, X-bracing usually laminated, some with black and white binding, back stripe

Top of the line models: 15" or larger, some with dreadnought shape, rosewood or maple back and sides, pearl soundhole inlay, recessed pickguard, some with pearl around top

PRAIRIE STATE

The Prairie State brand was used on guitars only.
The first Prairie State models were probably made around 1927, the year August Larson filed a patent application for an adjustable stabilizing tube.
All Prairie State brand instruments have the steel support rod; some instruments with the Maurer or Euphonon brand have the support tube through the body.

The only *f*-hole models the Larson Brothers made were Prairie State models. The tops are arched—not carved—with about the same degree of arch as typical Larson roundhole models. Prairie State *f*-hole models vary in width from 15" to 21" and in ornamentation. The Larsons made at least one cutaway *f*-hole model.

Prairie State models are similar to Maurer and Euphonon models, but with the following added specs: steel stabilizing tube running lengthwise through the body, adjustable neck rod either at the back of neck or inside the body at the neck, laminated neck.

12-fret body sizes: 13 1/2" concert, 14" grand concert and 15" auditorium

14-fret body sizes: 16" and 17" most common, some examples up to 21" wide

STAHL

The Wm. C. Stahl company of Milwaukee was marketing Stahl brand guitars made by the Larson Brothers by around 1904. Stahl labels typically read *Stahl— Maker, Milwaukee*, although there is no evidence that Stahl actually made any instruments. Virtually all Stahls with the logo stamped on the inside backstrip were made by the Larson Brothers. Some models with paper labels were made by the Larson Brothers; some were made by Regal or others.

Some Larson-made Stahl models have laminated braces; some have solid maple braces.

Stahl mandolin orchestra models, made by the Larsons, have maple back and sides with rosewood grain stain finish.

DYER

W.J. Dyer & Bro. of St. Paul marketed Dyer brand instruments made by the Larson Brothers beginning some time before 1912. Dyer labels typically identify Dyer as the maker, although there is no evidence Dyer actually made any instruments. Dyer also marketed Stetson brand guitars and guitars and mandolins made by Lyon and Healy, Harmony and others.

Most Larson-made Dyer guitars and virtually all mandolins have mahogany back and sides.

A special line of flat top harp instruments—mandolin, mandola, mandocello and guitar—was made for Dyer. Initially Dyer marketed harp instruments designed and built by Chris Knutsen (but not under the Dyer brand). By 1912 the Larsons had redesigned Knutsen's instruments and were producing them for Dyer under the Dyer brand. Knutsen's signature appears on the labels of his instruments and on those made by the Larsons prior to 1912, when Knutsen's patent expired. Knutsen's instruments typically have dot inlay on the fingerboard. Most Larson-made instruments have small ornamental fingerboard inlays, including snowflakes and diamonds, or more ornate tree-of-life patterns. Larson-made Dyer harp instruments have solid maple braces.

MAURER AND PRAIRIE STATE

The Larson Brothers published very few catalogs. The following models appear in a catalog of Maurer and Prairie State models published in the early 1930s.

All models have ebony bridge, ebony fingerboard and mahogany neck.

All guitar models have an inlaid backstripe, which is fancier on the more highly ornamented models.

Sizes	Width	Scale
Standard	12 3/4"	24 5/8"
Concert	13 1/2"	25"
Grand Concert	14"	25 3/8"
Auditorium	15"	25 5/8"

MAURER MODELS FROM EARLY 1930S CATALOG

487: size unspecified, oak back and sides, ladder bracing, multiple-bound top, "colored veneer" inlay around soundhole and edges, dot inlay

489: mahogany back and sides, otherwise same as Model 487

491: grand concert size, mahogany back and sides, multiple-bound top, colored wood inlaid around soundhole, dot inlay

493: auditorium size, otherwise same as Model 491

494: size unspecified, rosewood back and sides, multiple-bound top, colored wood and celluloid inlaid around soundhole, dot inlay

525: 3/4 size, otherwise same as Model 494

498: rosewood back and sides, multiple-bound top, bound back, colored-wood soundhole ring, dot inlay

493: curly maple back and sides, otherwise same as Model 498

541: concert size, rosewood back and sides, elaborate colored-wood purfling around soundhole and top edges, bound top and back, bound fingerboard, ornamental inlay, pearl ornamental peghead inlay

551: auditorium size, otherwise same as Model 541

562: standard size, rosewood back and sides, pearl and colored-wood purfling around soundhole and top edges, bound top and back, bound fingerboard, ornamental inlay, pearl ornamental peghead inlay

562 1/2: concert size, otherwise same as Model 562

564: auditorium size, otherwise same as Model 562

585: grand concert size, rosewood back and sides, pearl and colored-wood purfling around soundhole and top edges, pearl border on top around fingerboard, bound top and back, bound fingerboard, tree-of-life inlay, pearl ornamental peghead inlay, ivoroid tuner buttons

587: pearl tuner buttons, otherwise same as Model 585

590: auditorium size, ivoroid tuner buttons, otherwise same as Model 585

593: auditorium size, pearl tuner buttons, otherwise same as Model 585

15: mandolin, symmetrical pear-shaped body, oval hole, bent top, flat back, maple back and sides, colored-wood and celluloid inlay around soundhole and top edges, rosewood-grain stain finish

30: mandolin, symmetrical pear-shaped, oval hole, bent top, flat back, rosewood back and sides, ebony bridge with bone saddle, symmetrical pickguard under strings, pearl inlay around soundhole and in pickguard, fancy wood and celluloid inlay around top edges, ornamental fingerboard inlay, pearl peghead ornament

40: tenor mandola, symmetrical pear-shaped, oval hole, bent top, flat back, maple back and sides, ebony bridge with bone saddle, pickguard on treble side with pearl inlay, fancy wood inlay around top edges, bound top and back, ornamental fingerboard inlay, pearl peghead ornament, rosewood-grain stain finish

45: octave mandola, same ornamentation as Model 40 but larger

50: mandocello, same ornamentation as Model 40

Prairie State Models from Early 1930s Catalog

All models have support tube through body.

225: concert size, rosewood back and sides, fancy colored-wood inlay around soundhole and top edges, bound top and back, bound fingerboard, elaborate fingerboard inlay, pearl peghead ornament

425: auditorium size, otherwise same as Model 225

426: auditorium size, high nut for steel playing, otherwise same as Model 225

427: auditorium size, "gear pegs," reinforced neck, otherwise same as Model 225

428: auditorium size, "gear pegs," reinforced neck, high nut for steel playing, otherwise same as Model 225

235: concert size, rosewood back and sides, pearl and colored-wood purfling around soundhole and top edges, bound top and back, bound fingerboard, ornamental inlay, pearl peghead ornament, ivoroid tuner buttons

335: grand concert size, otherwise same as Model 235

435: auditorium size, otherwise same as Model 235

340: grand concert size, rosewood back and sides, pearl and colored-wood purfling around soundhole and top edges, pearl border on top around fingerboard, bound top and back, bound fingerboard, tree-of-life inlay, pearl peghead ornament, ivoroid tuner buttons

350: pearl tuner buttons, otherwise same as Model 340

440: auditorium size, ivoroid tuner buttons, otherwise same as Model 340

450: auditorium size, pearl tuner buttons, otherwise same as Model 340

COMMENTS

The Larsons' reputation today is based primarily on their flat top guitars, although their mandolins and *f*-hole archtops are also well-made. Workmanship, especially on later models, may be cruder than that of Martin or Gibson, and later bodies are sometimes slightly asymmetrical.

In the 1930s Larson flat tops were rivaled only by Martin and Gibson. The high-end guitar models are regarded as excellent instruments by players and are highly sought by collectors.

Harp-style guitars and mandolin family instruments are highly sought by collectors, in part because of their aesthetic appeal. Most modern harp guitar players prefer the Larson flat top design to the Gibson archtop harp guitar, and the Larson-Dyer models are considered by many players to be the finest harp guitars ever made.

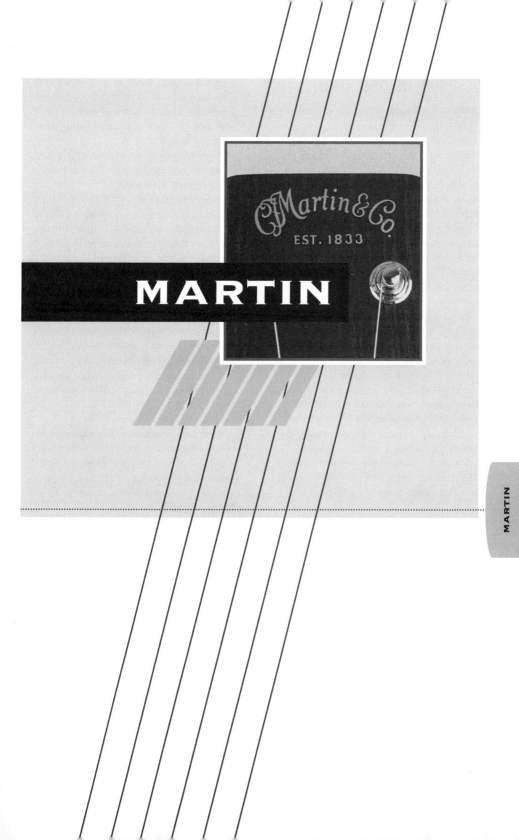

GENERAL INFORMATION

hristian Frederick Martin, son of an instrument maker from Mark Neukerkin, Germany, immigrated to the United States in 1833 and opened a full-line music store at 96 Hudson St. in New York City. Initially, guitar manufacturing and guitar sales accounted for only a small part of Martin's business; he sold all types of instruments at retail, and he also imported instruments for distribution to other dealers in the eastern United States. In 1839 Martin moved to Nazareth, PA, to devote full time to guitar making, although his labels and stamps continued to say "New York" until 1898. Consequently all Martin guitars made prior to 1898 are commonly referred to as New York Martins.

Martin had associations with John Coupa (a New York teacher), Charles Bruno and Henry Schatz. The names of Coupa, Bruno and Schatz appear with Martin's on some labels from this period.

Martin became the first American guitar manufacturer of real repute, and the company continues to be the most famous and respected maker of flat tops. The dreadnought body has become Martin's most popular flat top body style and has been widely imitated by other makers.

Company ownership remains in the Martin family. C.F. (Chris) Martin IV, great-great-great-grandson of the founder, is now chairman and CEO.

PERIODS

See comments at end of model descriptions for further analysis.

1833–1840s: Guitars show the influence of Martin's former employer, Johann Stauffer of Vienna, Austria. Typical Germanic features include hourglass body shape, some examples through the 1850s with laminated rosewood (outer) and spruce (inner) back and sides, pin bridge, separate neck heel in the shape of an ice cream cone, neck angle adjustable near heel by means of a "clock key" and 6-on-a-side tuners with the high E-string tuner closest to the nut.

Late 1840s–1850s: Martin develops a new American-style guitar, with body shapes, bracing pattern and ornamentation that define the modern flat top guitar. Body sizes are standardized by 1852. Standardized style numbers, corresponding to the wholesale price of the guitar, come into use in 1853. Some examples from the late 1840s and early 1850s have purfling around the middle of the sides.

Late 1850s–1927: Larger body sizes gradually replace the original sizes.

1928–late 1934: Martin develops steel string guitars and introduces the dreadnought body style (see Dreadnoughts, following).

1934–mid 1939: The golden era of the steel string guitar is led by Martin's dreadnoughts and 000-size models with 14-fret necks and "high-X" bracing.

Mid 1939–1944: Martin reduces the number of models offered, discontinuing all the pearl-trimmed models. The X-brace is moved away from the soundhole. Consequently, even though guitars from this period are still fine instruments, they are not as highly regarded as those of the earlier period.

1945–early 1947: Martins go through a transitional period from prewar to postwar styles.

Early 1947–late 1969: Martin quality remains stable as production gradually increases through the folk music boom of the 1960s. Brazilian rosewood is still used on the higher styles.

Late 1969–76: Indian rosewood replaces Brazilian. The Martin company expands with new acquisitions.

1976–current: Many vintage features are reintroduced, along with new features, new models and many custom and limited edition models.

MODEL NAMES

Beginning in the 1850s, model names of almost all Martin guitars and some mandolins consist of a body designation and a style designation, separated by a hyphen. Since October 1930 the model name is stamped along with the serial number on the neck block.

The Road Series models, introduced in 1995, do not follow this nomenclature system. Road Series model names consist of a body size followed by a letter, with no hyphen (00CME, 000R or DR, for example).

Body Designation, Flat Tops

By 1852, Martin offered flat tops in sizes (from largest to smallest) 1, 2, 2 1/2 and 3. Sizes 0 and 5 were added in 1854 and Size 4 in 1857. As larger models were introduced, they continued within the system: size 00 in 1877, size 000 in 1902.

Martin broke from an orderly system for body sizes with the introduction of the OM models in 1929. Since then, the following body designations have been used:

OM: Orchestra Model, 000-size body, 14-fret neck, 25.4" scale, introduced in 1929.

D: In 1916 Martin made a body size larger than 000—the D or dreadnought size, named after the largest class of battleships at the time. The D was initially available only on guitars made for the Ditson company. It first appeared in the Martin line in 1931.

M: In 1977 Martin introduced the equivalent of a 0000-size body (larger than the D) on a flat top guitar (the same body shape had been used on Martin archtops in the 1930s). It was designated M, according to Martin lore, because the neck stamper could not accommodate 0000.

7 or 7/8: Dimensions approximately 7/8 of D-size, introduced in 1980.

J: The Jumbo body style, introduced in 1985 (originally called Jumbo M) has the same 0000 body shape as the M but with the extra depth of the D.

B: Acoustic bass, introduced in 1992.

Other exceptions in the flat top line include C (cutaway or cedar top), H preceding a body size (herringbone binding) and N (classical). Additional prefixes are used for special models, including CEO, CMSH, CTSH and MTV.

Archtops and electrics generally do not conform strictly to the original size-style system.
Archtop prefixes include C, F and R
Electric prefixes include E, EB, GT and F.

Style Designation

The part of a model name after the hyphen refers to the ornamentation and type of wood. From the introduction of style numbers in the 1850s through the mid 1980s, Martin used an orderly, consistent system. The most popular models in the 1900s have been, from plainest to fanciest, 15, 16, 17, 18, 21, 28, 35, 42 and 45. Beginning in the mid 1980s, Martin's rapidly expanding model line (including many special limited-run models) resulted in new style numbers that that do not conform to the tradi-

tional system (Style 60 is less fancy than Style 45, for example), plus a long list of letter suffixes to delineate variations within styles.

60-series numbers denote a maple body.

4-digit style with *32* as last digits denotes a Shenandoah model, a budget line made overseas and finished out at the Martin factory in Nazareth, PA.

Letter suffixes include the initials of signature artists (EC = Eric Clapton, JC = Johnny Cash, etc.) and the following:

2R: 2 soundhole rings
A: ash
B: Brazilian rosewood
BK: black finish
C: classical or cutaway
DB: deep body
E: electric
FMG: figured mahogany
G: gut-string classical
GE: golden era
GM: Grand Marquis
H: Hawaiian
K: koa wood back and sides
K2: koa wood back, sides and top
L: left-handed
LE: limited edition
M: mahogany or (with J prefix) Jumbo M body size
MB: maple binding
MP: morado back and sides, low-profile neck
N: non-low profile neck (during period when low-profile neck is standard)
P: plectrum (pre-World War II), low-profile neck (1985–current) or Fishman Prefix pickup
Q: old-style nonadjustable neck (1985–current)
R: rosewood back and sides
S: special custom order (pre-World War II) or 12-fret neck (1967–current)
SE: signature edition
SW: special Wurlitzer
T: tenor or technology
V: vintage specs
W: walnut

Size	Width	Scale	Depth	Length
Early 1/4	6 3/16	17	2 7/8	12
Later 1/4	8 5/16	17	3 9/16	12 1/16
1/2	10 1/8	20 7/8	3 3/8	15 1/16
7 (7/8-D)	13 11/16	23	4 3/8	17 1/2
5, pre-c. 1924	11 1/4	21.4	3 7/8	16
5, c. 1924 and after	11 1/4	22	3 7/8	16
5T, pre-1929	11 1/4	22 5/8	3 7/8	16
5T, mid 1929 and after	11 1/4	23	3 7/8	16
4	11 1/2	22	3 3/4	16
3 1/2	10 11/16	22	3 7/8	16 7/8
3	11 1/4	23 7/8	3 13/16	17 3/8
2 1/2	11 5/8	24.5	3 7/8	17 7/8
2	12	24.5	4	18 1/4
1	12 3/4	24.9	4 3/16	18 7/8
0, 12-fret	13 1/2	24.9	4 3/16	19 1/8
0, 14-fret	13 1/2	24.9	4 1/4	18 3/8
00, 12-fret	14 1/8	24.9	4 1/16	19 5/8
00, 14-fret	14 5/16	24.9	4 1/8	18 7/8
000, pre-c. 1924 (12-fret)	15	24.9	4 1/16	20 7/16
000, c. 1924–34 (12-fret)	15	25.4	4 1/16	20 7/16
000, 14-fret	15	24.9*	4 1/8	19 3/8
OM	15	25.4	4 1/8	19 3/8
D, 12-fret	15 5/8	25.4	4 3/4	20 15/16
D, 14-fret	15 5/8	25.4	4 7/8	20
M	16	25.4	4 1/8	20 1/8
J-##M	16	25.4	4 7/8	20 1/8
N	14 7/16	26 3/8**	4 1/8	19 1/8
R	14 5/8	24.9	4 1/4	18 7/8
C	15	24.9	4 3/16	19 3/8
F acoustic	16	24.9	4 1/8	20 1/8
F electric	16	24.9	2	20 1/8
GT-70	16	24.9	2	19 3/4
GT-75	16	24.9	2	16 7/8

* 14-fret 000-18s and 000-28s from early 1934 (probably overlaps from the discontinued OM-18 and OM-28 designation) have a 25.4" scale.

** Early N-size guitars (1969) have 25.4" scale; from 1970 onward, N scale is 26 3/8".

LABELS AND STAMPS

Paper labels...

Christian Frederick Martin or C. F. Martin:
1833–1840s
Some with Martin & Schatz: **c. 1836**
Some with C. F. Martin and Bruno: **May–Nov. 1838**
Some with MARTIN & COUPA: **1840s**

Stamps...

C.F. MARTIN, New York on back of peghead, inside body on center backstrip and on neckblock; "ice-cream cone" heel (see neck section); guitars often stamped on outside of back by heel (not on back of peghead): **1833–66**

C.F. MARTIN, New York on back of peghead, C.F. MARTIN & Co, New York inside body on center backstrip and on neckblock—models with 2-piece neck: **1867–97**

C.F. MARTIN, New York on back of body near neck, C.F. MARTIN & Co, New York inside body on center backstrip and on neckblock—models with "ice-cream cone" heel: **1867–97**

C.F. MARTIN & Co, Nazareth, Pa on back of peghead and on inside center backstrip: **1898–mid 1935**

C.F. MARTIN & Co, Nazareth, Pa on inside center backstrip (no stamp on back of peghead): **mid 1935–1963**

Made in USA added to brand: **1963–current**

Serial number impressed into neck block (some from 1898–1902 impressed into top of peghead): **1898–current**

Model impressed into neck block: **Oct. 1930–current**

Top

Adirondack spruce: **pre-1946**

Sitka spruce (darker than Adirondack): **1946–current**

Occasional Adirondack tops: **1950s–60s**

Some with Engelman spruce, Engelman available on request: **current**

Rosewood

Brazilian rosewood replaced by Indian; most Brazilian is redder (vs. brown or purplish) and more figured than Indian…

D-size (some D-35s with combination of Indian and Brazilian rosewood into 1970): **late 1969**

000s and 00s: **early 1970**

Brazilian rosewood continues to be used on various limited edition and custom order instruments.

Bracing

Scalloped X-bracing introduced: **by late 1840s**

X-bracing on all models (except later G, C and N classicals and a few other examples): **1900**

Non-scalloped braces: **late 1944**

Scalloped braces reintroduced…

HD-28: **1976**

HD-35, M series, JM series: **from introduction**

D-45: **late 1985**

D-41: **1987**

Position of X on D models…

High X, X positioned 1" from soundhole: **before mid 1939**

X moved farther from soundhole (distance varies): **early 1939**

High X reintroduced, Style 16, special and custom models: **late 1980s**

Bridgeplate…

Maple: **pre-1968**

Rosewood: **1968**

Maple, models with scalloped bracing only: **1976**

Maple, all models: **1988**

Bridge

Ornamental with points at ends, metal fretwire saddle: **1830s–40s**

Point at bottom center, ivory saddle, some with separate ivory and pearl ornament: **1830s–40s**

Rectangular ebony pin bridge, some with pyramids at ends, introduced: **late 1840s**

Rectangular bridge with no pyramids, Style 21 and lower (Style 28 and higher stay with pyramid ends): **by 1920s**

Belly bridge…

Long rectangular saddle slot, Style 18 and higher: **late 1929**

Shorter bridge slot: **1965**

Pickguard

Tortoiseshell celluloid (a few early with genuine tortoiseshell) optional: **late 1929**

Black plastic: **1966**

Tortoiseshell celluloid reintroduced along with other vintage specs: **mid 1980s**

Binding

Abalone-trimmed models…

Wood purfling: **pre-World War II**

Plastic purfling: **1968–current**

Herringbone trim, Styles 21, Style 28 and pre-1898 Style 18…

First herringbone: **late 1860s**

Black-white plastic binding replaces herringbone: **early 1947**

Herringbone returns on HD-28: **1976**

Style 28 and higher…

Elephant ivory: **pre-1918**

Ivoroid, Style 28 and higher: **1918–66**

White non-grained plastic: **1966–current**

Styles 18 and 21…

Wood: **pre-1934**

Black plastic: **1934–36**

Tortoiseshell celluloid: **1936–66**

Black plastic returns: **1966–current**

MARTIN

NECK

3-piece neck, peghead grafted on with V-joint and no volute, separate "ice cream cone" neck heel with clock key fastening mechanism, some models: **1830s–90s**

2-piece cedar neck with grafted-on peghead and neck volute (much overlap with earlier style, depending on model): **late 1840s–1916**

1-piece mahogany neck, volute on Style 28 and higher models only: **1916–current**

14-fret neck...

Introduced with OM-28: **1929**

C-2 and C-3 archtops introduced with 14-fret neck: **1931**

0-17 and 0-18: **1932**

All Ds and all 000s, mahogany 00s and 0s (12-fret neck continues on rosewood 00s and 0s): **1934**

T-frets replace bar frets: **late 1934**

Neck reinforcement...

Ebony bar introduced: **mid 1920s**

Steel T-bar: **late 1934**

Ebony bar (due to wartime metal shortage): **1942**

Back to steel T-bar: **1946**

Square steel tube: **1967**

Adjustable truss rod with allen wrench adjustment inside body: **1985**

Neck width at nut...

12-fret models (size 2 1/2 and larger), 1 7/8": **throughout**

14-fret models, 1 3/4": **before mid 1939**

14-fret models, 1 11/16": **after mid 1939**

TUNERS

Models with slotted peghead have 3-on-a-plate tuners except in the 1930s, when they have individual Grover tuners slightly modified from solid-peghead style tuners. Models with solid peghead have individual tuners.

Stauffer-style, 6-on-a-side with high E-string tuner closest to nut: **1833–1840s**

Slotted peghead, 3-on-a-side tuners introduced (some still with Stauffer-style tuners): **1830s**

Many examples with 2-piece neck, solid peghead and ivory friction pegs: **1850s–early 1900s**

German-built tuners with gear wheel above worm gear: **into 1916**

American-built tuners with gear wheel above worm

gear and ivoroid buttons: **1916–c. 1925**

Gear wheel below worm gear: **c. 1925**

Grover planetary banjo tuners, Style OM only: **1929–c. 1931**

Open-back Grover tuners with rivet, thin metal buttons with seam in middle of button: **1931**

Open-back Grover tuners with adjustment screw, heavy metal buttons with no visible seam: **1935**

Sealed-back Grover tuners, heavy metal buttons with no visible seam, Style 28 and higher: **mid 1939–mid 1940**

Open-back Kluson tuners, no adjustment screw, plastic buttons, no peghead bushings: **1942–44**

Open-back Kluson tuners, adjustment screw, metal buttons, peghead bushings: **1945–46**

Kluson Deluxe tuners introduced, all D models, all Style 28s: **1947**

Open-back Grover Sta-tites, 0, 00 and 000 below Style 28: **1947**

Kluson sealed-back tuners introduced, Style 28: **1950**

Grover Rotomatic tuners introduced...

Style 28: **1958**

All D sizes: **1965**

All styles: **1967**

Sperzel, Schaller, Grover, some stamped with *Martin:* **1970s–current**

LOGO ON FRONT OF PEGHEAD

Vertical *Martin,* earliest C-1 archtop: **1931**

Vertical *CF Martin* inlay...

Introduced on C-2, C-3: **1931**

Style 45s with solid peghead: **late 1933**

F-7 and F-9 (from introduction): **1935**

CF Martin & Co, Est. 1833 ...

Silkscreen with black border around letters: **late 1931**

Decal: **mid 1932**

FINISH

French polish: **pre-1900**

Thin shellac: **1900**

Semi-gloss (thin shellac dulled by sanding): **1919**

"Satin," high-gloss shellac, varnish top coat on back and sides: **1923**

Clear nitro-cellulose lacquer, some models: **1926**

Nitro-cellulose lacquer, most models: **1929**

MARTIN

DREADNOUGHTS, 1916–87

Ditson models: made by Martin for Oliver Ditson company, with Ditson name and serial numbers, most early with brown-stain spruce top, mahogany back and sides (some custom-made with rosewood), 19 frets, fan-pattern bracing (on early series)

Model 111: plain, Style 18 trim except for no back trim

Model 222: plastic binding, plastic heel cap, inlaid ebony bridge pins

Model 333: pearl inlaid bridge, bound fingerboard and soundhole, German silver tuners

Ditson dreadnoughts introduced: **1916**
Martin serial numbers used after Ditson #571: **1921**
Ditson dreadnoughts discontinued: **1921**
Ditson dreadnought Model 111 reintroduced, X-bracing: **1923**
Ditson Model 111 discontinued (19 made, 1923–30): **1930**
Martin models introduced, mahogany body D-1 (becomes D-18) and rosewood body D-2 (becomes D-28), 12 frets clear of body: **1931**
D-18 and D-28 introduced: later **1931**
First D-45 produced (12-fret): **1933**
14 frets clear of body (except for approximately 16 D-18s, 24 D-28s and 2 D-45s, all with 12 frets clear of body): **1934**
2 widebody (16 1/4") D-45s: **1936**
D-45 catalogued: **1938**
D-45 discontinued: **1942**
12-fret neck available but not catalogued: **1954**
D-21 introduced: **1955**
D-28SW (Special Wurlitzer), 12-fret neck, slotted or solid peghead, available from E.U. Wurlitzer: **1962**
D12-20 12-string, 12-fret neck, introduced: **1964**
D-35 introduced (but not catalogued), D12-35 12-string introduced: **1965**
D-35 catalogued: **1966**
12-fret S models introduced in Martin line: **1967**
D-45 reintroduced: **1968**
Indian rosewood replaces Brazilian: **late 1969**
D12-41 12-string introduced: **1970**
D12-18 12-string introduced: **1973**
D-76 introduced: **early 1976**
HD-28, D-19 introduced: **late 1976**

HD-35 introduced: **1978**
D-25K, D-25K2, D-37K, D-37K2, D-19M introduced: **1980**
DC-28 introduced: **1981**
HD-37K2 introduced (1 shipped): **1982**
Shenandoah line introduced: **1983**
Custom D-28B and D-35B introduced: **1985**
HD-28B, HD-35B, D-41B, D-45B, D-16K, D-16M introduced: **1986**
HD-28BSE (Brazilian rosewood signature edition), D-45LE (limited edition), prototype D-62 (maple), D-16A (ash), and D-16W (walnut) introduced: **1987**

OMs, 1929–90

Style OM: 000 body, 14 frets clear of body, pyramid bridge, no pickguard, 25.4" scale, inlays at frets 5, 7 and 9, banjo tuning pegs, no decal, solid peghead
Introduced, Style 28: **1929**
Small pickguard: **late 1929**
Belly bridge: **very early 1930**
Styles 18 (dot inlay), 42, 45, and 45 DLX (snowflake inlays on bridge, abalone inlay on pickguard, engraved gold-plated tuners, pearl tuner buttons) introduced (only year for OM-42 and OM-45 DLX): **1930**
First appearance of silkscreen logo: **1930**
Large pickguard: **early 1931**
Right-angle tuners: **1931**
Inlay at frets 5, 7, 9, 12 and 15, decal logo standard, Styles 18 and 28: **late 1931**
Last original series OMs: **late 1933**
SOM-28 (reissue of OM-28) available: **1969 only**
SOM-45 (reissue of OM-45) introduced: **1977**
OM-28 reintroduced as limited edition: **1985**
HOM-35 offered as limited edition: **1989**
OM-28 reintroduced into regular production: **1990**

MADE BY MARTIN FOR OTHER COMPANIES

Since 1900, Martin has made instruments for many different companies and guitar teachers. Not all are included here.

Bacon: a few made for Bacon Banjo Co., sold under the Bacon brand, 1924.

Belltone: 15 guitars, 10 mandolins and 12 Style 3K ukes made with Belltone brand for sale by Perlberg and Halpin of New York.

Bitting Special: mandolins made for a Bethlehem, PA, teacher, 1916–19.

Ditson: 1917–21 and 1923–30, made for the Ditson Company in Boston in 3 sizes (standard, concert and dreadnought) and in 3 different styles, plus other instruments in standard Martin styles. Early examples have only a Ditson stamp, later have both Martin and Ditson. Instruments made from 1923–30 have Martin serial numbers. A total of 483 guitars with Ditson numbers have been documented through January 3, 1921.

Foden: 1912–17, made for concert guitarist William Foden, similar to standard Martin models but with a simple soundhole ring. Foden specified a 20-fret fingerboard, prompting Martin to switch all models from 19 to 20 frets. Foden Special models were made in 0 or 00 size and five different styles: Style A (similar to Martin Style 18), Style B (Style 21), Style C (Style 28), Style D (Style 30), and Style E (combination of Styles 40, 42, and 45). Only 27 instruments have been documented, but the frequency with which they turn up suggests that more may have been produced.

Jenkins: Style 1 and 2 ukes, made for Kansas City mail-order company, sold as Models 35 and 40, respectively.

Olcott-Bickford: 32 instruments made for concert guitarist Vahdah Olcott-Bickford. See Style 44 in model descriptions.

Paramount: c. 1930, around 36 made, unusual construction with Size 2 body mounted into larger rim and back, rims and back of rosewood, small round soundholes around "lip" that joins outer rims to inner rims, no soundhole in top (at least 1 with round soundhole in top), 14 frets clear of body, rosewood fingerboard, dot inlay to 15th fret, rounded-peak peghead, standard Paramount banjo peghead inlay, banjo-style tuners, some 4-string, some 6-string.

Schoenberg: 1987–94. Models include Soloist, cosmetically similar to OM-18 (also available as a cutaway); Concert Vintage, replica of 1930 OM-28;

Concert Standard, modernized version of 1930 OM-28; OM-45 Deluxe replica; plus some 12-fret 000 models and some dreadnoughts. Parts were constructed by Schoenberg's luthier (Dana Bourgeois from 1986–mid 1990, T.J. Thompson from mid 1990–94), assembled by Martin and then voiced and inlaid in Schoenberg's shop. From 1987–90 all have a metal plate on the neck block with a Martin serial number. In 1991 the metal plate was replaced by a brand stamp "Made expressly for Schoenberg Guitars by CF Martin Co." and a stamped Martin serial number. An additional stamp on the back of the peghead or on the main interior back brace reads "Schoenberg Guitars, T.J. Thompson, Eric Schoenberg."

The last Schoenberg/Martin guitar was numbered 541742 and completed in October 1994. Since then Schoenberg has been making guitars independently under his own name.

S.S. Stewart: ukes made under Stewart brand for sale by Buegeleisen and Jacobson of New York, 1923–25.

Rolando: made for Southern California Music Co., 1916–18, crest on peghead, similar to standard Martin koa wood styles, 261 total guitars consecutively numbered from #1, later examples with Martin serial numbers.

Vega: Martin acquired the Boston-based Vega banjo company in 1970 and moved production to Nazareth in 1971. Vega was sold to Galaxy Trading Co. of Santa Fe Springs, CA, in 1979. In 1998 Martin reissued a Deering-made Vega longneck banjo as part of the Kingston Trio set, which included an 0-18T tenor guitar and a D-28 guitar.

Weymann: ukes and taro-patches (but no guitars) made for Philadelphia-based banjo company, circa 1925.

Wurlitzer: 1922–24, standard Martin models but with single-ring soundhole ornamentation, Wurlitzer model number and Wurlitzer stamp on the back of the peghead, 297 total guitars.

MARTIN FLAT TOP BODY SIZES

All photos are shot from the same distance.

1989 M-36.

1939 D-28, 14 frets clear of body, herringbone trim around top edges, slotted-diamond fingerboard inlay.

1964 D-28SW, 12 frets clear of body, special-order model for the E.U. Wurlitzer company (courtesy Hank Sable).

1937 000-45.

1969 N-20.

1938 00-28G with custom-ordered 14-fret neck. Standard models have this body shape with 12 frets clear of body.

1967 00-21, 12 frets clear of body (courtesy Hank Sable).

1938 0-17H, straight-mounted bridge for Hawaiian playing.

1929 1-17P, plectrum.

1930 2-44, Olcott-Bickford model, pyramid bridge.

1930 21/2-17.

1929 5-17T, tenor.

1936 T-28, tiple.

425

SERIAL NUMBERS

All Martin guitars, basses and tiples made since 1898 (except for solidbody electric guitars from the 1970s) are numbered in one consecutive series. Beginning in 1991, mandolins were numbered in the guitar number series (see Martin Mandolins section).

Mandolins (prior to 1991) and a few early ukes have their own number series. Solidbody electrics, ukuleles and many instruments made for sale under other brands do not have Martin numbers.

The serial number is stamped on the neck block inside the instrument, except for some very early examples, which have the number stamped on the top of the peghead.

Numbers begin with #8000, which was Martin's estimate of the total number of instruments made before 1898.

SERIAL NUMBERS: GUITARS, BASSES AND TIPLES

YEAR	LAST NUMBER	YEAR	LAST NUMBER
1898	8349	1933	55084
1899	8716	1934	58679
1900	9128	1935	61947
1901	9310	1936	65176
1902	9528	1937	68865
1903	9810	1938	71866
1904	9988	1939	74061
1905	10120	1940	76734
1906	10329	1941	80013
1907	10727	1942	83107
1908	10883	1943	86724
1909	11018	1944	90149
1910	11203	1945	93623
1911	11413	1946	98158
1912	11565	1947	103468
1913	11821	1948	108269
1914	12047	1949	112961
1915	12209	1950	117961
1916	12390	1951	122799
1917	12988	1952	128436
1918	13450	1953	134501
1919	14512	1954	141345
1920	15848	1955	147328
1921	16758	1956	152775
1922	17839	1957	159061
1923	19891	1958	165576
1924	22008	1959	171047
1925	24116	1960	175689
1926	28689	1961	181297
1927	34435	1962	187384
1928	37568	1963	193327
1929	40843	1964	199626
1930	45317	1965	207030
1931	49589	1966	217215
1932	52590	1967	230095

YEAR	LAST NUMBER	YEAR	LAST NUMBER
1968	241925	1984	453300
1969	256003	1985	460575
1970	271633	1986	468175
1971	294270	1987	476216
1972	313302	1988	483952
1973	333873	1989	493279
1974	353387	1990	503309
1975	371828	1991	512487 (includes
1976	388800		11 mandolins)
1977	399625	1992	522655
1978	407800	1993	535223 (includes
1979	419900		6 mandolins)
1980	430300	1994	551696
1981	436474	1995	570434
1982	439627	1996	592930
1983	446101	1997	624799

FLAT TOPS KEY

Martin guitars from 1898 are branded *Nazareth, Pa.* on the inside back. Beginning in October, 1930, Martin guitars have the model name stamped on the neck block.

1833–1902

Rosewood soundhole rings
   Rosewood back and sides
      Straight-line binding (no decorative-pattern purfling) = **Style 17**
      Herringbone top edge purfling = **Style 28**
   Mahogany back and sides = **Style 16**
   Checkered-pattern soundhole ring = **Style 17**
Rope-pattern soundhole ring
   No decorative pattern edge purfling
      Unbound back (most in size 2 1/2 or 3) = **Style 17**
      Rosewood back binding (most in size 2) = **Style 18**
   Diagonal-pattern edge trim = **Style 24**
Herringbone soundhole ring
   White backstripe = **Style 17**
   Decorative marquetry backstripe
      Size 2 = **Style 20**
      Size 1 or 0: **Style 21**
      Specs unavailable: **Styles 22, 23**
Soundhole ring like Style 45 backstripe = **Style 26**
Pearl soundhole ring
   Pearl around top border
      No pearl on top around fingerboard = **Style 40**
      Pearl on top around fingerboard = **Style 42**

Pearl soundhole ring (*continued*)
    No pearl around top border
        Wood bridge
            Brass tuners = **Style 27**
            German silver tuners = **Style 30** or (00-size, late 1870s) **Style 33**
        Ivory bridge = **Style 34**

1902–31

No decorative marquetry on trim (other than binding lines)
    Unbound fingerboard
        1 to 4 soundhole rings = **Style 17**
        1-9-1 soundhole ring grouping = **Style 18**
    Bound fingerboard = **Style 44**
Herringbone soundhole ring = **Style 21**
Herringbone purfling around top border = **Style 28**
Pearl soundhole ring
    No pearl border around top
        Wood bridge
            Brass tuners = **Style 27**
            German silver tuners = **Style 30**
        Ivory bridge = **Style 34**
    Pearl border around top
        No pearl on top around fingerboard = **Style 40**
        Pearl on top around fingerboard
            Unbound peghead = **Style 42**
            Bound peghead = **Style 45**

1932–98

Beginning in the 1980s, Martin has made numerous
models that vary from these standard style specifications.

No top binding
    Hexagon outline inlay = **Concept-J**
    All single-dot fret markers = **Style 15**
    2 dots at 7th fret
        Herringbone soundhole ring = **Style 15**
        Plain soundhole rings = **Styles 17, #25 (2-17), 0-55 (00-17)**
1- or 3-ply binding with dark outer layer
    Plain soundhole ring = **Styles 1 (new style), 16**
    Soundhole rings in 5-9-5 grouping = **Style 21, 1992–current**
    Herringbone soundhole ring = **Style 16T**
    Pearl soundhole ring = **Style Special 16**
Multiple binding with dark outer layer
    Mahogany back and sides
        Natural spruce or koa top
            Non-12-string = **Style 18, D-1 old style**
            12-string = **D12-20**
        Dark-stained spruce top = **Style 19**

Rosewood back and sides
    No herringbone edge trim = **Style 21, 1932–92**
    Herringbone edge trim = **HD-28 CTB, HD-28GM, HD-28PSE**
Maple back and sides
    Unbound fingerboard
        Maple peghead face = **Style 60**
        Rosewood peghead face
            D size = **D-62**
            M size = **M-64**
    Tortoiseshell celluloid fingerboard binding
        Snowflake inlay = **D-62LE**
        Dot inlay = **Style 65**
Koa back and sides: **Style 25K**
Maple (light wood) outer binding = **D-18MB**
White body binding, no pearl edge trim
    Wood-marquetry soundhole rings (no herringbone)
        Mahogany back and sides = **N-10**
        Rosewood back and sides = **N-20**
    Non-pearl soundhole rings
        Unbound fingerboard
            2-piece rosewood back
                Star inlay = **D-76**
                Other inlay = **D-2 old style, 28, Custom 08, Custom 15**
            3-piece rosewood back = **CM-0089**
            Koa back = **28K**
            Mahogany back = **HD-28M**
        Bound fingerboard
            3-piece rosewood back = **Styles 35, 36**
            2-piece rosewood back = **Style 40 (1985 onward)**
            2-piece mahogany back = **Style 93**
            2-piece maple back = **Style 68**
    Pearl soundhole ring
        Bound peghead = **Style 38**
        Unbound peghead = **Style 37**
White body binding, pearl edge trim
    Unbound peghead
        No pearl on top around fingerboard = **Style 40, pre-1985**
        Pearl on top around fingerboard = **Style 42**
    Bound peghead
        No pearl on top around fingerboard = **Style 41**
        Pearl on top around fingerboard = **Style 45, Custom 17**

MARTIN

ARCHTOPS KEY

All roundhole archtop models have model name stamped on neckblock.

All acoustic *f*-hole archtop models have model name stamped on back center seam.

All electric archtops have model name stamped on back below soundhole.

Acoustic
  Dot inlay
    14 5/16" or less wide
      Spruce top = **R-18**
      Mahogany top = **R-17**
    15" wide = **C-1**
    16" wide = **F-1**
  Slotted-diamond inlay = **C-2, 1932–39**
  Snowflake inlay = **C-3**
  Hexagonal inlay
    Unbound peghead
      15" wide = **C-2, 1939–41**
      16" wide = **F-2**
    Bound peghead
      Fingerboard inlay at 6 frets
        Rosewood back and sides = **F-7**
        Maple back and sides = **F-5**
      Fingerboard inlay at 8 frets = **F-9**
Electric
  Single cutaway
    1 pickup = **F-50**
    2 pickups
      Standard square-corner peghead = **F-55**
      Flared-top peghead = **GT-70**
  Double cutaway
    Sunburst finish = **F-65**
    Burgundy or black finish
      6-string = **GT-75**
      12-string = **GT-75-12**

GUITARS

SECTION ORGANIZATION

Flat Top Styles
Hawaiian and Early Koa Models
12-Strings
Tenors and Plectrums
Classicals
Electric Flat Tops
Acoustic Basses
Acoustic Archtops

Electric Archtops
Electric Solidbodies

FLAT TOP STYLES

Models with no size or style designation are listed first.
  All other models are grouped according to style (example: D-28 is found under Style 28). Models within a particular style are listed in order of body size, starting with the smallest (see General Infor-

mation for size specs). All variations of a model are listed after the basic model in alphanumeric order.

This section includes Hawaiian and early koa models, 12-strings, tenors and plectrums, classicals and electric flat tops. Separate sections on those styles follow this section.

CEO: see appropriate style number (Style 1 for CEO-1, Style 2 for CEO-2, etc.)

C-MSH: see Classicals, following

Concept J Cutaway: J-size cutaway, maple back and sides, scalloped bracing, rounded body edges, no binding, no pickguard, abalone soundhole ring, ebony fingerboard, hexagon outline inlay on fingerboard and bridge, C.F. Martin IV signature inlay at 18th fret, active electronics, holographic finish changes color from different angles
Available: **1998**

C-TSH: see Classicals, following

D... models (no style number): see Road Series

EMP: see appropriate style number (Style 1 for EMP-1)

Road Series: no style number, laminated back and sides, A-frame (modified X) bracing, rosewood bridge, herringbone soundhole ring, tortoiseshell celluloid pickguard, black binding, no backstripe, U-shaped mortise-and-tenon neck joint, adjustable truss rod, low-profile neck, rosewood fingerboard, dot inlay, chrome-plated enclosed tuners, satin non-gloss finish

00CME: mahogany back and side, cutaway, piezo pickup, onboard controls: **1998–current**

000M: mahogany back and sides: **1997–current**

000R: rosewood back and sides: **1998–current**

DM: dreadnought, mahogany back and sides: **1995–current**

DR: dreadnought, rosewood back and sides: **1997–current**

DCM: dreadnought cutaway, mahogany back and sides: **1997–current**

DM12: 12-string dreadnought, mahogany back and sides: **1997–current**

JM: jumbo, mahogany back and sides: **1998–current**

Road Series X Models: X in model name, body of laminated wood-fiber material, A-frame top bracing with spruce reinforcement panels, decal soundhole ring, mahogany neck, Morado fingerboard, no inlay, gold epoxy screened peghead logo

000XM: 1999

DXM: 1998–current

DXB: DXM with gloss black finish: **1999**

DXBR: simulated Brazilian rosewood woodgrain on back and sides, gloss finish: **1999**

DXCM: cutaway version of DXM: **1999**

D12XM: 12-string: **1999**

SWD: dreadnought, Smartwood model, wood certified by Rainforest Alliance from environmentally friendly sources, cherry back and sides, cherry neck and interior blocks, katalox fingerboard and bridge, basswood interior linings, braces from uncertified reclaimed pulp logs
Available: **1998**

1/4 12-string: specs unavailable, 6 made: **1918**

Style 1, 1930s: solid mahogany back and sides, unbound ebony fingerboard, 12 frets clear of body

D-1: earliest version of D-18, soundhole rings in 1-9-1 grouping, rosewood binding, unbound ebony fingerboard, slotted peghead, 2 made: **1931**

DC-1: carved top, black binding, 2 made: **1934**

Style 1, 1990s: solid spruce top, solid mahogany back and sides or laminated rosewood back with solid rosewood sides (R models), laminated sides, A-frame (modified X) bracing, rosewood bridge, soundhole rings in 5-9-5 grouping, tortoiseshell celluloid pickguard, tortoiseshell celluloid binding, U-shaped (non-dovetail) neck joint, 14 frets clear of body, unbound rosewood fingerboard, dot inlay, enclosed chrome-plated tuners, satin (non-gloss) finish: **1992–current**

MARTIN

00-1 Grand Concert: mahogany back and sides, black backstripe: **1995–current**

00-1R Grand Concert: rosewood back and sides, no backstripe: **1995–current**

000-1 Auditorium: mahogany back and sides, black backstripe: **1995–current**

000-1R Auditorium: rosewood back and sides: **1995–current**

000C-1 Auditorium: cutaway, mahogany back and sides, black backstripe: **1997–current**

000C-1E Auditorium: transducer pickup: **1997–current**

OM-1: 1 3/4" nut width: **1999**

B-1 Acoustic Bass: see Acoustic Basses, following

C-1: see Acoustic Archtops, following

D-1 (D-1M): mahogany back and sides, black backstripe: **1992–current**

D-1ME: transducer pickup, onboard controls: **1997–current**

DC-1 (DC1-M): cutaway: **1995–current**

DC-1E (DC1-ME): cutaway, transducer pickup, onboard controls: **1997–current**

D-1ML: left-handed D-1: **1997–current**

D-1R: rosewood back and sides, no backstripe: **1994–current**

D-1RE: transducer pickup, onboard controls: **1997–current**

DC-1R: cutaway version of D-1R: **1998–current**

D12-1: 12-string, mahogany back and sides, black backstripe, 14 frets clear of body, 1 7/8" nut width: **1995–current**

0000-1 Grand Auditorium: mahogany back and sides: **1997–current**

J-1 Jumbo: mahogany back and sides: **1997–current**

JC-1: jumbo, cutaway, mahogany back and sides: **1998–current**

MTV-1 Unplugged: dreadnought, 2-piece back, treble half of body with mahogany back and side, bass half of body with rosewood back and side, ebony fingerboard, *Unplugged* inlay, MTV logo under Martin logo, ebony tuner buttons: **1996**

CEO-1: mahogany back and sides, scalloped braces, herringbone top border, abalone soundhole ring, hexagon outline inlays on fingerboard and bridge, ebony fingerboard, C.F. Martin IV signature at 20th fret, gold-plated tuners, ebony buttons, tweed case, limited run: **1997**

CEO-1R: solid rosewood back and sides: **1997**

C-1R: see Classicals, following

EMP-1: 000-size cutaway, ovangko wood sides, 3-piece back with rosewood center wedge and ovangko wings, soundhole ring of black and red marquetry, black saddle, ebony fingerboard, fingerboard inlay offset to bass side, pearl logo, label signed by C.F. Martin IV, limited run not to exceed 262: **1998**

Style 2

CEO-2: dreadnought, laminated striped Macassar ebony back and sides, scalloped bracing, herringbone top border, abalone soundhole ring, black binding with black-and-white side binding, ebony fingerboard, hexagon outline inlay on fingerboard and bridge ends, C.F. Martin IV signature inlay at 18th fret, gold-plated tuners, ebony buttons: **1998**

D-2: earliest version of D-28, solid Brazilian rosewood back and sides, soundhole rings in 5-9-5 grouping, herringbone top border, unbound ebony fingerboard, slotted-diamond inlay, 12 frets clear of body, slotted peghead: **1931–34** (4 in 1931, 2 in 1932, 1 in 1934)

D-2R: similar to D-28, laminated rosewood back and sides, A-frame (modified X) bracing, soundhole rings in 5-9-5 grouping, striped ebony bridge, black pickguard, white binding, white outer layer of binding, chainlink backstripe, U-shaped (non-dovetail) neck joint, striped ebony fingerboard, dot inlay, non-gloss finish: **1995–current**

Style 3: similar to Style 35, laminated rosewood back and sides, A-frame (modified X) bracing, ebony bridge, multiple-bound top and back with white outer layer, 3-piece back, white-black-white backstripes, U-shaped (non-dovetail) neck joint, bound ebony fingerboard, dot inlay, non-gloss finish

D-3R: similar to D-35: **1995–current**

Style 10: classical (see Classicals section, following)

Style 15: mahogany top, sides and back, soundhole ring of thin white-black-white lines, rectangular rosewood bridge, black bridge pins, no binding, rosewood fingerboard, dot inlay with no double-dots, semi-gloss finish

This version of Style 15 is almost identical to Style 17, with gloss or non-gloss finishes very hard to differentiate. Production of 5-15T does not overlap with 5-17T. All Style 15 models have a model stamp on the neck block.

Introduced: **1939**

Discontinued: **1964**

Reintroduced, solid mahogany top, back and sides, A-frame (modified X) bracing, herringbone soundhole ring decal, no binding, U-shaped mortise-and-tenon neck joint, rosewood fingerboard, dot inlay (2 at 12th fret), satin (non-gloss) finish: **1997**

Still in production

5-15T: tenor neck, 22" scale: **1949–63**

0-15: 1935 (2 made with maple and birch body), **1940–43**, **1948–61**

0-15H: Hawaiian, flat fingerboard, flush frets, high nut, non-slanted saddle: **1939**

0-15T: tenor neck: **1960–63**

00-15: rectangular bridge: **1998–current**

000-15: rectangular bridge: **1998–current**

000C-15E: cutaway, transducer pickup: **1999**

Custom 15: not a Style 15 model, dreadnought, rosewood back and sides, HD-28 with tortoiseshell celluloid pickguard, unbound ebony fingerboard, slotted-diamond inlay, V-neck, chrome-plated tuners: **1980–95**

Custom 15S: 12-fret neck: **1995**

D-15: 1997–current

DC-15E: cutaway, Fishman/Martin piezo pickup, onboard controls: **1998–current**

Style 16: mahogany back and sides, plain trim, bound top

Offered in sizes 2 1/2 and 3: **early 1850s**

Style number reintroduced, mahogany back and sides, multiple-bound top with dark outer layer, unbound back, unbound rosewood fingerboard, satin non-gloss finish

Introduced: **1961**

Dreadnought trade show specials, varying wood and trim, introduced: **1986**

16T-series (models listed by body size, following), scalloped braces, herringbone soundhole ring, tortoiseshell celluloid pickguard, tortoiseshell celluloid binding, herringbone backstripe, U-shaped mortise-and-tenon neck joint, extra-low profile neck, rosewood fingerboard, diamonds-and-squares inlay, semi-gloss finish, introduced: **1996**

Special 16T-series, SP prefix (models listed by body size, following), abalone soundhole ring, snowflake inlay on bridge and fingerboard, multi-colored backstripe, gold-plated tuners, gloss finish, introduced: **1997**

Still in production

5-16: soundhole rings in 1-9-1 grouping, dot inlay: **1962–63**

0-16: soundhole rings in 1-9-1 grouping, 3-ply top binding with black outer layer, tortoiseshell celluloid pickguard, rectangular (non-belly) bridge, black bridge pins, unbound rosewood fingerboard, dot inlay, 6 made: **1961**

0-16NY: soundhole rings in 1-9-1 grouping, no pickguard, unbound extra-wide rosewood fingerboard, no inlay, 12-fret neck, slotted peghead: **1961–95**

00-16C: classical (see Classical section, following): **1962–82**, 1 in **1988**

00-16AC: ash back and sides, X-bracing, soundhole rings in 5-9-5 grouping, black binding, tortoiseshell celluloid pickguard, black bridge pins with white dots, 25.4" scale: **1988**

00-16DB: "deep bodied" dreadnought depth, designed with Martin clinician Diane Ponzio, marketed as women's guitar, mahogany back and sides, slotted peghead, Waverly tuners, limited run of 97: **Jan. 1997**

00-16DBR: production model of 00-16DB but with rosewood back and sides: **1997–current**

00C-16DB: cutaway, small diamond inlay at frets 5 (2), 7 and 9 (2): **1998**

00-16M: soundhole rings in 5-9-5 grouping, X-bracing, tortoiseshell celluloid pickguard, 24.9" scale: **1988**

00-16CM: cutaway, X-bracing, soundhole rings in 5-9-5 grouping, tortoiseshell celluloid pickguard, 25.4" scale: **1988**

000-16: single layer of dark binding, scalloped braces, soundhole rings in 5-9-5 grouping, tortoiseshell celluloid binding on top and back, tortoiseshell celluloid pickguard, black bridge pins with white dots, black backstripe, 25.4" scale, diamonds-and-squares fingerboard inlay, chrome-plated tuners: **1989–95**

000-16M: designation for first year of 000-16: **1989**

000-16T: mahogany back and sides, scalloped braces, herringbone soundhole ring and backstripe, tortoiseshell celluloid-bound top, U-shaped mortise-and-tenon neck joint, extra-low profile neck, rosewood fingerboard, diamonds-and-squares inlay, semi-gloss finish: **1996–current**

000-16TR: rosewood back and sides, scalloped braces: **1996–current**

000-C16: cutaway, oval soundhole, 9-ply soundhole ring, small dot inlay: **1990–95**

000C-16TR: cutaway, rosewood back and sides, scalloped braces: **1996–current**

SP000-16T: scalloped braces, abalone soundhole ring, snowflake inlay on bridge and fingerboard, multi-colored backstripe, gold-plated tuners, gloss finish: **1997–current**

SP000CE-16: cutaway electric version of SP000 = 16: **1999**

SP000-16TR: rosewood back and sides, scalloped braces: **1997–current**

SP000C-16TR: cutaway, rosewood back and sides, scalloped braces, black body binding: **1997–current**

SP000C-16TREP: Fishman Prefix pickup, onboard electronics: **1997–current**

SPOM-16: 1 3/4" nut width: **1999**

D-16M: first version of D-16 (see following), mahogany back and sides, scalloped braces, satin (non-gloss) finish, tortoiseshell celluloid top binding: **1986, 1988–90**

D-16: replaces D-16M, mahogany back and sides, scalloped braces, black bridge pins, tortoiseshell

celluloid top binding, unbound back, unbound rosewood fingerboard, small dot inlay, chrome-plated Grover tuners, gloss finish
Introduced: **1989**
Black binding: **1994**
Last offered: **1995**

D-16H: mahogany back and sides, tortoiseshell celluloid top binding, satin finish, herringbone soundhole ring, herringbone backstripe, black bridge pins, chrome-plated Gotoh tuners, limited runs
Introduced: **1991**
Larger dot inlay: **1992**
Black bridge pins with white dots, abalone dot inlay: **1993**
Discontinued, replaced by **D-16T: 1996**

D-16A: ash back and sides, tortoiseshell celluloid top binding, limited runs: **1987–90**

D-16GT: D-16T (see following) with gloss top finish: **1999**

D-16K: koa back and sides, black binding, white bridge pins with black dots, gloss finish, limited run: **1986**

D-16T: mahogany back and sides, herringbone soundhole ring and backstripe, tortoiseshell celluloid-bound top, U-shaped mortise-and-tenon neck joint, extra-low profile neck, rosewood fingerboard, diamonds-and-squares inlay, semi-gloss finish: **1996–current**

D-16TR: rosewood back and sides, rosewood fingerboard, extra-low profile neck, semi-gloss finish: **1996–current**

D-16W: walnut back and sides, black binding on top and back, limited runs: **1987, 1990**

SPD-16 Maple: maple back and sides, "zipper" zigzag-pattern backstripe: **1998–current**

SPD-16 Walnut: walnut back and sides, multi-colored backstripe: **1998–current**

SPD-16T: mahogany back and sides, abalone soundhole ring, snowflake inlay on bridge and fingerboard, multi-colored backstripe, gold-plated tuners, gloss finish: **1996–current**

SPD-16TR: rosewood back and sides: **1997–current**

SPDC-16TR: cutaway, rosewood back and sides: **1997–current**

SPDC-16TREP: Fishman Prefix pickup, onboard electronics: **1997–current**

Style 17: rosewood back and sides, most with fan-braced top, 2 or 4 rosewood soundhole rings (earliest with checkered purfling in center of rings), 5-ply top binding with rosewood outer layer, unbound back, white backstripe, most with black neck and "ice cream cone" heel, brass tuner plates, ivory tuner buttons

Introduced, offered in sizes 2 1/2 and 3 (many Style 18s of the period are similar, but Style 18 was offered in size 2): **1856**

Green-and-white rope pattern in center of soundhole ring: **by 1870s**

X-braced top (most): **early 1890s**

No rope pattern in soundhole rings: **by 1897**

Discontinued: **1898**

Reintroduced, mahogany back and sides, spruce top, 3 black soundhole rings, 3-ply top binding of black line, light-colored wood line and (outer layer) rosewood, rosewood-bound back, standard neck (not painted black), unbound ebony fingerboard, small dot inlay at frets 5, 7 (2) and 9: **1906**

Rosewood bridge, rosewood fingerboard: **1909**

Discontinued: **1918**

Reintroduced, mahogany top, 3-layer top binding of black line, light wood line and (outer layer) rosewood, rosewood-bound back, thin black backstripe: **1922**

5-ply soundhole ring: **1927**

Binding variations (see individual models): **1929–30**

No binding: **by 1930**

Tortoiseshell celluloid pickguard optional: **1932**

Tortoiseshell celluloid pickguard standard: **1934**

Discontinued from catalog: **1957**

Discontinued: **1961**

Reintroduced, black pickguard: **1966–68**

Available by special order: **1982-88**

5-17: only 1800s listing: **1897**

Reintroduced, unbound ebony fingerboard: **1912**

Last made: **1916**

Reintroduced, rectangular (non-belly) bridge, rosewood fingerboard, double-dot inlays at 7th fret, thin black backstripe: **1927**

Unbound back: **1930**

Last made: **1943**

5-17T: tenor neck, no body binding, 22" scale: **1927–49**

3-17: **1856–1897**

1 made: **1909**

2 1/2-17: **1856–1897**

2-17: rectangular (non-belly) bridge throughout production, 6 made: **1910**

Reintroduced, braced for steel strings (Martin's first catalogued steel-string model), rectangular (non-belly) bridge: **1922**

"New style" 2-17, no binding (to drop list price to $25), referred to for a short time as **#25**, flat natural finish: **1929**

"Old style" 2-17 with binding last made: **1930**

Dark stain finish: **1935**

Gloss finish: **1936**

Last made: **1938**

2-17H: Hawaiian, flat fingerboard, flush frets, non-slanted saddle: **1927–31**

2-17T: tenor neck: **1927–28**

1-17: **1906–17, 1931–34**

1-17P: plectrum neck: **1928–31**

1-17P 5-string: 1 made: **1939**

0-17: **1906–17, 1929–48, 1966–68**

0-17H: Hawaiian, flat fingerboard, flush frets, non-slanted saddle: **1930–39**

0-17T: tenor neck: **1932–60**

00-17: **1908–17, 1930–60, 1982–88** (special order only)

0-55: special-ordered 00-17 by Rudick's of Akron, Ohio, all-mahogany body with Style 18 appointments, stamped 0-55 by request, 12 made: **1935**.

00-17H: Hawaiian, flat fingerboard, high nut, flush frets, non-slanted saddle: **1934–35**

00-17P: plectrum neck, 1 made: **1941**

000-17: **1911** (1 made), **1952**

Style 18: rosewood back and sides, rope-pattern colored-wood soundhole ring (some with herringbone soundhole ring), 5-ply top binding with rosewood outer layer, rosewood-bound back, unbound ebony fingerboard, brass tuner plates, ivory tuner buttons

Introduced in size 2 (similar to many Style 17s, but style 17 was offered in sizes 2 1/2 and 3): **1857**

Unbound back: **late 1890s**

Soundhole inlay of 9 alternating black-and-white rings

(white ring is actually the natural wood of the top) in between 2 single black rings, black backstripe, small dot inlay at frets 5, 7 and 9: **1902**

Mahogany back and sides: **1917**

Rosewood binding on top and back: **1918**

Shaded top optional: **by 1931**

Braced for steel strings: **1923**

5-ply top binding with black plastic outer layer, single-ply black plastic back binding, dot inlay through 15th fret, 2 inlays at 12th fret only: **early 1932**

Tortoiseshell celluloid pickguard: **1932**

Inlaid white layers in soundhole rings: **mid 1930s**

Shaded top optional: **1934**

Tortoiseshell celluloid outer binding: **1936**

Rosewood fingerboard and bridge, see individual models: **1935–47**

Small graduated-size dot inlay to 17th fret: **late 1944**

Large uniform-size dot inlay: **1946**

Large graduated-size dot inlay: **1947**

Black pickguard, black plastic outer binding: **1966**

Soundhole rings in 5-9-5 grouping: **1988**

Still in production

1/4-18: 1918–31

1/2-18: 1918-19

3/4-18: 4 made: **1921**

5-18: rectangular bridge, 12 frets clear of body, ebony fingerboard, slotted peghead

Introduced: **1898**

Rosewood fingerboard, some examples: **1935**

Rosewood fingerboard standard: **1940**

Solid peghead: **1948**

Last made: **1989**

5-18G: gut-string: 1 made in **1954**, 1 in **1956**

5-18K: koa back, sides and top, 3 made: **1921**, **1937**

5-18T: tenor neck, 1 made in each year: **1940**, **1954**, **1961**, **1962**

2 1/2-18: 1898–1923

2-18: 1857–1938

2-18G: gut-string, 1 made: **1954**

2-18T: tenor neck: **1928–30**

1-18: 1899–1927

1-18H: Hawaiian, flat fingerboard, high nut, flush frets, non-slanted saddle, 3 made: **1918**

1-18K: koa top, back and sides: **1917–19**

1-18P 5-string: 1 made: **1930**.

1-18T: tenor neck, 3 made: **1927**

0-18: rectangular (non-belly) bridge, unbound ebony fingerboard

Introduced: **1898**

Rosewood fingerboard, some examples: **1935**

Rosewood fingerboard standard: **1940**

Belly bridge: **early 1970s**

Discontinued: **1996**

0-18K: koa top, back and sides, most with Hawaiian setup: **1918–35**

0-18H: Hawaiian, flat fingerboard, high nut, flush frets, non-slanted saddle, 1 made: **1920**

0-18S: first 3 examples with 14-fret neck: **1932**

0-18T: tenor neck: **1929–95**

0-18T Carl Fisher: special order for New York dealer, 31 made: **1930**

0-18TD: specs unavailable, 1 made: **1977**

0-18TE: electric, tenor neck, single pickup, 2 made: **1959, 1962**

0-18T8: 8-string, tenor neck, 5 made: **1969–70**

Kingston Trio 0-18T: Nick Reynolds model, ebony fingerboard and bridge, sold with Kingston Trio D-28 and Vega banjo: **1997**

00-18: rectangular (non-belly) bridge, unbound ebony fingerboard

Introduced: **1898**

Belly bridge: **early 1930s**

Rosewood fingerboard, some examples: **1935**

Rosewood fingerboard standard: **1940**

Last offered: **1995**

00-18C: classical (see Classicals, following): **1962–95**

00-18E: electric: **1959–64**

00-18G: gut-string classical (see Classicals, following): **1936–62**

00-18H: Hawaiian, flat fingerboard, high nut, flush frets, non-slanted saddle: **1935–41**

00-18K: koa top, back and sides: **1918–34**

00-18S: earliest examples of R-18 archtop, 9 made: **1932**

00-18T: tenor neck, 6 made: **1931–40**

00-18V: aging toner on top, tortoiseshell celluloid outer binding, tortoiseshell celluloid pickguard, ebony fingerboard, V-neck, gold-plated tuners, 25.4" scale, Guitar of the Month, 9 made: **October 1984**

000-18: 1 made with maple back and sides: **1906**
Introduced into regular production, mahogany back and sides, 12 frets clear of body: **1911**
25.4" scale: **c. 1924**
000-size Style 18s available only as OM-18, with 25.4" scale: **1932–33**
000-18 reintroduced, 14 frets clear of body, 24.5" scale, earliest with 25.4" scale: **1934**
Rosewood fingerboard, some examples: **1935**
Rosewood fingerboard standard: **1940**
Still in production

000-18 12-string: 1 made: **1913**

000-18G: gut-string, 1 made: **1955**

000-18H: Hawaiian, flat fingerboard, high nut, flush frets, non-slanted saddle, 1 made: **1938**

000-18Q: non-adjustable truss rod (after adjustable truss rod became standard): **1986-1995**

000-18P: plectrum neck: **1930**

000-18S: 12-fret neck: **1976–77**

000-18T: tenor neck: **1930–41**

OM-18: small tortoiseshell celluloid pickguard, belly bridge, black bridge pins, black backstrip, 14-fret neck, 25.4" scale, solid peghead, no logo (a few with silkscreen logo), banjo tuners
Introduced: **1930**
Large pickguard: **early 1931**
Right-angle tuners: **1931**
Decal logo standard: **late 1931**
Black outer binding: **1932**
Last made: **late 1933**

OM-18P: plectrum neck, 15 frets clear of body: **1930–31**

OM-18T: tenor neck, 1 made: **1931**

OM-18V: vintage specs: **1999**

D-18: black bridge pins, black backstrip, 12-fret neck (first 29), unbound ebony fingerboard

Introduced: **1932**
14-fret neck: **1934**
Rosewood fingerboard: **1947**
Still in production

D-18E: 2 DeArmond pickups, ladder-braced top: **1958--59**

D-18GOM: Guitar of the Month, scalloped braces, rosewood binding, black bridge pins with pearl dots: **1989**

D-18H: Hawaiian, flat fingerboard, high nut, flush frets, non-slanted bridge, 3 made: **1934-36**

D-18H: specs unavailable, 2 made: **1966**

D-18LE: quilted or flamed mahogany back and sides, scalloped braces, tortoiseshell celluloid binding, black bridge pins with white dots, herringbone backstripe, ebony fingerboard and bridge, V-neck, gold-plated tuners with ebony buttons: **1986–87**

HD-18LE: Guitar of the Month, scalloped braces, tortoiseshell celluloid binding with herringbone top trim, black bridge pins with white dots, ebony tuner buttons: **Oct. 1987**

D-18M: specs unavailable, 1 made: **1961**

D-18MB: X brace 1" from soundhole, maple binding, white bridge pins with red dots, top signed by shop foremen, Guitar of the Month: **1990**

D-18P: P stands for low-profile neck (becomes standard version of D-18, P dropped from model name in 1989): **1987–88**

D-18Q: square non-adjustable truss rod: **1986-93**

D-18S: 12-fret neck, slotted peghead: **1967-93**

D-18T: tenor, 1 made: **1962**

D-18V: scalloped bracing, tortoiseshell celluloid binding, tortoiseshell celluloid pickguard, ebony fingerboard, V-neck: **1983–84**, then Guitar of the Month **Sept. 1985**

D-18VM: soundhole rings in 1-9-1 grouping, old-style squared peghead, V-neck, scalloped braces, X-brace 1" from soundhole, beveled-edge tortoiseshell celluloid pickguard, saddle extends to end of bridge slot, aged natural top, vintage style tuners: **1996–current**

D-18VMS: same as D-18VM except for, X-brace farther than 1" from soundhole, 12-fret neck, 1 3/4" nut width: **1996–current**

D12-18: 12-string, 14-fret neck, solid peghead: **1973-95**

HD18-JB Jimmy Buffett: scalloped braces, X-brace 1" from soundhole, grained ivoroid binding, herringbone top trim, abalone soundhole ring, herringbone backstripe, ebony fingerboard, snowflake inlay, Jimmy Buffett signature at 18th fret, palm tree peghead inlay of paua and abalone, gold foil logo, label signed by Jimmy Buffett and C.F. Martin IV, numbered run of 424 (corresponding with address of Margaritaville Cafe at 424 Fleming St., Key West)
Available: **summer 1998**

Vintage D-18: scalloped braces, tortoiseshell celluloid binding, low-profile neck, tortoiseshell celluloid pickguard, Guitar of the Month: **1992**

M-18: 1984–88

J-18: black bridge pins with white dots, tortoiseshell celluloid pickguard, enclosed chrome-plated tuners with ebony buttons, satin non-gloss finish, aging toner on top, 1987–89 examples labeled J-18M: **1987–current**

J-18M: original model name of J-18: **1987–89**

Style 19: mahogany back and sides, spruce top, rosewood bridge, soundhole rings in 5-9-5 grouping, 5-ply top binding with black outer layer, 3-ply back binding, rosewood fingerboard, dot inlay, dark-stained top finish: **1976–88**

D-19: 2 prototypes made: **1976**
Introduced: **1977**
Mahogany top optional: **1980**
Last listed: **April 1988**

Style 20: rosewood back and sides, herringbone soundhole ring of red, white and green wood, 5-ply top binding and 3-ply back with rosewood outer layer, herringbone backstripe of red, white and green wood, obscure style (little distinction between Style 20 and early Style 21 except for size)
Offered in size 2: **1850s–1897**

N-20: classical (see Classicals section, following)

N-20B: classical (see Classicals section, following)
D12-20: 12-string, mahogany back and sides, tortoiseshell celluloid binding, Style 28 checkered backstripe, 12 frets clear of body, black bridge pins with white dots, slotted peghead
Introduced: **1964**
Black binding and pickguard: **1967**
Last made: **1991**

SD6-20: six-string version of D12-20, 12-frets clear of body, 1 made: **1969**

Style 21: Brazilian rosewood back and sides, rosewood outer binding with 2 additional rosewood lines around top and back, colored-wood herringbone-pattern soundhole ring with 2 rosewood lines on either side, 5-ply top binding with rosewood outer layer, colored-wood herringbone backstripe, diamond-pattern figures on endpiece, unbound ebony fingerboard, engraved tuner plates, ivory buttons (little distinction between Style 20 and early Style 21 except for size)
Offered in size 1: **1860s**
Herringbone backstripe: **by late 1860s**
Double-rosewood soundhole rings replaced by groups of 5 rings: **1869**
Black-and-white herringbone inlay, herringbone soundhole ring between 2 groups of 5 rings, 5-ply top binding with rosewood outer layer, 2-ply back binding with rosewood outer layer, ebony endpiece: **by 1890s**
Slotted-diamond inlay at frets 5, 7 (2) and 9: **1901**
Inlays at frets 5, 7 (2), 9, 12 (2) and 15: **early 1932**
Black plastic binding: **mid 1932**
Tortoiseshell celluloid pickguard standard: **1932**
Tortoiseshell celluloid binding: **1936**
Rosewood fingerboard, see individual models: **1941–47**
Rosewood fingerboard, 00 and 000 size: **1947**
Small graduated-size dot inlay to 17th fret: **late 1944**
Large uniform-size dot inlay: **1946**
Large graduated-size dot inlay: **1947**
No herringbone soundhole ring, 1-9-1 ring grouping, rosewood fingerboard: **1947**
No herringbone backstripe: **early 1948**
Black pickguard, black outer binding: **1966**
Indian rosewood back and sides: **1970**
Soundhole rings in 5-9-5 grouping, tortoiseshell celluloid pickguard, tortoiseshell celluloid outer binding on top and back, no backstripe: **1992**
Still in production

1/2-21: 1 made: **1919**

3/4-21: 1 made: **1921**

5-21: standard Style 21 specs: **1902–27**; rosewood back and sides with Style 18 ornamentation, 1 made: **1977**

5-21T: tenor neck: **1927–28**

2 1/2-21: **1910–21**

2-21: mid 1880s–1929

2-21T: tenor neck, 1 made: **1928**

1-21: **1860s–1926**

1-21P: plectrum neck, 1 made: **1931**

0-21: 12-fret neck throughout production except for 3 with 14-fret neck in 1930
Introduced: **by 1890s**
Rosewood fingerboard: **1941**
Last made: **1948**

0-21H: Hawaiian, flat fingerboard, flush frets, non-slanted saddle, 1 made: **1918**

0-21K: koa top, back and sides: **1919–29**

0-21P: plectrum neck, 1 made: **1929**

0-21T: tenor neck, 5 made: **1929–35**

00-21: 12-fret neck throughout production, ebony fingerboard
Introduced: **1898**
Rosewood fingerboard: **1947**
Solid peghead: **1990**
Discontinued: **1996**

00-21B: Brazilian rosewood back and sides, 1 made: **1985**

00-21G: gut string, examples with X-bracing and fan-pattern, with pin bridge and with loop bridge, 3 made: **1937–38**

00-21GE Golden Era: pre-World War II specs, 12 frets clear of body, slotted-diamond inlay, slotted peghead, metal tuner buttons, limited run: **1998**

00-21H: Hawaiian, flat fingerboard, high nut, flush frets, non-slanted saddle, 3 made: **1914, 1952, 1955**

00-21LE: aging toner on top, scalloped braces, herringbone soundhole ring, tortoiseshell celluloid binding, tortoiseshell celluloid pickguard, black bridge pins with white dots, ebony fingerboard,

14-fret neck without diamond on back of peghead, slotted peghead, chrome 3-on-a-plate tuners, Guitar of the Month, 19 made: **Sept. 1987**

00-21NY: no pickguard, wide fingerboard, no fingerboard inlay: **1961–65**

00-21T: tenor neck, 2 made: **1934**

000-21: 12-fret neck
Introduced: **1902**
None made: **1932–33**
Reintroduced, 14-fret neck: **1934**
Rosewood fingerboard: **1947**
Discontinued: **1955**
1 made: **1965**
12 made: **1979**

000-21S: 12-fret neck, 1 made: **1977**

000-21 10-string: 2 made: **1902**

000-21 12-string: 1 made: **1921**

000-21 harp guitar: extra sub-bass strings, 4 made: **1902–09**

OM-21: black bridge pins with white dots, 1 3/4" nut width, chrome-plated tuners: **1992–current**

OM-21 Special: herringbone soundhole ring, striped rosewood bridge, tortoiseshell celluloid pickguard, ebonized rosewood fingerboard, slotted-diamond fingerboard inlay, black and white peghead binding with tortoiseshell celluloid outer layer, gold-plated tuners with pearl buttons, aging toner on top, Guitar of the Month: **1991**

D-21: **1955–69**

D-21LE: Indian rosewood back and sides, herringbone soundhole ring, tortoiseshell celluloid binding, tortoiseshell celluloid pickguard, V-neck, Guitar of the Month: **Nov. 1985**

D-21V: Brazilian rosewood back and sides, tortoiseshell celluloid binding, tortoiseshell celluloid pickguard, V-neck, ebony fingerboard, production: **1984**

D-21 Special Edition: Indian rosewood back and sides, black pickguard, bound fingerboard: **1985**

M-21 Custom: scalloped braces, soundhole rings in 5-9-5 grouping, 5-ply top binding and 1-ply back binding with tortoiseshell celluloid outer layer, tortoiseshell celluloid pickguard, black bridge pins

MARTIN

with white dots, low-profile neck, unbound rosewood fingerboard, slotted-diamond inlay, aging toner on top, Guitar of the Month: **Dec. 1984**

J-21: continuation of J-21M (see following): **1990–95**

J-21M: original name of J-21, tortoiseshell celluloid pickguard, black outer layer of binding, black bridge pins with white dots, chainlink backstripe: **1985–89**

J-21MC: cutaway, 9-ply soundhole ring, chrome-plated tuners with ebony buttons, Guitar of the Month: **1986**

Style 22: herringbone soundhole ring between 2 groups of 5 rings, 4-ply top binding with ivory outer layer (possibly with colored-wood purfling), ivory-bound back, very obscure style, no documented difference between Style 22 and Style 23
Available: **1850s**

Style 23: herringbone soundhole ring between 2 groups of 5 rings, 4-ply top binding with ivory outer layer (possibly with colored-wood purfling), ivory-bound back, very obscure style, no documented difference between Style 22 and Style 23
Available: **1850s**

Style 24: soundhole ring of green and white wood in Z-pattern (line of long diagonals between 2 short diagonal lines) between two groups of 5 rings, rosewood top binding, top purfling of green and brown wood in diagonal pattern (some with additional checkered-pattern lines), thin line of side binding, 2-ply back binding with rosewood outer layer, backstripe of red, green, brown and white wood in long arrow-pattern, engraved brass tuner plates, ivory tuner buttons, diamond-pattern figures on endpiece
Obscure style, offered in size 2: **1850s–1880s**

Style 25: stained spruce or koa top, koa back and sides, 2-piece back, rosewood bridge, soundhole rings in 5-9-5 grouping, tortoiseshell celluloid pickguard, black bridge pins with white dot, 5-ply top binding with black outer layer, black back binding, chainlink backstripe, rosewood fingerboard, dot inlay, chrome-plated tuners, available: **1980–89**

00-25K: spruce top, aging toner on top: **1980, 1985, 1988**

00-25K2: koa top, black pickguard: **1980–89**

D-25K: spruce top: **1980-89**

D-25K2: koa top, black pickguard: **1980–89**

#25: see Style 17, model 2-17, preceding

Style 26: rosewood back and sides, soundhole rings in 5-9-5 grouping, ivory-bound top, black-and-white rope-pattern top purfling, 1- or 3-ply back binding with ivory outer layer, "zipper" zigzag-pattern backstripe, obscure style
Offered in size 1: **c. 1850s–1880s**

Style 27: rosewood back and sides, soundhole rings of 4 groups of 5 rings with pearl ring in center, ivory-bound top, top purfling of green and brown wood in long diagonal pattern, 3-ply back binding with ivory outer layer, "zipper" zigzag-pattern backstripe, ivory-bound ebony fingerboard, brass tuner plates
Offered in size 2: **1857–1907**

2-27: 1857–1907

1-27: 1880s–1907

0-27: similar to Style 28, no abalone soundhole ring, unbound fingerboard: **1850s**

Style 28: Brazilian rosewood back and sides, soundhole inlay of black and white rings in groups of 5-9-5, ivory-bound top, 3-ply back binding with ivory outer layer, herringbone purfling around top edges, Style 45 backstripe of horizontal lines between 2 rows of diagonal lines, unbound ebony fingerboard
Introduced: **1870s**
Slotted-diamond inlay at frets 5 (2), 7 and 9 (2): **1901**
Ivoroid binding: **1919**
Braced for steel strings: **1925**
Shaded top optional: **by 1931**
Inlay at frets 5, 7 (2), 9, 12 (2) and 15: **early 1932**
Tortoiseshell celluloid pickguard standard: **1932**
Small graduated-size dot inlay to 17th fret: **late 1944**
Large uniform-size dot inlay: **1946**
Large graduated-size dot inlay: **1947**
No herringbone trim, 6-ply top binding with white outer layer, 3-ply back binding with white outer layer: **early 1947**
Narrow chainlink backstripe: **early 1947**
Wider chainlink backstripe: **1948**
Grover Rotomatic tuners: **1958**

Black pickguard (some with tortoiseshell celluloid pickguard to mid-year), non-grained white outer binding: **1966**

Indian rosewood, D-size: **late 1969**

Indian rosewood, all other sizes: **early 1970**

Still in production

1/4-28: 14 made: **1972**, **1981**

7-28: Baby D-28, 7/8 dreadnought size: **1980–95, 1997–current**

5-28: 1901–39 (slotted peghead), **1968–81** (solid peghead), 1 made in **1988**

5-28G: gut string, 1 made: **1939**

5-28T: tenor neck, 1 made: **1939**

2 1/2-28: 18 made: **1909–23**

2-28T: tenor neck, 35 made: **1929–30**

1-28: 1880s–1923

1-28P: plectrum neck, 19 made: **1928–30**

0-28: 1870s–1931, 6 in **1937**, 1 in **1969**

0-28E: electric, 1 made: **1963**

0-28H: Hawaiian, flat fingerboard, high nut, flush frets, non-slanted saddle, 2 made: **1928**

0-28K: koa top, back and sides, most with Hawaiian setup: **1917–31**, 1 in **1935**

0-28NY: no pickguard, no inlay, 12-fret neck, slotted peghead, 2 made: **1968–69**

0-28P: plectrum neck, 1 made: **1930**

0-28T: tenor neck: **1930–31**, 1 each in **1941**, **1961**, **1964**

00-28: mid 1880s–1941, 1 in **1958**, 1 in **1977**, 2 in **1984**

00-28C: classical (see Classicals section, following): **1966–95**

00-28G: gut string classical (see Classicals section, following): **1936–62**

00-28K: koa back and sides, Hawaiian setup, flat fingerboard, high nut, flush frets, non-slanted saddle: **1919–33**

00-28T: tenor neck, 2 made: **1931**, **1940**

000-28: 1902–current

Production: 1902–32 (12-fret): 349; 1931–46 (14-fret, herringbone): 1,193; 1947–93 (non-herringbone): 4,458.

000-28 10-string: 1 made: **1902**

000-28 12-fret Golden Era: Indian rosewood back and sides, Sitka spruce top, ebony pyramid bridge, herringbone top border, ivoroid binding, ebony fingerboard, 19 frets, abalone diamonds-and-squares inlay, Waverly-Sloane tuners, aging toner on top: **1996**

000-28 12-string: 1 made: **1936**

000-28-45: 000-28 body, Style 45 neck, 2 made: **1938–39**

000-28B: Brazilian rosewood, 6 made: **1985**

000-28C: classical, fan bracing: **1962–69**

000-28E: electric, 1 made: **1970**

000-28EC Eric Clapton: also see 000-42EC, Indian rosewood back and sides, tortoiseshell celluloid pickguard, herringbone soundhole ring, herringbone top border, top and back bound with grained ivoroid, 24.9" scale, ebony fingerboard, diamonds-and-squares inlay (originally specified for prewar style abalone snowflake inlay), nickel-plated openback tuners with "butterbean" buttons, vintage style squared headstock, decal logo, Geib style case: **1996–current**

000-28F: folk guitar, ivoroid binding, 24.9" or 25.4" scale, 12-fret neck, rounded ebony fingerboard, 19 frets, slotted peghead, 10 made: **1964–67**

000-28G: gut-string classical (see Classicals, following), 17 made: **1937–55**

000-28H: Hawaiian, flat fingerboard, high nut, flush frets, non-slanted saddle, 1 made: **1949**

000-28 harp guitar: extra sub-bass strings, 1 made: **1906**

000-28HX: specs unavailable, 2 made: **1965**

000-28K: koa top, back and sides, 1 made: **1921**

000-28NY: wide fingerboard, 12-fret neck, slotted peghead, 2 made: **1962**

000-28P: plectrum neck, 3 made: **1930**

000-28Q: non-adjustable truss rod (after adjustable truss rod became standard): **1986–95**

000-28S: 12-fret neck, 20 frets, slotted peghead: **1974–77**

000-28T: tenor neck, 1 made: **1929**

000-28V: Brazilian rosewood, scalloped braces, white bridge pins with red dots, tortoiseshell celluloid pickguard, ivoroid binding, herringbone trim, "zipper" zigzag-pattern backstripe, V-neck, chrome-plated tuners, aging toner on top, 17 made: **1983–84**

000-28VS: vintage specs, 12-fret neck: **1999**

OM-28: 14 frets clear of body, pyramid bridge, no pickguard, 25.4" scale, inlays at frets 5, 7 and 9, banjo tuning pegs, no decal, solid peghead
Introduced: **1929**
Small pickguard: **late 1929**
Belly bridge: **very early 1930**
First appearance of silkscreen logo: **1930**
Large pickguard: **early 1931**
Right-angle tuners: **1931**
Inlay at frets 5, 7, 9, 12 and 15, decal logo standard: **late 1931**
Last original series OM-28: **late 1933**
Reintroduced, 1 3/4" nut width: **1990**
Last offered: **1996**

OM-28T: tenor neck, 1 made: **1930**

OM-28P: plectrum neck, 5 made: **1931–32**

OM-28 Perry Bechtel: tortoiseshell celluloid pickguard, ivoroid binding, V-neck, aging toner on top, signed by Mrs. Perry Bechtel, Guitar of the Month: **1993**

OM-28LE: tortoiseshell celluloid pickguard, ivoroid binding, V-neck, aging toner on top, Guitar of the Month: **Oct. 1985**

OM-28V: Brazilian rosewood, tortoiseshell celluloid pickguard, ivoroid binding, V-neck, 1 made: **1984**

OMC-28: cutaway, X brace within 1" of soundhole, tortoiseshell celluloid pickguard, white bridge pins with red dots, low-profile neck, gold-plated tuners with small pearl buttons, Guitar of the Month: **1990**

OM-28VR: vintage reissue, scalloped braces, X-brace 1" from soundhole, old style long saddle slot, tortoiseshell celluloid pickguard, modified V-neck, 1 3/4" nut width, vintage style squared peghead, vintage style tuner buttons, aged natural top finish: **1996–current**

SOM 28: 000-28 with 25.4" scale, 6 made: **1969**

D-28: white bridge pins with black dots, 12-fret neck (first 41 examples), 14-fret neck from 1934 onward: **1931–current**

D-28 1935 Special: 1935 features, scalloped braces, V-neck, square tapered peghead, Guitar of the Month: **1993**

D-28 Cocobola: cocobola back and sides, 2 made: **1987**

D-28 Custom: scalloped braces, ebony fingerboard, snowflake inlay, torch peghead inlay, stamped logo on back of peghead, Guitar of the Month: **Nov. 1984**

D-28E: electric, 2 DeArmond pickups, ladder-braced top: **1959–64**

D-28G: gut string, 2 made: **1937**, **1961**

D-28H: Hawaiian, flat fingerboard, high nut, flush frets, non-angled saddle, 2 made: **1934**, **1936**

D-28HW Hank Williams Sr.: 1944 specs, Brazilian rosewood back and sides, soundhole inlay rings of wood, X-brace 1" from soundhole, "zipper" zigzag-pattern backstripe, diamonds-and-squares inlay, numbered run of 150, label signed by C.F. Martin IV: **1998**

D-28LF Lester Flatt: modeled after Flatt's 1950 D-28 modified by Mike Longworth in 1955, oversized pickguard, custom notched-diamond inlay, *L-5* at 17th fret: **1999**

D-28LSH: large soundhole, 2 pearl soundhole rings, ivoroid binding, herringbone top purfling, snowflake inlays on bridge ends, "zipper" zigzag-pattern backstripe, snowflake fingerboard inlay, gold-plated tuners with ebony buttons inlaid with snowflakes, Guitar of the Month: **1991**

D-28P: low-profile neck (standard on D-28 beginning in 1990): **1988–89**

D-28Q: non-adjustable square bar in neck (after adjustable truss rod became standard): **1986–93**

D-28S: 12-fret neck: **1954–93**

D-28SW: 12-fret neck, made for Wurlitzer, 30 made: **1962–68**

D-28T: tenor, 1 made: **1964**

D-28V: Brazilian rosewood, scalloped braces, X-brace *not* within 1" of soundhole, ivoroid binding, herringbone top purfling, tortoiseshell celluloid pickguard, white-black-white backstripe, slotted-diamond inlay: **1983–85**

D12-28: 12-string, 14-fret neck, 1 7/8" nut width: **1970–current**

DC-28: cutaway, oval hole, scalloped braces, 9-ply soundhole ring: **1981–current**

DC-28P: cutaway, low-profile neck, P designation dropped, 1 made: **1988**

CHD-28: cedar top, scalloped braces, herringbone trim, "zipper" zigzag-pattern backstripe: **1991–95**

Custom 08: see listing as Style 08 dreadnought

Custom 15: see listing as Style 15 dreadnought

HD-28: scalloped braces, herringbone top purfling, black pickguard, "zipper" zigzag-pattern backstripe: **1976–current**

HD-282R: large soundhole with double herringbone ring, "zipper" zigzag-pattern backstripe: **1994**

HD-28LSV: Large Soundhole Vintage, modeled after Clarence White's 1935 D-28 with soundhole enlarged to the first soundhole ring, 4 5/16" wide, herringbone trim, longer fingerboard bound in white, no inlay: **1997–current**

HD-28BLE: herringbone soundhole ring, tortoiseshell celluloid pickguard, white bridge pins with red dots, low-profile neck, chrome-plated tuners: 1 prototype for HD-28BSE without signatures made: **Dec. 1987**; 100 made for Guitar of the Month series: **1990**

HD-28BSE: signature edition (underneath top signed by C.F. Martin III, C.F. Martin IV and foremen), Brazilian rosewood back and sides, ivoroid binding, tortoiseshell celluloid pickguard, V-neck, slotted-diamond inlay, ebony tuner buttons, aging toner on top: **Dec. 1987**

HD-28C LSH: cutaway, scalloped braces, large soundhole, herringbone top purfling, tortoiseshell celluloid pickguard, white bridge pins with red dots, rosewood peghead overlay, sunburst top, built-in pickup, Guitar of the Month: **1993**

HD-28 Cocobola: cocobola back and sides, herringbone trim, 2 made: **1987**

HD-28 CTB: tortoiseshell celluloid binding, tortoiseshell celluloid pickguard, white bridge pins with red dots, herringbone backstripe, slotted diamonds at frets 3, 5, 7 and 9, *CFM* script inlay at 12th fret, slotted peghead, torch-pattern peghead inlay, brand stamp on back of peghead, gold-plated tuners with embossed *M* on buttons, Guitar of the Month: **1992**

HD-28GM: Grand Marquis model, scalloped braces, tortoiseshell celluloid binding, herringbone top purfling, herringbone soundhole ring and backstripe, tortoiseshell celluloid pickguard, black bridge pins with pearl dots, snowflakes inlaid on bridge, vertical pearl *CF Martin* peghead logo, *Grand Marquis* decal on back of peghead, gold-plated tuners, Guitar of the Month: **1989**

HD-28GM LSH: Grand Marquis model, large soundhole, double-herringbone soundhole ring, snowflake inlay, *Grand Marquis* inlay at 12th fret, pearl peghead logo: **1994**

HD-28LE: scalloped braces, X-brace 1" from soundhole, herringbone top purfling, tortoiseshell celluloid pickguard under the finish, white bridge pins with red dots, V-neck, diamonds-and-squares inlay, square peghead, aging toner on top, Guitar of the Month: **Dec. 1985**

HD-28M: mahogany back and sides, scalloped braces, aging toner on top, herringbone top purfling, tortoiseshell celluloid pickguard, white bridge pins with tortoiseshell celluloid dots, gold-plated tuners with pearl buttons, Guitar of the Month: **1988**

HD-28MP: Morado (Bolivian rosewood) back and sides, scalloped braces, herringbone top purfling, white bridge pins with black dots, "zipper" zigzag-pattern backstripe: **1990**

HD-28N: standard neck (not low-profile), scalloped braces, herringbone top purfling, white bridge pins with black dots, black pickguard, "zipper" zigzag-pattern backstripe: **1989–95**

HD-28P: scalloped braces, herringbone top purfling, black pickguard, white bridge pins with black dots, "zipper" zigzag-pattern backstripe, low-profile neck (standard on HD-28 beginning in 1987, P designation dropped in 1989): **1987–89**

HD-28PSE: signature edition, scalloped braces, aging toner on top, tortoiseshell celluloid binding, herringbone top purfling, tortoiseshell celluloid pickguard, white bridge pins with tortoiseshell celluloid dots, low-profile neck, tapered peghead, ebony tuner buttons, Guitar of the Month: **1988**

HD-28R: large soundhole, 2 herringbone soundhole rings: **1990**

HD-28SE: signature edition (underneath top signed by Martins and foremen), ivoroid binding, herringbone top purfling, tortoiseshell celluloid pickguard, diamonds-and-squares inlay, V-neck, ebony tuner buttons, Guitar of the Month: **Sept. 1986**

HD-28V: Brazilian rosewood back and sides, scalloped braces, X-brace 1" from soundhole, tortoiseshell celluloid pickguard, ivoroid binding, herringbone top purfling, 1 made: **1984**

HD-28VR: herringbone reissue, scalloped braces, X-brace 1" from soundhole, tortoiseshell celluloid pickguard, ivoroid binding, modified V-neck, vintage style squared peghead, open-back tuners, "butterbean" buttons, Geib style case: **1996–current**

HD-28VS: herringbone reissue, scalloped braces, X-brace 1" from soundhole, tortoiseshell celluloid pickguard, modified V-neck, 12-fret neck, 1 3/4" nut width, vintage style squared peghead, Geib style case: **1996–current**

Kingston Trio D-28: Bob Shane model, Indian rosewood back and sides, *The Kingston Trio/1957-1997* pearl fingerboard inlay, Brazilian rosewood peghead veneer, sold with Kingston Trio 0-18T and Vega banjo: **1997**

LHD-28: larch top (looks similar to spruce), scalloped braces, herringbone top purfling: **1991–92**

MC-28: cutaway, scalloped braces, oval soundhole: **1981–current**

MC-28N: cutaway, standard neck (not low-profile): **1989–95**

M2C-28: double cutaway, optional pickguard, white bridge pins with pearl dots, gold-plated self-locking tuners, Guitar of the Month: **1988**

0000-28H: scalloped braces, herringbone trim, same appointments as HD-28: **1997–current**

0000-28H AG Arlo Guthrie: 3-piece abalone soundhole ring, "zipper" zigzag-pattern backstripe, unbound ebony fingerboard, circles-and-arrows inlay, *Alice's Restaurant 30th* inlaid at frets 12, 13 and 14, gold foil logo, pearl peghead inlay engraved with depiction of Alice's Restaurant, label signed by Guthrie and

C.F. Martin IV, limited to 30: announced: **1997**; available: **1998**

000012-28H AG Arlo Guthrie: 12-string, limited to 30: announced: **1997**; available: **1998**

HJ-28: herringbone top purfling, ivoroid binding, tortoiseshell celluloid pickguard, white bridge pins with red dots, chrome-plated tuners with embossed *M* on buttons, aging toner on top

Available as Guitar of the Month: **1992**

Regular production model, scalloped bracing, HD-28 appointments, herringbone purfling: **1996**

Still in production

HJ-28M: herringbone top purfling, white bridge pins with tortoiseshell celluloid dots, Guitar of the Month: **1994**

Style 30: similar to Style 27, rosewood back and sides, ebony bridge, soundhole rings of 4 groups of 5 rings with pearl ring in center, ivory-bound top and back, herringbone top purfling, ivory-bound ebony fingerboard, no inlay, ivory-bound peghead, German silver tuner plates, some with pearl tuner buttons

Introduced: **by 1854**

Slotted-diamond inlay at frets 5 and 9, Maltese cross inlay at fret 7: **by 1898**

Ivoroid binding: **1918**

Discontinued: **1921**

5-30: 3 made: **1900–02**

2 1/2-30: **1850s–1914**

2-30: **1850s–1921**

1-30: **1890s–1919**

0-30: **1890s–1921**

00-30: **1890s–1921**

000-30: 1 made: **1919**

Style 33: obscure style, possibly early 00-version of Style 30 (first recorded 00 is a 00-33)

Available: **1877**

Style 34: pearl soundhole ring, top purfling of red, green and white herringbone (similar to Style 30), ivory-bound top, ivory bridge, 3-ply back binding

with ivory outer layer, backstripe of horizontal lines between 2 rows of diagonal lines (Style 45), ivory-bound fingerboard, ivory-bound peghead, German silver tuners, pearl tuner buttons.
Introduced: **early 1850s**
Multi-colored wood top border in diagonal pattern: **late 1800s**
Slotted-diamond inlay at frets 5 and 9, Maltese cross inlay at fret 7: **by 1898**
Last made: **1907**

5-34: 1 made: **1899**

3 1/2-34: 1857

2 1/2-34: 1850s–60s

2-34: 1850s–1898

1-34: 1880s–1904

0-34: 1870s–1899, 1 in **1907**

00-34: 6 made: **1898–99**

Style 35: Brazilian rosewood back and sides, 3-piece back, ebony bridge, soundhole rings in 5-9-5 grouping, 6-ply top binding and 3-ply back with white outer layer, 2 black lines on side binding, tortoiseshell celluloid pickguard, white bridge pins with black dots, white-black-white backstripes, bound ebony fingerboard, mitered corners on fingerboard binding, dot inlay, unbound peghead

Introduced: **April 1965**
Black pickguard: **1966**
1-piece fingerboard binding: **1968**
Transition to Indian rosewood, various combinations of Indian and Brazilian: **late 1969–70**
Indian rosewood replaces Brazilian: **1970**
Still in production

5-35: 1 made: **1971**

0012-35: 1 made: **1973**

HOM-35: Brazilian rosewood back and sides, white bridge pins with red dots, tortoiseshell celluloid pickguard, herringbone trim, ivoroid binding on top and back, 14-fret neck, 25.4" scale, ivoroid-bound fingerboard, gold-plated tuners, aging toner on top, Guitar of the Month: **1989**

D-35: bound ebony fingerboard, gloss finish: **1965–current**

D-35A: first version of D-35 (after X-35 prototype), D-size top braces, 000-size back braces, 6 made: **1965**

D-35B: second version of D-35 (after X-35 prototype), 00-size top braces, D-size back braces, 2 made: **1965**

D-35C: third (final) version of D-35 (after X-35 prototype), 00-size top braces, 000-size back braces, 2 made: **1965**

D12-35: 12-string, 12-fret neck, slotted peghead: **1965–95**

D-35P: low-profile neck, standard on D-35 beginning in 1987 (labeled until 1990): **1986–90**

D-35Q: non-adjustable truss rod (after adjustable truss rod became standard): **1986–93**

D-35S: 12-fret neck, slotted peghead: **1966–93**

D-35SW: 12-fret neck, slotted peghead, made for Wurlitzer, 3 made: **1966–68**

D-35V: Brazilian rosewood, tortoiseshell celluloid pickguard under the finish, mitered fingerboard binding, aging toner on top: **1984**

HD-35: scalloped braces, herringbone top trim, "zipper" zigzag-pattern backstripes: **1978–current**

HD-35P: low-profile neck (standard on HD-35 beginning in 1987, P dropped in 1989): **1987–89**

CHD-35: HD-35 with cedar top, scalloped braces, herringbone top purfling, "zipper" zigzag-pattern backstripes, locking tuners: **1992–95**

LHD-35: larch top (similar to spruce), scalloped braces, herringbone top purfling: **1992**

SD8-35: 8-string: **1969**

SD-35S9: 9-string, D12-35 body, made for Fats Johnson of the New Christy Minstrels, 1 made: **1968**

M-35: first version of M-36 (same specs), scalloped braces, low-profile neck, 26 made: **1978**

Style 36: M-size body, same as Style 35 except for rosewood bridge, Indian rosewood back and sides, 3-piece back, scalloped braces, soundhole rings in 5-9-5 grouping, 6-ply top binding and 3-ply back with white outer layer, tortoiseshell celluloid pick-

guard, rosewood bridge, white bridge pins with black dots, white-black-white backstripes, bound ebony fingerboard, dot inlay, aging toner on top: **1978–current**

M-36: first 26 stamped M-35: **1978-current**

M-36N: standard neck (not low-profile): **1988–95**

Style 37: stained spruce or koa top, flame-grained koa back and sides, ebony bridge, white pins with black dots, pearl soundhole ring, 6-ply top binding and 3-ply back binding with white outer layer, tortoiseshell celluloid pickguard, unbound ebony fingerboard, diamond-and-wedges inlay at frets 5 and 9, Maltese cross-type inlay at 7th fret: **1980–88**

7-37K: spruce top: **1980–87**

D-37K: spruce top: **1980-95**

D-37K2: koa top, black pickguard: **1980-95**

HD-37K2: herringbone top purfling, 1 made: **1982**

MC-37K: cutaway, spruce top, scalloped braces, oval soundhole: **1981–82**, **1988–93**

Style 38: rosewood back and sides, scalloped braces, rosewood bridge, abalone soundhole ring, tortoiseshell celluloid pickguard, 7-ply top binding and 3-ply back binding with white outer layer, tortoiseshell celluloid pickguard, white bridge pins with pearl dots, backstripe of horizontal lines between 2 rows of diagonal lines (Style 45), low-profile neck, ebony fingerboard with white-black-white binding, dot inlay, triple-bound peghead, decal logo, diamond volute on back of peghead, gold-plated tuners, stained top: **1977–current**

M-38: replaced by 0000-38: **1977–96**

M-38N: standard neck (not low-profile): **1989–95**

0000-38: formerly M-38: **1997–current**

Style 40: abalone inlay around top edge and soundhole but not on top around fingerboard, ivory bridge, ivory-bound fingerboard, backstripe of horizontal lines between 2 rows of diagonal lines (Style 45), German silver tuners, pearl tuner buttons
Introduced: **1860s**
Ivoroid-bound top and back, snowflake inlay at 5 frets

beginning at fret 5, unbound fingerboard and peghead: **1909–17**
Reintroduced, ebony bridge, backstripe of horizontal lines between 2 rows of diagonal lines (Style 45), ebony fingerboard, inlay at 5 frets: **1928**
Last listed: **1941**
Model number reintroduced, Indian rosewood back and sides, soundhole rings in 5-9-5 grouping, 8-ply top binding and 4-ply back with white outer layer, black pickguard, white bridge pins with pearl dots, chainlink backstripe, triple-bound ebony fingerboard, small hexagonal inlays, unbound peghead, gold-plated tuners: **1985**
Abalone soundhole ring, tortoiseshell celluloid pickguard, bound peghead, vertical *CF Martin* pearl peghead logo, gold-plated tuners: **1996**
Still in production

2-40: 1860s–98, 1 in **1909**

0-40: 1860s–98, 6 made **1912–13**

00-40: 1 made: **1913**; 4 made with koa top, back and sides (sold as model 00-40): **1917–18**; 15 made with koa top back and sides (sold as model 00-40): **1930**

00-40H: Hawaiian, flat fingerboard, high nut, flush frets, non-slanted saddle: **1928–39**

00-40 CFM/Stauffer: Indian rosewood back and sides, abalone top border, abalone soundhole ring, ivoroid-bound top and back, 12-fret neck, ebonized black neck finish, "ice cream cone" neck heel, unbound ebony fingerboard, snowflake inlay, unbound Stauffer-style scrolled peghead, pearl peghead logo, limited run of 75: **1997**

000-40: 1 made: **1909**

000-40H: Hawaiian, flat fingerboard, high nut, flush frets, non-slanted saddle, 1 made: **1933**

OM-40LE: herringbone and abalone top border, abalone soundhole ring, unbound ebony fingerboard, snowflake inlay, pearl peghead logo, gold-plated tuners with large ebony buttons and 4-point snowflake inlays: **1994**

D-40: scalloped braces: **1997–current**

D-40BLE: Brazilian rosewood back and sides, X-brace 1" from soundhole, white top binding, abalone pearl top border and soundhole ring, 3-ply back binding with white outer layer, 1 black line on side binding, tortoiseshell celluloid pickguard, 2 6-point snowflakes inlaid in bridge, white bridge pins with pearl dots, white-bound ebony fingerboard, snowflake inlay beginning at fret 1, white-bound peghead with pearl borders, engraved gold-plated tuners, label signed by C.F. Martin IV and Mike Longworth, Guitar of the Month: **1990**

D-40DM Don McLean: Engelmann spruce top, abalone soundhole ring, scalloped braces, X-brace 1" from soundhole, tortoiseshell celluloid pickguard with beveled edges, hexagon inlay engraved and tinted with images from "American Pie," pearl logo, modified torch peghead inlay, gold-plated tuners, pearloid tuner buttons, aging toner on top, limited run of 71: **1999**

HD-40MS Marty Stuart: Indian rosewood back and sides, scalloped bracing, X-brace 1" from soundhole, herringbone pattern soundhole ring of abalone and mother-of-pearl, top and back bound in grained ivoroid, herringbone backstripe, neck shape with extra low profile at 1st fret (modeled after D-45 currently owned by Stewart and previously owned by Hank Williams Jr. and Johnny Cash), ivoroid-bound fingerboard, fingerboard inlays of steer horns, horseshoes, dice, hearts and flowers, Marty Stuart signature inlaid at last fret, ivoroid-bound peghead, Martin logo in gold foil, gold-plated vintage style tuners with "butterbean" buttons, label signed by Stuart and C.F. Martin IV, vintage style case, limited run of 250: **1996**

J-40: continuation of J-40M: **1990–current**

J-40M: original name for J-40, scalloped braces: **1985–89**

J-40MBK: black pickguard, black finish, gold-plated tuners with large buttons: **1988–89**

J-40BK: black pickguard, black finish, gold-plated tuners with large buttons: **1990–current**

J-40MBLE: Brazilian rosewood back and sides, aging toner on top, tortoiseshell celluloid pickguard, gold-plated tuners with large pearl buttons, Guitar of the Month: **Nov. 1987**

J-40MC: original name for JC-40, cutaway, oval hole, 9-ply soundhole ring: **1987–89**

J12-40M: original name for J12-40, 12-string, non-scalloped braces, 14-fret neck, 1 13/16" nut width, solid peghead, ebony tuner buttons: **1985–89**

J12-40: 12-string, non-scalloped braces, 14-fret neck, solid peghead, ebony tuner buttons: **1990–current**

JC-40: cutaway, oval hole, 9-ply soundhole ring: **1990–current**

Style 41: rosewood back and sides, black pickguard, abalone inlay around top edge and soundhole (not on top around fingerboard), bound top and back with white outer layer, backstripe of horizontal lines between 2 rows of diagonal lines (Style 45), bound ebony fingerboard, Style 45 hexagonal abalone inlay from 3rd to 15th fret, triple-bound peghead, vertical pearl-inlaid *CF Martin* logo, gold-plated enclosed tuners

Introduced: **1969**
Scalloped braces, tortoiseshell celluloid pickguard, low-profile neck, smaller hexagonal inlay (7/8 of D-45-size inlay) from 1st to 17th fret: **1987**
Still in production

00-41: 5 made: **1972–75**

000-41: 2 made: **1975**

D-41: scalloped braces: **1969–current**

D-41S: black pickguard, 12-fret neck, slotted peghead, 17 made: **1970–93**

D-41N: standard (not low-profile) neck: **1989–95**

D-41BLE: Brazilian rosewood back and sides, aging toner on top, tortoiseshell celluloid pickguard, gold-plated tuners with large ebony buttons, Guitar of the Month: **1989**

D12-41: 12-string, 14-fret neck, solid peghead, 8 made: **1988–94**

D-41Q: retains non-adjustable truss rod, 7 made: **1986–93**

HPD-41: pearl herringbone trim around top and soundhole: **1999**

Style 42: rosewood back and sides, ivory bridge, inlaid bridge pins, ivory-bound top and back, abalone soundhole ring, abalone top border, abalone border on top around edge of fingerboard, ivory-bound ebony fingerboard, German silver

tuners, pearl tuner buttons
Introduced: **1858**
Backstripe of horizontal lines between 2 rows of diago-
nal lines (Style 45), snowflake inlay at frets 5, 7 and
9, non-adjustable neck, unbound peghead: **1898**
Snowflake inlay at frets 5, 7, 9, 12 and 15: **1901**
Ebony bridge, ivoroid binding: **1918**
Tortoiseshell celluloid pickguard standard: **1932**
Discontinued: **1948**
Indian rosewood, limited production: **1973**, **1985**, **1988**
Regular production, grained ivoroid outer binding,
snowflake inlay on bridge ends, snowflake inlay
beginning at fret 1, gold-plated tuners: **1996**
Still in production

5-42: 2 made: **1921–22**

2 1/2-42: 1 made: **1911**

2-42: **1858–1900**

1-42: **1858–1919**

0-42: 12-fret neck throughout production: **1870s–1942**

00-42: 12-fret neck throughout production
Introduced: **1898**
Last made: **1942**
1 made: **1973**
Reintroduced, tortoiseshell celluloid outer binding:
1994
Discontinued: **1996**

00-42G: gut string, may have X-bracing or fan pattern,
pin bridge or loop bridge, 3 made: **1936–39**

00-42K: koa back and sides, koa top, 1 made: **1919**

000-42: **1918–43**

000-42EC Eric Clapton: prewar style, snowflake
inlays on bridge ends, signature inlaid at last fret,
461 made: **1995**

OM-42: 14-fret neck, 25.4" scale, solid peghead with
ivoroid binding, gold-plated banjo tuners
1 made: **1930**
Regular production model, Indian rosewood back and
sides, snowflake inlay on bridge ends, grained
ivoroid binding, Style 45 snowflake inlay beginning
at fret 1, gold-plated open-back tuners with "butterbean" buttons: **1999**
Still in production

OM-42 PS Paul Simon: Indian rosewood back and
sides, tortoiseshell celluloid binding, tortoiseshell
celluloid fingerboard binding, snowflake inlay beginning at fret 1, signature inlay, vertical peghead
logo, nickel-plated Waverly open-back tuners: **1997**

D-42: Indian rosewood back and sides, scalloped
braces, X-brace 1" from soundhole, tortoiseshell celluloid pickguard, snowflake inlay on bridge ends,
grained ivoroid binding, Style 45 snowflake inlay
beginning at fret 1, gold-plated open-back tuners with
"butterbean" buttons, gloss finish: **1996–current**

D-42JC Johnny Cash: scalloped bracing, X brace
1" from soundhole, 3-piece back, backstripes of
horizontal lines between 2 rows of diagonal lines
(Style 45), neck shape with lower profile at 1st fret
(modeled after a D-45 formerly owned by Cash and
Hank Williams Jr.), ebony fingerboard, abalone star
inlay, pearl fingerboard border, Cash signature
inlaid at 19th fret, black finish (including headstock), label signed by Cash and C.F. Martin IV,
numbered limited run of 200, introduced: **1997**;
first production: **1998**

D-42K: koa back and sides, 150 made: **1998**

D-42LE: scalloped braces, white binding, tortoiseshell
celluloid pickguard, low-profile neck, gold-plated
tuners with large ebony buttons, Guitar of the
Month: **1988**

D-42S: left-handed, 1 made: **1934**

D-42V: Brazilian rosewood, scalloped braces, ivoroid
binding, V-neck, hexagonal inlay, 12 made: **1985**

Style 44: custom style for performer/teacher Vahdah
Olcott-Bickford, rosewood back and sides, soundhole rings in 5-9-5 grouping, 6-ply top binding of
white alternating with brown and/or black with ivory
outer layer (similar to later, non-herringbone Style
28), 3-ply back binding with ivory outer layer, backstripe of black and white lines with wide white line in
center, ivory-bound ebony fingerboard, no inlay,
ivory-bound peghead, some pegheads with *Soloist*
inlaid, some with *Olcott-Bickford Artist Model*
Introduced: **1913**
Ivoroid binding: **1918**
Last made: **1939**

2-44: 4 made: **1930**

0-44: 17 made: **1913–31**

00-44: 6 made: **1913–22**

00-44G: gut string, may have X or fan bracing, pin bridge or loop bridge, 2 made: **1938**

000-44: 3 made: **1917–19**

Style 45: rosewood back and sides, ivory bridge, inlaid bridge pins; ivory-bound top, back, fingerboard and peghead; abalone pearl borders with wood purfling on top, back, sides, by endpin, around end of fingerboard and around soundhole, backstripe of horizontal lines between 2 rows of diagonal lines, ebony fingerboard, snowflake inlay at frets 5, 9, 7, 12 and 15, scroll peghead inlay

Introduced as specially inlaid Style 42 models: **1902**
Style 45 first offered: **1904**
Torch or flowerpot peghead inlay: **by 1906**
Snowflake-pattern inlay at frets 1, 3, 5, 7, 9, 12, 15 and 17: **by 1910**
Ebony bridge, ivoroid binding: **1918**
Tortoiseshell celluloid pickguard: **1932**
C.F. Martin inlaid in pearl on peghead, 14-fret models only: **1934**
Hexagonal inlay on D-size: **by 1939**
Last listed: **1941**
Discontinued: **1942**
Reintroduced, black-and-white plastic purfling bordering abalone top and side inlay, hexagonal abalone inlay, "boxed" endpiece with abalone border (double abalone border where endpiece meets top and back): **1968**
Indian rosewood back and sides, old style endpiece with abalone mitered into side-border abalone: **1969–early 1970**
Scalloped bracing, low-profile neck: **1988**
Still in production

5-45: 1 made: **1922**

1-45: 6 made: **1904–1919**

2-45: 4 made: **1925–27**
2-45T: tenor neck, 2 made: **1927–28**

0-45: **1904–39**

0-45JB Joan Baez: modeled on Baez's 1929 0-45, Sitka spruce top, Indian rosewood back and sides, tortoiseshell celluloid pickguard, modified V neck

shape with diamond volute and pointed neck heel, 12 frets clear of body, Joan Baez signature at 18th fret, label signed by Joan Baez and C.F. Martin IV, numbered run of 59 (corresponding with Baez's debut in 1959): **summer 1998**

00-45: **1904–38, 1970–95**

00-45B: Brazilian rosewood, 2 made: **1985**

00-45K: koa top, back and sides, 1 made: **1919**

00-45N: non-scalloped braces, standard neck (not low-profile), 25.4" scale: **1989–95**

00-45 CFM/Stauffer: Brazilian rosewood back and sides, abalone top border, abalone soundhole ring, ivoroid-bound top and back, 12-fret neck, ebonized black neck finish, "ice cream cone" neck heel, bound ebony fingerboard, snowflake inlay, unbound Stauffer style scrolled peghead, pearl peghead logo, limited run of 25: **1997**

000-45: **1907–42, 1970–93** (7 with 12-fret neck in 1970, also 1 12-fret neck example stamped S-000-45 in 1975)

000-45 7-string: 1 made: **1911**; 1 Hawaiian made: **1929**; 1 left-handed made: **1931**

000-45B: Brazilian rosewood, 2 made: **1985**

000-45H: Hawaiian, flat fingerboard, high nut, flush frets, non-slanted saddle, 2 made: **1937**

000-45JR Jimmie Rodgers: Brazilian rosewood back and sides, Adirondack spruce top, *Thanks* in large block letters on back, *Jimmie Rodgers* fingerboard inlay, slotted peghead, *Blue Yodel* peghead inlay: **1997**

000-45 lyre head: 1 made: **1914**

000-45N: standard neck (not low-profile): **1989–95**

000-45S: 12-fret neck, 11 made: **1974–76**

000-45 vine fingerboard: 1 made: **1912**

S-000-45: 12-fret neck: **1975** (also 7 12-fret examples stamped 000-45 in 1970)

OM-45: small tortoiseshell celluloid pickguard, 14 frets clear of body, 25.4" scale, gold-plated banjo tuners
Introduced: **1930**
Large pickguard: **early 1931**
Right-angle tuners: **1931**
Discontinued: **late 1933**

MARTIN

449

Reintroduced (first 56 stamped SOM-45): **1977**
Discontinued: **1996**

OM-45 Deluxe: pearl inlay in pickguard and bridge, 14 made: **1930**

OM-45 Deluxe Golden Era: limited run of no more than 14: **1998**

SOM-45: first 56 examples of reissued OM-45: **1977**

Schoenberg/Martin OM: see General Information, Martins Made for Other Makers

D-45: 91 made: **1933–42**
Non-standard examples, compiled by Mike Longworth:
1st D-45, customized for Gene Autry, 12-fret neck: **1933**
2nd D-45, customized for Jackie "Kid" Moore, 12-fret neck: **1934**
3rd and 4th D-45s, stamped D-45S, 16 1/4" wide body, 14-fret neck: **1936**
5th D-45, 14-fret neck, double pickguards: **1937**
6th D-45, stamped D-45S, 12-fret neck, solid peghead: **1937**
D-45S, special neck: **1939**
D-45L, left-handed: **1940**
D-45S, "Austin": **1942**
D-45 reintroduced: **1968**
Still in production

Custom 17: see listing as Style 17 dreadnought

D-45 Deluxe: Brazilian rosewood back and sides, aging toner on top, ivoroid binding, fossilized ivory bridge pins with pearl dots, highly figured pearl fingerboard inlay, Guitar of the Month: **1993**

D-45 Gene Autry: 12-fret neck, *Gene Autry* in pearl script on fingerboard or snowflake fingerboard inlay with *Gene Autry* at 15th fret, torch peghead inlay: **1994**

D-45LE: Brazilian rosewood back and sides, tortoiseshell celluloid pickguard, hexagon outline at bridge ends, hexagon outline fingerboard inlays, gold-plated tuners with ebony buttons, Guitar of the Month: **Sept. 1987**

D-45N: standard neck (not low-profile): **1989–95**

D-45P: low-profile neck, 1 made: **1987**

D-45Q: retains non-adjustable truss rod, 32 made: **1986–93**

D-45S: 12-fret neck, slotted peghead (2 from 1936, see D-45, preceding): **1969–93**

D-45S Deluxe: ivoroid binding, tortoiseshell celluloid pickguard, 12-fret neck, snowflake inlay on fingerboard and bridge, slotted peghead, pearl inlay on side of peghead, gold-plated tuners with ebony buttons inlaid with pearl *M*, Guitar of the Month: **1992**

D-45SS Steven Stills: modeled on Stills's 1939 D-45, signature inlaid in fingerboard, abalone Southern Cross star constellation inlay in pickguard, limited run of 91: **1999**

D12-45: 12 string, 12-fret neck, slotted peghead: **1969–95**

D-45V: Brazilian rosewood, scalloped braces, aging toner on top, ivoroid binding, tortoiseshell celluloid pickguard under the finish, snowflake inlay: **1983–85**

D-45VR: scalloped braces, X-brace 1" from soundhole, snowflake inlay, adjustable truss rod, V-neck, C.F. Martin Sr. signature inlaid at 19th fret, aging toner on top, vintage style case: **1997–current**

SD12-45: 12-string, 14-fret neck, 2 made: **1971, 1973**

C.F. Martin Sr. Commemorative D-45: Indian rosewood back and sides, Sitka spruce top, hexagonal inlay, gold-plated open-back tuners with "butterbean" buttons, limited run of 200: **1996**

C.F. Martin Sr. Deluxe D-45: Brazilian rosewood back and sides, Sitka spruce top, abalone snowflake bridge inlay, snowflake fingerboard inlay, gold-plated open-back tuners with "butterbean" buttons, limited run of 91: **1996**

Custom J-45M Deluxe: tortoiseshell celluloid binding, tortoiseshell celluloid pickguard, black bridge pins with pearl dots, hexagonal inlay, gold-plated tuners with small ebony buttons, Guitar of the Month: **Oct.–Dec. 1986**

Style 55: see Style 17, 00-size, preceding

Style 60: birdseye maple back and sides, scalloped braces, tortoiseshell celluloid binding, tortoiseshell celluloid pickguard, white bridge pins with tortoiseshell celluloid dots, ebony fingerboard, gold-plated tuners with ebony buttons, aging toner on top
D-60: 1989–95

Style 62: flamed maple back and sides, scalloped braces, X-brace 1" from soundhole, soundhole rings in 1-9-1 grouping, tortoiseshell celluloid on top and back, tortoiseshell celluloid pickguard, white bridge pins with red dots, unbound ebony fingerboard, chrome-plated tuners with pearl buttons, aging toner on top
Introduced as D-62LE with different specs (see following): **1988**
Soundhole rings in 5-9-5 grouping: **1988**
Last made: **1995**

D-62: 1989–95

D-62LE: white bridge pins with tortoiseshell celluloid dots, snowflake inlay, label signed by C.F. Martin IV, Guitar of the Month: **Oct. 1986**

Style 64: flamed maple back and sides, scalloped braces, soundhole rings in 5-9-5 grouping, 6-ply top binding and 3-ply back binding with tortoiseshell celluloid outer layer, tortoiseshell celluloid pickguard, white bridge pins with tortoiseshell celluloid dots, backstripe of horizontal lines between 2 rows of diagonal lines (Style 45), low-profile neck, unbound ebony fingerboard, dot inlay, chrome-plated tuners, natural top finish

M-64: 1985–95

Style 65: flamed maple back and sides, ebony bridge, tortoiseshell celluloid pickguard, soundhole rings in 5-9-5 grouping, 6-ply top binding and 3-ply back binding with tortoiseshell celluloid outer layer, backstripe of horizontal lines between 2 rows of diagonal lines (Style 45), ebony fingerboard with tortoiseshell celluloid binding, dot inlay, gold-plated tuners with large pearl buttons
Available: **1985–current**

J-65: 1990-current

J-65M: original version of J-65: **1985–89**

CMJ-65 (Custom J-65): modeled after special guitar used by C.F. Martin IV at clinics, cherry sunburst finish, white binding, black pickguard, white bridge pins with pearl dots, hexagonal inlay, MEQ-932 active electronics: **1993–95**

J12-65: 12-string, 14-fret neck, solid peghead: **1991–95**

J12-65M: original version of J12-65 12-string: **1985–90**

Style 68: maple back and sides, 9-ply soundhole ring, 6-ply top binding and 3-ply back with white outer layer, 2 black lines on side binding, tortoiseshell celluloid pickguard, white bridge pins with pearl dots, chainlink backstripe, bound ebony fingerboard, abalone dot inlay, bound peghead, Style 45 vertical *CF Martin* peghead logo, carved diamond volute on back of peghead, gold-plated tuners

MC-68 cutaway body, oval soundhole, scalloped braces: **1985–95**

Style 76: Bicentennial limited edition, Indian rosewood back and sides, 3-piece back with herringbone backstripes, ebony bridge, white bridge pins with black dots, black pickguard, 6-ply top binding and 3-ply back binding with white outer layer, herringbone soundhole ring, unbound ebony fingerboard, pearl star inlay, engraved pearl eagle inlay on peghead, brass plate on neck block with ranking and serial number

D-76: 200 made: **1975**; 1,776 made: **1976**

D-76E: made for employees, label signed by C.F. Martin III, 98 made: **1976**

Style 89
CM-0089: forerunner of M-36, rosewood back and sides, 3-piece back, scalloped braces, soundhole rings in 5-9-5 grouping, 6-ply top binding and 3-ply back binding with white outer layer, tortoiseshell celluloid pickguard, white bridge pins with black dots, white-black-white backstripes, low-profile neck, unbound ebony fingerboard, unbound peghead, 25 made for Fantasy Records promotion of David Bromberg album: **1979**

Style 93
D-93: 160-year commemorative guitar, mahogany back and sides, X-brace 1" from soundhole, herringbone soundhole ring, diamond inlay at bridge ends, white binding, tortoiseshell celluloid pickguard, white bridgepins with red dots, herringbone backstripe, bound ebony fingerboard, *CFM* inlay at 3rd fret, bound peghead, Brazilian rosewood peghead veneer, gold-plated tuners with ebony buttons, aging toner on top, Guitar of the Month: **1993**

MARTIN

MARTIN

HAWAIIAN AND EARLY KOA MODELS

Most Hawaiians have frets flush with fingerboard,
bridge saddle mounted perpendicular to strings.
H after model name signifies Hawaiian, K signifies
koa wood construction. All H models have 12 frets
clear of body and slotted peghead.

2-17H: 1927–31

0-17H: 1930–40

0-18K (most with Hawaiian setup): **1918–35**

0-28K (most with Hawaiian setup): **1917–31**, 1 in **1935**

00-18H: 1935–41

00-40H: 1928–39

12-STRINGS

See listings under Flat Top Styles for complete
descriptions.

Model	Frets Clear	Peghead	Production
D12-1	14	solid	1997–current
D12-18	14	solid	1973–95
D12-20	12	slotted	1964–91
D12-28	14	solid	1970–current
D12-35	12	slotted	1965–93
D12-41	14	solid	1988–95
D12-45	12	slotted	1969–95
000012-28H AG	14	solid	1997
J12-40M	14	solid	1985–95
J12-65M	14	solid	1986–95

TENORS AND PLECTRUMS

Tenor and plectrum models are designated by T or P
after the model name. The first recorded Martin
tenor was a 5-17T in 1927. Many models have been
available as tenors, with scale lengths of 22 1/2"
before 1929, 23" from 1929 onward, and 14 frets
clear of body; and as plectrums with scale length of
27" and 15 frets clear of body. The 0-size tenor
body is 17 1/8" long, which is 1 1/4" shorter than
the 14-fret 0-size guitar body.

All tenor and plectrum models are listed with their
appropriate style number.

CLASSICALS

Prior to 1928, most Martin guitars were made for gut
strings but were not given classical model designations. The G-series models were the first attempt by
Martin to make a classical guitar that would appeal
to players of Spanish-made instruments.

00-16C: classical, 12-fret 00 body size, rounded
bridge ends, soundhole rings in 1-9-1 grouping, no
pickguard, black backstripe, 5-ply top binding with
tortoiseshell celluloid outer layer, unbound back, 25
1/4" scale, 12-fret neck, no fingerboard inlay, slotted peghead, non-gloss finish

Introduced: **1962**

Black plastic outer binding on top, 25.4" scale: **1966**

26 3/8" scale: **1970**

Discontinued: **1983**

00-18G: same body shape as 14-fret 00 but with
12-fret neck, examples with X-bracing or fan-pattern,
with pin bridge (rare) or loop bridge, ebony fingerboard, fingerboard 2" wide at nut, slotted peghead

Introduced: **1936**

Rosewood fingerboard: **c. 1940**

Last made: **1962**

00-18C: rounded bridge ends, 25 1/4" scale, 12 frets
clear of body, flat fingerboard, slotted peghead

Introduced: **1962**

25.4" scale: **1966**

26 3/8" scale: **1970**

Last offered: **1995**

00-28G: Style 28 materials and trim, same changes
as Style 28, same body shape as 14-fret 00 but only
12 frets clear of body, examples with X-bracing and
fan pattern, with pin bridge and with loop bridge,
fingerboard 2" wide at nut, slotted peghead: **1936–62**

00-28C: fan bracing, rounded bridge ends, no pickguard, 26.44" scale, 12-fret neck, slotted peghead:
1966–95

000-28C: rounded bridge ends, 12 frets clear of
body, slotted peghead: **1962–69**

000-28G: gut-string, Style 28 materials and trim,
same changes as Style 28, examples with X-bracing
and fan pattern, with pin bridge and with loop
bridge, 17 made: **1937–55**

N-10: Spanish-style body shape, mahogany back
and sides, fan bracing, loop bridge with rounded
ends, no pickguard, wood-marquetry soundhole
ring, 5-ply top binding and 3-ply back binding of
wood with black outer layer, 12-fret neck, 25.4"
scale, unbound rosewood fingerboard, solid peghead, pearloid tuner buttons

Introduced: **1968**
26.44" scale, slotted peghead with peaked top: **1970**
Last offered: **1995**

N-20: Brazilian rosewood back and sides, fan bracing, 5-ply top binding and 3-ply back binding of wood with black outer layer, black side stripe, wood marquetry soundhole ring, no pickguard, loop bridge with rounded ends, white-black-white backstripe, unbound ebony fingerboard, 12-fret neck, 25.4" scale, solid peghead, pearloid tuner buttons
Introduced: **1968**
Indian rosewood back and sides: **late 1969**
26.44" scale, slotted peghead with peaked top: **1970**
Last offered: **1995**

N-20B: Brazilian rosewood back and sides, 2 made: **1985–86**

N-20WN: Willie Nelson model, modeled after Nelson's 1969 N-20, piezo pickup, 25.4" scale, state of Texas inlay at 5th fret, *TRIGGER* inlay at 12th fret, squared-off peghead, limited run of 100, no more than 30 with Brazilian rosewood, remainder with East Indian rosewood: **1999**

C-1R: designed with Thomas Humphrey, western red cedar top, laminated rosewood back and sides, arched lattice-braced top, inlaid wood mosaic soundhole ring, negative neck-set angle, backstripe of horizontal lines between 2 rows of diagonal lines (Style 45), black-and-white binding with rosewood outer layer on top, back and sides, non-gloss finish: **1997–current**

C–TSH Martin/Humphrey: designed with Thomas Humphrey, Engelmann spruce top, solid rosewood back and sides, arched lattice-braced top, inlaid wood mosaic soundhole ring, negative neck-set angle, backstripe of horizontal lines between 2 rows of diagonal lines (Style 45), black-and-white binding with rosewood outer layer on top, back and sides, gloss finish: **1997–current**

ELECTRIC FLAT TOPS

00-18E: 00-18 with 1 DeArmond pickup at end of fingerboard, 2 knobs, X-bracing: **1959–64**

D-18E: D-18 with 2 DeArmond pickups, 3 knobs, toggle switch on upper treble bout, ladder bracing: **1958–59**

D-28E: D-28 with 2 DeArmond pickups, 4 knobs, toggle switch, ladder bracing: **1959–64**

Pickups on Acoustic Models
Since the mid 1970s, Martin has offered Frap, Barcus-Berry, Baggs and Fishman-made pickups, installed in various configurations on standard acoustic models. Current pickups include the Thinline (made by Fishman), Fishman Prefix and Baggs Dual Source.

ACOUSTIC BASSES

BM: Road Series model, J-size body, laminated mahogany back and sides, A-frame (modified X) bracing, rosewood bridge, herringbone soundhole ring, tortoiseshell celluloid pickguard, black binding, no backstripe, U-shaped mortise-and-tenon neck joint, adjustable truss rod, low-profile neck, rosewood fingerboard, dot inlay, chrome-plated enclosed tuners, satin non-gloss finish: **1998–current**

B-1: J-size body, solid mahogany back, laminated mahogany sides, ebony bridge, tortoiseshell celluloid pickguard, tortoiseshell celluloid binding, ebony fingerboard, 34" scale, aging toner on top, satin non-gloss finish: **1997–current**

B-1EP: Fishman Prefix pickup: **1997–current**

B-40: J-size body, rosewood back and sides, scalloped braces, soundhole rings in 5-9-5 grouping, black pickguard, white binding, chainlink backstripe, ebony fingerboard, fretless available by special order, no inlay, 1 37/64" nut width: **1992–96**

BC-40: cutaway: **1992–96**

B-540: 5-string, 1 3/4" nut width, custom-order only: **1994–96**

B-65: J-size body, maple back and sides, tortoiseshell celluloid pickguard, tortoiseshell celluloid binding, ebony fingerboard, fretless available by special order: **1992–95**

ACOUSTIC ARCHTOPS

All *f*-hole archtops have serial number and model number stamped on the inside center backstripe. Round-hole models are stamped on neck block.

Style C: 000-size body, 15" wide, carved spruce top, back arched by braces (not carved)

C-1: round hole, mahogany back and sides, black outer binding on top and back, trapeze tailpiece, earliest with inlaid vertical *Martin* peghead logo, darkened top finish
Introduced: **1931**
f-holes introduced (round-hole examples still produced): **1932**
Martin inlaid vertically on peghead with *C* and *F* on either side: **1932**
Last roundholes produced: **1933**
Decal logo, shaded top finish: **1934**
3-ply binding with ivoroid outer layer: **1935**
Last made: **1942**

C-1T: tenor neck: **1931–38**

C-1P: plectrum neck: 9 made (round hole) **1931–33**; 1 made in **1939**

C-1 12-string: round hole, 1 made: **1932**

C-2: rosewood back and sides, round hole, multiple-bound top and back with white outer layer, unbound elevated pickguard of tortoiseshell celluloid, "zipper" zigzag-pattern backstripe, unbound bony fingerboard, slotted-diamond inlay, vertical *Martin* peghead inlay, darkened top finish
Introduced: **1931**
f-holes introduced (round-hole examples still produced): **1932**
Martin inlaid vertically on peghead with *C* and *F* on either side: **1932**
Last roundholes produced: **1933**
Shaded top finish: **1934**
Ivoroid-bound fingerboard: **1935**
Hexagonal inlay on frets 3, 5, 7, 9, 12 and 15: **1939**
1 made with maple body: **1939**
Last made: **1942**

C-2 12 string: *f*-hole, 1 made: **1932**

C-2T: tenor neck: **1931–34**, **1936**

C-2P: plectrum neck, round hole, 2 made: **1931**

C-2 mandocello: round hole, 2 made: **1932**

C-3: rosewood back and sides, round hole, gold-plated tailpiece, 5-ply top binding with ivoroid outer layer, elevated tortoiseshell celluloid pickguard with black-and-white binding, backstripe of horizontal lines between 2 rows of diagonal lines (Style 45), ivoroid-bound ebony fingerboard, Style 45 pattern snowflake inlay, ivoroid-bound peghead with vertical

Martin logo, gold-plated tuners, darkened top finish
Introduced: **1931**
f-holes introduced (round-hole examples still produced): **1932**
Martin inlaid vertically on peghead with *C* and *F* on either side: **1932**
Last roundholes produced: **1933**
Shaded top finish: **1934**
Last made: **1934**

C-3T: tenor neck, *f*-holes, 1 made: **1934**

Style R: 00 body size, 14 5/16" wide, arched top, mahogany back arched by braces (not carved)

R-18: 12-fret 00-size body, spruce top arched by braces (not carved), round hole, 4-ply top binding with black outer layer, 14 frets clear of body, sunburst top finish
Introduced, first 9 stamped 00-18S: **1932**
14-fret 00-size body, round hole: **1933**
3-piece *f*-holes: **late 1933**
Carved top, 1-piece *f*-holes: **1937**
Last made: **1942**

R-18T: tenor neck: **1934–41**

R-18P: plectrum neck, 4 made: **1934–36**

R-17: arched (not carved) mahogany top, 14-fret 00-size body, 3-segment *f*-holes
Introduced: **1934**
1-piece *f*-holes: **1937**
Last made: **1942**

R-15: maple or birch back and sides, spruce top arched by braces (not carved), 3-segment *f*-holes, elevated pickguard, rosewood fingerboard, sunburst top finish, 2 made: **1934**

R-21: 12-fret 000 body size, rosewood back and sides, carved spruce top, arched back, 4-ply top binding with black outer layer, *f*-holes, 14-fret neck, sunburst top finish, 1 made: **1938**

Style F: 16" wide, carved top, back arched by braces (not carved), *f*-holes

F-1: mahogany back and sides, multiple-bound top and back with ivoroid outer layer, unbound elevated plastic pickguard, unbound ebony fingerboard, unbound peghead, sunburst top finish: **1940–42**

F-1 12-string: 1 made: **1941**

F-2: rosewood back and sides, 3-ply top and back binding with white outer layer, ivoroid-bound elevated plastic pickguard, "zipper" zigzag-pattern backstripe, ivoroid-bound ebony fingerboard, hexagonal inlay beginning at fret 3, unbound peghead with vertical *CF Martin* logo: **1940–42**, 1 with maple body in **1941**

F-5: maple back and sides, elevated tortoiseshell celluloid pickguard with white-black-white binding, ebony fingerboard, hexagonal inlay beginning at fret 3, maple neck and peghead, natural finish, 2 made: **1940**

F-7: Brazilian rosewood back and sides, 7-ply top binding with ivoroid outer layer, ivoroid-bound elevated tortoiseshell celluloid pickguard, backstripe of horizontal lines between 2 rows of diagonal lines (Style 45), ivoroid-bound ebony fingerboard, 2 white lines inlaid down length of fingerboard, ivoroid hexagonal inlays at frets 3, 5, 7, 9, 12 and 15, 3-ply peghead binding with ivoroid outer layer, *Martin* inlaid vertically on peghead with *C* and *F* on either side, chrome-plated tuner buttons, sunburst top finish
Introduced: **1935**
Pearloid hexagonal inlay: **1937**
Discontinued: **1942**

F-7S: round hole, 1 made: **1936**

F-9: rosewood back and sides, 7-ply top binding with ivoroid outer layer, elevated tortoiseshell celluloid pickguard with white-black-white binding, backstripe of horizontal lines between 2 rows of diagonal lines (Style 45), white-black-white lines inlaid down length of fingerboard, abalone hexagonal inlays (a few pearloid) at frets 1, 3, 5, 7, 9, 12, 15 and 17, tortoiseshell celluloid peghead veneer, 3-ply peghead binding with ivoroid outer layer, *Martin* inlaid vertically on peghead with *C* and *F* on either side, Grover tuners with *CMF* engraved on tuner buttons, gold-plated hardware, sunburst top finish
Available: **1935–41**

ELECTRIC ARCHTOPS

F series: 16" wide, thin hollowbody of laminated maple, DeArmond pickups, *f*-holes, adjustable plexiglass bridge, elevated pickguard of dark plas-

tic, unbound fingerboard, standard Martin peghead shape

F-50: single cutaway, 1 pickup, 2 knobs, shaded top finish: **1961–65**

F-55: single cutaway, 2 pickups, 4 knobs, toggle switch: **1961–65**

F-65: double cutaway, 2 pickups, 4 knobs, toggle switch, vibrato tailpiece: **1961–65**

X series: prototypes

XTE-70: prototype of GT-70 (see following), 3 made: **1965**

XTE-75: prototype of GT-75 (see following), 3 made: **1965**

XGT-85: prototype of GT style guitar, specs unavailable, 1 made: **1965**

GT Series: 16" wide, thin hollowbody of laminated maple, *f*-holes, 2 pickups, 4 knobs, toggle switch, vibrato tailpiece, white elevated pickguard, bound fingerboard, adjustable truss rod with truss rod cover on peghead, larger peghead than standard Martin with pointed corners (a few late examples with peghead tapering toward top), single-bound peghead, burgundy or black finish (a few late examples with red finish)

GT-70: single cutaway: **1965–66**

GT-75: double cutaway: **1965–67**

GT-7512: 12-string, no vibrato, peghead tapers toward top, 3 made: **1966**

GT-75R: specs unavailable, 1 made: **1965**

ELECTRIC SOLIDBODIES

Style 18: maple body with rosewood, walnut or mahogany laminate stripes, unbound rosewood fingerboard, asymmetrical scroll-shaped peghead, adjustable truss rod with cover on peghead, *CFM* monogram logo, serial numbers beginning with 1000

E-18: 2 Di Marzio pickups with 1 row of poles visible, 4 knobs, 1 selector switch on upper bass horn, 1 mini-switch for phase control near knobs: **1979–83**

EM-18: 2 exposed-coil humbucking pickups with white coils (2 rows of polepieces visible), 4 knobs, 1 selector switch on upper bass horn, 2 mini-switches for phase control and coil-tap near knobs: **1979–83**

EB-18: electric bass, 1 pickup: **1979–83**

Style 28:
solid mahogany body with contoured edges, neck-through body construction, unbound ebony fingerboard, asymmetrical scroll-shaped peghead, *CFM* monogram logo shaded finish

E-28: 2 uncovered Seymour Duncan humbucking pickups with black coils, 4 knobs, active electronics, 1 selector switch above knobs, 2 switches for phase control and active-bypass below knobs: **1980–83**

EB-28: electric bass, 2 pickups: **1980–83**

COMMENTS

Flat tops (by period):

Stauffer style flat tops display extremely fine workmanship. They have considerable appeal to collectors but are not sought after as utility instruments. Prices vary depending on condition and ornamentation but these models generally sell for less money than prime examples from the 1929–44 period.

Models from the 1840s to the early 1900s represent the earliest appearances of modern flat top designs. They exhibit superb workmanship, but they have relatively small bodies designed for gut strings only. These models do not appeal to steel-string players due to the gut-string design; they do not appeal to classical players because the body and neck dimensions differ from those of modern classicals. They appeal primarily to collectors, and despite their historical appeal, current market values are less than for later steel-string models.

Twelve-fret steel-string models and 14-fret models from the mid 1920s to 1944 are characterized by superb workmanship and extremely fine sound and playability. They are of great interest to collectors and musicians. Some musicians prefer the sound and feel of the 12-fret neck, and these are equal in value to 14-fret guitars of the same period (up to 1939). The 14-fret models are considered by most collectors and musicians to represent the golden era of the flat top Martin. D-45s bring some of the highest prices of any vintage fretted instruments. All high-end styles, all Ds and all OMs from this period are highly sought.

Flat tops from 1944–46 represent the transition from prewar style to postwar. They bring prices lower than prewar models but higher than postwar models.

Flat tops from 1947–69 are regarded as instruments of good quality and playability, although they are not as highly sought as those of earlier periods. Rosewood models are of Brazilian rosewood, which is in greater demand than Indian rosewood. D-size models in particular command good prices and are highly respected by musicians.

The 1970–76 period was Martin's period of greatest annual production. Guitars from this period are considered to be excellent utility instruments but are of little interest to collectors.

From 1976 to the present, Martin has been undergoing considerable changes, with numerous reissues, new models, limited editions, new features, specification changes and a large number of custom-made guitars. Many new model names do not fit into the traditional model numbering system, so that higher style numbers no longer necessarily mean a higher grade of wood or ornamentation. Workmanship is generally superior to that of the 1970–76 period. While not currently regarded as collector's items, these instruments have the workmanship, playability and sound to be potential future collectibles.

Martin has been the premier maker of flat top acoustic guitars since the mid 1800s. Martin's other styles are interesting and in many cases quite rare, but they have not achieved the reputation, collector appeal or market value of the flat top steel-string guitars.

Classicals are equal in workmanship to steel-string models, but the sound and feel is not such that they appeal to most serious classical players. They do not have the market or collectible appeal of equivalent steel-string models.

Acoustic archtops do not have the traditional look, feel and sound of instruments by other makers with carved maple backs and elevated fingerboards. They have the workmanship equivalent to flat tops and they are rare, but they have not achieved the market recognition or value of equivalent flat top models.

On flat top electrics the DeArmond pickup system interferes with the acoustic sound, and the magnetic pickups do not produce a faithful acoustic sound. These models are historically interesting but not highly regarded.

Archtop electrics are interesting primarily because they were made by Martin. Their designs and electronics were outdated at the time they were introduced. They are of little interest to players or collectors.

Solidbody electrics are not highly sought and are interesting primarily as a footnote in Martin history.

UKULELES, TIPLES, TAROPATCHES AND BANJOS

GENERAL INFORMATION

The first Martin ukes, built in the first half of 1916, are serial numbered beginning with #1 and ending before #200. Ukes made after mid 1916 do not have a serial number and must be dated by specification changes.

Peghead decals appear on ukes in the 1930s.

Ukes have the Martin stamp on the back of the peghead until 1935.

SECTION ORGANIZATION

Standard (Soprano) Ukuleles

Other Uke Sizes, Including Taropatch

Tiples

Tenor Banjo

Vega Banjos

STANDARD (SOPRANO) UKULELES

All are 6 3/8" wide with 13 5/8" scale.

Style 0: mahogany body, no body binding, 12-fret rosewood fingerboard, small dot inlay, wood friction pegs

Introduced: **1922**

Ebony nut, nickel patent pegs: **1927**

Available by special order only, mahogany or koa: **1990s**

Style 1: mahogany body, rosewood outer binding with black and white wood binding around top, 12-fret rosewood fingerboard, small dot inlay, wood friction pegs

Introduced: **1918**

Patent pegs: **1927**

Dark plastic binding: **1934**

Last listed: **1965**

1K: koa wood: **1920–42**

Style 2: mahogany body, triple-bound top with ivoroid outer binding, single-bound back, 12-fret fingerboard, small dot inlay

Introduced: **1918**

Nickel patent pegs: **1923**

Style 2 last listed: **1965**

2K: koa wood: **1920–33**

Style 3: mahogany body, 7-ply top binding, 3-ply back binding, 5-ply soundhole ring, celluloid (or bone) ornament lower edge of top, 17-fret ebony fingerboard extends to soundhole, small pearl paired-diamond inlay at frets 5, 7 and 9, diamonds joined at 7th fret, 3 lines inlaid down center of fingerboard, 3-ply plastic nut, 4-point celluloid (or bone) peghead ornament, friction pegs

Introduced: **1918**

Unjoined diamond inlays at 7th fret, no peghead ornament, nickel patent pegs: **1923**

Style 3K last listed: **1939**

No celluloid ornament at lower edge of top: **late 1940s**

Available by special order only, mahogany or koa: **1990s**

3K: koa wood: **1920–39**

Style 5K: koa wood body, ivoroid-bound top and back with abalone trim, abalone pearl and black-and-white wood around soundhole, ivoroid-bound ebony fingerboard, 17-fret fingerboard extends to soundhole, snowflake inlay, koa peghead veneer with pearl-inlaid flowerpot, patent pegs

Introduced: **1922**

Abalone on sides: **1925**

No abalone on sides: **1927**

Last listed: **1940**

Style 5: mahogany body, same trim as Style 5K: **1941–42**

OTHER UKE SIZES

Taropatch: 8 strings arranged in pairs, 7 5/8" wide, 14 7/8" scale

Introduced in Styles 1, 2, and 3: **1918**

Koa wood taropatches, Styles 1K, 2K and 3K, introduced: **1922**

All discontinued except 1 and 2K: **1930**

Styles 1 and 2K discontinued: **1932**

1-C: concert ukulele, 7 5/8" wide (same body as taropatch), 14 3/4" scale, trimmed like Style 1 uke
Introduced: **1925**
Last listed: **1965**
Available by special order only: **1990s**

1-T: tenor ukulele, 8 15/16" wide, 17" scale, mahogany body, rosewood fingerboard and bridge, ebony nut, ivory saddle, pin bridge, rosewood binding, 12 frets clear of body
Introduced: **1928**
Black plastic binding: **1934**
Tortoiseshell celluloid binding: **1936**
14 frets clear of body: **by 1960s**
Black plastic binding: **1966**
Available by special order only: **1990s**

Style 51: baritone ukulele, 10" wide, 20 1/8" scale, mahogany body, white-black-white soundhole rings, 2-ply top binding with dark outer layer, single-ply dark back binding, pin bridge, 14 frets clear of body, rosewood fingerboard
Introduced: **1960**
Available by special order only: **1990s**

TIPLES

All are 8 15/16" wide with 17" scale, 10 strings grouped 2-3-3-2, tuned like a ukulele but with octaves on 3 lowest-pitched groups. Specs change as equivalent guitar styles change.

T-15: all-mahogany, ring of black and white lines around soundhole
Available: **1949–66**

T-17: all-mahogany, ring of black and white lines around soundhole
Available: **1926–48**

T-18: mahogany back and sides, spruce top, rosewood binding
Introduced: **1923**
Black plastic binding: **1934**
Available by special order only: **1990s**

T-28: rosewood back and sides, spruce top, white outer binding
Introduced: **1924**
Available by special order only: **1990s**

TENOR BANJO

Style 1: maple rim with 12 1/2" diameter, 11" head diameter, Grover "hub-cap" metal resonator recessed into rim, 24 brackets, tension hooks through rim, tension nuts recessed into back, maple neck, 17 frets, dot inlay
96 total sold: **1923–26**

VEGA BANJOS

Martin acquired the Vega Co. of Boston in 1970. In 1971, Vega banjo production was moved to the Martin factory in Nazareth. Vega was sold to an Asian manufacturer in 1979. Martin-made Vegas have a Martin decal on the back of the peghead and on the inside of the body. The Vega brand is now owned by Deering.

Vega longneck reissue: Dave Guard model, part of Kingston Trio set (with D-28 and 0-18T), made by Deering
Available: **1998**

COMMENTS

Ukuleles were popular from the 1910s into the 1930s, with a strong appeal carrying into the 1960s. Production during some periods was as great as for Martin guitars. Martin ukes are considered to be among the finest ever made for workmanship and sound. Demand for vintage Martin ukes has increased dramatically in recent years, with koa wood models bringing more than mahogany models, and fancier styles bringing more than plain styles. All sizes are sought by players and collectors.

Tiples, adapted from a South American instrument, achieved some popularity in the 1930s and have also been used in modern Hawaiian music. Current interest among players is extremely limited. Although they do have excellent sound, they appeal primarily to collectors.

The original Martin banjo model is of interest only as a historical footnote.

Martin-made Vega banjos are equivalent in quality of workmanship to Martin guitars of the same period and are superior in workmanship to the Vega banjos made in Boston in the 1960s. However, most banjo collectors still regard the Boston Vega as the authentic original and the Martin-made Vega as a utility instrument.

MANDOLIN SERIAL NUMBERS

YEAR	LAST NUMBER	YEAR	LAST NUMBER
1895	23	1943–45	none
1896	112	1946	17641
1897	155	1947	18303
1898	359	1948	19078
1899	577	1949	19559
1900	800	1950	20065
1901	881	1951	20496
1902	1171	1952	20902
1903	1348	1953	21452
1904	1507	1954	21952
1905	1669	1955	22254
1906	2026	1956	22629
1907	2357	1957	22985
1908	2510	1958	23111
1909	2786	1959	23262
1910	3098	1960	23512
1911	3431	1961	23663
1912	3847	1962	23938
1913	4162	1963	24139
1914	4462	1964	24339
1915	4767	1965	24439
1916	5007	1966	24564
1917	5752	1967	24639
1918	6370	1968	24839
1919	7237	1969	24989
1920	8761	1970	25039
1921	9627	1971	25139
1922	10196	1972	25289
1923	11020	1973	25339
1924	11809	1974	25679
1925	12520	1975	25895
1926	13359	1976	26045 (also #259996–#260020)
1927	13833		
1928	14170	1977	26101
1929	14630	1978	none
1930	14892	1979	26112
1931	15290	1980	26156
1932	15476	1981	26215
1933	15528	1982	26225
1934	15729	1983	26247
1935	15887	1984	26254
1936	16156	1985	26263
1937	16437	1986	26273
1938	16580	1987	26279
1939	16747	1988	26281
1940	16957	1989	none
1941	17263	1990	none
1942	17405		

MARTIN

Beginning in 1991 mandolins are numbered in the same series with guitars:

YEAR	LAST NUMBER
1991	512487 (includes 11 mandolins)
1992	522655
1993	535223 (includes 6 mandolins)
1994	551696
1995	570434
1996	592930
1997	624799

MANDOLINS

SERIAL NUMBER AND MODEL PLACEMENT

Bowlback: serial number on neck block

Flat back: model letter (1931 and after) and serial number on inside center strip

Carved back...

Serial number on inside back: **pre-1931**

Style number and serial number on inside back: **1931 and after**

SECTION ORGANIZATION

Bowlback, Bent Top Models
Flat Back, Bent Top Models
Carved Top and Back, Oval Hole Models
Carved Top and Back, *f*-Hole Models
Mandolas
Mandocellos

BOWLBACK, BENT TOP MODELS

All with oval hole, 13" scale

G1: 27 rosewood ribs, symmetrical pickguard under strings with ornamental inlay, 2 ornamental tuner plates on front of peghead, ornamental peghead cutout
Only catalog listing: **1896**

G2: rosewood ribs, symmetrical pickguard under strings with ornamental inlay, ornamental peghead cutout, tuner plates on back of peghead
Only catalog listing: **1896**

G3: rosewood ribs, ivory bridge, symmetrical pickguard under strings with ornamental inlay, tuner plate covers peghead
Only catalog listing: **1896**

G5: rosewood ribs, ivory bridge, butterfly-shaped tortoiseshell pickguard under strings with abalone and pearl inlay, pearl fingerboard with abalone inlays, tuner plate covers peghead, point on top of peghead
Only catalog listing: **1896**

Style 1: 18 ribs, ebony bridge and fingerboard, no fingerboard inlay, symmetrical pickguard under strings with ornamental inlay, German silver tuners, tuner plates on front of peghead, ornamental peghead cutout
Introduced: **1898**
20 ribs, no inlay on pickguard, dot inlay, tuners installed from back: **1904**
22 ribs: **1909**
Pickguard on treble side: **1917**
Last made: **1924**

Style 2: 26 rosewood ribs, fancier soundhole and binding than Style 1, symmetrical pickguard under strings with ornamental inlay, colored-wood soundhole ring, ornamental peghead cutout
Introduced: **1898**
Light and dark wood binding with rosewood on outer edge: **1901**
Pickguard on treble side: **1917**
Last made: **1924**

Style 3: 26 rosewood ribs, symmetrical pickguard with inlay mounted under strings, ivory-bound top with colored-wood purfling, abalone and ivory soundhole border, pearl tuner buttons, ornamental peghead cutout
Introduced: **1898**
Ivory tuner buttons: **1901**
Black and white binding with ivory on outer edge, snowflake inlay: **1904**
Last made: **1922**

Style 4: 34 rosewood ribs, symmetrical pickguard with inlay mounted under strings, ivory-bound top with abalone border, abalone and ivory soundhole border, ivory-bound fingerboard, German silver peghead plate, pearl tuner buttons, ornamental peghead cutout
Introduced: **1898**

30 ribs, ivory tuner buttons: **1901**
Last made: **1921**

Style 5: 34 rosewood ribs, symmetrical pickguard with inlay mounted under strings, alternating pearl and tortoiseshell top binding, ivory-bound fingerboard, vine inlay, ornamental peghead cutout
Introduced: **1898**
Ivory tuner buttons, ornamental peghead inlay: **1901**
Last made: **1920**

Style 6: 42 rosewood ribs fluted and joined with ivory, ivory bridge, symmetrical pickguard under strings with ornamental inlay, ivory-bound top with abalone border, abalone border on top around fingerboard, ivory-bound fingerboard, vine inlay, ornamental peghead cutout
Introduced: **1898**
Ornamental peghead inlay: **1901**
Ivory-bound side border: **1904**
Snowflake inlay: **1914**
Last made: **1921**

Style 6A: (not catalogued) same as Style 6 but with pickguard on treble side, some with multiple black-and-white top binding and no peghead inlay
Available: **1903–20**

Style 7: 42 fluted rosewood ribs, symmetrical pickguard under strings with ornamental inlay, elaborate pearl inlay on wide border around top and soundhole, ivory and abalone side border, vine fingerboard inlay crosses at 7th fret, floral peghead inlay, ornamental peghead cutout
First made: **1899**
Catalogued: **1904**
Last made: **1917**

Style 000: 9 mahogany ribs, pickguard on treble side extends to edge, dot inlay, solid peghead
Only year catalogued: **1914**

Style 00: 9 rosewood ribs, plain symmetrical pickguard mounted under strings, rosewood binding, dot inlay, solid peghead
Introduced: **1908**
Teardrop pickguard on treble side: **1917**
Mahogany bowl, 14 ribs: **1923**
Last made: **1925**

Style 0: 18 rosewood ribs, rope-pattern soundhole

ring, plain symmetrical pickguard mounted under strings, ivory saddle, rosewood binding, dot inlay, solid peghead
Introduced: **1905**
Teardrop pickguard on treble side: **1917**
Last made: **1925**

FLAT BACK, BENT TOP MODELS

All have oval hole, 13" scale.

A: rosewood back and sides, spruce top, pickguard on treble side with pointed "tail," rosewood-bound top, dot inlay, solid guitar-style peghead
Introduced: **1914**
Mahogany back and sides, rosewood-bound top and back, ebony bridge, teardrop pickguard, ebony fingerboard, dot inlay: **1917**
Black binding: **1935**
Shaded top optional: **1937**
Rosewood fingerboard and bridge: **mid 1940s**
Offered by special order only: **1995**

AK: koa wood body: **1920–37**

B: rosewood back and sides, spruce top, herringbone soundhole ring and backstripe, pickguard on treble side with pointed "tail," multiple rosewood and white holly binding on top and back, slotted-diamond inlays at frets 5, 7 and 10, ornamental peghead cutout
Introduced: **1914**
Teardrop pickguard: **1917**
Discontinued: **1946**
Reintroduced: **1981**
Discontinued: **1987**

BK: koa wood body, available: **1921**, **1925**

C: rosewood back and sides, spruce top, colored wood purfling on top, abalone soundhole ring, teardrop pickguard, ivory-bound top and back, Style 42 inlay from 3rd fret to 17th, ornamental peghead cutout
Introduced: **1914**
Abalone border on top: **1917**
Celluloid binding: **1919**
Colored wood around top border: **1921**
Last made: **1934**

D: rosewood back and sides, spruce top, ebony bridge, pickguard on treble side with pointed "tail," ivory-bound top with abalone border, purfling on

sides, ivory-bound ebony fingerboard, Style 45 snowflake inlay from 1st fret to 17th, engraved silver-plated tuners, ornamental peghead cutout
Available: **1914–16**

E: rosewood back and sides, spruce top, pickguard on treble side with pointed "tail," ivory bridge, ivory-bound top, back and peghead, abalone borders on top, back and sides, ivory-bound ebony fingerboard, Style 45 snowflake inlay from 1st fret to 17th, ornamental peghead inlay, German silver tuners, inlaid tuner buttons, ornamental peghead cutout
Introduced: **1915**
Teardrop pickguard: **1917**
Celluloid binding: **1919**
Discontinued: **1937**

CARVED TOP AND BACK, OVAL HOLE MODELS

All have carved spruce top, maple back and sides, 13" scale.

15: maple back and sides, spruce top, celluloid-bound top and back, ebony fingerboard and bridge, small dot inlay, solid peghead with rounded peak, natural top finish, antique brown finish on back and sides
Available: **1929–41**

20: symmetrical 2-point body shape, maple back and sides, spruce top, ebony bridge, elevated pickguard follows body point, multiple-bound top and back, ebony fingerboard, dot inlay, ornamental peghead cutout
Introduced: **1929**
Bound fingerboard: **1930**
Decal on peghead: **1935**
Discontinued: **1942**

CARVED TOP AND BACK, ƒ-HOLE MODELS

All have carved spruce top, maple back and sides, 13 3/4" scale.

2-15: maple back and sides, spruce top, elevated pickguard, triple-bound top, single-bound back, solid peghead with rounded peak, peghead decal, sunburst top finish, brown stain back and sides
Available: **1936–64**

2-20: symmetrical 2-point body, maple back and

sides, spruce top, triple-bound top, single-bound back, ebony bridge, single-bound fingerboard, dot inlay, ornamental peghead cutout, tortoiseshell celluloid peghead overlay, decal logo, shaded top finish
Available: **1936–41**

2-30: symmetrical 2-point body, ƒ-holes, maple back and sides, spruce top, single-bound elevated pickguard, multiple-bound top and back, single-bound fingerboard with treble-side extension, slotted diamonds-and-squares inlay, single-bound peghead with ornamental peghead cutout, peghead decal
Available: **1937–41**

MANDOLAS

Style 1: same wood and trim as Style 1 mandolin: **1902–14**

Style 2: same wood and trim as Style 2 mandolin: **1901**

Style AA: same wood and trim as Style A mandolin: **1915–31**, **1935**, **1941**

Style BB: same wood and trim as Style B mandolin: **1917–21**, **1932–39**

MANDOCELLOS

4 bowlback models made: **1909**
3 with C-1 archtop guitar body: **1932**
2 with C-1 archtop guitar body: **1935**
2 with C-2 archtop guitar body: **1932**

COMMENTS

Martin bowlbacks are regarded as excellent instruments by those modern classical mandolinists who prefer traditional Italian style bowlback construction.

Martin's flat back models and carved models have never achieved great recognition from collectors or musicians. They are of interest primarily to Martin collectors and, in the cases of the fancier models, to those who regard them as works of art.

The carved models exhibit excellent workmanship but are not as ornate as the high-end bowlback or flat-back models. The carved Styles 20 and 30 are sought by collectors but, despite their workmanship and rarity, do not command prices equivalent to artist-model Gibsons.

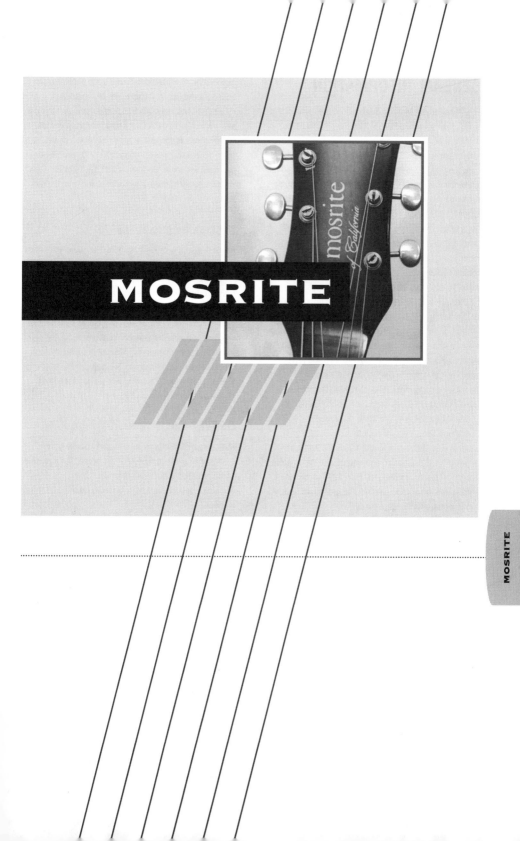

MOSRITE

GENERAL INFORMATION

The earliest Mosrite guitars bore the name of the man who made them: Moseley. Semie Moseley was born in Oklahoma on June 13, 1935. During the 1950s, based in Bakersfield, CA, he divided his time between building guitars and preaching. He worked for Rickenbacker from 1953–55 and built his first double-neck Spanish electric for country musician Joe Maphis around 1955. It had what would become typical Mosrite features: slant-mounted pickup in the neck position, three notches in the peghead to create the letter *M*, and a vibrato. He also built a doubleneck electric for rockabilly artist Larry Collins and supplied necks to Los Angeles guitar maker Paul Bigsby.

Moseley went into guitar making full time in Bakersfield in 1963. His success was based almost entirely on the endorsement of The Ventures (the pop instrumental group), who also had exclusive world-wide distribution rights for Mosrite. In 1965 Moseley acquired the rights to the Dobro name and, after using up existing parts stock, began making Dobro resonator guitars in Bakersfield (see Dobro section).

Moseley's ties with the Ventures ended in 1969, and after a short-lived distribution deal with Vox, Mosrite was shut down in late 1969. Mosrite was revived in 1972 under an agreement with the Kustom company that lasted until 1975. In 1975 Moseley entered into an agreement with Pacific Music Supply, but few instruments were made.

Moseley built some Original Ventures models for the Japanese market beginning in 1977. He also introduced a line of Brass Rail models at the 1977 National Association of Music Merchants trade show. He continued production in Carson City, NV, in 1980.

By 1988 Moseley was building guitars, including a new Ventures model, in the small mountain community of Jonas Ridge, NC. By the time of his death from bone marrow cancer on August 7, 1992, production had been moved to Booneville, AR. By 1994 his widow Loretta had resumed production on a limited basis in Jonas Ridge.

MISCELLANEOUS SPECS

All electric guitar models have 24 1/2" scale, rosewood fingerboard, zero fret, chrome-plated "bowler hat" knobs.

Unless otherwise specified, all electric models in 1968 were offered in sunburst, cherryburst, metallic red, metallic blue, pearl white, deep black, transparent cherry red and transparent sunburst.

Vibrato, solidbody models: *Mosrite of California* logo between vibrato base and bridge

Vibrato, hollowbody models: vibrato separate from bridge with no plate in between

DATING

Mosrite serial numbers are pressed into the fingerboard near the body end of the board, but a reliable number list is not available.

Many examples have a date stamped on the end of the neck.

Early Ventures can be dated by specs. Other models can be best dated by pot codes (see Appendix).

MOSRITE MODELS

Ventures: body shape resembles a mirror-image of a Fender Stratocaster

Ventures Mark I: 2 slant-mounted pickups with no logo stamp on covers, lever-action string mute, metal knobs with no logo, glued-in neck, bound fingerboard, triple-bound top, side-mounted jack, bound end of fingerboard, small dot inlay, *The Ventures* peghead decal
Introduced: **1963**

Vibra-Mute tailpiece with 3 screws at base: **late 1963**
Top-mounted jack (into pickguard), bolt-on neck with 4 bolts: **by early 1964**
Plastic knobs with logo: **1964**
Mosrite embossed on pickups, unbound top, no binding at end of fingerboard, truss rod adjustment at body end: **1965**
Moseley on tailpiece, 2 screws at tailpiece base: **1966**
Truss rod adjustment at peghead: **1966**
No *Ventures* logo: **1968**
Discontinued: **1969**

Reintroduced as **V-1** (see following): **1972**

Discontinued: **1975**

Reintroduced as **Ventures Model 1988:** similar to Ventures but with white pickup covers, no pickguard, 2 knobs, jack in top, switch near knobs, unbound fingerboard, woodgrain finish, 1988 on peghead: **1988**

Renamed **V-89: 1989**

Ventures Mark II: smaller body than Mark I, straight-mounted pickups with no visible polepieces

Ventures Mark V: specs unavailable

After 1969 the only authorized use of The Ventures' name was on a guitar made for the Rock and Roll Hall of Fame. However, Moseley built a number of Ventures models for private sale that did bear The Ventures name.

JOE MAPHIS MODELS

Joe Maphis Doubleneck: standard neck and octave neck, plastic knobs

Introduced: **1960s**

Production model: 6-string and 12-string neck (octave neck still available), *Joe Maphis Model* on 6-string peghead, 2 pickups per neck, 3 switches, available: **late 1960s**

Early style with octave neck reintroduced, 1 pickup on short neck, 2 pickups on standard neck, decorative armrest, 2 knobs: **late 1980s**

Joe Maphis Mark I, Model 501: larger than Ventures body, 1 1/2" deep, semi-hollowbody with no sound-holes, spruce top, walnut back and sides, 2 single-coil pickups with visible poles, 2 knobs, 1 toggle switch on upper treble bout, all controls mounted into pickguard, adjustable string saddles, single-bound top, fingerboard with slanted end, zero fret, metal nut, metal tuner buttons, *Joe Maphis Model* on peghead, natural or sunburst finish: **1968**

Joe Maphis Mark X (bass), Model 502: bridge cover/handrest, stop tailpiece, 30 1/4" scale, metal tuner buttons with notched ends: **1968**

Joe Maphis Mark XII, Model 503: 12-string, stop tailpiece: **1968**

Joe Maphis Mark XVIII (doubleneck), Model 105: widened body shape, 1 1/4" deep, 6- and 12-string necks, 2 switches on upper treble bout, 1 switch on

upper bass bout, unbound top: **1968**

Celebrity (CE) models: symmetrical double cutaway, 2 single-coil pickups with visible poles, 2 knobs and toggle switch on small plate, vibrato, small pickguard, bound fingerboard, zero fret, metal nut, bound peghead

Available: **1968**

CE I Mark I, Model 202: 2 3/4" deep, adjustable string saddles, vibrato, double-bound *f*-holes, single-bound top and back, metal tuner buttons

Introduced: **1968**

Discontinued: **1969**

Reintroduced as **Celebrity I** (see following): **1972**

CE I Mark X (bass), Model 203: non-roller saddles, no vibrato, bridge cover/handrest, short trapeze tailpiece, 30 1/4" scale: **1968**

CE I Mark XII, Model 204: 12-string, roller saddles, no vibrato, 30 1/4" scale: **1968**

CE II Mark I, Model 211: 1 17/18" deep, otherwise same as CE I Mark I: **1968**

CE II Mark X (bass), Model 212: non-roller saddles, no vibrato, bridge cover/handrest, short trapeze tailpiece, 30 1/4" scale: **1968**

CE II Mark XII, Model 213: 12-string, roller saddles, no vibrato: **1968**

CE III Mark I, Model 220: 1 7/8" deep, no visible pickup poles, non-roller string saddles, trapeze tailpiece, optional vibrato, single-bound top and back, plastic tuner buttons

Introduced: **1968**

Discontinued: **1969**

Reintroduced as **Celebrity III** (see following): **1972**

CE III Mark X (bass), Model 221: non-roller saddles, no vibrato, bridge cover/handrest, short trapeze tailpiece, 30 1/4" scale, metal tuner buttons

CE III Mark XII, Model 222: 12-string, trapeze tailpiece, plastic tuner buttons

Combo (CO) Series: Maphis shape, semi-hollowbody with 1 *f*-hole, 2 single-coil pickups with visible poles, 2 knobs, toggle switch on upper treble bout, controls into pickguard, bound *f*-hole, single-bound top and back, bound fingerboard, metal nut

MOSRITE

Available: **1968**

CO Mark I, Model 300: vibrato

CO Mark X, Model 301: non-roller bridge, no vibrato, bridge cover/handrest, stop tailpiece, 30 1/4" scale

CO Mark XII (12-string), Model 302: vibrato optional

Mark Series: semi-hollow body with 1 ƒ-hole, 2 pickups with visible poles, 2 knobs, toggle switch on upper treble bout, all controls into pickguard
Available: **1968**

Mark I, Model 102: 1 1/4" deep, adjustable string saddles, vibrato, unbound ƒ-holes, unbound top and back, bound fingerboard, metal tuner buttons

Mark X (bass), Model 103: 1 1/4" deep, non-roller bridge, no vibrato, bridge cover/handrest, stop tailpiece, 30 1/4" scale

Mark XII (12-string), Model 104: optional vibrato

Mark V, Model 101: 1 1/8" deep, non-roller bridge, unbound fingerboard, plastic tuner buttons

Gospel Series: symmetrical double cutaway, 2 3/4" deep, 2 single-coil pickups with visible poles, 4 knobs and toggle switch on small control plate, vibrato, single-bound ƒ-holes, triple-bound top and back, single-bound fingerboard, metal tuner buttons, natural finish, shaded brown peghead finish
Available: **1968**

Gospel Guitar Mark I, Model 600: adjustable string saddles

Gospel Guitar Mark X (bass), Model 601: non-roller bridge, no vibrato, bridge cover/handrest, stop tailpiece, 30 1/4" scale

Gospel Guitar Mark XII (12-string), Model 602: roller bridge, optional vibrato

Balladere I, Model 401: acoustic, small-bodied dreadnought shape, mahogany back and sides, 3 5/16" deep, pickguard with tail and point even with soundhole, points at bridge ends, recessed belly of bridge, 4 dots on bridge, single-bound top and back, 24 1/2" scale, unbound fingerboard, white tuner buttons, natural or transparent sunburst finish
Available: **1968**

Balladere II, Model 402: rosewood back and sides,

5" deep, double-bound top and back, metal tuner buttons: **1968**

Celebrity Series: thin double-cutaway, 16 1/2" wide, laminated maple body, ƒ-holes, small tortoiseshell celluloid pickguard, bound ƒ-holes, 4-ply top binding, bound back, single-bound rosewood fingerboard, large dot inlay, zero fret, 3 notches in top of peghead, metal tuner buttons

Celebrity I: 2 3/4" deep, maple body, 2 humbucking pickups, 4 knobs mounted into top, 2 pushbuttons near bridge pickup (pickup bypass switches), toggle switch on upper bass bout, individually adjustable string saddles, vibrato, transparent gold, cherry sunburst, or black finish: **1972–74**

Celebrity II Standard: 1 3/4" deep, 2 knobs, no bypass switches, no vibrato, trapeze tailpiece, transparent gold, sunburst, transparent cherry, cherry sunburst, or black finish: **1972–74**

Celebrity II Standard Bass: 2 knobs, no bypass switches: **1972–74**

Celebrity II Deluxe: 4 knobs, no bypass switches: **1972–74**

Celebrity II Deluxe Bass: 4 knobs: **1972–74**

V Series: solidbody (same shape as Ventures model), asymmetrical double cutaway with treble horn longer than bass horn, toggle switch on upper treble bout, all controls mounted through pickguard, beveled body edges, single-bound fingerboard with slanted end, large dot inlay, zero fret, 3 notches on top of peghead, metal tuner buttons

V-I: 2 pickups identical to Ventures but without Ventures logo, 2 knobs, individually adjustable string saddles, no vibrato: **1972–74**

V-II: 4 knobs, 2 pushbuttons near bridge pickup (pickup bypass switches), Moseley vibrato: **1972–74**

V-I Bass: handrest/bridge cover, 30 1/4" scale: **1972–74**

V-II Bass: handrest/bridge cover, 30 1/4" scale: **1972–74**

300 Series: solidbody, tulip-shape cutaway on treble side, slight cutaway on bass side, single-bound

MOSRITE

fingerberg, natural mahogany or walnut finish

300: 1 humbucking pickup, 2 knobs, stop tailpiece: **1974**

300 Bass: bridge cover/handrest: **1974**

350 Stereo: 2 pickups, 4 knobs, slide switch, 2 jacks: **1974**

350 Stereo Bass: 2 pickups, 4 knobs, slide switch, 2 jacks, bridge cover/handrest: **1974**

Blues Bender, Model 500: solidbody, horns of equal length, deeper cutaway on treble side, beveled body edges, 2 humbucking pickups mounted straight across, 4 knobs, 2 jacks, stereo electronics, stop tailpiece, tortoise grain pickguard, bound fingerboard, metal tuner buttons, dark burgundy finish
Available: **1974**

Brass Rail: 1/4" x 3/4" brass rail in maple neck, neck-through-body construction

Standard: solidbody guitar

Standard Bass: solidbody bass

Deluxe: solidbody guitar with preamp

Gospel: semi-hollowbody double-cutaway guitar

COMMENTS

Semie Moseley's early instruments, which were handmade custom instruments for celebrity performers, are highly sought by collectors even though some of the handwork is relatively crude.

The early versions of the Ventures model are highly sought by collectors. Most others are regarded as good utility instruments. The Ventures model inspired a number of Japanese-made fakes in the late 1960s, identifiable by Japanese tuners and generally inferior quality.

MOSRITE

NATIONAL/ VALCO

GENERAL INFORMATION

John Dopyera registered the National String Instrument Corporation in California on August 16, 1926, to make resonator instruments. Through the years his brothers Rudy, Robert, Louis and Emil (Ed) would be involved in various financial and manufacturing roles. On January, 26, 1928, the Dopyeras traded their interest for stock in a corporation whose principals included George Beauchamp, Paul Barth and Ted Kleinmeyer.

John Dopyera resigned on February 19, 1929, and formed the Dobro Manufacturing company with his brothers to make instruments under the Dobro brand. He returned to National in 1932 following the departure of Beauchamp and Barth. Dobro merged with National to form the National-Dobro company in 1935.

National-Dobro held patents on several styles of resonator instruments that produced greater volume than conventional acoustic instruments. Both National and Dobro lines include woodbody and metalbody instruments. National-brand resonator instruments have 1 or 3 cones, with the cones opening toward the back of the instrument. Single-cone models have a "biscuit bridge" (bridge mounted on a biscuit-size piece of wood) sitting on the peak of the cone. Dobro-brand resonator instruments, including those licensed to Regal, have the resonator cone opening toward the top of the instrument and a 4- or 8-armed "spider" supporting the bridge.

National marketed its first electric instruments in 1935. The Supro brand was introduced in late 1935 as a budget electric line. By the late 1930s, emphasis was shifting from acoustic resonator instruments to electric archtops and lap steels. According to Ed Dopyera, no resonator models of any type were made after 1939. The 1942 National catalog still listed several National models.

National-Dobro began a move from California to Chicago in 1936. Victor Smith, Al Frost and Louis Dopyera gained controlling interest, and they changed the company name to Valco (combining the first letters of their first names) in 1943.

The Chicago Musical Instrument company (which would acquire Gibson in 1944) began distributing Valco instruments in 1941, and some National instruments from the late 1930s through the 1950s have bodies made by Gibson. In the late 1940s Gibson also supplied necks and fingerboards to Valco. Some bodies were made by Harmony or Regal (also based in Chicago). Gibson bodies can be identified by their distinctive shape, by a work order number ink-stamped on the inside of the body and by their workmanship.

From the 1940s through the mid 1960s, Valco made instruments and amps under various brands for other companies. The most commonly seen are Gretsch, Oahu, Silvertone (for Sears) and Airline (for Montgomery Ward). Others include Norman English, Dwight, Atlas and St. Louis Music.

National introduced many innovative designs throughout the company's history, although not all were successful. In addition to resonator instruments, National's innovations include electric archtops with no soundholes, the first double-pickup electric, a magnesium-core neck with no neck heel, a 6-coil pickup and guitar bodies of molded fiberglass.

Valco absorbed the Kay company in 1967 and announced a new line of acoustic and electric models that same year. The company went bankrupt, however, and the last instruments were sold at a bankruptcy auction in summer 1968.

The National brand name was used in the early-to-mid 1970s on electric and acoustic instruments made in Asia and marketed by the Strum and Drum company.

National Reso-phonic Guitars was formed in San Luis Obispo, CA, in 1988 by Don Young and McGregor Gaines, former plant supervisor and shop foreman, respectively, for the Original Musical Instrument company (see Dobro/Regal/OMI section). All National Reso-phonic models have the National type cone. The company began producing woodbody instruments in 1989 and introduced metalbody models in 1991. These instruments have a shield decal with *National* and *Reso-phonic*.

TERMS

Ebonoid: black polished celluloid

Ebonized: black-stained wood, typically poplar or maple, to simulate ebony

Pearlette or pearloid: celluloid with light areas to simulate mother-of-pearl

GUITAR PICKUPS

Blade in oval housing: **1935–37**

Blade in rectangular housing: **1937–39**

Metal-covered, 2 rows of poles, 3 poles per row:

1939–51

Bridge pickup, integrated into bridge (wire coming out of bridge), some models: **1947–65**

Floating, vinyl-covered, 1 row of poles: **1951–55**

Metal-covered, 1 row of poles…

No mounting ring: **1951–late 1950s**

Plastic mounting ring, set screws on sides of ring: **1954–57**

Plastic mounting ring, no set screws on side, height-adjustable by Phillips-head E-string pole pieces: **1958–59**

Plastic mounting ring, no set screws on side, height adjustable by slotted-head E-string polepieces: **1960–68**

Silkscreen design on pickup: **1962–65**

STEEL GUITAR PICKUPS

Strings through pickup…

National steels: **early 1940s only**

Supro steels: **1939–68**

Strings over pickup, 1 row of 6 poles, National models: **1942–68**

PEGHEADS

National…

Rounded top: **1928–55**

Wavy top edge: **1956–57**

Asymmetrical shape, longer on treble side: **1958–68**

Angular top, 6-on-a-side tuners: **1966–68**

Supro…

Pointed top (Kay shape) or rounded top: **1936–55**

Narrow asymmetrical shape, longer on bass side: **1955–62**

Wider asymmetrical shape, longer on bass side: **1962–68**

Rounded top, 6-on-a-side tuners: **1966–68**

Airline…

Narrow asymmetrical shape, longer on treble side: **1958–63**

Wider asymmetrical shape, longer on treble side (but not as long as Nationals from same period): **1964–65**

Rounded top, 6-on-a-side tuners (like Supro from same period): **1966–68**

NATIONAL LOGOS

Shield…

Decal: **1927–40**

Nickeled and enameled plate, black and silver: **1940–51**

Brass plate with light blue enamel: **1951–60**

Script…

Some with silkscreen logo: **1951–55**

Raised metal (plated pot metal): **1956–60**

Molded plastic, most models: **1960–68**

Some low-end models with foil sticker logo, some steels with plated pot metal logo: **1960–68**

SUPRO LOGO PLATES

Black logo on silver field, black border: **1936–47**

Blue logo on gold field, bronze border: **1948–early 1960s**

Early 1930s Style O, standard resonator coverplate with 9 diamond-shaped hole clusters (no ribs), straight-cut f-holes, 12 frets clear of body, Dobro style tailpiece.

Mid 1930s Style O, small diamond-hole pattern resonator cover, edges of f-holes rolled into body, 14 frets clear of body.

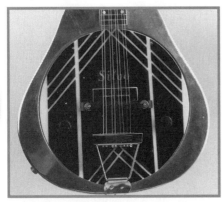

Rectangular pickup with split blade, on a Silvo mandolin, used on Silvo models and other electrics in the late 1930s.

Square control plate, strings-through-pickup design, used on almost all Supro lap steels.

Floating vinyl-covered pickup, used on National and Supro models in the early 1950s.

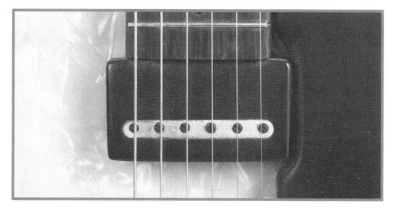

Metal-covered pickup with screws in side of mounting ring, used from 1954–57. Earlier models with this pickup have no mounting ring. Later models have no screws in side of mounting ring.

Silkscreened design on pick-ups, 1962–65.

Shield decal on a 1930s Triolian mandolin.

Ebonoid peghead veneer with etched logo, on a late 1930s Silvo mandolin.

Supro peghead shape from 1962–68, with plastic logo. Earlier (1955–62) pegheads are narrower. National pegheads from 1958–68 are longer on the treble side.

Metal serial number plate used on all Valco-made instruments and amps from 1941–63.

Foil serial number sticker used on Valco-made instruments from 1964–68.

SERIAL NUMBERS

PATENTS ON NATIONAL MODELS

NUMBER	GRANTED	FOR
1,741,453	Dec. 21, 1929	tri-cone resonator
1,808,756	June 9, 1931	biscuit resonator

SERIAL NUMBERS, 1927–35

From 1927–35, National used various serial number series for different models.

On single-cone models, the number is usually stamped onto the top of the peghead, except on Style Os with S-prefix numbers, which are usually stamped into the body by the endpin.

On roundneck tri-cone models, the number is stamped into the body by the endpin up until #2400. On squareneck tri-cone models, the number is stamped into the back of the metal neck near the peghead up until #2400. After #2400 on both models the number is stamped on the top of the peghead.

Numbers in these tables are arranged by the following priority: all numerals, numerals with letter suffix, numerals with letter prefix.

This information and number list was compiled by Bob Brozman.

NUMBER RANGE	DESCRIPTION	DATE RANGE
Tri-Cones		
0100–01002	roundneck	1928–30
100–3323	squareneck	1927–34
S prefix	roundneck	1930–33
Tenors, Styles 1–3		
100–600	tri-cone	1928
600–850	pear-shape, 1 cone	1929
850–1400	guitar-shape, 1 cone	1939–34
Other, Styles 1–3		
100–602	mandolin	1928–34
100–405	uke.	1928–34
Triolian		
0100–0202	yellow	1929
1107–1443	woodbody	1928–29 (many with no number)
A223–A1814*	Bakelite neck**	1930
1B–87B	green, 12-fret.	1933
26P–2249P	yellow, 12-fret	1930–33
2250P–2311P	yellow, 14-fret	1934–35
50W–3173W	brown, 12-fret	1928–35
3174W–3346W	brown, 14-fret	1935–39

* A-prefix numbers are used on other models in 1938 (see following).

** As many as half of the approximately 1800 Bakelite-neck Triolians were returned to the factory for a wood neck. Renecked examples may have a serial number from a later date than other specs would indicate.

NATIONAL/VALCO

NUMBER RANGE	DESCRIPTION	DATE RANGE
Triolian Tenor		
800–1483		1928–early 1930s
W or P suffix		1928–early 1930s
Duolian		
2402–7580	14-fret	1936–37
01236–06123	12-fret	1930–35
07919–09464	14-fret	1935–36
C1–C6500*	12-fret, straight *f*-holes	1930–33
C6500–C7500*	12-fret, rolled *f*-holes	1933–34
C7501–C9721*	14-fret, slot-head	1935–36
E7580–E7807	14-fret	1935–36
R60–R572	12-fret, made for Sears	1930–32

* C-prefix numbers are used on other models in 1938 (see following).

Style O		
290–5659	14-fret, slot-head	1935
5659–7027	14-fret, solid-head	1936–37
S1–S4400	12-fret, straight *f*-holes	1930–33
S4401–S5401	12-fret, rolled *f*-holes	1933–34
S5401–S6205	14-fret	1934–35

El Trovador	
K prefix	1933

Trojan	
T001–T2025	1934–35

Serial Numbers, 1936–42

From 1936–42, a single series was used for all instruments. The 1936–42 numbers are referred to as Chicago numbers. Information for 1936–42 numbers was provided by Bob Brozman and Mike Newton.

LETTER	ACOUSTICS	ELECTRICS
A prefix*	1937	1936–37
B prefix	1936	1937–38
C prefix*	1938	1938–40
FS suffix	factory second	
G prefix		1941–42
G suffix		1943–47
L prefix	1939	
N prefix		1935
S prefix		1935–36

*A and C prefixes also occur in some pre-1936 number series.

SERIAL NUMBER PLATES, 1947–63

Beginning in 1941, Valco put the serial number on a small oblong aluminum plate, nailed onto the back of the neck near the peghead. These plates were also put on amplifiers. All Valco-made instruments and amps—including those made for Sears (Silvertone), Montgomery Ward (Airline), Gretsch, Oahu and others—are numbered in a single series. This information and number list was compiled by Mike Newton.

YEAR	APPROX. RANGE	YEAR	APPROX. RANGE
1947	V100–V7500	1958	X85000–X99000
1948	V7500–V15000		T100–T5000
1949	V15000–V25000	1959	T5000–T25000
1950	V25000–V35000	1960	T25000–T50000
1951	V35000–V38000	1961	T50000–T75000
	X100–X7000	1962	T75000–T90000
1952	X7000–X17000		G100–G5000
1953	X17000–X30000	1963	T90000–T99000
1954	X30000–X43000		G5000–G15000
1955	X43000–X57000	1964	G15000–G38000
1956	X57000–X71000	1965	G39000–G39999
1957	X71000–X85000		

SERIAL NUMBER STICKERS, 1964–68

In 1964, Valco replaced the aluminum serial number plate with a rectangular foil sticker. Stickers have numeric prefixes.

PREFIX	RANGE
1	1965–early 1968
2	early–mid 1968

NATIONAL RESO-PHONIC, 1989–CURRENT

Serial numbers are on a paper label on the inside back. Some also have a penciled production code number that may include a year and a month.

All woodbody instruments except Radio-Tone Model B and ResoLectric are numbered in one consecutive series. All other models have their own number series.

YEAR	APPROX. LAST NUMBER	YEAR	APPROX. LAST NUMBER
Woodbody Models		*Radio-Tone B*	
1989	86	1996	2
1990	156	1997	42
1991	241	1998	75
1992	335		
1993	404	*ResoLectric*	
1994	492	1990	40
1995	523	1991	120
1996	546	1992	181
1997	613	1993	211
1998	623	1994	263
		1995	282
		1996	290
		1997	379
		1998	523

PREWAR RESONATOR MODELS

YEAR	APPROX. LAST NUMBER		YEAR	APPROX. LAST NUMBER
Styles O, O Deluxe			1996	235
1992	50		1997	325
1993	195		1998	422
1994	290			
1995	425		*Style 1 1/2*	
1996	611		1994	3
1997	753		1995	5
1998	870		1996	11
			1997	22
Delphi			1998	26
1993	10			
1994	84		*Style 2*	
1995	158		1996	7
1996	289		1997	9
1997	426		1998	11
1998	603			
			Style 3	
Duolian			1994	5
1992–93	111		1995	25
			1996	31
Style N			1997	35
1993	1		1998	40
1994	6			
1995	22		*Style 4*	
1996	39		1996	11
1997	89		1997	none
1998	129		1998	13
Ukes			*Polychrome Tricone*	
1997	67		1994	58
1998	171		1995	112
			1996	178
Style 1			1997	228
1994	43		1998	338
1995	127			

PREWAR RESONATOR MODELS KEY

Plastic-covered solid wood body
    Cutaway, bound fingerboard = **Resophonic (No. 1133)**
    Non-cutaway, square neck = **Resophonic (No. 1033)**
Molded plastic hollowbody
    White = **Bluegrass 35**
    Red = **(Supro) Folk Star**
    Black = **(Montgomery Ward) Airline**
    Sunburst = **model name unknown**

Woodbody
    Yellow-painted body = **Triolian wood body**
    Magnolia body = **California**
    Mahogany top
        Varied pattern inlay = **Estralita**
        Dot inlay = **El Trovador**
    Maple top
        Bound fingerboard = **Trojan**
        Unbound fingerboard = **Rosita**
    Spruce top
        Dot inlay = **Havana**
        Double-parallelogram inlay = **Aragon de Luxe**
Metalbody
    Tri-cone resonator
        Plain nickel-plate finish = **Style 1**
        Wriggly engraving around borders = **Style "1 1/2"**
        Rose pattern engraving
            No roses on coverplate = **Style 2**
            Roses on coverplate = **Style "2 1/2"**
        Lily of the Valley engraving = **Style 3**
        Chrysanthemum engraving = **Style 4**
        Musician scene on back = **Style 35**
        Surfer scene on back = **Style 97**
        Maple-grain paint finish = **M-3 (Marino)**
    Single-cone resonator
        Chrome plating
            Don on bridge cover
                Plain body = **Don Style 1**
                Sheaf of flowers engraving = **Don Style 2**
                Other elaborate engraving = **Don Style 3**
            No Don on bridge cover
                Palm tree etching (8 variations) = **Style O**
                No etching = **Style N**
        Paint finish
            Bound fingerboard = **Triolian**
            Unbound fingerboard
                Gray or brown finish = **Duolian**
                Maple finish = **Collegian**

NATIONAL NON-RESONATOR ACOUSTICS, 1940s AND 1950s KEY

Round hole, flat top
    17" wide = **N-1111**
    16" wide = **N-66 or 1155**
    14 1/4" wide
        Neck heel = **N-33 or 1160**
        No neck heel = **1150**
    13 1/4" wide = **Student model No. 1191**

ƒ-holes, archtop
> Split half-circle inlay = **N-150 or 1135**
> Dot inlay
>> Gibson L-50 body shape
>>> Clear pickguard = **N-100 or 1145**
>>> Opaque pickguard = **1140**
>> Harmony or Kay body shape = **N-50 or NA-35**

NATIONAL ACOUSTICS

SECTION ORGANIZATION

Tri-plates or "Silvers"
Other Tri-cones
Single-Cone Resonator, Metalbody, 1928–43
Single-Cone Resonator, Woodbody, 1928–43
Single-Cone Resonator, 1950s–60s
Non-Resonator Models
National Reso-Phonic, 1989–Current

TRI-PLATES OR "SILVERS"

German silver body (solid nickel alloy with nickel plating), tri-cone resonator with 2 cones on bass side and 1 on treble, T-shaped bridge cover and handrest, grid-pattern soundholes on upper body, Hawaiian (squareneck) or Spanish (roundneck), 12 frets clear of body, mahogany neck, slotted peghead

Earliest examples: cone configuration offset from the 2 cones on bass side and 1 on treble side arrangement, different shape bridge cover/handrest, grid holes on upper body actually woven with separate pieces of metal soldered to body

Style 1: plain body, early examples with unbound fingerboard, later with bound fingerboard, dot inlay, squareneck model has 1 dot at 12th fret

"Style 1 1/2" (collectors' term): many examples of Style 1 with wriggly line engraved around borders

Style 2: Wild Rose or Wild Irish Rose engraving, no engraving on coverplate, dot inlay

"Style 2 1/2" (collectors' term): some 1927–28 examples of Style 2 with roses engraved on coverplate as well as on body

Style 3: Lily of the Valley engraving, bound ebony fingerboard, diamond inlay, some with ebony peghead veneer and pearl logo, some with celluloid peghead veneer and etched logo

Style 4: Chrysanthemum engraving, bound ebony fingerboard, diamond inlay, some with ebony peghead veneer and pearl logo, some with celluloid peghead veneer and engraved logo

Styles 1 and 2, Spanish and Hawaiian, introduced: **1927**
Styles 3 and 4, Spanish and Hawaiian, introduced: **1928**
Style 4, clear pickguard: **1936**
Style 3 referred to as **Artist (S-3)**, with squareneck, dot inlay: **1937**
Style 4, ebonoid peghead veneer: **by 1938**
Style 4 discontinued: **1940**
Styles 1, 2 and 3 discontinued: **1943**

Tenor (23" scale) or **plectrum** (26" scale): triangular body shape, tri-cone resonator, no upper body holes, coverplate like guitars, 3-piece maple neck (earliest with mahogany neck), straight-through banjo-type tuners, banjo-type peghead
Introduced in Styles 1, 2 and 3 only; no Style 4: **1928**
Pear-shaped body, single-cone resonator: **by 1930**
Guitar-shaped body: **1931**
Styles 1 and 2 discontinued; Style 3 only: **1936**
Clear pickguard: **1937**
Style 3 discontinued: **by 1939**

Mandolin: triangular body shape, tri-cone resonator, no upper body holes, coverplate like guitars
Introduced in Styles 1, 2 and 3 only; no Style 4: **1928**
Single-cone resonator: **1928**
Styles 1 and 2 discontinued; Style 3 only: **1936**
Clear pickguard: **1937**
Style 3 discontinued: **by 1939**

Ukulele: guitar-shaped body, single-cone resonator, no upper body holes, 5 diamond-shaped hole clusters in coverplate
Introduced in Styles 1, 2, and 3 only; no Style 4: **1928**
Smaller body: **by 1931**
Styles 1 and 2 discontinued; Style 3 only: **1936**
Style 3 discontinued: **by 1939**

OTHER TRI-CONES

Triolian woodbody: earliest examples with round coverplate and 3 cones (see Single-Cone Resonator, Woodbody, following)
Available: **late 1928**

Style 35: nickel-plated brass body, etching of Renaissance musician under willow tree on back, airbrushed enamel coloring, maple neck, 12 frets clear of body, bound ebonoid fingerboard on Hawaiian model, bound rosewood fingerboard on Spanish model, dot inlay, solid peghead (tenor and mandolin mentioned in literature but not produced)
Introduced: **1936**
Ebonoid peghead veneer: **1937**
Etched body but with no color: **by 1939**
Discontinued: **by 1942**

Style 97: nickel-plated brass body, etching of surf rider on back, airbrushed enamel coloring, 12 frets clear of body, bound ebony fingerboard, mahogany neck, slotted peghead with point at top, ebonoid peghead veneer, shield logo with 3 vertical lines
Tenor: guitar-shaped body, single resonator, 4 ribs on coverplate, opaque pickguard, maple neck
Mandolin: triangular body shape, single-cone resonator, 4 ribs on cover plate
Style 97 guitar, tenor and mandolin introduced: **1936**
Clear pickguard: **1937**
Also referred to as **Marino 97**: **1940**
Discontinued: **1940**

M-3 Hawaii: nickel-plated brass body
Introduced: **c. 1937**
woodgrain enamel finish: **by 1942**
Discontinued: **1943**

SINGLE-CONE RESONATOR, METALBODY, 1928–43

All have coverplate with 9 diamond-shaped hole clusters, unless otherwise noted. Some coverplates have 4 raised "ribs" radiating from center.

Triolian: woodbody (see Single-Cone Resonator, Woodbody, following)
Introduced: **late 1928**
Triolian metalbody replaces woodbody, steel body, round shoulders, upper *f*-holes with straight-cut edges, 12 frets clear of body, bound ebonized fingerboard, slotted peghead, brown "2-tone walnut" sunburst finish or yellow finish with stenciled tropical scene on back, tenor, mandolin and uke available: **1929**
Shaded walnut, "polychrome" maple sunburst or yellow/green finish, palm tree scene stenciled on back, many yellow/green examples with Bakelite neck: **1930**
Squareneck available by special order: **1933**
Rolled edges of *f*-holes: **1933**
Shorter body, square shoulders, straight-cut *f*-holes, 14 frets clear of body, 2-tone walnut sunburst finish: **by 1935**
Solid peghead: **1936**
Pickguard with diagonal stripes and letter *N*, rosewood fingerboard, ebonoid peghead veneer, painted mahogany-grain finish: **1937**
Discontinued: **1940**

Duolian: steel body, round shoulders, upper *f*-holes with straight-cut edges, unbound fingerboard of ebonized maple, 12 frets clear of body, "frosted duco" paint finish with crystal-like texture, finish varies in color from light gray to greenish gray to black, some with walnut-grain finish
Introduced: **1930**
Squareneck available by special order: **1933**
Rolled edges on *f*-holes, mahogany neck: **1933**
Shorter body, squared shoulders, straight-cut *f*-holes, rosewood fingerboard, 14 frets clear of body, solid peghead standard (slotted still available): **by 1935**
5 large round "sieve-holes" in coverplate, solid peghead: **1936**
Plain black pickguard (Spanish only), "red bean" fingerboard, unspecified hardwood neck, walnut grain paint finish: **by 1937**
Discontinued: **1939**

Style O: nickel-plated brass body, upper *f*-holes with straight-cut edges, Hawaiian scenes sandblasted on front and back, palm trees to right of resonator, canoe on left side of back, sandblasted sides, 12 frets clear of body, maple neck, single-bound fingerboard of ebonized maple, dot inlay, slotted peghead, decal logo
Early examples: nickel-plated steel body, front palm trees to bass side of resonator
Introduced: **July 1930**
Tenor, mandolin and uke available: **by 1932**
Rolled *f*-hole edges, squareneck available: **1933**

Shorter body, 14 frets clear of body, front palm trees on both sides of resonator, canoe on right side of back, no side etching: **by Dec. 1934**

Small diamond-shaped hole patterns in coverplate: **1935**

Pickguard with flower, bound ebony fingerboard, block inlay, solid peghead with block-letter *National* etched in pearloid block, some with slotted peghead: **1936**

Clear pickguard, unspecified hardwood neck, parallelogram inlay, ebonoid peghead veneer, metal shield logo plate: **1937**

Palm trees etched on sides: **by 194**0

Uke discontinued: **by 1942**

All Style O models discontinued: **1943**

Style N: plain body version of Style O, nickel-plated brass body, no etching, 12 frets clear of body, bound ebonoid fingerboard, pearloid peghead veneer

Introduced: **1930–31**

Collegian: similar to Duolian, steel body, round holes in coverplate, clear pickguard, 14 frets clear of body, dot inlay, solid peghead, metal logo plate, maple-yellow finish, round or square neck

Introduced in Supro line: **1938**

Moved to National line, tenor and mandolin available: **by 1942**

Discontinued: **1943**

"Don" Silver Guitars: nickel-plated brass body, upper *f*-holes, single-cone resonator, *Don* on bridge cover, 14 frets clear of body, bound fingerboard, slotted peghead

Don Style 1: plain body except for engraved borders, pearl dot inlay, mahogany neck, white pearlette peghead veneer

Don Style 2: "modernistic" body engraving somewhat resembling sheaves of flowers, block inlay specified but some with dot

Don Style 3: same with more elaborate engraving than Don Style 2, described as "conventional" pattern, diamond-shaped inlay

Don series introduced: **by 193**4

Discontinued: **1936**

SINGLE-CONE RESONATOR, WOODBODY, 1928–43

California: magnolia body, mahogany neck

14 prototypes made: **1928**

Triolian woodbody: upper *f*-holes, earliest examples with diamond-shape screen holes in coverplate and 3 resonator cones, later with 1 cone and standard single-cone coverplate, 12 frets clear of body, bound ebonized fingerboard specified but most with yellow body finish on fingerboard, yellow finish with red and blue highlights, *PATAPPFOR* on body (not on plate), ocean scene decal on front, Hawaiian girl decal on back, tenor available

Introduced: **late 1928**

Discontinued, replaced by Triolian metalbody (see Single-Cone Resonator, Metalbody, 1928–43, preceding): **1929**

Rosita: maple or birch veneer body probably made by Harmony, lyre-shaped holes in upper body, trapeze tailpiece, bound top and back, 14 frets clear of body, ebonized fingerboard, dot inlay, slotted peghead, 2-tone mahogany finish, round or square neck

Introduced: **1933**

f-holes in upper body: **by 1937**

Discontinued: **1939**

El Trovador: body made by Kay, mahogany top, 2-piece matched mahogany back, upper *f*-holes, triple-bound top and back, trapeze tailpiece, 12 frets clear of body, bound fingerboard, dot inlay, slotted peghead, serial number beginning with *K*

Available for 8 months: **1933**

Trojan: maple veneer body, upper *f*-holes, trapeze tailpiece, bound top, 14 frets clear of body, bound fingerboard, slotted peghead, shaded walnut finish

Introduced: **1934**

Unbound fingerboard, shaded walnut finish: **by 1935**

Opaque pickguard: **1936**

Dobro-type tailpiece, ebonoid pickguard with stripes and letter *N* (Spanish only), bound top and back, rosewood fingerboard, solid peghead, bound ebonoid peghead veneer: **by 1937**

Discontinued: **by 1942**

Estralita: mahogany top, 2-piece matched mahogany back, upper *f*-holes, 4-ply binding around coverplate hole, 4-ply binding on top and back, unbound fingerboard, 14 frets clear of body, varied-pattern inlay, solid peghead, shaded brown finish, tenor, mandolin and uke available

Introduced: **by 1934**
Discontinued: **by 1942**

Havana: spruce top, upper *f*-holes, roundneck or
squareneck, bound fingerboard, dot inlay, some
with 3 dots at 5th and 9th frets, ebonoid peghead
veneer, natural top finish, sunburst back finish
Introduced: **1938**
Clear pickguard: **by 1939**
Discontinued: **1942**

Aragon de Luxe/Aragon No. 5: archtop,
spruce top, maple back and sides, bound upper *f*-
holes, radial pattern coverplate with semi-rectangular holes in groups of 3, broad plate tailpiece, clear
pickguard, triple-bound top and back, bound rosewood fingerboard, double-parallelogram inlay, rosewood peghead veneer, bound peghead,
chrome-plated hardware, light brown sunburst finish, similar in appearance to a fancy Kay guitar
Available: **1939–42**

SINGLE-CONE RESONATOR, 1950S–60S

After World War II, National/Valco announced its intent
to market the following models: Collegian, Aragon,
Style O, M-3 and S-3. However, there is no evidence that these or any other metalbody instruments were made after World War II. None appears
on the National price list of February 1948.

Reso-phonics

No. 1133: 12" wide, semi-solid woodbody, single
cutaway, small resonator coverplates on front and
back, plastic coverplate on upper bouts, shield logo
plate on upper bass bout, Dobro-type tailpiece,
22" scale, dot inlay, shield logo plate on peghead,
rounded peghead corners, body covered with black,
white or maroon pearloid

Reso-phonic: white pearloid version of No. 1133,
model name on plastic plate on upper body

No. 1033: Hawaiian style, non-cutaway with small
upper bouts, small resonator coverplates on front
and back, no plastic plate on upper bouts, Dobro-
type tailpiece, 22" scale, diagonal stairstep markers
(like lap steels), shield logo plate on peghead, body
covered with black, white or maroon pearloid
Introduced as "Student Instruments": **1956**
Discontinued from catalogs: **1958**

Sold as late as: **1964**
Some assembled from old parts for bankruptcy auction, no logo plate, squared-off peghead, serial
number on a foil sticker: **1968**

Bluegrass 35: 15" wide, molded Res-o-glas (fiberglass) body, non-cutaway, no upper soundholes,
small diamond-shaped holes in coverplate, stickpin
logo on upper bass bout, quarter-circle inlay, Arctic
white
Available: **1963–64**

Folk Star: red fiberglass body, Supro logo, see
Supro Guitars, Basses, and Mandolins

Airline: black fiberglass body, Airline (Montgomery
Ward) model, see Airline section

Sunburst resonator model (name unknown):
15" wide, molded Res-O-Glas (fiberglass) body,
2 screen holes on upper bouts, dot or block inlay,
scroll-shaped peghead, tortoiseshell celluloid peghead veneer, sunburst finish sprayed over red fiberglass body
Available: **1960s**

NON-RESONATOR MODELS

In 1947, National announced three 17"-wide archtops
available in natural or sunburst finish, two
16 1/4"-wide archtops, three sizes (unspecified) of
flat tops, and two mandolins.
The following postwar bodies (and possibly some necks)
were made by Gibson, except where noted. Also,
some non-catalog examples exist with combinations
of National and Gibson specs and ornamentation.
All of National's Spanish style guitars were fitted with
the Stylist Hand-Fit neck, a heel-less design not
made by Gibson, beginning in 1949.

ARCHTOPS

N-275: 17" wide, sunburst or blond finish (only
specs available)
Only listing: **1947**

N-150/1135: Gibson L-7 body (some with Gibson
neck), 17" wide, clear pickguard, triple-bound top and
back, bound fingerboard, split half-circle inlay, bound
peghead, ebonoid peghead veneer, shield logo, sunburst or blond finish

Introduced as **N-150: 1947**
Renamed **1135: 1948**
Stylist hand-fit heel-less neck: **1949**
Triple-bound rosewood peghead veneer: **1951**
Dark pickguard: **c. 1951**
Discontinued: **1954**

N-125: 17" wide, sunburst or blond (only specs
available)
Only listing: **1947**

N-100/1140/Cameo: Gibson L-50 body (some
with Gibson neck), 16 1/4" wide, clear pickguard,
metal endpin, bound top and back, dot inlay, wide
shield logo, sunburst finish
Introduced as **N-100: 1947**
Renamed **1145: 1948**
Stylist hand-fit heel-less neck: **1949**
Replaced by **1140**, opaque pickguard: **1951**
Renamed **Cameo**: 15 1/2" wide: **1957**
Discontinued: **1958**

N-50: archtop, 16 1/4" wide, sunburst finish, probably made by Kay (only specs available)
Only listing: **1947**

NA-35: archtop, 16 1/4" wide, sunburst finish, probably made by Kay (only specs available)
Only listing: **1947**

FLAT TOPS

N-111: body shape like Gibson SJ-200, 17" wide,
sunburst finish
Only listing: **1947**

N-66/1155: Gibson J-45 body (some with Gibson
neck), 16" wide, round-shouldered dreadnought,
mahogany back and sides, triple-bound top, single-
bound back, dot inlay, wide shield logo, sunburst
finish
Introduced as **N-66: 1947**
Renamed **1155: 1948**
Stylist hand-fit heel-less neck: **1949**
Natural finish optional: **by 1951**
Natural finish standard: **1954**
Factory-installed pickup (No. 1155E) with poles
through fingerboard optional (see Hollowbody
Electrics section): **1954**

Discontinued: **1961**

N-33/1150: Gibson LG-1 body, 14 1/4" wide,
mahogany back and sides, dot inlay, shield logo
plate, natural top finish
Introduced as **N-33: 1947**
Renamed **1160: 1948**
Replaced by **1150**, rounder body shape more like 000
Martin, body probably made by Harmony or Kay,
wide shield logo plate: **1951**
Discontinued: **1958**

Student Model No. 1191/Student Trial:
non-Gibson body, 13 1/4" wide, compensating
height-adjustable bridge, Dobro-type tailpiece, dot
inlay, wide shield logo, sunburst finish
Introduced: **1952**
Listed as **Student Trial Guitar: 1954**
Discontinued: **1955**

1967 FLAT TOPS

N-700: 15 1/2" wide, square-shouldered dreadnought, maple back and sides, point on belly of
bridge, butterfly (diamond enclosed by block) inlay,
asymmetrical peghead

N-730: 15 1/2" wide, jumbo shape (rounded bouts),
maple back and sides, point on belly of bridge,
butterfly (diamond enclosed by block) inlay, asymmetrical peghead

N-720: 15 1/2" wide, dreadnought shape, mahogany
back and sides, fancy bridge with whale fluke shape
at each end, wide soundhole ring, block inlay,
asymmetrical peghead

N-710: 15 1/2" wide, mahogany back and sides, point
on belly of bridge, block inlay, asymmetrical peghead

N-55/N-550: 14" wide, classical, rectangular
bridge, wide soundhole ring, no inlay, symmetrical
slotted peghead, no peghead logo

N-580: 15 3/4" wide, 12-string, trapeze tailpiece,
block inlay, symmetrical peghead, sunburst finish
Available: **1967–early 1968**

MANDOLINS

N-51: carved top, sunburst or blond finish (only

specs available)

N-31: carved top, sunburst finish (only specs available)
Only listing: **1947**

Banjos

N-575: maple resonator and neck, bound finger-board, dot inlay, 3-tone sunburst finish, 5-string, tenor (**N-575T**) or plectrum (**N-575P**)
Available: **early 1968**

National Reso-Phonic, 1989–Current

All have 12 frets clear of body, round neck.

Jazz Blues JB-1: single cone, woodbody, maple neck, rosewood fingerboard, amber-to-walnut sun-burst, ivoroid binding
225 made: **1989–94**

Islander: single cone, woodbody, no binding, maple neck, rosewood fingerboard, pink top finish with stenciled trim, painted island scene of surfers and Diamond Head on back
82 made: **1989–92**

Deluxe Islander: pearloid peghead veneer, pearloid binding on body and fingerboard
41 made: **1989–92**

M-1 Mahogany: single cone, 5-ply mahogany top, solid mahogany back and sides, mahogany neck, ebony fingerboard, 3-ply bound top and back with ivoroid outer layer, pearloid peghead veneer, engraved logo
73 made: **1990–94**

Style O: single cone, nickel-plated brass body, etched palm tree scene, 12 frets clear of body, ivo-roid-bound ebony fingerboard, dot inlay, squared-off slotted peghead, approx. 920 made as of Feb. 1999
Available: **1992–current**

Style O gold-plated: available by special order, 8 made: **1993–94**

Style O Deluxe: double-line with wriggle engraved around top border, ebony fingerboard, diamond inlay, 10 made as of Feb. 1999: **1994–current**

Style N: similar to Style O but with plain (non-etched) body, 137 made as of Feb. 1999
Available: **1993–current**

ResoLectric: single cutaway, single-cone style coverplate, small thin body, alder back, maple top veneer, 2 pointer knobs on upper bass bout, ivoroid-bound top, maple neck, dot inlay, solid peaked peghead narrows toward top

R-1 ResoLectric: coverplate on top and back, Chandler lipstick pickup in neck position, L.R. Baggs acoustic under-saddle pickup, 206 made: **1990–93**

R-2 ResoLectric: no coverplate on back, pearloid or tortoiseshell celluloid pickguard, otherwise similar to R-1, approx. 90 made: **1993–96**

R-3 ResoLectric: Seymour Duncan P-90 cream soap-bar pickup in neck position, Highlander transducer pickup under saddle, 3 pointer knobs and selector switch on upper bass bout, 243 made as of Feb. 1999: **late 1996–current**

Duolian/Delphi: single cone, steel body, mahog-any neck, unbound rosewood fingerboard, dot inlay, squared-off slotted peghead with *National Duolian* stamp, baked paint "appliance" finish on body and coverplate, deep green, charcoal grey or dark brown finish
Introduced as **Duolian**, 111 made: **1992–93**
Renamed **Delphi:** bound rosewood fingerboard, dot inlay, shield logo variety of baked paint "appliance" finishes: **late 1993**
Still in production, 603 made as of Feb. 1999

Radio-Tone Bendaway/Model B: single cone, single cutaway, laminated top and back of unspecified wood, solid maple sides, 3 soundhole slots on both upper bouts, unbound fingerboard, dot inlay, 1930s style rounded-top peghead with ebonoid veneer, 79 made as of Feb. 1999
Available: **late 1996–current**

Radio-Tone: symmetrical body, 218 made: **1994–98**

Estralita: single cone, laminated top and back of unspecified wood, solid maple sides, bound top, maple neck, bound fingerboard, dot inlay, squared-off slotted peghead with ivoroid veneer, 60 made as of Feb. 1999

Available: **1997–current**

Style 1 Tricone: nickel-plated brass body, mahogany neck, bound ebony fingerboard, dot inlay, slotted peghead with point at top, vintage-style tuners, 432 made as of Feb. 1999
Available: **1994–current**

Style 1 1/2/Wriggle Tricone: similar to Style 1 but with added wriggle lines around edges, nickel- or silver-plated, 26 made as of Feb. 1999
Available: **1994–current**

Style 3 Tricone: nickel-plated brass body, engraved on front, back and sides with lily pattern, mahogany neck, bound ebony fingerboard, pearl diamond inlay, ivoroid peghead veneer, engraved 3-on-a-plate tuners, slotted peghead with point at top, vintage 41 made as of Feb. 1999
Introduced: **1994**
Approx. 5 with silver-plated body: **1995**
Still in production

Style 4 Tricone: engraved on front, back and sides with chrysanthemum pattern, mahogany neck, ivoroid heel cap, bound ebony fingerboard, pearl diamond inlay, ivoroid peghead veneer, engraved 3-on-a-plate tuners, slotted peghead with point at top, 13 made as of Feb. 1999
Available: **1995–current**

Style 2 Tricone: rose-pattern engraving, 11 made as of Feb. 1999
Available: **1996–current**

Style 3 Single Cone/SLO Model 3: engraved on front, back and sides with lily pattern, figured maple neck, bound ebony fingerboard, pearl diamond inlay, ivoroid peghead veneer, engraved 3-on-a-plate tuners, slotted squared-off peghead, 13 made as of Feb. 1999
Available: **1993–current**

Polychrome Tricone: steel body, mahogany neck, bound ebony fingerboard, dot inlay, solid peaked peghead with ebonoid veneer (late 1930s style), variety of baked paint "appliance" finishes, 338 made as of Nov. 1999
Available: **1994–current**

Ukuleles: soprano size, metal body, 7 1/8 " wide, single cone, bound ebony fingerboard, rounded-top peghead, 180 made (about half with nickel-plated body, half with paint finish) as of Feb. 1999

Nickel-plated: brass body, dot inlay, *NATIONAL* block-letter peghead logo: **1997–current**

Painted: steel body, dot inlay, *NATIONAL* block-letter peghead logo: **1997–current**

Style 3: nickel-plated brass body, engraved with lily pattern, diamond inlay, ebonoid peghead veneer, shield logo: **1997–current**

COMMENTS

National's resonator instruments produced significantly more volume than conventional acoustic guitars and were highly popular in the late 1920s and early 1930s, with tri-cone models appealing to Hawaiian-style performers and single-cone models appealing to blues players.

All of the tri-cone models are highly sought by collectors, with the rarer, more ornate Styles 2, 3 and 4 bringing more than plainer models. Roundneck tri-cones are rarer than squarenecks and bring much higher prices. Squareneck tri-cones are highly sought by those Hawaiian style players who play metalbody instruments. (Hawaiian style players who play woodbody guitars prefer Dobro models.)

Of the single-cone metalbody models, Style 0 is the most highly regarded by collectors. The Triolian and the plainer Duolian are very highly regarded by blues players, many of whom feel that the steel-body sound has yet to be surpassed for Delta blues music. The Don models are so rare that it is difficult to estimate their appeal, but they exceed the Style 0 in value.

Woodbody resonator models have some appeal to collectors but generally do not bring as much as a Duolian in equivalent condition, except for the early woodbody Triolian.

Postwar resonator models, with semi-solid wood or hollow fiberglass construction, have some appeal to collectors and players because of their unique design and funky sound, but they bring less than woodbody resonator models from the prewar period.

Some of the archtop models are interesting for historic and aesthetic reasons, but they are not highly regarded by collectors or players.

NATIONAL ELECTRIC HOLLOWBODIES KEY

Metalbody = **Silvo**
Flat top woodbody = **1155E**
Archtop
    Pointed cutaway = **Bel-Aire**
    Rounded cutaway = **Debonaire**
    Non-cutaway
        1 pickup with poles
            Block inlay
                Pickup in neck position = **California**
                Pickup near bridge = **Princess**
            Parallelogram inlay = **New Yorker Spanish, 1938–47**
            Dot inlay
                No soundholes = **Chicago**
                f-holes
                    Natural finish, 16 1/4" wide = **New Yorker, 1947–58**
                    Sunburst finish, 15 1/4" wide = **Dynamic**
        1 blade pickup
            Dot inlay = **Electric Spanish, 1935–36**
            Block inlay
                No soundholes = **Electric Spanish, late 1936–late 1938**
                f-holes = **Aristocrat, c. 1941–42**
        1 standard pickup and 1 bridge pickup = **Aristocrat, 1942–53**
        2 standard pickups = **Sonora**

ELECTRIC HOLLOWBODIES

All National archtop electrics have the Stylist heel-less neck by 1949.

Some models from the late 1940s and 1950s have bodies made by Gibson or Harmony. Gibson bodies can be identified by their distinctive shape, the presence of an ink-stamped work order number inside the body and workmanship.

SECTION ORGANIZATION

Archtops
Flat Tops
Other Electric Instruments (except steel guitars)

ARCHTOPS

Electric Spanish/New Yorker: body and neck made by Regal, 15 1/2" wide, spruce top, laminated maple back and sides, 3-segment *f*-holes, blade pickup in oblong "airplane" housing pointing toward bridge, pickup stamped *Pat. Appl'd.*, pickup in bridge position, volume control and jack on top next to tailpiece (some late examples of this version have jack on rim), trapeze tailpiece, single-bound top, unbound back, dovetail neck joint, bound rosewood fingerboard, multiple dots-and-diamonds inlay, rosewood peghead veneer, National shield decal logo, Harmony-made tuners with metal "butterbean" buttons, sunburst finish

Introduced as **Electric Spanish** (similar model introduced earlier under Dobro brand, see Dobro section): **April 1935**

Tone control added, jack on rim on treble side: **late 1935**

Extended pickup mounting "ears" with 2 knobs to adjust pickup height, *Pat. Pending* stamped on pickup coil housing, pickguard cut out to accommodate pickup, knobs on opposite sides, Harmony Tone-Rite tuners with hexagonal base plates and 5-sided metal buttons: **early 1936**

Pickup cover points toward neck, volume and tone knobs on lower treble bout: **early to mid 1936**

Volume and tone knobs on upper bass bout, bound tortoiseshell celluloid pickguard with engraved flower, pickguard stops short of pickup, screw-on jack on lower bass bout: **mid 1936**

Ebonoid pickguard with stripes and letter *N* triple-bound ebony fingerboard, large pearl block inlay, larger peghead with angled corners, ebonoid peghead veneer with binding simulated by beveled edge, *National* engraved on peghead: **late 1936**

Engraved shield peghead logo: **later 1936**

Rectangular pickup bolted to saddle and suspended through top, volume and tone knobs on lower treble bout, triple-bound top, non-angled corners on peghead, open-back Kluson tuners with metal buttons: **mid 1937**

Body made by Kay, no soundholes, 7-ply neck by National-Dobro, bolt-on neck tenon (similar to woodbody Dobro neck): **late 1937**

Renamed **New Yorker Spanish**: rectangular pickup with 2 rows of 3 poles (6 separate coils), pickup in neck position, ebony bridge, bound ebonoid pickguard, triple-bound top and back, 1-piece neck, bound ebony fingerboard, single-parallelogram inlay, single-bound peghead with ebonoid veneer, shield logo plate, natural or sunburst finish: **late 1938**

Pickup in bridge position, triple-bound top, single-bound back, 2-ply pickguard with binding simulated by beveled edge, rosewood fingerboard, block inlay to 10th fret, dot inlay at frets 15 (2) and 17, beveled peghead veneer to let maple peghead show along edges, long tuner enclosures: **c. 1941**

16 1/4" wide, *f*-holes, rectangular pickup with 6 poles in a single line, scalloped-edge pickguard with 2 knobs, trapeze tailpiece, double-bound top and back, dot inlay, wide shield logo plate, natural finish: **1947**

Designated No. 1120: **1954**

2 knobs into top, script logo, natural finish: **1955**

Model name on pickguard: **1956**

Discontinued: **1958**

Electric Tenor: 4-string tenor, similar to Spanish Electric but with dot inlay, logo straight across peghead, floral peghead ornament under logo: **1935–41**

Sonora: *f*-holes, blade pickup in neck position, rectangular pickup in bridge position, 2 knobs, screw-on jack on lower bass side, flat plate tailpiece, clear pickguard, bound fingerboard, double-parallelo-gram inlay, bound peghead, enclosed tuners, sunburst finish

Available: **1939–41**

Chicago: spruce top, no soundholes, rectangular pickup with 2 rows of 3 poles, pickup near bridge, jack on lower bass side, Dobro style tailpiece, dark pickguard, dark binding on top and back, dot inlay, natural finish

Available: **1942**

Princess: 15" wide, *f*-holes, rectangular pickup near bridge, 2 knobs, jack on upper bass side, trapeze tailpiece, tortoiseshell celluloid pickguard, triple-bound top and back, rosewood fingerboard, block inlay, tortoiseshell celluloid peghead veneer, natural finish

Introduced: **by 1942**

Sunburst finish optional: **1947**

Discontinued: **1948**

Aristocrat: 17" wide, spruce top, rectangular pickup near bridge, screw-on jack on lower bass side, double-bound top and back, brown pickguard, trapeze tailpiece, unbound rosewood fingerboard, large block inlay, bound peghead, natural top finish

Introduced: **by 1941**

Bound fingerboard, split half-circle inlay: **1942**

Large bridge/pickup assembly with 2 knobs on opposite sides of bridge (1 pickup only), jack into bridge, clear pickguard, triple-parallelogram inlay, logo with *National* through shield, 3 vertical lines below logo, appears in advertisement but with no model name: **early 1947**

Maple top, 1 standard pickup in neck position and 1 pickup integrated into bridge, 1 round black knob and 1 black pointer knob on lower treble bout, knobs on square plates, screw-on jack on lower treble side, plate tailpiece with *f*-hole cutout, clear pickguard, triple-parallelogram inlay, 3 vertical lines through peghead logo, natural or sunburst finish: **1947**

Designated No. 1111, no plates under knobs, sunburst finish only: **1948**

Body made by Gibson, maple back and sides, spruce top, triple-bound top, split half-circle inlay, bolt-on neck, sunburst finish: **by 1950** Body made by Kay, white knobs, dark pickguard with wavy edge extends below bridge, block inlay, stickpin figure

below logo: **1951**
Discontinued: **1954**

California (No. 1100): body made by Kay, 17" wide, laminated spruce top, laminated maple back and sides, 1 pickup in neck position with 6 poles in a line, controls in pickguard with screw-on jack, trapeze tailpiece, bound *f*-holes, double-bound top and back (some triple-bound), block inlay, wide logo plate, natural finish
Introduced: **1949**
Black plastic-covered floating pickup, script logo: **1953**
Discontinued: **1955**

Dynamic (No. 1125): 15 1/4" wide, metal-covered pickup in neck position, straight-edge pickguard with 2 knobs, trapeze tailpiece, single-bound top and back, single-bound *f*-holes, dot inlay, ebonoid peghead veneer, wide logo plate, sunburst finish
Introduced: **1951**
2 knobs into top, jack on side, script logo: **1955**
Model name on pickguard: **1956**
Discontinued: **by 1959**

Club Combo (No. 1170): 16 1/4" wide, rounded cutaway, 2 plastic-covered floating pickups, 4 knobs and 1 lever switch mounted in pickguard, short trapeze bridge, bound top, large block inlay, script logo, sunburst finish
Introduced: **1952**
Discontinued: **1955**
Reintroduced (No. 1185), tapered *f*-holes with smooth lines and no curl at ends, 2 pickups mounted into top, 2 knobs on lower treble bout, 1 lever switch on cutaway bout, asymmetrical plate tailpiece, blond finish: **1959**
Discontinued: **1961**

Debonaire (No. 1107): rounded cutaway, 1 pickup, 2 knobs on cutaway bout, trapeze tailpiece, bound top and back, bound *f*-holes, dot inlay, script logo, sunburst finish
Available: **1953–60**

Bel-Aire (No. 1109): Gibson ES-175 body, 16 1/4" wide, pointed cutaway, 2 pickups, 3 knobs on bass side, lever switch on cutaway bout, master tone knob and jack on lower treble bout, trapeze tailpiece, bound top and back, block inlay, script logo, sunburst finish

Introduced: **1953**
Model name on pickguard: **1956**
Renumbered 1198, 3 pickups, 4 knobs and jack on lower treble bout, 3-way slotted switch on cutaway bout, 3 knobs on upper bass bout, plate tailpiece with stairstep edges, metal tuner buttons: **1958**
Discontinued: **1961**

Del-Mar (No. 1103): 17" wide, rounded cutaway, 2 metal-covered pickups, 2 knobs and jack on lower treble bout, 1 lever switch on cutaway bout, adjustable bridge, plate tailpiece with 2 *f*-shaped cutouts, bound top and back, butterfly (diamond enclosed by block) inlay, butterfly tuner buttons, peghead logo plate, stickpin figure below logo, sunburst finish
Available: **1954–57**

Bobbie Thomas: thin double-cutaway body, stylized *f*-holes with 2 points at each end, 2 pickups, 4 knobs on lower treble cout, master volume control on upper treble bout, selector switch on upper bass bout, Bigsby vibrato, bound fingerboard, diamond-in-rectangle inlay, Grover Rotomatic tuners, signature on pickguard, sunset orange (**N-800**), cherry shade (**N-801**) or natural blond (**N-802**) finish
Available: **early 1968**

N-820/N821: similar to Bobbie Thomas but with adjustable bridge, non-Bigsby vibrato with flat arm, block inlay, no signature, emerald green (**N-820**) or sunburst (**N-821**) finish
Available: **early 1968**

N-830: similar to Bobbie Thomas but with vibrato mounted on top (not to endpin), tubular vibrato arm, no master volume control, no signature, block inlay, tuners with plastic butterfly buttons, cherry shade finish
Available: **early 1968**

FLAT TOPS

The Silvo style round ebonoid coverplate and electronics were available as optional equipment or replacement part for all National single-cone resonator guitars.

Tri-cones: a few tri-cone resonator models fitted with pickups: **mid 1930s**

Silvo: nickel-plated metalbody, upper *f*-holes, *Silvo* on round ebonoid coverplate, squareneck, 23" scale, ebonoid fingerboard and peghead veneer, Roman numeral parallelogram markers

Tenor and mandolin available, both with Dobro style tailpiece, both roundneck

Available: **1937–42**

Jumbo Flat Top Electric Spanish (No.

1155E): similar body to Gibson J-45, 16" wide, round-shouldered dreadnought shape, mahogany back and sides, pickup poles through fingerboard, knobs mounted into side near neck, bridge tapers to point below pins, triple-bound top, single-bound back, natural top finish

Available: **1954–61**

OTHER ELECTRIC INSTRUMENTS

Violelectric: violin, 1 knob on top

Introduced: **by 1936**

Discontinued: **by 1942**

New Yorker Mandolin: A-style body shape, 1 knob mounted on top, Dobro-type tailpiece, bound fingerboard

Introduced with no model name: **by 1936**

Named **New Yorker**, rectangular pickup cover, 2 knobs, shield logo: **by 1938**

Discontinued: **1942**

New Yorker Banjo: tenor neck, round body, spruce top, maple sides, arched back, 2 knobs, Dobro-type tailpiece, parallelogram inlay, shield logo

Introduced with no model name: **by 1936**

Named **New Yorker: by 1938**

Discontinued: **1942**

COMMENTS

National electric archtops have never been highly regarded by most players. Some models with innovative designs, such as archtops with no *f*-holes, are sought by collectors for historic and aesthetic reasons.

The metalbody Silvo model is highly sought by collectors.

NATIONAL ELECTRIC SOLIDBODIES KEY

Map-shaped body
 Butterfly (diamond enclosed by block) inlay (fiberglass body)
  Red finish = **Glenwood 95**
  White body finish
   Black neck finish = **Glenwood 98**
   White neck finish = **Glenwood 99, 1962**
  Sea foam green finish = **Glenwood 99, 1963–65**
 Block inlay (woodbody)
  1 pickup (blond or cherry finish) = **Westwood 72**
  1 pickup plus bridge pickup (black-to-cherry sunburst) = **Westwood 75**
  2 standard pickups plus bridge pickup (cherry finish) = **Westwood 77**
 Quarter-circle inlay (fiberglass body)
  Rounded upper treble horn
   Red finish (1 pickup) = **Val-Pro 82**
   White finish (1 standard pickup plus one bridge pickup) = **Val-Pro 84**
   Black finish (2 standard pickups plus bridge pickup) = **Val-Pro 88**
  Pointed upper treble horn
   Red finish = **Newport 82**
   Sea foam green finish = **Newport 84**
   Black finish = **Newport 88**

Non-map body shape
  Parallelogram inlay = **Town and Country**
  Butterfly (diamond enclosed by block) inlay
    Slight cutaway on bass side = **Val-Trol Custom**
    No cutaway on bass side
      Lever tone selector switch = **Glenwood, 1954–57**
      Slotted tone selector switch = **Glenwood Deluxe**
  Block inlay
    Long bass horn (body shape like Fender Jazzmaster)
      3 pickups = N-644
      2 pickups = N-634
      1 pickup - N-624
    Slight cutaway on bass side = **Val-Trol Baron**
    No cutaway on bass side
      Controls in pickguard = **No. 1124**
      Knobs into top
        2 knobs = **Avalon**
        4 knobs = **Stylist**
Dot inlay
  24 3/4" (standard) scale
    Vinyl-covered pickup
      Cutaway = **No. 1123**
      Non-cutaway = **No. 1122**
    Metal-covered pickup
      Sunburst finish
        6-string = **Bolero**
        12-string = **N-654**
      Beige fiberglass body = **Studio 66**
  22" scale
    Pickup in neck position (plus bridge pickup) = **Val-Trol Jr.**
    Pickup in bridge position = **Westwood**

NATIONAL ELECTRIC SOLIDBODIES

SECTION ORGANIZATION
Non-Map Body Shape
Map-Shaped Models

NON-MAP BODY SHAPE
Solid Body Electric Spanish/Cosmopolitan: 11 1/4" wide, adjustable rosewood bridge, short trapeze tailpiece, 24 3/4" scale, unbound fingerboard, dot inlay, symmetrical peghead, script logo, sunburst finish

Non-cutaway model: 1 vinyl-covered floating pickup in neck position, 2 knobs mounted on pickguard
Introduced as **Solid Body Electric Spanish** (No. 1122): **1952**

Renamed **Cosmopolitan: 1954**
Discontinued: **1956**

Cutaway model introduced as **Solid Body Electric Spanish** (No. 1123): **1952**
Discontinued, replaced by Bolero (No. 1132): **1956**

Double-pickup cutaway model, 2 vinyl-covered floating pickups, 4 knobs and 1 lever switch mounted on pickguard, block inlay, introduced as **Solid Body Electric Spanish** (No. 1124): **1952**
Blond finish optional (No. 1124B): **1954**
Discontinued, replaced by Avalon (No. 1134) (see following): **1956**

Town and Country (No. 1104): 12 1/4" wide, rounded cutaway, 2 metal-covered pickups, 6 knobs in single line on bass side, 1 lever switch on treble side, adjustable bridge, trapeze tailpiece, single-parallelogram inlay, butterfly tuner buttons, script logo, natural top finish, black finish on sides, white plastic backplate

Introduced: **1954**

13 5/8" wide, pointed cutaway on treble side, shallower pointed cutaway on bass side, 3 pickups, 6 knobs on bass side, 1 knob and 3-way slotted switch on treble side, asymmetrical plate tailpiece, sunburst finish: **1958**

Discontinued: **by 1961**

Glenwood (Deluxe) (No. 1105): 12 1/4" wide, rounded cutaway, white plastic backplate, 2 rectangular pickups, 6 knobs on bass side, 1 lever switch on treble side, some with *Glenwood* on pickguard, adjustable rosewood bridge, plate tailpiece with 2 *f*-shaped cutouts, bound top, bound fingerboard, butterfly (diamond enclosed by block) inlay, triple-bound symmetrical peghead, metal stairstep tuner buttons, logo with *National* through shield, stickpin figure below logo, gold-plated hardware, natural top finish, black sides finish, white plastic backplate

Introduced as No. 1105: **1954**

Small script peghead logo above shieldlike ornament, plastic butterfly tuner buttons: **1957**

Renamed **Glenwood Deluxe**, 13 5/8" wide, 6 knobs on bass side, 1 knob and 3-way slotted switch on treble side, bridge with individually adjustable saddles, Bigsby vibrato, metal tuner buttons: **1958**

Discontinued, model name continues on map-shaped models (see following): **1961**

Bolero (No. 1132): 12" wide, cutaway with point not as sharp as No. 1124 (see preceding), 1 metal-covered pickup, 2 knobs mounted on pickguard, adjustable rosewood bridge, short trapeze tailpiece, unbound fingerboard, dot inlay, symmetrical peghead, plastic butterfly tuner buttons, script logo, sunburst top finish, black finish on back and sides

Available: **1956–57**

Avalon (No. 1134): 12" wide, cutaway with point not as sharp as No. 1124 (see preceding), 2 metal-covered pickups, 2 knobs on lower treble bout, 1 lever switch on cutaway bout, adjustable rosewood bridge, short trapeze tailpiece, bound fingerboard, block inlay, symmetrical rounded-top peghead (necks left over from No. 1124), plastic butterfly tuner buttons, script logo, blond top finish, black finish on back and sides

Available: **1956–57**

Stylist (No. 1102): 13 1/4" wide, single cutaway, 2 pickups, 4 knobs on lower treble bout, lever switch on cutaway bout, asymmetrical plate tailpiece, large block inlay, asymmetrical peghead longer on treble side, black finish

Available: **1958–60**

Val-Trol Junior (No. 1122): 13 5/8" wide, rounded cutaway on treble side, shallower cutaway on bass side, beveled-edge wood body, 1 standard pickup and 1 bridge pickup, 3 knobs on bass side, 1 knob and 3-way slotted switch on treble side, plate tailpiece, 22" scale, dot inlay, plastic butterfly tuner buttons, ivory finish

Available: **1958–60**

Westwood (No. 1101): 12" wide, single cutaway, 1 pickup in bridge position, 2 knobs, Dobro-type tailpiece, 22" scale, dot inlay, rectangular peghead shape, gold-to-black sunburst finish

Available: **1958–60**

Model name continues on map-shaped models (see following)

Val-Trol Custom (No. 1199): 13 3/4" wide, pointed cutaway on treble side, shallower pointed cutaway on bass side, 2 standard pickups and 1 bridge pickup, 6 knobs in pairs on bass side (1 pair below bridge), 1 knob and 3-way slotted switch on treble side, model name on pickguard, plate tailpiece with stairstep edges, bound fingerboard, butterfly (diamond enclosed by block) inlay, gold-plated hardware, black finish

Available: **1959–60**

Val-Trol Baron (No. 1106): 13 1/2" wide, cutaway on treble side with rounded horn, shallow pointed cutaway on bass side, 2 standard pickups and 1 bridge pickup, 6 knobs in pairs on bass side (1 pair below bridge), 1 knob and 3-way slotted switch on treble side, asymmetrical plate tailpiece, bound fingerboard, large block inlay, black finish

Available: **1959–60**

Studio 66/Varsity 66: molded Res-o-glas (fiberglass) body, single cutaway, 1 pickup, 2 knobs, trapeze tailpiece, dot inlay, desert buff (beige) finish
Introduced as **Studio 66: 1961**
Smaller body, slight cutaway on bass side, black finish: **1963**
Listed as **Varsity 66: 1964**
Discontinued: **1965**

ResoLectric: see National Reso-Phonic, National Hollow Acoustic section

N-600 Series: body shape similar to Fender Jazzmaster with elongated bass horn, unbound rosewood fingerboard, block inlay, 6-on-a-side tuner configuration, sunburst finish

N-624: 1 pickup, 2 knobs, bar bridge, handrest covering tailpiece: **early 1968**

N-634: 2 pickups, 3 knobs, 2 switches, adjustable bridge, vibrato with large square base: **early 1968**

N-644: 3 pickups, 4 knobs, 3 switches, adjustable bridge, vibrato on 5-sided base plate: **early 1968**

N-654: 12-string, 2 pickups, 2 knobs, 2 rocker switches, dot inlay, 6 tuners per side: **early 1968**

MAP-SHAPED MODELS

Body is shaped roughly like a map of the U.S. with upper treble bout corresponding to Florida. All have asymmetrical peghead longer on treble side. Any color within a model group was offered in catalogs as optional on all models within that group, but few if any variations from standard colors exist. The standard National vibrato has a rectangular coverplate and thin tubular arm. A top-mounted Bigsby vibrato was optional. A few examples have a Burns vibrato.
Map-shaped models appeared in a late 1961 catalog, but no instruments were produced until 1962.

Glenwood 99: molded Res-o-glas (fiberglass) body, pointed treble horn, 2 standard pickups and 1 bridge pickup, 3 knobs and 3-way slotted switch on bass side, 3 knobs on treble side, plate tailpiece with stairstep sides, butterfly (diamond enclosed by block) inlay, peghead veneer edges beveled to show wide black line, snow white finish on body and back of neck
Introduced: **1962**

Bigsby vibrato, gold-plated hardware, sea foam green finish: **1963**
Master volume knob added near jack: **1964**
Discontinued: **1965**

Glenwood 95: molded Res-o-glas (fiberglass) body, pointed treble horn, 2 standard pickups, 3 knobs and 3-way slotted switch on bass side, 3 knobs on treble side, plate tailpiece with stairstep sides, butterfly (diamond enclosed by block) inlay, vermillion red finish
Available: **1962–64**

Glenwood 98: molded Res-o-glas (fiberglass) body, pointed treble horn, 2 standard pickups and 1 bridge pickup, 3 knobs and 3-way slotted switch on bass side, 3 knobs on treble side, Bigsby vibrato, butterfly (diamond enclosed by block) inlay, peghead veneer edges beveled to show white-black-white lines, chrome-plated hardware, pearl white body finish, black finish on back of neck
Introduced: **1962**
Master volume knob added near jack: **1964**
Discontinued: **1965**

Val-Pro 88/Newport 88: molded Res-o-glas (fiberglass) body, rounded treble horn, 2 standard pickups, 1 bridge pickup, 6 knobs and 3-way slotted switch on treble side, quarter-circle inlay, raven black finish
Introduced as **Val-Pro 88: 1962**
Renamed **Newport 88:** pointed treble horn, 6 knobs on bass side in groups of 2, vibrato: **1963**
Discontinued: **1965**
Some assembled from leftover parts (some with Italian hardware) for bankruptcy auction: **1968**

Val-Pro 84/Newport 84: molded Res-o-glas (fiberglass) body, rounded upper treble horn, 1 standard pickup, 1 bridge pickup, 3 knobs and 3-way slotted switch on treble side, quarter-circle inlay, arctic white finish
Introduced as **Val-Pro 84: 1962**
Renamed **Newport 84:** pointed treble horn, vibrato, sea foam green finish: **1963**
Discontinued: **1965**
Some assembled from leftover parts (some with Italian hardware) for bankruptcy auction: **1968**

Val-Pro 82/Newport 82: molded Res-o-glas (fiberglass) body, rounded treble horn, 1 pickup, 3 knobs and 3-way slotted switch on treble side, quarter-circle inlay, scarlet finish

Introduced as **Val-Pro 82:** 1962

Renamed **Newport 82:** pointed treble horn, knobs and switch on bass side, vibrato, pepper red finish: **1963**

Discontinued: **1965**

Some assembled from leftover parts (some with Italian hardware) for bankruptcy auction: **1968**

Westwood 77: solid hardwood body heavily routed from back, rounded treble horn, 2 standard pickups and 1 bridge pickup, 6 knobs on bass side, 3-way slotted switch and 1 knob on treble side, clear lucite bridge base, bound fingerboard, block inlay, cherry finish

Available: **1962–64**

Some assembled from leftover parts (some with Italian hardware) for bankruptcy auction: **1968**

Westwood 75: 1 standard pickup and 1 bridge pickup, 3 knobs on bass side, 3-way slotted switch on treble side, block inlay, cherry-to-black sunburst finish

Available: **1962–64**

Some assembled from leftover parts (some with Italian hardware) for bankruptcy auction: **1968**

Westwood 72: 1 pickup, 3 knobs on treble side, 3-way slotted switch on bass side, block inlay, blond-ivory finish

Introduced: **1962**

Cherry finish: **1963**

Last made: **1964**

Some assembled from leftover parts (some with Italian hardware) for bankruptcy auction: **1968**

COMMENTS

National electric solidbodies are not highly regarded by players. Some models, especially the map shapes, are sought by collectors for their unique aesthetic appeal.

NATIONAL BASSES KEY

Solidbody
  Map-shaped body
    Rounded upper treble bout = **Val-Pro Bass 85**
    Pointed upper treble bout = **National 85 Bass**
    Symmetrical double cutaway = **National Electric Bass**
  Semi-hollowbody = **N-850**

NATIONAL BASSES

Val-Pro 85/National 85: molded Res-o-glas (fiberglass) body shaped like map of United States (upper treble bout corresponds to Florida), rounded treble horn, 1 standard pickup and 1 bridge pickup, 2 knobs, 24 3/4" scale, quarter-circle inlay, snow white finish

Introduced as **Val-Pro 85:** 1961

Renamed **National 85:** pointed treble horn, ermine white finish: **1963**

Discontinued: **1965**

National Electric Bass: woodbody, double cutaway, 1 standard pickup and 1 bridge pickup, 2 knobs, trapeze tailpiece, 2 fin-shaped elevated finger rests, 24 3/4" scale, dot inlay, white plastic peghead veneer, sunburst finish

Available: **early 1960s–1964**

N-850: semi-hollowbody, double cutaway with rounded horns, modernistic soundholes, 2 pickups, block inlay, 3-tone sunburst finish

Available: **1967–early 1968**

COMMENTS

National basses are not highly regarded by players or collectors.

NATIONAL STEELS

Electric Hawaiian (no other model name): cast aluminum body, round body shape 10 5/8" in diameter, 7 decorative recessed "panels" on top, *National* on body near neck, blade pickup, 1 knob and jack on bass side of body near neck, metal bridge cover, square neck, rosewood fingerboard, 20 frets, dot inlay, cutout in center of peghead, clear lacquer finish, 7 strings optional
Introduced: **1935**
1 knob and jack in lower top panel on treble side: **late 1935**
Height-adjustable pickup, 2 knurled adjustment knobs in top, 2 control knobs, control knobs and adjustment knobs in middle panels, jack recessed in side: **early 1936**
Control knobs in lower panel: **1936**
Optional 26-fret fingerboard extends over *National* on body: **1936**
Discontinued: **1937**

New Yorker: square-end body, stairstep body sides, 3-pickup "sextet" arrangement (large pickup/bridge combination with bar pickup with notch at 3rd string, 2 additional pickups beneath fingerboard extending to 12th fret), 2 control knobs on treble side labeled *Full Treble* and *Master Control*, 2 knobs on bass side labeled *Natural Haw.* and *Full Bass*, screw-on jack on bass side even with 17th fret marker, chrome pickup cover attached by 4 screws, 23" scale (25" by special order), ebonoid fingerboard, *Electric* etched into fingerboard between bridge and fret markers, white parallelogram markers with Roman numerals (some without numerals), shield logo etched into ebonoid peghead veneer, metal tuner buttons, white-black-white stairstep finish, 7 or 8 strings
Introduced as Electric Hawaiian Model (no other name): **1935**
Visible pickup with split bar, 2 concealed pickups, white pointer knob on tone control (actually a pickup selector switch) below bridge, *Hawaiian-chimes-harp* tone settings, black volume knob on treble side, no *Electric* on fingerboard: **early 1937**
Some without Roman numerals in markers: **c. 1938**
Named **New Yorker: by 1939**
Rectangular pickup with poles in straight line, no concealed pickups, tone control potentiometer (not pickup selector switch), black-painted wooden handrest/pickup cover attached by 2 knurled nuts,

metal fingerboard, multi-colored Roman numeral markers: **by 1942**
Clear plastic bridge cover, metal logo plate, plastic tuner buttons: **1946**
Lucite fingerboard with back-painted Roman numerals: **1948**
Large square pickup, 3-way tone switch with *bass-mellow-brilliant* settings, *New Yorker* below tone switch: **1949**
Rectangular pickup: **1951**
Rounded stairstep corners on body, model name and art deco design on pickup cover, totem pole markers, stickpin peghead logo, angled (non-stairstep) peghead corners: **1956**
Discontinued: **1967**

Professional Hawaiian: maple body, stairstep body design like New Yorker (preceding), 4 knobs (2 on each side), *The New Yorker* and shield logo on body under strings, parallelogram markers with Roman numerals, *National* diagonally across peghead with 3 vertical lines, natural finish
Available: **1936–39**

Silvo: nickel-plated metal guitar body, flat top, upper *f*-holes, round ebonoid coverplate with rectangular pickup, *Silvo* on coverplate, square metal neck, 23" scale, ebonoid fingerboard and peghead veneer, Roman numeral parallelogram markers
Available: **1937–41**

Console: 2 8-string necks, *Console* on side, 2 white pointer knobs, 2 black round knobs at bridge end, black handrest extends across both necks, pegheads at different angles, ebonoid fingerboard, open parallelogram markers (some with Roman numerals), shield logo between necks near peghead, black top finish, white finish on sides, 6-string to 10-string necks optional
Available: **1939–41**

Woodbody (model name unknown): symmetrical woodbody, points near neck, rounded bottom end, strings pass through pickup, knobs on square plates with radial markings, rosewood fingerboard, inlaid celluloid frets flush with fingerboard, inlaid dot markers, shield logo plate, mahogany stain finish
Available: **early 1940s**

Dynamic: stairstep body design like New Yorker, cord hard-wired into body, clear plastic pickup cover, knobs on opposite sides mounted on arrow-shaped plates, 23" scale, Roman numeral markers, rounded peghead, white ebonoid top plates, black sides and back, 8 strings optional

Introduced: **by 1942**

Non-stairstep body side extensions, pointed control plates, jack into side, black-and-white stairstep markers in octave patterns with multi-colored geometric figures: **1947**

Side pieces beveled in toward body, black pickup cover, white plastic body covering (some with olive and white), black control plates: **by 1951**

Stickpin logo, knobs on same side, body insets for 3 screw-in legs, wine red and white finish: **by 1956**

Discontinued: **1964**

Reintroduced (N-425), script logo reads upside down to player: **1967**

Last made: **early 1968**

Chicago: square-end body, scooped graduation to neck, strings pass through pickup, knobs on opposite sides, knobs mounted on square plates with radial markings, 23" scale, parallelogram outline markers, "iridescent" black pearlette covering

Introduced: **by 1942**

Large square pickup, no control knob plates, stairstep marker pattern with numbers: **c. 1945**

Discontinued: **1948**

Princess: 1-piece stairstep body, strings pass through pickup, 1 round knob on treble side, 1 pointer knob below bridge, knobs mounted on square plates with radial design, parallelogram outline markers, white pearlette covering

Available: **1942–47**

Waikiki: slightly rounded bottom end, rounded graduation to neck, strings pass through pickup, large square control plate with knobs on opposite sides, 23" scale, light-colored fingerboard, Roman numeral markers, "blonde walnut" finish

Available: **1942–47**

Grand Console: 2 8-string necks, staggered tiers, heads at same angle, large square pickups, clear plastic pickup covers, logo between necks in center, controls (1 pointer knob, 1 round knob, 1 selector switch) between necks, totem pole markers, wood peghead covers, cream and copper/brown finish

Introduced: **1947**

Non-staggered tiers optional: **1949**

Cream colored plastic pickup covers: **1950**

4 legs optional: **1954**

Listed as **Console:** 2 round knobs and 1 selector switch between necks, 1 knob at each bridge, gold-colored control plate and markers, black and white finish: **by 1961**

Listed as model N-450, last made: **early 1968**

Electra-Chord: rectangular body, single center-support stand with 2 pedals; pitch-changers, tuners, and pickup at same end; clear plastic pitch-changers cover, totem pole markers, 6 strings

Available: **1948**

Special/Console 8: 8 strings, symmetrical body with side extensions (like Dynamic), large square pickup, 1 pointer knob and 1 round knob mounted on pointed plates, clear plastic pickup cover, shield logo plate on body extension below string anchors, 23" scale, Lucite fingerboard with back-painted Roman numeral markers, wooden peghead cover, black and white finish

Introduced as Special: **1948**

Replaced by **Console 8:** stairstep extensions on treble side only, totem pole markers, stickpin logo, 3 legs: **1958**

Discontinued: **1961**

Trailblazer: square end with rounded corners, slight body waists, sharp points at neck, metal handrest, 1 pointer knob, 1 round knob, knobs on opposite sides, 23" scale, numbered markers enclosed in hexagonal figures, model name on peghead, black lacquer finish

Available: **1948–49**

Chicagoan: metal handrest, 1 pointer knob, 1 round knob, 23" scale, numbered musical-note markers, oyster (gray) pearloid covering

Available: **1948–60**

Triplex Chord Changer: asymmetrical stairstep body of maple and walnut, lever-controlled tuning changer, 2 round white knobs, white plastic pickup cover, Lucite fingerboard back-painted white, totem pole markers, rounded top peghead, wide shield

logo plate, natural finish
Introduced: **1949**
Variation: fingerboard back-painted brown, geometric markers, standard shield logo: **c. 1955**
Script logo, shield with V-like sides below logo: **1956**
Discontinued: **1958**

Clipper: elongated guitar-shaped body, white plastic pickup cover, 2 knobs, jack into top, bound top and back, black-and-white stairstep markers in octave patterns, peghead wider at top than at nut, shield logo plate, sunburst finish
Available: **1952–55**

Triple-neck Hawaiian: 3 8-string necks, staggered tiers, individual pickup covers, 2 knobs, 1 selector switch, peghead covers, 4 legs, black and white finish
Available: **1953–60**

Rocket One Ten: rocket fin-shaped body side extensions, model name on bridge cover, white body finish, red or black control plates

Available: **1956–57**

Studio 76: rounded bottom end, rounded shoulders, 2 knobs on opposite sides, stairstep pattern markers (or black-white diagonally split rectangular markers), stickpin logo, onyx black pearloid finish
Available: **1963**

Console 16: 2 8-string necks joined by large tubes, large handrest extends over both necks, 1 knob on each neck, 1 switch on handrest, geometric markers, 4 legs
Introduced as a Supro model: **1958**
Discontinued: **1961**
Reintroduced in National line: **1967**
Discontinued: **1968**

COMMENTS

Early aluminum body National (and Supro and Dobro) lap steels are of interest to collectors for historical reasons. Some later high-end models have a strong aesthetic appeal and make excellent wall-hangers.

SUPRO ELECTRIC HOLLOWBODIES KEY

Non-cutaway
    1 pickup on square control plate (flat top guitar) = **Rio**
    1 pickup in bridge position = **Electric Spanish, Avalon Spanish**
    1 pickup in middle position
        3-segment *f*-holes = **Capitan**
        Standard *f*-holes = **El Capitan, 1948–53**
    1 pickup in neck position
        Bound fingerboard = **El Capitan, 1953–55**
        Unbound fingerboard = **Ranchero**
    2 pickups = **Del-Mar**
Single cutaway
    1 pickup = **Westwood**
    2 pickups
        White finish = **Sierra**
        Natural top, black back and sides = **Coronado, 1960–62**
    2 standard pickups and 1 bridge pickup = **Coronado, 1958–60**
Double cutaway
    2 pickups
        No vibrato = **Croydon**
        Vibrato
            Dot inlay = **Clermont**
            Block inlay = **Carlisle**
    3 pickups = **Stratford**

SUPRO SOLIDBODIES KEY

1 floating vinyl-covered pickup
    Non-cutaway = **Ozark, 1952–55**
    Cutaway
        White finish = **Ozark Cutaway**
        Black finish = **Ozark Jet**
1 pickup with strings-through-pickup design
    Ozark on body or pickguard = **Ozark 1958–61**
    60 or no name on body = **Sixty**
1 metal-covered pickup (strings pass over pickup)
    Single cutaway, no cutaway on bass side
        White finish = **Super, 1958 or 1962**
        Red finish = **Belmont, 1955–61**
        Gold finish = **Special**
        White-to-black sunburst finish = **Super, 1959–61**
    Single cutaway with slight cutaway on bass side
        Fire bronze finish = **Ozark, 1962**
        Red finish = **Belmont 1962–63**
        Sand buff (beige) finish
            Stairstep tailpiece = **Sahara, 1960–62**
            Dobro style tailpiece = **Kingston**
        Blue finish = **Sahara, 1963–64**
        White finish = **Holiday**
    Asymmetrical double cutaway (similar to Fender Jazzmaster)
        Vibrato = **Lexington S625**
        No vibrato
            3-tone sunburst finish = **Shaded Guitar S525**
            Cherry-to-black sunburst finish = **Normandy S601**
            Cherry finish
                24 3/4" scale = **Normandy S611**
                22" scale = **Colt**
    Full double cutaways
        24 3/4" (standard) scale
            No vibrato = **Ozark, 1963–65**
            Vibrato = **Supersonic (Suprosonic)**
        22" scale = **Super Seven**
1 standard pickup and 1 bridge pickup = **Rhythm Tone**
2 standard pickups
    White finish = **Dual-Tone**
    Natural finish wood top = **Coronado, 1961**
    Black finish = **Coronado II, 1962–65**
    Red finish
        Slight cutaway on bass side = **Bermuda**
        Double cutaway, similar to Fender Jazzmaster
            No vibrato = **Normandy S612**
            Vibrato = **Normandy S613**
    Blue finish = **Tremo-Lectric**
    Ivory-to-black sunburst finish = **Super Twin**

Sunburst finish

Tortoiseshell celluloid pickguard

No vibrato = **12-string**

Large rectangular vibrato base = **Lexington S635**

Burns vibrato (small pyramid on base) = **Shaded Guitar S535**

White pickguard = **Normandy S602**

2 standard pickups and 1 bridge pickup

No cutaway on bass side = **Silverwood**

Slight cutaway on bass side

Sunburst finish = **Rhythm Master**

White finish = **Martinique**

Asymmetrical double cutaway, similar to Fender Jazzmaster

Butterfly (diamond enclosed by block) inlay

Sunburst finish = **Arlington S665**

White finish = **Arlington S655**

Dot inlay = **Fiberglass Guitar S555**

3 pickups

Single cutaway = **Triple-Tone**

Asymmetrical double cutaway, similar to Fender Jazzmaster

Large rectangular vibrato base = **Lexington S645**

Burns vibrato (small pyramid on base) = **Shaded Guitar S545**

SUPRO GUITARS, BASSES, MANDOLINS

SECTION ORGANIZATION

Acoustic Models
Resonator Models
Electric Flat Top
Electric Archtops
Thinlines
Electric Solidbodies
Electric Basses
Mandolins and Ukulele

ACOUSTIC MODELS

S700: flat top, 15 1/2" wide, dreadnought shape, mahogany back and sides, large bridge with 3 points at each end, 4-point pickguard, wide rosette, wide top and back binding, bound fingerboard, block inlay, asymmetrical peghead longer on bass side

S710: flat top, 15 1/2" wide, rounded bouts (similar to Gibson J-185 or Everly Brothers), rectangular bridge, 2 points on pickguard, tortoiseshell celluloid binding, bound fingerboard, block inlay, asymmetrical peghead longer on bass side

S720: flat top, 14" wide, classical, rectangular bridge with string-loop anchoring, wide soundhole ring, unbound rosewood fingerboard, slotted peghead, no logo

Available: **1967–early 1968**

S6109: flat top, 15 3/4" wide, dreadnought shape, laminated mahogany back and sides, rectangular bridge, double-bound top, single-bound back, dot inlay, symmetrical peghead

S6102: flat top, 15 3/4" wide, dreadnought shape, mahogany back and sides, rectangular bridge, double-bound top, single-bound back, wide rosette, bound fingerboard, dot inlay, symmetrical peghead

S7008: flat top, 14 1/4" wide, classical, laminated mahogany back and sides, bound top and back, slotted peghead

S7005: flat top, 14 1/4" wide, classical, mahogany back and sides, bound top and back, wide rosette, slotted peghead

S5113: flat top, 15" wide, rounded lower bout, laminated mahogany back and sides, rectangular bridge, tortoiseshell celluloid binding on top and back, no rosette, dot inlay, symmetrical peghead

S6160: flat top, 15 3/4" wide, rounded lower bout, laminated mahogany back and sides, triple-bound top, single-bound back, wide rosette, rectangular bridge, dot inlay, symmetrical peghead

S6170: flat top, 15 3/4" wide, rounded lower bout, laminated mahogany back and sides, bridge with small point on belly, triple-bound top, single-bound back, wide rosette, bound fingerboard, block inlay, symmetrical peghead

S7900: flat top, 12-string, 15 3/4" wide, laminated mahogany back and sides, bridge with 3 points on belly, wide rosette, triple-bound top, single-bound back, dot inlay, symmetrical peghead
Only catalog appearance: **1968**

S6835: arched top, 15 1/2" wide, laminated maple body, bound top and back, dot inlay, symmetrical peghead, cherry sunburst finish

S6840: same as S6835 but with golden sunburst finish

S8900: 17 1/4" wide, otherwise same as S6840, golden sunburst finish
Only catalog appearance: **1968**

RESONATOR MODELS

Collegian Spanish (No. 25): metal body similar to National Duolian, round holes in coverplate, clear pickguard, 12 frets clear of body, maple yellow finish
Introduced: **1939**
Moved to National line: **1942**
Discontinued: **1943**

Collegian Hawaiian (No. 26): squareneck: **1939–42**

Collegian Tenor (No. 27): tenor neck: **1939–42**

Arcadia (No. 23): 3-ply birch body made by Harmony, 14 1/4" wide, *f*-holes, round holes in coverplate, black-and-silver painted top edges to simulate binding, 12 frets clear of body, dot inlay, solid peghead, metal logo plate, sunburst finish
Available: **1939–42**

Folk Star/Vagabond: molded Res-o-glas (fiberglass) body, standard National single-cone resonator and coverplate, screen holes in upper body, stairstep tailpiece, dot inlay (some with block), "gay festival red" finish

Introduced: **1964**
Renamed **Vagabond:** 1967
Discontinued (some assembled with parts leftover from National Bluegrass 35 and Airline resonator models, sold at bankruptcy auction): **1968**

ELECTRIC FLAT TOP

Rio (No. 130): 13" wide, body and neck by Regal, electronics and bridge mounted on square plate (same plate used on Clipper lap steel), strings pass through pickup, 2 knobs on opposite sides, hardwired cord, 12 frets clear of body, dot inlay, slotted peghead, natural finish
Available: **1941–43**

ELECTRIC ARCHTOPS

Supro Electric Spanish/Avalon Spanish:
14 3/4" wide, body and neck by Regal, *f*-holes, bar pickup with oblong housing mounted near bridge, 1/4" jack, ebonoid pickguard, rosewood adjustable bridge, trapeze tailpiece, 3-piece neck, 20-fret rosewood fingerboard, dot inlay, Harmony Tune-Rite tuners with metal buttons, block-letter logo stenciled across top of peghead
Tenor neck available
Introduced as **Supro Electric Spanish: late 1935**
No *f*-holes: **1936**
Body by Kay, bolt-on National/Dobro neck, rectangular pickup housing, pickup attached to bridge, screw-on jack, Dobro style tailpiece, plastic tuner buttons: **1937**
Renamed **Avalon Spanish: 1938**
Discontinued: **1941**

Capitan (No. 140): 15 3/4" wide, body by Regal, spruce top, maple back and sides, 3-segment *f*-holes, 1 rectangular pickup with 6 separate coils, pickup in middle position, 2 knobs, Dobro style tailpiece, adjustable bridge, bolt-on neck, ebonized fingerboard, black body binding, pearl dot inlay, plastic tuner buttons, oval logo plate, natural finish
Available: **1941–43**

El Capitan: 15 1/2" wide, 1 pickup in middle position, trapeze tailpiece, clear pickguard, single-bound top and back, single-bound *f*-holes, single-bound rosewood fingerboard, dot inlay, point at top of peghead, metal logo plate, sunburst finish
Introduced: **1948**

Floating vinyl-covered pickup in neck position, knobs mounted on pickguard: **1953**
Discontinued: **1955**

Ranchero: 15 1/2" wide, unspecified hardwood construction, 3-segment *f*-holes, 1 pickup in neck position, 2 knobs, Dobro style tailpiece, black pickguard, bound top and back, dot inlay, rounded-peak peghead, metal logo plate, sunburst finish
Introduced: **1948**
Standard *f*-holes, floating vinyl-covered pickup in neck position, knobs mounted into white plastic pickguard, point at top of peghead, natural finish: **1953**
Metal-covered pickup in neck position, controls into top, model name on black pickguard, 3-point pickguard shape, trapeze tailpiece, enclosed tuners, asymmetrical peghead longer on bass side, black peghead veneer, plastic butterfly tuner buttons: **1955**
White 3-point pickguard follows contour of body, sunburst finish: **1958**
Discontinued: **1960**

Sierra: 15 3/8" wide, rounded cutaway, 2 pickups, 2 knobs, lever switch on cutaway bout, stairstep tailpiece, wing-shape pickguard with straight edge on treble side, black binding, block inlay, plastic butterfly tuner buttons, enclosed tuners, asymmetrical peghead longer on bass side, Arctic white finish
Available: **1955–57**

Westwood: 15 3/8" wide, rounded cutaway, 1 pickup in neck position, 2 knobs, bound top and back, bound *f*-holes, stairstep tailpiece, wing-shaped pickguard with straight edge on treble side, rosewood fingerboard, dot inlay, butterfly tuner buttons, enclosed tuners, asymmetrical peghead longer on bass side, sunburst finish
Available: **1955–58**

Coronado: 16" wide, 2 3/4" deep, rounded cutaway, 2 standard pickups and 1 bridge pickup, 1 knob near bridge, 3-way slotted switch on cutaway bout, stairstep tailpiece, small beveled-edge pickguard, multiple-bound top and back, large block inlay, asymmetrical peghead longer on bass side, black finish
Introduced: **1958**
15 1/2 wide, 2" deep, deeper cutaway, no bridge pickup, 4 knobs, 3-way slotted switch on cutaway bout, natural top finish, black finish on neck, back

and sides: **1960**
Discontinued: **1962**

Del-Mar: 15 7/8" wide, non-cutaway, maple back and sides, tapered *f*-holes with smooth lines and no curl at ends, 2 pickups, 2 knobs on lower treble bout, 3-way slotted switch on upper treble bout, stairstep tailpiece, triple-bound top and back, block inlay, natural finish
Available in Supro line (moved from National line): **1959**

THINLINES

Stratford: thinline double cutaway, 3 pickups, 6 knobs, 3 rocker switches, vibrato, block inlay, 6-on-a-side tuner arrangement, sunburst finish
Introduced: **1967**
Symmetrical peghead, 3-on-a-side tuner arrangement: **1968**
Discontinued: **1968**

Carlisle: thinline double cutaway, 2 pickups, 4 knobs, 1 toggle switch, vibrato, block inlay, 6-on-a-side tuner arrangement, cherry finish
Introduced: **1967**
Symmetrical peghead, 3-on-a-side tuner arrangement: **1968**
Discontinued: **1968**

Clermont: thinline double cutaway, 2 pickups, 4 knobs, 1 toggle switch, vibrato, dot inlay, 6-on-a-side tuner arrangement, cherry finish
Introduced: **1967**
Symmetrical peghead, 3-on-a-side tuner arrangement: **1968**
Discontinued: **1968**

Croydon: thinline double cutaway, 2 pickups, 4 knobs, 1 toggle switch, no vibrato, dot inlay, 6-on-a-side tuner arrangement, cherry finish
Introduced: **1967**
Symmetrical peghead, 3-on-a-side tuner arrangement: **1968**
Discontinued: **1968**

ELECTRIC SOLIDBODIES

Ozark: 11 1/4" wide, non-cutaway, floating vinyl-covered pickup, 2 knobs mounted into pickguard, rosewood bridge, short trapeze tailpiece, dot inlay, metal logo plate, point at top of peghead (some with plastic logo and rounded-top peghead), white pearloid body covering

Available: **1952–54**

Ozark Cutaway: single cutaway: **1953–54**

Ozark model name reintroduced on Sixty model (see following), 12" wide, single cutaway, strings pass through pickup, pickup and controls mounted on plate with rounded corners, model name on body below pickup, dot inlay, narrow asymmetrical peghead longer on bass side, butterfly tuner buttons, Arctic white finish: **1958**
Model name on pickguard, gold-to-black sunburst finish: **1959**
13 1/2" wide: **1960**
Single cutaway with slight cutaway on bass side, 1 pickup in middle position, strings pass over pickup, Dobro style tailpiece, fire bronze finish: **1962**
Double cutaway, beveled body edges, 1 pickup, stud tailpiece with metal cover, dot inlay, narrow asymmetrical peghead longer on bass side, poppy red finish: **1963**
Discontinued: **1967**

Ozark Jet: 11 1/4" wide, single-cutaway, 1 floating pickup with light-colored vinyl covering, 2 knobs mounted into white plastic pickguard, rosewood bridge, short trapeze tailpiece, bound fingerboard, dot inlay, plastic logo, symmetrical peghead, black finish
Available: **1952–54**

Dual-Tone: 11 1/4" wide, single cutaway, 2 pickups, 4 knobs in straight line, lever switch on cutaway bout, dark wing-shape pickguard surrounds rhythm pickup, elevated fin-shaped finger rest on treble side, rosewood bridge, short trapeze tailpiece, dot inlay, symmetrical peghead, white plastic body covering
Introduced: **1954**
12" wide, reverse stairstep tailpiece with highest step on bass side, model name on black pickguard, large block inlay, plastic butterfly tuner buttons, asymmetrical peghead longer on treble side, black peghead veneer, metal logo plate, Arctic white plastic covering: **1955**
13" wide, 3-way slotted switch near neck pickup: **1958**
13 1/2" wide: **1960**
Fiberglass body, slight cutaway on bass side, beveled body edges, 1 knob and 3-way slotted switch on treble side, 4 knobs in groups of 2 on bass side, standard stairstep tailpiece, no model name on pickguard, plastic logo, wider peghead with point more toward center: **1962**

Discontinued: **1966**

Belmont: 12" wide, single cutaway, 1 pickup in neck position, 2 knobs on treble side mounted into pickguard, elevated fin-shape finger rest on treble side, reverse stairstep tailpiece with highest step on bass side, model name on white pickguard, dot inlay, butterfly tuner buttons, asymmetrical peghead longer on treble side, black peghead plate, gold-plated hardware, sherry maroon (red) plastic covering
Introduced: **1955**
Beveled top edges, pickup near bridge, Dobro style tailpiece, no elevated finger rest: **1958**
13 1/2" wide: **1960**
Fiberglass body, single cutaway, slight cutaway on bass side, 1 pickup in bridge position, 2 knobs, 1 slide switch, Dobro style tailpiece, optional vibrato with rectangular coverplate and tubular arm, plastic logo, wider peghead with point more toward center, white peghead veneer, cherry red finish: **1962**
Teardrop pickguard: **1963**
Discontinued: **1964**

Sixty: 12 1/4" wide, single cutaway, pickup and controls on plate with rounded corners, strings pass through pickup, 2 knobs on opposite sides, jack in control plate, black pickguard, dot inlay, asymmetrical peghead longer on bass side, white plastic covering
Introduced: **by 1955**
Large *60* on lower treble bout, pin-striping on finish: **1957**
Sixty model name discontinued, model continues as Ozark (see preceding): **1958**

Rhythm Tone: 13" wide, single cutaway, beveled top edges, 1 standard pickup and 1 bridge pickup, 3 knobs in straight line, 3-way slotted switch on cutaway bout, reverse stairstep tailpiece with highest step on bass side, elevated fin-shape finger rest on treble side, dot inlay, asymmetrical peghead longer on bass side, black finish
Only catalog appearance: **1958**

Rhythm Master: 13 1/2" wide, single cutaway with slight cutaway on bass side, beveled top edges, 2 standard pickups and 1 bridge pickup, 1 knob, 3-way slotted switch, reverse stairstep tailpiece with highest step on bass side, rosewood

fingerboard, block inlay, asymmetrical peghead longer on bass side, plastic butterfly tuner buttons, sunburst finish
Available: **1958–59**

Special: 12" wide, single cutaway, 1 pickup near neck, 2 knobs, 1 switch, Dobro style tailpiece, 22" scale, dot inlay, gold finish
Available: **1958–59**

Super: 12" wide, single cutaway, 1 pickup near bridge, 2 knobs, 1 switch, Dobro style tailpiece, 22" scale, dot inlay, symmetrical peghead with rounded top edge, metal logo plate, fawn ivory finish
Introduced: **1958**
Rectangular peghead, plastic logo, ivory-to-black sunburst finish: **1960**
2 knobs, no switch, *Supro* on pickguard, white finish: **1962**
Discontinued: **1964**

Super Twin: 2 pickups, 2-position slide switch: **1959–60**

Triple-Tone: 13" wide, single cutaway, beveled top edges, 3 pickups, 4 knobs, 3-way slotted switch, reverse stairstep tailpiece with highest step on bass side, elevated fin-shaped finger rest on treble side, block inlay, black finish
Only catalog appearance: **1959**

Silverwood: 13 1/2" wide, single cutaway, 2 standard pickups and 1 bridge pickup, 6 small knobs in pairs on bass side, 1 knob and 3-way slotted switch on treble side, beveled-edge pickguard with *Val Trol*, bound fingerboard, large block inlay, asymmetrical peghead longer on bass side, white peghead veneer, plastic logo, plastic butterfly tuner buttons, blond finish
Available: **1960–61**

Sahara (70): 13 1/2" wide, single cutaway with slight cutaway on bass side, 1 pickup, 3 knobs on treble side, 1 knob and 3-way slotted switch on bass side, reverse stairstep tailpiece with highest step on bass side, dot inlay, asymmetrical peghead longer on bass side, plastic logo, sand buff (beige) finish
Introduced: **1960**
13 3/4" wide, fiberglass body, beveled edges, 2 knobs,

Dobro style tailpiece, model name and palm tree on pickguard, Wedgewood blue finish: **1963**
Renamed **Sahara 70: 1964**
Discontinued: **1967**

Coronado (II): 15 1/2" wide, 2" deep, arched top, single rounded cutaway, spruce top, 2 pickups, 4 knobs on lower treble bout, 3-way slotted switch on cutaway bout, stairstep tailpiece, double-bound top and back, bound fingerboard, block inlay, plastic logo, natural top finish, black finish on back and sides
Introduced as **Coronado: 1961**
Renamed **Coronado II:** fiberglass body, beveled edges, single cutaway, slight cutaway on bass side, 3-way slotted switch on upper bass bout, vibrato, *Coronado* on pickguard, raven black finish: **1962**
Discontinued: **1967**

Bermuda: 15 1/4" wide, single cutaway, slight cutaway on bass side, slab fiberglass body, 2 pickups, 2 knobs, 1 slide switch, electronic tremolo under pickguard operated by toggle switch, stairstep tailpiece, dot inlay, asymmetrical peghead longer on bass side, plastic logo, "polyester cherry" finish
Only catalog appearance: **1962**

Martinique: single cutaway, slight cutaway on bass side, beveled body edges, 2 standard pickups and 1 bridge pickup, 1 knob and 3-way slotted switch on lower treble bout, 6 knobs in pairs on bass side, Bigsby vibrato optional, *Val-Trol* on pickguard, bound fingerboard, block inlay, asymmetrical peghead longer on bass side, plastic logo, butterfly tuner buttons, ermine white finish
Introduced: **1962**
Non-Bigsby vibrato: **1965**
Discontinued: **1967**

Kingston: Res-o-glas (fiberglass) body, single cutaway with slight cutaway on bass side, slab body, 1 pickup near bridge, 2 knobs, 1 slide switch, Dobro style tailpiece, asymmetrical peghead longer on bass side, dot inlay, plastic butterfly tuner buttons, sand buff finish
Available: **1962–63**

Super Seven: asymmetrical double rounded cutaway, pickup in middle position, *Supro* on pickup, stud tailpiece with metal cover, dot inlay, asymmet-

rical peghead slightly longer on bass side, oval logo, poppy red finish
Available: **1963–66**

Tremo-Lectric: beveled fiberglass body, single cutaway with slight cutaway on bass side, 2 pickups, 4 knobs on control plate, 2 switches near bridge pickup, electronic tremolo under pickguard operated by toggle switch, stairstep tailpiece, dot inlay, asymmetrical peghead longer on bass side, Wedgewood blue finish
Available: **1963–66**

Supersonic/Suprosonic: beveled fiberglass body, symmetrical double cutaway, 1 pickup near neck, vibrato, dot inlay, asymmetrical peghead longer on bass side, holly red finish
Introduced as **Supersonic: 1963**
Renamed **Suprosonic 30: 1964**
Discontinued: **1967**

Holiday/White Holiday: beveled fiberglass body, single cutaway with slight cutaway on bass side, 1 pickup near bridge, slide switch on bass side, 3 knobs on treble side, vibrato, teardrop pickguard, bound fingerboard, block inlay, asymmetrical peghead longer on bass side, white finish
Introduced as **Holiday: 1963**
Renamed **White Holiday: 1964**
Discontinued: **1967**

Shaded Guitars (no other model name): asymmetrical double cutaway shape somewhat like Fender Jazzmaster, tortoiseshell celluloid pickguard, dot inlay, 6-on-a-side tuner arrangement, sunburst finish

S525: 1 pickup, 2 knobs: **1966**

S535: 2 pickups, 4 rocker switches on bass side, Burns vibrato: **1966**

S545: 3 pickups, 6 rocker switches on bass side, Burns vibrato: **1966**

Fiberglass Guitar (no other model name) (No. S555): asymmetrical double cutaway shape somewhat like Fender Jazzmaster, 2 standard pickups and 1 bridge pickup, 3 knobs on treble side, 6 rocker switches on bass side, Bigsby vibrato, dot inlay, 6-on-a-side tuner arrangement, white finish

Only catalog appearance: **1966**

Arlington: asymmetrical double cutaway shape somewhat like Fender Jazzmaster, 2 standard pickups and 1 bridge pickup, Bigsby vibrato, 6 rocker switches, butterfly (diamond enclosed by rectangle) inlay, 6-on-a-side tuner arrangement, sunburst (No. S665) or white (No. S655) finish
Only catalog appearance: **1967**

Lexington: asymmetrical double cutaway shape somewhat like Fender Jazzmaster, individually adjustable bridge saddles, vibrato with large rectangular base, tortoiseshell celluloid pickguard, dot inlay, 6-on-a-side tuner arrangement, 3-tone sunburst finish

S645: 3 pickups, 6 rocker switches, 3 knobs: **1967**

S635: 2 pickups, 4 rocker switches, 2 knobs: **1967**

S625: 1 pickup, 2 knobs: **1967**

Normandy: asymmetrical double cutaway shape somewhat like Fender Jazzmaster, black rectangular pickup(s) with oval shape in center, metal height-adjustable bridge, white pickguard, dot inlay, 6-on-a-side tuners

S603: 2 pickups, vibrato, cherry-to-black sunburst finish: **1967**

S613: 2 pickups, vibrato, cherry finish: **1967**

S602: 2 pickups, no vibrato, cherry-to-black sunburst finish: **1967**

S612: 2 pickups, no vibrato, cherry finish: **1967**

S601: 1 pickup, cherry-to-black sunburst finish: **1967**

S611: 1 pickup, cherry finish: **1967**

Colt: asymmetrical double-cutaway shape somewhat like Fender Jazzmaster, black rectangular pickup with oval shape in center, white pickguard, 22" scale, dot inlay, 6-on-a-side tuners, red finish
Only catalog appearance: **1967**

12-string: asymmetrical double-cutaway shape somewhat like Fender Jazzmaster, 2 pickups, 4 rocker switches on bass side, 2 knobs on treble side, tortoiseshell celluloid pickguard, dot inlay, symmetrical peghead, sunburst finish
Only catalog appearance: **1967**

ELECTRIC BASSES

Pocket Bass: 13 1/2" wide, symmetrical double cutaway, beveled top edges, 1 rectangular pickup in neck position and 1 bridge pickup, trapeze tailpiece, 1 finger rest bar, 24 3/4" scale, dot inlay, jet black finish
Introduced: **1960**
2 elevated fin-shaped finger rests: **1961**
No bridge pickup, no finger rests, 4-on-a-side tuner arrangement: **1967**
Discontinued: **1968**

Taurus: asymmetrical double cutaway somewhat similar to Fender Jazzmaster, 1 standard pickup and 1 bridge pickup, 4-on-a-side tuner arrangement, sunburst finish
Available: **1967–early 1968**

MANDOLINS AND UKULELE

Electric Mandolin: conventional woodbody construction, body by Regal, symmetrical A-style body shape, no soundholes, bar pickup with oblong housing mounted near bridge, Dobro style tailpiece, bound fingerboard, dot inlay, Harmony Tune-Rite tuners with metal buttons, block-letter logo across peghead
Available: **late 1935–37**

Collegian Mandolin (No. 28): metalbody, resonator, maple yellow finish
Available: **1939–41**

S464: A-style, arched top, pear-shape body, laminated maple body, white pickguard, dot inlay, symmetrical peghead

S345: asymmetrical body, body point on each upper bout, arched spruce top, laminated maple back and sides, black pickguard, block inlay, symmetrical peghead
Only catalog appearance: **1968**

S395 (electric): asymmetrical body, body point on each upper bout, arched spruce top, laminated maple back and sides, thin bar pickup mounted near neck, 2 knobs on lower treble bout, black pickguard, block inlay, symmetrical peghead
Only catalog appearance: **1968**

Collegian Ukulele (No. 29): metalbody, resonator, maple yellow finish
Available: **1939–41**

COMMENTS

Supro was National's budget brand, and the same relation between Supro and National generally holds true today in the vintage market, with the exception of some lap steel models. Few players have high regard for Supro electrics. A few models have some appeal to collectors but primarily on the basis of oddity.

SUPRO STEELS

All models have strings passing through pickup and 23" scale unless otherwise noted.

Electric Hawaiian (no other model name): cast aluminum body, round body shape 6 7/8" in diameter, blade pickup, strings pass over pickup, 1 knob on treble side, rosewood fingerboard, dot inlay, cutout in peghead
Available: **late 1935–37**

Hawaiian Electric (no other model name): symmetrical woodbody, wider body than any other Supro model, rounded bottom corners, 2 body points near neck, metal handrest, strings pass over pickup, round knob mounted on treble-side extension of pickup cover, screw-on jack on bass-side extension of pickup cover, elevated wood pickguard, *Supro/Electric* decal between pickup and neck, bound top, ebonoid fingerboard, dot inlay, numbered frets, mahogany sunburst finish
Introduced: **1937**
Rectangular extension of pickup cover on treble side only, jack in side, no pickguard, small parallelogram markers: **mid 1937**
Discontinued: **1939**

Avalon Hawaiian: square bottom end, scooped graduation to neck, enameled handrest, 2 knobs mounted on rectangular plates, *Supro* on knob plates, knobs on opposite sides, aluminum fingerboard, parallelogram markers, black finish
Available: **1938–40**

No. 20: symmetrical body, strings pass over pickup,

1 knob on square plate on treble side, black finger-board, silver "pearlette" paint finish

No. 30: same with sunburst mahogany finish

No. 60: guitar/amp-in-case outfit, No. 20 guitar with 110 volt A.C. amp in case

No. 70: guitar/amp-in-case outfit, No. 30 guitar with battery powered amp in case
Introduced: **1938**
Discontinued: **c. 1941**

Hawaiian (no other model name): square bottom end, scooped graduation to neck, 2 knobs on oppo-site sides, pickup and knobs on square metal con-trol plate, diamonds-and-dots markers
Available: **1939–40**

Baton: square-end woodbody with 2 points near neck, pickup and controls on square metal plate, 21" scale, diamond-shaped markers, grained walnut finish
Available: **1941–43**

Clipper: square corners with rounded belly, 2 points near neck, pickup and controls on square plate, bound rosewood fingerboard, plastic frets flush with fingerboard, pearl dot inlay, brown pearlette covering
Available: **1941–43**

Irene: square end, sharp points at neck, pickup and controls on square plate, 23 1/2" scale, painted-on fingerboard, Roman numeral markers, cream pearlette covering
Available: **1942–43**

Supreme: square corners with rounded belly, 2 points near neck, pickup and controls on square plate, bound plastic fingerboard top-painted brown, geometric markers, long V-shaped figures on tuner enclosures, brown pearlette covering
Introduced as Hawaiian (no other model name): **1946**
Named Supreme: **1947**
Lucite fingerboard back-painted brown, Kluson Deluxe tuners: **1948**
Cream-colored plastic pickup cover: **1949**
Butterfly tuner buttons, accordion red finish: **1955**
Tulip yellow finish: **1958**
Discontinued: **1960**

Comet: symmetrical body, straight bottom with rounded corners, beveled around fingerboard, pickup and controls on square plate, 1 round knob, 1 pointer knob, hard-wired cord, painted-on black fingerboard, geometric markers, rounded-top peg-head narrower at top than at nut, grey pearlette covering
Introduced: **c. 1947**
Standard jack, Arctic white plastic covering: **1948**
Black plastic pickup cover, brown painted control plate, plastic logo below control plate on treble side: **1952**
Discontinued: **1966**

Varsity: symmetrical body with slight waists, sharp points near neck, wide handrest, rectangular peg-head, lacquer finish
Available: **1948–51**

Twin/Console: 2 6-string necks, pickups on square control plates, 3 knobs, logo below control plate on neck farthest from player, geometric mark-ers, rounded-top pegheads, pearlette covering
Introduced as **Twin: 1948**
Renamed **Console:** black bridge covers and control plates, Lucite fingerboards, black-and-silver stairstep markers in octave pattern, Arctic white fin-ish, 4 legs: **by 1955**
Logo below control plate: **1966**
Discontinued: **1969**

Airline/Jet Airliner: asymmetrical body with straight edge on bass side, black plastic bridge/pickup cover with *Supro* logo, 2 knobs on treble side, black control plate, black fingerboard (some with *Airline* on fingerboard), totem pole markers, rounded peghead, black plastic covering on main body (some with white fingerboard and grey pearlette main body covering), white plastic on treble-side body extension
Introduced by: **1952**
8-string available: **1961**
Renamed **Jet Airliner: 1962**
Renamed **Airline: 1963**
Renamed **Jet Airliner: 1964**
Discontinued: **1965**

Spectator: symmetrical woodbody, rounded points near neck, pickup and controls on round-cornered plate, painted-on fingerboard, totem pole markers,

rectangular peghead, natural finish
Available: **1952–54**

Student De Luxe: straight-line body sides, 1
knob, pickup and controls on metal plate, 21" scale,
stairstep-pattern fingerboard markers, *Student
Special* in script near bridge, black and white
pearlette covering, wood finish optional
Introduced: **1952**
Renamed **Special**, wine-maroon finish: **1955**
White plastic covering: **1958**
Discontinued: **by 1962**

Studio: symmetrical body, rounded points at neck,
pickup and controls on metal plate with rounded
corners, 2 knobs on treble side, jack in control plate
on bass side, gold plastic fingerboard, totem pole
markers, peghead wider at top than at nut, opales-
cent blue pearlette covering
Introduced: **by 1955**
Painted-on fingerboard, totem pole markers, ivory-to-
black sunburst finish: **1959**
Ivory finish: **1961**
Discontinued: **1964**

De Luxe: straightline body shape, slight bevel
around neck, 1 knob, 21" scale, stairstep-pattern
fingerboard markers, *Student De Luxe* in script near
bridge, mottled red and white finish, no logo, tool-
box style case contains amp
Available: **1955**

Studio Four: guitar-shaped body, pickup and controls in metal plate with rounded corners, black
control plate, painted-on black fingerboard,
Bermuda red lacquer finish
Available: **1960–64**

Console 8: similar to Airline but with 8 strings and
3 legs, asymmetrical body straight on bass side,
black plastic pickup cover, black control plate, black
plastic covering on main body, white covering on
treble-side extension
Available: **1958–60**

Console 16: 2 8-string necks joined by large tubes,
large handrest covers both pickups, 1 knob on each
neck, switch on handrest, geometric markers, 4 legs
Available: **1958–60**
Reintroduced in National line, only catalog listing: **1967**

12-string Console: 2 6-string necks: **1960–64**

COMMENTS

The Supro lap steel pickup—with strings-through-
pickup design and separate coils for bass and treble
strings—has a dirty sound that appeals to some
players of blues and rock music. For that reason,
some players prefer Supro models over National
models. Most collectors regard National models
more highly than Supros.

AIRLINE MODELS MADE BY VALCO

Airline was a house brand of the Montgomery Ward
company. Not all instruments with the Airline logo
were made by National/Valco.

SECTION ORGANIZATION

Acoustic
Solidbodies, Single Cutaway
Angular-Shape Woodbody
Angular-Shape Fiberglass Body
Basses
Lap Steels

ACOUSTIC
Acoustic Resonator Model: described as

"extra volume folk guitar," single-cone resonator,
molded Res-o-glas (fiberglass) body, 15" wide, 8
stylized M- or lyre-shaped holes in resonator coverplate, 2 holes in upper bouts with screen inserts or
plastic inserts, dot inlay (some with block), asymmetrical peghead longer on treble side, plastic logo,
white peghead veneer, black finish
Available: **1964–67**

SOLIDBODIES, SINGLE CUTAWAY

All similar to Supro models, single cutaway with slight
cutaway on bass side, beveled body edges, 2 fin-
shaped finger rests, bound fingerboard, no backplate, white plastic block inlay, asymmetrical

peghead longer on treble side, sticker logo, goldoid (lacquered brass) metal parts, models available:

- 1 pickup
- 2 pickups
- 3 pickups
- 3 pickup deluxe, blond finish, Bigsby vibrato

Introduced: **1958**
Backplate, plastic logo, chrome-plated hardware: **1960**
Slightly thinner body, body edges more rounded, most with black pickup mounting rings and knobs, most with sunburst finish, some with cream finish: **1962**
Replaced by angular-shape woodbody models: **1963**

- Model similar to Supro White Holiday, single cut-away with slight cutaway on bass side, 1 pickup, 3 knobs on bass side, 3-way slotted switch on treble side, white finish
Available: **c. 1961**

ANGULAR-SHAPE WOODBODY

All with straight-line body edges, longer upper bass horn than treble horn, 2 fin-shaped finger rests, models available:
- 1 pickup, dot inlay
- 2 pickups, block inlay
Available: **1963–64**

ANGULAR-SHAPE FIBERGLASS BODY

Models with 24 3/4" scale
- 3 pickups, 6 knobs and 3-way slotted switch on bass side, Bigsby vibrato, block inlay, white fiberglass, available: **1963–64**
- 2 pickups: 4 knobs and 3-way slotted switch on treble side, 1 knob on bass side, plate tailpiece, bound fingerboard, block inlay, red finish, available: **1965–68**
- 1 pickup: yellow finish, available: **1965–68**

Models with short 22" scale, amp in case
- 1 pickup
- 2 pickups
Available: **c. 1963**

BASSES

- Model similar to Supro Pocket Bass, double cut-away, 1 standard pickup and 1 bridge pickup, 2 knobs, 2 fin-shaped finger rests, dot inlay, sunburst finish
Available: **1961–65**

Violin-shape basses: body material unavailable, dot inlay, 4-on-a-side tuner arrangement, 2 models available:
- 1 pickup
- 1 standard pickup and 1 bridge pickup
Available: **1966–67**

LAP STEELS

Hawaiian steel: straight-line body sides, controls and pickup on plate with rounded corners, strings pass through pickup, 2 knobs on bass side, 20" scale, painted-on fingerboard, split black/white parallelogram markers, logo between pickup and neck, black finish
Available: **1965–67**

Deluxe Pro: similar to National Rocket 110, body shaped like rocket with finlike side extensions and control plates, white pickup cover with *Rocket*, 23" scale, Roman numeral markers, plastic peghead logo, black and white finish
Available: **1965**

COMMENTS

The fiberglass angular-shape Airline guitars have some aesthetic appeal to collectors due to their unique body shape.
The fiberglass resonator model is essentially the same instrument with the same funky sound as the red Supro Folk Star and has the same appeal. (The white National Bluegrass 35 is rarer and more highly sought.)

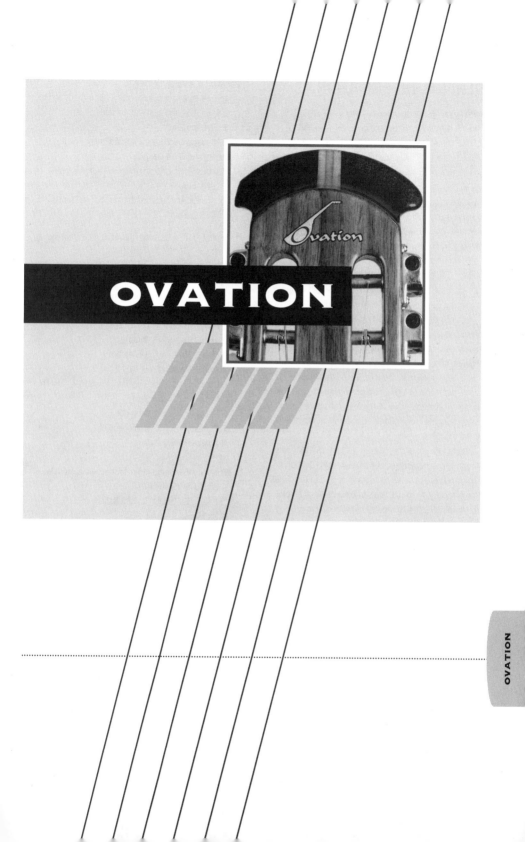

OVATION

GENERAL INFORMATION

Ovation was founded in 1965 by Charles H. Kaman, an aerospace engineer who had started Kaman Aircraft to make helicopters in 1945. Using technology developed for testing aircraft, Kaman sought to quantify sound quality and to utilize space-age materials in guitars. Production of a new "round-back" design, with a fiberglass bowl for the back and sides and conventional spruce top, began in North Hartford, CT, in 1966 and moved into a former cotton mill in New Hartford in 1967.

Ovation quickly established a reputation for durable guitars. The company's early success was based in part on endorsement models from folksinger Josh White and country/pop artist Glen Campbell.

In 1970 Ovation introduced the first high-quality piezo crystal pickup system for acoustic guitars, and acoustic/electric models would eventually dominate Ovation sales.

In 1976 Ovation introduced the Adamas model, with a top made of a graphite composite material, featuring small soundholes in the extreme upper bouts rather than the conventional round hole in the middle of the top.

Charlie Kaman's son Charles William (Bill) Kaman II took over as president of Kaman Music (Ovation's parent company) in July 1986 and retired in late 1998. The company, headquartered in Bloomfield, CT, continues to make Ovation instruments and also produces or distributes Hamer and Takamine guitars and various other brands of instruments and accessories.

4-DIGIT MODEL NUMBERS

Ovation introduced 4-digit model numbers in September 1967. A K-prefix was used from November 1968 to June 1972.

A numeral or letter(s) following the 4-digit code (separated by a hyphen) denotes finish color.

By the 1990s the increasing number of Ovation models had outgrown the four-digit system, and some model codes from circa 1990 onward do not conform to the original system.

1st digit:
1 All models until 1990s
5 Super shallow bowl
6 Mid-depth bowl

2nd digit is type of guitar:
1* Acoustic roundbacks, semi-hollowbody electrics
2 Solidbody and semi-hollowbody electrics
3 Ultra acoustics
5 Acoustic/electric cutaway Adamas; Adamas II, Elite and Ultra electrics
6 Acoustic/electric roundbacks (Adamas only, 1985–current)
7 Acoustic electric roundbacks, non-Adamas, 1985–current

* Beginning in 1996, all Ovations come with a pickup system.

3rd digit denotes bowl style and depth on acoustic and acoustic/electrics (except super shallow and mid-depth bowls, which are denoted by the 1st digit):
1 Standard bowl, 5 11/16" deep
2 Artist bowl, 5 1/8" deep
3 Elite/Matrix electric deep bowl
4 Matrix shallow bowl
5 Custom Balladeer, Legend, Legend 12, Custom Legend 12, Anniversary
6 Cutaway electric, deep bowl
7 Cutaway electric, shallow bowl
8 Adamas, 6 1/16" deep

4th digit denotes model, for first acoustic models:
1 Balladeer (Standard)
2 Deluxe Balladeer/Custom Balladeer
3 Classic
4 Josh White, later Country Artist and Folklore
5 12-string
6 Contemporary Folk Classic
7 Glen Campbell Artist Balladeer, Deluxe Balladeer (later Adamas and Anniversary)
8 Glen Campbell 12-string (later Adamas 12-string)
9 Custom Legend

Finish code follows hyphen after model number. Adamas models have a separate finish code.
1 Sunburst
2 Red
4 Natural
5 Black
6 White
7 LTD Nutmeg/Anniversary Brown/Beige/Tan
8 Blue
9 Brown

ASB Aspen blue
B Barnwood (gray-to-black sunburst)
BCB Black cherryburst
CCB Cherry cherryburst
CG Cadillac green
CGB Cadillac greenburst
CS Cherry sunburst
H (HB) Honeyburst
M Mahogany
NEB New England burst
OB Opaque burgundy
P Plum burst

RRB Ruby redburst
RR Ruby red
W Walnut stain
WB Wineburst

Misc. Changes

Larger floral leaf soundhole ring appears: **Sept. 1967**
Shallow "Artist" bowl introduced: **Nov. 1968**
Supershallow bowl introduced: **1983**
Mid-depth bowl introduced: **1998**

SERIAL NUMBERS

1967–72

These numbers were researched and compiled by Paul Bechtoldt.

RANGE	DATE	COMMENT
006—319	1966	3 digits in red ink
320—999	Feb.–Nov. 1967	New Hartford factory, 3 digits in red ink
1000s	Nov. 1967–July 1968	4 digits in black ink, no letter prefix
10000s	Feb.–May 1970	5 digits, no letter prefix
A + 3 digits	July–Nov. 1968	
B + 3 digits	Nov. 1968–Feb. 1969	
B + 5 digits	1974–79	Solidbody bass Magnum series
C + 3 digits	Feb. 1969–Sept. 1969	
D + 3 digits	Sept. 1969–Feb. 1970	
E + 4 digits	Jan. 1973–Feb. 1975	Solidbodies
E + 5 digits	Feb. 1975–1980	Solidbodies
E + 6 digits	late 1980–81	Some UK-IIs (does not reflect production)
F prefix	July 1968–Feb. 1970	
G prefix	July 1968–Feb. 1970	
H, I, J, L prefix	1970–73	Storm series

General Series, 1972–Current (except Adamas)

Numbers were provided by the Ovation company.

RANGE	DATE
000001–007000	May–Dec. 1972
007001–020000	1973
020001–039000	1974
039001–067000	1975
067001–086000	1976
086001–103000	Jan.–Sept. 1977
103001–126000	Sept. 1977–Apr. 78
126001–157000	Apr.–Dec. 1978
157001–203000	1979
211011–214933	1980

RANGE	DATE
214934–263633	1981
263634–291456	1982
291457–302669	1983
302760–303319	1984, Elites only
315001–339187	May–Dec. 1984, Balladeers only
303320–356000	1985–86
357000–367999	1987
368000–382106	1988
382107–392900	1989

OVATION

BOWLBACK (FIBERGLASS-BACK) MODELS

RANGE	DATE
400001–403676	1991
403760–420400	1990
421000–430680	1990
430681–446000	1991
402700–406000	1992
446001–457816	1992

RANGE	DATE
457810–470769	1993
470770–484400	1994
484401–501470	1995
501471–518689	1996
518690–528368	1997

ADAMAS SERIAL NUMBERS

Series starts with 0077 in Sept. 1977.

RANGE	YEAR
0077–0099	1977
0100–0608	1978
0609–1058	1979
1059–1670	1980
1671–2668	1981
2669–3242	1982
3243–3859	1983
3860–4109	1984
4110–4251	1985
4252–4283	1986

RANGE	YEAR
4284–4427	1987
4428–4696	1988
4697–4974	1989
4975–5541	1990
5542–6278	1991
6279–7088	1992
7089–8159	1993
8160–9778	1994
9779–11213	1995
11214–12000	1996

BOWLBACK (FIBERGLASS-BACK) MODELS

Standard Balladeer: modified X-bracing, white-black-white binding, unbound ebony fingerboard, dot inlay, Grover Rotomatic tuners, chrome-plated tuners, natural top, less than 100 made before February 1967 move to New Hartford factory
Variations:
- Very early with no soundhole ring
- Early with small or thin soundhole ring with figure-8 chainlink motif and grape bunch at 4 o'clock position
- Some with extra diamond fret markers at 12th fret

Deep bowl, non-cutaway, acoustic (**1111**): **1966–still 83, 1993–current**
Deep bowl, non-cutaway, acoustic/electric (**1611, 1711**): **1983–85, 1993–current**
Deep bowl, cutaway, acoustic/electric (**1661, 1761**): **1982–98**
Super shallow bowl, acoustic/electric (**1561/1861**): **1984–current**
Mid-depth bowl, cutaway, acoustic/electric (**1771**): **1998–current**

12-string, deep bowl, acoustic (**1151**): **1996–current**
12-string, deep bowl, acoustic/electric (**1751**): **1996–98**
12-string, mid-depth bowl (**6751**): **1998–current**

Artist Balladeer: shallow bowl version of Balladeer: (**1121**): **Nov. 1968–c. 1990**

Electric Artist: shallow bowl version of acoustic/electric Balladeer: (**1621**): **May 1971–c. 1990**

Balladeer Special: inlaid rosette, thin hand-rubbed natural finish
Mid-depth bowl, cutaway, acoustic/electric (**S771**): **1999–current**
Super shallow bowl, cutaway, acoustic/electric (**S771**): **1999–current**

Custom Balladeer: cedar top optional, modified X-bracing, dot inlay on bridge, unbound ebony fingerboard, diamond inlays, chrome-plated hardware
Introduced: **by 1976**
No bridge inlays: **1994**
Discontinued: **1996**

Deep bowl, acoustic (**1112**): **1976–c. 1990**

Deep bowl, acoustic/electric (**1612/1712**): **1976–c. 1990**

Super shallow bowl, acoustic/electric, cedar top optional (**1862/1860**): **1989–96**

12-string, deep bowl, acoustic (**1155**): **1982–94**

12-string, deep bowl, electric/acoustic (**1655/1755**): **1982–94**

Deluxe Balladeer/Legend: same as Balladeer but with 5-ply top binding, bound ebony fingerboard, diamond inlays at 12th fret, 5-piece maple/mahogany neck, Grover Rotomatic tuners, gold-plated tuners

Introduced as **Deluxe Balladeer: Feb. 1967**

Renamed **Legend: June 1972**

Still in production

Deep bowl, acoustic (**1117**): **Feb. 1967–current**

Deep bowl, acoustic/electric (**1617, 1717**): **June 1972–98**

Deep bowl, cutaway, acoustic/electric (**1667, 1767**): **1982–96**

Shallow bowl, cutaway, acoustic/electric (**1677**): **1982–c. 1990**

Mid-depth bowl, cutaway, acoustic/electric (**1777**): **1996–current**

Super shallow bowl (**1567, 1867**): **1984–current**

12-string, deep bowl, acoustic (**1156**): **1982–93**

12-string, deep bowl, acoustic/electric (**1656, 1756**): **1982–93**

12-string, super shallow bowl, cutaway, acoustic/electric (**1866**): **1989–current**

Legend Ltd.: deep bowl, stereo electronics, nutmeg finish (**1651**): **1979–88**

Nylon-String Legend: see Classic, deep bowl, cutaway (following)

Thunderbolt: super shallow bowl, 6-on-a-side tuner arrangement: **1988–90**

Classic: rectangular string loop bridge, 12 frets clear of body, unbound ebony fingerboard, no inlay, flat fingerboard 2" wide at nut, fingerboard extends 1 extra fret on treble side, slotted peghead, gold-plated tuners

Deep bowl, non-cutaway, acoustic (**1113**): **Sept. 1967–93**

Deep bowl, non-cutaway, acoustic/electric (**1613/1713**): **1972–93**

Deep bowl, cutaway, acoustic/electric (**1663/1763**): **1982–current**

Super shallow bowl, cutaway (**1863**): **1989–current**

Artist Classic: shallow bowl (**1123**): **Nov. 1968–75**

Classic Balladeer: Balladeer bracing, shallow bowl, rectangular string-loop bridge, 12 frets clear of body, flat fingerboard, no inlay, slotted peghead (**1122**): **June 1972–78**

Josh White/Folklore: deep bowl, 12 frets clear of body, steel strings, dot inlay with diamonds at 12th fret, flat fingerboard, 1 7/8" nut width, slotted peghead, chrome-plated tuners (**1114**)

Introduced: **Sept. 1967**

Discontinued after Josh White's death: **1970**

Reintroduced as Folklore (**1114**) and Electric Folklore (**1614**): **June 1972**

Discontinued: **1983**

Folklore reintroduced, cutaway, steel strings, X bracing, mid-depth body, 5-piece maple/mahogany neck, ebony fingerboard, 1 7/8" nut width (**6774**): **1994**

Still in production

Country Artist: shallow bowl, 12 frets clear of body, rectangular bridge, nylon strings tie to bridge, flat fingerboard, no inlay, 1 7/8" nut width, slotted peghead, chrome-plated tuners: **May 1971**

Discontinued: **by 1993**

Reintroduced, nylon strings, 1 7/8" nut width, VT-8 pattern top bracing, mid-depth body, 5-piece maple/mahogany neck, ebony fingerboard: **1994**

Still in production

Shallow bowl, non-cutaway, acoustic (**1124**): **May 1971–c. 1990**

Shallow bowl, non-cutaway, acoustic/electric (**1624**): **May 1971–c. 1990**

Shallow bowl, cutaway, acoustic/electric (**1674**): **1982–c. 1990**

Mid-depth body (**6773**): **1994–current**

12-string/Pacemaker: unbound ebony fingerboard, dot and diamond inlay, chrome-plated tuners

Introduced: **Jan. 1968**

Renamed **Pacemaker: June 1972**

Discontinued: **1982**

BOWLBACK (FIBERGLASS-BACK) MODELS

Acoustic (**1115**): **Jan. 1968–82**
Acoustic/electric (**1615**): **June 1972–82**

Contemporary Folk Classic: appears in catalog but only produced as a prototype (probably during development of Glen Campbell model) with red, green or blue bowl color option (**1116**): **July 1968**

Concert Classic: 12 frets clear of body, unbound ebony fingerboard, no inlay, flat fingerboard 2" wide at nut, fingerboard extends 1 extra fret on treble side, slotted peghead, chrome-plated tuners, natural or sunburst finish

Acoustic (**1116**): **1974–c. 1990**
Acoustic/electric (**1616**): **1974–c. 1990**

Glen Campbell Artist Balladeer: shallow bowl version of Legend model, bound ebony fingerboard, diamond inlay, gold-plated tuners

Acoustic (**1127**): **Nov. 1968–c. 1990**
Acoustic/electric (**1627**): **1971–c. 1990**
12-string, acoustic (**1118**): **Nov. 1968–82**
12-string, acoustic/electric (**1618**): **1971–82**

Custom Legend: carved walnut bridge, abalone top border, engraved abalone soundhole ring, bound ebony fingerboard, fancy floral abalone inlay, pearloid tuner buttons, gold-plated tuners, natural or sunburst finish
Introduced: **1974**
Abalone trim added: **1988**
Still in production

Deep bowl, non-cutaway, acoustic (**1119**): **1974–c. 1990**
Deep bowl, non-cutaway, acoustic/electric (**1619/1719**): **1974–96**
Deep bowl, cutaway, acoustic/electric, black finish offered as **Al DiMeola Model** (**1669, 1769**): **1982–93, 1996–current**
Deep bowl, cutaway, Roland GR synthesizer installed (**R-869**): **1998–current**
Super shallow bowl, cutaway, acoustic/electric (**1569/1869**): **1984–current**

12-string, acoustic (**1159**): **1980–93**
12-string, electric (**1659/1759**): **1980–current**

Patriot Bicentennial: limited run of 1,776 guitars, fancy version of Custom Legend with drum-and-flag decal and *1776*1976* on lower treble bout
Available: **1976**

Adamas: laminated top of carbon graphite material, 22 soundholes in upper treble bouts, decorative leaf pattern of various woods around soundholes, walnut neck and fingerboard, carved bridge ends and top of peghead, labels signed by Charles H. Kaman up to #600, labels signed by C.W. (Bill) Kaman II thereafter (until late 1998), suffix after model name is guitar's natural frequency resonance
Introduced in prototype form for artists and select dealers: **Sept. 1976**
The first 26 are prototypes; #27–#61 are a non-tooling production run; #62–#76 have a new headstock design and the Kaman bar neck reinforcement; early examples have wooden epaulettes around soundholes, later with a photographic mylar material
Tooling for production run: **Sept. 1977**
First production models received by dealers (first production Adamas sold is Model 1687, #0077-95): **Dec. 1977**
Still in production

Deep bowl, non-cutaway, acoustic (**1187**): **1977–c. 1990**
Deep bowl, non-cutaway, acoustic, wide neck (**1189**): **1979–93**
Deep bowl, non-cutaway, acoustic/electric (**1687**): **1977–98**
Deep bowl, non-cutaway, acoustic/electric, wide neck (**1689**): **1979–93**
Deep bowl, cutaway (**1587**): **1979–98**
Deep bowl, cutaway, acoustic/electric (**6581**): **1998–current**
Super shallow bowl, cutaway, red, black or blue finish (**1881**): **1993**
12-string, deep bowl, acoustic (**1188**): first example is #213: **1978–c. 1990**
12-string, deep bowl, acoustic/electric (**1688**): **1978–98**
12-string, super shallow bowl, cutaway, red, black or blue finish (**1885**): **1993**

BOWLBACK (FIBERGLASS-BACK) MODELS

Adamas Q: top, back and neck of black carbon fiber material, non-cutaway, 8 soundholes in upper bouts curving with contour of body edge (**Q181**) Available: **1998–current**

Adamas SMT: mid-depth bowl, cutaway, acoustic/electric, ebony bridge, mahogany neck, ebony fingerboard, spruce-grain graphite top finish (**1597**): **1998–current**

Round soundhole (**6591**): **1998–current**
12-string (**1598**): **1998–current**

Anniversary (**1157**): deep bowl, carved walnut bridge, herringbone top border, bound ebony fingerboard, abalone inlay, gold-plated tuners, natural or antique brown finish

Acoustic (**1157**): **1978–c. 1990**
Acoustic/electric (**1657**): **1978–c. 1990**

Parlor: narrow waist "salon" body, mid-depth bowl, solid Sitka spruce top, round soundhole, 5-piece maple/mahogany neck, unbound ebony fingerboard, piezo pickup
Available: **1998–current**

Adamas II: similar to Adamas except for standard Ovation walnut bridge, no peghead carving, 5-piece mahogany/maple neck, available as acoustic/electric only, no soundholes on cutaway side
Introduced: **1981**
Soundholes added on cutaway side: **1994**
Discontinued: **1998**

Deep bowl, non-cutaway (**1681**): **1981–98**
Deep bowl, cutaway (**1581**): **1982–98**
Super shallow bowl, cutaway (**1881**): **1993–98**
12-string (**1685**): **1981–98**
12-string, super shallow bowl, cutaway (**1885**): **1993–98**

Elite: Adamas II with solid spruce top, cedar top optional, prototype is Adamas #N-19-82WTSL (WTSL for Wood Top Super Legend): **1982**
Introduced on price list (production begins shortly thereafter): **Oct. 1982**
Cedar top optional on 1768 and 1868: **1993**
Still in production

Deep bowl, non-cutaway (**1718**): **1982–97**
Deep bowl, cutaway (**1768**): **c. 1990–98**
Mid-depth bowl, cutaway (**1778**): **1998–current**
Super shallow bowl, cutaway (**1868**): **1983–current**
Super shallow bowl, cutaway angel step walnut (**5868**): **1993**
12-string acoustic/electric (**1758**): **1989–93**
12-string, shallow bowl, cutaway, acoustic/electric (**1858**): **1993–current**
12-string, shallow bowl, cutaway, angel step walnut finish, acoustic/electric (**5858**): **1993**

Legend Elite: deep bowl, Sitka spruce top, 5-piece maple/mahogany neck, rosewood fingerboard

Acoustic/electric (**1735**): **1985–c. 1990**
12-string (**1736**): **1985–c. 1990**

Elite Standard: 3-band EQ, no fingerboard inlay

Deep bowl, non-cutaway (**6718**): **1993–96**
Deep bowl, cutaway (**6768**): **1994–98**
Mid-depth bowl, non-cutaway (**6758**): **1998–current**
Mid-depth bowl, cutaway (**6778**): **1998–current**
Super shallow bowl, cutaway (**6868**): **1994–current**

Elite Bass: deep bowl, cutaway

4 strings (**D-868/B-768**): **1990–current**
5 strings (**B-5768**): **1995–98**

Custom Elite: AAA-grade Sitka spruce top, rosewood fingerboard, inlaid ebony/maple peghead logo

Deep bowl (**CE-768**): **1996–current**
Super shallow bowl (**CE-868**): **1996–current**
Mid-depth bowl (**CE-778**): **1998–current**

Ultra: deep bowl, laminated spruce top, "urelite" (urethane) neck, rosewood fingerboard, dot inlay
Introduced: **1983**
Wood neck: **1985**
Discontinued: **1993**

Acoustic (**1311/1312**): **1983–93**
Acoustic/electric (**1511/1512**): **1983–93**

Ultra Deluxe: spruce top, preamp, 1-piece mahogany neck, bound rosewood fingerboard, abalone diamonds-and-dots inlay

OVATION

Deep bowl, non-cutaway, acoustic, maple top optional (**1317/1312-D**): **1984–96**

Deep bowl, non-cutaway, acoustic/electric, flame maple top optonal, (**1517-D**): **1985–96**

Deep bowl, cutaway, acoustic/electric (**1527-D**): **1984–93**

Super shallow bowl, cutaway, acoustic/electric (**1528-D**): **1989–95**

12 string, acoustic (**1315-D**): **1990–93**

12-string, acoustic/electric (**1515-D**): **1989–95**

Celebrity: built overseas, laminated spruce top, no preamp (except where noted), mahogany neck, bound rosewood fingerboard

Introduced: **1984**

Preamp added: **1997**

Still in production

Deep bowl, acoustic, black fingerboard binding, dot inlay (**CC-11**): **1984–96**

Deep bowl, acoustic/electric, DJ-4 bridge pickup (**CC-01**): **1997–current**

Deep bowl, acoustic/electric, piezo bridge pickup, white fingerboard binding, diamonds-and-dots inlay (**CC-67**): **1984–96**

Deep bowl, classical (nylon strings), acoustic, 12-fret neck, 26" scale, 2" nut width, black fingerboard binding, no inlay, gold-plated hardware, natural finish (**CC-13/1113**): **1984–96**

Deep bowl, classical (nylon strings), piezo bridge pickup (**CC-63/1613/1713**): **1984–96**

Deep bowl, cutaway, acoustic/electric (**CC-68**): **1991–96**

Deep bowl, cutaway, acoustic/electric, preamp (**CC-268**): **1994–96**

Deep bowl, cutaway, classical (nylon strings), (**CC-63/1663**): c. **1990–96**

Mid-depth bowl, cutaway (**CC-47**): **1997–98**

Super shallow bowl, classical, cutaway, acoustic/electric (**CC-53**): c. **1990–96**

Shallow bowl, (**CC-57**): c. **1990–93**

Super shallow bowl, cutaway, acoustic/electric (**CC-57**): **1996–current**

Super shallow bowl, cutaway, preamp (**CC-157**): c. **1990–96**

Compact mini-body, short scale (**Celebrity Trekker CC-12**): **1998–current**

12-string acoustic (**CC-15**): c. **1990–96**

12-string acoustic/electric (**CC-65**); c. **1990–96**

Bass deep bowl, cutaway (**CC-77**): c. **1990–93**

Bass, round soundhole (**CC-74**): **1993–96, 1998–current**

Bass, deep bowl, Elite soundholes (**CC-75**): **1994**

Celebrity Deluxe: cutaway body, spruce top, pre-amp and graphic-EQ control, Elite soundholes, nato neck, rosewood fingerboard, dot and diamond inlay, gold-plated tuners, sunburst, natural or black finish

Deep bowl, non-cutaway, cedar top, spruce or sycamore top optional (**CC-267**): **1992–96**

Mid-depth bowl (**CS-247**): **1998–current**

Super shallow bowl (**CC-257/CS-257**): **1992–current**

Compact mini-body, short scale (**CS-212**): **1998–current**

12-string, mid-depth bowl (**CS-245**): **Jan. 1994–current**

Bass, 4 strings (**CS-274**): **Jan. 1994–96**

Bass, 5 strings (**CS-275**): **1994–98**

Pinnacle: made in Japan, spruce top, 3-band EQ, mahogany neck, rosewood fingerboard, dot inlay

Introduced internationally: **1987**

Introduced to U.S. market: **1990**

Discontinued: **1994**

Deep bowl, non-cutaway (**3712**): **1991–93**

Deep bowl, non-cutaway, torch top (figured horse chestnut) (**3711**): **1991–93**

Super shallow bowl, cutaway (**3862**): **1990–94**

Super shallow bowl, cutaway, torch top (figured horse chestnut) (**386T**): **1991–93**

12-string, torch top (figured horse chestnut) (**385T**): **1990–93**

Viper: solidbody cutaway, mahogany back with tone chambers, back encased in fiberglass with shallow bowlback shape, spruce top, Adamas soundholes, no fingerboard inlay

Steel strings (**EA68**): **Jan. 1994–current**

Nylon strings (**EA69**): **Jan. 1994–current**

12-string (**EA58**): **1994–98**

Bass (**EAB68**): **1994–current**

D Guitar/Longneck (DS768): long scale
Available: **Jan. 1994–current**

Mandolin (MM68): small cutaway body, 8 strings, Elite top
Available: **Jan. 1994–current**

5-string acoustic bass: guitar body
Available: **Jan. 1994–98**

Mandocello: guitar body, 8 strings, Adamas (composite) or Elite top
MC868 Adamas composite top: **1994–current**
MCS868 Elite spruce top: **1994–current**

Al DiMeola Model: Custom Legend 1769 (see preceding) with black finish
Available: **1998–current**

COLLECTORS SERIES

Model number is the year (except for 12-strings and two 199S models in 1990), followed by finish code.

1982-8: deep bowl non-cutaway, round soundhole, blueburst finish, $995 list, 1908 made

1983-B: supershallow cutaway, round soundhole, ebony fingerboard, barnboard (grey/black sunburst) finish, $995 list, 2754 made

1984-5: supershallow cutaway, Elite style, ebony stain finish, $995 list, 2637 made

1985-1: supershallow cutaway, Elite style, autumnburst finish, $1095 list, 2198 made

2985-1: 12-string supershallow cutaway, Elite style, autumnburst finish, $1195 list, 715 made

1986-6: supershallow cutaway, round soundhole, pearl white finish, $1095 list, 1858 made

2986-6: 12-string supershallow cutaway, round soundhole, pearl white finish, $1195 list, 392 made

1987-7: deep bowl cutaway, Elite style, nutmeg finish, $1800 list, 820 made
1987-5: deep bowl cutaway, Elite style, black finish, $1800 list, 108 made

1988-P: supershallow cutaway, Elite style, pewter finish, $1195 list, 1177 made

1989-8: supershallow cutaway, round soundhole, blue pearl finish, $1299 list, 981 made

1990-7: deep bowl cutaway, bird's eye maple Elite style, nutmeg finish, $1599 list, 500 made
199S-7: supershallow cutaway, bird's eye maple Elite style, nutmeg finish, $1599 list, 750 made
1990-1: deep bowl cutaway, bird's eye maple Elite style, sunburst finish, $1599 list, 50 made

199S-1: supershallow cutaway, bird's eye maple Elite style, sunburst finish, $1599 list, 100 made

1991-4: deep bowl cutaway, round soundhole, natural finish, $1159 list, 1464 made
1991-5: deep bowl cutaway, round soundhole, black metallic finish, $1159 list, 1464 made

1992-H: super shallow cutaway, quilted ash Elite style, honeyburst finish, $1699 list, 1995 made

1993-4: mid-depth cutaway, Elite style, natural finish, 1537 made

1994-7: mid-depth cutaway, round soundhole, nutmeg finish, 1763 made

1995-7: mid-depth cutaway, round soundhole, nutmeg finish, 1502 made

1996-TPB: mid-depth cutaway, round soundhole, burgundy finish, 1280 made

1997-7N: narrow waist, walnut-bound Sitka spruce top, round soundhole, maple leaf soundhole ring, unbound fingerboard, nutmeg stain finish

1998: mid-depth cutaway, figured maple top, Adamas soundholes, New England sunburst finish

1999: mid-depth cutaway, bubinga top, Adamas soundholes, 5-piece maple/mahogany neck, red waterfall finish

OVATION

SEMI-HOLLOW AND SOLIDBODY ELECTRICS

SEMI-HOLLOW AND SOLIDBODY ELECTRICS

SECTION ORGANIZATION

Electric Storm Semi-Hollowbody Series
Solidbody Models

ELECTRIC STORM SEMI-HOLLOWBODY SERIES

Original Storm colors: Natural, Nutmeg or Black
Storm color codes, beginning May 1971:
2 red
4 natural nutmeg
5 black

Thunderhead (K-1360): double cutaway, 2 hum-bucking pickups, phase switch on upper bass bout, master volume, separate tone controls, pickup balance/blend control on lower treble bout, gold-plated hardware, natural, nutmeg or walnut green finish.

Thunderhead (K-1460): vibrato
Introduced: **July 1968**
Thunderhead K-1160 renumbered **K-1213**, Thunderhead K-1260 renumbered **K-1214: Mar. 1970**
Thunderhead K-1213 renumbered **K-1233**, Thunderhead K-1214 renumbered **K-1234: May 1971**
Discontinued: **June 1972**

Tornado (K-1160): same as Thunderhead except no phase switch and separate volume and tone controls for each pickup, chrome-plated hardware

Tornado (K-1260): vibrato
Introduced: **July 1968**
Tornado K-1160 renumbered **K-1211**, Tornado K-1260 renumbered **K-1212: Mar. 1970**
Tornado K-1211 renumbered **K-1231**, Tornado K-1212 renumbered **K-1232: May 1971**
Discontinued: **Jan. 1973**

Hurricane (K-1120): 12-string: **July 1968–mid 1969**

Typhoon I Bass (K-1140): double cutaway, smaller body with shorter horns than Thunderhead, 1 pickup

Typhoon II Bass (K-1240): 2 pickups, catalogued as **Williwaw** (means Mountain Wind) but never sold under that name
Introduced: **July 1968**
Same body size as Thunderhead: **mid 1969**
Typhoon I discontinued: **Aug. 1969**
Typhoon II K-1240 renumbered K-1222: **Mar. 1970**
Discontinued: **June 1972**

Typhoon III: double cutaway, fretless: **late 1969**

Typhoon IV (K-1216): fretless : **March 1970–June 1972**

Typhoon V (K-1217): **May 1971–June 1972**

Eclipse (K-1235): 6-string economy model, black finish
Available: **May 1971–Jan. 1973**

SOLIDBODY MODELS

Breadwinner (1251): mahogany back and neck, 2 very large single-coil pickups, dot fret markers, textured finish (like fiberglass bowls). Colors: 5 black, 6 white, 7 tan, 8 blue
Available: **June 1972–82**

Deacon (1252): diamond inlay, sunburst finish
First listed: **June 1972**
First available: **Jan. 1973**
Humbucking pickup: **1975**
Last offered: **1982**

Deacon 12-string (1253): a few made: **1975**

Preacher (1281): double cutaway, 2 mahogany body, humbuckers, 24 1/2" scale
Available: **1975–82**

Preacher Deluxe (1282): series/parallel pickup switch and mid-range control: **late 1975–82**

Preacher 12-string (1285): 1975–82

Viper (1271): single cutaway, 2 single-coil pickups, 25" scale, most are ash, some maple or mahogany

Viper III (1273): 3 single-coil pickups
Available: **1975–82**

OVATION

MAGNUM BASS

Magnum I (1261): 1974–82

Magnum II (1262): 3-band EQ: **1974–82**

Magnum III (1263): 2 pickups but less radical body than Magnum I, split-coil humbucking bridge pickup with string grooves in polepieces, 4 separate pickups in neck position with access holes in pickup cover to balance individual string volume: **1978–82**

Magnum IV (1264): 1978–82

UK-II 1291: body of Urelite (urethane) on aluminum frame
Available: **1980–82**

Ultra Hard Body: made in Japan, solidbodies in 3 styles:

GP Series: double cutaway with pointed bass-side horn, 3-on-a-side tuner configuration

GF Series: double cutaway with rounded horns, Fender Stratocaster shape, 6-on-a-side tuner configuration

UB Series: bass, double cutaway with rounded horns, Fender Precision shape, 4-on-a-side tuner configuration
Available: **1985–late 1980s**

COMMENTS

None of Ovation's conventional electric models was commercially successful, and all are relatively rare, with the semi-hollowbody models the rarest. They are of interest primarily to Ovation collectors.

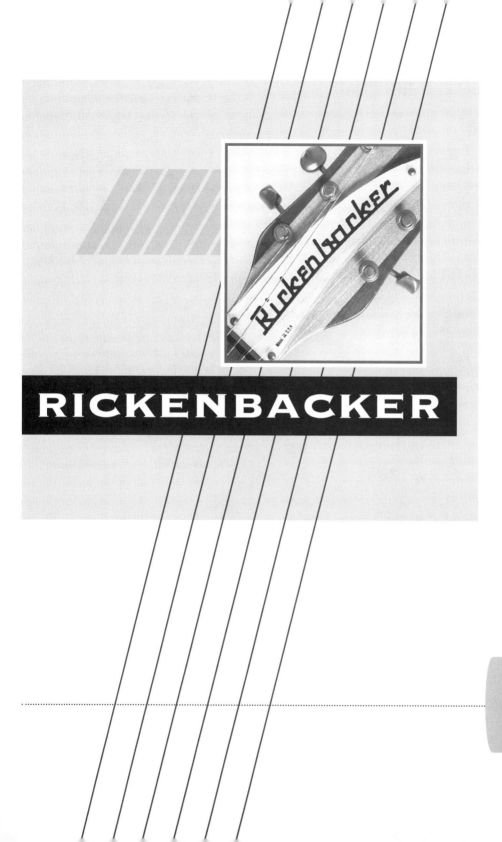

RICKENBACKER

GENERAL INFORMATION

Adolph Rickenbacker, a distant cousin of World War I flying ace Eddie Rickenbacker, was born in Switzerland in 1892. He emigrated to America as a child and moved to Los Angeles in 1918. He and two partners formed the Rickenbacker Manufacturing Company, a metal stamping shop, in 1925. He invested in the original National company in 1928 and was contracted to provide metal guitar bodies to National.

Rickenbacker, George Beauchamp (founding partner and general manager of National) and other figures from National formed the Ro-Pat-In Corporation on October 15, 1931, to develop Beauchamp's design for an electric guitar with a magnetic pickup. Rickenbacker was president of Ro-Pat-In; Beauchamp was secretary-treasurer. Rickenbacker's metal shop continued to supply parts to National, but Beauchamp was ousted from National on November 10, 1931.

Ro-Pat-In's first guitars were electric models—Hawaiian guitars with cast aluminum bodies and Spanish models with conventional archtop wood bodies—introduced in 1932 under the Electro String Instruments brand. The company name was changed to the Electro String Instrument Corporation in 1934, and the brand name was changed to Rickenbacker, although many instrument decals say Rickenbacher with an *h*, which was the original family spelling.

The company introduced a lap steel with Bakelite neck and body in 1935, and by 1936 the line included electric mandolins, bass viols, violins, cellos, and violas—all with the horseshoe pickup. Lap steels accounted for the majority of Rickenbacker's sales prior to World War II.

In July 1942 the company diverted its production efforts to war-related products. Instrument production resumed in early 1946.

Adolph Rickenbacker sold the company in 1953 to F. C. Hall, founder of the Radio and Television Equipment Company (Radio-Tel), an electronics company that had been the exclusive distributor for Fender products. Hall shifted Rickenbacker's emphasis to Spanish electrics, although Hawaiians continued to sell well, due in a large part to an endorsement by Jerry Byrd. Hall expanded the guitar line with the solidbody Combo series in 1954. German-born Roger Rossmeisl designed a new solidbody line in 1957 and the hollowbody Capri series in 1958.

In 1962, the factory was moved to Santa Ana, CA, and Radio-Tel was renamed Rickenbacker, Inc.

Rickenbacker's image was heightened considerably by the Beatles' use of Rickenbackers in the mid 1960s. By the late 1960s Rickenbacker was the premier maker of electric 12-strings. In the 1970s, basses played a prominent role in enhancing the Rickenbacker reputation. Vintage Series reissues, introduced in 1984, are now a vital part of the company's continuing success.

In 1984 F.C. Hall passed control of the company to his son, John C. Hall, who combined all the manufacturing and distribution under the name Rickenbacker International Corporation (RIC).

EXPORT MODELS

From 1964–69, Rickenbacker exported some models to Rose, Morris & Co, Ltd. in England for sale in Europe. Most of the export models have an equivalent U.S. model. Many hollowbody export models have *f*-holes rather than slash holes or no holes. Rickenbacker designated export models with an *S* after the model number. Rose, Morris assigned a different set of numbers. See model descriptions for individual model specs.

Rickenbacker Model	Rose, Morris Model
325	1996
335	1997
336-12	3262
345	1998
360-12	1993
615	1995
4000-4001	1999
4005	3261

PICKUPS

Horseshoe magnet wraps over strings, magnet 1 1/2" wide, all models: **1932–43**

Horseshoe magnet wraps over strings, magnet 1 1/4" wide...

Guitars: **1946–59**

Basses...

U.S. models: **1957–64**

Export models: **1964–66**

Vintage reissues: **1984–current**

Lap steels: **1946–71**

Oblong metal plate in center of pickup: **1956–57**

Rectangular metal plate in center of pickup: **1957–58**
Metal bar (part of housing) across middle of pickup,
   black metal housing: **early 1957–Oct. 1957**
"Chrome bar," same as above but with chrome-plated
   housing: **Oct. 1957–70**
Rick-O-Sound stereo (extra jack) on deluxe models:
   1960–current
Hi-Gain, exposed polepieces: **1969 only**
Hi-Gain, black polepiece covers: **1970–current**
Humbucking, poles near edge: **1970s–current**
Hybrid, blackface, no visible poles: **1980s–current**
Reissue of chrome bar, vintage reissues: **1984–current**

KNOBS, 1954–CURRENT

Changes are transitional from model to model.
Solidbodies…
   Metal: **1954–57**
   Small black plastic: **1958–current**
Hollowbodies…
   Metal chrome-plated: **1954–58**
   "Kitchen oven," black plastic with elongated gold
      diamond design on top: **1958–c. 1963, reissues**
   Small black plastic: **c. 1961–current**

VIBRATOS AND TAILPIECES

Kauffman side-to-side, no roller bridges: **1932–57**
Kauffman with roller bridges: **1957–late 1960**
Ac'cent vibrato (name on cover plate on early examples),
   arm attached by slot-head screw, roller bridge,
   adjustable saddles: **early 1961–75, 1985–current**
Boyd (rare), some with pitch-changing levers: **1962–65**
Bigsby, some vintage reissues: **1984–current**
Torsion, like Ac'cent but with no rollers or coil springs:
   1980s–current
Bigsby, 325V59 (reissue model): **1984–current**
R tailpiece, some non-vibrato models: **1963–current**

PICKGUARDS

Plastic or metal, one piece (see model descriptions):
   1954–early 1960s
Two-piece split-level design, hollowbody models: **late
   1958–current**
Gold-backed Lucite…
   Some solidbody models: **1958–62**
   Some hollowbody models: **1958–63**
White plastic standard…
   Solidbody models: **1962–current**
   Hollowbody models: **1963–current**

ORNAMENTATION, 1956–CURRENT

Standard trim: dot inlay, no binding on fingerboard or
   body
Deluxe trim…
   Bound top and back, bound fingerboard, triangular
      inlay goes completely across fingerboard:
      1957–69
   Rounded top edges with no binding on Models
      360–375 (bound top available as Old Style trim
      through 1969), bound fingerboard, sparkle
      "crushed pearl" fingerboard inlay: **1964–69**
   Bound top or rounded edge top with no binding,
      bound fingerboard, non-sparkle triangular inlay
      with rounded corners, triangular inlay does not
      extend across fingerboard: **1970–current**
Checkered binding…
   Rounded-top deluxe examples and Model 381: **late
      1950s–64**
   All rounded top (New Style) deluxe guitar models,
      solidbody bass models: **1964–70**
   4002 bass (from introduction): **1981–current**

LOGO

Rickenbacher with an *h* …
   All models: **1934–49**
   A few examples (old decals): **1950s**
Rickenbacker with a *k*: **1950–current**

FINISHES, MID 1950S–CURRENT

Sunburst, 2-tone brown: **mid to late 1950s**
Fireglo, shaded red with some yellow: **1960–current**
Autumnglo (shaded with red and brown): **1960–80**
Official custom finishes (custom color finishes available
   from mid 1950s–current, more finishes available
   than listed)…
   Fireglo, Mapleglo (natural), Azureglo (blue), Jetglo
      (black), Burgundyglo (red): **by 1968**
   Fireglo, Azureglo, Jetglo, Burgundy (standard);
      White, Walnut Brown, Mapleglo, Autumnglo
      (custom): **by 1971**
   Fireglo, Azureglo, Jetglo, Burgundy (standard);
      Ruby Walnut, Mapleglo, White (custom glossy);
      Natural, Black Brown (custom matte): **by 1981**
   Midnight Blue (metallic), Metallic Silver, Ruby
      (metallic), White, Red, Mapleglo, Fireglo, Jetglo:
      late 1980s

1957 Combo 800, double cutaway with cutaway 4 frets deeper on treble side, 1 double-coil horseshoe pickup (courtesy Shane's Music).

Early 1957 Combo 450, tulip-shaped body (courtesy Wagner Swanson).

Early 1960s Combo 900, modified-tulip body shape with deeper treble-side cutaway.

Late 1950s Combo 850, extreme cutaway body shape, non-original Bigsby vibrato (courtesy Lloyd Chiate).

Model 360, New Style (1964 and after) rounded top edges, deluxe triangular fingerboard inlay.

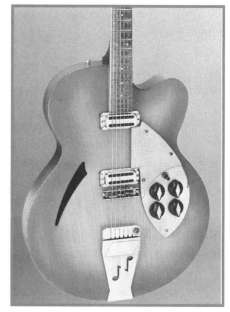

Model 330F with standard trim: unbound body, dot inlay (courtesy Eugene's).

Cresting wave body shape on a 4001V63 bass.

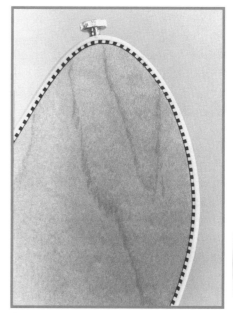

Checkered trim on the back of a New Style Model 360.

RICKENBACKER

Standard Rickenbacker peghead shape.

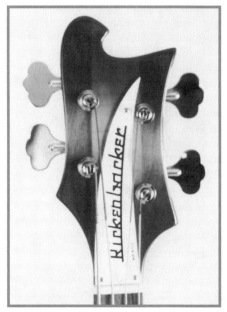

Cresting wave peghead shape.

Split-level pickguard.

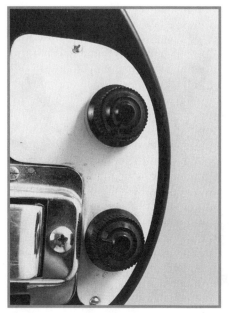

"Flying saucer" knobs on a Bakelite lap steel.

RICKENBACKER

526

Deluxe triangular inlay from 1964–70, with "crushed pearl" sparkle inlay extending completely across fingerboard.

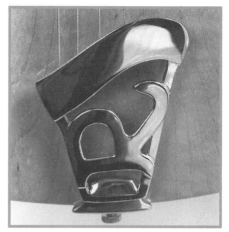

R tailpiece

Horseshoe pickup on a late 1930s Electro Spanish (Bakelite round-neck) model, with prewar style magnet (1 1/2" wide).

Postwar horse-shoe magnet (1 1/4" wide) on a Bakelite lap steel.

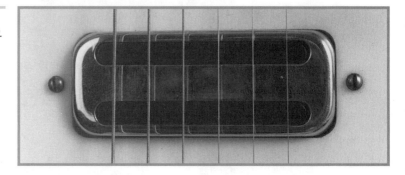

Chrome bar pickup, 1957–70.

SERIAL NUMBERS

1932–54

Serial numbers on early models are unreliable, but patent numbers give the earliest possible date of manufacture (date patent was granted).

1954–Oct. 1960

Number is stamped on jackplate or bridge.

Solidbodies, 1954–Sept. 1959

Number configuration **m(m)Cy###**

Numeral(s) **m(m)** before letter designate model: 4 = 400 or 425, 6 = 600, 65 = 650, 8 = 800

Letter **C** is type of instrument: C = Combo (guitar), B = bass, M = mandolin, V = 3/4 size

First numeral **y** after letter is year. Examples: 65C7### = 1957 Combo 650, 4C6### = 1956 Combo 400

Last 3 numerals **###** are ranking. Each model has its own series.

Exceptions:

Model 450s have **4C####A** configuration.

3/4 size models have **V###**, **V####** or **####A** configuration through Oct. 1960. First numeral is still last digit of year.

Basses have **B####** configuration.

Mandolins have **M###** configuration.

Some examples have **#C##** configuration and are not dateable by serial number.

Solidbodies (Except 3/4 Sizes) Sept. 1959–Oct. 1960

Number configuration **#(#)A###**

Only 3 numerals after letter. Numbers do not contain dating information.

Hollowbodies, 1958–Oct. 1960

Number configuration **pV##** (early 1958) or **pV###**

Numeral **p** before letter is number of pickups (2 or 3).

Letter **V** is for vibrato, **T** for standard tailpiece or (after June 1960) **R** for deluxe model.

Last digits **##** or **###** are ranking. Series starts over with 001 in Jan. 1960.

1958 range of numbers: V80–3V254

Highest Capri series number in 1959: 2T835

First Capri series number in 1960: 3V706

Oct. 1960–86

Numbers on jackplate with configuration: **YM** (2 letters) above jack hole; **##** or **###** (2 or 3 digits) below hole.

First letter **Y** (ranging from A–Z) denotes year:

A 1961	H 1968	O 1975	V 1982
B 1962	I 1968	P 1976	W 1983
C 1963	J . . . . 1960 or 1970	Q 1977	X 1984
D 1964	K 1971	R 1978	Y 1985
E 1965	L 1972	S 1979	Z 1986
F 1966	M 1973	T 1980	
G 1967	N 1974	U 1981	

Second letter **M** (ranging from A–L) denotes month:

A . . . . January	D . . . . April	G . . . . July	J . . . . October
B . . . . February	E . . . . May	H . . . . August	K . . . . November
C . . . . March	F . . . . June	I . . . . September	L . . . . December

Digits **##** or **###** are ranking.

1987–96

Numbers on jackplate with configuration **Ay** (letter and numeral) above jack hole; **##** or **###** (2 or 3 digits) below hole.
Letter **A** (ranging from A–L) denotes month (see preceding table for letter-month code).
Numeral **y** after letter denotes year:

0 1987	4 1991	8 1995
1 1988	5 1992	9 1996
2 1989	6 1993	
3 1990	7 1994	

Digits **##** or **###** are ranking.

1997–Nov. 1998

Numbers on jackplate with configuration **Ay** (letter and numeral) above jack hole; **####** (4 digits) below hole.
Letter **A** (ranging from M–X with no letter O) denotes month:

M . . . . January	Q . . . . April	T . . . . July	W . . . . October
N . . . . February	R . . . . May	U . . . . August	X . . . . November
P . . . . March	S . . . . June	V . . . . September	

Numeral **y** after letter denotes year:
0 1997
1 1998

Digits **####** are ranking.

Nov. 1998–Current

Numbers on jackplate with configuration: **yy** (2 digits) above jack hole; **ww###** (4 digits) below hole.
yy = last 2 digits of year
ww = week of the year
= ranking

HOLLOWBODIES KEY

All 1932–50 hollowbody models, archtop and flat top, are identifiable by a horseshoe pickup. The only postwar guitar models with horseshoe pickup are solidbody models 650 and 850.

Most examples in the 310–325 series have no soundholes and the same body shape
   as solidbody models 650 and 850. Except for a few custom examples, the 650
   and 850 have a horseshoe-magnet pickup; no 310-325 series models have horseshoe-magnet pickups. The 650 and 850 have a carved top; the 310-325s do not
   have a carved top.

Models in parentheses were never in production, although prototypes exist for
   some models.
Limited edition and vintage reissue models (except for 381-12V69) are not
   included in this key.

Full-depth body
   Non-cutaway
      Archtop
         ƒ-holes on lower bouts = **S-59**
         ƒ-holes on upper bouts = **Rickenbacker Spanish (SP)**
      Flat top
         ƒ-holes on lower bouts = **Ken Roberts Electro Spanish**
         ƒ-holes on upper bouts = **Electro Spanish**
         Round hole
            No pickup = **385**
            2 pickups
               No vibrato = (386)
               Vibrato = (387)
            3 pickups
               No vibrato = (388)
               Vibrato = (389)
   Single cutaway
      Archtop
         No pickup = (390)
         2 pickups
            No vibrato = (391)
            Vibrato = (392)
         3 pickups
            No vibrato = (393)
            Vibrato = (394)
   Double cutaway
      No pickup = (380)
      2 pickups
         6-string
            No vibrato = **381**
            Vibrato = (382) some sold as **381**
         12-string = **381-12V69**
      3 pickups
         No vibrato = (383)
         Vibrato = (384)

Thinbody
    Double cutaway
        3/4 scale, body 12 3/4" wide
            2 pickups
                No vibrato = **310**
                Vibrato = **315**
            3 pickups
                No vibrato
                    6-string = **320**
                    12-string = **325-12**
                Vibrato = **325**
        Full scale, body 15 1/4" wide
            Standard ornamentation (dot inlay)
                2 pickups
                    Gold-plated hardware = **380L Laguna**
                    Chrome-plated hardware
                      No vibrato
                        6-string
                          Wood top = **330**
                          Plastic top = **331**
                        12-string
                          6-12 converter = **336-12**
                        No converter = **330-12**
                    Vibrato = **335**
                3 pickups
                  No vibrato
                    Slash holes = **340**
                    No holes = **350**
                Vibrato = **345**
            Deluxe ornamentation (triangular inlay)
                2 pickups
                    6-string
                      No vibrato = **360**
                      Vibrato = **365**
                    12-string
                      6-12 converter = **366-12**
                      No converter = **360-12**
                3 pickups
                  6-string
                      No vibrato = **370**
                      Vibrato = **375**
                  12-string = **370-12**
    Single cutaway
        Standard ornamentation (dot inlay)
            2 pickups
                No vibrato = **330F**
                Vibrato = **335F**
            3 pickups
                No vibrato = **340F**
                Vibrato = **345F**

Thinbody, single cutaway (*continued*)
Deluxe ornamentation (triangular inlay)
2 pickups
6-string
No vibrato = **360F**
Vibrato = **365F**
12-string = **360F-12**
3 pickups
No vibrato = **370F**
Vibrato = **375F**

HOLLOWBODIES

All models from 1958 and after have standard ornamentation—unbound top and back, unbound fingerboard and dot inlay—unless otherwise noted. See General Information for more on ornamentation.

SECTION ORGANIZATION

Pre-1950 Models
Capri Series (300 series, thinbody, double cutaway)
Export Thin Hollowbody Models
Thin Full-body, F-Series (single cutaway)
Thick Body Series (fullbody)
Acoustic 1990s Models
Doubleneck Model

PRE-1950 MODELS

Electro Spanish: 3-ply mahogany flat top body made by Harmony, small *f*-holes in upperbouts, horseshoe-magnet pickup, no volume knob, straight bridge, 25" scale, 14 frets clear of body, dot inlay, slotted peghead (tenor available with solid peghead), plastic peghead veneer
Introduced: **1932**
Volume knob added: **c. 1934**
Bound top: **1934**
Replaced by Ken Roberts model (see following):
late 1935

Electro Spanish Guitar (Model B): see Solidbodies section

Ken Roberts Electro Spanish: 3-ply mahogany flat top body made by Harmony, *f*-holes in lower

bouts, horseshoe-magnet pickup, 1 octagonal knob on treble side near pickup, compensating bridge, Kauffman vibrato, bound top and back, 17 frets clear of body, bound fingerboard, dot inlay, rounded-peak peghead, shaded brown finish
Introduced: **late 1935**
Round knob with ridges: **1938**
Discontinued: **1940**

Vibrola Spanish Guitar: see Solidbodies section

S-59: archtop body made by Kay, *f*-holes in lower bouts, large screw-on pickup unit with horseshoe magnet spans waist to waist (pickup unit also available as accessory), 1 knob on pickup bracket, trapeze tailpiece, multiple-bound top and back, 14 frets clear of body, alternating 2-dots and single-diamond inlay, point at top peghead, blond finish
Available: **1940–42**

Rickenbacker Spanish (SP): archtop body made by Harmony, *f*-holes in upper bouts, horseshoe-magnet pickup, 2 white knobs, adjustable bridge, 3-ply or 4-ply binding on top, unbound or single-bound back, 25" scale, 14 frets clear of body, bound rosewood fingerboard, block inlay, rounded-peak peghead
Available: **1946–49**

CAPRI SERIES

310-375: thin hollowbody, double cutaway with pointed horns, bass horn slightly longer than treble, flat top recessed at tailpiece, top not beveled around bass side like solidbody models with same shape, chrome bar pickups

	12 3/4" wide		15 1/4" wide	
	3/4 scale	Full scale	Standard trim	Deluxe trim
2 pickups	310		330	360
2 pickups, vib.	315		335	365
3 pickups	320	350	340	370
3 pickups, vib.	325	355	345	375

310–325 series: 12 3/4" wide, most with no soundholes, single-piece pickguard of gold-backed Lucite, 2 knobs, 1 switch, 21-fret fingerboard does not extend over body, standard trim, short scale

Introduced: **Jan. 1958**

4 knobs, split-level 2-piece gold pickguard: **late 1958**

Some with ƒ-hole: **1961**

5 knobs (blend control added), white split-level pickguard: **1963**

ƒ-holes standard: **1964**

24-fret fingerboard extends over body: **1969**

315 and 325 discontinued: **1975**

Hi-Gain pickups: **by 1975**

No soundholes standard, ƒ-holes optional: **1979**

Still in production

310: Jan. 1958–70, 1981–late 1985

315: Jan. 1958–74

320: Jan. 1958–92

320B: early 1960s style reissue, 4 knobs: **late 1982–84**

320VB: vibrato (same as earlier 325): **1985–92**

320S: ƒ-hole: **1982**

325: Jan. 1958–74

325B: early 1960s style reissue, 4 knobs: **1983–84**

325S: domestic version of export model 1996 (see following), ƒ-hole: **1964–67**

325-12: 12-string (1 custom made for John Lennon in 1964): **1985–86**

John Lennon Special Edition 325 (325JL): chrome bar pickups, 5 knobs, Torsion vibrato, signature and drawing on pickguard, black finish, limited edition of 953 right-handed and 21 left-handed: **1989–93**

325-12JL: 12-string, John Lennon model, signature and drawing on pickguard, chrome bar pickups, slanted plate tailpiece, limited edition, available: **1990–91**

325V59/Hamburg: reissue of John Lennon's modified 1959 325, no soundholes, chrome bar pickups, 4 diamond-shaped knobs, Bigsby vibrato, Kluson style tuners

Introduced as **325V59: 1984**

Renamed **325V59 Hamburg: 1997**

Still in production

325V63/Miami: reissue of John Lennon 1963 style 325, chrome bar pickups, 5 knobs, Torsion vibrato, Kluson style tuners

Introduced as **325V63: 1984**

Renamed **325V Miami: 1997**

Still in production

330–345 series: 15 1/4" wide, 2" deep, most with slash soundhole, 2 knobs, 1 switch, single-piece pickguard of gold-backed lucite, 21-fret fingerboard does not extend over body, standard trim, brown sunburst or natural finish

Introduced: **Feb. 1958**

4 knobs, split-level 2-piece pickguard: **late 1958**

Thinner body, 1 1/2" deep: **1961**

5 knobs (blend control added), white split-level 2-piece pickguard: **1963**

R tailpiece on non-vibrato models: **1963**

24-fret fingerboard extends over body: **1969**

Some with slanted frets: **late 1969**

330: Feb. 1958–current

330S-12: domestic version of export model 1993 (see following), ƒ-hole, double-bound top: **1964–67**

330VB: vibrato (same as earlier 335): **1985–97**

330-12: 12-string: **1965–97**

331: "Light Show" model, same as Model 330 but with translucent plastic top, colored lights inside body (earliest with white lights and colored filters) activated by musical tones, bound fingerboard, dot inlay, external power box provided: **1970–75**

332/12: 12-string version of 331 "Light Show": **1971–75**

335: Feb. 1958–1977 (available as 330VB: **1985–97**)

335S: domestic version of export model 1997 (see following), ƒ-hole: **1964–67**

336-12: 330-12 with comblike 6-12 converter: **1966–74**

336S-12: domestic version of import model 3262 (see following): **1967–69**

340: Feb. 1958–1997

340VB: vibrato (same as earlier 345): **1985–97**

340-12: 12-string version of 340: **1985–97**

345: Feb. **1958–1974** (available as 340VB: **1985–97**)

345S: domestic version of export model, 1998 (see following), f-hole: **1964–67**

350–355 series: 12 3/4" wide (same body as 310-325 series), full-length scale

350 Liverpool: no soundhole, standard trim, 24 frets: **1983–97**

350VB: vibrato (same as earlier 355 Liverpool Plus): **1985–97**

350SH: Susanna Hoffs (of the Bangles) model, 2 chrome bar pickups and 1 humbucking pickup, signature on pickguard, deluxe trim with checkered binding, 24 frets, limited edition of 250: **1988–91**

350V63/Liverpool: same as 355JL but without signature and drawing on pickguard, 21 frets
Introduced as **350V63: 1994**
Renamed **350V63 Liverpool: 1997**
Still in production

350V63 Liverpool 12: 12-string: **1997–current**

350-12V63/Liverpool: same as 355-12JL but without signature and drawing on pickguard
Introduced as **350-12V63: 1994**
Renamed **350 Liverpool: 1997**

355JL: John Lennon model, signature and drawing on pickguard, no vibrato, standard trim, 21 frets, black finish, limited edition of 660 right-handed and 8 left-handed, available: **1989–93**

355JLVB: John Lennon model, same as 355JL but with vibrato, limited edition of 23, available: **1989–93**

355-12JL: John Lennon model, same as 355JL but 12-string, limited edition of 329 right-handed and 5 left-handed, available: **1989–93**

355 Liverpool Plus: no soundhole, standard trim, 24 frets, vibrato, available: **1983–85**

360–75 series: 15 1/4" wide, slash soundhole, 2 knobs, 1 switch, single-piece pickguard of gold-backed lucite, 21-fret fingerboard does not extend over body, deluxe trim, early natural finish models with brown wood binding
Introduced: **1958**
4 knobs, split-level 2-piece pickguard: **late 1958**
Rick-O-Sound stereo with 2 output jacks, optional: **1960**

Thinner body, 1 1/2" deep: **1961**

5 knobs (blend control added), white split-level 2-piece pickguard: **1963**

R tailpiece on non-vibrato models: **1963**

New Style, more rounded horns, rounded top edges, no top binding, checkered back binding, bound slash hole: **June 1964**

Old Style, pointed horns and top binding, still available through: **1968**

Roller bridge on vibrato models: **1968**

24-fret fingerboard extends over body: **1969**

Checkered-binding discontinued: **early 1970s**

Series still in production

360: 1958–91

360VB: vibrato (same as earlier 365), Old Style trim (bound top and back), Hi-Gain pickups, R tailpiece
Introduced: **1984**
Renamed **360WB: 1991**
Discontinued: **1998**

360V64: Old Style trim (bound top and back), chrome bar pickups, slanted plate tailpiece: **1991–current**

360-12 Deluxe: 2 pickups, Rick-O-Sound stereo, flat plate tailpiece, fireglo or natural finish
Introduced: **1964**
New Style: rounded top edge, no top binding, checkered back binding, R tailpiece: **fall 1964**
Plain back binding: **early 1970s**
Discontinued: **1990**

360-12 OS: continuation of 360-12 with Old Style trim, bound top, non-checkered back binding: **fall 1964**
Renamed **360-12 w/WBBS**
Renamed **360-12B WB:** chrome bar pickups: **1983**
Discontinued: **1984** (model continues as 360-12WB with Hi-Gain pickups)

360-12WB: continuation of 360-12 with Old Style body and trim, Hi-Gain pickups: **1984**
Renamed **360-12**, Hi-Gain pickups, R tailpiece: **1990**
Discontinued: **1998**

360-12V64: Old Style body and trim, chrome bar pickups, slanted plate tailpiece: **1985–current**

365: 1958–74 (available as 360VB: **1984–97**)

366-12: 360-12 with comblike 6-12 converter: **1966–74**

370: 1958–90

370VB: vibrato (same as earlier 375), Old Style trim (bound top and back), Hi-Gain pickups, R tailpiece: **1984–90**

70-12: Roger McGuinn (of the Byrds) model, limited

edition of 1000, available: **1988**

375: 1958–74 (available as 370VB: 1984–90)

380L Laguna: same body as 360-375 series, 2 humbucking pickups, optional piezo bridge pickup, individually adjustable saddles, bridge mounted into body, 5 knobs, 1 switch, rounded top edges with no binding, maple fingerboard, dot inlay, natural finish 5-piece peghead of maple and walnut, gold-plated hardware, walnut stain finish: **1998–current**

EXPORT THIN HOLLOWBODY MODELS

Distributed in Europe by Rose, Morris & Co., Ltd., export versions of existing models but with *f*-hole instead of slash hole, fireglo finish standard
Introduced: **1964**
Black and autumnglo finishes available: **1965**
Last distributed by Rose, Morris: **1969**
Reissues and signature model introduced in U.S.: **1987**
Still in production

1993: export version of Model 330-12 but with double-bound body, earliest with flat tailpiece, later with *R* tailpiece, some sold in the U.S. and Canada: **1964–69**

1996: export version of Model 325: **1964–69**

1997: export version of Model 335: **1964–69**
Reissued for U.S. and world market, 2 chrome bar pickups, slanted plate tailpiece: **1987**
Still in production

1997SPC: 3 pickups: **1993–97**

1997VB: same as 1997 reissue, with Torsion vibrato: **1987–90**

1998: export version of Model 345: **1964–69**

1998PT: Pete Townshend (of The Who) model, name on pickguard, reissue of export model 1998 but without vibrato, limited edition of 250: **1987–88**

3262: export version of 336-12: **1967–69**

THIN FULL-BODY, F-SERIES

330F-345F, 360F-375F: thin semi-hollowbody 17" wide, 2 1/2" deep, full body width, single rounded cutaway, 4 diamond-shaped knobs, 1

switch, controls mounted on split-level pickguard, same trim and feature patterns as regular 330 and 360 series, 14 frets clear of body, sunburst or natural finish

	Standard	Deluxe
2 pickups	330F	360F
2 pickups, vibrato	335F	365F
3 pickups	340F*	370F
2 pickups, vibrato	345F	375F

* No 340Fs appear on shipping totals.

Introduced: **1959**
Thinner body (eventually less than 2"): **early 1960s**
5 knobs (blend control added), white split-level 2-piece pickguard: **1963**
Controls mounted into top: **1968**
Discontinued: **1981**

330F: 1959–60 (listed through 1968), total production 13 instruments

335F: 1959–60 (listed through 1968), total production 14 instruments

345F: 1959–63 (listed through 1968), total production 11 instruments

360F: 1959–72

360F-12: 12-string: **1973–80**

365F: 1959–72

370F: 1959–72

375F: 1959–72

THICK BODY SERIES

All have full-depth body and full scale.

380L Laguna: thinbody, see preceding

380–384: carved top and back, extreme double cutaways, 1 slash hole, triangular inlay

385–389: flat top, dreadnought body shape, round hole, pin bridge

390–394: carved top and back, single cutaway, slash holes

Most of the models in the thick body series never went into production for obvious reasons (Model 389, for example, would have 3 pickups and a vibrato on a flat top acoustic). Only those in boldface were pro-

RICKENBACKER

duction models. Some prototypes exist of non-production models.

	Double-cut archtop	Non-cut flat top	Single-cut flat top
No pickups	(380)	385	(390)
2 pickups	381	(386)	(391)
2 pickups, vibrato	(382)	(387)	(392)
3 pickups	(383)	(388)	(393)
3 pickups, vibrato	(384)	(389)	(394)

381: 2 prototypes (one with flat back and top), double cutaway with pointed horns, slash soundhole, 2 pickups, 2 switches, 2 knobs, 1-piece pickguard shaped like split-level, checkered binding on top and back, dot or triangular inlay, brown sunburst or natural, several variations
Introduced: **1958**
Discontinued: **1963**
Reintroduced, double split-level pickguard, 5 knobs: **1969**
Some examples with vibrato sold as Model 381 (rather than 382): **late 1960s**
Discontinued: **1974**

381V68: reissue: **1987**
Renamed **381V69: 1991**
Discontinued: **1998**

381-12: 12-string: **1969–73**

381-12V69: 12-string, deluxe trim, checkered binding, *R* tailpiece: **1989–current**

381JK: John Kay (of Steppenwolf) model, 2 humbucking pickups, mini phaser switch, active electronics, stereo, black finish, limited edition of 250: **1988–97**

382: some examples sold as 381: **late 1960s**

385: dreadnought body shape, variants include Gibson J-200 body shape (rounded bouts) and classical body shape (**385S**)
Available: **1958–71**

ACOUSTIC 1990s MODELS

700: flat top, body shape similar to Gibson J-200, with circular lower bout, belly bridge with 3 notches on belly, checkered top binding, bound fingerboard, triangle inlay, 5-piece peghead

700 Shasta: rosewood back and sides: **1998–current**

700-12 Shasta: 12-string, rosewood back and sides: **1998–current**

700 Comstock: maple back and sides: **1998–current**

700-12 Comstock: 12-string, maple back and sides: **1998–current**

730: flat top, dreadnought body shape, belly bridge with 3 notches on belly, checkered top binding, bound fingerboard, triangle inlay, 5-piece peghead

730 Shiloh: rosewood back and sides: **1998–current**

730-12 Shiloh: 12-string, rosewood back and sides: **1998–current**

730 Laramie: maple back and sides: **1998–current**

730-12 Laramie: 12-string, maple back and sides: **1998–current**

760J Jazz-bo: single cutaway, carved spruce top, maple back and sides, slash soundholes bound top and back, adjustable rosewood bridge, trapeze tailpiece, bound fingerboard, reverse-trianglular inlay (widest side of triangle on treble side of fingerboard), sunburst finish
Available: **1998–current**

DOUBLENECK MODEL

362/12: 6-string and 12-string guitar necks, Model 360 features, 2 pickups, 5 knobs, 2 switches, stereo electronics, *R* tailpiece, deluxe trim, checkered top binding, standard pegheads
Available: **1975–92**

COMMENTS

Rickenbacker was the first company to successfully market electric guitars, but the prewar models most highly sought by collectors and players are lap steels. Spanish-neck models are relatively rare and appeal to collectors primarily for historical reasons.

The most highly sought hollowbody models are those from the 1950s and 1960s, particularly those with old style pickups and fancier ornamentation. The export models are also highly regarded by collectors.

Vintage reissues are among the finest of any manufacturers in terms of faithfulness to original designs.

SOLIDBODIES KEY

Standard ornamentation: unbound body and fingerboard, dot inlay
Deluxe ornamentation: bound body and fingerboard, triangular inlay

Horseshoe-magnet pickup
    Non-cutaway (Bakelite body)
        4 metal plates on top = **Vibrola Spanish Guitar**
        5 metal plates on top = **Electro Spanish Guitar (Model B)**
    Cutaway deeper on treble side than bass
        1 single-coil pickup, 1 switch = **600, 1954–59**
        1 double-coil pickup, 2 switches = **800, 1954–59**
        1 horseshoe-magnet pickup and 1 bar pickup = **800, 1957–59**
    Double cutaway with pointed horns
        1 single-coil pickup, 1 switch = **650, 1957–59**
        1 double-coil pickup, 2 switches = **850, 1953–57**
        1 horseshoe-magnet pickup and 1 bar pickup = **850, 1957–59**
Understring (non-horseshoe magnet) pickup(s)
    Cresting wave body shape
        1 pickup
          Vibrato = **425, 1965–73**
          No vibrato
            Full scale = **425, 1958–64** or **420, 1965–84**
            3/4 scale = **900, 1969–80***
        2 pickups
          Strings anchor through saddles (no tailpiece)
            Gold-plated hardware
              Walnut body wings = **650S Sierra**
              Vermillion body wings = **650E Excalibur**
            Chrome-plated hardware
              Blue/green-finish body wings = **650A Atlantis**
              Black finish = **650C Colorado**
              Walnut body wings = **650D Dakota**
          Strings anchor at tailpiece
            Dot inlay
              Boyd vibrato = **450**
              Ac'cent vibrato = **615, 1962-77** or **610VB, 1985–current**
              No vibrato
                Standard peghead shape
                  Full scale
                    5 knobs
                      6-string = **610**
                      12-string = **610-12**
                    4 knobs
                      6-string = **450, 1958–84**
                      12-string = **450-12**
                      6-12 converter = **456–12**
                3/4 scale = **950, 1969-80***
              Cresting wave peghead shape = **480**

Understring pickups, cresting wave body, 2 pickups, strings anchor at tailpiece (*continued*)

    Triangular inlay

        Ac'cent vibrato = **625, 1962–77** or **620VB, 1985–current**

        No vibrato

            12-string

                Standard binding = **620–12**

                Deluxe binding = **660/12TP**

            6-string

                Standard peghead shape

                    Mono = **460**

                    Stereo = **460, 1961-76** or **620, 1977–current**

                Cresting wave peghead shape = **481**

    3 pickups

        Standard ornamentation = **450****, **1962-77** or **615****

        Deluxe ornamentation

            Standard peghead shape = **460**** or **625****

            Cresting wave peghead shape = **483**

Tulip body shape

    Full scale

        1 pickup = **400**

        2 pickups = **450, 1957–58**

    3/4 scale

        1 pickup

            21 frets = **900, 1957–74***

            18 frets = **1000**

        2 pickups = **950, 1957–74***

Asymmetrical double cutaway with rounded horns (similar to Fender Strat)

    4 knobs

        Bound body = **250 El Dorado**

        Unbound body

            Unbound fingerboard = **430**

            Bound fingerboard = **230 Hamburg**

    2 knobs

        Chrome-plated hardware = **220Hamburg**

        Gold-plated hardware = **260 El Dorado**

        Black hardware = **230GF**

* Transition from tulip body shape to cresting wave
body shape occurs from 1969–74
** 3rd pickup optional

SOLIDBODIES

All post-World War II models have standard ornamentation—unbound top and back, unbound fingerboard, dot inlay—unless otherwise noted.

SECTION ORGANIZATION

Pre-World War II Models (Bakelite Body)
Cutaway Body with Slight Cutaway on Bass Side
Tulip Body Shape

- **"Sweeping Crescent" Extreme Cutaway (both sides to 20th fret)**
- **Cresting Wave Body Shape**
- **Asymmetrical Double Cutaway, Rounded Horns (similar to Fender Stratocaster)**
- **Export Model**
- **Non-Rickenbacker Brand Solidbodies: Electro, Ryder, and Contello**
- **Doublenecks**

PRE–WORLD WAR II MODELS

Electro Spanish Guitar (Model B): black
Bakelite body, horseshoe-magnet pickup, some with Kauffman vibrato, 5 decorative chrome plates, body hollow underneath plates, 1 octagonal knob on lower bass bout, strings anchor through body, detachable Bakelite neck with integral molded fret ridges
Tenor available with wood neck and standard frets
Introduced: **mid 1935**
2 round knobs with ridges (some with 1 black knob, 1 white): **1938**
White enameled plates: **by 1940**
Named **Model B: by 1941**
Discontinued: **1943**

Vibrola Spanish Guitar: black Bakelite body,
horseshoe-magnet pickup, 4 decorative chrome plates, 6 small holes on upper treble plate, body hollow underneath plates, motorized electric vibrola unit, 1 knob on upper bass bout, 1 knob on lower bass bout (at least 1 example with knobs on lower bouts), detachable Bakelite neck with integral molded fret ridges
Introduced: **Dec. 1937**
1 knob on lower bass bout, 1 knob on lower treble bout, small holes in upper-bout plates: **c. 1939**
Discontinued (90 total produced): **1943**

CUTAWAY BODY WITH SLIGHT CUTAWAY ON BASS SIDE

Carved top, cutaway to 19th fret on treble side, cutaway to 15th fret on bass side, earliest with routed back and metal backplate, controls mounted into body, small black pickguard does not extend below pickup, jack in side, square-corner peghead, blond finish

Combo 600: 1 horseshoe-magnet pickup, 1 tone
switch, 2 chrome knobs, single-piece saddle
Introduced: **1954**
Asymmetrical peghead, vertical logo: **late 1954**
Black or gold pickguard extends below bridge but does not cover treble horn: **1956**
Larger pickguard covers treble horn, black plastic knobs mounted into pickguard, individual saddles, turquoise blue finish optional: **1957**
Last produced (but still catalogued): **1959**
Offered in catalog with cresting wave cutaway body shape but none produced: **1964**
Discontinued from price list: **1969**

Combo 800: double-coil horseshoe-magnet pickup,
1 tone switch, 1 selector switch, 2 chrome knobs, individual saddles
Introduced: **1954**
Asymmetrical peghead, vertical logo: **late 1954**
Black or gold pickguard extends below bridge but does not cover treble horn: **1956**
Larger pickguard covers treble horn, black plastic knobs mounted into pickguard, turquoise blue finish optional: **1957**
1 horseshoe-magnet pickup and 1 bar pickup: **by late 1957**
Last produced (but still catalogued): **1959**
Offered in catalog with cresting wave cutaway body shape but none produced: **1964**
Discontinued from price list: **1969**

TULIP BODY SHAPE

Combo 400: symmetrical tulip-shaped body, neck-
through-body construction, 1 rectangular pickup with oblong metal plate in center, pickup in neck position, 1 tone switch in upper treble bout, large anodized aluminum pickguard covers most of body but does not completely surround pickup, jack in pickguard, 21 frets, Cloverfield green (blue-green), Montezuma brown (golden) or jet black finish
Introduced: **1956**
2 knobs, 2 switches: **late 1957**
Discontinued, replaced by **425** (see Cresting Wave Body Shape, following): **1958**

Combo 450: symmetrical tulip-shaped body, neck-
through-body construction, 2 rectangular pickups with rectangular metal plate in center, 2 knobs, rotary selector switch with pointed knob on upper treble bout, large anodized aluminum pickguard covers most of top but does not completely surround pickup, jack in pickguard, 21 frets, Cloverfield green (blue-green), Montezuma brown (golden) or jet black finish
Introduced: **early 1957**
3-way (toggle) selector switch: **by late 1957**
2 chrome bar pickups, 2 knobs and 1 selector switch on lower treble bout: **early 1958**
Cresting wave body shape (see following): **Mar. 1958**

Model 900: 3/4-size, symmetrical tulip-shaped
body, neck-through-body construction (some with glued neck), 1 rectangular pickup with rectangular

RICKENBACKER

chrome plate in center, pickup in middle position, 2 knobs, 1 toggle switch, 21 frets, black finish
Introduced: **1957**
Deeper cutaway shape on treble side, brown, black, gray or natural finish: **late 1957**
Chrome bar pickup: **1958**
Fireglo finish optional: **1961**
Rocker bridge: **1968**
Body changed to cresting wave cutaway shape (see following), transitional period: **1969–74**

Model 950: same as Model 900 but with 2 pickups, 2 knobs, rotary selector switch, 21 frets, same changes as model 900 including change to cresting wave cutaway shape (see following): **1957–74**

Model 1000: same as Model 900 but with 18 frets, same changes as model 900 but does not change to cresting wave body shape: **1957–70**

"Sweeping Crescent" Extreme Cutaway

Double cutaway with pointed horns, both cutaways to 20th fret, top beveled around bass side (semi-hollowbody models with similar shape have no bass-side bevel), some with neck-through-body construction

Combo 650: 1 horseshoe-magnet pickup, 2 knobs, 1 switch, natural maple or turquoise finish
Introduced: **1957**
Chrome-bar pickup: **late 1957**
Last produced (but still offered): **1959**
Discontinued from price list: **1960**

Combo 850: 1 double-coil horseshoe-magnet pickup, 2 knobs, 2 switches, natural maple or turquoise finish
Introduced: **1957**
1 horseshoe and 1 chrome bar pickup: **late 1957**
Last produced (but still offered): **1959**
Discontinued from price list: **1967**

Cresting Wave Body Shape

Double cutaway, elongated bass-side horn, horns do not come to a point

Combo 450: 1 5/8" deep, 2 chrome bar pickups, metal pickguard, sunburst finish, model name continued from tulip-body series (see preceding)

Introduced: **Mar. 1958**
4 knobs, fireglo, black or natural finish: **by 1960**
Thinner body: **1961**
White plastic pickguard: **1962**
Boyd vibrato offered, a few (if any) examples made: **late 1962**
3 pickups optional: **1962–77**
Hi-Gain pickups: **1970**
Discontinued: **1984**

450-12: 12-string, 4 knobs, 1 switch: **1964–85**

456-12: 12-string with comblike converter for 6-string playing: **1968–78**

Combo 425: 1 5/8" deep, 1 chrome bar pickup, white pickguard, sunburst finish
Introduced: **late 1958**
Thinner body: **1961**
A few with Boyd vibrato (very rare): **1965**
Discontinued: **1973**

Combo 420: non-vibrato version of 425, 1 chrome bar pickup
Available: **1965–83**

Combo 460: neck-through-body, 2 chrome bar pickups, 5 knobs (extra mixer control), 1 switch, anodized aluminum pickguard, deluxe trim, black, natural or fireglo finish
Introduced: **late 1961**
Rick-O-Sound stereo standard, white plastic pickguard: **1962**
Stereo discontinued: **1968**
Discontinued: **1985**

615: top carved out in tailpiece area to accommodate vibrato, 2 pickups, roller bridge, Ac'cent vibrato, fireglo, natural maple or black diamond finish
Introduced: **early 1962**
Adjustable-height pickguard: **late 1963**
Discontinued: **1977**
Reissued as **610VB** (see following): **1985**

615S: Rickenbacker designation for British export Model 1995: **1964**

625: deluxe trim version of 615
Introduced: **early 1962**
Adjustable-height pickguard: **late 1963**
Discontinued: **1977**
Reissued as **620VB** (see following): **1985**

620: neck-through-body construction, 2 pickups, 5 knobs, 1 switch, triangular inlay
Available: **1974–current**

620-12: 12-string, standard trim: **1981–current**

620VB: deluxe trim, vibrato: **1985–97**

610: neck-through-body construction, 2 pickups, 5 knobs, no vibrato, split-level pickguard
Available: **1985–97**

610VB: vibrato: **1985–97**

610-12: 12-string: **1988–97**

650 series: neck-through-body construction, 2 pickups, 4 knobs, 1 switch, controls on pickguard, top routed to accommodate bridge unit, no tailpiece, individually adjustable string saddles, metal pickguard, 24 frets, dot inlay
Introduced: **1991**
Vibrato optional: **1994–97**
Still in production

650E Excalibur: maple neck/body, gold-plated hardware, vermillion brown body wings: **1991–97**

650A Atlantis: maple neck/body, maple body wings with blue/green finish, chrome-plated hardware: **1992–current**

650C Colorado: maple neck/body, chrome-plated hardware, all black finish: **1993–current**

650D Dakota: maple neck/body, walnut body wings, chrome-plated hardware, oiled satin finish: **1993–current**

650S Sierra: maple neck/body, gold-plated hardware, dark walnut body wings, oiled satin finish: **1993–current**

660-12TP: Tom Petty model, 12-string, 2 chrome bar pickups, slanted plate tailpiece, deluxe trim, checkered binding, fireglo or jetglo finish, limited edition of 1000
Available: **1991–97**

900: 3/4 scale, 1 pickup, 2 knobs, jack in pickguard

950: 3/4 scale, 2 pickups, 4 knobs, jack in pickguard
Model names continued from tulip-body series, transition period to cresting wave body shape: **1969–71**
900 and 950 discontinued: **1980**

480: bass horn longer than that of other cresting wave models (similar to Model 4000 bass), 2 pickups, 4 knobs, 1 switch, bolt-on neck, 25" scale, bound fingerboard, dot inlay, cresting wave peghead shape
Available: **1973–83**

483: bass horn longer than that of other cresting wave models (similar to Model 4000 bass), 3 humbucking pickups, 4 knobs, 1 switch, 25" scale, bound fingerboard, dot inlay, cresting wave peghead shape
Available: **1973–83**

481: bass horn longer than that of other cresting wave models (similar to Model 4000 bass), 2 humbucking pickups, 3 humbucking pickups available by special order, 4 knobs, 1 selector switch, phase reversal switch, deluxe trim, 25" scale, slanted frets, cresting wave peghead shape
Available: **1973–83**

ASYMMETRICAL DOUBLE CUTAWAY, ROUNDED HORNS

Body shape is similar to Fender Stratocaster.

430: 2 oblong pickups with plastic covers and no visible poles, 2 knobs, 1 switch, jack into top, laminated beveled-edge pickguard surrounds pickups, bolt-on neck, 25" scale, unbound rosewood fingerboard, dot inlay
Introduced: **1971**
Pickups with visible polepieces, 4 knobs, 1 switch, single-ply pickguard does not surround pickups: **by 1975**
Discontinued: **1982**

230 Hamburg: 2 shielded single-coil pickups, 4 knobs, 1 switch, jack on side, unbound top and back, 25" scale, bound rosewood fingerboard, dot inlay, chrome-plated hardware
Available: **1983–91**

250 El Dorado: 2 shielded single-coil pickups, 4 knobs, 1 switch, jack on side, double-bound top and back, 25" scale, bound rosewood fingerboard, dot inlay, gold-plated hardware
Available: **1983–92**

220 Hamburg: 2 pickups, 2 knobs, 1 switch, controls on white plastic pickguard, bolt-on neck, 25" scale, maple fingerboard, dot inlay
Available: **1992–97**

260 El Dorado: 2 pickups, 2 knobs, 1 switch, chrome-plated metal pickguard, bolt-on neck, 25" scale, maple fingerboard, gold-plated hardware
Available: **1992–97**

230GF Glenn Frey: contoured body, 2 pickups with black covers and visible polepieces, 2 knobs, 1 switch, controls mounted on silver plastic pickguard, signature on pickguard, bolt-on neck, 25" scale, black fingerboard, pin dot inlay, black hardware, black finish, limited edition of 1000
Available: **1992–97**

EXPORT MODEL

Model 1995: distributed in Europe by Rose Morris & Co., same as Model 615, designated Model 615S by Rickenbacker
101 instruments sold (only year): **1964**

NON-RICKENBACKER BRAND SOLIDBODIES

All models sold by Radio-Tel (Rickenbacker's distribution company).

Electro ES-16: similar to model 1000 but with pickup in middle position and glued-in neck, 3/4-size, extreme double cutaways with pointed horns, 1 chrome bar pickup, 2 knobs, 1 switch, pickguard covers most of top, dot inlay, peghead logo of *Electro* with lightning bolt crossing *t*, fireglo, black or natural finish
Available: **1964–71**

Electro ES-17: similar to Model 425 but with pickup in middle position and set neck, full scale, cresting wave cutaway shape, 1 chrome bar pickup, 2 knobs, 1 switch, pickguard covers most of top, dot inlay, *Electro* with lightning bolt crossing *t* on peghead, fireglo, black or natural finish
Available: **1964–75**

Ryder: same as Model 425 (cresting wave body) with Ryder label
Available: **1963**

Contello: same as Model 425 (cresting wave body) with Contello logo
Available: **1962**

Astro AS-51: 1 pickup, offset dot inlay, sold as a kit
Available: **1963–64**

DOUBLENECKS

Custom doublenecks available as early as 1961.

4080: bolt-on guitar and bass necks, cresting wave body shape, stereo electronics, guitar with Model 480 features, 2 pickups, *R* tailpiece, bass with 4001 features, 2 pickups, deluxe trim, cresting wave pegheads
Available: **1975–92**

4080/12: bolt-on 12-string guitar and 4-string bass necks, cresting wave body shape, 2 pickups per neck, deluxe trim, cresting wave pegheads: **1977–92**

COMMENTS

The Bakelite Electro Spanish, which is the first production solidbody electric guitar, and the rare Vibrola Spanish models have considerable historic appeal although they are not regarded as good utility instruments.

The most highly sought Rickenbacker solidbodies are the early Combo models, particularly those with horseshoe-magnet pickups.

Ironically, Rickenbacker was a late entry into the postwar electric guitar market, but its designs for solidbody and hollowbody models were (and still are) unique and distinctive from those of all other makers. The Rickenbacker sound, too, is considered unique. Rickenbackers from the 1970s are not as highly sought by collectors but are considered fine utility instruments by those who prefer the Rickenbacker sound.

Considering Rickenbacker's history and reputation, it has remained a very small company compared to Fender or Gibson. Before 1966, which was a boom year for Rickenbacker, almost all models could be called rare in comparison to most Fender and Gibson models.

BASSES KEY

Solidbody
  Cresting wave body shape
    1 pickup = **4000**
    2 pickups
      Dot inlay
        Black hardware = **4003S/SPC Blackstar**
        Gold-plated hardware = **4004C Cheyenne**
        Chrome-plated hardware
          Non-horseshoe magnet pickup = **4004L Laredo**
          Horseshoe-magnet pickup
            Cream finish = **4001CS**
            Other finish = **4001S**
      Triangular inlay = **4001** or **4003**
    Double cutaway with rounded horns (similar to Fender Stratocaster)
      Rosewood fingerboard
        1 pickup
          30" scale = **3000**
          33 1/2" scale = **3001**
        2 pickups
          Chrome-plated hardware = **2030 Hamburg**
          Gold-plated hardware = **2050 El Dorado**
        Black fingerboard = **2030GF**
      Maple fingerboard = **2020**
Hollowbody
  No top binding = **4005**
  Top binding = **4005WB**
  Plastic top with colored lights = **4000L Light Show**

BASSES

SECTION ORGANIZATION

Solidbody
Hollowbody

SOLIDBODY

4000: cresting wave body shape, horseshoe-magnet pickup, 2 knobs, mahogany neck-through-body, maple side wings, Lucite pickguard with gold back, 33 1/2" scale, unbound rosewood fingerboard, dot inlay, cresting wave peghead, natural woodgrain or 2-tone brown sunburst finish
Introduced: **June 1957**
Sliding bridge cover plate with string mute: **late 1957**
Walnut neck: **by 1958**
Gold-backed or white plastic pickguard: **1958**
Maple neck with walnut peghead "wings": **1960**
Fireglo finish optional: **1960**

Black or autumnglo finish optional: **early 1960s**
Slimmer, more contoured body: **1961**
Tailpiece with under-string mutes, white plastic pickguard only (later black optional): **1963**
Metal pickup cover, non-horseshoe magnet pickup: **1964**
Discontinued: **1985**

4000FL: fretless, available by special order: **late 1960s**

4001: deluxe 2-pickup version of 4000, 1 horseshoe-magnet pickup, 1 bar pickup, 4 knobs, white pickguard, checkered body binding, 33 1/2" scale, bound rosewood fingerboard, triangular inlay, walnut "wings" on peghead, fireglo finish
Introduced: **Nov. 1961**
Natural finish optional: **1965**
Metal pickup cover, non-horseshoe-magnet pickup: **1964**
Discontinued: **1987**

4001FL: fretless
Available by special order: **late 1960s**
Reintroduced, dot inlay: **1989**
Discontinued: **1998**

4001S: export model, sold as **Model 1999** in Europe by
Rose, Morris & Co., Ltd., same as 4001 but with no
binding, dot inlay
Export model introduced: **1964**
Metal pickup cover, understring (non-horseshoe mag-
net) pickup: **1967**
Last sold by Rose, Morris: **1969**
Some sold by special order in the U.S.: **early 1970s**
Introduced as standard U.S. model: **1980**
Discontinued: **1985**

4001V63: reissue of 1963 version 4001S, horseshoe-
magnet pickup: **1984–current**

4001CS: Chris Squire model, cresting wave body
shape, 1 horseshoe-magnet pickup and 1 understring pickup, 1-piece peghead and fingerboard of
padauk wood (dark), 33 1/2" scale, dot inlay, cresting wave peghead shape, cream finish, limited edition of 1000: **1991–97**

4008: 8 strings, cresting wave body shape, 33 1/2"
scale, cresting wave peghead, available by special
order only: **1975–83**

4003: like 4001 (deluxe trim), designed for round-
wound strings, little visible difference from 4001,
split pickguard, rosewood fingerboard, truss rod
adjustment at body
Introduced: **1979**
1-piece pickguard, truss rod adjustment at peghead:
1984
Discontinued: **1998**

4003S: standard trim version of 4003, 1-piece pickguard: **1980–97**

4003S5: 5 strings: **1987–97**

4003S8: 8 strings: **1987–97**

4003S Tuxedo: white body, neck and fingerboard, black
pickguard, black hardware: **1987–97**

4003S/SPC Blackstar: Mike Mesaros (of the
Smithereens) model, 33 1/2" scale, black fingerboard, pin dot fingerboard inlay, black knobs, limited
edition of 200: **1988–97**

3000: double cutaway with rounded horns, similar
body shape to Fender Stratocaster, 1 humbucking
pickup, 2 knobs, 30" scale, standard trim, standard
peghead shape
Available: **1975–84**

3001: 33 1/2" scale, 3 knobs, otherwise same as 3000:
1975–84

4002: cresting wave body shape, curly maple top,
2 humbucking pickups, 4 knobs, 3 jacks (mono,
stereo, low impedance), laminated black pickguard,
checkered body binding, 33 1/2" scale, bound ebony
fingerboard, triangular inlay, cresting wave peghead,
mapleglo or walnut finish, limited edition
Available: **1967–85**

4004: cresting wave body shape, maple neck-
through-body, 2 knobs, 1 switch, no pickguard,
unbound body, dot inlay

4004C Cheyenne: walnut wings, gold-plated hardware:
1993–97

4004L Laredo: dot inlay, chrome-plated hardware,
black finish: **1993–97**

2030 Hamburg: double cutaway with rounded
horns, body shape similar to Fender Stratocaster, 2
pickups, 4 knobs, active circuitry, contoured top, 33
1/2" scale, rosewood fingerboard, dot inlay
Available: **1984–97**

2050 El Dorado: double cutaway with rounded
horns, body shape similar to Fender Stratocaster, 2
pickups, 4 knobs, active circuitry, bound top, 33 1/2"
scale, rosewood fingerboard, dot inlay, gold-plated
hardware
Available: **1984–97**

2030GF: bass version of 230GF Glenn Frey model
guitar:
Available: **1992–97**

2020: bass version of 220 Hamburg guitar
Available: **1992–97**

HOLLOWBODY

4005: 360 guitar body with New Style rounded top
edges, double cutaway with rounded points,
2 understring pickups, *R* tailpiece, 33 1/2" scale, single-bound fingerboard, triangular inlay, cresting
wave peghead shape, fireglo or natural finish

Introduced: **1965**

Standard Colorglo finishes optional: **1970s**

Last offered: **1984**

4005WB and **4005-6WB:** Old Style, white binding on top and back: **1966–83**

4005-6: 6-string: **1965–77**

4005-8: 8-string model, asymmetrical peghead longer on bass side but not cresting wave shape (rare): **late 1960s**

4005S: export model, sold as **Model 3261** in Europe by Rose, Morris & Co., Ltd.: **1965–69**

STEELS

SECTION ORGANIZATION

Singleneck Models (no pedals)

Doublenecks

Consoles

Pedal Models

SINGLENECK MODELS (NO PEDALS)

Electro Hawaiian Guitar (Frying Pan): circular cast aluminum body, horseshoe-magnet pickup, magnet 1 1/2" wide, no knobs, dot markers, slotted peghead, metal Electro nameplate (early with engraved logo)

A-25: 25" scale

A-22: 22 1/2" scale

Introduced: **1932**

Volume control knob added: **1934**

Rickenbacher added to nameplate: **1934**

Magnet 1 1/4" wide, chrome tailpiece, Phillips-head pickup adjustment screws: **1946**

Discontinued: **1950**

A-22 reintroduced, Bakelite back plate, decal on peghead: **1954**

Discontinued: **1958**

Model B: Bakelite body and neck, horseshoe-magnet pickup, magnet 1 1/2" wide, knurled adjustment nuts on pickup, 1 octagonal knob on bass side, strings anchor through body, 5 decorative chrome plates, bolt-on neck with integral molded frets

Custom variations include rounded-edge body, silver- or gold-plated hardware

Introduced: **July 1935**

Pointer knob on treble side, round knob on bass side: **by 1937**

4000L: like 331 light show guitar

Available: **early 1970s**

COMMENTS

Early examples of Models 4000 and 4001, with horseshoe-magnet pickup, are among the most highly sought of all electric basses. They are far rarer than the most highly sought Fender basses.

Unlike Rickenbacker guitars, the most highly regarded Rick basses are the solidbody models. Hollowbody models are rarer and bring more money than any but the early solidbodies.

Frets outlined in white: **by 1938**

2 round knobs with arrows, some with plastic control plates: **1938**

Knobs on same side: **by 1939**

7- and 8-string models available: **1940**

10-string model, metal neck, available: **1940**

Black painted plates: **c. 1940**

White painted plates: **1940**

6-string referred to as Model E in mail-order literature, 7-string referred to as Model B: **1940 only**

Magnet 1/14" wide, chrome tailpiece, strings anchor at tailpiece, Phillips-head pickup adjustment screws, T-shaped aluminum logo plate (transitional examples may not have all of these features): **1946**

Some with white plastic plates with molded numbers around tone and volume controls: **late 1940s**

Some with vertical blade-shaped logo plate: **c. 1949**

Last T-shaped logo plate: **1950**

Discontinued: **by 1955**

BD: deluxe version of Model B, metal peghead cover: **Mar. 1949–70**

Silver Hawaiian/Model 100/NS: chrome-plated body stamped from sheet metal (usually brass), horseshoe-magnet pickup, 1 knob, strings anchor through holes in top, referred to as Model NS (for New Style) in prewar literature (see Model S, following, for postwar NS specs)

Introduced: **1937**

1 black knob, 1 white knob, knobs on same side: **1939**

8-string available: **by 1940**

Discontinued: **1943**

Model 59: body stamped from sheet metal, fixed-height horseshoe-magnet pickup with 2 screws on each end, 1 knob, ivory or black crinkled paint finish
Introduced: **late 1937**
2 knobs on opposite sides, most with 1 black knob and 1 white knob: **c. 1938**
Shaded gray finish: **1939**
Discontinued: **1943**

Model S/NS (New Style): body stamped from sheet metal, horseshoe-magnet pickup, 2 knobs, black dots or open holes for fingerboard markers, decal logo, shaded gray finish, some with slightly crinkled finish, doubleneck available (see following), referred to as Model NS (for New Style) in postwar literature (see Silver Hawaiian, preceding, for prewar NS specs)
Introduced: **1946**
White dot markers, smooth finish: **by 1948**
Discontinued: **early 1950s**

Academy: Bakelite body, horseshoe-magnet pickup, 2 knobs, *Academy* on peghead, brown mahogany or maroon finish
Introduced: **1946**
Discontinued, replaced by Ace (see following): **by 1948**

Ace: Bakelite body, horseshoe-magnet pickup, 2 knobs, plastic pickup cover, *Ace* on peghead, brown mahogany or maroon finish
Introduced: **by 1948**
Discontinued: **1953**

Model SD: deluxe version of NS, body stamped from sheet metal, 2 knobs, Lucite fingerboard, peghead cover, 2-tone tan/mahogany enamel finish, 6, 7 or 8 strings
Available: **c. 1949–late 1953**

Model G/Deluxe Hawaiian: ornate version of Silver Hawaiian, chrome-plated body, Lucite fingerboard back-painted gold, gold-plated peghead cover, gold-plated hardware, 6 or 8 strings
Available: **late 1940s–1957**

SW: woodbody, straight-line body sides with bevels around fingerboard, control plate extends to include knobs, metal fingerboard, block markers, peghead cover, dark or blond finish, 6 or 8 strings, 3 legs optional
Introduced: **by 1956**
Discontinued: **1962**

TW: 10-string, large rectangular body, separate control plate for knobs, blond finish only: **1956–60**

CW: woodbody, 3 knobs, angled front edge, grille cloth on front edge, 2-tone walnut or maple finish, 3 legs

CW-6: 6-string, 22 1/2" scale: **1957–60**

CW-7: 7-string, 22 1/2" scale: **1957–60**

CW-8: 8-string, 22 1/2" scale: **1957–60**

CW-10: 10-string, 22 1/2" scale: **1957–60**
22-1/2"-scale models continue as JB model (see following)

CW-61: 6-string, 25" scale: **1958–70**

CW-71: 7-string, 25" scale: **1958–70**

CW-81: 8-string, 25" scale: **1958–70**

CW-101: 10-string, 25" scale: **1958–70**

JB: Jerry Byrd model, woodbody, angled front edge, grille cloth on front with *Jerry Byrd* plate, 22 1/2" scale, 6, 7, 8 or 10 strings, 3 legs
Available (replaces 22-1/2" scale CW models: **1961–70**

100 series: 6 strings, woodbody, straight-line body sides with bevels around fingerboard, 1-piece triangular control plate for knobs, block markers, early with black-and-white speckled finish

Model 100: light or silver gray finish: **by 1956–70**

Model 102: natural finish
Introduced: **1957**
Fireglo finish optional: **1961 only**
Last offered: **1970**

Model 105: gray or natural, 3 legs: **1959–70**

J-6: 6 strings, gray or brown metalbody (only specs available)
Available: **1957–61**

J-8: 8 strings: **1961**

Bronson Model 52: distributed by the Bronson company based in Detroit, brown Bakelite body, decorative metal plates, peghead cover with horizontal *Bronson* and vertical *Melody King*
Introduced: **by 1948**
Discontinued: **early 1950s**

DOUBLENECKS

Most doublenecks, regardless of body style, were designated by the letter D followed by a hyphen, followed by the number of strings.

D-12: double 6-string

D-14: double 7-string

D-16: double 8-string
Any combination of 6-, 7- and 8-string necks was available.

Electro double-neck: stamped metalbody, Bakelite necks
Introduced: **by 1940**
Discontinued: **by 1953**

NS style: stamped metalbody, metal necks
Introduced: **by 1942**
Discontinued: **by 1953**

Deluxe model: referred to as **DC-12** and **DC-16**, stamped metalbody, metal necks, Lucite fingerboards, peghead covers
Introduced: **c. 1950**
Discontinued: **by 1953**

DW: woodbody, bevels around fingerboards, dark or blond finish, 2 6-string or 2 8-string necks, 3 legs optional
Available: **1954–61**

CONSOLES

Console 200 series: 22 1/2" scale, metal edge trim, metal tuner covers, opaque blond finish or natural walnut or maple finish, 4 legs

Console 206: 2 6-string necks: **1956–70**

Console 208: 2 8-string necks: **1956–70**

Console 208: 8- and 10-string necks: **1956–70**

Console 500 Series: 22 1/2" scale, 3 necks, natural walnut or maple finish, 4 legs

Console 508: 2 8-string necks, 10-string middle neck: **1956–70**

Console 518: 3 8-string necks: **1956–70**

Console 700 Series: 25" scale, 2 knobs per neck, 1 or 2 pedals optional, walnut or blond finish

Console 706: 2 6-string necks: **1957–70**

Console 708: 2 8-string necks: **1957–70**

Console 718: 1 8-string and 1 10-string neck: **1957–70**

Console 758: 3 8-string necks: **1957–70**

Console 768: 2 8-string necks, 10-string middle neck: **1957–70**

PEDAL MODELS
700 Series
Pedal 780: 25" scale, 8 strings, 6 pedals, natural finish: **1961–70**

Pedal 785: 10 strings, 6 pedals: **1961–70**

Pedal 790: 2 8-string necks, 6 pedals: **1962–70**

COMMENTS

Rickenbacker's prewar (1 1/2" wide) horseshoe-magnet pickup is considered by many players to be the finest pickup ever made for the electric Hawaiian guitar. The prewar Frying Pan model, the first production electric instrument by any maker, is rare and highly sought by collectors. The Bakelite model, especially the prewar version with wide pickup and strings anchoring through the body, is not as rare as the Frying Pan but is one of the most highly sought lap steels by players and collectors. Models with sheet metal bodies are not highly regarded, except for the aesthetically appealing chrome-plated Silver Hawaiian and the more ornate Model G.

Postwar models are of less interest to collectors although they are considered fine utility instruments, with the Jerry Byrd model the most highly sought. Rickenbacker's pedal steels are not highly regarded.

OTHER INSTRUMENTS

Electro Mandolin: flat top and back, oval body shape, body made by Harmony and similar to Harmony Patrician, 10 3/8" wide, 2 5/8" deep at neck, mahogany top, back and sides, oval hole, horseshoe-magnet pickup, 5-ply binding above and below horseshoe, 1 knob, low bridge, 4-ply top binding, single-bound back, single-bound asymmetrical fingerboard, dot inlay, pearloid peghead veneer
Introduced: **mid 1930s**
Arched spruce top, maple back and sides: **late 1930s**
Arched back, vibrato available: **by 1940**
Discontinued: **1943**

Electric Mandolin: solid body, wide lower bout, 1 understring pickup, shaded walnut finish, 4-string (**Model 5000**), 5-string (**Model 5001**), or 8-string (**Model 5002**)
Introduced: **1958**
Fireglo finish available: **1959**
Last price list appearance: **1961**

5002V58 Mandolin: reissue of 8-string model: **1998–current**

Bantar: electric 5-string banjo, 2 chrome bar pickups, 4 knobs, *R* tailpiece, deluxe or standard trim (both catalogued as **Model 6000**), fireglo or mapleglo finish
Introduced: **1966**Standard trim model discontinued: **1968**
Deluxe trim model discontinued: **mid 1970s**

Banjoline: 360-style body, 6 strings (2 paired, 2 singles), 2 chrome bar pickups, vibrato, plectrum banjo neck, standard (**6005**) or deluxe (**6006**) trim, woodgrain fireglo, woodgrain mapleglo or solid azureglo finish
Available: **1968–mid 1970s**

Electro Violin, Viola, Cello: Bakelite body and neck, horseshoe pickup, tuners on chinrest, no peghead
Introduced: **1935**
Tubular aluminum body, bent horseshoe pickup, conventional peghead, ebony fingerboard, bakelite chinrest: **1939**
Discontinued: **1941**

Electro Bass Viol: metal body, double-coil horseshoe pickup, 1 volume knob, ebony fingerboard, adjustable end pin, amplifier used as support stand
Introduced: **1935**
Tubular aluminum body, volume and tone controls: **1938**
Discontinued: **1941**

COMMENTS

Rickenbacker's prewar instruments are sought for historical reasons. The postwar mandolin, Bantar and Banjoline are regarded as curiosities.

INDEPENDENT MAKERS

BENEDETTO

GENERAL INFORMATION

Robert Benedetto began making archtop guitars in Hopatcong, NJ, in 1968 and relocated to Clearwater, FL, in 1976. He moved to East Stroudsburg, PA, in 1990 and then to Plant City, FL, in early 1999.

In 1982, with a guitar co-designed with Chuck Wayne, Benedetto initiated what would become a modern school of archtop design characterized by minimalist ornamentation and the use of wood instead of plastic or metal for tailpieces, bindings, peghead veneers, etc. Benedetto's innovations and trademark features include the "honey blonde" finish, solid ebony tailpiece, exotic/burl woods for peghead veneers (front and back) and violin-style finishes (oil varnish, spirit varnish and French polish).

With the booming interest in archtop guitars in the 1990s, Benedetto emerged as the leader of a new generation of makers as well as the leading maker of 7-string archtop guitars. He is also the only archtop guitarmaker who is a prolific violin maker. He wrote the only comprehensive book on archtop guitar construction, *Making an Archtop Guitar*, in 1994 and released a 9 1/2-hour instructional video, *Archtop Guitar Design & Construction*, in 1996.

In early 1999 Benedetto entered into an agreement with Fender/Guild to design a custom Benedetto archtop line to be produced at the Guild custom shop in Nashville and also to consult on the existing Guild archtop line produced at the Guild factory in Westerly, RI. Additionally, Guild has the option to produce the standard Benedetto models. Under the terms of the agreement, Benedetto will complete his backlog of orders and then make only custom "one-off" guitars.

As of early 1999, Benedetto has made a total of 715 instruments, 435 of which are archtop guitars. He made 6 unique semi-hollowbody electric guitars from 1982–86 and an additional 5 (3 prototypes and 2 finished) examples of his "benny" model. From 1986 through spring 1987, he made 209 solidbody electrics (157 guitars and 52 basses) with John Buscarino. He has also made 1 classical guitar, 2 mandolins, 51 violins, 5 violas and 1 cello.

MODELS

All models, unless otherwise noted: 16", 17" or 18" wide, 3" deep, Venetian (rounded) cutaway, spruce top, maple back and sides, optional Benedetto float-

ing pickup, ebony bridge, tailpiece, fingerboard and pickguard, 25" scale

Specs listed here are standard models. Benedetto has made many instruments with custom features that may vary from standard specs.

All models were discontinued in early 1999 as part of Benedetto's consulting agreement with Fender/Guild (see preceding).

Cremona: no inlay on tailpiece, string anchor-holes at an angle, fine-line binding on top, back, fingerboard and peghead, bound narrow pickguard with straight edges, no fingerboard inlay, large flared peghead, exotic burl veneer on front and back of peghead, small scroll peghead inlay with engraved model name, ornamental peghead cutout, gold-plated tuners with metal or ebony tuner buttons
Introduced: **1972**

Fratello: black-white binding on top, back, fingerboard and peghead, delicate inlay on tailpiece, string anchor-holes at an angle, bound pickguard, 3-piece maple neck, square-end fingerboard, block inlay, ornamental floral peghead inlay under logo, center-dip peghead
Introduced: **1980**

Manhattan: black-white binding on top, back, fingerboard and peghead, no inlay on tailpiece, string anchor-holes at an angle, narrow pickguard with straight edges, 3-piece maple neck, no fingerboard inlay, elongated triangular peghead inlay underlining logo, gold-plated or black chrome tuners with ebony buttons
Introduced: **1989**

Limelite: early version 16" wide, otherwise similar to Cremona: **1980–84**
Later version, ornamental inlay on tailpiece, fine-line binding throughout, string-anchor holes at an angle, pointed-end fingerboard, split-block (blocks have slight "waist" indentions) inlay, large flared peghead, tied-scroll peghead ornament with model name engraved, ornamental cutout at top of peghead, gold-plated tuners with gold or ebony tuner buttons: **1990**
Delicate inlay above and below model name: **1993**

7-String: no inlay on tailpiece, string anchor-holes at an angle, narrow pickguard with straight edges, no fingerboard inlay, delicate ornamental peghead inlays above and below logo, asymmetrical peg-

head with point at top, 4 tuners on bass side, 3 tuners on treble side
Introduced: **1977**

La Venezia: derived from prototype co-designed with Chuck Wayne in 1982, no body binding, large flared peghead (serpentine style peghead in early 1999), ebony nut, no pickguard, ebony endpin, no fingerboard inlay, black chrome tuners with ebony buttons
Introduced: **1993**

Americana: 18" wide, non-cutaway, co-designed with author Tom Van Hoose, narrow pickguard, black-white binding on top, back, fingerboard and peghead, no fingerboard inlay, large flared peghead, gold-plated tuners with ebony buttons
Introduced: **1994**

Renaissance Series: one-offs, non-cutaway, delicate floral-pattern sound openings and unique appointments, 2 instruments made
Il Fiorentino: **1994**
Il Palissandro: **1996**

the benny electric: carved spruce top, no sound-holes, Florentine (pointed) cutaway, 2 custom Kent Armstrong black humbucking pickups, 2 ebony knobs and selector switch on lower treble bout, stud-mounted tailpiece with individual string adjustments, unbound fingerboard, no fingerboard inlay except for delicate leaf inlay at 12th fret, rounded-peak peghead, gold-plated tuners with metal buttons
Introduced: **1998**

Kenny Burrell: limited edition, Florentine (pointed) cutaway, 2 5/8" deep at neck, 3 7/16" deep at endpin, 1 Benedetto humbucking pickup, ebony tone and volume knobs, black-white binding on top, back, fingerboard and peghead, square-end fingerboard, delicate abalone inlay motif, Hipshot "D" tuner, gold-plated tuners with ebony buttons, honey blonde, sunburst or blue finish
Introduced: **1998**

COMMENTS

Benedetto is the foremost living maker of archtop guitars. His instruments are played by many noted musicians, including Kenny Burrell, Jimmy Bruno, Andy Summers and Earl Klugh. His guitars bring the highest prices of any living maker.

SERIAL NUMBERS
General

All Benedetto archtop guitars (except the first 2), plus his 11 semi-hollowbody electrics and 1 classical, are numbered in a single series.

Electric solidbodies and basses each have their own separate series, beginning with #1001.

Violins, violas and cello have their own series, beginning with #101.

Mandolins are not numbered.

Archtops, Semi-Hollow Electrics and Classical

4- or 5-digit serial number with configuration **##(#)yy** (adopted with third guitar, #0372).

1st 2 (or 3) digits **##(#)** = ranking, beginning with #1 in 1968.

Last 2 digits **yy** = year.

Example: 43599 was made in 1999 and is the 435th archtop made since 1968.

NUMBER	YEAR SHIPPED
1	1968
2	1970
0372	1972
0473	1973
0575–0676	1976
0777–1177	1977
1277–2778	1978
2879–4279	1979
4380–5580	1980
5681–7381	1981
7482–9582	1982
9682–10983	1983
11084–11984	1984
12085–12885	1985
12986–13586	1986
13686–13987-A	1987
14087–16488	1988
16588–19189	1989
19289–22490-A	1990
22591–25091	1991
25192–28092	1992
28193–30293	1993
30393–32994	1994
33095–36595	1995
36696–39496	1996
39597–40697	1997
40798–43498	1998
43599	1999

INDEPENDENT

COLLINGS

GENERAL INFORMATION

Bill Collings began making flat top guitars in Houston in 1975. He relocated to Austin in 1980. By the late 1980s he had begun making archtops. By the mid 1990s Collings had emerged as the premier independent maker of flat top guitars.

LABELS AND OTHER MARKINGS

No label, signature on inside back strip in green ink: **1975–79**

Light brown oval label, brown ink, *Bill Collings, Luthier*, illustration showing logs floating in river: **1979–84**

Parchment-colored oval label (darker than previous label), brown ink, *Bill Collings, Luthier*, illustration showing logs and guitars floating in river: **1984–late 1989**

Light brown oval label, black ink, *Collings, Austin, Texas*, illustration showing logs and guitars floating in river: **late 1989–current**

STANDARD MODELS

Numerous options of wood and inlays are available.

Dreadnoughts: 15 5/8" wide, 1 11/16" nut width, 25 1/2" scale, based on Martin-style square-shouldered dreadnought

D1: mahogany back and sides, scalloped braces, tortoiseshell celluoid binding, ebony bridge, black-white binding, tortoiseshell celluloid pickguard, mahogany neck, ebony fingerboard, pearl logo, pearl dot inlay

D2: Indian rosewood, grained ivoroid binding, scalloped braces, black-white binding with ivoroid outer layer, mahogany neck, ebony fingerboard, ebony bridge, pearl logo, diamond-and-squares inlay

D2H: herringbone purfling around top edge

DS2H: 12-fret neck, slotted peghead, Waverly vintage style tuners, otherwise same materials and ornamentation as D2

D3: same as D-2 but with abalone soundhole ring, double-bound peghead and fingerboard, no inlay, gold-plated tuners

Orchestra: based on Martin OM, 15" wide, 25 1/2" scale

OM-1: same materials and ornamentation as D1

OM-2: same materials and ornamentation as D2

OM-2H: same materials and ornamentation as D2H

000-2H: 12-neck, pyramid bridge, slotted peghead, waverly vintage style tuners, otherwise same materials and trim as OM2H and D2H

OM-3: same materials and ornamentation as D3

Baby: 12 1/2" wide, 14 1/8" scale, same materials and ornamentation as D2

Small Jumbo (SJ): based on Gibson J-185, circular lower bout, 16" wide, 25 1/2" scale, 1 11/16" nut width, maple back and sides, scalloped bracing, ivoroid binding, black-white binding, black-white soundhole ring, tortoise pickguard, ebony bridge, maple neck, double-bound ebony fingerboard, double-bound peghead with off-center notch, slotted diamond inlay, vertical diamond peghead inlay, pearl logo, gold Schaller mini-tuners

C: based on Gibson L-00, 1 11/16" nut, 25 1/2" scale, 14 3/4" wide

C10: mahogany back and sides, scalloped braces, ivoroid binding, tortoiseshell celluloid pickguard, ebony bridge, mahogany neck, ebony fingerboard, pearl logo, small dot inlay, various finish colors

C10 Deluxe: rosewood back and sides, double-bound peghead, peghead with off-center notch, double-bound bony fingerboard, small dot inlay, pearl logo, Schaller mini-tuners

CJ (Collings Jumbo): 16" wide, 25 1/2" scale, round-shouldered dreadnought, rosewood back and sides, scalloped braces, multi-ply binding with ivoroid outer layer, tortoiseshell celluloid pickguard, mahogany neck, ivoroid-bound ebony fingerboard, peghead with off-center notch in top, pearl logo, Waverly vintage style tuners

Archtops: available 16", 17" and 18" wide, S-holes

GRUHN FLAT TOPS

Collings made a series of flat top guitars designed by George Gruhn, available in dreadnought (D) or jumbo (F) shape, with plain (Style 1) or fancy (Style 2) ornamentation. These have a *Gruhn* logo on the peghead and a Collings label inside. All were made in 1989. They are numbered from 001–021.

SERIAL NUMBERS

Collings guitars made from 1975 into 1987 do not have serial numbers. Many have a handwritten date under the top.

Collings began numbering some (but not all) guitars in 1987.

Flat Tops

In 1988 Collings began numbering all flat top guitars in one consecutive series, beginning with approximately #175. As of January 1999, serial numbers had reached 4700.

Beginning in 1991, archtops are numbered in the same series with flat tops, but with a different number configuration (see following).

Serial number, month and year are handwritten by Bill Collings on the label.

Archtops

Prior to 1991, Collings archtops have a separate serial number series. Beginning in 1991, archtops have a 2-part serial number. The first part is the instrument's ranking in the general series (with flat tops); the suffix is the ranking in the separate archtop series.

Example: 343-30 is the 343rd instrument and the 30th archtop.

COMMENTS

Collings is the most successful of current independent makers. Although his operation is no longer a one-man shop, his instruments maintain the quality associated with a small operation. His flat top guitars are very highly regarded by players.

D'ANGELICO

John D'Angelico was born in New York City in 1905. At age nine he was apprenticed to a granduncle who made violins, mandolins and flat top guitars. D'Angelico established his own shop in New York in 1932 to make violins, mandolins and archtop guitars. He began using model names around 1934 and standardized his models around 1937.

Early examples were modeled on Gibson's 16"-wide L-5, but with a 16 1/2"-wide body, different inlay and no truss rod. Some archtops from the 1940s have a round or oval soundhole.

D'Angelico died September 1, 1964. He built a total of 1,164 guitars, the last 10 of which were finished by his apprentice James L. D'Aquisto and bear D'Aquisto's name on the peghead and tailpiece. His total mandolin production is estimated at 300–350.

General Changes

First cutaway model: **May 9, 1947**

f-holes...

    Standard shape: **1932**

    Straight angle rather than point at mid-f: **mid 1930s**

    Standard shape holes except on Excel: **1937**

    Standard shape holes, all models: **late 1930s**

Tailpieces...

    Straight-across string anchor piece: **1932**

    Slanted (but not stairstep) design...

        New Yorker: **mid 1937**

        Excel: **c. 1938**

    Stairstep tailpiece introduced: **c. 1940**

Necks...

    Reinforced but non-adjustable neck (no truss rod cover): **1932–c. 1940**

    Adjustable truss rod, truss rod cover, introduced: **c. 1940**

Models

Model specs vary due to custom orders and to D'Angelico's gradual evolution of designs.

Style A: 17" wide, parallel bracing, a few with X-braced top, unbound f-holes, smooth edge pickguard, block inlay, some early with dot inlay, rounded peak and 2 small points on top of peghead (some with no points)

First mentioned in D'Angelico's notebook: **1936**

Last made (#1690): **Sept. 14, 1945**

Style A-1: specs unavailable

First mentioned in D'Angelico's notebook: **1936**

Last made (#1661): **Nov. 20, 1943**

Style B: 17" wide, parallel bracing (a few with X-braced top), block inlay, unbound f-holes, peghead with broken-scroll pediment framing ornamental cupola, pointed angles on scroll

First mentioned in D'Angelico's notebook: **1936**

Last made (#1782): **Feb. 17, 1948**

New Yorker: 18" wide, X-braced top, triple-bound f-holes, black binding lines on body sides and side of fingerboard, split-block inlay, gold-plated hardware, skyscraper logo, peghead with dip in center

First recorded New Yorker: **1936**

Peghead with broken-scroll pediment framing ornamental cupola, rounded angles on scroll, some examples: **1937**

Center-dip peghead on some examples as late as: **1958**

Excel: 17" wide, X-braced top, bound f-holes, multiple-bound top and back, single-bound f-holes, block inlay, rounded-top peghead

First recorded Excel: **1936**

Peghead with broken-scroll pediment framing ornamental cupola, rounded angles on scroll: **by 1937**

Rounded-top peghead on some examples as late as: **1939**

Stairstep tailpiece: **by 1943**

Excel Special: 17" wide, New Yorker trim

First Excel Special (recorded as Small New Yorker): **1943**

G-7: electric hollowbody, plywood body supplied by Code or United (New Jersey-based companies), necks by D'Angelico, no D'Angelico serial number

COMMENTS

Players and collectors consider D'Angelico's Excel and New Yorker models to be among the finest archtop guitars ever made. They are (along with certain Stromberg models) the most sought after and most expensive archtops on the vintage market.

SERIAL NUMBERS

D'Angelico serial numbers are not strictly chronological. Some overlaps in date ranges occur.

Guitars

RANGE	APPROX. YEAR
No number	1932–34
1005–1097	1932–34
1105–1235	1936
1234–1317	1937
1318–1385	1938
1388–1456	1939
1457–1508	1940
1509–1562	1941
1563–1621	1942
1622–1658	1943
1659–1681	1944
1682–1702	1945
1703–1740	1946
1738–1781	1947
1782–1804	1948
1805–1831	1949
1832–1855	1950
1856–1885	1951
1886–1908	1952
1909–1936	1953
1933–1962	1954
1961–1988	1955
1989–2017	1956
2018–2040	1957
2041–2067	1958
2068–2098	1959
2099–2122	1960
2123–2164	1961–64
2211–2214	1955–56

Mandolins

RANGE	YEARS
No number	1932–39
125–135	1940
136–148	1941
149–168	1942–44

D'AQUISTO

James L. D'Aquisto (1935–95) apprenticed to John D'Angelico. After D'Angelico's death in 1964, D'Aquisto finished out the last 10 guitars that D'Angelico had started and then opened his own shop. Many of his instruments are custom made, with variations including round holes, oval holes, S-shaped holes, 7-strings, flat tops and tenor guitars.

The first 16 D'Aquistos have peghead features—including logo, truss rod cover, cutout at top and ornamental button—similar to those of a D'Angelico New Yorker. D'Aquisto's cutout at the top of the peghead evolved from D'Angelico's broken-scroll (inverted-T) shape to a more circular shape.

In the 1990s D'Aquisto concentrated on new designs (Solo, Avant Garde, Centura and Advance) that featured minimalist ornamentation and, wherever feasible, all-wood materials.

D'Aquisto-designed guitars have also been manufactured by Hagstrom, beginning in 1968, and by Fender/Japan in the 1980s.

GENERAL CHANGES

Evolution to S-shaped soundholes: **1967–69**
Evolution to circular peghead cutout: **1967–69**
Transition to ebony tailpiece and pickguard: **1970–73**

ARCHTOP MODELS
New Yorker Special: 17" wide

New Yorker Deluxe: 18" wide
First New Yorker: **May 1965**
Later examples have model name engraved on pearl
scroll inlaid on peghead

Excel: 17" wide
First Excel: Aug. **1965**

New Yorker Classic: 17" or 18" wide, unbound
S-holes or oval hole, wood binding, no fingerboard
inlay, wood peghead veneer
First New Yorker Classic: **1985**

Avant Garde: unbound S-holes or oval hole, wood
binding, wood peghead veneer
First Avant Garde: **1987**

Solo: large 2-segment soundholes, slotted peghead

Centura: smaller body, wide soundholes

Advance: large wide soundholes, each with 2
removable inserts

MISC. MODELS

First solidbody: **1976**
First flat top, 16" wide: **1975**
First hollowbody electric, plywood construction: **1976**

COMMENTS

D'Aquisto was the most highly regarded builder of
archtop guitars at the time of his death in 1995. His
reputation is based on archtops, but all instruments
made by him are of value.

SERIAL NUMBERS

Standard Archtops (Except Centura)

Occasional overlaps occur.

RANGE	YEAR
1001–1005	1965
1006–1014	1966
1015–1022	1967
1023–1029	1968
1030–1036	1969
1037–1043	1970
1044–1050	1971
1051–1063	1972
1064–1073	1973
1074–1084	1974
1085–1094	1975
1095–1102	1976
1103–1112	1977
1113–1125	1978
1126–1133	1979
1134–1142	1980
1143–1151	1981
1152–1160	1982
1161–1164	1983
1166–1175	1984
1176–1183	1985
1185–1192	1986
1192–1202	1987
1201–1210	1988
1211–1217	1989
1218–1228	1990
1229–1231	1991
1235	1992
1236	1992
1237–1238	no date entered
1239–1246	1993
1247–1252	1994
1253–1254	1995
1255	1994
1256–1257	no information

OTHER MODELS

Centuras: 5 produced from 1993–95, numbered 1001–1005

Plywood hollowbody electrics:

001-004: 1976

25 with no number: 1977–80

128–130: 1981

New body style, beginning with #101: 1982

Solidbody electrics: 29 produced from 1976–91, numbered E101–E110 and 111–129 (no E-prefix).

Flat tops: 16 produced from 1973–83, numbered from 101–116.

Mandolins: 3 produced, numbered 101, 102 and 103, the last in 1972.

GILCHRIST

GENERAL INFORMATION

Stephen Gilchrist, based in Warrnambool, Victoria, Australia, began making instruments in 1976. He spent 1980 in the United States, refining his designs while working at Gruhn Guitars in Nashville. He is best known for mandolins, mandolas and mandocellos. His mandolins are modeled after the Gibson F-5. His mandolas and mandocellos are larger than traditional Gibson-size instruments.

Gilchrist has also made some acoustic and electric guitars. Most of the electric guitars were made from 1987–88. Some do not bear the Gilchrist name anywhere on the instrument, and none has a serial number.

Like many individual makers, many of Gilchrist's instruments have custom features. His catalog models are listed here.

MANDOLINS, MANDOLAS AND MANDOCELLOS
Ornamental Options
The following ornamental options are available on Models 5, 4 and 3:

Standard: flowerpot peghead inlay, dot fingerboard inlay

Artist: flamed hard rock maple back, sides and neck, parallel top bracing, bound soundholes, pearl block inlay, fern peghead inlay, gold-plated hadware, light blond finish

Basic: plain maple back, sides and neck, deep mahogany brown finish, ivoroid-bound top, unbound peghead, ivoroid tuner buttons, nickel-plated hardware, black finish

Classical: softer maple back, black binding, cam clamp pickguard bracket, unbound fingerboard, no inlay, ebony tuner buttons, black chrome hardware, deep amber finish

Model 5: F-style scroll body, f-holes, parallel or X-braced top

Model 4: F-style scroll body, oval hole

Model 3: A-style pear-shaped body, f-holes, longneck, snakehead peghead, extended fingerboard

Model 2: A-style pear shaped body, not longneck, oval soundhole, square-end fingerboard, sunburst top finish

Model 1: A-style pear-shaped body, not longneck, oval soundhole, unbound square-end fingerboard, snakehead peghead with no logo, blond top finish

GUITARS
Model 16: f-hole archtop, 16" wide, engraved tailpiece, multiple-bound top, back and fingerboard, bound ebony fingerboard, stylized V inlay, snakehead peghead, peghead inlay similar to fingerboard inlay

Model 17: f-hole archtop, 17" wide, engraved tailpiece, multiple-bound top, back and fingerboard, bound ebony fingerboard, dot inlay, snakehead peghead, flowerpot peghead inlay

Model 18: f-hole archtop, 18" wide multiple-bound top, back and fingerboard, ebony fingerboard, stylized V inlay, snakehead peghead, peghead inlay similar to fingerboard inlay, engraved tailpiece

COMMENTS

Gilchrist's F-style mandolins, mandolas and mandocellos are regarded by players as among the finest by any current maker.

SERIAL NUMBERS

From 1978–82 and from mid 1993–current, the serial number is preceded by the last 2 digits of the year.

RANGE	SHIPPING DATE
1–9	1976–77
7810–7849	1978
7950–7954	May 1979
7955–7962	June 1979
7963–7965	Aug. 1979
7966–7972	Oct. 1979
7973–7980	Nov. 1979
8081	Mar. 1980
8082	Apr. 1980
8083	June 1980
8084–8087	Aug. 1980
8088–8094	Oct. 1980
8095–8099	Dec. 1980
81100–81101	Apr. 1981
81102	June 1981
81103–81104	July 1981
81105–81108	Sept. 1981
81109–81117	Dec. 1981
82118–82120	May 1982
82121–82122	Mar. 1982
82123	Feb. 1982
82124–82125	Sept. 1982
82126	June 1982
82127–82128	Mar. 1982
82129–82131	Sept. 1982
82132–82144	Dec. 1982
145–152	Dec. 1983
153–160	July 1984
161–170	Jan. 1985
(none made in 1986)	
171–174	July 1987
175	May 1987

RANGE	SHIPPING DATE
176	June 1988
177–183	July 1987
184–185	June 1988
186	May 1989
187–192	Dec. 1989
193	Apr. 1990
194	Dec. 1989
195	July 1989
196–202	July 1990
203–209	Jan. 1991
210–211	Oct. 1990
212–217	Sept. 1991
218–226	Feb. 1992
227–241	Jun. 1992
243–250	Nov. 1992
251–258	Mar. 1993
93259–93268	Aug. 1993
93269–93274	Dec. 1993
93275–93283	Mar. 1994
94284–94290	July 1994
94291–94304	Oct. 1994
94305–94311	Mar. 1995
95312–95319	June 1995
95320–95327	Oct. 1995
95328–95336	Jan 1996
96337–96344	Apr. 1996
96345–96354	Aug 1996
96355–96365	Jan 1997
97366–97375	May 1997
97376–97386	Aug. 1997
97387–98396	Jan. 1998
98397	Sept. 1988
98398–97401	Jan. 1998
98402–98411	May 1998
98412–98423	Sept. 1998
98424–98436	Jan. 1999

MONTELEONE

John Monteleone's first instruments were two dreadnought-size flat top guitars he made in the 1970s. He began repairing and restoring vintage instruments for Mandolin Brothers (a prominent vintage dealer) in Staten Island, NY, in 1973. He completed his first mandolin in August 1974. He opened his own shop in Bayshore, NY, in 1976 and relocated to Islip, NY, in 1990.

Monteleone's first mandolins were replicas of the Gibson F-5, with the Gibson logo. He has become best known for his Grand Artist models—F-style mandolin family instruments identifiable by his "relaxed" body-scroll design—and more recently for his archtop guitars. He has also made mandolas, mandocellos and 10-string mandolins.

Monteleone's first six guitars were flat top models (including the prototype for the Hexaphone model). He began making archtops in 1978 and by the 1990s was building more guitars than mandolins.

Like many individual makers, Monteleone has made many instruments with custom features that do not conform to strict model specifications. Only standard models are listed here.

LABELS

Label with *Monteleone Master Model*, signed and dated, through mandolin #8: **1974–77**

Label with *John Monteleone, 41 Degnon Blvd. Bayshore, NY.*, beginning with mandolin #9: **1977–90**

No label, number and date stamped into inside back on almost all instruments, beginning with instruments made in new shop in Islip: **1977–current**

MANDOLINS

Style F/M-1: replica of Gibson F-5

First example, designated **F-5 replica**, with Gibson logo: **1974**

Designated **M-1**, with mandolin #2: **1976**

First use of Monteleone logo, #5: **1977**

Last use of Gibson logo, #8: **1977**

Designated **Style F**, #11: **1977**

Last Style F: **1985**

39 total produced

Grand Artist: scroll body with opened scroll,

extended fingerboard, dot inlay, also mandolin and mandocello, prototype completed: **1977**

Style B: symmetrical rounded body, extended fingerboard, dot inlay, S-holes, prototype completed: **1982**

Baby Grand: symmetrical body with 2 points, extended fingerboard, dot inlay, prototype completed: **1983**

Radio Flyer: companion to Radio Flyer guitar (see following), prototype completed: **1996**

ARCHTOP GUITARS

Options available on all models:

- 16", 17" or 18" wide
- Elliptical (oval) soundhole
- 1 3/4" or 1 7/8" nut width
- 7 strings
- Custom binding and inlay

Eclipse: 16 3/4" wide, 20 1/2" long body, rounded cutaway, no inlay, S-holes, black-and-white binding, prototype completed: **1978**

Hot Club Model A: 15 5/8" wide, rounded cutaway at right angle to neck (similar to Selmer cutaway shape used by Django Reinhardt), S-holes, no inlay, slotted peghead, prototype completed: **1985**

Radio City: 18" wide, 21 5/8" long body, rounded cutaway, deco ornamentation, pearl inlays on bridge and tailpiece, black-and-white binding, ebony fingerboard, ebony peghead veneer with pearl and abalone inlay on front and back, metal tuner buttons with *M*, brass truss rod cover, prototype completed: **1992**

Radio Flyer: 17" wide, 21 1/2" long body or 18" wide, 21 5/8" long body, slash soundholes, black-and-white wood binding, ebony fingerboard with ebony binding, Schaller tuners, ebony buttons, first made: **1993**

Grand Artist: companion to Grand Artist mandolin, 17" wide, 22 1/4" long body, scrolled upper bass bout , black-and-white binding, extended ebony fingerboard, prototype completed: **1994**

FLAT TOP GUITARS

Hot Club Model F: elliptical (long oval) soundhole, flat spruce top, no fingerboard inlay, solid
tapered peghead, prototype completed: **1987**

Hexaphone: 17" wide, non-cutaway standard, cutaway available, elliptical soundhole, dot inlay, prototype completed: **1977**
Second example made: **1998**

COMMENTS

Monteleone's instruments are highly regarded for
craftsmanship as well as aesthetics, and he has
achieved equal success with archtop guitars and
mandolins. His mandolins are well-respected by
musicians (although bluegrass mandolinists generally prefer a closer replica of the Gibson F-5 to
Monteleone's Grand Artist model). His guitars are
highly regarded by jazz musicians.

SERIAL NUMBERS

There are some inconsistencies and overlaps in these
lists.

Mandolins

RANGE	YEAR
1	1974
2–3	1976
4–18	1977
19–24	1978
25–37	1979
38–54	1980
55–66	1981
67–85	1982
86–97	1983
98–107	1984
108–117	1985
118–127	1986
128–131	1987
132–138	1988
139–148	1989
149–155	1990

RANGE	YEAR
156–158	1991
159–162	1992
163–164	1993
165	1996
166	1993
171	1994
173–175	1996
176–186	1996–98

Guitars

RANGE	YEAR
1	1965
2–3	1974
104	1975
105	1976
106	1976
107–108	1978
109	1979
110	1981
111	1982
112	1983
113–115	1984
116–117	1985
118–119	1986
120–121	1987
122–125	1988
126–127	1987
128–129	1988
130	1991
131–132	1989
133–135	1990
136	1989
137–145	1992–93
146–149	1994
150–151	1993
152–155	1994–95
156–157	1996
158–159	1995
160–161	1996
162–165	1997
166	1996
167–168	1995
170–183	1997–98

STROMBERG

Charles Stromberg opened an instrument business in Boston around 1905, producing banjos and drums. His son Elmer, born July 14, 1895, joined him in the business in 1910, and they began making guitars in the 1930s. Elmer Stromberg died in 1955, a few months after his father's death.

The shop of Chas. Stromberg and Son produced banjos as well as guitars but is best known for the large-bodied archtop Master 300 and Master 400 models. Their great volume made them attractive to guitarists who had to compete with horn sections in jazz bands.

Total production of Stromberg guitars is estimated at about 640 instruments.

GENERAL CHANGES

16" wide, 3-segment *f*-holes, criss-cross top bracing (2 parallel and 3 ladder braces): **into 1930s**
17" wide, 3-segment *f*-holes, 2 parallel braces: **c. 1940**
Standard *f*-holes, 2 parallel braces: **early 1940s**
1 diagonal brace from upper bass bout to lower treble: **mid to late 1940s**
Cutaway available on G-3 and DeLuxe models: **1940s**
Adjustable truss rod with adjustment under nut (nut is removable), introduced: **c. late 1940s**

LABELS

Some student-grade instruments from the 1920s and early 1930s were marketed under the Stromberg-Voisinet brand, which was a forerunner of the Kay brand and unrelated to Charles and Elmer Stromberg. Instruments made by Charles and Elmer Stromberg are labeled Chas. Stromberg and Son with a Boston address.

Stromberg's labels were actually business cards, so instruments can be roughly dated by the telephone numbers on the labels.

Phone Number	Date
Bowdoin 1228R or 1728M	1920–27
Bowdoin 6559W or 1242W	1927–29
Bowdoin 1878R	1929–32
CA 3174	1932–45
CA 7-3174	by 1949–55

PEGHEADS

Almost all Stromberg guitars have an engraved plastic peghead veneer. Very few examples have pearl peghead inlay.

MODELS

Specs for Deluxe, G-1, and G-3 are for later versions of these models. Specs for all models vary due to custom orders and evolution of designs.

Master 400: 19" wide, non-cutaway (a few cutaways made), heavy tailpiece with 5 cutouts, bound pickguard with stairstep treble side, bound *f*-holes, pointed-end ebony fingerboard, slashed-block inlay (custom patterns optional), plastic peghead veneer, *400* on peghead, gold-plated hardware, sunburst or natural finish

Master 300: 19" wide, bound stairstep pickguard, block inlay

Deluxe, Deluxe Cutaway: 17 3/8" wide, tailpiece with 3 cutouts and Y-shaped center section, bound pickguard (optional) with stairstep treble side, bound *f*-holes, bound ebony fingerboard with pointed end, gold-plated hardware, *Deluxe* on peghead, natural or sunburst finish

G-1 (early G-100): tailpiece with 2 horizontal plates and 4 vertical tubes, triple-bound top and back, bound pickguard, notched-diamond or 4-point inlay, bound peghead, nickel-plated hardware

G-3, G-3 Cutaway: 17 3/8" wide, bound pickguard with straight edges, ebony fingerboard, slashed-block inlay, gold-plated hardware, natural or sunburst finish

COMMENTS

Stromberg's reputation is based on his large-body Master models, particularly the later examples and the rare cutaway examples. Although Stromberg's workmanship is generally regarded as not equal to that of D'Angelico, the later Strombergs have such superb sound that they bring prices on a par with D'Angelicos. The early models with multiple top braces are not highly regarded by most players but are of interest to collectors because of the Stromberg reputation.

APPENDIX

Many electric instruments and amplifiers can be dated by the numbers on the potentiometers (pots), speaker chassis or other electronic parts. The Electronic Industries Association has a standardized "source-date" code that indicates the company, year and week of manufacture. Although EIA was formed in 1924, codes on pots and speakers do not appear until after World War II.

The code is a 6- or 7-digit number. Sometimes there is a space after the first 3 digits, sometimes a hyphen, sometimes no space. On pots it is impressed (except for some ink-stamped in the early 1950s) straight across, arced around the edge of the back or on the side. On speakers, it is painted on the speaker chassis.

Codes have configuration **mmmyww** or **mmmyyww**

First 3 digits **mmm** signify the maker. Among the most common are:
106=Allen-Bradley Corp.
134=CentraLab
137=CTS
140=Clarostat
220=Jensen
304=Stackpole
328=Utah/Oxford
381=Bourns Networks
465=Oxford

4th digit **y** in a 6-digit code corresponds to the last digit of the year of manufacture. Pot makers used a 6-digit code prior to 1961 and a 7-digit code from 1961 onward. Some other components, however, continued with a 6-digit code.

4th and 5th digits **yy** in a 7-digit code correspond to the last 2 digits of the year of manufacture.

Final 2 digits **ww** correspond to the week of the year in which the part was made. A series of numbers ending with 2 digits greater than 53 can not be a dating code.

Examples:
304-6320 was made by Stackpole in the 20th week of 1963.
1377633 was made by CTS in the 33rd week of 1976.
304731 was made by Stackpole in the 31st week of either 1947 or 1957.

The pot must be original, of course, for the date to be of use.

The pot date signifies only the earliest possible date that the instrument could have been made. A pot dated the 50th week of 1952, for example, probably means the instrument was not finished until 1953.

FENDER

Many early '50s Fenders have Clarostat pots with codes stamped in blue ink.

Practically all Fenders from 1966–69 have 1966 pots. (CBS apparently bought a huge supply of pots after acquiring Fender in 1965.)

For Fenders, better-selling models usually have pot dates closer to neck dates. Lap steels often have pots with dates as far as two years apart.

GIBSON

Coded pots made by CentraLab: **1953–67**
Coded pots made by CTS: **1968–94**
Custom-coded pots by CGE: **1995–current**

In 1995 Gibson began using custom made pots from CGE (formerly CentraLab). The top surface of the pot is stamped with a Gibson logo. The code, stamped on the side, has this configuration:

my 440-#####

m: The first digit or letter corresponds to the month. 1=January, 9=September, X=October, Y=November, Z=December.

y: The second digit corresponds to the last digit of the year. 6=1996, 7=1997, etc.

OTHER MAKERS

All Guild electrics from 1979 to the early 1990s have 1979 pots.

National used coded pots by Stackpole as early as 1945. Up until circa 1955, codes are on the back. After that, codes are on the side.

A patent number on an instrument gives the earliest possible date that the instrument or part could have been made.

A patent pending notice predates an actual patent number. Patents typically take a year or more from the application to the granting of the patent. Even after a patent has been granted, parts with a patent pending notice may be used up before new parts with a patent number are introduced.

Year	First Number of Year	Year	First Number of Year	Year	First Number of Year	Year	First Number of Year
1836	1	1877	185,813	1918	1,251,458	1959	2,866,973
1837	110	1878	198,733	1919	1,290,027	1960	2,919,443
1838	546	1879	211,078	1920	1,326,899	1961	2,966,681
1839	1,061	1880	223,211	1921	1,364,063	1962	3,015,103
1840	1,465	1881	236,137	1922	1,401,948	1963	3,070,801
1841	1,923	1882	251,685	1923	1,440,362	1964	3,116,487
1842	2,413	1883	269,820	1924	1,478,996	1965	3,163,865
1843	2,901	1884	291,016	1925	1,521,590	1966	3,226,729
1844	3,395	1885	310,163	1926	1,568,040	1967	3,295,143
1845	3,873	1886	333,494	1927	1,612,700	1968	3,360,800
1846	4,348	1887	355,291	1928	1,654,521	1969	3,419,907
1847	4,914	1888	375,720	1929	1,696,897	1970	3,487,470
1848	5,409	1889	395,305	1930	1,742,181	1971	3,551,909
1849	5,993	1890	418,665	1931	1,787,424	1972	3,631,539
1850	6,981	1891	443,987	1932	1,839,190	1973	3,707,729
1851	7,865	1892	466,315	1933	1,892,663	1974	3,781,914
1852	8,622	1893	488,976	1934	1,941,449	1975	3,858,241
1853	9,512	1894	511,744	1935	1,985,878	1976	3,930,271
1854	10,358	1895	531,619	1936	2,026,516	1977	4,000,520
1855	12,117	1896	552,502	1937	2,066,309	1978	4,065,812
1856	14,009	1897	574,369	1938	2,104,004	1979	4,139,952
1857	16,324	1898	596,467	1939	2,142,080	1980	4,180,867
1858	19,010	1899	616,871	1940	2,185,170	1981	4,242,757
1859	22,477	1900	640,167	1941	2,227,418	1982	4,308,622
1860	26,642	1901	664,827	1942	2,268,540	1983	4,366,579
1861	31,005	1902	690,385	1943	2,307,007	1984	4,423,523
1862	34,045	1903	717,521	1944	2,338,081	1985	4,490,855
1863	37,266	1904	748,567	1945	2,366,154	1986	4,562,596
1864	41,047	1905	778,834	1946	2,391,856	1987	4,633,526
1865	45,685	1906	808,618	1947	2,413,675	1988	4,716,594
1866	51,784	1907	839,799	1948	2,433,824	1989	4,794,652
1867	60,658	1908	875,679	1949	2,457,797	1990	4,890,335
1868	72,959	1909	908,436	1950	2,492,944	1991	4,982,447
1869	85,503	1910	945,010	1951	2,563,016	1992	5,077,836
1870	98,460	1911	980,178	1952	2,580,379	1993	5,175,886
1871	110,617	1912	1,013,095	1953	2,624,046	1994	5,274,846
1872	122,304	1913	1,049,326	1954	2,664,562	1995	5,377,359
1873	134,504	1914	1,083,267	1955	2,698,434	1996	5,479,658
1874	146,120	1915	1,123,212	1956	2,728,913	1997	5,590,420
1875	158,350	1916	1,166,419	1957	2,775,762		
1876	171,641	1917	1,210,389	1958	2,818,567		

APPENDIX

esearch on vintage instruments is ongoing, with new discoveries being made almost every day. Some of the books listed here were considered to be thorough, all-encompassing works when they were first published, yet several are now into third editions and/or paperback editions—an indication that this field of study is still being expanded, revised and refined.

There are many more books available than those listed here, and there is seldom a music-related book, article or photograph that doesn't hold some useful information.

We feel that the following books are among the most accurate, comprehensive and useful.

GENERAL

Bacon, Tony, and Barry Moorhouse, *The Bass Book*. San Francisco: Miller Freeman Books, 1995.

Bacon, Tony, and Paul Day, *The Ultimate Guitar Book*. New York: Alfred A. Knopf, Inc., 1991.

Duchossoir, A. R. *Guitar Indentification*. 3rd ed. Milwaukee: Hal Leonard Publishing Corporation (distributor), 1990.

Gruhn, George, and Walter Carter. *Acoustic Guitars and Other Fretted Instruments: A Photographic History*. San Francisco: Miller Freeman, 1993.

Gruhn, George, and Walter Carter. *Electric Guitars and Basses: A Photographic History*. San Francisco: Miller Freeman, 1994.

Wheeler, Tom. *American Guitars*. New York: Harper-Perennial (HarperCollins), 1990.

D'ANGELICO/D'AQUISTO

Schmidt, Paul William. *Acquired of the Angels: The Lives and Works of Master Guitar Makers John D'Angelico and James D'Aquisto*. Metuchen, NJ: The Scarecrow Press, Inc., 1991.

EPIPHONE

Carter, Walter. *Epiphone: The Complete History*. Milwaukee: Hal Leonard, 1995.

Fred, L.B., and Jim Fisch. *Epiphone: The House of Stathopoulo*. New York: Amsco Publications, 1996.

FENDER

Bacon, Tony, and Paul Day, *The Fender Book*. San Francisco: Miller Freeman Books, 1992.

Duchossoir, A. R. *The Fender Stratocaster*. Rev. ed. Milwaukee: Hal Leonard Publishing Corporation (distributor), 1990.

_____. *The Fender Telecaster*. Milwaukee: Hal Leonard Publishing Corporation (distributor), 1991.

Morrish, John. *The Fender Amp Book*. San Francisco: Miller Freeman Books, 1995.

Smith, Richard. *Fender: The Sound Heard Round the World*. Fullerton, CA: Garfish, 1995.

Teagle, John, and John Sprung. *Fender Amps: The First Fifty Years*. Milwaukee: Hal Leonard Corporation, 1995.

GIBSON

Bacon, Tony, and Paul Day. *The Gibson Les Paul Book*

Carter, Walter. *Gibson Guitars, 100 Years of an American Icon*. Santa Monica, CA: General Publishing Group, 1994.

Duchossoir, A. R. *Gibson Electrics, Vol. 1* . Milwaukee: Hal Leonard Publishing Corporation (distributor), 1981.

Van Hoose, Thomas A. *The Gibson Super 400: Art of the Fine Guitar*. San Francisco: Miller Freeman Books, 1991.

Whitford, Eldon, David Vinopal and Dan Erlewine. *Gibson's Fabulous Flat-Top Guitars*. San Francisco: Miller Freeman Books, 1994.

GUILD

Moust, Hans. *The Guild Guitar Book*. Breda, The Netherlands: GuitArchives, 1995.

GRETSCH

Bacon, Tony, and Paul Day. *The Gretsch Book*. San Francisco: Miller Freeman Books, 1996.

Scott, Jay. *Gretsch: The Guitars of the Fred Gretsch Company*. Fullerton, CA: Centerstream, 1992.

LARSON BROTHERS

Hartman, Robert Carl. *Guitars and Mandolins in America, Featuring the Larsons' Creations*. Rev. ed. Hoffman Estates, IL: Maurer & Co., 1988.

MARTIN

Carter, Walter. *The Martin Book*. San Francisco: Miller Freeman Books, 1995.

Longworth, Mike. *Martin Guitars: A History.* 3rd ed. Nazareth, PA: Mike Longworth, 1988.

Washburn, Jim, and Richard Johnston. *Martin Guitars: An Illustrated Celebration of America's Premier Guitarmaker.* Emmaus, PA: Rodale Press, Inc., 1997.

NATIONAL

Brozman, Bob. *The History and Artistry of National Resonator Instruments.* Fullerton, CA: Centerstream, 1993.

OVATION

Carter, Walter. *The History of the Ovation Guitar.* Milwaukee: Hal Leonard, 1996.

RICKENBACKER

Bacon, Tony, and Paul Day. *The Rickenbacker Book.* San Francisco: Miller Freeman Books, 1994.

Smith, Richard. *The Complete History of Rickenbacker Guitars.* Fullerton, CA: Centerstream Publishing, 1987.

MODEL INDEX

A

Airline...
Acoustic Resonator Model, 507
Basses, 509
Deluxe Pro, 509
Extra Volume Folk Guitar, 507
Fiberglass bodies, 509
Resonator model, 507
Solidbodies, Supro shapes, 507
Steels, 509
Woodbodies, angular shape, 508,
Ambassador, Gibson-made, 300
Astro AS-51, 542

B

Bacon, Martin-made, 421
Belltone, Martin-made, 421
Benedetto, 550
Bitting Special, Martin-made, 422
Bronson Melody King, 547

C

Capital, Gibson-made, 300
Coast Wholesale (Mason), 307
Collings, 552
Contello, 542
Cromwell, Gibson-made...
EG amp, 302
EG-5, 302
EG-H, Hawaiian, 302
G-series, guitars, 301,
GM-series, mandolins, 302

D

D'Angelico, 554
D'Aquisto, 556
Ditson, Martin-made...
Dreadnoughts, 421,
General, 422
Dobro...
1, Hawaiian electric, 16
2, Standard electric, 16
5, mandolin, 15
5, Regal, 14
5-string, 26
6, Regal, 13
7, mandolin, 15
10, mandolin, 15
10, OMI, 22
12, OMI, 22
14 (Silver), 14
15 (Silver), 14
15, OMI mandolin , 26

15, uke, 15
16 (Silver), 14
19, 12
20, OMI, 23
25, Regal, 14
25 1/2, Regal tenor, 14
27 (27G), 13
27 Cyclops, 12
27 Deluxe, 22
27, OMI, 22
27, Regal, 13
27G, 13
27 1/2, Regal tenor, 13
30, Dopera's Original, 20
30, OMI, 24
30, uke, 15
32, Regal, 14
32/35, Regal, 14
33 Wood, 23
33, OMI, 24
36, 12
36, Dopera's Original, 20
36, OMI, 24
37, Regal, 13
37G, 13
37M, mandolin, 15
37 1/2, Regal tenor, 13,
40, uke, 15
45, 11
45 Cyclops, 12
45, Regal, 13
45G, 13,
45-S, OMI, 22
45 1/2, Regal tenor, 13,
46, 14
47M, mandolin, 15
45/50 Tenortrope, 15
50, OMI, 22
50, tenor, 11
55, Regal, 13
55/56, 11
60, 11
60 Classic, 20
60 Cyclops, 12
60, mandolin, 15
60, OMI, 20,
60/75 Tenortrope, 15
62, 14
62, OMI (60M), 21,
63, OMI, 22
64, OMI (60W-S), 21
65/66, 11
66, OMI, 22
66B, 11
75, OMI, 24
75, tenor, 12
75/100 Tenortrope, 15
76, 12
85/86, 11

88 (33 Painted), 24
88, OMI, 24
90, woodbody, 22
90, metalbody, 25
95, OMI, 25
100/106, 12
114, OMI, 22
114C, OMI, 22
125, 11
150/156, 12
175, 12
206, 12
210, mandolin, 15
250, mandolin, 15
270, mandolin, 15
320, mandolin, 15
370, mandolin, 15
450, mandolin, 15
1000, OMI, 25
3000, OMI, 25
All-Electric, 16
Amplifier, 17
Ampliphonic Mandolin, 26
Angelus, 12
Angelus, Regal, 13
Artist, 14
Avalon, 18
Basses, 26
Blue Grass, 18
Blues Special, 22
Bluesmaker, 25
Bottleneck, 25
Brumfield, Deacon, DB Original, 17
C-3, Mosrite, 18
C-60, Mosrite, 18
C-60, OMI, 21
C-65, Mosrite, 19
California Girl, 24
Californian, 19
Chrysanthemum, 25
Columbia, 19
Custom Deluxe (75), 25
Custom Walnut, 11
Cyclops, 12
D-8, Mosrite, 19
D-12, Mosrite, 19
D-40, Mosrite, 18
D-50, Mosrite, 18
D-100, Mosrite, 19
D Bass, 26
D Dobro, OMI, 24
DB Original, 17
De Luxe, 11
De Luxe Tenortrope, 15
Deco, 23
Dobro Jr., 13
Dobro Special, 25
Dobro, Inc. (Gardena), 17

DobroLektric, 25
Dopera's Original, 19
Double-Cyclops, 12
Douglas, Jerry, 23
Duolian, 25
E-3, 25
E-45, 25
Electric Resonator, 16
F Bass, 26
F Deluxe Bass, 26
F-60, OMI, 21
Gardena (Mosrite), 17,
Graves, Josh (see Uncle Josh), 23
Hawaiian woodbody, 17
Hound Dog, 19
Hound Dog 101, 23
Hula Blues, 22
Josh, OMI, 20
Jr., 13
Kahuna, 23
Kirby, Pete "Oswald", 23
Kona, 23
Leader, 14
Lexington, 19
Lily of the Valley, 24
Mandolin, electric, 17
Mandolins, 15
Memphis, 19
Mesa, 24
Mobro Standard, 19
Mobro Steel, 19
Monterey, 18
Mosrite, 18
Oahu, 25
Perkins, Al, 23
Plainsman, 19
Professional, 15 Silver, 14
Professional, 85/86, 11
Professional Tenortrope, 15,
Regal metalbody, 14, ,
Regal Silver, 14
Regal uke, 16,
Regal woodbody, 13
Replica 66, 19
Resonator Electric, 16
Richmond, 18
Rose, 24
Sailboat, 24
Silver Guitar Series, 14
Soft Cutaway (90), 23
Spanish Electric, 16
Special, 25
Special De Luxe, 12
Swatzell, Tom, 23
Tenortropes, 15
Texarkana, 18
Troubadour, 23
Uke, Regal, 16

MODEL INDEX

MODEL INDEX

When it Comes to Guitars We Wrote the Book